Why do you need this new edition?

6 good reasons why you should buy this new edition of *Society: The Basics* by John Macionis!

1. Personalized Learning—The new MySocLab delivers proven results in helping you succeed, provides engaging experiences that personalize learning, and comes from a trusted partner with educational expertise and a deep commitment to helping students and instructors achieve their goals.

2. New Media Activities—MySocLab now features videos, readings, and interactive map activities for each chapter that bring the content to life.

3. Improve Critical Thinking—Six new learning objectives per chapter help readers build critical thinking and study skills. The learning objectives are revisited throughout the chapter to help you read effectively.

4. New Design—*Society: The Basics* has been redesigned for a new generation of learners to help you see sociology come alive!

5. Seeing Sociology in *Your* Everyday Life—New activities in MySocLab empower you to utilize what you've learned in the chapter in your own everyday life.

6. Pearson Choices—We know you want greater value, innovation, and flexibility in products. You can choose from a variety of text and media formats to match your learning style and your budget.

PEARSON

This book is offered to teachers of sociology in the hope that it will help our students understand their place in today's society and in tomorrow's world.

John J. Macionis

Society: The Basics

Twelfth Edition

John J. Macionis

KENYON COLLEGE

PEARSON

Boston   Columbus   Indianapolis   New York   San Francisco   Upper Saddle River
Amsterdam   Cape Town   Dubai   London   Madrid   Milan   Munich   Paris   Montréal   Toronto
Delhi   Mexico City   São Paulo   Sydney   Hong Kong   Seoul   Singapore   Taipei   Tokyo

If you purchased this text within the United States or Canada you should be aware that it has been imported without the approval of the Publisher or the Author.

Editorial Director: *Craig Campanella*
Editor in Chief: *Dickson Musslewhite*
Acquisitions Editor: *Brita Mess*
Assistant Editor: *Seanna Breen*
Development Editor: *Jenn Auvil*
Editorial Assistant: *Zoe Lubitz*
Director of Marketing: *Brandy Dawson*
Executive Marketing Manager: *Kelly May*
Marketing Assistant: *Frank Alarcon*
Managing Editor: *Denise Forlow*
Production Editor: *Barbara Reilly*
Data Researcher: *Kimberlee Klesner*
Senior Manufacturing and Operations Manager
  for Arts & Sciences: *Mary Fischer*

Operations Specialist: *Alan Fischer*
Design Manager: *John Christiana*
Art Director: *Anne Bonanno Nieglos*
Interior Designer: *Ilze Lemesis*
Digital Imaging Specialist: *Corin Skidds*
Cover Designer: *Jodi Notowitz*
Media Director: *Brian Hyland*
Media Editor: *Rachel Comerford*
Lead Media Project Manager: *Nikhil Bramhaver*
Full-Service Project Management: *Kathleen Allain, PreMediaGlobal*
Printer/Binder: *Courier Companies, Inc.*
Cover Printer: *Courier Companies, Inc.*
Text Font: *10/12 Minion*

Credits and acknowledgments borrowed from other sources and reproduced, with permission, in this textbook appear on appropriate page within text (or on pages 506–7).

Many of the designations by manufacturers and seller to distinguish their products are claimed as trademarks. Where those designations appear in this book, and the publisher was aware of a trademark claim, the designations have been printed in initial caps or all caps.

10 9 8 7 6 5 4 3 2

ISBN 10:   0-205-91371-7
ISBN 13:   978-0-205-91371-8

brief contents

contents

4 Social Interaction in Everyday Life 86

5 Groups and Organizations 106

6 Sexuality and Society 128

14 Education, Health, and Medicine 372

15 Population, Urbanization, and Environment 408

16 Social Change: Modern and Postmodern Societies 438

boxes

Seeing Sociology in Everyday Life

Controversy & Debate

maps

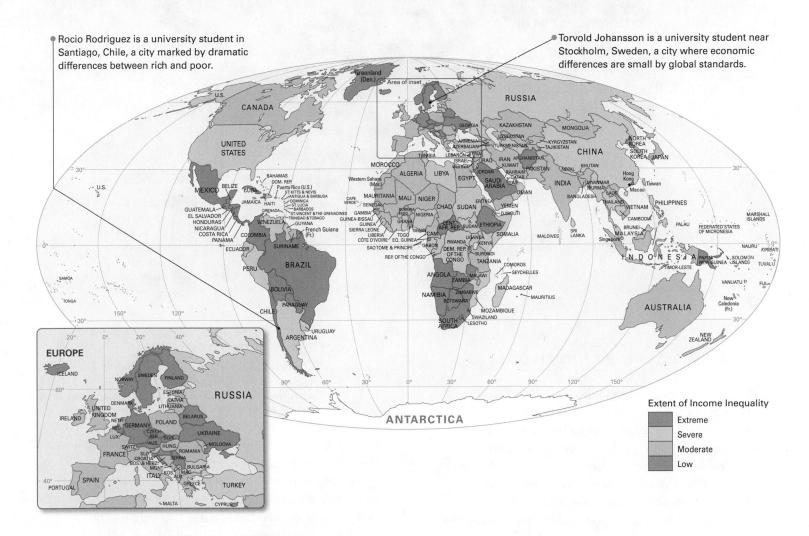

Rocio Rodriguez is a university student in Santiago, Chile, a city marked by dramatic differences between rich and poor.

Torvold Johansson is a university student near Stockholm, Sweden, a city where economic differences are small by global standards.

Extent of Income Inequality
- Extreme
- Severe
- Moderate
- Low

GLOBAL MAPS: Window on the World

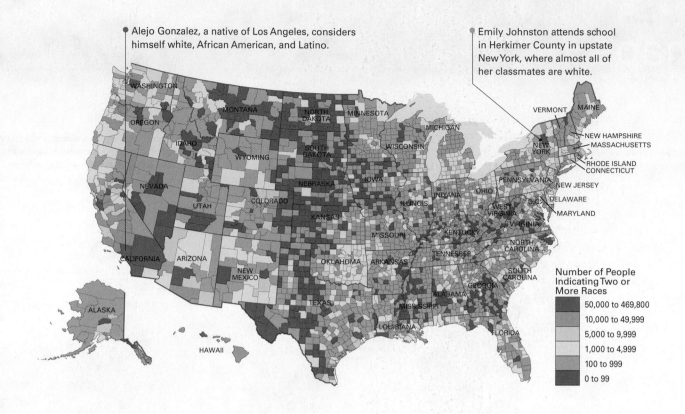

Alejo Gonzalez, a native of Los Angeles, considers himself white, African American, and Latino.

Emily Johnston attends school in Herkimer County in upstate New York, where almost all of her classmates are white.

Number of People Indicating Two or More Races

50,000 to 469,800
10,000 to 49,999
5,000 to 9,999
1,000 to 4,999
100 to 999
0 to 99

NATIONAL MAPS: Seeing Ourselves

preface

Today's world challenges us like never before. Several years into the present recession, the economy remains uncertain, not only here in the United States but around the world. During recent decades, income inequality has steadily increased. There is a lot of anger about how our national leaders in Washington are doing—or not doing—their jobs. Technological disasters of our own making threaten the natural environment, and the mild winter of 2011–2012 in the United States only adds to of the mounting evidence of global warming. Perhaps no one should be surprised to read polls that tell us most people are anxious about their economic future, unhappy with government, and worried about the state of the planet. Many of us simply feel overwhelmed, as if we were up against forces we can barely understand—much less control.

That's where sociology comes in. For more than 150 years, sociologists have been working to better understand how society operates. We sociologists may not have all the answers, but we have learned quite a lot that we can share with you. A beginning course in sociology is your introduction to the fascinating and very useful study of the social world. After all, we all have a stake in understanding our world and doing all we can to improve it.

Society: The Basics, Twelfth Edition, provides you with comprehensive understanding of how this world works. You will find this book to be informative, engaging, and even entertaining. Before you have finished the first chapter, you will discover that sociology is not only useful—it is also fun. *Sociology is a field of study that can change the way you see the world and open the door to many new opportunities*. What could be more worthwhile than that?

The Text and MySocLab®
A Powerful and Interactive Learning Package

Society: The Basics, Twelfth Edition, is the heart of an interactive, multimedia learning program that includes both a thorough revision of the leading text as well a new interactive learning lab. As the fully involved text author, I have been personally responsible for revising the text and writing both the Test Item File and the instructor annotations that are found in the Annotated Instructor's Edition. Now, convinced of the high potential of Pearson's MySocLab technology to transform learning, *I have taken personal responsibility for all the content of the MySocLab that accompanies my texts*. To ensure the highest level of quality, I have written the Social Explorer interactive map exercises, authored all the learning assessment questions, and personally selected all the readings and short videos that are keyed to each chapter. I have written both the book and the lab material to ensure that the two are linked seamlessly and transparently. This may well be the most substantial revision of our material ever!

Why all the hard work? The answer is all about better learning. *Society: The Basics, Twelfth Edition*, when used together with MySocLab, can raise the level of cognitive reasoning in students through interactive learning that encourages greater discovery and creativity. To track this learning process, the new edition makes use of the familiar Bloom's taxonomy, which I have adapted for students of sociology to include the following cognitive skills:

Remember: *The ability to recall facts and define important concepts*

Understand: *The ability to explain social patterns, trends, or problems*

Apply: *The ability to apply ideas, including theoretical approaches, to new topics or situations*

Analyze: *The ability to identify elements of social structure and patterns of social inequality, including their causes and consequences*

Evaluate: *The ability to make judgments as to the strengths and weaknesses of arguments or social arrangements*

Create: *The ability to combine elements or ideas to envision something new*

Each chapter of the text begins with six specific **learning objectives** based on these six cognitive skill levels, and each major section of the chapter is tagged as to the level of the material it covers. Of course, any conventional textbook inevitably focuses on student learning on the lower intellectual levels—remembering and understanding the material so as to be able to explain it in one's own words. But the interactivity found in text exercises and especially in MySocLab expands the opportunities for students to gain higher cognitive skills. The lab's **Social Explorer exercises**, for example, give students the opportunity to analyze social patterns presented in maps and to reach conclusions on their own. In addition, the lab's **Sociology in Focus** student blog gives readers the chance to evaluate many of today's debates and controversies, sharing their opinions and experiences and finding out what others think. For each chapter of the text, I've also written a new **Seeing Sociology in *Your* Everyday Life** essay, which shows the "everyday life" relevance of sociology by explaining how the material in the chapter can empower students in their personal and professional lives. Each of these essays includes learning activities designed at three intellectual levels (a "remember" exercise, an "apply" exercise, and a "create" exercise).

If you have not examined the new version of MySocLab that accompanies *Society: The Basics, Twelfth Edition*, you should take a look. You will be excited by what you find!

The revised text and the new lab together operate as a powerful learning program, and one that offers flexibility to you as an instructor. By using *Society: The Basics, Twelfth Edition*, and MySocLab, you may choose to allow students to do lab exercises on their own, or you can use the lab material for powerful in-class presentations. You decide the extent of integration into your course—from independent self-assessment to total course management. The lab is accompanied by an instructor's manual featuring easy-to-read media grids, activities, sample syllabi, and tips for integrating technology into your course.

Here are some of the learning tools you will find in MySocLab:

- **Social Explorer®** activities, written by John Macionis, provide easy access to sociological maps containing rich demographic data—many based on the 2010 census—about the United States. An exercise, which leads students on a journey of sociological discovery, is provided for every chapter of the text (look for the "Explore" logo in each chapter).

- **Videos**, selected for each chapter by John Macionis, bring concepts to life and stimulate class discussion (look for the "Watch" logo in each chapter of the text, which identifies the specific video that is part of the assessment program for that chapter).

- **MySocLibrary** is a virtual bookshelf of classic and contemporary readings. John Macionis has selected and linked readings to every chapter (look for the "Read" logo in each chapter, which identifies the specific reading that is part of the assessment program for that chapter).

- The **Sociology in Focus blog**, which is linked to a similarly titled feature box found in every chapter of the text, gives students the chance to evaluate their world, to take a stand on current controversies, and to suggest new possibilities.

- **Seeing Sociology in *Your* Everyday Life** essays, written by John Macionis, explain how the material found in every chapter of the text can personally and professionally benefit students in their everyday lives.

- **Writing tutorials** and a searchable **research database** are at students' fingertips.

- **Practice tests** and **flashcards** help students prepare for quizzes and exams.

What's New in This Edition?

Here's a quick summary of the new material found throughout *Society: The Basics, Twelfth Edition.*

- **Learning Objectives** Each chapter identifies six specific learning objectives at various levels of cognitive reasoning.

- **Enhanced Attention to Feminist Theory** In many chapters, feminist theory is now presented not simply as a subtype of social-conflict theory but on its own terms in expanded form.

- **Focus on Increasing Economic Inequality in the United States** Many chapters explore how the increasing economic inequality in the United States has affected various aspects of social life. An entirely new section in Chapter 8, "Social Stratification," thoroughly analyzes this trend.

- **Census 2010 and All the Latest Data** Each and every statistic in all the Macionis texts is the most current available at the time of publication. This revision is thoroughly informed by results of the Census 2010 and has many statistics for 2011.

- **Current events** are discussed throughout the book as a way to link sociological concepts to the world familiar to today's students. This revision includes discussion of the economic recession, the "jobless recovery," record levels of poverty in the United States, increasing economic inequality, the Occupy Wall Street movement, debate surrounding public employee unions, popular television shows and films, the Arab democracy uprisings, the Japanese nuclear disaster, the rise of China and other nations around the world, and even the significance of Prince William's marriage to Catherine Middleton.

- **Sociology = Student Empowerment** Each chapter has an added online essay that highlights ways in which specific sociological learning empowers students to more effectively deal with their everyday lives, including their careers.

- **Seamless Linkage between Text and MySocLab** Because the author has both revised the text and written or selected all material for the MySocLab, the two elements now work together to produce an unprecedented level of student learning.

- **New Student Blog** Each chapter of this revised text now has a Sociology in Focus box that highlights a high-interest issue such as interracial dating and marriage, affirmative action, the question of when young people are really "grown up," the chances of achieving the "American Dream," and the political movements that have changed the Arab world. Students can go to MySocLab and share their experiences and opinions on these issues and also see what others think.

- **New Design** *Society: The Basics, Twelfth Edition,* has been redesigned to be even more attractive and visually engaging. Check out the new look of the Making the Grade chapter summaries.

Here is a brief summary of some of the material that is new, chapter by chapter:

Chapter 1: Sociology: Perspective, Theory, and Method

More on the "rise of the rest" and how economic development abroad is reshaping life here in the United States. New data show how race is linked to player position in major sports. The discussion of research is revised to show how various approaches can be blended. A Sociology in Focus box on the popular press now invites students to assess the mass media on an Internet blog. The new student empowerment essay found in MySocLab explains the power that students gain by learning to apply the sociological perspective to their everyday lives and a second essay explains how they can be more critical consumers of information.

Chapter 2: Culture

A Sociology in Focus box on the Yąnomamö now includes an Internet blog that invites students to share experiences of culture shock. Updates focus on the extent of text messaging by young people, immigration, the "official English" movement, and changing student attitudes about life goals. There is updating of the discussion of key cultural values. There is expanded feminist analysis of culture. A new student empowerment essay found in MySocLab helps students explore the experience of confronting cultural differences in everyday life.

Chapter 3: Socialization: From Infancy to Old Age

There are updates on the share of multiracial people in the United States, how social class affects which traits parents desire most in their children, the extent of child labor around the world, and the social and physical state of older people in the United States. A Sociology in Focus box on how our society defines adulthood now includes an online student blog, which encourages students to explain why they do or do not feel "grown-up." The revised chapter has expanded coverage of the mass media and additional critical discussion of the death and dying research of Elisabeth Kübler-Ross. A student empowerment essay found in MySocLab encourages student to appreciate the power of human "agency" by which we become co-creators of our lives.

Chapter 4: Social Interaction in Everyday Life

There are new global data on who performs housework, showing how gender shapes everyday life. There is expanded discussion of gender and personal "performances." The discussion of women changing their names when they marry men is informed by new research. A Sociology in Focus box on gender and communication now invites students to join a student blog. A new student empowerment essay found in MySocLab explains the important part we all play in the social construction of everyday reality.

Chapter 5: Groups and Organizations

The revised chapter has updates on the expansion of McDonald's, the process of groupthink, network ties, and how race and gender shape the labor force. There is expanded and updated discussion of the erosion of personal privacy. A Sociology in Focus box on computer technology, large organizations, and personal privacy now invites students to join a student blog found on MySocLab. A new student empowerment essay in MySocLab helps students critically evaluate the high level of rationality that animates modern societies and suggests ways they might create a more personal social world.

Chapter 6: Sexuality and Society

There are updates on laws regulating first-cousin marriage and sex and the military, as well as updates on all aspects of sexual behavior, including premarital sex, extramarital sex, homosexuality, pornography, rape, teen pregnancy, and abortion. The discussion of levels of sexual activity across the life course now reflects new research. Find a new discussion on the history of celibacy among clergy. The discussion of gay rights includes a recent declaration by the American Psychological Association that therapy should not be used to try to make gay men or lesbians straight. The discussion of prostitution is both updated and expanded and includes comparative discussion of public policy. A Sociology in Focus box on "hooking up" invites students to share their opinions on a blog found on MySocLab. The discussion of date rape has been expanded and updated with results from recent research. The new student empowerment essay found in MySocLab helps students appreciate how the social construction of sexuality results in so much diversity in sexual attitudes and practices.

Chapter 7: Deviance

There are updates on sending white-collar criminals to prison, the number of hate crimes, hate-crime legislation across the United States, the convergence in the arrest rates for women and men, the use of capital punishment in the United States and around the world, the number of police in the United States, the extent of plea bargaining, the number of people incarcerated in the United States, and the rate of criminal recidivism. The medicalization of deviance has been expanded with discussion of the national trend toward the "medicalization of marijuana." The discussion of Hirschi's control theory has been revised for greater clarity. All criminal statistics contained in the chapter are the latest available. A Sociology in Focus box on "breaking the rules" invites students to join an online blog. A new student empowerment essay found in MySocLab provides a lesson in tolerance as it explains how societies construct notions of right and wrong.

Chapter 8: Social Stratification

The chapter provides expanded discussion of the extent of economic inequality in the United States with 2010 data for income and wealth and new data showing trends over the last several decades. There is a major new section on the Occupy Wall Street movement and evidence that the U.S. public is becoming more concerned about the extent of economic inequality. Chapter updates include analysis of Prince William's 2011 marriage to commoner Catherine Middleton, new data on longevity and economic well-being in the former Soviet Union, numerous discussions of the Occupy Wall Street movement, the link between income and health, the link between class position and what parents spend raising children, and the declining share of people in the United States who think they can achieve the American Dream. Significant additions have been made to the discussion on meritocracy. The discussion of China's standard of living and economic performance has been revised to reflect the latest trends and data. There are new data from a *Forbes* magazine study of the richest 400 families in the United States in 2011. The data on poverty in the United States are all new and show that the number of people living in poverty has reached a historical record. In addition, new discussion explains that almost half of the U.S. population is now living either in poverty or with low income. A Sociology in Focus box on social mobility invites students to join an online blog. A new student empowerment essay found in MySocLab encourages students to appreciate how the personal traits we link to social standing say less about individuals than about how our society is organized. A second essay offers suggestions about how to relate to people whose social background differs from your own.

Chapter 9: Global Stratification

The revised chapter has the latest on the global distribution of income, the extent of slavery worldwide, and the world's richest people. The distribution of the world's 195 nations into high-, middle-, and low-income categories has been recalculated using the latest available data from the United Nations and the World Bank, and the profiles of these categories of nations have been thoroughly updated. A Sociology in Focus box now invites students to share their opinions and experiences about extreme poverty in the United States. A new student empowerment essay in MySocLab helps students appreciate the difficulty faced by travelers when they encounter people of very different social standing as well as the difficulty of people in poor nations who try to relate to us.

Chapter 10: Gender Stratification

The chapter has updates on the occupations that claim the highest percentage of women, the number of U.S. women in the military who have lost their lives in the wars in Iraq and Afghanistan, the prevalence of sexual harassment in the United States, the highest-paid female and male television actors, the incidence of female genital mutilation worldwide, and the number of nations that have adopted gender quotas for positions of political leadership. Find the latest ranking of nations according to their degree of gender equality, including the declining ranking of the United States. New data reveal the academic fields with the largest share of bachelor's degrees earned by women and by men. The chapter now includes a new discussion of unemployment for women and men. There is expanded application of symbolic-interaction theory to gender. Find expanded discussion of intersection theory. A new Sociology in Focus box asks whether men are being "left behind" on the campus and invites students to share their experiences and opinions on an online blog. A new student empowerment essay in MySocLab helps students see that the social arrangements most of us think of as "natural" are socially constructed, and asks them to envision what they see as a just world in terms of gender.

Chapter 11: Race and Ethnicity

The chapter has updates on the size of all racial and ethnic categories of the U.S. population, the number of people speaking a language other than English in the home, the number of immigrants entering the country each year, and the income, poverty rate, and educational attainment of all racial and ethnic categories. There is expanded focus on multiracial and multiethnic people. A new Sociology in Focus box on affirmative action invites students to join an online blog at MySocLab. A new student empowerment essay in MySocLab encourages students to create a new vision of society beyond racial categories constructed in terms of superiority and inferiority.

Chapter 12: Economics and Politics

The revised chapter has updates on the increasing size of the global Walmart corporation, the extent of government control of the economy in high-income nations, the size and gender breakdown of the U.S. labor force, the types of jobs held by this country's workers, and the share of U.S. workers in a labor union. Find the latest debate over the power of public employee unions and new discussion of the Occupy Wall Street movement and the emergence of super PACs, as well as updates on state laws regulating voting among convicted felons, the number of terrorist attacks worldwide, and the annual military expenditure for the United States and for the entire world. A new discussion of "the jobless recovery" explains why the economic recovery has not reduced joblessness very much. A new Sociology in Focus box highlights the public employee union battle beginning in 2011 and invites students to share their opinions at an online blog. A new Controversy and Debate box asks whether our all-volunteer army amounts to having a warrior caste made up of working-class people. The uprisings in the Arab world are included with updates to the beginning of 2012. Two new student empowerment essays at MySocLab suggest how students can apply chapter information to their own careers and how they can encourage greater democracy in the United States.

Chapter 13: Family and Religion

The revised chapter has updates, including 2011 data, on the number of households and families in the United States, the size of families, the cost of raising children, average income for families of various racial and ethnic categories, the average age of first marriage, the incidence of domestic violence, the share of one-parent families, the number of cohabiting couples, the increasing number of states and nations recognizing same-sex marriage, the increasing share of young women who are single, the share of the U.S. population that identifies with a religious organization, and the debate over the teaching of religion in public schools. New discussion highlights how the recent recession has affected families. There is expanded discussion of the effects of religious belief on social life. A new Sociology in Focus box highlights the declining importance of race and ethnicity in dating and marriage and invites students to share their opinions and experiences using an online blog. Two new student empowerment essays at MySocLab explain how students can use sociological thinking to make better relational choices and also how sociological analysis of religion differs from holding religious beliefs.

Chapter 14: Education, Health, and Medicine

The revised chapter has the latest data on the schooling of the world's children, global rates of illiteracy, the extent of schooling here in the United States, the share of high school graduates who enroll in college, differences in salaries for public school teachers across the country, the average costs of public and private colleges, the average earnings of men and women with various levels of schooling, the high school dropout rate, average student performance on the SAT, and the increasing availability of teaching jobs. Find updated discussion of the leading causes of death in the past and today, gender differences in patterns of health, income differences in patterns of health, smoking by U.S. adults, trends in the incidence of various sexually transmitted diseases, and the rising cost of health care. A Sociology in Focus box on the dearth of men on the typical college campus invites students to share their opinions at an online student blog. There is expanded discussion of why the United States has not embraced a national, government-based health care system and also expanded discussion of the nursing shortage. New student empowerment essays at MySocLab highlight the personal benefits of advanced education and how students can benefit from sociological analysis of health.

Chapter 15: Population, Urbanization, and Environment

A new chapter-opening story focuses on the planet's unprecedented population of 7 billion at the beginning of 2012. The revised chapter has the latest data on our country's population size, fertility, mortality, infant mortality, life expectancy, and sex ratio, as well as the rising urban population, the number and size of urban regions, the latest on the rural rebound, the increasing number of large cities with a "minority majority" population, the high rates of material consumption in the United States, our society's high level of solid waste and what happens to it, the global supply of water, and the state of the world's rainforests. The recent recession and housing crisis has been incorporated into the discussion of migration. The environment section of the revised chapter now includes the concern over the planet's declining bee population. A Sociology in Focus box on the danger of global population increase invites students to share their opinions on the MySocLab blog. A new student empowerment essay suggests ways in which students can promote a more sustainable national culture.

Chapter 16: Social Change: Modern and Postmodern Societies

The revised chapter has updates on cell phone use while driving, our population's longevity, the Japanese nuclear disaster, public attitudes toward modern life, and a number of changes that distinguish our society today from that which existed a century ago. A new Seeing Sociology in Everyday Life box explores the evolution of a modern type of clothing—jeans—that turns out to be more traditional than most people think. There are factual updates to the story of Kitty Genovese in the Controversy & Debate box. A Sociology in Focus box on personal freedom and social responsibility encourages students to share their opinions and experiences on a blog found at MySocLab. A new student empowerment essay highlights ways in which sociological thinking can help students face the challenges of modern living. A second essay asks students to think about how they can make a difference in today's world.

Supplements for the Instructor

ANNOTATED INSTRUCTOR'S EDITION   (0-205-89919-6) The AIE is a complete student text with author-written annotations on every page. The annotations are especially useful to new instructors, but they are written to be helpful to even the most seasoned teachers. Margin notes include summaries of research findings, statistics from the United States and other nations, insightful quotations, information highlighting patterns of social diversity in the United States, and high-quality survey data from the General Social Survey conducted by the National Opinion Research Center (NORC) and from the World Values Survey conducted by the World Values Survey Association.

INSTRUCTOR'S MANUAL WITH TEST BANK (0-205-89916-1) This text offers an instructor's manual that will be of interest even to those who have never chosen to use one before. The manual—now revised by John Macionis—goes well beyond the expected detailed chapter outlines and discussion questions to provide summaries of important developments, recent articles from *Teaching Sociology* that are relevant to classroom discussions, suggestions for classroom activities, and supplemental lecture material for every chapter of the text.

The Test Bank—again, written by the author—reflects the material in the textbook—both in content and in language—far better than the testing file available with any other introductory sociology textbook. The file contains more than 100 items per chapter—in multiple-choice, true/false, and essay formats. For all of the questions, the correct answer is provided, as well as the page number in the text where the material is found and the Bloom's level of cognitive reasoning the question requires of the student.

MYTEST (0-205-89918-8) This online, computerized software allows instructors to create their own personalized exams, to edit any or all of the existing test questions, and to add new questions. Other special features of this program include random generation of test questions, creation of alternative versions of the same test, scrambling question sequence, and test preview before printing.

TESTGEN (0-205-92672-X) The test item file is also available through TestGen EQ. This fully networkable test-generating software works with both Windows™ and Macintosh™ computers.

POWERPOINT® LECTURE SLIDES (0-205-89955-2) These Power-Point slides combine graphics and text in a colorful format to help you convey sociological principles in a visual and engaging way. Each chapter of the textbook has between fifteen and twenty-five slides that effectively communicate the key concepts in that chapter.

Supplements for the Student

STUDY GUIDE (0-205-92923-0) This complete guide helps students review and reflect on the material presented in *Society: The Basics, Twelfth Edition*. Each of the sixteen chapters in the Study Guide provides an overview of the corresponding chapter in the student text, summarizes its major topics and concepts, offers applied exercises, and features end-of-chapter tests with answers.

MYSOCLAB (0-205-89992-7) As mentioned before, MySocLab is a learning and assessment tool that enables instructors to assess student performance and adapt course content—without invest-

ing additional time or resources. MySocLab is designed with instructor flexibility in mind—you decide the extent of integration into your course, from independent self-assessment to total course management. The lab is accompanied by an instructor's manual featuring easy-to-read media grids, activities, sample syllabi, and tips for integrating technology into your course.

A Word about Language

This text has a commitment to describe the social diversity of the United States and the world. This promise carries with it the responsibility to use language thoughtfully. In most cases, the book uses the terms "African American" and "person of color" rather than the word "black." Similarly, we use the terms "Latino," "Latina," and "Hispanic" to refer to people of Spanish descent. Most tables and figures refer to "Hispanics" because this is the term the Census Bureau uses when collecting statistical data about our population.

Students should realize, however, that many individuals do not describe themselves using these terms. Although the word "Hispanic" is commonly used in the eastern part of the United States and "Latino" and the feminine form "Latina" are widely heard in the West, across the United States people of Spanish descent identify with a particular ancestral nation, whether it be Argentina, Mexico, some other Latin American country, or Spain or Portugal in Europe.

The same holds for Asian Americans. Although this term is a useful shorthand in sociological analysis, most people of Asian descent think of themselves in terms of a specific country of origin, say, Japan, the Philippines, Taiwan, or Vietnam.

In this text, the term "Native American" refers to all the inhabitants of the Americas (including Alaska and the Hawaiian Islands) whose ancestors lived here prior to the arrival of Europeans. Here again, however, most people in this broad category identify with their historical society, such as Cherokee, Hopi, Seneca, or Zuni. The term "American Indian" refers to only those Native Americans who live in the continental United States, not including Native peoples living in Alaska or Hawaii.

On a global level, this text avoids the word "American"—which literally designates two continents—to refer to just the United States. For example, referring to this country, the term "the U.S. economy" is more precise than "the American economy." This convention may seem a small point, but it implies the significant recognition that we in this country represent only one society (albeit a very important one) in the Americas.

In Appreciation

The usual practice of crediting a book to a single author hides the efforts of dozens of women and men who have helped create *Society: The Basics, Twelfth Edition*. I offer my deep and sincere thanks to the Pearson editorial team, including Yolanda de Rooy, division president; Craig Campanella, editorial director; Dickson Musslewhite, editor-in-chief; and Brita Mess, senior acquisitions editor in sociology, for their steady enthusiasm in the pursuit of both innovation and excellence.

Day-to-day work on the book is shared by the author and the production team. Barbara Reilly, Pearson production editor, is a key member of the group; indeed, if anyone "sweats the details" as much as I do, it is Barbara! Kimberlee Klesner works with me to ensure that all the data in this revision are the very latest available. Kimberlee brings enthusiasm that matches her considerable talents, and I thank her for both.

I also want to thank the members of the Pearson sales staff, the men and women who have represented this text with such enthusiasm over the years. My hat goes off especially to Brandy Dawson and Kelly May, who share responsibility for our marketing campaign.

Thanks, also, to Anne Nieglos for managing the design and to Kathleen Allain of PreMediaGlobal for managing the production process. Copy editing of the manuscript was skillfully done by Paula Bonilla and Amy Macionis.

It goes without saying that every colleague knows more about a number of topics covered in this book than the author does. For that reason, I am grateful to the hundreds of faculty and the many students who have written to me to offer comments and suggestions. I especially wish to thank the following colleagues for sharing their wisdom in ways that have improved this book over the years:

Doug Adams (Ohio State University), Kip Armstrong (Bloomsburg University), Rose Arnault (Fort Hays State University), Robert Atkins (North Seattle Community College), William Beaver (Robert Morris University), Scott Beck (Eastern Tennessee State University), Lois Benjamin (Hampton University), Philip Berg (University of Wisconsin, La Crosse), Kimberly H. Boyd (Germanna Community College), Robert Brainerd (Highland Community College), John R. Brouillette (Colorado State University), Cathryn Brubaker (DeKalb College), Brent Bruton (Iowa State University), Richard Bucher (Baltimore City Community College), Evandro Camara (Emporia State University), Bill Camp (Lucerne County Community College), Karen Campbell (Vanderbilt University), Francis N. Catano (Saint Anselm College), Harold Conway (Blinn College), Dave Conz (Arizona State University), Allison Cotton (Prairie View A&M University), Gerry Cox (Fort Hays State University), Lovberta Cross (Shelby State Community College), James A. Davis (Harvard University), Sumati Devadutt (Monroe Community College), Keith Doubt (Northeast Missouri State University), Thomas Dowdy (Oklahoma Baptist University), William Dowell (Heartland Community College), Doug Downey (Ohio State University), Denny Dubbs (Harrisburg Area Community College), Travis Eaton (Northeast Louisiana State University), Helen Rose Fuchs Ebaugh (University of Houston), John Ehle (Northern Virginia Community College), Roger Eich (Hawkeye Community College), Heather FitzGibbon (College of Wooster), Kevin Fitzpatrick (University of Alabama, Birmingham), Dona C. Fletcher (Sinclair Community College), Charles Frazier (University of Florida), Karen Lynch Frederick (Saint Anselm College), Patricia Gagné (University of Kentucky, Louisville), Pam Gaiter (Collin County Community College), Jarvis Gamble (Owens Technical College), Patricia L. Gibbs (Foothill College), Steven Goldberg (City College, City University of New York), Charlotte Gotwald (York College of Pennsylvania), Norma B. Gray (Bishop State Community College), Rhoda Greenstone (DeVry Institute), Jeffrey Hahn (Mount Union College), Harry Hale (Northeast Louisiana State University), Dean Haledjian (Northern Virginia Community College), Dick Haltin (Jefferson Community College), Marvin Hannah (Milwaukee Area Technical College), Chad Hanson (Casper College), Charles Harper (Creighton University), Rudy Harris (Des Moines Area Community College), Michael Hart (Broward College), Jennifer Heneghan (Jones College), Gary Hodge (Collin County Community College), Elizabeth A. Hoisington (Heartland Community College), Kathleen Holmes (Darton College), Sara Horsfall (Stephen F. Austin State University), Dale Howard (NorthWest Arkansas Community College), Peter Hruschka (Ohio Northern University), Glenna Huls (Camden County College), Jeanne Humble (Lexington Community College), Cynthia Imanaka (Seattle Central Community College), Craig Jenkins (Ohio State University), Sam Joseph (Lucerne County Community College), Ed Kain (Southwestern University), Audra Kallimanis (Mount Olive College), Paul Kamolnick (Eastern Tennessee State University), Irwin Kantor (Middlesex County College), Judi Kessler (Monmouth College), Thomas Korllos (Kent State University), Rita Krasnow (Virginia Western Community College), Donald Kraybill (Elizabethtown College), Howard Kurtz (Oklahoma City University), Michael Lacy (Colorado State University), Tom Lake (Dutchess Community College), Carol A. Landry (Oakland Community College); George Lowe (Texas Tech University), Don Luidens (Hope College), Larry Lyon (Baylor University), Li-Chen Ma (Lamar University), Setma Maddox (Texas Wesleyan University), Errol Magidson (Richard J. Daley College), Kooros Mahmoudi (Northern Arizona University), Mehrdad Mashayekhi (Georgetown University), Allan Mazur (Syracuse University), Karen E. B. McCue (University of New Mexico, Albuquerque), Rodney A. McDanel (Benedictine University), Doug McDowell (Rider University), Ronald McGriff, (College of the Sequoias), Meredith McGuire (Trinity College), Karla McLucas (Bennett College), Lisa McMinn (Wheaton College), Jack Melhorn (Emporia State University), Will Melick (Kenyon College), Ken Miller (Drake University), Linda Miller (Queens University of Charlotte), Richard Miller (Navarro College), Joe Morolla (Virginia Commonwealth University), Peter B. Morrill (Bronx Community College), Craig Nauman (Madison Area Technical College), Dina B. Neal (Vernon College), Jody Nedley-Newcomb (Southwestern Community College), Therese Nemec (Fox Valley Technical College), Joong-Hwan Oh (Hunter College), Richard Perkins (Houghton College), Marla A. Perry (Iowa State University), Anne Peterson (Columbus State Community College), Marvin Pippert (Roanoke College), Lauren Pivnik (Monroe Community College), Scott Potter (Marion Technical College), Nevel Razak (Fort Hays State College), Lee Reineck (Stautzenberger College), George Reim (Cheltenham High School), Virginia Reynolds (Indiana University of Pennsylvania), Laurel Richardson (Ohio State University), Rebecca Riehm (Jefferson Community College), Heather Rimes (Florida Southern College-Orlando), Keith Roberts (Hanover College), Ellen Rosengarten (Sinclair Community College), Frederick Roth (Marshall University), Mark Rubinfeld (Westminster College, Salt Lake City), Paulina Ruf (University of Tampa), Bill Ruth (Paris Junior College); Michael Ryan (Dodge City Community College), Marvin Scott (Butler University), Ray Scupin (Linderwood College), Steve Severin (Kellogg Community College), Tim Sexton (Chippewa Valley Technical College), Harry Sherer (Irvine Valley College), Walt

Shirley (Sinclair Community College), Anson Shupe (Indiana University–Purdue University at Fort Wayne), Brenda Silverman (Onondaga Community College), Ree Simpkins (Missouri Southern State University), Scott Simpson (Arkansas Northeastern College), Glen Sims (Glendale Community College), Toni Sims (University of Louisiana, Lafayette), Sherry Smith (Georgia Perimeter College-Clarkston Campus), Sylvia Kenig Snyder (Coastal Carolina University), Thomas Soltis (Westmoreland Community College), Nancy Sonleitner (University of Oklahoma), Leslie Stanley-Stevens (Tarleton State University), Larry Stern (Collin County Community College), Randy Ston (Oakland Community College), Richard Sweeney (Modesto Junior College), Vickie H. Taylor (Danville Community College), Don Thomas (Ohio State University), Mark J. Thomas (Madison Area Technical College), Len Tompos (Lorain County Community College), Christopher Vanderpool (Michigan State University), Phyllis Watts (Tiffin University), Murray Webster (University of North Carolina, Charlotte), Debbie White (Collin County Community College), Marilyn Wilmeth (Iowa University), Stuart Wright (Lamar University), William Yoels (University of Alabama, Birmingham), Dan Yutze (Taylor University), Wayne Zapatek (Tarrant County Community College), Jin-kun Wei (Brevard Community College), William Wood (California State University Fullerton), Amy Wong (San Diego State University), and Frank Zulke (Harold Washington College).

In addition, I am greatful to the following people who have reviewed MySocLab:

Sharon Bjorkman (Pikes Peak Community College), Sonia Brown (College of Lake County), Gina Carreno-Lukasik (Florida Atlantic University), Brenda Chaney (Ohio State University at Marion), Susan Claxton (Georgia Highlands College), Joanna Cohen (Temple University), Marian Colello (Bucks County Community College), Theodore Cohen (Ohio Wesleyan University), David Curtis (Park University), Rose De Luca (Emmanuel College), Silvio Dobry (Hostos Community College), Mark Eckel (McHenry County College), Roberta Farber (Stern College, Yeshiva University), Karen Fischer (Finger Lakes Community College), Tammie Foltz (Des Moines Area Community College), Mara Fryar (Wake Technical Community College), Bonnie Galloway (Rider University), Jeff Gingerich (Cabrini College), Karen Harrington (North Central University), Jennifer Haskin (Washtenaw Community College), Pati Hendrickson (Tarleton State University), Marta Henriksen (Central New Mexico Community College), Alexander Hernandez (Boston College), Jennifer Holland (Clemson University), Kristin Holster (Dean College), Erica Hunter (University at Albany), Daniel Jasper (Moravian College), Shelly Jeffy (University of North Carolina Greensboro), Art Jipson (University of Dayton), Faye Jones (Mississippi Gulf Coast Community College JC Campus), Peter Kaufman (SUNY New Paltz), Shirley Keeton (American University of Afghanistan), Lloyd Klein (York College, CUNY), Mike Klemp-North (Northcentral Technical College), Brian Klockc (SUNY Plattsburgh), Amy Lane (Kalamazoo College), Mitchell Mackinem (Claflin University), Aubrey Maples-Saus (Wright State University), Amanda Miller (University of Central Oklahoma), Monica Miller (Kirkwood Community College), Richard Miller (Missouri Southern State University), Zachary Miner (University at Albany), Lisa Munoz (Hawkeye Community College), Michael O'Connor (Hawkeye Community College), Aurea Osgood (Winona State University), Leon Ragonesi (CSU Dominguez Hills), Carolyn Read (Copiah-Lincoln Junior College), Paul Rhoads (Williams Baptist College), Rebecca Riehm (Jefferson Community College), Daniel Roddick (Rio Hondo College), Judith Rosenstein (United States Naval Academy), Sharon Sarles (Austin Community College), Leslie Scoby (Sabetha High School), Greg Scott (Kuyper College), Laurence Segall (Southern Ct. State University), Mark Sherry (The University of Toledo), Steve Shuecraft (St Charles Community College), Tamara Sniezek (CSU Stanislaus), Karrie Snyder (Northwestern University), LaRoyce Sublett (Georgia Perimeter College), Donna Sullivan (Marshall University), Jennifer Sullivan (Mitchell College), Connie Veldink (Everett Community College), Yvonne Vissing (Salem State College), Stan Weeber (McNeese State University), Jene' Wilkerson (Paul D. Camp Community College), Carlos Zeisel (North Shore Community College).

Finally, I dedicate this twelfth edition to the memory of my father, John Joseph Macionis (1916–2012). Dad, you taught me so many things, including the importance of hard work, the need to listen to people, and always, to do whatever you can to help others. You touched so many lives and your achievements were matched by your humility. May you find peace on your journey!

With best wishes to my colleagues and with love to all,

John J. Macionis

1 Sociology: Perspective, Theory, and Method

Learning Objectives

Remember the definitions of the key terms highlighted in boldfaced type throughout the chapter, including the sociological perspective and sociology's major theoretical approaches.

Understand the sociological perspective and how it differs from what we think of as "common sense." Also understand the importance of a global perspective.

Apply sociology's theoretical approaches to specific social patterns, such as sports. Identify the benefits of sociological thinking to your personal life and your career.

Analyze why researchers decide to use a particular research method or sometimes combine methods to answer their research questions.

Evaluate the strengths and weaknesses of a researcher's methodology when reading about any sociological study.

Create the ability to critically assess all the information that you encounter every day by gaining a thorough understanding of the sociological perspective and the logic of research.

CHAPTER OVERVIEW

You are about to begin a course that could change your life. Sociology is a new and exciting way of understanding the world around you. It will change what you see, how you think about the world, and it may well change how you think about yourself. Chapter 1 of this text introduces the discipline of sociology. The most important skill to gain from this course is the ability to use what we call the *sociological perspective*. This chapter next introduces *sociological theory*, which helps us build understanding from what we see using the sociological perspective. The chapter continues by explaining how sociologists "do" sociology, describing three general approaches to conducting research and four specific methods of data collection. ■

From the moment he first saw Tonya step off the subway train, Dwayne knew she was "the one." As the two walked up the stairs to the street and entered the building where they were both taking classes, Dwayne tried to get Tonya to stop and talk. At first, she ignored him. But after class, they met again, and she agreed to join him for coffee. That was three months ago. Today, they are engaged to be married.

If you were to ask people in the United States, "Why do couples like Tonya and Dwayne marry?" it is a safe bet that almost everyone would reply, "People marry because they fall in love." Most of us find it hard to imagine a happy marriage without love; for the same reason, when people fall in love, we expect them to think about getting married.

But is the decision about whom to marry really just a matter of personal feelings? There is plenty of evidence to show that if love is the key to marriage, Cupid's arrow is carefully aimed by the society around us.

Society has many "rules" about whom we should and should not marry. In all states but Massachusetts, Vermont, New Hampshire, Connecticut, Iowa, New York, Washington, Maryland, and also the District of Columbia, the law rules out half the population, banning people from marrying someone of the same sex, even if the couple is deeply in love. But there are other rules as well. Sociologists have found that people, especially when they are young, are very likely to marry someone close in age, and people of all ages typically marry someone of the same race, of similar social class background, of much the same level of education, and with a similar degree of physical attractiveness (Chapter 13, "Family and Religion," gives details). People end up making choices about whom to marry, but society narrows the field long before they do.

When it comes to love, our decisions do not simply result from what philosophers call "free will." Sociology teaches us that the social world guides our life choices in much the same way that the seasons influence our choice of clothing.

The Sociological Perspective

● **Understand**

Sociology is *the systematic study of human society*. At the heart of this discipline is a distinctive point of view called the *sociological perspective*.

Seeing the General in the Particular

One good way to define the **sociological perspective** is *seeing the general in the particular* (Berger, 1963). This definition tells us that sociologists look for *general* patterns in the behavior of *particular* people. Although every individual is unique, society shapes the lives of people in various *categories* (such as children and adults, women and men, the rich and the poor) very differently. We begin to see the world sociologically by realizing how the general categories into which we fall shape our particular life experiences.

 **Watch** the video "Sociologists at Work" on **mysoclab.com**

We can easily see the power of society over the individual by imagining how different our lives would be had we been born in place of any of these children from, respectively, Kenya, Ethiopia, Myanmar, Peru, South Korea, and India.

For example, does social class position affect what women look for in a spouse? In a classic study of women's hopes for their marriages, Lillian Rubin (1976) found that higher-income women typically expected the men they married to be sensitive to others, to talk readily, and to share feelings and experiences. Lower-income women, she found, had very different expectations and were looking for men who did not drink too much, were not violent, and held steady jobs. Obviously, what women expect in a marriage partner has a lot to do with social class position.

This text explores the power of society to guide our actions, thoughts, and feelings. We may think that marriage results simply from the personal feeling of love. Yet the sociological perspective shows us that factors such as our sex, age, race, and social class guide our selection of a partner. It might be more accurate to think of love as a feeling we have for others who match up with what society teaches us to want in a mate.

Seeing the Strange in the Familiar

At first, using the sociological perspective may seem like *seeing the strange in the familiar*. Consider how you might react if someone were to say to you, "You fit all the right categories, which means you would make a wonderful spouse!" We are used to thinking that people fall in love and decide to marry based on personal feeling and the things that make us unique. But the sociological perspective reveals to us the initially strange idea that society shapes what we think and do in patterned ways.

Seeing Society in Our Everyday Lives

The society in which we live has a lot to do with our everyday choices in food, clothing, music, schooling, jobs, and just about everything else. Even the most "personal" decisions we make turn out to be shaped by society. To see how society shapes personal choices, consider the decision by women to bear children. Like the selection of a mate, the choice of having a child—or how many children to have— would seem to be very personal. Yet there are social patterns here as well. As shown in Global Map 1–1 on page 4, the average woman in the United States has just about two children during her lifetime. In Guatemala, however, the "choice" is about three; in Kenya, about four; in Nigeria, about five; in Afghanistan, about six; and in Niger, almost seven (United Nations Development Programme, 2011).

---

sociology the systematic study of human society

sociological perspective sociology's special point of view that sees general patterns of society in the lives of particular people

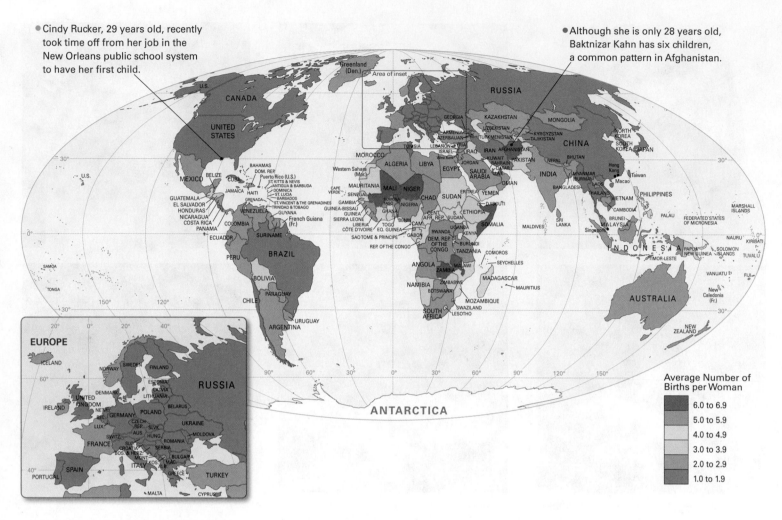

Cindy Rucker, 29 years old, recently took time off from her job in the New Orleans public school system to have her first child.

Although she is only 28 years old, Baktnizar Kahn has six children, a common pattern in Afghanistan.

Average Number of Births per Woman

	6.0 to 6.9
	5.0 to 5.9
	4.0 to 4.9
	3.0 to 3.9
	2.0 to 2.9
	1.0 to 1.9

Window on the World

GLOBAL MAP 1–1 Women's Childbearing in Global Perspective

Is childbearing simply a matter of personal choice? A look around the world shows that it is not. In general, women living in poor countries have many more children than women in rich nations. Can you point to some of the reasons for this global disparity? In simple terms, such differences mean that if you had been born into another society (whether you are female or male), your life might be quite different from what it is now.

Sources: Data from Martin et al. (2011), Population Reference Bureau (2011), United Nations Development Programme (2011).

What accounts for these striking differences? Because poor countries provide women with less schooling and fewer economic opportunities, women's lives are centered in the home, and they are less likely to use contraception. The strange truth is that society has much to do with the familiar decisions that women and men make about childbearing.

Another example of the power of society to shape even our most private choices comes from the study of suicide. What could be more personal than the lonely decision to end your own life? Emile Durkheim (1858–1917), one of sociology's pioneers, showed that even here, social forces are at work.

Examining official records in and around his native France, Durkheim (1966, orig. 1897) found that some categories of people were more likely than others to take their own lives. He found that men, Protestants, wealthy people, and the unmarried each had much higher suicide rates than women, Catholics and Jews, the poor, and married people. Durkheim explained these differences in terms of *social integration:* Categories of people with strong social ties had low suicide rates, and more individualistic people had high suicide rates.

In Durkheim's time, men had much more freedom than women. But despite its advantages, freedom weakens social ties and thus increases the risk of suicide. Likewise, more individualistic Protestants were more likely to commit suicide than more tradition-bound Catholics and Jews, whose rituals encourage stronger social ties. The wealthy have much more freedom than the poor—but once again, at the cost of a higher suicide rate.

A century later, Durkheim's analysis still holds true. Figure 1–1 shows suicide rates for four categories of the U.S. population. In 2008, there were 13.3 recorded suicides for every 100,000 white people, which is more than twice the rate for African Americans (5.2). For both races, suicide was more common among men than among women. White men (21.2) are almost four times as likely as white women (5.5) to take their own lives. Among African Americans, the rate for men (9.1) was more than five times that for women (1.6) (Miniño et al., 2011). Applying Durkheim's logic, the higher suicide rate among white people and men reflects their greater wealth and freedom, just as the lower rate among women

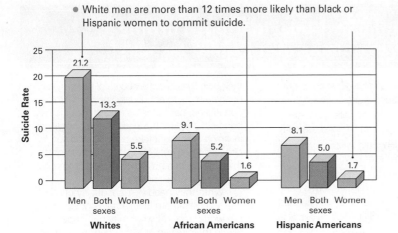

● White men are more than 12 times more likely than black or Hispanic women to commit suicide.

Suicide Rate

Whites: Men 21.2, Both sexes 13.3, Women 5.5
African Americans: Men 9.1, Both sexes 5.2, Women 1.6
Hispanic Americans: Men 8.1, Both sexes 5.0, Women 1.7

Diversity Snapshot

FIGURE 1–1 Rate of Death by Suicide, by Race and Sex, for the United States

Suicide rates are higher for white people than for black and Hispanic people. Among all categories of the population, rates are several times higher for men than for women. Rates indicate the number of deaths by suicide for every 100,000 people in each category for 2008.

Source: Miniño et al. (2011).

and people of color reflects their limited social choices. Just as Durkheim did a century ago, we can see general sociological patterns in the personal actions of particular individuals.

Seeing Sociologically: Marginality and Crisis

Anyone can learn to see the world using the sociological perspective. But two situations help people see clearly how society shapes individual lives: living on the margins of society and living through a social crisis.

Living on the Edge

From time to time, everyone feels isolated, as if we are living on the edge. For some categories of people, however, being an *outsider*—not part of the dominant category—is an everyday experience. The greater people's social marginality, the better they are able to use the sociological perspective.

For example, no African American grows up in the United States without understanding the importance of race in shaping people's lives. Songs by rapper Jay-Z express the anger he feels, not only about the poverty he experienced growing up but also about the many innocent lives lost to violence in a society of such wide racial disparities. His lyrics, and those of many similar artists,

People with the greatest privileges tend to see individuals as responsible for their own lives. Those at the margins of society, by contrast, are quick to see how race, class, and gender can create disadvantages. The rap artist Jay-Z has given voice to the frustration felt by many African Americans living in this country's inner cities.

which are spread throughout the world by the mass media, show that some people of color—especially African Americans living in the inner city—feel that their hopes and dreams are crushed by society. But white people, as the dominant majority, think less often about race and the privileges it provides, believing that race affects only people of color and not themselves, despite the privileges provided by being white in a multiracial society. People at the margins of social life, including not only racial minorities but also women, gays and lesbians, people with disabilities, and the very old, are aware of social patterns that others rarely think about. To become better at using the sociological perspective, we must step back from our familiar routines and look at our own lives with a new curiosity.

Periods of Crisis

Periods of rapid change or crisis make everyone feel a little off balance, encouraging us to use the sociological perspective. The sociologist C. Wright Mills (1959) illustrated this idea using the Great Depression of the 1930s. As the unemployment rate soared to 25 percent, people without jobs could not help but see general social forces at work in their particular lives. Rather than saying, "Something is wrong with me; I can't find a job," they took a sociological approach and realized, "The economy has collapsed; there are no jobs to be found!" Mills believed that using what he called the "sociological imagination" in this way helps people understand their society and how it affects their own lives. The Seeing Sociology in Everyday Life box on page 6 takes a closer look.

The Importance of a Global Perspective

● **Understand**

As new information technology draws even the farthest reaches of the planet closer together, many academic disciplines are taking a **global perspective,** *the study of the larger world and our society's place in it.* What is the importance of a global perspective for sociology?

First, global awareness is a logical extension of the sociological perspective. Sociology shows us that our place in society shapes our life experiences. It stands to reason, then, that the position of our society in the larger world system affects everyone in the United States.

The world's 195 nations can be divided into three broad categories according to their level of economic development (see Global Map 9–1 on page 227). **High-income countries** are the *nations with the highest overall standards of living.* The seventy-two countries in this category include the United States and Canada, Argentina, the nations of Western Europe, Israel, Saudi Arabia, Japan, and Australia. Taken together, these nations generate most of the world's goods and services, and the people who live in them own

The Sociological Imagination: Turning Personal Problems into Public Issues

As Mike opened the envelope, he felt the tightness in his chest. The letter he dreaded was in his hands—his job was finished at the end of the day. After eleven years! Years in which he had worked hard, sure that he would move up in the company. All those hopes and dreams were now suddenly gone. Mike felt like a failure. Anger at himself—for not having worked even harder, for having wasted so many years of his life in what had turned out to be a dead-end job—swelled up inside him.

But as he returned to his workstation to pack his things, Mike soon realized that he was not alone. Almost all his colleagues in the tech support group had received the same letter. Their jobs were moving to India, where the company was able to provide telephone tech support for less than half the cost of employing workers in California.

By the end of the weekend, Mike was sitting in the living room with a dozen other ex-employees. Comparing notes and sharing ideas, they now realized that they were simply a few of the victims of a massive outsourcing of jobs that is part of what analysts call the "globalization of the economy."

In good times and bad, the power of the sociological perspective lies in making sense of our individual lives. We see that many of our particular problems (and our successes, as well) are not unique to us but are the result of larger social trends. Half a century ago, the sociologist C. Wright Mills pointed to the power of what he called the sociological imagination to help us understand everyday events. As he saw it, society—not people's personal failings—is the main cause of poverty and other social problems. By turning personal problems into public issues, the sociological imagination also is the key to bringing people together to create needed change. In this excerpt,* Mills (1959:3–5) explains the need for a sociological imagination:

> When society becomes industrialized, a peasant becomes a worker; a feudal lord is liquidated or becomes a businessman. When classes rise or fall, a man is employed or unemployed; when the rate of investment goes up or down, a man takes new heart or goes broke. When wars happen, an insurance salesman becomes a rocket launcher; a store clerk, a radar man; a wife lives alone; a child grows up without a father. Neither the life of an individual nor the history of a society can be understood without understanding both.
>
> Yet men do not usually define the troubles they endure in terms of historical change. . . . The well-being they enjoy, they do not usually impute to the big ups and downs of the society in which they live. Seldom aware of the intricate connection between the patterns of their own lives and the course of world history, ordinary men do not usually know what this connection means for the kind of men they are becoming and for the kinds of history-making in which they might take part. They do not possess the quality of mind essential to grasp the interplay of men and society, of biography and history, of self and world. . . .
>
> What they need . . . is a quality of mind that will help them [see] what is going on in the world and . . . what may be happening within themselves. It is this quality . . . [that] may be called the sociological imagination.

What Do You Think?

1. As Mills sees it, how are personal troubles different from public issues? Explain this difference in terms of what happened to Mike in the story above.

2. Living in the United States, why do we often blame ourselves for the personal problems we face?

3. How can using the sociological imagination give us the power to change the world?

---

*In this excerpt, Mills uses "man" and male pronouns to apply to all people. As far as gender is concerned, even this outspoken critic of society reflected the conventional writing practices of his time.

---

most of the planet's wealth. Economically speaking, people in these countries are very well off, not because they are smarter or work harder than anyone else but because they were lucky enough to be born in a rich region of the world.

A second category is **middle-income countries,** *nations with a standard of living about average for the world as a whole.* People in any of these seventy nations—many of the countries of Eastern Europe, South Africa and some other African nations, and almost all of Latin America and Asia—are as likely to live in rural villages as in cities and to walk or ride tractors, scooters, bicycles, or animals as they are to drive automobiles. On average, they receive eight years of schooling. Most middle-income countries also have considerable social inequality within their own borders, meaning that some people are extremely rich (members of the business elite in nations across North Africa, for example) but many more lack safe housing and adequate nutrition (people living in the shanty settlements that surround Lima, Peru, or Mumbai, India).

The remaining fifty-three nations of the world are **low-income countries,** *nations with a low standard of living in which most people are poor.* Most of the poorest countries in the world are in Africa, and a few are in Asia. Here again, a few people are very rich, but the majority struggle to get by with poor housing, unsafe water, too little food, and perhaps most serious of all, little chance to improve their lives.

Chapter 9 ("Global Stratification") explains the causes and consequences of global wealth and poverty. But every chapter of this text makes comparisons between the United States and other nations for five reasons:

1. **Where we live shapes the lives we lead.** As you saw in Global Map 1–1 on page 4, women living in rich and poor countries have very different lives, as suggested by the number of children they have. To understand ourselves and appreciate how others live, we must understand something about how countries differ, which is one good reason to pay attention to the global maps found throughout this text.

---

global perspective the study of the larger world and our society's place in it

high-income countries the nations with the highest overall standards of living	**middle-income countries** nations with a standard of living about average for the world as a whole	**low-income countries** nations with a low standard of living in which most people are poor

2. **Societies throughout the world are increasingly interconnected.** Historically, people in the United States took only passing note of the countries beyond our own borders. In recent decades, however, the United States and the rest of the world have become linked as never before. Electronic technology now transmits pictures, sounds, and written documents around the globe in seconds.

One effect of this new technology is that people all over the world now share many of the same tastes in food, clothing, movies, and music. Rich countries such as the United States influence other nations, whose people are ever more likely to gobble up our Big Macs and Whoppers, dance to the latest hip-hop music, and speak English.

But the larger world also has an impact on us. We all know the contributions of famous immigrants such as Arnold Schwarzenegger (who came to the United States from Austria) and Gloria Estefan (who came from Cuba). About 1.25 million immigrants enter the United States each year, bringing their skills and talents, along with their fashions and foods, greatly increasing the racial and cultural diversity of this country (U.S. Department of Homeland Security, 2011; Hoefer et al., 2011).

3. **What happens in the rest of the world affects life here in the United States.** As trade has increased across national boundaries, the world has developed a global economy. Large corporations make and market goods worldwide. Stock traders in New York pay close attention to the financial markets in Tokyo and Hong Kong even as wheat farmers in Kansas watch the price of grain in the former Soviet republic of Georgia. Because most new U.S. jobs involve international trade, greater global understanding has never been more important.

In the last several decades, the power and wealth of the United States has been challenged by what some analysts have called "the rise of the rest," meaning the increasing power and wealth of the rest of the world. As nations such as Brazil, Russia, India, and China have expanded their economic production, many of the manufacturing and also office jobs that once supported a large share of our labor force have moved overseas. One consequence of this trend is that, as the country struggles to climb out of the recent recession, the unemployment rate remains high and may stay high for years to come. As many analysts see it, our current "jobless recovery" is one result of a new global economy that is reshaping societies all around the world (Zakeria, 2008).

4. **Many social problems that we face in the United States are far more serious elsewhere.** Poverty is a serious problem in the United States, but as Chapter 9 ("Global Stratification") explains, poverty in Latin America, Africa, and Asia is both more common and more serious. In the same way, although women have lower social standing than men in the United States, gender inequality is much greater in the world's poor countries.

5. **Thinking globally helps us learn more about ourselves.** We cannot walk the streets of a distant city without thinking about what it means to live in the United States. Comparing life in various settings often leads to unexpected lessons. For instance, in Chapter 9, we visit a squatter settlement in Chennai, India. There, despite desperate lack of basic material goods, people thrive in the love and support of family members. Why, then, are so many poor people in the United States angry and alone? Are material things—so central to our definition of a "rich" life—the best way to measure human well-being?

In sum, in an increasingly interconnected world, we can understand our way of life and ourselves only to the extent that we understand others and the societies in which they live. Sociology is an invitation to learn a new way of looking at the world around us. But is this invitation worth accepting? What are the benefits of applying the sociological perspective?

Applying the Sociological Perspective

 Apply

Applying the sociological perspective is useful in many ways. First, sociology is at work guiding many of the laws and policies that shape our lives. Second, on an individual level, making use of the sociological perspective leads to important personal growth and expanded awareness. Third, studying sociology is excellent preparation for the world of work.

Sociology and Public Policy

Sociologists have helped shape public policy—the laws and regulations that guide how people in communities live and work—in countless ways, from racial desegregation and school busing to laws regulating divorce. For example, in her study of how divorce affects people's income, the sociologist Lenore Weitzman (1985, 1996) discovered that women who leave marriages typically experience a dramatic loss of income. Recognizing this fact, many states passed laws that have increased women's claims to marital property and enforced fathers' obligations to provide support for women raising their children.

Sociology and Personal Growth

By applying the sociological perspective, we are likely to become more active and aware and to think more critically in our everyday lives. Using sociology pays off in four ways:

1. **The sociological perspective helps us assess the truth of "common sense."** We all take many things for granted, but that does not make them true. One example is the idea that we are free individuals who are personally responsible for our own lives. If we think we decide our own fate, we may be quick to praise successful people as superior and consider others with fewer achievements personally deficient. A sociological approach, by contrast, encourages us to ask whether common beliefs are really true and, to the extent that they are not, why they are so widely held.

2. **The sociological perspective helps us see the opportunities and constraints in our lives.** Sociological thinking leads us to see that in the game of life, we have a say in how to play our cards, but it is society that deals us the hand. The more we understand the game, the better players we will be. Sociology helps us learn more about the world so that we can pursue our goals more effectively.

3. **The sociological perspective empowers us to be active participants in our society.** The better we understand how society operates, the more effective citizens we become. As C. Wright Mills explained in the box on page 6, it is the sociological perspective that turns a private problem (such as being out of work) into a public issue (a lack of good jobs). As we come to see how society affects us, we may decide to support society as it is, or we may set out with others to change it.

4. **The sociological perspective helps us live in a diverse world.** North Americans represent just 5 percent of the world's population, and as the remaining chapters of this book explain, many of the other 95 percent live very differently than we do. Still, like people everywhere, we tend to view our own way of life as "right," "natural," and "better." The sociological perspective prompts us to think critically about the relative strengths and weaknesses of all ways of life, including our own.

Careers: The "Sociology Advantage"

Most students at colleges and universities today are very interested in getting a good job. A background in sociology is excellent preparation for the working world. Of course, completing a bachelor's degree in sociology is the right choice for people who decide they would like to go on to graduate work and eventually become a secondary school teacher, college professor, or researcher in this field. Throughout the United States, tens of thousands of men and women teach sociology in universities, colleges, and high schools. But just as many professional sociologists work as researchers for government agencies or private foundations and businesses, gathering important information on social behavior and carrying out evaluation research. In today's cost-conscious world, agencies and companies want to be sure that the products, programs, and policies they create get the job done at the lowest cost. Sociologists, especially those with advanced research skills, are in high demand for this kind of work (Deutscher, 1999).

In addition, a smaller but increasing number of people work as clinical sociologists. These women and men work, much as clinical psychologists do, with the goal of improving the lives of troubled clients. A basic

difference is that sociologists focus on difficulties not in the personality but in the individual's web of social relationships.

But sociology is not just for people who want to be sociologists. People who work in criminal justice—including jobs in police departments, probation offices, and corrections facilities—gain the "sociology advantage" by learning what categories of people are most at risk of becoming criminals or victims, how effective various policing policies and programs are at preventing crime, and why people turn to crime in the first place. Similarly, people who work in the health care field—including physicians, nurses, and technicians—also gain a sociology advantage by learning about patterns of health and illness within the population, as well as how factors such as race, ethnicity, gender, and social class affect human health.

The American Sociological Association (2002, 2011a, 2011b) reports that sociology is also excellent preparation for jobs in dozens of fields, including advertising, banking, business, education, government, journalism, law, public relations, and social work. In almost any type of work, success depends on understanding how various categories of people differ in beliefs, family patterns, and other ways of life. Unless you have a job that never involves dealing with people, you should consider the workplace benefits of learning more sociology.

The Origins of Sociology

 Analyze

Like the "choices" people make, major historical events rarely just "happen." Even sociology itself is the result of powerful social forces.

Social Change and Sociology

Striking changes in Europe during the eighteenth and nineteenth centuries made people think more about society and their place in it, spurring the development of sociology. Three kinds of change were especially important in the development of sociology: the rise of a factory-based economy, the explosive growth of cities, and new ideas about democracy and political rights.

A New Industrial Economy

During the Middle Ages, most people in Europe plowed fields near their homes or engaged in small-scale *manufacturing* (a term derived from Latin words meaning "to make by hand"). By the end of the eighteenth century, inventors used new sources of energy—the power of moving water and then steam—to operate large machines in mills and factories. As a result, instead of laboring at home or in tightly knit groups, workers became part of a large and anonymous labor force, under the control of strangers who owned the factories. This change in the system of production took people away from their homes, weakening the traditions that had guided community life for centuries.

The Growth of Cities

Across Europe, landowners took part in what historians call the *enclosure movement*—they fenced off more

---

Just about every job in today's economy involves working with people. For this reason, studying sociology is good preparation for your future career. In what ways does having "people skills" help police officers perform their job?

and more farmland to create grazing areas for sheep, the source of wool for the thriving textile mills. Without land, countless tenant farmers had little choice but to head to the cities in search of work in the new factories.

As cities grew larger, these urban migrants faced many social problems, including pollution, crime, and homelessness. Moving through streets crowded with strangers, they faced a new, impersonal social world.

Political Change

Economic development and the growth of cities also brought new ways of thinking. In the writings of Thomas Hobbes (1588–1679), John Locke (1632–1704), and Adam Smith (1723–1790), we see a shift in focus from people's moral duties to God and king to the pursuit of self-interest. Philosophers now spoke of *personal liberty* and *individual rights.* Echoing these sentiments, our own Declaration of Independence clearly states that each citizen has "certain unalienable rights," including "life, liberty, and the pursuit of happiness."

The French Revolution, which began in 1789, was an even greater break with political and social tradition. As the French social analyst Alexis de Tocqueville (1805–1859) declared, the change in society in the wake of the French Revolution amounted to "nothing short of the regeneration of the whole human race" (1955:13, orig. 1856).

A New Awareness of Society

Huge factories, exploding cities, and a new spirit of individualism— these changes combined to make people more aware of their surroundings. The new discipline of sociology was born in England, France, and Germany—precisely the countries where these changes were greatest.

Science and Sociology

Throughout history, the nature of society has fascinated people, including the brilliant philosopher K'ung Fu-tzu, or Confucius (551–479 B.C.E.), in China and the Greek philosophers Plato (c. 427–347 B.C.E.) and Aristotle (384–322 B.C.E.).[1] Later, the Roman emperor Marcus Aurelius (121–180), the medieval thinkers Saint Thomas Aquinas (c. 1225–1274) and Christine de Pizan (c. 1363–1431), and the great English playwright William Shakespeare (1564–1616) wrote about the workings of society.

Yet these thinkers were more interested in imagining the ideal society than they were in studying society as it really was. It was the

What we see depends on our point of view. When gazing at the stars, lovers see romance, but scientists see thermal reactions. How does using the sociological perspective change what we see in the world around us?

French social thinker Auguste Comte (1798–1857) who coined the term *sociology* in 1838 to describe this new way of thinking. This makes sociology among the youngest of the academic disciplines— far newer than history, physics, or economics, for example.

Comte (1975, orig. 1851–54) saw sociology as the product of three stages of historical development. During the earliest *theological stage,* from the beginning of human history up to the end of the European Middle Ages about 1350 C.E., people took the religious view that society expressed God's will.

With the dawn of the Renaissance in the fifteenth century, Comte explained, the theological stage gave way to a *metaphysical stage* in which people came to see society as a natural rather than a supernatural phenomenon. The English philosopher Thomas Hobbes (1588–1679), for example, suggested that society reflected not the perfection of God so much as the failings of a selfish human nature.

What Comte called the *scientific stage* began with the work of early scientists such as the Polish astronomer Copernicus (1473–1543), the Italian astronomer and physicist Galileo (1564–1642), and the English physicist and mathematician Isaac Newton (1642–1727). Comte's contribution came in applying the scientific approach—first used to study the physical world—to the study of society.[2]

Comte's approach is called **positivism**, *a scientific approach to knowledge based on "positive" facts as opposed to mere speculation.* Comte thought that knowledge based on tradition or metaphysics was really only speculation. A positivist approach to knowledge, however, is based on *science.* As a positivist, Comte believed that society operates according to certain laws, just as the physical world operates according to gravity and other laws of nature. Comte believed that by using science, people could come to understand the laws not only of the physical world but of society as well.

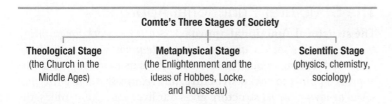

Comte's Three Stages of Society

Theological Stage	Metaphysical Stage	Scientific Stage
(the Church in the Middle Ages)	(the Enlightenment and the ideas of Hobbes, Locke, and Rousseau)	(physics, chemistry, sociology)

---

[1]The abbreviation B.C.E. means "before the common era." We use this throughout the text instead of the traditional B.C. ("before Christ") to reflect the religious diversity of our society. Similarly, in place of the traditional A.D. (*anno Domini*, or "in the year of our Lord"), we use the abbreviation C.E. ("common era").

[2]Illustrating Comte's stages, the ancient Greeks and Romans viewed the planets as gods; Renaissance metaphysical thinkers saw them as astral influences (giving rise to astrology); by the time of Galileo, scientists understood planets as natural objects moving according to natural laws.

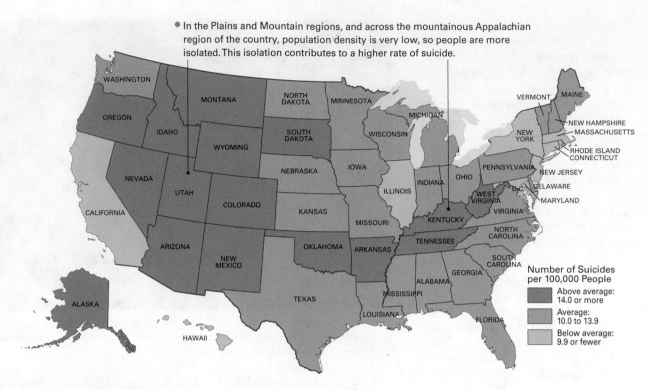

In the Plains and Mountain regions, and across the mountainous Appalachian region of the country, population density is very low, so people are more isolated. This isolation contributes to a higher rate of suicide.

Number of Suicides per 100,000 People

- Above average: 14.0 or more
- Average: 10.0 to 13.9
- Below average: 9.9 or fewer

Seeing Ourselves

NATIONAL MAP 1–1 Suicide Rates across the United States

This map shows which states have high, average, and low suicide rates. Look for patterns. By and large, high suicide rates occur where people live far apart from one another. More densely populated states have low suicide rates. Do these data support or contradict Durkheim's theory of suicide? Why?

 Explore the relationship between population density and suicide in your own state and across the United States on **mysoclab.com**

Source: Centers for Disease Control and Prevention (2011).

By the beginning of the twentieth century, sociology had taken hold in the United States and showed the influence of Comte's ideas. Today, most sociologists continue to consider science a crucial part of sociology, but we now realize that human behavior is far more complex than the movement of planets. We are creatures of imagination and spontaneity, so human behavior can never be explained by any rigid "laws of society." In addition, early sociologists such as Karl Marx (1818–1883) were troubled by the striking inequalities of industrial society. They hoped that the new discipline of sociology would not just help us understand society but also lead to change toward greater social justice.

Sociological Theory

● Apply

The desire to translate observations into understanding brings us to the important part of sociology known as *theory*. A **theory** is *a statement of how and why specific facts are related*. The job of sociological theory is to explain social behavior in the real world. For example, recall Durkheim's theory that categories of people with low social integration (men, Protestants, the wealthy, and the unmarried) are at higher risk of suicide.

Sociologists conduct research to test and refine their theories. National Map 1–1 shows the suicide rates for each of the fifty states and gives you a chance to do some theorizing of your own.

In deciding which theory to use, sociologists face two basic questions: What issues should we study? And how should we connect the facts? Making a decision to use one theoretical approach over another, sociologists are choosing a "road map" to guide their thinking. In other words, a **theoretical approach** is *a basic image of society that guides thinking and research*. Sociologists make use of three major theoretical approaches: *the structural-functional approach*, *the social-conflict approach*, and *the symbolic-interaction approach*.

The Structural-Functional Approach

The **structural-functional approach** is *a framework for building theory that sees society as a complex system whose parts work together to promote solidarity and stability*. As its name suggests, this approach points to **social structure**, *any relatively stable pattern of social behavior*. Social structure gives our lives shape in families, the workplace, or the college classroom. This approach also looks for each structure's **social functions**, *the consequences of a social pattern for the operation of society as a whole*. All social patterns, from a simple handshake to complex religious rituals, function to tie people together and to keep society going, at least in its present form.

social functions the consequences of a social pattern for the operation of society as a whole

manifest functions the recognized and intended consequences of any social pattern

latent functions the unrecognized and unintended consequences of any social pattern

social dysfunction any social pattern that may disrupt the operation of society

The structural-functional approach owes much to Auguste Comte, who pointed out the need to keep society unified when many traditions were breaking down. Emile Durkheim, who helped establish sociology in French universities, also based his work on this approach. A third structural-functional pioneer was the English sociologist Herbert Spencer (1820–1903). Spencer compared society to the human body: Just as the structural parts of the human body—the skeleton, muscles, and internal organs—each carry out certain functions to help the entire organism survive, social structures operate together to preserve society. The structural-functional approach, then, leads sociologists to identify various structures of society and investigate their functions.

The U.S. sociologist Robert K. Merton (1910–2003) expanded our understanding of social function by pointing out that any social structure probably has many functions, some more obvious than others. He distinguished between **manifest functions**, *the recognized and intended consequences of any social pattern,* and **latent functions**, *the unrecognized and unintended consequences of any social pattern.* For example, the obvious function of this country's system of higher education is to give young people the information and skills they will need to hold jobs after graduation. Perhaps just as important, although less often acknowledged, is college's function as a "marriage broker," bringing together young people of similar social backgrounds. Another latent function of higher education is to limit unemployment by keeping millions of people out of the labor market, where many of them might not easily find jobs.

But Merton also recognized that not all the effects of social structure are good. Thus a **social dysfunction** is *any social pattern that*

may disrupt the operation of society. Globalization of the economy, a rising flow of immigrants, and increasing inequality of income are all factors that—in the eyes of some people—disrupt existing social patterns. As these examples suggest, what is helpful and what is harmful for society is a matter about which people often disagree. In addition, what is functional for one category of people (say, a banking system that provides high profits for Wall Street executives) may well be dysfunctional for other categories of people (workers who lose pension funds invested in banks that fail or people who cannot pay their mortgages and end up losing their homes).

Evaluate The main idea of the structural-functional approach is its vision of society as stable and orderly. The main goal of the sociologists who use this approach, then, is to figure out "what makes society tick."

In the mid-1900s, most sociologists favored the structural-functional approach. In recent decades, however, its influence has declined. By focusing on social stability and unity, critics point out, structural-functionalism is not critical of inequalities based on social class, race, ethnicity, and gender, all of which cause tension and conflict. In general, its focus on stability at the expense of conflict makes this approach somewhat conservative. As a critical response, sociologists developed the social-conflict approach.

CHECK YOUR LEARNING How do manifest functions differ from latent functions? Give an example of a manifest function and a latent function of automobiles in the United States.

The Social-Conflict Approach

The **social-conflict approach** is *a framework for building theory that sees society as an arena of inequality that generates conflict and change.* Unlike the structural-functional emphasis on solidarity and stability, this approach highlights how factors such as class, race, ethnicity, gender, and age are linked to inequality in terms of money, power, education, and social prestige. A conflict analysis rejects the idea that social structure promotes the operation of society as a whole, focusing instead on how any social pattern benefits some people while hurting others.

Sociologists using the social-conflict approach look at ongoing conflict between dominant and disadvantaged categories of people—the rich in relation to the poor, white people in relation to people of color, and men in relation to women. Typically, people on top try to protect their privileges, while the disadvantaged try to gain more for themselves.

The social-conflict approach points out patterns of inequality in everyday life. The TV series *Real Housewives of Orange County* takes a close-up look at the lives of extremely affluent women. In what ways do they depend on the work of people of lower social position?

We can use the sociological perspective to look at sociology itself. All of the most widely recognized pioneers of the discipline were men. This is because in the nineteenth century, it was all but unheard of for women to be college professors, and few women took a central role in public life. But Jane Addams was an early sociologist in the United States who founded Hull House, a Chicago settlement house where she spent many hours helping young people.

A social-conflict analysis of our educational system shows how schooling reproduces class inequality from one generation to the next. For example, secondary schools assign students to either college preparatory or vocational training programs. From a structural-functional point of view, such "tracking" benefits everyone by providing schooling that fits students' abilities. But conflict analysis argues that tracking often has less to do with talent than with social background, meaning that well-to-do students are placed in higher tracks, while poor children end up in lower tracks.

In this way, young people from privileged families get the best schooling, which leads them to college and later to high-income careers. The children of poor families, by contrast, are not prepared for college and, like their parents before them, typically get stuck in low-paying jobs. In both cases, the social standing of one generation is passed on to the next, with schools justifying the practice in terms of individual merit (Bowles & Gintis, 1976; Oakes, 1982, 1985).

Many sociologists use social-conflict theory not just to understand society but also as part of their efforts to reduce inequality. Karl Marx championed the cause of workers in what he saw as

their battle against factory owners. In a well-known statement (inscribed on his monument in London's Highgate Cemetery), Marx declared, "The philosophers have only interpreted the world, in various ways; the point, however, is to change it."

Feminism and Gender-Conflict Theory

One important social-conflict theory is **gender-conflict theory** (or **feminist theory**), *the study of society that focuses on inequality and conflict between women and men*. The gender-conflict approach is closely linked to **feminism**, *support of social equality for women and men*.

The importance of gender-conflict theory lies in making us aware of the many ways in which our society places men in positions of power over women, in the home (where men are usually considered "head of the household"), in the workplace (where men earn more income and hold most positions of power), and in the mass media (how many hip-hop stars are women?).

Another contribution of feminist theory is making us aware of the importance of women to the development of sociology. Harriet Martineau (1802–1876) is regarded as the first woman sociologist. Born to a wealthy English family, Martineau made her mark in 1853 by translating the writings of Auguste Comte from French into English. She later documented the evils of slavery and argued for laws to protect factory workers, defending workers' right to unionize. She was particularly concerned about the position of women in society and fought for changes in education policy so that women could look forward to more in life than being a wife and mother in the home.

In the United States, Jane Addams (1860–1935) was a sociological pioneer who in 1889 helped found Hull House, a Chicago settlement house that provided assistance to immigrant families. Although widely published—Addams wrote eleven books and hundreds of articles—she chose the life of a public activist over that of a university sociologist, speaking out on issues involving inequality, immigration, and the pursuit of peace. Though her pacifism during World War I was the subject of much controversy, she was awarded the Nobel Peace Prize in 1931.

All chapters of this book consider the importance of gender and gender inequality. For an in-depth look at feminism and the social standing of women and men, see Chapter 10 ("Gender Stratification").

Race-Conflict Theory

Another important type of social-conflict theory is **race-conflict theory**, *the study of society that focuses on inequality and conflict between people of different racial and ethnic categories*. Just as men have power over women, white people have numerous social advantages over people of color, including, on average, higher incomes, more schooling, better health, and longer life expectancy.

Race-conflict theory also points out the contributions to the development of sociology made by people of color. Ida Wells Barnett

social-conflict approach a framework for building theory that sees society as an arena of inequality that generates conflict and change

gender-conflict theory a point of view that focuses on inequality and conflict between women and men

feminism support of social equality for women and men

race-conflict theory a point of view that focuses on inequality and conflict between people of different racial and ethnic categories

One of sociology's pioneers in the United States, William Edward Burghardt Du Bois saw sociology as a key to solving society's problems, especially racial inequality. Du Bois earned a Ph.D. in sociology from Harvard University and established the Atlanta Sociological Laboratory, one of the first centers of sociological research in the United States. He helped his colleagues in sociology—and people everywhere—see the deep racial divisions in the United States. White people can simply be "Americans," Du Bois explained, but African Americans have a "double consciousness," reflecting their status as citizens who are never able to escape identification based on the color of their skin.

In his sociological classic *The Philadelphia Negro: A Social Study* (1899), Du Bois explored Philadelphia's African American community, identifying both the strengths and the weaknesses of people wrestling with overwhelming social problems on a day-to-day basis. He challenged the belief—widespread at that time—that blacks were inferior to whites, and he blamed white prejudice for the problems African Americans faced. He also criticized successful people of color for being so eager to win white acceptance that they gave up all ties with the black community, which needed their help.

Despite notable achievements, Du Bois gradually grew impatient with academic study, which he felt was too detached from the everyday struggles of people of color. Du Bois wanted change. It was the hope of sparking public action against racial separation that led Du Bois, in 1909, to participate in the founding of the National Association for the Advancement of Colored People (NAACP), an organization that has been active in supporting racial equality for more than a century. As the editor of the organization's magazine, *Crisis*, Du Bois worked tirelessly to challenge laws and social customs that deprived African Americans of the rights and opportunities enjoyed by the white majority.

Du Bois described race as the major problem facing the United States in the twentieth century. Early in his career, he was hopeful about overcoming racial divisions. By the end of his life, however, he had grown bitter, claiming that little had changed. At the age of ninety-three, Du Bois left the United States for Ghana, where he died two years later.

What Do You Think?

1. If he were alive today, do you think Du Bois would still consider race a major problem in the twenty-first century? Why or why not?

2. How much do you think African Americans today experience "double consciousness"?

3. In what ways can sociology help us understand and reduce racial conflict?

Sources: Based on Baltzell (1967), Du Bois (1967, orig. 1899), Wright (2002a, 2002b), and personal communication with Earl Wright II.

(1862–1931) was born to slave parents but rose to become a teacher and then a journalist and newspaper publisher. She campaigned tirelessly for racial equality and, especially, to put an end to the lynching of black people. She wrote and lectured about racial inequality throughout her life (Lengerman & Niebrugge-Brantley, 1998).

An important contribution to understanding race in the United States was made by William Edward Burghardt Du Bois (1868–1963). Born to a poor Massachusetts family, Du Bois enrolled at Fisk University in Nashville, Tennessee, and then at Harvard University, where he earned the first doctorate awarded by that university to a person of color. Du Bois then founded the Atlanta Sociological Laboratory, which was an important center of sociological research in the early decades of the last century. Like most people who follow the social-conflict approach (whether focusing on class, gender, or race), Du Bois believed that scholars should not simply learn about society's problems but also try to solve them. He therefore studied the black communities across the United States, pointing to numerous social problems ranging from educational inequality, a political system that denied people their right to vote, and the terrorist practice of lynching. Du Bois spoke out against racial inequality and participated in the founding of the National Association for the Advancement of Colored People (NAACP) (E. Wright, 2002a, 2002b). The Thinking About Diversity box takes a closer look at the ideas of W. E. B. Du Bois.

Evaluate The various social-conflict theories have gained a large following in recent decades, but like other approaches, they have met with criticism. Because any social-conflict analysis focuses on inequality, it largely ignores how shared values and interdependence can unify members of a society. In addition, say critics, to the extent that it pursues political goals, a social-conflict approach cannot claim scientific objectivity. Supporters of social-conflict approaches respond that *all* theoretical approaches have political consequences.

A final criticism of both structural-functional and social-conflict theories is that they paint society in broad strokes—in terms of "family," "social class," "race," and so on. A third theoretical approach

Major Theoretical Approaches

	Structural-Functional Approach	Social-Conflict and Feminist Approach	Symbolic-Interaction Approach
What is the level of analysis?	Macro-level	Macro-level	Micro-level
What image of society does the approach have?	Society is a system of interrelated parts that is relatively stable. Each part works to keep society operating in an orderly way. Members generally agree about what is morally right and morally wrong.	Society is a system of social inequalities based on class (Marx), gender (gender-conflict theory and feminism), and race (race-conflict theory). Society operates to benefit some categories of people and harm others. Social inequality causes conflict that leads to social change.	Society is an ongoing process. People interact in countless settings using symbolic communications. The reality people experience is variable and changing.
What core questions does the approach ask?	How is society held together? What are the major parts of society? How are these parts linked? What does each part do to help society work?	How does society divide a population? How do advantaged people protect their privileges? How do disadvantaged people challenge the system seeking change?	How do people experience society? How do people shape the reality they experience? How do behavior and meaning change from person to person and from one situation to another?

views society less in general terms and more as the specific, everyday experiences of individual people. The Applying Theory table summarizes the contributions of each of these approaches.

CHECK YOUR LEARNING Why do you think sociologists characterize the social-conflict approach as "activist"? What is it actively trying to achieve?

The Symbolic-Interaction Approach

Both the structural-functional approach and the social-conflict approach share a **macro-level orientation**, meaning *a broad focus on social structures that shape society as a whole*. Macro-level sociology takes in the big picture, rather like observing a city from a helicopter and seeing how highways help people move from place to place or how housing differs from rich to poor neighborhoods. Sociology also uses a **micro-level orientation**, *a close-up focus on social interaction in specific situations*. Exploring city life in this way occurs at street level, where you might watch how children invent games on a school playground or observe how pedestrians respond to homeless people they pass on the street. The **symbolic-interaction approach**, then, is *a framework for building theory that sees society as the product of the everyday interactions of individuals*.

How does "society" result from the ongoing experiences of tens of millions of people? One answer, detailed in Chapter 4 ("Social Interaction in Everyday Life"), is that society is nothing more than the reality that people construct for themselves as they interact with one another. That is, we human beings live in a world of symbols, and we attach meaning to virtually everything, from the words on this page to the wink of an eye. We create "reality," therefore, as we define our surroundings, decide what we think of others, and shape our own identities.

Symbolic-interaction theory has roots in the thinking of Max Weber (1864–1920), a German sociologist who emphasized understanding a particular setting from the point of view of the people in it. Since Weber's time, sociologists have taken micro-level sociology in a number of directions. Chapter 3 ("Socialization: From Infancy to Old Age") discusses the ideas of George Herbert Mead (1863–1931), who explored how our personalities develop as a result of social experience. Chapter 4 ("Social Interaction in Everyday Life") presents the work of Erving Goffman (1922–1982), whose *dramaturgical analysis* describes how we resemble actors on a stage as we play out our various roles. Other contemporary sociologists, including George Homans and Peter Blau, have developed *social-exchange analysis*, the idea that interaction is guided by what each person stands to gain and lose from others. In the ritual

---

macro-level orientation a broad focus on social structures that shape society as a whole

structural-functional approach a framework for building theory that sees society as a complex system whose parts work together to promote solidarity and stability

social-conflict approach a framework for building theory that sees society as an arena of inequality that generates conflict and change

micro-level orientation a close-up focus on social interaction in specific situations

symbolic-interaction approach a framework for building theory that sees society as the product of the everyday interactions of individuals

Sports: Playing the Theory Game

Who doesn't enjoy sports? Children and teens may play as many as two or three organized sports. For adults who don't participate themselves, weekend television is filled with sporting events, and whole sections of our newspapers are devoted to teams and players and scores. What can we learn by applying sociology's three theoretical approaches to this familiar element of life in the United States?

The Structural-Functional Approach According to the structural-functional approach, the manifest functions of sports include recreation, getting in shape, and letting off steam in a relatively harmless way. Sports have important latent functions as well, from building social relationships to creating jobs. Perhaps the most important latent function of sports is to encourage competition, which is central to our society's way of life.

Of course, sports also have dysfunctional consequences. For example, colleges and universities that try to field winning teams sometimes recruit students for their athletic skill rather than their academic ability. This practice not only lowers a school's academic standards but also shortchanges athletes, who spend little time doing the academic work that will prepare them for future careers (Upthegrove, Roscigno, & Charles, 1999).

The Social-Conflict Approach A social-conflict analysis points out how sports are linked to social inequality. Some sports—tennis, swimming, golf, skiing—are expensive, so participation is largely limited to the well-to-do. Football, baseball, and basketball, however, are accessible to people at almost all income levels. Thus the games people play are not simply a matter of choice but also a reflection of their social standing.

Gender-conflict or **feminist theory** leads us to recognize that, throughout history, men have dominated the world of sports. The first modern Olympic Games, held in 1896, excluded women from competition. Through most of the twentieth century, Little League teams barred girls based on the traditional ideas that girls and women lack the strength and the stamina to play sports and that they risk losing their femininity if they do. Both the Olympics and the Little League are now open to females as well as males, but even today, women still take a back seat to men, particularly in sports with the greatest earnings and social prestige.

Race-conflict theory reminds us that our society has long excluded people of color from professional sports. Even so, opportunities have expanded in recent decades.

In 1947, Jackie Robinson crossed the "color line" to become the first African American player in Major League Baseball. More than fifty years later, professional baseball retired the legendary Robinson's number 42 on *all* teams. In 2010, African Americans (13 percent of the U.S. population) accounted for 10 percent of Major League Baseball players, 67 percent of National Football League (NFL) players, and 78 percent of National Basketball Association (NBA) players (Lapchick, 2011).

But racial discrimination still exists in professional sports. For one thing, race is linked to the positions athletes play on the field, in a pattern called "stacking." The figure shows the results of a 2011 study of race in Major League Baseball. Notice that white players are most concentrated in the central "thinking" positions of pitcher (64 percent white) and catcher (63 percent white). By contrast, African Americans represent only 5 percent of pitchers, and there were no black catchers. At the same time, 11 percent of infielders are African Americans, as are 29 percent of outfielders (positions characterized as requiring "speed and reactive ability") (Lapchick, 2011).

Outfield

Infield

Pitcher

Catcher

| ■ Whites | ☐ African Americans | ☐ Latinos | ■ Asians |

"Stacking" in Professional Baseball

Does race play a part in professional sports? Looking at the various positions in professional baseball, we see that white players are more likely to play the central positions in the infield, while people of color are more likely to play in the outfield. What do you make of this pattern?

Source: Lapchick (2011).

More broadly, African Americans have a large share of players in only five major sports: basketball, football, baseball, boxing, and track. And across all professional sports, the vast majority of managers, head coaches, and team owners are white (Lapchick, 2011).

Who benefits most from professional sports? Although some players get sky-high salaries and millions of fans enjoy following their teams, the vast profits that sports generate are controlled by a small number of people—predominantly white men. In sum, sports in our country are bound up with inequalities based on gender, race, and wealth.

The Symbolic-Interaction Approach At the micro-level, a sporting event is a complex, face-to-face interaction. In part, play is guided by the players' assigned positions and the rules of the game. But players are also spontaneous and unpredictable. Following the symbolic-interaction approach, we see sports less as a system and more as an ongoing process.

From this point of view, too, we would also expect each player to understand the game a little differently. Some players enjoy stiff competition; for others, love of the game may be greater than the need to win. In addition, the behavior of any single player is likely to change over time. A rookie in professional baseball, for example, may feel self-conscious during the first few games in the big leagues but go on to develop a comfortable sense of fitting in with the team. Coming to feel at home on the field was slow and painful for Jackie Robinson, who knew that many white players and millions of white fans resented his presence. In time, however, his outstanding ability and his confident, cooperative manner won him the respect of the entire nation.

The three theoretical approaches provide different insights into sports, and none is entirely correct. Applied to any issue, each approach provides part of a complex picture. To fully appreciate the power of the sociological perspective, you should become familiar with all three.

What Do You Think?

1. Describe how a macro-level approach to sports differs from a micro-level approach.

2. Make up three questions about sports that reflect the focus of each of the three theoretical approaches.

3. How might you apply the three approaches to other social patterns, such as the workplace or family life?

of courtship, for example, people seek mates who offer at least as much—in terms of physical attractiveness, intelligence, and social background—as they offer in return.

🔵 **Evaluate** Without denying the existence of macro-level social structures such as the family and social class, symbolic-interaction theory reminds us that society basically amounts to *people interacting*. That is, micro-level sociology shows us how individuals construct and experience society. However, by emphasizing what is unique in each social scene, this approach risks overlooking the widespread influence of culture, as well as factors such as class, gender, and race.

CHECK YOUR LEARNING How does a micro-level analysis differ from a macro-level analysis? Provide an illustration of a social pattern at both levels.

Keep in mind that each of the major theoretical approaches leads you to recognize particular facts as important and to answer questions in particular ways. As the Seeing Sociology in Everyday Life box exploring social patterns in sports on page 15 shows, the fullest understanding of society comes from using all three approaches.

Three Ways to Do Sociology

🔵 **Understand**

All sociologists want to learn about the social world. But just as some may prefer one theoretical approach to another, many sociologists favor one research orientation. The following sections describe three ways to do sociological research: positivist, interpretive, and critical sociology.

Positivist Sociology

One popular way to do sociological research is **positivist sociology**, which is *the study of society based on scientific observation of social behavior*. As explained earlier, positivist research discovers facts through the use of **science**, *a logical system that develops knowledge from direct, systematic observation*. Positivist sociology is sometimes called *empirical sociology* because it is based on **empirical evidence**, which is *information we can verify with our senses*.

Scientific research often challenges what we accept as "common sense." Here are three examples of widely held beliefs that are not supported by scientific evidence:

1. **"Differences in the behavior of females and males are just 'human nature.'"** Wrong. Much of what we call "human nature" is constructed

positivist sociology the study of society based on scientific observation of social behavior

empirical evidence information we can verify with our senses

science a logical system that develops knowledge from direct, systematic observation

by the society in which we live. We know this because researchers have found that definitions of "feminine" and "masculine" change over time and vary from one society to another (see Chapter 10, "Gender Stratification").

2. **"The United States is a middle-class society in which most people are more or less equal."** Not true. As Chapter 8 ("Social Stratification") explains, the richest 5 percent of U.S. families control 60 percent of the country's wealth, while almost half of all families have scarcely any wealth at all. In fact, recent research shows that the gap between the richest people and average people in the United States has never been greater (Wolff, 2010; Economic Policy Institute, 2011).

3. **"People marry because they are in love."** Not exactly. In U.S. society, as already discussed, many social rules guide the selection of mates. Around the world, as Chapter 13 ("Family and Religion") explains, research indicates that marriages in most societies are arranged by parents and have little to do with love.

These examples confirm the old saying that "it's not what we *don't* know that gets us into trouble as much as the things *we do* know that *just aren't so.*" The Sociology in Focus box explains why we also need to think critically about the "facts" we find in the mass media and on the Internet.

We have all been brought up hearing many widely accepted "truths," being bombarded by "expert" advice in the popular media, and feeling pressure to accept the opinions of those around us. As adults, we need to evaluate more critically what we see, read, and hear. Sociology can help us do that. Sociologists (and everyone else) can use science to assess many kinds of information.

As the television show *Make It or Break It* makes clear, sports are an important element of social life in countless communities across the United States. Sociology's three theoretical approaches all contribute to our understanding of the role of sports in society.

Every day, we see stories in newspapers and magazines that tell us what people think and how they behave. But a lot of what you might read turns out to be misleading or even untrue.

Take the issue of extramarital sex, meaning married people having sex with someone other than their spouse. A look at the cover of many of the "women's magazines" you find in the checkout aisle at the supermarket or a quick reading of the advice column in your local newspaper might lead you to think that extramarital sex is a major issue facing married couples. The popular media seem full of stories about how to keep your spouse from "cheating" or pointing out clues to tip you off that your spouse is having an affair. Most of the studies reported in the popular press and on Internet Web sites suggest that more than half of married people—women as well as men—cheat on their spouses.

But is extramarital sex really that widespread? No. Researchers who conduct sound sociological investigation have found that in a given year, only 3 to 4 percent of married people have an extramarital relationship, and no more than 15 to 20 percent of married people have *ever* done so. Why, then, do surveys in the popular media report rates of extramarital sex that are so much higher? We can answer this question by taking a look at who fills out "pop" surveys.

First, it is people with a personal interest in some topic who are most likely to respond to an offer in the mass media or to complete a survey online. For this reason, people who have some personal experience with extramarital sex (either their own behavior or their partner's) are more likely to show up in these studies. In contrast, studies correctly done by skilled researchers carefully select subjects so that the results are representative of the entire population.

Second, because the readership of the magazines and online sources that conduct these surveys is, on average, young, these surveys attract a high proportion of young respondents. And one thing we know about young people—married or unmarried—is that they are more likely to have sex. For example, the typical married person who is thirty years of age is more than twice as likely to have had an extramarital relationship than the typical married person over age sixty.

TRIXIE
August 2012
"How Much Cheating? New Survey Tells All!"

Third, women are much more likely than men to read the popular magazines that feature sex surveys. Therefore, women are more likely to fill out the surveys. In recent decades, the share of women, especially younger women, who have had extramarital sex has gone up. Why are today's younger women more likely than women a generation or two earlier to have had extramarital sex? Probably because women today are working out of the home and many are traveling as part of their jobs. In general, today's women have a wider social network that brings them into contact with more men.

Chapter 8 ("Sexuality and Society") takes a close look at sexual patterns, including extramarital relationships. For now, just remember that a lot of what you read in the popular media and online may not be as true as some people think.

Join the Blog!

Can you think of other issues in which pop media surveys may give misleading information? What are they? Do you think that the popular media are a source of accurate information about the world? Go to MySocLab and join the Sociology in Focus blog to share your opinions and experiences and to see what others think.

Sources: T. W. Smith (2006), Black (2007), Parker-Pope (2008).

Concepts, Variables, and Measurement

Let's take a closer look at how science works. A basic element of science is the **concept**, *a mental construct that represents some part of the world in a simplified form*. Sociologists use concepts to label aspects of social life, including "the family" and "the economy," and to categorize people in terms of their "gender" or "social class."

A **variable** is *a concept whose value changes from case to case*. The familiar variable "height," for example, has a value that varies from person to person. The concept "social class" can describe people's social standing using the values "upper class," "middle class," "working class," or "lower class."

The use of variables depends on **measurement**, *a procedure for determining the value of a variable in a specific case*. Some variables are easy to measure, as when a nurse checks our blood pressure. But measuring sociological variables can be far more difficult. For example, how would you measure a person's social class? You might start by looking at the clothing people wear, listening to how they speak, or noting where they live. Or trying to be more precise, you might ask about income, occupation, and education. Because there are many ways to measure a complex variable like social class, researchers must make decisions about how to *operationalize* a variable, stating exactly what they are measuring.

Statistics

Sociologists also face the problem of dealing with large numbers of people. For example, how do you report income for thousands or even millions of individuals? Listing streams of numbers would carry little meaning and tells us nothing about the people as a whole. To solve this problem, sociologists use *descriptive statistics* to state what is "average" for a large population. The most commonly used descriptive statistics are the *mean* (the arithmetic average of all measures, which you calculate by adding all the values and dividing

concept a mental construct that represents some aspect of the world in a simplified form

variable a concept whose value changes from case to case

measurement a procedure for determining the value of a variable in a specific case

reliability consistency in measurement

validity actually measuring exactly what you intend to measure

by the number of cases), the *median* (the score at the halfway point in a listing of numbers from lowest to highest), and the *mode* (the score that occurs most often).

Reliability and Validity

For a measurement to be useful, it must be reliable and valid. **Reliability** refers to *consistency in measurement*. A measurement is reliable if repeated measurements give the same result time after time. But consistency does not guarantee **validity**, which is *actually measuring exactly what you intend to measure*. Valid measurement means more than hitting the same spot somewhere on a target again and again; it means hitting the exact target, the bull's-eye.

Say you want to know just how religious the students at your college are. You might ask students how often they attend religious services. But is going to a house of worship really the same thing as being religious? Maybe not, because people take part in religious rituals for many reasons, some of them having little to do with religion; in addition, some strong believers avoid organized religion altogether. Thus even when a measurement yields consistent results (meaning that it is reliable), it can still miss the intended target (and therefore lack validity). Good sociological research depends on careful measurement, which is always a challenge to researchers.

Correlation and Cause

The real payoff in scientific research is determining how variables are related. **Correlation** means *a relationship in which two (or more) variables change together*. But sociologists want to know not just how variables change but which variable changes the other. The scientific ideal is to determine **cause and effect**, *a relationship in which change in one variable causes change in another*. As noted earlier, Emile Durkheim found that the degree of social integration (the cause) affected the suicide rate (the effect) among categories of people. Scientists refer to the cause as the *independent variable* and the effect as the *dependent variable*. Understanding cause and effect is valuable because it allows researchers to *predict* how one pattern of behavior will produce another.

correlation a relationship in which two (or more) variables change together

cause and effect a relationship in which change in one variable (the independent variable) causes change in another (the dependent variable)

Just because two variables change together does not necessarily mean that they have a cause-and-effect relationship. For instance, the marriage rate in the United States falls to its lowest point in January, which also happens to be the month when the national death rate is highest. Does this mean that people drop dead because they don't marry or that they don't marry because they die? Of course not. More likely, it is the cold and often stormy weather across much of the country in January (perhaps combined with the postholiday blues) that is responsible for both the low marriage rate and the high death rate.

When two variables change together but neither one causes the other, sociologists describe the relationship as a *spurious*, or false, correlation. A spurious correlation between two variables usually results from some third factor. For example, delinquency rates are high where young people live in crowded housing, but this is not because crowded housing causes youngsters to "turn bad." Both crowded housing and delinquency result from a third factor: poverty. To be sure of a real cause-and-effect relationship, we must show that (1) variables are correlated, (2) the independent (causal) variable occurs before the dependent variable, and (3) there is no evidence that a third variable has been overlooked, causing a spurious correlation.

The Ideal of Objectivity

A guiding principle of science is *objectivity*, or personal neutrality, in conducting research. Ideally, objective research allows the facts to speak for themselves and not be influenced by the personal values and biases of the researcher. In reality, of course, achieving total neutrality is impossible for anyone. But carefully observing the rules of scientific research will maximize objectivity.

The German sociologist Max Weber noted that people usually choose *value-relevant* research topics—topics they care about. But once their work is under way, he cautioned, researchers should try to be *value-free*. That is, we must be dedicated to finding truth as it *is* rather than as we think it *should be*. For Weber, this difference sets science apart from politics. Researchers (unlike politicians) must stay open-minded and be willing to accept whatever results come from their work, whether they personally agree with them or not.

Weber's argument still carries much weight in sociology, although most researchers realize that we can never be completely value-free or even aware of all our biases (Demerath, 1996). In addition, keep in mind that sociologists are not "average" people: Most are highly educated white men and women who are more politically

One principle of scientific research is that sociologists and other investigators should try to be objective in their work, so that their personal values and beliefs do not distort their findings. But such a detached attitude may discourage the connection needed for people to open up and share information. Thus sociologists have to decide how much to pursue objectivity and how much to show their own feelings.

research orientations

positivist sociology the study of society based on systematic observation of social behavior

interpretive sociology the study of society that focuses on discovering the meanings people attach to their social world

critical sociology the study of society that focuses on the need for social change

liberal than the population as a whole. Sociologists need to remember that they, too, are influenced by their social backgrounds.

Interpretive Sociology

Not all sociologists agree that science is the only way—or even the best way—to study human society. This is because, unlike planets or other elements of the natural world, humans are much more than objects moving around in ways that can be measured. Of course we are active creatures, but our humanity lies in the fact that we attach *meaning* to our actions, and meaning is not easy to observe directly. Therefore, sociologists have developed a second research orientation, known as **interpretive sociology**, *the study of society that focuses on discovering the meanings people attach to their social world*. Max Weber, the pioneer of this framework, argued that the proper focus of sociology is *interpretation*, or understanding the meaning people create in their everyday lives. Sociologists who use this approach may well measure behavior, making use of the positivist approach, but their greater goal is discovering what people *mean* by what they do.

The Importance of Meaning

Interpretive sociology differs from positivist sociology in three ways. First, positivist sociology focuses on actions—on what people do—because this is what we can observe directly. Interpretive sociology focuses on people's understanding of their actions. Second, positivist sociology claims that objective reality involves what can be observed, so that reality exists "out there." Interpretive sociology counters that reality is subjective, involving the meanings that people construct in the course of their everyday lives. Third, positivist sociology, with a focus on outward behavior, tends to favor *quantitative* data, numerical measurements of what can be observed. Interpretive sociology, with a focus on "inside" meaning, favors *qualitative* data by which researchers try to discover how people understand their world.

In sum, the positivist orientation, which is very close to science, is well suited for research in a laboratory, where investigators stand back and take careful measurements of what people do. The interpretive orientation, while not rejecting science outright, claims that we learn more by interacting with people, trying to uncover subjective meaning, and learning how people make sense of their everyday lives. This type of research is best carried out in a natural setting.

Weber's Concept of *Verstehen*

Max Weber claimed that the key to interpretive sociology lies in *Verstehen* (pronounced "fair-SHTAY-in"), the German word for "understanding." It is the interpretive sociologist's job not just to observe *what* people do but also to share in their world of meaning, coming to appreciate *why* they act as they do. Subjective thoughts and feelings, which scientists tend to dismiss because they are difficult to measure, are the focus of the interpretive sociologist's attention.

Critical Sociology

Like the interpretive orientation, critical sociology developed in reaction to what many sociologists saw as the limitations of positivist sociology. In this case, however, the problem involves the central principle of scientific research: objectivity. Positivist sociology holds that reality is "out there" and that the researcher's job is to study and document how society works. But Karl Marx, who founded the critical orientation, rejected the idea that society exists as a "natural" system. To assume that society is somehow "fixed," he claimed, is the same as saying that society cannot be changed. With a focus on society as it exists, positivist sociology, from this point of view, ends up supporting the status quo. **Critical sociology**, by contrast, is *the study of society that focuses on the need for social change*.

The Importance of Change

Critical sociology does not ignore "facts." Researchers using this approach may well make use of scientific methods to learn, for example, how much income inequality there is in the United States. But rather than asking the positivist question "How much inequality *is* there?" critical sociologists ask moral and political questions, such as "*Should* we have this much inequality?" or "*Should* society exist in its present form?"

Their answer, typically, is that it should not. So critical sociology does not reject using science to learn about what's going on in the social world. But critical sociology does reject the scientific neutrality that requires researchers to try to be "objective" and limit their work to studying the status quo.

One recent account of the critical orientation, echoing Marx, claims that the point of this type of sociology is "not just to research the social world but to change it in the direction of democracy and social justice" (Feagin & Hernán, 2001:1). In making value judgments about how society should be improved, critical sociology rejects Weber's goal that sociology be a value-free science and emphasizes instead that sociologists should be social activists in pursuit of greater social equality.

Sociologists using the critical orientation seek to change not only society but also the character of research itself. They often identify personally with their research subjects and encourage them to help decide what to study and how to do the work. Often, researchers and subjects use their findings to provide a voice for less powerful people and to advance the political goal of a more equal society (Hess, 1999; Feagin & Hernán, 2001; Perrucci, 2001).

Sociology as Politics

Positivist sociologists object to researchers taking sides in this way. The positivist claim is that to the extent that critical sociology (whether feminist, Marxist, or of some other critical orientation) becomes political, it gives up scientific objectivity, and therefore cannot correct for its own biases. The critical sociology response is that *all* research is political in that either it calls for change or it does not. As critical sociology sees it, sociologists thus have no choice about their work being political, but they can choose *which* positions to support.

Three Research Orientations in Sociology

	Positivist Sociology	Interpretive Sociology	Critical Sociology
What is reality?	Society is an orderly system. There is an objective reality "out there."	Society is ongoing interaction. People construct reality as they attach meanings to their behavior.	Society is patterns of inequality. Reality is that some categories of people dominate others.
How do we conduct research?	Using a scientific orientation, the researcher carefully observes behavior, gathering empirical, ideally quantitative, data. Researcher tries to be a neutral observer.	Seeking to look "deeper" than outward behavior, the researcher focuses on subjective meaning. The researcher gathers qualitative data, discovering the subjective sense people make of their world. Researcher is a participant.	Seeking to go beyond positivism's focus on studying the world as it is, the researcher is guided by politics and uses research as a strategy to bring about desired social change. Researcher is an activist.
Corresponding theoretical approach	Structural-functional approach	Symbolic-interaction approach	Social-conflict approach

Critical sociology is an activist approach that ties knowledge to action and seeks not just to understand the world as it exists but also to improve it. In general, positivist sociology tends to appeal to researchers who try to be nonpolitical or who have more conservative political views; critical sociology appeals to those whose politics range from liberal to radical left.

Research Orientations and Theory

We have now considered various research orientations as well as various theoretical approaches. Is there a link between research orientations and sociological theory? The connection is not precise, but each of the three ways to do sociology—positivist, interpretive, and critical—does stand closer to one of the theoretical approaches presented earlier in this chapter. The positivist orientation is linked to the structural-functional approach, and this is because both are concerned with the scientific goal of understanding society as it is. The interpretive orientation is linked to the symbolic-interaction approach by the fact that both focus on the meanings people attach to their social world. Finally, the critical orientation is connected to the social-conflict approach because both are animated by the goal of reducing social inequality.

The Summing Up table provides a quick review of the differences among the three ways to do sociology. Many sociologists favor one orientation over another; however, because each provides useful insights, it is a good idea to become familiar with all three.

Gender and Research

 Analyze

In recent years, sociologists have become aware that research is affected by **gender**, *the personal traits and social positions that members of a society attach to being female or male.* Gender can affect sociological research in five ways (Eichler, 1988; Giovannini, 1992):

1. **Androcentricity.** Androcentricity (literally, "focus on the male") means approaching an issue from a male perspective. Sometimes researchers act as if only men's activities are important, ignoring what women do. For years, sociologists studying occupations focused on the paid labor of men and overlooked the housework and child care traditionally performed by women. Research that seeks to explain human behavior cannot ignore half of humanity.

    Gynocentricity—seeing the world from a female perspective—can also limit good sociological investigation. However, in our male-dominated society, this problem arises less often.

2. **Overgeneralizing.** This problem occurs when sociologists gather data only from men but then use that information to draw conclusions about all people. For example, a researcher might speak to a handful of male public officials and then form conclusions about an entire community.

3. **Gender blindness.** Failing to consider gender at all is called *gender blindness*. The lives of men and women differ in many ways. A study of growing old in the United States might suffer from gender blindness if it overlooked the fact that most elderly men live with spouses but elderly women generally live alone.

4. **Double standards.** Researchers must be careful not to judge men and women by different standards. For example, a family researcher who labels a couple "man and wife" may define the man as the "head of the household" and treat him as important while assuming that the woman simply engages in family "support work."

5. **Interference.** Another way gender can distort a study is if a subject reacts to the sex of the researcher, interfering with the research operation. While studying a small community in Sicily, for instance, Maureen Giovannini (1992) found that many men treated her as a *woman* rather than as a *researcher*.

Some thought it inappropriate for an unmarried woman to speak privately with a man. Others denied Giovannini access to places they considered off-limits to women.

There is nothing wrong with focusing research on people of one sex or the other. But all sociologists, as well as people who read their work, should be mindful of how gender can affect an investigation.

Research Ethics

 Analyze

Like all other scientific investigators, sociologists must be aware that their work can harm as well as help subjects or communities. For this reason, the American Sociological Association (ASA)—the major professional association of sociologists in North America—has established formal guidelines for conducting research (1997).

Sociologists must try to be skillful and fair-minded in their work. They must disclose all research findings without omitting significant data. They should make their results available to other sociologists who may want to conduct a similar study.

Sociologists must also make sure that subjects taking part in a research project are not harmed, and they must stop their work right away if they suspect that any subject is at risk of harm. Researchers are also required to protect the privacy of individuals involved in a research project, even if they come under pressure from authorities, such as the police or the courts, to release confidential information. Researchers must also get the *informed consent* of participants, which means that the subjects must fully understand their responsibilities and the risks that the research involves before agreeing to take part.

Another guideline concerns funding. Sociologists must include in their published results all sources of financial support. They must avoid accepting money from a source if there is any question of a conflict of interest. Researchers must never accept funding from any organization that seeks to influence the research results for its own purposes.

The federal government also plays a part in research ethics. Every college and university that seeks federal funding for research involving human subjects must have an *institutional review board* (IRB) that examines grant applications and ensures that research will not violate ethical standards.

Finally, there are global dimensions to research ethics. Before beginning research in another country, an investigator must become familiar enough with that society to understand what people *there* are likely to regard as a violation of privacy or a source of personal danger. In a diverse society such as our own, the same rule applies to studying people whose cultural background differs from that of the researcher. The Thinking About Diversity box on page 22 offers tips on the sensitivity outsiders should apply when studying Hispanic communities.

Research Methods

 Analyze

A **research method** is *a systematic plan for doing research.* Four commonly used methods of sociological investigation are experiments, surveys, participant observation, and the use of existing data. None is better or worse than any other. Rather, just as a carpenter chooses a particular tool for a particular job, researchers select a method according to whom they want to study and what they want to learn.

Testing a Hypothesis: The Experiment

The **experiment** is *a research method for investigating cause and effect under highly controlled conditions.* Experiments closely follow the logic of science, testing a *specific hypothesis,* a statement of how two (or more) variables are related. A hypothesis is really an educated guess about how variables are linked, usually expressed as an *if-then* statement: *If* this particular thing were to happen, *then* that particular thing will result.

An experimenter gathers the evidence needed to reject or not to reject the hypothesis in four steps: (1) State which variable is the *independent variable* (the "cause" of the change) and which is the dependent variable (the "effect," the thing that is changed). (2) Measure the initial value of the dependent variable. (3) Expose the dependent variable to the independent variable (the "cause" or "treatment"). (4) Measure the dependent variable again to see what change, if any, took place. If the expected change took place, the experiment supports the hypothesis; if not, the hypothesis must be modified.

Successful experiments depend on careful control of all factors that might affect what the experiment is trying to measure. Control is easiest in a research laboratory. But experiments in an everyday location— "in the field," as sociologists say—have the advantage of letting researchers observe subjects in their natural settings.

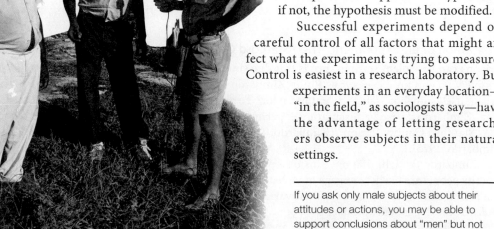

If you ask only male subjects about their attitudes or actions, you may be able to support conclusions about "men" but not more generally about "people." What would a researcher have to do to ensure that research data support conclusions about all of society?

Jorge: If you are going to include Latinos in your research, you need to learn a little about their culture.

Mark: I'm interviewing lots of different families. What's special about interviewing Latinos?

Jorge: Sit down and I'll tell you a few things you need to know. . . .

Because our society is socially diverse, sociologists often find themselves studying people who differ from themselves. Learning, in advance, the ways of life of any category of people can ease the research process and ensure that no hard feelings are caused along the way.

Gerardo Marín and Barbara Van Oss Marín (1991) have identified five areas of concern when conducting research with Hispanic people, currently the largest minority in the United States.

1. **Be careful with terms.** The Maríns point out that "Hispanic" is a label of convenience used by the U.S. Census Bureau. Few people from Spanish- and Portuguese-speaking cultures think of themselves as "Hispanic"; most identify with a particular country, such as Peru, Cuba, Argentina, or Spain.

2. **Be aware of cultural differences.** By and large, the U.S. population is individualistic and competitive. Many Hispanics, by contrast, place

more value on cooperation and community. An outsider may judge the behavior of a Hispanic subject as conformist or overly trusting when in fact the person is simply trying to be helpful. Researchers should also realize that Hispanic respondents might agree with a particular statement merely out of politeness.

3. **Anticipate family dynamics.** Hispanic cultures have strong family loyalties. Asking subjects to reveal information about another family member may make them uncomfortable or even angry. The Maríns add that a researcher's request to speak privately with a Hispanic woman in the home may provoke suspicion or outright disapproval from her husband or father.

4. **Take your time.** Spanish cultures, the Maríns explain, tend to place the quality of relationships above simply getting a job done. A non-Hispanic researcher who tries to hurry an interview with a Hispanic family out of a desire

not to delay the family's dinner may be considered rude for not proceeding at a more sociable and relaxed pace.

5. **Think about personal space.** Finally, Hispanics typically maintain closer physical contact than many non-Hispanics. Therefore, researchers who seat themselves across the room from their subjects may seem standoffish. Researchers might also wrongly label Hispanics "pushy" if they move closer than a non-Hispanic researcher finds comfortable.

Of course, Hispanics differ among themselves just as people in any category do, and these generalizations apply to some more than to others. But investigators should be aware of cultural dynamics when carrying out any research, especially in the United States, where hundreds of distinctive categories of people make up our multicultural society.

What Do You Think?

1. Give a specific example of damage to a study that might take occur if researchers are not sensitive to the culture of their subjects.

2. What do researchers need to do to avoid the kinds of problems noted in this box?

3. Discuss the research process with classmates from various cultural backgrounds. In what ways are the concerns raised by people of different cultural backgrounds similar? In what ways do they differ?

Illustration of an Experiment: The "Stanford County Prison"

Prisons can be violent settings, but is this due simply to the "bad" people who end up there? Or as Philip Zimbardo suspected, does prison itself somehow cause violent behavior? To answer this question, Zimbardo devised a fascinating experiment, which he called the "Stanford County Prison" (Zimbardo, 1972; Haney, Banks, & Zimbardo, 1973).

Zimbardo thought that once inside a prison, even emotionally healthy people are likely to engage in violence. So Zimbardo treated the *prison setting* as the independent variable capable of causing *violence,* the dependent variable.

To test this hypothesis, Zimbardo and his research team first constructed a realistic-looking "prison" in the basement of the psychology building on the campus of Stanford University. Then they placed an ad in a local newspaper, offering to pay young men to

help with a two-week research project. To each of the seventy who responded they administered a series of physical and psychological tests and then selected the healthiest twenty-four.

The next step was to assign randomly half the men to be "prisoners" and half to be "guards." The plan called for the guards and prisoners to spend the next two weeks in the mock prison. The prisoners began their part of the experiment when real police officers "arrested" them at their homes. After searching and handcuffing the men, the police drove them to the local police station, where they were fingerprinted. Then police transported their captives to the Stanford prison, where the guards locked them up. Zimbardo started his video camera and watched to see what would happen next.

The experiment turned into more than anyone had bargained for. Both guards and prisoners soon became embittered and hostile toward one another. Guards humiliated the prisoners by assigning them jobs such as cleaning toilets with their bare hands. The prisoners resisted and insulted the guards. Within four days, the researchers had removed five prisoners who displayed "extreme emotional depression, crying, rage and acute anxiety" (Haney, Banks, & Zimbardo, 1973:81). Before the end of the first week, the situation had become so bad that the researchers had to end the experiment.

The events that unfolded at the "Stanford County Prison" supported Zimbardo's hypothesis that prison violence is rooted in the social character of the jails themselves, not in the personalities of individual guards and prisoners. This finding raises questions about our society's prisons, leading to some basic reforms. Zimbardo's experiment also shows the potential of research to threaten the physical and mental well-being of subjects. Such dangers are not always as obvious as they were in this case. Therefore, researchers must carefully consider the potential harm to subjects at all stages of their work and halt any study, as Zimbardo did, if subjects suffer harm of any kind.

● **Evaluate**   In carrying out the "Stanford County Prison" study, the researchers chose to do an experiment because they were interested in testing a hypothesis. In this case, Zimbardo and his colleagues wanted to find out if the prison setting itself (rather than the personalities of individual guards and prisoners) is the cause of prison violence. The fact that the "prison" erupted in violence—even using guards and prisoners who had "healthy" profiles—supports their hypothesis.

CHECK YOUR LEARNING   How might Zimbardo's findings help explain the abuse of Iraqi prisoners by U.S. soldiers after the 2003 invasion?

Asking Questions: Survey Research

A **survey** is *a research method in which subjects respond to a series of statements or questions on a questionnaire or in an interview.* The most widely used of all research methods, the survey is well suited to studying what cannot be observed directly, such as political attitudes or religious beliefs.

A survey targets some *population*, for example, unmarried mothers or adults living in rural counties in Wisconsin. Sometimes every adult in the country is the survey population, as in polls taken during national political campaigns. Of course, contacting a vast number of people is all but impossible, so researchers usually study a *sample*, a much smaller number of subjects selected to represent the entire population. Surveys using samples of as few as 1,500 people commonly give accurate estimates of public opinion for the entire country.

Beyond selecting subjects, the survey must have a specific plan for asking questions and recording answers. The most common way to do this is to give subjects a *questionnaire* with a series of written statements or questions. Often the researcher lets subjects choose possible responses to each item, as on a multiple-choice test. Sometimes, though, a researcher may want subjects to respond freely, to permit all opinions to be expressed. Of course, this free-form approach means that the researcher later has to make sense out of what can be a bewildering array of answers.

In an *interview*, a researcher personally asks subjects a series of questions, thereby solving one problem common to the questionnaire method: the failure of some subjects to return the questionnaire to the researcher. A further difference is that interviews give participants freedom to respond as they wish. Researchers often ask follow-up questions to clarify an answer or to probe a bit more deeply. In doing this, however, a researcher must avoid influencing the subject even in subtle ways, such as by raising an eyebrow as the subject offers an answer.

Illustration of Survey Research: Studying the African American Elite

Do highly successful African Americans escape the sting of racism? The sociologist Lois Benjamin—herself a successful college professor and the first African American faculty member at the University of Tampa—thought the answer was no. To investigate the effects of racism on talented African American men and women, Benjamin set out to conduct survey research.

Benjamin (1991) chose to interview subjects rather than distribute a questionnaire because she wanted to enter into a conversation with her subjects, to ask follow-up questions, and to be able to pursue topics that might come up in conversation. Another reason Benjamin favored interviews over questionnaires is that racism is a sensitive topic. A supportive researcher can make it easier for subjects to answer painful questions more freely.

Because conducting interviews takes a great deal of time, Benjamin had to limit the number of people in her study. She settled for 100 men and women. Even this small number kept Benjamin busy for more than two years of scheduling, traveling, and meeting with respondents. She spent another two years transcribing the tapes of her interviews, sorting out what the hours of talk told her about racism, and writing up her results.

Benjamin began by interviewing people she knew and asking them to suggest others. This strategy is called *snowball sampling* because the number of individuals included grows rapidly over time. Snowball sampling is appealing because it is an easy way to do research: We begin with familiar people, who provide introductions to their friends and colleagues. The drawback, however, is that snowball sampling rarely produces a sample that is representative of the larger population. Benjamin's sample probably contained many like-minded individuals, and it was certainly biased toward people willing to talk openly about race. She understood these problems and tried to include in her sample people of both sexes, of different ages, and representing different regions of the country. The Thinking About Diversity box on page 25 presents a statistical profile of Benjamin's respondents and offers some tips on how to read tables.

Benjamin based all her interviews on a series of questions and allowed her subjects to answer however they wished. As usually happens, the interviews took place in a wide range of settings. She met subjects in offices (hers or theirs), in hotel rooms, and in cars. In each case, Benjamin recorded the conversation, which lasted from two-and-one-half to three hours, so that she would not be distracted by taking notes.

As research ethics demand, Benjamin offered complete anonymity to participants. Even so, many of the women and men in her study—including notables such as Vernon E. Jordan Jr., the former president of the National Urban League, and Yvonne Walker-Taylor, the first woman president of Wilberforce University—were accustomed to being in the public eye and permitted Benjamin to use their names.

What surprised Benjamin most about her research was how eagerly many subjects responded to her request for an interview. These normally busy men and women appeared go out of their way to contribute to her project. Furthermore, once the interviews were under way, many of her subjects became very emotional. Benjamin reports that at some point in the conversation, about 40 of her 100 subjects cried. For them, apparently, the research provided an opportunity to release feelings and share experiences that they had never revealed to anyone before. How did Benjamin respond to the expression of such sentiments? She reports that she cried along with her respondents.

Of the research orientations described earlier in this chapter, you will see that Benjamin's research fits best under interpretive sociology (she wanted to find out what race meant to her subjects) and critical sociology (she undertook the study partly to document that racial prejudice still exists). Many of her subjects reported fearing that race might someday undermine their success, and others spoke of a race-based "glass ceiling" preventing them from reaching the highest positions in U.S. society. Summarizing her findings, Benjamin concluded that despite the improving social standing of African Americans, black people in the United States still suffer the sting of racial hostility.

⬤ **Evaluate** Professor Benjamin chose the survey as her method because she wanted to ask a lot of questions and gather information from her subjects. Certainly, some of the information she collected could have been obtained using a questionnaire. But she decided to carry out interviews because she was dealing with a complex and sensitive topic. Interacting with her subjects one on one for several hours, Benjamin could put them at ease, discuss personal matters, and ask them follow-up questions.

CHECK YOUR LEARNING Could this research have been carried out by a white sociologist? Why or why not?

In the Field: Participant Observation

Participant observation is *a research method in which investigators systematically observe people while joining them in their routine activities.* This method lets researchers study everyday social life in any natural setting, from a nightclub to a religious seminary. Cultural anthropologists use participant observation to study other societies, calling this method *fieldwork.*

At the beginning of a field study, most researchers do not have a specific hypothesis in mind. In fact, they may not yet realize what the important questions will turn out to be. This makes most participant observation *exploratory* and *descriptive*, falling within interpretive sociology and producing mostly qualitative, rather than quantitative, data. Compared with experiments and surveys, participant observation has few hard-and-fast rules. But this flexibility allows investigators to explore the unfamiliar and adapt to the unexpected.

Participant observers try to gain entry into a setting without disturbing the routine behavior of others. Their role is twofold: To gain an insider's viewpoint, they must become participants in the setting, "hanging out" for months or even years, trying to act, think, and even feel the same way as the people they are observing; at the same time, they must remain observers, standing back from the action and applying the sociological perspective to social patterns that others take for granted.

Because the personal impressions of a single researcher play such a central role, critics claim that participant observation falls short of scientific standards. Yet its personal approach is also a strength: Where a high-profile team of sociologists administering a formal survey might disrupt a setting, a sensitive participant observer often can gain important insight into people's behavior.

Illustration of Participant Observation: Street Corner Society

Did you ever wonder what everyday life was like in an unfamiliar neighborhood? In the late 1930s, a young graduate student at Harvard University named William Foote Whyte (1914–2000) set out to study social life in a rather rundown section of Boston. His curiosity led him to carry out four years of participant observation in this neighborhood, which he called "Cornerville."

At the time, Cornerville was home to first- and second-generation Italian immigrants. Most were poor, and many Bostonians considered Cornerville a place to avoid, a slum inhabited by criminals. Wanting to learn the truth, Whyte set out to discover for himself exactly what life was like inside this community. His celebrated book, *Street Corner Society* (1981, orig. 1943), describes Cornerville as a community with its own code of values, complex social patterns, and particular social conflicts.

Focus groups are a type of survey in which a small number of people representing a target population are asked for their opinions about some issue or product. Here a sociology professor asks students to evaluate textbooks for use in her introductory class.

Lois Benjamin's African American Elite: Using Tables in Research

Say you want to present a lot of information about a diverse population. How do you do it quickly and easily? The answer is by using a table. A table provides a lot of information in a small amount of space, so learning to read tables can increase your reading efficiency. When you spot a table, look first at the title to see what information it contains. The title of the table presented here provides a profile of the 100 subjects participating in Lois Benjamin's research. Across the top of the table, you will see eight variables that describe these men and women. Reading down each column, note the categories within each variable; the percentages in each column add up to 100.

Starting at the top left, we see that Benjamin's sample was mostly men (63 percent, versus 37 percent women). In terms of age, most of the respondents (68 percent) were in the middle stage of life, and most grew up in a predominantly black community in the South or in the North or Midwest region of the United States.

These individuals are indeed a professional elite. Notice that half have earned either a doctorate (32 percent) or a medical or law degree (17 percent). Given their extensive education (and Benjamin's own position as a professor), we should not be surprised that the largest share (35 percent) work in academic institutions. In terms of income, these are wealthy individuals, with most (64 percent) earning more than $50,000 annually back in 1990 (a salary that only 41 percent of full-time workers make even today).

Finally, we see that these 100 individuals are generally left-of-center in their political views. In part, this reflects their extensive schooling (which encourages progressive thinking) and the tendency of academics to fall on the liberal side of the political spectrum.

What Do You Think?

1. Why are statistical data, such as those in this table, an efficient way to convey a lot of information?

2. Looking at the table, can you determine how long it took most people to become part of this elite? Explain your answer.

3. Do you see any ways in which this African American elite might differ from a comparable white elite? If so, what are they?

The Talented One Hundred: Lois Benjamin's African American Elite

Sex	Age	Childhood Racial Setting	Childhood Region	Highest Educational Degree	Job Sector	Income	Political Orientation
Male 63%	35 or younger 6%	Mostly black 71%	West 6%	Doctorate 32%	College or university 35%	More than $50,000 64%	Radical left 13%
Female 37%	36 to 54 68%	Mostly white 15%	North or Midwest 32%	Medical or law 17%	Private, for-profit 17%	$35,000 to $50,000 18%	Liberal 38%
	55 or older 26%	Racially mixed 14%	South 38%	Master's 27%	Private, nonprofit 9%	$20,000 to $34,999 12%	Moderate 28%
			Northeast 12%	Bachelor's 13%	Government 22%	Less than $20,000 6%	Conservative 5%
			Other 12%	Less 11%	Self-employed 14%		Depends on issue 14%
					Retired 3%		Unknown 2%
100%	100%	100%	100%	100%	100%	100%	100%

Source: Adapted from Lois Benjamin, *The Black Elite: Facing the Color Line in the Twilight of the Twentieth Century* (Chicago: Nelson-Hall, 1991), p. 276.

To start, Whyte considered a range of research methods. He could have taken questionnaires to one of Cornerville's community centers and asked local people to fill them out. Or he could have invited members of the community to come to his Harvard office for interviews. But it is easy to see that such formal strategies would have gained little cooperation from the local people and produced few insights. Whyte decided, therefore, to ease into Cornerville life and slowly build a personal understand of this rather mysterious place.

Soon enough, Whyte discovered the challenges of even getting started in field research. As an upper-middle-class WASP graduate student from Harvard, he stood out on the streets of Cornerville. Even a friendly overture from an outsider could seem pushy and rude. Early on, Whyte dropped in at a local bar, hoping to buy a woman a drink and encourage her to talk about Cornerville. Looking around the room, he could find no woman alone. He thought he might have an opportunity when he saw a man sit down with two women. He walked over and asked, "Pardon me. Would you mind if I joined you?" Instantly, he realized his mistake:

> There was a moment of silence while the man stared at me. Then he offered to throw me down the stairs. I assured him that this would not be necessary, and demonstrated as much by walking right out of there without any assistance. (1981:289)

As this incident suggests, gaining entry to a community is the vital—and sometimes hazardous—first step in field research. "Breaking in" requires patience, ingenuity, and a little luck. Whyte's big break came in the form of a young man named "Doc," whom he met in a local social service agency. Whyte explained to Doc how hard it was to make friends in Cornerville. Doc responded by taking Whyte

Participant observation is a method of sociological research that allows a researcher to investigate people as they go about their everyday lives in some "natural" setting. At its best, participant observation makes you a star in your own reality show; but living in what may be a strange setting far from home for months at a time is always challenging.

you can just hang around, and you'll learn the answers in the long run without even having to ask the questions." (1981:303)

In the months and years that followed, Whyte became familiar with everyday life in Cornerville and even married a local woman with whom he would spend the rest of his life. In the process, he learned that the common stereotypes were wrong. In Cornerville, most people worked hard, many were quite successful, and some even boasted of sending children to college. Even today, Whyte's book is a fascinating story of the deeds, dreams, and disappointments of immigrants and their children living in one ethnic community, and it contains the rich detail that can come only from years of participant observation.

Evaluate To study the community he called Cornerville, Professor Whyte chose participant observation—a good choice because he did not have a specific hypothesis to test, nor did he know at the outset exactly what the questions were. By moving into this community for several years, Whyte was able to come to know the place and able to paint a complex picture of social life there.

CHECK YOUR LEARNING Give an example of a topic for sociological research that would be best studied using (1) an experiment, (2) a survey, and (3) participant observation.

Using Available Data: Existing Sources

Not all research requires investigators to collect new data. Sometimes sociologists make use of existing sources, data collected by others.

The data most widely used by researchers are gathered by government agencies such as the U.S. Census Bureau. Data about other nations in the world are found in various publications of the United Nations and the World Bank.

Using available information saves time and money. This method has special appeal to sociologists with low budgets. And in fact, government data are usually more extensive and more accurate than what most researchers could obtain on their own.

But using available data has problems of its own. Data may not be available in the exact form that is needed. For example, you may be able to find the average salaries paid to professors at your school but not separate figures for the amounts paid to women and men. Further, there are always questions about how accurate the existing data are. In his nineteenth-century study of suicide, described earlier, Emile Durkheim used official records. But Durkheim had no way to know if a death classified as a suicide was really an accident or vice versa.

under his wing and introducing him to others in the community. With Doc's help, Whyte soon became a neighborhood regular.

Whyte's friendship with Doc illustrates the importance of a *key informant* in field research. Such people not only introduce a researcher to a community but also often remain a source of information and help. But using a key informant also has its risks. Because any person has a particular circle of friends, a key informant's guidance is certain to "spin" the study in one way or another. Moreover, in the eyes of others, the reputation of the key informant, for better or worse, usually rubs off on the investigator. So although a key informant is helpful early on, a participant observer must seek a broader range of contacts.

Having entered the Cornerville world, Whyte quickly learned another lesson: A field researcher needs to know when to speak up and when to shut up. One evening, he joined a group discussing neighborhood gambling. Wanting to get the facts straight, Whyte asked innocently, "I suppose the cops were all paid off?"

> The gambler's jaw dropped. He glared at me. Then he denied vehemently that any policeman had been paid off and immediately switched the conversation to another subject. For the rest of that evening I felt very uncomfortable.

The next day, Doc offered some sound advice:

> "Go easy on that 'who,' 'what,' 'why,' 'when,' 'where' stuff, Bill. You ask those questions and people will clam up on you. If people accept you,

---

research method a systematic plan for doing research

experiment a research method for investigating cause and effect under highly controlled conditions

survey a research method in which subjects respond to a series of statements or questions on a questionnaire or in an interview

participant observation a research method in which investigators systematically observe people while joining them in their routine activities

use of existing sources a research method in which a researcher uses data already collected by others

Illustration of the Use of Existing Sources: A Tale of Two Cities

Why might one city have been home to many famous people and another have produced hardly any famous people at all? To those of us living in the present, historical data offer a key to unlocking secrets of the past. The award-winning study *Puritan Boston and Quaker Philadelphia,* by E. Digby Baltzell (1979), shows how a researcher can use available data to do historical research.

This story begins with Baltzell making a chance visit to Bowdoin College in Maine. As he walked into the college library, he saw on the wall three large portraits—of the celebrated author Nathaniel Hawthorne, the famous poet Henry Wadsworth Longfellow, and Franklin Pierce, the fourteenth president of the United States. He soon learned that all three men were members of the same class at Bowdoin, graduating in 1825. How could it be, Baltzell wondered, that this small college had graduated more famous people in a single year than his own, much bigger, University of Pennsylvania had graduated in its entire history? To answer this question, Baltzell was soon paging through historical documents to see whether New England states had really produced more famous people than his native Pennsylvania.

What were Baltzell's data? He turned to the *Dictionary of American Biography,* twenty volumes profiling more than 13,000 outstanding men and women in fields such as politics, law, and the arts. The dictionary told Baltzell who was great, and he realized that the longer the biography, the more important the person is thought to be.

By the time Baltzell had identified the seventy-five individuals with the longest biographies, he saw a striking pattern. Massachusetts had the most by far, with twenty-one of the seventy-five top achievers. The New England states, combined, claimed thirty-one entries. By contrast, Pennsylvania could boast of only two, and all the states in the Middle Atlantic region had just twelve. Looking more closely, Baltzell discovered that most of New England's great achievers had grown up in and around the city of Boston. Again, in

stark contrast, almost no one of comparable standing came from his own Philadelphia, a city with many more people than Boston.

What could explain this remarkable pattern? Baltzell drew inspiration from the German sociologist Max Weber (1958, orig. 1904–05), who argued that a region's record of achievement was influenced by its major religious beliefs (see Chapter 13, "Family and Religion"). In the religious differences between Boston and Philadelphia, Baltzell found the answer to his puzzle. Boston was a Puritan settlement, founded by people who highly valued the pursuit of excellence and public achievement. Philadelphia, by contrast, was settled by Quakers, who believed in equality and avoided public notice.

Both the Puritans and the Quakers had fled religious persecution in England, but once people settled in the new land, the two religious traditions produced quite different cultural patterns. Convinced of humanity's innate sinfulness, Boston Puritans built a rigid society in which family, church, and school regulated people's behavior. They celebrated hard work as a means of glorifying God and viewed public success as a reassuring sign of God's blessing. In short, Puritanism fostered a disciplined and ambitious life in which people both sought and respected achievement.

Philadelphia's Quakers, by contrast, built their way of life on the belief that all human beings are basically good. They saw little need for strong social institutions to "save" people from sinfulness. They believed in equality, so even those who became rich considered themselves no better than anyone else. Thus rich and poor alike lived modestly and discouraged one another from standing out by seeking fame or running for public office.

In Baltzell's sociological imagination, Boston and Philadelphia took the form of two social "test tubes": Puritanism was poured into one, Quakerism into the other. Centuries later, we can see that different "chemical reactions" occurred in each case. The two belief systems apparently led to different attitudes toward personal achievement, which in turn shaped the history of each region. Today, we can see that Boston's Kennedys (despite being Catholic) are only

Summing Up

Four Research Methods

	Experiment	Survey	Participant Observation	Existing Sources
Application	For explanatory research that specifies relationships between variables Generates quantitative data	For gathering information about issues that cannot be directly observed, such as attitudes and values Useful for descriptive and explanatory research Generates quantitative or qualitative data	For exploratory and descriptive study of people in a "natural" setting Generates qualitative data	For exploratory, descriptive, or explanatory research whenever suitable data are available
Advantages	Provides the greatest opportunity to specify cause-and-effect relationships Replication of research is relatively easy.	Sampling, using questionnaires, allows surveys of large populations. Interviews provide in-depth responses.	Allows study of "natural" behavior Usually inexpensive	Saves time and expense of data collection Makes historical research possible
Limitations	Laboratory settings have an artificial quality. Unless the research environment is carefully controlled, results may be biased.	Questionnaires must be carefully prepared and may yield a low return rate. Interviews are expensive and time-consuming.	Time-consuming Replication of research is difficult. Researcher must balance roles of participant and observer.	Researcher has no control over possible biases in data. Data may only partially fit current research needs.

Jena: (*raising her eyes from her notebook*) Today, in sociology class, we talked about stereotypes.

Marcia: (*trying to focus on her science lab*) OK, here's one: Roommates don't like to be disturbed when they're studying.

Jena: Seriously, my studious friend, we all have stereotypes, even professors.

Marcia: (*becoming faintly interested*) Like what?

Jena: Professor Chandler said today in class that Protestants are most likely to kill themselves. And later Yannina—this girl from, I think, Ecuador—said something like "You Americans are rich, but you don't take marriage seriously, and you love to divorce!"

Marcia: My brother said to me last week that "everybody knows you have to be black to play professional basketball." Now there's a stereotype!

College students, like everyone else, are quick to make generalizations about people. As this chapter explains, sociologists, too, love to generalize by looking for social patterns in everyday life. However, beginning students of sociology may wonder if sociological generalizations aren't really the same thing as stereotypes. For example, are the statements reported by Jena and Marcia true generalizations or false stereotypes?

A **stereotype** is *a simplified description applied to every person in some category*. Each of the statements the students made is a stereotype that is false, for three reasons. First, rather than describing averages, each statement describes every person in some category in exactly the same way; second, even though many stereotypes often contain an element of truth, each of these three statements leaves out relevant facts and distorts reality; and third, each statement is motivated by bias, spoken more as a put-down than as a fair-minded observation.

Good sociology makes generalizations, but they must meet three conditions. First, sociologists do not carelessly apply any generalization to everyone in a category. Second, sociologists make sure that a generalization squares with all available facts. And third, sociologists make generalizations fair-mindedly, in the interest of getting at the truth.

Jena remembered her professor saying (although not in quite the same words) that the suicide rate among Protestants is higher than among Catholics or Jews. Based on information presented earlier in this chapter, that is a true statement. However, the way Jena incorrectly reported the classroom remark—"If you're a Protestant, you're likely to kill yourself"—is not good sociology. It is not a true generalization because the vast majority of Protestants do no such thing. It would be just as wrong to jump to the conclusion that a particular friend, because he is a Protestant male, is about to end his own life. (Imagine refusing to lend money to a roommate who happens to be a Baptist, explaining, "Well,

A sociology classroom is a good place to get at the truth behind common stereotypes.

given the way people like you commit suicide, I might never get paid back!")

Second, sociologists shape their generalizations to available facts. A more factual version of the statement Yannina made is that by world standards, the U.S. population has a very high standard of living, that almost everyone in our society does marry at some point with every intention of staying married, and that even though our divorce rate is among the world's highest, few people take pleasure in divorcing.

Third, sociologists try to be fair-minded and want to get at the truth. The statements made by Marcia's brother about African Americans and basketball is a stereotype and therefore not good sociology for two reasons. First, as stated it is simply not true, and second, it seems motivated by racial bias rather than truth-seeking.

The bottom line, then, is that good sociological generalizations are *not* the same as stereotyping. But a college sociology course is an excellent setting for getting at the truths behind common stereotypes. The classroom encourages discussion and offers the factual information you need to decide whether a particular statement is a valid sociological generalization or a harmful or unfair stereotype.

What Do You Think?

1. Can you think of a common stereotype of sociologists? What is it? After reading this box, do you still think it is valid?

2. Do you think taking a sociology course can help correct people's stereotypes? Why or why not?

3. Can you think of a stereotype of your own that might be challenged by sociological analysis?

one of that city's many families that exemplify the Puritan pursuit of recognition and leadership. By contrast, there has never been even one family with such stature in the entire history of Philadelphia.

Baltzell's study uses scientific logic, but it also illustrates the interpretive approach by showing how people make sense of their world. His research reminds us that sociological investigation often involves mixing research orientations to fit a particular problem. The Summing Up table on page 27 provides a quick review of the four major methods of sociological investigation.

 Evaluate The main reason Professor Baltzell chose to use existing sources is that this is a good way to learn about history. The *Dictionary of American Biography* offers a great deal of information about people who lived long ago and obviously are not available for an interview. At the same time, existing sources were not created with the purpose of answering a modern-day sociologist's questions. For this reason, using such documents requires a critical eye and a good deal of creative thinking.

CHECK YOUR LEARNING What other questions about life in the past might you wish to answer using existing sources?

Putting It All Together: Ten Steps in Sociological Research

 Evaluate

The following ten questions will guide you through a research project in sociology.

1. **What is your topic?** Being curious and using the sociological perspective can generate ideas for social research at any time and in any place. Pick a topic you find interesting and that you think is important to study.

2. **What have others already learned?** You are probably not the first person with an interest in some issue. Visit the library and search the Internet to see what theories and methods other researchers have applied to your topic. In reviewing the existing research, note problems that have come up to avoid repeating past mistakes.

3. **What, exactly, are your questions?** Are you seeking to explore an unfamiliar social setting? To describe some category of people? To investigate cause and effect among variables? Clearly state the goals of your research, and operationalize all variables.

4. **What will you need to carry out research?** How much time and money are available to you? What special equipment or skills does the research require? Can you do all the work yourself?

5. **Are there ethical concerns?** Might the research harm anyone? How can you minimize the chances for injury? Will you promise your subjects anonymity? If so, how will you ensure that anonymity will be maintained?

6. **What method will you use?** Consider all major research strategies and combinations of methods. The most suitable method will depend on the kinds of questions you are asking and the resources available to you.

7. **How will you record the data?** The research method you use guides your data collection. Be sure to record information accurately and in a way that will make sense to you later on (it may be months before you write up the results of your work). Watch out for any personal bias that may creep into your work.

8. **What do the data tell you?** Determine what the data say about your initial questions. If your study involves a specific hypothesis, you should be able to confirm, reject, or modify it on the basis of your findings. Keep in mind that there will be several ways to interpret your results, depending on the theoretical approach you apply, and you should consider them all.

9. **What are your conclusions?** Prepare a final report explaining what you have learned. Also, evaluate your own work. What problems arose during the research process? What questions were left unanswered?

10. **How can you share what you've learned?** Consider making a presentation to your class or maybe even to a meeting of professional sociologists. The point is to share what you have learned with others and to let them respond to your work.

The Controversy & Debate box discusses the use of the sociological perspective and reviews many of the ideas presented in this chapter. This box will help you apply what you have learned to the important question of how the generalizations made by sociologists differ from the common stereotypes we hear every day.

Seeing Sociology in Everyday Life

Why do couples marry?

We asked this question at the beginning of this chapter. The commonsense answer is that people marry because they are in love. But as this chapter has explained, society guides our everyday lives, affecting what we do, think, and feel. Look at the three photographs, each showing a couple that, we can assume, is "in love." In each case, can you provide some of the rest of the story? By looking at the categories that the people involved represent, explain how society is at work in bringing the two people together.

Hint Society is at work on many levels. Consider (1) rules about same-sex and other-sex marriage, (2) laws defining the number of people who may marry, (3) the importance of race and ethnicity, (4) the importance of social class, (5) the importance of age, and (6) the importance of social exchange (what each partner offers the other). All societies enforce various rules that state who should or should not marry whom.

Beyoncé Giselle Knowles, widely known as Beyoncé, performs in New York's Madison Square Garden with her husband Jay-Z (Shawn Corey Carter). Looking at this couple, who married in 2008, what social patterns do you see?

In 1997, during the fourth season of her hit TV show, *Ellen*, Ellen DeGeneres "came out" as a lesbian, which put her on the cover of *Time* magazine. Since then, she has been an activist on behalf of gay and lesbian issues. Following California's brief legalization of same-sex marriage in 2008, she married her longtime girlfriend, Australian actress Portia de Rossi.

In 2011, 85-year-old Hugh Hefner planned to marry 25-year-old Crystal Harris, only to have her call off the wedding a few days before the scheduled June event. The July issue of *Playboy* magazine featured Harris on the cover with the line "Introducing Mrs. Crystal Hefner" covered at the last minute with a sticker stating "Runaway Bride in This Issue!" What social patterns do you see in this relationship?

Seeing Sociology in *Your* Everyday Life

1. Analyze the marriages of your parents, other family members, and friends in terms of class, race, age, and other factors. What evidence can you find that society guides the feelings that we call "love"?

2. Figure 13–2 on page 351 shows the U.S. divorce rate over the past century. Using the sociological perspective, and with an eye to the timeline inside the back cover of this book, try to identify societal factors that caused the divorce rate to rise or fall.

3. As this chapter has explained, the time in human history when we are born, the society in which we are born, as well as our class position, race, and gender all shape the personal experiences we have throughout our lives. Does this mean we have no power over our own destiny? No, in fact, the more we understand how society works, the more power we have to shape our own lives. Go to the "Seeing Sociology in *Your* Everyday Life" feature on MySocLab to learn more about how the material in this chapter can help deepen your understanding of yourself and others around you so that you can more effectively pursue your life goals. A second feature shows ways that what you have learned about sociological research enhances your ability for critical thinking.

What Is the Sociological Perspective?

The **sociological perspective** reveals the power of society to shape individual lives.
- C. Wright Mills called this point of view the "sociological imagination," which transforms personal troubles into public issues.
- Being an outsider or experiencing a social crisis can encourage the sociological perspective. **pp. 2–7**

Applying the sociological perspective has many benefits:
- helping us understand the barriers and opportunities in our lives
- giving us an advantage in our careers
- guiding public policy **pp. 7–8**

Global awareness is an important part of the sociological perspective because our society's place in the world affects us all.

sociology (p. 2) the systematic study of human society

sociological perspective (p. 2) the special point of view of sociology that sees general patterns of society in the lives of particular people

👁️ Watch the Video on **mysoclab.com**

📖 Read the Document on **mysoclab.com**

global perspective (p. 5) the study of the larger world and our society's place in it
high-income countries (p. 5) the nations with the highest overall standards of living
middle-income countries (p. 6) nations with a standard of living about average for the world as a whole
low-income countries (p. 6) nations with a low standard of living, in which most people are poor

Origins of Sociology

Rapid social change helped trigger the development of sociology:
- rise of an industrial economy
- explosive growth of cities
- new political ideas. **pp. 8–10**

Auguste Comte named the discipline of sociology in 1838.
- Early philosophers had tried to describe the ideal society, but Comte wanted to understand society as it really is.
- Karl Marx and many later sociologists used sociology to try to make society better. **p. 9**

positivism (p. 9) a scientific approach to knowledge based on "positive" facts as opposed to mere speculation

Theory: Linking Facts to Create Meaning

 ·········· **macro-level** ··········

The **structural-functional approach** explores how social structures work together to help society operate.
- Auguste Comte, Emile Durkheim, and Herbert Spencer helped develop the structural-functional approach. **pp. 10–11**

The **social-conflict approach** shows how inequality creates conflict and causes change.
- Two important types of conflict analysis are **gender-conflict theory**, which is also called **feminism**, and **race-conflict theory**.
- Karl Marx helped develop the social-conflict approach. **pp. 11–14**

 ·········· **micro-level** ··········

The **symbolic-interaction approach** studies how people, in everyday interaction, construct reality.
- Max Weber and George Herbert Mead helped develop of the social-interaction approach. **pp. 14, 16**

✳️ Explore the Map on **mysoclab.com**

theory (p. 10) a statement of how and why specific facts are related

theoretical approach (p. 10) a basic image of society that guides thinking and research

structural-functional approach (p. 10) a framework for building theory that sees society as a complex system whose parts work together to promote solidarity and stability

social structure (p. 10) any relatively stable pattern of social behavior

social functions (p. 10) the consequences of a social pattern for the operation of society as a whole

manifest functions (p. 11) the recognized and intended consequences of any social pattern

latent functions (p. 11) the unrecognized and unintended consequences of any social pattern

social dysfunction (p. 11) any social pattern that may disrupt the operation of society

social-conflict approach (p. 11) a framework for building theory that sees society as an arena of inequality that generates conflict and change

gender-conflict theory (feminist theory) (p. 12) the study of society that focuses on inequality and conflict between women and men

feminism (p. 12) support of social equality for women and men

race-conflict theory (p. 12) the study of society that focuses on inequality and conflict between people of different racial and ethnic categories

macro-level orientation (p. 14) a broad focus on social structures that shape society as a whole

micro-level orientation (p. 14) a close-up focus on social interaction in specific situations

symbolic-interaction approach (p. 14) a framework for building theory that sees society as the product of the everyday interactions of individuals

---

positivist sociology (p. 16) the study of society based on scientific observation of social behavior

science (p. 16) a logical system that bases knowledge on direct, systematic observation

empirical evidence (p. 16) information we can verify with our senses

concept (p. 17) a mental construct that represents some aspect of the world in a simplified form

variable (p. 17) a concept whose value changes from case to case

measurement (p. 17) a procedure for determining the value of a variable in a specific case

reliability (p. 18) consistency in measurement

validity (p. 18) actually measuring exactly what you intend to measure

correlation (p. 18) a relationship in which two (or more) variables change together

cause and effect (p. 18) a relationship in which change in one variable (the independent variable) causes change in another (the dependent variable)

interpretive sociology (p. 19) the study of society that focuses on the meanings people attach to their social world

critical sociology (p. 19) the study of society that focuses on the need for social change

gender (p. 20) the personal traits and social positions that members of a society attach to being female or male

Research: Doing Sociology

Positivist sociology uses the logic of science to understand how variables are related.
- tries to establish cause and effect
- demands that researchers try to be objective
- linked to structural-functional theory   **pp. 16–18**

Interpretive sociology focuses on the meanings that people attach to behavior.
- people construct reality in their everyday lives.
- Weber's *Verstehen* is learning how people understand their world.
- linked to symbolic-interaction theory   **p. 19**

Critical sociology uses research to bring about social change.
- focuses on inequality
- rejects the principle of objectivity, claiming that all research is political
- linked to social-conflict theory   **pp. 19–20**

Methods: Strategies for Doing Research

The **experiment** allows researchers to study cause and effect between two or more variables in a controlled setting.
- example of an experiment: Zimbardo's "Stanford County Prison"   **pp. 22–23**

Survey research uses questionnaires or interviews to gather subjects' responses to a series of questions.
- example of a survey: Benjamin's "Talented One Hundred"   **pp. 23–25**

Through **participant observation**, researchers join with people in a social setting for an extended period of time.
- example of participant observation: Whyte's *Street Corner Society*   **pp. 24, 26**

Researchers use data collected by others from **existing sources** to save time and money.
- example of using existing sources: Baltzell's *Puritan Boston and Quaker Philadelphia*   **pp. 26–27**

research method (p. 21) a systematic plan for doing research

experiment (p. 21) a research method for investigating cause and effect under highly controlled conditions

survey (p. 23) a research method in which subjects respond to a series of statements or questions on a questionnaire or in an interview

participant observation (p. 24) a research method in which investigators systematically observe people while joining them in their routine activities

stereotype (p. 29) a simplified description applied to every person in some category

2 Culture

Learning Objectives

Remember the definitions of the key terms highlighted in boldfaced type throughout this chapter.

Understand the historical process through which human beings came to live within a symbolic world we call "culture."

Apply sociology's macro-level theoretical approaches to culture in order to better understand our way of life.

Analyze popular television programming and films to see how they reflect the key values of U.S. culture.

Evaluate cultural differences, informed by an understanding of two important sociological concepts: ethnocentrism and cultural relativism.

Create a broader vision of U.S. culture by studying cultural diversity, including popular culture as well as subcultural and countercultural patterns.

This chapter focuses on the concept of "culture," which refers to a society's entire way of life. The root of the word "culture" is the same as that of the word "cultivate," a link that suggests people living together actually "grow" their way of life over time. ■

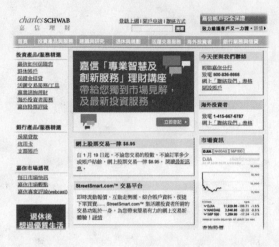

It's late on a Tuesday night, but Fang Lin gazes intently at her computer screen. Dong Wang, who is married to Fang, walks up behind the chair.

"I'm trying to finish organizing our investments," Fang explains, speaking in Chinese.

"I didn't realize that we could do all this online in our own language," Dong says, reading the screen. "That's great. I like that a lot."

Fang and Dong are not alone in feeling this way. Back in 1990, executives of Charles Schwab & Co., a large investment brokerage corporation, gathered at the company's headquarters in San Francisco to discuss ways to expand their business. They came up with the idea that the company would profit by giving greater attention to the increasing cultural diversity of the United States. Why? Pointing to data collected by the U.S. Census Bureau, they saw that the number of Asian Americans was rising rapidly, not just in San Francisco but all over the country. The data also showed that Asian Americans, on average, were doing pretty well financially. That's still true, with more than half of today's Asian American families earning more than $75,000 a year.

Based on such data, Schwab launched a diversity initiative, assigning executives to work on building awareness of the company among Asian Americans. Since then, the scope of the program has grown so that Schwab now employs more than 300 people who speak Chinese, Japanese, Korean, Vietnamese, or some other Asian language. Having account executives who speak languages other than English is smart because research shows that most immigrants who come to the United States prefer to communicate in their first language, especially when dealing with important matters like investing their money. In addition, the company has launched Web sites using Korean, Chinese, and other Asian languages. Fang Lin and Dong Wang are just two of the millions of people who have opened accounts with companies that reach out to them in a familiar language other than English.

This initiative has been extremely successful for Schwab, which now manages a much larger share of investments made by Asian Americans. Asian Americans spent $290 billion in 2010, so any company would do well to follow the lead Schwab has taken. Other racial and ethnic categories that represent even larger markets in the United States are Hispanic Americans and African Americans (each spending more than $500 billion in 2010) (Fattah, 2002; Karrfalt, 2003; U.S. Census Bureau, 2011; U.S. Bureau of Labor Statistics, 2011).

Businesses like Schwab have learned that the United States is the most *multicultural* of all the world's nations. This cultural diversity reflects our long history of receiving immigrants from all over the world. The ways of life found around the world differ not only in terms of languages and forms of dress but also in preferred foods, musical tastes, family patterns, and beliefs about right and wrong. Some of the world's people have many children, while others have few; some honor the elderly, while others seem to glorify youth. Some societies are peaceful and others warlike, and they embrace thousands of different religious beliefs and ideas about what is polite and rude, beautiful and ugly, pleasant and repulsive. This amazing human capacity for so many different ways of life is a matter of human culture.

What Is Culture?

● Understand

Culture is *the ways of thinking, ways of acting, and material objects that together form a people's way of life.* When studying culture, sociologists consider both thoughts and things. **Nonmaterial culture** consists of *the ideas created by members of a society,* ranging from

Human beings around the globe create diverse ways of life. Such differences begin with outward appearance: Contrast the women shown here from Ethiopia, India, Kenya, Thailand, South Yemen, and the United States and the men from Taiwan (Republic of China), Ecuador, and Papua New Guinea. Less obvious but of even greater importance are internal differences, since culture also shapes our goals in life, our sense of justice, and even our innermost personal feelings.

art to Zen. By contrast, **material culture** refers to *the physical things created by members of a society*, everything from armchairs to zippers.

The terms "culture" and "society" obviously go hand in hand, but their precise meanings differ. Culture is a shared way of life or social heritage; **society** refers to *people who interact in a defined territory and share a culture*. Neither society nor culture could exist without the other.

Culture shapes not only what we do but also what we think and how we feel—elements of what we commonly, but wrongly, describe as "human nature." The warlike Yąnomamö of the Brazilian rain forest think aggression is natural, but halfway around the world, the Semai of Malaysia live quite peacefully. The cultures of the United States and Japan both stress achievement and hard work, but members of our society

Confronting the Yąnomamö: The Experience of Culture Shock

A small aluminum motorboat chugged steadily along the muddy Orinoco River, deep within South America's vast tropical rain forest. The anthropologist Napoleon Chagnon was nearing the end of a three-day journey to the home territory of the Yąnomamö, one of the most technologically simple societies on Earth.

Some 12,000 Yąnomamö live in villages scattered along the border of Venezuela and Brazil. Their way of life could not be more different from our own. The Yąnomamö wear little clothing and live without electricity, cars, or other conveniences most people in the United States take for granted. They use bows and arrows for hunting and warfare, as they have for centuries. Many of the Yąnomamö have had little contact with the outside world, so Chagnon would be as strange to them as they would be to him.

By 2:00 in the afternoon, Chagnon had almost reached his destination. The hot sun and humid air were becoming unbearable. Chagnon's clothes were soaked with sweat, and his face and hands were swollen from the bites of gnats swarming around him. But he scarcely noticed, so focused was he that in just a few moments, he would be face to face with people unlike any he had ever known.

Chagnon's heart pounded as the boat slid onto the riverbank. He and his guide climbed from the boat and walked toward the Yąnomamö village, stooping as they pushed their way through the dense undergrowth. Chagnon describes what happened next:

> I looked up and gasped when I saw a dozen burly, naked, sweaty, hideous men staring at us down the shafts of their drawn arrows! Immense wads of green tobacco were stuck between their lower teeth and lips, making them look even more hideous, and strands of dark green slime dripped or hung from their nostrils—strands so long that they clung to their [chests] or drizzled down their chins.

My next discovery was that there were a dozen or so vicious, underfed dogs snapping at my legs, circling me as if I were to be their next meal. I just stood there holding my notebook, helpless and pathetic. Then the stench of the decaying vegetation and filth hit me and I almost got sick. I was horrified. What kind of welcome was this for the person who came here to live with you and learn your way of life, to become friends with you? (1992:11–12)

Fortunately for Chagnon, the Yąnomamö villagers recognized his guide and lowered their weapons. Reassured that he would survive the afternoon, Chagnon still was shaken by his inability to make any sense of these people. And this was going to be his home for the next year and a half! He wondered why he had given up physics to study human culture in the first place.

Join the Blog!

Can you think of an experience of your own similar to the one described here? Do you think you may ever have *caused* culture shock in others? Go to MySocLab and join the Sociology in Focus blog to share your experiences and opinions and to see what others think.

---

value individualism more than the Japanese, who value collective harmony.

Given the extent of cultural differences in the world and people's tendency to view their own way of life as "natural," it is no wonder that we often feel **culture shock**, *personal disorientation when experiencing an unfamiliar way of life*. People can experience culture shock right here in the United States when, say, African Americans shop in an Iranian neighborhood in Los Angeles, college students visit the Amish countryside in Ohio, or New Yorkers travel through small towns in the Deep South. But culture shock can be intense when we travel abroad: The Sociology

in Focus box tells the story of a U.S. researcher making his first visit to the home of the Yąnomamö living in the Amazon region of South America.

> January 2, high in the Andes Mountains of Peru. In the rural highlands, people are poor and depend on one another. The culture is built on cooperation among families and neighbors who have lived nearby for many generations. Today, we spend an hour watching a new house being built. A young couple invited their families and friends, who arrived about 6:30 in the morning, and right away everyone began building. By midafternoon, most of the work had been done, and the couple then provided a large meal, drinks, and music that continued for the rest of the day.

No particular way of life is "natural" to humans, even though most people around the world view their own behavior that way. The cooperation that comes naturally in small communities high in the Andes Mountains of Peru is very different from the competitive lifestyle that is natural to so many people living in, say, Chicago or New York. Such variations come from the fact that we are creatures of culture who join

---

culture the ways of thinking, the ways of acting, and the material objects that together from a people's way of life

nonmaterial culture the ideas created by members of a society

material culture the physical things created by members of a society

together to create our own way of life. Every other animal, from ants to zebras, behaves very much the same all around the world because behavior is guided by instincts, biological programming over which the species has no control. A few animals—notably chimpanzees and related primates—have some capacity for culture, as researchers have learned by observing them using tools and teaching simple skills to their offspring. But the creative power of humans is far greater than that of any other form of life. In short, *only humans rely on culture rather than instinct to create a way of life and ensure our survival* (Harris, 1987; Morell, 2008). To understand how human culture came to be, we need to look back at the history of our species.

Culture and Human Intelligence

Scientists tell us that our planet is 4.5 billion years old (see the timeline inside the back cover of this text). Life appeared about 1 billion years later. Fast-forward another 2 to 3 billion years, and we find dinosaurs ruling Earth. It was only after these giant creatures disappeared—some 65 million years ago—that our history took a crucial turn with the appearance of the animals we call primates.

The importance of primates is that they have the largest brains relative to body size of all living creatures. About 12 million years ago, primates began to evolve along two different lines, leading humans away from the great apes, our closest relatives. Some 5 million years ago, our distant human ancestors climbed down from the trees of Northeast Africa to move around in the tall grasses. There, walking upright, they learned the advantages of hunting in groups and made use of fire, tools, and weapons; built simple shelters; and fashioned basic clothing. These Stone Age achievements mark the point at which our ancestors embarked on a distinct evolutionary course, making culture their primary strategy for survival. By about 250,000 years ago, our own species, *Homo sapiens*—Latin for "intelligent person"—had emerged. Humans continued to evolve so that by about 40,000 years ago, people who looked more or less like us roamed the planet. With larger brains, these "modern" *Homo sapiens* developed culture rapidly, as the wide range of tools and cave art that have survived from this period suggests.

By 12,000 years ago, the founding of permanent settlements and the creation of specialized occupations in the Middle East (in portions of modern-day Iraq and Egypt) marked a turning point. About this time, the biological forces we call instincts had almost disappeared, replaced by a more efficient survival scheme: *fashioning the natural environment to our purposes.* Ever since, humans have made and remade their world in countless ways, resulting in today's fascinating cultural diversity.

How Many Cultures?

How many cultures are there in the United States? One indicator of culture is language; the Census Bureau lists more than 300 languages spoken in this country, most of which were brought by immigrants from nations around the world (U.S. Census Bureau, 2011).

All societies contain cultural differences that can provoke a mild case of culture shock. This woman traveling on a British subway is not sure what to make of the woman sitting next to her, who is wearing the Muslim full-face veil known as the *niqab*.

Globally, experts document almost 7,000 languages, suggesting the existence of as many distinct cultures. Yet the number of languages spoken around the world is declining, and more than half are now spoken by fewer than 10,000 people (Lewis, 2009). Experts expect that the coming decades may see the disappearance of hundreds of these languages, and perhaps half the world's languages may even disappear before the end of this century (Crystal, 2010). Languages on the endangered list include Gullah, Pennsylvania German, and Pawnee (all spoken in the United States), Han (northwestern Canada), Oro in the Amazon region (Brazil), Sardinian (Sardinia, Italy), Aramaic (the language of Jesus of Nazareth in the Middle East), Nu Shu (a language of southern China that is the only one known to be spoken exclusively by women), and Wakka Wakka and several other Aboriginal tongues spoken in Australia. What accounts for the decline? Likely reasons include high-technology communication, increasing international migration, and an expanding global economy, all of which are reducing global cultural diversity (UNESCO, 2001; Barovick, 2002; Hayden, 2003; Lewis, 2009).

The Elements of Culture

 Understand

Although cultures vary greatly, they all have common elements, including symbols, language, values, and norms. We begin our discussion with the one that is the basis for all the others: symbols.

Symbols

Like all creatures, human beings sense the surrounding world, but unlike others, we also give the world *meaning*. Humans transform

New Symbols in the World of Instant Messaging

Molly: gr8 to c u!

Greg: u 2

Molly: jw about next time

Greg: idk, lotta work!

Molly: no prb, xoxoxo

Greg: thanx, bcnu

The world of symbols changes all the time. One reason that people create new symbols is that we develop new ways to communicate. Today, 83 percent of adults in the United States own cell phones and three-quarters of them—especially those who are young—use mobile text-messaging on a regular basis. Researchers report that cell phone owners between 18 and 24 years of age typically send or receive about 100 text messages a day (Pew Research Center, 2011).

Here are some of the most common text-messaging symbols:

b be
bc because
b4 before
b4n 'bye for now
bbl be back later
bcnu be seeing you
brb be right back
cu see you
def definitely
g2g got to go
gal get a life
gmta great minds think alike

gr8 great
hagn have a good night
h&k hugs and kisses
idc I don't care
idt I don't think
idk I don't know
imbl it must be love
jk just kidding
jw just wondering
j4f just for fun
kc keep cool
l8r later
lmao laugh my ass off
ltnc long time no see
myob mind your own business
no prb no problem
omg oh my gosh
pcm please call me

plz please
prbly probably
qpsa ¿Que pasa?
rt right
thanx thanks
u you
ur you are
w/ with
w/e whatever
w/o without
wan2 want to
wtf what the freak
y why
2l8 too late
? question
2 to, two
4 for, four

What Do You Think?

1. What does the creation of symbols such as these suggest about culture?

2. Do you think that using such symbols is a good way to communicate? Does it lead to confusion or misunderstanding? Why or why not?

3. What other kinds of symbols can you think of that are new to your generation?

Sources: J. Rubin (2003), Berteau (2005), Bacher (2009), and Lenhart (2010).

the elements of the world into *symbols*. A **symbol** is *anything that carries a particular meaning recognized by people who share a culture.* A word, a whistle, a wall of graffiti, a flashing red light, a raised fist—all serve as symbols. The human capacity to create and manipulate symbols is almost limitless—think of the variety of meanings associated with the simple act of winking an eye, which can convey such messages as interest, understanding, or insult.

Societies create new symbols all the time. The Seeing Sociology in Everyday Life box describes some of the "cyber-symbols" that have developed along with our increasing use of computers for communication.

We are so dependent on our culture's symbols that we often take them for granted. We become keenly aware of the importance of a symbol, however, when it is used in an unconventional way, as when someone burns a U.S. flag during a political demonstration. Entering an unfamiliar culture also reminds us of the power of symbols; culture shock is really the inability to "read" meaning in

unfamiliar surroundings. Not understanding the symbols of a culture leaves a person feeling lost and isolated, unsure of how to act, and sometimes frightened.

Culture shock is a two-way process. On one hand, the traveler *experiences* culture shock when meeting people whose way of life is dramatically different. For example, North Americans who consider dogs beloved household pets might be put off by the Masai of eastern Africa, who ignore dogs and never feed them. The same travelers might be horrified to find that in parts of Indonesia and the People's Republic of China, people roast dogs for dinner.

On the other hand, a traveler can *inflict* culture shock on others by acting in ways that offend them. The North American who asks for a steak in an Indian restaurant is likely to offend Hindus working there because they consider cows sacred and never to be eaten. Global travel provides endless opportunities for misunderstanding.

Symbolic meanings also vary within a single society. In the debate about flying the Confederate flag over the South Carolina statehouse a few years ago, some people saw the flag as a symbol of regional pride, while others saw it as a symbol of racial oppression.

Language

The heart of a symbolic system is **language**, *a system of symbols that allows people to communicate with one another.* Humans have created many alphabets to express the hundreds of languages we speak. Several examples are shown in Figure 2–1. Even rules for writing differ: Most people in Western societies write from left to right, people in northern Africa and western Asia write from right to left, and people in eastern Asia write from top to bottom. Global Map 2–1 on page 42 shows where in the world we find the three most widely spoken languages: English, Chinese, and Spanish.

Language allows much more than communication; it is the key to **cultural transmission**, *the process by which one generation passes culture to the next.* Just as our bodies contain the genes of our ancestors, our cultural heritage contains countless symbols created by those who came before us. Language is the key that unlocks centuries of accumulated wisdom.

Language skills may link us to the past, but they also spark the human imagination to connect symbols in new ways, creating an almost limitless range of future possibilities. Language sets humans apart as the only creatures who are self-conscious, aware of our limitations and ultimate mortality, yet are able to dream and hope for a future better than the present.

Does Language Shape Reality?

Does someone who speaks Cherokee, an American Indian language, experience the world differently from other North Americans who think in English or Spanish? Edward Sapir and Benjamin Whorf claimed that the answer is yes, because each language has its own distinctive symbols that serve as the building blocks of reality (Sapir, 1929, 1949; Whorf, 1956, orig. 1941). Further, they noted that each symbolic system has words or expressions not found in any other symbolic system. Finally, all languages connect symbols with distinctive emotions, so as multilingual people know, a single idea may "feel" different when spoken in Spanish rather than in English or Chinese.

Formally, the **Sapir-Whorf thesis** holds that *people see and understand the world through the cultural lens of language.* In the decades since Sapir and Whorf published

People throughout the world communicate not just with spoken words but also with bodily gestures. Because gestures vary from culture to culture, they can occasionally be the cause of misunderstandings. For instance, the commonplace "thumbs up" gesture we use to express "Good job!" can get a person from the United States into trouble in Greece, Iran, and a number of other countries, where people take it to mean "Up yours!"

FIGURE 2–1 **Human Languages: A Variety of Symbols**
Here the English word "read" is written in twelve of the hundreds of languages humans use to communicate with one another.

their work, however, scholars have taken issue with this proposition. The widespread belief that, for example, Eskimos experience "snow" differently because they have many words for it is not true; Inuit speakers have about the same number of words for snow as English speakers do.

So how does language affect our reality? Current thinking is that although we do fashion reality out of our symbols, evidence supports the claim that language does not *determine* reality in the way Sapir and Whorf claimed. For example, we know that children understand the idea of "family" long before they learn that word; similarly, adults can imagine new ideas or things before devising a name for them (Kay & Kempton, 1984; Pinker, 1994).

Values and Beliefs

What accounts for the popularity of movie characters such as James Bond, Neo, Erin Brockovich, "Dirty Harry," Lara Croft, and Rocky Balboa? Each is ruggedly individualistic, going it alone and relying on personal skill and savvy to challenge "the system." In admiring such characters, we are supporting certain **values**, *culturally defined standards that people use to decide what is desirable, good, and beautiful and that serve as broad guidelines for social living.* Values are what people who share a culture use to make choices about how to live.

Values are broad principles that underlie **beliefs**, *specific ideas that people hold to be true.* In other words, values are abstract standards of goodness, and beliefs are particular matters that people accept as true or false. For example, because most U.S. adults share

GLOBAL MAP 2–1 Language in Global Perspective

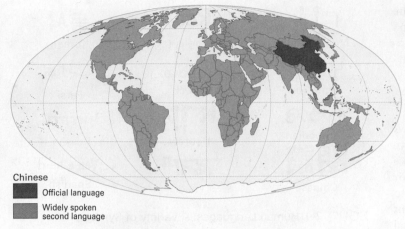

Chinese (including Mandarin, Cantonese, and dozens of other dialects) is the native tongue of one-fifth of the world's people, almost all of whom live in Asia. Although all Chinese people read and write with the same characters, they use several dozen dialects. The "official" dialect, taught in schools throughout the People's Republic of China and the Republic of Taiwan, is Mandarin (the dialect of Beijing, China's capital). Cantonese, the language of Canton, is the second most common Chinese dialect; it differs in sound from Mandarin roughly the way French differs from Spanish.

Chinese
- Official language
- Widely spoken second language

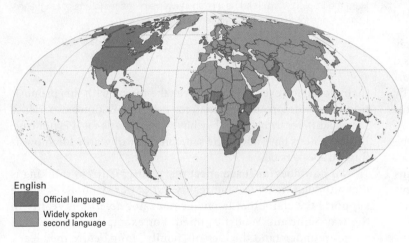

English is the native tongue or official language in several world regions (spoken by 5 percent of humanity) and has become the preferred second language in most of the world.

English
- Official language
- Widely spoken second language

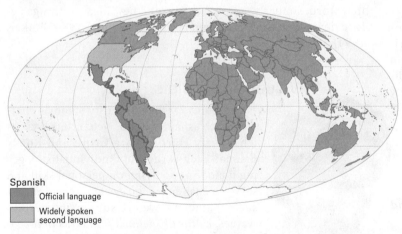

The largest concentration of Spanish speakers is in Latin America and, of course, Spain. Spanish is also the second most widely spoken language in the United States.

Sources: Lewis (2009), and Central Intelligence Agency (2009).

Spanish
- Official language
- Widely spoken second language

the value of providing equal opportunity for all, they believe that a qualified woman could serve as president of the United States, as the 2008 presidential campaign of Hillary Rodham Clinton demonstrated (NORC, 2011:393).

Key Values of U.S. Culture

In a classic study of U.S. culture, sociologist Robin Williams Jr. (1970) identified ten values as central to our way of life:

1. **Equal opportunity.** People in the United States believe that everyone should have a chance to get ahead based on talent and

---

language a system of symbols that allows people to communicate with one another

cultural transmission the process by which one generation passes culture to the next

Sapir-Whorf thesis the idea that people see and understand the world through the cultural lens of language

values culturally defined standards that people use to decide what is desirable, good, and beautiful and that serve as broad guidelines for social living

beliefs specific ideas that people hold to be true

---

effort. Our society does not endorse *equality of condition* in which everyone is exactly the same social standing but *equality of opportunity* in which social standing reflects people's abilities and how hard they try to get ahead. This means that society should provide the opportunity for schooling and work so people can earn social standing that reflects individual talent and effort.

2. **Individual achievement and personal success.** Our way of life encourages competition as the means for people to show what they can do. We tend to believe that the rewards people receive should more or less reflect their personal merit. A successful person is given the respect due a "winner."

3. **Material comfort.** Success in the United States generally means making money and enjoying what it will buy. Although people sometimes remark that "money won't buy happiness," most of us would love to "hit it big" all the same.

4. **Activity and work.** Our heroes, from Olympic gold medalists to the winners of television's *American Idol,* are "doers" who get the job done. Our culture values action over reflection and taking control of events over passively accepting fate.

5. **Practicality and efficiency.** We value the practical over the theoretical, what will "get us somewhere" over what is interesting "for its own sake." Many young people hear their parent give the advice: "It's good to enjoy what you study, but major in something that will help you get a job!"

6. **Progress.** We are an optimistic people who, despite waves of nostalgia, believe that the present is better than the past. We celebrate progress, viewing the "very latest" as the "very best."

7. **Science.** We expect scientists to solve problems and to improve our lives. We believe that we are rational people, and our focus on science probably explains our cultural tendency (especially among men) to devalue emotion and intuition as sources of knowledge.

8. **Democracy and free enterprise.** Members of our society recognize numerous individual rights that governments should not take away. We believe that a just political system is based on free elections in which adults elect government leaders and on an economy that responds to the choices of individual consumers.

9. **Freedom.** We favor individual initiative over collective conformity.

How does the popularity of the television show *American Idol* illustrate many of the key values of U.S. culture listed here?

While we accept the idea that everyone has at least some responsibilities to others, we believe that people should look out for themselves and be free to pursue their personal goals.

10. **Racism and group superiority.** Despite strong ideas about individualism and freedom, most people in the United States still judge individuals according to gender, race, ethnicity, and social class. In general, U.S. culture values males over females, whites over people of color, people with northwestern European backgrounds over those whose ancestors came from other parts of the world, and rich over poor. Although we describe ourselves as a nation of equals, there is little doubt that some of us are "more equal" than others.

Values: Often in Harmony, Sometimes in Conflict

In many ways, cultural values go together. Williams's list includes examples of *value clusters* in our way of life. For instance, our way of life values activity and hard work because members of our society expect effort to lead to achievement and success and result in material comfort.

Sometimes, however, one core cultural value contradicts another. Take the first and last items on Williams's list, for example: Members of our society say they believe in equality of opportunity, yet many also look down on others because of their sex or race. Value conflict causes strain and often leads to awkward balancing acts in our beliefs. Sometimes we decide that one value is more important than another by, for example, supporting equal opportunity while opposing same-sex marriage. In these cases, we simply learn to live with the contradictions.

Values: Change Over Time

Like all elements of culture, values change over time. People in the United States have always valued hard work. But, in recent years, more people wonder whether hard work is really enough to "get ahead." For many people, too, a single-minded focus on work is giving way to increasing importance on leisure—having time off from the job to do things such as reading, travel, or community service that provide enjoyment and satisfaction. Similarly, although the importance of material comfort remains strong, more people are seeking personal growth through meditation and other spiritual activity.

Values: A Global Perspective

Values vary from culture to culture around the world. In general, the values that are important in higher-income countries differ somewhat from those common in lower-income countries.

People in lower-income nations develop cultures that value survival. This means that people place a great deal of importance on physical safety and economic security. They worry about having enough to eat and a safe

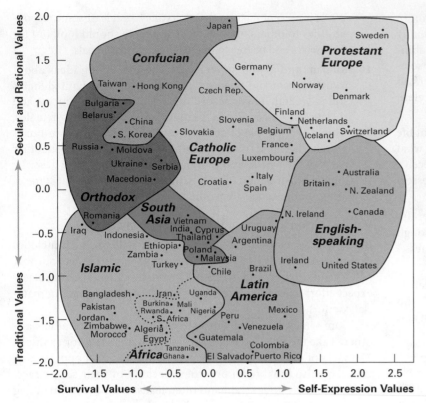

Global Snapshot

FIGURE 2–2 Cultural Values of Selected Countries

A general global pattern is that higher-income countries tend to be secular and rational and favor self-expression. By contrast, the cultures of lower-income countries tend to be more traditional and concerned with economic survival. Each region of the world has distinctive cultural patterns, including religious traditions, that affect values. Looking at the figure, what patterns can you see?

Sources: Ronald Inglehart and Christian Welzel (2010).

place to sleep at night. In addition, lower-income nations tend to be traditional, with values that celebrate the past and emphasize the importance of family and religious beliefs. These nations, in which men have most of the power, typically discourage or forbid practices such as divorce and abortion.

People in higher-income countries develop cultures that value individualism and self-expression. These countries are rich enough that most of the people take survival for granted, focusing their attention instead on which "lifestyle" they prefer and how to achieve the greatest personal happiness. In addition, these countries tend to be secular and rational, placing less emphasis on family ties and religious beliefs and more on people thinking for themselves and being tolerant of others who differ from them. In higher-income countries, women have social standing more equal to men, and there is widespread support for practices such as divorce and abortion

Watch the video "Individual Rights vs. the Common Good" on mysoclab.com

(World Values Survey, 2011). Figure 2–2 shows how selected countries of the world compare in terms of cultural values.

Norms

Most people in the United States are eager to gossip about "who's hot" and "who's not." Members of American Indian societies, however, typically condemn such behavior as rude and divisive. Both patterns illustrate the operation of **norms,** *rules and expectations by which a society guides the behavior of its members.* In everyday life, people respond to each other with *sanctions,* rewards or punishments that encourage conformity to cultural norms.

Mores and Folkways

William Graham Sumner (1959, orig. 1906), an early U.S. sociologist, coined the term **mores** (pronounced "MORE-ayz") to refer to *norms that are widely observed and have great moral significance.* Certain mores include *taboos,* such as our society's insistence that adults not engage in sexual relations with children.

People pay less attention to **folkways,** *norms for routine or casual interaction.* Examples include ideas about appropriate greetings and proper dress. A man who does not wear a tie to a formal dinner party may raise an eyebrow for violating folkways or "etiquette." If he were to arrive at the party wearing *only* a tie, however, he would violate cultural mores and invite a more serious response.

As we learn cultural norms, we gain the capacity to evaluate our own behavior. Doing wrong (say, downloading a term paper from the Internet) can cause both *shame*—the painful sense that others disapprove of our actions—and also *guilt*—a negative judgment we make of ourselves. Only cultural creatures can experience shame and guilt. This is what the writer Mark Twain had in mind when he remarked that people are the only animals that blush—or need to.

Ideal and Real Culture

Values and norms do not describe actual behavior so much as they suggest how we *should* behave. We must remember that *ideal* culture always differs from *real* culture, which is what actually occurs in everyday life. For example, most women and men agree on the importance of sexual faithfulness in marriage. Even so, in one study, 17 percent of married people reported having been sexually unfaithful to their spouse at some point in the marriage (NORC, 2011:2666). But a culture's moral standards are important all the same, calling to mind the old saying "Do as I say, not as I do."

---

norms rules and expectations by which a society guides the behavior of its members

mores norms that are widely observed and have great moral significance

folkways norms for routine or casual interaction

Technology and Culture

● **Analyze**

In addition to symbolic elements such as values and norms, every culture includes a wide range of physical human creations called *artifacts*. The Chinese eat with chopsticks rather than forks, the Japanese place mats rather than rugs on the floor, and many men and women in India prefer flowing robes to the close-fitting clothing common in the United States. The material culture of a people can seem as strange to outsiders as their language, values, and norms.

A society's artifacts partly reflect underlying cultural values. The warlike Yąnomamö carefully craft their weapons and prize the poison tips on their arrows. By contrast, our society's emphasis on individualism and independence helps explain our high regard for the automobile: We own more than 250 million motor vehicles—more than one for every licensed driver. In recent years as gas prices have climbed, more of these cars are fuel-efficient models. Still, large heavy pickup trucks and SUVs continue to sell well, a trend no doubt encouraged by our cultural emphasis on rugged individualism.

In addition to expressing values, material culture also reflects a society's level of **technology**, *knowledge that people use to make a way of life in their surroundings*. The more complex a society's technology, the easier it is for members of that society to shape the world for themselves.

Standards of beauty—including the color and design of everyday surroundings—vary significantly from one culture to another. This Ndebele couple in South Africa dresses in the same bright colors with which they decorate their home. Members of North American and European societies, by contrast, make far less use of bright colors and intricate detail, so their housing appears much more subdued.

Gerhard Lenski argued that a society's level of technology is crucial in determining what cultural ideas and artifacts emerge or are even possible (Nolan & Lenski, 2010). He pointed to the importance of *sociocultural evolution*—the historical changes in culture brought about by new technology—which unfolds in terms of four major levels of development: hunting and gathering, horticulture and pastoralism, agriculture, and industry.

Hunting and Gathering

The oldest and most basic way of living is **hunting and gathering**, *the use of simple tools to hunt animals and gather vegetation for food*. From the time of our earliest ancestors 3 million years ago until about 1800, most people in the world lived as hunters and gatherers. Today, however, this technology supports only a few societies, including the Kaska Indians of northwestern Canada, the Pygmies of Central Africa, the Khoisan of southwestern Africa, the Aborigines of Australia, and the Semai of Malaysia. Typically, hunters and gatherers spend most of their time searching for game and edible plants. Their societies are small, generally with several dozen people living in a nomadic, familylike group, moving on as they use up an area's vegetation or follow migratory animals.

Everyone helps search for food, with the very young and the very old doing what they can. Women usually gather vegetation—the primary food source for these peoples—while men do most of the hunting. Because the tasks they perform are of equal value, the two sexes are regarded as having about the same social importance (Leacock, 1978).

Hunters and gatherers do not have formal leaders. They may look to one person as a *shaman*, or priest, but holding such a position does not excuse the person from the daily work of finding food. Overall, hunting and gathering is a simple and egalitarian way of life.

Limited technology leaves hunters and gatherers vulnerable to the forces of nature. Storms and droughts can easily destroy their food supply, and they have few effective ways to respond to accidents or disease. Looking back at these societies, we see that many children died in childhood, and only half lived to the age of twenty.

As people with powerful technology steadily close in on them, hunting and gathering societies are vanishing. Fortunately, studying their way of life has provided us with valuable information about our sociocultural history and our fundamental ties to the natural environment.

Horticulture and Pastoralism

Horticulture, *the use of hand tools to raise crops*, appeared around 10,000 years ago. The hoe and the digging stick (used to punch holes in the ground for planting seeds) first turned up in fertile regions of the Middle East and Southeast Asia, and by 6,000 years ago, these tools were in use from Western Europe to China. Central and South Americans also learned to cultivate plants, but rocky soil and mountainous land forced members of many societies to continue to hunt and gather even as they adopted this new technology (Fisher, 1979; Chagnon, 1992).

What would it be like to live in a society with simple technology? That's the premise of the television show *Survivor*. What advantages do societies with simple technology afford their members? What disadvantages do you see?

In especially dry regions, societies turned not to raising crops but to **pastoralism,** *the domestication of animals.* Throughout the Americas, Africa, the Middle East, and Asia, many societies combine horticulture and pastoralism.

Growing plants and raising animals allows societies to feed hundreds of members. Pastoral peoples remain nomadic, but horticulturalists make permanent settlements. In a horticultural society, a material surplus means that not everyone has to produce food; some people are free to make crafts, become traders, or serve as full-time priests. Compared with hunters and gatherers, pastoral and horticultural societies are more unequal, with some families operating as a ruling elite.

Because hunters and gatherers have little control over nature, they generally believe that the world is inhabited by spirits. As they gain the power to raise plants and animals, however, people come to believe in one God as the creator of the world. The pastoral roots of Judaism and Christianity are evident in the term "pastor" and the common view of God as a "shepherd" who stands watch over all.

Agriculture

Around 5,000 years ago, technological advances led to **agriculture,** *large-scale cultivation using plows harnessed to animals or more powerful energy sources.* Agrarian technology first appeared in the Middle East and gradually spread throughout the world. The invention of the animal-drawn plow, the wheel, writing, numbers, and new metals changed societies so much that historians call this era the "dawn of civilization."

By turning the soil, plows allow land to be farmed for centuries, so agrarian people can live in permanent settlements. With large food surpluses that can be transported by animal-powered wagons, populations grow into the millions. As members of agrarian societies become more and more specialized in their work, money is used as a form of common exchange, replacing the earlier system of barter. Although the development of agrarian technology expands human choices and fuels urban growth, it also makes social life more individualistic and impersonal.

Agriculture also brings about a dramatic increase in social inequality. Most people live as serfs or slaves, but a few elites are freed from labor to cultivate a "refined" way of life based on the study of philosophy, art, and literature. At all levels, men gain pronounced power over women.

People with only simple technology live much the same the world over, with minor differences caused by regional variations in climate. But agrarian technology gives people enough control over the world that cultural diversity dramatically increases (Nolan & Lenski, 2010).

Industry

Industrialization occurred as societies replaced the muscles of animals and humans with new forms of power. Formally, **industry** is *the production of goods using advanced sources of energy to drive large machinery.* The introduction of steam power, starting in England about 1775, greatly boosted productivity and transformed culture in the process.

Agrarian people work in or near their homes, but most people in industrial societies work in large factories under the supervision of strangers. In this way, industrialization pushes aside the traditional cultural values that guided family-centered agrarian life for centuries.

technology knowledge that people use to make a way of life in their surroundings

hunting and gathering the use of simple tools to hunt animals and gather vegetation for food

horticulture the use of hand tools to raise crops

pastoralism the domestication of animals

agriculture large-scale cultivation using plows harnessed to animals or more powerful energy sources

industry the production of goods using advanced sources of energy to drive large machinery

postindustrialism the production of information using computer technology

Industry also made the world seem smaller. In the nineteenth century, railroads and steamships carried people across land and sea faster and farther than ever before. In the twentieth century, this process continued with the invention of the automobile, the airplane, radio, television, and computers.

Industrial technology also raises living standards and extends the human life span. Schooling becomes the rule because industrial jobs demand more and more skills. In addition, industrial societies reduce economic inequality and steadily extend political rights.

It is easy to see industrial societies as "more advanced" than those relying on simpler technology. After all, industry raises living standards and stretches life expectancy to the seventies and beyond—about twice that of the Yąnomamö. But as industry intensifies individualism and expands personal freedom, it weakens human community. Also, industry has led people to abuse the natural environment, which threatens us all. And although advanced technology gives us laborsaving machines and miraculous forms of medical treatment, it also contributes to unhealthy levels of stress and has created weapons capable of destroying in a flash everything that our species has achieved.

Postindustrial Information Technology

Going beyond the four categories discussed by Lenski, we see that many industrial societies, including the United States, have now entered a postindustrial era in which more and more economic production makes use of *new information technology*. **Postindustrialism** refers to *the production of information using computer technology*. Production in industrial societies centers on factories that make things, but postindustrial production centers on computers and other electronic devices that create, process, store, and apply *ideas and information*.

The emergence of an information economy changes the skills that define a way of life. No longer are mechanical abilities the only key to success. People find that they must learn to work with symbols by speaking, writing, computing, and creating images and sounds. One result of this change is that our society now has the capacity to create symbolic culture on an unprecedented scale as people work with computers to generate new words, music, and images.

Cultural Diversity

 Analyze

In the United States, we are aware of our cultural diversity when we hear several different languages being spoken while riding a subway in New York, Washington, D.C., or Los Angeles. Compared to a country like Japan, whose historic isolation makes it the most *monocultural* of all high-income nations, centuries of immigration have

Sometimes the distinction between high culture and popular is not so clear. Bonham's Auction House in England recently featured spray-painted works by the graffiti artist Banksy. This particular one was expected to sell for more than $250,000.

made the United States the most *multicultural* of all high-income countries.

Between 1820 (when the government began keeping track of immigration) and 2011, almost 80 million people came to our shores from other nations. This cultural mix continues as more than 1.25 million additional people arrive each year. A century ago, almost all immigrants came from Europe; today, almost 80 percent of newcomers arrive from Latin America and Asia. To understand the reality of life in the United States, we must move beyond shared cultural patterns to consider cultural diversity.

High Culture and Popular Culture

Cultural diversity can involve social class. In fact, in everyday talk, we usually use the term "culture" to mean art forms such as classical literature, music, dance, and painting. We describe people who attend the opera or the theater as "cultured," thinking that they appreciate the "finer things in life."

We speak less kindly of ordinary people, assuming that everyday culture is somehow less worthy. We are tempted to judge the music of Haydn as "more cultured" than hip-hop, couscous as better than cornbread, and polo as more polished than Ping-Pong.

high culture cultural patterns that distinguish a society's elite

popular culture cultural pattens that are widespread among a society's population

These differences arise because many cultural patterns are readily available to only some members of a society. Sociologists use the term **high culture** to refer to *cultural patterns that distinguish a society's elite* and **popular culture** to designate *cultural patterns that are widespread among a society's population.*

Common sense may suggest that high culture is superior to popular culture, but sociologists are uneasy with such judgments, for two reasons. First, neither elites nor ordinary people share all the same tastes and interests; people in both categories differ in numerous ways. Second, do we praise high culture because it is really better than popular culture or simply because its supporters are more privileged in terms of money, power, and prestige? For example, there is no difference between a violin and a fiddle; however, we name the instrument one way when it is used to produce a type of music typically enjoyed by a person of higher social position and the other when it produces music appreciated by people with lower social standing.

Subculture

The term **subculture** refers to *cultural patterns that set apart some segment of a society's population.* People who ride "chopper" motorcycles, traditional Korean Americans, New England "Yankees," Ohio State football fans, the southern California "beach crowd," Elvis impersonators, and wilderness campers all display subcultural patterns.

It is easy but often inaccurate to put people in subcultural categories because almost everyone participates in many subcultures without having much commitment to any one of them. In some cases, ethnicity and religion can be strong enough to set people apart from one another, with tragic results. Consider the former nation of Yugoslavia in southeastern Europe. The 1990s' civil war there was fueled by extreme cultural diversity. This *one* small country with a population about equal to the Los Angeles metropolitan area made use of *two* alphabets, embraced *three* major religions, spoke *four* major languages, was home to *five* major nationalities, was divided into *six* separate republics, and absorbed the cultural influences of *seven* surrounding countries. The cultural conflict that plunged this nation into civil war shows that subcultures are a source not only of pleasing variety but also of tension and even violence.

Many people view the United States as a melting pot where many nationalities blend into a single "American" culture (Gardyn, 2002). But given so much cultural diversity, how accurate is the melting pot image? For one thing, subcultures involve not just *difference* but also *hierarchy*. Too often what we view as dominant or "mainstream" culture are patterns favored by powerful segments of the population, and we view the lives of disadvantaged people as "subculture." But are the cultural patterns of rich skiers on the slopes of Aspen, Colorado, any less a subculture than the cultural patterns of skateboarders on the streets of Los Angeles? Some sociologists therefore prefer to level the playing field of society by emphasizing multiculturalism.

Multiculturalism

Multiculturalism is *a perspective recognizing the cultural diversity of the United States and promoting equal standing for all cultural traditions.* Multiculturalism represents a sharp change from the past, when U.S. society downplayed cultural diversity, defining itself in terms of European and especially English immigrants. Today there is a spirited debate about whether we should continue to focus on historical traditions or highlight contemporary diversity.

E pluribus unum, the Latin phrase that appears on each U.S. coin, means "out of many, one." This motto symbolizes not only our national political union but also the idea that the varied experiences of immigrants from around the world come together to form a new way of life.

But from the outset, the many cultures did not melt together so much as harden into a hierarchy. At the top were the English, who formed a majority and established English as the nation's dominant language. Further down, people of other backgrounds were advised to model themselves after "their betters" so that the "melting" was really a process of Anglicization—adoption of English ways. As multiculturalists see it, early in its history, U.S. society set up the English way of life as an ideal that everyone else should imitate and by which everyone should be judged.

Since then, historians have reported events from the point of view of the English and others of European ancestry, paying little attention to the perspectives and accomplishments of Native Americans and people of African and Asian descent. Multiculturalists criticize this as **Eurocentrism**, *the dominance of European (especially English) cultural patterns.* Molefi Kete Asante, a supporter of multiculturalism, argues that "like the fifteenth-century Europeans who could not cease believing that the Earth was the center of the universe, many [people] today find it difficult to cease viewing European culture as the center of the social universe" (1988:7).

One controversial issue involves language. Some people believe that English should be the official language of the United States; by 2011, legislatures in thirty-one states had enacted laws making it the official language (ProEnglish, 2011). But almost 60 million men and women—one in five—speak a language other than English at home. Spanish is the second most commonly spoken language in the United States, and several hundred other tongues are heard across the country, including Italian, German, French, Filipino, Japanese, Korean, Vietnamese, Russian, and a host of Native American languages. National Map 2–1 on page 50 shows where in the United States large numbers of people speak a language other than English at home.

---

multiculturalism a perspective recognizing the cultural diversity of the United States and promoting equal standing for all cultural traditions

Eurocentrism the dominance of European (especially English) cultural patterns

Afrocentrism emphasizing and promoting African cultural patterns

---

subculture cultural patterns that set apart some segment of a society's population

Supporters of multiculturalism say it is a way of coming to terms with our country's increasing social diversity. With the Asian American and Hispanic American populations increasing rapidly, almost half of the country's children under the age of five represent some minority category. Analysts predict that today's young people will live to see people of African, Asian, and Hispanic ancestry become the *majority* of this country's entire population.

Supporters also claim that multiculturalism is a good way to strengthen the academic achievement of African American children. To counter Eurocentrism, some multicultural educators call for **Afrocentrism,** *emphasizing and promoting African cultural patterns,* which they see as a strategy for correcting centuries of ignoring the cultural achievements of African societies and African Americans.

Although multiculturalism has found favor in recent years, it has drawn criticism as well. Opponents say it encourages divisiveness rather than unity because it urges people to identify with only their own category rather than with the nation as a whole. In addition, critics say, multiculturalism actually harms minorities themselves. Multicultural policies (from African American studies departments to all-black dorms) seem to support the same racial segregation that our nation has struggled so long to overcome. Furthermore, in the early grades, an Afrocentric curriculum may deny children important knowledge and skills by forcing them to study only certain topics from a single point of view.

Finally, the global war on terrorism has drawn the issue of multiculturalism into the spotlight. In 2005, British Prime Minister Tony Blair responded to a terrorist attack in London, stating, "It is important that the terrorists realize [that] our determination to defend our values and our way of life is greater than their determination to … impose their extremism on the world." He went on to warn that the British government would expel Muslim clerics who encouraged hatred and terrorism (Barone, 2005; Carle, 2008). Of course, there are also many people in other parts of the world who believe that Britain and the United States have imposed their way of life on others. In a world of cultural difference and conflict, we have much to learn about tolerance and peacemaking.

Counterculture

Cultural diversity also includes outright rejection of conventional ideas or behavior. **Counterculture** refers to *cultural patterns that strongly oppose those widely accepted within a society.*

During the 1960s, for example, a youth-oriented counterculture rejected mainstream culture as too competitive, self-centered, and materialistic. Instead, hippies and other counterculturalists favored a collective and cooperative lifestyle in which "being" was more important than "doing" and the capacity for personal growth—or "expanded consciousness"—was prized more highly than material possessions like fancy homes and cars. Such differences led some people to "drop out" of the larger society.

Countercultures continue to flourish. At the extreme, small militaristic communities (made up of people born and bred in this country) or bands of religious militants (from other countries) exist in the United States, some of them engaging in violence intended to threaten our way of life.

Cultural Change

Perhaps the most basic human truth is that "all things shall pass." Even the dinosaurs, which thrived on this planet for 160 million years, exist today only as fossils. Will humanity survive for millions of years to come? All we can say with certainty is that given our reliance on culture, the human record will show continuous change.

Although we can see general patterns of "U.S. culture," this country is actually a mosaic of diverse cultural patterns shaped by factors including social class, ethnicity, age, and geographical region. What general U.S. cultural patterns do you see in a television show such as *Jersey Shore*? Is this an example of high culture or popular culture? What subcultural patterns do you see in the show?

Figure 2–3 on page 51 shows changes in attitudes among first-year college students between 1969 (the height of the 1960s' counterculture) and 2010. Some attitudes have changed only slightly: Today, as a generation ago, most men and women look forward to raising a family. But today's students are much less concerned with developing a philosophy of life and are much more interested in making money.

Change in one dimension of a cultural system usually sparks changes in others. For example, today's college women are far more interested in making money because women are much more likely to be in the labor force than their mothers or grandmothers were. Working for income may not change their interest in having a family, but it does increase their age at first marriage and the divorce rate. Such connections

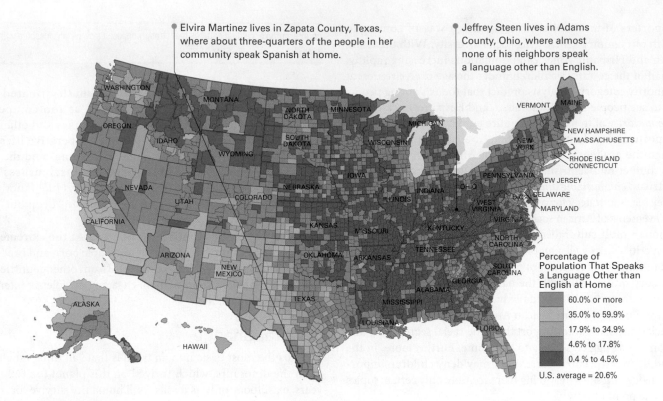

Elvira Martinez lives in Zapata County, Texas, where about three-quarters of the people in her community speak Spanish at home.

Jeffrey Steen lives in Adams County, Ohio, where almost none of his neighbors speak a language other than English.

Percentage of Population That Speaks a Language Other than English at Home

- 60.0% or more
- 35.0% to 59.9%
- 17.9% to 34.9%
- 4.6% to 17.8%
- 0.4% to 4.5%

U.S. average = 20.6%

Seeing Ourselves

NATIONAL MAP 2–1 Language Diversity across the United States

Of more than 289 million people age five or older in the United States, the Census Bureau reports that nearly 60 million (20.6 percent) speak a language other than English at home. Of these, 62 percent speak Spanish and 15.7 percent use an Asian language (the Census Bureau lists thirty-nine languages and language categories, each of which is favored by more than 100,000 people). The map shows that non–English speakers are concentrated in certain regions of the country. Which ones? What do you think accounts for this pattern?

✱ **Explore** the percentage of foreign-born people in your local community and in counties across the United States on **mysoclab.com**

Source: U.S. Census Bureau (2010).

illustrate the principle of **cultural integration**, *the close relationships among various elements of a cultural system.*

Cultural Lag

Some parts of a cultural system change faster than others. William Ogburn (1964) observed that technology moves quickly, generating new elements of material culture (such as test-tube babies) faster than nonmaterial culture (such as ideas about parenthood) can keep up with them. Ogburn called this inconsistency **cultural lag**, *the fact that some cultural elements change more quickly than others, disrupting a cultural system.* In a world in which a woman can give birth to a child by using another woman's egg, which has been

fertilized in a laboratory with the sperm of a total stranger, how are we to apply traditional ideas about motherhood and fatherhood?

Causes of Cultural Change

Cultural changes are set in motion in three ways. The first is *invention,* the process of creating new cultural elements. Invention has given us the telephone (1876), the airplane (1903), and the computer (late 1940s), each of which changed our way of life. The process of invention goes on all the time, as indicated by the thousands of applications submitted every year to the U.S. Patent Office. The timeline inside the back cover of this book shows other inventions that have helped change our culture.

Discovery, a second cause of change, involves recognizing and understanding more fully something already in existence, from a distant star or the foods of another culture to women's athletic

---

cultural integration the close relationships among various elements of a cultural system

cultural lag the fact that some cultural elements change more quickly than others, disrupting a cultural system

📖● **Read** "Gangstas, Thugs, and Hustlas: The Code of the Street in Rap Music" by Charis Kubrin on **mysoclab.com**

ability. Many discoveries result from painstaking scientific research, and others happen by a stroke of luck, as in 1898, when Marie Curie unintentionally left a rock on a piece of photographic paper, noticed that emissions from the rock had exposed the paper, and thus discovered radium.

The third cause of cultural change is *diffusion,* the spread of objects or traits from one society to another. Because new technology sends information around the globe in seconds, cultural diffusion has never been greater than it is today.

Our own way of life has contributed many significant cultural elements to the world, ranging from computers to jazz music. Of course, diffusion works the other way, too, so that much of what we assume is "American" actually comes from elsewhere. Most of the clothing we wear and the furniture we use, as well as the watch we carry and the money we spend, all had their origins in other cultures (Linton, 1937a).

It is certainly correct to talk about "American culture," especially when we are comparing our way of life to the culture of some other society. But this discussion of cultural change shows us that culture is always complex and always changing. The Thinking About Diversity box on page 52 offers a good example of the diverse and dynamic character of culture with a brief look at the history of rock-and-roll music.

Ethnocentrism and Cultural Relativism

December 10, a small village in Morocco. Watching many of our fellow travelers browsing through a tiny ceramics factory, we have little doubt that North Americans are among the world's greatest shoppers. We delight in surveying hand-woven carpets in China or India, inspecting finely crafted metals in Turkey, or collecting the beautifully colored porcelain tiles we find here in Morocco. Of course, all these items are wonderful bargains. But one major reason for the low prices is unsettling to people living in rich countries: Many products from the world's low- and middle-income countries are produced by children—some as young as five or six—who work long days for pennies per hour.

We think of childhood as a time of innocence and freedom from adult burdens such as work. In poor countries throughout the world, however, families depend on income earned by their children. So what people in one society think of as right and natural, people elsewhere find puzzling and even immoral. Perhaps the Chinese philosopher Confucius had it right when he noted that "all people are the same; it's only their habits that are different."

Just about every imaginable idea or behavior is commonplace somewhere in the world, and this cultural variation causes travelers both excitement and distress. North Americans turn on a light by flipping a light switch up, but Australians flip the light switch down. North Americans name city streets, but the Japanese name city blocks. North Americans are used to maintaining several feet of "personal space," but Egyptians in conversation stand very close to each other. For this reason, members of our society can find much that confuses or even offends us when we travel to other societies. In rural Morocco, for example, bathrooms typically lack toilet paper, a fact that causes considerable discomfort for North Americans, who recoil at the thought of using the left hand for bathroom hygiene, as the locals do.

Given that a particular culture is the basis for everyday experience, it is no wonder that people everywhere exhibit **ethnocentrism**,

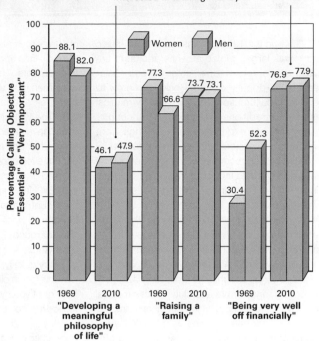

• Compared to college students 40 years ago, today's students are less interested in developing a philosophy of life and more interested in making money.

Student Snapshot

FIGURE 2–3 Life Objectives of First-Year College Students, 1969 and 2010

Researchers have surveyed first-year college students every year since 1969. While attitudes about some things such as the importance of family have stayed about the same, attitudes about other life goals have changed dramatically.

Sources: Astin et al. (2002) and Pryor et al. (2011).

the practice of judging another culture by the standards of one's own culture. Some small degree of ethnocentrism is necessary for people to be emotionally attached to their way of life. But ethnocentrism also generates misunderstanding and sometimes conflict.

Members of every cultural system tend to prefer what they know and are wary about what is different. The ancient Romans took this view of difference to an extreme, using the same word for both "stranger" and "enemy." Even language is culturally biased. Years ago, people in North America or Europe referred to China as the "Far East." But this term, unknown to the Chinese, is an ethnocentric term for a region that is far to the east *of us.* The Chinese name for their country translates as "Central Kingdom," suggesting that they, like us, see their society as the center of the world.

The alternative to ethnocentrism is **cultural relativism**, *the practice of judging a culture by its own standards.* Cultural relativism can be difficult for travelers to adopt: It requires not only openness to unfamiliar values and norms but also the ability to put aside cultural standards we have known all our lives. Even so, as people of the world increasingly come into contact with one another, the importance of understanding other cultures will become ever greater.

Early in the 1950s, mainstream "pop" music was largely aimed at white adults. In the 1950s, rock-and-roll emerged as a major part of U.S. popular culture. Rock soon grew to become a cultural tide that swept away musical tastes and traditions and changed the country in ways we still experience today. Songs were written by professional composers, recorded by long-established record labels, and performed by well-known artists including Perry Como, Eddie Fisher, Doris Day, and Patti Page. Just about every big-name performer was white.

At that time, the country was rigidly segregated racially, which created differences in the cultures of white people and black people. In the subcultural world of African Americans, music had different sounds and rhythms, reflecting jazz, gospel singing, and rhythm and blues. These musical styles were created by African American composers and performers working with black-owned record companies and broadcast on radio stations to an almost entirely black audience.

Class, too, divided the musical world of the 1950s, even among whites. A second musical subculture was country and western, a musical style popular among poorer whites, especially people living in the South. Like rhythm and blues, country and western music had its own composers and performers, its own record labels, and its own radio stations.

"Crossover" music was rare, meaning that very few performers or songs moved from one musical world to gain popularity in another. But this musical segregation began to break down about 1955 with the birth of rock-and-roll. Rock was a new mix of other musical patterns, drawing on mainstream pop but including country and western and, especially, rhythm and blues.

The new rock-and-roll music drew together musical traditions, but it soon divided society in a new way—by age. Rock-and-roll was the first music clearly linked to the emergence of a youth culture—rock was all the rage among teenagers but was little appreciated or even understood by their parents. The new rock-and-roll performers were men (and a few women) who looked young and took a rebellious stand against "adult" culture. The typical rocker looked like what parents might have called a "juvenile delinquent" and who claimed to be "cool," an idea that most parents did not even understand.

The first band to make it big in rock-and-roll was Bill Haley and the Comets. Emerging from the country and western tradition, Haley's first big hits in 1954—"Shake, Rattle, and Roll" and "Rock around the Clock"—were "covers" of earlier rhythm and blues songs.

Very quickly, however, young people began to lose interest in older performers such as Bill Haley in favor of younger performers sporting sideburns, turned-up collars, and black leather jackets. By 1956, the undisputed star of rock-and-roll was a poor white southern boy from Tupelo, Mississippi, named Elvis Aron Presley. With rural roots, Elvis Presley knew country and western music, and after he moved to Memphis, Tennessee, he learned black gospel and rhythm and blues.

Presley became the first superstar of rock-and-roll not just because he had talent but also because he had great crossover power. With early hits including "Hound Dog" (a rhythm and blues song originally recorded by Big Mama Thornton) and "Blue Suede Shoes" (written by country and western star Carl Perkins), Presley broke down many of the walls based on race and class.

By the end of the 1950s, popular musical styles developed in many new directions, creating soft rock (Ricky Nelson, Pat Boone), rockabilly (Johnny Cash), and dozens of doo-wop groups, both black and white (often named for birds—the Falcons, the Penguins, the Flamingos—or cars—the Imperials, the Impalas, the Fleetwoods). In the 1960s, rock expanded further, including folk music (the Kingston Trio; Peter, Paul, and Mary; Bob Dylan), surf music (the Beach Boys, Jan and Dean), and the "British invasion" led by the Beatles.

Starting on the clean-cut, pop side of rock, the Beatles soon shared the spotlight with another British band proud of its "delinquent" clothing and street-fighter looks—the Rolling Stones. During the 1960s, the hard rock of the Beatles and Stones was joined by softer "folk rock" performed by the Byrds, the Mamas and the Papas, Simon and Garfunkel, and Crosby, Stills, and Nash. In addition, "Motown" (named after the "motor city," Detroit) and "soul" music, launched the careers of dozens of African American stars, including James Brown, Aretha Franklin, the Four Tops, the Temptations, and Diana Ross and the Supremes.

On the West Coast, San Francisco developed a more political rock music performed by Jefferson Airplane, the Grateful Dead, and Janis Joplin. West Coast spin-off styles included "acid rock," influenced by drug use, performed by The Doors and Jimi Hendrix. The jazz influence also returned to the world of rock, creating such "jazz rock" groups as Chicago and Blood, Sweat, and Tears.

This brief look at the early decades of rock-and-roll shows the power of race and class to shape subcultural patterns. It also shows that the production of culture—music as well as movies and music videos—became a megabusiness. Most of all, it shows us that culture does not stand still but is a living process, changing, adapting, and reinventing itself over time.

What Do You Think?

1. Many dimensions of our way of life shaped rock-and-roll. In what ways do you think the emergence of rock-and-roll changed U.S. culture?

2. Throughout this period of musical change, most musical performers were men. What does this tell us about our way of life? Is today's popular music still dominated by men?

3. Can you carry on the story of musical change in the United States to the present? (Think of disco, heavy metal, punk rock, rap, and hip-hop.)

Source: Based on Stuessy & Lipscomb (2008).

Elvis Presley (*center*) drew together the music of rhythm and blues singers, such as Big Mama Thornton (*left*), and country and western stars, including Carl Perkins (*right*). The development of rock-and-roll illustrates the ever-changing character of U.S. culture.

As the opening to this chapter explained, businesses in the United States are learning the value of marketing to a culturally diverse population. Similarly, businesses now know that success in the global economy depends on awareness of cultural patterns around the world. IBM, for example, now provides technical support for its products on Web sites in more than thirty languages (IBM, 2011).

This embrace of difference is a change from the past, when many companies used marketing strategies that lacked sensitivity to cultural diversity. The translation of Coors beer's phrase "Turn It Loose" startled Spanish-speaking customers by proclaiming that the beer would cause diarrhea. Braniff Airlines translated its slogan "Fly in Leather" into Spanish so carelessly that it read "Fly Naked"; similarly, Eastern Airlines' slogan "We Earn Our Wings Every Day" became "We Fly Daily to Heaven," which is hardly comforting to air travelers. Even the poultry giant Frank Perdue fell victim to poor marketing when his pitch "It Takes a Tough Man to Make a Tender Chicken" was transformed into the Spanish phrase "A Sexually Excited Man Will Make a Chicken Affectionate" (Helin, 1992).

But cultural relativism introduces problems of its own. If almost any kind of behavior is the norm *somewhere* in the world, does that mean everything is equally right? Does the fact that some Indian and Moroccan families benefit from having their children work long hours justify child labor? Because we are all members of a single human species, surely there must be some universal standards of proper conduct. But what are they? And in trying to develop them, how can we avoid imposing our own standards on others? There are no simple answers to these questions. But when confronting an unfamiliar cultural practice, it is best to resist making judgments before grasping what people in that culture understand the issue to be. Remember also to think about your own way of life as others might see it. After all, what we gain most from studying others is better insight into ourselves.

In the world's low-income countries, most children must work to provide their families with needed income. These young girls work long hours in a brick factory in the Kathmandu Valley, Nepal. Is it ethnocentric for people living in high-income nations to condemn the practice of child labor because we think youngsters belong in school? Why or why not?

A Global Culture?

Today more than ever, we can observe many of the same cultural practices the world over. Walking the streets of Seoul, South Korea; Kuala Lumpur, Malaysia; Chennai, India; Cairo, Egypt; or Casablanca, Morocco, we see people wearing jeans, hear familiar music, and read ads for many of the same products we use at home. Are we witnessing the birth of a single global culture?

Societies around the world now have more contact with one another than ever before, thanks to the flow of goods, information, and people:

1. **Global economy: The flow of goods.** International commerce is at an all-time high. The global economy has spread many consumer goods—from cars and TV shows to music and fashion—throughout the world.

2. **Global communications: The flow of information.** The Internet and satellite-assisted communications enable people to experience events taking place thousands of miles away, often as they happen. Access to the Internet is spreading—about 60 percent of global Internet users live outside of high-income countries—and online they encounter web pages typically written in English (ITU World Telecommunication, 2011). This fact helps explain why, as shown in Global Map 2–1 on page 42, English is rapidly emerging as the preferred second language around the world.

3. **Global migration: The flow of people.** Knowledge about the rest of the world motivates people to move to where they imagine life will be better, and modern transportation technology, especially air travel, makes relocating easier than ever before. As a result, in most countries, significant numbers of people were born elsewhere, including some 40 million people in the United States, 13 percent of the total population (U.S. Census Bureau, 2011).

These global links help make the cultures of the world more similar. But there are three important limitations to the global culture thesis. First, the global flow of information, goods, and people is uneven in different parts of the world. Generally speaking, urban areas (centers of commerce, communication, and people) have stronger ties to one another, while rural villages remain isolated. In addition, the greater economic and military power of North America and Western Europe means that these regions influence the rest of the world more than the rest of the world influences them.

Second, the global culture thesis assumes that people everywhere are able to *afford* the new goods and services. As Chapter 9 ("Global Stratification") explains, desperate poverty in much of the world deprives people of even the basic necessities of a safe and secure life.

Third, although many cultural elements have spread throughout the world, people everywhere do not attach the same meanings to them. Do children in Tokyo draw the same lessons from reading the Harry Potter books as children in New York or London?

Similarly, we enjoy foods from around the world while knowing little about the lives of the people who created them. In short, people everywhere look at the world through the lens of their own culture.

Theories of Culture

 Apply

Sociologists investigate how culture helps us make sense of ourselves and the surrounding world. Here we will examine several macro-level theoretical approaches to understanding culture. A micro-level approach to the personal experience of culture, which emphasizes how individuals not only conform to cultural patterns but also create new patterns in their everyday lives, is the focus of Chapter 4 ("Social Interaction in Everyday Life").

The Functions of Culture: Structural-Functional Theory

The structural-functional approach explains culture as a complex strategy for meeting human needs. Drawing from the philosophical doctrine of *idealism,* this approach considers values to be the core of a culture (Parsons, 1966; R. M. Williams, 1970). In other words, cultural values direct our lives, give meaning to what we do, and bind people together. Countless other cultural traits have various functions that support the operation of society.

Thinking functionally helps us understand unfamiliar ways of life. Consider the Amish farmer in central Ohio plowing hundreds of acres with a team of horses. His methods may violate the U.S. cultural value of efficiency, but from the Amish point of view, hard work functions to develop the discipline necessary for a devoutly religious way of life. Long days of working together not only make the Amish self-sufficient but also strengthen family ties and unify local communities.

Of course, Amish practices have dysfunctions as well. The hard work and strict religious discipline are too demanding for some, who end up leaving the community. Also, strong religious beliefs sometimes prevent compromise, and as a result, slight differences in religious practices have caused the Amish to divide into different communities (Kraybill, 1989; Kraybill & Olshan, 1994).

If cultures are strategies for meeting human needs, we would expect to find many common patterns around the world. **Cultural universals** are *traits that are part of every known culture.* Comparing hundreds of cultures, George Murdock (1945) identified dozens of cultural universals. One common element is the family, which functions everywhere to control sexual reproduction and to oversee the care of children. Funeral rites, too, are found everywhere, because all human communities cope with the reality of death. Jokes are another cultural universal, serving as a safe means of releasing social tensions.

● **Evaluate** The strength of structural-functional analysis lies in showing how culture operates to meet human needs. Yet by emphasizing a society's dominant cultural patterns, this approach largely ignores cultural diversity. Also, because this approach emphasizes cultural stability, it downplays the importance of change. In short, cultural systems are neither as stable nor as universal as structural-functional analysis leads us to believe. The Applying

Theory table summarizes this theoretical approach's main lessons about culture and places it alongside two other approaches that we consider next.

CHECK YOUR LEARNING In the United States, what are some of the functions of sports, Fourth of July celebrations, and Black History Month?

Inequality and Culture: Social-Conflict Theory

The social-conflict approach draws attention to the link between culture and inequality. From this point of view, any cultural trait benefits some members of society at the expense of others.

Why do certain values dominate a society in the first place? Many conflict theorists, especially Marxists, argue that culture is shaped by a society's system of economic production. Social-conflict theory, then, is rooted in the philosophical doctrine of *materialism,* which holds that a society's system of material production (such as our own capitalist economy) has a powerful effect on the rest of the culture. This materialist approach contrasts with the idealist leanings of structural functionalism.

Social-conflict analysis ties our society's cultural values of competitiveness and material success to our country's capitalist economy, which serves the interests of the nation's wealthy elite. The culture of capitalism teaches us to think that rich and powerful people work harder or longer than others and that they therefore deserve their wealth and privileges. It also encourages us to view capitalism as somehow "natural," discouraging us from trying to reduce economic inequality.

Eventually, however, the strains of inequality erupt into movements for social change. Two historical examples are the civil rights movement and the women's movement. A more recent example is the Occupy Wall Street movement, which has focused on our society's increasing economic inequality. All these movements seek greater equality, and all have encountered opposition from defenders of the status quo.

Gender and Culture: Feminist Theory

As Marx saw it, culture is rooted in economic production. Therefore, our society's culture largely reflects the capitalist economic system. Feminists agree with Marx's claim that culture is an arena of conflict, but they see this conflict as being rooted in gender.

Gender refers to *the personal traits and social positions that members of a society attach to being female or male.* From a feminist point of view, gender is a crucial dimension of social inequality, a topic that Chapter 10, "Gender Stratification" examines in detail. As that chapter explains, men have greater access to the workforce than women do and so men earn more income. In addition, men have greater power, both in our national political system; for example, all of this country's presidents have been men. In addition, on the level of everyday experience, men exercise the most power in the typical household.

Feminist theory claims that our culture is "gendered." This means that our way of life reflects the ways in which our society defines what is male as more important than what is female. This inequality is evident right in the language we use. We tend to say "man and wife,"

Culture

	Structural-Functional Theory	Social-Conflict and Feminist Theories	Sociobiology Theory
What is the level of analysis?	Macro-level	Macro-level	Macro-level
What is culture?	Culture is a system of behavior by which members of societies cooperate to meet their needs.	Culture is a system that benefits some people and disadvantages others.	Culture is a system of behavior that is partly shaped by human biology.
What is the foundation of culture?	Cultural patterns are rooted in a society's core values and beliefs that tend to remain fairly stable over time.	Marx claimed that culture is rooted in a society's system of economic production; feminist theory sees cultural conflict as rooted in gender.	Cultural patterns, especially cultural universals, are rooted in humanity's biological evolution.
What core questions does the approach ask?	How does a cultural pattern help society operate? What cultural patterns are found in all societies?	How does a cultural pattern benefit some people and harm others? How does a cultural pattern support social inequality?	How does a cultural pattern help a species adapt to its environment?

a phrase used in traditional wedding vows; we almost never hear the phrase "woman and husband." Similarly, the masculine word "king" conveys power and prestige, with a meaning that is almost entirely positive. The comparable feminine word "queen" has a range of meanings, some which are negative.

Not only does our culture define what is masculine as dominant in relation to what is feminine, but our way of life also defines this male domination as "natural." Such a system of beliefs serves to justify gender inequality by claiming it cannot be changed. In short, cultural patterns reflect and support gender inequality. Cultural patterns also perpetuate this inequality to the extent that they carry it forward into the future.

● **Evaluate** The social-conflict theory suggests that cultural systems do not address human needs equally, allowing some people to dominate others. Marx focused on economic inequality, and analyzed culture as an expression of capitalism. Feminists focus on gender and understand culture as a reflection of male domination. All these dimensions of inequality are "built into" our way of life. But, at the same time, such inequality also generates pressure toward change.

Yet by stressing the divisiveness of culture, all social conflict analysis understates the ways in which cultural patterns integrate members of society. Thus we should consider both social-conflict and structural-functional insights for a fuller understanding of culture.

CHECK YOUR LEARNING How might a social-conflict analysis of college fraternities and sororities differ from a structural-functional analysis?

Evolution and Culture: Sociobiology

We know that culture is a human creation, but does human biology influence how this process unfolds? A third way of thinking, standing with one foot in biology and one in sociology, is **sociobiology**, *a theoretical approach that explores ways in which human biology affects how we create culture.*

Sociobiology rests on the theory of evolution proposed by Charles Darwin in his book *On the Origin of Species* (1859). Darwin asserted that living organisms change over long periods of time as a result of *natural selection,* a matter of four simple principles. First, all living things live to reproduce themselves. Second, the blueprint for reproduction is in the genes, the basic units of life that carry traits of one generation into the next. Third, some random variation in genes allows a species to "try out" new life patterns in a particular environment. This variation enables some organisms to survive better than others and to pass on their advantageous genes to their offspring. Fourth and finally, over thousands of generations, the genes that promote reproduction survive and become dominant. In this way, as biologists say, a species *adapts* to its environment, and dominant traits emerge as the "nature" of the organism.

Sociobiologists claim that the large number of cultural universals reflects the fact that all humans are members of a single biological species. It is our common biology that underlies, for example, the apparently universal "double standard" of sexual behavior. As the sex researcher Alfred Kinsey put it, "Among all people everywhere in the world, the male is more likely than the female to desire sex with a variety of partners" (quoted in Barash, 1981:49). But why?

We all know that children result from joining a woman's egg with a man's sperm. But the biological importance of a single sperm is very different from that of a single egg. For healthy men, sperm is a "renewable resource" produced by the testes throughout most of the life course. A man releases hundreds of millions of sperm in a single ejaculation (Barash, 1981:47). A newborn female's ovaries,

Using an evolutionary perspective, sociobiologists explain that different reproductive strategies give rise to a double standard: Men treat women as sexual objects more than women treat men that way. While this may be so, many sociologists counter that behavior—such as that shown here—is more correctly understood as resulting from a culture of male domination.

say, sociobiology unites all humanity because all people share a single evolutionary history. Sociobiology does assert that men and women differ biologically in some ways that culture cannot easily overcome. But far from claiming that males are somehow more important than females, sociobiology emphasizes that both sexes are vital to human reproduction and survival.

Second, say the critics, sociobiologists have little evidence to support their theories. Research to date suggests that biological forces do not *determine* human behavior in any rigid sense. Rather, humans *learn* behavior within a culture. The contribution of sociobiology, then, includes explaining why some cultural patterns are more common and seem easier to learn than others (Barash, 1981).

CHECK YOUR LEARNING Using the sociobiology approach, explain why some cultural patterns, such as sibling rivalry (the fact that children in the same family often compete and even fight with one another), are widespread.

Because any analysis of culture requires a broad focus on the workings of society, the major theoretical approaches discussed in this chapter are macro-level in scope. The symbolic-interaction approach, with its micro-level focus on people's behavior in specific situations, will be explored in Chapter 4 ("Social Interaction in Everyday Life").

Culture and Human Freedom

 Evaluate

This chapter leads us to ask an important question: To what extent are human beings, as cultural creatures, free? Does culture bind us to each other and to the past? Or does it enhance our capacity for individual thought and independent choice?

Culture as Constraint

As symbolic creatures, humans cannot live without culture. But the capacity for culture does have some drawbacks. We may be the only animals who name ourselves, but living in a symbolic world means that we are also the only creatures who experience alienation. In addition, culture is largely a matter of habit, which limits our choices and drives us to repeat troubling patterns, such as racial prejudice and gender discrimination, in each new generation.

Our society's emphasis on personal achievement urges us toward excellence, yet this same competitive behavior also isolates us from one another. Material things comfort us in some ways but divert us from the security and satisfaction that come from close relationships and spiritual strength.

Culture as Freedom

For better or worse, human beings are cultural creatures, just as ants and bees are prisoners of their biology. But there is a crucial difference. Biological instincts create a ready-made world; culture forces us to choose as we make and remake a world for ourselves. No better evidence of this freedom exists than the cultural diversity

however, contain her entire lifetime supply of follicles, or immature eggs. A woman releases a single egg cell from the ovaries each month. So although men are biologically capable of fathering thousands of offspring, a woman is able to bear only a relatively small number of children.

Given this biological difference, men reproduce their genes most efficiently by being promiscuous—readily engaging in sex. But women look differently at reproduction. Each of a woman's relatively few pregnancies demands that she carry the child, give birth, and provide care for some time afterward. Efficient reproduction on the part of the woman depends on selecting a man whose qualities (beginning with the likelihood that he will simply stay around) will contribute to her child's survival and, later, successful reproduction.

The double standard certainly involves more than biology and is tangled up with the historical domination of women by men. But sociobiology suggests that this cultural pattern, like many others, has an underlying "bio-logic." Simply put, the double standard exists around the world because women and men everywhere tend toward distinctive reproductive strategies.

 Evaluate Sociobiology has generated intriguing insights into the biological roots of some cultural patterns. But the approach remains controversial for two main reasons.

First, some critics fear that sociobiology may revive the biological arguments of a century ago that claimed the superiority of one race or sex. But defenders counter that sociobiology rejects the past pseudoscience of racial and gender superiority. In fact, they

The United States and Canada: How Do These National Cultures Differ?

The United States and Canada are two of the largest high-income countries in the world, and they share a common border of about 4,000 miles. But do the United States and Canada share the same culture?

One important point to make right away is that both nations are *multicultural*. Not only do both countries have hundreds of Native American societies, but immigration has also brought people from all over the world to both the United States and Canada. In both countries, most early immigrants came from Europe, but in recent years most immigrants have come from nations in Asia and Latin America. The Canadian city of Vancouver, for example, has an Asian community that is almost the same size as the Latino community in Los Angeles.

Canada differs from the United States in one important respect—historically, Canada has had *two* dominant cultures: French (about 16 percent of the population) and British (roughly 36 percent). Almost one-third of people in the provinces of Quebec (where French is the official language) and New Brunswick (which is officially bilingual) claim some French ancestry.

Are the dominant values of Canada much the same as those we have described for the United States? Seymour Martin Lipset (1985) finds that they differ to some degree. The United States declared its independence from Great Britain in 1776; Canada did not formally separate from Great Britain until 1982, and the British monarch is still Canada's official head of state. Thus, Lipset continues, the dominant culture of Canada lies between the culture of the United States and that of Great Britain.

The culture of the United States is more individualistic, and Canada's is more collective. In the United States, individualism is seen in the historical importance of the cowboy, a self-sufficient loner, and even outlaws such as Jesse James and Billy the Kid are regarded as heroes because they challenged authority. In Canada, by contrast, it is the Mountie—Canada's well-known police officer on horseback—who is looked on with great respect. Canada's greater emphasis on collective life is also evident in stronger unions: Canadian workers are almost three times as likely to be members of a union as workers in the United States (Steyn, 2008; Statistics Canada, 2011; U.S. Department of Labor, 2011).

Politically, people in the United States tend to think that individuals ought to do things for themselves. In Canada, much as in Great Britain, there is a strong sense that government should look after the interests of everyone. The U.S. Constitution emphasizes the importance of "life, liberty, and the pursuit of happiness" (words that place importance on the individual), while Canadian society is based on "peace, order, and good government" (words that place importance on the

government) (Steyn, 2008). One clear result of this difference today is that Canada has a much broader social welfare system (including universal health care) than the United States (the only high-income nation without such a program). It also helps explain the fact that about one-third of all households in the United States own one or more guns, and the idea that individuals are entitled to own a gun, although controversial, is widespread. In Canada, by contrast, few households have a gun, and the government restricts gun ownership, as in Great Britain.

What Do You Think?

1. Why do you think some Canadians feel that their way of life is overshadowed by that of the United States?

2. Ask your friends to name the capital city of Canada. (The correct answer is Ottawa, in the province of Ontario.) Are you surprised by how few know the answer? Why or why not?

3. Why do many people in the United States not know very much about either Canada or Mexico, countries with which we share long borders?

The individuals that a society celebrates as heroic are a good indication of that society's cultural values. In the United States, outlaws such as Jesse James (and later, Bonnie and Clyde) were regarded as heroes because they represented the individual standing strong against authority. In Canada, by contrast, people have always looked up to the Mountie, who symbolizes society's authority over the individual.

of our own society and the even greater human diversity found around the world.

Learning more about this cultural diversity is one goal shared by sociologists. The Thinking Globally box offers some contrasts

between the cultures of the United States and Canada. Wherever we may live, the better we understand the workings of the surrounding culture, the better prepared we will be to use the freedom it offers us.

Seeing Sociology in Everyday Life

What clues do we have to a society's cultural values?

The values of any society—that is, what that society thinks is important—are reflected in various aspects of everyday life, including the things people have and the ways they behave. An interesting way to "read" our own culture's values is to look at the "superheroes" that we celebrate. Take a look at the characters in the three photos shown here and, in each case, describe what makes the character special and what each character represents in cultural terms.

Hint Superman (as well as all superheroes) defines our society as good; after all, Superman fights for "truth, justice, and the American way." Many superheroes have stories that draw on great people in our cultural history, including religious figures such as Moses and Jesus: They have mysterious origins (we never really know their true families), they are "tested" through great moral challenges, and they finally succeed in overcoming all obstacles. (Today's superheroes, however, are likely to win the day using force and often violence.) Having a "secret identity" means superheroes can lead ordinary lives (and means we ordinary people can imagine being superheroes). But to keep their focus on fighting evil, superheroes must place their work ahead of any romantic interests ("Work comes first!"). Sookie also illustrates the special challenge to "do it all" faced by women in our society: Besides using her special powers to fight evil, she still has to hold down a full-time job.

Superman first appeared in an *Action Comics* book in 1938, as the United States struggled to climb out of economic depression and faced the rising danger of war. Since then, Superman has been featured in a television show as well as in a string of Hollywood films. One trait of most superheroes is that they have a secret identity; in this case, Superman's everyday identity is "mild-mannered news reporter" Clark Kent.

In the television drama, *True Blood,* Sookie Stackhouse (Anna Paquin), a waitress with telepathic abilities and other special powers, inhabits a world in which you never know if your customer is a vampire. Heroic humans with special abilities as portrayed in the mass media rarely include women.

Another longtime superhero important to our culture is Spider-Man. In the *Spider-Man* movies, Peter Parker (who transforms into Spider-Man when he confronts evil) is secretly in love with Mary Jane Watson. Again and again the male hero rescues the female from danger. But, in true superhero style, Spider-Man does not allow himself to follow his heart because with great power comes great responsibility, and that must come first.

Seeing Sociology in *Your* Everyday Life

1. Members of every culture, as they decide how to live their lives, look to "heroes" for role models and inspiration. In modern societies, the mass media play a big part in creating heroes. What traits define popular culture heroes such as Clint Eastwood's film character "Dirty Harry," Sylvester Stallone's film characters "Rocky" as well as "Rambo," and Arnold Schwarzenegger's character "the Terminator"?

2. Watch an animated Disney film such as *Finding Nemo, The Lion King, The Little Mermaid, Aladdin,* or *Pocahontas*. One reason for the popularity of these films is that they all share many of the same distinctive cultural themes that appeal to members of our society. Using the list of key values of U.S. culture on pages 42 and 43 as a guide, identify the cultural values that make the film you selected especially "American."

3. Do you know someone on your campus who has lived in another country or a cultural setting different from what is familiar to you? Try to engage in conversation with someone whose way of life is significantly different from your own. Try to discover something that you accept or take for granted in one way that the other person sees in a different way and try to understand why. Go to the "Seeing Sociology in *Your* Everyday Life" feature on MySocLab to learn more about cultural diversity and how we can all learn from experiencing cultural differences.

What Is Culture?

Culture is a **way of life**.

- Culture is shared by members of a society. **p. 37**
- Culture shapes how we act, think, and feel. **p. 37**

Culture is a **human trait**.

- Although several species display a limited capacity for culture, only human beings rely on culture for survival. **p. 39**

Culture is a **product of evolution**.

- As the human brain evolved, culture replaced biological instincts as our species' primary strategy for survival. **p. 39**

We experience **culture shock** when we enter an unfamiliar culture and are not able to "read" meaning in our new surroundings. We create culture shock for others when we act in ways they do not understand. **pp. 39–40**

culture (p. 36) the ways of thinking, the ways of acting, and the material objects that together from a people's way of life

nonmaterial culture (p. 36) the ideas created by members of a society

material culture (p. 37) the physical things created by members of a society

society (p. 37) people who interact in a defined territory and share a culture

culture shock (p. 38) personal disorientation when experiencing an unfamiliar way of life

The Elements of Culture

Culture relies on **symbols** in the form of words, gestures, and actions to express meaning. **p. 39**

- The fact that different meanings can come to be associated with the same symbol (for example, a wink of an eye) shows the human capacity to create and manipulate symbols. **p. 40**
- Societies create new symbols all the time (for example, new computer technology has sparked the creation of new cyber-symbols). **p. 40**

Language is the symbolic system by which people in a culture communicate with one another. **p. 41**

- People use language—both spoken and written—to transmit culture from one generation to the next. **p. 41**
- Because every culture is different, each language has words or expressions not found in any other language. **p. 41**

Values are abstract standards of what *ought* to be (for example, equality of opportunity).

- Values can sometimes be in conflict with one another. **p. 43**
- Lower-income countries have cultures that value survival; higher-income countries have cultures that value individualism and self-expression. **p. 43**

Beliefs are specific statements that people who share a culture hold to be true (for example, "A qualified woman could be elected president"). **p. 41**

◉─┤**Watch** the **Video** on **mysoclab.com**

Norms, which guide human behavior, are of two types:

- **mores** (for example, sexual taboos), which have great moral significance **p. 44**
- **folkways** (for example, greetings or dining etiquette), which are matters of everyday politeness **p. 44**

symbol (p. 40) anything that carries a particular meaning recognized by people who share a culture

language (p. 41) a system of symbols that allows people to communicate with one another

cultural transmission (p. 41) the process by which one generation passes culture to the next

Sapir-Whorf thesis (p. 41) the idea that people see and understand the world through the cultural lens of language

values (p. 41) culturally defined standards that people use to decide what is desirable, good, and beautiful and that serve as broad guidelines for social living

beliefs (p. 41) specific ideas that people hold to be true

norms (p. 44) rules and expectations by which a society guides the behavior of its members

mores (p. 44) norms that are widely observed and have great moral significance

folkways (p. 44) norms for routine or casual interaction

Technology and Culture

Culture is shaped by **technology**. We understand technological development in terms of stages of **sociocultural evolution**:

- hunting and gathering
- horticulture and pastoralism
- agriculture
- industry
- postindustrial information technology **pp. 45–47**

technology (p. 45) knowledge that people use to make a way of life in their surroundings

hunting and gathering (p. 45) the use of simple tools to hunt animals and gather vegetation for food

horticulture (p. 45) the use of hand tools to raise crops

pastoralism (p. 46) the domestication of animals

agriculture (p. 46) large-scale cultivation using plows harnessed to animals or more powerful energy sources

industry (p. 46) the production of goods using advanced sources of energy to drive large machinery

postindustrialism (p. 47) the production of information using computer technology

Cultural Diversity

We live in a **culturally diverse society**.

- This diversity is due to our country's history of immigration. **p. 47**
- Diversity reflects regional differences. **p. 47**
- Diversity reflects differences in social class that set off **high culture** (available only to elites) from **popular culture** (available to average people). **pp. 47–48**

A number of values are central to our way of life. But **cultural patterns** are not the same throughout our society.

Subculture is based on differences in interests and life experiences.

- Hip-hop fans and jocks are two examples of youth subcultures in the United States. **p. 48**

Multiculturalism is an effort to enhance appreciation of cultural diversity.

- Multiculturalism developed as a reaction to the earlier "melting pot" idea, which was thought to result in minorities' losing their identity as they adopted mainstream cultural patterns. **p. 48**

✳ Explore the Map on mysoclab.com

Counterculture is strongly at odds with conventional ways of life.

- Militant religious fundamentalist groups in the United States who plot to destroy Western society are examples of a counterculture. **p. 49**

📖 Read the Document on mysoclab.com

Cultural change results from

- **invention** (examples include the telephone and the computer) **p. 50**
- **discovery** (for example, the recognition that women are capable of political leadership) **p. 50**
- **diffusion** (for example, the growing popularity of various ethnic foods and musical styles). **p. 51**

Cultural lag results when some parts of a cultural system change faster than others. **p. 50**

How do we understand cultural differences?

- **Ethnocentrism** links people to their society but can cause misunderstanding and conflict between societies. **p. 51**
- **Cultural relativism** is increasingly important as people of the world come into more and more contact with each other. **pp. 51–53**

high culture (p. 48) cultural patterns that distinguish a society's elite

popular culture (p. 48) cultural patterns that are widespread among a society's population

subculture (p. 48) cultural patterns that set apart some segment of a society's population

multiculturalism (p. 48) a perspective recognizing the cultural diversity of the United States and promoting equal standing for all cultural traditions

Eurocentrism (p. 48) the dominance of European (especially English) cultural patterns

Afrocentrism (p. 49) emphasizing and promoting African cultural patterns

counterculture (p. 49) cultural patterns that strongly oppose those widely accepted within a society

cultural integration (p. 50) the close relationships among various elements of a cultural system

cultural lag (p. 50) the fact that some cultural elements change more quickly than others, disrupting a cultural system

ethnocentrism (p. 51) the practice of judging another culture by the standards of one's own culture

cultural relativism (p. 51) the practice of judging a culture by its own standards

Theories of Culture

Structional-functional theory views culture as a relatively stable system built on core values. All cultural patterns play some part in the ongoing operation of society. **p. 54**

Social conflict theory sees culture as a dynamic arena of inequality and conflict. Cultural patterns benefit some categories of people more than others. Marx claimed that cultural patterns reflect the operation of a society's economic system. **p. 54**

Feminist theory is a type of social-conflict theory that sees culture as a system of inequality based on gender. **pp. 54–55**

Sociobiology theory explores how the long history of evolution has shaped patterns of culture in today's world. **pp. 55–56**

cultural universals (p. 54) traits that are part of every known culture

gender (p. 54) the personal traits and social positions that members of a society attaches to being female or male

sociobiology (p. 55) a theoretical approach that explores ways in which human biology affects how we create culture

Culture and Human Freedom

- Culture can limit the choices we make.
- As cultural creatures, we have the capacity to shape and reshape our world to meet our needs and pursue our dreams. **pp. 56–57**

3 Socialization: From Infancy to Old Age

Learning Objectives

Remember the definitions of the key terms highlighted in boldfaced type throughout this chapter.

Understand the nature-nurture debate about human development.

Apply the sociological perspective to see how society defines behavior at various stages of the life course.

Analyze the contribution of the family, schooling, the peer group, and the mass media to personality development.

Evaluate the contributions of six important thinkers to our understanding of the socialization process.

Create a complex appreciation for the fact that our personalities are not fixed at birth but develop and change as we interact with others over the life course.

Having completed a macro-level look at the world of culture (Chapter 2, "Culture"), we turn now to a micro-level look at how individuals become members of society through the process of socialization. ■

On a cold winter day in 1938, a social worker walked quickly to the door of a rural Pennsylvania farmhouse. Sent to investigate a case of possible child abuse, the social worker entered the home and soon discovered a five-year-old girl hidden in a second-floor storage room. The child, whose name was Anna, was wedged into an old chair with her arms tied securely above her head so that she couldn't move. She was wearing filthy clothes, and her arms and legs were as thin as matchsticks (K. Davis, 1940).

Anna's situation can only be described as tragic. She was born in 1932 to an unmarried and mentally impaired woman of twenty-six who lived with her strict father. Angry about his daughter's "illegitimate" motherhood, the grandfather did not even want the child in his house, so for the first six months of her life, Anna was passed among several welfare agencies. But her mother could not afford to pay for her care, and Anna returned to the hostile home of her grandfather.

To lessen the grandfather's anger, Anna's mother kept the child in the storage room and gave her just enough milk to keep her alive. There she stayed—day after day, month after month, with almost no human contact—for five long years.

Learning about Anna's rescue, the sociologist Kingsley Davis immediately went to see the child. He found her with local officials at a county home. Davis was stunned by the emaciated girl, who could not laugh, speak, or even smile. Anna was completely unresponsive, as if alone in an empty world.

Social Experience: The Key to Our Humanity

 **Understand**

Socialization is so basic to human development that we sometimes overlook its importance. But in this terrible case of an isolated child, we can see what humans would be like without social contact. Although physically alive, Anna hardly seems human. We can see that without social experience, a child is not able to act or communicate in a meaningful way and seems to be as much an object as a person.

Sociologists use the term **socialization** to refer to *the lifelong social experience by which people develop their human potential and learn culture.* Unlike other species, whose behavior is biologically set, humans need social experience to learn their culture and to survive. Social experience is also the basis of **personality**, *a person's fairly consistent patterns of acting, thinking, and feeling.* We build a personality by internalizing—taking in—our surroundings. But without social experience, as Anna's case shows, personality hardly develops at all.

Human Development: Nature and Nurture

Anna's case makes clear the fact that humans depend on others to provide the care needed not only for physical growth but also for personality to develop. A century ago, however, people mistakenly believed that humans were born with instincts that determined their personality and behavior.

The Biological Sciences: The Role of Nature

Charles Darwin's groundbreaking study of evolution, described in Chapter 2 ("Culture"), led people to think that human behavior was instinctive, simply our "nature." Such ideas led to claims that the U.S. economic system reflects "instinctive human competitiveness," that some people are "born criminals," or that women are "naturally" emotional while men are "naturally" more rational.

People trying to understand cultural diversity also misunderstood Darwin's thinking. Centuries of world exploration had taught Western Europeans that people around the world behaved quite differently from one society to another. But Europeans linked these differences to biology rather than culture. It was an easy, although incorrect and very damaging, step to claim that members of technologically simple

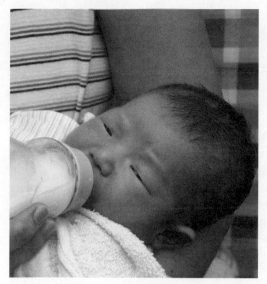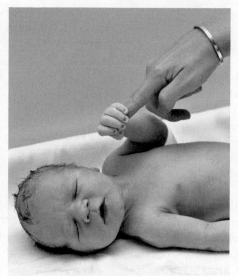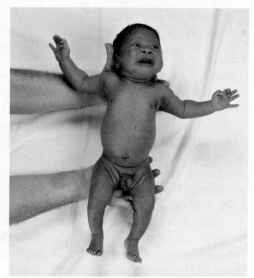

Human infants display various *reflexes*—biologically based behavior patterns that enhance survival. The sucking reflex, which actually begins before birth, enables the infant to obtain nourishment. The grasping reflex, triggered by placing a finger on the infant's palm, causing the hand to close, helps the infant to maintain contact with a parent and, later on, to grasp objects. The Moro reflex, activated by startling the infant, has the infant swinging both arms outward and then bringing them together across the chest. This action, which disappears after several months of life, probably developed among our evolutionary ancestors so that a falling infant could grasp the body hair of a parent.

societies were biologically less evolved and therefore "less human." This ethnocentric view helped justify colonialism: Why not take advantage of others if they seem not to be as "fully human" as you are?

The Social Sciences: The Role of Nurture

In the twentieth century, biological explanations of human behavior came under fire. The psychologist John B. Watson (1878–1958) developed a theory called *behaviorism,* which held that behavior is not instinctive but learned. Thus people everywhere are equally human, differing only in their cultural patterns. In short, Watson rooted human behavior not in nature but in *nurture.*

Today, social scientists are cautious about describing *any* human behavior as instinctive. This does not mean that biology plays no part in human behavior. Human life, after all, depends on the functioning of the body. We also know that children often share biological traits (such as height and hair color) with their parents and that heredity plays a part in intelligence, musical and artistic talent, and personality (such as how you deal with frustration). However, whether you develop your inherited potential depends on how you are raised. For example, if children do not use their brain early in life, the brain fails to develop fully (Goldsmith, 1983; Begley, 1995).

Without denying the importance of nature, then, nurture matters more in shaping human behavior. More precisely, *nurture is our nature.*

Social Isolation

As the story of Anna shows, cutting people off from the social world is very harmful. For ethical reasons, researchers can never place human beings in total isolation to study what happens. But in the past, they have studied the effects of social isolation on nonhuman primates.

Research with Monkeys

In a classic study, the psychologists Harry and Margaret Harlow (1962) placed rhesus monkeys—whose behavior is in some ways surprisingly similar to human behavior—in various conditions of social isolation. They found that complete isolation (with adequate nutrition) for even six months seriously disturbed the monkeys' development. When returned to their group, these monkeys were passive, anxious, and fearful.

The Harlows then placed infant rhesus monkeys in cages with an artificial "mother" made of wire mesh with a wooden head and the nipple of a feeding tube where the breast would be. These monkeys also survived but were unable to interact with others when placed in a group.

But monkeys in a third category, isolated with an artificial "mother" covered with soft terry cloth, did better. Each of these monkeys would cling to the "mother" closely. Because these monkeys showed less developmental damage than the earlier groups, the Harlows concluded that the monkeys benefited from this closeness. The experiment confirmed how important it is that adults cradle infants affectionately.

Finally, the Harlows discovered that infant monkeys could recover from as much as three months of isolation. But after about six months, isolation caused irreversible emotional and behavioral damage.

Read "Final Note on an Extreme Case of Isolation" by Kingsley Davis on **mysoclab.com**

Studies of Isolated Children

The rest of Anna's story squares with the Harlows' findings. After her discovery, Anna received extensive social contact and soon showed improvement. When Kingsley Davis (1940) revisited her after ten days, he found her more alert and even smiling (perhaps for the first time in her life). Over the next year, Anna made slow but steady progress, showing more interest in other people and gradually learning to walk. After a year and a half, she could feed herself and play with toys.

But as the Harlows might have predicted, Anna's five years of social isolation had caused permanent damage. At age eight, her mental development was still less than that of a two-year-old. Not until she was almost ten did she begin to use words. Because Anna's mother was mentally retarded, perhaps Anna was also. The riddle was never solved, however, because Anna died at age ten of a blood disorder, possibly related to the years of abuse she suffered (K. Davis, 1940, 1947).

A more recent case of childhood isolation involves a California girl abused by her parents (Curtiss, 1977; Rymer, 1994). From the time she was two, Genie was tied to a potty chair in a dark garage. In 1970, when she was rescued at age thirteen, Genie weighed only 59 pounds and had the mental development of a one-year-old. With intensive treatment, she became physically healthy, but her language ability remains that of a young child. Today, Genie lives in a home for developmentally disabled adults.

● **Evaluate** All evidence points to the crucial role of social experience in forming personality. Human beings can sometimes recover from abuse and short-term isolation. But there is a point—exactly when is unclear from the small number of cases studied—at which isolation in infancy causes permanent developmental damage.

CHECK YOUR LEARNING What do studies of isolated children teach us about the importance of social experience?

Understanding Socialization

 Understand

Socialization is a complex, lifelong process. The following sections highlight the work of six researchers—Sigmund Freud, Jean Piaget, Lawrence Kohlberg, Carol Gilligan, George Herbert Mead, and Erik H. Erikson—who made lasting contributions to our understanding of human development.

Sigmund Freud's Elements of Personality

Sigmund Freud (1856–1939) lived in Vienna at a time when most Europeans considered human behavior biologically fixed. Trained as a physician, Freud turned to the study of personality and eventually developed the celebrated theory of psychoanalysis.

Basic Human Needs

Freud claimed that biology plays a major part in human development, although not in terms of specific instincts, as is the case in other species. Rather, he theorized that humans have two basic needs or drives that are present at birth. First is a need for bonding, which he called the "life instinct," or *eros* (named after the Greek god of love). Second, we share an aggressive drive he called the "death instinct," or *thanatos* (the Greek word for "death"). These opposing forces, operating at an unconscious level, create deep inner tension.

Freud's Model of Personality

Freud combined basic human drives and the influence of society into a model of personality with three parts: id, ego, and superego. The **id** (Latin for "it") represents *the human being's basic drives,* which are unconscious and demand immediate satisfaction. Rooted in biology, the id is present at birth, making a newborn a bundle of demands for attention, touching, and food. But society opposes the self-centered id, which is why one of the first words a child usually learns is "no."

To avoid frustration, a child must learn to approach the world realistically. This is done through the **ego** (Latin for "I"), which is *a person's conscious efforts to balance innate pleasure-seeking drives with the demands of society.* The ego arises as we gain awareness of our distinct existence and face the fact that we cannot have everything we want.

In the human personality, **superego** (Latin for "above or beyond the ego") is *the cultural values and norms internalized by an individual.* The superego operates as our conscience, telling us *why*

The personalities we develop depend largely on the environment in which we live. When a child's world is shredded by violence, the damage (including losing the ability to trust) can be profound and lasting. This drawing was made by a child in the Darfur region of Sudan, where armed militia have killed more than 300,000 people since 2003. What are the likely effects of such experiences on a young person's self-confidence and capacity to form trusting ties?

we cannot have everything we want. The superego begins to form as a child becomes aware of parental demands and matures as the child comes to understand that everyone's behavior should take account of cultural norms.

Personality Development

To the id-centered child, the world is a jumble of physical sensations that bring either pleasure or pain. As the superego develops, however, the child learns the moral concepts of right and wrong. Initially, in other words, children can feel good only in a physical way (as when being held and cuddled), but after three or four years, they feel good or bad according to how they judge their behavior against cultural norms (doing "the right thing").

The id and the superego remain in conflict, but in a well-adjusted person, the ego manages these opposing forces. If conflicts are not resolved during childhood, they may surface as personality disorders later on.

Culture, in the form of superego, *represses* selfish demands, forcing people to look beyond their own desires. Often the competing demands of self and society result in a compromise Freud called *sublimation*, which changes selfish drives into socially acceptable behavior. For example, marriage makes the satisfaction of sexual urges socially acceptable, and competitive sports are an outlet for aggression.

Evaluate In Freud's time, few people were ready to accept sex as a basic drive. More recent critics have charged that Freud's work presents humans in male terms and devalues women (Donovan & Littenberg, 1982). Freud's theories are also difficult to test scientifically. But Freud influenced everyone who later studied human personality. Of special importance to sociology are his ideas that we internalize social norms and that childhood experiences have a lasting impact on personality.

CHECK YOUR LEARNING What are the three elements in Freud's model of personality? What does each one mean?

Jean Piaget's Theory of Cognitive Development

The Swiss psychologist Jean Piaget (1896–1980) studied human *cognition,* how people think and understand. As Piaget watched his own three children grow, he wondered not just what they knew but how they made sense of the world. Piaget went on to identify four stages of cognitive development.

The Sensorimotor Stage

Stage one is the **sensorimotor stage**, *the level of human development at which individuals experience the world only through their senses.* For about the first two years of life, the infant knows the world only by touching, tasting, smelling, looking, and listening. "Knowing" to very young children amounts to what their senses tell them.

The Preoperational Stage

About age two, children enter the **preoperational stage**, *the level of human development at which individuals first use language and other symbols.* Now children begin to think about the world using

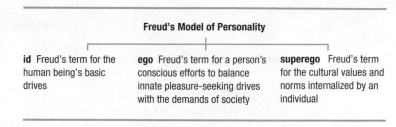

Freud's Model of Personality

| **id** Freud's term for the human being's basic drives | **ego** Freud's term for a person's conscious efforts to balance innate pleasure-seeking drives with the demands of society | **superego** Freud's term for the cultural values and norms internalized by an individual |

their imagination. But "pre-op" children between about two and six attach meaning only to specific experiences and objects. They can identify a toy as their "favorite" but cannot explain what *types* of toys they like.

Lacking abstract concepts, a child cannot judge size, weight, or volume. In one of his best-known experiments, Piaget placed two identical glasses containing equal amounts of water on a table. He asked several five- and six-year-olds whether the amount in each was the same. They nodded that it was. The children then watched Piaget take one of the glasses and pour its contents into a taller, narrower glass, raising the level of the water. He asked again whether each glass held the same amount. The typical five- or six-year-old now insisted that the taller glass held more water. By about age seven, children are able to think abstractly and realize that the amount of water stays the same.

The Concrete Operational Stage

Next comes the **concrete operational stage**, *the level of human development at which individuals first see causal connections in their surroundings.* Between the ages of seven and eleven, children focus on how and why things happen. In addition, they attach more than one symbol to an event or object. If, for example, you say to a child of five, "Today is Wednesday," she might respond, "No, it's my birthday!" indicating that she can use just one symbol at a time. But an older child at the concrete operational stage would be able to respond, "Yes, and it's also my birthday."

The Formal Operational Stage

The last stage in Piaget's model is the **formal operational stage**, *the level of human development at which individuals think abstractly and critically.* At about age twelve, young people begin to reason in the abstract rather than think only of concrete situations. For example, if you ask a child of seven, "What would you like to be when you grow up?" you will get a concrete response such as "a teacher." But most teenagers can consider the question more abstractly and might respond, "I would like a job that helps others." As they gain the capacity for abstract thought, young people also learn to understand metaphors. Hearing the phrase "A penny for your thoughts" might lead a child to ask for a coin, but a teenager will recognize a gentle invitation to intimacy.

Evaluate Freud saw human beings torn by opposing forces of biology and culture. Piaget saw the mind as active and creative. He saw an ability to engage the world unfolding in stages as the result of both biological maturation and social experience.

But do people in all societies pass through all four of Piaget's stages? Living in a traditional society that changes slowly probably limits the capacity for abstract and critical thought. Even in the

Piaget's Stages of Development

sensorimotor stage Piaget's term for the level of human development at which individuals experience the world only through their senses	preoperational stage Piaget's term for the level of human development at which individuals first use language and other symbols	concrete operational stage Piaget's term for the level of human development at which individuals first see causal connections in their surroundings	formal operational stage Piaget's term for the level of human development at which individuals think abstractly and critically

United States, perhaps 30 percent of people never reach the formal operational stage (Kohlberg & Gilligan, 1971).

CHECK YOUR LEARNING What are Piaget's four stages of cognitive development? What does his theory teach us about socialization?

Lawrence Kohlberg's Theory of Moral Development

Lawrence Kohlberg (1981) built on Piaget's work to study *moral reasoning,* how people come to judge situations as right or wrong. Here again, development occurs in stages.

Young children who experience the world in terms of pain and pleasure (Piaget's sensorimotor stage) are at the *preconventional* level of moral development. At first, "rightness" amounts to "what feels good to me." For example, a child may reach for something on a table that looks shiny, which is the reason parents of young children have to "childproof" their homes.

The *conventional* level, Kohlberg's second stage, appears by the teens (corresponding to Piaget's final, formal operational stage). At this point, young people lose some of their selfishness as they learn to define right and wrong in terms of what pleases parents and conforms to cultural norms. At this stage, individuals also become aware of not just action but also intention. They might realize, for example, that stealing food for hungry children is not the same as stealing an iPod to sell for pocket change.

In Kohlberg's final stage of moral development, the *postconventional* level, people move beyond their society's norms to consider abstract ethical principles. As they think about ideas such as liberty, freedom, or justice, they may argue that what is lawful still may not be right. When the African American civil rights activist Rosa Parks refused to give up her seat on a Montgomery, Alabama, bus back in 1955, she violated that city's segregation laws in order to call attention to the racial injustice of the law.

Childhood is a time to learn principles of right and wrong. According to Carol Gilligan, however, boys and girls define what is "right" in different ways. After reading about Gilligan's theory, can you suggest what these two children might be arguing about?

Evaluate Like the work of Piaget, Kohlberg's model explains moral development in terms of distinct stages. But whether this model applies to people in all societies remains unclear. Further, many people in the United States apparently never reach the postconventional level of moral reasoning, although exactly why is still an open question.

Another problem with Kohlberg's research is that all his subjects were boys. He committed a common research error, described in Chapter 1 ("Sociology: Perspective, Theory, and Method"), by generalizing the results of male subjects to all people. This problem led a colleague, Carol Gilligan, to investigate how gender affects moral reasoning.

CHECK YOUR LEARNING What are Kohlberg's three stages of moral development? What does his theory teach us about socialization?

Carol Gilligan's Theory of Gender and Moral Development

Carol Gilligan (1982) set out to compare the moral development of girls and boys and concluded that the two sexes use different standards of rightness. Boys, she claims, have a *justice perspective,* relying on formal rules to define right and wrong. Girls, by contrast, have a *care and responsibility perspective,* judging a situation with an eye toward personal relationships and loyalties. For example, as boys see it, stealing is wrong because it breaks the law. Girls are more likely to wonder why someone would steal and to be sympathetic toward someone who steals, say, to feed her family.

Kohlberg treats rule-based male reasoning as morally superior to the person-based female approach. Gilligan notes that impersonal rules have long governed men's lives in the workplace, but personal relationships are more relevant to women's lives as mothers and caregivers. Why, then, Gilligan asks, should we set up male standards as the norms by which to judge everyone?

Evaluate Gilligan's work sharpens our understanding of both human development and gender issues in research. Yet the question remains, does nature or nurture account for the differences between females and males? In Gilligan's view, cultural conditioning is at work, a view that finds support in other research. For example, Nancy Chodorow (1994) claims that children grow up in homes in which, typically, mothers do much more nurturing than fathers. As girls learn to identify with mothers, they become more concerned with care and responsibility to others. By contrast, boys become more like fathers, who are often detached from the home, and they may develop more detached personalities and a greater concern for abstract rules. Perhaps the moral reasoning of females and males will become more similar as more women organize their lives around the workplace.

CHECK YOUR LEARNING According to Gilligan, how do boys and girls differ in their approach to understanding right and wrong?

George Herbert Mead's Theory of the Social Self

George Herbert Mead (1863–1931) developed the theory of *social behaviorism* to explain how social experience develops an individual's personality (1962, orig. 1934).

The Self

Mead's central concept is the **self**, *the part of an individual's personality composed of self-awareness and self-image.* Mead's genius lay in seeing the self as the product of social experience.

First, said Mead, *the self develops only with social experience.* The self is not part of the body and does not exist at birth. Mead rejected the idea that personality is guided by biological drives (as Freud asserted) or even biological maturation (as Piaget claimed). For Mead, self develops only as the individual interacts with others. Without interaction, as we see from cases of isolated children, the body grows, but no self emerges.

Second, Mead explained, *social experience is the exchange of symbols.* Only people use words, a wave of the hand, or a smile to create meaning. We can train a dog using reward and punishment, but the dog attaches no meaning to its actions. By contrast, human beings find meaning in action by imagining people's underlying intentions. In short, a dog responds *to what you do*, but a human responds to *what you have in mind* as you do it. You can train a dog to go to the hallway and bring back an umbrella. But without understanding intention, if the dog cannot find the umbrella, it is incapable of the *human* response: to look for a raincoat instead.

Third, Mead continues, *understanding intention requires imagining a situation from the other's point of view.* Using symbols, we imagine ourselves in another person's shoes and see ourselves as that person does. This capacity lets us anticipate how others will respond to us even before we act. A simple toss of a ball, for example, requires stepping outside yourself to imagine how the other person will catch your throw. All symbolic interaction, then, involves seeing ourselves as others see us, a process Mead called *taking the role of the other.*

The Looking-Glass Self

In effect, others are a mirror (which people used to call a "looking glass") in which we see ourselves. What we think of ourselves, then, depends on how we think others see us. For example, if we think others see us as clever, we will think of ourselves in the same way. But if we feel they think of us as clumsy, then that is how we will see ourselves. Charles Horton Cooley (1864–1929) used the phrase **looking-glass self** to mean *a self-image based on how we think others see us* (1964, orig. 1902).

The I and the Me

Mead's fourth point is that *by taking the role of the other, we become self-aware.* Another way of saying this is that the self has two parts. One part of the self operates as the subject, being active and spontaneous. Mead called the subjective side of the self the "I" (the subjective form of the personal pronoun). The other part of the self works as an object, the way we imagine others see us. Mead called the objective side of the self the "me" (the objective form of the personal pronoun). All social experience has both components: We initiate an action (the I-phase, or subjective side, of the self), and then we evaluate the action based on how others respond to us (the me-phase, or objective side, of the self).

Development of the Self

According to Mead, the key to developing the self is learning to take the role of the other. With limited social experience, infants can

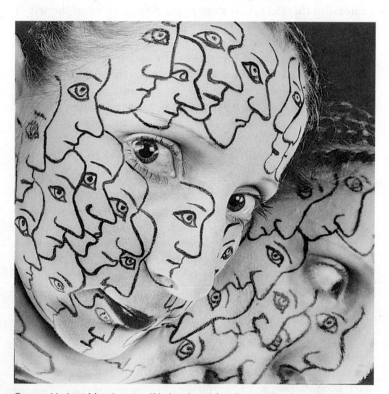

George Herbert Mead wrote, "No hard-and-fast line can be drawn between our own selves and the selves of others." The artwork *Manyness* by Rimma Gerlovina and Valeriy Gerlovin conveys this important truth. Although we tend to think of ourselves as unique individuals, each person's characteristics develop in an ongoing process of interaction with others.

Rimma Gerlovina and Valeriy Gerlovin, *Manyness*, 1990. © the artists, New City, N.Y.

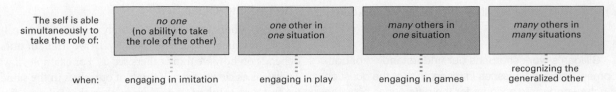

The self is able simultaneously to take the role of:	*no one* (no ability to take the role of the other)	*one* other in *one* situation	*many* others in *one* situation	*many* others in *many* situations
when:	engaging in imitation	engaging in play	engaging in games	recognizing the generalized other

FIGURE 3–1   Building on Social Experience

George Herbert Mead described the development of the self as a process of gaining social experience. That is, the self develops as we expand our capacity to take the role of the other.

do this only through *imitation.* They mimic the behavior of other people without understanding underlying intention, and so at this point, they have no self.

As children learn to use language and other symbols, the self emerges in the form of *play.* Play involves assuming roles modeled on **significant others**, *people, such as parents, who have special importance for socialization.* Playing "mommy and daddy" begins to teach children to imagine the world from a parent's point of view.

Gradually, children learn to take the roles of several others at once. This skill lets them move from simple play (say, playing catch) involving one other person to complex *games* (such as baseball) involving many others. By about age seven, most children have the social experience needed to engage in team sports.

Figure 3–1 charts the progression from imitation to play to games. But there is a final stage in the development of the self. A game involves dealing with a limited number of other people in just one situation. Everyday life demands that we see ourselves in terms of cultural norms as *any* member of our society might. Mead used the term **generalized other** to refer to *widespread cultural norms and values we use as references in evaluating ourselves.*

As life goes on, the self continues to change along with our social experiences. But no matter how much the world shapes us, we always remain creative beings, able to react to the world around us. Thus, Mead concluded, we play a key role in our own socialization.

🔵 **Evaluate**   Mead's work explores the character of social experience itself. In the symbolic interaction of human beings, he believed he had found the root of both self and society.

Mead's view is completely social, allowing no biological element at all. This is a problem for followers of Freud (who said our drives are rooted in the body) and Piaget (whose stages of development are tied to biological maturity).

Be careful not to confuse Mead's concepts of the I and the me with Freud's id and superego. For Freud, the id originates in our biology, but Mead rejected any biological element of self (although he never clearly spelled out the origin of the I). In addition, the id and the superego are locked in continual combat, but the I and the me work cooperatively together (Meltzer, 1978).

CHECK YOUR LEARNING   Explain the meaning and importance of Mead's concepts of the I and the me. What did Mead mean by "taking the role of the other"? Why is this process so important to socialization?

Erik H. Erikson's Eight Stages of Development

Although some analysts discussed in this chapter (including Freud) point to childhood as the crucial time when personality takes shape, Erik H. Erikson (1902–1994) took a broader view of socialization. He explained that we face challenges throughout the life course (1963, orig. 1950).

Stage 1: Infancy—the challenge of trust (versus mistrust). Between birth and about eighteen months, infants face the first of life's challenges: to establish a sense of trust that their world is a safe place. Family members play a key part in how any infant meets this challenge.

Stage 2: Toddlerhood—the challenge of autonomy (versus doubt and shame). The next challenge, up to age three, is to learn skills to cope with the world in a confident way. Failure to gain self-control leads children to doubt their abilities.

Stage 3: Preschool—the challenge of initiative (versus guilt). Four- and five-year-olds must learn to engage their surroundings—including people outside the family—or experience guilt at having failed to meet the expectations of parents and others.

Stage 4: Preadolescence—the challenge of industriousness (versus inferiority). Between ages six and thirteen, children enter school, make friends, and strike out on their own more and more. They either feel proud of their accomplishments or fear that they do not measure up.

Stage 5: Adolescence—the challenge of gaining identity (versus confusion). During the teen years, young people struggle to establish their own identity. In part, teens identify with others, but they also want to be unique. Almost all teens experience some confusion as they struggle to establish an identity.

Stage 6: Young adulthood—the challenge of intimacy (versus isolation). The challenge for young adults is to form and keep intimate relationships with others. Making close friends (and especially falling in love) involves balancing the need to bond with the need to have a separate identity.

Stage 7: Middle adulthood—the challenge of making a difference (versus self-absorption). The challenge of middle age is to contribute to the lives of others in the family, at work, and in the larger world. Failing at this, people become self-centered, caught up in their own limited concerns.

Stage 8: Old age—the challenge of integrity (versus despair). Near the end of their lives, people hope to look back on what they have accomplished with a sense of integrity and satisfaction. For those who have been self-absorbed, old age brings only a sense of despair over missed opportunities.

● **Evaluate** Erikson's theory views personality formation as a lifelong process, with success at one stage (say, an infant gaining trust) preparing us to meet the next challenge. However, not everyone faces these challenges at the exact order presented by Erikson. Nor is it clear that failure to meet a challenge at one stage of life means that a person is doomed to fail in life's later stages. A broader question, raised earlier in our discussion of Piaget's ideas, is whether people in other cultures and at other times in history would define a successful life in Erikson's terms.

In sum, Erikson's model points out how several factors, including the family and school, shape our personalities. In the next section, we take a close look at these important agents of socialization.

CHECK YOUR LEARNING In what ways does Erikson take a broader view of socialization than other thinkers presented in this chapter?

Agents of Socialization

● **Analyze**

Every social experience we have affects us in at least a small way. However, several familiar settings have special importance in the socialization process. These include the family, the school, the peer group, and the mass media.

The Family

The family affects socialization in many ways. For most people, the family may be the most important socialization agent of all.

Nurture in Early Childhood

Responsibility for the care of infants, who are totally dependent on others, typically falls on parents and other family members. For several years—at least until children begin school—the family has the job of teaching children skills, values, and beliefs. Overall, research suggests, nothing is more likely to produce a happy, well-adjusted child than a loving family (Gibbs, 2001).

Not all family learning results from intentional teaching by parents. Children also learn from the type of environment adults create. Whether children learn to see themselves as strong or weak, smart or stupid, loved or simply tolerated—and as Erik Erikson suggests, whether they see the world as trustworthy or dangerous—depends largely on the quality of the surroundings provided by parents and other caregivers.

Race and Class

The family also gives children a social identity to children. In part, social identity involves race. Racial identity is complex because, as Chapter 11 ("Race and Ethnicity") explains, societies define race in various ways. In addition, in 2010, more than 8 million people (2.7 percent of the population) said they consider

Sociological research indicates that wealthy parents tend to encourage creativity in their children while poor parents tend to foster conformity. Although this general difference may be valid, parents at all class levels can and do provide loving support and guidance by simply involving themselves in their children's lives. Henry Ossawa Tanner's painting *The Banjo Lesson* stands as a lasting testament to this process.

Henry Ossawa Tanner, *The Banjo Lesson*, 1893. Oil on canvas. Hampton University Museum, Hampton, Virginia.

themselves to be in two or more racial categories. This number is rising and 4 percent of all births in the United States are now recorded as interracial. National Map 3–1 on page 72 shows where people who describe themselves as racially mixed live.

Social class, like race, plays a large part in shaping a child's personality. Whether born into families of high or low social position, children gradually come to realize that their family's social standing affects how others see them and, in time, how they come to see themselves.

In addition, research shows that the class position of parents affects not just how much money parents have to spend on their children but also what parents expect of them (Ellison, Bartkowski, & Segal, 1996). When people in the United States were asked to pick from a list of traits they thought most desirable in a child, parents of all social class backgrounds claim that they want their child to be "popular." But almost 60 percent of parents from the lower class

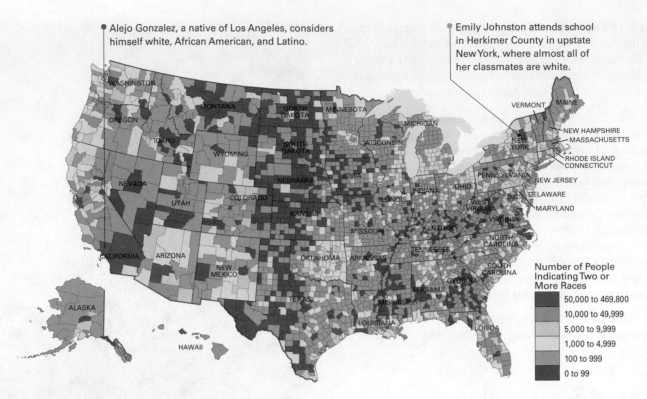

Alejo Gonzalez, a native of Los Angeles, considers himself white, African American, and Latino.

Emily Johnston attends school in Herkimer County in upstate New York, where almost all of her classmates are white.

Number of People Indicating Two or More Races

50,000 to 469,800
10,000 to 49,999
5,000 to 9,999
1,000 to 4,999
100 to 999
0 to 99

Seeing Ourselves

NATIONAL MAP 3–1 **Racially Mixed People across the United States**

This map shows, for 2010, the county-by-county distribution of people who described themselves as racially mixed. How do you think growing up in an area with a high level of racially mixed people (such as Los Angeles or Miami) would be different from growing up in an area with few such people (for example, in upstate New York or the Plains States in the middle of the country)?

✴ **Explore** the percentage of racially mixed people in your local community and in counties across the United States on **mysoclab.com**

Source: U.S. Census Bureau (2011).

point to "obedience" as a key trait in a child, compared to only about 40 percent of parents in the upper class. By contrast, well-to-do parents are more likely than low-income parents to praise children who can "think for themselves" (NORC, 2011).

What accounts for the difference? Melvin Kohn (1977) explains that people of lower social standing usually have only limited education and hold jobs that involve performing routine tasks under close supervision. Expecting that their children will grow up to take similar positions, they encourage obedience and may even use physical punishment such as spanking to get it. Because well-off parents generally have had more schooling, they usually have jobs that demand imagination and creativity, so they try to inspire the same qualities in their children. Consciously or not, all parents act in ways that encourage their children to follow in their footsteps.

Wealthier parents typically provide their children with an extensive program of leisure activities, including sports, vacation travel, and music lessons. These enrichment activities—far less available to children growing up in low-income families—build *cultural capital*, which advances learning and creates a sense of confidence in these children that they will be successful throughout their lives (Lareau, 2002).

Social class also affects how long the process of growing up takes, as the Sociology in Focus box explains.

The School

Schooling enlarges children's social world to include people with backgrounds different from their own. It is only as they encounter people who differ from themselves that children come to understand the importance of factors such as race and social position. As they do, they are likely to cluster in playgroups made up of their own class, race, and gender.

Gender

Schools join with families in socializing children into gender roles. Studies show that at school, boys engage in more physical activities and spend more time outdoors, and girls are more likely to help teachers with various housekeeping chores. Boys also engage in more aggressive behavior in the classroom, while girls are typically quieter and better behaved (Best, 1983; Jordan & Cowan, 1995).

Solly: *(seeing several friends walking down the dorm hallway, just returned from dinner)* Yo, guys! Jeremy's twenty-one today. We're going down to the Box Car to celebrate.

Matt: *(shaking his head)* Dunno, dude. I got a lab to finish up. It's just another birthday.

Solly: Not just any birthday, my friend. He's twenty-one—an *adult*!

Matt: *(sarcastically)* If turning twenty-one would make me an adult, I wouldn't still be clueless about what I want to do with my life!

Are you an adult or still an adolescent? Does turning twenty-one make you a "grown-up"? According to the sociologist Tom Smith (2003), in our society, no one factor announces the onset of adulthood. In fact, the results of his survey—using a representative sample of 1,398 people over the age of eighteen—suggest that many factors play a part in our decision to consider a young person as "grown up."

According to the survey, the single most important transition in claiming adult standing in the United States today is the completion of schooling. But other factors are also important: Smith's respondents linked adult standing

What significance does graduating from college have in the process of becoming an adult?

to taking on a full-time job, gaining the ability to support a family financially, no longer living with parents, and finally, marrying and becoming a parent. In other words, almost everyone in the United States thinks a person who has done *all* of these things is fully "grown up."

At what age are these transitions likely to be completed? On average, about age twenty-six. But such an average masks an important difference based on social class. People who do not attend college (more commonly among people growing up in lower-income families) typically finish school before age twenty, and a full-time job, independent living, marriage, and parenthood may follow in a year or two. Those from more privileged backgrounds are likely to attend college and may even go on to graduate or professional school, delaying the process of becoming an adult for as long as ten years, past the age of thirty.

Join the Blog!

Do you consider yourself an adult? At what age do you think adulthood begins? Why? Go to MySocLab and join the Sociology in Focus blog to share your opinions and experiences and to see what others think.

What Children Learn

Schooling is not the same for children living in rich and poor communities. As Chapter 14 ("Education, Health, and Medicine") explains, children from well-off families typically have a far richer experience in school than those whose families are poor.

What children learn in school goes beyond the formally planned lessons. Schools informally teach many things, which together might be called the *hidden curriculum*. Activities such as spelling bees, for example, teach children not only how to spell and to think on their feet but also that society divides the population into "winners" and "losers." Sports help students develop their strength and skills and also teach children important lessons in cooperation and competition.

For most children, school is also their first experience with bureaucracy. The school day is based on impersonal rules and a strict time schedule. Not surprisingly, these are also the traits of the large organizations that will employ them later in life.

The Peer Group

By the time they enter school, children have also discovered the **peer group,** *a social group whose members have interests, social position, and age in common.* Unlike the family and the school, the peer group allows children to escape the direct supervision of adults. Among their peers, children learn how to form relationships on

their own. Peer groups also offer the chance to discuss interests that adults may not share (such as clothing and popular music) or permit (such as drugs and sex).

It is not surprising, then, that parents often express concern about who their children's friends are. In a rapidly changing society, peer groups have great influence, and the attitudes of young and old may be different enough to form a "generation gap." The importance of peer groups typically peaks during adolescence, when young people begin to break away from their families and think of themselves as adults.

Even during adolescence, however, parental influence on children remains strong. Peers may affect short-term interests such as music or television shows, but parents have greater influence on long-term goals such as going to college (Davies & Kandel, 1981).

Finally, any neighborhood or school is made up of many peer groups. As Chapter 5 ("Groups and Organizations") explains, individuals tend to view their own group in positive terms and put down other groups. In addition, people are influenced by peer groups they would like to join, a process sociologists call **anticipatory socialization,** *learning that helps a person achieve a desired position.* In school, for example, young people may copy the styles and slang of a group they hope will accept them. Later in life, a young lawyer who hopes to move up may conform to the attitudes and behavior of the firm's partners in order to be accepted.

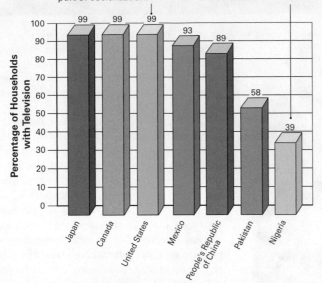

- In high-income countries such as the United States, television is an important part of socialization.

- In low-income countries such as Nigeria, the mass media play a smaller role in socialization.

Global Snapshot

FIGURE 3–2   Television Ownership in Global Perspective

Television is popular in high- and middle-income countries, where almost every household owns at least one TV.

Sources: TVB (2011), World Bank (2011).

The Mass Media

August 30, Isle of Coll, off the west coast of Scotland. The last time we visited this remote island, there was no electricity and most people spoke the ancient Gaelic language. Now that a power cable comes from the mainland, homes have lights, appliances, television, and the Internet! Almost with the flip of a switch, this tiny place has been pulled ahead into the modern world. With the culture of the larger world flowing in through the mass media, it is no surprise that traditions are fast disappearing. A rising share of the island's population is now mainlanders who ferry over with their cars to spend time in their vacation homes. And everyone now speaks English.

The **mass media** are *the means for delivering impersonal communications to a vast audience.* The term *media* (plural of *medium*) comes from the Latin word for "middle," suggesting that the media connect people. *Mass* media resulted as communications technology (first newspapers and then radio, television, films, and the Internet) spread information on a massive scale. The mass media are important not only because they are so powerful but also because their influence is likely to differ from that of the family, the local school, and the peer group. In short, the mass media introduce people to ideas and images that reflect the larger society and the entire world.

In the United States, television, introduced in the 1930s, quickly became the dominant medium after World War II. Today, 82 percent of U.S. households have a personal computer,

and 77 percent of households are connected to the Internet (TVB, 2011). Even more widespread is television ownership: 99 percent of U.S. households have at least one TV, and 84 percent have two or more. As Figure 3–2 indicates, the United States has one of the highest rates of television ownership in the world.

The Extent of Mass Media Exposure

Just how "glued to the tube" are we? National survey data tells us that, although just 40 percent of adults claim television watching is a "necessity," 80 percent of both men and women say they watch television every day. The typical U.S. household has a television on for more than eight hours a day, with the average adult watching television for about five hours. That means that, each week, people in the United States spend about as much time watching television as they do on the job.

The extent of television viewing varies among categories of the population. Men, on average, watch television for just under five hours a day; women watch for about five and one-half hours. Older people watch more television, with seniors averaging about seven hours a day. School-age children top the list, with about seven and one-half hours of daily viewing, if we count playing video games as well watching television programming. Generally, minorities watch more television that non-minorities, and people with lower incomes spend more time watching TV than affluent people do (Kaiser Family Foundation, 2010; Pew Research Center, 2010; Rideout, Foehr, & Roberts, 2010; TVB, 2011; U.S. Bureau of Labor Statistics, 2011; U.S. Census Bureau, 2011).

In today's society, years before children learn to read, television watching is a part of their daily routine. As they grow, children spend as many hours in front of a television as they do in school or interacting with their parents. This extensive viewing shows no signs of change despite the fact that, according to research, the more children watch television the slower their cognitive development, the more passive they become, the less they use their imagination, and the higher their risk of obesity. It is not that television is directly harmful to children; rather, extensive television takes time away from interaction with parents and peers, as well as exercise and other activities that are more likely to promote development and health (American Psychological Association, 1993; Fellman, 1995; Shute, 2010).

Television and Politics

The comedian Fred Allen once quipped that we call television a "medium" because it is "rarely well done." For a variety of reasons, television (as well as other mass media) provokes plenty of criticism, and about 80 percent of U.S. adults claim that the mass media are biased in one way or another. Some liberal critics argue that for most of television's history, racial and ethnic minorities have been invisible or have been shown only in stereotypical roles (such as African Americans playing butlers, Asian Americans playing gardeners, or Hispanics playing new immigrants). In recent years, however, minorities have moved closer to center stage on television. There are now far more Hispanic actors on prime-time television than there were a generation ago, and they play a far wider range of characters (Lichter & Amundson, 1997; Fetto, 2003b).

From another perspective, conservative critics charge that the television and film industries are dominated by a liberal "cultural elite." In recent years, they claim, "politically correct" media have advanced liberal causes, including feminism and gay rights. But not everyone agrees, and some counter that the popularity of the Fox Network, home to Sean Hannity, Bill O'Reilly, and other conservative commentators, suggests that television programming offers "spin" from both sides of the political spectrum (Rothman, Powers, & Rothman, 1993; B. Goldberg, 2002; Pew Center for People and the Press, 2011).

Television and Violence

In 1996, the American Medical Association (AMA) issued the startling statement that violence in television and films had reached such a high level that it posed a hazard to our health. Surveys confirm that three-fourths of U.S. adults say they have either walked out of a movie or turned off television because of too much violence. Almost two-thirds of television programs contain violence, and in most such scenes, characters engaging in violence show no remorse and are not punished (Rideout, 2007).

Public concern about violence in the mass media is especially high when it comes to children. About two-thirds of parents say that they are "very concerned" that their children are exposed to too much media violence. Research has found a correlation between the amount of time school children spend watching television and using video games and aggressive behavior such as fighting, the early use of alcohol and other illegal drugs, and even trouble sleeping. In 2011, the American Academy of Pediatrics issued a recommendation that children's television time be limited to two hours a day, and that parents not permit children under the age of two to watch television at all (Robinson et al., 2001; Centers for Disease Control, 2011; Garrison, et al, 2011).

In 1997, the television industry adopted a rating system for programs. But we are left to wonder whether watching sexual or violent programming is itself the cause of harm to young people or whether, for example, children who receive little attention from parents or who suffer from other risk factors end up watching more television. In any case, we might well ask why the mass media contain so much sex and violence in the first place?

Television and the other mass media have enriched our lives with entertaining and educational programming. The media also increase our exposure to other cultures and provoke discussion of current issues. At the same time, the power of the media—especially television—to shape how we think remains controversial.

 Evaluate This section shows that socialization is complex, and that many factors shape our personalities as we grow. In addition, the various agents of socialization do not always work together, with children learning things from peer groups and the mass media that may conflict with what they learn at home.

Concern with violence and the mass media extends to the world of video games, especially those popular with young boys. Among the most controversial games, which include high levels of violence, is "Call of Duty." Do you think the current rating codes are sufficient to guide parents and children who buy video games, or would you support greater restrictions on game content?

Beyond family, school, peer group, and the media, other spheres of life also play a part in social learning. For most people in the United States, these include religious organizations, the workplace, the military, and social clubs. In the end, socialization is not a simple learning process but a complex balancing act as we absorb information from a variety of sources. In the process of sorting and weighing all the information we receive, we form our own distinctive personalities.

CHECK YOUR LEARNING Identify all the major agents of socialization discussed in this section. What are some of the unique ways that each helps us develop our individual personalities?

Socialization and the Life Course

Apply

Although childhood has special importance in the socialization process, learning continues throughout our lives. An overview of the life course reveals how society organizes human experience according to age—namely, the stages of life we know as childhood, adolescence, adulthood, and old age.

Childhood

The next time you go shopping for athletic shoes, check where the shoes on display are made. Most brands are manufactured in countries such as Taiwan and Indonesia where wages are far lower than they are in the United States. What is not stated anywhere on the shoes is that many are made by children who spend their days working in factories instead of going to school. More than 150 million of the world's children work, half of them full time, and one-third of these boys and girls

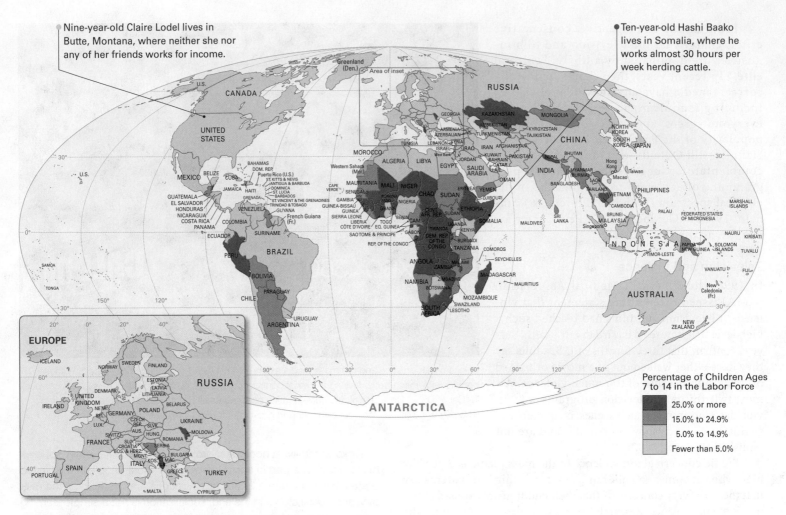

Nine-year-old Claire Lodel lives in Butte, Montana, where neither she nor any of her friends works for income.

Ten-year-old Hashi Baako lives in Somalia, where he works almost 30 hours per week herding cattle.

Percentage of Children Ages 7 to 14 in the Labor Force

- 25.0% or more
- 15.0% to 24.9%
- 5.0% to 14.9%
- Fewer than 5.0%

Window on the World

GLOBAL MAP 3–1 Child Labor in Global Perspective

Because industrialization extends childhood and discourages children from working and other activities considered suitable only for adults, child labor is uncommon in the United States and other high-income countries. In less economically developed nations of the world, however, children are a vital economic asset, and they typically begin working as soon as they are able. How would childhood in, say, the African nation of Chad or Sudan differ from that in the United States or Canada?

Sources: UNICEF (2011).

do work that is dangerous to their physical and mental health. For their efforts, they earn very little—typically, about 50 cents an hour (International Labour Organization, 2011; U.S. Department of Labor, 2010). Global Map 3–1 shows that child labor is most common in the nations of Africa and Asia.

The idea of children working long days in factories may be disturbing to people who live in high-income nations because we think of *childhood*—roughly the first twelve years of life—as a carefree time of learning and play. In fact, as the historian Philippe Ariès (1965) explains, the whole idea of "childhood" is fairly new. In the Middle Ages, children of four or five were treated like adults and expected to fend for themselves.

We defend our view of childhood by pointing out that youngsters are biologically immature. But a look back in time and around the world shows that the concept of childhood is grounded not in biology but in culture (LaRossa & Reitzes, 2001). In rich countries

today, not everyone has to work, so childhood is extended to allow time for young people to learn the skills they will need in a high-technology workplace.

Because childhood in the United States lasts such a long time, some people worry when children seem to be growing up too fast. In part, this "hurried child" syndrome results from changes in the family—including high divorce rates and both parents in the labor force—that leave children with less supervision. In addition, "adult" programming on television, in films, and on the Internet carries grown-up concerns such as sex, drugs, and violence into young people's lives. Today's ten- to twelve-year-olds, says one executive of a children's television channel, have about the same interests and experiences typical of twelve- to fourteen-year-olds a generation ago. Perhaps this is why today's children, compared to kids fifty years ago, have higher levels of stress and anxiety (K. S. Hymowitz, 1998; Gorman, 2000; Hoffman, 2010).

Adolescence

At the same time that industrialization created childhood as a distinct stage of life, adolescence emerged as a buffer between childhood and adulthood. Today, we generally link *adolescence,* or the teenage years, with emotional and social turmoil as young people develop their own identities. Again, we are tempted to attribute teenage rebelliousness and confusion to the biological changes of puberty. But it really comes from cultural inconsistency. For example, the mass media glorify sex and schools hand out condoms, even as parents urge restraint. Consider, too, that an eighteen-year-old may face the adult duty of going to war but lacks the adult right to drink a beer. In short, adolescence is a time of social contradictions, when people are no longer children but not yet adults.

Like all stages of life, adolescence varies according to social background. Most young people from working-class families move right from high school to the adult world of work and parenting. Such men and women are typically considered adults by the time they reach age twenty. Wealthier teens, however, have the resources to attend college and perhaps graduate school, thereby stretching adolescence to the late twenties and even the thirties (T. W. Smith, 2003). The Thinking About Diversity box on page 78 provides an example of how race and ethnicity can shape the academic performance of high school students.

Adulthood

If stages of the life course were based on biological changes, it would be easy to define *adulthood*. Regardless of exactly when it begins, adulthood is the time of life when most accomplishments take place, including pursuing a career and raising a family. Personalities are largely formed by then, although dramatic change in a person's environment—such as unemployment, divorce, or serious illness—may cause significant changes to the self.

Early Adulthood

During early adulthood—until about age forty—young adults learn to manage day-to-day affairs for themselves, often juggling conflicting priorities: parents, partner, children, schooling, work, and leisure activities. Women are especially likely to try to "do it all" because our culture gives them major responsibility for child rearing and household chores even if they have demanding jobs outside the home.

Middle Adulthood

In middle adulthood—roughly ages forty to sixty-five—people sense that their life circumstances are pretty well set. They also become more aware of the fragility of health, which the young typically take for granted. Women who have devoted many years to raising a family can find middle adulthood emotionally trying. Children grow up and require less attention, and husbands become absorbed in their careers, leaving some women with spaces in their lives that are difficult to fill. Many women

who divorce during middle adulthood also face serious financial problems (Weitzman, 1985, 1996). For all these reasons, an increasing number of women in middle adulthood return to school and seek new careers.

For everyone, growing older means experiencing physical decline, a prospect our culture makes especially painful for women. Because good looks are considered more important for women, the appearance of wrinkles and graying hair can be traumatic. Men have their own particular difficulties as they get older. Some must admit that they are never going to reach earlier career goals. Others realize that the price of career success has been neglect of family or personal health.

Old Age

Old age—the later years of adulthood and the final stage of life—begins around the mid-sixties. With people living longer, the elderly population is growing nearly as fast as the U.S. population as a whole. As Figure 3–3 on page 79 shows, about one person in eight is over age sixty-five, and the elderly now outnumber teenagers. By 2030, the number of seniors will double 72 million, and the "average" person in the United States will be almost forty (U.S. Census Bureau, 2010).

We can only begin to imagine the full consequences of the "graying of the United States." As more and more people retire from the labor force, the share of nonworking adults—already ten times greater than in 1900—will go up, increasing demand for health care and other social products and services. But perhaps most important, elderly people will be more visible in everyday life. As the twenty-first century goes on, the young and the old will interact more and more.

In recent decades, some people have become concerned that U.S. society is shortening childhood, pushing children to grow up faster and faster. In the television show *Pretty Little Liars*, this young woman in high school is having an affair with her teacher. Do television programs and films like this contribute to a "hurried child syndrome"? Do you see this as a problem or not? Why?

Adolescence is a time when people ask questions like "Who am I?" and "What do I want to become?" In the end, we all have to answer these questions for ourselves. But race and ethnicity are likely to have an effect on what our answers turn out to be.

Grace Kao (2000) investigated the identity and goals of students enrolled in Johnstown High School, a large (3,000-student) school in a Chicago suburb. Johnstown High is considered a good school with above-average test scores. It is also racially and ethnically diverse: 47 percent of the students are white, 43 percent are African American, 7 percent are Hispanic, and 3 percent are of Asian descent.

Kao interviewed sixty-three Johnstown students, female and male, both individually and in small groups with others of the same race and ethnicity. Talking with them, she learned how important racial and ethnic stereotypes are in young people's developing sense of self.

What are these stereotypes? White students are seen as hardworking in school and concerned about getting high grades. African American students are thought to study less, either because they are not as smart or because they just don't try as hard. In any case, students see African Americans at high risk of failure in school.

Because the stereotype says that Hispanics are headed for manual occupations—as gardeners or laborers—they are seen as not caring very much about doing well. Finally, Asian American students are seen as hardworking high achievers, either because they are smarter or because they focus on academics rather than, say, sports.

From her interviews, Kao learned that most students think these stereotypes are true and take them personally. They expect people, including themselves, to perform in school more or less the way the stereotype predicts. In addition, young people—whether white, black, Hispanic, or Asian—mostly hang out with others like

themselves, which gives them little chance to find out that their assumptions are wrong.

Students of all racial and ethnic categories say they *want* to do well in school. But not getting to know those who differ from themselves means that they measure success *only in relation to their own category*. To African American students, in other words, "success" means doing as well as other black students and not flunking out. To Hispanics, "success" means avoiding manual labor and ending up with any job in an office. Whites and Asians define "success" as earning high grades and living up to the high-achievement stereotype. For all these young people, then, "self" develops to reflect how our society defines race and ethnicity.

What Do You Think?

1. Were you aware of racial and ethnic stereotypes similar to those described here in your high school? What about your college?

2. Do you think gender stereotypes affect the performance of women and men in school as much as racial and ethnic stereotypes? Explain.

3. What can be done to reduce the damaging effects of racial and ethnic stereotypes?

The aging of the U.S. population is the focus of **gerontology** (*geron* in Greek means "old person"), *the study of aging and the elderly*. Gerontologists study both the physical and the social dimensions of growing old.

Aging and Biology

For most of our population, gray hair, wrinkles, and declining energy begin in middle age. After about age fifty, bones become more brittle, injuries take longer to heal, and the risks of chronic illnesses (such as arthritis and diabetes) and life-threatening conditions (such as heart disease and cancer) rise steadily. Sensory abilities—taste, sight, touch, smell, and especially hearing—become less sharp with age (Treas, 1995; Metz & Miner, 1998).

Even so, most older people are neither disabled nor discouraged by their physical condition. In 2010, only 15.5 percent of seniors said that they could not walk a quarter mile by themselves, and fewer than five percent required assisted care in a hospital or nursing home. About 13 percent needed help with shopping, chores,

or other daily activities. Overall, only 30 percent of people over age seventy-five characterize their health as "fair" or "poor"; 70 percent consider their overall condition "good" to "excellent." On average, the health of U.S. seniors is steadily improving (Adams, Martinez, & Vickerie, 2010; CDC, 2011).

Aging and Culture

Culture shapes how we understand growing old. In low-income countries, old age gives people great influence and respect because elders control the most land and have wisdom gained over the course of a lifetime. For these reasons, a preindustrial society usually takes the form of a **gerontocracy**, *a form of social organization in which the elderly have the most wealth, power, and prestige*.

Industrialization lessens the social standing of the elderly, giving more wealth, power, and prestige to younger people. This trend seems to be continuing: The average age of today's corporate executives, which was fifty-nine back in 1980, was just fifty-four in 2008 (Spencer Stuart, 2008). In an industrial society, older people typically live apart

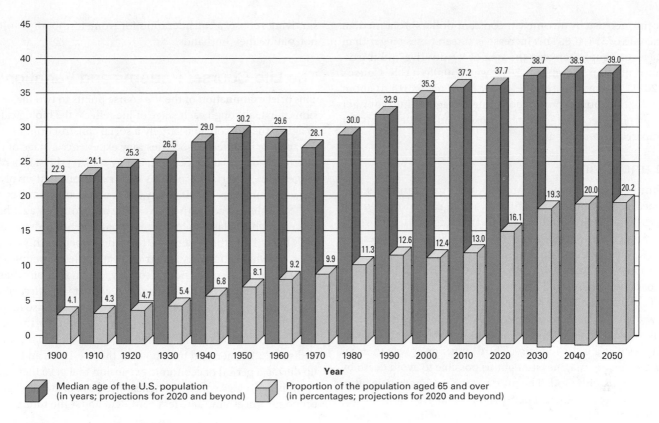

FIGURE 3–3 The Graying of U.S. Society

The proportion of the U.S. population over the age of sixty-five tripled during the last century. The median age of the U.S. population has now passed thirty-five years and will continue to rise.

Source: U.S. Census Bureau (2010).

from their grown children, and rapid social change makes much of what seniors know obsolete, at least from the point of view of younger people. A problem common to industrial societies, then, is **ageism**, *prejudice and discrimination against older people.*

> **November 1, approaching Kandy, Sri Lanka.** Our little van struggles up the steep mountain incline. Breaks in the lush vegetation offer spectacular views that interrupt our conversation about growing old. "Then there are no old-age homes in your country?" I ask. "In Colombo and other cities, I am sure," our driver responds, "but not many. We are not like you Americans." "And how is that?" I ask, stiffening a bit. His eyes remain fixed on the road: "We would not leave our fathers and mothers to live alone."

Not surprisingly, growing old in the United States is challenging. When we're young, becoming older means taking on new roles and responsibilities. In old age, the opposite happens as people leave behind roles that have given them identity, pleasure, and prestige.

gerontology the study of aging and the elderly

gerontocracy a form of social organization in which the elderly have the most wealth, power, and prestige

ageism prejudice and discrimination against older people

When people retire from familiar work routines, some find restful recreation or new activities, but others lose their sense of self-worth and suffer outright boredom.

Aging and Income

Reaching old age means living with less income. But today, the U.S. elderly population is doing better than ever. In 1960, some 35 percent of the elderly were poor; by 2010, this figure had fallen to 9.0 percent—less than the poverty rate of 15.1 percent for the population as a whole (U.S. Census Bureau, 2011). A generation ago, old age carried the highest risk of poverty; today, that is true of young people under eighteen.

What changed? An increasing share of older couples earned double incomes during their working years, which helped them save more. In addition, better health allows older people to continue to work for income. Government programs have become more generous, so that almost half of all government spending now goes to programs that assist the elderly even as spending on children has remained more or less flat. But the recent economic downturn has canceled out many of these advantages as people have lost some of the pension income they were counting on, and more of today's workers are not receiving pension benefits at all.

If many seniors are struggling, they are doing better than many younger people. Since 1980, on average, seniors have posted a 42 percent increase in income (in constant dollars) to a median annual income of $31,408. This increase is fifteen times bigger than the increase for people between the ages of twenty-five and thirty-four, whose median income in 2010 was $50,059 (U.S. Census Bureau, 2011). Today, the average senior has a net worth of about $237,000. So, although seniors continue to lag behind younger adults in income, recent decades have provided greater gains for them compared to younger adults.

Death and Dying

Throughout most of human history, low living standards and limited medical technology meant that death, caused most often by disease or accident, could come at any stage of life. Today, however, 85 percent of people in the United States die after age fifty-five (Kochanek et al., 2011).

After observing many dying people, the psychologist Elisabeth Kübler-Ross (1969) described death as an orderly transition involving five distinct stages. Typically, a person first reacts to the prospect of dying with *denial,* perhaps to be expected in a culture that doesn't like to talk about death. The second phase is *anger* as the person facing death sees it as a gross injustice. Third, anger gives way to *negotiation* as the person imagines it might be possible to avoid death by striking a bargain with God. The fourth stage, *resignation,* is often accompanied by psychological depression. Finally, a complete adjustment to death requires *acceptance.* At this point, no longer paralyzed by fear and anxiety, the person whose life is ending sets out to find peace and makes the most of whatever time remains.

More recent research has shown that Kübler-Ross simplified the process of dying—not everyone passes through these stages or does so in the order that she presents them (Konigsberg, 2011). At the same time, this research has helped to draw attention to the process of dying. As the share of men and women in old age increases, we can expect our culture to become more comfortable with the idea of death. In recent years, people in the United States have started talking about death more openly, and the trend is toward viewing dying as preferable to prolonged suffering. More married couples are taking steps to prepare for death with legal and financial planning; this openness may help ease the pain of the

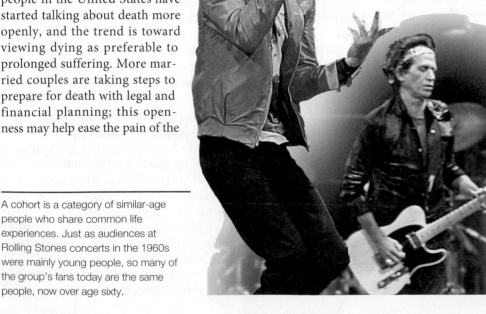

A cohort is a category of similar-age people who share common life experiences. Just as audiences at Rolling Stones concerts in the 1960s were mainly young people, so many of the group's fans today are the same people, now over age sixty.

surviving spouse, a consideration for women who, more often than not, outlive their husbands.

The Life Course: Patterns and Variations

This brief examination of the life course points to two major conclusions. First, although each stage of life reflects the biological process of aging, the life course is largely a social construction. For this reason, people in different societies may experience a stage of life quite differently or not at all. Second, in any society, the stages of the life course present certain problems and transitions that involve learning something new and, in many cases, unlearning familiar routines.

Societies organize the life course according to age, but other forces, such as class, race, ethnicity, and gender also shape people's lives. Thus the general patterns described in this chapter apply somewhat differently to various categories of people.

People's life experiences also vary, depending on when, in the history of the society, they are born. A **cohort** is *a category of people with something in common, usually their age.* Because members of a particular age cohort are generally influenced by the same economic and cultural trends, they tend to develop similar attitudes and values. Women and men born in the late 1940s and 1950s grew up during a period of economic expansion that gave them a sense of optimism. Today's college students, who have grown up in an age of economic uncertainty, are less confident about the future.

Resocialization: Total Institutions

● **Apply** ....

A final type of socialization, experienced by more than 2.5 million people in the United States at any one time, involves being confined—often against their will—in prisons or mental hospitals. This is the world of the **total institution**, *a setting in which people are isolated from the rest of society and controlled by an administrative staff.*

According to Erving Goffman (1961), total institutions have three important characteristics. First, staff members supervise all aspects of daily life, including where residents (often called "inmates") eat, sleep, and work. Second, life in a total institution is controlled and standardized, with the same food, uniforms, and activities for everyone. Third, formal rules dictate when, where, and how inmates perform their daily routines.

The purpose of such rigid routines is **resocialization**, *radically changing an inmate's personality by carefully controlling the environment.* Prisons and mental hospitals physically isolate inmates behind fences, barred windows, and locked doors and control their access to the telephone, computers, mail, and visitors. The institution

Mike: Sociology is a good course. Since my professor started telling us how to look at our lives using the a sociological perspective, I'm realizing that a lot of who, what, and where I am is because of society.

Kim: (*teasingly*) Oh, so *society* is responsible for making you so smart and witty and handsome?

Mike: No, that's all me. But I'm seeing that being at college and playing football is maybe not all me.

What do you think? How free are we, really? This chapter stresses one key theme: Society shapes how we think, feel, and act. If this is so, then in what sense are we free? To answer this important question, consider the Muppets, puppet stars of television and film that many of us remember from childhood. Watching the antics of Kermit the Frog, Miss Piggy, and the rest of the troupe, we almost believe they are real rather than objects controlled from offstage. As the sociological perspective points out, human beings are like puppets in that we, too, respond to offstage forces. Society gives us a culture and shapes our lives according to class, race, and gender. If this is so, can we really claim to be free?

Sociologists answer this question with many voices. The politically liberal response is that individuals are *not* free of society—in fact, as social creatures, we never could be. But if we are condemned to live in a society with power over us, it is important to do what we can to make our world as just as possible, by working to lessen class differences and other barriers to opportunity for minorities, including women. Conservatives agree that society shapes our lives but also point out that we *are* free because society can never dictate our dreams or stand in our way if we are determined to succeed. Our history as a nation, right from the revolutionary act that led to its founding, is one story after another of individuals pursuing their personal goals despite great odds.

Does understanding more about how society shapes our lives give us greater power to "cut the strings" and choose for ourselves how to live?

Both attitudes are found in George Herbert Mead's analysis of socialization. Mead recognized that society makes demands on us, sometimes limiting our options. But he also reminded us that human beings are spontaneous and creative, capable of acting on society and bringing about change. Mead noted the power of society while still affirming the human capacity to evaluate, criticize, and ultimately choose and change.

In the end, we may seem like puppets, but only on the surface. A crucial difference is that we can stop, look up at the "strings" that make us move, and even yank on them defiantly (Berger, 1963:176). If our pull is strong enough, we may accomplish more than we might think. As Margaret Mead is said to have remarked, "Never doubt that a small group of thoughtful, committed citizens can change the world. Indeed, it is the only thing that ever has."

What Do You Think?

1. Do you think that our society gives more freedom to males than to females? Why or why not?

2. When we all face hard economic times, as we have in the past few years, do you think most people feel that they have some control over their lives or not? Why?

3. Has learning about the process of socialization increased or decreased your feeling of freedom? Why?

becomes their entire world, making it easier for the staff to bring about personality change—or at least obedience—in the inmate.

Resocialization is a two-part process. First, the staff breaks down a new inmate's existing identity. For example, an inmate must surrender personal possessions, including clothing and grooming articles used to maintain a distinctive appearance. Instead, the staff provides standard-issue clothes so that everyone looks alike. The staff subjects new inmates to "mortifications of self," which can include searches, medical examinations, head shaving, fingerprinting, and assignment of a serial number. Once inside the walls, individuals also give up their privacy as guards routinely inspect their living quarters.

In the second part of the resocialization process, the staff tries to build a new self in the inmate through a system of rewards and punishments. Having a book to read, watching television, or making a telephone call may seem like minor pleasures to the outsider, but in the rigid environment of the total institution, the opportunity to gain such simple privileges as these can be a powerful motivation to conform. The length of confinement typically depends on how well the inmate cooperates with the staff.

Total institutions affect people in different ways. Some inmates may end up "rehabilitated" or "recovered," but others may change little, and still others may become hostile and bitter. Over a long period of time, living in a rigidly controlled environment can leave some *institutionalized,* without the capacity for independent living.

But what about the rest of us? Does socialization crush our individuality or empower us to reach our creative potential? The Controversy & Debate box takes a closer look at this question.

Seeing Sociology in Everyday Life

Socialization: From Infancy to Old Age

When do we grow up and become adults?

As this chapter explains, many factors come into play in the process of moving from one stage of the life course to another. In global perspective, what makes our society unusual is that there is no one event that clearly tells everyone (and us, too) that the milestone of adulthood has been reached. We have important events that say, for example, when someone completes high school (graduation ceremony) or gets married (wedding ceremony). Look at the photos below. In each case, what do we learn about how the society defines the transition from one stage of life to another?

Hint Societies differ in how they structure the life course, including which stages of life are defined as important, what years of life various stages correspond to, and how clearly movement from one stage to another is marked. Given our cultural emphasis on individual choice and freedom, many people tend to say "You're only as old as you feel" and let people decide these things for themselves. When it comes to reaching adulthood, our society is not very clear—the Sociology in Focus box on page 73 points out many factors that figure into becoming an adult. So there is no widespread "adult ritual" as we see in these photos. Keep in mind that, for us, class matters a lot in this process, with young people of higher social standing staying in school and delaying full adulthood until well into their twenties or even their thirties. Finally, in these tough economic times, the share of young people in their twenties living with parents goes way up, which can delay adulthood for an entire cohort.

Among the Hamer people in the Omo Valley of Ethiopia, young boys must undergo a test to mark their transition to manhood. Usually the event is triggered by the boy's expressing a desire to marry. In this ritual, witnessed by everyone in his society, the boy must jump over a line of bulls selected by the girl's family. If he succeeds in doing this three times, he is declared a man and the wedding can take place (marking the girl's transition to womanhood). Does our society have any ceremony or event similar to this to mark the transition to adulthood?

On the San Carlos Reservation in Arizona, young Apache girls perform the Sunrise Dance to mark their transition to adulthood. Carefully painted by an elder according to Apache tradition, each girl holds a special staff, which symbolizes her hope for a long and healthy life and spiritual happiness. Many of the world's societies time these coming-of-age rituals to correspond to a girl's first menstrual cycle. Why do you think this is so?

These young men and women in Seoul, South Korea, are participating in a Confucian ceremony to mark their becoming adults. This ritual, which takes place on the twentieth birthday, defines young people as full members of the community and also reminds them of all the responsibilities they are now expected to fulfill. If we had such a ritual in the United States, at what age would it take place? Would a person's social class affect the timing of this ritual?

Seeing Sociology in *Your* Everyday Life

1. Across the United States, many families plan elaborate parties to celebrate a daughter's or son's graduation from high school. In what respects is this a ritual that marks reaching adulthood? How does social class affect whether or not people define this event the beginning of adulthood?

2. In the United States, when does the stage of life we call "old age" begin? Is there an event that marks the transition to old age? Does social class play a part in this process? If so, how?

3. In what sense are human beings free? After reading through this chapter, develop a personal statement of the extent to which you think you are able to guide your own life. Notice that some of the thinkers discussed in this chapter (such as Sigmund Freud) argued that there are sharp limits on our ability to act freely; by contrast, others (especially George Herbert Mead) claimed that human beings have significant ability to be creative. What is your personal statement about the extent of human freedom? Go to the "Seeing Sociology in *Your* Everyday Life" feature on MySocLab to learn more about the extent of personal freedom in society as well as suggestions about ways of making the most of the freedom we have.

What Is Socialization?

Socialization is a **lifelong process**.

- Socialization develops our humanity as well as our particular personalities.
- The importance of socialization is seen in the fact that extended periods of social isolation result in permanent damage (cases of Anna and Genie). **pp. 64–66** ⬛ Read the **Document** on **mysoclab.com**

Socialization is a matter of **nurture** rather than **nature**.

- A century ago, most people thought human behavior resulted from biological instinct.
- For us as human beings, it is our nature to nurture. **p. 65**

socialization (p. 64) the lifelong social experience by which people develop their human potential and learn culture

personality (p. 64) a person's fairly consistent patterns of acting, thinking, and feeling

Important Contributions to Our Understanding of Socialization

Sigmund Freud's model of the human personality has three parts:

- **id:** innate, pleasure-seeking human drives
- **superego:** the demands of society in the form of internalized values and norms
- **ego:** our efforts to balance innate, pleasure-seeking drives and the demands of society **pp. 66–67**

Jean Piaget believed that human development involves both biological maturation and gaining social experience. He identified four stages of cognitive development:

- The **sensorimotor stage** involves knowing the world only through the senses.
- The **preoperational stage** involves starting to use language and other symbols.
- The **concrete operational stage** allows individuals to understand causal connections.
- The **formal operational stage** involves abstract and critical thought. **pp. 67–68**

Lawrence Kohlberg applied Piaget's approach to stages of moral development:

- We first judge rightness in **preconventional** terms, according to our individual needs.
- Next, **conventional** moral reasoning takes account of parental attitudes and cultural norms.
- Finally, **postconventional** reasoning allows us to criticize society itself. **p. 68**

Carol Gilligan found that gender plays an important part in moral development, with males relying more on abstract standards of rightness and females relying more on the effects of actions on relationships. **pp. 68–69**

👁 Watch the **Video** on **mysoclab.com**

To **George Herbert Mead:**

- The **self** is part of our personality and includes self-awareness and self-image.
- The self develops only as a result of social experience.
- Social experience involves the exchange of symbols.
- Social interaction depends on understanding the intention of another, which requires taking the role of the other.
- Human action is partly spontaneous (the I) and partly in response to others (the me).
- We gain social experience through imitation, play, games, and understanding the **generalized other**. **pp. 69–70**

Charles Horton Cooley used the term **looking-glass self** to explain that we see ourselves as we imagine others see us. **p. 69**

Erik H. Erikson identified challenges that individuals face at each stage of life from infancy to old age. **pp. 70–71**

id (p. 66) Freud's term for the human being's basic drives

ego (p. 66) Freud's term for a person's conscious efforts to balance innate pleasure-seeking drives with the demands of society

superego (p. 66) Freud's term for the cultural values and norms internalized by an individual

sensorimotor stage (p. 67) Piaget's term for the level of human development at which individuals experience the world only through their senses

preoperational stage (p. 67) Piaget's term for the level of human development at which individuals first use language and other symbols

concrete operational stage (p. 67) Piaget's term for the level of human development at which individuals first see causal connections in their surroundings

formal operational stage (p. 67) Piaget's term for the level of human development at which individuals think abstractly and critically

self (p. 69) George Herbert Mead's term for the part of an individual's personality composed of self-awareness and self-image

looking-glass self (p. 69) Cooley's term for a self-image based on how we think others see us

significant others (p. 70) people, such as parents, who have special importance for socialization

generalized other (p. 70) Mead's term for widespread cultural norms and values we use as references in evaluating ourselves

Agents of Socialization

The **family** is usually the first setting of socialization.

- Family has the greatest impact on attitudes and behavior.
- A family's social position, including race and social class, shapes a child's personality.
- Ideas about gender are learned first in the family. **pp. 71–72**

✴ Explore the Map on **mysoclab.com**

Schools give most children their first experience with bureaucracy and impersonal evaluation.

- Schools teach knowledge and skills needed for later life.
- Schools expose children to greater social diversity.
- Schools reinforce ideas about gender. **pp. 72–73**

The **peer group** helps shape attitudes and behavior.

- The peer group takes on great importance during adolescence.
- The peer group frees young people from adult supervision. **p. 73**

The **mass media** have a huge impact on socialization in modern, high-income societies.

- The average U.S. child spends about 7.5 hours a day watching television and playing video games—as much time as attending school and interacting with parents.
- Research suggests that excessive television viewing can be harmful to children.
- The mass media often reinforce stereotypes about gender and race.
- The mass media expose people to a great deal of violence. **pp. 74–75**

peer group (p. 73) a social group whose members have interests, social position, and age in common

anticipatory socialization (p. 73) learning that helps a person achieve a desired position

mass media (p. 74) the means for delivering impersonal communications to a vast audience

Socialization and the Life Course

The concept of **childhood** is grounded not in biology but in culture. In high-income countries, childhood is extended. **pp. 75–76**

The emotional and social turmoil of **adolescence** results from cultural inconsistency in defining people who are not children but not yet adults. Adolescence varies by social class. **p. 77**

Adulthood is the stage of life when most accomplishments take place. Although personality is now formed, it continues to change with new life experiences. **p. 77**

Old age is defined as much by culture as biology.

- Traditional societies give power and respect to elders.
- In high-income countries, old age is a time of disengagement and loss of social importance.
- The "graying of the United States" means that our country's average age is going up. **pp. 77–80**

Acceptance of **death and dying** is part of socialization for the elderly. This process typically involves five stages: denial, anger, negotiation, resignation, and acceptance. **p. 80**

gerontology (p. 78) the study of aging and the elderly

gerontocracy (p. 78) a form of social organization in which the elderly have the most wealth, power, and prestige

ageism (p. 79) prejudice and discrimination against older people

cohort (p. 80) a category of people with something in common, usually their age

Total Institutions

Total institutions include prisons, mental hospitals, and monasteries.

- Staff members supervise all aspects of life.
- Life is standardized, with all inmates following set rules and routines. **pp. 80–81**

Resocialization is a two-part process:

- breaking down inmates' existing identity
- building a new self through a system of rewards and punishments **pp. 81–82**
- Why is social experience the key to human personality?
- What familiar social settings have special importance to how we live and grow?
- How do our experiences change over the life course?

total institution (p. 80) a setting in which people are isolated from the rest of society and controlled by an administrative staff

resocialization (p. 80) radically changing an inmate's personality by carefully controlling the environment

4 Social Interaction in Everyday Life

Learning Objectives

Remember the definitions of the key terms highlighted in boldfaced type throughout this chapter.

Understand how everyday interaction is based on various statuses and roles.

Apply the process we call the social construction of reality to issues including emotions, gender, and humor.

Analyze everyday social interaction using dramaturgical analysis.

Evaluate the importance of culture, class, and gender in the social construction of reality.

Create a deeper ability to "read" patterns and meaning in countless situations we experience every day.

CHAPTER OVERVIEW

This chapter takes a micro-level look at society, examining patterns of everyday social interaction. First, the chapter identifies important social structures, including status and role. Then it explains how people construct reality in social interaction. Finally, it applies the lessons learned to three important dimensions of everyday life: emotions, gender, and humor. ■

Harold and Sybil are on their way to another couple's home in an unfamiliar area near Fort Lauderdale, Florida. For the last twenty minutes, as Sybil sees it, they have been driving in circles, searching in vain for Coconut Palm Road.

"Look, Harold," says Sybil. "There are some people up ahead. Let's ask for directions."

Harold, gripping the wheel ever more tightly, begins muttering under his breath. "I know where I am. I don't want to waste time talking to strangers. Just let me get us there."

"I'm sure you know where you are, Harold," Sybil responds, looking straight ahead. "But I don't think you know where you're going."

Harold and Sybil are lost in more ways than one: Not only can't they find where their friends live, but they also cannot understand why they are growing angrier with each other with each passing minute.

What's going on? Like most men, Harold cannot stand getting lost. The longer he drives around, the more incompetent he feels. Sybil can't understand why Harold doesn't pull over to ask someone the way to Coconut Palm Road. If she were driving, she thinks to herself, they would already be comfortably settled in with their friends.

Why don't men like to ask for directions? Because men value their independence, they are uncomfortable asking for any type of help and are reluctant to accept it. To ask another person for assistance is the same as saying, "You know something I don't know." If it takes Harold a few more minutes to find Coconut Palm Road on his own—and to keep his sense of being in control—he thinks that's the way to go.

Women are more in tune with others and strive for connectedness. From Sybil's point of view, asking for help is right because sharing information builds social bonds and at the same time gets the job done. Asking for directions seems as natural to her as searching on his own is to Harold. Obviously, getting lost is sure to create conflict for Harold and Sybil as long as neither one of them understands the other's point of view.

Such everyday social patterns are the focus of this chapter. The central concept is **social interaction**, *the process by which people act and react in relation to others.* We begin by presenting the rules and building blocks of everyday experience and then explore the almost magical way in which face-to-face interaction creates the reality in which we live.

Social Structure: A Guide to Everyday Living

● **Understand**

October 21, Ho Chi Minh City, Vietnam. This morning we leave the ship and make our way along the docks toward the center of Ho Chi Minh City, known to an earlier generation as Saigon. Government security officers wave us through the heavy iron gates. Pressed against the fence are dozens of men who operate cyclos (bicycles with small carriages attached to the front), the Vietnamese version of taxicabs. We spend the next twenty minutes shaking our heads at several persistent drivers who pedal alongside us, pleading for our business. The pressure is uncomfortable. We decide to cross the street but realize suddenly that there are no stop signs or signal lights—and the street is an unbroken stream of bicycles, cyclos, motorbikes, and small trucks. The locals don't bat an eye; they just walk at a steady pace across the street, parting waves of vehicles that immediately close in again behind them. Walk right into traffic? With our small children on our backs? Yup, we did it; that's the way it works in Vietnam.

status a social position that a person holds

ascribed status a social position a person receives at birth or takes on involuntarily later in life

achieved status a social position a person takes on voluntarily that reflects personal ability and effort

status set all the statuses a person holds at a given time

master status a status that has special importance for social identity, often shaping a person's entire life

Members of every society rely on social structure—cultural patterns of thought and action—to make sense out of daily situations. As our family's introduction to the streets of Vietnam suggests, the world can be disorienting, even frightening, when society's rules are unclear. Let's take a closer look at the ways in which societies organize everyday life.

Status

 Understand

In every society, people build their lives using the idea of **status**, *a social position that a person holds*. In everyday use, the word *status* generally refers to prestige, as when a college president is said to have more "status" than a newly hired assistant professor. But sociologically speaking, both "president" and "professor" are statuses, or positions, within the collegiate organization.

Status is part of our social identity and defines our relationships to others. As Georg Simmel (1950:307, orig. 1902), one of the founders of sociology, pointed out, before we can deal with anyone, we need to know who the person is.

Each of us holds many statuses at once. The term **status set** refers to *all the statuses a person holds at a given time*. A teenage girl may be a daughter to her parents, a sister to her brother, a student at her school, and a goalie on her soccer team.

Status sets change over the life course. A child grows up to become a parent, a student graduates to become a lawyer, and a single person marries to become a husband or wife, sometimes becoming single again as a result of death or divorce. Joining an organization or finding a job enlarges our status set; retirement or withdrawing from activities makes it smaller. Over a lifetime, people gain and lose dozens of statuses.

Ascribed and Achieved Status

Sociologists classify statuses in terms of how people attain them. An **ascribed status** is *a social position a person receives at birth or takes on involuntarily later in life*. Examples of ascribed statuses include being a daughter, a Cuban, a teenager, or a widower. Ascribed statuses are matters about which we have little or no choice.

By contrast, an **achieved status** refers to *a social position a person takes on voluntarily*

Members of our society celebrate the achievements of athletes such as Manny ("Pac-Man") Pacquiao not only because of the many boxing titles that have made him a national hero in the Philippines, but also because he overcame the unbeatable odds of a childhood in poverty during which he had to drop out of elementary school to sell doughnuts on the street to support his family.

that reflects personal ability and effort. Achieved statuses in the United States include honors student, Olympic athlete, software writer, and thief.

In the real world, of course, most statuses involve a combination of ascription and achievement. That is, people's ascribed statuses influence the statuses they achieve. People who achieve the status of lawyer, for example, are likely to share the ascribed benefit of being born into relatively well-off families. By the same token, many less desirable statuses, such as convicted criminal, drug addict, or unemployed worker, are more easily achieved by people who were born into poverty.

Master Status

Some statuses matter more than others. A **master status** is *a status that has special importance for social identity, often shaping a person's entire life*. For most people, a job is a master status because it reveals a great deal about social background, education, and income. In a few cases, a person's name is a master status; being in the Bush or Kennedy family attracts attention and creates opportunities.

A master status can be negative as well as positive. Take, for example, serious illness. Sometimes people, even lifelong friends, avoid cancer patients or people with AIDS because of their illnesses. As another example, the fact that all societies limit opportunities for women makes gender a master status.

Sometimes a physical disability serves as a master status to the point where we dehumanize people by seeing them only in terms of their disability. The Thinking About Diversity box on page 90 shows how.

Role

 Understand

A second important social structure is **role**, *behavior expected of someone who holds a particular status*. A person *holds* a status and *performs* a role (Linton, 1937b). For example, holding the status of student leads you to perform the role of attending classes and completing assignments.

Both statuses and roles vary by culture. In the United States, the status "uncle" refers to the brother of either

Physical disability works in much the same ways as class, gender, or race in defining people in the eyes of others. In the following interviews, two women explain how a physical disability can become a master status—a trait that overshadows everything else about them. The first voice is that of twenty-nine-year-old Donna Finch, who lives with her husband and son in Muskogee, Oklahoma, and holds a master's degree in social work. She is also blind.

> Most people don't expect handicapped people to grow up; they are always supposed to be children. . . . You aren't supposed to date; you aren't supposed to have a job; somehow you're just supposed to disappear. I'm not saying this is true of anyone else, but in my own case I think I was more intellectually mature than most children, and more emotionally immature. I'd say that not until the last four or five years have I felt really whole.

Rose Helman is an elderly woman who is retired and lives near New York City. She suffers from spinal meningitis and is also blind.

> You ask me if people are really different today than in the '20s and '30s. Not too much.

They are still fearful of the handicapped. I don't know if fearful is the right word, but

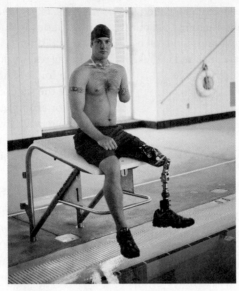
Modern technology means that most soldiers who lose limbs in war now survive. How do you think the loss of an arm or a leg affects a person's social identity and sense of self?

uncomfortable at least. But I can understand it somewhat; it happened to me. I once asked a man to tell me which staircase to use to get from the subway out to the street. He started giving me directions that were confusing, and I said, "Do you mind taking me?" He said, "Not at all." He grabbed me on the side with my dog on it, so I asked him to take my other arm. And he said, "I'm sorry, I have no other arm." And I said, "That's all right, I'll hold onto the jacket." It felt funny hanging onto the sleeve without the arm in it.

What Do You Think?

1. Have you ever had a disease or disability that became a master status? If so, how did others react?

2. How might such a master status affect someone's personality?

3. Can being very fat or very thin serve as a master status? Why or why not?

Source: Based on Orlansky & Heward (1981).

---

mother or father; in Vietnam, however, the word for "uncle" is different when referring to the mother's or father's side of the family, and the two men have different responsibilities. In every society, actual role performance varies according to a person's unique personality, although some societies permit more individual expression of a role than others.

Because we hold many statuses at once in our status set, everyday life is a mix of many roles. Robert Merton (1968) introduced the term **role set** to identify *a number of roles attached to a single status.*

Figure 4–1 shows four statuses of one person, each status linked to a different role set. First, as a professor, this woman interacts with students (the teacher role) and with other academics (the colleague role). Second, as a researcher, she gathers and analyzes data (the fieldwork role) that she uses in her publications (the author role). Third, the same woman holds the status of "wife," with a marital role (such as confidante and sexual partner) toward her spouse, with whom she shares a domestic role toward the household. Fourth, she holds the status of "mother," with routine responsibilities for her children (the maternal role), as well as involvement in their school and other organizations (the civic role).

A global perspective shows us that the roles people use to define their lives differ from society to society. In low-income countries, people spend fewer years as students, and family roles are typically very

important to social identity. In high-income nations, people spend more years as students, and family roles may or may not be very important to social identity. Another dimension of difference involves housework. As Global Map 4–1 on page 92 shows, especially in poor nations of the world, doing housework is an important role that falls heavily on women.

Role Conflict and Role Strain

People in modern, high-income countries juggle many responsibilities demanded by their various statuses and roles. As most mothers can testify, being a parent and working outside the home both involve physically and emotionally draining roles. Sociologists thus recognize **role conflict** as *conflict among the roles connected to two or more statuses.*

We experience role conflict when we find ourselves pulled in various directions as we try to respond to the many statuses we hold. One response to role conflict is deciding that "something has to go." More than one politician, for example, has decided not to run for office because of the conflicting demands of a hectic campaign schedule and family life. In other cases, people put off having children in order to stay on the "fast track" for career success.

Even roles linked to a single status may make competing demands on us. **Role strain** is *tension among the roles connected to a single status.* A college professor may enjoy being friendly with students. At the same time, however, the professor must maintain the personal distance needed to evaluate students objectively and fairly. In short, performing the roles of even a single status can be something of a balancing act.

One strategy for minimizing role conflict is separating parts of our lives so that we perform roles for one status at one time and place and carry out roles for another status in a completely different setting. A familiar example of this pattern is deciding to "leave the job at work" before heading home to the family.

Role Exit

After she left the life of a Catholic nun to become a university sociologist, Helen Rose Fuchs Ebaugh began to study her own experience of *role exit,* the process by which people disengage from important social roles. In studying a range of "exes," including ex-nuns, ex-doctors, ex-husbands, and ex-alcoholics, Ebaugh saw a pattern in the process of becoming an "ex."

According to Ebaugh (1988), the process begins as people come to doubt their ability to continue in a certain role. As they imagine alternative roles, they ultimately reach a tipping point when they decide to pursue a new life. Even at this point, however, a past role can continue to influence their lives. Exes carry with them a self-image shaped by an earlier role, which can interfere with building a new sense of self. For example, an ex-nun may hesitate to wear stylish clothing and makeup.

Exes must also rebuild relationships with people who knew them in their earlier life. Learning new social skills is another challenge. For example, Ebaugh reports, ex-nuns who enter the dating scene after decades in the church are often surprised to learn that today's sexual norms are very different from those they knew when they were teenagers.

The Social Construction of Reality

🔘 **Analyze**

In 1917, the Italian playwright Luigi Pirandello wrote a play titled *The Pleasure of Honesty,* about a character named Angelo Baldovino, a brilliant man with a checkered past. Baldovino enters the fashionable home of the Renni family and introduces himself in a peculiar way:

> Inevitably we construct ourselves. Let me explain. I enter this house and immediately I become what I have to become, what I can become: I construct myself. That is, I present

Flirting is an everyday experience in reality construction. Each person offers information to the other and hints at romantic interest. Yet the interaction proceeds with a tentative and often humorous air so that either individual can withdraw at any time without further obligation.

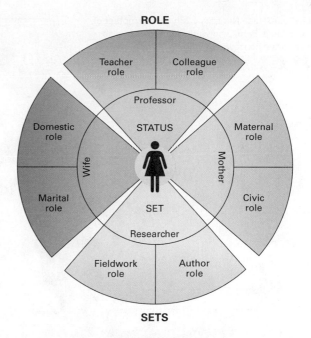

ROLE

SETS

FIGURE 4–1 Status Set and Role Sets

A status set includes all the statuses a person holds at a given time. The status set defines *who we are* in society. The many roles linked to each status define *what we do.*

myself to you in a form suitable to the relationship I wish to achieve with you. And, of course, you do the same with me. (act 1, scene 1; 1962:157–58)

Baldovino suggests that although behavior is guided by status and role, we have considerable ability to shape what happens from moment to moment. In other words, "reality" is not as fixed as we may think.

The **social construction of reality** is *the process by which people creatively shape reality through social interaction.* This idea is the foundation of the symbolic-interaction approach, described in Chapter 1 ("Sociology: Perspective, Theory, and Method"). As Baldovino's remark suggests, quite a bit of "reality" remains unclear in everyone's mind, especially in unfamiliar situations. So we present ourselves in terms that suit the setting and our purposes, and as others do the same, reality takes shape.

Social interaction, then, is a complex negotiation that builds reality. Most everyday situations involve at least some agreement about what's going on. But how people see events depends on their different backgrounds, interests, and intentions.

✳ **Explore** how education shapes reality construction on **mysoclab.com**

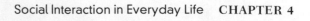

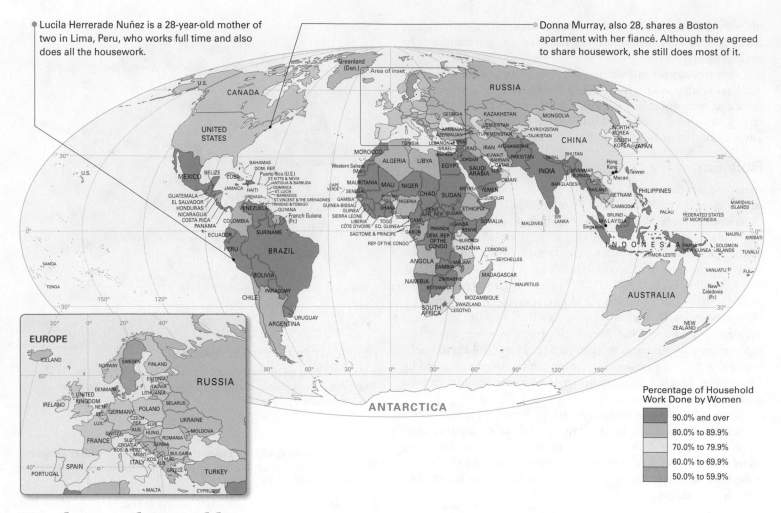

Lucila Herrerade Nuñez is a 28-year-old mother of two in Lima, Peru, who works full time and also does all the housework.

Donna Murray, also 28, shares a Boston apartment with her fiancé. Although they agreed to share housework, she still does most of it.

Percentage of Household Work Done by Women

- 90.0% and over
- 80.0% to 89.9%
- 70.0% to 79.9%
- 60.0% to 69.9%
- 50.0% to 59.9%

Window on the World

GLOBAL MAP 4–1 Housework in Global Perspective

Throughout the world, housework is a major part of women's routines and identities. This is especially true in poor nations of Latin America, Africa, and Asia, where the social position of women is far below that of men. But our society also defines housework and child care as "feminine" activities, even though women and men have the same legal rights and most women work outside the home.

Source: United Nations (2010).

"Street Smarts"

What people commonly call "street smarts" is actually a form of constructing reality. In his autobiography, *Down These Mean Streets*, Piri Thomas recalls moving to a new apartment in Spanish Harlem. Returning home one evening, young Piri found himself cut off by Waneko, the leader of the local street gang, who was flanked by a dozen others.

"Whatta ya say, Mr. Johnny Gringo," drawled Waneko.

Think man, I told myself, *think your way out of a stomping. Make it good.* "I hear you 104th Street coolies are supposed to have heart," I said. "I don't know this for sure. You know there's a lot of streets where a whole 'click' is made out of punks who can't fight one guy unless they all jump him for the stomp." I hoped this would push Waneko into giving me a fair one. His expression didn't change.

"Maybe we don't look at it that way."

Crazy, man, I cheer inwardly, *the* cabron *is falling into my setup.* . . . . . "I wasn't talking to you," I said. "Where I come from, the pres is president 'cause he got heart when it comes to dealing."

Waneko was starting to look uneasy. He had bit on my worm and felt like a sucker fish. His boys were now light on me. They were no longer so much interested in stomping me as seeing the outcome between Waneko and me. "Yeah," was his reply. . . .

I knew I'd won. Sure, I'd have to fight; but one guy, not ten or fifteen. If I lost, I might still get stomped, and if I won I might get stomped. I took care of this with my next sentence. "I don't know you or your boys," I said, "but they look cool to me. They don't feature as punks."

I had left him out purposely when I said "they." Now his boys were in a separate class. I had cut him off. He would have to fight me on his own, to prove his heart to himself, to his boys, and most important, to his turf. He got away from the stoop and asked, "Fair one, Gringo?" (1967:56–57)

This situation reveals the drama—sometimes subtle, sometimes savage—by which human beings creatively build everyday reality. Of course, not everyone enters a situation with equal power. Should a police officer on patrol have come upon the fight that took place between Piri and Waneko, both young men might have ended up in jail.

The Thomas Theorem

By using his wits and fighting with Waneko until they both tired, Piri Thomas won acceptance by the gang. What took place that evening in Spanish Harlem is an example of the **Thomas theorem**, named after W. I. Thomas and Dorothy Thomas (1928; Thomas, 1966:301, orig. 1931): *Situations that are defined as real are real in their consequences.*

Applied to social interaction, the Thomas theorem means that although reality is "soft" as it is being shaped, it can become "hard" in its effects. In the situation just described, local gang members saw Piri Thomas act in a worthy way, so in their eyes, he *became* worthy.

Ethnomethodology

Most of the time, we take social reality for granted. To become more aware of the social world we help create, Harold Garfinkel (1967) came up with **ethnomethodology**, *the study of the way people make sense of their everyday surroundings.* This approach begins by pointing out that everyday behavior rests on a number of assumptions. For instance, when you ask someone the simple question "How are you?" you usually want to know how someone is doing in general, but you might be wondering how the person is dealing with a specific physical, mental, spiritual, or financial challenge. However, the person being asked probably assumes that you are not really interested in the details about any of these things and that you are just "being polite."

One good way to investigate the assumptions we make about everyday reality is to break the rules. For example, the next time someone asks, "How are you?" offer details from your last physical examination or explain all the good and bad things that have happened since you woke up that morning and see how the person reacts.

The results are predictable, because we all have some idea of what the "rules" of everyday interaction are. The person will most likely become confused or irritated by your unexpected behavior—a reaction that helps us see not only what the rules are but how important they are to everyday reality.

Reality Building: Class and Culture

People do not build everyday experience out of thin air. In part, how we act or what we see in our surroundings depends on our interests. Gazing at the sky on a starry night, for example, lovers discover romance and scientists see hydrogen atoms

People build reality from their surrounding culture. Yet because cultural systems are marked by diversity and even outright conflict, reality construction always involves tensions and choices. Turkey is a nation with a mostly Muslim population, but it has also embraced Western culture. Here women confront starkly different definitions of what is "feminine."
Staton R. Winter, *The New York Times.*

fusing into helium. Social background also affects what we see, which is why the residents of Spanish Harlem experience a different world than people living on Manhattan's pricey Upper East Side.

In global perspective, reality construction varies even more. Consider these everyday situations: People waiting for a bus in London typically "queue up" in a straight line; people in New York City are rarely so orderly. The law in Saudi Arabia forbids women to drive cars, a ban unthinkable in the United States. In this country, a "short walk" means a few blocks or a few minutes; in the Andes Mountains of Peru, this same phrase means a few miles.

The point is that people build reality from the surrounding culture. Chapter 2 ("Culture") explains how people the world over find different meanings in specific gestures, so inexperienced travelers can find themselves building an unexpected and unwelcome reality. Similarly, in a study of popular culture, JoEllen Shively (1992) screened films set in the American West to men of European descent and to Native American men. The men in both categories claimed to enjoy the films, but for different reasons. White men interpreted the films as praising rugged people striking out for the frontier and conquering the forces of nature. Native American men saw in the same films a celebration of land and nature. Given their different cultures, it is as if people in the two categories saw two different films.

Films also have an effect on the reality we all experience. The 2009 film *Adam,* for example, about a young man with Asperger syndrome, is one of a series of recent films that have changed people's awareness of the struggle of coping with mental disorders.

Dramaturgical Analysis: The "Presentation of Self"

 Analyze

Erving Goffman (1922–1982) was another sociologist who analyzed social interaction, explaining how people live their lives much like actors performing on a stage. If we imagine ourselves as directors observing what goes on in the theater of everyday life, we are doing what Goffman called **dramaturgical analysis**, *the study of social interaction in terms of theatrical performance.*

Dramaturgical analysis offers a fresh look at the concepts of status and role. A status is like a part in a play, and a role is a script, supplying dialogue and action for the characters. Goffman described each person's performance as the **presentation of self**, *a person's efforts to create specific impressions in the minds of others.* This process, sometimes called *impression management,* begins with the idea of personal performance (Goffman, 1959, 1967).

Performances

As we present ourselves in everyday situations, we reveal information to others both consciously and unconsciously. Our performances include the way we dress (in theatrical terms, our costume), the objects we carry (props), and our tone of voice and the way we carry ourselves (our demeanor). In addition, we vary our performances according to where we happen to be (the set). We may joke loudly in a restaurant or at a sporting event, for example, but we lower our voice when entering

Read "The Presentation of Self in Everyday Life" by Erving Goffman on **mysoclab.com**

a house of worship. People design settings, such as homes or offices, to bring about desired reactions in others.

An Application: The Doctor's Office

Consider how the operation of a physician's office conveys important information to an audience of patients. The fact that medical doctors enjoy high prestige and power in the United States is clear upon entering a doctor's office. First, the doctor is nowhere to be seen. Instead, in what Goffman describes as the "front region" of the setting, the patient encounters a receptionist, who works as a gatekeeper, deciding whether and when the patient can meet the doctor. A simple glance around the doctor's waiting room, with patients (often impatiently) waiting to be invited into the inner sanctum, leaves little doubt that the doctor and the staff are in charge.

The "back region" is composed of the examination rooms as well as the doctor's private office. Once inside the office, the patient can see a wide range of props, such as medical books and framed degrees, that give the impression that the doctor has the specialized knowledge necessary to call the shots. The doctor is usually seated behind a desk—the larger the desk, the greater the statement of power—and the patient is given only a chair.

The doctor's appearance and manner offer still more information. The usual white lab coat (costume) may have the practical function of keeping clothes from becoming dirty, but its social function is to let others know the physician's status at a glance. A stethoscope around the neck and a black medical bag in hand (more props) have the same purpose. The doctor uses highly technical language that is often mystifying to the patient, again emphasizing that the doctor is in charge. Finally, patients use the title "doctor," but they, in turn, are often addressed only by their first names, which further shows the doctor's dominant position. The overall message of a doctor's performance is clear: "I will help you, but you must allow me to take charge."

Nonverbal Communication

The novelist William Sansom describes the performance of a character named Mr. Preedy, an English vacationer on a beach in Spain:

> He took care to avoid catching anyone's eye. First, he had to make it clear to those potential companions of his holiday that they were of no concern to him whatsoever. He stared through them, round them, over them—eyes lost in space. The beach might have been empty. If by chance a ball was thrown his way, he looked surprised; then let a smile of amusement light his face (Kindly Preedy), looked around dazed to see that there were people on the beach, tossed it back with a smile to himself and not a smile *at* the people. . . .
> [He] then gathered together his beach-wrap and bag into a neat sand-resistant pile (Methodical and Sensible Preedy), rose slowly to stretch his huge frame (Big-Cat Preedy), and tossed aside his sandals (Carefree Preedy, after all). (1956:230–31)

Without saying a single word, Mr. Preedy offers a great deal of information about himself to anyone watching him. This is the process of **nonverbal communication**, *communication using body movements, gestures, and facial expressions rather than speech.*

Many parts of the body can be used to generate *body language,* that is, to convey information to others. Facial expressions are the most significant form of body language. Smiling, for example, shows pleasure, although we distinguish among the deliberate smile of Kindly Preedy on the beach, a spontaneous smile of joy at seeing a friend, a pained smile of embarrassment, and the full, unrestrained smile of self-satisfaction that we often associate with winning some important contest.

Eye contact is another crucial element of nonverbal communication. Generally, we use eye contact to invite social interaction. Someone across the room "catches our eye," sparking a conversation. Avoiding another's eyes, by contrast, discourages communication. Hands also speak for us. Common hand gestures within our culture convey, among other things, an insult, a request for a ride, an invitation for someone to join us, or a demand that others stop in their tracks. Gestures also add meaning to spoken words. For example, pointing in a threatening way gives greater emphasis to a word of warning, shrugging the shoulders adds an air of indifference to the phrase "I don't know," and rapidly waving the arms lends urgency to the single word "Hurry!"

Body Language and Deception

As any actor knows, it is very difficult to pull off a perfect performance in front of others. In everyday life, unintended body language can contradict our planned meaning: A teenage boy explains why he is getting home so late, for example, but his mother doubts his words because he avoids looking her in the eye; the movie star on a television talk show claims that her recent flop at the box office is "no big deal," but the nervous swing of her leg suggests otherwise. Because nonverbal communication is hard to control, it provides clues to deception, in much the same way that changes in breathing, pulse rate, perspiration, and blood pressure recorded on a lie detector suggest that a person is lying.

Recognizing dishonest performances is difficult because no single bodily gesture tells us for sure that someone is lying. But because any performance involves so many bits of body language, few people can keep up a lie without some slip-up, raising the suspicions of a careful observer. Therefore, the key to detecting lies is to view the whole performance with an eye for inconsistencies.

Gender and Performances

Because women are socialized to respond to others, they tend to be more sensitive than men to nonverbal communication. Research suggests that women "read" men better than men "read" women (Farris et al., 2008). Gender is also one of the key elements in the presentation of self, as the following sections explain.

Demeanor

Demeanor—the way we act and carry ourselves—is a clue to social power. Simply put, powerful people enjoy more freedom in how they act. Off-color remarks, swearing, or putting your feet on the desk may be acceptable for the boss but rarely for employees. Similarly, powerful people can interrupt others, but less powerful people are expected to show respect through silence (Smith-Lovin & Brody, 1989; Henley, Hamilton, & Thorne, 1992; C. Johnson, 1994).

Because women generally occupy positions of lesser power, demeanor is a gender issue as well. As Chapter 10 ("Gender Stratification") explains, 39 percent of all working women in the United States hold secretarial or service jobs under the control of supervisors who are usually men. Women, then, learn to craft their personal performances more carefully than men and to defer to men more often in everyday interaction (U.S. Department of Labor, 2011).

Personal Space

How much space does a personal performance require? Power plays a key role here; the more power you have, the more space you use. Men typically command more space than women, whether pacing back and forth before an audience or casually stretching out on a bench. Why? Our culture has traditionally measured femininity by how *little* space women occupy—the standard of "daintiness"—and masculinity by how *much* territory a man controls—the standard of "turf" (Henley, Hamilton, & Thorne, 1992).

For both sexes, the concept of **personal space** is *the surrounding area over which a person makes some claim to privacy*. In the United States, people generally stay several feet apart when speaking; throughout the Middle East, by contrast, people stand much closer. But just about everywhere, men (with their greater social power) often intrude into women's personal space. If a woman moves into a man's personal space, however, he is likely to take it as a sign of sexual interest.

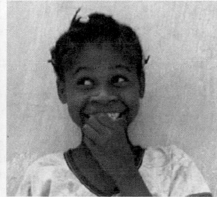

Hand gestures vary widely from one culture to another. Yet people everywhere chuckle, grin, or smirk to indicate that they don't take another person's performance seriously. Therefore, the world over, people who cannot restrain their mirth tactfully cover their faces.

To most people in the United States, these expressions convey anger, fear, disgust, happiness, surprise, and sadness. But do people elsewhere in the world define them in the same way? Research suggests that all human beings experience the same basic emotions and display them to others in the same basic ways. But culture plays a part by specifying the situations that trigger one emotion or another.

Staring, Smiling, and Touching

Eye contact encourages interaction. In conversations, women hold eye contact more than men. But men have their own brand of eye contact: staring. When men stare at women, they are claiming social dominance and defining women as sexual objects.

Although it often shows pleasure, smiling can also be a sign of trying to please someone or of submission. In a male-dominated world, it is not surprising that women smile more than men (Henley, Hamilton, & Thorne, 1992).

Finally, mutual touching suggests intimacy and caring. Apart from close relationships, however, touching is generally something men do to women (but rarely, in our culture, to other men). A male doctor touches the shoulder of his female nurse as they examine a report, a young man touches the back of his woman friend as he guides her across the street, or a male tennis instructor touches the arms of young women as he teaches them how to serve. In such examples, the intent of touching may be harmless and may bring little response, but it amounts to a subtle ritual by which men claim dominance over women.

Idealization

People behave the way they do for many, often complex reasons. Even so, Goffman suggests, we construct performances to *idealize* our intentions. That is, we try to convince others (and perhaps ourselves) that our actions reflect ideal cultural standards rather than selfish motives.

Idealization is easily illustrated by returning to the world of doctors and patients. In a hospital, doctors engage in a performance known as "making rounds." Upon entering a patient's room, the doctor often stops at the foot of the bed and silently examines the patient's chart. Afterward, doctor and patient talk briefly. In ideal terms, this routine represents a personal visit to check on a patient's condition.

In reality, the picture is not so perfect. A doctor may see dozens of patients a day and remember little about many of them. Reading the chart is a chance to recall the patient's name and medical problems, but revealing the impersonality of the patient's care would undermine the cultural ideal of the doctor as deeply concerned about the welfare of others.

Doctors, college professors, and other professionals typically idealize their motives for entering their chosen careers. They are quick to describe their work as "making a contribution to science," "serving the community," or even "answering a calling from God." Rarely do people admit the more common, less honorable, motives: the income, power, prestige, and leisure time that these occupations provide.

We all use idealization to some degree. When was the last time you smiled and made polite remarks to someone you did not like? Such little lies ease our way through social interactions. Even when we suspect that others are putting on an act, we are unlikely to challenge their performance, for reasons that we shall examine next.

Embarrassment and Tact

The famous speaker giving a campus lecture keeps mispronouncing the college president's name; the head coach rises to speak at the team's end-of-season banquet, unaware of the napkin still tucked in her dress; the student enters the lecture hall late and soaking wet, attracting the gaze of hundreds of classmates. As carefully as individuals may try to craft their performances, slip-ups of all kinds happen. The result is *embarrassment,* or discomfort after a spoiled performance. Goffman describes embarrassment as "losing face."

Embarrassment is an ever-present danger because idealized performances typically contain some deception. In addition, most performances involve juggling so many elements that one thoughtless moment can shatter the intended impression.

A curious fact is that an audience often overlooks flaws in a performance, allowing the actor to avoid embarrassment. If we do point out a misstep ("Excuse me, but your fly is open"), we do it quietly and only to help someone avoid even greater loss of face. In Hans Christian Andersen's classic fable "The Emperor's New Clothes," the child who blurts out the truth, pointing out to everyone that the emperor is parading about naked, is scolded for being rude.

Often members of an audience actually help the performer recover from a flawed performance. *Tact* is helping someone "save face." After hearing a supposed expert make an embarrassingly inaccurate remark, for example, we might ignore the comment, as if it had never been spoken. Or with mild laughter we could treat what was said as a joke. Or we could simply respond, "I'm sure you didn't mean that," hearing the statement but not allowing it to destroy the performance. With these options in mind, it is easier to understand Abraham Lincoln's observation that "tact is the ability to describe others the way they see themselves."

Why is tact so common? Embarrassment creates discomfort not only for the actor but also for everyone else. Just as the entire audience feels uneasy when an actor forgets a line, people who observe the awkward behavior of others are reminded of how fragile their own performances often are. Socially constructed reality thus functions like a dam holding back a sea of chaos. Should one person's performance spring a leak, others tactfully help make repairs. After all, everyone lends a hand in building reality, and no one wants it suddenly swept away.

In sum, Goffman's research shows that although behavior is spontaneous in some respects, it is more patterned than we like to think. Almost 400 years ago, William Shakespeare captured this idea in lines that still ring true:

> All the world's a stage,
> And all the men and women merely players:
> They have their exits and their entrances;
> And one man in his time plays many parts.
> (*As You Like It,* act 2, scene 7)

Many of us think that emotions are simply part of our biological makeup. While there is a biological foundation to human emotion, sociologists have learned that what triggers an emotion—as well as when, where, and to whom the emotion is displayed—is shaped by culture. Similarly, every society has situations or settings in which some people are forbidden to display any emotion at all. Look at each of these photos and explain why members of the palace guard, courtside assistants at professional tennis matches, and soldiers facing those of higher rank typically must "keep a straight face."

Interaction in Everyday Life: Three Applications

 Apply

The final sections of this chapter illustrate the major elements of social interaction by focusing on three important dimensions of everyday life: emotions, language, and humor.

Emotions: The Social Construction of Feeling

Emotions, more commonly called *feelings,* are an important dimension of everyday life. Indeed, what we *do* often matters less than how we *feel* about it. Emotions seem very personal because they are "inside." Even so, just as society guides our behavior, it guides our emotional life.

The Biological Side of Emotions

Studying the social interaction of men and women all over the world, Paul Ekman (1980a, 1980b) reports that people everywhere express six basic emotions: happiness, sadness, anger, fear, disgust, and surprise. In addition, Ekman found that people in every society use much the same facial expressions to show these emotions. Ekman believes that some emotional responses seem to be "wired" into human beings; that is, they are biologically programmed in our facial features, muscles, and central nervous system.

Why might this be so? Over centuries of evolution, emotions developed in the human species because they serve a social purpose: supporting group life. Emotions are powerful forces that allow us to overcome our individualism and build connections with others. Thus the capacity for emotion arose in our ancestors along with the development of culture (Turner, 2000).

The Cultural Side of Emotions

But culture does play an important role in guiding human emotions. First, Ekman explains, culture defines *what triggers* an emotion. Whether people define the departure of an old friend as joyous (causing happiness), insulting (arousing anger), a loss (creating sadness), or mystical (causing surprise and awe) has a lot to do with the culture. Second, culture provides rules for the *display* of emotions. For example, most people in the United States express emotions more freely with family members than with others in the workplace. Similarly, we expect children to express emotions to parents, although parents tend to hide their emotions from their children. Third, culture guides how we *value* emotions. Some societies encourage the expression of emotion, while others expect members to control their feelings and maintain a "stiff upper lip." Gender also plays a part; traditionally, at least, many cultures expect women to show emotions while condemning emotional expression by men as a sign of weakness. In some cultures, of course, this pattern is less pronounced or even reversed.

Emotions on the Job

In the United States, most people are freer to express their feelings at home than on the job. This is because, as Arlie Russell Hochschild (1979, 1983) explains, the typical corporation or other place of business does indeed try to control not only the behavior of its employees but also their emotions. Take the case of an airline flight attendant who offers passengers a drink, a snack, and a smile. Do you think that this smile may convey real pleasure at serving the customer? It may. But Hochschild's study of flight attendants

Liz: I just *can't* be pregnant! I'm going to see my doctor tomorrow about an abortion. There's no way I can deal with a baby at this point in my life!
Jen: I can't believe you'd do that, Liz! How are you going to feel in a couple of years when you think of what that *child* would be doing if you'd let it live?

Few issues today generate as much emotion as abortion. In a study of women's abortion experiences, the sociologist Jennifer Keys (2002) discovered emotional scripts or "feeling rules" that guide how women feel about ending a pregnancy.

Keys explains that different emotional scripts arise from the political controversy surrounding abortion. The antiabortion movement defines abortion as a personal tragedy, the "killing of an unborn child." Given this definition, which we see in Jen's comment above, women who end a pregnancy through abortion are doing something very wrong and can expect to feel grief, guilt, and regret. So intense are these feelings, according to supporters of this position, that such women often suffer from "postabortion syndrome."

Those who take the pro-choice position have an opposing view of abortion. From this point of view, illustrated by Liz's comment, the woman's problem is the *unwanted pregnancy*; abortion is an acceptable medical solution. Therefore, the emotion to be expected in a woman who ends a pregnancy is not guilt but relief.

In her research, Keys conducted in-depth interviews with forty women who had recently had abortions and found that all of them used such scripts to "frame" their situation in an antiabortion or pro-choice manner. In part, this construction of reality reflected the woman's own attitude about abortion. In addition, however,

women's partners and friends typically encouraged specific feelings about the event. Ivy, one young woman in the study, had a close friend who was also pregnant. "Congratulations!" she exclaimed when she learned of Ivy's condition. "We're going to be having babies together!" Such a statement established one "feeling rule"—having a baby is *good*—which sent the message to Ivy that her planned abortion should trigger guilt. Working in the other direction, Jo's partner was horrified at the news that she was pregnant. Doubting his own ability to be a father, he blurted out, "I would rather put a gun to my head than have this baby!" His panic not only defined having the child as a mistake but alarmed Jo as well. Clearly, her partner's reaction made the decision to end the pregnancy a matter of relief from a terrible problem.

Medical personnel also play a part in the process of reality construction by using specific terms. Nurses and doctors who talk about

"the baby" encourage the antiabortion framing of abortion and provoke grief and guilt. On the other hand, those who use language such as "pregnancy tissue," "fetus," or "the contents of the uterus" encourage the pro-choice framing of abortion as a simple medical procedure leading to relief. Olivia began using the phrase "products of conception," which she picked up from her doctor. Denise spoke of her procedure as "taking the extra cells out of my body. Yeah, I did feel some guilt when I thought that this was the beginning of life, but my body is full of life—you have lots of cells in you."

After the procedure, most women reported actively trying to manage their feelings. Explained Ivy, "I never used the word 'baby.' I kept saying to myself that it was not formed yet. There was nothing there yet. I kept that in my mind." On the other hand, Keys found that all of the women in her study who had undergone abortions but nevertheless leaned toward the antiabortion position did use the term "baby." When interviewed, Gina explained, "I do think of it as a baby. The truth is that I ended my baby's life and I should not have done that. Thinking that makes me feel guilty. But—considering what I did—maybe I *should* feel guilty." Believing that what she had done was wrong, in other words, Gina actively called out the feeling of guilt—in part, Keys concluded, to punish herself.

What Do You Think?

1. In your own words, explain "emotional scripts" or "feeling rules."
2. Can you apply the idea of "scripting feelings" to the experience of getting married?
3. In light of this discussion, to what extent is it correct to say that our feelings are not as personal as we may think they are?

The words that doctors and nurses use guide whether a woman having an abortion defines the experience in positive or negative terms.

points to a different conclusion: The smile is an emotional script demanded by the airline as the right way to do the job. Therefore, from Hochschild's research we see an added dimension of the "presentation of self" described by Erving Goffman. Not only do our everyday life presentations to others involve surface acting but they also involve the "deep acting" of emotions.

With these patterns in mind, it is easy to see that we socially construct our emotions as part of our everyday reality, a process sociologists call *emotion management*. The Controversy & Debate box relates the very different emotions displayed by women who

decide to have an abortion, depending on their personal view of terminating a pregnancy.

Language: The Social Construction of Gender

As Chapter 2 ("Culture") explains, language is the thread that weaves members of a society in the symbolic web we call culture. Language conveys not only a surface message but also deeper levels of meaning. One important level involves gender. Language defines men and women differently in terms of both power and value (Henley, Hamilton, & Thorne, 1992; Thorne, Kramarae, & Henley, 1983).

Language and Power

A young man proudly rides his new motorcycle up his friend's driveway and asks, "Isn't she a beauty?" On the surface, the question has little to do with gender. Yet why does he use the pronoun *she* rather than *he* or *it* to refer to his prized possession?

The answer is that language helps men establish control over their surroundings. That is, a man attaches a female pronoun to a motorcycle (or car, boat, or other object) because doing so reflects *ownership*. Perhaps this is also why, in the United States and elsewhere, traditionally a woman who marries takes the last name of her husband. This pattern still has support from about three-fourths of adults. But some women today (currently about 6 percent of women who marry) are asserting their independence by keeping their own name or combining the two family names (Gooding & Kreider, 2010; Hamilton, Geist, & Powell, 2011).

Language and Value

Typically, the English language treats as masculine whatever has greater value, force, or significance. For instance, the adjective *virtuous,* meaning "morally worthy" or "excellent," is derived from the Latin word *vir,* meaning "man." On the other hand, the adjective *hysterical,* meaning "emotionally out of control," comes from the Greek word *hystera,* meaning "uterus."

In many familiar ways, language also confers a different value on the two sexes. Traditional masculine terms such as *king* or *lord* have a positive meaning, while comparable terms, such as *queen,* *madam,* and *dame,* can have negative meanings. Similarly, the use of the suffixes *-ess* and *-ette* to indicate femininity usually devalues the words to which they are added. For example, a *major* has higher standing than a *majorette,* as does a *host* in relation to a *hostess* or a *master* to a *mistress.* Thus, language both mirrors social attitudes and helps perpetuate them.

Given the importance of gender in everyday life, perhaps we should not be surprised that women and men sometimes have trouble communicating with each other. In the Sociology in Focus box on page 100, Harold and Sybil, whose misadventures finding their friends' home were described in the opening to this chapter, return to illustrate how the two sexes often seem to be speaking different languages.

Reality Play: The Social Construction of Humor

Humor plays an important part in everyday life. Everyone laughs at a joke, but few people think about what makes something funny. We can apply many of the ideas developed in this chapter to explain how, by using humor, we "play with reality" (Macionis, 1987).

The Foundation of Humor

Humor is produced by the social construction of reality; specifically, it arises as people create and contrast two different realities.

Generally, one reality is *conventional,* that is, what people in a specific situation expect. The other reality is *unconventional,* an unexpected violation of cultural patterns. In short, humor arises from the contradictions, ambiguities, and double meanings found in differing definitions of the same situation.

There are countless ways to mix realities and thereby generate humor. Contrasting realities emerge from statements that contradict themselves, such as "Nostalgia is not what it used to be"; statements that repeat themselves, such as Yogi Berra's line, "It's *déjà vu* all over again"; or statements that mix up words, such as Oscar Wilde's line, "Work is the curse of the drinking class." Even switching around syllables does the trick, as in the case of the country song "I'd Rather Have a Bottle in Front of Me than a Frontal Lobotomy."

You can also build a joke the other way around, leading the audience to expect an unconventional answer and then delivering a very ordinary one. When a reporter asked the famous criminal Willy Sutton why he robbed banks, for example, he replied dryly, "Because that's where the money is." Regardless of how a joke is constructed, the greater the opposition or difference between the two definitions of reality, the greater the humor.

When telling jokes, the comedian uses various strategies to strengthen this opposition and make the joke funnier. One common technique is to present the first, or conventional, remark in conversation with another actor but then turn toward the audience or the camera to deliver the second, unexpected line. In a Marx Brothers movie, Groucho remarks, "Outside of a dog, a book is a man's best friend." Then, raising his voice and turning to the camera, he adds, "And *inside* of a dog, it's too dark to read!" Such "changing channels" emphasizes the difference between the conventional and unconventional realities. Following the same logic, many stand-up comedians also "reset" the audience to conventional expectations by adding, "But seriously, folks, . . ." between jokes. Monty Python comedian John Cleese did this with his trademark line, "And now for something completely different."

Comedians pay careful attention to their performances—the precise words they use and the timing with which they deliver their lines. A joke is well told if the comic times the lines to create the sharpest possible opposition between the realities; in a careless performance, the joke falls flat. Because the key to humor lies in the collision of realities, we can see why the climax of a joke is termed the "*punch* line."

The Dynamics of Humor: "Getting It"

After hearing a joke, did you ever say, "I don't get it"? To "get" humor, members of an audience must understand the two realities involved well enough to appreciate their difference. A comedian may make getting a joke harder by leaving out some important information. In such cases, the audience must pay attention to the stated elements of the joke and fill in the missing pieces. As a simple example, consider the comment of movie producer Hal Roach upon reaching his hundredth birthday: "If I had known I would live to be

Watch the video "The Role of Humor" on **mysoclab.com**

In the story that opened this chapter, Harold and Sybil faced a situation that rings all too true to many people: When they are lost, men grumble to themselves and perhaps blame their partners but avoid asking for directions. For their part, women can't understand why men refuse help when they need it.

Deborah Tannen (1990) explains that men typically define most everyday encounters as competitive. Therefore, getting lost is bad enough without asking for help, which lets someone else get "one up." By contrast, because women have traditionally had a subordinate position, they find it easy to ask for help. Sometimes, Tannen points out, women ask for assistance even when they don't need it.

A similar gender-linked pattern involves what women consider "trying to be helpful" and men call "nagging." Consider the following exchange (adapted from Adler, 1990):

Sybil: What's wrong, honey?

Harold: Nothing.

Sybil: Something is bothering you. I can tell.

Harold: I told you nothing is bothering me. Leave me alone.

Sybil: But I can see that something is wrong.

Harold: OK. Just why do you think something is bothering me?

Sybil: Well, for one thing, you're bleeding all over your shirt.

Harold: (*now irritated*) Yeah, well, it doesn't bother me.

Sybil: (*losing her temper*) WELL, IT SURE IS BOTHERING ME!

Harold: (*walking away*) Fine. I'll go change my shirt.

The problem couples face in communicating is that what one partner *intends* by a comment is not always what the other *hears* in the words. To Sybil, her opening question is an

effort at cooperative problem solving. She can see that something is wrong with Harold (who has cut himself while doing yard work), and she wants to help him. But Harold interprets her pointing out his problem as belittling him and tries to close off the discussion. Sybil, confident that Harold would be more positive toward her if he just understood that she only wants to be helpful, repeats her question. This sets in motion a vicious circle in which Harold, thinking his wife is trying to make him feel incapable of looking after himself, responds by digging in his heels. This, in turn, makes his wife all the more sure that she needs to do something. And around it goes until somebody gets really angry.

In the end, Harold agrees to change his shirt but still refuses to discuss the original problem. Defining his wife's concern as "nagging," Harold just wants Sybil to leave him alone. For her part, Sybil fails to understand her husband's view of the situation and walks away convinced that he is a stubborn grouch.

Join the Blog!

What differences have you noticed in the ways men and women communicate? Go to MySocLab and join the Sociology in Focus blog to share your opinions and experiences and to see what others think.

---

one hundred, I would have taken better care of myself!" Here, getting the joke depends on realizing the unstated fact that Roach must have taken pretty good care of himself because he did make it to one hundred. Or take one of W. C. Fields's lines: "Some weasel took the cork out of my lunch!" "What a lunch!" we think to ourselves to "finish" the joke.

Here is an even more complex joke: What do you get if you cross an insomniac, a dyslexic, and an agnostic? Answer: A person who stays up all night wondering if there is a dog. To get this one, you must know that insomnia is an inability to sleep, that an agnostic doubts the existence of God, and that dyslexia causes a person to reverse letters in words.

Why would a comedian require the audience to make this sort of effort to understand a joke? Our enjoyment of a joke is increased by the pleasure of figuring out all the pieces needed to "get it." In addition, "getting" the joke makes you an "insider" compared to those who don't get it. We have all experienced the frustration of not getting a joke: fear of being judged stupid, coupled with a sense of being excluded from a pleasure shared by others. Sometimes someone may tactfully explain the joke so the other person doesn't feel left

out. But as the old saying goes, if a joke has to be explained, it isn't very funny.

The Topics of Humor

All over the world, people smile and laugh, making humor a universal element of human culture. But because the world's people live in different cultures, humor rarely travels well.

October 1, Kobe, Japan. Can you share a joke with people who live halfway around the world? At dinner, I ask two Japanese college women to tell me a joke. "You know 'crayon'?" Asako asks. I nod. "How do you ask for a crayon in Japanese?" I respond that I have no idea. She laughs out loud as she says what sounds like "crayon crayon." Her companion Mayumi laughs too. My wife and I sit awkwardly, straight-faced. Asako relieves some of our embarrassment by explaining that the Japanese word for "give me" is *kureyo*, which sounds like "crayon." I force a smile.

What is humorous to the Japanese, then, may be lost on the Chinese, Brazilians, or people in the United States. Even the social diversity of this country means that people will find humor in different situations. New Englanders, southerners, and westerners have their own brands of humor, as do Latinos and Anglos, fifteen- and fifty-year-olds, Wall Street bankers and rodeo riders.

But for everyone, topics that lend themselves to double meanings or controversy generate humor. For example, in the United States, the first jokes many of us learned as children concerned bodily functions kids are not supposed to talk about. The mere mention of "unmentionable acts" or even certain parts of the body can dissolve young faces in laughter.

Are there jokes that can break through the culture barrier? Yes, but they must touch on universal human experiences such as, say, turning on a friend:

> I think of a number of jokes, but none seems likely to work. Understanding jokes about the United States is difficult for people who know little about our culture. Is there something more universal? Inspiration: "Two men are walking in the woods and come upon a huge bear. One guy leans over and tightens up the laces on his running shoes. 'Jake,' says the other, 'what are you doing? You can't outrun that bear!' 'I don't have to outrun the bear,' responds Jake. 'I just have to outrun *you*!" Smiles all around.

The controversy found in humor often walks a fine line between what is funny and what is "sick." During the Middle Ages, people used the word "humors" (derived from the Latin *humidus,* meaning "moist") to mean a balance of bodily fluids that regulated a person's health. Researchers today document the power of humor to reduce stress and improve health. One recent study of cancer patients, for example, found that the greater a patient's sense of humor, the greater the odds of surviving the disease. Such findings confirm the old saying "Laughter is the best medicine" (Bakalar, 2005; Sven Svebak, cited in M. Elias, 2007). At the extreme, however, people who always take conventional reality lightly risk being defined as deviant or even mentally ill (a common stereotype shows insane people laughing uncontrollably, and for a long time mental hospitals were known as "funny farms").

Then, too, every social group considers certain topics too sensitive for humorous treatment. If you joke about such things, you risk criticism for telling a "sick" joke (and being labeled "sick" yourself). People's religious beliefs, tragic accidents, or appalling crimes are some of the subjects of "sick" jokes or no jokes at all. Even years later, there have been no jokes about the victims of the September 11, 2001, terrorist attacks.

The Functions of Humor

Humor is found everywhere because it works as a safety valve for potentially disruptive statements and ideas. Put another way, humor provides an acceptable way to discuss a sensitive topic without appearing to be serious or being offensive. Having said something controversial, people often use humor to defuse the situation by simply stating, "I didn't mean anything by what I said—it was just a joke!"

People also use humor to relieve tension in uncomfortable situations. One study of medical examinations found that most patients try to joke with doctors to ease their own nervousness (Baker et al., 1997).

Humor and Conflict

Humor holds the potential to liberate those who laugh, but it can also be used to put down other people. Men who tell jokes about women, for example, are typically expressing some measure of hostility toward them. Similarly, jokes about gay people reveal tensions about sexual orientation. Real conflict can be masked by humor when people choose not to bring the conflict out into the open (Primeggia & Varacalli, 1990).

"Put-down" jokes make one category of people feel good at the expense of another. After collecting and analyzing jokes from many societies, Christie Davies (1990) confirmed that ethnic conflict is a driving force behind humor in most of the world. The typical ethnic joke makes fun of some disadvantaged category of people, at the same time making the joke teller feel superior. Given the Anglo-Saxon traditions of U.S. society, Poles and other ethnic and racial minorities have long been the butt of jokes, as have Newfoundlanders in eastern Canada, Scots in England, Irish in Scotland, Sikhs in India, Turks in Germany, Hausas in Nigeria, Tasmanians in Australia, and Kurds in Iraq.

Disadvantaged people also make fun of the powerful, although usually with some care. Women in the United States joke about men, just as African Americans find humor in white people's ways and poor people poke fun at the rich. Throughout the world, people target their leaders with humor, and officials in some countries take such jokes seriously enough to arrest those who do not show proper respect (Speier, 1998).

In sum, humor is much more important than we may think. It is a means of mental escape from a conventional world that is not entirely to our liking (Flaherty, 1984, 1990; Yoels & Clair, 1995). This fact helps explain why so many of our nation's comedians come from the ranks of historically marginalized peoples, including Jews and African Americans. As long as we maintain a sense of humor, we assert our freedom and are never prisoners of reality. By putting a smile on our faces, we change ourselves and the world just a little and for the better.

Because humor involves challenging established conventions, most U.S. comedians—including George Lopez—have been social "outsiders," members of racial or ethnic minorities.

Seeing Sociology in Everyday Life

How do we all construct the reality we experience?

This chapter suggests that Shakespeare might have had it right when he said, "All the world's a stage." And if so, then the Internet may be the latest and greatest stage so far. When we use Web sites such as Facebook, as Goffman explains, we present ourselves as we want others to see us. Everything we write about ourselves as well as how we arrange our page creates an impression in the mind of anyone interested in "checking us out." Take a look at the Facebook page below, paying careful attention to all the details. What is the young man explicitly saying about himself? What can you read "between the lines"? That is, what information can you identify that he may be trying to conceal, or at least purposely not be mentioning? How honest do you think his "presentation of self" is? Why? Do a similar analysis of the young woman's Facebook profile shown on the next page.

Hint Just about every element of a presentation conveys information about us to others, so all the information found on a Web site like this one is significant. Some information is intentional—for example, what people write about themselves and the photos they choose to post. Other information may be unintentional but is nevertheless picked up by the careful viewer, who may be noting the following things:

- The length and tone of the person's profile (Is it a long-winded list of talents and accomplishments or humorous and modest?)
- The language used (Poor grammar may be a clue to educational level.)

- What hour of the day or night the person wrote the material (A person creating his profile at 11 P.M. on a Saturday night may not be quite the party person he describes himself to be.)

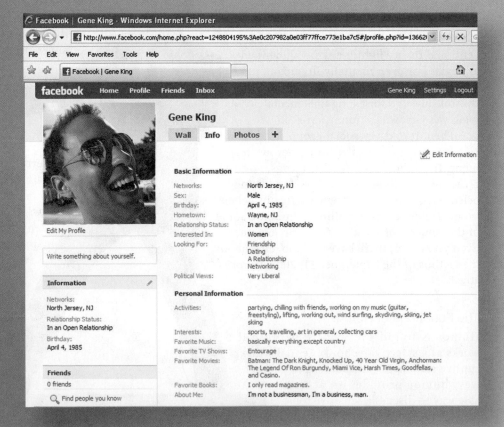

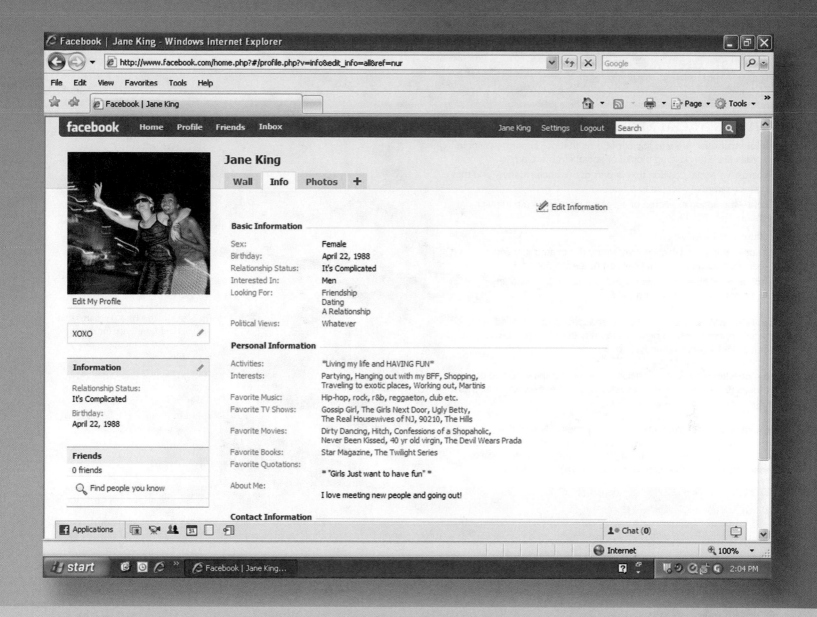

Seeing Sociology in *Your* Everyday Life

1. Identify five important ways in which you "present yourself" to others including, for example, the way you decorate your dorm room, apartment, or house; the way you dress; and the way you behave in the classroom. In each case, think about what you are trying to say about yourself. Do you present a different self to various others, such as friends, professors, and parents? If so, how do you account for the differences?

2. During one full day, every time somebody asks, "How are you?" or "How's it goin'?" stop and try to actually give a complete, truthful answer. What happens when you respond to a polite question in an honest way? Listen to how people respond, and also watch their body language. What can you conclude?

3. This chapter has explained that we all engage in a process called the social construction of reality. What that means is that each of us plays a part in shaping the reality we experience. Let's apply this idea to the issue of personal freedom. To what extent does the material presented in this chapter support a claim that humans are free to shape their own lives? Go to the "Seeing Sociology in *Your* Everyday Life" feature on MySocLab to learn more about the social construction of reality as well as suggestions for ways you can help construct a more positive social world.

What Is Social Structure?

Social structure refers to social patterns that guide our behavior in everyday life. The building blocks of social structure are

- **status**—a social position that is part of our social identity and that defines our relationships to others
- **role**—the action expected of a person who holds a particular status   **pp. 88–89**

A status can be either an

- **ascribed status**, which is involuntary (for example, being a teenager, an orphan, or a Mexican American), or an
- **achieved status**, which is earned (for example, being an honors student, a pilot, or a thief).

A **master status**, which can be either ascribed or achieved, has special importance for a person's identity (for example, being blind, a doctor, or a Kennedy).   **p. 89**

Role conflict results from tension among roles linked to two or more statuses (for example, a woman who juggles her responsibilities as a mother and a corporate CEO).

Role strain results from tension among roles linked to a single status (for example, the college professor who enjoys personal interaction with students but at the same time knows that social distance is necessary in order to evaluate students fairly).   **pp. 90–91**

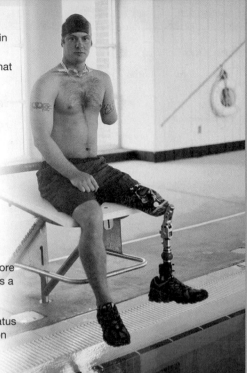

social interaction (p. 88) the process by which people act and react in relation to others

status (p. 89) a social position that a person holds

status set (p. 89) all the statuses a person holds at a given time

ascribed status (p. 89) a social position a person receives at birth or takes on involuntarily later in life

achieved status (p. 89) a social position a person takes on voluntarily that reflects personal ability and effort

master status (p. 89) a status that has special importance for social identity, often shaping a person's entire life

role (p. 89) behavior expected of someone who holds a particular status

role set (p. 90) a number of roles attached to a single status

role conflict (p. 90) conflict among the roles connected to two or more statuses

role strain (p. 90) tension among the roles connected to a single status

The Social Construction of Reality

Through **social interaction**, we construct the reality we experience.

- For example, two people interacting both try to shape the reality of their situation.

※ **Explore** the **Map** on **mysoclab.com**   **pp. 91–93**

The **Thomas theorem** says that the reality people construct in their interaction has real consequences for the future.

- For example, a teacher who believes a certain student to be intellectually gifted may well encourage exceptional academic performance.   **p. 93**

Ethnomethodology is a strategy to reveal the assumptions people have about their social world.

- We can expose these assumptions by intentionally breaking the "rules" of social interaction and observing the reactions of other people.   **p. 93**

Both **culture** and **social class** shape the reality people construct.

- For example, a "short walk" for a New Yorker is a few city blocks, but for a peasant in Latin America, it could be a few miles.   **p. 93**

social construction of reality (p. 91) the process by which people creatively shape reality through social interaction

Thomas theorem (p. 93) W. I. Thomas's claim that situations defined as real are real in their consequences

ethnomethodology (p. 93) Harold Garfinkel's term for the study of the way people make sense of their everyday surroundings

Dramaturgical Analysis: The "Presentation of Self"

Dramaturgical analysis explores social interaction in terms of theatrical performance: A status operates as a part in a play and a role is a script.

[●] Read the **Document** on **mysoclab.com**

Performances are the way we present ourselves to others.
- Performances are both conscious (intentional action) and unconscious (nonverbal communication).
- Performances include costume (the way we dress), props (objects we carry), and demeanor (tone of voice and the way we carry ourselves). **p. 94**

Gender affects performances because men typically have greater social power than women. Gender differences involve *demeanor*, *use of space*, and *staring*, *smiling*, and *touching*.
- **Demeanor**—With greater social power, men have more freedom in how they act.
- **Use of space**—Men typically command more space than women.
- **Staring** and **touching** are generally done by men to women.
- **Smiling**, as a way to please another, is more commonly done by women. **pp. 95–96**

Idealization of performances means we try to convince others that our actions reflect ideal culture rather than selfish motives. **p. 96**

Embarrassment is the "loss of face" in a performance. People use **tact** to help others "save face." **pp. 96–97**

dramaturgical analysis (p. 94) Erving Goffman's term for the study of social interaction in terms of theatrical performance

presentation of self (p. 94) Erving Goffman's term for a person's efforts to create specific impressions in the minds of others

nonverbal communication (p. 94) communication using body movements, gestures, and facial expressions rather than speech

personal space (p. 95) the surrounding area over which a person makes some claim to privacy

Interaction in Everyday Life: Three Applications

Emotions: The Social Construction of **Feeling**

The same basic emotions are biologically programmed into all human beings, but culture guides what triggers emotions, how people display emotions, and how people value emotions. In everyday life, the presentation of self involves managing emotions as well as behavior. **pp. 97–98**

Language: The Social Construction of **Gender**

Gender is an important element of everyday interaction. Language defines women and men as different types of people, reflecting the fact that society attaches greater power and value to what is viewed as masculine. **pp. 98–99**

Reality Play: The Social Construction of **Humor**

Humor results from the difference between conventional and unconventional definitions of a situation. Because humor is a part of culture, people around the world find different situations funny. **pp. 99–101**

(◉) Watch the **Video** on **mysoclab.com**

5 Groups and Organizations

Learning Objectives

Remember the definitions of the key terms highlighted in boldfaced type throughout this chapter.

Understand that, over the course of history, our society has gradually become more reliant on large, formal organizations.

Apply research about group conformity to familiar events in everyday life.

Analyze the growing concern about personal privacy in our modern society.

Evaluate the benefits and challenges of living in a highly rational society.

Create a greater ability to live effectively and more happily within a world of large, formal organizations.

We spend most of our lives within the collectivities that sociologists call social groups and formal organizations. This chapter begins by analyzing social groups, both small and large, highlighting the differences between them. Then the focus shifts to formal organizations that carry out various tasks in our modern society. ■

With the workday over, Juan and Jorge pushed through the doors of the local McDonald's restaurant. "Man, am I hungry," announced Juan, heading right into line. "Look at all the meat I'm gonna eat." But Jorge, a recent immigrant from a small village in Guatemala, is surveying the room with a sociological eye. "There is much more than food to see here. This place is all about America!"

And so it is, as we shall see. But back in 1948, when the story of McDonald's began, people in Pasadena, California, paid little attention to the opening of a new restaurant by brothers Maurice and Richard McDonald. The McDonald brothers' basic concept, which was soon called "fast food," was to serve meals quickly and cheaply to large numbers of people. The brothers trained employees to do highly specialized jobs: One person grilled hamburgers while others "dressed" them, made French fries, whipped up milkshakes, and handed the food to the customers in assembly-line fashion.

As the years went by, the McDonald brothers prospered, and they opened several more restaurants, including one in San Bernardino. It was there, in 1954, that Ray Kroc, a traveling blender and mixer salesman, paid them a visit.

Kroc was fascinated by the efficiency of the McDonald brothers' system and saw the potential for expanding into a nationwide chain of fast-food restaurants. The three launched the plan as partners. Soon, Kroc bought out the McDonalds (who returned to running their original restaurant) and went on to become one of the great success stories of all time. Today, McDonald's is one of the most widely known brand names in the world, with more than 33,000 restaurants serving 64 million people daily throughout the United States and in 118 other countries (McDonald's, 2011).

The success of McDonald's points to more than just the popularity of burgers and French fries. The organizational principles that guide this company are coming to dominate social life in the United States and elsewhere. As Jorge correctly observed, this one small business not only transformed the restaurant industry but also changed our way of life.

We begin this chapter by looking at *social groups,* the clusters of people with whom we interact in our daily lives. As you will learn, the scope of group life expanded greatly during the twentieth century. From a world of families, local neighborhoods, and small businesses, our society now relies on the operation of huge corporations and other bureaucracies that sociologists describe as *formal organizations.* Understanding this expansion of social life and appreciating what it means for us as individuals are the main objectives of this chapter.

Social Groups

Understand

Almost everyone wants a sense of belonging, which is the essence of group life. A **social group** is *two or more people who identify with and interact with one another.* Human beings come together in couples, families, circles of friends, churches, clubs, businesses, neighborhoods, and large organizations. Whatever the form, groups contain people with shared experiences, loyalties, and interests. While keeping their individuality, members of social groups also think of themselves as a special "we."

Not every collection of individuals forms a group. People with a status in common, such as women, African Americans, homeowners, soldiers, millionaires, college graduates, and Roman Catholics, are not a group but a *category*. Though they know that others hold the same status, most are strangers to one another. Similarly, students sitting in a large stadium interact to a very limited extent. Such a loosely formed collection of people in one place is a *crowd* rather than a group.

However, the right circumstances can quickly turn a crowd into a group. Events from power failures to terrorist attacks can make people bond quickly with strangers.

Primary and Secondary Groups

Friends often greet one another with a smile and the simple phrase "Hi! How are you?" The response is usually "Fine, thanks. How about you?" This answer is often more scripted than sincere. Explaining how you are *really* doing might make people feel so awkward that they would beat a hasty retreat.

Social groups are of two types, based on their members' degree of personal concern for one another. According to Charles Horton Cooley (1864–1929), a **primary group** is *a small social group whose members share personal and lasting relationships.* Joined by *primary relationships,* people spend a great deal of time together, engage in a wide range of activities, and feel that they know one another pretty well. In short, they show real concern for one another. The family is every society's most important primary group.

Cooley called personal and tightly integrated groups "primary" because they are among the first groups we experience in life. In addition, family and friends have primary importance in the socialization process, shaping our attitudes, behavior, and social identity.

Members of primary groups help one another in many ways, but they generally think of their group as an end in itself rather than as a means to other ends. In other words, we tend to think that family and friendship link people who "belong together." Members of a primary group also tend to view each other as unique and irreplaceable. Especially in the family, we are bound to others by emotion and loyalty. Brothers and sisters may not always get along, but they always remain "family."

In contrast to the primary group, the **secondary group** is *a large and impersonal social group whose members pursue a specific goal or activity.* In most respects, secondary groups have characteristics opposite to those of primary groups. *Secondary relationships* involve weak emotional ties and little personal knowledge of one another. Many secondary groups exist for only a short time, beginning and ending without particular significance. Students

As human beings, we live our lives as members of groups. Such groups may be large or small, temporary or long-lasting, and can be based on kinship, cultural heritage, or some shared interest.

---

social group two or more people who identify with and interact with one another

primary group a small social group whose members share personal and lasting relationships

secondary group a large and impersonal social group whose members pursue a specific goal or activity

---

enrolled in the same course at a large university—people who may or may not see one another again after the semester ends—are one example of a secondary group.

Secondary groups include many more people than primary groups. For example, dozens or even hundreds of people may work in the same company, yet most of them pay only passing attention to one another. Sometimes the passage of time transforms a group from secondary to primary, as with co-workers who share an office for many years and develop closer relationships. But generally, members of a secondary group do not think of themselves as "we." Secondary ties need not be hostile or cold, of course. Interactions among students, co-workers, and business associates are often quite pleasant even if they are impersonal.

Unlike members of primary groups, who display a *personal orientation,* people in secondary groups have a *goal orientation.* Primary group members define each other according to *who* they are in terms of family ties or personal qualities, but people in secondary groups look to one another for *what* they are, that is, what they can do for each other. In secondary groups, we tend to "keep score," aware of what we give others and what we receive in return. This goal orientation means that secondary group members usually remain formal and polite. It is in a secondary relationship, therefore, that we ask the question "How are you?" without expecting a truthful answer.

The Summing Up table on page 110 reviews the characteristics of primary and secondary groups. Keep in mind that these traits define two types of groups in ideal terms; most real groups contain elements of both. For example, a women's group on a university campus may be quite large (and therefore secondary), but its members may identify strongly with one another and provide lots of mutual support (making it seem primary).

Many people think that small towns and rural areas emphasize primary relationships and that large cities are characterized by secondary ties. This generalization is partly true, but some urban neighborhoods—especially those populated by people of a single ethnic or religious category—can be very tightly knit.

Group Leadership

How do groups operate? One important element of group dynamics is leadership. Although a small circle of friends may have no leader at all, most large secondary groups place leaders in a formal chain of command.

Two Leadership Roles

Groups typically benefit from two kinds of leadership. **Instrumental leadership** refers to *group leadership that focuses on the completion of tasks*. Members look to instrumental leaders to make plans, give orders, and get things done. **Expressive leadership**, by contrast, is *group leadership that focuses on the group's well-being*. Expressive leaders take less interest in achieving goals and focus on promoting the well-being of members and minimizing tension and conflict among members.

Because they concentrate on performance, instrumental leaders usually have formal, secondary relationships with other members. These leaders give orders and reward or punish people according to how much they contribute to the group's efforts. Expressive leaders build more personal, primary ties. They offer sympathy to members going through tough times, keep the group united, and lighten serious moments with humor. Typically, successful instrumental leaders enjoy more *respect* from members and expressive leaders generally receive more personal *affection*.

Three Leadership Styles

Sociologists also describe leadership in terms of its decision-making style. *Authoritarian leadership* focuses on instrumental concerns, takes personal charge of decision making, and demands that group members obey orders. Although this leadership style may win little affection from the group, a fast-acting authoritarian leader is appreciated in a crisis.

Democratic leadership is more expressive, making a point of including everyone in the decision-making process. Although less successful in a crisis situation, when there is little time for discussion, democratic leaders generally draw on the ideas of all members to develop creative solutions to problems.

Laissez-faire leadership allows the group to function more or less on its own (*laissez-faire* in French means "leave it alone"). This style is typically the least effective in promoting group goals (White & Lippitt, 1953; Ridgeway, 1983).

Group Conformity

Groups influence the behavior of their members, often promoting conformity. "Fitting in" provides a secure feeling of belonging, but at the extreme, group pressure can be unpleasant and even dangerous. Interestingly, as experiments by Solomon Asch and Stanley Milgram showed, even strangers can encourage group conformity.

Asch's Research

Solomon Asch (1952) recruited students for what he told them was a study of visual perception. Before the experiment began, he explained to all but one member of a small group that their real purpose was to put pressure on the remaining person. Placing six to eight students around a table, Asch showed them a "standard" line, as drawn on Card 1 in Figure 5–1, and asked them to match it to one of three lines on Card 2.

Anyone with normal vision can see that the line marked "A" on Card 2 is the correct choice. Initially, as planned, everyone made the matches correctly. But then Asch's secret accomplices began answering incorrectly, leaving the uninformed student (seated at the table so as to answer next to last) bewildered and uncomfortable.

What happened? Asch found that one-third of all subjects chose to conform by answering incorrectly. Apparently, many of us are willing to compromise our own judgment to avoid the discomfort of being different, even from people we do not know.

Milgram's Research

Stanley Milgram, a former student of Solomon Asch's, conducted conformity experiments of his own. In Milgram's controversial study (1963, 1965; A. G. Miller, 1986), a researcher explained to male recruits that they would be taking part in a study of how punishment affects learning. One by one, he assigned them to the role of teacher and placed another person—actually an accomplice of Milgram's—in a connecting room to pose as a learner.

The teacher watched as the learner sat down in what looked like an electric chair. The researcher applied electrode paste to one of the learner's wrists, explaining that this would "prevent blisters and burns." The researcher then attached an electrode to the wrist and secured the leather straps, explaining that they would "prevent

---

Summing Up

Primary Groups and Secondary Groups

	Primary Group	Secondary Group
Quality of relationships	Personal orientation	Goal orientation
Duration of relationships	Usually long-term	Variable; often short-term
Breadth of relationships	Broad; usually involving many activities	Narrow; usually involving few activities
Perception of relationships	Ends in themselves	Means to an end
Examples	Families, circles of friends	Co-workers, political organizations

excessive movement while the learner was being shocked." Although the shocks would be painful, the researcher reassured the teacher, they would cause "no permanent tissue damage."

The researcher then led the teacher back into the adjoining room, pointing out that the "electric chair" was connected to a "shock generator," actually a phony but realistic-looking piece of equipment with a label that read "Shock Generator, Type ZLB, Dyson Instrument Company, Waltham, Mass." On the front was a dial that supposedly regulated electric current from 15 volts (labeled "Slight Shock") to 300 volts ("Intense Shock") to 450 volts ("Danger: Severe Shock").

Seated in front of the "shock generator," the teacher was told to read aloud pairs of words. Then the teacher was to repeat the first word of each pair and wait for the learner to recall the second word. Whenever the learner failed to answer correctly, the teacher was told to apply an electric shock.

The researcher directed the teacher to begin at the lowest level (15 volts) and to increase the shock by 15 volts every time the learner made a mistake. And so the teacher did. At 75, 90, and 105 volts, the teacher heard moans from the learner; at 120 volts, shouts of pain; by 270 volts, screams; at 315 volts, pounding on the wall; after that, dead silence. Only a few of the forty subjects assigned to the role of teacher during the initial research even questioned the procedure before reaching the dangerous level of 300 volts, and twenty-six of the subjects—almost two-thirds—went all the way to the potentially lethal 450 volts. Even Milgram was surprised at how readily people obeyed authority figures.

Milgram (1964) then modified his research to see whether ordinary people—not authority figures—could pressure strangers to administer electrical shocks, in the same way that Asch's groups had pressured individuals to match lines incorrectly.

This time, Milgram formed a group of three teachers, two of whom were his accomplices. Each of the teachers was to suggest a shock level when the learner made an error; the rule was that the group would then administer the *lowest* of the three suggested levels. This arrangement gave the person not in on the experiment the power to deliver a lesser shock regardless of what the others said.

The accomplices suggested increasing the shock level with each error the learner made, putting pressure on the third person to do the same. The subjects in these groups applied voltages three to four times higher than those applied by subjects acting alone. Thus Milgram's research suggests that people are likely to follow the directions not only of legitimate authority figures but also of groups of ordinary individuals, even if doing so means harming another person.

Janis's "Groupthink"

Experts also cave in to group pressure, says Irving L. Janis (1972, 1989). Janis argues that a number of U.S. foreign policy blunders, including the failure to foresee the Japanese attack on Pearl Harbor during World War II and our ill-fated involvement in the Vietnam War, resulted from group conformity among our highest-ranking political leaders.

Common sense tells us that group discussion improves decision making. Janis counters that group members often seek agreement that closes off other points of view. Janis called this process **groupthink**, *the tendency of group members to conform, resulting in a narrow view of some issue.*

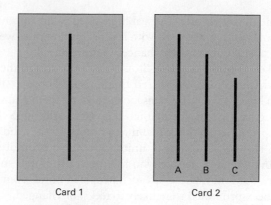

FIGURE 5–1 Cards Used in Asch's Experiment in Group Conformity

In Asch's experiment, subjects were asked to match the line on Card 1 to one of the lines on Card 2. Many subjects agreed with the wrong answers given by others in their group.

Source: Asch (1952).

A classic example of groupthink resulted in the disastrous U.S. invasion of the Bay of Pigs in Cuba in 1961. Looking back, Arthur Schlesinger Jr., an adviser to President Kennedy at the time, confessed to feeling guilty for "having kept so quiet during those crucial discussions in the Cabinet Room," adding that the group discouraged anyone from challenging what, in hindsight, Schlesinger considered "nonsense" (quoted in Janis, 1972:30, 40). Groupthink may also have been a factor in the U.S. invasion of Iraq in 2003, when U.S. leaders were led to believe—erroneously—that Iraq had stockpiles of weapons of mass destruction. Closer to home, one professor suggests that college faculties are subject to groupthink because they share political attitudes that are overwhelmingly liberal (Klein, 2010).

Reference Groups

How do we assess our own attitudes and behavior? Frequently, we use a **reference group**, *a social group that serves as a point of reference in making evaluations and decisions.*

A young man who imagines his family's response to a woman he is dating is using his family as a reference group. A supervisor who tries to predict her employees' reaction to a new vacation policy is using them in the same way. As these examples suggest, reference groups can be primary or secondary. In either case, our need to conform shows how others' attitudes affect us.

We also use groups that we do *not* belong to for reference. Being well prepared for a job interview means showing up dressed the way people in that company dress for work. Conforming to groups we do not belong to is a strategy to win acceptance and illustrates the process of *anticipatory socialization*, described in Chapter 3 ("Socialization: From Infancy to Old Age").

Stouffer's Research

Samuel Stouffer and his colleagues (1949) conducted a classic study of reference groups during World War II. Researchers asked soldiers to rate their own, or any competent soldier's, chances of promotion in their army unit. You might guess that soldiers serving in outfits with high promotion rates would be optimistic about advancement. Yet Stouffer's research pointed to the opposite conclusion: Soldiers in army units with low promotion rates were actually more positive about their chances to move ahead.

The key to understanding Stouffer's results lies in the groups against which soldiers measured themselves. Those assigned to units with lower promotion rates looked around them and saw people making no more headway than they were. Although they had not been promoted, neither had many others, so they did not feel deprived. However, soldiers in units with higher promotion rates could think of many people who had been promoted sooner or more often than they had. With such people in mind, even soldiers who had been promoted were likely to feel shortchanged.

The point is that we do not make judgments about ourselves in isolation, nor do we compare ourselves with just anyone. Regardless of our situation in *absolute* terms, we form a subjective sense of our well-being by looking at ourselves *relative* to specific reference groups.

In-Groups and Out-Groups

Each of us favors some groups over others, whether because of political outlook, social prestige, or just manner of dress. On some college campuses, for example, left-leaning student activists may look down on fraternity members, whom they view as conservative; fraternity members, in turn, may snub the "nerds" who work too hard. People in just about every social setting make similar positive and negative evaluations of members of other groups.

Such judgments illustrate another key element of group dynamics: the opposition of in-groups and out-groups. An **in-group** is *a social group toward which a member feels respect and loyalty*. An

out-group, by contrast, is *a social group toward which a person feels a sense of competition or opposition*. In-groups and out-groups are based on the idea that "we" have valued traits that "they" lack.

Tensions between groups sharpen the groups' boundaries and give people a clearer social identity. However, members of in-groups generally hold overly positive views of themselves and unfairly negative views of various out-groups.

Power also plays a part in intergroup relations. A powerful in-group can define others as a lower-status out-group. Historically, in countless U.S. towns and cities, many white people viewed people of color as an out-group and subordinated them socially, politically, and economically. Internalizing these negative attitudes, minorities often struggled to overcome negative self-images. In this way, in-groups and out-groups foster loyalty but also generate conflict (Tajfel, 1982; Bobo & Hutchings, 1996).

Group Size

The next time you go to a party, try to arrive first. If you do, you will be able to observe some fascinating group dynamics. Until about six people enter the room, every person who arrives usually joins in a single conversation. As more people arrive, the group divides into two or more clusters, and it divides again and again as the party grows. This process shows that group size plays a crucial role in how group members interact.

To understand why, note the mathematical number of relationships among two to seven people. As shown in Figure 5–2, two people form a single relationship; adding a third person results in three relationships; adding a fourth person yields six. Increasing the number of people further boosts the number of relationships much more rapidly because every new individual can interact with everyone already there. Thus by the time seven people join one conversation, twenty-one "channels" connect them. With so many open channels, at this point the group usually divides into smaller conversation groups.

The Dyad

The German sociologist Georg Simmel (1858–1918) explored the dynamics in the smallest social groups. Simmel (1950, orig. 1902) used the term **dyad** (Greek for "pair") to designate *a social group with two members*. Simmel explained that social interaction in a dyad is typically more intense than in larger groups because neither member must share the other's attention with anyone else. In the United States, love affairs, marriages, and the closest friendships are dyadic.

But like a stool with only two legs, dyads are unstable. Both members of a dyad must work to keep the relationship going; if either withdraws, the group collapses. To make marriage more stable, society supports the marital dyad with legal, economic, and often religious ties.

The Triad

Simmel also studied the **triad**, *a social group with three members*. A triad contains three relationships, each of which unites two of the three people. A triad is more stable than a dyad because one member can act as a mediator if relations between the other two become strained. This analysis of group dynamics helps explain why members of a dyad (say, spouses having conflict) often seek out a third person (such as a marriage counselor) to discuss tensions between them.

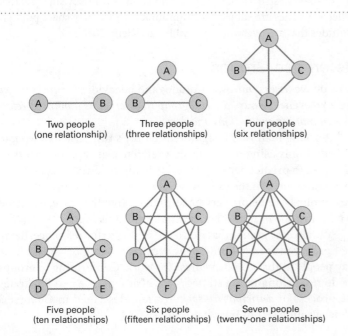

FIGURE 5–2 Group Size and Relationships

As the number of people in a group increases, the number of relationships that link them increases much faster. By the time six or seven people share a conversation, the group usually divides into two. Why are relationships in smaller groups typically more intense?

Source: Created by the author.

The triad, illustrated by Jonathan Green's painting *Friends*, includes three people. A triad is more stable than a dyad because conflict between any two persons can be mediated by the third member. Even so, should the relationship between any two become more intense in a positive sense, those two are likely to exclude the third.

Jonathan Green, *Friends*, 1992. Oil on masonite, 14 in. × 11 in. © Jonathan Green, Naples, Florida. Collection of Patric McCoy.

On the other hand, two of the three can pair up to press their views on the third, or two may intensify their relationship, leaving the other feeling left out. For example, when two of the three members of a triad develop a romantic interest in each other, they will come to understand the meaning of the old saying, "Two's company, three's a crowd."

As groups grow beyond three people, they become more stable and capable of withstanding the loss of one or more members. At the same time, increases in group size reduce the intense interaction possible in only the smallest groups. This is why larger groups are based less on personal attachment and more on formal rules and regulations.

Social Diversity: Race, Class, and Gender

Race, ethnicity, class, and gender each play a part in group dynamics. Peter Blau (1977; Blau, Blum, & Schwartz, 1982; South & Messner, 1986) points out three ways in which social diversity influences intergroup contact:

1. **Large groups turn inward.** Blau explains that the larger a group is, the more likely its members are to concentrate relationships among themselves. Say a college is trying to enhance social diversity by increasing the number of international students. These students may add a dimension of difference, but as their numbers rise they become more likely to form their own social group. Thus efforts to promote social diversity may have the unintended effect of promoting separatism.

2. **Heterogeneous groups turn outward.** The more socially diverse a group is, the more likely its members are to interact with outsiders. Campus groups that recruit people of both sexes and various social backgrounds typically have more intergroup contact than those with members of one social category.

3. **Physical boundaries create social boundaries.** To the extent that a social group is physically segregated from others (by having its own dorm or dining area, for example), its members are less likely to interact with other people.

Networks

A **network** is *a web of weak social ties*. Think of a network as a "fuzzy" group containing people who come into occasional contact but lack a sense of boundaries and belonging. If you think of a *group* as a "circle of friends," think of a *network* as a "social web" expanding outward, often reaching great distances and including large numbers of people.

The largest network of all is the World Wide Web of the Internet. But the Internet has expanded much more in some global regions than in others. Global Map 5–1 on page 114 shows that Internet use is high in rich countries such as the United States and the countries of Western Europe and far less common in poor nations in Africa and Southeast Asia.

Some networks come close to being groups, as in the case of college friends who stay in touch years after graduation by e-mail and telephone. More commonly, however, a network includes people we know of or who know of us but with whom we interact rarely, if at all. As one woman known as a community organizer puts it, "I get calls at home, [and] someone says, 'Are you Roseann Navarro? Somebody told me to call you. I have this problem . . . .'" (quoted in Kaminer, 1984:94).

Network ties often give us the sense that we live in a "small world." In a classic experiment, Stanley Milgram (1967; Watts, 1999) gave letters to subjects in Kansas and Nebraska intended for specific people in Boston who were unknown to the original subjects. No addresses were given, and the subjects in the study were told to send the letters to others they knew personally who might know the target people. Milgram found that the target people received the letters with, on average, six subjects passing them on. This result led Milgram to conclude that everyone is connected to everyone else by "six degrees of separation." Later research, however, has cast doubt on Milgram's conclusions. Examining Milgram's original data, Judith Kleinfeld noted that most of Milgram's letters (240 out of 300) never arrived at all (Wildavsky, 2002). Most of those that did reach their destination had been given to people who were wealthy, a fact that led Kleinfeld to conclude that rich people are better connected across the country than ordinary men and women. Illustrating this assertion, convicted swindler Bernard Madoff was able to recruit more than 5,000 clients entirely through his extensive business networks, with one new client encouraging others to sign up. In the end, these people and organizations lost some $50 billion in the largest Ponzi pyramid scheme of all time (Lewis, 2010).

Network ties may be weak, but they can be a powerful resource. For immigrants who are trying to become established in a new community, businesspeople seeking to expand their operations, or new

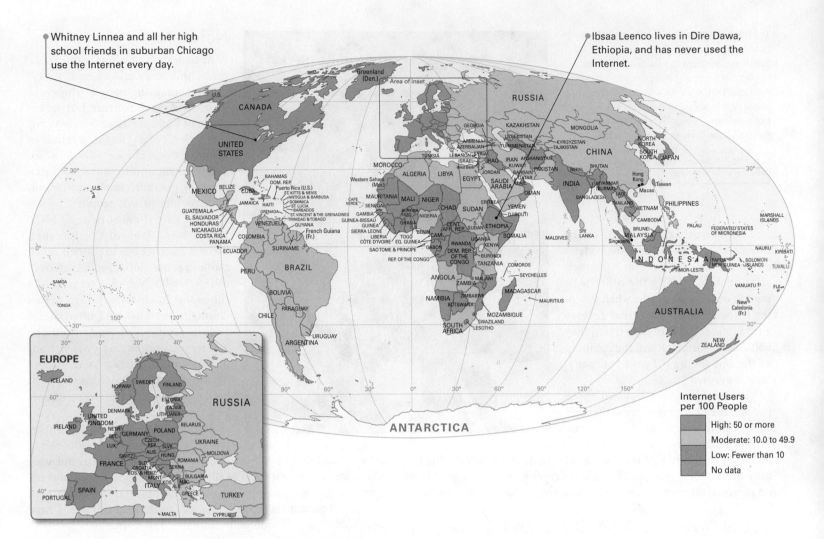

Whitney Linnea and all her high school friends in suburban Chicago use the Internet every day.

Ibsaa Leenco lives in Dire Dawa, Ethiopia, and has never used the Internet.

Internet Users per 100 People

- High: 50 or more
- Moderate: 10.0 to 49.9
- Low: Fewer than 10
- No data

Window on the World

GLOBAL MAP 5–1 Internet Users in Global Perspective

This map shows how the Information Revolution has affected countries around the world. In most high-income nations, at least one-half of the population uses the Internet. By contrast, only a small share of people in low-income nations does so. What effect does this pattern have on people's access to information? What does this mean for the future in terms of global inequality?

Source: International Telecommunications Union (2011).

college graduates looking for a job, *whom* you know is often just as important as *what* you know (Hagan, 1998; Petersen, Saporta, & Seidel, 2000).

Networks are based on people's colleges, clubs, neighborhoods, political parties, religious organizations, and personal interests. Obviously, some networks are made up of people with more wealth, power, and prestige than others; that explains the importance of being "well connected." The networks of more privileged categories of people—such as the members of a country club—are a valuable form of "social capital," which is more likely to lead people in these categories to higher-paying jobs (Green, Tigges, & Diaz, 1999; Lin, Cook, & Burt, 2001).

Some people also have denser networks than others; that is, they are connected to more people. Typically, the largest social networks include those who are affluent, young, well educated, and living in large cities. Typically, about half of the

individuals in a person's social network change over a period of seven years (Fernandez & Weinberg, 1997; Podolny & Baron, 1997; Mollenhorst, 2009).

Gender also shapes networks. Although the networks of men and women are typically of the same size, women include more relatives (and more women) in their networks, and men include more co-workers (and more men). Women's ties, therefore, may not be quite as powerful as typical "old-boy" networks. But research suggests that as gender equality increases in the United States, the networks of men and women are becoming more alike (Reskin & McBrier, 2000; Torres & Huffman, 2002).

Explore membership in one of our country's largest formal organizations—the military—in your local community and in counties across the United States on **mysoclab.com**

Formal Organizations

● Understand

As noted earlier, a century ago, most people lived in small groups of family, friends, and neighbors. Today, our lives revolve more and more around **formal organizations**, *large secondary groups organized to achieve their goals efficiently.* Formal organizations, such as corporations and government agencies, differ from small primary groups in their impersonality and their formally planned atmosphere.

When you think about it, organizing more than 300 million members of U.S. society is truly remarkable, whether it involves paving roads, collecting taxes, schooling children, or delivering the mail. To carry out most of these tasks, we rely on large formal organizations.

Types of Formal Organizations

Amitai Etzioni (1975) identified three types of formal organizations, distinguished by the reasons people participate in them: utilitarian organizations, normative organizations, and coercive organizations.

Utilitarian Organizations

Just about everyone who works for income belongs to a *utilitarian organization,* one that pays people for their efforts. Becoming part of a utilitarian organization—a business, government agency, or school system, for example—is usually a matter of individual choice, although most people must join one or another such organization to make a living.

Normative Organizations

People join *normative organizations* not for income but to pursue some goal they think is morally worthwhile. Sometimes called *voluntary associations,* these include community service groups (such as Amnesty International, the PTA, the League of Women Voters, and the Red Cross), political parties, and religious organizations. In global perspective, people in the United States and in other high-income nations are the most likely to join voluntary associations. A recent study found that 73 percent of first-year college students in the United States said they had participated in some organized volunteer activity within the past year (Pryor et al., 2010; see also Curtis, Baer, & Grabb, 2001; Schofer & Fourcade-Gourinchas, 2001).

Coercive Organizations

Coercive organizations have involuntary memberships. People are forced to join these organizations as a form of punishment (prisons) or treatment (some psychiatric hospitals). Coercive organizations have special physical features, such as locked

The 2010 film *The Social Network* depicts the birth of Facebook, now one of the largest social networking sites in the world. In what ways have Internet-based social networks changed social life in the United States?

---

rationalization of society the historical change from tradition to rationality as the main type of human thought

tradition values and beliefs passed from generation to generation

rationality a way of thinking that emphasizes deliberate, matter-of-fact calculation of the most efficient way to accomplish a particular task

---

doors and barred windows, and are supervised by security personnel. They isolate people (whom they label "inmates" or "patients") for a period of time in order to radically change their attitudes and behavior. Recall from Chapter 3 ("Socialization: From Infancy to Old Age") the power of a total institution to change a person's sense of self.

It is possible for a single organization to fall into *all* of these categories from the point of view of different individuals. For example, a mental hospital serves as a coercive organization for a patient, a utilitarian organization for a psychiatrist, and a normative organization for a hospital volunteer.

Origins of Formal Organizations

Formal organizations date back thousands of years. Elites who controlled early empires relied on government officials to collect taxes, undertake military campaigns, and build monumental structures, from the Great Wall of China to the pyramids of Egypt.

However, early organizations had two limitations. First, they lacked the technology to travel over large distances, to communicate quickly, and to gather and store information. Second, the preindustrial societies they were trying to rule had traditional cultures. **Tradition**, according to the German sociologist Max Weber, consists of *values and beliefs passed from generation to generation.* Tradition makes a society conservative, Weber explained, because it limits an organization's efficiency and ability to change.

By contrast, Weber described the modern worldview as **rationality**, *a way of thinking that emphasizes deliberate, matter-of-fact calculation of the most efficient way to accomplish a particular task.* A rational worldview pays little attention to the past and is open to any changes that might get the job done better or more quickly.

The rise of the "organizational society" rests on what Weber called the **rationalization of society**, *the historical change from tradition to rationality as the main type of human thought.* Modern society, he claimed, becomes "disenchanted" as sentimental ties give way to a rational focus on science, complex technology, and the organizational structure called bureaucracy.

Characteristics of Bureaucracy

Bureaucracy is *an organizational model rationally designed to perform tasks efficiently.* Bureaucratic officials regularly create and revise policy to increase efficiency. To appreciate the power and scope of bureaucratic organization, consider that any one of more than 400 million telephones in the United States can connect you within seconds to any other phone in a home, a business, an automobile, or even a hiker's backpack on a remote trail in the Rocky Mountains. Such instant communication is beyond the imagination of people who lived in the ancient world.

Our telephone system depends on technology such as electricity, fiber optics, and computers. But the system could not exist without the organizational capacity to keep track of every telephone call—recording which phone called which other phone, when, and for how long—and presenting all this information to more than 300 million telephone users in the form of a monthly bill (FCC, 2010; CTIA, 2011).

What specific traits promote organizational efficiency? Max Weber (1978, orig. 1921) identified six key elements of the ideal bureaucratic organization:

1. **Specialization.** Our ancestors spent most of their time looking for food and finding shelter. Bureaucracy, by contrast, assigns individuals highly specialized jobs.

2. **Hierarchy of offices.** Bureaucracies arrange workers in a vertical ranking. Each person is thus supervised by someone "higher up" in the organization while in turn supervising others in lower positions. Usually, with few people at the top and many at the bottom, bureaucratic organizations take the form of a pyramid.

3. **Rules and regulations.** Rationally enacted rules and regulations guide a bureaucracy's operation. Ideally, a bureaucracy seeks to operate in a completely predictable way.

4. **Technical competence.** Bureaucratic officials have the technical competence to carry out their duties. Bureaucracies typically hire new members according to set standards and then monitor their performance. Such impersonal evaluation contrasts with the ancient custom of favoring relatives, whatever their talents, over strangers.

5. **Impersonality.** Bureaucracy puts rules ahead of personal whim so that both clients and workers are all treated in the same way. From this impersonal approach comes the commonplace image of the "faceless bureaucrat."

6. **Formal, written communications.** It is often said that the heart of bureaucracy is not people but paperwork. Rather than casual, face-to-face talk, bureaucracy depends on formal, written memos and reports, which accumulate in vast files.

Bureaucratic organization promotes efficiency by carefully hiring workers and limiting the unpredictable effects of personal taste and opinion. The Summing Up table reviews the differences between small social groups and large formal organizations.

Organizational Environment

All organizations exist in the larger world. How well any organization performs depends not only on its own goals and policies but also on the **organizational environment**, *factors outside an organization that affect its operation.* These factors include technology, economic and political trends, current events, the available workforce, and other organizations.

Modern organizations are shaped by *technology*, including copiers, telephones, and computer equipment. Computers give employees access to more information and people than ever before. At the same time, computer technology allows managers to monitor the activities of workers much more closely than in the past (Markoff, 1991).

Economic and political trends affect organizations. All organizations are helped or hurt by periodic economic growth or recession. Most industries also face competition from abroad as well as changes in laws—such as new environmental standards—at home.

Population patterns also affect organizations. The average age, typical level of education, social diversity, and size of a local community determine the available workforce and sometimes the market for an organization's products or services.

Current events can have significant effects even on organizations that are far away. Events such as the economic instability in Europe, the sweeping political changes in the Middle East, and the current level of consumer confidence affect the operation of both government and business organizations.

Other organizations also contribute to the organizational environment. To be competitive, a hospital must be responsive to the insurance industry and to organizations representing doctors, nurses, and other health care workers. It must also be aware of the medical equipment, health care procedures, and prices available at nearby facilities.

The Informal Side of Bureaucracy

Weber's ideal bureaucracy deliberately regulates every activity. In real-life organizations, however, human beings are creative (and stubborn) enough to resist bureaucratic regulation. Informality may amount to cutting corners on the job at times, but it can also provide the flexibility needed for an organization to adapt and be successful.

In part, informality comes from the personalities of organizational leaders. Studies of U.S. corporations document that the qualities and quirks of individuals—including personal charisma, interpersonal skills, and the ability to recognize problems—can have a great effect on organizational performance (Halberstam, 1986; Baron, Hannan, & Burton, 1999).

Authoritarian, democratic, and laissez-faire types of leadership (described earlier in this chapter) reflect individual personality as

Weber described the operation of the ideal bureaucracy as rational and highly efficient. In real life, actual large organizations often operate very differently from Weber's model, as can be seen on the television show *30 Rock*.

Summing Up

Small Groups and Formal Organizations

	Small Groups	Formal Organizations
Activities	Much the same for all members	Distinct and highly specialized
Hierarchy	Often informal or nonexistent	Clearly defined, corresponding to offices
Norms	General norms, informally applied	Clearly defined rules and regulations
Membership criteria	Variable; often based on personal affection or kinship	Technical competence to carry out assigned tasks
Relationships	Variable and typically primary	Typically secondary, with selective primary ties
Communications	Typically casual and face-to-face	Typically formal and in writing
Focus	Person-oriented	Task-oriented

much as any organizational plan. Then, too, in the "real world" of organizations, leaders sometimes seek to benefit personally through abuse of organizational power. From the news media, we learn that many corporate leaders of banks and insurance companies that collapsed since the financial meltdown of 2008 walked off with multimillion-dollar "golden parachutes." Throughout the business world, leaders take credit for the efforts of the people who work for them, at least when things go well. For example, the importance of many secretaries is much greater than most people think, and certainly greater than a secretary's official job title and salary suggest.

Communication offers another example of organizational informality. Memos and other written documents are the formal way to spread information throughout an organization. Typically, however, people create informal networks, or "grapevines," that spread information quickly, if not always accurately. Grapevines, using word of mouth and e-mail, are particularly important to rank-and-file workers because higher-ups often try to keep important information from them.

The spread of e-mail has "flattened" organizations somewhat, allowing even the lowest-ranking employee to bypass immediate superiors and communicate directly with the organization's leader or all fellow employees at once. Some organizations consider such "open-channel" communication unwelcome and limit the use of e-mail. Leaders may also seek to protect themselves from a flood of messages each day. Microsoft Corporation (whose founder, Bill Gates, has an unlisted e-mail address that helps him limit his mail to a few hundred messages each day) has developed screens that filter out all messages except those from approved people (Gwynne & Dickerson, 1997).

Using new information technology together with age-old human ingenuity, members of formal organizations often find ways to personalize their work and surroundings. Such efforts suggest that we should take a closer look at some of the problems of bureaucracy.

Problems of Bureaucracy

We rely on bureaucracy to manage everyday life efficiently, but many people are uneasy about large organizations gaining too

much influence. Bureaucracy can dehumanize and manipulate us, and some say it poses a threat to political democracy. These dangers are discussed in the following sections.

Bureaucratic Alienation

Max Weber held up bureaucracy as a model of productivity. Yet Weber was keenly aware of bureaucracy's potential to *dehumanize* the people it is supposed to serve. The impersonality that fosters efficiency also keeps officials and clients from responding to each other's unique personal needs. Typically, officials treat each client impersonally as a standard "case." Sometimes the tendency toward dehumanization goes too far, as in 2008 when the U.S. Army accidentally sent letters to family members of soldiers killed in Iraq and Afghanistan, addressing the recipients as "John Doe" ("Army Apologizes," 2009).

Formal organizations create *alienation,* according to Weber, by reducing the human being to "a small cog in a ceaselessly moving mechanism" (1978:988, orig. 1921). Although formal organizations are designed to benefit humanity, Weber feared that people might well end up serving formal organizations.

Bureaucratic Inefficiency and Ritualism

On Labor Day 2005, as people in New Orleans and other coastal areas were battling to survive in the wake of Hurricane Katrina, 600 firefighters from around the country assembled in a hotel meeting room in Atlanta awaiting deployment. Officials of the Federal Emergency Management Agency (FEMA) explained to the crowd that they were first going to be given a lecture on "equal opportunity, sexual harassment, and customer service." Then, the official continued, they would each be given a stack of FEMA pamphlets with the agency's phone number to distribute to people in the devastated areas. A firefighter stood up and shouted, "This is ridiculous! Our fire departments and mayors sent us down here to save lives, and you've got us doing *this*?" The FEMA official thundered back, "You are now employees of FEMA, and you will follow orders and do what you are told!" ("Places," 2005:39).

People sometimes describe inefficiency by saying that an organization has too much "red tape," meaning that important work does not get done. The term "red tape" is derived from the ribbon used by slow-working eighteenth-century English administrators to wrap official parcels and records (Shipley, 1985).

To Robert Merton (1968), red tape amounts to a new twist on the already familiar concept of group conformity. He coined the term **bureaucratic ritualism** to describe *focusing on rules and regulations to the point of undermining an organization's goals*. In short, rules and regulations should be a means to an end, not an end in themselves that takes the focus away from the organization's stated goals. After the terrorist attacks of September 11, 2001, the U.S. Postal Service continued to help deliver mail addressed to Osama bin Laden to a post office in Afghanistan, despite the objections of the FBI. It took an act of Congress to change the policy (Bedard, 2002).

Bureaucratic Inertia

If bureaucrats sometimes have little reason to work very hard, they have every reason to protect their jobs. Thus officials typically work to keep an organization going even when its original goal has been realized. As Weber put it, "Once fully established, bureaucracy is among the social structures which are hardest to destroy" (1978:987, orig. 1921).

Bureaucratic inertia refers to *the tendency of bureaucratic organizations to perpetuate themselves*. Formal organizations tend to take on a life of their own beyond their formal objectives. For example, the U.S. Department of Agriculture has offices in nearly every county in all fifty states, even though only about one county in seven has any working farms and just 1 percent of the population works in farming. This governmental department now has an annual budget (about $130 billion) that exceeds the net farm income for the entire country (Hanson, 2011). Usually, an organization manages to stay in business by redefining its goals; for example, the Agriculture Department now performs a broad range of work not directly related to farming, including nutritional and environmental research.

Oligarchy

Early in the twentieth century, Robert Michels (1876–1936) pointed out the link between bureaucracy and political **oligarchy**, *the rule of the many by the few* (1949, orig. 1911). According to what Michels called the "iron law of oligarchy," the pyramid shape of bureaucracy places a few leaders in charge of the resources of the entire organization.

Weber believed that a strict hierarchy of responsibility resulted in high organizational efficiency. But Michels countered that hierarchy also weakens democracy because officials can and often do use their access to information, resources, and the media to promote their own personal interests.

Furthermore, bureaucracy helps distance officials from the public, as in the case of the corporate president or public official who is "unavailable for comment" to the local press or the national president who withholds documents from Congress claiming "executive privilege." Oligarchy, then, thrives in the hierarchical structure of bureaucracy and reduces leaders' accountability to the people.

Political competition, term limits, a system of checks and balances, and the law prevent the U.S. government from becoming an out-and-out oligarchy. Even so, in U.S. political races, candidates who have the visibility, power, and money that come with already being in office enjoy a significant advantage. In recent congressional elections, nearly 90 percent of congressional officeholders running for reelection were able to win reelection (Center for Responsive Politics, 2011).

The Evolution of Formal Organizations

 Analyze

The problems of bureaucracy—especially the alienation it produces and its tendency toward oligarchy—stem from two organizational traits: hierarchy and rigidity. To Weber, bureaucracy is a top-down system: Rules and regulations made at the top guide every part of people's work down the chain of command. A century ago in the United States, Weber's ideas took hold in an organizational model called *scientific management*. We take a look at this model and then examine three challenges over the course of the twentieth century that gradually have led to a new model: the *flexible organization*.

Scientific Management

Frederick Winslow Taylor (1911) had a simple message: Most businesses in the United States were sadly inefficient. Managers had little idea of how to increase their business's output, and workers relied on the same tired skills of earlier generations. To increase efficiency, Taylor explained, business should apply the principles of science. **Scientific management**, then, is *the application of scientific principles to the operation of a business or other large organization*.

⊙—⌐Watch the video "Frederick Taylor and Scientific Management" on mysoclab.com

Scientific management involves three steps. First, managers carefully observe the job performed by each worker, identifying all the operations involved and measuring the time needed for each. Second, managers analyze their data, trying to discover ways for workers to perform each job more efficiently. For example, managers might decide to give workers different tools or to reposition various work operations within the factory. Third, management provides guidance and incentives for workers to do their jobs more efficiently. If a factory worker moves 20 tons of pig iron in one day, for example, management would show the worker how to do the job more efficiently and then provide higher wages as the worker's productivity rises. Taylor concluded that if scientific principles were applied to all the steps of the production process, companies would become more profitable, workers would earn higher wages, and consumers would pay lower prices.

A century ago, the auto pioneer Henry Ford put it this way: "Save ten steps a day for each of 12,000 employees, and you will have saved fifty miles of wasted motion and misspent energy" (Allen & Hyman, 1999:209). In the early 1900s, the Ford Motor Company and many other businesses followed Taylor's lead and made improvements in efficiency. Today, corporations review every aspect of their operations in an effort to increase efficiency and profitability.

The principles of scientific management do lead to greater productivity. But by breaking down work into small steps and giving managers close control over the working process, scientific management also leads to greater social inequality between managers and workers, a pattern that remains with us today.

As the decades passed, formal organizations faced other important challenges involving race and gender, rising competition from abroad, and the changing nature of work. We now take a brief look at each of these challenges and how they prompted organizations to change.

The First Challenge: Race and Gender

In the 1960s, critics claimed that big businesses and other organizations engaged in unfair hiring practices. Rather than hiring on the basis of competence as Weber had proposed, they routinely excluded women and other minorities, especially from positions of power. Hiring on the basis of competence is only partly a matter of fairness; it is also a matter of enlarging an organization's talent pool to promote efficiency.

Patterns of Privilege and Exclusion

In the early twenty-first century, as shown in Figure 5–3, non-Hispanic white men in the United States—32 percent of the working-age population—still held 64 percent of senior-level management jobs. Non-Hispanic white women made up 32 percent of the population, but they held just 24 percent of executive positions (U.S. Equal Employment Opportunity Commission, 2012). The members of other minorities lagged further behind.

Rosabeth Moss Kanter (1977; Kanter & Stein, 1979) points out that excluding women and minorities from the workplace ignores the talents of more than half the population. Furthermore, underrepresented people in an organization often feel like socially isolated out-groups: uncomfortably visible, taken less seriously, and with fewer chances for promotion. Sometimes what passes for "merit," or good work, in an organization is simply being of the right social category (Castilla, 2008).

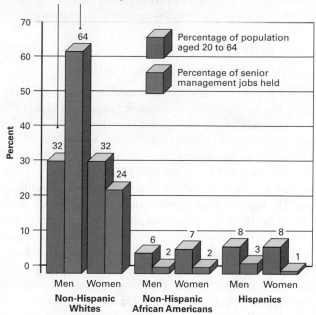

• Compared to their percentage of the total population, white men are overrepresented in senior management positions.

Diversity Snapshot

FIGURE 5–3 U.S. Managers in Private Industry by Race, Sex, and Ethnicity, 2010

White men are more likely than their population size suggests to be managers in private industry. The opposite is true for white women and other minorities. What factors do you think may account for this pattern?

Sources: U.S. Census Bureau (2011) and U.S. Equal Employment Opportunity Commission (2012).

Opening up an organization so that change and advancement happen more often, Kanter claims, improves everyone's on-the-job performance by motivating employees to become "fast-trackers" who work harder and are more committed to the company. By contrast, an organization with many dead-end jobs turns workers into less productive "zombies" who are never asked for their opinion on anything. An open organization encourages leaders to seek out the input of all employees, which usually improves decision making.

The "Female Advantage"

Some organizational researchers argue that women bring special management skills that strengthen an organization. According to Deborah Tannen (1994), women have a greater "information focus" and more readily ask questions in order to understand an issue. Men, by contrast, have an "image focus" that makes them wonder how asking questions in a particular situation will affect their reputation.

In another study of women executives, Sally Helgesen (1990) found three other gender-linked patterns. First, women place greater value on communication skills and share information more than men do. Second, women are more flexible leaders who typically give their employees greater freedom. Third, compared to men, women tend to emphasize the interconnectedness of all organizational operations. These patterns, which Helgesen dubbed the *female advantage*, help make companies more flexible and democratic.

In sum, one challenge to conventional bureaucracy is to become more open and flexible in order to take advantage of the experience, ideas, and creativity of everyone, regardless of race or gender. The result goes right to the bottom line: greater profits.

The Second Challenge: The Japanese Work Organization

In 1980, the corporate world in the United States was shaken to discover that the most popular automobile model sold in this country was not a Chevrolet, Ford, or Plymouth but the Honda Accord, made in Japan. Recently, the Japanese corporation Toyota passed General Motors to become the largest carmaker in the world (BBC, 2011). Ironically, as late as the 1950s, the label "Made in Japan" generally indicated that a product was cheap and poorly made. But times have changed. The success of the Japanese auto industry, as well as companies making electronics, cameras, and many other products, has drawn attention to the "Japanese work organization." How has so small a country been able to challenge the world's economic powerhouse?

Japanese organizations reflect that nation's strong collective spirit. In contrast to the U.S. emphasis on rugged individualism, the Japanese value cooperation. In effect, formal organizations in Japan are more like large primary groups. A generation ago, William Ouchi (1981) highlighted differences between formal organizations in Japan and in the United States. First, Japanese companies hired new workers in groups, giving everyone the same salary and responsibilities. Second, many Japanese companies hired workers for life, fostering a strong sense of loyalty. Third, with the idea that employees would spend their entire careers there, many Japanese organizations trained workers in all phases of their operations. Fourth, although Japanese corporate leaders took ultimate responsibility for their organization's performance, they involved workers in "quality circles" to discuss decisions that affected them. Fifth, Japanese companies played a large role in the lives of workers, providing home mortgages, sponsoring recreational activities, and scheduling social events. Together, such policies encourage much more loyalty among members of Japanese organizations than is typically the case in their U.S. counterparts.

Not everything has worked out well for Japanese corporations. About 1990, the Japanese economy entered a recession that has lasted for two decades. During this downturn, many Japanese companies changed their policies, no longer offering workers jobs for life or many of the other benefits noted by Ouchi. But the long-term outlook for Japanese business organizations remains bright.

In recent years, the widely admired Toyota corporation has also seen challenges. After expanding its operations to become the world's largest auto company, in 2010 Toyota was forced to announce recalls of millions of its vehicles due to mechanical problems, suggesting that one consequence of its rapid growth was losing focus on what had been the key to its success all along—quality (Saporito, 2010).

The Third Challenge: The Changing Nature of Work

Beyond rising global competition and the need to provide equal opportunity for all, pressure to modify conventional work organizations is also coming from changes in the nature of work itself. Over the past few decades, the economy of the United States has moved from industrial to postindustrial production. Rather than working in factories using heavy machinery to make *things,* more people today are using computers and other electronic technology to create or process *information.* A postindustrial society, then, is characterized by information-based organizations.

Frederick Taylor developed his concept of scientific management at a time when most jobs involved tasks that, though often backbreaking, were routine. Workers shoveled coal, poured liquid iron into molds, welded body panels to automobiles on an assembly line, or shot hot rivets into steel girders to build skyscrapers. In addition, a large part of the U.S. labor force in Taylor's day was made up of immigrants, most of whom had little schooling and many of whom knew little English. The routine nature of industrial jobs, coupled with the limited skills of the labor force, led Taylor to treat work as a series of fixed tasks set down by management and followed by employees.

Many of today's information age jobs are very different: The work of designers, artists, consultants, writers, editors, composers, programmers, business owners, and others now demands creativity and imagination. What does this mean for formal organizations? Here are several ways in which today's organizations differ from those of a century ago:

1. **Creative freedom.** As one Hewlett-Packard executive put it, "From their first day of work here, people are given important responsibilities and are encouraged to grow" (cited in Brooks, 2000:128). Today's organizations treat employees with information age skills as a vital resource. Executives can set production goals but cannot dictate how to accomplish tasks that require imagination and discovery. This gives highly skilled workers *creative freedom,* which means they are subject to less day-to-day supervision as long as they generate good results in the long run.

2. **Competitive work teams.** Many organizations allow several groups of employees to work on a problem and offer the greatest rewards to the group that comes up with the best solution. Competitive work teams—a strategy first used by Japanese organizations—draw out the creative contributions of everyone and at the same time reduce the alienation often found in conventional organizations (Maddox, 1994; Yeatts, 1994).

3. **A flatter organization.** By spreading responsibility for creative problem solving throughout the workforce, organizations take on a flatter shape. That is, the pyramid shape of conventional bureaucracy is replaced by an organizational form with fewer levels in the chain of command, as shown in Figure 5–4. Fiat recently assumed control of Chrysler Corporation, for example, and the new corporate leadership paid less attention to rank, encouraging people at lower levels of management to speak directly to the CEO. Making Chrysler a flatter organization has helped lift the performance of that company (Saporito, 2011).

4. **Greater flexibility.** The typical industrial age organization was a rigid structure guided from the top. Such organizations may accomplish a good deal of work, but they are not especially creative or able to respond quickly to changes in the larger environment. The ideal model in the information age is a *more open and flexible* organization that both generates new ideas and adapts quickly to the rapidly changing global marketplace.

What does this all mean for organizations? As David Brooks puts it, "The machine is no longer held up as the standard that healthy organizations should emulate. Now it's the ecosystem" (2000:128). Today's "smart" companies seek out intelligent, creative people (AOL calls its main buildings "Creative Centers") and nurture the growth of their talents.

Keep in mind, however, that many of today's jobs do not involve creative work at all. More correctly, the postindustrial economy has created two very different types of work: high-skill creative work and low-skill service work. Work in the fast-food industry, for example, is routine and highly supervised and thus has much more in common with the factory work of a century ago than with the creative teamwork typical of today's information organizations. Therefore, at the same time that some organizations have taken on a flatter, more flexible form, others continue to use a rigid chain of command.

The "McDonaldization" of Society

As noted in the opening to this chapter, McDonald's has enjoyed enormous success, now operating more than 33,000 restaurants in the United States and around the world. Japan has more than 3,300 Golden Arches, and the world's largest McDonald's, which seats more than 1,500 customers, is found in London.

McDonald's is far more than a restaurant chain; it is a symbol of U.S. culture. Not only do people around the world associate McDonald's with the United States, but also here at home, one poll found that 98 percent of schoolchildren could identify Ronald McDonald, making him as well known as Santa Claus.

Even more important, the organizational principles that underlie McDonald's are coming to dominate our entire society. Our culture is becoming "McDonaldized,"[1] an awkward way of saying that we model many aspects of life on the approach taken by this restaurant chain: Parents buy toys at worldwide chain stores all carrying identical merchandise; we drop in at a convenient shop for a ten-minute drive-through oil change; face-to-face communication is being replaced more and more with electronic methods such as voice mail, e-mail, and instant messaging; more vacations take the form of resorts and tour packages; television packages the news in the form of ten-second sound bites; college admissions officers size up applicants they have never met by glancing at their GPA and SAT scores; and professors assign ghost-written textbooks[2] and evaluate students using tests mass-produced for them by publishing companies.

Can you tell what all these developments have in common?

Four Principles

According to George Ritzer (1993), the McDonaldization of society involves four basic organizational principles:

1. **Efficiency.** Ray Kroc, the marketing genius behind the expansion of McDonald's, set out to serve a hamburger, French fries, and a milkshake to a customer in fifty seconds. Today, one of the company's most popular items is the Egg McMuffin, an

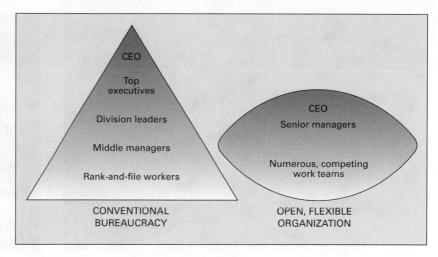

FIGURE 5–4 Two Organizational Models

The conventional model of bureaucratic organizations has a pyramid shape, with a clear chain of command. Orders flow from the top down, and reports of performance flow from the bottom up. Such organizations have extensive rules and regulations, and their workers have highly specialized jobs. More open and flexible organizations have a flatter shape, more like a football. With fewer levels in the hierarchy, responsibility for generating ideas and making decisions is shared throughout the organization. Many workers do their jobs in teams and have a broad knowledge of the entire organization's operation.

Source: Created by the author.

entire breakfast packaged into a single sandwich. In the restaurant, customers pick up their meals at a counter, dispose of their own trash, and stack their own trays as they walk out the door or, better still, drive away from the pickup window taking whatever mess they make with them. Such efficiency is now central to our way of life. We tend to think that anything done quickly is, for that reason alone, good.

2. **Predictability.** An efficient organization wants to make everything it does as predictable as possible. McDonald's prepares all food using set formulas. Company policies guide the performance of every job.

3. **Uniformity.** The first McDonald's operating manual declared the weight of a regular raw hamburger to be 1.6 ounces, its size to be 3.875 inches across, and its fat content to be 19 percent. A slice of cheese weighs exactly half an ounce, and French fries are cut precisely 9/32 inch thick.

   Think about how many of the objects we see every day around the home, the workplace, and the campus are designed and mass-produced uniformly according to a standard plan. Not just our environment but our everyday life experiences—from traveling the nation's interstates to sitting at home viewing national TV shows—are more standardized than ever before.

Read "The McDonaldization of Society" by George Ritzer on **mysoclab.com**

---

[1]The term "McDonaldization" was coined by Jim Hightower (1975); much of this discussion is based on the work of George Ritzer (1993, 1998, 2000) and Eric Schlosser (2002).
[2]A number of popular sociology books were not written by the person whose name appears on the cover. This book is not one of them. This is an anti-McDonald's textbook, researched, written, revised, and designed visually by a passionate author and a small dedicated editorial team. Even the test bank and the MySocLab online learning material that accompanies this text were written by the author.

The best of today's information age jobs—including working at Google, the popular search engine Web site—allow people lots of personal freedom, as long as they produce good ideas. At the same time, many other jobs, such as working the counter at McDonald's, involve the same routines and strict supervision found in factories a century ago.

Almost anywhere in the world, a person can walk into a McDonald's restaurant and buy the same sandwiches, drinks, and desserts prepared in the same way.[3] Uniformity results from a highly rational system that specifies every action and leaves nothing to chance.

4. **Control.** The most unreliable element in the McDonald's system is human beings. After all, people have good and bad days, and they sometimes let their minds wander or decide to do something a different way. To minimize the unpredictable human element, McDonald's has automated its equipment to cook food at a fixed temperature for a set length of time. Even the cash registers at McDonald's are keyed to pictures of the menu items so that ringing up a customer's order is as simple as possible.

Similarly, automatic teller machines are replacing bank tellers, highly automated bakeries produce bread while people stand back and watch, and chickens and eggs (or is it eggs and chickens?) emerge from automated hatcheries. In supermarkets, laser scanners at self-checkouts are phasing out human checkers. Much of our shopping now occurs in malls, where everything from temperature and humidity to the kinds of stores and products sold are subject to continuous control and supervision (Ide & Cordell, 1994).

Can Rationality Be Irrational?

There is no doubt about the popularity or efficiency of McDonald's. But there is another side to the story. Max Weber was alarmed at the increasing rationalization of the world, fearing that formal organizations would cage our imaginations and crush the human spirit. As he saw it, rational systems are efficient but dehumanizing. McDonaldization

bears him out. Each of the principles we have just discussed limits human creativity, choice, and freedom. Echoing Weber, Ritzer states that "the ultimate irrationality of McDonaldization is that people could lose control over the system and it would come to control us" (1993:145). Perhaps even McDonald's understands the limits of rationalization—the company has now expanded its offerings of more upscale foods, such as premium roasted coffee and salad selections that are more sophisticated, fresh, and healthful (Philadelphia, 2002).

The Future of Organizations: Opposing Trends

Evaluate

Early in the twentieth century, ever-larger organizations arose in the United States, most taking on the bureaucratic form described by Max Weber. In many respects, these organizations were like armies led by powerful generals who issued orders to their captains and lieutenants. Ordinary soldiers, working in the factories, did what they were told.

With the emergence of the postindustrial economy after 1950, as well as rising competition from abroad, many organizations evolved toward the flatter, more flexible model that encourages communication and creativity. Such "intelligent organizations" (Pinchot & Pinchot, 1993; Brooks, 2000) have become more productive than ever. Just as important, for highly skilled people who enjoy creative freedom, these organizations create less of the alienation that so worried Weber.

But this is only half the story. Although the postindustrial economy created many highly skilled jobs, it created even more routine service jobs, such as those offered by McDonald's. Fast-food companies now represent the largest pool of low-wage labor, aside from migrant workers, in the United States (Schlosser, 2002). Work of this kind, which Ritzer terms "McJobs," offers few of the benefits that today's highly skilled workers enjoy. On the contrary, the automated routines that define work in the fast-food industry, telemarketing, and similar fields are not very different from those that Frederick Taylor described a century ago.

---

[3]As McDonald's has "gone global," a few products have been added or changed according to local tastes. For example, in Uruguay, customers enjoy the McHuevo (a hamburger with poached egg on top); Norwegians can buy McLaks (grilled salmon sandwiches); the Dutch favor the Groenteburger (vegetable burger); in Thailand, McDonald's serves Samurai pork burgers; the Japanese can purchase a Chicken Tatsuta Sandwich (chicken seasoned with soy and ginger); Filipinos eat McSpaghetti (spaghetti with tomato sauce and bits of hot dog); and in India, where Hindus eat no beef, McDonald's sells a vegetarian Maharaja Mac (B. Sullivan, 1995).

Jake: I'm doing the best Facebook page ever. It's really cool and tells my whole story!

Duncan: Why do you want to put your whole life out there for everyone to see?

Jake: Ummm, to be famous?

Duncan: Famous? Ha! You're throwing away whatever privacy you have left.

Jake completes a page on Facebook, which includes his name and college, e-mail, photo, biography, and current personal interests. It can be accessed by billions of people around the world.

Late for a meeting with a new client, Sarah drives her car through a yellow light as it turns red at a main intersection. A computer linked to a pair of cameras notes the violation and takes one picture of her license plate and another of her sitting in the driver's seat. Seven days later, she receives a summons to appear in traffic court.

Julio looks through his mail and finds a letter from a Washington, D.C., data services company telling him that he is one of about 145,000 people whose name, address, Social Security number, and credit file have recently been sold to criminals in California posing as businesspeople. With this information, other people can obtain credit cards or take out loans in his name.

These are all cases showing that today's organizations—which know more about us than ever before and more than most of us realize—pose a growing threat to personal privacy. Large organizations are necessary for today's society to operate. In some cases, organizations using information about us may actually be helpful. But cases of identity theft are on the rise, and personal privacy is on the decline.

In the past, small-town life gave people little privacy. But at least if people knew something about you, you were just as likely to know something about them. Today, unknown people "out there" can access information about each of us all the time without our learning about it.

In part, the loss of privacy is a result of increasingly complex computer technology. Are you aware that every e-mail you send and every

Web site you visit leaves a record in one or more computers? These records can be retrieved by people you don't know as well as by employers and other public officials.

Another part of today's loss of privacy reflects the number and size of formal organizations. As explained in this chapter, large organizations tend to treat people impersonally, and they have a huge appetite for information. Mix large organizations with ever more complex computer technology, and it is no wonder that most people in the United States are concerned about who knows what about them and what people are doing with this information.

For decades, the level of personal privacy in the United States has been declining. Early in the twentieth century, when state agencies began issuing driver's licenses, for example, they generated files for every licensed driver. Today, officials can send this information at the touch of a button not only to the police but also to all sorts of other organizations. The Internal Revenue Service and the Social Security Administration, as well as government agencies that benefit veterans, students, the unemployed, and the poor, all collect mountains of personal information.

Business organizations now do much the same thing, and many of the choices we make end up in a company's database. Most of us use credit—the U.S. population now has more than 1 billion credit cards, an average of five per adult—but the companies that do "credit checks" collect and distribute information about us to almost anyone who asks, including criminals planning to steal our identity.

Then there are the small cameras found not only at traffic intersections but also in stores, public buildings, and parking garages and across college campuses. The number of surveillance cameras that monitor our movements is rapidly increasing with each passing year. So-called security cameras may increase public safety in some ways—say, by discouraging a mugger or even a terrorist—at the cost of the little privacy we have left. In the United Kingdom, probably the world leader in the use of security cameras with 4 million of them, the typical resident of London appears on closed-circuit television about 300 times every day,

and all this "tracking" is stored in computer files. Here in the United States, New York City already has 4,000 surveillance cameras in the subway system and city officials plan to have cameras installed in 1,500 city buses by 2013.

Government monitoring of the population in the United States has been expanding steadily in recent years. After the September 11, 2001, terrorist attacks, the federal government took steps (including the USA PATRIOT Act) to strengthen national security. Today, government officials closely monitor not only people entering the country but also the activities of all of us. These activities may increase national security, but they certainly erode personal privacy.

Some legal protections remain. Each of the fifty states has laws that give citizens the right to examine some records about themselves kept by employers, banks, and credit bureaus. The federal Privacy Act of 1974 also limits the exchange of personal information among government agencies and permits citizens to examine and correct most government files. In response to rising levels of identity theft, Congress is likely to pass more laws to regulate the sale of credit information. But so many organizations, private as well as public, now have information about us—experts estimate that 90 percent of U.S. households are profiled in databases somewhere—that current laws simply cannot effectively address the privacy problem.

Join the Blog!

Do you believe that the use of surveillance cameras in public places enhances or significantly reduces personal privacy? Is the cost worth the gains in personal security? What about automatic toll payment on our nation's roads, such as the E-ZPass system, which allows motorists to move quickly through toll gates, but also records information about where you go and when you got there? Go to MySocLab and join the Sociology in Focus blog to share your opinions and experiences and to see what others think.

Sources: "Online Privacy" (2000), J. Rosen (2000), A. Hamilton (2001), Heymann (2002), O'Harrow (2005), Tingwall (2008), Werth (2008), Hui (2010), and Stein (2011).

Today, organizational flexibility gives better-off workers more freedom but often means the threat of "downsizing" for many rank-and-file employees. Organizations facing global competition are eager to attract creative employees, but they are also eager to cut costs by using technology to eliminate as many routine jobs as possible. The net result is that some people are better off than ever while others worry about holding their jobs and struggle to make ends meet—a trend that Chapter 8 ("Social Stratification") explores in detail.

U.S. organizations remain the envy of the world for their productive efficiency. Indeed, there are few places on Earth where the mail arrives as quickly and dependably as it does in this country. But we should remember that the future is far brighter for some people than for others. In addition, as the Sociology in Focus box explains, formal organizations pose a mounting threat to our privacy, something to keep in mind as we envision our organizational future.

Seeing Sociology in Everyday Life

To what extent is the concept of McDonaldization a part of our everyday lives?

This chapter explains that since the opening of the first McDonald's restaurant in 1948, the principles that underlie the fast food industry—efficiency, predictability, uniformity, and control—have spread to many aspects of our everyday lives. Here is a chance to identify aspects of McDonaldization in several familiar routines. In each of the two photos on the facing page, can you identify specific elements of McDonaldization? That is, in what ways does the organizational pattern or the technology involved increase efficiency, predictability, uniformity, and control? In the photo below, what elements do you see that are clearly not McDonaldization? Why?

Hint This process, which is described as the "McDonaldization of society," has made our lives easier in some ways, but it has also made our society ever more impersonal, gradually diminishing our range of human contact. Also, although this organizational pattern is intended to serve human needs, it may end up doing the opposite by forcing people to live according to the demands of machines. Max Weber feared that our future would be an overly rational world in which we all might lose much of our humanity.

Small, neighborhood businesses like this one were once the rule in the United States. But the number of "mom and pop" businesses is declining as "big box" discount stores and fast-food chains expand. Why are small stores disappearing? What social qualities of these stores are we losing in the process?

Automated teller machines became common in the United States in the early 1970s. A customer with an electronic identification card can complete certain banking operations (such as withdrawing cash) without having to deal with a human bank teller. What makes the ATM one example of McDonaldization? Do you enjoy using an ATM? Why or why not?

At checkout counters in many supermarkets, customers lift each product through a laser scanner linked to a computer in order to identify what the product is and what it costs. The customer then inserts a credit or debit card to pay for the purchases.

Seeing Sociology in *Your* Everyday Life

1. Have colleges and universities been affected by the process called McDonaldization? Do large, anonymous lecture courses qualify as an example? Why? What other examples of McDonaldization can you identify on the college campus?

2. Visit any large public building with an elevator. Observe groups of people as they approach the elevator, and enter the elevator with them. Watch their behavior: What happens to conversations as the elevator doors close? Where do people fix their eyes? Can you explain these patterns?

3. What experiences do you have that are similar to using an ATM or a self-checkout at a discount store? Identify several examples and explain ways that you benefit from using them. In what ways might you be harmed by using these devices? Go to the "Seeing Sociology in *Your* Everyday Life" feature on MySocLab to learn more about the advantages and disadvantages of living in a highly rational society as well as suggestions about ways of making choices that enhance the quality of your own life.

What Are Social Groups?

Social groups are two or more people who identify with and interact with one another.

- **A primary group** is small, personal, and lasting (examples include family and close friends).
- **A secondary group** is large, impersonal, goal-oriented, and often of shorter duration (examples include a college class or a corporation). **pp. 108–9**

Elements of Group Dynamics

Group leadership

- *Instrumental leadership* focuses on completing tasks.
- *Expressive leadership* focuses on a group's well-being.
- *Authoritarian leadership* is a "take charge" style that demands obedience; *democratic leadership* includes everyone in decision making; *laissez-faire leadership* lets the group function mostly on its own. **p. 110**

Group conformity

- The Asch, Milgram, and Janis research shows that group members often seek agreement and may pressure one another toward conformity.
- Individuals use *reference groups*—including both *in-groups* and *out-groups*—to form attitudes and make evaluations. **pp. 110–12**

Group size and diversity

- Georg Simmel described the *dyad* as intense but unstable; the *triad*, he said, is more stable but can dissolve into a dyad by excluding one member.
- Peter Blau claimed that larger groups turn inward, socially diverse groups turn outward, and physically segregated groups turn inward. **pp. 112–13**

Networks are relational webs that link people with little common identity and limited interaction. Being "well connected" in networks is a valuable type of social capital. **pp. 113–14**

social group (p. 108) two or more people who identify with and interact with one another

primary group (p. 109) a small social group whose members share personal and lasting relationships

secondary group (p. 109) a large and impersonal social group whose members pursue a specific goal or activity

instrumental leadership (p. 110) group leadership that focuses on the completion of tasks

expressive leadership (p. 110) group leadership that focuses on the group's well-being

groupthink (p. 111) the tendency of group members to conform, resulting in a narrow view of some issue

reference group (p. 111) a social group that serves as a point of reference in making evaluations and decisions

in-group (p. 112) a social group toward which a member feels respect and loyalty

out-group (p. 112) a social group toward which a person feels a sense of competition or opposition

dyad (p. 112) a social group with two members

triad (p. 112) a social group with three members

network (p. 113) a web of weak social ties

What Are Formal Organizations?

Formal organizations are large secondary groups organized to achieve their goals efficiently.

- **Utilitarian organizations** pay people for their efforts (examples include businesses or government agencies).
- **Normative organizations** have goals people consider worthwhile (examples include voluntary associations such as the PTA).
- **Coercive organizations** are organizations people are forced to join (examples include prisons and mental hospitals). **p. 115**

✳ Explore the Map on **mysoclab.com**

All formal organizations operate in an **organizational environment** that is influenced by

- technology
- political and economic trends
- current events
- population patterns
- other organizations **pp. 115–16**

formal organization (p. 115) a large secondary group organized to achieve its goals efficiently

tradition (p. 115) values and beliefs passed from generation to generation

rationality (p. 115) a way of thinking that emphasizes deliberate, matter-of-fact calculation of the most efficient way to accomplish a particular task

rationalization of society (p. 115) Weber's term for the historical change from tradition to rationality as the main type of human thought

Modern Formal Organizations: Bureaucracy

Bureaucracy, which Max Weber saw as the dominant type of organization in modern societies, is based on

- specialization
- hierarchy of offices
- rules and regulations
- technical competence
- impersonality
- formal, written communications **pp. 115–17**

Problems of bureaucracy include

- bureaucratic alienation
- bureaucratic inefficiency and ritualism
- bureaucratic inertia
- oligarchy **pp. 117–18**

The Evolution of Formal Organizations

Conventional Bureaucracy

- In the early 1900s, Frederick Taylor's **scientific management** applied scientific principles to increase productivity. **pp. 118–19**

 **Watch** the **Video** on **mysoclab.com**

More Open, Flexible Organizations

- In the 1960s, Rosabeth Moss Kanter proposed that opening up organizations for all employees, especially women and other minorities, increased organizational efficiency.
- In the 1980s, global competition drew attention to the Japanese work organization's collective orientation. **pp. 119–20**

The Changing Nature of Work

Recently, the rise of a postindustrial economy has created two very different types of work:

- highly skilled and creative work (examples include designers, consultants, programmers, and executives)
- low-skilled service work associated with the "McDonaldization" of society, based on efficiency, uniformity, and control (examples include jobs in fast-food restaurants and telemarketing) **pp. 120–22**

 **Read** the **Document** on **mysoclab.com**

bureaucracy (p. 115) an organizational model rationally designed to perform tasks efficiently

organizational environment (p. 116) factors outside an organization that affect its operation

bureaucratic ritualism (p. 118) a focus on rules and regulations to the point of undermining an organization's goals

bureaucratic inertia (p. 118) the tendency of bureaucratic organizations to perpetuate themselves

oligarchy (p. 118) the rule of the many by the few

scientific management (p. 118) the application of scientific principles to the operation of a business or other large organization

6 Sexuality and Society

Learning Objectives

Remember the definitions of the key terms highlighted in boldfaced type throughout this chapter.

Understand how sexuality involves biology but is also a creation of society.

Apply sociology's major theoretical approaches to the topic of sexuality.

Analyze why humans are the only living species that recognizes the incest taboo.

Evaluate various controversial issues such as teen pregnancy, pornography, prostitution, and "hooking up" on campus.

Create a more critical and complex appreciation for the many connections between sexuality and society.

Sex. No one can doubt that it is an important dimension of our lives. But, as this chapter explains, sex is far from a simple biological process linked to reproduction. Society, including culture and patterns of inequality, shapes human sexuality and guides the meaning of sexuality in our everyday lives. ■■

Pam Goodman walks along the hallway with her friends Jennifer Delosier and Cindy Thomas. The three young women are sophomores at Jefferson High School, in Jefferson City, a small town in the Midwest.

"What's happening after school?" Pam asks.

"Dunno," replies Jennifer. "Maybe Todd is coming over."

"Got the picture," adds Cindy. "We're so gone."

"Shut up!" Pam stammers, smiling. "I hardly know Todd."

"OK, but . . ." The three girls break into laughter.

It is no surprise that young people spend a lot of time thinking and talking about sex. But as the sociologist Peter Bearman discovered, sex involves more than just talk. Bearman and two colleagues (Bearman, Moody, & Stovel, 2004) conducted confidential interviews with 832 students at the high school in a midwestern town they called Jefferson City, learning that 573 (69 percent of the students) had had at least one "sexual and romantic relationship" during the previous eighteen months. So most, but not all, of these students were sexually active.

Bearman wanted to learn about sexual activity in order to understand the problem of sexually transmitted diseases (STDs) among young people. Why are the rates of STDs so high? And why can there be sudden "outbreaks" of disease that involve dozens of young people in a community?

To find the answers to these questions, Bearman and colleagues asked the students to identify their sexual partners (promising, of course, not to reveal any confidential information). This information allowed them to trace connections between individual students in terms of sexual activity and produced a surprising pattern: Sexually active students were linked to each other through common partners much more than anyone might have expected. In all, common partners linked half of the sexually active students, as shown in the diagram.

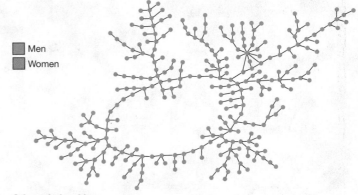

■ Men
■ Women

Other relationships
(If a pattern was observed more than once, numeral indicates frequency.)

Source: Bearman, Moody, & Stovel (2004).

Awareness of the connections among people can help us understand how STDs spread from one infected person to another in a short period of time. Bearman's study also shows that research can teach us a great deal about human sexuality, which is an important dimension of social life. You will also see that sexual attitudes and behavior have changed dramatically over the past century in the United States.

Understanding Sexuality

● **Understand**

How much of your thoughts and actions every day involve sexuality? If you are like most people, the answer is "quite a lot," because sexuality is about much more than just having sex.

We claim that beauty is in the eye of the beholder, which suggests the importance of culture in setting standards of attractiveness. All of the people pictured here—from Kenya, Arizona, Saudi Arabia, Thailand, Ethiopia, and Ecuador—are considered beautiful by members of their own society. At the same time, sociobiologists point out that in every society on Earth, people are attracted to youthfulness. The reason, as sociobiologists see it, is that attractiveness underlies our choices about reproduction, which is most readily accomplished in early adulthood.

Sexuality is a theme found almost everywhere—in sports, on campus, in the workplace, and especially in the mass media. There is also a sex industry that includes pornography and prostitution, both of which are multibillion-dollar businesses in this country. The bottom line is that sexuality is an important part of how we think about ourselves as well as how others think about us. For this reason, there are few areas of social life in which sexuality does not play some part.

Nevertheless, U.S. culture has long treated sex as taboo; even today, many people avoid talking about it. As a result, although sex can produce much pleasure, it also causes confusion, anxiety, and sometimes outright fear. Even scientists long considered sex off limits as a topic to study. It was not until the middle of the twentieth century that researchers turned their attention to this vital dimension of social life. Since then, as this chapter explains, we have discovered a great deal about human sexuality.

Sex: A Biological Issue

Sex refers to *the biological distinction between females and males.* From a biological point of view, sex is the way humans reproduce. A female ovum and a male sperm, each containing twenty-three chromosomes (biological codes that guide physical development), combine to form an embryo. To one of these pairs of chromosomes—the pair that determines the child's sex—the mother contributes an X chromosome and the father contributes either an X or a Y. An X from the father produces a female (XX) embryo; a Y from the father produces a male (XY) embryo. A child's sex is thus determined biologically at the moment of conception.

The sex of an embryo guides its development. If the embryo is male, the growth of testicular tissue starts to produce large amounts of testosterone, a hormone that triggers the development of male genitals (sex organs). If little testosterone is present, the embryo develops female genitals.

Sex and the Body

Some differences in the body set males and females apart. Right from birth, the two sexes have different **primary sex characteristics**, namely, *the genitals, organs used for reproduction.* At puberty, as people reach sexual maturity, additional sex differentiation takes place. At this point, people develop **secondary sex characteristics**, *bodily development, apart from the genitals, that distinguishes biologically mature females and males.* Sexually mature females have wider hips for giving birth, milk-producing breasts for nurturing infants, and soft, fatty tissue that provides a reserve supply of nutrition during pregnancy and breast feeding. Sexually mature males typically develop more muscle in the upper body, more extensive body hair, and deeper voices. Of course, these are general differences; some males are smaller and have less body hair and higher voices than some females.

Keep in mind that sex is not the same thing as gender. *Gender* is an element of culture and refers to the personal traits and patterns of behavior (including responsibilities, opportunities, and privileges) that a culture attaches to being female or male. Chapter 10 ("Gender Stratification") explains that gender is an important dimension of social inequality.

Intersexual People

Sex is not always as clear-cut as has just been described. The term **intersexual people** refers to *people whose bodies (including genitals) have both female and male characteristics.* Intersexuality is both natural and very rare, involving well below 1 percent of a society's population. An older term for an intersexual person is *hermaphrodite* (derived from Hermaphroditus, the child of the mythological Greek gods Hermes and Aphrodite, who embodied both sexes). A true hermaphrodite has both a female ovary and a male testis.

However, our culture demands that sex be clear-cut, a fact evident in the requirement that parents record the sex of their child at birth as either female or male. In the United States, some people respond to intersexual people with confusion or even disgust. But attitudes in other cultures are quite different: The Pokot of eastern Africa, for example, pay little attention to what they consider a simple biological error, and the Navajo look on intersexual people with awe, seeing in them the full potential of both the female and the male (Geertz, 1975).

Transsexuals

Transsexuals are *people who feel they are one sex even though biologically they are*

We are used to thinking of sex as a clear-cut issue of being female or male. But transgender people do not fit such simple categories. In 2008, Thomas Beatie, age 34, became pregnant and gave birth to a healthy baby girl; a year later, he gave birth to a second child, a boy. Beatie, who was born a woman, had surgery to remove his breasts and legally changed his sex from female to male, but nonetheless chose to bear a child. What is your response to cases such as this?

the other. Estimates suggest that one or two of every 1,000 people who are born have experienced the feeling of being trapped in a body of the wrong sex and a desire to be the other sex. Sometimes called transgender people, many begin to disregard conventional ideas about how females and males should look and behave. Some also go one step further and undergo *gender reassignment,* surgical alteration of their genitals, which is usually accompanied by hormone treatments. This medical process is complex and takes months or even years, but it helps many people gain a joyful sense of finally becoming on the outside who they feel they are on the inside (Gagné, Tewksbury, & McGaughey, 1997; Olyslager & Conway, 2007).

Sex: A Cultural Issue

Sexuality has a biological foundation. But like all other elements of human behavior, sexuality is also very much a cultural issue. Biology may explain some animals' mating rituals, but humans have no similar biological program. Although there is a biological "sex drive" in the sense that people find sex pleasurable and may seek to engage in sexual activity, our biology does not dictate any specific ways of being sexual any more than our desire to eat dictates any particular foods or table manners.

Cultural Variation

Almost every sexual practice shows considerable variation from one society to another. In his pioneering research study of sexuality in the United States, Alfred Kinsey and his colleagues (1948) found that most couples reported having intercourse in a single position: face to face, with the woman on the bottom and the man on top. Halfway around the world, in the South Seas, most couples *never* have sex in this way. In fact, when the people of the South Seas learned of this practice from Western missionaries, they poked fun at it as the strange "missionary position."

Even the simple practice of displaying affection varies from society to society. Most people in the United States kiss in public, but the Chinese kiss only in private. The French kiss publicly, often twice (once on each cheek), and the Belgians kiss three times (starting on either cheek). The Maori of New Zealand rub noses, and most people in Nigeria don't kiss at all.

Modesty, too, is culturally variable. If a woman stepping into a bath is disturbed, what body parts does she cover? Helen Colton (1983) reports that an Islamic woman covers her face,

In Montana, marriage between first cousins is against the law.

In Indiana, first cousins Shawn and Delia Dawson were able to marry only because they are both 70 years old.

First-Cousin Marriages
- Allowed
- Allowed with restrictions
- Not allowed

Seeing Ourselves

NATIONAL MAP 6–1 First-Cousin Marriage Laws across the United States

There is no single view on first-cousin marriages in the United States: Twenty-five states forbid such unions, nineteen allow them, and six allow them with restrictions.* In general, states that permit first-cousin marriages are found in New England, the Southeast, and the Southwest.

*Of the six states that allow first-cousin marriages with restrictions, five permit them only when couples are past childbearing age.

Source: National Conference of State Legislatures (2011).

a Laotian woman covers her breasts, a Samoan woman covers her navel, a Sumatran woman covers her knees, and a European woman covers her breasts with one hand and her genital area with the other.

Around the world, some societies restrict sexuality, and others are more permissive. In China, for example, societal norms so closely regulate sexuality that few people have sexual intercourse before they marry. In the United States, at least in recent decades, intercourse prior to marriage has become the norm, and some people choose to have sex even without strong commitment.

The Incest Taboo

When it comes to sex, do all societies agree on anything? The answer is yes. One cultural universal—an element found in every society the world over—is the **incest taboo**, *a norm forbidding sexual relations or marriage between certain relatives.* In the United States, the law, reflecting cultural mores, prohibits close relatives (including brothers and sisters, parents and children) from having sex or marrying. But in another example of cultural variation, exactly which family members are included in our society's incest taboo varies from state to state. National Map 6–1 shows that about half

the states outlaw marriage between first cousins and about half do not; a few states permit this practice but with restrictions (National Conference of State Legislatures, 2011).

Some societies (such as the North American Navajo) apply incest taboos only to the mother and others on her side of the family. There are also societies on record (including ancient Peru and Egypt) that have approved brother-sister marriages among the nobility as a strategy to keep power within a single family (Murdock, 1965, orig. 1949).

Why does some form of incest taboo exist everywhere? Part of the reason is biology: Reproduction between close relatives of any species increases the odds of producing offspring with mental or physical problems. But why, of all living species, do only humans observe an incest taboo? This fact suggests that controlling sexuality between close relatives is a necessary element of *social* organization. For one thing, the incest taboo limits sexual competition in families by restricting sex to spouses (ruling out, for example, sex between parent and child). Second, because family ties define people's rights and obligations toward one another, reproduction between close relatives would hopelessly confuse kinship; if a mother and son had a daughter, would the child consider the male a father or a brother? Third, by requiring people to marry outside their immediate families, the incest taboo integrates the

Over the course of the past century, social attitudes in the United States have become more accepting of most aspects of human sexuality. What do you see as some of the benefits of this greater openness? What are some of the negative consequences?

larger society as people look beyond their close kin when seeking to form new families.

The incest taboo has long been a sexual norm in the United States and throughout the world. But in this country, many other sexual norms have changed over time. In the twentieth century, as the next section explains, our society experienced both a sexual revolution and a sexual counterrevolution.

Sexual Attitudes in the United States

 **Understand**

What do people in the United States think about sex? Our culture's attitudes toward sexuality have always been somewhat contradictory. The early Puritan settlers of New England demanded strict conformity in attitudes and behavior, and they imposed severe punishment for any sexual misconduct, even if it took place in the privacy of the home. Later on, most European immigrants arrived with rigid ideas about "correct" sexuality, typically limiting sex to reproduction within marriage. Some regulation of sexual activity has continued ever since. As late as the 1960s, for example, some states legally prohibited the sale of condoms in stores. Until 2003, when the Supreme Court struck them down, thirteen states had laws banning sexual acts between partners of the same sex. Even today, "fornication" laws, which forbid intercourse by unmarried couples, are still on the books in eight states.

But this is just one side of the story. As Chapter 2 ("Culture") explains, because U.S. culture is individualistic, many of us believe that people should be free to do pretty much as they wish, as long as they cause no direct harm to others. The idea that what people do in the privacy of their own homes is no one else's business makes sex a matter of individual freedom and personal choice.

When it comes to sexuality, is the United States restrictive or permissive? The answer is both. On one hand, many people in the United States still view sexual conduct as an important indicator of personal morality. On the other hand, sex is increasingly a part of popular culture carried by the mass media—one recent report concluded that the number of scenes in television shows with sexual content doubled in a mere ten years (Kunkel et al., 2005). Within this complex framework, we turn now to changes in sexual attitudes and behavior that have occurred over the course of the past century.

The Sexual Revolution

Over the past century, the United States witnessed profound changes in sexual attitudes and practices. The first indications of this change came in the 1920s as millions of people migrated from farms and small towns to rapidly growing cities. There, living apart from their families and meeting new people in the workplace, young men and women enjoyed considerable sexual freedom, one reason that decade became known as the "Roaring Twenties."

In the 1930s and 1940s, the Great Depression and World War II slowed the rate of change. But in the postwar period, after 1945, Alfred Kinsey set the stage for what later came to be known as the *sexual revolution*. In 1948, Kinsey and his colleagues published their first study of sexuality in the United States, and it raised eyebrows everywhere. The national uproar resulted mostly from the fact that scientists were actually studying sex, a topic many people were uneasy talking about even in the privacy of their homes.

Kinsey also had some interesting things to say. His two books (Kinsey, Pomeroy, & Martin, 1948; Kinsey et al., 1953) became best-sellers partly because they revealed that people in the United States, on average, were far less conventional in sexual matters than most had thought. These books encouraged a new openness toward sexuality, which helped set the sexual revolution in motion.

In the late 1960s, the sexual revolution truly came of age. Youth culture dominated public life, and expressions such as "sex, drugs, and rock-and-roll" and "if it feels good, do it!" summed up the new, freer attitude toward sex. The baby boom generation, born between 1946 and 1964, became the first cohort in U.S. history to grow up with the idea that sex was part of people's lives, whether they were married or not.

New technology also played a part in the sexual revolution. The birth control pill, introduced in 1960, not only prevented pregnancy but also made having sex more convenient. Unlike a condom or a diaphragm, which has to be applied at the time of intercourse, the pill could be taken like a daily vitamin supplement. Now women as well as men could engage in sex spontaneously without any special preparation.

Because women were historically subject to greater sexual regulation than men, the sexual revolution had special significance for them. Society's "double standard" allows (and even encourages) men to be sexually active but expects women to be virgins until marriage and faithful to their husbands afterward. The survey data in Figure 6–1 show the narrowing of the double standard as a result of the sexual revolution. Among people born between 1933 and 1942 (that is, people who are in their seventies today), 56 percent of men but just 16 percent of women report having had two or more sexual partners by age twenty. Compare this wide gap with the pattern among those born between 1953 and 1962 (people now in their fifties), who came of age after the sexual revolution. In this category, 62 percent of men and 48 percent of women say they had two or more sexual partners by age twenty (Laumann et al., 1994:198). The sexual revolution increased sexual activity overall, and it changed women's behavior more than men's.

Greater openness about sexuality develops as societies become richer and the opportunities for women increase. With these facts in mind, look for a pattern in the global use of birth control shown in Global Map 6–1 on page 136.

The Sexual Counterrevolution

The sexual revolution made sex a topic of everyday discussion and sexual activity more a matter of individual choice. However, by 1980, the climate of sexual freedom that had marked the late 1960s and 1970s was criticized by some people as evidence of our country's moral decline, and the *sexual counterrevolution* began.

Politically speaking, the sexual counterrevolution was a conservative call for a return to "family values" and a change from sexual freedom back toward what critics saw as the sexual responsibility valued by earlier generations. Critics of the sexual revolution objected not just to the idea of "free love" but also to trends such as cohabitation (heterosexual couples living together without being married) and unmarried couples having children.

Looking back, the sexual counterrevolution did not greatly change the idea that people should decide for themselves when and with whom to have a sexual relationship. But whether for moral reasons or concerns about sexually transmitted diseases, more people began choosing to limit their number of sexual partners or not to have sex at all.

Is the sexual revolution over? It is true that people are making more careful decisions about sexuality. But as the rest of this

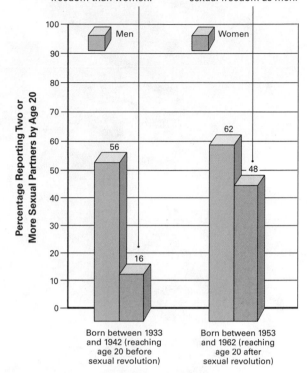

• Nancy Houck, now 76 years old, has lived most of her life in a social world where men have had much more sexual freedom than women.

• Sarah Roholt, 50, is a baby boomer who feels that she and her women friends have pretty much the same sexual freedom as men.

Diversity Snapshot

FIGURE 6–1 **The Sexual Revolution: Closing the Double Standard**

A larger share of men than women reports having had two or more sexual partners by age twenty. But the sexual revolution greatly reduced this gender difference.

Source: Laumann et al. (1994:198).

chapter explains, the ongoing sexual revolution is evident in the fact that there is now greater acceptance of premarital sex as well as increasing tolerance for various sexual orientations.

Premarital Sex

In light of the sexual revolution and the sexual counterrevolution, how much has sexual behavior in the United States really changed? One interesting trend involves premarital sex—sexual intercourse before marriage—among young people.

Consider, first, what U.S. adults *say* about premarital intercourse. Table 6–1 on page 137 shows that about 29 percent characterize sexual relations before marriage as "always wrong" or "almost always wrong." Another 17 percent consider premarital sex "wrong only sometimes," and about 52 percent say premarital sex is "not wrong at all" (NORC, 2011:410). Public opinion is far more accepting of premarital sex today than was the case a generation ago, but our society clearly remains divided on this issue.

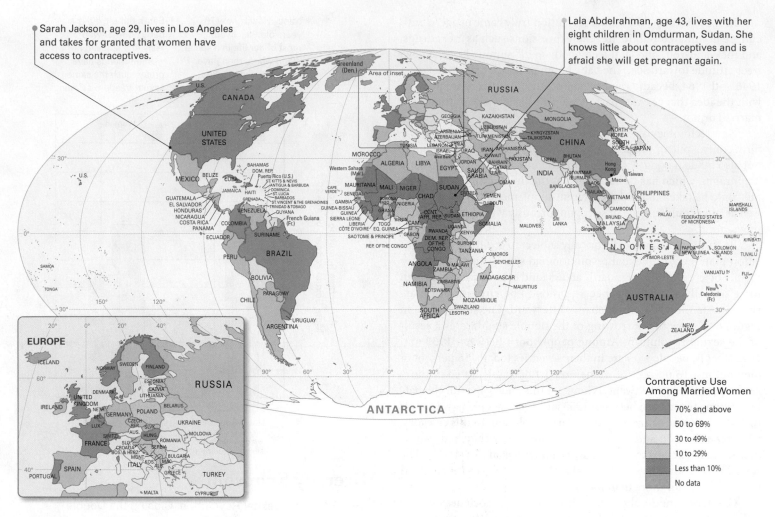

Sarah Jackson, age 29, lives in Los Angeles and takes for granted that women have access to contraceptives.

Lala Abdelrahman, age 43, lives with her eight children in Omdurman, Sudan. She knows little about contraceptives and is afraid she will get pregnant again.

Contraceptive Use Among Married Women

- 70% and above
- 50 to 69%
- 30 to 49%
- 10 to 29%
- Less than 10%
- No data

Window on the World

GLOBAL MAP 6–1 Contraceptive Use in Global Perspective

The map shows the percentage of married women using modern contraceptive methods (such as barrier methods, contraceptive pill, implants, injectables, intrauterine devices, or sterilization). In general, how do high-income nations differ from low-income nations? Can you explain this difference?

Sources: Data from United Nations (2008) and Population Reference Bureau (2011).

Now let's look at what young people *do*. For women, there has been marked change over time. The Kinsey studies reported that for people born in the early 1900s, about 50 percent of men but just 6 percent of women had had premarital sexual intercourse before age nineteen. Studies of baby boomers, born after World War II, show a slight increase in premarital sex among men but a large increase—to about one-third—among women. The most recent studies show that by the time they are seniors in high school, 46 percent of young men and women have had premarital sexual intercourse. In addition, sexual experience among high school students who are sexually active is limited—only 14 percent of students report four or more sexual partners. Other research reports that, among young people between the ages of fifteen and twenty-four, 70 percent of women and 68 percent of men say they have had sexual intercourse. Over the last decade, the share of young people who report this type of sexual activity

has declined (Laumann et al., 1994; Centers for Disease Control and Prevention, 2010; Chandra et al., 2011; Martinez, Copen, and Abma, 2011; National Center for Health Statistics, 2011).

A common belief is that an even larger share of young people engage in oral sex. This choice reflects the fact that this practice avoids the risk of pregnancy; in addition, many young people see oral sex as something less than "going all the way." Recent research suggests that the share of young people who say they have had oral sex is almost the same as the share reporting having had sexual intercourse. Therefore, mass media claims of an "oral sex epidemic" among people in the United States are almost certainly exaggerated.

Finally, a significant minority of young people choose abstinence (not having sexual intercourse). Many also choose not to have oral sex, which, like intercourse, can transmit disease. Even so, research confirms the fact that premarital sex is widely accepted among young people today.

Sex between Adults

Judging from the mass media, people in the United States are very active sexually. But do popular images reflect reality? The Laumann study (1994), the largest study of sexuality since Kinsey's groundbreaking research, found that frequency of sexual activity varies widely in the U.S. population. One-third of adults report having sex with a partner a few times a year or not at all, another one-third have sex once or several times a month, and the remaining one-third have sex with a partner two or more times a week. In short, no single stereotype accurately describes sexual activity in the United States.

Despite the widespread image of "swinging singles" promoted on television shows such as *Sex and the City,* it is married people who have sex with partners the most. In addition, married people report the highest level of satisfaction—both physical and emotional—with their partners (Laumann et al., 1994).

Extramarital Sex

What about married people having sex outside of marriage? This practice, commonly called "adultery" (sociologists prefer the more neutral term *extramarital sex*), is widely condemned in the United States. Table 6–1 shows that more than 90 percent of U.S. adults consider a married person having sex with someone other than the marital partner "always wrong" or "almost always wrong." The norm of sexual fidelity within marriage has been and remains a strong element of U.S. culture.

But actual behavior falls short of the cultural ideal. The Laumann study reports that about 25 percent of married men and 10 percent of married women have had at least one extramarital sexual experience. Stating this the other way around, it means that 75 percent of men and 90 percent of women have remained sexually faithful to their partners. Research indicates that the incidence of extramarital sex is higher among the young than the old, higher among men than among women, and higher among people of low social position than among those who are financially well-off. In addition, the odds of extramarital sex are higher among those who report no religious affiliation and, as we might expect, the odds rise among those who report a low level of happiness in their marriage (Laumann et al., 1994:214; T. W. Smith, 2006; NORC, 2011:411).

Sex over the Life Course

Patterns of sexual activity change with age. In the United States, most young men become sexually active by the time they reach sixteen and women by the age of seventeen. By the time they reach their mid-twenties, about 90 percent of both women and men reported being sexually active with a partner at least once during the past year (Reece et al., 2010; Chandra et al., 2011).

TABLE 6–1 How We View Premarital and Extramarital Sex

Survey Question: "There's been a lot of discussion about the way morals and attitudes about sex are changing in this country. If a man and a woman have sexual relations before marriage, do you think it is always wrong, almost always wrong, wrong only sometimes, or not wrong at all? What about a married person having sexual relations with someone other than the marriage partner?"

	Premarital Sex	Extramarital Sex
"Always wrong"	21.3%	77.1%
"Almost always wrong"	8.1	13.1
"Wrong only sometimes"	16.9	6.3
"Not wrong at all"	51.9	2.0
"Don't know"/No answer	1.8	1.4

Source: *General Social Surveys, 1972–2010: Cumulative Codebook* (Chicago: National Opinion Research Center, 2011), pp. 410–11.

Overall, adults report having sexual intercourse about sixty-two times a year, which is slightly more than once a week. Young adults report the highest frequency of sexual intercourse at eighty-four times a year. This number falls to sixty-four times for adults in their forties and declines further to about ten times a year for adults in their seventies.

From another angle, by about age sixty, less than half of adults (54 percent of men and 42 percent of women) say they have had sexual intercourse one or more times during the past year. By age seventy, just 43 percent of men and 22 percent of women report the same behavior (T. W. Smith, 2006; Herbenick et al., 2010).

Sexual Orientation

 Analyze

In recent decades, public opinion about sexual orientation has shown a remarkable change. **Sexual orientation** is *a person's romantic and emotional attraction to another person.* The norm in all human societies is **heterosexuality** (*hetero* is Greek for "the other of two"), meaning *sexual attraction to someone of the other sex.* Yet in every society, a significant share of people experience **homosexuality** (*homo* is Greek for "the same"), *sexual attraction to someone of the same sex.* Keep in mind that people do not necessarily fall into just one of these categories; they may have varying degrees of attraction to both sexes.

The idea that sexual orientation is often not clear-cut points to the existence of a third category: **bisexuality,** *sexual attraction to people of both sexes.* Some bisexual people are attracted equally to males and females; many others are attracted more strongly to one sex than the other. Finally, **asexuality** refers to *a lack of sexual attraction to people of either sex.* Figure 6–2 on page 138 places each of these sexual orientations in relation to the others.

---

sexual orientation a person's romantic and emotional attraction to another person

heterosexuality sexual attraction to someone of the other sex

homosexuality sexual attraction to someone of the same sex

bisexuality sexual attraction to people of both sexes

asexuality a lack of sexual attraction to people of either sex

High Opposite-Sex Attraction

	High Same-Sex Attraction
Heterosexuality	Bisexuality
Asexuality	Homosexuality

Low Same-Sex Attraction

Low Opposite-Sex Attraction

Diversity Snapshot

FIGURE 6–2 Four Sexual Orientations

A person's levels of same-sex attraction and opposite-sex attraction are two distinct dimensions that combine in various ways to produce four major sexual orientations.

Source: Adapted from Storms (1980).

It is important to remember that sexual *attraction* is not the same thing as sexual *behavior*. Many people have experienced some attraction to someone of the same sex, but far fewer ever actually engage in same-sex behavior. This is in large part because our culture discourages such actions.

In the United States and around the world, heterosexuality is the norm because, biologically speaking, heterosexual relations permit human reproduction. Even so, most societies tolerate homosexuality. Among the ancient Greeks, upper-class men considered homosexuality the highest form of relationship, partly because they looked down on women as intellectually inferior. As men saw it, heterosexuality was necessary only so they could have children, and "real" men preferred homosexual relations (Kluckhohn, 1948; Ford & Beach, 1951; Greenberg, 1988).

What Gives Us a Sexual Orientation?

The question of how people come to have a particular sexual orientation is strongly debated. The arguments cluster into two general positions: sexual orientation as a product of society and sexual orientation as a product of biology.

Sexual Orientation: A Product of Society

This approach argues that people in any society attach meanings to sexual activity, and these meanings differ from place to place and over time. As Michel Foucault (1990, orig. 1978) points out, for example, there was no distinct category of people called "homosexuals" until a century ago, when scientists and eventually the public as a whole began defining people that way. Throughout history, many people no doubt had what we would call "homosexual experiences." But neither they nor others saw in this behavior the basis for any special identity.

Anthropological studies show that patterns of homosexuality differ greatly from one society to another. In Siberia, for example, the Chukchee Eskimo perform a ritual during which one man dresses as a female and does a woman's work. The Sambia, who dwell in the Eastern Highlands of New Guinea, have a ritual in which young boys perform oral sex on older men in the belief that eating semen will make them more masculine. In southeastern Mexico, a region in which religions recognize gods who are both female and male, the local culture defines people not only as female and male but also as *muxes* (MOO-shays), a third sexual category. *Muxes* are men who dress and act as women, some only on ritual occasions, some all the time. The Thinking About Diversity box takes a closer look at this pattern. Such diversity around the world shows that sexual expression is socially constructed (Blackwood & Wieringa, 1999; Grave, 2005; Lacey, 2008; Rosenberg, 2008).

Sexual Orientation: A Product of Biology

A growing body of evidence suggests that sexual orientation is innate, or rooted in human biology, in much the same way that people are born right-handed or left-handed. Arguing this position, Simon LeVay (1993) links sexual orientation to the structure of a person's brain. LeVay studied the brains of both homosexual and heterosexual men and found a small but important difference

One factor that has advanced the social acceptance of homosexuality is the inclusion of openly gay characters in the mass media, especially films and television shows. In the popular musical-drama series *Glee*, Chris Colfer plays Kurt Hummel, who came out as being gay during the first season of the show. How would you assess the portrayal of homosexuality in the mass media?

A Third Gender: The *Muxes* of Mexico

Alejandro Taledo, sixteen years old, stands on a street corner in Juchitán, a small town in the state of Oaxaca, in southeastern Mexico. Called Alex by her friends, she has finished a day of selling flowers with her mother and now waits for a bus to ride home for dinner.

As you may know, Alejandro is commonly a boy's name. In fact, this young Mexican was born a boy. But several years ago, Alex decided that, whatever her sex, she felt like she was a girl and she decided to live according to her own feelings.

In this community, she is not alone. Juchitán and the surrounding region is well known not only for beautiful black pottery and delicious food but also for the large number of gays, lesbians, and transgender people who live there. At first glance, this fact may surprise people who think of Mexico as a traditional country, especially when it comes to gender and sexuality. In Mexico, the stereotype goes, men control the lives of women, especially their sexuality. But like all stereotypes, this one misses some important facts. Nationally, Mexico has become more tolerant of diverse sexual expression. In 2009, Mexico City, the nation's capital, began recognizing same-sex marriages. And nowhere is tolerance for sexual orientation greater than it is in the region around Juchitán.

There, transgender people are called *muxes* (pronounced MOO-shays), which is based on the Spanish word *mujer,* meaning "woman." *Muxes* are considered neither male nor female but of a third gender. Some *muxes* wear women's clothing and act almost entirely in a feminine way. Others adopt a feminine look and behavior only on special occasions. One of the most popular events is the region's grand celebration, which is held every November and is attended by more than 2,000 *muxes* and their families. A highlight of this event is a competition for the title of "transvestite of the year."

The acceptance of transgender people in central Mexico has its roots in the culture that existed before the Spanish arrived. At that time, anyone with ambiguous gender was viewed as especially wise and talented. The region's history includes accounts of Aztec priests and Mayan gods who cross-dressed or were considered to be both male and female. In the sixteenth century, the coming of the Spanish colonists and the influence of the Catholic Church reduced much of this gender tolerance. But acceptance of mixed sexual identity continues today in this region, where many people hold so tightly to their traditions that they speak only their ancient Zapotec language rather than Spanish.

And so it is in Juchitán that *muxes* are respected, accepted, and even celebrated. *Muxes* are successful in business and take leadership roles in the church and in politics. Most important, they are commonly accepted by friends and family alike. Alejandro lives with her parents and five siblings and helps her mother, both selling flowers on the streets and also at home. Her father, Victor Martinez Jimenez, is a local construction worker who speaks only Zapotec. He still refers to Alex as "him" but says "it was God who sent him, and why would I reject him? He helps his mother very much. Why would I get mad?" Alex's mother, Rosa Taledo Vicente, adds, "Every family considers it a blessing to have one gay son. While daughters marry and leave home, a *muxe* cares for his parents in their old age."

What Do You Think?

1. Do you think that U.S. society is tolerant of people wishing to combine masculine and feminine dress and behavior? Why or why not?

2. *Muxes* are people who were born biologically male. How do you think the local people in this story would feel about women who wanted to dress and act like men? Would you expect equal tolerance for such people? Why or why not?

3. How do you personally feel about the existence of a third category of sexual identity? Explain your views.

Sources: Gave (2005), Lacey (2008), and Rosenberg (2008).

---

in the size of the hypothalamus, a part of the brain that regulates hormones. Such an anatomical difference, he claims, plays a part in shaping sexual orientation.

Genetics may also influence sexual orientation. One study of forty-four pairs of brothers, all homosexual, found that thirty-three pairs had a distinctive genetic pattern involving the X chromosome. Moreover, the gay brothers had an unusually high number of gay male relatives—but only on their mother's side. Such evidence leads some researchers to think there may be a "gay gene" located on the X chromosome (Hamer & Copeland, 1994).

● **Evaluate** Mounting evidence supports the conclusion that sexual orientation is rooted in biology, although the best guess at present is that both nature and nurture play a part. Remember that sexual orientation is not a matter of neat categories. Most people who think of themselves as homosexual have had one or more heterosexual experiences, just as many people who think of themselves as heterosexual have had one or more homosexual experiences. Explaining sexual orientation, then, is not easy.

There is also a political issue here with great importance for gay men and lesbians. To the extent that sexual orientation is based in

Watch the video "Alternative Sexual Orientation" on **mysoclab.com**

FIGURE 6–3 Sexual Orientation in the United States: Survey Data

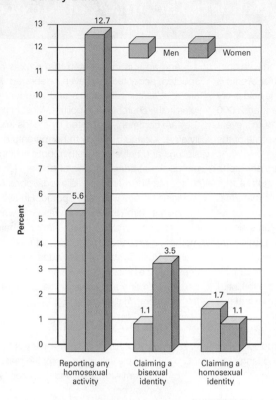

(a) Share of the Population That Is Bisexual or Homosexual

Although more women than men report having had a homosexual experience, more men than women claim to have a homosexual identity.

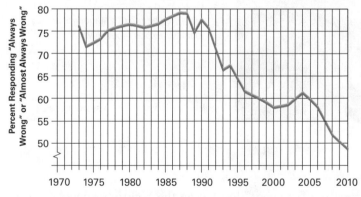

(b) Attitudes toward Homosexual Relations, 1973–2010

Source: (a) Chandra et al. (2011); (b) NORC (2011:411).

biology, homosexuals have no more choice about their sexual orientation than they do about their skin color. If this is so, shouldn't gay men and lesbians expect the same legal protection from discrimination as African Americans?

CHECK YOUR LEARNING What evidence supports the position that sexual behavior is constructed by society? That sexual orientation is rooted in biology?

How Many Gay People Are There?

What share of our population is gay? This is a hard question to answer because, as noted earlier, sexual orientation is not a matter of neat categories. In addition, people are not always willing to discuss their sexuality with strangers or even family members. Alfred Kinsey estimated that about 4 percent of males and 2 percent of females have an exclusively same-sex orientation, although he pointed out that most people experience same-sex attraction at some point in their lives.

Some social scientists put the gay share of the population at 10 percent. But research surveys show that how homosexuality is defined makes a big difference in the result (Chandra et al., 2011). As part (a) of Figure 6–3 shows, 5.6 percent of men and 12.7 percent of women between the ages of eighteen and forty-four reported engaging in homosexual activity *at some time in their lives.* At the same time, just 1.7 percent of men and 1.1 percent of women defined themselves as "partly" or "entirely" homosexual.

In recent surveys, about 1.1 percent of men and 3.5 percent of women described themselves as bisexual. But bisexual experiences appear to be more common among younger people, especially while they live on college and university campuses (Laumann et al., 1994; Chandra et al., 2011). Many bisexuals do not think of themselves as either gay or straight, and their behavior reflects aspects of both gay and straight living.

The Gay Rights Movement

The public's attitude toward homosexuality has been moving toward greater acceptance. Back in 1973, as shown in part (b) of Figure 6–3, about three-fourths of U.S. adults claimed that homosexual relations were "always wrong" or "almost always wrong." Although that percentage changed little in the 1970s and 1980s, by 2010 it had dropped to 47 percent (NORC, 2011:411). Among college students, who are generally more tolerant of homosexual relationships than the population as a whole, we see a similar trend. In 1980, about half of college students supported laws prohibiting homosexual relationships; by 2008, as Figure 6–4 shows, roughly one-quarter felt the way (Astin et al., 2002; Pryor et al., 2009).

In large measure, this change was brought about by the gay rights movement, which arose in the middle of the twentieth century. Up to that time, most people in this country did not discuss homosexuality, and it was common for companies (including the federal government and the armed forces) to fire anyone who was accused of being gay. Mental health professionals also took a hard line, describing homosexuals as "sick" and sometimes placing them in mental hospitals, where, it was hoped, they might be "cured." It is no surprise that most lesbians and gay men remained "in the closet," closely guarding the secret of their sexual orientation. But the gay rights movement gained strength during the 1960s. One early milestone for the movement occurred in 1973 when the American Psychiatric Association (APA) declared that homosexuality was not an illness but simply "a form of sexual behavior." In 2009, the APA declared that psychological therapy should not be used in an effort to make gay people straight (Cracy, 2009).

The gay rights movement also began using the term **homophobia** to describe *discomfort over close personal interaction with people* *thought to be gay, lesbian, or bisexual* (Weinberg, 1973). The concept of homophobia turns the tables on society: Instead of asking "What's wrong with gay people?" the question becomes "What's wrong with people who can't accept a different sexual orientation?"

In 2004, a number of cities and towns began to allow gay couples to marry, although these unions were later declared illegal. But gay marriage became legal in Massachusetts in 2004 and is also legal in Connecticut (2008), Vermont (2009), Iowa (2009), New Hampshire (2009), New York (2011), Washington (2012), Maryland (2012), and the District of Columbia (2009). Eight other states, including California (which briefly legalized gay marriage in 2008), Oregon, Nevada, Delaware, Illinois, Rhode Island, New Jersey, and Hawaii recognize either "domestic partnerships" or "civil unions" that provide most or all of the benefits of marriage. At the same time, a majority of the states have enacted laws that forbid gay marriage and prohibit recognizing such marriages performed elsewhere (National Conference of State Legislatures, 2012).

Sexual Issues and Controversies

🌑 Evaluate

Sexuality lies at the heart of a number of controversies in the United States today. Here we take a look at four key issues: teen pregnancy, pornography, prostitution, and sexual violence.

Teen Pregnancy

All sexual activity—but especially engaging in sexual intercourse, which can lead to pregnancy—demands a high level of responsibility. Teenagers may be biologically mature enough to conceive, but many are not emotionally secure enough to appreciate the consequences of their actions. Surveys show that there are some 750,000 teen pregnancies in the United States each year, most of them unplanned. This country's rate of births to teenage women is higher than that of all other high-income countries and is twice the rate in Canada (Ventura et al., 2009; Alan Guttmacher Institute, 2010; Population Reference Bureau, 2011).

For young women of all racial and ethnic categories, weak families and low income sharply increase the likelihood of becoming sexually active and having an unplanned child. To make matters worse, having unplanned children raises the risk that young women (as well as young fathers-to-be) will not complete a high school education and will end up living in poverty (Alan Guttmacher Institute, 2010).

Pregnancy among unmarried teenage women, once a social taboo, has become part of the mass media with shows like MTV's *Teen Mom* and *16 and Pregnant*. Such shows clearly convey the many challenges that face young mothers-to-be. Would you expect these shows to have any effect on the country's teen pregnancy rate? Explain.

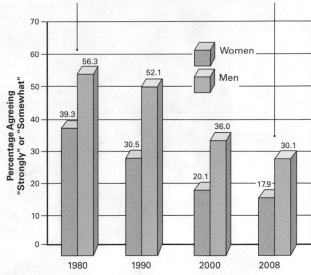

● Since 1980, college students' opposition to homosexual relationships has declined sharply.

Statement: "It is important to have laws prohibiting homosexual relationships."

Student Snapshot

FIGURE 6–4 **Opposition to Homosexual Relationships: Attitudes of First-Year College Students, 1980–2008**

The historical trend among college students is toward greater tolerance of homosexual relationships, a view held by a large majority.

Sources: Astin et al. (2002) and Pryor et al. (2009).

Did the sexual revolution raise the rate of teenage pregnancy? Surprisingly, perhaps, the answer is no. The rate of pregnancy among teens in 1950 was higher than it is today, partly because people back then married at a younger age. In addition, because abortion was against the law, many pregnancies led to quick marriages. As a result, many teens became pregnant, but almost 90 percent were married. Today, the number of pregnant teens is lower, but in about 80 percent of all cases, these women are unmarried. In a slight majority (58 percent) of such cases, these women keep their babies; in the remainder, they have abortions (27 percent) or miscarriages (15 percent) (Alan Guttmacher Institute, 2010). National Map 6–2 on page 142 shows pregnancy rates for women between the ages of fifteen and nineteen throughout the United States.

Pornography

Pornography is *sexually explicit material intended to cause sexual arousal*. But what is and is not pornographic has long been a matter of debate. Recognizing that different people view portrayals of sexuality differently,

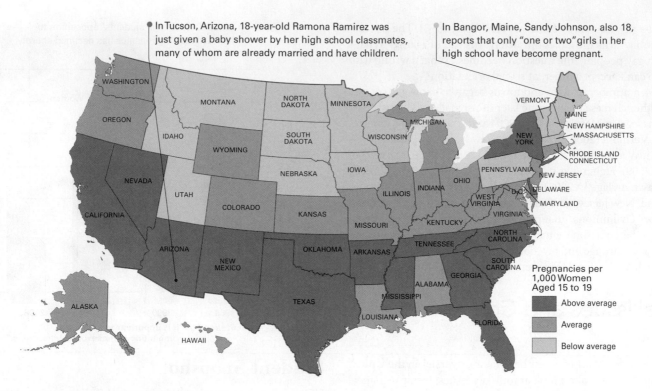

In Tucson, Arizona, 18-year-old Ramona Ramirez was just given a baby shower by her high school classmates, many of whom are already married and have children.

In Bangor, Maine, Sandy Johnson, also 18, reports that only "one or two" girls in her high school have become pregnant.

Pregnancies per 1,000 Women Aged 15 to 19

Above average

Average

Below average

Seeing Ourselves

NATIONAL MAP 6–2 Teenage Pregnancy Rates across the United States

The map shows pregnancy rates for women aged fifteen to nineteen in 2010. In what regions of the country are rates high? Where are they low? What explanation can you offer for these patterns?

Explore the percentage of 15- to 17-year-olds who are married in your local community and in counties across the United States on **mysoclab.com**

Source: Alan Guttmacher Institute (2010).

the U.S. Supreme Court gives local communities the power to decide for themselves what type of material violates "community standards" of decency and lacks "redeeming social value."

Definitions aside, pornography is very popular in the United States: X-rated videos, telephone "sex lines," sexually explicit movies and magazines, and thousands of Internet Web sites make up a thriving industry that takes in more than $10 billion each year. Most pornography in the United States is created in California, and the vast majority of people who consume pornography—who are found throughout the country—are men (Steinhauer, 2008).

Traditionally, people have criticized pornography on *moral* grounds. National surveys confirm the concern of 60 percent of U.S. adults that "sexual materials lead to a breakdown of morals" (NORC, 2011:413). Today, however, pornography is also seen as a *political* issue because most of it degrades women, portraying them as the sexual playthings of men.

Some critics also claim that pornography is a cause of violence against women. Although it is difficult to prove a scientific cause-and-effect relationship between what people view and how they act, the public shares a concern about pornography and violence, with almost half of adults holding the opinion that pornography encourages people to commit rape (NORC, 2011:413).

Although people everywhere object to sexual material they find offensive, many also value the principle of free speech and the protection of artistic expression. Nevertheless, pressure to restrict pornography is building from an unlikely coalition of conservatives, who oppose pornography on moral grounds, and liberals as well as feminists, who condemn it for political reasons.

Prostitution

Prostitution is *the selling of sexual services*. Often called "the world's oldest profession," prostitution has existed throughout recorded history. In the United States today, about one in six adult men reports having paid for sex at some time (NORC, 2011). Because most people think that sex should be an expression of intimacy, they find the idea of sex for money disturbing. As a result, prostitution is against the law everywhere in the United States except for parts of rural Nevada.

Around the world, prostitution is greatest in poor countries where patriarchy is strong and traditional cultural norms limit women's ability to earn a living. Global Map 6–2 shows where prostitution is most widespread.

Types of Prostitution

Most prostitutes (many prefer the morally neutral term "sex workers") are women, and they fall into different categories. *Call girls* are elite prostitutes, typically young, attractive, and well-educated

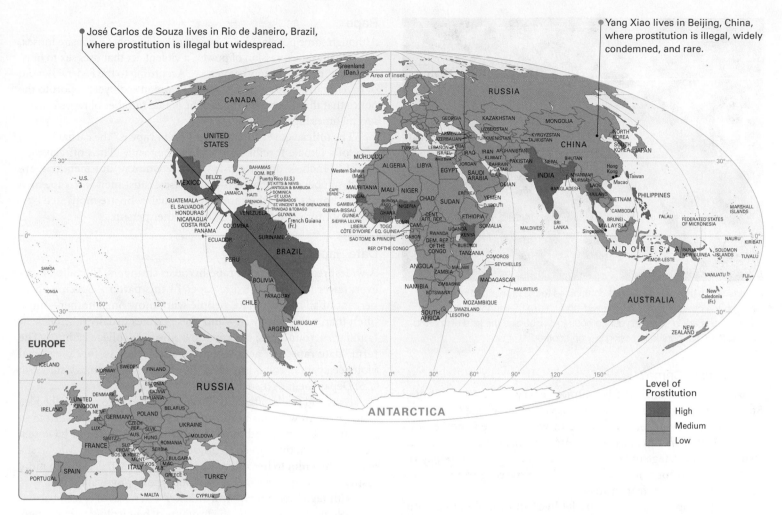

José Carlos de Souza lives in Rio de Janeiro, Brazil, where prostitution is illegal but widespread.

Yang Xiao lives in Beijing, China, where prostitution is illegal, widely condemned, and rare.

Level of Prostitution
- High
- Medium
- Low

Window on the World

GLOBAL MAP 6–2 Prostitution in Global Perspective

Generally speaking, prostitution is widespread in societies where women have low standing. Officially, at least, the People's Republic of China boasts of gender equality, including the elimination of "vice" such as prostitution, which oppresses women. By contrast, in much of Latin America, where patriarchy is strong, prostitution is common. In many Islamic societies, patriarchy is also strong, but religion is a counterbalance, so prostitution is limited. Western, high-income nations have a moderate amount of prostitution.

Sources: *Peters Atlas of the World* (1990) and Mackay (2000).

women who arrange their own "dates" with clients by telephone. The classified pages of any large city newspaper contain numerous ads for "escort services," by which women and men offer both companionship and sex for a fee.

In the middle category are prostitutes who are employed in "massage parlors" or brothels under the control of managers. These sex workers typically have less choice about their clients, receive less money for their services, and get to keep no more than half of the money they make.

At the bottom of the sex worker hierarchy are *streetwalkers*, women and men who "work the streets" of large cities. Some female streetwalkers are under the control of male pimps who take most of their earnings. Many others are addicted to drugs and sell sex to buy the drugs they need. Both types of people are at high risk of becoming the victims of violence (Davidson, 1998; Estes, 2001).

The lives of sex workers, then, are diverse, with some earning more than others and some at greater risk of violence. But studies point to one thing that most of these women and men have in common: They consider their work degrading. As one researcher suggested, one minute the sex worker is adored as "the most beautiful woman," while the next she is condemned as a "slut" (Barton, 2006).

Most prostitutes offer heterosexual services. However, gay prostitutes also trade sex for money. Researchers report that many gay prostitutes end up selling sex after having suffered rejection by family and friends because of their sexual orientation (Weisberg, 1985; Boyer, 1989; Kruks, 1991).

Read "Human Rights, Sex Trafficking, and Prostitution" by Alice Leuchtag on **mysoclab.com**

Experts agree that one factor that contributes to the problem of sexual violence on the college campus is the widespread use of alcoholic beverages. What policies are in force on your campus to discourage the kind of drinking that leads to one person imposing sex on another?

A Victimless Crime?

Prostitution is against the law almost everywhere in the United States, but many people consider it a victimless crime (defined in Chapter 7, "Deviance," as a crime in which there is no obvious victim). Consequently, instead of enforcing prostitution laws consistently, police stage only occasional crackdowns. This policy reflects a desire to control prostitution while also recognizing that it is impossible to eliminate it entirely.

Many people take a "live and let live" attitude about prostitution and say that adults ought to be free to do as they please so long as no one is forced to do anything. But is prostitution really victimless? The sex trade subjects many women to abuse and outright violence and also plays a part in spreading sexually transmitted diseases, including AIDS. In addition, many poor women, especially in low-income nations, become trapped in a life of selling sex. Thailand, in Southeast Asia, has as many as 2 million prostitutes, representing about 10 percent of all women in the labor force. Many of these women begin working before they are teenagers, are often subjected to physical abuse, and run a high risk of contracting HIV (Wonders & Michalowski, 2001; Kapstein, 2006; UNAIDS, 2010).

In the past, the focus of law enforcement has been on the women who earn money as sex workers. But prostitution would not exist without demand on the part of men. For this reason, police officers are now more likely to target "johns" when they attempt to buy sex. Sweden has adopted this approach to prostitution. Since 1999, the *selling* of sex has been legal; however, the *buying* of sex is not. Therefore, almost all of the enforcement of prostitution laws in that country is directed toward men (Ritter, 2008; Women's Justice Center, 2008).

Sexual Violence: Rape and Date Rape

Ideally, sexual activity occurs within a loving relationship between consenting adults. In reality, however, sex can sometimes be twisted by hatred and violence. Here we consider two types of sexual violence: rape and date rape.

Rape

Although some people think rape is motivated only by a desire for sex, it is actually an expression of power, a violent act that uses sex to hurt, humiliate, or control another person. According to the Federal Bureau of Investigation (2011), about 85,000 women each year report to the police that they have been raped. The actual number of rapes is likely several times higher.

The official government definition of rape is "the carnal knowledge of a female forcibly and against her will." Thus official rape statistics include only victims who are women. But men, too, are raped—in perhaps 10 percent of all cases. Most men who rape men are not homosexual; they are heterosexuals who are motivated by a desire not for sex but to dominate another person.

Date Rape

A widespread myth is that rape involves strangers. In reality, however, fewer than one-third of rapes fit this pattern. Seventy-three percent of all rapes involve people who know one another—more often than not, pretty well—and these crimes usually take place in familiar surroundings, such as the home or a college campus. The term "date rape" or "acquaintance rape" refers to forcible sexual violence against women by men they know (Laumann et al., 1994; U.S. Department of Justice, 2011).

A second myth, often linked specifically to date rape, is the idea that a woman who has been raped must have done something to encourage the man and make him think she wanted to have sex. Perhaps the victim agreed to go out with the offender. Maybe she even invited him to her room. But, of course, such actions no more justify rape than they would any other type of physical assault.

Although rape is a physical attack, it often leaves emotional and psychological scars. Beyond the brutality of being physically violated, rape by an acquaintance also affects a victim's ability to trust others. Psychological scars are especially serious among the two-thirds of sexual assault victims who are under eighteen and even more so among the one-third who are under the age of twelve. The home is no refuge from rape: One-third of all victims under the age of eighteen are attacked by their own fathers or stepfathers (Snyder, 2000).

How common is date rape? One study found that about 10 percent of a sample of high school girls reported being the victim of sexual or physical violence inflicted by boys they were dating. About 10 percent of high school girls and 5 percent of high school boys reported being forced into having sexual intercourse against their will. The risk of abuse is especially high among girls who become sexually active before reaching the age of fifteen (Dickinson, 2001; Centers for Disease Control and Prevention, 2010).

Nowhere has the issue of date rape been more widely discussed in recent years than on college campuses, where the danger of date rape is high. The collegiate environment promotes easy friendships and encourages trust. At the same time, many young students have much to learn about relationships and about themselves. As the Sociology in Focus box explains, although college life encourages communication, it provides few social norms to help guide young people's sexual experiences. To counter the problem, many schools now actively address myths about rape. In addition, greater attention is now focused on the use of alcohol, which increases the likelihood of sexual violence.

When Sex Is Only Sex: The Campus Culture of "Hooking Up"

Brynne: My mom told me once that she didn't have sex with my dad until after they were engaged.

Katy: I guess times have really changed!

Have you ever been in a sexual situation and not been sure of the right thing to do? Most colleges and universities highlight two important rules. First, sexual activity must take place only when both participants have given clear statements of consent. The consent principle is what makes "having sex" different from date rape. Second, no one should knowingly expose a partner to a sexually transmitted disease, especially when the partner is unaware of the danger.

These rules are very important, but they say little about the larger issue of what sex *means*. For example, when is it "right" to have a sexual relationship? How well do you have to know the other person? If you do have sex, are you obligated to see the person again?

Two generations ago, there were informal rules for campus sex. Dating was considered part of the courtship process. That is, "going out" was a way in which women and men evaluated each other as possible marriage partners while they sharpened their own sense of what they wanted in a mate. Because, on average, marriage took place in the early twenties, many college students became engaged and married while they were still in school. In this cultural climate, sex was viewed by college students as part of a

relationship along with a commitment—a serious interest in the other person as a possible marriage partner.

Today, the sexual culture of the campus is very different. Partly because people now marry much later, the culture of courtship has declined dramatically. About three-fourths of women in a recent national survey point to a new campus pattern, the culture of "hooking up." What exactly is "hooking up"? Most describe it in words like these: "When a girl and a guy get together for a physical encounter—anything from kissing to having sex—and don't necessarily expect anything further."

Student responses to the survey suggest that "hookups" have three characteristics. First, most couples who hook up know little about each other. Second, a typical hookup involves people who have been drinking alcohol, usually at a campus

party. Third, most women are critical of the culture of hooking up and express little satisfaction with these encounters. Certainly, some women (and men) who hook up simply walk away, happy to have enjoyed a sexual experience free of further obligation. But given the powerful emotions that sex can unleash, hooking up often leaves someone wondering what to expect next: "Will you call me tomorrow?" "Will I see you again?"

The survey asked women who had experienced a recent hookup to report how they felt about the experience a day later. A majority of respondents said they felt "awkward," about half felt "disappointed" and "confused," and one in four felt "exploited." Clearly, for many people, sex is more than a physical encounter. Further, because today's campus climate is very sensitive to charges of sexual exploitation, there is a need for clearer standards of fair play.

Join the Blog!

How extensive is the pattern of hooking up on your campus? What do you see as the advantages of sex without commitment? What are the disadvantages of this type of relationship? Are men and women likely to answer these questions differently? Go to MySocLab and join the Sociology in Focus blog to share your opinions and experiences and to see what others think.

Source: Based in part on Marquardt & Glenn (2001).

Theories of Sexuality

 Apply

Applying sociology's various theoretical approaches gives us a better understanding of human sexuality. The following sections discuss the three major approaches. The Applying Theory table on page 146 highlights the key insights of each approach.

Structural-Functional Theory

The structural-functional approach explains the contribution of any social pattern to the overall operation of society. Because sexuality can have such important consequences, society regulates this type of behavior.

The Need to Regulate Sexuality

From a biological point of view, sex allows our species to reproduce. But culture and social institutions regulate *with whom* and *when* people reproduce. For example, most societies condemn married people who have sex with someone other than a spouse. To allow sexual passion to go unchecked would threaten family life, especially the raising of children.

The fact that the incest taboo exists everywhere shows clearly that no society permits a completely free choice of sexual partners. Reproduction by family members other than married partners would break down the kinship system and hopelessly confuse human relationships.

Historically, the social control of sexuality was strong, mostly because sex often led to childbirth. We see these controls at work

The control of women's sexuality is a common theme in human history. During the Middle Ages, Europeans devised the "chastity belt"—a metal device locked about a woman's groin that prevented sexual intercourse (and probably interfered with other bodily functions as well). While such devices are all but unknown today, the social control of sexuality continues. Can you point to examples?

in the old-fashioned distinction between "legitimate" reproduction (within marriage) and "illegitimate" reproduction (outside marriage). But once a society develops the technology to control births, its sexual norms become more permissive. This occurred in the United States, where over the course of the twentieth century, sex moved beyond its basic reproductive function and became mainly a form of intimacy and even recreation (Giddens, 1992).

Latent Functions: The Case of Prostitution

It is easy to see that prostitution is harmful because it spreads disease and exploits women. But does it have latent functions that help explain why prostitution is so widespread? According to Kingsley Davis (1971), prostitution is one way to meet the sexual needs of a large number of people who do not have ready access to sex, including soldiers, travelers, and people who are not physically attractive or are too poor to attract a marriage partner. Some people favor prostitution because they want sex without the "hassle" of a relationship. As a number of analysts have pointed out, "Men don't pay for sex; they pay so they can *leave*" (Miracle, Miracle, & Baumeister, 2003:421).

● **Evaluate** The structural-functional approach helps us see the important role sexuality plays in the organization of society. The incest taboo and other cultural norms also suggest that society has

always paid attention to who has sex with whom and, especially, who reproduces with whom.

Functionalist analysis sometimes ignores gender; when Kingsley Davis wrote of the benefits of prostitution for society, he was really talking about the benefits to *men*. In addition, the fact that sexual patterns change over time, just as they differ around the world, is ignored by this perspective. To appreciate the varied and changeable character of sexuality, we now turn to the symbolic-interaction approach.

CHECK YOUR LEARNING Compared to traditional societies, why do modern societies give people more choice about matters involving sexuality?

Symbolic-Interaction Theory

The symbolic-interaction approach highlights how, as people interact, they construct everyday reality. As explained in Chapter 4 ("Social Interaction in Everyday Life"), different people construct different realities, so the views of one group or society may well differ from those of another. In the same way, our understanding of sexuality can and does change over time, just as it differs from one society to another.

The Social Construction of Sexuality

Almost all social patterns involving sexuality saw a lot of change over the course of the past century. One good illustration is the changing importance of virginity. A century ago, our society's norm—for women, at least—was virginity before marriage. This norm was strong because there was no effective means of birth control available, and virginity was the only assurance a man had that his bride-to-be was not carrying another man's child.

APPLYING THEORY

Sexuality

	Structural-Functional Theory	Symbolic-Interaction Theory	Social-Conflict and Feminist Theories
What is the level of analysis?	Macro-level	Micro-level	Macro-level
What is the importance of sexuality for society?	Society depends on sexuality for reproduction. Society uses the incest taboo and other norms to control sexuality in order to maintain social order.	Sexual practices vary among the many cultures of the world. Some societies allow individuals more freedom than others in matters of sexual behavior.	Sexuality is linked to social inequality. U.S. society regulates women's sexuality more than men's, which is part of the larger pattern of men dominating women.
Has sexuality changed over time? How?	Yes. As advances in birth control technology separate sex from reproduction, societies relax some controls on sexuality.	Yes. The meanings people attach to virginity and other sexual matters are all socially constructed and subject to change.	Yes and no. Some sexual standards have relaxed, but society still defines women in sexual terms, just as homosexual people are harmed by society's heterosexual bias.

Today, because we have gone a long way toward separating sex from reproduction, the virginity norm has weakened. In the United States, among people born between 1963 and 1974, just 16.3 percent of men and 20.1 percent of women reported being virgins at first marriage (Laumann et al., 1994:503). Of course, among some categories of people, the virginity norm is likely to be considered important; among others, it may not be observed at all.

In the same way, the rule that priests in the Catholic Church should be celibate is officially defended as a means to ensure that, by giving up marriage and children, a priest will have greater commitment to the work of the Church. Yet, the Catholic Church did not enact this rule until the 12th century—more than a thousand years after Christ. Clearly, whether members of the clergy should be celibate is a matter of disagreement from one religious organization to another (Stephey, 2009).

A final example of our society's construction of sexuality involves young people. A century ago, childhood was a time of innocence in sexual matters. In recent decades, however, thinking has changed. Although few people encourage sexual activity between children, most people believe that children should be educated about sex so that they can make intelligent choices about their behavior as they grow older.

Global Comparisons

Around the world, different societies attach different meanings to sexuality. For example, Ruth Benedict (1938), an anthropologist who spent years learning the ways of life of the Melanesian people of southeastern New Guinea, reported that adults paid little attention when young children engaged in sexual experimentation with one another. Parents in Melanesia shrugged off such activity because before puberty, sex cannot lead to reproduction. Is it likely that most parents in the United States would respond the same way?

Sexual practices also vary from culture to culture. Circumcision of infant boys (the practice of removing all or part of the foreskin of the penis) is common in the United States but rare in most other parts of the world. A practice sometimes referred to as female circumcision (removal of the clitoris) is rare in the United States but common in parts of Africa and the Middle East (Crossette, 1995; Huffman, 2000). (For more about this practice, more accurately

From a social-conflict point of view, sexuality is not so much a "natural" part of our humanity as it is a socially constructed pattern of behavior. Sexuality plays an important part in social inequality: By defining women in sexual terms, men devalue them as objects. Would you consider the behavior shown here to be "natural" or socially directed? Why?

called "female genital mutilation," see the Thinking About Diversity box on page 261.)

● **Evaluate** The strength of the symbolic-interaction approach lies in revealing the constructed character of familiar social patterns. Understanding that people "construct" sexuality, we can better appreciate the variety of sexual attitudes and practices found over the course of history and around the world.

One limitation of this approach is that not all sexual practices are so variable. Men everywhere have always been more likely to see women in sexual terms than the other way around. Some broader social structure must be at work in a pattern that is this widespread, as we shall see in the following section on the social-conflict approach.

CHECK YOUR LEARNING What evidence can you provide that human sexuality is socially constructed?

Social-Conflict and Feminist Theories

As you have seen in earlier chapters, social-conflict theories highlight dimensions of inequality. This approach reveals how sexuality both reflects patterns of social inequality and helps perpetuate them. Feminist theory, a social-conflict approach focusing on gender inequality, links sexuality to the domination of women by men.

Sexuality: Reflecting Social Inequality

Recall our discussion of prostitution, a practice outlawed almost everywhere in our society. Enforcement of prostitution laws is uneven at best, especially when it comes to who is and is not likely to be arrested. Gender bias is evident here: Although two people are involved, the record shows that police are far more likely to arrest (less powerful) female prostitutes than (more powerful) male clients. Class inequality, too, is involved: It is streetwalkers—women with the least income and most likely to be minorities—who face the highest risk of arrest (Saint James & Alexander, 2004). A feminist approach also leads us to ask whether so many women would be involved in prostitution in the first place if they had economic opportunities equal to those of men.

More generally, which categories of people in U.S. society are most likely to be defined in terms of their sexuality? The answer, once again, is those with less power: women compared to men, people of color compared

Frank: The abortion people are marching again across campus.

Marvin: For or against?

Frank: Both. I'm not sure which came first, but somebody said there have already been some fights . . .

A black van pulls up in front of the storefront in a busy section of the city. Two women get out of the front seat and cautiously look up and down the street. After a moment, one nods to the other, and they open the rear door to let a third woman out of the van. Standing to the right and left of the woman, the two quickly escort her inside the building.

This scene might describe two federal marshals taking a convict to a police station, but it is actually an account of two clinic workers helping a woman who has decided to have an abortion. Why are they so cautious? Anyone who has read the papers in recent years knows about the angry confrontations at abortion clinics across North America. Some opponents have even targeted and killed doctors who carried out abortions, some 1.2 million of which are performed in the United States each year (Ventura et al., 2009). It is one of the most hotly debated issues of our day.

Abortion has not always been so controversial. In colonial times, midwives and other healers performed abortions with little community opposition and with full approval of the law. But controversy arose about 1850, when early medical doctors wanted to eliminate the competition they faced from midwives and other traditional health providers, whose income came largely from ending pregnancies. By 1900, medical doctors had succeeded in getting every state to pass a law banning abortion.

Such laws greatly reduced the number of abortions. Those that did occur were performed "underground," as secretly as possible. Many women who wanted abortions—especially those who were poor—had little choice but to seek help from unlicensed "back alley" abortionists, sometimes with tragic results due to unsanitary conditions and the use of medically dangerous techniques.

By the 1960s, opposition to antiabortion laws was rising. In 1973, the U.S. Supreme Court made a landmark decision (in the cases of *Roe* v. *Wade* and *Doe* v. *Bolton*), striking down all state laws banning abortion. In effect, this action established a woman's legal access to abortion nationwide.

Even so, the abortion controversy continues. On one side of the issue are people who describe themselves as "pro-choice," supporting a woman's right to choose abortion. On the other side are those who call themselves "pro-life," opposing abortion as morally wrong; these people would like to see the Supreme Court reverse its 1973 decision.

How strong is the support for each side of the abortion controversy? A recent national survey asked a sample of adults the question "Should it be possible for a pregnant woman to obtain a legal abortion if the woman wants it for any reason?" In response, 42 percent said yes (placing them in the pro-choice camp) and 54 percent said no (expressing the pro-life position); the remaining 4 percent offered no opinion (NORC, 2011:399).

A closer look shows that circumstances make a big difference in how people see this issue. The figure shows that large majorities of U.S. adults favor legal abortion if a pregnancy seriously threatens a woman's health, if the pregnancy is a result of rape, or if a fetus is likely to have a serious defect. The bottom line is that about 42 percent support access to abortion under *any* circumstances, but 83 percent support access to abortion under *some* circumstances.

Many of those who take the pro-life position feel strongly that abortion amounts to killing unborn children—nearly 50 million since *Roe* v. *Wade* was passed. To them, people never have the right to end innocent life in this way. But pro-choice advocates are no less committed to the position that women must have control over their own bodies. If pregnancy decides the course of women's lives, women will never be able to compete with men on equal terms, whether it is on campus or in the workplace. Therefore, access to legal, safe abortion is a necessary condition to women's full participation in society (Alan Guttmacher Institute, 2011).

What Do You Think?

1. The more conservative, pro-life position sees abortion as a moral issue, and the more liberal, pro-choice position views abortion as a power issue. Compare these positions to how conservatives and liberals view the issue of pornography.

2. Surveys show that men and women have almost the same opinions about abortion. Does this surprise you? Why or why not?

3. Why do you think the abortion controversy is often so bitter? Is there some reasonable middle ground on this issue? Explain.

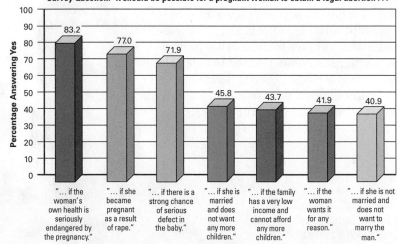

Survey Question: "It should be possible for a pregnant woman to obtain a *legal abortion* . . ."

Percentage Answering Yes

- 83.2 — ". . . if the woman's own health is seriously endangered by the pregnancy."
- 77.0 — ". . . if she became pregnant as a result of rape."
- 71.9 — ". . . if there is a strong chance of serious defect in the baby."
- 45.8 — ". . . if she is married and does not want any more children."
- 43.7 — ". . . if the family has a very low income and cannot afford any more children."
- 41.9 — ". . . if the woman wants it for any reason."
- 40.9 — ". . . if she is not married and does not want to marry the man."

When Should the Law Allow a Woman to Choose Abortion?

The extent of public support for legal abortion depends on how the issue is presented.

Source: NORC (2011:397–399).

queer theory a body of research findings that challenges the heterosexual bias in U.S. society

heterosexism a view that labels anyone who is not heterosexual as "queer"

to whites, and gays and lesbians compared to heterosexuals. In this way, sexuality, a natural part of human life, is used by society to define some people as less worthy.

Sexuality: Creating Social Inequality

Social-conflict theorists, especially feminists, point to sexuality as the root of inequality between women and men. Defining women in sexual terms devalues them from full human beings to objects of men's interest and attention. Is it any wonder that the word "pornography" comes from the Greek word *porne,* meaning "harlot" or "prostitute"?

If men define women in sexual terms, it is easy to see pornography—almost all of which is consumed by males—as a power issue. Because pornography typically shows women focused on pleasing men, it supports the idea that men have power over women.

Some radical critics doubt that this element of power can ever be removed from heterosexual relations (A. Dworkin, 1987). Most social-conflict theorists do not reject heterosexuality, but they do agree that sexuality can and does degrade women. Our culture often describes sexuality in terms of sport (men "scoring" with women) and violence ("slamming," "banging," and "hitting on," for example, are verbs used for both fighting and sex).

Queer Theory

Social-conflict theory has taken aim not only at the domination of women by men but also at heterosexuals dominating homosexuals. In recent years, as many lesbians and gay men have sought public acceptance, a gay voice has risen in sociology. The term **queer theory** refers to *a body of research findings that challenges the heterosexual bias in U.S. society.*

Queer theory begins with the claim that our society is characterized by **heterosexism**, *a view that labels anyone who is not heterosexual as "queer."* Our heterosexual culture victimizes a wide range of people, including gay men, lesbians, bisexuals, intersexuals, transsexuals, and even asexual people. Furthermore, although most people agree that bias against women (sexism) and people of color (racism) is wrong, heterosexism is widely tolerated and sometimes well within the law. For example, U.S. military forces cannot legally discharge a female soldier simply for "acting like a woman" because this would be a clear case of gender discrimination. But, from 1916 when the ban was enacted until the law changed at the end of 2010, the military forces could and did discharge women and men for homosexuality if they were sexually active (Webley, 2010).

Heterosexism is also part of everyday culture (Kitzinger, 2005). When we describe something as "sexy," for example, don't we really mean attractive to *heterosexuals*?

● **Evaluate** The social-conflict and feminist approaches show how sexuality is both a cause and an effect of inequality. In particular, they help us understand men's power over women and heterosexual people's domination of homosexual people.

At the same time, these approaches overlook the fact that many people do not see sexuality as a power issue. On the contrary, many couples enjoy a vital sexual relationship that deepens their commitment to one another. In addition, these social-conflict approaches pay little attention to steps our society has made toward reducing inequality. Today's men are less likely to describe women as sex objects than they were a few decades ago. One of the most important issues in the workplace today is ensuring that all employees remain free from sexual harassment. Rising public concern (see Chapter 10, "Gender Stratification") has reduced sex abuse in the workplace. There is also ample evidence that the gay rights movement has won greater opportunities and social acceptance for gay people.

CHECK YOUR LEARNING How does sexuality play a part in creating social inequality?

This chapter closes with a look at what is perhaps the most divisive issue involving sexuality: **abortion,** *the deliberate termination of a pregnancy.* There seems to be no middle ground in the debate over this controversial issue. The Controversy & Debate box helps explain why.

Seeing Sociology in Everyday Life

How do the mass media play into our society's views of human sexuality?

Far from it being a "natural" or simply "biological" concept, cultures around the world attach all sorts of meanings to human sexuality. The photos below show how the mass media—in this case, popular magazines—reflect our own culture's ideas about sexuality. In each case, can you "decode" the magazine cover and explain its messages? To what extent do you think the messages are true?

Hint The messages we get from mass media sources like these not only tell us about sexuality but also tell us what sort of people we ought to be. There is a lot of importance attached to sexuality for women, placing pressure on women to look good to men and to define life success in terms of attracting men with their sexuality. Similarly, being masculine means being successful, sophisticated, in charge, and able to attract desirable women. When the mass media endorse sexuality, it is almost always according to the norm of heterosexuality.

Magazines like this one are found at the checkout lines of just about every supermarket and discount store in the United States. Looking just at the cover, what can you conclude about women's sexuality in our society?

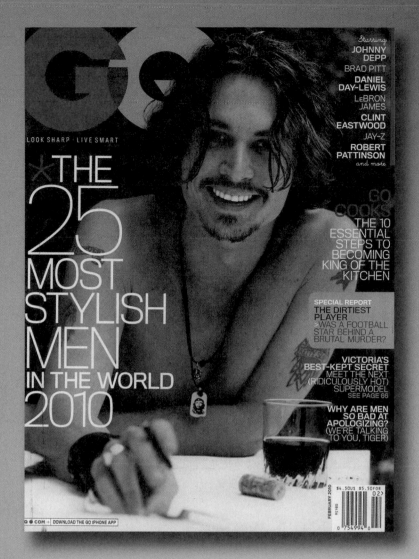

Messages about sexuality are directed to men as well as to women. Here is a recent issue of *GQ*. What messages about masculinity can you find? Do you see any evidence of heterosexual bias?

Seeing Sociology in *Your* Everyday Life

1. Looking at the *Cosmopolitan* cover, what evidence of heterosexual bias do you see? Explain.

2. Contact your school's student services office, and ask for information about the extent of sexual violence on your campus. Do people typically report such crimes? What policies and procedures does your school have to respond to sexual violence?

3. Based on what you have read in this chapter, what evidence supports the argument that sexuality is constructed by society? For more on how sexuality is a societal issue, go to the "Seeing Sociology in *Your* Everyday Life" feature on MySocLab, where you will also find suggestions about the benefits of seeing sexuality using the socio-logical perspective.

What Is Sexuality?

Sex is biological, referring to bodily differences between females and males.

Gender is cultural, referring to behavior, power, and privileges a society attaches to being female or male.

Sexuality is a **biological issue**.

- Sex is determined at conception as a male sperm joins a female ovum.
- Males and females have different genitals (*primary sex characteristics*) and bodily development (*secondary sex characteristics*).
- *Intersexual people (hermaphrodites)* have some combination of male and female genitalia.
- *Transsexual people* feel they are one sex although biologically they are the other.
  pp. 131–32

Sexuality is a **cultural issue**.

- For humans, sex is a matter of cultural meaning and personal choice rather than biological programming.
- Sexual practices vary considerably from one society to another (examples include kissing, ideas about modesty, and standards of beauty).
- The *incest taboo* exists in all societies because regulating sexuality, especially reproduction, is a necessary element of social organization. Specific taboos vary from one society to another.   **pp. 132–34**

sex (p. 131) the biological distinction between females and males

primary sex characteristics (p. 131) the genitals, organs used for reproduction

secondary sex characteristics (p. 131) bodily development, apart from the genitals, that distinguishes biologically mature females and males

intersexual people (p. 132) people whose bodies (including genitals) have both female and male characteristics

transsexuals (p. 132) people who feel they are one sex even though biologically they are the other

incest taboo (p. 133) a norm forbidding sexual relations or marriage between certain relatives

Sexual Attitudes in the United States

The **sexual revolution**, which peaked in the 1960s and 1970s, drew sexuality out into the open. Baby boomers were the first generation to grow up with the idea that sex was a normal part of social life.   **pp. 134–35**

The **sexual counterrevolution**, which was evident by 1980, aimed criticism at "permissiveness" and urged a return to more traditional "family values."   **p. 135**

Beginning with the work of Alfred Kinsey, researchers have studied sexual behavior in the United States and reached many interesting conclusions:

- Premarital sexual intercourse became more common during the twentieth century.
- Almost half of young men and women have intercourse by their senior year in high school.
- Among all U.S. adults, sexual activity varies: One-third report having sex with a partner a few times a year or not at all; another one-third have sex once to several times a month; the remaining one-third have sex two or more times a week.
- Extramarital sex is widely condemned, and just 25 percent of married men and 10 percent of married women report being sexually unfaithful to their spouses at some time.   **pp. 135–37**

Sexual Orientation

👁—Watch the Video on mysoclab.com

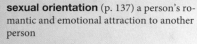

Sexual orientation is a person's romantic or emotional attraction to another person. Four sexual orientations are
- heterosexuality
- homosexuality
- bisexuality
- asexuality   **pp. 137–38**

Most research supports the claim that sexual orientation is rooted in biology in much the same way as being right-handed or left-handed.   **pp. 138–40**

Sexual orientation is not a matter of neat categories because many people who think of themselves as heterosexual have homosexual experiences; the reverse is also true.
- The share of the U.S. population that is homosexual depends on how you define "homosexuality."
- 5.6% of adult men and 12.7% of adult women report engaging in homosexual activity at some point intheir lives; 1.7% of men and 1.1% of women define themselves as homosexual; 1.1% of men and 3.5% of women claim a bisexual identity.   **p. 140**

The gay rights movement helped change public attitudes toward greater acceptance of homosexuality. Still, 47 percent of U.S. adults say homosexuality is wrong.   **pp. 140–41**

sexual orientation (p. 137) a person's romantic and emotional attraction to another person

heterosexuality (p. 137) sexual attraction to someone of the other sex

homosexuality (p. 137) sexual attraction to someone of the same sex

bisexuality (p. 137) sexual attraction to people of both sexes

asexuality (p. 137) a lack of sexual attraction to people of either sex

homophobia (p. 140) discomfort over close personal interaction with people thought to be gay, lesbian, or bisexual

Sexual Issues and Controversies

Teen Pregnancy About 750,000 U.S. teenagers become pregnant each year. The rate of teenage pregnancy has dropped since 1950, when many teens married and had children. Today, most pregnant teens are not married and are at high risk of dropping out of school and being poor.   **pp. 141–42**

✳—Explore the Map on mysoclab.com

Pornography The law allows local communities to set standards of decency. Conservatives condemn pornography on moral grounds; liberals view pornography as a power issue, condemning it as demeaning to women.   **pp. 141–42**

Prostitution The selling of sexual services is illegal almost everywhere in the United States. Many people view prostitution as a victimless crime, but it victimizes women and spreads sexually transmitted diseases.   **pp. 142–44**

📖—Read the Document on mysoclab.com

Sexual Violence About 85,000 rapes are reported each year in the United States, but the actual number is probably several times higher. About 10 percent of rape cases involve men as victims. Rape is a violent crime in which victim and offender typically know one another.   **pp. 144–45**

Abortion Laws banned abortion in all states by 1900. Opposition to these laws rose during the 1960s, and in 1973, the U.S. Supreme Court declared these laws unconstitutional. Today, some 1.2 million abortions are performed each year. People who describe themselves as "pro-choice" support a woman's right to choose abortion; people who call themselves "pro-life" oppose abortion on moral grounds.   **pp. 148–49**

pornography (p. 141) sexually explicit material intended to cause sexual arousal

prostitution (p. 142) the selling of sexual services

abortion (p. 149) the deliberate termination of a pregnancy

Theories of Sexuality

Structural-functional theory highlights society's need to regulate sexual activity and especially reproduction. One universal norm is the incest taboo, which keeps family relations clear.   **pp. 145–46**

Symbolic-interaction theory emphasizes the various meanings people attach to sexuality. The social construction of sexuality can be seen in sexual differences between societies and in changing sexual patterns over time.   **pp. 146–47**

Social-conflict theory links sexuality to social inequality. *Feminist theory* claims that men dominate women by devaluing them to the level of sexual objects. *Queer theory* claims our society has a heterosexual bias, defining anything different as "queer."   **pp. 147–49**

queer theory (p. 149) a body of research findings that challenges the heterosexual bias in U.S. society

heterosexism (p. 149) a view that labels anyone who is not heterosexual as "queer"

7 Deviance

Learning Objectives

Remember the definitions of the key terms highlighted in boldfaced type throughout this chapter.

Understand deviance as not the action of bad people but part of the way society is organized.

Apply sociology's major theoretical approaches to deviance.

Analyze the operation of major parts of the criminal justice system.

Evaluate the importance and limitation of official criminal statistics provided by the FBI.

Create the ability to move beyond commonsense ideas about right and wrong.

CHAPTER OVERVIEW

Common sense may suggest that some things are "right" and some are "wrong" and that most of us, at least most of the time, know the difference. But the line between "good" and "bad" is highly variable because it is constructed by society. This chapter explains how and why society creates and encourages both conformity and deviance. The chapter also introduces the concept of crime and surveys the operation of the criminal justice system. ■

"I was like the guy lost in another dimension, a stranger in town, not knowing which way to go." With these words, Bruce Glover recalls the day he returned to his hometown of Detroit, Michigan, after being away for twenty-six years—a long stretch in a state prison. Now fifty-six years of age, Glover was a young man of thirty when he was arrested for running a call girl ring. Found guilty at trial, he was given a stiff jail sentence.

"My mother passed while I was gone," Glover continues, shaking his head. "I lost everything." On the day he walked out of prison, he realized just how true that statement was. He had nowhere to go and no way to get there. He had no valid identification, which he would need to find a place to live and a job. He had no money to buy the clothes he needed to go out and start looking. He turned to a prison official and asked for help. Only with the assistance of a state agency was he finally able to get some money and temporary housing (C. Jones, 2007).

This chapter explores issues involving crime and criminals, asking not only how our criminal justice system handles offenders but also why societies develop standards of right and wrong in the first place. As you will see, law is simply one part of a complex system of social control: Society teaches us all to conform, at least most of the time, to countless rules. We begin our investigation by defining several basic concepts.

What Is Deviance?

 **Understand**

Deviance is *the recognized violation of cultural norms.* Norms guide virtually all human activities, so the concept of deviance is quite broad. One category of deviance is **crime**, *the violation of a society's formally enacted criminal law.* Even criminal deviance spans a wide range, from minor traffic violations to prostitution, sexual assault, and murder.

Most familiar examples of nonconformity are negative instances of rule breaking, such as stealing from a campus bookstore, assaulting a fellow student, or driving a car while intoxicated. But we also define especially righteous people—students who speak up too much in class or people who are overly enthusiastic about new computer technology—as deviant, even if we give them a measure of respect. What all deviant actions or attitudes, whether negative or positive, have in common is some element of *difference* that causes us to think of another person as an "outsider" (H. S. Becker, 1966).

Not all deviance involves action or even choice. The very *existence* of some categories of people can be troublesome to others. To the young, elderly people may seem hopelessly "out of touch," and to some whites, the mere presence of people of color may cause discomfort. Able-bodied people often view people with disabilities as an out-group, just as rich people may shun the poor for falling short of their high-class standards.

Social Control

All of us are subject to **social control**, *attempts by society to regulate people's thoughts and behavior.* Often this process is informal, as when parents praise or scold their children or when friends make fun of a classmate's choice of music. Cases of serious deviance, however, may bring action by the **criminal justice system**, *the organizations—police, courts, and prison officials—that respond to alleged violations of the law.*

How a society defines deviance, *who* is branded as deviant, and *what* people decide to do about deviance all have to do with the way a society is organized. Only gradually, however, have people come to understand that the roots of deviance are deep in society, as this chapter will explain.

The Biological Context

Chapter 3 ("Socialization: From Infancy to Old Age") explained that a century ago, most people understood—or more correctly, misunderstood—human behavior to be the result of biological instincts.

Early interest in criminality therefore focused on biological causes. In 1876, Cesare Lombroso (1835–1909), an Italian physician who worked in prisons, theorized that criminals stand out physically, with low foreheads, prominent jaws and cheekbones, protruding ears, hairy bodies, and unusually long arms. All in all, Lombroso claimed that criminals look like our apelike ancestors.

Had Lombroso looked more carefully, he would have found the physical features he linked to criminality throughout the entire population. We now know that no physical traits distinguish criminals from noncriminals.

In the middle of the twentieth century, William Sheldon took a different approach, suggesting that body structure might predict criminality (Sheldon, Hartl, & McDermott, 1949). He cross-checked hundreds of young men for body type and criminal history and concluded that delinquency was most common among boys with muscular, athletic builds. Sheldon Glueck and Eleanor Glueck (1950) confirmed that conclusion but cautioned that a powerful build does not necessarily *cause* or even *predict* criminality. Parents, they suggested, tend to be somewhat distant from powerfully built sons, who in turn grow up to show less sensitivity toward others. In a self-fulfilling prophecy, people who expect muscular boys to be bullies may act in ways that bring about the aggressive behavior they expect.

Today, genetics research seeks possible links between biology and crime. In 2003, scientists at the University of Wisconsin reported results of a twenty-five-year study of crime among 400 boys. The researchers collected DNA samples from each boy and noted any history of trouble with the law. The researchers concluded that genetic factors (especially defective genes that, say, make too much of an enzyme) together with environmental factors (especially abuse early in life) were strong predictors of adult crime and violence. They noted, too, that these factors together were a better predictor of crime than either one alone (Lemonick, 2003; Pinker, 2003).

● **Evaluate** Biological theories offer a limited explanation of crime. The best guess at present is that biological traits in combination with environmental factors explain some serious crime. Most of the actions we define as deviant, however, are carried out by people who are physically quite normal.

In addition, because a biological approach looks at the individual, it offers no insight into how some kinds of behaviors come to be defined as deviant in the first place. Therefore, although there is much to learn about how human biology may

Deviance is always a matter of difference. Deviance emerges in everyday life as we encounter people whose appearance or behavior differs from what we consider "normal." Who is the "deviant" in this photograph? From whose point of view?

affect behavior, research currently puts far greater emphasis on social influences.

CHECK YOUR LEARNING What does biological research add to our understanding of crime? What are the limitations of this approach?

Personality Factors

Like biological theories, psychological explanations of deviance focus on individual abnormality. Some personality traits are inherited, but most psychologists think personality is shaped primarily by social experience. Deviance, then, is viewed as the result of "unsuccessful" socialization.

Classic research by Walter Reckless and Simon Dinitz (1967) illustrates the psychological approach. Reckless and Dinitz began by asking teachers to categorize twelve-year-old male students as either likely or unlikely to get into trouble with the law. They then interviewed both the boys and their mothers to assess each boy's self-concept and how he related to others. Analyzing their results, Reckless and Dinitz found that the "good boys" displayed a strong conscience (what Freud called superego), could handle frustration, and identified with conventional cultural norms and values. The "bad boys," by contrast, had a weaker conscience, displayed little tolerance of frustration, and felt out of step with conventional culture.

As we might expect, the "good boys" went on to have fewer runins with the police than the "bad boys." Because all the boys lived in an area where delinquency was widespread, the investigators

Why is it that street-corner gambling like this is usually against the law but playing the same games in a fancy casino is not?

The Social Foundations of Deviance

Although we tend to view deviance as the free choice or personal failings of individuals, all behavior—deviance as well as conformity—is shaped by society. Three social foundations of deviance identified here will be detailed later in this chapter:

1. **Deviance varies according to cultural norms.** No thought or action is inherently deviant; it becomes deviant only in relation to particular norms. Public nudity breaks the law almost everywhere but is common in some San Francisco neighborhoods; automobile radar detectors are legal in every state except for Virginia. Rural areas of Nevada permit prostitution, a practice outlawed in the rest of the United States. Fifteen states have gambling casinos, twenty-nine have casinos on Indian reservations, and thirteen states have casinos at race tracks. In all other states, casino gambling is illegal. Text messaging while driving is legal in eleven states but against the law in thirty-five others (four other states forbid the practice for young drivers). Ten states even ban the sale of raw milk (Ozersky, 2010; American Gaming Association, 2011; National Conference of State Legislatures, 2011).

    Further, most cities and towns have at least one unique law. For example, Mobile, Alabama, outlaws the wearing of stiletto-heeled shoes; Pine Lawn, Missouri, bans saggy, "low-rider" pants; South Padre Island, Texas, bans the wearing of neckties; Mount Prospect, Illinois, has a law against keeping pigeons or bees; Topeka, Kansas, bans snowball fights; Hoover, South Dakota, does not allow fishing with a kerosene lantern; and Beverly Hills, California, regulates the number of tennis balls allowed on the court at one time (R. Steele, 2000; Wittenauer, 2007).

    Around the world, deviance is even more diverse. Albania outlaws any public display of religious faith, such as "crossing" oneself; Vietnam can prosecute citizens for meeting with foreigners; Malaysia does not allow tight-fitting jeans for women; Saudi Arabia bans the sale of red flowers on Valentine's Day; Iran does not allow women to wear makeup and forbids the playing of rap music (Chopra, 2008).

2. **People become deviant as others define them that way.** Everyone violates cultural norms at one time or another. Have you ever walked around talking to yourself or "borrowed" a pen from your workplace? Whether such behavior defines us as mentally ill or criminal depends on how others perceive, define, and respond to it.

3. **Both norms and the way people define rule breaking involve social power.** The law, claimed Karl Marx, is the means by which powerful people protect their interests. A homeless person who stands on a street corner speaking out against the government risks arrest for disturbing the peace; a mayoral candidate during an election campaign doing exactly the same thing gets police protection. In short, norms and how we apply them reflect social inequality.

attributed staying out of trouble to a personality that controlled deviant impulses. Based on this conclusion, Reckless and Dinitz called their analysis *containment theory.*

In a more recent study, researchers followed 500 nonidentical twin boys from birth until they reached the age of thirty-two. Twins were used so that researchers could compare each of the twins to his brother, controlling for social class and family environment. Observing the boys when they were young, parents, teachers, and the researchers assessed their level of self-control, ability to withstand frustration, and ability to delay gratification. Echoing the earlier conclusions of Reckless and Dinitz, the researchers found that the brother who had lower scores on these measures in childhood almost always went on to get into more trouble, including criminal activity (Moffitt et al., 2011).

Evaluate Psychologists have shown that personality patterns have some connection to deviance. Some serious criminals are psychopaths who do not feel guilt or shame, have no fear of punishment, and have little or no sympathy for the people they harm (Herpertz & Sass, 2000). More generally, the capacity for self-control and the ability to withstand frustration do seem to be skills that promote conformity. However, as noted in the case of the biological approach, most serious crimes are committed by people whose psychological profiles are normal.

Both biological and psychological research views deviance as a trait of individuals. The reason these approaches have limited value in explaining deviance is that wrongdoing has more to do with the organization of society. We now turn to a sociological approach, which explores where ideas of right and wrong come from, why people define some rule breakers but not others as deviant, and what role power plays in this process.

CHECK YOUR LEARNING Why do biological and psychological analyses not explain deviance very well?

The Functions of Deviance: Structural-Functional Theories

● Apply

The key insight of the structural-functional approach is that deviance is a necessary part of social organization. This point was made a century ago by Emile Durkheim.

Durkheim's Basic Insight

In his pioneering study of deviance, Emile Durkheim (1964a, orig. 1893; 1964b, orig. 1895) made the surprising statement that there is nothing abnormal about deviance. In fact, it performs four essential functions:

1. **Deviance affirms cultural values and norms.** As moral creatures, people must prefer some attitudes and behaviors to others. But any definition of virtue rests on an opposing idea of vice: There can be no good without evil and no justice without crime. Deviance is needed to define and support morality.

2. **Responding to deviance clarifies moral boundaries.** By defining some individuals as deviant, people draw a boundary between right and wrong. For example, a college marks the line between academic honesty and cheating by disciplining students who cheat on exams.

3. **Responding to deviance brings people together.** People typically react to serious deviance with shared outrage. In doing so, Durkheim explained, they reaffirm the moral ties that bind them. For example, after the 2012 shooting death of Florida high-school student Trayvon Martin, people across the United States were joined by a common desire to see that a full investigation of the shooting was carried out by authorities and that justice was done.

4. **Deviance encourages social change.** Deviant people push a society's moral boundaries, suggesting alternatives to the status quo and encouraging change. Today's deviance, declared Durkheim, can become tomorrow's morality (1964b:71, orig. 1895). For example, rock-and-roll, condemned as immoral in the 1950s, became a multibillion-dollar industry just a few years later (see the Thinking About Diversity box on page 52). In recent decades, hip-hop music has followed the same path toward respectability.

An Illustration: The Puritans of Massachusetts Bay

Kai Erikson's classic study of the Puritans of Massachusetts Bay brings Durkheim's theory to life. Erikson (2005b, orig. 1966) shows that even the Puritans, a disciplined and highly religious group, created deviance to clarify their moral boundaries. In fact, Durkheim might well have had the Puritans in mind when he wrote:

> Imagine a society of saints, a perfect cloister of exemplary individuals. Crimes, properly so called, will there be unknown; but faults which appear [insignificant] to the layman will create there the same scandal that the ordinary offense does in ordinary consciousness. . . . For the same reason, the perfect and upright man judges his smallest failings with a severity that the majority reserve for acts more truly in the nature of an offense. (1964b:68–69, orig. 1895)

Deviance is thus not a matter of a few "bad apples" but a necessary condition of "good" social living.

Deviance may be found in every society, but the *kind* of deviance people generate depends on the moral issues they seek to clarify. The Puritans, for example, experienced a number of "crime waves," including the well-known outbreak of witchcraft in 1692. With each response, the Puritans answered questions about the range of proper beliefs by celebrating some of their members and condemning others as deviant.

Erikson discovered that even though the offenses changed, the proportion of the population the Puritans defined as deviant remained steady over time. This stability, he concluded, confirms Durkheim's claim that society creates deviants to mark its changing moral boundaries. In other words, by constantly defining a small number of people as deviant, the Puritans maintained the moral shape of their society.

Merton's Strain Theory

Some deviance may be necessary for a society to function, but Robert Merton (1938, 1968) argued that too much deviance results from particular social arrangements. Specifically, the extent and type of deviance depend on whether a society provides the *means* (such as schooling and job opportunities) to achieve cultural *goals* (such as financial success). Merton's strain theory is illustrated in Figure 7–1 on page 160.

Conformity lies in pursuing cultural goals through approved means. Therefore, the U.S. "success story" is someone who gains

Durkheim claimed that deviance is a necessary element of social organization, serving several important functions. After a man convicted of killing a child settled in their New Hampshire town, residents came together to affirm their community ties as well as their understanding of right and wrong. Has any event on your campus caused a similar reaction?

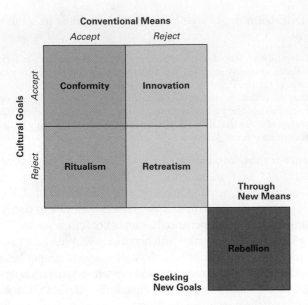

Conventional Means

	Accept	*Reject*
Accept	Conformity	Innovation
Reject	Ritualism	Retreatism

Cultural Goals

Through New Means

Rebellion

Seeking New Goals

FIGURE 7–1 Merton's Strain Theory of Deviance

Combining a person's view of cultural goals and the conventional means to obtain them allowed Robert Merton to identify various types of deviance.

Source: Merton (1968).

wealth and prestige through talent, schooling, and hard work. But not everyone who wants conventional success has the opportunity to attain it. For example, people living in poverty may see little hope of becoming successful if they play by the rules. According to Merton, the strain between our culture's emphasis on wealth and the lack of opportunities to get rich may encourage some people, especially the poor, to engage in stealing, drug dealing, and other forms of street crime. Merton called this type of deviance *innovation*—using unconventional means (street crime) rather than conventional means (hard work at a "straight" job) to achieve a culturally approved goal (wealth).

The inability to reach a cultural goal may also prompt another type of deviance that Merton calls *ritualism*. For example, people who believe they cannot achieve the cultural goal of becoming rich may stick rigidly to the rules (the conventional means) anyway in order to at least feel respectable.

A third response to the inability to succeed is *retreatism*: rejecting both cultural goals and means so that one in effect "drops out." Some alcoholics, drug addicts, and street people are retreatists. The deviance of retreatists lies in their unconventional lifestyles and, perhaps more seriously, in what seems to be their willingness to live this way.

Young people cut off from legitimate opportunity often form subcultures that many people view as deviant. Gang subcultures are one way young people gain the sense of belonging and respect denied to them by the larger culture.

The fourth response to failure is *rebellion*. Like retreatists, rebels such as radical "survivalists" reject both the cultural definition of success and the conventional means of achieving it but go one step further by forming a counterculture supporting alternatives to the existing social order.

Deviant Subcultures

Richard Cloward and Lloyd Ohlin (1966) extended Merton's theory, proposing that crime results not simply from limited legitimate (legal) opportunity but also from readily accessible illegitimate (illegal) opportunity. In short, deviance or conformity depends on the *relative opportunity structure* that frames a person's life.

The life of Al Capone, a notorious gangster, illustrates Cloward and Ohlin's theory. As a son of poor immigrants, Capone faced barriers of poverty and ethnic prejudice, which lowered his odds of achieving success in conventional terms. Yet as a young man during the Prohibition era (the years between 1920 and 1933, when alcoholic beverages were banned in the United States), Capone found in his neighborhood people who could teach him how to sell alcohol illegally—a source of illegitimate opportunity. Where the structure of opportunity favors criminal activity, Cloward and Ohlin predict the development of *criminal subcultures,* such as Capone's criminal organization or today's inner-city street gangs.

But what happens when people are unable to find *any* opportunity, legal or illegal? Then deviance may take one of two forms. One is *conflict subcultures,* such as armed street gangs that regularly engage in violence, ignited by frustration and a desire for respect. Another possible outcome is the development of *retreatist subcultures,* in which deviants drop out and abuse alcohol or other drugs.

Albert Cohen (1971, orig. 1955) suggests that criminality is most common among lower-class youths because they have the least opportunity to achieve success by conventional means. Neglected by society, they seek self-respect by creating a delinquent subculture that defines as worthy the traits these youths do have. Being feared on the street may win few points with society as a whole, but it may satisfy a youth's desire to "be somebody" in a local neighborhood.

Walter Miller (1970, orig. 1958) adds that deviant subcultures are characterized by (1) *trouble,* arising from frequent conflict with teachers and police; (2) *toughness,* the value placed on physical size, strength, and agility, especially among males; (3) *smartness,* the ability to succeed on the streets, to outsmart or "con" others; (4) *a need for excitement,* the search for thrills, risk, or danger; (5) *a belief in fate,* a sense that people lack control over their own lives; and (6) *a desire for freedom,* often expressed as anger toward authority figures.

Watch the video "Crips and Bloods, clip 1" on **mysoclab.com**

Astrid: Simon! You're downloading that music illegally. You'll get us both into trouble!

Simon: Look, everyone cheats. Rich CEOs cheat in business. Ordinary people cheat on their taxes. Politicians lie. What else is new?

Astrid: So it's OK to steal? Is that what you really believe?

Simon: I'm not saying it's OK. I'm just saying everyone does it. . . .

It's been a bad couple of years for the idea of playing by the rules. First, we learn that the executives of not just one but many U.S. corporations are guilty of fraud and outright stealing on a scale most of us cannot even imagine. More recently, we realize that the Wall Street leaders running the U.S. economy not only did a pretty bad job of it but also paid themselves tens of millions of dollars for doing so. And, of course, even the Catholic church, which we hold up as a model of moral behavior, is still trying to recover from the charges that hundreds of priests have sexually abused parishioners (most of them under the age of consent) for decades while church officials covered up the crimes.

There are plenty of theories offered about what is causing this widespread wrongdoing. Some suggest that the pressure to win—by whatever means necessary—in the highly competitive world of business and politics can be overwhelming. As one analyst put it, "You can get away with your embezzlements and your lies, but you can never get away with *failing*."

Such thinking helps explain the wrongdoing among many CEOs in the corporate world and the conviction of several members of Congress for ethics violations, but it offers little insight into the problem of abusive priests. In some ways at least, wrongdoing seems to have become a way of life for just about everybody. For example, the Internal Revenue Service reports that Simon is right—millions of U.S. taxpayers cheat on their taxes, failing to pay an estimated $345 billion each year.

The music industry claims that it has lost billions of dollars to illegal piracy of recordings, a practice especially common among young people. Perhaps most disturbing of all, surveys of students in high school, college, and also graduate school show that about half say they cheated on a test at least once during the past year (Gallup, 2004; Morin, 2006).

Emile Durkheim viewed society as a moral system, built on a set of rules about what people should and should not do. Years earlier, another French thinker named Blaise Pascal made the opposite claim that "cheating is the foundation of society." Today, which of the two statements is closer to the truth?

Join the Blog!

In your opinion, how widespread is wrongdoing in U.S. society today? Is the problem getting worse? Have you downloaded music illegally? What about cheating on college assignments or tests? Go to MySocLab and join the Sociology in Focus blog to share your opinions and experiences and to see what others think.

Do you consider cheating in school wrong? Would you turn in someone you saw cheating? Why or why not?

Sources: "Our Cheating Hearts" (2002), Bono (2006), and Lohr (2008).

Finally, Elijah Anderson (1994, 2002; Kubrin, 2005) explains that in poor urban neighborhoods, most people manage to conform to conventional or "decent" values. Yet faced every day with neighborhood crime and violence, indifference or even hostility from police, and sometimes even neglect from their own parents, some young men decide to live by the "street code." To show that he can survive on the street, a young man displays "nerve," a willingness to stand up to any threat. Following this street code, the young man believes that a violent death is better than being "dissed" (disrespected) by others. Some manage to escape the dangers, but the risk of ending up in jail—or worse—is very high for these young men, who have been pushed to the margins of our society.

● **Evaluate** Durkheim made an important contribution by pointing out the functions of deviance. However, there is evidence that a community does not always come together in reaction to crime; sometimes fear of crime causes people to withdraw from public life (Liska & Warner, 1991; Warr & Ellison, 2000).

Merton's strain theory also has been criticized for explaining some kinds of deviance (stealing, for example) better than others (crimes of passion or mental illness). Furthermore, not everyone seeks success in the conventional terms of wealth, as strain theory suggests.

The general argument of Cloward and Ohlin, Cohen, and Miller—that deviance reflects the opportunity structure of society—has been confirmed by subsequent research (Allan & Steffensmeier, 1989; Uggen, 1999). However, these theories fall short by assuming that everyone shares the same cultural standards for judging right and wrong. If we define crime as including not just burglary and auto theft but also fraud and other crimes carried out by corporate executives and Wall Street tycoons, many more high-income people will be counted among criminals. There is evidence that people of all social backgrounds have become more casual about breaking the rules, as the Sociology in Focus box explains.

Finally, all structural-functional theories suggest that everyone who breaks the rules will be labeled deviant. However, becoming deviant is actually a highly complex process, as the next section explains.

CHECK YOUR LEARNING Why do you think many of the theories just discussed seem to say that crime is more common among people with lower social standing?

Defining Deviance: Symbolic-Interaction Theories

 Apply

The symbolic-interaction approach explains how people come to see deviance in everyday situations. From this point of view, definitions of deviance and conformity are surprisingly flexible.

Labeling Theory

The central contribution of symbolic-interaction analysis is **labeling theory**, *the idea that deviance and conformity result not so much from what people do as from how others respond to those actions.* Labeling theory stresses the relativity of deviance, meaning that people may define the same behavior in any number of ways.

Consider these situations: A college student takes a sweater off the back of a roommate's chair and packs it for a weekend trip, a married woman at a convention in a distant city has sex with an old boyfriend, and a mayor gives a big city contract to a major campaign contributor. We might define the first situation as carelessness, borrowing, or theft. The consequences of the second case depend largely on whether the woman's behavior becomes known back home. In the third situation, is the mayor choosing the best contractor or paying off a political debt? The social construction of reality is a highly variable process of detection, definition, and response.

Primary and Secondary Deviance

Edwin Lemert (1951, 1972) observed that some norm violations—say, skipping school or underage drinking—may provoke some reaction from others, but this process has little effect on a person's self-concept. Lemert calls such passing episodes *primary deviance.*

But what happens if people take notice of someone's deviance and really make something of it? After an audience has defined some action as primary deviance, the individual may begin to change, taking on a deviant identity by talking, acting, or dressing in a different way, rejecting the people who are critical, and repeatedly breaking the rules. Lemert (1951:77) calls this change of self-concept *secondary deviance.* He explains that "when a person begins to employ . . . deviant behavior

In 2012, 24-year-old Benjamin Colton Barnes was found dead in the wilderness near Washington's Mount Ranier. He is thought to have shot and killed National Park Ranger Margaret Anderson after she stopped his vehicle at a roadblock. The fact that Barnes was a veteran of the Iraq War who had difficulty making the transition to civilian life may have played a part in his alleged actions. In such cases, are you more likely to think of a suspect as "sick" rather than as "bad"? Why?

as a means of defense, attack, or adjustment to the . . . problems created by societal reaction . . . , deviance [becomes] secondary." For example, say that people have begun describing a young man as an "alcohol abuser," which establishes primary deviance. These people may then exclude him from their friendship network. His response may be to become bitter toward them, start drinking even more, and seek the company of others who approve of his drinking. These actions mark the beginning of secondary deviance, a deeper deviant identity.

Stigma

Secondary deviance marks the start of what Erving Goffman (1963) calls a *deviant career.* As people develop a deeper commitment to deviant behavior, they typically acquire a **stigma**, *a powerfully negative label that greatly changes a person's self-concept and social identity.*

A stigma operates as a master status (see Chapter 4, "Social Interaction in Everyday Life"), overpowering other dimensions of identity so that a person is discredited in the minds of others and consequently becomes socially isolated. Often a person gains a stigma informally as others begin to see the individual in deviant terms. Sometimes, however, an entire community stigmatizes a person in a public way through what Harold Garfinkel (1956) calls a *degradation ceremony.* A criminal prosecution is one example, operating much like a high school graduation ceremony in reverse: A person stands before the community to be labeled in negative rather than positive terms.

Retrospective and Projective Labeling

Once people stigmatize a person as deviant, they may engage in *retrospective labeling,* a reinterpretation of the person's past in light of some present deviance (Scheff, 1984). For example, after discovering that a priest has sexually molested a child, others rethink his past, perhaps offering comments such as "He always did want to be around young children." Retrospective labeling, a process of selecting out certain facts about a person's biography, typically deepens a deviant identity.

Similarly, people may engage in *projective labeling* of a stigmatized person, using a deviant identity to predict the person's future actions. Regarding the priest, people might say, "He's going to keep at it until he's caught." The more people in someone's social world think such things and act accordingly, the more these definitions affect the individual's self-concept, and the greater the chance that the predictions will come true.

Labeling Difference as Deviance

Is a homeless man who refuses to allow police to take him to a city shelter on a cold night simply trying to live independently, or is he "crazy"? People have a tendency to treat behavior that irritates or threatens them not simply as "different" but as deviance or even mental illness.

The psychiatrist Thomas Szasz (1961, 1970, 2003, 2004) claims that people are too quick to apply the label of mental illness to conditions that simply amount to differences we don't like. The only way to avoid this troubling practice, Szasz concludes, is to stop using the idea of mental illness entirely. The world is full of people whose differences in thought or action may irritate us, but such differences are not grounds for defining someone as mentally ill. Such labeling, Szasz claims, simply enforces conformity to the standards of people powerful enough to impose their will on others.

Most mental health professionals reject the idea that mental illness does not exist. But they agree that it is important to think carefully about how we define "difference." First, people who are mentally ill are no more to blame for their condition than people who suffer from cancer or some other physical problem. Therefore, having a mental or physical illness is no grounds for a person being labeled "deviant." Second, people (especially those without the medical knowledge to diagnose mental illness) should avoid applying such labels just to make others conform to their own standards of behavior.

The Medicalization of Deviance

Labeling theory, particularly the ideas of Szasz and Goffman, helps explain an important shift in the way our society understands deviance. Over the past fifty years, the growing influence of psychiatry and medicine in the United States has led to the **medicalization of deviance**, *the transformation of moral and legal deviance into a medical condition.*

Medicalization amounts to swapping one set of labels for another. In moral terms, we judge people or their behavior as "bad" or "good." However, the scientific objectivity of medicine passes no moral judgment, instead using clinical diagnoses such as "sick" or "well."

To illustrate this idea, until the mid-twentieth century, most people viewed alcoholics as morally weak people easily tempted by the pleasure of drink. Gradually, however, medical specialists redefined alcoholism so that most people now consider it a disease, leading us to define alcoholics as "sick" rather than "bad."

Another example of the medicalization of deviance involves the medical use of marijuana. What used to be seen as a moral and criminal issue is more and more becoming a medical issue. By 2012, a dozen states had enacted medical marijuana laws. The "medicalization of marijuana" is shifting the use of this drug from a law enforcement issue to a health issue under the control of physicians. As the "illegal drug" is redefined as "medicine," the "dealer" becomes a "caregiver," and the "user" becomes a "patient" (Ferguson, 2010).

In the same way, obesity, drug addiction, child abuse, and sexual promiscuity are all behaviors that used to be strictly moral matters. To varying degrees, all are now defined as illnesses for which people need help rather than punishment.

---

labeling theory the idea that deviance and conformity result not so much from what people do as from how others respond to those actions

stigma a powerfully negative label that greatly changes a person's self-concept and social identity

medicalization of deviance the transformation of moral and legal deviance into a medical condition

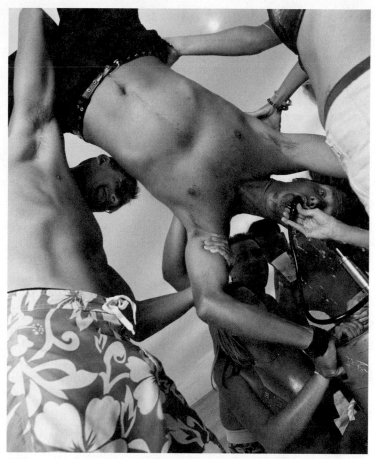

All social groups teach their members skills and attitudes that encourage certain behavior. In recent years, discussion on college campuses has focused on the dangers of binge drinking, which results in several dozen deaths each year among young people in the United States. How much of a problem is binge drinking on your campus?

The Difference Labels Make

Whether we define deviance as a moral or a medical issue has three consequences. First, it affects *who responds* to deviance. An offense against common morality typically brings a reaction from members of the community or the police. A medical label, however, places the situation under the control of clinical specialists, including counselors, psychiatrists, and physicians.

A second issue is *how people respond* to deviance. A moral approach defines deviants as offenders subject to punishment. Medically, however, they are patients who need treatment. Punishment is designed to fit the crime, but treatment programs are tailored to the patient and may involve any therapy that a specialist thinks might prevent future illness.

Third, and most important, the two labels differ on the issue of *the competence of the deviant person.* From a moral standpoint, whether we are right or wrong, at least we take responsibility for our own behavior. Once we are defined as sick, however, we are seen as unable to control (or if "mentally ill," perhaps even to understand) our actions. Once labeled incompetent, people are subjected to treatment, often against their will. For this reason alone, defining deviance in medical terms should be done with extreme caution.

Sutherland's Differential Association Theory

Learning any social pattern, whether conventional or deviant, is a process that takes place in groups. According to Edwin Sutherland (1940), a person's tendency toward conformity or deviance depends on the amount of contact with others who encourage or reject conventional behavior. This is Sutherland's theory of *differential association.*

A number of studies confirm the idea that young people are more likely to engage in delinquent behavior if they believe that members of their peer group encourage such activity (Akers et al., 1979; Miller & Mathews, 2001). One recent investigation focused on sexual activity among eighth-grade students. Two strong predictors of such behavior in young girls were having a boyfriend who encouraged sexual relations and having girlfriends they believed would approve of such activity. Similarly, boys were encouraged to become sexually active by friends who rewarded them with high status in their peer group (Little & Rankin, 2001).

Hirschi's Control Theory

The sociologist Travis Hirschi (1969; Gottfredson & Hirschi, 1995) developed *control theory,* which states that social control depends on people's anticipating the consequences of their behavior. Hirschi assumes that everyone finds at least some deviance tempting. But the thought of a ruined career keeps most people from breaking the rules; for some, just imagining the reactions of family and friends is enough. On the other hand, individuals who think they have little to lose from deviance are likely to become rule breakers.

Specifically, Hirschi links conformity to four different types of social control:

1. **Attachment.** Strong social and emotional attachments encourage conformity. The stronger the individual's attachment to parents, teachers, friends, schools or other institutions, the less the risk of engaging in deviance.

2. **Commitment.** The greater a person's stake in conformity, the lower the risk of deviance. In other words, access to legitimate opportunity encourages conformity and discourages deviance.

By contrast, someone with little confidence in future success is more likely to drift toward deviance.

3. **Involvement.** Extensive involvement in legitimate activities—such as holding a job, going to school, or playing sports—inhibits deviance (Langbein & Bess, 2002). By contrast, people with little to do who spend time "hanging out" waiting for something to happen have time and energy to engage in deviant activity.

4. **Belief.** Strong beliefs in conventional morality and respect for authority figures encourages conformity and restrains tendencies toward deviance. By contrast, people with a weak conscience (especially when they are left unsupervised) are more open to temptation (Stack, Wasserman, & Kern, 2004).

Hirschi's analysis calls to mind our earlier discussions of the causes of deviant behavior. Here again, a person's relative social privilege and the family and community environment affect the risk of deviant behavior (Hope, Grasmick, & Pointon, 2003).

● **Evaluate** The various symbolic-interaction theories all see deviance as a process. Labeling theory links deviance not to the action but to the *reaction* of others. Thus, some people are defined as deviant but others who think or behave in the same way are not. The concepts of secondary deviance, deviant career, and stigma show how being labeled deviant can become a lasting self-concept.

Yet labeling theory has several limitations. First, because it takes a highly relative view of deviance, labeling theory ignores the fact that some kinds of behavior—such as murder—are condemned just about everywhere. Therefore, labeling theory is most usefully applied to less serious issues, such as sexual promiscuity or mental illness. Second, research on the consequences of deviant labeling does not clearly show whether deviant labeling produces further deviance or discourages it (Smith & Gartin, 1989; Sherman & Smith, 1992). Third, not everyone resists being labeled deviant; some people actively seek it (Vold & Bernard, 1986). For example, people engage in civil disobedience and willingly subject themselves to arrest in order to call attention to social injustice.

APPLYING THEORY

Deviance

	Structural-Functional Theory	Symbolic-Interaction Theory	Social-Conflict Theory	Race-Conflict and Feminist Theories
What is the level of analysis?	Macro-level	Micro-level	Macro-level	Macro-level
What is deviance? What part does it play in society?	Deviance is a basic part of social organization. By defining deviance, society sets its moral boundaries.	Deviance is part of socially constructed reality that emerges in interaction. Deviance comes into being as individuals label something deviant.	Deviance results from social inequality. Norms, including laws, reflect the interests of powerful members of society.	Deviance reflects racial and gender inequality. Deviant labels are more readily applied to women and other minorities.
What is important about deviance?	Deviance is universal: It exists in all societies.	Deviance is variable: Any act or person may or may not be labeled deviant.	Deviance is political: People with little power are at high risk of being labeled deviant.	Deviance is a means of control: Dominant categories of people discredit others as a means to dominate them.

Sociologists consider Sutherland's differential association theory and Hirschi's control theory important contributions to our understanding of deviance. But why do society's norms and laws define certain kinds of activities as deviant in the first place? This important question is addressed by social-conflict analysis, the focus of the next section.

CHECK YOUR LEARNING   Clearly define primary deviance, secondary deviance, deviant career, and stigma.

Deviance and Inequality: Social-Conflict Theories

 Apply

The social-conflict approach, summarized in the Applying Theory table, links deviance to social inequality. That is, who or what is labeled "deviant" depends on which categories of people hold power in a society.

Deviance and Power

Alexander Liazos (1972) points out that the people we tend to define as deviants—the ones we dismiss as "nuts" and "sluts"—are typically not as bad or harmful as they are *powerless*. Bag ladies and unemployed men on street corners, not corporate polluters or international arms dealers, carry the stigma of deviance.

Social-conflict theory explains this pattern in three ways. First, all norms—especially the laws of any society—generally reflect the interests of the rich and powerful. People who threaten the wealthy are likely to be labeled deviant, whether it's by taking people's property ("common thieves") or advocating a more egalitarian society ("political radicals"). Karl Marx, a major architect of the social-conflict approach, argued that the law and all social institutions support the interests of the rich. Or as Richard Quinney puts it, "Capitalist justice is by the capitalist class, for the capitalist class, and against the working class" (1977:3).

Second, even if their behavior is called into question, the powerful have the resources to resist deviant labels. The majority of the corporate executives who were involved in the corporate scandals of recent years have yet to be arrested; only a few have gone to jail.

Third, the widespread belief that norms and laws are "just" and "good" masks their political character. For this reason, although we may condemn the unequal application of the law, most of us give little thought to whether the laws themselves are really fair or not.

Deviance and Capitalism

In the Marxist tradition, Steven Spitzer (1980) argues that deviant labels are applied to people who interfere with the operation of capitalism. First, because capitalism is based on private control of property, people who threaten the property of others—especially the poor who steal from the rich—are prime candidates for being labeled deviant. Conversely, the rich who take advantage of the poor are less likely to be labeled deviant. For example, landlords who charge poor tenants high rents and evict those who cannot pay are not considered criminals; they are simply "doing business."

Perhaps no one better symbolized the greed that drove the Wall Street meltdown of 2008 than Bernard Madoff, who swindled thousands of people and organizations out of some $50 billion. In 2009, after pleading guilty to eleven felony counts, Madoff was sentenced to 150 years in prison. Do you think white-collar offenders are treated fairly by our criminal justice system? Why or why not?

Second, because capitalism depends on productive labor, people who cannot or will not work risk being labeled deviant. Many members of our society think people who are out of work, even through no fault of their own, are somehow deviant.

Third, because the operation of the capitalist system depends on respect for authority figures, people who resist authority are likely to be labeled deviant. Examples are children who skip school or talk back to parents or teachers and adults who do not cooperate with employers or police.

Fourth, anyone who directly challenges the capitalist status quo is likely to be defined as deviant. Such has been the case with labor organizers, radical environmentalists, and antiwar activists.

On the other side of the coin, society positively labels whatever supports the operation of capitalism. For example, winning athletes enjoy celebrity status because they make money and express the values of individual achievement and competition, both vital to capitalism. Also, Spitzer notes, we condemn using drugs of escape (marijuana, psychedelics, heroin, and crack) as deviant but promote drugs (such as alcohol and caffeine) that promote adjustment to the status quo.

The capitalist system also tries to control people who don't fit into the system. The elderly, people with mental or physical disabilities, and Robert Merton's retreatists (people addicted to alcohol or other drugs) are a "costly yet relatively harmless burden" to society. Such people, claims Spitzer, are subject to control by social welfare agencies. But people who openly challenge the capitalist system, including the inner-city underclass and revolutionaries—Merton's innovators and rebels—are controlled by the criminal justice system and, if necessary, military forces such as police SWAT teams and the National Guard.

Note that both the social welfare and criminal justice systems blame individuals, not the system, for social problems. Welfare

The television series *Boardwalk Empire* offers an inside look at the lives of gangsters in this country's history. How accurately do you think the mass media portray organized crime? Explain.

responsibilities to society. In practice, someone who loses a civil case pays for damage or injury but is not labeled a criminal. Furthermore, corporate officials are protected by the fact that most charges of white-collar crime target the organization rather than individuals.

In the rare cases that white-collar criminals are charged and convicted, they usually escape punishment. A government study found that those convicted of fraud and punished with a fine ended up paying less than 10 percent of what they owed; most managed to hide or transfer their assets to avoid paying up. Among white-collar criminals convicted of embezzlement, only about half ever served a day in jail. One accounting found that just 54 percent of the embezzlers convicted in the U.S. federal courts served prison sentences; the rest were put on probation or issued a fine (U.S. Bureau of Justice Statistics, 2011). As some analysts see it, until courts impose more prison terms, we should expect white-collar crime to remain widespread (Shover & Hochstetler, 2006).

recipients are considered unworthy freeloaders, poor people who rage at their plight are labeled rioters, anyone who actively challenges the government is branded a radical or a communist, and those who try to gain illegally what they will never get legally are rounded up as common criminals.

White-Collar Crime

In a sign of things to come, a Wall Street stockbroker named Michael Milken made headlines back in 1987 when he was jailed for business fraud. Milken attracted attention because not since the days of Al Capone had anyone made so much money in one year: $550 million—about $1.5 million a day (Swartz, 1989).

Milken engaged in **white-collar crime**, defined by Edwin Sutherland (1940) as *crime committed by people of high social position in the course of their occupations*. White-collar crime does not involve violence and rarely brings police with guns drawn to the scene. Rather, white-collar criminals use their powerful offices illegally to enrich themselves or others, often causing significant public harm in the process. For this reason, sociologists sometimes call white-collar offenses "crime in the suites" as opposed to "crime in the streets."

The most common white-collar crimes are bank embezzlement, business fraud, bribery, and violating antitrust laws that require businesses to be competitive. Sutherland (1940) explains that such white-collar offenses typically end up in a civil hearing rather than a criminal courtroom. *Civil law* regulates business dealings between private parties; *criminal law* defines a person's moral

Corporate Crime

Sometimes whole companies, not just individuals, break the law. **Corporate crime** consists of *the illegal actions of a corporation or people acting on its behalf.*

Corporate crime ranges from knowingly selling faulty or dangerous products to deliberately polluting the environment (Derber, 2004). The collapse of a number of corporations in recent years, linked to criminal conduct on the part of company officials, has cost tens of thousands of people their jobs and their pensions.

In addition, companies often violate safety regulations, resulting in injury or death. Between 2006 and 2011, 177 people died in underground coal mines in the United States, in many cases amid allegations of safety violations. We might also wonder whether any "safe" mines really exist in light of the fact that hundreds more people died from "black lung" disease resulting from years of inhaling coal dust. The death toll for all job-related hazards in the United States runs into the thousands, and almost 2 million people are injured on the job seriously enough to require time away from work (Jafari, 2008; U.S. Department of Labor, 2011; Mine Safety and Health Administration, 2011).

Organized Crime

Organized crime is *a business supplying illegal goods or services*. Sometimes crime organizations force people to do business with them, as when a gang extorts money from shopkeepers for "protection." In most cases, however, organized crime involves selling illegal goods and services—often sex, drugs, and gambling—to willing buyers.

Organized crime has flourished in the United States for more than a century. The scope of its operations expanded among immigrants who found that this society was not willing to share its opportunities with them. Thus some ambitious minorities (such as Al Capone, mentioned earlier) made their own success, especially during Prohibition, when the government banned the production and sale of alcohol.

white-collar crime crime committed by people of high social position in the course of their occupations

corporate crime the illegal actions of a corporation or people acting on its behalf

organized crime a business supplying illegal goods or services

In the fall of 2010, Tyler Clementi, an eighteen-year-Rutgers University freshman, jumped off the George Washington Bridge and ended his life three days after his roommate had used a webcam to view Clementi engaged in a same-sex encounter with another young man. The roommate, who was also found to have sent out Twitter messages encouraging others to watch the video, was later convicted of a number of charges including invasion of privacy and bias intimidation. Because the intent in committing the crime was ruled to be bias based on the victim's sexual orientation, the roommate faces a possible sentencing—set to take place in May, 2012—of ten or more years in prison (DeFalco, 2011; Zernike, 2012).

As this case illustrates, hate crime laws punish a crime more severely if the offender is motivated by bias against some category of people. Supporters make three arguments in favor of hate crime legislation. First, the offender's intentions are always important in weighing criminal responsibility, so considering hatred as an intention is nothing new. Second, victims of hate crimes typically suffer more serious injuries than victims of crimes with other motives. Third, a crime motivated by racial or other bias is more harmful because it can inflame an entire community more than a crime carried out, say, for money.

Critics counter that while some hate crime cases involve hard-core racism, most are impulsive acts by young people. Even more important, critics maintain, hate crime laws are a threat to First

Do you think this example of vandalism should be prosecuted as a hate crime? In other words, should the punishment be more severe than if the spray painting were just "normal" graffiti? Why or why not?

Amendment guarantees of free speech. Hate crime laws allow courts to sentence offenders not just for their actions but also for their attitudes. As the Harvard University law professor Alan Dershowitz cautions, "As much as I hate bigotry, I fear much more the Court attempting to control the minds of its citizens." In short, according to critics, hate crime laws open the door to punishing beliefs rather than behavior.

In 1993, the U.S. Supreme Court upheld the sentence handed down to Todd Mitchell, an African American youth, for assaulting a white youth with a motivation of racial bias. In a unanimous decision, the justices reaffirmed that the government should not punish an individual's beliefs. But, they reasoned, a belief is no longer protected when it becomes the motive for a crime.

What Do You Think?

1. Do you think crimes motivated by hate are more harmful than those motivated by, say, greed? Why or why not?

2. Do you think minorities such as African Americans should be subject to the same hate crime laws as white people? Why or why not?

3. On balance, do you favor or oppose hate crime laws? Why?

Sources: Terry (1993), A. Sullivan (2002), and Hartocollis (2007).

The Italian Mafia is a well-known example of organized crime. But other criminal organizations involve African Americans, Chinese, Colombians, Cubans, Haitians, Nigerians, and Russians, as well as others of almost every racial and ethnic category. Organized crime today involves a wide range of activities, from selling illegal drugs to prostitution to credit card fraud and selling false identification papers to illegal immigrants (Valdez, 1997; Federal Bureau of Investigation, 2010).

 Evaluate According to social-conflict theory, a capitalist society's inequality in wealth and power shapes its laws and how they are applied. The criminal justice and social welfare systems thus act as political agents, controlling categories of people who are a threat to the capitalist system.

Like other approaches to deviance, social-conflict theory has its critics. First, this approach implies that laws and other cultural norms are created directly by the rich and powerful. At the very least, this is an oversimplification because the law also protects workers, consumers, and the environment, sometimes opposing the interests of corporations and the rich.

Second, social-conflict analysis argues that criminality springs up only to the extent that a society treats its members unequally. However, as Durkheim noted, deviance exists in all societies, whatever the economic system and their degree of inequality.

CHECK YOUR LEARNING Define white-collar crime, corporate crime, and organized crime.

Deviance, Race, and Gender: Race-Conflict and Feminist Theories

● **Apply**

What people consider deviant reflects the relative power and privilege of different categories of people. Drawing on race-conflict theory and feminist theory, the following sections explain how racial and ethnic hostility motivates hate crimes and how gender is linked to deviance.

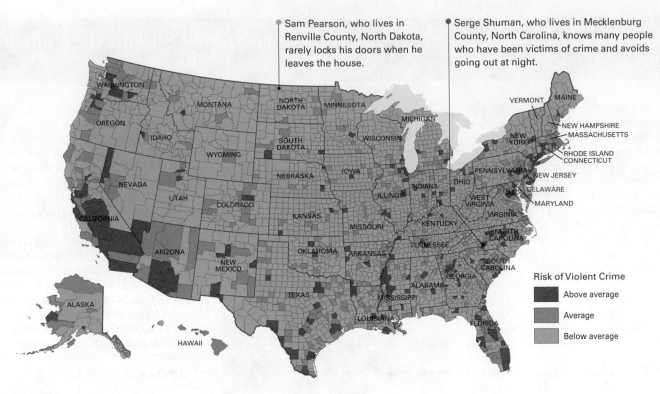

Sam Pearson, who lives in Renville County, North Dakota, rarely locks his doors when he leaves the house.

Serge Shuman, who lives in Mecklenburg County, North Carolina, knows many people who have been victims of crime and avoids going out at night.

Risk of Violent Crime

Above average

Average

Below average

Seeing Ourselves

NATIONAL MAP 7–1 **The Risk of Violent Crime across the United States**

This map shows the risk of becoming a victim of violent crime. In general, the risk is highest in low-income, rural counties that have a large population of men between the ages of fifteen and twenty-four. After reading this section of the text, see whether you can explain this pattern.

Explore the share of the population in prison in your local community and in counties across the United States on **mysoclab.com**

Source: CAP Index, Inc. (2009).

Race-Conflict Theory: Hate Crimes

A **hate crime** is *a criminal act against a person or a person's property by an offender motivated by racial or other bias*. A hate crime may express hostility toward someone based on race, religion, ancestry, sexual orientation, or physical disability. The federal government recorded 6,628 hate crimes in 2010 (U.S. Department of Justice, 2011).

In 1998, people across the country were stunned by the brutal killing of Matthew Shepard, a gay student at the University of Wyoming, by two men filled with hatred toward homosexuals. But such crimes are far from isolated cases. The National Coalition of Anti-Violence Programs reported that, in 2010, twenty-seven murders occurred in which racial or other bias was involved. Surveys indicate that 40 percent of lesbians and gay men in the United States say that they have been the victims of hate violence in their adult lifetimes, and about 90 percent of such people report experiencing verbal abuse. People who contend with multiple stigmas, such as gay men of color, are especially likely to be victimized (Dang & Vianney, 2007; National Coalition of Anti-Violence Programs, 2011). Yet hate crimes can happen to anyone: In 2010, almost 20 percent of hate crimes based on race targeted white people (Federal Bureau of Investigation, 2011).

By 2011, forty-five states and the federal government had enacted legislation that raises penalties for crimes motivated by hatred. Supporters are gratified, but opponents charge that such laws, which increase the penalty for a crime based on the attitudes of the offender, amount to punishing "politically incorrect" thoughts. The Thinking About Diversity box on page 167 takes a closer look at the issue of hate crime laws.

Feminist Theory: Deviance and Gender

In 2009, a number of women in Sudan were convicted of "dressing indecently." The punishment was imprisonment and, in several cases, ten lashes. The crime was wearing trousers (BBC, 2009).

This is an exceptional case, but the fact is that virtually every society in the world places stricter controls on the behavior of women than men. Historically, our own society has centered women's lives on the home. In the United States even today, women's opportunities in the workplace, in politics, in athletics, and in the military are more limited than men's.

Gender also figures into the theories about deviance noted earlier. For example, Robert Merton's strain theory defines cultural goals in terms of financial success. Traditionally at least, this goal has had more to do with the lives of men, because women have been socialized to define success in terms of relationships, particularly marriage and motherhood (E. B. Leonard, 1982). A more woman-focused theory might recognize the "strain" that results from the cultural ideal of equality clashing with the reality of gender-based inequality.

According to labeling theory, gender influences how we define deviance because people commonly use different standards to judge the behavior of females and males. Further, because society puts men in positions of power over women, men often escape direct responsibility for actions that victimize women. In the past, at least, men who sexually harassed or assaulted women were labeled only mildly deviant and sometimes escaped punishment entirely.

By contrast, women who are victimized may have to convince others—even members of a jury—that they are not to blame for their own sexual harassment or assault. Research confirms an important truth: Whether people define a situation as deviant—and, if they do, who in the situation is defined as deviant—depends on the sex of both the audience and the actors (King & Clayson, 1988).

Finally, despite its focus on inequality, much social-conflict analysis does not address the issue of gender. If economic disadvantage is a primary cause of crime, as conflict theory suggests, why do women (whose economic position is much worse than men's) commit far *fewer* crimes than men?

Crime

Understand
....

Crime is the violation of criminal laws enacted by a locality, a state, or the federal government. All crimes are composed of two elements: the *act* itself (or in some cases, the failure to do what the law requires) and *criminal intent* (in legal terminology, *mens rea*, or "guilty mind"). Intent is a matter of degree, ranging from willful conduct to negligence. Someone who is negligent does not set out deliberately to hurt anyone but acts (or fails to act) in a way that results in harm. Prosecutors weigh the degree of intent in deciding whether, for example, to charge someone with first-degree murder, second-degree murder, or negligent manslaughter. Alternatively, they may consider a killing justifiable, as in self-defense.

Types of Crime

In the United States, the Federal Bureau of Investigation (FBI) gathers information on criminal offenses and regularly reports the results in a publication called *Crime in*

Julian Assange is the founder of WikiLeaks, which tries to hold governments and other powerful organizations accountable for their behavior. Not surprisingly, Assange has found himself in trouble with the law. He is shown here in 2010, having been released on bail pending future prosecution.

---

crimes against the person (violent crimes) crimes that direct violence or the threat of violence against others

crimes against property (property crimes) crimes that involve theft of money or property belonging to others

victimless crimes violations of law in which there are no obvious victims

---

the United States. Two major types of crime make up the FBI "crime index."

Crimes against the person, also referred to as *violent crimes,* are *crimes that direct violence or the threat of violence against others.* Violent crimes include murder and manslaughter (legally defined as "the willful killing of one human being by another"), aggravated assault ("an unlawful attack by one person on another for the purpose of inflicting severe or aggravated bodily injury"), forcible rape ("the carnal knowledge of a female forcibly and against her will"), and robbery ("taking or attempting to take anything of value from the care, custody, or control of a person or persons, by force or threat of force or violence and/or putting the victim in fear"). National Map 7–1 shows the risk of violent crime for all the counties in the United States.

Crimes against property, also referred to as *property crimes,* are *crimes that involve theft of money or property belonging to others.* Property crimes include burglary ("the unlawful entry of a structure to commit a [serious crime] or a theft"), larceny-theft ("the unlawful taking, carrying, leading, or riding away of property from the possession of another"), motor vehicle theft ("the theft or attempted theft of a motor vehicle"), and arson ("any willful or malicious burning or attempt to burn the personal property of another").

A third category of offenses, not included in major crime indexes, is **victimless crimes,** *violations of law in which there are no obvious victims.* Also called *crimes without complaint,* they include illegal drug use, prostitution, and gambling. The term "victimless crime" is misleading, however. How victimless is a crime when young drug users embark on a life of crime to support their drug habit? What about a pregnant woman who, by smoking crack, permanently harms her baby? Or a gambler who loses the money needed to support himself and his family? Perhaps it is more correct to say that people who commit such crimes are both offenders and victims.

Because public views of victimless crimes vary greatly, laws differ from place to place. Although gambling and prostitution are legal in only limited areas, both activities are common across the country.

Criminal Statistics

Statistics gathered by the FBI show crime rates rising from 1960 to 1990 and then declining after that. Even so, police count more than 10 million

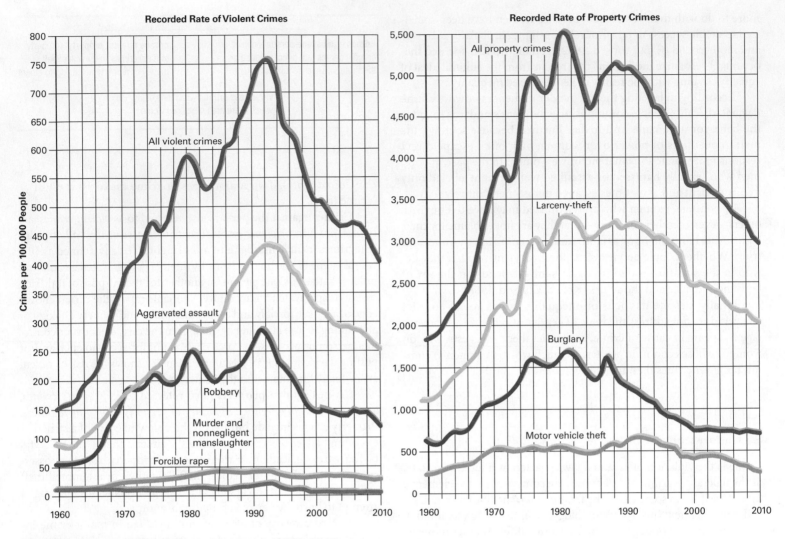

Recorded Rate of Violent Crimes

Crimes per 100,000 People

All violent crimes

Aggravated assault

Robbery

Murder and
nonnegligent
manslaughter

Forcible rape

Recorded Rate of Property Crimes

All property crimes

Larceny-theft

Burglary

Motor vehicle theft

FIGURE 7–2 Crime Rates in the United States, 1960–2010

The graphs show the rates for various violent crimes and property crimes during recent decades. Since about 1990, the trend has been downward.

Source: Federal Bureau of Investigation (2011).

serious crimes each year. Figure 7–2 shows the trends for various serious crimes.

Always read crime statistics with caution, however, because they include only crimes known to the police. Almost all murders are reported, but other assaults—especially between people who know one another—often are not. Police records include an even smaller proportion of property crimes, especially when the losses are small.

Researchers check official crime statistics by conducting *victimization surveys,* in which they ask a representative sample of people about their experiences with crime. Victimization surveys carried out in 2010 showed that the actual number of serious crimes was almost twice as high as police reports indicate (Truman, 2010).

The Street Criminal: A Profile

Using government crime reports, we can gain a general description of the categories of people most likely to be arrested for crimes.

Gender

Although each sex makes up roughly half the population, police collared males in 62.4 percent of all property crime arrests in 2010; the other 37.6 percent of arrests involved women. In other words, men are arrested almost twice as often as women for property crimes. In the case of violent crimes, the difference is even greater, with 80 percent of arrests involving males and just 20 percent females (a four-to-one ratio).

It may be that law enforcement officials are reluctant to define women as criminals. In global perspective, the greatest gender difference in crime rates occurs in societies that most severely limit the opportunities of women. In the United States, the difference in arrest rates for women and men has been narrowing, which probably indicates increasing gender equality in our society. Between 2001 and 2010, there was a 10.5 percent *increase* in arrests of women and a 6.8 percent *drop* in arrests of men (Federal Bureau of Investigation, 2011).

Age

Official crime rates rise sharply during adolescence, peak in the late teens, and fall as people get older. People between the ages of fifteen and twenty-four represent just 14 percent of the U.S. population, but in 2010, they accounted for 39.4 percent of all arrests for violent crimes and 47.6 percent of arrests for property crimes.

Social Class

The FBI does not assess the social class of arrested persons, so no statistical data of the kind given for gender and age are available. But research has long indicated that street crime is more widespread among people of lower social position (Thornberry & Farnsworth, 1982; Wolfgang, Thornberry, & Figlio, 1987).

Yet the connection between class and crime is more complicated than it appears on the surface. For one thing, many people see the poor as less worthy than the rich, whose wealth and power confer "respectability" (Tittle, Villemez, & Smith, 1978; Elias, 1986). And although crime—especially violent crime—is a serious problem in the poorest inner-city communities of the United States, most of these crimes are committed by a few hard-core offenders. The majority of people in inner-city neighborhoods have no criminal record at all (Wolfgang, Figlio, & Sellin, 1972; Elliott & Ageton, 1980; Harries, 1990).

The connection between social standing and criminality also depends on the type of crime. If we expand our definition of crime beyond street offenses to include white-collar crime, the "common criminal" suddenly looks much more affluent and may live in a $10 million home.

Race and Ethnicity

Both race and ethnicity are strongly linked to crime rates, although the reasons are many and complex. Official statistics show that 69.4 percent of arrests for index crimes in 2010 involved white people. However, arrests of African Americans are higher in proportion to their share of the general population. African Americans make up 13 percent of the population of the United States but account for 28.9 percent of the arrests for property crimes (versus 68.4 percent for whites) and 38.1 percent of arrests for violent crimes (versus 59.3 percent for whites) (Federal Bureau of Investigation, 2011).

There are several reasons for the disproportionate number of arrests among African Americans. First, in the United States, race is closely linked to social standing, which, as already explained, affects the likelihood of engaging in street crimes. Many poor people living in the midst of wealth come to see society as unjust and therefore are more likely to turn to crime to get their share (Blau & Blau, 1982; E. Anderson, 1994; Martinez, 1996).

Second, black and white family patterns differ: 73 percent of non-Hispanic black children (compared with 29 percent of non-Hispanic white children) are born to single mothers. There are two risks associated with single parenting: Children get less supervision, and they are at greater risk of living in poverty. With almost 40 percent of African American children growing up in poor

Read "Race and Class in the American Criminal Justice System" by David Cole on mysoclab.com

families (compared with 12 percent of white children), no one should be surprised at proportionately higher crime rates for African Americans (Courtwright, 1996; Jacobs & Helms, 1996; Martin et al., 2011; U.S. Census Bureau, 2011).

Third, prejudice prompts white police to arrest black people more readily and leads citizens to report African Americans more willingly, so people of color are overly criminalized (Chiricos, McEntire, & Gertz, 2001; Quillian & Pager, 2001; Demuth & Steffensmeier, 2004).

Fourth, remember that the official crime index does not include arrests for offenses ranging from drunk driving to white-collar violations. This omission contributes to the view of the typical criminal as a person of color. If we broaden our definition of crime to include drunk driving, business fraud, embezzlement, stock swindles, and cheating on income tax returns, the proportion of white criminals rises dramatically.

Keep in mind, too, that categories of people with high arrest rates are also at higher risk of being victims of crime. In the United States, for example, African Americans are six times as likely to die as a result of homicide as white people (Rogers et al., 2001; Xu et al., 2010).

Finally, some categories of the population have unusually low rates of arrest. People of Asian descent, who account for 4.9 percent of the population, figure in only 1.2 percent of all arrests. As Chapter 11 ("Race and Ethnicity") explains, Asian Americans enjoy higher than average educational achievement and income. Also, Asian American culture emphasizes family solidarity and discipline, both of which keep criminality down.

"You look like this sketch of someone who's thinking about committing a crime."

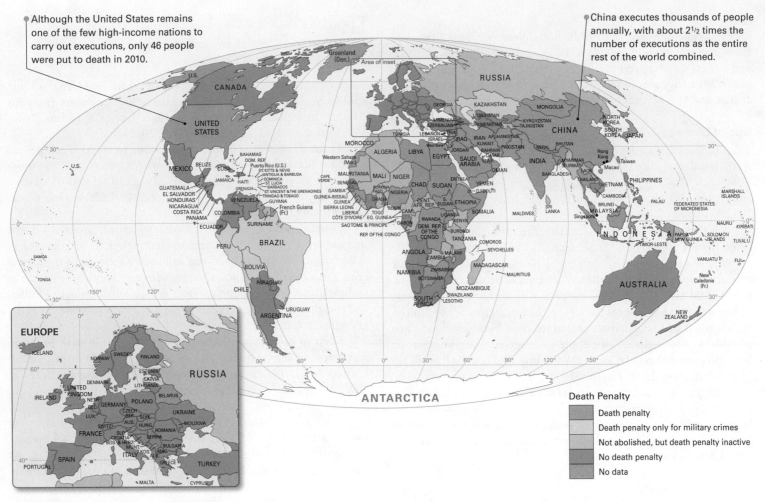

Although the United States remains one of the few high-income nations to carry out executions, only 46 people were put to death in 2010.

China executes thousands of people annually, with about 2½ times the number of executions as the entire rest of the world combined.

Death Penalty

- Death penalty
- Death penalty only for military crimes
- Not abolished, but death penalty inactive
- No death penalty
- No data

Window on the World

GLOBAL MAP 7–1 Capital Punishment in Global Perspective

The map identifies fifty-eight countries in which the law allows the death penalty for ordinary crimes; in nine more, the death penalty is reserved for exceptional crimes under military law or during times of war. The death penalty does not exist in ninety-six countries; in thirty-four more, although the death penalty remains in law, no execution has taken place in more than ten years. Compare rich and poor nations: What general pattern do you see? In what way are the United States and Japan exceptions to this pattern?

Source: Amnesty International (2011).

Crime in Global Perspective

By world standards, the U.S. crime rate is high. Although recent crime trends are downward, there were 14,748 murders in this country in 2010, which amounts to one every half hour around the clock. In large cities such as New York, never does a week go by without someone being killed.

The rate of violent crime (but not property crime) in the United States is several times higher than in Europe. The contrast is even greater between our country and the nations of Asia, especially India and Japan, where violent and property crime rates are among the lowest in the world.

Elliott Currie (1985) suggests that crime arises from our culture's emphasis on individual economic success, often at the expense of strong families and neighborhoods. The United States also has extraordinary cultural diversity—a result of centuries of immigration—that can lead to conflict. In addition, economic inequality is higher in this country than in most other high-income nations. Our society's relatively weak social fabric, combined with considerable frustration among the poor, increases the level of criminal behavior.

Another factor contributing to violence in the United States is extensive private ownership of guns. Two-thirds of murder victims in the United States die from shootings. The U.S. rate of handgun homicides is more than five times higher than in Canada, a country that strictly limits handgun ownership (Federal Bureau of Investigation, 2011; Statistics Canada, 2011).

Surveys show that about one-third of all adults in the United States claim they personally own a firearm and almost half of U.S. households have at least one gun (Gallup, 2011). In fact, there are more guns (about 285 million) than adults in this country, and

When economic activity takes place outside of the law, people turn to violence rather than courts to settle disagreements. In Central America, drug violence has pushed the homicide rate to the highest level in the world.

40 percent of these weapons are handguns, which are commonly used in violent crimes. In large part, gun ownership reflects people's fear of crime, yet easy availability of guns in this country makes crime more deadly (Brady Campaign, 2011; NORC, 2011).

Supporters of gun control claim that restricting gun ownership would reduce the number of murders in the United States. For example, the number of murders each year in Canada, where the law prevents most people from owning guns, is about the same as the number of murders in just the U.S. city of New York. But as critics of gun control point out, laws regulating gun ownership do not keep guns out of the hands of criminals, who almost always obtain guns illegally. They also claim that gun control is no magic bullet in the war on crime: The number of people in the United States killed each year by knives alone is three times the number of Canadians killed by weapons of all kinds (J. D. Wright, 1995; Munroe, 2007; Federal Bureau of Investigation, 2011; Statistics Canada, 2011).

By the end of 2008, gun sales to private citizens were up sharply, reflecting the fears on the part of many gun owners that the Obama administration would act to curtail gun ownership. Changes in the law may or may not occur in the next few years, but debate over the consequences of widespread gun ownership will continue (Potter, 2008).

> **December 24–25, traveling through Peru.** In Lima, Peru's capital city, the concern with crime is obvious. Almost every house is fortified with gates, barbed wire, or broken glass embedded in cement at the top of a wall. Private security forces are everywhere in the rich areas along the coast, where we find the embassies, expensive hotels, and the international airport.
>
> The picture is very different as we pass through small villages high in the Andes to the east. The same families have lived in these communities for generations, and people know one another. No gates and fences here. And we've seen only one police car all afternoon.

Crime rates are high in some of the largest cities of the world, such as Manila, Philippines, and São Paulo, Brazil, which have rapid population growth and millions of desperately poor people. Outside of big cities, however, the traditional character of low-income societies and their strong family structure allow local communities to control crime informally.

Some types of crime have always been multinational, such as terrorism, espionage, and arms dealing. But today, the globalization we are experiencing on many fronts also extends to crime. A case in point is the illegal drug trade. In part, the problem of illegal drugs in the United States is a *demand* issue. That is, the demand for cocaine and other drugs in this country is high, with high rates of addiction and many young people who are willing to risk arrest or even violent death for a chance to get rich in the drug trade. But the *supply* side of the issue is just as important.

In the South American nation of Colombia, at least 20 percent of the people depend on cocaine production for their livelihood. Not only is cocaine Colombia's most profitable export, but it represents four times what that nation earns from exporting coffee. Clearly, then, drug dealing and many other crimes are closely related to social conditions both in this country and elsewhere.

Different countries have different strategies for dealing with crime. The use of capital punishment (the death penalty) is one example. According to Amnesty International (2011), although China does not release official statistics, that nation executes more people each year than the rest of the world combined. Of the 527 documented executions in 2010, more than 80 percent were in five nations: Iran, North Korea, Saudi Arabia, Yemen, and the United States. Global Map 7–1 shows which countries currently use capital punishment. The global trend is toward abolishing the death penalty: Amnesty International reports that since 1985, sixty-six nations have ended this practice.

The U.S. Criminal Justice System

 Analyze

The criminal justice system is a society's formal response to crime. We shall briefly examine the key elements of the U.S. criminal justice system: police, the courts, and the system of punishment and corrections. First, however, we must understand an important principle that underlies the entire system, the idea of due process.

Due Process

Due process is a simple but very important idea: The criminal justice system must operate according to law. Criminal law is grounded in the first ten amendments to the U.S. Constitution—known as the Bill of Rights—adopted by Congress in 1791. The Constitution offers various protections to any person charged with a crime. Among these are the right to counsel, the right to refuse to testify against

Police

The police generally serve as the point of contact between a population and the criminal justice system. In principle, the police maintain public order by enforcing the law. Of course, there is only so much that the 705,009 full-time police officers across the United States can do to monitor the activities of more than 308 million people. As a result, the police use a great deal of personal judgment in deciding which situations warrant their attention and how to handle them. Police also face danger on a daily basis. In most years, more than 100 U.S. police officers die in the line of duty.

Given these facts, how do police officers carry out their duties? In a study of police behavior in five cities, Douglas Smith and Christy Visher (1981; D. A. Smith, 1987) concluded that because they must act swiftly, police officers quickly size up situations in terms of six factors. First, the more serious they think the situation is, the more likely they are to make an arrest. Second, police take account of the victim's wishes in deciding whether or not to make an arrest. Third, the odds of arrest go up the more uncooperative a suspect is. Fourth, police are more likely to take into custody someone they have arrested before, presumably because this suggests guilt. Fifth, the presence of bystanders increases the chances of arrest. According to Smith and Visher, the presence of observers prompts police to take stronger control of a situation, if only to move the encounter from the street (the suspect's turf) to the police department (where law officers have the edge). Sixth, all else being equal, police officers are more likely to arrest people of color than to arrest whites, perceiving people of African or Latino descent as either more dangerous or more likely to be guilty.

Courts

After arrest, a court determines a suspect's guilt or innocence. In principle, U.S. courts rely on an adversarial process involving attorneys—one representing the defendant and another the state—in the presence of a judge who monitors legal procedures.

In practice, however, about 97 percent of criminal cases are resolved before court appearance through **plea bargaining**, *a legal negotiation in which a prosecutor reduces a charge in exchange for a defendant's guilty plea.* For example, the state may offer a defendant charged with burglary a lesser charge, perhaps possession of burglary tools, in exchange for a guilty plea (U.S. Department of Justice, 2011).

Plea bargaining is widespread because it spares the system the time and expense of trials. A trial is usually unnecessary if there is little disagreement as to the facts of the case. Moreover, because of the number of cases entering the system, prosecutors could not bring every case to trial even if they wanted to. By quickly resolving most of their work, then, the courts can channel their resources into the most important cases.

But plea bargaining pressures defendants (who are presumed innocent) to plead guilty. A person can exercise the right to a trial, but only at the risk of receiving a more severe sentence if found guilty. Furthermore, low-income defendants must often rely on a public defender—typically an overworked and underpaid attorney who may devote little time to even the most serious cases (Novak, 1999). Plea bargaining may be efficient, but it undercuts both the adversarial process and the rights of defendants.

Police must be allowed discretion if they are to handle effectively the many different situations they face every day. At the same time, it is important that the police treat people fairly. Here we see a police officer deciding whether or not to charge a young woman with driving while intoxicated. What factors do you think enter into this decision?

oneself, and the right to confront all accusers, as well as freedom from being tried twice for the same crime and freedom from being "deprived of life, liberty, or property without due process of law." Furthermore, the Constitution gives all people the right to a speedy and public trial by jury and freedom from excessive bail and from "cruel and unusual" punishment.

In general terms, the concept of due process means that anyone charged with a crime must receive (1) fair notice of the proceedings, (2) a hearing on the charges conducted according to law and with the ability to present a defense, and (3) a judge or jury that weighs evidence impartially (Inciardi, 2000).

Due process limits the power of government, with an eye toward this nation's cultural support of individual rights and freedoms. Deciding exactly how far government can go makes up much of the work of the judicial system, especially the U.S. Supreme Court.

Punishment

In 2011, on a sunny morning in Tucson, Arizona, Congressional Representative Gabrielle Giffords sat down behind a folding table positioned in front of a supermarket. At two minutes before 10 o'clock, she tweeted "My 1st Congress on Your Corner starts now. Please stop by to let me know what's on your mind." Shortly after that, a taxi pulled to the curb nearby and dropped off a single passenger, a troubled young man who had violence on his mind. He paid the cab fare with a $20 bill, and then walked toward Ms. Giffords and pulled out a Glock 19 pistol loaded with thirty-one cartridges. For fifteen deadly seconds, gunshots rang out. The human toll: twenty people shot, including six who died (von Drehle, 2011).

Such cases force us to wonder about the reasons that drive some people to deadly violence and also to ask how a society should respond to such acts. In the case of the Tucson shootings, the offender appears to have been suffering from serious mental illness, so there is some question about the extent to which he is responsible for his actions (Cloud, 2011). But typically, of course, the question of responsibility is resolved when a suspect is apprehended and put on trial. If found guilty, the next step is punishment.

What does a society gain through the punishment of wrongdoers? Scholars answer with four basic reasons, which are described in the following sections: retribution, deterrence, rehabilitation, and societal protection.

Television shows like *Law & Order: Special Victims Unit* suggest that the criminal justice system carefully weighs the guilt and innocence of defendants. But as explained here, only 3 percent of criminal cases are actually resolved through a formal trial.

Retribution

The oldest justification for punishment is to satisfy people's need for **retribution**, *an act of moral vengeance by which society makes the offender suffer as much as the suffering caused by the crime.* Retribution rests on the view that society exists in a moral balance. When criminality upsets this balance, punishment in equal measure restores the moral order, as suggested in the ancient code calling for "an eye for an eye, a tooth for a tooth."

In the Middle Ages, most people viewed crime as sin—an offense against God as well as society—that required a harsh response. Although critics point out that retribution does little to reform the offender, many people still consider vengeance reason enough for punishment.

Deterrence

A second justification for punishment is **deterrence**, *the attempt to discourage criminality through the use of punishment.* Deterrence is based on the eighteenth-century Enlightenment idea that as calculating and rational creatures, humans will not break the law if they think that the pain of the punishment will outweigh the pleasure of the crime.

Deterrence emerged as a reform measure in response to harsh punishments based on retribution. Why put someone to death for stealing if theft can be discouraged by a prison sentence? As the concept of deterrence gained acceptance in industrial nations, execution and physical mutilation of criminals were replaced by milder forms of punishment such as imprisonment.

Punishment may deter crime in two ways. *Specific deterrence* convinces an individual offender that crime does not pay. Through *general deterrence*, punishing one person serves as an example to others.

Rehabilitation

The third justification for punishment, **rehabilitation**, is *a program for reforming the offender to prevent later offenses.* Rehabilitation arose along with the social sciences in the nineteenth century. Since then, sociologists have claimed that crime and other deviance spring from a social environment marked by poverty or lack of parental supervision. Logically, then, if offenders learn to be deviant, they can also learn to obey the rules; the key is controlling their environment. *Reformatories* or *houses of correction* provided a controlled setting where people could learn proper behavior (recall the description of total institutions in Chapter 3, "Socialization: From Infancy to Old Age").

Four Justifications for Punishment

retribution an act of moral vengeance by which society makes the offender suffer as much as the suffering caused by the crime	**deterrence** the attempt to discourage criminality through the use of punishment	**rehabilitation** a program for reforming the offender to prevent later offenses	**societal protection** rendering an offender incapable of further offenses temporarily through imprisonment or permanently by execution

Four Justifications for Punishment

Retribution	The oldest justification for punishment.
	Punishment is society's revenge for a moral wrong.
	In principle, punishment should be equal in severity to the crime itself.
Deterrence	An early modern approach.
	Crime is considered social disruption, which society acts to control.
	People are viewed as rational and self-interested; deterrence works because the pain of punishment outweighs the pleasure of crime.
Rehabilitation	A modern strategy linked to the development of social sciences.
	Crime and other deviance are viewed as the result of social problems (such as poverty) or personal problems (such as mental illness).
	Social conditions are improved; treatment is tailored to the offender's condition.
Societal protection	A modern approach easier to carry out than rehabilitation.
	Even if society is unable or unwilling to rehabilitate offenders or reform social conditions, people are protected by the imprisonment or execution of the offender.

Like deterrence, rehabilitation motivates the offender to conform. In contrast to deterrence and retribution, which simply make the offender suffer, rehabilitation encourages constructive improvement. Unlike retribution, which demands that the punishment fit the crime, rehabilitation tailors treatment to each offender. Thus identical crimes would prompt similar acts of retribution but different rehabilitation programs.

Societal Protection

A final justification for punishment is **societal protection**, *rendering an offender incapable of further offenses temporarily through imprisonment or permanently by execution*. Like deterrence, societal protection is a rational approach to punishment intended to protect society from crime.

Currently, about 2.3 million people are jailed in the United States. Although the crime rate has gone down in recent years, the number of offenders locked up across the country has gone up, quadrupling since 1980. This rise in the prison population reflects tougher public attitudes toward crime, stiffer sentences handed down by courts, and an increasing number of drug-related arrests. As a result, the United States now imprisons about one in every one hundred adults, a larger share of its population than any other country in the world. One in every thirty-one adults in the United States is either in prison, on probation, or on parole. Critics of this trend claim that this country now has a policy of *mass incarceration* (Gottschalk, 2006, 2011; Sentencing Project, 2008; Pew Center on the States, 2011; U.S. Bureau of Justice Statistics, 2011).

Evaluate The Summing Up table reviews the four justifications for punishment. However, an accurate assessment of the consequences of punishment is no simple task.

The value of retribution lies in Durkheim's claim that punishing the deviant person increases society's moral awareness. For this reason, punishment was traditionally a public event. Although the last public execution in the United States took place in Kentucky more than seventy years ago, today's mass media ensure public awareness of executions carried out inside prison walls (Kittrie, 1971).

Does punishment deter crime? Despite our extensive use of punishment, our society has a high rate of **criminal recidivism**, *later offenses by people previously convicted of crimes*. A recent study reported that 45.4 percent of people released from prison in 1999 and 43.3 percent of those released in 2004 were back in jail within three years, either for committing a new crime or for violating conditions governing their release. Other research tells us that about three-fourths of current state prisoners have been incarcerated before (DeFina & Arvanites, 2002; Langan & Levin, 2002; Pew Center on the States, 2011). So does punishment really deter crime? Fewer than one-half of all crimes are known to police, and of these, only about one in five results in an arrest. Most crimes, therefore, go unpunished, leading us to conclude, perhaps, that the old saying "crime doesn't pay" may not be entirely true.

Prisons provide short-term societal protection by keeping offenders off the streets, but they do little to reshape attitudes or behavior in the long term (Carlson, 1976; R. A. Wright, 1994). Perhaps rehabilitation is an unrealistic expectation, because according to Sutherland's theory of differential association, locking up criminals together for years probably strengthens criminal attitudes and skills. Imprisonment also breaks whatever social ties inmates may have in the outside world, which, following Hirschi's control theory, makes inmates more likely to commit new crimes upon release.

CHECK YOUR LEARNING What are society's four justifications for punishment? Does sending offenders to prison accomplish each of them? How?

The Death Penalty

Perhaps the most controversial issue involving punishment is the death penalty. Between 1977 and 2011, about 7,500 people were sentenced to death in U.S. courts; 1,234 executions were carried out. In thirty-four states, the law allows the state to execute offenders convicted of very serious crimes such as first-degree murder. But while a majority of states do permit capital punishment, only a few states are likely to carry out executions. Across the United States, half of the 3,173 people on death row at the beginning of 2010 were in just four states: California, Texas, Florida, and Pennsylvania (U.S. Bureau of Justice Statistics, 2011).

Opponents of capital punishment point to research suggesting that the death penalty has limited value as a crime deterrent. Countries such as Canada, where the death penalty has been abolished, have not seen a rise in the number of murders. Critics also point out that the United States is the only Western, high-income nation that routinely executes offenders. As public concern about the death penalty has increased, the use of capital punishment has declined from as many as ninety-eight executions in 1999 to thirty-seven in 2008 but rising again in 2010 to forty-six.

Public opinion surveys reveal that the share of U.S. adults who claim to support the death penalty as a punishment for murder remains high (63.5 percent) and has been fairly stable over time (NORC, 2011:248). College students hold about the same attitudes as everyone else, with about two-thirds of first-year students expressing support for the death penalty (Pryor et al., 2008).

But judges, criminal prosecutors, and members of trial juries are less and less likely to call for the death penalty. One reason is that because the crime rate has come down in recent years, the public now has less fear of crime and is less interested in applying the most severe punishment.

A second reason is public concern that the death penalty may be applied unjustly. The analysis of DNA evidence—a recent advance—from old crime scenes has shown that many people were wrongly convicted of a crime. Across the country, between 1975 and 2012, 139 people who had been sentenced to death were released from death row after new DNA evidence demonstrated their innocence. Such findings were one reason that in 2000, the governor of Illinois stated that he could no longer support the death penalty, leading him to commute the death sentences of every person on that state's death row (S. Levine, 2003; Death Penalty Information Center, 2011).

A third reason for the decline in the use of the death penalty is that more states now permit judges and juries to sentence serious offenders to life in prison without the possibility of parole. Such punishment offers to protect society from dangerous criminals, who can be "put away" forever without requiring an execution.

Fourth and finally, many states now shy away from capital punishment because of the high cost of prosecuting capital cases. Death penalty cases require more legal work and demand superior defense lawyers, often at public expense. In addition, such cases commonly include testimony by various paid "experts," including physicians and psychiatrists, which also runs up the costs of trial. Then there is the cost of many appeals that almost always follow a conviction leading to the sentence of death. When all these factors are put together, the cost of a death penalty case typically exceeds the cost of sending an offender to prison for life. So it is easy to see why states often choose not to seek the death penalty. One accounting, for example, reveals that the state of New Jersey has been spending more

To increase the power of punishment to deter crime, capital punishment was long carried out in public. Here is a photograph from the last public execution in the United States, with twenty-two-year-old Rainey Bethea standing on the scaffold moments from death in Owensboro, Kentucky, on August 16, 1937. Children as well as adults were in the crowd. Now that the mass media report the story of executions across the country, states carry out capital punishment behind closed doors.

than $10 million a year prosecuting death penalty cases that have yet to result in a single execution (Thomas & Brant, 2007).

Organizations opposed to the death penalty are challenging this punishment in court. In 2008, for example, the U.S. Supreme Court upheld the use of lethal injection against the charge that this procedure amounts to cruel and unusual punishment, which would be unconstitutional (Greenhouse, 2008). There is no indication at present that the United States will end the use of the death penalty. But the trend is away from this type of punishment.

Community-Based Corrections

Prison is at the center of our system of corrections. Prisons keep convicted criminals off the streets. The thought of prison probably deters many people from committing serious crime. But the evidence suggests that locking people up does little to rehabilitate most offenders. Further, prisons are expensive, costing about $30,000 per year to support each inmate, in addition to the high costs of building the facilities.

A recent alternative to prison that has been adopted by cities and states across the country is **community-based corrections**, *correctional programs operating within society at large rather than behind prison walls.* Community-based corrections have three main advantages: They reduce costs, they reduce overcrowding in prisons, and they allow for supervision of convicts while eliminating the hardships of prison life and the stigma that accompanies going to jail. In general, the idea of community-based corrections is not so much to punish as to reform; such programs are therefore usually

Duane: I'm a criminal justice major, and I want to be a police officer. Crime is a huge problem in the United States and police are what keeps the crime rate low.

Sandy: I'm a sociology major. As for combatting crime, I'm not sure it's quite that simple. . . .

During the 1980s, crime rates shot upward. Just about everyone lived in fear of violent crime, and in many large cities, the numbers of people killed and wounded made whole neighborhoods seem like war zones. There seemed to be no solution to the problem.

Yet in the 1990s, serious crime rates began to fall so that in recent years they have returned to levels not seen in more than a generation. Why? Researchers point to several reasons:

1. **A reduction in the youth population.** It was noted earlier that young people (particularly males) are responsible for much violent crime. Between 1990 and 2000, the share of the population aged fifteen to twenty-four dropped by about 5 percent (in part because of the legalization of abortion in 1973).

2. **Changes in policing.** Much of the drop in crime (like the earlier rise in crime) has taken place in large cities. In New York City, the number of murders was 2,245 in 1990, falling to 471 in 2009 (the lowest figure since the city started keeping reliable records in 1963) and rising to 536 in 2010. Part of the reason for the decline is that the city has adopted a policy of *community policing,* which means that police are concerned not just with making arrests but with preventing crime before it happens. Officers get to know the areas they patrol and frequently stop young men for jaywalking or other minor infractions so they can check them for concealed weapons (the word has gotten around that you

risk arrest if you carry a gun). In addition, there are more police at work in large cities. For example, Los Angeles added more than 2,000 police in the 1990s, and it, too, saw its violent crime rate fall during that period.

3. **More prisoners.** Between 1985 and 2010, the number of inmates in U.S. prisons soared from 750,000 to more than 2.3 million. The main reason for this increase is tough new laws that demand prison time for many crimes, especially drug offenses. As one analyst put it, "When you lock up an extra million people, it's got to have some effect on the crime rate" (Franklin Zimring, quoted in Witkin, 1998:31).

4. **A better economy.** The U.S. economy boomed during the 1990s. With unemployment down, more people were working, reducing the likelihood that some would turn to crime out of economic desperation. The logic here is simple: More jobs, fewer crimes. Notice, however, that despite the recession

that started by the end of 2007, government data show crime rates have continued to fall through the end of 2010. It may be that the recent economic downturn will soon send crime rates back upward.

5. **The declining drug trade.** Many analysts think that the most important factor in reducing rates of violent crime is the decline of crack cocaine. Crack came on the scene around 1985, and violence spread, especially in the inner cities, as young people—facing few legitimate job opportunities and increasingly armed with guns—became part of a booming drug trade. By the early 1990s, however, the popularity of crack had begun to fall as people saw the damage the drug was causing to entire communities. This realization, coupled with steady economic improvement and stiffer sentences for drug offenses, helped bring about the turnaround in violent crime.

The current picture looks better relative to what it was a decade or two ago. But one researcher cautions, "It looks better, but only because the early 1990s were so bad. So let's not fool ourselves into thinking everything is resolved. It's not."

What Do You Think?

1. Do you support the policy of community policing? Why or why not?
2. What do you see as the pros and cons of building more prisons?
3. Of all the factors mentioned here, which do you think is the most important in crime control? Which is least important? Why?

One reason that crime has gone down is that there are more than 2 million people incarcerated in this country. This has caused severe overcrowding of facilities such as this Maricopa County, Arizona, prison.

Sources: Winship & Berrien (1999), Donahue & Leavitt (2000), Rosenfeld (2002), Liptak (2008), C. Mitchell (2008), Antlfinger (2009), and Federal Bureau of Investigation (2011).

---

offered to individuals who have committed less serious offenses and who appear to be good prospects for avoiding future criminal violations (Inciardi, 2000; Pew Center on the States, 2009).

Probation

One form of community-based corrections is *probation,* a policy of permitting a convicted offender to remain in the community

under conditions imposed by a court, including regular supervision. Courts may require that a probationer receive counseling, attend a drug treatment program, hold a job, avoid associating with "known criminals," or anything else a judge thinks is appropriate. Typically, a probationer must check in with an officer of the court (the probation officer) on a regular schedule to make sure the guidelines are being followed. Should the probationer fail to live

In recent years, the inmate population of U.S. prisons has soared to 2.3 million people. Courts have ruled that some prisons in the United States are now overcrowded. In 2011, the U.S. Supreme Court ordered California to release more than 30,000 prisoners over the next two years to prevent "needless suffering and death" that might result from severely overcrowded conditions. Do you agree with critics of our prison system who claim that the United States now practices a policy of "mass incarceration"? Why or why not?

up to the conditions set by the court or commit a new offense, the court may revoke probation and send the offender to jail.

Shock Probation

A related strategy is *shock probation,* a policy by which a judge orders a convicted offender to prison for a short time and then suspends the remainder of the sentence in favor of probation. Shock probation is thus a mix of prison and probation that is intended to impress on the offender the seriousness of the situation while still withholding full-scale imprisonment. In some cases, shock probation takes place in a special "boot camp" facility where offenders might spend up to three months in a military-style setting intended to teach discipline and respect for authority (Cole & Smith, 2002).

Parole

Parole is a policy of releasing inmates from prison to serve the remainder of their sentences in the local community under the supervision of a parole officer. Although courts may sometimes sentence an offender to prison without the possibility of parole, most other inmates become eligible for parole after serving a certain portion of their sentence. At that time, a parole board evaluates the risks and benefits of an inmate's early release from prison. If parole is granted, the parole board then monitors the offender's conduct until the sentence is completed. Should the offender not comply with the conditions of parole or be arrested for another crime, the board can revoke parole, returning the offender to prison to complete the sentence.

Evaluate Researchers hare carefully studied both probation and parole to see how well these programs work. Evaluations of these policies are mixed. There is little question that community-based programs are much less expensive than conventional imprisonment; they also free up room in prisons for people who commit more serious crimes. Yet research suggests that although probation and shock probation do seem to work for some people, they do not significantly reduce criminal recidivism. Similarly, parole is useful to prison officials as a means to encourage good behavior among prison inmates who hope for early release. Yet levels of crime among those released on parole are so high that a number of states have ended their parole programs entirely (Inciardi, 2000).

CHECK YOUR LEARNING What are three types of community-based corrections? What are their advantages?

Such evaluations point to a sobering truth: By itself, the criminal justice system cannot eliminate crime. As the Controversy & Debate box explains, although police, courts, and prisons do affect crime rates, crime and other deviance are not just the acts of "bad people" but reflect the operation of society itself.

Seeing Sociology in Everyday Life

Why do most of us—at least most of the time— obey the rules?

As this chapter has explained, every society is a system of social control that encourages conformity to certain norms and discourages deviance or norm breaking. One way society does this is through the construction of heroes and villains. Heroes, of course, are people we are supposed to look up to and use as role models. Villains are people whom we look down on and reject their example, allowing them to become "anti-heroes" who point us in the opposite direction. Organizations of all types create heroes and villains that serve as guides to everyday behavior. In each case that follows, who is being made into a hero? Why? What are the values or behaviors that we are encouraged to copy in our own lives?

Hint A society without heroes and villains would be one in which no one cared what people thought or how they acted. Societies create heroes as role models that should inspire us to be more like them. Societies create heroes by emphasizing one aspect of someone's life and ignoring lots of other things. For example, Babe Ruth was a great ball player, but his private life was sometimes less than inspiring. Perhaps this is why the Catholic church never considers anyone a candidate for sainthood until after—usually long after—the person has died.

Colleges and universities create heroes in various ways. Here we see the president of Washington College (Maryland) awarding the Sophie Kerr Prize at a recent graduation ceremony. This prize, which included a check for more than $50,000, recognized English major Claire Tompkins's ability to write outstanding short stories. What is heroic in this case? What does graduating with honors or cum laude define as heroic? What about villains—how do colleges and universities create these, as well?

Religious organizations, too, use heroes to encourage certain behavior and beliefs. The Roman Catholic Church has defined the Virgin Mary and more than 10,000 other men and women as "saints." For what reasons might someone be honored in this way? What do saints do for the rest of us?

Most sports have a "hall of fame." A larger-than-life-size statue of the legendary slugger Babe Ruth attracts these New York City children on their visit to the Baseball Hall of Fame in Cooperstown, New York. What are the qualities that make an athlete "legendary"? Isn't it more than just how far someone hits a ball?

Seeing Sociology in *Your* Everyday Life

1. Do athletic teams, fraternities and sororities, and even people in a college classroom create heroes and villains? Explain how and why.

2. Watch an episode of any real-action police show such as *Cops.* Based on what you see, how would you profile the people who commit street crimes? What types of crimes do you typically *not* see on police reality shows?

3. Based on the material presented in this chapter, we might say that "Deviance is a difference that makes a difference." That is, deviance is constructed as part of social life because, as Emile Durkheim argued, it is a necessary part of society. Make a (private) list of ten negative traits that have been directed at you (or that you have directed at yourself). Then look at your list and try to determine what it says about the society we live in. Why, in other words, do these differences make a difference to members of our society? Go to the "Seeing Sociology in *Your* Everyday Life" feature on MySocLab to learn more about how sociological thinking can give you a deeper understanding of right and wrong and find suggestions for how to respond to difference.

What Is Deviance?

Deviance refers to norm violations ranging from minor infractions, such as bad manners, to major infractions, such as serious violence.   **p. 156**

Theories of Deviance

Biological theories

- focus on individual abnormality
- explain human behavior as the result of biological instincts

Lombroso claimed criminals have apelike physical traits; later research links criminal behavior to certain body types and genetics.

pp. 156–57

Psychological theories

- focus on individual abnormality
- see deviance as the result of "unsuccessful socialization"

Reckless and Dinitz's *containment theory* links delinquency to weak conscience.

pp. 157–58

Sociological theories view all behavior—deviance as well as conformity—as products of society. Sociologists point out that

- what is deviant varies from place to place according to cultural norms
- behavior and individuals become deviant as others define them that way
- what and who a society defines as deviant reflect who has and does not have social power   **p. 158**

deviance (p. 156) the recognized violation of cultural norms

crime (p. 156) the violation of a society's formally enacted criminal law

social control (p. 156) attempts by society to regulate people's thoughts and behavior

criminal justice system (p. 156) the organizations—police, courts, and prison officials—that respond to alleged violations of the law

Theories of Deviance

The Functions of Deviance: Structural-Functional Theories

Durkheim claimed that deviance is a normal element of society that

- affirms cultural norms and values
- clarifies moral boundaries
- brings people together
- encourages social change   **p. 159**

Merton's **strain theory** explains deviance in terms of a society's cultural goals and the means available to achieve them.

Deviant subcultures are discussed by Cloward and Ohlin, Cohen, Miller, and Anderson.

 Watch the Video on mysoclab.com   **pp. 159–61**

Defining Deviance: Symbolic-Interaction Theories

Labeling theory claims that deviance depends less on what someone does than on how others react to that behavior. If people respond to primary deviance by stigmatizing a person, secondary deviance and a deviant career may result.   **pp. 162–63**

The **medicalization of deviance** is the transformation of moral and legal deviance into a medical condition. In practice, this means a change in labels, replacing "good" and "bad" with "well" and "sick."   **p. 163**

Sutherland's **differential association theory** links deviance to how much others encourage or discourage such behavior.   **p. 164**

Hirschi's **control theory** states that imagining the possible consequences of deviance often discourages such behavior. People who are well integrated into society are less likely to engage in deviant behavior.   **p. 164**

labeling theory (p. 162) the idea that deviance and conformity result not so much from what people do as from how others respond to those actions

stigma (p. 162) a powerfully negative label that greatly changes a person's self-concept and social identity

medicalization of deviance (p. 163) the transformation of moral and legal deviance into a medical condition

Deviance and Inequality: Social-Conflict Theories

Based on Karl Marx's ideas, social-conflict theory holds that laws and other norms operate to protect the interests of powerful members of any society.

- **White-collar offenses** are committed by people of high social position as part of their jobs. Sutherland claimed that such offenses are rarely prosecuted and are most likely to end up in civil rather than criminal court.
- **Corporate crime** refers to illegal actions by a corporation or people acting on its behalf. Although corporate crimes cause considerable public harm, most cases of corporate crime go unpunished.
- **Organized crime** has a long history in the United States, especially among categories of people with few legitimate opportunities. **pp. 165–67**

Deviance, Race, and Gender: Race-Conflict and Feminist Theories

- Race-conflict theory and feminist theory explain that what people consider deviant reflects the relative power and privilege of different categories of people.
- **Hate crimes** are crimes motivated by racial or other bias; they target people who are already disadvantaged based on race, gender, or sexual orientation.
- In the United States and elsewhere, societies control the behavior of women more closely than that of men. **pp. 167–68**

white-collar crime (p. 166) crime committed by people of high social position in the course of their occupations

corporate crime (p. 166) the illegal actions of a corporation or people acting on its behalf

organized crime (p. 166) a business supplying illegal goods or services

hate crime (p. 168) a criminal act against a person or a person's property by an offender motivated by racial or other bias

What Is Crime?

Crime is the violation of criminal laws enacted by local, state, or federal governments. There are two major categories of serious crime:

- crimes against the person (violent crime), including murder, aggravated assault, forcible rape, and robbery
- crimes against property (property crime), including burglary, larceny-theft, auto theft, and arson **p. 169**

✳ **Explore** the **Map** on **mysoclab.com**

Patterns of Crime in the United States

- About 62% of people arrested for property crimes and 80% of people arrested for violent crimes are male.
- Official statistics show that arrest rates peak in late adolescence and drop steadily with age.
- Street crime is more common among people of lower social position. Including white-collar and corporate crime makes class differences in criminality smaller.
- More whites than African Americans are arrested for street crimes. However, African Americans are arrested more often than whites in relation to their population size. Asian Americans have a lower-than-average rate of arrest.

📖 **Read** the **Document** on **mysoclab.com**

- By world standards, the U.S. crime rate is high. **pp. 170–73**

crimes against the person (p. 169) crimes that direct violence or the threat of violence against others; also known as *violent crimes*

crimes against property (p. 169) crimes that involve theft of money or property belonging to others; also known as *property crimes*

victimless crimes (p. 169) violations of law in which there are no obvious victims

The U.S. Criminal Justice System

Police

The police maintain public order by enforcing the law.

- Police use personal discretion in deciding whether and how to handle a situation.
- Research suggests that police are more likely to make an arrest if the offense is serious, if bystanders are present, or if the suspect is African American or Latino. **p. 174**

Courts

Courts rely on an adversarial process in which attorneys—one representing the defendant and one representing the state—present their cases in the presence of a judge who monitors legal procedures.

- In practice, U.S. courts resolve most cases through plea bargaining. Though efficient, this method puts less powerful people at a disadvantage. **p. 174**

Punishment

There are four justifications for punishment:

- retribution
- deterrence
- rehabilitation
- societal protection **pp. 175–76**

The **death penalty** remains controversial in the United States, the only high-income Western nation that routinely executes serious offenders. The trend is toward fewer executions. **pp. 176–77**

Community-based corrections include probation and parole. These programs lower the cost of supervising people convicted of crimes and reduce prison overcrowding but have not been shown to reduce recidivism. **pp. 177–79**

plea bargaining (p. 174) a legal negotiation in which a prosecutor reduces a charge in exchange for a defendant's guilty plea

retribution (p. 175) an act of moral vengeance by which society makes the offender suffer as much as the suffering caused by the crime

deterrence (p. 175) the attempt to discourage criminality through the use of punishment

rehabilitation (p. 175) a program for reforming the offender to prevent later offenses

societal protection (p. 176) rendering an offender incapable of further offenses temporarily through imprisonment or permanently by execution

criminal recidivism (p. 176) later offenses by people previously convicted of crimes

community-based corrections (p. 177) correctional programs operating within society at large rather than behind prison walls

8 Social Stratification

Learning Objectives

Remember the definitions of the key terms highlighted in boldfaced type throughout the chapter.

Understand that social stratification is a trait of society, not simply a reflection of individual differences.

Apply sociology's major theoretical approaches to social stratification.

Analyze evidence to assess the extent of inequality in our society and how common social mobility in the United States really is.

Evaluate how ideology operates to support social inequality.

Create a more precise vision of social class differences in the United States, including what is unequal and how unequal it is.

This chapter introduces the concept of social stratification, which is important because our social standing affects almost everything about our lives. This chapter defines social stratification, surveys systems of inequality through history and in various societies today, and then takes a close-up look at inequality in the United States. You will see that the extent of social inequality in the United States is greater than most people imagine. ■

On April 10, 1912, the ocean liner *Titanic* slipped away from the docks of Southampton, England, on its first voyage across the North Atlantic to New York. A proud symbol of the new industrial age, the towering ship carried 2,300 men, women, and children, some of them enjoying more luxury than most travelers today could imagine. Many poor immigrants crowded the lower decks, journeying to what they hoped would be a better life in the United States.

Two days out, the crew received radio warnings of icebergs in the area but paid little notice. Then, near midnight, as the ship steamed swiftly westward, a stunned lookout reported a massive shape rising out of the dark ocean directly ahead. Moments later, the *Titanic* collided with a huge iceberg, as tall as the ship itself, that split open its side as if the grand vessel were a giant tin can.

Seawater flooded into the ship's lower levels, pulling the ship down by the bow. Within twenty-five minutes of impact, people were rushing for the lifeboats. By 2:00 A.M., the bow was completely submerged, and the stern rose high above the water. Clinging to the deck, quietly observed by those huddled in lifeboats, hundreds of helpless passengers and crew solemnly passed their final minutes before the ship disappeared into the frigid Atlantic (W. Lord, 1976).

The tragic loss of more than 1,600 lives in the Titanic disaster made news around the world. Looking back on this terrible event with a sociological eye, we see that some categories of passengers had much better odds of survival than others. In keeping with that era's traditional ideas about gender, women and children boarded the lifeboats first, with the result that 80 percent of the people who died were men. Class was also a factor in who survived and who did not. More than 60 percent of the passengers traveling on first-class tickets were saved because they were on the upper decks, where warnings were sounded first and lifeboats were accessible. Only 36 percent of the second-class passengers survived, and of the third-class passengers on the lower decks, only 24 percent escaped drowning. On board the *Titanic,* class meant more than the quality of accommodations; it was a matter of life or death.

The fate of the passengers on the *Titanic* dramatically illustrates how social inequality affects the way people live—and sometimes whether they live at all. This chapter explores the important concept of social stratification and examines social inequality in the United States.

What Is Social Stratification?

● Understand

Every society is marked by inequality, with some people having significantly more money, schooling, health, and power than others. **Social stratification**, defined as *a system by which a society ranks categories of people in a hierarchy,* is based on four important principles:

1. **Social stratification is a trait of society, not simply a reflection of individual differences.** Many of us think of social standing in terms of personal talent and effort, and as a result, we often exaggerate the extent to which we control our own fate. Did a higher percentage of the first-class passengers on the *Titanic* survive because they were better swimmers than second- and third-class passengers? No. They did better because of their privileged position on the ship. Similarly, children born into wealthy families are more likely than children born into poverty to enjoy good health, do well in school, succeed in a career, and live a long life. Neither the rich nor

the poor created social stratification, yet this system shapes the lives of us all.

2. **Social stratification carries over from generation to generation.** We have only to look at how parents pass their social position on to their children to see that stratification is a trait of societies rather than individuals. Some people, especially in industrial societies, do experience **social mobility,** *a change in position within the social hierarchy.* Social mobility may be upward or downward. We celebrate the achievements of rare individuals such as Gisele Bundchen (from Brazil), talent show host Simon Cowell (Great Britain), and rapper Jay-Z (United States), none of whom ever finished high school but nevertheless managed to rise to fame and fortune. Some people also move downward in the social hierarchy because of business setbacks, unemployment, or illness. More often people move *horizontally;* they switch one job for another at about the same social level. The social standing of most people remains much the same over their lifetime.

3. **Social stratification is universal but variable.** Social stratification is found everywhere. Yet *what* is unequal and *how* unequal it is vary from one society to another. In some societies, inequality is mostly a matter of prestige; in others, wealth or power is the key element of difference. In addition, some societies contain more inequality than others.

4. **Social stratification involves not just inequality but beliefs as well.** Any system of inequality not only gives some people more than others but also defines these arrangements as fair. Like the *what* of social inequality, the explanations of *why* people should be unequal differ from society to society.

Caste and Class Systems

 **Understand**

When comparing societies in terms of inequality, sociologists distinguish between *closed systems,* which allow little change in social position, and *open systems,* which permit much more social mobility. Closed systems are called *caste systems*, and more open systems are called *class systems.*

The Caste System

A **caste system** is *social stratification based on ascription, or birth.* A pure caste system is closed because birth alone determines a person's entire future, with little or no social mobility based on individual effort. People live out their lives in the rigid categories into which they were born, without the possibility for change for the better or worse.

An Illustration: India

Many of the world's agrarian societies are caste systems. Although India's economy is growing rapidly, much of the population still lives in traditional villages, where the caste system is part of

The personal experience of poverty is clear in this photograph of mealtime in a homeless shelter. The main sociological insight is that although we feel the effects of social stratification personally, our social standing is largely the result of the way society (or a world of societies) structures opportunity and reward. To the core of our being, we are all products of social stratification.

everyday life. The traditional Indian system includes four major castes (or *varnas,* from a Sanskrit word that means "color"): Brahmin, Kshatriya, Vaishya, and Sudra. On the local level, however, each of these is composed of hundreds of subcaste groups (*jatis*).

From birth, caste position determines the direction of a person's life. First, with the exception of farming, which is open to everyone, families in each caste perform one type of work, as priests, soldiers, barbers, leather workers, street sweepers, and so on.

Second, a caste system demands that people marry others of the same ranking. If people were to have "mixed" marriages with members of other castes, what rank would their children hold? Sociologists call this pattern of marrying within a social category *endogamous* marriage (*endo-* stems from the Greek word for "within"). According to tradition—this practice is now rare and found only in remote rural areas—Indian parents select their children's future marriage partners, often before the children reach their teens.

Third, caste guides everyday life by keeping people in the company of "their own kind." Norms reinforce this practice by teaching, for example, that a "purer" person of a higher caste position is "polluted" by contact with someone of lower standing.

Fourth, caste systems rest on powerful cultural beliefs. Indian culture is built on the Hindu tradition that doing the caste's life work and accepting an arranged marriage are moral duties.

Caste and Class Systems

caste system social stratification based on ascription, or birth	**class system** social stratification based on both birth and individual achievement	**meritocracy** social stratification based on personal merit

In rural India, the traditional caste system still shapes people's lives. This girl is a member of the "untouchables," a category below the four basic castes. She and her family are clothes washers, people who clean material "polluted" by blood or human waste. Such work is defined as unclean for people of higher caste position. In the cities, by contrast, caste has given way to a class system where achievement plays a greater part in social ranking and income and consumption are keys to social standing.

Caste and Agrarian Life

Caste systems are typical of agrarian societies because agriculture demands a lifelong routine of hard work. By teaching a sense of moral duty, a caste system ensures that people are disciplined for a lifetime of work and are willing to perform the same jobs as their parents. Thus the caste system has hung on in rural India more than seventy years after being formally outlawed. People living in the industrial cities of India have many more choices about work and marriage partners than people in rural areas.

Another country long dominated by caste is South Africa, although the racial system of *apartheid* is no longer legal and is now in decline. The Thinking Globally box takes a closer look.

The Class System

Because a modern economy must attract people to work in many occupations other than farming, it depends on developing people's talents in diverse fields. This process of schooling and specialization gives rise to a **class system**, *social stratification based on both birth and individual achievement.*

Class systems are more open than caste systems, so people who gain schooling and skills may experience social mobility. As a result, class distinctions become blurred, and even blood relatives may have different social standings. Categorizing people according to their color, sex, or social background comes to be seen as wrong in modern societies as all people gain political rights and, in principle, equal standing before the law. In addition, work is no longer fixed at birth but involves some personal choice. Greater individuality also translates into more freedom in selecting a marriage partner.

Meritocracy

The concept of **meritocracy** refers to *social stratification based on personal merit.* Because industrial societies need to develop a broad range of abilities beyond farming, stratification is based not just on the accident of birth but also on *merit* (from a Latin word meaning "earned"), which includes a person's knowledge, abilities, and effort. A rough measure of merit is the importance of a person's job and how well it is done. To increase meritocracy, industrial societies expand equality of opportunity and teach people to expect unequal rewards based on individual performance.

A pure meritocracy has never existed, but in such a system social position would depend entirely on a person's performance, reflecting both ability and effort. Such a system would have ongoing social mobility, blurring social categories as individuals continuously move up or down in the system, depending on their latest performance.

Caste societies define merit in different terms, emphasizing loyalty to the system—that is, dutifully performing whatever job comes with the social position a person has at birth. Because they assign jobs before anyone can know anything about a person's talents or interests, caste systems waste human potential. On the other hand, because caste systems clearly assign everyone a "place" in society and a general type of work, they are very orderly. A need for some amount of order is the reason that even industrial and postindustrial societies keep some elements of caste—such as letting wealth pass from generation to generation—rather than becoming complete meritocracies. A pure meritocracy would have individuals moving up and down the social ranking all the time. Such social volatility would pull apart families and other social groupings. After all, economic performance is not everything: Would we want to evaluate our friends or family members solely on how successful they are in their jobs outside of the home? Probably not. Class systems in industrial societies move toward meritocracy to promote productivity and efficiency; but at the same time, they keep caste elements, such as family, to maintain order and social unity.

Status Consistency

Status consistency is *the degree of uniformity in a person's social standing across various dimensions of social inequality.* A caste system has little social mobility and therefore has high status consistency. This means that, remaining in the same social category, the typical person has the same relative standing with regard to

Jerome: Wow. I've been reading about racial caste in South Africa. I'm glad that's over.

Reggie: But racial inequality is far from over. . . .

At the southern tip of the African continent lies South Africa, a country about the size of Alaska with a population of about 50 million. For 300 years, the native Africans who lived there were ruled by white people, first by the Dutch traders and farmers who settled there in the mid-seventeenth century and then by the British, who colonized the area early in the nineteenth century. By the early 1900s, the British had taken over the entire country, naming it the Union of South Africa.

In 1961, the nation declared its independence from Britain, calling itself the Republic of South Africa, but freedom for the black majority was still decades away. To ensure their political control over the black population, whites instituted the policy of *apartheid*, or racial separation. Apartheid, written into law in 1948, denied blacks national citizenship, ownership of land, and any voice in the nation's government. As a lower caste, blacks received little schooling and performed menial, low-paying jobs. White people with even average wealth had at least one black household servant.

The members of the white minority claimed that apartheid protected their cultural traditions from the influence of people they considered inferior. When blacks resisted apartheid, whites used brutal military repression to maintain their power. Even so, steady resistance—especially from younger blacks, who demanded a political voice

and economic opportunity—gradually forced the country to change. Criticism from other industrial nations added to the pressure. By the mid-1980s, the tide began to turn as the South African government granted limited political rights to people of mixed race and Asian ancestry. Next, all people gained the right to form labor unions, to enter occupations once limited to whites, and to own property. Officials also repealed apartheid laws that separated the races in public places.

The pace of change increased in 1990 with the release from prison of Nelson Mandela, who led the fight against apartheid. In 1994, the first national election open to all races made Mandela president, ending centuries of white minority rule.

Despite this dramatic political change, social stratification in South Africa is still based on race. Even with the right to own property, one-fourth of black South Africans have no work, and one-fourth of the population lives below the poverty line. The worst off are some 7 million *ukuhleleleka,*

which means "marginal people" in the Xhosa language. Soweto-by-the-Sea may sound like a summer getaway, but it is a shantytown, home to hundreds of thousands of people crammed into shacks made of packing crates, corrugated metal, cardboard, and other discarded materials. Recent years have seen some signs of prosperity; some shopping centers have been built, and most streets are now paved. But many families still live without electricity for lights or refrigeration. Some also lack plumbing, forcing people to use buckets to haul sewage. In some communities, women line up to take a turn at a single water tap that serves as many as 1,000 people. Jobs are hard to come by, and those who do find work are lucky to earn $250 a month.

South Africa's current president, Jacob Zuma, who was elected in 2009, leads a nation still crippled by its history of racial caste. Tourism is up and holds the promise of an economic boom in years to come, but the country can break free from the past only by providing real opportunity to all its people.

What Do You Think?

1. How has race been a form of caste in South Africa?

2. Although apartheid is no longer law, why does racial inequality continue to shape South African society?

3. Does race operate as an element of caste in the United States? Explain your answer.

Sources: Mabry & Masland (1999), Murphy (2002), Perry (2009), and World Bank (2011).

---

wealth, power, and prestige as everyone else in that caste group. However, the greater mobility of class systems moves people up and down and therefore produces less status consistency. In the United States, for example, most college professors with advanced degrees enjoy high social prestige but earn only modest incomes. Low status consistency means that it is more difficult to define people's social position. Therefore, *classes* are much harder to define than *castes*.

Caste and Class: The United Kingdom

The mix of caste and meritocracy in class systems is well illustrated by the United Kingdom (Great Britain—composed of England, Wales, and Scotland—and Northern Ireland), an industrial nation with a long agrarian history.

Aristocratic England

In the Middle Ages, England had a system of aristocracy that resembled a caste. The aristocracy included the leading members of the church, who were thought to speak with the authority of God. Some clergy were local priests, who were not members of the aristocracy and who lived simple lives. But the highest church officials lived in palaces and presided over an organization that owned much land, which was the major source of wealth. Church leaders, who were typically referred to as the *first estate* in France and other European countries, also had a great deal of power to shape the political events of the day.

The rest of the aristocracy, which in France and other European countries was called the *second estate,* was a hereditary nobility that made up barely 5 percent of the population. The royal family—the king and queen at the top of the power structure—as well as lesser nobles (including several hundred families headed by men titled as dukes, earls, and barons) together owned most of the nation's land. Most of the men and women within the aristocracy were wealthy due to their land, and they had many servants for their homes as well as ordinary farmers to work their fields. With all their work done for them by others, members of the aristocracy had no occupations and thought that engaging in any work for income was beneath them. They used their time to develop skills in horseback riding and warfare and to cultivate refined tastes in art, music, and literature.

To prevent their vast landholdings from being divided by heirs when they died, aristocrats devised the law of *primogeniture* (from the Latin meaning "firstborn"), which required that all property pass to the oldest son or other male relation. Younger sons had to find other means of support. Some of these men became leaders in the church, where they would live as well as they were used to, and helped tie together the church and the state by having members of the same families running both. Other younger sons within the aristocracy became military officers or judges or took up other professions considered honorable for gentlemen. In an age when no woman could inherit her father's property and few women had the opportunity to earn a living on their own, a noble daughter depended for her security on marrying well.

Below the high clergy and the rest of the aristocracy, the vast majority of men and women were called *commoners* or, in France and other European countries, the *third estate*. Most commoners were serfs working land owned by nobles or the church. Unlike members of the aristocracy, most commoners had little schooling and were illiterate.

As the Industrial Revolution expanded England's economy, some commoners living in cities made enough money to challenge the nobility. More emphasis on meritocracy, the growing importance of money, and the expansion of schooling and legal rights eventually blurred the differences between aristocrats and commoners and gave rise to a class system.

Perhaps it is a sign of the times that these days, traditional titles are put up for sale by aristocrats who need money. In 1996, for example, Earl Spencer—the brother of Princess Diana—sold one of his titles, Lord of Wimbledon, to raise the $300,000 he needed to redo the plumbing in one of his large homes (McKee, 1996).

In 2011, Prince William, second in line to the British throne, married commoner Catherine Middleton, who then took the title, "Her Royal Highness the Duchess of Cambridge." They now take their place as part of a royal family that traces its ancestry back more than a thousand years—an element of caste that remains in the British class system.

The United Kingdom Today

The United Kingdom has a class system today, but caste elements of the past are still evident. A small number of British families have aristocratic backgrounds and many still hold inherited wealth and enjoy high prestige, schooling at excellent universities, and substantial political influence. A traditional monarch, Queen Elizabeth II, is the United Kingdom's head of state, and Parliament's House of Lords is composed of "peers," about half of whom are of noble birth. However, control of government has passed to the House of Commons, where the prime minister and other leaders reach their positions by achievement—winning an election— rather than by birth. Another sign of a more open system is the fact that in 2011, Prince William, the queen's grandson, married Catherine Middleton, a woman who was a commoner (although from a relatively privileged family) and thus might be said to have "earned" her new position.

Lower in the class hierarchy, roughly one-fourth of the British people fall into the middle class. Some earn comfortable incomes from professions and businesses and are likely to have investments in the form of stocks and bonds. Below the middle class, perhaps half of all Britons consider themselves "working-class," earning modest incomes through service work or manual labor. The remaining one-fourth of the British people make up the lower class, the poor who lack steady work or who work full time but are paid too little to live comfortably. Most lower-class Britons live in the nation's northern and western regions, which have been plagued by closings of mines and factories.

The British mix of caste elements and meritocracy has produced a highly stratified society with some opportunity to move upward or downward, much the same as exists in the United States (Long & Ferrie, 2007). Historically, British society has been somewhat more castelike than is the case in the United States, a fact reflected in the importance attached to linguistic accent. Distinctive patterns of speech develop in any society when people are set off from one another over several generations. People in the United States treat accent as a clue to where a person lives or grew up (we can easily identify a midwestern "twang" or a southern "drawl"). In the United Kingdom, however, accent is more a mark of social class (upper-class people speak "the King's English," but most people speak "like commoners"). So different are these two accents that the British seem to be, as the saying goes, "a single people divided by a common language."

Classless Societies? The Former Soviet Union

Nowhere in the world do we find a society without some degree of social inequality. Yet some nations have claimed to be classless.

The Russian Revolution

The Union of Soviet Socialist Republics (USSR), which rivaled the United States as a military superpower in the mid- to late twentieth century, was born out of a revolution in Russia in 1917. The Russian Revolution ended the feudal estate system ruled by a hereditary nobility and transferred most farms, factories, and other productive property from private ownership to state control. Following the lead of Karl Marx, who believed that private ownership of property was the source of social stratification, Soviet leaders boasted of becoming a classless society.

Critics, however, pointed out that based on their jobs, the Soviet people were actually stratified into four unequal categories. At the top were high government officials, known as *apparatchiks.* Next came the Soviet intelligentsia, including lower government officials, college professors, scientists, physicians, and engineers. Below them were manual workers and, at the lowest level, the rural peasantry.

In reality, the Soviet Union was not classless at all, and political power was concentrated in only a small percentage of the population. But putting factories, farms, colleges, and hospitals under state control did create greater economic equality (although with sharp differences in power) than in capitalist societies such as the United States.

One of the major events of the twentieth century was the socialist revolution in Russia, which led to the creation of the Soviet Union. Following the ideas of Karl Marx, the popular uprising overthrew a feudal aristocracy, as depicted in the 1920 painting *Bolshevik* by Boris Mikhailovich Kustodiev.

The Modern Russian Federation

In 1985, Mikhail Gorbachev came to power with a new economic program known as *perestroika* ("restructuring"). Gorbachev saw that although the Soviet system had significantly reduced economic inequality, overall living standards lagged far behind those of other industrial nations. Gorbachev tried to generate economic growth by reducing the centralized control of the economy, which had proved to be inefficient.

Gorbachev's economic reforms turned into one of the most dramatic social movements in history. People throughout Eastern Europe blamed their poverty and lack of basic freedoms on the repressive ruling class of Communist party officials. Beginning in 1989, people throughout Eastern Europe toppled their socialist governments, and in 1991, the Soviet Union itself collapsed, with its largest republic remaking itself as the Russian Federation.

The Soviet Union's story shows that social inequality involves more than economic resources. Soviet society may not have had the extremes of wealth and poverty found in the United Kingdom and the United States. But an elite class existed all the same, based on political power rather than wealth.

What about social mobility in so-called classless societies? In the twentieth century, there was as much upward social mobility in the Soviet Union as in the United Kingdom or the United States. Rapidly expanding industry and government drew many poor rural peasants into factories and offices. This trend illustrates what sociologists call **structural social mobility**, *a shift in the social position of large numbers of people due more to changes in society itself than to individual efforts.*

> **November 24, Odessa, Ukraine.** The first snow of our voyage flies over the decks as our ship docks at Odessa, the former Soviet Union's southern port on the Black Sea. Not far from the dock, we gaze up at the Potemkin Steps, the steep stairway up to the city, where the first shots of the Russian Revolution rang out. It has been six years since our last visit, and much has changed; indeed, the Soviet Union itself has collapsed. Has life improved? For some people, certainly. There are now chic boutiques in which well-dressed shoppers buy fine wines, designer clothes, and imported perfumes. Outside, shiny new Volvos, Mercedeses, and even a few Cadillacs stand out against the small Ladas from the "old days." But for most people, life seems much worse. Flea markets line the curbs as families sell their home furnishings. When meat sells for $4 a pound and the average person earns about $30 a month, people become desperate. Even the city has to save money by turning off streetlights after 8:00 P.M. The spirits of most people seem as dim as Odessa's streets.

During the 1990s, structural social mobility in the Russian Federation turned downward as that country experienced something similar to the Great Depression of the 1930s in the United States. One indicator is that the average life span for men dropped by five years and for women by two years. Many factors contributed to this decline, including Russia's poor health care system, but the Russian people clearly have suffered in the turbulent period of economic change that began in 1991 (Bohlen, 1998; Gerber & Hout, 1998; Mason, 2004).

The hope was that in the long run, closing inefficient state industries would improve the nation's economic performance. The economy has expanded, but for many Russians, living standards have fallen and millions face hard times. Some people have made huge fortunes, although some of this new wealth vanished in the recent recession. Now, economic indicators have been on their way up, with lower unemployment and a falling poverty rate. The government has gained greater control over the Russian economy, which has caused economic inequality to decline but also raised questions about what a return to a more socialist society will mean for political freedoms (Wendle, 2009; World Bank, 2011).

China: Emerging Social Classes

Sweeping political and economic change has affected not just the Russian Federation but also the People's Republic of China. After the Communist revolution in 1949, the state took control of all farms, factories, and other productive property. Communist party leader Mao Zedong declared all work to be equally important, so officially, social classes no longer existed.

The new program greatly reduced economic inequality. But as in the Soviet Union, social differences remained. The country was ruled by a political elite with enormous power and considerable privilege; below them were managers of large factories and skilled professionals; next came industrial workers; at the bottom were rural peasants, who were not even allowed to leave their villages to migrate to cities.

Further economic change came in 1978 when Mao died and Deng Xiaoping became China's leader. The state gradually loosened its hold on the economy, allowing a new class of business owners to emerge. Communist party leaders remain in control of the country, and some have prospered as they have joined the ranks of the small but wealthy elite who control new, privately run industries. China's economy has experienced rapid growth, and the nation has now moved into the middle-income category. Much of this new prosperity has been concentrated in coastal areas where living standards have soared far above those in China's rural interior. A sign of the times is that the luxury car company Bentley now sells more of its cars in China than in Great Britain (Richburg, 2011; United Nations, 2011).

Since the late 1990s, the booming cities along China's coast have become home to many thousands of people made rich by the expanding economy. In addition, these cities have attracted more than 100 million young migrants from rural areas in search of better jobs and a better life. Many more have wanted to move to the booming cities, but the government still restricts movement, which has the effect of slowing upward social mobility. For those who have been able to move, the jobs that are available are generally better than the work that people knew before. But many of these new jobs are dangerous, and most pay wages that barely meet the higher costs of living in the city, so the majority of the migrants remain poor. But, in general, China's population has experienced structural upward mobility as the economy has expanded by about 10 percent annually over the past three decades. China is now the world's second largest economy (after the United States), reflecting in part how much of the world's manufacturing now takes place there (Wu & Treiman, 2007; Chang, 2008; Powell, 2008; World Bank, 2011).

A new category in China's social hierarchy consists of the *hai gui*, a term derived from words meaning "returned from overseas" or "sea turtles." The ranks of the "sea turtles" are increasing by tens of thousands each year as young women and men return from educations in other countries, in many cases from college and university campuses in the United States. These young people, most of whom were from privileged families to begin with, typically return to China to find many opportunities and soon become very influential (Liu & Hewitt, 2008).

China's emerging new class system is a mix of the old political hierarchy and a new business hierarchy. Economic inequality in China has increased as members of the new business elite have become millionaires and even billionaires. As Figure 8–1 shows, economic inequality in China is greater than in Sweden, the United Kingdom, or Canada, although it remains less then the inequality found in the United States. With ongoing change in China, patterns of social stratification are likely to remain in flux for some time to come (Bian, 2002; Kuhn, 2007; Wines & Johnson, 2011; World Bank, 2011).

Ideology: The Power behind Stratification

How do societies persist without sharing their resources more equally? The highly stratified British aristocracy lasted for centuries, and for 2,000 years people in India accepted the idea that they should be privileged or poor based on the accident of birth.

A major reason that social hierarchies endure is **ideology,** *cultural beliefs that justify particular social arrangements, including patterns of inequality.* A belief—for example, the idea that the rich are smart and the poor are lazy—is ideological to the extent that it supports inequality by defining it as fair.

Plato and Marx on Ideology

According to the ancient Greek philosopher Plato (427–347 B.C.E.), every culture considers some type of inequality fair. Although Karl Marx understood this, he was far more critical of inequality than Plato. Marx criticized capitalist societies for defending wealth and power in the hands of a few as a "law of the marketplace." Capitalist law, he continued, defines the right to own property, which encourages money to remain within the same families from one generation to the next. In short, Marx concluded, culture and institutions combine to support a society's elite, which is why established hierarchies last such a long time.

China has the fastest-growing economy of all the major nations and currently manufactures more products than even the United States. With more and more money to spend, the Chinese are now a major consumer of automobiles—a fact that probably saved the Buick brand from extinction.

Historical Patterns of Ideology

Ideology changes along with a society's economy and technology. Because agrarian societies depend on most of their people performing a lifetime of labor, they develop caste systems that make carrying out the duties of a person's social position or "station" a moral responsibility. With the rise of industrial capitalism, an ideology of meritocracy arises, defining wealth and power as prizes to be won by the individuals who perform the best. This change means that the poor—often given charity under feudalism—are looked down on as personally undeserving. This harsh view is linked to the ideas of Herbert Spencer, as explained in the Thinking About Diversity box on page 194.

History shows how difficult it is to change social stratification. However, challenges to the status quo always arise. Traditional ideas about "a woman's place in the home," for example, have given way to economic opportunity for women in societies today. The continuing progress toward racial equality in South Africa is another case of widespread rejection of the ideology of apartheid. The popular uprisings against political dictatorships across the Middle East that began in 2011 show us that this process of challenging particular patterns of inequality continues.

Explaining Stratification: Structural-Functional Theory

 Apply

Why does social stratification exist at all? According to the structural-functional approach, social stratification plays a vital part in the operation of society. This argument was presented many years ago by Kingsley Davis and Wilbert Moore (1945).

The Davis-Moore Thesis

The **Davis-Moore thesis** states that *social stratification has beneficial consequences for the operation of a society.* How else, ask Davis and Moore, can we explain the fact that some form of social stratification has been found in every society?

Davis and Moore note that modern societies have hundreds of occupational positions of varying importance. Certain jobs—say, washing cars or answering a telephone—are fairly easy and can be performed by almost anyone. Other jobs—such as designing a new generation of computers or transplanting human organs—are very difficult and demand the scarce talents of people with extensive and expensive training.

Therefore, Davis and Moore explain, the greater the functional importance of a position, the more rewards a society attaches to it. This strategy promotes productivity and efficiency because rewarding important work with income, prestige, power, or leisure encourages people to do these jobs and to work better, longer, and harder. In short, unequal rewards (which is what social stratification is) benefit society as a whole.

Davis and Moore claim that any society could be egalitarian, but only to the extent that people are willing to let *anyone* perform *any* job. Equality also demands that someone who performs a job

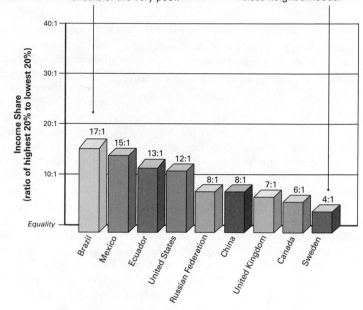

- Driving to work in São Paulo, Brazil, Fabio Campos passes both gated mansions of the very rich and rundown shacks of the very poor.
- On her way to work in Stockholm, Sweden, Sylvia Arnbjörg passes through mostly middle-class neighborhoods.

Global Snapshot

FIGURE 8–1 Economic Inequality in Selected Countries, 2010

Many low- and middle-income countries are marked by greater economic inequality than the United States. But the United States has more economic inequality than most high-income nations.

Sources: U.S. Census Bureau (2011) and World Bank (2011).

poorly be rewarded just as much as someone who performs the job well. Such a system clearly offers little incentive for people to try their best, reducing the society's productive efficiency.

The Davis-Moore thesis suggests the reason stratification exists; it does not state precisely what rewards a society should give to any occupational position or how unequal rewards should be. It merely points out that positions a society considers crucial must offer enough rewards to draw talented people away from less important work.

● **Evaluate** Although the Davis-Moore thesis is an important contribution to understanding social stratification, it has provoked criticism. Melvin Tumin (1953) wondered, first of all, how we assess the importance of a particular occupation. Perhaps the high rewards our society gives to physicians result partly from deliberate efforts by medical schools to limit the supply of physicians and thereby increase the demand for their services.

Furthermore, do rewards actually reflect the contribution someone makes to society? With an annual income of about $315 million, Oprah Winfrey earns more in one day than the president of the United States earns all year. Oprah is certainly a celebrity, but would anyone argue that the work she has done in television is more important than leading a country? And what about members of the U.S. military serving in Iraq or Afghanistan? Although they face the daily risk of combat, newly enlisted

Jake: "My dad is amazing. He's really smart!"

Frank: "You mean he's rich. He owns I don't know how many fast food places."

Jake: "Do you think people get rich without being smart?"

It's a question we all wonder about. How much is our social position a matter of intelligence? What about hard work? Being born to the "right family"? Even "dumb luck"?

More than in most societies, in the United States we link social standing to personal abilities, including intelligence. In 2010, *Time* magazine put Mark Zuckerberg on the cover and announced that he was "Person of the Year" for developing Facebook. For this achievement, and amassing a fortune of some $10 billion, it is easy to imagine that this Harvard dropout is a pretty smart guy (Grossman, 2010).

This idea goes back a long time. We have all heard the words "the survival of the fittest," which describe our society as a competitive jungle in which the "best" survive and the rest fall behind. The phrase was coined by one of sociology's pioneers, Herbert Spencer (1820–1903), whose ideas about social inequality are still widespread today.

Spencer, who lived in England, eagerly followed the work of the natural scientist Charles Darwin (1809–1882). Darwin's theory of biological evolution held that a species changes physically over many generations as it adapts to the natural environment. Spencer incorrectly applied Darwin's theory to the operation of society, which does not operate according to biological principles. In Spencer's distorted view, society became the "jungle," with the "fittest" people rising to wealth and the "failures" sinking into miserable poverty.

It is no surprise that Spencer's views, as wrong as they were, were popular among the rising U.S. industrialists of the day. John D. Rockefeller (1839–1937), who made a vast fortune building the oil industry, recited Spencer's "social gospel" to young children in Sunday school. As Rockefeller saw it, the growth of giant corporations—and the astounding wealth of their owners—was merely the result of the survival of the fittest, a basic fact of nature. Neither Spencer nor Rockefeller had much sympathy for the poor, seeing poverty as evidence of individuals' failing to measure up in a competitive world. Spencer opposed social welfare programs because he thought they penalized society's "best"

people (through taxes) and rewarded its "worst" members (through welfare benefits). By incorrectly using Darwin's theory, the rich could turn their backs on everyone else, assuming that the existing inequality was inevitable and somehow "natural."

Today, sociologists point out that our society is far from a meritocracy, as Spencer claimed. And it is not the case that companies or individuals who generate lots of money necessarily benefit society. The people who made hundreds of millions of dollars selling subprime mortgages in recent years certainly ended up hurting just about everyone. But Spencer's view that the "fittest" rise to the top remains widespread in our very unequal and individualistic culture.

What Do You Think?

1. How much do you think inequality in our society can correctly be described as "the survival of the fittest"? Why?

2. Why do you think Spencer's ideas are still popular in the United States today?

3. Is how much you earn a good measure of your importance to society? Why or why not?

---

privates first class in the United States Army earned a base salary of $21,000 in 2011 (Defense Finance and Accounting Service, 2011). And what about the heads of the big Wall Street financial firms that collapsed in 2008? It seems reasonable to conclude that these corporate leaders made some bad decisions, yet their salaries were astronomical. Even after finishing its worst year ever, with losses of $27 billion, Merrill Lynch paid bonuses of more than $1 million to each of more than 700 employees (Fox, 2009). The top people in the financial industry made out even better. In 2010, a year in which Goldman Sachs recorded a decline in profit of 37 percent, CEO Lloyd Blankfein made more than $14 million—an amount it would take a typical U.S. Army private more than 679 years to earn. As the Occupy Wall Street movement of 2011 has asked, do corporate executives deserve such megasalaries for their contributions to society?

Oprah Winfrey reported income of $315 million in 2010. Guided by the Davis-Moore thesis, why would societies reward some people with so much more fame and fortune than others? How would Karl Marx answer this question?

Second, Tumin claimed that Davis and Moore ignore how the caste elements of social stratification can *prevent* the development of individual talent. Born to privilege, rich children have opportunities to develop their abilities, which is something many gifted poor children never have.

Third, living in a society that places so much emphasis on money, we tend to overestimate the importance of high-paying work; how much do stockbrokers or people who trade international currencies really contribute to the well-being of people in our society? For the same reason, it is difficult for us to see the value of any work not oriented toward making money, such as parenting, creative writing, playing in a symphony, or just being a good friend to someone in need (Packard, 2002).

Read "Some Principles of Stratification" by Kingsley Davis and Wilbert E. Moore, and the response by Melvin Tumin, on **mysoclab.com**

Finally, by suggesting that social stratification benefits all of society, the Davis-Moore thesis ignores how social inequality can harm society and even promote conflict. Some amount of inequality may encourage people to reach for more—to work harder or gain more schooling so they can find a better-paying job. But too much inequality, especially with limited upward mobility, can smother ambition and harden people's beliefs that they will never get ahead or even gain economic security. In this way, people come to see their society as fundamentally unjust, a belief that may encourage them to seek more radical change (Kaiser, 2010). This criticism leads to the social-conflict approach, which provides a very different explanation for social inequality.

CHECK YOUR LEARNING State the Davis-Moore thesis in your own words. What are Tumin's criticisms of this thesis?

Back in the Great Depression of the 1930s, "tent cities" that were home to desperately poor people could be found in much of the United States. The depression came to an end, but poverty persisted. The recent recession sparked a resurgence of tent cities, including this one in Fresno, California. How would structural-functional analysis explain such poverty? What about the social-conflict approach?

Explaining Stratification: Social-Conflict Theory

● Apply

Social-conflict analysis argues that rather than benefiting society as a whole, social stratification benefits some people and disadvantages others. This analysis draws heavily on the ideas of Karl Marx, with contributions from Max Weber.

Karl Marx: Class Conflict

As Marx saw it, the Industrial Revolution promised humanity a society free from want. Yet during Marx's lifetime, the capitalist economy had done little to improve the lives of most people. Marx set out to explain a glaring contradiction: how, in a society so rich, so many could be so poor.

In Marx's view, social stratification is rooted in people's relationship to the means of production. People either own productive property (such as factories and businesses) or sell their labor to others. In feudal Europe, the aristocracy and the church owned the productive land; the peasants toiled as farmers. Under industrial capitalism, the aristocracy was replaced by **capitalists** (sometimes called the *bourgeoisie*, a French word meaning "town dwellers"), *people who own and operate factories and other businesses in pursuit of profits*. Peasants became the **proletarians**, *people who sell their labor for wages*. Capitalists and proletarians have opposing interests and are separated by a vast gulf of wealth and power, making class conflict inevitable.

Marx lived during the nineteenth century, a time when a small number of industrialists in the United States were amassing great fortunes. Andrew Carnegie, J. P. Morgan, and John Jacob Astor (one of the few very rich passengers to drown on the *Titanic*) lived in fabulous mansions that were filled with priceless works of art and staffed by dozens of servants. Even by today's standards, their incomes were staggering. For example, Carnegie earned more than $20 million in 1900 (roughly $536 million in today's dollars), when the average worker earned roughly $500 a year (Baltzell, 1964; Williamson, 2011).

In time, Marx believed, the working majority would overthrow the capitalists once and for all. Capitalism would bring about its own downfall, Marx reasoned, because it makes workers poorer and poorer and gives them little control over what they make or how they make it. Under capitalism, work produces only **alienation**, *the experience of isolation and misery resulting from powerlessness*.

To replace capitalism, Marx imagined a *socialist* system that would meet the needs of all rather than just the needs of the elite few: "The proletarians have nothing to lose but their chains. They have a world to win" (Marx & Engels, 1972:362, orig. 1848).

● **Evaluate** Marx has had enormous influence on sociological thinking. But his revolutionary ideas, calling for the overthrow of capitalist society, also make his work highly controversial.

One of the strongest criticisms of the Marxist approach is that it ignores a central idea of the Davis-Moore thesis: that a system of unequal rewards is needed to place people in the right jobs and to motivate people to work hard. Marx separated reward from performance; his egalitarian ideal was based on the principle "from each according to his ability, to each according to his needs" (Marx & Engels, 1972:388, orig. 1848). However, failure to reward individual performance may be precisely what caused the low productivity of the former Soviet Union and other socialist economies around the world. Defenders respond to such criticism by asking why we assume that humanity is inherently selfish rather than social; individual rewards are not the only way to motivate people to perform their social roles (M. S. Clark, 1991).

A second problem is that the revolutionary change Marx predicted has failed to happen, at least in advanced capitalist societies. The next section explains why.

CHECK YOUR LEARNING How does Marx's view of social stratification differ from the Davis-Moore thesis?

Why No Marxist Revolution?

During 2011, widespread talk of the rich 1 percent versus the 99 percent, who are the rest of us, echoes the vision of Karl Marx and shows his influence remains today. Even so, despite Marx's prediction, capitalism is still thriving. Why have industrial workers not overthrown capitalism? Ralf Dahrendorf (1959) suggested four reasons:

1. **Fragmentation of the capitalist class.** Today, tens of millions of stockholders, rather than single families, own most large companies. Day-to-day corporate operations are in the hands of a large class of managers, who may or may not be major stockholders. With stock widely held—about half of U.S. households own at least some stocks—more and more people have a direct stake in the capitalist system (U.S. Census Bureau, 2011).

2. **A higher standard of living.** As Chapter 12 ("Economics and Politics") explains, a century ago, most U. S. workers were in factories or on farms in **blue-collar occupations**, *lower-prestige jobs that involve mostly manual labor*. Today, most workers are in **white-collar occupations**, *higher-prestige jobs that involve mostly mental activity*. These jobs are in sales, customer support, management, and other service fields. Most of today's white-collar workers do not think of themselves as an "industrial proletariat." Just as important, the average income in the United States rose almost tenfold over the course of the twentieth century, even allowing for inflation. During

this period, in addition, the number of hours in the workweek actually decreased. Therefore, despite recent tough times economically, the typical worker today is far better off than the typical worker was a century ago, an example of structural social mobility. One consequence of this rising standard of living is that more people support the status quo.

3. **More worker organizations.** Workers today have the right to form labor unions and other organizations that make demands of management, backed by threats of work slowdowns and strikes. As a result, labor disputes are settled without threatening the capitalist system.

4. **Greater legal protections.** Over the past century, new laws made the workplace safer, and unemployment insurance, disability protection, and Social Security now provide workers with greater financial security.

A Counterpoint

These developments suggest that U.S. society has smoothed many of capitalism's rough edges. Yet many observers claim that Marx's analysis of capitalism is still largely valid (Domhoff, 1983; Stephens, 1986; Boswell & Dixon, 1993; Hout, Brooks, & Manza, 1993). First, wealth remains highly concentrated, with the richest 1 percent of the U.S. population owning 35 percent of all privately owned property (Keister, 2000; Wolff, 2010). Second, many of today's white-collar jobs offer no more income, security, or satisfaction than factory work did a century ago. Third, many benefits enjoyed by today's workers came about through the class conflict Marx described; workers still struggle to hold on to what they have; and in recent years, many workers have actually lost pensions and other benefits. Fourth, although workers have gained legal protections, ordinary people still face disadvantages that the law cannot overcome. Fifth, as this chapter will explain, income and wealth are becoming more unequal, just as Marx claimed they would. The "Occupy" movement is only the most visible expression of a widespread belief that our economic system does not serve the interests of most people. Therefore, social-conflict theorists conclude, even though a socialist revolution has not taken place in the United States, Marx was still mostly right about capitalism.

Max Weber: Class, Status, and Power

Max Weber agreed with Karl Marx that social stratification causes social conflict, but he viewed Marx's two-class model as too simple. Instead, he claimed that social stratification involves three distinct dimensions of inequality.

The first dimension, economic inequality—the issue so important to Marx—Weber called *class* position. Weber did not think of classes as well-defined categories but as a continuum ranging from high to low. Weber's second dimension is *status*, or social prestige, and the third is *power*.

Weber's Socioeconomic Status Hierarchy

Marx viewed social prestige and power as simple reflections of economic position and did not treat them as distinct dimensions of inequality. But Weber noted that status consistency in modern societies is often quite low: A local official might exercise great power yet have little wealth or social prestige.

The extent of social inequality in agrarian systems is greater than that found in industrial societies. One indication of the unchallenged power of rulers is the monumental structures built over years with the unpaid labor of common people. Although the Taj Mahal in India is among the world's most beautiful buildings, it was built as a tomb for a single individual.

Weber, then, characterizes social stratification in industrial societies as a multidimensional ranking rather than a hierarchy of clearly defined classes. In line with Weber's thinking, sociologists use the term **socioeconomic status (SES)** to refer to *a composite ranking based on various dimensions of social inequality.*

Inequality in History

Weber observed that each of his three dimensions of social inequality stands out at a different time in the history of human societies. Status or social prestige is the main dimension of difference in agrarian societies, taking the form of honor. Members of these societies gain prestige by conforming to cultural norms that apply to their particular rank.

Industrialization and the development of capitalism eliminate traditional rankings based on birth but create striking financial inequality. Thus in an industrial society, the crucial difference between people is the economic dimension of class.

Over time, industrial societies witness the growth of a bureaucratic state. Bigger government and the spread of all types of other organizations make power more important in the stratification system. Especially in socialist societies, where government regulates many aspects of life, high-ranking officials become the new ruling elite.

This historical analysis points to a final difference between Weber and Marx. Marx thought societies could eliminate social stratification by abolishing private ownership of productive property. Weber doubted that overthrowing capitalism would significantly lessen social stratification. It might reduce economic differences, he reasoned, but socialism would increase inequality by expanding government and concentrating power in the hands of a political elite. The popular uprisings against socialist bureaucracies in Eastern Europe and the former Soviet Union show that discontent can be generated by socialist political elites and thus support Weber's position.

● **Evaluate** Weber's multidimensional view of social stratification greatly influenced sociologists and made the concept of socioeconomic status hierarchy popular. But critics (particularly those who favor Marx's ideas) argue that although social class boundaries may have blurred, industrial and postindustrial societies still show striking patterns of social inequality.

As we have all heard during the 2012 presidential campaign, economic inequality has increased recently in the United States. Although some people favor Weber's multidimensional hierarchy, others think, in light of this trend toward greater economic inequality, that Marx's view of the rich versus the poor is closer to the truth.

CHECK YOUR LEARNING What are Weber's three dimensions of social inequality? According to Weber, which of them would you expect to be most important in the United States? Why?

Explaining Stratification: Symbolic-Interaction Theory

● **Apply**

Because social stratification has to do with the way an entire society is organized, sociologists (Marx and Weber included) typically treat it as a macro-level issue. But a micro-level analysis of social stratification is also important because people's social standing affects their everyday interactions. The Applying Theory table summarizes the contributions of the three theoretical approaches to social stratification.

APPLYING THEORY

Social Stratification

	Structural-Functional Theory	Social-Conflict Theory	Symbolic-Interaction Theory
What is the level of analysis?	Macro-level	Macro-level	Micro-level
What is social stratification?	Stratification is a system of unequal rewards that benefits society as a whole.	Stratification is a division of a society's resources that benefits some people and harms others.	Stratification is a factor that guides people's interactions in everyday life.
What is the reason for our social position?	Social position reflects personal talents and abilities in a competitive economy.	Social position reflects the way society divides resources.	The products we consume all say something about social position.
Are unequal rewards fair?	Yes. Unequal rewards boost economic production by encouraging people to work harder and try new ideas. Linking greater rewards to more important work is widely accepted.	No. Unequal rewards only serve to divide society, creating "haves" and "have-nots." There is widespread opposition to social inequality.	Maybe. People may or may not define inequality as fair. People may view their social position as a measure of self-worth, justifying inequality in terms of personal differences.

When Class Gets Personal: Picking (with) Your Friends

The sound of banjo music drifted across the field late one summer afternoon. I laid my brush down, climbed over the fence I had been painting, and walked toward the sound of the music to see what was going on. That's how I met my neighbor Max, a retired factory worker who lived just up the road. Max was a pretty good "picker," and within an hour, I was back on his porch with my guitar. I called Howard, a friend who teaches at the college, and he showed up a little while later, six-string in hand. The three of us jammed for a couple of hours, smiling all the while.

The next morning, I was mowing the grass in front of the house when Max came walking down the road. I turned off the mower as he came down the driveway. "Hi, Max," I said. "Thanks for having us over last night. I really had fun."

"Don't mention it," Max responded. Then he shook his head a little and added, "Ya know, I was thinkin' after you guys left. I mean, it was really

somethin' how you guys looked like you were having a great time. With somebody like *me!*"

"Well, yeah," I replied, not sure what he meant. "You sure played better than we did."

Max looked down at the ground, embarrassed by the compliment. Then he added, "What I mean is that you guys were having a good time with somebody like *me.* You're both professors, right? *Doctors*, even . . ."

What Do You Think?

1. Why do you think Max felt that two college teachers would not enjoy spending time with him?

2. How does his reaction suggest that people take social position personally?

3. Can you think of a similar experience you have had with someone of a different social position?

In most communities, people interact primarily with others of about the same social standing. This pattern begins with the fact that due to social stratification, people tend to live with others like themselves. In larger public spaces, such as a large shopping mall, we often see couples or groups made up of individuals whose appearance and shopping habits are similar. At the same time, people with very different social standing commonly keep their distance from one another. Well-dressed people walking down the street on their way to an expensive restaurant, for example, might move across the sidewalk or even cross the street to avoid getting close to others they think are homeless people. The Seeing Sociology in Everyday Life box gives another example of how differences in social class position can affect interaction.

Finally, just about everyone realizes that the way we dress, the car we drive (or the bus we ride), and even the food and drink we order at the campus snack bar say something about our resources and personal tastes. Sociologists use the term **conspicuous consumption** to refer to *buying and using products because of the "statement" they make about social position*. Ignoring the water fountain in favor of paying for bottled water tells people that you have extra money to spend. And no one needs a $100,000 automobile to get around, of course, but driving up in such a vehicle says "I have arrived" in more ways than one.

Evaluate A micro-level analysis of social stratification helps us see patterns of social inequality in our everyday lives. At the same time, the limitation of this approach is that it has little to say about how and why broad patterns of social inequality exist, which was the focus of the structural-functional and social-conflict approaches.

CHECK YOUR LEARNING Point to several ways in which social stratification shapes the way people of different social positions behave in the course of a typical day.

Stratification and Technology: A Global Perspective

Apply

We can weave together a number of observations made in this chapter by considering the relationship between a society's technology and its type of social stratification. This analysis draws on Gerhard Lenski's model of sociocultural evolution discussed in Chapter 2 ("Culture").

Hunting and Gathering Societies

With simple technology, hunters and gatherers produce only what is necessary for day-to-day living. Some people may produce more than others, but the group's survival depends on all sharing what they have. Thus no categories of people are better off than others.

Horticultural, Pastoral, and Agrarian Societies

As technological advances create a surplus, social inequality increases. In horticultural and pastoral societies, a small elite controls most of the surplus. Large-scale agriculture is more productive still, and striking inequality—as great as at any time in history—places the nobility in an almost godlike position over the masses.

Industrial Societies

Industrialization pushes inequality downward. Prompted by the need to develop people's talents, meritocracy takes hold and weakens the power of traditional elites. Industrial productivity also raises the living standards of the historically poor majority. Specialized work demands schooling for all, sharply reducing illiteracy. A literate population demands a greater voice in political decision making, reducing social inequality and lessening men's domination of women.

Over time, even wealth becomes somewhat less concentrated (contradicting Marx's prediction). In the 1920s, the richest 1 percent of U.S. families owned about 40 percent of all wealth, a figure that fell to 30 percent by the 1980s as taxes—with higher rates for people with higher incomes—paid for new government programs benefiting the poor (Williamson & Lindert, 1980; Beeghley, 1989; U.S. House of Representatives, 1991). Such trends help explain why Marxist revolutions occurred in *agrarian* societies, such as Russia (1917), Cuba (1959), and Nicaragua (1979), where social inequality is most pronounced, rather than in *industrial* societies as Marx predicted. However, wealth inequality turned upward again after 1990 and is once again at about the same level as it was in the 1920s (Keister, 2000; Wolff, 2010). This is one important reason that the Occupy Wall Street movement has gained support in cities all across the United States. In addition, economic inequality has greater importance in the 2012 presidential campaign than it has since the Great Depression (Bivens, 2011; Mishel, 2011).

The Kuznets Curve

In human history, then, technological advances first increase but then moderate the intensity of social stratification. Greater inequality is functional for agrarian societies, but industrial societies benefit from a more equal system. This historical trend, recognized by the Nobel Prize–winning economist Simon Kuznets (1955, 1966), is illustrated by the Kuznets curve, shown in Figure 8–2.

Social inequality around the world generally supports the Kuznets curve. Global Map 8–1 on page 200 shows that high-income nations that have passed through the industrial era (including the United States, Canada, and the nations of Western Europe) have somewhat less income inequality than nations in which a larger share of the labor force remains in farming (as is common in Latin America and Africa). At the same time, it is important to remember that income inequality reflects not just technological development but also the political and economic priorities of a country. Income inequality in the United States has been increasing in recent decades due to political decisions about tax rates as well as other policies. As a result, this country still has more economic inequality than Canada, countries throughout Europe, and Japan.

Another criticism of the Kuznets curve is that it was developed by comparing societies at different levels of economic development (using what sociologists call "cross-sectional data"). Such data do not tell us about the future of any one society. In the United States, the recent trend showing increases in economic inequality suggests that the Kuznets curve may require serious revision—represented

by the broken line in Figure 8–2 corresponding to the postindustrial era. The fact that U.S. society is now experiencing greater economic inequality suggests that the long-term trend may differ from what Kuznets projected half a century ago.

Inequality in the United States

 Understand

Recently, there's been a lot of talk about economic inequality in the United States. The Occupy Wall Street Movement claims that 1 percent of the population is running away with the country while the remaining 99 percent of us are being left behind. The mass media provide almost daily accounts of increasing inequality. In addition, the 2012 presidential campaign has fueled an intense debate over how to help average families find and keep jobs as the economy continues to struggle. This part of the chapter provides all the facts about the state of social inequality in the United States.

Historically, a widespread view has been that there are not class differences in the United States. This country differs from most European nations and Japan in never having had a titled nobility. With the significant exception of our racial history, we have never known a caste system that rigidly ranks categories of people. Even so, U.S. society is highly stratified. Not only do the rich have most of the money, but they also receive the most schooling, enjoy the best health, and consume the most goods and services. Such privilege contrasts sharply with the poverty of millions of women

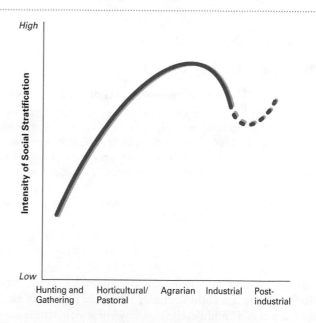

FIGURE 8–2 Social Stratification and Technological Development: The Kuznets Curve

The Kuznets curve shows that greater technological sophistication is generally accompanied by more pronounced social stratification. The trend reverses itself as industrial societies relax rigid, castelike distinctions in favor of greater opportunity and equality under the law. Political rights are more widely extended, and there is even some leveling of economic differences. However, the emergence of postindustrial society has brought an upturn in economic inequality, as indicated by the broken line added by the author.

Sources: Based on Kuznets (1955) and Lenski (1966).

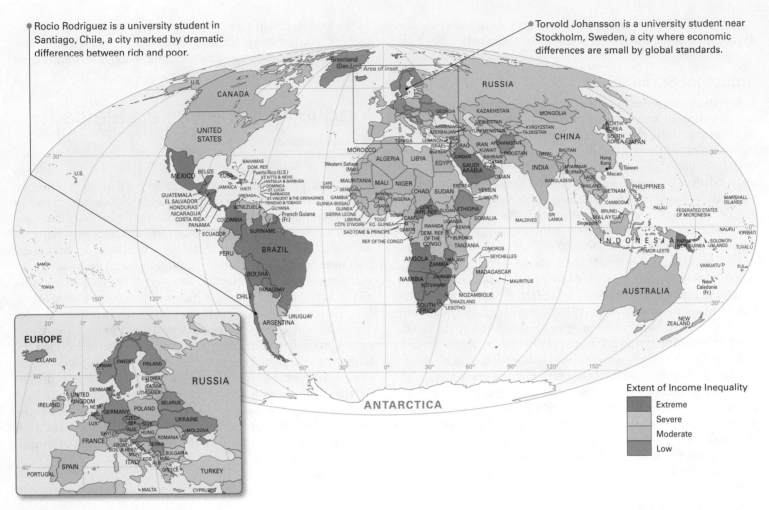

Rocio Rodriguez is a university student in Santiago, Chile, a city marked by dramatic differences between rich and poor.

Torvold Johansson is a university student near Stockholm, Sweden, a city where economic differences are small by global standards.

Extent of Income Inequality

- Extreme
- Severe
- Moderate
- Low

Window on the World

GLOBAL MAP 8–1 Income Inequality in Global Perspective

Societies throughout the world differ in the rigidity and extent of their social stratification and their overall standard of living. This map highlights income inequality. Generally speaking, the United States stands out among high-income nations, such as Great Britain, Sweden, Japan, and Australia, as having greater income inequality. The less economically developed countries of Latin America and Africa, including Colombia, Brazil, and the Central African Republic, as well as Saudi Arabia, exhibit the most pronounced inequality of income. Is this pattern consistent with the Kuznets curve?

Source: Based on Gini coefficients obtained from World Bank (2011).

and men who worry about finding next month's rent or paying a doctor's bill when a child becomes ill. Many people think of the United States as a "middle-class society" in which people are more or less alike. But is this really the case?

Income, Wealth, and Power

One important dimension of economic inequality is **income**, *earnings from work or investments*. The Census Bureau reports that the median U.S. family income in 2010 was $60,395. The pie chart in the middle of Figure 8–3 shows the distribution of income among all U.S. families.[1] The richest 20 percent of families (earning at least $114,000 annually, with a mean of about $187,000) received 47.8 percent of all

income, and the bottom 20 percent (earning less than $27,000, with a mean of about $15,000) received only 3.8 percent.

The table at the left in Figure 8–3 takes a closer look at income distribution. In 2010, the highest-paid 5 percent of U.S. families earned at least $200,000 (averaging more than $313,000), or 20 percent of all income. In terms of share of all income, this top-earning

---

[1] The Census Bureau reports both mean and median incomes for families ("two or more persons related by blood, marriage, or adoption") and households ("two or more persons sharing a living unit"). In 2010, mean family income was $78,361, higher than the median family income ($60,395) because high-income families pull up the mean but not the median. For households, these figures are somewhat lower—a mean of $67,530 and a median of $49,445—because families average 3.18 people and households average 2.58.

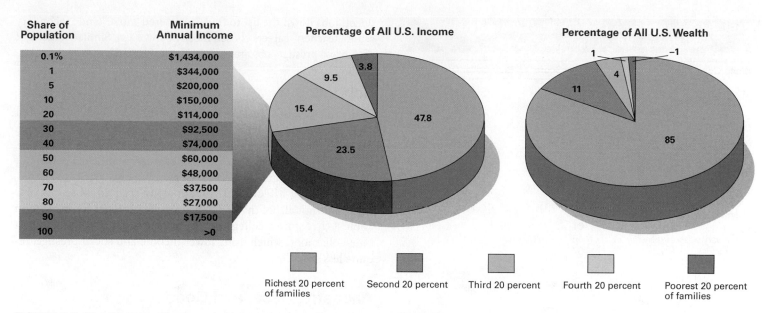

Share of Population	Minimum Annual Income
0.1%	$1,434,000
1	$344,000
5	$200,000
10	$150,000
20	$114,000
30	$92,500
40	$74,000
50	$60,000
60	$48,000
70	$37,500
80	$27,000
90	$17,500
100	>0

Percentage of All U.S. Income

3.8 · 9.5 · 15.4 · 47.8 · 23.5

Percentage of All U.S. Wealth

1 · −1 · 4 · 11 · 85

Richest 20 percent of families · Second 20 percent · Third 20 percent · Fourth 20 percent · Poorest 20 percent of families

FIGURE 8–3 **Distribution of Income and Wealth in the United States, 2010**

Income, and especially wealth, are divided unequally in U.S. society.

Sources: Income data from U.S. Census Bureau (2011); wealth data based on Keister (2000), Bucks et al. (2009), Wolff (2010), and author estimates.

5 percent received more than the lowest-paid 40 percent. The top 1 percent of the families earned at least $344,000. At the very top of the pyramid, the richest 0.1 percent earned at least $1.4 million. In short, while a small number of people earn very high incomes, the majority make do with far less.

Income is only one part of a person's or family's **wealth**, *the total value of money and other assets, minus outstanding debts.* Wealth—including stocks, bonds, and real estate—is distributed even more unequally than income.

The pie chart at the right in Figure 8–3 shows the approximate distribution of wealth in the United States. The richest 20 percent of U.S. families own roughly 85 percent of the country's entire wealth. High up in this privileged category are the top 5 percent of families, the "very rich," who own 62 percent of all private property. Richer still, with wealth into the tens of millions of dollars, are the 1 percent of families that qualify as "super-rich" and possess about 35 percent of the nation's privately held resources (Keister, 2000; Keister & Moller, 2000; Bucks et al., 2009; Wolff, 2010). At the top of the wealth pyramid, the ten richest individuals in our society have a combined net worth of more than $291 billion (Forbes, 2011). This amount equals the total property of 2.4 million average families, enough people to fill the cities of Chicago, Dallas, and Los Angeles.

The wealth of the average U.S. family is about $120,300 (Bucks et al., 2009). Family wealth reflects the total value of homes, cars, investments, insurance policies, retirement pensions, furniture, clothing, and all other personal property, minus a home mortgage

and other debts. The wealth of average people is not only less than that of the rich but also different in kind. Most people's wealth centers on a home and a car—property that generates no income—but the greater wealth of the rich is mostly in the form of stocks and other income-producing investments.

When financial assets are balanced against debts, the lowest-ranking 40 percent of families have virtually no wealth at all. The negative percentage shown in Figure 8–3 for the poorest 20 percent means that these families actually live in debt.

In the United States, wealth is an important source of power. The small proportion of families that controls most of the country's wealth also has the ability to shape the agenda of the entire society. As explained in Chapter 12 ("Economics and Politics"), some sociologists argue that such concentrated wealth weakens democracy because the political system primarily serves the interests of the super-rich.

Occupational Prestige

In addition to generating income, work is also an important source of social prestige. We commonly evaluate each other according to the kind of work we do, giving greater respect to those who do what we consider to be more important work and less to others with more modest jobs.

Sociologists measure the relative social prestige of various occupations (NORC, 2011). Table 8–1 on page 202 shows that people give high prestige to occupations, such as medicine, law, and engineering, that require extensive training and generate high income. By contrast, less prestigious work—as a waitress or janitor, for example—not only pays less but requires less ability and schooling. Occupational prestige rankings are much the same in all high-income nations (Lin & Xie, 1988).

In any society, high-prestige occupations go to privileged categories of people. In Table 8–1, for example, the highest-ranking occupations are dominated by men. We have to go more than a

income earnings from work or investments   **wealth** the total value of money and other assets, minus outstanding debts

TABLE 8–1 The Relative Social Prestige of Selected Occupations in the United States

White-Collar Occupations	Prestige Score	Blue-Collar Occupations
Physician	86	
College/university professor	74	
Lawyer	75	
Dentist	72	
Physicist, astronomer	73	
Architect	73	
Psychologist	69	
Airplane pilot	61	
Electrical engineer	64	
Member of the clergy	69	
Pharmacist	68	
Sociologist	61	
Secondary school teacher	66	
Optometrist	67	
Registered nurse	66	
Dental hygienist	52	
	60	Police officer
Elementary school teacher	66	
Veterinarian	62	
Actor	58	
Accountant	65	
Economist	63	
	51	Electrician
Painter, sculptor	52	
Librarian	54	
	53	Aircraft mechanic
	53	Firefighter
Social worker	52	
Athlete	65	
Computer programmer	61	
Editor, reporter	60	
Radio or TV announcer	55	
	49	
Real estate agent	49	
Bookkeeper	47	
	47	Machinist
Musician, composer	47	
	46	Secretary
	47	Mail carrier
Photographer	45	
Bank teller	43	
	42	Tailor
	40	Farmer
	39	Carpenter
	31	Auto body repairer
	36	Bricklayer, stonemason
	35	Baker
	34	Bulldozer operator
	36	Hairdresser
	30	Truck driver
Cashier	29	
Retail apparel salesperson	30	
	28	Waiter, waitress
	25	Bartender
	36	Child care worker
	23	Household laborer
	22	Door-to-door salesperson
	22	Janitor
	28	Taxi driver
	28	Garbage collector
	27	Bellhop
	9	Shoe shiner

Source: Adapted from *General Social Surveys, 1972–2010: Cumulative Codebook* (Chicago: National Opinion Research Center, 2011), pp. 3211–18.

dozen jobs down the list to find "registered nurse" and "secondary school teacher," careers chosen mostly by women. Similarly, many of the lowest-prestige jobs are commonly performed by people of color.

Schooling

Industrial societies have expanded opportunities for schooling, but some people still receive much more than others. In 2010, although 87 percent of women and men aged twenty-five and older had completed high school, just 29.6 percent of women and 30.3 percent of men were college graduates (U.S. Census Bureau, 2011).

Schooling affects both occupation and income because most (but not all) of the better-paying white-collar jobs shown in Table 8–1 require a college degree or other advanced study. Most blue-collar jobs, which bring lower income and social prestige, require less schooling.

Ancestry, Race, and Gender

A class system rewards individual talent and effort. But nothing affects social standing as much as birth into a particular family, which has a strong bearing on future schooling, occupation, and income. Research suggests that more than one-third of our country's richest individuals—those with hundreds of millions of dollars in wealth—derived their fortunes mostly from inheritance (Miller & Newcomb, 2005; Harford, 2007). Inherited poverty shapes the future of tens of millions of others.

Also closely linked to social position in the United States is race. White people have a higher overall occupational standing than African Americans and also receive more schooling. The median African American family income was $38,500 in 2010, just 56 percent of the $68,961 earned by non-Hispanic white families. This difference in income makes a real difference in people's lives. For example, 74 percent of non-Hispanic white families own their homes compared to 45 percent of black families (U.S. Census Bureau, 2011).

Some of the racial difference in income results from the larger proportion of single-parent families among African Americans. Comparing only families that include a married couple, African American families earned 79 percent as much as non-Hispanic white families.

Over time, this income difference builds into a huge wealth gap (Altonji, Doraszelski, & Segal, 2000). A survey of families by the government's Federal Reserve found that median wealth for minority families, including African Americans, Hispanics, and Asian Americans ($27,800), is just 16 percent of the median ($170,400) for non-Hispanic white families (Bucks et al., 2009).

Social ranking involves ethnicity as well. People of English ancestry have enjoyed the most wealth and wielded the greatest power in U.S. society. The Latino population—the largest U.S. racial or ethnic minority—has long been disadvantaged. In 2010, the median income among Hispanic families was $39,538, which is 57 percent of the median income for non-Hispanic white families. A detailed examination of how race and ethnicity affect social standing is presented in Chapter 11 ("Race and Ethnicity").

Of course, both men and women are found in families at every social level. Yet on average, women have less income, wealth, and occupational prestige than men. Among single-parent families, those headed by a woman are twice as likely to be poor as those headed by a man. Chapter 10 ("Gender Stratification") examines the link between gender and social stratification.

Social Classes in the United States

 Analyze

As noted earlier, rankings in a caste system are rigid and obvious to all. Defining social categories in a more fluid class system such as ours, however, is not so easy. Followers of Karl Marx see two major social classes: capitalists and proletarians. Other sociologists find as many as six classes (Warner & Lunt, 1941) or even seven (Coleman & Rainwater, 1978). Still others side with Max Weber, believing that people form not clear-cut classes but a multidimensional status hierarchy.

Defining classes in the United States is difficult because of the relatively low level of status consistency. Especially toward the middle of the hierarchy, people's social position on one dimension may not be the same as their standing on another. For example, a government official may have the power to administer a multimillion-dollar budget yet earn only a modest personal income. Similarly, many members of the clergy enjoy ample prestige but only moderate power and low pay. Or consider the casino poker player who wins little respect but makes a lot of money.

Finally, the social mobility characteristic of class systems—again, most pronounced around the middle—means that social position may change during a person's lifetime, further blurring class boundaries. With these issues in mind, we will examine four general rankings: the upper class, the middle class, the working class, and the lower class.

The Upper Class

Families in the upper class—the top 5 percent of the U.S. population—earn at least $200,000 a year, and some earn ten times that much or more. In 2011, *Forbes* magazine profiled the richest 400 people in the United States, who were

These women have appeared on the television program *Real Housewives of Atlanta*. Using the categories discussed in the pages that follow, within which social class category do you think they fall? Why?

worth at least $1.05 billion (and as much as $59 billion) (*Forbes*, 2011). These people form the core of the upper class, or Karl Marx's "capitalists"—the owners of the means of production and thus of most of the nation's private wealth. Many of these people spend much of their time managing their own wealth. Many upper-class people with smaller fortunes are business owners, top executives in large corporations, or senior government officials. Historically, the upper class has been composed of white Anglo-Saxon Protestants, but this is less true today (Pyle & Koch, 2001).

As a general rule, the more a family's income exceeds $200,000 a year, the stronger their claim is to being upper class. But more than the *size* of income is involved. Also important is the *source* of income. The larger the share of income that comes from inherited wealth in the form of stocks and bonds, real estate, and other investments, the stronger a family's claim to being upper-class. The distinction between earning money and inheriting money brings us to the difference between "upper-uppers" and "lower-uppers."

Upper-Uppers

The *upper-upper class,* sometimes called "blue bloods" or simply "society," includes less than 1 percent of the U.S. population (Baltzell, 1995). Membership is almost always the result of birth, as suggested by the old remark that the easiest way to become an upper-upper is to be born one. Most of these families possess enormous wealth that is primarily inherited. For this reason, members of the upper-upper class are said to have "old money."

Set apart by their wealth, upper-uppers live in exclusive neighborhoods such as Beacon Hill in Boston, the Rittenhouse Square section of Philadelphia, the Gold Coast of Chicago, and Nob Hill in San Francisco. Their children typically attend private schools with others of similar background and complete their formal education at high-prestige colleges and universities. In the historical pattern of European aristocrats, they study liberal arts rather than vocational skills.

Women of the upper-upper class often do volunteer work for charitable organizations. Such activities serve a dual purpose: They help the larger community, and they build networks that broaden this elite's power (Ostrander, 1980, 1984).

Lower-Uppers

Most upper-class people actually fall into the *lower-upper class.* And lower-uppers include some of the richest people in the world. The queen of England is in the upper-upper class based not only on her fortune of $650 million but on her family tree. J. K. Rowling, author of the Harry Potter books, is worth almost twice as much—more

People often distinguish between the "new rich" and families with "old money." Men and women who suddenly begin to earn high incomes tend to spend their money on status symbols because they enjoy the new thrill of high-roller living and they want others to know of their success. Those who grow up surrounded by wealth, by contrast, are used to a privileged way of life and are more quiet about it. Thus the conspicuous consumption of the lower-upper class (*left*) can differ dramatically from the more private pursuits and understatement of the upper-upper class (*right*).

than $1 billion—but this self-made woman (who was once on welfare) stands at the top of the lower-upper class. The major difference, in other words, is that members of the lower-upper class are the "working rich" who get their money mostly by earning it rather than inheritance. These "new rich" families—who make up 3 to 4 percent of the U.S. population—generally live in large homes in expensive neighborhoods, own vacation homes near the water or in the mountains, and send their children to private schools and good colleges. Yet most do not gain entry into the clubs and associations of "old money" families.

The Middle Class

Made up of 40 to 45 percent of the U.S. population, the large middle class has a tremendous influence on our culture. Television and movies usually show middle-class people, and most commercial advertising is directed at these average consumers. The middle class contains far more racial and ethnic diversity than the upper class.

Upper-Middles

People near the top of this category are called the *upper-middle class,* based on their above-average income in the range of $114,000 to $200,000 a year. Such income allows upper-middle-class families to live in a comfortable house in a fairly expensive area, own several nice automobiles, and build investments. Two-thirds of upper-middle-class children graduate from college, and about one-third have postgraduate degrees. Many go on to high-prestige occupations as physicians, engineers, lawyers, accountants, and business executives. Lacking the power of the richest people to influence national or international events, upper-middles often play an important role in local political affairs.

Average-Middles

The rest of the middle class falls close to the center of the U.S. class structure. *Average-middles* typically work at less prestigious white-collar jobs as bank branch managers or high school teachers or in highly skilled blue-collar jobs such as electrical work and carpentry. Family income falls between $48,000 and $114,000 a year, which is roughly the national average.[2]

Middle-class people generally build up a small amount of wealth over the course of their working lives, mostly in the form of a house and a retirement account. Most average-middle-class men and women are likely to be high school graduates, but the odds are just fifty-fifty that they will complete a four-year college degree, usually at a less expensive, state-supported school.

The Working Class

About one-third of the population falls within the working class (sometimes called the *lower-middle class*). In Marxist terms, the working class forms the core of the industrial proletariat. The blue-collar jobs held by members of the working class yield a family income of between $27,000 and $48,000 a year, somewhat below the national average. Working-class families have little or no wealth and are vulnerable to financial problems caused by unemployment or illness.

Many working-class jobs provide little personal satisfaction—requiring discipline but rarely imagination—and subject workers to continual supervision. These jobs also offer fewer benefits, such as medical insurance and pension plans. The data show that 56 percent of working-class families own their own homes, which are

---

[2]In some parts of the United States where the cost of living is very high (say, San Francisco), a family might need as much as $150,000 in annual income to reach the middle class.

Nickel and Dimed: On (Not) Getting By in America

All of us know people who work at low-wage jobs as waitresses at diners, clerks at drive-throughs, or sales associates at discount stores such as Walmart. We see such people just about every day. Many of us actually *are* such people. In the United States, "common sense" tells us that the jobs people have and the amount of money they make reflect their personal abilities as well as their willingness to work hard.

Barbara Ehrenreich (2001) had her doubts. To find out what the world of low-wage work is really like, the successful journalist and author decided to leave her comfortable upper-middle-class life to live and work in the world of low-wage jobs. She began in Key West, Florida, taking a job as a waitress for $2.43 an hour plus tips. Right away, she found out she had to work much harder than she ever imagined. By the end of a shift, she was exhausted, but after sharing tips with the kitchen staff, she averaged less than $6.00 an hour. This was barely above the national minimum wage at the time and provided just enough income to pay the rent on her tiny apartment, buy food, and cover other basic expenses. She had to hope that she didn't get sick, because the job did not provide health insurance and she couldn't afford to pay for a visit to a doctor's office.

After working for more than a year at a number of other low-wage jobs, including cleaning motels in Maine and working on the floor of a Walmart in Minnesota, she had rejected quite a bit of "common sense." First, she now knew that tens of millions of people with low-wage jobs work very hard every day. If you don't think so, Ehrenreich says, take on one of these jobs for yourself. Second, these jobs require not only hard work (imagine thoroughly cleaning three motel rooms every hour all day long) but also special skills and real intelligence (try waiting on ten tables in a restaurant at the same time and keeping everybody happy). She found that the people she worked with were, on average, just as smart, clever, and funny as others she knew who wrote books for a living or taught at a college.

Why, then, do we think of low-wage workers as lazy or as having less ability? It surprised Ehrenreich to learn that many low-wage workers felt this way about themselves. In a society that teaches us to believe that personal ability is everything, we learn to size people up by their job. Ehrenreich discovered that many low-wage workers, subject to constant supervision, random drug tests, and other rigid rules that usually come with such jobs, end up feeling unworthy, even to the point of not trying for anything better. Such beliefs, she concludes, help support a society of extreme inequality in which some people live very well because of the low wages paid to the rest.

What Do You Think?

1. Have you ever held a low-wage job? If so, would you say you worked hard? What was your pay? Were there any benefits?

2. Ehrenreich claims that most well-off people in the United States are dependent on low-wage workers. What does she mean by this?

3. How much of a chance do most people with jobs at Wendy's or Walmart have to enroll in college and to work toward a different career? Explain.

---

typically in lower-cost neighborhoods. College becomes a reality for only about one-third of working-class children.

The Lower Class

The remaining 20 percent of our population make up the lower class. Low income makes their lives insecure and difficult. In 2010, the federal government classified 46.2 million people (15.1 percent of the population) as poor. Millions more—called the "working poor"—are slightly better off, holding low-prestige jobs that provide little satisfaction and minimal income. Barely half manage to complete high school, and only one in four ever reaches college. In the Seeing Sociology in Everyday Life box, one sociologist describes the experience of trying to survive day-to-day doing low-wage work.

Society segregates the lower class, especially when the poor are racial or ethnic minorities. About 44 percent of lower-class families own their own homes, typically in the least desirable neighborhoods. Although poor neighborhoods are often found in inner cities, lower-class families also live in rural communities, especially across the South.

The Difference Class Makes

🔴 **Apply**

Social stratification affects nearly every dimension of our lives. In the following sections, we will briefly examine some of the ways social standing is linked to our health, values, politics, and family life.

Health

Health is closely related to social standing. Children born into poor families are twice as likely to die from disease, neglect, accidents, or violence during their first year of life than children born into privileged families. Among adults, people with above-average incomes are almost twice as likely as low-income people to describe their health as excellent. In addition, on average, richer people live five years longer because they eat more nutritious food, live in safer and less stressful environments, and receive better medical care (Congressional Budget Office, 2008; U.S. Department of Health and Human Services, 2011).

Compared to high-income people, low-income people are half as likely to report good health and, on average, live about five fewer years. The toll of low income—played out in inadequate nutrition, little medical care, and high stress—is easy to see on the faces of the poor, who look old before their time.

Values and Attitudes

Some values and attitudes vary from class to class. The "old rich" have an unusually strong sense of family history because their position is based on wealth passed down from generation to generation. Secure in their birthright privileges, upper-uppers also favor understated manners and tastes; many "new rich" engage in conspicuous consumption, using homes, cars, and even airplanes as status symbols to make a statement about their social position.

Affluent people with greater education and financial security are also more tolerant of controversial behavior such as homosexuality. Working-class people, who grow up in an atmosphere of greater supervision and discipline and are less likely to attend college, tend to be less tolerant (Lareau, 2002; NORC, 2007).

Social class has a great deal to do with an individual's self-concept. People with higher social standing experience more confidence in everyday interaction for the simple reason that others tend to view them as having greater importance. The Thinking About Diversity box describes the challenges faced by one young woman from a poor family attending a college where most students are from elite families.

Politics

Do political attitudes follow class lines? The answer is yes, but the pattern is complex. A desire to protect their wealth prompts well-off people to take a more conservative approach to *economic* issues, favoring, for example, lower taxes. But on *social* matters such as abortion and gay rights, highly educated, more affluent people are more liberal. People of lower social standing, by contrast, tend to be economic liberals, favoring government social programs that benefit them, but typically hold more conservative views on social issues (NORC, 2009).

A clearer pattern emerges when it comes to political involvement. Higher-income people, who are better served by the system, are more likely to vote and to join political organizations than people with low incomes. In the 2008 presidential election, more than 80 percent of adults with family incomes of at least $100,000 voted, compared to 57 percent of adults with family incomes of less than $40,000 (U.S. Census Bureau, 2009).

Family and Gender

Social class also shapes family life. Generally, lower-class families are somewhat larger than middle-class families because of earlier marriage and less use of birth control. Another family pattern is that working-class parents encourage children to conform to conventional norms and respect authority figures. Parents of higher social standing pass on a different "cultural capital" to their children, teaching them to express their individuality and imagination more freely (Kohn, 1977; McLeod, 1995; Lareau, 2002).

The more money a family has, the more opportunities parents have to develop their children's talents and abilities. An affluent family earning more than $99,730 a year will spend $477,100 raising a child born in 2010 to the age of eighteen. Middle-class people, with an average annual income of about $75,000, will spend $286,860, and a lower-income family, earning less than $57,600, will spend $206,180 (Lino, 2011). Privilege leads to privilege as family life reproduces the class structure in each generation.

Class also shapes our world of relationships. In a classic study of married life, Elizabeth Bott (1971, orig. 1957) found that most working-class couples divide their responsibilities according to traditional gender roles; middle-class couples, by contrast, are more egalitarian, sharing more activities and expressing greater intimacy. More recently, Karen Walker (1995) discovered that working-class friendships typically serve as sources of material assistance; middle-class friendships are likely to involve shared interests and leisure pursuits.

Social Mobility

 Evaluate

Ours is a dynamic society marked by quite a bit of social movement. Earning a college degree, landing a higher-paying job, or marrying someone who earns a good income contributes to *upward social mobility;* dropping out of school, losing a job, or becoming divorced (especially for women) may result in *downward social mobility.*

Marcella grew up without the privileges that most other students on the campus of this private, liberal arts college take for granted. During her senior year, she and I talked at length about her college experiences and why social class presented a huge challenge to her. Marcella is not her real name; she wishes to remain anonymous. I have summarized what she has said about her college life in the story that follows.

When I came here, I entered a new world. I found myself in a strange and dangerous place. All around me were people with habits and ideas I did not understand. A thousand times I thought to myself, I hope all of you will realize that there are other worlds out there and that I am from one of them. Will you accept me?

I am a child of poverty, a young woman raised in a world of want and violence. I am now on the campus of an elite college. I may have a new identity as a college student. But my old life is still going on in my head. I have not been able to change how I think of myself.

Do you want to find out more about me? Learn more about the power of social class to shape how we feel about ourselves? Here is what I want to say to you.

When I was growing up, I envied most of you. You lived in a middle-class bubble, a world that held you, protected you, and comforted you. Not me. While your parents were discussing current events, planning family trips, and looking out for you, my father and mother were screaming at each other. I will never be able to forget summer nights when I lay in my bed, sticky with sweat, biting my fingernails as a telephone crashed against the wall that separated my room from theirs. My father was drunk and out of control; my mother ducked just in time.

Your fathers and mothers work in office buildings. They have good jobs, as doctors, lawyers, and architects; they are corporate managers; they run small businesses. Your mothers and fathers are people who matter. My mom takes the bus to a hospital where she works for $10 an hour cleaning up after people. She spends her shift doing what she is told. My dad? Who knows. He was a deadbeat, a drunk, a drug addict. I don't know if he still is or not. I haven't heard from him in eight years.

You grew up in a neighborhood and probably lived for many years in one house. My family lived in low-cost rental housing. We moved a lot. When there was no money for rent, we packed up our stuff and moved to a new place. It seemed like we were always running away from something.

You grew up with books, with trips to the library, with parents who read to you. You learned how to speak well and have an impressive vocabulary. I never heard a bedtime story, and I had maybe one inspiring teacher. Most of what I know I had to learn on my own. Maybe that's why I always feel like I am trying to catch up to you.

You know how to use forks, knives, and spoons the right way. You know how to eat Chinese food and what to order at a Thai restaurant. You have favorite Italian dishes. You know how to order wine. You know about German beers, Danish cheeses, and French sauces. Me? I grew

up having Thanksgiving dinner on paper plates, eating turkey served by social service volunteers. When you ask me to go with you to some special restaurant, I make some excuse and stay home. I can't afford it. More than that, I am afraid you will find out how little I know about things you take for granted.

How did I ever get to this college? I remember one of my teachers telling me that I "have promise." The college admission office accepted me. But I am not sure why. I was given a scholarship that covers most of my tuition. That solved one big problem, and now I am here. But sometimes I am not sure I will stay. I have to study more than many of you to learn things you already know. I have to work two part-time jobs to make the money I needed to buy a used computer, clothes, and the occasional pizza at the corner place where many of you spend so much time.

It's amazing to me that I am here. I realize how lucky I am. But now that I am here, I realize that the road is so much longer than I thought it would be. Getting to this college was only part of the journey. The scholarship was only part of the answer. The biggest challenge for me is what goes on every day—the thousands of ways in which you live a life that I still don't really understand, the thousands of things that I won't know or that I will do wrong that will blow my cover, and show me up for the fraud I am.

What Do You Think?

1. How does this story show that social class involves much more than how much money a person has?

2. Why does Marcella worry that other people will think she is a "fraud"? If you could speak to her about this fear, what would you say?

3. Have you ever had similar feelings about being less important than—or better than—someone else based on social class position? Explain.

Over the long term, though, social mobility is not so much a matter of individual changes as changes in society itself. In the first half of the twentieth century, for example, industrialization expanded the U.S. economy, pushing up living standards. Even people who were not good swimmers rode the rising tide of prosperity. More recently, the "outsourcing" of jobs and the closing of U.S. factories and other business operations have brought downward structural mobility, dealing economic setbacks to many people. The

How likely is it to move up in U.S. society? What about the odds of moving down? What share of people, as adults, end up staying right where they started as children? To answer these questions, Lisa A. Keister used data from the National Longitudinal Survey of Youth (NLSY), a long-term study of 9,500 men and women. These people were first studied in 1979 during their youth—when they were between fourteen and twenty-two years old and living at home with one or both parents. The same people were studied again as adults in 2000, when they ranged in age from thirty-five to forty-three years old. About 80 percent of the subjects were married and all had households of their own.

What Keister wanted to know was how the economic standing of the subjects may have changed over their lifetimes, which she measured by estimating (from NLSY data) their amount of wealth at two different times. In 1979, because the subjects were young and living at home, she measured the family wealth of the subjects' parents. Keister placed each subject's family in one of five wealth quintiles—from the richest 20 percent down to the poorest 20 percent—and these quintiles are shown in the vertical axis of the accompanying table. In 2000, she measured the wealth of the same people, who were now living in households of their own. Wealth rankings in 2000 are shown in the horizontal axis of the table.

So what did Keister learn? How much social mobility, in terms of household wealth, took place over the course of twenty-one years? Looking at the table, we can learn a great deal. The cell in the upper left corner shows us that, of the

richest 20 percent of subjects in 1979, 55 percent of these young people went on to remain in the top wealth category in 2000. Obviously, because these people were starting out in the top category, there could be no upward movement (although some of the subjects were richer as adults than they were when they were young). Twenty-five percent of the richest subjects in 1979 had dropped one level to the second quintile. That means that 80 percent of the richest people in 1979 were still quite well off in 2000; only 20 percent of the richest people were downwardly mobile across two or more categories (9 percent who fell two levels, 6 percent who fell three levels, and 5 percent who fell to the lowest wealth level).

A similar pattern is seen as we begin with the poorest subjects—those who were in the lowest wealth quintile in 1979. Obviously, again, because these people started out in the lowest category, they had nowhere to go but up. But 45 percent of these men and women remained in the lowest wealth category as adults (the bottom-right box), and 27 percent moved up one quintile. Another 28 percent of the poorest people moved up two or more quintiles as adults (11 percent who rose two levels, 9 percent who rose three levels, and 8 percent who rose to the richest level).

For subjects in the middle ranges, the data show that mobility was somewhat more

pronounced. For those who started in the second richest quintile, just 33 percent ended up in the same place. The remaining 67 percent moved up or down at least one level, although the most common move was rising or falling one level. Of those in the third (or middle) quintile, 35 percent ended up in the same rank as adults, and 65 percent moved up or down at least one level. Again, most of those who moved shifted just one level. Similarly, of those who started out in the fourth quintile, 35 percent ended up in the same ranking as adults, and 65 percent moved in most cases one level up or down.

So what can we conclude about patterns of wealth mobility over a generation between 1979 and 2000? The first conclusion is that a majority of people did experience mobility, moving up or down one or more levels. So mobility was the rule rather than the exception. Second, movement downward was about as common as movement upward. Third, movement was somewhat more common among people closer to the middle of the wealth hierarchy—the largest share of people who "stayed put" (55 percent among those who started out at the top and 45 percent of those who started out at the bottom) were at one or the other extreme.

Join the Blog!

What about the results presented here surprises you? Overall, how well do the data square with what you imagine most people in this country think about mobility? Go to MySocLab and join the Sociology in Focus blog to share your opinions and experiences and to see what others think.

Childhood Standing, 1979	Adult Standing, 2000				
	Richest 20%	Second 20%	Third 20%	Fourth 20%	Poorest 20%
Richest 20% →	55	25	9	6	5
Second 20% →	25	33	23	11	8
Third 20% →	13	21	35	20	11
Fourth 20% →	7	14	20	35	24
Poorest 20% →	8	9	11	27	45

economic downturn that hit hard at the end of 2007 and continues several years later reduced the income and economic opportunities of millions of people.

Sociologists distinguish between shorter- and longer-term changes in social position. **Intragenerational social mobility** is *a change in social position occurring during a person's lifetime* (*intra* is Latin for "within"). **Intergenerational social mobility**, *upward or downward social mobility of children in relation to their parents,* is important because it reveals long-term changes in society that affect everyone (*inter* is Latin for "between").

Research on Mobility

In few societies do people think about "getting ahead" as much as in the United States. Moving up, after all, is the American dream. But is there as much social mobility in our country as we like to think?

One recent study of intergenerational mobility shows that about 32 percent of U.S. men had the same type of work as their fathers, 37 percent were upwardly mobile (for example, a son born to a father with a blue-collar job ends up doing white-collar work), and 32 percent were downwardly mobile (for example, the father has a white-collar job and the son does blue-collar work). Among women, 46 percent were upwardly mobile, 28 percent were downwardly mobile, and 27 percent showed no change compared to their fathers (Beller & Hout, 2006). The Sociology in Focus box provides the results of another study of long-term social mobility.

Horizontal social mobility—changing jobs at the same class level—is even more common. Overall, about 80 percent of children show some type of social mobility in relation to their parents (Hout, 1998; Beller & Hout, 2006).

Research points to four general conclusions about social mobility in the United States:

1. **Social mobility over the past century has been fairly high.** A high level of mobility is what we would expect in an industrial class system.

2. **Within a single generation, social mobility is usually small.** Most young families increase their income over time as they gain education and skills. A typical family headed by a thirty-year-old earned about $55,000 in 2010; a typical family headed by a fifty-year-old earned $75,000 (U.S. Census Bureau, 2011). Yet only a few people move "from rags to riches" (the way J. K. Rowling did) or lose a lot of money (a number of rock stars who made it big had little money left a few years later). Most social mobility involves small movement within one class level rather than large movement between classes.

3. **The long-term trend in social mobility has been upward.** Industrialization, which greatly expanded the U.S. economy, and the growth of white-collar work over the course of the twentieth century have raised living standards. In recent decades, however, mobility has been downward about as often as it has been upward (Keister, 2005).

4. **Since the 1970s, social mobility has been uneven.** Real income (adjusted for inflation) rose during the twentieth century until the 1970s. Since then, as shown in Figure 8–4, real income has risen and fallen, with overall smaller gains than was the case before 1970. Most recently, the economic recession that began in 2007 resulted in several years of declining incomes for most people.

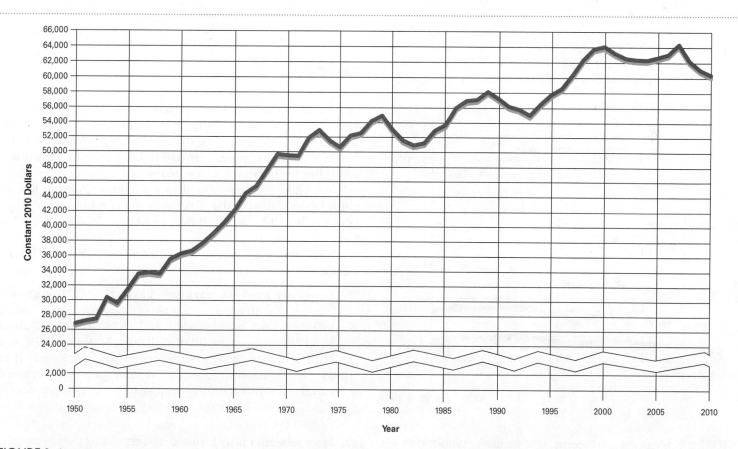

FIGURE 8–4

Median Annual Income, U.S. Families, 1950–2010

Average family income in the United States grew rapidly between 1950 and 1970. Since then, however, the increase has been smaller.

Source: U.S. Census Bureau (2011).

Mobility by Income Level

The experience of social mobility depends on where in the social class system you happen to be. Figure 8–5 shows how U.S. families at different income levels made out between 1980 and 2010. Well-to-do families (the highest 20 percent, but not all the same families over the entire period) saw their incomes jump 51 percent, from an average of $124,069 in 1980 to $187,395 in 2010. People in the middle of the population also had gains, but more modest ones. The lowest-income 20 percent actually lost ground, making an average of $1,160 less in 2010 than in 1980 (adjusted for inflation).

For families at the top of the income scale (the highest 5 percent), recent decades have brought a windfall. These families, with average income of about $176,000 in 1980, were making $313,298 in 2010—seventy-seven percent more than they had made in 1980 (U.S. Census Bureau, 2011).

Mobility: Race, Ethnicity, and Gender

White people in the United States have always been in a more privileged position than people of African or Hispanic descent. Through the economic expansion of the 1980s and 1990s, many more African Americans entered the ranks of the wealthy. But overall, the real income of African Americans has changed little in three decades. African American family income as a percentage of white family income has fallen slightly to 56 percent in 2010 from 61 percent in 1975. Compared with white families, Latino families lost ground between 1975 (when their average income was 66 percent of that of white families) and 2010 (when it slipped to 57 percent) (Pomer, 1986; U.S. Census Bureau, 2011).

Feminists point out that historically, women have had less chance for upward mobility than men because most working women held clerical jobs (such as secretary) and service positions (such as food server) that offer few opportunities for advancement.

Over time, however, the earnings gap between women and men has been narrowing. Women working full time in 1980 earned 60 percent as much as men working full time; by 2010, women were earning 77 percent as much (U.S. Census Bureau, 2011).

Mobility and Marriage

Research points to the conclusion that marriage has an important effect on social standing. In a study of women and men in their forties, Jay Zagorsky (2006) found that people who marry and stay married accumulate about twice as much wealth as people who remain single or who divorce. Reasons for this difference include the fact that couples who live together typically enjoy double incomes and also pay only half the bills the two partners would have if they were single and living in separate households.

It is also likely that compared to single people, married men and women work harder in their jobs and save more money. Why? Primarily because they are working not just for themselves but to support children and spouses who are counting on them (Popenoe, 2006).

Just as marriage pushes social standing upward, divorce usually makes social position go down. Couples who divorce take on the financial burden of supporting two households, which leaves them with less money for savings or other investment. After divorce, women are hurt more than men because typically the man earns more. Many women who divorce lose not only most of their income but also benefits such as health care and insurance coverage (Weitzman, 1996).

The American Dream: Still a Reality?

The expectation of upward social mobility is deeply rooted in U.S. culture. Through much of our history, the economy has grown steadily, raising living standards. Today, at least for some people, the American dream is alive and well. In 2010, one in four U.S. families earned $100,000 or more (in dollars controlled for inflation), compared with just one in fifteen back in 1967. There are now more than 8 million millionaire households in the United States, five times the number a decade ago (Rank & Hirschl, 2001; L. Eisenberg, 2007; Wolff, 2010; U.S. Census Bureau, 2011).

Yet not all indicators are so positive. Note these disturbing trends:

1. **For many workers, earnings have stalled.** The annual income of a fifty-year-old man working full time climbed by 65 percent between 1958 and 1974 (from $29,716 to $48,979 in constant 2010 dollars). Between 1974 and 2010, however, this worker's income *fell* by 7.3 percent to $45,420, even as the number of hours worked increased and the cost of necessities such as housing, education, gasoline, and medical care went way up (Russell, 1995a; U.S. Census Bureau, 2011).

2. **More jobs offer little income.** The expanding global economy has moved many industrial jobs overseas, reducing the availability of high-paying factory jobs here in the United States. At the same time, the expansion of our service economy means more of today's jobs—in fast-food restaurants or large discount

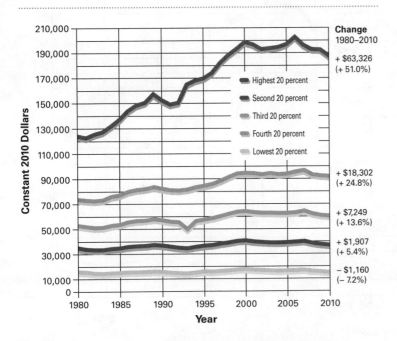

FIGURE 8–5 Mean Annual Income, U.S. Families, 1980–2010
(in 2010 dollars, adjusted for inflation)

The gap between high-income and low-income families is wider today than it was in 1980.

Source: U.S. Census Bureau (2011).

I grew up in Elkins Park, Pennsylvania, an older Philadelphia suburb that is a mostly middle-class community, although like most of suburbia, some neighborhoods boast bigger houses than others. What made Elkins Park special was that a century ago, a handful of great mansions were built by early Philadelphia industrialists. Back then, all there was to the town was these great "estates," separated by fields and meadows. By about 1940, however, most of this land was split off into lots for the homes of newer middle-class suburbanites. The great mansions suddenly seemed out of place, with heirs disagreeing over who should live there and how to pay the rising property taxes. As a result, many of the great mansions were sold, the buildings taken down, and the land subdivided.

In the 1960s, when I was a teenager, a short bike ride could take me past the Breyer estate (built by the founder of the ice-cream company, now the township police building), the Curtis estate (built by a magazine publisher and transformed into a community park), and the Wanamaker estate (built by the founder of a large Philadelphia department store, now the site of high-rise apartments). Probably the grandest of them all was the Wiedner estate, modeled after a French chateau, complete with doorknobs and window pulls covered in gold; it now stands empty.

In their day, these magnificent structures were not just home to a family and many servants; they were also monuments in steel and stone to a time when the rich were, well, *really* rich. By contrast, the community that emerged on the grounds once owned by these wealthy families is middle class, with modest homes built on much smaller lots.

But did the so-called Gilded Age of great wealth disappear forever? No. By the 1980s, a new wave of great mansions was being built in the United States. Take the architect Thierry Despont, who designs huge houses for the super-rich. One of Despont's "smaller" homes might be 20,000 square feet (about ten times the size of the average U.S. house), and they go all the way up to 60,000 square feet (as big as any of the Elkins Park mansions built a century ago and almost the size of the White House). These megahomes have kitchens as large as college classrooms, exercise rooms, indoor swimming pools, and even indoor tennis courts (Krugman, 2002).

Megahouses are being built by newly rich chief executive officers (CEOs) of large corporations. Although CEOs have always made more money than most people, recent years have seen executive compensation soar. Between 1970 and 2010, the average U.S. family saw only a modest increase in income (about 22 percent after inflation is taken into account). During the same period, the average compensation for the 100 highest-paid CEOs skyrocketed from $1.3 million to $26 million. From another angle, the typical CEO is now making about the same annual income as the entire 454-person staff of the White House, which includes the nation's president. Richer still, the twenty highest-earning investment fund managers in 2010 had, on average, $882 million *each* in income, earning more in 38 minutes than an average worker made all year and more than 2,000 times as much as the country's president (Corporate Library, 2011; Creswell, 2011; O'Toole, 2011; U.S. Census Bureau, 2011).

What Do You Think?

1. Do you consider increasing economic inequality a problem? Why or why not?

2. How many times more than an average worker should a CEO earn? Explain your answer.

3. Does very high CEO pay help or hurt stockholders? What about the general public? Explain your reasoning.

---

stores—offer relatively low wages. Of all the people who lost their jobs during the recession that began in 2007 and were lucky enough to find another job, half took pay cuts (Foroohar, 2011).

3. **Young people are remaining at home.** In 2011, 55 percent of young people aged eighteen to twenty-four were still living with their parents, in most cases because they are unable to support a household of their own. Since 1975, the average age at first marriage has moved upward five years (to 26.5 years for women and 28.7 years for men).

Over the past generation, more people have become rich, and the rich have become richer. At the very top of the pile, as the Seeing Sociology in Everyday Life box explains, the highest-paid corporate executives have enjoyed a runaway rise in their earnings. Yet the increasing share of low-paying jobs has brought downward mobility for millions of families, feeding the fear that the chance to enjoy a middle-class lifestyle is slipping away. As a glance back at Figure 8–4 on page 209 shows, although median family income doubled between 1950 and 1973, it has grown by only 14 percent over two generations since then (U.S. Census Bureau, 2011).

The Global Economy and the U.S. Class Structure

Underlying the shifts in U.S. class structure over recent decades is global economic change. Much of the industrial production that gave U.S. workers high-paying jobs a generation ago has moved overseas, where wages are cheaper. With less industry at home, the United States now serves as a vast consumer market for industrial goods such as cars, stereos, cameras, and computers made in China, India, Japan, South Korea, Brazil, and elsewhere.

High-paying jobs in manufacturing, held by 28 percent of the U.S. labor force in 1960, support just 9 percent of workers today. In their place, the economy offers service work, which pays far less. Traditionally high-paying corporations such as USX (formerly United States Steel) now employ fewer people than the expanding McDonald's chain, and fast-food clerks make only a fraction of what steelworkers earn.

The global reorganization of work has not been bad news for everyone. The global economy is driving upward social mobility for educated people who specialize in law, finance, marketing, and computer technology. Even allowing for the downturn that began at the end of 2007, the global economic expansion also helped push up the stock market more than tenfold between 1980 and 2011, reaping profits for families with money to invest.

But the same trend has hurt many average workers, who have lost their factory jobs and now perform low-wage service work. In addition, many companies (General Motors and Ford are recent examples) have downsized—cutting the ranks of their workforce—in an attempt to stay competitive in world markets. As a result, although 53 percent of all married-couple families today contain two or more people in the labor force—more than twice the share in 1950—many families are working harder than ever before simply to hold on to what they have (A. L. Nelson, 1998; Sennett, 1998; U.S. Census Bureau, 2011; Wall Street Journal, 2011).

Poverty in the United States

 Analyze

Social stratification creates both "haves" and "have-nots." All systems of social inequality create poverty, or at least **relative poverty**, *the lack of resources of some people in relation to those who have more*. A more serious but preventable problem is **absolute poverty**, *a lack of resources that is life-threatening*.

As Chapter 9 ("Global Stratification") explains, about 1.4 billion human beings around the world—one person in five—are at risk of absolute poverty. Even in the affluent United States, families go hungry, sleep in parked cars or on the streets, and suffer from poor health simply because they are poor.

The Extent of Poverty

In 2010, the government classified 46.2 million men, women, and children as poor, the largest number since the tracking began more than fifty years ago. The poor now represent 15.1 percent of the U.S. population. To be counted among the poor, families or individuals must report income below an official poverty line, which, for a family of four, was set that year at $22,314. The poverty line is about three times what the government estimates people will spend for food. But the income of the average poor family was just 59 percent of this amount. This means that the typical poor family had to get by on $13,000 in 2010 (U.S. Census Bureau, 2011).

absolute poverty a lack of resources that is life-threatening

relative poverty the lack of resources of some people in relation to those who have more

Who Are the Poor?

Although no single description fits all poor people, poverty is greater among certain categories of our population. Where these categories overlap, the problem is especially serious.

Age

A generation ago, the elderly were the category of the population at greatest risk for poverty. But thanks to better retirement programs offered today by private employers and the government, the poverty rate for people over age sixty-five fell from 30 percent in 1967 to 9 percent—well below the national average—in 2010. Looking at it from another angle, about 7.6 percent (3.5 million) of the poor are elderly (U.S. Census Bureau, 2011).

Today the burden of poverty falls most heavily on children and young adults. In 2010, some 22 percent of people under age eighteen (16.4 million children) and 21.9 percent of people ages eighteen to twenty-four (6.5 million young adults) were poor. Put another way, one-half of the U.S. poor are young people under the age of twenty-five.

Race and Ethnicity

Seventy-one percent of all poor people are white (including some who also describe themselves as Hispanic); 23 percent are African American (also including some who say they are also Hispanic). But in relation to their overall numbers, African Americans are almost three times as likely as whites to be poor. In 2010, some 27.4 percent of African Americans (10.7 million people) lived in poverty, compared to 26.6 percent of Hispanics (13.2 million), 12.1 percent of Asian Americans (1.7 million), and 9.9 percent of non-Hispanic whites (19.6 million). The poverty gap between whites and minorities has changed little since 1975.

People of color have especially high rates of child poverty. Among African American children, 39.1 percent are poor; the comparable figures are 35 percent among Hispanic children and 12.4 percent among non-Hispanic white children (U.S. Census Bureau, 2011).

Gender and Family Patterns

Of all poor people age eighteen or older, 58 percent are women and 42 percent are men. This difference reflects the fact that women who head households are at high risk of poverty. Of all poor families, 52 percent are headed by women with no husband present, and just 10 percent of poor families are headed by single men.

The United States has experienced a **feminization of poverty,** which is defined as *the trend of women making up an increasing proportion of the poor*. In 1960, only 25 percent of all poor households were headed by women; the majority of poor families had both wives and husbands in the home. By 2010, however, the proportion of poor families headed by single women had more than doubled to 52 percent.

The feminization of poverty is one result of a larger trend: the rapidly increasing number of households at all class levels headed by single women. This trend, coupled with the fact that households headed by women are at high risk of poverty, helps explain why women and their children make up an increasing share of the U.S. poor.

In 2010, the poverty rate for households headed by a single woman was 31.6 percent. By contrast, for married couple families, the poverty rate was just 6.2 percent.

Urban and Rural Poverty

In the United States, the greatest concentration of poverty is found in central cities, where the 2010 poverty rate stood at 19.7 percent. The poverty rate in suburbs is 11.8 percent. Thus the poverty rate for urban areas as a whole is 14.9 percent, lower than the 16.5 percent found in rural areas. National Map 8–1 on page 214 shows that most of the U.S. counties with the highest poverty rate are rural.

Explaining Poverty

The richest nation on Earth contains tens of millions of poor people, a fact that raises serious questions. It is true, as some analysts remind us, that most poor people in the United States are far better off than the poor in other countries: 33 percent of U.S. poor families own a home, 64 percent own a car, and only about 17 percent say they often go without food (U.S. Census Bureau, 2011; U.S. Department of Agriculture, 2011). But there is little doubt that poverty harms the overall well-being of millions of people in this country.

Why is there poverty in the first place? We will examine two opposing explanations for poverty that lead to a lively and important political debate.

One View: Blame the Poor

One view holds that *the poor are mostly responsible for their own poverty.* Throughout this nation's history, people have placed a high cultural value on self-reliance, convinced that a person's social standing is mostly a matter of individual talent and effort. According to this view, society offers plenty of opportunities to anyone who is able and willing to take advantage of them, and the poor are people who cannot or will not work due to a lack of skills, schooling, or motivation.

In his study of poverty in Latin American cities, the anthropologist Oscar Lewis (1961) concluded that the poor become trapped in a *culture of poverty,* a lower-class subculture that can destroy people's ambition to improve their lives. Socialized in poor families, children become resigned to their situation, producing a self-perpetuating cycle of poverty.

In 1996, hoping to free people from what some saw as a culture of poverty in the United States, Congress changed the welfare system, which had provided a federal guarantee of financial assistance to poor

Henry Ossawa Tanner captured the humility and humanity of impoverished people in his painting *The Thankful Poor.* This insight is important in a society that tends to define poor people as morally unworthy and deserving of their bitter plight.

Henry Ossawa Tanner (1859–1937), *The Thankful Poor.* Private collection. Art Resource, New York.

people since 1935. The federal government continues to send money to the states to distribute to needy people, but benefits carry strict time limits—in most cases, no more than two years at a stretch and a total of five years if a person moves in and out of the welfare system. The stated purpose of this reform was to force people to be self-supporting and move them away from dependency on government.

Another View: Blame Society

A different position, argued by William Julius Wilson (1996a, 1996b; see also Mouw, 2000), holds that *society is primarily responsible for poverty.* Wilson points to the loss of jobs in our inner cities as the primary cause of poverty, claiming that there is simply not enough work to support families. Wilson sees any apparent lack of trying on the part of the poor as a result of little opportunity rather than as a cause of poverty. From Wilson's point of view, Lewis's analysis amounts to *blaming the victim,* that is, saying that victims are responsible for their own suffering.

To combat poverty and reduce the need for welfare, Wilson argues, the government must take the lead by investing in people and their communities. Such investments include funding jobs, providing affordable child care for low-income mothers and fathers, ensuring that schools teach both the language skills and work skills that will prepare them for the types of jobs that will be available looking forward, and even expanding regional public transportation to help people get from where they live to the places where the jobs are.

The recent recession, along with increasing income inequality, has swelled the ranks of the poor to some 46 million people. In addition, another 95 million people have income at less than twice the poverty rate, which can be described as *low-income* or *near poor.* When you add these categories together, about 140 million

Watch the video "Consequences of Poverty" on **mysoclab.com**

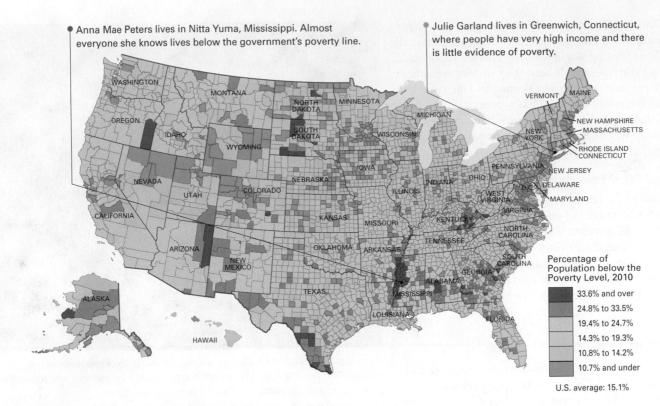

Anna Mae Peters lives in Nitta Yuma, Mississippi. Almost everyone she knows lives below the government's poverty line.

Julie Garland lives in Greenwich, Connecticut, where people have very high income and there is little evidence of poverty.

Percentage of Population below the Poverty Level, 2010

	33.6% and over
	24.8% to 33.5%
	19.4% to 24.7%
	14.3% to 19.3%
	10.8% to 14.2%
	10.7% and under

U.S. average: 15.1%

Seeing Ourselves

NATIONAL MAP 8–1 Poverty across the United States, 2010

This map shows that the poorest counties in the United States—where the poverty rate is more than twice the national average—are in Appalachia, across the Deep South, along the border with Mexico, near the Four Corners region of the Southwest, and in the Dakotas. Can you suggest some reasons for this pattern?

✳ **Explore** the percentage of people living in poverty in your local community and in counties across the United States on **mysoclab.com**

Source: U.S. Census Bureau (2011).

people—approaching half the U.S. population—is either poor or low-income. Put another way, about half of adults in the United States say that they could not raise $2,000 in cash within a month without selling some of what they own. Such statistics suggest that something more than people themselves—that is, traits of society—is at work (Foroohar, 2011; U.S. Census Bureau, 2011; Yen, 2011).

Evaluate The U.S. public is evenly divided over whether the government or people themselves should take responsibility for reducing poverty (NORC, 2011:499). Government statistics show that 56 percent of the heads of poor families did not work at all during 2010, and an additional 31 percent worked only part time (U.S. Census Bureau, 2011). To some people, such facts might seem to support the "blame the poor" side of the argument, because one major cause of poverty is not holding a job.

But the reasons that people do not work are more in step with the "blame society" position. Middle-class women may be able to combine working and child rearing, but this is much harder for poor women who cannot afford child care, and few employers provide child care programs. As William Julius Wilson explains, many people are jobless not because they are avoiding work but because there are not enough jobs to go around. In short, the most effective way to reduce poverty is to ensure a greater supply of jobs as well as child care for parents who work (W. J. Wilson, 1996a; Bainbridge, Meyers, & Waldfogel, 2003).

CHECK YOUR LEARNING Explain the view that the poor should take responsibility for poverty and the view that society is responsible for poverty. Which is closer to your own view?

The Working Poor

Not all poor people are jobless, and the *working poor* command the sympathy and support of people on both sides of the poverty debate. In 2010, some 14 percent of heads of poor families (1.3 million women and men) worked at least fifty weeks of the year and yet could not escape poverty. Another 31 percent of these heads of families (2.8 million people) remained poor despite having part-time employment. Put differently, 3.4 percent of heads of families who work full time earn so little that they remain poor. Since July 2009, the federal minimum wage has been $7.25 per hour. (Some states or municipalities set higher wage levels; in 2012, the nation's highest minimum wage was $10.24 per hour in San Francisco.) But at the federal minimum wage of $7.25, working is no guarantee of escaping poverty—even earning $8.00 per hour, a full-time worker cannot lift an urban family of four above the poverty line. Looking back in time, today's minimum wage

Marco: *(rushing in the door)* Sorry I'm late. I stopped at the store and got stuck behind some welfare mother in the checkout line.

Sergei: *(looking back with a confused grin)* Exactly what does a person on welfare look like?

What is *your* image of a "welfare recipient"? If you are like many people in the United States, you might think of a middle-aged African American woman. But you would be wrong. In truth, the typical person receiving welfare in this country is a child who is white.

There is a lot of confusion about welfare. There is also disagreement about whether this type of assistance is a good or bad idea. In 1996, Congress debated the issue and enacted a new law that ended the federal government's role in providing income assistance to poor households. In place of this federal program, new state-run programs now offer limited help to the poor, but they require people who receive aid to get job training or find work—or have their benefits cut off.

To understand how we got to where we are, let's begin by explaining what, exactly, welfare is. The term "welfare" refers to an assortment of policies and programs designed to improve the well-being of some low-income people. Until the welfare reform of 1996, most people used the term to refer to just one part of the overall system: Aid for Families with Dependent Children (AFDC), a federal program of monthly financial support for parents (mostly single women) to care for themselves and their children. In 1996, about 5 million households in the United States received AFDC for at least some part of the year.

Conservatives opposed AFDC, claiming that rather than reducing child poverty, AFDC made the problem worse, in two ways. First, they claimed that AFDC weakened families, because for years after the program began, it paid benefits to poor mothers only if no husband lived in the home. As a result, the government was actually providing an economic incentive to women to have children outside of marriage, and they blame it for the rapid rise of out-of-wedlock births among poor people. To conservatives, marriage is one key to reducing poverty: Only about one in sixteen married-couple families is poor; more than nine in ten AFDC families were headed by an unmarried woman.

Second, conservatives believe that welfare encourages poor people to become dependent on government handouts, the main reason that eight out of ten poor heads of households did not have full-time jobs. Furthermore, only 5 percent of single mothers receiving AFDC worked full time, compared to more than half of nonpoor single mothers. Conservatives say that welfare gradually moved well beyond its original purpose of short-term help to nonworking women with children (say, after divorce or death of a husband) and gradually became a way of life. Once trapped in dependency, poor women would raise children who were themselves likely to be poor as adults.

Liberals have a different view. Why, they ask, do people object to government money going to poor mothers and children when most "welfare" actually goes to richer people? The cost of AFDC was as high as $25 billion annually—no small sum, to be sure, but much less than the $585 billion in annual Social Security benefits Uncle Sam provides to more than 43 million of our senior citizens, most of whom are not poor. And it is just a small fraction of the more than $1 trillion "bailout money" Congress voted in 2008 and 2009 to assist the struggling financial industry.

Liberals insist that most poor families who turn to public assistance are truly needy. Most of the people who are helped in this way are children. And they don't get very much. The typical household receives only about $500 per month in assistance, hardly enough to attract people to a life of welfare dependency. Even adding some additional money in the form of food stamps, households assisted by welfare still struggle well below the poverty line everywhere in the country. Therefore, liberals see public assistance as a "Band-Aid approach" to the serious social problems of too few jobs and too much income inequality in the United States. As for the charge that public assistance weakens families, liberals agree that the share of families with one parent has gone up, but they see single parenting as a broad trend found at all class levels in many countries.

Back in 1996, the conservative arguments carried the day, ending the AFDC program. Our society's individualistic culture has always encouraged us to blame people themselves (rather than society) for poverty, which becomes a sign not of need but of laziness and personal failure (Inglehart et al., 2000). This view of the poor is probably the biggest reason that led Congress to replace the federal AFDC program with state-run programs called Temporary Assistance for Needy Families (TANF), requiring poor adults to get job training and limiting income assistance to two consecutive years with a lifetime limit of five years.

By 2008, the new TANF policy had cut the number of households receiving income assistance by about 60 percent. This means that many single parents who were once on welfare have taken jobs or are receiving job training. With this in mind, conservatives who supported welfare reform see the new program as a huge success. The welfare rolls have been cut, and more people have moved from receiving a check to working to support themselves. But liberals claim that the reform is far from successful. They point out that many of the people who are now working earn so little pay that they are hardly better off than before. In other words, the reform has greatly reduced the number of people receiving welfare, but it has done little to reduce the extent of poverty.

What Do You Think?

1. How does our cultural emphasis on self-reliance help explain the controversy surrounding public assistance? Why do people not criticize benefits (such as home mortgage interest deductions) for people who are better off?

2. Do you approve of the time limits on benefits built into the TANF program? Why or why not?

3. Why do you think the welfare reforms have done little to reduce poverty?

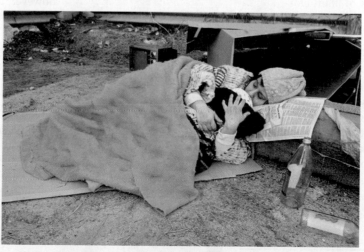

Is society responsible for poverty or are individuals themselves to blame? When it comes to homeless families, most people think society should do more.

Sources: Lichter & Crowley (2002), Lichter & Jayakody (2002), Von Drehle (2008), and U.S. Census Bureau (2011).

would have to rise to $10.60 an hour just to match the inflation-controlled value of the minimum wage back in 1968. In different terms, half of all of today's workers now earn less than about $26,000 a year, which puts most people below, at, or close to the poverty line for a family of four (Raum, 2011; U.S. Census Bureau, 2011).

Individual ability and personal effort do play a part in shaping social position. However, the weight of sociological evidence points toward society, not individual character traits, as the primary source of poverty because more and more available jobs offer only low wages. In addition, the poor are *categories* of people—female heads of families, people of color, people in inner-city neighborhoods isolated from the larger society—who face special barriers and limited opportunities.

The Controversy & Debate box on page 215 takes a closer look at the current welfare debate. Understanding this important social issue can help us decide how our society should respond to the problem of poverty, as well as the problem of homelessness discussed next.

Homelessness

Each year, the government's Department of Housing and Urban Development conducts a national survey of cities and towns to find out how many people in the United States are homeless. The 2010 survey found about 649,917 people living in shelters, in transitional housing, and on the street on a single night in January. But, the government estimates, a much larger number—approximately 1.6 million people—are homeless for at least some time during the course of the year (U.S. Department of Housing and Urban Development, 2011). As with earlier estimates of the homeless population, critics claimed that the HUD estimate undercounted the homeless, who may well have numbered several million people. Some estimates suggest that as many as 3 million people are homeless for at least one night in a given year. In addition, they add, evidence suggests that the number of homeless people in the United States is increasing (L. Kaufman, 2004; National Coalition for the Homeless, 2009).

The familiar stereotypes of homeless people— men sleeping in doorways and women pushing rickety shopping carts containing everything they own—have been replaced by the "new homeless": people thrown out of work because of plant closings, women who take their children and leave home to escape domestic violence, women and men forced out of apartments by rent increases, and others unable to meet mortgage or rent payments because of low wages or no work at all. Today, no stereotype paints a complete picture of the homeless.

The large majority of homeless people report that they do not work, although about 20 percent have at least a part-time job (U.S. Conference of Mayors, 2010). Working or not, all homeless people have one thing in common: poverty. For that reason, the explanations of poverty just presented also apply to homelessness. Some people blame the *personal traits* of the homeless. More than one-third of

In 2011, with economic inequality increasing, the Occupy Wall Street movement emerged. This groundswell of anger and activism put much of the blame for the recent recession on the very rich.

homeless people are substance abusers, and one-fourth have a serious mental illness. More broadly, a fraction of 1 percent of our population, for one reason or another, seems unable to cope with our complex and highly competitive society (U.S. Department of Housing and Urban Development, 2011).

Others see homelessness resulting from *societal factors,* including low wages and a lack of affordable housing. Supporters of this position point out that 35 percent of the homeless consist of families (typically a single mother with young children), and since the recession began in 2007, the share of families among the homeless has been rising. From another angle, children are the fastest-growing category of the homeless (Kozol, 1988; Bohannan, 1991; L. Kaufman, 2004; U.S. Department of Housing and Urban Development, 2011).

No one disputes that a large proportion of homeless people are personally impaired to some degree, but cause and effect are difficult to untangle. Long-term structural changes in the U.S. economy, cutbacks in social service budgets, and the recent economic downturn have all contributed to the problem of homelessness.

Increasing Inequality, Increasing Controversy

Evaluate

There is a rising level of debate about income inequality in the United States. The reason for the increasing controversy is simple—economic inequality has reached levels not seen in this country since 1929, just before the Great Depression. As shown in Figure 8–6, the 1920s was a decade that saw steady gains in income for the highest earning 1 percent of the population who, just before the stock market crash, were receiving almost 25 percent of all income.

For several decades following the Depression, the trend was toward greater income equality. By the 1970s, as the figure shows, the richest 1 percent received less than 10 percent of all income. During the last thirty years, however, the trend has reversed direction. Today, the highest-paid 1 percent of the population enjoy about the same share of all income that the top earners received in 1929.

The United States has always been a nation in which most people expect some degree of economic inequality. This country's core values of competitive individualism and personal responsibility support the idea that people should receive rewards in proportion to their talents, abilities, and efforts.

Even so, people are now losing confidence that this is, in fact, the case. In a recent survey, U.S. adults were presented with the statement, "Differences in income in America are too large." In response, 63 percent agreed and only 16 percent disagreed (the remainder said that they neither agreed nor disagreed or that they did not know) (NORC, 2011:2270).

Other surveys find that a large majority of people agree with the statement, "This is a country in which the rich get richer and the poor get poorer" (Kohut, 2011).

Are the Very Rich Worth the Money?

Such widespread concern about economic inequality suggests serious problems. First, in a society in which most think there is too much income inequality, people doubt that the highest-paid individuals are really worth the money they are paid. Certainly, there are some very smart, very talented, and very hard-working women and men in our country who are rewarded with high incomes. People in the entertainment industry, like television personalities Mariska Hargitay (who is paid about $10 million a year), Conan O'Brien ($14 million), and Jay Leno ($30 million) earn more money than most of us may ever see. Even bigger stars like Johnny Depp and Beyoncé bring home far more (each earns close to $100 million a year). Such rewards are what we have come to expect very popular media stars to receive, and we may justify such pay because of the power these celebrities have to attract viewers and advertising money.

But we should be careful not to assume that income is directly related to talent, ability, and effort. In 2011, Alex Rodriguez of the New York Yankees took home the biggest paycheck among major league ball players, at $32 million. This amount almost equals the money paid that season to the entire Kansas City Royals team, who surely offer more talent, ability, and effort than even the single best player on the Yankees. Another Yankee—Babe Ruth—who was arguably the greatest ballplayer of all time earned only $80,000 (or $1.2 million in today's dollars) in his highest-paid seasons (1930 and 1931) on the Yankees.

The Occupy Wall Street movement gained support across the nation and inspired citizen action around the world for criticizing the very high pay that a small share of corporate leaders receive. In 2011, according to *Forbes* magazine, John Hammergren, CEO of McKesson Pharmaceuticals, was the highest-earning CEO, receiving total compensation of $131 million in salary, bonus, stock options, and other perks. That year, the country's ten highest-paid CEOs averaged just over $60 million each in earnings. Noteworthy, in light of the movement's focus on Wall Street, is the fact that no Wall Street CEOs made it into the top ten (although Wall Street's top hedge-fund managers made much more). Surveying U.S. corporations, CEOs are earning more than ever. Back in 1970, the compensation of top CEOs was about 40 times what the average company employee earned. In 2011, top CEOs earned about 400 times the company average and took home pay increases of about 25 percent, so the upward trend shows no sign of ending (Corporate Library, 2011; Helman, 2011; Roth, 2011; U.S. Census Bureau, 2011).

Defenders of such high pay claim that companies pay what it takes to attract the most talented people to top leadership, which helps companies perform better. Critics counter that company performance is not clearly linked to CEO rewards—half of the companies paying top salaries to CEOs actually lost money in their most recent year (Helman, 2011; NORC, 2011).

Can the Rest of Us Get Ahead?

A second problem that accompanies increasing inequality is rising doubt that people who are willing to work hard can get ahead. The idea that those willing to make the effort can enjoy economic security and expect

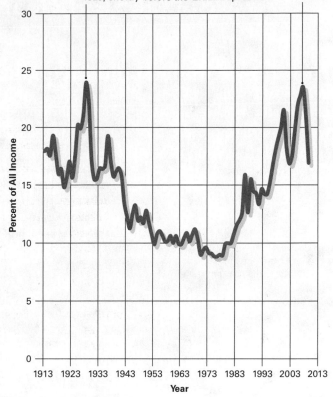

● In 2007, the highest-paid 1 percent of the population received almost the same share of all income as in 1929, shortly before the Great Depression.

FIGURE 8–6 Share of All Income Earned by the Richest 1 Percent, 1913–2009

In 1929, the richest 1 percent of the U.S. population earned almost one-fourth of all income. This share declined in the decades after that, dropping below 10 percent by the mid-1970s. In recent decades, however, the trend has been toward greater income inequality. By 2007, the top 1 percent was earning almost one-fourth of all income once again, although this share fell with the onset of the recession.

Sources: Saez & Piketty (2009) and Internal Revenue Service (2011).

to improve social standing over time is at the heart of the American Dream. But, in recent decades, while people at the top of the income hierarchy have been generously rewarded, average people who work hard have been struggling to hang on to what they have. With good-paying jobs harder to find, it is not surprising that the share of people who say that they believe their family can achieve the American Dream has declined—from 76 percent in 2001 to 57 percent in 2010 (Zogby, 2010).

Today, the public's awareness of economic inequality is as high as it has been since the Great Depression of the 1930s. Should the trend toward greater economic inequality persist, and should the loss of confidence in our system of social inequality continue, the demands for basic change to our society are sure to intensify.

Finally, as we debate the shape of inequality here at home, we must remember that the drama of social stratification extends far beyond the borders of the United States. The most striking social inequality is found not by looking inside one country but by comparing living standards in various parts of the world. In Chapter 9, we broaden our focus by investigating global stratification.

Seeing Sociology in Everyday Life

How do we understand inequality in the United States?

This chapter sketches the class structure of the United States and how people end up in their positions in our system of social inequality. How accurately do you think the mass media reflect the reality of inequality in our society? Look at the three photos of television shows, one from back in the 1950s and the other two from today. What messages about social standing, and how we get there, does each show convey?

Hint In general, the mass media present social standing as a reflection of an individual's personal traits and sometimes sheer luck. In *The Millionaire*, wealth was visited on some people for no apparent reason at all. In *The Bachelor*, women try to gain the approval of a man. In *America's Next Top Model*, the key to success is good looks and personal style. But social structure is also involved in ways that we easily overlook. Is there any significance to the fact that (as of 2011) all the bachelors on that show have been white? Does "good looks" matter as much to men as it does to women? Is becoming a millionaire really a matter of luck? Does social standing result from personal competition as much as television shows suggest?

In *The Millionaire*, a popular television show that ran from 1955 until 1960, a very rich man (who was never fully shown on camera) had the curious hobby of giving away $1 million to other people he had never even met. Each week, he gave his personal assistant, Michael Anthony, a check to pass along to "the next millionaire." Anthony tracked down the person and handed over the money, and the story went on to reveal how such great wealth from out of nowhere changed someone's life for better (or sometimes for worse). What does this story line seem to suggest about social class position?

In the TV show *The Bachelor,* first aired in 2002, a young bachelor works his way through a collection of twenty-five attractive young women, beginning with group dates, moving on to overnight visits with three "finalists," and (in most cases) proposing to his "final selection." Much of the interaction takes place in a lavish, 7,500-square-foot home somewhere in southern California. What does this show suggest is the key to social position? What message does this show promote about the importance of marriage for women?

In 2003, Tyra Banks created *America's Next Top Model*, and she also stars in the show. Each season, up to thirteen young women demonstrate their talents as models to a panel of judges, including Banks; one contestant is eliminated each week until only one remains as the "winner." What messages about social position and achieving success does this show present to young women?

Seeing Sociology in *Your* Everyday Life

1. During an evening of television viewing, assess the social class level of the characters you see on various shows. In each case, explain why you assign someone a particular social position. Do you find many clearly upper-class people? Middle-class people? Working-class people? Poor people? Describe the patterns you find.

2. Develop several questions that together will let you measure social class position. The trick is to decide what you think social class really means. Then try your questions on several adults, refining the questions as you proceed.

3. Social stratification involves how a society distributes resources. It also has a relational dimension—social inequality guides *with whom* we do and do not interact and also *how* we interact with people. Can you give examples of how social class differences guide social interaction in your everyday life? Go to the "Seeing Sociology in *Your* Everyday Life" feature on MySocLab for additional discussion of the relational aspects of social stratification, including suggestions for how to relate to people whose social backgrounds differ from your own. A second "Seeing Sociology in *Your* Everyday Life" feature explores the interplay of caste and meritocracy and why members of our society tend to see social class standing as simply the result of personal abilities and effort.

What Is Social Stratification?

Social stratification is a system by which a society ranks categories of people in a hierarchy, so that some people have more money, power, and prestige than others.

Social stratification

- is a trait of society, not simply a reflection of individual differences
- carries over from one generation to the next
- is supported by a system of cultural beliefs that defines certain kinds of inequality as just
- takes two general forms: caste systems and class systems   **pp. 186–87**

Caste Systems

- are based on birth (ascription)
- permit little or no social mobility
- shape a person's entire life, including occupation and marriage
- are common in traditional, agrarian societies   **pp. 187–89**

Class Systems

- are based on both birth (ascription) and **meritocracy** (individual achievement)
- permit some social mobility
- are common in modern industrial and postindustrial societies   **pp. 188–93**

social stratification (p. 186) a system by which a society ranks categories of people in a hierarchy

social mobility (p. 187) a change in position within the social hierarchy

caste system (p. 187) social stratification based on ascription, or birth

class system (p. 188) social stratification based on both birth and individual achievement

meritocracy (p. 188) social stratification based on personal merit

status consistency (p. 188) the degree of uniformity in a person's social standing across various dimensions of social inequality

structural social mobility (p. 191) a shift in the social position of large numbers of people due more to changes in society itself than to individual efforts

ideology (p. 192) cultural beliefs that justify particular social arrangements, including patterns of inequality

Theories of Social Stratification

Structural-functional theory points to ways social stratification helps society operate.

- The **Davis-Moore thesis** states that social stratification is universal because of its functional consequences.
- In caste systems, people are rewarded for performing the duties of their position at birth.
- In class systems, unequal rewards attract the ablest people to the most important jobs and encourage effort.   **pp. 193–95**

Read the Document on mysoclab.com

Social-conflict theory claims that stratification divides societies in classes, benefiting some categories of people at the expense of others and causing social conflict.

- Karl Marx claimed that capitalism places economic production under the ownership of capitalists, who exploit the proletarians, who sell their labor for wages.
- Max Weber identified three distinct dimensions of social stratification: economic class, social status or prestige, and power. Conflict exists between people at various positions on a multidimensional hierarchy of **socioeconomic status (SES)**.   **pp. 195–97**

Symbolic-interaction theory, a micro-level analysis that explores how inequality shapes everyday life, explains that we size people up by looking for clues to their social standing. **Conspicuous consumption** refers to buying and displaying products that make a "statement" about social class. Most people tend to socialize with others whose social standing is similar to their own.   **pp. 197–98**

Davis-Moore thesis (p. 193) the functional analysis claiming that social stratification has beneficial consequences for the operation of society

capitalists (p. 195) people who own and operate factories and other businesses in pursuit of profits

proletarians (p. 195) people who sell their labor for wages

alienation (p. 195) the experience of isolation and misery resulting from powerlessness

blue-collar occupations (p. 196) lower-prestige jobs that involve mostly manual labor

white-collar occupations (p. 196) higher-prestige jobs that involve mostly mental activity

socioeconomic status (SES) (p. 197) a composite ranking based on various dimensions of social inequality

conspicuous consumption (p. 198) buying and using products because of the "statement" they make about social position

Social Stratification and Technology: A Global Perspective

Hunting and Gathering → Horticultural and Pastoral → Agrarian → Industrial → Postindustrial

- Gerhard Lenski explains that advancing technology initially increases social stratification, which is most intense in agrarian societies.

- Industrialization reverses the trend, reducing social stratification.

- In postindustrial societies, social stratification again increases.   **pp. 198–99**

Inequality in the United States

Social stratification involves many dimensions:

- *Income*—Earnings from work and investments are unequal, with the richest 20% of families earning more than twelve times as much as the poorest 20% of families.
- *Wealth*—The total value of all assets minus debts, wealth is distributed more unequally than income, with the richest 20% of families holding 85% of all wealth.
- *Power*—Income and wealth are important sources of power.
- *Occupational Prestige*—Work generates not only income but also prestige. White-collar jobs generally offer more income and prestige than blue-collar jobs. Many lower-prestige jobs are performed by women and people of color.
- *Schooling*—Schooling affects both occupation and income. Some categories of people have greater opportunities for schooling than others.
- *Family ancestry, race and ethnicity,* and *gender* all affect social standing. **pp. 199–203**

income
(p. 200) earnings from work or investments

wealth
(p. 201) the total value of money and other assets, minus outstanding debts

Social Classes in the United States

$200,000

upper class—5% of the population. Most members of the *upper-upper class*, or "old rich," inherited their wealth; the *lower-upper class*, or "new rich," work at high-paying jobs.

$200,000

$48,000

middle class—40% to 45% of the population. People in the *upper-middle class* have significant wealth; *average-middles* have less prestige, do white-collar work, and most attend college.

$48,000

$27,000

working class—30% to 35% of the population. People in the *lower-middle class* do blue-collar work; only about one-third of children attend college.

$27,000

lower class—20% of the population. Most people in the lower class lack financial security due to low income; many live below the poverty line; half do not complete high school. **pp. 203–5**

- People with higher social standing generally have better health, hold certain values and political attitudes, and pass on advantages in the form of "cultural capital" to their children.
- Social mobility is common in the United States, as it is in other high-income countries, but typically only small changes occur from one generation to the next.
- Due to the expansion of the global economy, the richest families now earn more than ever; families near the bottom of the class system have seen only small increases. **pp. 205–12**

intragenerational social mobility
(p. 208) a change in social position occurring during a person's lifetime

intergenerational social mobility
(p. 208) upward or downward social mobility of children in relation to their parents

Poverty in the United States

Poverty Profile

- The government classifies 46.2 million people—15.1% of the population—as poor.
- About 50% of the poor are under age 25.
- About 70% of the poor are white, but in relation to their population, African Americans and Hispanics are more likely to be poor.
- The **feminization of poverty** means that more poor families are headed by women.
- About 45% of the heads of poor families are among the "working poor" who work at least part time but do not earn enough to lift a family of four above the poverty line.
- Estimates place the number of people who are homeless at some time over the course of a year at between 1.6 and 3 million.
- The fact that almost half of the U.S. population is either poor or low-income (living with income at less than twice the poverty level) suggests that society more than individual traits is the main cause of poverty. **pp. 212–16**

relative poverty
(p. 212) the lack of resources of some people in relation to those who have more

absolute poverty
(p. 212) a lack of resources that is life-threatening

feminization of poverty (p. 212) the trend of women making up an increasing proportion of the poor

※ **Explore** the **Map** on **mysoclab.com**   ◉ **Watch** the **Video** on **mysoclab.com**

Explanations of Poverty

- Blame individuals: The *culture of poverty* thesis states that poverty is caused by shortcomings in the poor themselves (Oscar Lewis).
- Blame society: Poverty is caused by society's unequal distribution of wealth and lack of good jobs (William Julius Wilson). **pp. 213–14**

Increasing Social Inequality

- In recent decades, income inequality has increased.
- Surveys show most people think income differences are too large.
- Many people also are concerned that hard work may not be enough to get ahead. **pp. 216–17**

9 Global Stratification

Learning Objectives

Remember the definitions of the key terms highlighted in boldfaced type throughout this chapter.

Understand that social stratification involves not just people within our society but inequality among the nations of the world.

Apply two different theoretical approaches to gain insights about the causes of global stratification.

Analyze the social standing of women in global perspective.

Evaluate the common claim that slavery has been abolished in the modern world.

Create an appreciation for the extent of social inequality in our world, which is far greater than what is readily observed in the United States.

CHAPTER OVERVIEW

Social stratification involves not just inequality among people within a single country; it is also a worldwide pattern, with some nations far more economically productive than others. This chapter shifts the focus from inequality within the United States to inequality in the world as a whole. The chapter begins by describing global inequality and then provides two theoretical models that explain global stratification. ■

More than 1,000 workers were busily sewing together polo shirts on the fourth floor of the garment factory in Narsingdi, a small town about 30 miles northeast of Bangladesh's capital city of Dhaka. The thumping beats of hundreds of sewing machines produced a steady roar throughout the long working day.

But in an instant everything changed when an electric gun used to shoot spot remover onto stained fabric gave off a spark, which ignited the flammable liquid. Suddenly, a worktable burst into flames. People rushed to smother the fire with shirts, but there was no stopping the blaze: In a room filled with combustible materials, the flames spread quickly.

The workers scrambled toward the narrow staircase that led to the street. At the bottom, however, the human wave pouring down the steep steps collided with a folding metal gate across the doorway that was kept locked to prevent workers from leaving during working hours. Panicked, the people turned, only to be pushed back by the hundreds behind them. In a single terrifying minute of screaming voices, thrusting legs, and pounding hearts, dozens were crushed and trampled. By the time the gates were opened and the fire was put out, fifty-two garment workers lay dead.

Garment factories like this one are big business in Bangladesh, where clothing accounts for 77 percent of the country's total economic exports. One-third of these garments end up in stores in the United States. The reason so much of the clothing we buy is made in poor countries like Bangladesh is simple economics—Bangladeshi garment workers labor for as many as twelve hours a day, often seven days a week, and most earn the minimum wage of only $500 a year, which is just a few percent of what a garment worker makes in the United States.

Tanveer Chowdhury manages this garment factory, which his family owns. Speaking to reporters, he complained bitterly about the tragedy. "This fire has cost me $586,373, and that does not include $70,000 for machinery and $20,000 for furniture. I made commitments to meet deadlines, and I still have the deadlines. I am now paying for air freight at $10 a dozen when I should be shipping by sea at 87 cents a dozen."

There was one other cost Chowdhury did not mention. To compensate families for the loss of their loved ones in the fire, the factory eventually agreed to pay $1,952 per person. In Bangladesh, life—like labor—is cheap (based on Bearak, 2001; Bajaj, 2010; and World Bank, 2011).

Garment workers in Bangladesh are part of the roughly 1.4 billion of the world's people who work hard every day and yet remain poor. As this chapter explains, although poverty is a reality in the United States and other nations, the greatest social inequality is not *within* nations but *between* them (Goesling, 2001; Chen & Ravallion, 2008; Milanovic, 2011). We can understand the full dimensions of poverty only by exploring **global stratification**, *patterns of social inequality in the world as a whole.*

Global Stratification: An Overview

 Understand

Chapter 8 ("Social Stratification") described inequality in the United States. In global perspective, however, social stratification is far greater. The left pie chart in Figure 9–1 divides the world's total income by quintiles (fifths) of the population. Recall from Chapter 8

that the richest 20 percent of the U.S. population earns about 48 percent of the national income (see Figure 8–3 on page 201). The richest 20 percent of the global population, however, receives about 77 percent of world income. At the other extreme, the poorest 20 percent of the U.S. population earns 4 percent of our national income; the poorest fifth of the world's people, by contrast, struggles to survive on just 2 percent of global income (Milanovic, 2011).

In terms of wealth, as the chart at the right in Figure 9–1 shows, global inequality is even greater. A rough estimate is that the richest 20 percent of the world's adults own 84 percent of the planet's wealth. About half of all wealth is owned by less than 5 percent of the world's adult population; about 30 percent, by the richest 1 percent. On the other hand, the poorest half of the world's adults own barely 3 percent of all global

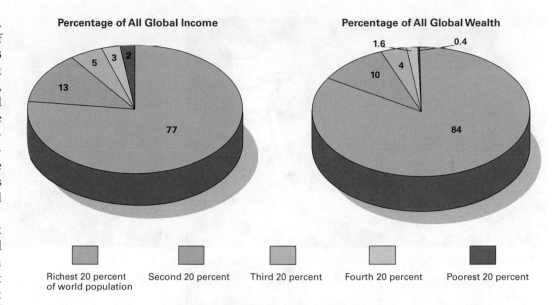

Percentage of All Global Income

Percentage of All Global Wealth

Richest 20 percent of world population Second 20 percent Third 20 percent Fourth 20 percent Poorest 20 percent

FIGURE 9–1 Distribution of Global Income and Wealth

Global income is very unequal, with the richest 20 percent of the world's people earning almost forty times as much as the poorest 20 percent. Global wealth is even more unequally divided, with the richest 20 percent owning 84 percent of private wealth and the poorest half of the world's people having barely anything at all.

Sources: Author calculations based on Davies et al. (2009) and Milanovic (2009, 2011).

wealth. In terms of dollars, about half the world's families have less than $8,600 in total wealth, far less than the $120,300 in wealth for the typical family in the United States (Bucks et al., 2009; Davies et al., 2009).

Because some countries are so much richer than others, even people in the United States with income below the government's poverty line live far better than the majority of people on the planet. The average person in a rich nation such as the United States is extremely well off by world standards. Any one of the world's richest *people* (in 2011, the world's three richest people—Bill Gates and Warren Buffett in the United States and Carlos Slim Helú in Mexico—were *each* worth more than $50 billion) has more personal wealth than the total economic output of the world's 122 poorest *countries* (*Forbes*, 2011; Milanovic, 2011; World Bank, 2011).

A Word about Terminology

Classifying the 195 nations on Earth into categories ignores many striking differences. These nations have rich and varied histories, speak different languages, and take pride in their distinctive cultures. However, various models have been developed that classify countries in order to study global stratification (U.S. Department of State, 2011).

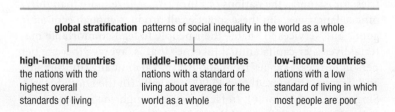

global stratification patterns of social inequality in the world as a whole

high-income countries the nations with the highest overall standards of living

middle-income countries nations with a standard of living about average for the world as a whole

low-income countries nations with a low standard of living in which most people are poor

One global model, developed after World War II, labeled the rich, industrial countries the "First World"; the less industrialized, socialist countries the "Second World"; and the nonindustrialized, poor countries the "Third World." But the "three worlds" model is less useful today. For one thing, it was a product of Cold War politics, when the capitalist West (the First World) faced off against the socialist East (the Second World) while other nations (the Third World) remained more or less on the sidelines. But the sweeping changes in Eastern Europe and the collapse of the Soviet Union in the early 1990s mean that a distinctive Second World no longer exists.

Another problem is that the "three worlds" model lumped together more than 100 countries as the Third World. In reality, some better-off nations of the Third World (such as Chile in South America) have thirteen times the per-person productivity seen in the poorest countries of the world (such as Ethiopia in East Africa).

These facts call for a modestly revised system of classification. The seventy-two **high-income countries** are defined as *the nations with the highest overall standards of living*. These nations have a per capita gross domestic product (GDP) greater than $12,000. The world's seventy **middle-income countries** are not as rich; they are *nations with a standard of living about average for the world as a whole*. Their per capita GDP is less than $12,000 but greater than $2,500. The remaining fifty-three **low-income countries** are *nations with a low standard of living in which most people are poor*. In these nations, per capita GDP is less than $2,500 (United Nations Development Programme, 2011; World Bank, 2011).

Watch the video "Globalization" on **mysoclab.com**

The United States is among the world's high-income countries, in which industrial technology and economic expansion have produced material prosperity. The presence of market forces is evident in this view of New York City (*above, left*). India has recently become one of the world's middle-income countries (*above, right*). An increasing number of motor vehicles fill city streets. Afghanistan (*left*) is among the world's low-income countries. As the photograph suggests, these nations have limited economic development. Combined with rapidly increasing population, the result is widespread poverty.

This model has two advantages over the "three worlds" system. First, it focuses on economic development rather than political system (capitalist or socialist). Second, it gives a better picture of the relative economic development of various countries because it does not lump together all lower-income nations into a single "Third World."

Research confirms that *where you live* has a larger effect on income and standard of living than class position *within* any country (Milanovic, 2011). At the same time, when ranking countries, keep in mind that there is social stratification within every nation. In Bangladesh, for example, members of the Chowdhury family, who own the garment factory described in the chapter-opening story, earn as much as $1 million per year, which is several thousand times more than one of their workers earns.

To grasp the full extent of global inequality, you need to consider that the wealthiest people in rich countries such as the United States live worlds apart from the poorest people in low-income countries such as Bangladesh, Haiti, and Sudan. That's why, as noted earlier, the richest people in the world have more annual income than the total economic output of most of the world's countries.

High-Income Countries

In nations where the Industrial Revolution first took place more than two centuries ago, productivity increased more than 100-fold. To understand the power of industrial and computer technology,

consider that any number of rich nations (including the United States, Canada, the United Kingdom, France, Germany, or Japan) is more productive than the whole continent of Africa south of the Sahara, where industrialization and Internet connections are limited.

Global Map 9–1 shows that the high-income nations of the world include the United States, Canada, and Mexico, Argentina and Chile, the nations of Western Europe, Israel, Saudi Arabia, Singapore, Hong Kong (part of the People's Republic of China), Japan, South Korea, the Russian Federation, Malaysia, Australia, and New Zealand.

These countries cover roughly 47 percent of Earth's land area, including parts of five continents, and lie mostly in the Northern Hemisphere. In 2011, the population of these nations was about 1.58 billion, or about 23 percent of the world's people. About three-fourths of the people in high-income countries live in or near cities (Population Reference Bureau, 2011; World Bank, 2011).

Significant cultural differences exist among high-income countries; for example, the nations of Europe recognize more than thirty official languages. But these societies all produce enough economic goods and services to enable their people to lead comfortable material lives. Per capita annual income (that is, average income per person per year) ranges from about $13,000 annually (in Romania and Panama) to more than $45,000 annually (in the United States, Singapore, and Norway). In fact, people in high-income countries enjoy 75 percent of the world's total income.

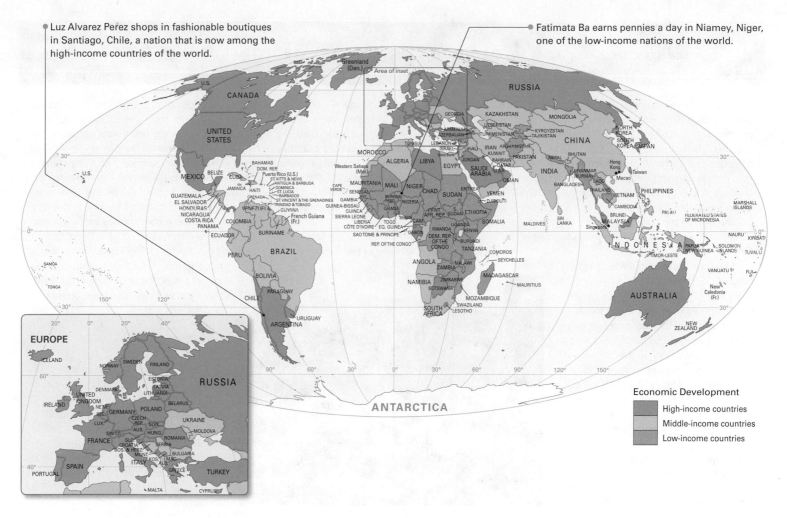

Luz Alvarez Perez shops in fashionable boutiques in Santiago, Chile, a nation that is now among the high-income countries of the world.

Fatimata Ba earns pennies a day in Niamey, Niger, one of the low-income nations of the world.

Economic Development

- High-income countries
- Middle-income countries
- Low-income countries

Window on the World

GLOBAL MAP 9–1 Economic Development in Global Perspective

In high-income countries—including the United States, Canada, Mexico, Chile, Argentina, the nations of Western Europe, Israel, Saudi Arabia, Singapore, Hong Kong, South Korea, Malaysia, Australia, the Russian Federation, Japan, and New Zealand—a highly productive economy provides people, on average, with material plenty. Middle-income countries—including most of Latin America and Asia—are less economically productive, with a standard of living about average for the world as a whole but far below that of the United States. These nations also have a significant share of poor people who are barely able to feed and house themselves. In the low-income countries of the world, poverty is severe and widespread. Although small numbers of elites live very well in the poorest nations, most people struggle to survive on a small fraction of the income common in the United States.

Note: Data for this map are provided by the United Nations. Each country's economic productivity is measured in terms of its gross domestic product (GDP), which is the total value of all the goods and services produced by a country's economy within its borders in a given year. Dividing each country's GDP by the country's population gives us the per capita (per-person) GDP and allows us to compare the economic performance of countries of different population sizes. High-income countries have a per capita GDP of more than $12,000. Many are far richer than this, however; the figure for the United States exceeds $45,000. Middle-income countries have a per capita GDP ranging from $2,500 to $12,000. Low-income countries have a per capita GDP of less than $2,500. Figures used here reflect the United Nations' "purchasing power parities" system, which is an estimate of what people can buy using their income in the local economy.

Source: Data from United Nations Development Programme (2011).

Keep in mind that high-income countries have many low-income people. The Sociology in Focus box on page 228 profiles the striking poverty that exists in *las colonias* along our country's southern border.

Production in rich nations is capital-intensive. This means that it is based on the use of factories, big machinery, and advanced technology. Most of the largest corporations that design and market computers, as well as most computer users, are located in high-income countries. In addition, high-income countries also control the world's financial markets, so daily events on the stock exchanges of New York, London, and Tokyo affect people throughout the world. In short, rich nations are very productive because of their advanced technology and also because they control the global economy.

Middle-Income Countries

Middle-income countries have per capita annual incomes ranging from $2,500 to $12,000, roughly the median ($7,737) for the world's nations taken together. About 54 percent of the people in

"We wanted to have something for ourselves," explains Olga Ruiz, who has lived in the border community of College Park, Texas, for two decades. There is no college in College Park, nor does this dusty stretch of rural land have sewer lines or even running water. Yet this town is one of some 1,800 settlements that have sprouted up in southern Texas along the 1,200-mile border with Mexico that runs from El Paso to Brownsville. Together, they are home to roughly 500,000 people.

Many people speak of *las colonias* (Spanish for "the colonies") as "America's Third World" because these desperately poor communities look much like their counterparts in Mexico or many other middle- or low-income nations. But almost all of the people living in the *colonias* are Latino, 85 percent of them are legal residents, and more than half are U.S. citizens.

Anastacia Ledsema, seventy-two years old, moved to a *colonia* called Sparks more than forty years ago. Born in Mexico, Ledsema married a Texas man, and together they paid $200 for a quarter-acre lot in a new border community. For months, they camped out on their land. Step by step, however, they invested their labor and

their money to build a modest house. Not until 1995 did their small community get running water—a service promised by developers years before. After the water line came, things changed more than they expected. "When we got water," recalls Ledsema, "that's when so many people came in." The population of Sparks quickly doubled to about 3,000, overwhelming the water supply so that sometimes the faucet does not run at all.

The residents of all the *colonias* know that they are poor, and with annual per capita income

of about $6,000, they are poor even by global standards. Indeed, the Census Bureau declared the county surrounding one border community to be the poorest in the United States. Concerned over the lack of basic services in so many of these communities, Texas officials have banned any new settlements. But most of the people who move here—even those who start off sleeping in their cars or trucks—see these communities as the first step on the path to the American dream. Oscar Solis, a neighborhood leader in Panorama Village, with a population of about 150, is proud to show visitors around the small but growing town. "All of this work we have done ourselves," he says with a smile, "to make our dream come true."

Join the Blog!

Are you surprised that such intense poverty exists in a rich country like the United States? Why or why not? Go to MySocLab and join the Sociology in Focus blog to share your opinions and experiences and to see what others think.

Source: Based on Schaffer (2002) and *The Economist* (2011).

middle-income countries live in or near cities, and industrial jobs are common. The remaining 46 percent of the people live in rural areas, where most are poor and lack access to schools, medical care, adequate housing, and even safe drinking water.

Looking at Global Map 9–1, we see that seventy of the world's nations fall into the middle-income category. At the high end are Venezuela (Latin America), Bulgaria (Europe), and Iran (Asia), where annual income is about $11,000. At the low end are Nicaragua (Latin America), Cape Verde (Africa), and Vietnam (Asia), with roughly $3,000 annually in per capita income.

One cluster of middle-income countries used to be part of the Second World. These countries, found in Eastern Europe and Western Asia, had mostly socialist economies until popular revolts between 1989 and 1991 swept their governments aside. Since then, these nations have introduced more free-market economies. These middle-income countries include Ukraine, Kazakhstan, Georgia, and Turkmenistan.

Other middle-income nations include Peru and Brazil in South America and Namibia and Angola in Africa. Both India and the People's Republic of China have entered the middle-income category, which now includes most of Asia.

Taken together, middle-income countries span roughly 36 percent of the world's land area and are home to about 4.2 billion

people, or about 61 percent of humanity. Some very large countries (such as China) are far less crowded than others (such as El Salvador), but compared to high-income countries, these societies are densely populated (Population Reference Bureau, 2011; World Bank, 2011).

Low-Income Countries

Low-income countries, where most people are very poor, are mostly agrarian societies with some industry. Fifty-three nations, identified in Global Map 9–1, are spread across Central and East Africa and Asia. Low-income countries cover 18 percent of the planet's land area and are home to 17 percent of its people. Population density is generally high, although it is greater in Asian countries (such as Bangladesh) than in Central African nations (such as Chad and the Democratic Republic of the Congo).

In poor countries, 36 percent of the people live in cities; a majority inhabits villages and farms as their ancestors have done for centuries. In fact, half the world's people are farmers, most of whom follow cultural traditions. With limited industrial technology, they cannot be very productive—one reason that many endure severe poverty. Hunger, disease, and unsafe housing shape the lives of the world's poorest people.

In general, when natural disasters strike high-income nations, property damage is great, but loss of life is low. The triple disaster that struck Japan in 2011 (*left*)—a massive earthquake followed by a major tsunami and then the spread of radiation from a damaged nuclear power plant—was certainly an economic calamity, but it also left more than 20,000 people dead or missing. Even so, the less powerful earthquake that hit Haiti in 2010 (*right*) killed three times that number of people.

Those of us who live in rich nations such as the United States find it hard to understand the scope of human need in much of the world. From time to time, televised pictures of famine in very poor countries such as Ethiopia and Bangladesh give us shocking glimpses into the poverty that makes every day a life-and-death struggle for many in low-income nations. Behind these images lie cultural, historical, and economic forces that we shall explore in the remainder of this chapter.

Global Wealth and Poverty

 Analyze

October 14, Manila, Philippines. What caught my eye was how clean she was—a girl no more than seven or eight years old, wearing a freshly laundered dress with her hair carefully combed. She followed us with her eyes: Camera-toting Americans stand out here, in one of the poorest neighborhoods in the entire world.

Fed by methane from decomposing garbage, the fires never go out on Smokey Mountain, the vast garbage dump on the north side of Manila. Smoke covers the hills of refuse like a thick fog. But Smokey Mountain is more than a dump; it is a neighborhood that is home to thousands of people. It is hard to imagine a setting more hostile to human life. Amid the smoke and the squalor, men and women do what they can to survive. They pick plastic bags from the garbage and wash them in the river, and they collect cardboard boxes or anything else they can sell. What chance do their children have, coming from families that earn only a few hundred dollars a year, with hardly any opportunity for schooling, year after year breathing this foul air? Against this backdrop of human tragedy, one lovely little girl has put on a fresh dress and gone out to play.

Now our taxi driver threads his way through heavy traffic as we head for the other side of Manila. The change is amazing: The smoke and smell of the dump give way to neighborhoods that could be in Miami or Los Angeles. A cluster of yachts floats on the bay in the distance.

No more rutted streets; now we glide quietly along wide boulevards lined with trees and filled with expensive Japanese cars. We pass shopping plazas, upscale hotels, and high-rise office buildings. Every block or so we see the gated entrance to an exclusive residential community with security guards standing watch. Here, in large, air-conditioned homes, the rich of Manila live—and many of the poor work.

Low-income nations are home to some rich and many poor people. The fact that most people live with incomes of a few

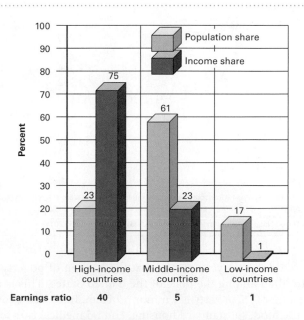

FIGURE 9–2 **The Relative Share of Income and Population by Level of Economic Development**

For every dollar earned by people in low-income countries, people in high-income countries earn $40.

Source: Based on Population Reference Bureau (2011) and United Nations Development Programme (2011).

TABLE 9-1 Wealth and Well-Being in Global Perspective, 2011

Country	Gross Domestic Product (US$ billions)	GDP per Capita (PPP US$)*	Quality of Life Index
High-Income			
Norway	415	58,278	.943
Australia	925	40,286	.929
United States	14,582	46,653	.910
Canada	1,574	39,035	.908
Sweden	458	36,139	.904
Japan	5,498	33,649	.901
South Korea	1,015	29,326	.897
United Kingdom	2,246	34,342	.863
Middle-Income			
Eastern Europe			
Bulgaria	48	11,547	.771
Albania	12	7,737	.739
Ukraine	138	6,591	.729
Latin America			
Cuba	63	9,700	.776
Ecuador	59	8,170	.720
Brazil	2,088	10,847	.718
Asia			
People's Republic of China	5,879	7,206	.687
Thailand	319	8,328	.682
India	1,729	3,354	.547
Middle East			
Iran	331	11,891	.707
Syria	59	4,857	.632
Africa			
Algeria	159	8,477	.698
Namibia	12	6,474	.625
Low-Income			
Latin America			
Haiti	7	1,040	.454
Asia			
Laos	7	2,404	.524
Cambodia	11	1,952	.523
Bangladesh	100	1,458	.500
Africa			
Ethiopia	30	991	.363
Guinea	5	1,037	.345
Democratic Republic of the Congo	13	327	.286

*These data are the United Nations' purchasing power parity (PPP) calculations, which avoid currency rate distortion by showing the local purchasing power of each domestic currency.

Source: United Nations Development Programme (2011) and World Bank (2011).

hundred dollars a year means that the burden of poverty is far greater than among the poor of the United States. This is not to suggest that U.S. poverty is a minor problem. In so rich a country, too little food, substandard housing, and no medical care for tens of millions of people—almost half of them children—amount to a national tragedy.

Read "The Global Economy and the Privileged Class" by Robert Perrucci and Earl Wysong on **mysoclab.com**

The Severity of Poverty

Poverty in poor countries is more severe than it is in rich countries. A key reason that quality of life differs so much around the world is that economic productivity is lowest in precisely the regions where population growth is highest. Figure 9–2 on page 229 shows the proportion of world population and global income for countries at each level of economic development. High-income countries are by far the most advantaged, with 75 percent of global income supporting just 23 percent of humanity. In middle-income nations, 61 percent of the world's people earn 23 percent of global income. This leaves 17 percent of the planet's population with just 1 percent of global income (Population Reference Bureau, 2011; World Bank, 2011). For every dollar received by an individual in a low-income country, someone in a high-income country takes home $40.

Table 9–1 shows the extent of wealth and well-being in specific countries around the world. The first column of figures gives the gross domestic product (GDP) for a number of high-, middle-, and low-income countries.[1] The United States, a large industrial nation, had a 2010 GDP of more than $14 trillion; Japan's GDP that same year was more than $5 trillion. A comparison of GDP figures shows that the world's richest nations are thousands of times more productive than the poorest countries.

The second column of figures in Table 9–1 divides GDP by the entire population size to give an estimate of what people can buy using their income in the local economy. The per capita GDP for the richest high-income countries, including the United States, Norway, and Australia, is very high, exceeding $40,000. For middle-income countries, the figures range from just over $3,000 in India to more than $10,000 in Brazil and more than $11,000 in Bulgaria. In the world's lowest-income countries, per capita GDP is less than a thousand dollars. In the Democratic Republic of the Congo or Ethiopia, a typical person labors all year to make what the average worker in the United States earns in a week.

The last column of Table 9–1 is a measure of quality of life in the various nations. This index, calculated by the United Nations, combines income, education (extent of adult literacy and average years of schooling), and longevity (how long people typically live). Index values are decimals that fall between extremes of 1 (highest) and 0 (lowest). By this calculation, Norwegians enjoy the highest quality of life (.943), with residents of the United States close behind (.910). At the other extreme, people in the African nation of the Democratic Republic of the Congo have the lowest quality of life (.286).

Relative versus Absolute Poverty

The distinction between relative and absolute poverty, made in Chapter 8 ("Social Stratification"), has an important application to global inequality. People living in rich countries generally focus on *relative poverty,* meaning that some people lack resources that are taken for granted by others. By definition, relative poverty exists in every society, rich or poor.

More important in global perspective, however, is *absolute poverty,* a lack of resources that is life-threatening. Human beings in absolute poverty lack the nutrition necessary for health and long-term survival. To be sure, some absolute poverty exists in the United States.

----

[1]Gross domestic product is the value of all the goods and services produced by a country's economy within its borders in a given year.

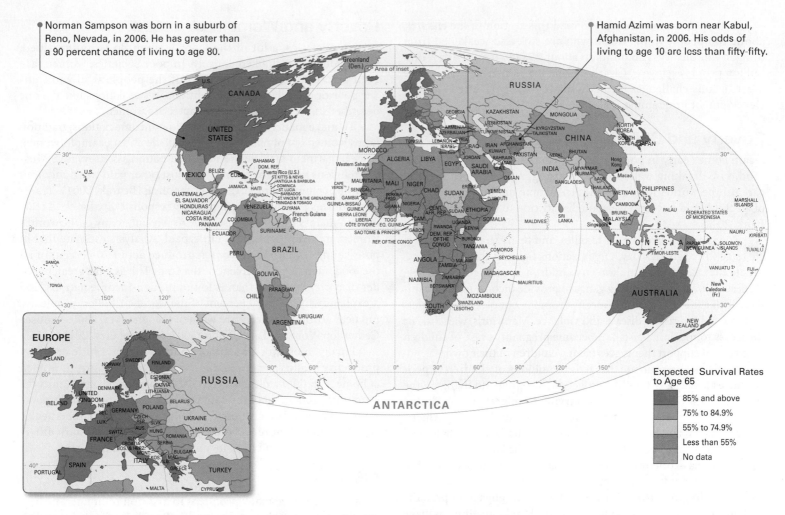

Norman Sampson was born in a suburb of Reno, Nevada, in 2006. He has greater than a 90 percent chance of living to age 80.

Hamid Azimi was born near Kabul, Afghanistan, in 2006. His odds of living to age 10 are less than fifty-fifty.

Expected Survival Rates to Age 65

- 85% and above
- 75% to 84.9%
- 55% to 74.9%
- Less than 55%
- No data

Window on the World

GLOBAL MAP 9–2 The Odds of Surviving to the Age of Sixty-Five in Global Perspective

This map identifies expected survival rates to the age of sixty-five for nations around the world. In high-income countries, including the United States, more than 85 percent of people live to this age. But in low-income nations, death often comes early, with just one-third of people reaching the age of sixty-five.

Source: United Nations (2009).

But such immediately life-threatening poverty strikes only a small proportion of the U.S. population; in low-income countries, by contrast, one-third or even half of the people are in desperate need.

Because absolute poverty is deadly, people in low-income nations face an elevated risk of dying young. Global Map 9–2 lets us explore this pattern by presenting the odds of living to the age of sixty-five that are typical for the nations of the world. In rich societies, more than 85 percent of people reach this age. In the world's poorest countries, however, the odds of living to age sixty-five are less than one in three, and two in ten children do not survive to the age of five (United Nations, 2009; UN Inter-agency Group for Child Mortality Estimation, 2010).

The Extent of Poverty

Poverty in poor countries is more widespread than it is in rich nations such as the United States. Chapter 8 ("Social Stratification") noted that the U.S. government officially classifies 15.1 percent of

the population as poor. In low-income countries, however, most people live no better than the poor in the United States, and many are far worse off. As Global Map 9–2 shows, the low odds of living to the age of sixty-five in the countries of sub-Saharan Africa indicate that absolute poverty is greatest there, where 27 percent of the population is malnourished. In the world as a whole, at any given time, 13 percent of the people—about 925 million—suffer from chronic hunger, which leaves them less able to work and puts them at high risk of disease (Chen & Ravallion, 2008; United Nations Food and Agriculture Organization, 2011).

The typical adult in the United States consumes about 3,750 calories a day, which is actually too much and leads to obesity and related health problems. The typical adult in a low-income country not only does more physical labor but consumes just 2,100 calories a day. The result is undernourishment: too little food or not enough of the right kinds of food (United Nations Food and Agriculture Organization, 2011).

In the ten minutes it takes to read this section of the chapter, about 100 people in the world who are sick and weakened from hunger will die. This amounts to about 25,000 people a day, or 9 million people each year. Clearly, easing world hunger is one of the most serious challenges facing humanity today (United Nations Development Programme, 2008).

Poverty and Children

Death comes early in poor societies, where families lack adequate food, safe drinking water, secure housing, and access to medical care. In the world's low- and middle-income nations, one-quarter of all children do not receive enough nutrition to be healthy (World Bank, 2011).

Poor children live in poor families, and many share in the struggle to get through each day. Organizations fighting child poverty estimate that at least 100 million city children in poor countries beg, steal, sell sex, or work for drug gangs to provide income for their families. Such a life almost always means dropping out of school and puts children at high risk of disease and violence. Many girls, with little or no access to medical assistance, become pregnant, a case of children who cannot support themselves having children of their own.

Analysts also estimate that tens of millions of children in poor countries leave their families altogether, sleeping and living on the streets as best they can or perhaps trying to migrate to the United States. Roughly half of all street children are found in Latin American cities such as Mexico City and Rio de Janeiro, where half of all children grow up in poverty. Many people in the United States know these cities as exotic travel destinations, but they are also home to thousands of children living in makeshift huts, under bridges, or in alleyways. In cities around the world, officials engage in periodic "urban cleansing," rounding up street children in an effort to make the city more attractive to high-income visitors (United Nations Development Programme, 2000; Collymore, 2002; Leopold, 2007; Thomas de Benitez, 2011).

Poverty and Women

In rich societies, a lot of the work women do is undervalued, underpaid, or overlooked entirely. In poor societies, women face even greater disadvantages. Most of the people who work under poor or even dangerous conditions in sweatshops like the one described in the opening to this chapter are women.

To make matters worse, in many low-income nations, tradition keeps women out of many jobs. In Bangladesh, for example, women work in garment factories because that nation's conservative Muslim religious norms bar them from most other paid work and limit their opportunities for advanced schooling (Bearak, 2001). Traditional norms also give women primary responsibility for child rearing and maintaining the household. As a result, many of the world's women are overworked and underpaid. Analysts estimate that in poor countries, although women produce about 70 percent of all the food, men own 90 percent of the land. This is a far greater gender disparity in wealth than is found in high-income nations, and it explains why about 70 percent of the world's 1 billion people living near absolute poverty are women (Moghadam, 2005; Landsea Center for Women's Land Rights, 2007; Hockenberry, 2011).

Finally, most women in poor countries receive little or no reproductive health care. Limited access to birth control keeps women at home with their children, keeps the birth rate high, and limits the economic production of the country. In addition, the world's poorest women typically give birth without help from trained health care personnel. Figure 9–3 on page 234 illustrates the stark difference between low- and high-income countries in this regard.

Slavery

Poor societies have many problems in addition to hunger, including illiteracy, warfare, and slavery. The British Empire banned slavery in 1833, followed by the United States in 1865. But slavery is a reality for at least 12.3 million men, women, and children, and as many as 215 million children are working as child laborers, half of whom are forced to do hazardous work (International Labour Organization, 2010, 2011; U.S. Department of Labor, 2011).

Anti-Slavery International (ASI) describes five types of slavery. First is *chattel slavery,* in which one person owns another. In spite of the fact that this practice is against the law almost everywhere, several million people fall into this category. The buying and selling of slaves—generally people of one ethnic or caste group enslaving members of another—still takes place in many countries throughout Asia, the Middle East, and especially Africa. In the African nation of Mauritania, perhaps 500,000 people are enslaved, which represents about 20 percent of the entire population. People who are enslaved are the property of another; they cannot own property themselves, nor can they even have custody of their own children (Fisher, 2011). The Thinking Globally box describes the reality of one slave's life in Mauritania.

Tens of millions of children fend for themselves every day on the streets of poor cities, where many fall victim to disease, drug abuse, and violence. What do you think should be done to ensure that children like these in Bangalore, India, receive adequate nutrition and a quality education?

"God Made Me to Be a Slave"

Fatma Mint Mamadou is a young woman living in North Africa's Islamic Republic of Mauritania. Asked her age, she pauses, smiles, and shakes her head. She has no idea when she was born. Nor can she read or write. What she knows is tending camels, herding sheep, hauling bags of water, sweeping, and serving tea to her owners. This young woman is one of perhaps 500,000 slaves in Mauritania.

In the central region of this nation, having very dark skin almost always means being a slave to an Arab owner. Fatma accepts her situation; she has known nothing else. She explains in a matter-of-fact voice that she is a slave, like her mother before her and her grandmother before that. "Just as God created a camel to be a camel," she shrugs, "he created me to be a slave."

Fatma, her mother, and her brothers and sisters live together in a squatter settlement on the edge of Nouakchott, Mauritania's capital city. Their home is a 9-by-12-foot hut that they built from wood scraps and other materials taken from construction sites. The roof is nothing more than a piece of cloth; there is no plumbing or furniture. The nearest water comes from a well a mile down the road.

In this region, slavery began more than 500 years ago, about the time Columbus sailed west toward the Americas. As Arab and Berber tribes moved across the African continent spreading Islam, they raided local villages and made slaves of the people, a practice that was continued for dozens of generations. In 1905, the French colonial rulers of Mauritania banned slavery. After the nation gained independence in 1961, the new government reaffirmed the ban.

Human slavery continues to exist in the twenty-first century.

However, slavery was not officially abolished until 1981, and even then, it was not made a crime. In 2007, the nation passed legislation making the practice of slavery punishable by up to ten years in prison, and the government now provides monetary compensation to victims of slavery. But the new laws have done little to change strong traditions. The sad truth is that people like Fatma still have no idea of the concept of "freedom to choose."

The next question is more personal: "Are you and other girls ever raped?" Again, Fatma hesitates. With no hint of emotion, she responds, "Of course, in the night the men come to breed us. Is that what you mean by rape?"

What Do You Think?

1. How does tradition play a part in keeping people in slavery?
2. What might explain the fact that the world still tolerates slavery?
3. Explain the connection between slavery and poverty.

Sources: Based on Burkett (1997) and Fisher (2011).

A second type of bondage is *slavery imposed by the state*. In this case, a government imposes forced labor on people for criminal violations or simply because the government needs their labor. In China, for example, people who are addicted to drugs or who engage in prostitution or other crimes are subject to forced labor. In North Korea, the government can force people to work for almost any reason at all.

A third and common form of bondage is *child slavery,* in which desperately poor families let their children take to the streets to do what they can to survive. The International Labour Organization estimates that 215 million children are at work, at least 115 million of whom are in forced and hazardous forms of labor. In 2011, the U.S. Department of Labor identified 130 goods—including cotton, sugarcane, tobacco, and coffee—produced in more than seventy-one nations with forced labor, mostly by children.

Fourth, *debt bondage* is the practice by which an employer pays wages to workers that are less than what the employer charges the workers for company-provided food and housing. Under such an arrangement, workers can never pay their debts so, for practical purposes, they are enslaved. Many sweatshop workers in low-income nations fall into this category.

Fifth, *servile forms of marriage* may also amount to slavery. In India, Thailand, and some African nations, families marry off women against their will. Many end up as slaves working for their husband's family; some are forced into prostitution.

An additional form of slavery is *human trafficking,* the moving of men, women, and children from one place to another for the purpose of performing forced labor. Women or men are brought to a new country with the promise of a job and then forced to become prostitutes or farm laborers. In other cases, "parents" adopt children from another country and then force them to work in sweatshops. Such activity is big business: Next to trading in guns and drugs, trading in people brings the greatest profits to organized crime around the world (Orhant, 2002; International Labour Organization, 2010; Anti-Slavery International, 2011; U.S. Department of Labor, 2011).

In 1948, the United Nations issued the Universal Declaration of Human Rights, which states, "No one shall be held in slavery or servitude; slavery and the slave trade shall be prohibited in all their forms." Unfortunately, more than six decades later, this social evil still exists.

Explanations of Global Poverty

What accounts for severe and widespread poverty in so much of the world? The rest of this chapter provides answers to this question using the following facts about poor societies:

1. **Technology.** About one-quarter of people in low-income countries farm the land using human muscles or animal power. With limited energy sources, agricultural production is modest.

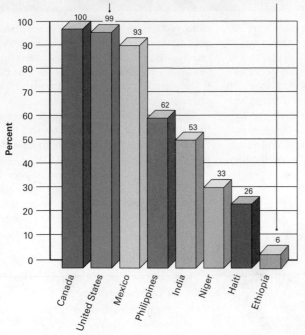

• Compared to a woman in the United States, an Ethiopian woman is far less likely to give birth with the help of medical professionals and is much more likely to die in childbirth.

Global Snapshot

FIGURE 9–3 Percentage of Births Attended by Skilled Health Staff

In the United States, most women give birth with the help of medical professionals, but this is usually not the case in low-income nations.

Source: World Bank (2010).

2. **Population growth.** As Chapter 15 ("Population, Urbanization, and Environment") explains, the poorest countries have the world's highest birth rates. Despite the death toll from poverty, the populations of poor countries in Africa double their numbers every twenty-five years. In sub-Saharan Africa, 43 percent of the people are under the age of fifteen. With such a large share of the population just entering the childbearing years, the wave of population growth will continue to roll into the future. For example, in recent years, the population of Uganda has swelled by an average of 5 percent annually, so even with economic development, living standards have fallen (Population Reference Bureau, 2011).

3. **Cultural patterns.** Poor societies are culturally traditional. People who hold to long-established ways of life resist change—even change that promises a richer material life.

---

colonialism the process by which some nations enrich themselves through political and economic control of other nations

neocolonialism a new form of global power relationships that involves not direct political control but economic exploitation by multinational corporations

4. **Social stratification.** Low-income nations distribute their wealth very unequally. Chapter 8 ("Social Stratification") explained that social inequality is greater in agrarian societies than in industrial societies. In Brazil, for example, 75 percent of all farmland is owned by just 4 percent of the people (Galano, 1998; Frayssinet, 2009).

5. **Gender inequality.** Extreme gender inequality in poor societies keeps women from holding jobs, which typically means they have many children. An expanding population, in turn, slows economic development. Many analysts conclude that raising living standards in much of the world depends on improving the social standing of women.

6. **Global power relationships.** A final cause of global poverty lies in the relationships between the nations of the world. Historically, wealth flowed from poor societies to rich nations through **colonialism**, *the process by which some nations enrich themselves through political and economic control of other nations.* The countries of Western Europe colonized much of Latin America beginning roughly 500 years ago. Such global exploitation allowed some nations to develop economically at the expense of other nations.

Although 130 former colonies gained their independence during the twentieth century, exploitation continues through **neocolonialism**, *a new form of global power relationships that involves not direct political control but economic exploitation by multinational corporations.* A **multinational corporation** is *a large business that operates in many countries.* Corporate leaders can impose their will on countries in which they do business to create favorable economic conditions, just as colonizers did in the past (Bonanno, Constance, & Lorenz, 2000).

Global Stratification: Applying Theory

● Apply

There are two major explanations for the unequal distribution of the world's wealth and power: *modernization theory* and *dependency theory.* Each theory suggests a different solution to the suffering of hungry people in much of the world.

Modernization Theory

Modernization theory is *a model of economic and social development that explains global inequality in terms of technological and cultural differences between nations.* Modernization theory, which follows the structural-functional approach, emerged in the 1950s, a time when U.S. society was fascinated with new developments in technology. To showcase the power of protective technology and also to counter the growing influence of the Soviet Union and socialism in much of the world, U.S. policymakers drafted a market-based foreign policy that has been with us ever since (Rostow, 1960, 1978; Bauer, 1981; Berger, 1986; Firebaugh, 1996; Firebaugh & Sandhu, 1998).

Historical Perspective

Until a few centuries ago, the entire world was poor. Because poverty has been the norm throughout human history, modernization theory proposes that it is *affluence* that demands an explanation.

Affluence came within reach of a growing share of people in Western Europe during the late Middle Ages as world exploration and trade expanded. Soon the Industrial Revolution was under way, transforming first Western Europe and then North America. Industrial technology, together with the spirit of capitalism, created new wealth as never before. At first, this new wealth benefited only a few individuals. But industrial technology was so productive that gradually the living standards of even the poorest people began to improve. Absolute poverty, which had plagued humanity throughout history, was finally in decline.

In high-income countries where the Industrial Revolution began, the standard of living jumped at least fourfold during the twentieth century. As middle-income nations in Asia and Latin America have industrialized, they too have become richer. But with limited industrial technology, low-income countries have changed much less.

The Importance of Culture

Why didn't the Industrial Revolution sweep away poverty the world over? Modernization theory points out that not every society wants to adopt new technology. Doing so takes a cultural environment that emphasizes the benefits of innovation as well as material wealth.

Modernization theory identifies *tradition* as the greatest barrier to economic development. A reverence for the past may discourage people from adopting new technologies that would raise their living standards. Even today, many people—from the Amish in North America to traditional Islamic people in the Middle East to the Semai of Malaysia—oppose new technology because they see it as a threat to their family relationships, customs, and religious beliefs.

Max Weber (1958, orig. 1904–1905) found that at the end of the Middle Ages, Western Europe's cultural environment favored change. As Chapter 13 ("Family and Religion") explains, the Protestant Reformation reshaped traditional Catholic beliefs to generate a progress-oriented way of life. Wealth—looked on with suspicion by the Roman Catholic Church—became a sign of personal virtue, and the growing importance of individualism steadily replaced the traditional emphasis on family and community. These new cultural patterns laid the groundwork for the Industrial Revolution.

Rostow's Stages of Modernization

Modernization theory holds that the door to affluence is open to all. As technological advances spread around the world, all societies should gradually industrialize. According to Walt Rostow (1960, 1978), modernization occurs in four stages:

1. **Traditional stage.** Socialized to honor the past, people in traditional societies cannot easily imagine that life can or should be any different. They therefore build their lives around families and local communities, following well-worn paths that allow little individual freedom or change. Life is often spiritually rich but lacking in material goods.

   A century ago, much of the world was in this initial stage of economic development. Nations such as Bangladesh, Niger, and Somalia are still at the traditional stage and remain poor. Even in countries such as India that have recently joined the ranks of middle-income nations, certain segments of the population have remained highly traditional. The Seeing Sociology in Everyday Life box on page 236 takes a look at traditional life in India.

2. **Take-off stage.** As a society shakes off the grip of tradition, people start to use their talents and imagination, sparking economic growth. A market emerges as people produce goods not just for their own use but also to trade with others for profit. Greater individualism, a willingness to take risks, and a desire for material goods also take hold, often at the expense of family ties and time-honored norms and values.

   Great Britain reached take-off by about 1800, the United States by 1820. Thailand, a middle-income country in eastern Asia, is now in this stage. Such development is typically speeded by progressive influences from rich nations, including foreign aid, the availability of advanced technology and investment capital, and opportunities for schooling abroad.

In rich nations such as the United States, most parents expect their children to enjoy their childhood years, largely free from the responsibilities of adult life. This is not the case in poor nations across Latin America, Africa, and Asia. Poor families depend on whatever income their children can earn, and many children as young as six or seven work full days weaving or performing other kinds of manual labor. Child labor lies behind the low prices of many products imported for sale in this country.

Although India has become a middle-income nation, its per capita GDP is only $3,354, about 7 percent as large as that in the United States. For this reason, India is home to more than one-quarter of the world's hungry people.

But most North Americans do not easily understand the reality of poverty in India. Many of the country's 1.2 billion people live in conditions far worse than those our society labels "poor." A traveler's first experience of Indian life can be shocking. Chennai (formerly known as Madras), for example, one of India's largest cities with 7 million inhabitants, seems chaotic to the outsider, with streets choked by motorbikes, trucks, carts pulled by oxen, and waves of people. Along the roadway, vendors sit on burlap cloths selling fruits, vegetables, and cooked food while people a few yards away work, talk, bathe, and sleep.

Although some people live well, Chennai is dotted by more than 1,000 shanty settlements, home to half a million people from rural villages who have come in search of a better life. Shantytowns are clusters of huts built with branches, leaves, and pieces of discarded cardboard and tin. These dwellings offer little privacy and lack refrigeration, running water, and bathrooms. A visitor from the United States may feel uneasy in such

an area, knowing that the poorest sections of our own inner cities seethe with frustration and sometimes explode with violence.

But India's people understand poverty differently than we do. No restless young men hang out at the corner, no drug dealers work the streets, and there is little danger of violence. In the United States, poverty often means anger and isolation; in India, even shantytowns are organized around strong families—children, parents, and often grandparents—who offer a smile of welcome to a stranger.

For traditional people in India, life is shaped by *dharma*, the Hindu concept of duty and destiny that teaches people to accept their fate, whatever

it may be. Mother Teresa, a Catholic nun who worked among the poorest of India's people, went to the heart of the cultural differences: "Americans have angry poverty," she explained. "In India, there is worse poverty, but it is a happy poverty."

Perhaps we should not describe anyone who clings to the edge of survival as happy. But the pain of poverty in India is eased by the strength and support of families and communities, a sense that life has a purpose, and a worldview that encourages each person to accept whatever life offers. As a result, a visitor may come away from a first encounter with Indian poverty rather confused: "How can people be so poor and yet seem content, active, and *joyful*?"

What Do You Think?

1. What did Mother Teresa mean when she said that in India there is "happy poverty"?

2. How might a visit to an Indian shantytown change the way members of a high-income society think of being "rich"?

3. Do you know of any poor people in the United States who have attitudes toward poverty similar to these people in India? What would make people seem to accept their poverty?

---

3. **Drive to technological maturity.** As this stage begins, "growth" is a widely accepted idea that fuels a society's pursuit of higher living standards. A diversified economy drives a population eager to enjoy the benefits of industrial technology. At the same time, people begin to realize (and sometimes regret) that industrialization is weakening traditional family and local community life. Great Britain entered this stage by about 1840, the United States by 1860. Today, Mexico, the U.S. territory of Puerto Rico, and Poland are among the nations driving to technological maturity.

At this stage of development, absolute poverty is greatly reduced. Cities swell with people who have left rural villages in search of economic opportunity. Specialization gives rise to the wide range of jobs that we find in our economy today. An increasing focus on work makes relationships less personal. Growing individualism generates social movements demanding greater political rights. Societies approaching technological maturity also provide basic schooling for all their people and advanced training for some. The newly educated consider tradition "backward" and push for further change. The social position of women steadily approaches that of men.

4. **High mass consumption.** Economic development continues to raise living standards as mass production stimulates mass consumption. Simply put, people soon learn to "need" the expanding array of goods that their society produces. The United States, Japan, Australia, and the nations of Western Europe entered this stage by 1900. Reaching this level of economic prosperity today are two former British colonies in eastern Asia: Hong Kong (part of the People's Republic of China since 1997) and Singapore (independent since 1965).

✳ **Explore** which areas of the United States have attracted large numbers of immigrants seeking the high standard of living available in a country at this stage of modernization on **mysoclab.com**

The Role of Rich Nations

Modernization theory claims that high-income countries play four important roles in global economic development:

1. **Controlling population increase.** Because population growth is greatest in the poorest societies, rising population can overtake economic advances. Rich nations can help limit population

increase by exporting birth control technology and promoting its use. Once economic development is under way, birth rates should decline, as they have in industrialized nations, because children are no longer an economic asset and now cost a great deal of money to raise.

2. **Increasing food production.** Rich nations can export high-tech farming methods to poor nations to help increase agricultural yields. Such techniques, collectively referred to as the Green Revolution, include new hybrid seeds, modern irrigation methods, chemical fertilizers, and pesticides for insect control.

3. **Introducing industrial technology.** Rich nations can encourage economic growth in poor societies by introducing machinery and information technology, which raise productivity. Industrialization also shifts the labor force from farming to skilled industrial and service jobs.

4. **Providing foreign aid.** Investment capital from rich nations can boost the prospects of poor societies trying to reach Rostow's take-off stage. Foreign aid can raise farm output by making it possible for poor countries to buy more fertilizer and build irrigation projects. In addition, financial and technical assistance to build power plants and factories improves industrial output. Each year, the United States provides about $34 billion in foreign aid to developing countries (U.S. Census Bureau, 2011).

🌑 **Evaluate** Modernization theory has many influential supporters among social scientists (Parsons, 1966; Moore, 1977, 1979; Berger, 1986; Firebaugh, 1996; Firebaugh & Sandu, 1998). For decades, it has shaped the foreign policy of the United States and other rich nations. Supporters point to rapid economic development in Latin America (especially Mexico), South America (especially Chile, Argentina, and Brazil), and Asia (especially South Korea, Taiwan, Singapore, and Hong Kong) as proof that the affluence created in Western Europe and North America is within the reach of all countries.

But modernization theory faces criticism from socialist countries (and left-leaning analysts in the West) as little more than a defense of capitalism. Its most serious flaw, according to critics, is that modernization has simply not occurred in many poor countries. The United Nations reported that living standards in a number of nations, including Haiti and Nicaragua in Latin America and Sudan, Ghana, and Rwanda in Africa, have changed little—and are in some cases worse today than they were in 1960 (United Nations Development Programme, 2008).

A second criticism of modernization theory is that it fails to recognize how rich nations, which benefit from the status quo, often block the path to development for poor countries. Centuries ago, rich countries industrialized from a position of global strength. Can we expect poor countries today to do so from a position of global weakness?

Third, modernization theory treats rich and poor societies as separate worlds, ignoring the fact that a single global economy affects all nations. Many countries in Latin America and Asia are still struggling to overcome the harm caused by colonialism, which boosted the fortunes of Europe.

Fourth, modernization theory holds up the world's most developed countries as the standard for judging the rest of humanity, revealing an ethnocentric bias. We need to remember that our Western idea of "progress" has caused us to rush headlong into a competitive, materialistic way of life, which uses up the world's scarce resources and pollutes the natural environment.

Fifth and finally, modernization theory suggests that the causes of global poverty lie almost entirely within the poor societies themselves. Critics see this analysis as little more than blaming the victims for their own problems. Instead, they argue, an analysis of global inequality should focus just as much on the behavior of rich nations as it does on the behavior of poor ones and also on the global economic system.

Concerns such as these reflect a second major approach to understanding global inequality, dependency theory.

CHECK YOUR LEARNING State the main ideas of modernization theory, including Rostow's four stages of economic development. Point to strengths and weaknesses of this theory.

Dependency Theory

Dependency theory is *a model of economic and social development that explains global inequality in terms of the historical exploitation of poor nations by rich ones.* This analysis, which follows the

Modernization theory claims that corporations that build factories in low-income nations help people by providing them with jobs and higher wages than they had before; dependency theory views these factories as "sweatshops" that exploit workers. In response to the Olympic Games selling sports clothing produced by sweatshops, these women staged a protest in Athens, Greece; they are wearing white masks to symbolize the "faceless" workers who make much of what we wear. Is any of the clothing you wear made in sweatshop factories?

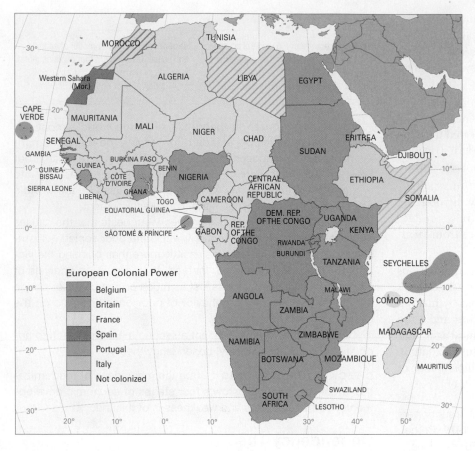

FIGURE 9–4 Africa's Colonial History

For more than a century, most of Africa was colonized by European nations, with France dominating in the northwest region of the continent and Great Britain dominating in the east and south.

establish colonies. They were so successful that a century ago, Great Britain controlled about one-fourth of the world's land, boasting that "the sun never sets on the British Empire." The United States, itself originally a patchwork of small British colonies on the eastern seaboard of North America, soon pushed across the continent, purchased Alaska, and gained control of Haiti, Puerto Rico, Guam, the Philippines, the Hawaiian Islands, and Guantanamo Bay in Cuba.

As colonialism spread, there emerged a brutal form of human exploitation—the international slave trade—from about 1500 until 1850. Even as the world was turning away from slavery, Europeans took control of most of the African continent, as Figure 9–4 shows, and dominated most of the continent until the early 1960s.

Formal colonialism has almost disappeared from the world. However, according to dependency theory, political liberation has not translated into economic independence. Far from it—the economic relationship between poor and rich nations continues the colonial pattern of domination. This *neocolonialism* is the heart of the capitalist world economy.

Wallerstein's Capitalist World Economy

Immanuel Wallerstein (1974, 1979, 1983, 1984) explains global stratification using a model of the "capitalist world economy." Wallerstein's term "world economy" suggests that the prosperity of some nations and the poverty and dependency of other countries result from a global economic system. He traces the roots of the global economy to the beginning of colonization more than 500 years ago, when Europeans began gathering wealth from the rest of the world. Because the global economy is based in high-income countries, it is capitalist in character (Frank, 1980, 1981; Delacroix & Ragin, 1981; Bergesen, 1983; Dixon & Boswell, 1996; Kentor, 1998).

Wallerstein calls the rich nations the *core* of the world economy. Colonialism enriched this core by funneling raw materials from around the world to Western Europe, where they fueled the Industrial Revolution. Today, multinational corporations operate profitably worldwide, channeling wealth to North America, Western Europe, Australia, and Japan.

Low-income countries are the *periphery* of the global economy. Drawn into the world economy by colonial exploitation, poor nations continue to support rich ones by providing inexpensive labor and a vast market for industrial products. The remaining countries are the *semiperiphery* of the world economy. They include middle-income countries such as India and Brazil that have closer ties to the global economic core.

According to Wallerstein, the world economy benefits rich societies (by generating profits for them) and harms the rest of the world (by causing poverty). The world economy thus makes poor nations dependent on rich ones. This dependency involves three factors:

social-conflict approach, puts primary responsibility for global poverty on rich nations, which for centuries have systematically impoverished low-income countries and made them dependent on the rich ones. This destructive process continues today.

Historical Perspective

Everyone agrees that before the Industrial Revolution, there was little affluence in the world. However, dependency theory asserts that people living in poor countries were actually better off economically in the past than their descendants are now. André Gunder Frank (1975), a noted supporter of this theory, argues that the colonial process that helped develop rich nations also *underdeveloped* poor societies.

Dependency theory is based on the idea that the economic positions of the rich and poor nations of the world are linked and cannot be understood apart from one another. Poor nations are not simply lagging behind rich ones on the "path of progress"; rather, the prosperity of the most developed countries came largely at the expense of less developed ones. In short, some nations became rich only because others became poor. Both are the result of the global economic system that began to take shape five centuries ago.

The Importance of Colonialism

Late in the fifteenth century, Europeans began surveying the Americas to the west, Africa to the south, and Asia to the east in order to

1. **Narrow, export-oriented economies.** Poor nations produce only a few crops for export to rich countries. Examples include

coffee and fruit from Latin American nations, oil from Nigeria, hardwoods from the Philippines, and palm oil from Malaysia. Today's multinational corporations buy raw materials cheaply in poor societies and transport them to core nations, where factories process them for profitable sale. Thus poor nations develop few industries of their own.

2. **Lack of industrial capacity.** Without an industrial base, poor societies face a double bind: They count on rich nations to buy their inexpensive raw materials, and they must then try to buy from the rich nations whatever expensive manufactured goods they can afford. In a classic example of this dependency, British colonialists encouraged the people of India to raise cotton but prevented them from weaving their own cloth. Instead, the British shipped Indian cotton to English textile mills in Birmingham and Manchester, manufactured the cloth, and shipped finished goods back to India, where the very people who harvested the cotton bought the garments.

   Dependency theorists claim that the Green Revolution—widely praised by modernization theorists—works the same way. Poor countries sell cheap raw materials to rich nations and then try to buy expensive fertilizers, pesticides, and machinery in return. Typically, rich countries profit from this exchange more than poor nations.

3. **Foreign debt.** Unequal trade patterns have plunged poor countries into debt. Collectively, the poor nations of the world owe rich countries some $3.5 trillion; hundreds of billions of dollars are owed to the United States alone. Such staggering debt paralyzes a country, causing high unemployment and rampant inflation (World Bank, 2011).

The Role of Rich Nations

Modernization theory and dependency theory assign very different roles to rich nations. Modernization theory holds that rich countries *produce wealth* through capital investment and new technology. Dependency theory views global inequality in terms of how countries *distribute wealth,* arguing that rich nations have *overdeveloped* themselves as they have *underdeveloped* the rest of the world.

Dependency theorists dismiss the idea that programs developed by rich countries to control population and boost agricultural and industrial output raise living standards in poor countries. Instead, they claim, such programs actually benefit rich nations and the ruling elites, not the poor majority, in low-income countries (Kentor, 2001).

Frances Moore Lappé and Joseph Collins (1986) maintain that the capitalist culture of the United States encourages people to think of poverty as somehow inevitable. In this line of reasoning, they explain, poverty results from "natural"

processes, including people having too many children, and from natural disasters such as droughts. But global poverty is far from inevitable; in their view, it results from deliberate government policies. Lappé and Collins point out that the world already produces enough food to allow every person on the planet to become quite fat. In fact, most of Africa actually exports food, even though many people in African nations go hungry.

According to Lappé and Collins, the contradiction of poverty amid plenty stems from the rich-nation policy of producing food for profit, not people. That is, corporations in rich nations cooperate with elites in poor countries to grow and export profitable crops such as coffee, which means using land that could otherwise produce basics such as beans and corn for local families. Governments of poor countries support the practice of growing for export because they need food profits to repay foreign debt. According to Lappé and Collins, the capitalist corporate structure of the global economy is at the core of this vicious cycle.

Evaluate The main idea of dependency theory is that no nation becomes rich or poor in isolation because a single global economy shapes the future of all nations. Pointing to continuing poverty in Latin America, Africa, and Asia, dependency theorists claim that development simply cannot proceed under the constraints now imposed by rich countries. Rather, they call for radical reform of the entire world economy so that it operates in the interests of the majority of people.

Critics charge that dependency theory wrongly treats wealth as if no one gets richer without someone else getting poorer. Farmers, small business owners, and corporations can and do create new wealth through hard work and imaginative use of new technology. After all, they point out, look at how the manufacturing that once took place in the United States now takes place in lower-income nations where it is helping what are now called "emerging markets" to expand. More broadly, they add, despite the fact that some have prospered more than others, how can there be a "zero sum" when the entire world's wealth has increased tenfold since 1950?

Although the world continues to grow richer, billions of people are being left behind. This shantytown of Cité Soleil, Haiti, is typical of many cities in low-income countries. What can you say about the quality of life in such a place?

Global Poverty

	Modernization Theory	Dependency Theory
Which theoretical approach is applied?	Structural-functional approach	Social-conflict approach
How did global poverty come about?	The whole world was poor until some countries developed industrial technology, which allowed mass production and created affluence.	Colonialism moved wealth from some countries to others, making some nations poor as it made other nations rich.
What are the main causes of global poverty today?	Traditional culture and a lack of productive technology.	Neocolonialism—the operation of multinational corporations in the global, capitalist economy.
Are rich countries part of the problem or part of the solution?	Rich countries are part of the solution, contributing new technology, advanced schooling, and foreign aid.	Rich countries are part of the problem, making poor countries economically dependent and in debt.

Second, dependency theory is wrong in blaming rich nations for global poverty because many of the world's poorest countries (such as Ethiopia) have had little contact with rich nations. On the contrary, a long history of trade with rich countries has dramatically improved the economies of nations including Sri Lanka, Singapore, and Hong Kong (all former British colonies), as well as South Korea and Japan. In short, say the critics, most evidence shows that foreign investment by rich nations encourages economic growth, as modernization theory claims, and not economic decline, as dependency theory holds (E. F. Vogel, 1991; Firebaugh, 1992).

Third, critics call dependency theory simplistic for pointing the finger at a single factor—the capitalist market system—as the cause of global inequality (Worsley, 1990). Dependency theory views poor societies as passive victims and ignores factors inside these countries that contribute to their economic problems. Sociologists have long recognized the vital role of culture in shaping people's willingness to embrace or resist change. Under the rule of the ultratraditional Muslim Taliban, for example, Afghanistan became economically isolated, and its living standards sank to among the lowest in the world. Is it reasonable to blame high-income, capitalist societies for that country's stagnation?

Nor can rich societies be held responsible for the reckless behavior of foreign leaders whose corruption and militarism impoverish their countries. Examples include the regimes of Ferdinand Marcos in the Philippines, François Duvalier in Haiti, Manuel Noriega in Panama, Mobutu Sese Seko in Zaire (today's Democratic Republic of the Congo), and Saddam Hussein in Iraq. Some leaders even use food supplies as weapons in internal political struggles, leaving the masses starving, as in the African nations of Ethiopia, Sudan, and Somalia. Likewise, many countries throughout the world have done little to improve the status of women or control population growth.

Fourth, critics say dependency theory is wrong to claim that global trade always makes rich nations richer and poor nations poorer. For example, in 2010, the United States had a trade deficit of $647 billion, meaning that this nation imports that much more goods than it sells abroad. Our country's single greatest debt was to China, whose profitable trade has now pushed that country into the ranks of the world's middle-income nations (U.S. Census Bureau, 2011).

Fifth, critics fault dependency theory for offering only vague solutions to global poverty. Most dependency theorists urge poor nations to end all contact with rich countries, and some call for nationalizing foreign-owned industries. In other words, dependency theory is really an argument for some sort of world socialism. In light of the difficulties that socialist countries (even better-off socialist countries such as Russia) have had in meeting the needs of their own people, critics ask, should we really expect such a system to rescue the entire world from poverty?

The Applying Theory table summarizes the main arguments of modernization theory and dependency theory.

CHECK YOUR LEARNING State the main ideas of dependency theory. What are several strengths and weaknesses of this theory?

Global Stratification: Looking Ahead

 Evaluate

Among the most important trends in recent decades is the development of a global economy. In the United States, rising production and sales abroad bring profits to many corporations and their stockholders, especially those who already have substantial wealth. At the same time, the global economy has moved manufacturing jobs abroad, closing factories in this country and hurting many average workers. The net result: greater economic inequality in the United States.

People who support the global economy claim that the expansion of trade results in benefits for all countries involved. For this reason, they endorse policies such as the North American Free Trade Agreement (NAFTA) signed by the United States, Canada, and Mexico, which took effect in 1994. Critics of expanding globalization make other claims: Manufacturing jobs are being lost in the United States, and more manufacturing now takes place abroad in factories where workers are paid little and few laws ensure workplace safety. In addition, other critics of expanding globalization point to the ever-greater stresses that our economy places on the natural environment.

But perhaps the greatest concern is the vast economic inequality that exists between the world's countries. The concentration of wealth in high-income countries, coupled with grinding poverty in low-income nations, may well be the biggest problem facing humanity in the twenty-first century.

Both modernization theory and dependency theory offer some understanding of this urgent problem. In evaluating these theories, we must consider empirical evidence. Over the course of the twentieth century, living standards rose in most of the world. Even the economic output of the poorest 25 percent of the world's people increased fourfold during those 100 years. As a result, the number of people living on less than $1.25 a day fell from about 1.9 billion in 1981 to about 1.4 billion in 2005 (Chen & Ravallion, 2008). In short, most people around the world are better off than ever before in *absolute* terms.

The greatest reduction in poverty has taken place in Asia, a region generally regarded as an economic success story. In 1981, almost 80 percent of global $1.25-per-day poverty was in East Asia; by 2005, that figure had fallen to 17 percent. Since then, two very large Asian countries—India and China—have joined the ranks of the middle-income nations. The economic growth in India and China has been so great that in the last two decades, global economic inequality has actually decreased as economic prosperity has spread from Europe and North America to Asia (Sala-i-Martin, 2002; Bussollo et al., 2007; Chen & Ravallion, 2008; Davies et al., 2008).

Latin America represents a mixed case. In the 1970s, this world region enjoyed significant economic growth; during the 1980s and 1990s, however, there was little overall improvement. The share of the global $1.25-per-day poverty was slightly higher in 2005 (3 percent) than it was in 1981 (2 percent) (Chen & Ravallion, 2008).

In Africa, about half of the nations are showing economic growth greater than in the past. In many countries, however, especially those south of the Sahara, the extent of extreme poverty has become worse. In 1981, sub-Saharan Africa accounted for 11 percent of $1.25-per-day poverty; by 2005, this share had risen to 28 percent (Sala-i-Martin, 2002; Chen & Ravillion, 2008).

Over the course of the last century, economic output has increased for both rich and poor nations. But this increase in output has not been at the same rate. As a result, in 2010, the gap between the rich and the poor in the world was almost six times bigger than it was back in 1900. Figure 9–5 shows that the poorest of the world's people are being left behind.

Recent trends suggest the need to look critically at both modernization theory and dependency theory. The fact that governments have played a large role in the economic growth that has occurred in Asia and elsewhere challenges modernization theory and its free-market approach to development. On the other hand, since the upheavals in the former Soviet Union and Eastern Europe, a global reevaluation of socialism has also been taking place. Because socialist nations have a record of poor economic performance and political repression, many low-income nations are unwilling to follow the advice of dependency theory and place economic development entirely under government control.

Although the world's future is uncertain, we have learned a great deal about global stratification. One major insight, offered by modernization theory, is that poverty is partly a *problem of technology*. A higher standard of living for a growing world population

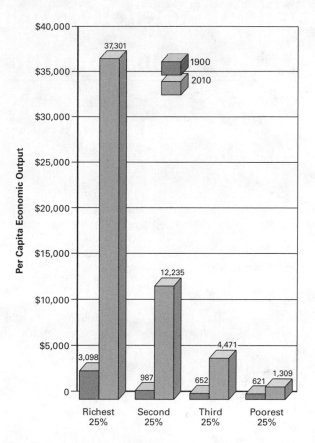

Global Snapshot

FIGURE 9–5 The World's Increasing Economic Inequality

The gap between the richest and poorest people in the world in 2010 was nearly six times bigger than it was in 1900.

Source: United Nations Development Programme (2010).

depends on the ability of poor nations to raise their agricultural and industrial productivity. A second insight, derived from dependency theory, is that global inequality is also a *political issue*. Even with higher productivity, the human community must address crucial questions concerning the distribution of resources, both within societies and around the globe.

Although economic development raises living standards, it also places greater strains on the natural environment. As nations such as India and China—with a combined population of 2.6 billion—become more affluent, their people will consume more energy and other natural resources. In fact, China now has the world's second largest economy, and this nation is now the world's largest market for new automobiles. China is also the second largest consumer of oil, which is one reason that global gasoline prices have been high. Richer nations, in which people consume more, also produce more solid waste and create more pollution.

Finally, the vast gulf that separates the world's richest and poorest people puts everyone at greater risk of war and terrorism as the poorest people challenge the social arrangements that threaten their existence (Lindauer & Weerapana, 2002). In the long run, it is probably true that we can achieve peace on this planet only by ensuring that all of the world's people enjoy a significant measure of dignity and security.

Seeing Sociology in Everyday Life

CHAPTER 9 **Global Stratification**

How much social inequality can we find if we look around the world?

This chapter explains that a global perspective reveals even more social stratification than we find here in the United States. Around the world, an increasing number of people in lower-income countries are traveling to higher-income nations in search of jobs. As "guest workers," they perform low-wage work that the country's own more well-off citizens do not wish to do. In such cases, the rich and poor truly live "worlds apart."

Hint Dubai's recent building boom has been accomplished using the labor of about 1 million guest workers, who actually make up about 85 percent of the population of the United Arab Emirates. Recent years have seen a rising level of social unrest, including labor strikes, which has led to some improvements in working and living conditions and better health care. But guest workers have no legal rights to form labor unions, nor do they have any chance to gain citizenship.

Many guest workers come to Dubai from India to take jobs building this country's new high-rise hotels and business towers. With very little income, they often sleep six to a small room. How do you think living in a strange country, with few legal rights, affects these workers' ability to improve their working conditions?

Oil wealth has made some of the people of Dubai, in the United Arab Emirates, among the richest in the world. Dubai's wealthiest people can afford to ski on snow—in one of the hottest regions of the world—on enormous indoor ski slopes like this one. Is there anything about this picture that makes you uncomfortable? Explain your reaction.

Guest workers in Dubai labor about twelve hours a day but earn only between $50 and $175 a month. Do you think the chance to take a job like this in a foreign country is an opportunity (income is typically twice what people can earn at home), or is it a form of exploitation?

Seeing Sociology in *Your* Everyday Life

1. What comparisons can you make between the pattern of guest workers coming to places like Dubai in the Middle East and workers coming to the United States from Mexico and other countries in Latin America?

2. Page through several issues of any current newsmagazine or travel magazine to find any stories or advertising mentioning lower-income countries (selling, say, coffee from Colombia or exotic vacations to India). What picture of life in low-income countries does the advertising present? In light of what you have learned in this chapter, how accurate does this image seem to you?

3. Have you ever traveled in a low-income nation? Do you think people from a high-income nation such as the United States should feel guilty when seeing the daily struggles of the world's poorest people? Why or why not? Go to the "Seeing Sociology in *Your* Everyday Life" feature on MySocLab to learn more about global stratification and also to read some suggestions for travelers who have the chance to interact with people in low-income nations.

Global Stratification: An Overview

High-Income Countries

- contain 23% of the world's people
- receive 75% of global income
- have a high standard of living based on advanced technology
- produce enough economic goods to enable their people to lead comfortable lives
- include 72 nations, among them the United States, Canada, Mexico, Argentina, Chile, the nations of Western Europe, Israel, Saudi Arabia, the Russian Federation, Japan, South Korea, Malaysia, and Australia **pp. 226–27**

Middle-Income Countries

- contain 61% of the world's people
- receive 23% of global income
- have a standard of living about average for the world as a whole
- include 70 nations, among them the nations of Eastern Europe, Peru, Brazil, Namibia, Egypt, Indonesia, India, and the People's Republic of China **pp. 227–28**

Low-Income Countries

- contain 17% of the world's people
- receive 1% of global income
- have a low standard of living due to limited industrial technology
- include 53 nations, generally in Central and East Africa and Asia, among them Chad, the Democratic Republic of the Congo, Ethiopia, and Bangladesh **pp. 228–29**

Watch the **Video** on **mysoclab.com**

global stratification (p. 224) patterns of social inequality in the world as a whole

high-income countries (p. 225) the nations with the highest overall standards of living

middle-income countries (p. 225) nations with a standard of living about average for the world as a whole

low-income countries (p. 225) nations with a low standard of living, in which most people are poor

Global Wealth and Poverty

All societies contain **relative poverty**, but low-income nations face widespread **absolute poverty** that is life-threatening.

- Worldwide, about 925 million people are at risk due to poor nutrition.
- About 9 million people die each year from diseases caused by poverty.
- Throughout the world, women are more likely than men to be poor. Gender bias is strongest in poor societies.
- As many as 12.3 million men, women, and children live in conditions that can be described as slavery, and estimates place upwards of 215 million children working as child laborers, many in hazardous conditions. **pp. 229–33**

Read the **Document** on **mysoclab.com**

Factors Causing Poverty

- Lack of technology limits production.
- High birth rates produce rapid population increase.
- Traditional cultural patterns make people resist change.
- Extreme social inequality distributes wealth very unequally.
- Extreme gender inequality limits the opportunities of women.
- Colonialism allowed some nations to exploit other nations; neocolonialism continues today. **pp. 233–34**

colonialism (p. 234) the process by which some nations enrich themselves through political and economic control of other nations

neocolonialism (p. 234) a new form of global power relationships that involves not direct political control but economic exploitation by multinational corporations

multinational corporation (p. 234) a large business that operates in many countries

Global Stratification: Applying Theory

Modernization theory maintains that nations achieve affluence by developing advanced technology. This process depends on a culture that encourages innovation and change toward higher living standards.

Walt Rostow identified four stages of development:

- *Traditional stage*—People's lives are built around families and local communities. (Example: Bangladesh)
- *Take-off stage*—A market emerges as people produce goods not just for their own use but to trade with others for profit. (Example: Thailand)
- *Drive to technological maturity*—The ideas of economic growth and higher living standards gain widespread support; schooling is widely available; the social standing of women improves. (Example: Mexico)
- *High mass consumption*—Advanced technology fuels mass production and mass consumption as people now "need" countless goods. (Example: the United States)   **pp. 234–36**

 **Explore the Map on mysoclab.com**

Modernization theory claims . . .

- Rich nations can help poor nations by providing technology to control population size, increase food production, and expand industrial and information economy output and by providing foreign aid to pay for new economic development.
- Rapid economic development in Asia shows that affluence is within reach of other nations of the world.   **pp. 236–37**

Critics claim . . .

- Rich nations do little to help poor countries and benefit from the status quo. Low living standards in much of Africa and South America result from the policies of rich nations.
- Because rich nations, including the United States, control the global economy, many poor nations struggle to support their people and cannot follow the path to development taken by rich countries centuries ago.   **p. 237**

Dependency theory maintains that global wealth and poverty were created by the colonial process beginning 500 years ago that overdeveloped rich nations and underdeveloped poor nations. This capitalist process continues today in the form of neocolonialism—economic exploitation of poor nations by multinational corporations.

Immanuel Wallerstein's model of the capitalist world economy identified three categories of nations:

- *Core*—the world's high-income countries, which are home to multinational corporations
- *Semiperiphery*—the world's middle-income countries, with ties to core nations
- *Periphery*—the world's low-income countries, which provide low-cost labor and a vast market for industrial products   **pp. 237–38**

Dependency theory claims . . .

- Three key factors—export-oriented economies, a lack of industrial capacity, and foreign debt—make poor countries dependent on rich nations and prevent their economic development.
- Radical reform of the entire world economy is needed so that it operates in the interests of the majority of people.   **pp. 238–39**

Critics claim . . .

- Dependency theory overlooks the tenfold increase in global wealth since 1950 and that the world's poorest countries have had weak, not strong, ties to rich countries.
- Rich nations are not responsible for cultural patterns and political corruption that block economic development in many poor nations.   **pp. 239–40**

modernization theory (p. 234) a model of economic and social development that explains global inequality in terms of technological and cultural differences between nations

dependency theory (p. 237) a model of economic and social development that explains global inequality in terms of the historical exploitation of poor nations by rich ones

245

10 Gender Stratification

Learning Objectives

Remember the definitions of the key terms highlighted in boldfaced type throughout this chapter.

Understand that gender is not a simple matter of biology but an idea created by society.

Apply sociology's major theoretical approaches to the concept of gender.

Analyze the ways in which gender is a dimension of social stratification.

Evaluate today's society using various feminist approaches.

Create a vision of a society in which women and men would have the same overall social standing.

CHAPTER OVERVIEW

We live in a world organized around not only the differences of social class but also around the concepts of feminine and masculine, which sociologists call "gender." This chapter examines gender, explores the meaning societies attach to being female or male, and explains why gender is an important dimension of social stratification. ■

At first we traveled quite alone . . . but before we had gone many miles, we came on other wagonloads of women, bound in the same direction. As we reached different cross-roads, we saw wagons coming from every part of the country and, long before we reached Seneca Falls, we were a procession.

So wrote Charlotte Woodward in her journal

as she made her way in a horse-drawn wagon along the rutted dirt roads leading to Seneca Falls, a small town in upstate New York. The year was 1848, a time when slavery was legal in much of the United States and the social standing of all women, regardless of color, was far below that of men. Back then, in much of the country, women could not own property, keep their own wages if they were married, draft a will, file lawsuits in a court (including lawsuits seeking custody of their own children), or attend college, and husbands were widely viewed as having unquestioned authority over their wives and children.

Some 300 women gathered at Wesleyan Chapel in Seneca Falls to challenge this second-class citizenship. They listened as their leader, Elizabeth Cady Stanton, called for expanding women's rights and opportunities, including the right to vote. At that time, most people considered such a proposal absurd and outrageous. Even many of those attending the conference were shocked by the idea: Stanton's husband, Henry, rode out of town in protest (Gurnett, 1998).

Much has changed since the Seneca Falls convention, and many of Stanton's proposals are now accepted as matters of basic fairness. But as this chapter explains, women and men still lead different lives in the United States and elsewhere in the world; in most respects, men are still in charge. This chapter explores the importance of gender and explains that gender, like class position, is a major dimension of social stratification.

Gender and Inequality

 Understand

Chapter 6 ("Sexuality and Society") explained that biological differences divide the human population into categories of female and male. **Gender** refers to *the personal traits and social positions that members of a society attach to being female or male.* Gender, then, is a dimension of social organization, shaping how we interact with others and even how we think about ourselves. More important, gender also involves *hierarchy,* placing men and women in different positions in terms of power, wealth, and other resources. This is why sociologists speak of

gender stratification, *the unequal distribution of wealth, power, and privilege between men and women.* In short, gender affects the opportunities and constraints we face throughout our lives.

Male-Female Differences

Many people think there is something "natural" about gender distinctions because biology does make one sex different from the other. But we must be careful not to think of social differences in biological terms. In 1848, for example, women were denied the vote because many people assumed that women did not have enough intelligence or any interest in politics. Such attitudes had nothing to do with biology; they reflected the *cultural* patterns of that time and place.

Another example is athletic performance. In 1925, most people—both women and men—believed that the best women runners could never compete with men in a marathon. Today, as Figure 10–1 shows, the gender gap has greatly narrowed, and the best women runners routinely post better times than the fastest men of decades past. Here again, most of the differences between men and women turn out to be socially created.

Differences in physical ability between the sexes do exist. On average, males are 10 percent taller than females, 20 percent heavier, and 30 percent stronger, especially in the upper body. On the other hand, women outperform men in the ultimate game of life itself: Life expectancy for men is 75.7 years, and women can expect to live 80.6 years (Ehrenreich, 1999; McDowell et al., 2008; Kochanek et al., 2011).

In adolescence, males do a bit better on the mathematics and reading parts of the SAT, while females show stronger writing skills, differences that reflect both biology and socialization (Lewin, 2008; College Board, 2011). However, research does not point to any overall differences in intelligence between males and females.

Biologically, then, men and women differ in limited ways, with neither one naturally superior. But culture can define the two sexes differently, as the global study of gender described in the next section shows.

Gender in Global Perspective

The best way to see how gender is based in culture is by comparing one society to another. Three important studies highlight just how different "masculine" and "feminine" can be.

The Israeli Kibbutz

In Israel, collective settlements are called *kibbutzim*. The *kibbutz* (the singular form of the word) has been an important setting for gender research because gender equality is one of its stated goals; men and women share in both work and decision making.

In recent decades, kibbutzim have become less collective and thus less distinctive organizations. But for much of their history, both sexes shared most everyday jobs. Many men joined women in taking care of children, and women joined men in repairing buildings and providing armed security. Both sexes made everyday decisions for the group. Girls and boys were raised in the same way; in many cases, young children were raised together in dormitories away from parents. Women and men in the kibbutzim achieved remarkable (although not complete) social equality, evidence that cultures define what is feminine and what is masculine.

Margaret Mead's Research

The anthropologist Margaret Mead carried out groundbreaking research on gender. If gender is based in the biological differences between men and women, she reasoned, people everywhere should define "feminine" and "masculine" in the same way; if gender is cultural, these concepts should vary.

Mead (1963, orig. 1935) studied three societies in New Guinea. In the mountainous home of the Arapesh, Mead observed men and women with remarkably similar attitudes and behavior. Both sexes, she reported, were cooperative and sensitive to others—in short, what our culture would label "feminine."

Moving south, Mead then studied the Mundugumor, whose headhunting and cannibalism stood in striking contrast to the

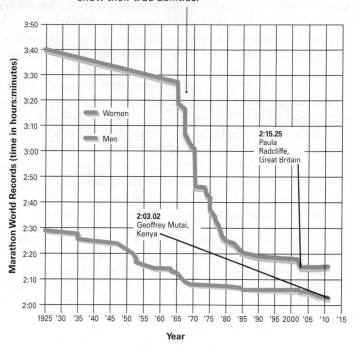

• The women's movement of the 1960s encouraged women to show their true abilities.

Diversity Snapshot

FIGURE 10–1 Men's and Women's Athletic Performance

Do men naturally outperform women in athletic competition? The answer is not obvious. Early in the twentieth century, men outpaced women by more than an hour in marathon races. But as opportunities for women in athletics have increased, women have been closing the performance gap. Only twelve minutes separate the current world marathon records for women (set in 2003) and for men (set in 2011).

Source: Marathonguide.com (2011).

gentle ways of the Arapesh. In this culture, both sexes were typically selfish and aggressive, traits we define as "masculine."

Finally, traveling west to the Tchambuli, Mead discovered a culture that, like our own, defined females and males differently. But, Mead reported, the Tchambuli *reversed* many of our ideas of gender: Females were dominant and rational, and males were submissive, emotional, and nurturing toward children. Based on her observations, Mead concluded that culture is the key to gender distinctions, because what one society defines as masculine another may see as feminine.

Some critics view Mead's findings as "too neat," as if she saw in these societies just the patterns she was looking for. Deborah Gewertz (1981) challenged what she called Mead's "reversal hypothesis," pointing out that Tchambuli males are really the more aggressive sex. Gewertz explains that Mead visited the Tchambuli (who themselves spell their name Chambri) during the 1930s, after they had lost much of their property in tribal wars, and observed men rebuilding their homes, a temporary role for Chambri men.

gender the personal traits and social positions that members of a society attach to being female or male

gender stratification the unequal distribution of wealth, power, and privilege between men and women

Watch the video "Similarities and Differences between Men and Women" on **mysoclab.com**

George Murdock's Research

In a broader study of more than 200 preindustrial societies, George Murdock (1937) found some global agreement on which tasks are feminine and which masculine. Hunting and warfare, Murdock observed, generally fall to men, and home-centered tasks such as cooking and child care tend to be women's work. With their simple technology, preindustrial societies apparently assign roles reflecting men's and women's physical characteristics. With their greater size and strength, men hunt game and protect the group; because women bear children, they do most of the work in the home.

Beyond this general pattern, Murdock found much variety. Consider agriculture: Women did the farming in about the same number of societies as men; in most societies, the two sexes divided this work. When it came to many other tasks, from building shelters to tattooing the body, Murdock found that preindustrial societies of the world were as likely to turn to one sex as the other.

⬤ Evaluate Global comparisons show that, overall, societies do not consistently define tasks as feminine or masculine. With industrialization, the importance of muscle power declines, further reducing gender differences (Nolan & Lenski, 2010). In sum, gender is too variable to be a simple expression of biology; what it means to be female and male is mostly a creation of society.

CHECK YOUR LEARNING By comparing many cultures, what do we learn about the origin of gender differences?

Patriarchy and Sexism

Conceptions of gender vary, and there is evidence of societies in which women have greater power than men. One example is the Musuo, a very small society in southwestern China's Yunnan province, in which women control most property, select their sexual partners, and make most decisions about everyday life. The Musuo appear to be a case of **matriarchy** ("rule by mothers"), *a form of social organization in which females dominate males*, which has only rarely been documented in human history.

The pattern found almost everywhere in the world is **patriarchy** ("rule by fathers"), *a form of social organization in which males*

dominate females. Global Map 10–1 shows the great variation in the relative power and privilege of women that exists from country to country. According to the United Nations' gender development index, Sweden, the Netherlands, and Denmark give women the highest social standing; by contrast, women in Mali, Niger, Chad, and Yemen have the lowest social standing compared with men. Of the world's 195 nations, the United States was ranked 47th in terms of gender equality (United Nations Development Programme, 2011).

The justification for patriarchy is **sexism**, *the belief that one sex is innately superior to the other.* Sexism is not just a matter of individual attitudes; it is built into the institutions of society. *Institutional sexism* is found throughout the economy, with women highly concentrated in low-paying jobs. Similarly, the legal system has long excused violence against women, especially on the part of boyfriends, husbands, and fathers.

The Costs of Sexism

Sexism limits the talents and the ambitions of the half of the human population who are women. Although men benefit in some respects from sexism, their privilege comes at a high price. Masculinity in our culture encourages men to engage in many high-risk behaviors: using tobacco and alcohol, playing dangerous sports, and even driving recklessly. As Marilyn French (1985) argues, patriarchy drives men to relentlessly seek control, not only of women but also of themselves and their world. Thus masculinity is linked not only to accidents but also to suicide, violence, and stress-related diseases. The *Type A personality*—marked by chronic impatience, driving ambition, competitiveness, and free-floating hostility—is one cause of heart disease and an almost perfect match with the behavior our culture considers masculine (Ehrenreich, 1983).

Finally, as men seek control over others, they lose opportunities for intimacy and trust. As one analyst put it, competition is supposed to "separate the men from the boys." In practice, however, it separates men from men and from everyone else (Raphael, 1988).

Must Patriarchy Go On?

In preindustrial societies, women have little control over pregnancy and childbirth, which limits the scope of their lives. In those same societies, men's

In every society, people assume that certain jobs, patterns of behavior, and ways of dressing are "naturally" feminine while others are just as obviously masculine. But in global perspective, we see remarkable variety in such social definitions. These men, Wodaabe pastoral nomads who live in the African nation of Niger, are proud to engage in a display of beauty most people in our society would consider feminine.

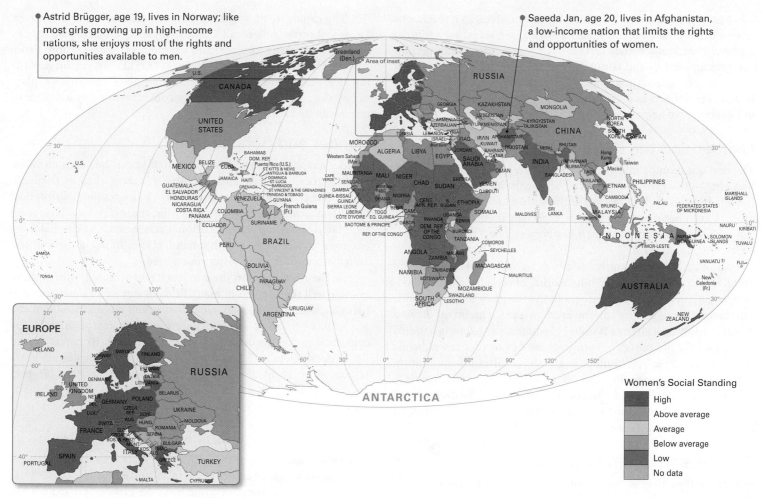

Astrid Brügger, age 19, lives in Norway; like most girls growing up in high-income nations, she enjoys most of the rights and opportunities available to men.

Saeeda Jan, age 20, lives in Afghanistan, a low-income nation that limits the rights and opportunities of women.

Women's Social Standing
- High
- Above average
- Average
- Below average
- Low
- No data

Window on the World

GLOBAL MAP 10–1 Women's Power in Global Perspective

Women's social standing in relation to men's varies around the world. In general, women live better in rich countries than in poor countries. Even so, some nations stand out: In Sweden, the Netherlands, and Denmark, women come closest to social equality with men.

Source: Data from United Nations Development Programme (2011).

---

greater height and physical strength are valued resources that give them power. But industrialization, including birth control technology, increases people's choices about how to live. In societies like our own, biological differences offer little justification for patriarchy.

But males are dominant in the United States and elsewhere. Does this mean that patriarchy is inevitable? Some researchers claim that biological factors such as differences in hormones and slight differences in brain structure "wire" the two sexes with different motivations and behaviors—especially aggressiveness in males—making patriarchy difficult or perhaps even impossible to change (S. Goldberg, 1974; Rossi, 1985; Popenoe, 1993b; Udry, 2000). However, most sociologists believe that gender is socially constructed and *can* be changed. The fact that no society has completely eliminated patriarchy does not mean that we must remain prisoners of the past.

To understand why patriarchy continues today, we must examine how gender is rooted and reproduced in society, a process that begins in childhood and continues throughout our lives.

Gender and Socialization

 **Understand**

From birth until death, gender shapes human feelings, thoughts, and actions. Children quickly learn that their society considers females and males different kinds of people; by about age three, they begin to think of themselves in these terms.

In the past, many people in the United States traditionally described women using terms such as "emotional," "passive," and "cooperative." By contrast, men were described as "rational," "active," and "competitive." It is curious that we were taught for so long to think of gender in terms of one sex being opposite to the other, especially because women and men have so much in common and also because research suggests that most people develop personalities that are a mix of feminine and masculine traits (Bem, 1993).

Just as gender affects how we think of ourselves, so it teaches us how to behave. **Gender roles** (also known as **sex roles**) are *attitudes and activities that a society links to each sex*. A culture that defines males as ambitious and competitive encourages them to seek out positions of leadership and play team sports. To the extent that females are defined as deferential and emotional, they are expected to be supportive helpers and quick to show their feelings.

Gender and the Family

The first question people usually ask about a newborn—"Is it a boy or a girl?"—has great importance because the answer involves not just sex but the likely direction of the child's life. In fact, gender is at work even before a child is born, especially in lower-income nations, because parents hope their firstborn will be a boy rather than a girl (Pappas, 2011).

Soon after birth, family members welcome infants into the "pink world" of girls or the "blue world" of boys (Bernard, 1981). People even send gender messages in the way they handle infants. One researcher at an English university presented an infant dressed as either a boy or a girl to a number of women; her subjects handled the "female" child tenderly, with frequent hugs and caresses, while treating the "male" child more aggressively, often lifting him up high in the air or bouncing him on a knee (Bonner, 1984; Tavris & Wade, 2001). The lesson is clear: The female world revolves around cooperation and emotion, and the male world puts a premium on independence and action.

Gender and the Peer Group

About the time they enter school, children begin to move outside the family and make friends with others of the same age. Considerable research points to the fact that young children tend to form single-sex play groups (Martin & Fabes, 2001).

Peer groups teach additional lessons about gender. After spending a year watching children at play, Janet Lever (1978) concluded that boys favor team sports with complex rules and clear objectives such as scoring runs or making touchdowns. Such games nearly always have winners and losers, reinforcing masculine traits of aggression and control.

Girls, too, play team sports. But, Lever explains, girls also play hopscotch, jump rope, or simply talk, sing, or dance. These activities have few rules, and rarely is victory the ultimate goal. Instead of teaching girls to be competitive, Lever explains, female peer groups promote the interpersonal skills of communication and cooperation, presumably the basis for girls' future roles as wives and mothers.

Sex is a biological distinction that develops prior to birth. Gender is the meaning that a society attaches to being female or male. Gender differences are a matter of power, because what is defined as masculine typically has more importance than what is defined as feminine. Infants begin to learn the importance of gender by the way parents treat them. Do you think this child is a girl or a boy? Why?

The games we play offer important lessons for our later lives. Lever's observations recall Carol Gilligan's gender-based theory of moral reasoning, discussed in Chapter 3 ("Socialization: From Infancy to Old Age"). Boys, Gilligan (1982) claims, reason according to abstract principles. For them, "rightness" amounts to "playing by the rules." By contrast, girls consider morality a matter of responsibility to others.

Gender and Schooling

Gender shapes our interests and beliefs about our own abilities, guiding areas of study and, eventually, career choices (Correll, 2001). The types of courses people take in high school still reflect traditional gender patterns. For example, more girls than boys learn secretarial skills and take vocational classes such as cosmetology and food services. On the other hand, classes in woodworking and auto mechanics attract mostly young men.

As their numbers on the campus have increased, women have become well represented in many fields of study that once excluded them, including mathematics, chemistry, and biology. But men still predominate in many fields, including engineering (earning 82 percent of all bachelor's degrees), computer science (82 percent), and the physical sciences (59 percent). Women tend to cluster in library science (90 percent of all bachelor's degrees), education (79 percent), psychology (77 percent), and sociology (52 percent) (National Center for Education Statistics, 2011).

Gender and the Mass Media

Since television captured the public imagination in the early 1950s, white males have held center stage; racial and ethnic minorities were all but absent from television until the early 1970s. Even when both sexes appeared on camera, men generally played the brilliant detectives, fearless explorers, and skilled surgeons. Women played the less capable characters, often unnecessary except for the sexual interest they added to the story. In recent years, more women have taken starring roles, but female stars earn less than their male counterparts. Before he left the show *Two and a Half Men*, for example, Charlie Sheen was the highest-paid male television actor, earning $875,000 an episode. Mariska Hargitay has been the highest-paid female actor, earning $400,000 an episode for *Law & Order: SVU*.

Historically, advertisements have shown women in the home, cheerfully using cleaning products, serving food, trying out appliances, and modeling clothes. Men predominate in ads for cars, travel, banking services, industrial companies, and alcoholic beverages. The authoritative voiceover—the voice that describes a product on television and radio—is almost always male (D. M. Davis, 1993; Coltrane & Messineo, 2000; Messineo, 2008).

A careful study of gender in advertising reveals that men usually appear taller than women, implying male superiority. Women, by contrast, are more frequently presented lying down (on sofas and beds) or, like

In our society, the mass media have enormous influence on our attitudes and behavior, and what we see shapes our views of gender. In the 2009 film *Twilight,* we see a strong, "take charge" male playing against a more passive female. Do you think the mass media create these gender patterns? Or it is more correct to say that they reproduce them? Is there another option?

children, seated on the floor. Men's facial expressions and behavior give off an air of competence and imply dominance; women often appear childlike, submissive, and sexual. Men focus on the products being advertised, and women often focus on the men (Goffman, 1979; Cortese, 1999).

Advertising also perpetuates what Naomi Wolf (1990) calls the "beauty myth." The Seeing Sociology in Everyday Life box on page 254 takes a closer look at how this myth affects both women and men.

Gender and Social Stratification

● Apply

Gender involves more than how people think and act. It is also about how society is organized, how our lives are affected by social hierarchy. The reality of gender stratification can be seen in just about every aspect of our everyday lives. We look, first, to the world of working women and men.

Working Women and Men

In 1900, just 20 percent of women but 80 percent of men were in the U.S. labor force. Today, the share of women has tripled, to almost 60 percent, while the share of men has fallen to 71 percent. In addition, 67 percent of working women and 78 percent of working men work full time. From another angle, 47 percent of all U.S. jobs are held by women, and 53 percent are held by men (U.S. Department of Labor, 2011). Any way you look at it, the once common view that earning income is a man's role no longer holds true.

Factors that have contributed to change in the U.S. labor force include the decline of farming, the growth of cities, shrinking family size, and a rising divorce rate. In the United States, along with most other nations of the world, women working for income is now the rule rather than the exception. Women make up almost half the U.S. paid labor force, and 53 percent of U.S. married couples depend on two incomes.

In the past, many younger women in the labor force were childless. But today, 59 percent of married women with children under age six are in the labor force, as are 71 percent of married women with children between six and seventeen years of age. For widowed, divorced, or separated women with children, the comparable figures are 60 percent of women with younger children and 72 percent of women with older children (U.S. Department of Labor, 2011).

Gender and Occupations

Although women are closing the gap with men as far as working for income is concerned, the work done by the two sexes remains very different. The U.S. Department of Labor (2011) reports a high concentration of women in two types of jobs. Administrative support work draws 23 percent of working women, most of whom are secretaries or other office workers. These are called "pink-collar jobs" because 74 percent are filled by women. Another 16 percent of employed women perform service work. Most of these jobs are in the food service industries, child care, and health care.

Table 10–1 shows the ten occupations with the highest concentrations of women. These jobs tend to be at the low end of the pay scale, with limited opportunities for advancement and with men as supervisors (U.S. Department of Labor, 2011).

Men dominate most other job categories, including the building trades, where 99 percent of brickmasons, stonemasons, and heavy-equipment mechanics are men. Likewise, men make up 87 percent of engineers, 87 percent of police officers, 69 percent of lawyers, 68 percent of physicians and surgeons, and 57 percent of corporate managers. According to a recent survey, just 16 of the *Fortune* 500 companies in the United States have a woman as their chief executive officer, and just 16 percent of the seats on corporate boards of directors are held by women. Only one of the twenty-five highest-paid business executives in the United States is a woman. Even so, increasing the leadership role of women in the business world is not just a matter of fairness; research into the earnings of this country's 500 largest corporations showed that the companies with more women on the board also are the most profitable (Graybow, 2007; Loomis, 2007; U.S. Department of Labor, 2011; Catalyst, 2011; *Fortune*, 2011).

Gender stratification in everyday life is easy to see: Female nurses assist male physicians, female secretaries serve male executives, and female flight attendants are under the command of male

TABLE 10–1 Jobs with the Highest Concentrations of Women, 2010

Occupation	Number of Women Employed	Percentage in Occupation Who Are Women
1. Dental assistant	289,000	97.5
2. Preschool or kindergarten teacher	691,000	97.0
3. Speech-language pathologist	127,000	96.3
4. Secretary or administrative assistant	2,962,000	96.1
5. Dental hygienist	134,000	95.1
6. Child care worker	1,181,000	94.7
7. Receptionist or information clerk	1,188,000	92.7
8. Word processor or typist	133,000	92.5
9. Teacher assistant	893,000	92.4
10. Dietitian and nutritionist	97,000	92.3

Source: U.S. Department of Labor (2011).

The Beauty Myth

Beth: "I can't eat lunch. I need to be sure I can get into that black dress for tonight."

Sarah: "Maybe eating is more important than looking good for Tom."

Beth: "That's easy for you to say. You're a size 2, and Jake adores you!"

The Duchess of Windsor once remarked, "A woman cannot be too rich or too thin." The first half of her observation might apply to men as well, but certainly not the second. After all, the vast majority of ads placed by the $10-billion-a-year U.S. cosmetics industry and the $60-billion diet industry target women.

According to Naomi Wolf (1990), certain cultural patterns add up to a "beauty myth" that is damaging to women. First, the foundation of the beauty myth is the notion, taught from an early age, that women should measure their worth in terms of physical appearance or, more specifically, how physically attractive they are *to men*. Of course, the standards of beauty embodied by the *Playboy* centerfold or the 100-pound New York fashion model are out of reach for most women.

Second, our society teaches women to prize relationships with men, whom they presumably attract with their beauty. Striving for beauty not only drives women to be extremely disciplined but also forces them to be highly attentive to and responsive to men. In short, beauty-minded women try to please men and avoid challenging male power.

Belief in the beauty myth is one reason that so many young women are focused on body image, particularly being as thin as possible, often to the point of endangering their health. During the past

One way our culture supports the beauty myth is through beauty pageants for women; over the years, contestants have become thinner and thinner.

several decades, the share of young women who develop an eating disorder such as anorexia nervosa (dieting to the point of starvation) or bulimia (binge eating followed by vomiting) has risen dramatically.

The beauty myth, then, is the idea that striving to be physically attractive to men is the key to women's happiness. As Wolf sees it, however, such efforts are more likely to end up standing between women and their power and worthwhile accomplishments.

The beauty myth affects males as well: Men are told repeatedly that they should want to possess beautiful women. Such ideas about beauty reduce women to objects and motivate thinking about women as if they were dolls rather than human beings.

There can be little doubt that the idea of beauty is important in everyday life. According to Wolf, the question is whether beauty is about how we look or how we act.

What Do You Think?

1. Is there a "money myth" that states that people's income is a simple reflection of their talent? Does it apply more to one sex than to the other?

2. Can you see a connection between the beauty myth and the rise of eating disorders among young women in the United States?

3. Among people with physical disabilities, do you think that issues of "looking different" are more serious for women or for men? Why?

---

airline pilots. In any field, the greater a job's income and prestige, the more likely it is to be held by a man. For example, women represent 97 percent of kindergarten teachers, 82 percent of elementary and middle school teachers, 57 percent of secondary school educators, 46 percent of professors in colleges and universities, and 23 percent of college and university presidents (*Chronicle of Higher Education*, 2007; U.S. Department of Labor, 2011).

How are women kept out of certain jobs? By defining some kinds of work as "men's work," society defines women as less competent than men. In a study of coal mining in southern West Virginia, Suzanne Tallichet (2000) found that most men considered it "unnatural" for women to work in the mines. Women who did so were defined as deviant and subject to labeling as "sexually loose" or as lesbians. Such labeling made these women outcasts, presented a challenge to holding the job, and made advancement all but impossible.

In the corporate world, too, the higher in the company we look, the fewer women we find. You hardly ever hear anyone say out loud

Read "Maid to Order: The Politics of Other Women's Work" by Barbara Ehrenreich on **mysoclab.com**

that women don't belong at the top levels of a company. But many people seem to feel this way, which can prevent women from being promoted. Sociologists describe this barrier as a *glass ceiling* that is not easy to see but blocks women's careers all the same.

One challenge to male domination in the workplace comes from women who are entrepreneurs. In 2008, there were more than 10 million woman-owned businesses in the United States, double the number of a decade ago; they employed more than 13 million people and generated $2 trillion in sales. By starting their own businesses, women have shown that they can make opportunities for themselves apart from large, male-dominated companies (Center for Women's Business Research, 2009).

Gender and Unemployment

The unemployment rates for women and men typically rise and fall together, with men having a slightly higher level of joblessness. By the end of 2011, the unemployment rate for adult women stood at 7.9 percent, below the figure of 8.4 percent for adult men (U.S. Department of Labor, 2011).

High unemployment among men reflects the fact that men's work is heavily in manufacturing, and many factory jobs have moved abroad. But during the recent recession, there have also been job losses in the administrative support and service jobs that are held mostly by women. During the last two years, as the nation has struggled to climb out of recession, the unemployment rate for men has fallen faster than the rate among women (Kochlar, 2011; U.S. Department of Labor, 2011).

Gender, Income, and Wealth

In 2010, the median earnings for women working full time were $36,931, and men working full time earned $47,715. This means that for every dollar earned by men, women earned about 77 cents. These earnings differences are greatest among older workers because older working women typically have less education and seniority than older working men. Earning differences are smaller among younger workers because younger men and women tend to have similar schooling and work experience.

Among all full-time workers of all ages, 24 percent of women earned less than $25,000 in 2010, compared with 15 percent of comparable men. At the upper end of the income scale, men were twice as likely as women (24 percent versus 12 percent) to earn more than $75,000 (U.S. Census Bureau, 2011).

The main reason women earn less is the *type* of work they do: largely clerical and service jobs. In effect, jobs and gender interact. People still perceive jobs with less clout as "women's work," just as people devalue certain work simply because it is performed by women (England, Hermsen, & Cotter, 2000; Cohen & Huffman, 2003).

In recent decades, supporters of gender equality have proposed a policy of "comparable worth," paying people not according to the historical double standard but according to the level of skill and responsibility involved in the work. As an example of the problem, consider the case of floral designers, the people who make attractive displays of flowers. These workers—most of whom are women—earn about $12 an hour. At the same time, the people who drive the vans and other small trucks to deliver these flower arrangements—most of whom are men—earn about $15.45 an hour (U.S. Bureau of Labor Statistics, 2010). It is hard to see why floral arrangers would earn just 78 percent as much as van drivers. Is there a difference in the level of skill or training required? Or does the disparity reflect gender stratification?

In response to such patterns, several nations, including Great Britain and Australia, have adopted comparable worth policies, but these policies have found limited acceptance in the United States. As a result, women in this country lose as much as $1 billion in income annually.

A second cause of gender-based income disparity has to do with society's view of the family. Both men and women have children, of course, but our culture gives more of the responsibility of parenting to women. Pregnancy and raising small children keep many younger women out of the labor force at a time when their male peers are making significant career advancements. When women workers return to the labor force, they have less job experience and seniority than their male counterparts (Stier, 1996; Waldfogel, 1997).

In addition, women who choose to have children may be unable or unwilling to take on fast-paced jobs that tie up their evenings and weekends. To avoid role strain, they may take jobs that offer shorter commuting distances, more flexible hours, and employer-provided child care services. Women pursuing both a career and a family are torn between their dual responsibilities in ways that men are not. One study found that almost half of women in competitive jobs took time off to have children, compared to about 12 percent of men. Similarly, later in life, women are more likely than men to take time off from work to care for aging parents (Hewlett, 2005; Hewlett & Luce, 2010). Role conflict is also experienced by women on campus: Several studies confirm that young female professors with at least one child are less likely to have tenure than comparable men in the same field (Shea, 2002; Ceci & Williams, 2011).

The two factors noted so far—type of work and family responsibilities—account for about two-thirds of the earnings difference between women and men. A third factor—discrimination against women—accounts for most of the remainder (Fuller & Schoenberger, 1991). Because overt discrimination is illegal, it is practiced in subtle ways. Women on their way up the corporate ladder often run into the glass ceiling described earlier; company officials may deny its existence, but it effectively prevents many women from rising above middle management.

For all these reasons, women earn less than men in all major occupational categories. Even so, many people think that women own most of the country's wealth, perhaps because women typically outlive men. Government statistics tell a different story: Fifty-seven percent of people with $1.5 million or more in assets are men, although widows are highly represented in this elite club (Johnson & Raub,

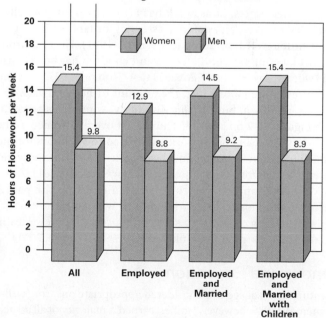

● On average, women spend considerably more time doing housework than men.

Diversity Snapshot

FIGURE 10–2 Housework: Who Does How Much?

Regardless of employment or family status, women do more housework than men. What effect do you think the added burden of housework has on women's ability to advance in the workplace?

Source: U.S. Bureau of Labor Statistics (2011).

Gender Today: Are *Men* Being Left Behind?

Looking around the college campus, it would be easy to think that gender stratification favors females. The latest data show that 57 percent of college students are women and, because they are more likely to complete their program of study, women earn 59 percent of all associate and bachelor's degrees. In addition, on most campuses, when it comes to academic awards, women are overly represented among the winners.

As many analysts see it, the pattern of women outperforming men is not limited to college. In the early grades, boys are twice as likely as girls to be diagnosed with a learning disability, receive prescribed medication, or be placed in a special education class. Most disciplinary problems in the schools involve boys; just about all the school shootings and other acts of serious violence are carried out by boys. Boys earn grades that fall below those earned by girls. Later on, a smaller share of boys will graduate from high school. Even the suicide rate for young men is almost five times higher than that for young women. Taken together, such data have led some people to charge that our society has launched a war on boys.

So what's happening to the men? One argument is that the rise of feminism has directed a great deal of support and attention to girls and women, ignoring the needs of boys and men. Others claim that too many boys suffer from the absence of a father in their lives; girls can use their mothers as role models but what are fatherless boys to do? Still others suggest that our industrial way of life (which favored masculine strength and skills manipulating objects) has given way to an information-age culture that is far more verbal, favoring females.

Not everyone is convinced that boys and men are so bad off. It is true that most violent crime involves males, but for the last fifteen years crime rates have fallen. Girls may be outperforming boys in the classroom and on some standardized tests, but the scores boys earn have never been higher. And, when all is said and done, don't men still run the country? And the whole world?

Join the Blog!

Are males being left behind? What do *you* think? Go to MySocLab and join the Sociology in Focus blog to share your opinions and experiences and to see what others think.

Sources: Sommers (2000), von Drehle (2007), Lamm (2010), and Paton (2010).

2006; Internal Revenue Service, 2008). Just 10 percent of the people identified by *Forbes* magazine as the richest people in the United States in 2011 were women (*Forbes*, 2011).

Housework: Women's "Second Shift"

In the United States, housework has always presented a cultural contradiction: We claim that it is essential for family life, but people get little reward for doing it (Bernard, 1981). Here, as around the world, taking care of the home and children has been considered "women's work" (see Global Map 4–1 on page 92). As women have entered the labor force, the amount of housework women do has gone down, but the *share* done by women has stayed the same. Figure 10–2 on page 255 shows that overall, women average 15.4 hours a week of housework, compared to 9.8 hours for men. As the figure shows, women in all categories do significantly more housework than men (U.S. Bureau of Labor Statistics, 2011).

Men do support the idea of women entering the paid labor force, and most count on the money women earn. But many men resist taking on an equal share of household duties (Heath & Bourne, 1995; Harpster & Monk-Turner, 1998; Stratton, 2001).

Gender and Education

A century ago, college was considered appropriate only for (well-to-do) men. By 1980, however, women earned a majority of all associate and bachelor's degrees. In 2009, women were a majority (57 percent) of the students on college and university campuses across the United States, earning 59 percent of all associate and bachelor's degrees (National Center for Education Statistics, 2011).

According to recent research, women have a more positive view of the value of a college degree compared to men. This is a gender-linked difference that holds among all major racial and ethnic categories. As a result, among U.S. adults between the ages of twenty-five and twenty-nine, 36 percent of women have completed a four-year college degree, compared to just 28 percent of men (Wang & Parker, 2011).

As college doors have opened wider to women in recent decades, differences in men's and women's majors have become smaller. In 1970, for example, women accounted for just 17 percent of bachelor's degrees in the natural sciences, computer science, and engineering; by 2009, the proportion had more than doubled to 36 percent.

In 1992, for the first time, women earned a majority of postgraduate degrees, which are often a springboard to high-prestige jobs. In all areas of study in 2009, women earned 60 percent of all master's degrees and 52 percent of all doctorates (including 60 percent of all Ph.D. degrees in sociology). Women have also broken into many graduate fields that used to be almost all male. For example, in 1970, only a few hundred women received a master's of business administration (M.B.A.) degree, compared to more than 76,000 women in 2009 (45 percent of all such degrees) (National Center for Education Statistics, 2011).

Despite this progress, men still predominate in some professional fields. In 2009, men received 54 percent of law degrees (LL.B. and J.D.), 51 percent of medical degrees (M.D.), and 54 percent of dental degrees (D.D.S. and D.M.D.) (National Center for Education Statistics, 2011). Many people in our society may still define high-paying professions (and the drive and competitiveness needed to succeed in them) as masculine. But the share of women in all these professions has risen and is now close to half. When will statistical parity be reached? Probably not for at least a few more years. For example, the American Bar Association (2011) reports that in 2010, men still accounted for 53 percent of law school students across the United States.

Based on the educational gains women have made, some analysts suggest that education is the one social institution where women rather than men predominate. More broadly, women's relative advantages in school performance have prompted a national debate about whether men are in danger of being left behind. The Sociology in Focus box takes a closer look.

Gender and Politics

A century ago, almost no women held elected office in the United States. In fact, women were legally barred from voting in national elections until the passage of the Nineteenth Amendment to the Constitution in 1920. However, a few women were candidates for political office even before they could vote. The Equal Rights party supported Victoria Woodhull for the U.S. presidency in 1872; perhaps it was a sign of the times that she spent election day in a New York City jail. Table 10–2 identifies milestones in women's gradual movement into U.S. political life.

Today, thousands of women serve as mayors of cities and towns across the United States, and tens of thousands hold responsible administrative jobs in the federal government. At the state level, 24 percent of state legislators in 2011 were women (up from just 5 percent in 1971). National Map 10–1 on page 258 shows where in the United States women have made the greatest political gains.

Change is coming more slowly at the highest levels of power, although a majority of U.S. adults claim they would support a qualified woman for any office, including the presidency. In 2008, Hillary Clinton came close to gaining the presidential nomination of the Democratic party, losing out to Barack Obama, who became the nation's first African American president. In 2011, 6 of 50 state governors were women (12 percent), and in Congress, women held 73 of 435 seats in the House of Representatives (17 percent) and 17 of 100 seats in the Senate (17 percent) (Center for American Women and Politics, 2011).

Women make up half of Earth's population, but they hold just 19 percent of seats in the world's 187 parliamentary governments. This number is considerably higher than the 3 percent of seats women held fifty years ago. In part, this rise reflects the fact that more than 100 countries have adopted some form of gender quota (either constitutional, enacted into legislation, or a voluntary goal of political parties) that ensures women a greater political voice. Even so, only in twenty countries, among them Sweden and Norway, do women represent more than one-third of the members of parliament (Paxton, Hughes, & Green, 2006; Inter-Parliamentary Union, 2011).

Gender and the Military

Since colonial times, women have served in the U.S. armed forces. Yet in 1940, at the outset of World War II, just 2 percent of armed forces personnel were women. In the fall of 2011, women represented 14 percent of all deployed U.S. troops as well as people serving in all capacities in the armed forces.

Clearly, women make up a growing share of the U.S. military, and almost all military assignments are now open to both women and men. But law prevents women from engaging in offensive warfare. Even so, the line between troop support and outright combat is easily crossed, as women serving in Iraq have learned. In fact,

TABLE 10–2 Significant Firsts for Women in U.S. Politics

1869	Law allows women to vote in Wyoming Territory.
1872	First woman to run for the presidency (Victoria Woodhull) represents the Equal Rights party.
1917	First woman elected to the House of Representatives (Jeannette Rankin of Montana).
1924	First women elected state governors (Nellie Taylor Ross of Wyoming and Miriam "Ma" Ferguson of Texas); both followed their husbands into office. First woman to have her name placed in nomination for the vice-presidency at the convention of a major political party (Lena Jones Springs, a Democrat).
1931	First woman to serve in the Senate (Hattie Caraway of Arkansas); completed the term of her husband upon his death and won reelection in 1932.
1932	First woman appointed to the presidential cabinet (Frances Perkins, secretary of labor in the cabinet of President Franklin D. Roosevelt).
1964	First woman to have her name placed in nomination for the presidency at the convention of a major political party (Margaret Chase Smith, a Republican).
1972	First African American woman to have her name placed in nomination for the presidency at the convention of a major political party (Shirley Chisholm, a Democrat).
1981	First woman appointed to the U.S. Supreme Court (Sandra Day O'Connor).
1984	First woman to be successfully nominated for the vice-presidency (Geraldine Ferraro, a Democrat).
1988	First woman chief executive to be elected to a consecutive third term (Madeleine Kunin, governor of Vermont).
1992	Political "Year of the Woman" yields record number of women in the Senate (six) and the House (forty-eight), as well as first African American woman to win election to U.S. Senate (Carol Moseley-Braun of Illinois), first state (California) to be served by two women senators (Barbara Boxer and Dianne Feinstein), and first woman of Puerto Rican descent elected to the House (Nydia Velazquez of New York).
1996	First woman appointed secretary of state (Madeleine Albright).
2000	First former First Lady to win elected political office (Hillary Rodham Clinton, senator from New York).
2001	First woman to serve as national security adviser (Condoleezza Rice); first Asian American woman to serve in a presidential cabinet (Elaine Chao).
2005	First African American woman appointed secretary of state (Condoleezza Rice).
2007	First woman elected as Speaker of the House (Nancy Pelosi).
2008	For the first time, women make up a majority of a state legislature (New Hampshire).
2009	Record number of women in the Senate (seventeen) and the House (seventy-three).

between May 2003 and January 2012, the wars in Iraq and Afghanistan claimed the lives of 143 female soldiers.

The debate on women's role in the military has been going on for centuries. Some people object to opening doors in this way, claiming that women lack the physical strength of men. Others reply that military women are better educated and score higher on intelligence tests than military men. But the heart of the issue is our society's deeply held view of women as *nurturers*—people who give life and help others—which clashes with the image of women trained to kill.

Whatever our views of women and men, the reality is that military women are in harm's way. In part, this fact reflects the strains of a military short of personnel. In addition, the type of insurgency that surrounds our troops in Iraq and Afghanistan can bring violent combat to any soldier at any time. Finally, our modern warfare technology blurs the distinction between combat and noncombat

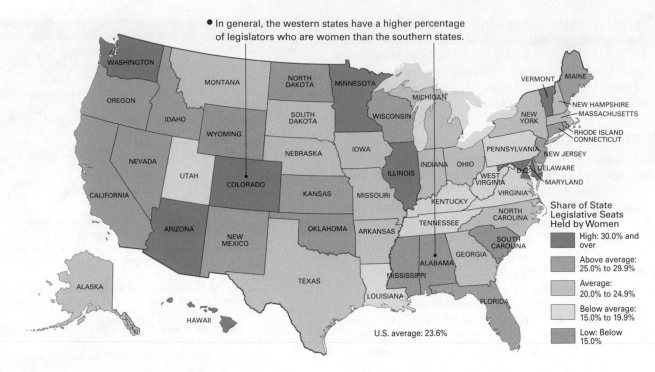

In general, the western states have a higher percentage of legislators who are women than the southern states.

Share of State Legislative Seats Held by Women

- High: 30.0% and over
- Above average: 25.0% to 29.9%
- Average: 20.0% to 24.9%
- Below average: 15.0% to 19.9%
- Low: Below 15.0%

U.S. average: 23.6%

Seeing Ourselves

NATIONAL MAP 10–1 Women in State Government across the United States

Although women make up half of U.S. adults, just 24 percent of the seats in state legislatures are held by women. Look at the state-by-state variations in the map. In which regions of the country have women gained the greatest political power? What do you think accounts for this pattern?

✹ Explore the percentage of women in management, business, and finance in your local community and in counties across the United States on **mysoclab.com**

Source: Center for American Women and Politics (2011).

personnel. A combat pilot can fire missiles at a target miles away; by contrast, non-fighting medical evacuation teams must travel directly into the line of fire (Segal & Hansen, 1992; Wilcox, 1992; Kaminer, 1997; McGirk, 2006).

Are Women a Minority?

A **minority** is *any category of people distinguished by physical or cultural difference that a society sets apart and subordinates.* Given the clear economic disadvantage of being a woman in our society, it seems reasonable to say that women are a minority in the United States even though they outnumber men.[1]

Even so, most white women do not think of themselves in this way. This is partly because, unlike racial minorities (including African Americans) and ethnic minorities (say, Hispanics), white women are well represented at all levels of the class structure, including the very top.

Bear in mind, however, that at every class level, women typically have less income, wealth, education, and power than men. Patriarchy makes women dependent on men—first their fathers and later their husbands—for their social standing (Bernard, 1981).

---

[1]Sociologists use the term "minority" instead of "minority group" because, as explained in Chapter 5 ("Groups and Organizations"), women make up a *category,* not a group. People in a category share a status or identity but generally do not know one another or interact.

Violence against Women

In the nineteenth century, men claimed the right to rule their households, even to the point of using physical discipline against their wives, and a great deal of "manly" violence is still directed against women. A government report estimates that 304,720 aggravated assaults against women occur annually. To this number can be added 169,370 rapes or sexual assaults and perhaps 1.2 million simple assaults (U.S. Department of Justice, 2011).

Gender violence is also an issue on college and university campuses. According to research carried out by the U.S. Department of Justice, in a given academic year, about 3 percent of female college students become victims of rape (either attempted or completed). Projecting these figures over a typical five-year college career, about 20 percent of college women experience rape. In 90 percent of all cases, the victim knew the offender, and most of the assaults took place in the woman's living quarters (National Institute of Justice, 2011).

Off campus as well, most gender-linked violence occurs where men and women interact most: in the home. Richard Gelles (cited in Roesch, 1984) argues that with the exception of the police and the military, the family is the most violent organization in the United States, and it is women who suffer most of the injuries. The risk of violence is especially great for low-income women living in families that face a great deal of stress; low-income women also

have fewer options to get out of a dangerous home (Smolowe, 1994; Frias & Angel, 2007).

Violence toward women also occurs in casual relationships. As noted in Chapter 7 ("Deviance"), most rapes involve men known, and often trusted, by their victims. Dianne Herman (2001) claims that abuse of women is built into our way of life. All forms of violence against women—from the catcalls that intimidate women on city streets to a pinch in a crowded subway to physical assaults that occur at home—express what she calls a "rape culture" of men trying to dominate women. Feminists explain that sexual violence is fundamentally about *power,* not sex, and therefore should be understood as a dimension of gender stratification.

In global perspective, violence against women is built into other cultures in many different ways. One case in point is the practice of female genital mutilation, a painful and often dangerous surgical procedure that is performed in more than two dozen countries and is also known to occur in the United States, as shown in Global Map 10–2 on page 260. The Thinking About Diversity box on page 261 describes an instance of female genital mutilation that took place in California and asks whether this practice, which some people defend as promoting "morality," amounts to a case of violence against women.

Violence against Men

If our way of life encourages violence against women, it may encourage even more violence against men. As noted in Chapter 7 ("Deviance"), in more than 80 percent of cases in which a police makes an arrest for a violent crime, including murder, robbery, and assault, the offender is a male. In addition, 77 percent of murder victims (and 51 percent of the victims of all of violent crime) are men (Federal Bureau of Investigation, 2011; U.S. Bureau of Justice Statistics, 2011).

Our culture tends to define masculinity in terms of aggression and violence. "Real men" work and play hard, speed on the highways, and let nothing stand in their way. A higher crime rate is one result. But even when no laws are broken, men's lives involve more stress and isolation than women's lives, which is one reason that the suicide rate for men is four times higher than for women (Xu et al., 2010). In addition, as noted earlier, men live, on average, about five fewer years than women.

Violence is not simply a matter of choices made by individuals. It is cultural—that is, built into our very way of life, with resulting harm to both men and women. In short, the way any society constructs gender plays an important part in how violent or peaceful that society will be.

Sexual Harassment

Sexual harassment refers to *comments, gestures, or physical contacts of a sexual nature that are deliberate, repeated, and unwelcome.* During the 1990s, sexual harassment became an issue of national importance that rewrote the rules for workplace interaction between women and men.

Most (but not all) victims of sexual harassment are women. The reason is that, first, our culture encourages men to be sexually assertive and to see women in sexual terms. As a result, social interaction between men and women in the workplace, on campus, and elsewhere can easily take on sexual overtones. Second, most people in positions of power—including business executives, doctors, bureau chiefs, assembly line supervisors, professors, and military officers—are men who oversee the work of women. Surveys carried out in widely different work settings show that about 3 percent of women claim that they have been harassed on the job in the last year and about half of women say they receive unwanted sexual attention (NORC, 2011:1508).

Sexual harassment is sometimes obvious and direct: A supervisor may ask for sexual favors from an employee and make threats if the advances are refused. Courts have declared that such *quid pro quo* sexual harassment (the Latin phrase means "one thing in return for another") is a violation of civil rights.

More often, however, the problem of unwelcome sexual attention is a matter of subtle behavior—sexual teasing, off-color jokes, comments about someone's looks—that may or may not be intended to harass anyone. But based on the *effect* standard favored by many feminists, such actions add up to creating a *hostile environment* for women in the workplace. Incidents of this kind are far more complex because they involve different perceptions of the same behavior. For example, a man may think that repeatedly complimenting a co-worker on her appearance is simply being friendly. The co-worker, on the other hand, may believe that the man is

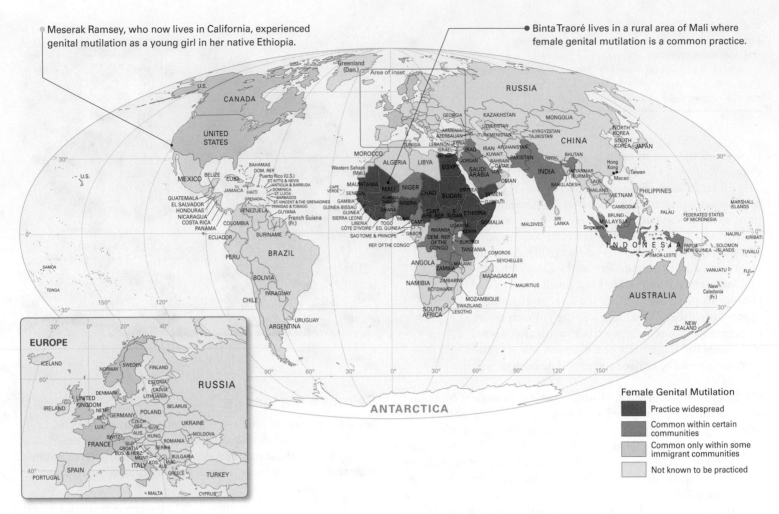

Meserak Ramsey, who now lives in California, experienced genital mutilation as a young girl in her native Ethiopia.

Binta Traoré lives in a rural area of Mali where female genital mutilation is a common practice.

Female Genital Mutilation

- Practice widespread
- Common within certain communities
- Common only within some immigrant communities
- Not known to be practiced

Window on the World

GLOBAL MAP 10–2 Female Genital Mutilation in Global Perspective

Female genital mutilation is known to be performed in at least twenty-eight countries around the world. Across Africa, the practice is common and affects a majority of girls in the eastern African nations of Sudan, Ethiopia, and Somalia. In several Asian nations, including India, the practice is limited to a few ethnic minorities. In the United States, Canada, several European nations, and Australia, there are reports of the practice among some immigrants.

Sources: Seager (2003), Population Reference Bureau (2010), United Nations (2011), and World Health Organization (2011).

thinking of her in sexual terms and is not taking her work seriously, an attitude that could harm her job performance and prospects for advancement.

Pornography

Chapter 6 ("Sexuality and Society") defined *pornography* as sexually explicit material that causes sexual arousal. However, people take different views of exactly what is and what is not pornographic; the law gives local communities the power to define whether sexually explicit material violates "community standards of decency" and lacks "any redeeming social value."

Traditionally, people have raised concerns about pornography as a *moral* issue. But pornography also plays a part in gender stratification. From this point of view, pornography is really a *power*

issue because most pornography dehumanizes women, depicting them as the playthings of men.

In addition, there is widespread concern that pornography encourages violence against women by portraying them as weak and undeserving of respect. Men show contempt for women defined in this way by striking out against them. Surveys show that about half of U.S. adults think that pornography encourages people to commit rape (NORC, 2011:413).

Like sexual harassment, pornography raises complex and sometimes conflicting concerns. Despite the fact that some material may offend just about everyone, many people defend the rights of free speech and artistic expression. Nevertheless, pressure to restrict pornography has increased in recent decades, reflecting both the longstanding concern that pornography weakens morality and the more recent concerns that it is demeaning and threatening to women.

Meserak Ramsey, a woman born in Ethiopia and now working as a nurse in California, paid a visit to an old friend's home. Soon after arriving, she noticed her friend's eighteen-month-old daughter huddled in the corner of a room in obvious distress. "What's wrong with her?" she asked.

Ramsey was shocked when the woman said her daughter had recently had a clitoridectomy, the surgical removal of the clitoris. This type of female genital mutilation—performed by a midwife, a tribal practitioner, or a doctor and typically without anesthesia—is common in Nigeria, Sierra Leone, Senegal, Sudan, Ethiopia, Somalia, and Egypt, and is known to be practiced in certain cultural groups in other nations around the world. It is illegal in the United States.

Among members of highly patriarchal societies, husbands demand that their wives be virgins at marriage and remain sexually faithful thereafter. The point of female genital mutilation is to eliminate sexual feeling, which, people assume, makes women less likely to violate sexual norms and thus be more desirable to men to seek to control them. In about one-fifth of all cases, an even more severe procedure, called infibulation, is performed, in which the entire external genital area is removed and the surfaces are stitched together, leaving only a small hole for urination and menstruation. Before marriage, a husband retains the right to open the wound and ensure himself of his bride's virginity.

How many women have undergone female genital mutilation? Worldwide, estimates suggest that at least 3 million girls (most in Africa) undergo this procedure annually; globally, the number of women who have been cut in this way exceeds 100 million (Kristof & WuDunn, 2009; World Health Organization, 2011). In the United States, hundreds or even thousands of such procedures are performed every year. In most cases, immigrant mothers and grandmothers who have themselves been mutilated insist that young girls in their family follow their example. Indeed, many immigrant women demand the procedure *because* their daughters now live in the United States, where sexual mores are more lax. "I don't have to worry about her now," the girl's mother explained to Meserak Ramsey. "She'll be a good girl."

Medically, the consequences of genital mutilation include more than the loss of sexual pleasure. Pain is intense and can persist for years. There is also danger of infection, infertility, and even death. Ramsey knows the anguish all too well: She herself underwent genital mutilation as a young girl. She is one of the lucky ones who has had few medical problems since. But the extent of her suffering is suggested by this story: She invited a young U.S. couple to stay at her home. Late at night, she heard the woman's cries and burst into their room to investigate, only to learn that the couple was making love and the woman had just had an orgasm. "I didn't understand," Ramsey recalls. "I thought that there must be something wrong with American girls. But now I know that there is something wrong with me." Or with a system that inflicts such injury in the name of traditional morality.

What Do You Think?

1. Is female genital mutilation a medical procedure or a means of social control? Explain your answer.

2. Can you think of other examples of physical mutilation imposed on women? What are they?

3. What do you think should be done about female genital mutilation in places where it is widespread? Do you think respect for human rights should override respect for cultural differences in this case?

These young women have just undergone female genital mutilation. What do you think should be done about this practice?

Sources: Crossette (1995), Boyle, Songora, & Foss (2001), and Sabatini (2011).

Theories of Gender

 Apply

Why does gender exist in all known societies? Sociology's macro-level approaches—the structural-functional and social-conflict approaches—address the central place of gender in social organization. In addition, the symbolic-interaction approach helps us see the importance of gender in everyday life. The Applying Theory table on page 263 summarizes the important insights offered by each of these approaches.

Structural-Functional Theory

The structural-functional approach views society as a complex system of many separate but integrated parts. From this point of view, gender serves as a means to organize social life.

As Chapter 2 ("Culture") explained, the earliest hunting and gathering societies had little power over biology. Lacking effective birth control, women could do little to prevent pregnancy, and the responsibilities of child care kept them close to home. At the same time, men's greater strength made them better suited for warfare and hunting. Over the centuries, this sex-based division of labor became institutionalized and largely taken for granted (Lengermann & Wallace, 1985; Freedman, 2002).

Industrial technology opens up a much greater range of cultural possibilities. With human muscle power no longer the main energy source, the physical strength of men becomes less important. In addition, the ability to control reproduction gives women greater choices about how to live. Modern societies relax traditional gender roles as the societies become more meritocratic because

In the 1950s, Talcott Parsons proposed that sociologists interpret gender as a matter of *differences*. As he saw it, masculine men and feminine women formed strong families and made for an orderly society. In recent decades, however, social-conflict theory has reinterpreted gender as a matter of *inequality*. From this point of view, U.S. society places men in a position of dominance over women.

rigid roles waste an enormous amount of human talent. Yet change comes slowly because gender is deeply rooted in culture.

Gender and Social Integration

As Talcott Parsons (1942, 1951, 1954) observed, gender helps integrate society, at least in its traditional form. Gender forms a *complementary* set of roles that links women and men into family units and gives each sex responsibility for carrying out important tasks. Women take the lead in managing the day-to-day life of the household and raising children. Men connect the family to the larger world as they participate in the labor force.

Thus gender plays an important part in socialization. Society teaches boys—presumably destined for the labor force—to be rational, self-assured, and competitive. Parsons called this complex of traits *instrumental* qualities. To prepare girls for child rearing, socialization stresses *expressive* qualities, such as emotional responsiveness and sensitivity to others.

Society encourages gender conformity by instilling in men and women a fear that straying too far from accepted standards of masculinity or femininity will cause rejection by the opposite sex. In simple terms, women learn to reject nonmasculine men as sexually unattractive, and men learn to reject unfeminine women. In sum, gender integrates society both structurally (in terms of what we do) and morally (in terms of what we believe).

⬤ **Evaluate** Influential in the 1950s, this approach has lost much of its standing today. First, structural-functionalism assumes a singular vision of society that is not shared by everyone. For example, historically, many women have worked outside the home because of economic necessity, a fact not reflected in Parsons's conventional, middle-class view of social life. Second, Parsons's analysis ignores the personal strains and social costs of rigid gender roles. Third, in the eyes of those seeking sexual equality,

Parsons's gender "complementarity" amounts to little more than women submitting to male domination.

CHECK YOUR LEARNING In Parsons's analysis, what functions does gender perform for society?

Symbolic-Interaction Theory

The symbolic-interaction approach takes a micro-level view of society, focusing on face-to-face interaction in everyday life. As suggested in Chapter 4 ("Social Interaction in Everyday Life"), gender affects everyday interaction in a number of ways.

Gender and Everyday Life

If you watch women and men interacting, you will probably notice that women typically engage in more eye contact than men do. Why? Holding eye contact is a way of encouraging the conversation to continue; in addition, looking directly at someone clearly shows the other person that you are paying attention.

This pattern is an example of sex roles, defined earlier as the way a society defines how women and men should think and behave. To understand such patterns, consider the fact that people with more power tend to take charge of social encounters. When men and women engage one another, as they do in families and in the workplace, it is men who typically initiate the interaction. That is, men speak first, set the topics of discussion, and control the outcomes. With less power, women are expected to be more *deferential*, meaning that they show respect for others of higher social position. In many cases, this means that women (just like children or others with less power) spend more time being silent and also encouraging men (or others with more power) not just with eye contact but by smiling or nodding in agreement. As a technique to control a conversation, men often interrupt others, just as they typically feel less need to ask the opinions of other people, especially those with less power (Tannen, 1990, 1994; Henley, Hamilton, & Thorne, 1992; Ridgeway & Smith-Lovin, 1999).

Gender and Reality Construction

If a woman is planning to marry a man, should she take his last name or keep her own? This decision is about more than how she will sign a check: It also affects how employers will see her and even her future pay.

In the United States today, about 18 percent of women who marry men keep their own name. This is a decline from the 1990s, when the share peaked at about 23 percent. Research shows that women who marry in their thirties (after they have started a career) are much more likely to keep their own name than women who marry in their early twenties. Research also shows that subjects asked to assess women's personal traits typically perceive those who take their husband's last name as more caring, dependent, and emotional (traditional feminine qualities). By contrast, they assess women who keep their maiden names as more ambitious, talented, and capable (more competitive against others, including men). Data on salaries reveal a significant difference in pay: Married women who keep their own name end up earning about 40 percent more than those who adopt their husband's name (Shellenbarger, 2011).

Such patterns demonstrate how gender shapes the reality we experience in everyday life. They also suggest that women who face a decision about surnames when they marry may consider the choice they make will carry particular meaning to others and have important consequences.

Gender

	Structural-Functional Theory	Symbolic-Interaction Theory	Social-Conflict and Intersection Theories
What is the level of analysis?	Macro-level	Micro-level	Macro-level
What does gender mean?	Parsons described gender in terms of two complementary patterns of behavior: masculine and feminine.	Numerous sociologists have shown that gender is part of the reality that guides social interaction in everyday situations.	Engels described gender in terms of the power of one sex over the other. Gender interacts with class, race, and ethnicity to create various levels of disadvantage.
Is gender helpful or harmful?	Helpful. Gender gives men and women distinctive roles and responsibilities that help society operate smoothly. Gender builds social unity as men and women come together to form families.	Hard to say; gender is both helpful and harmful. In everyday life, gender is one of the factors that help us relate to one another. At the same time, gender shapes human behavior, placing men in control of social situations. Men tend to initiate most interactions, while women typically act in a more deferential manner.	Harmful. Gender limits people's personal development. Gender divides society by giving power to men to control the lives of women. Intersection theory explains that minority women face multiple disadvantages.

Evaluate The strength of the symbolic-interaction approach is helping us see how gender plays a part in shaping almost all our everyday experiences. Our society defines men (and everything we consider to be masculine) as having more value than women (and what is defined as feminine). For this reason, just about every familiar social encounter is "gendered" so that men and women interact in distinctive and unequal ways.

The symbolic-interaction approach suggests that individuals socially construct the reality they experience as they interact every day, using gender-linked traits such as clothing and demeanor (and, for women, also last name) as elements of their personal "performances" that shape ongoing reality.

Gender plays a part in the reality we experience. Yet, as a structural dimension of society, gender is at least largely beyond the immediate control of any of us as individuals as it gives some people power over others. In other words, patterns of everyday social interaction reflect our society's gender stratification. Everyday interaction also helps reinforce this inequality. For example, to the extent that fathers take the lead in dinner table discussions, the entire family learns to expect men to "display leadership" and "show their wisdom." As mothers do the laundry, children learn that women are expected to do household chores.

A limitation of the symbolic-interaction approach is that by focusing on situational social experience, it says little about the broad patterns of inequality that set the rules for our everyday lives. To understand the roots of gender stratification, we have to "kick it up a level" to see more closely how society makes men and women unequal. We will do this using the social-conflict approach.

CHECK YOUR LEARNING Point to several ways that gender shapes the everyday face-to-face interactions of individuals.

Social-Conflict Theory

From a social-conflict point of view, gender involves much more than differences in behavior—gender is a structural system of *power* that provides privilege to some and disadvantage to others. Consider the striking similarity between the way traditional ideas about gender benefit men and harm women and the way ideas about race benefit men and disadvantage racial and ethnic minorities. Conventional ideas about gender do not make society operate smoothly, as a structural-functional analysis suggests. On the contrary, gender is a societal structure that creates division and tension, with men seeking to protect their privileges as women challenge the status quo.

As earlier chapters noted, the social-conflict approach draws heavily on the ideas of Karl Marx. Yet as far as gender is concerned, Marx was a product of his times, and his writings focused almost entirely on men. However, his friend and collaborator Friedrich Engels did develop a theory of gender stratification.

Gender and Class Inequality

Looking back through history, Engels saw that in hunting and gathering societies, the activities of women and men, though different, had equal importance. A successful hunt brought men great prestige, but the vegetation gathered by women provided most of a group's food supply. As technological advances led to a productive surplus, social equality and communal sharing gave way to private property and ultimately a class hierarchy, and men gained significant power over women. With surplus wealth to pass on to heirs, upper-class men needed to be sure that their sons were their own, which led them to control the sexuality of women. The desire to control both women's sexuality and private property brought about monogamous marriage and the family. Women were taught to remain virgins until marriage, to remain faithful to their husbands thereafter, and to build their lives around bearing and raising one man's children.

Family law ensures that property is transmitted within families from one generation to the next, keeping the class system intact.

According to Engels (1902, orig. 1884), the rise of capitalism makes male domination even stronger. First, capitalism uses trade and industrial production to create more wealth, which gives greater power to men as income earners and owners of property. Second, an expanding capitalist economy depends on turning people, especially women, into consumers who seek personal fulfillment by buying and using products. Third, society assigns women the task of maintaining the home to free men to work in factories. The double exploitation of capitalism, as Engels saw it, lies in paying low wages for male labor and paying women no wages at all.

● **Evaluate** Social-conflict analysis is strongly critical of conventional ideas about gender, claiming that society would be better off if we minimized or even did away with this dimension of social structure. That is, this approach regards conventional families, which traditionalists consider personally and socially positive, as a social evil. A problem with social-conflict analysis, then, is that it minimizes the extent to which women and men live together cooperatively and often happily in families. A second problem lies in the assertion that capitalism is the basis of gender stratification. In fact, agrarian societies are typically more patriarchal than industrial-capitalist societies. In addition, although socialist nations, including the People's Republic of China and the former Soviet Union, did move women into the labor force, by and large they provided women with very low pay in sex-segregated jobs (Rosendahl, 1997; Haney, 2002).

CHECK YOUR LEARNING According to Engels, how does gender support social inequality in a capitalist class system?

Intersection Theory

In recent years, an additional social-conflict approach has gained great importance in sociology: intersection theory. The key insight of intersection theory is that there are multiple systems of stratification based on race, class, and gender, and these systems do not operate independently of one another. On the contrary, these dimensions of inequality intersect and interact. Formally, then, **intersection theory** is *analysis of the interplay of race, class, and gender, which often results in multiple dimensions of disadvantage.* Research shows that disadvantages

The basic insight of intersection theory is that various dimensions of social stratification—including race and gender—can add up to great disadvantages for some categories of people. Just as African Americans earn less than whites, women earn less than men. Thus African American women confront a "double disadvantage," earning just 62 cents for every dollar earned by non-Hispanic white men. How would you explain the fact that some categories of people are much more likely to end up in low-paying jobs like this one?

linked to race and gender often combine to produce especially low social standing for some people (Ovadia, 2001).

Income data confirm the basic claim of intersection theory. Looking first at race and ethnicity, the median income in 2010 for African American women working full time was $32,332, which is 80 percent as much as the $40,495 earned by non-Hispanic white women; Hispanic women earned $28,149—just 70 percent as much as their white counterparts. Looking at gender, African American women earned 88 percent as much as African American men, and Hispanic women earned 89 percent as much as Hispanic men.

To explore the "intersection" of these dimensions of inequality, we find that some categories of women experience greater disadvantages. African American women earned only 62 percent as much as non-Hispanic white men, and Hispanic women earned just 54 percent as much (U.S. Census Bureau, 2011). These income differences reflect minority women's lower positions in the occupational and educational hierarchies.

Intersection theory helps us to see that although gender has a powerful effect on our lives, it does not operate alone. Class position, race and ethnicity, gender, and sexual orientation form a multilayered system that provides disadvantages for some and privileges for others (Saint Jean & Feagin, 1998).

● **Evaluate** If it is true that women are disadvantaged, it is also the case that some women are disadvantaged more than others. This insight is the first contribution of intersection theory. In addition, this approach helps us understand that, although the lives of all women are shaped by gender, there is no single "woman's experience." Rather, white women, Hispanic women, women of color (and also older women, women with disabilities, and lesbians) all have particular social standing and experiences that must be understood on their own terms.

A remaining issue that must be addressed is what people should *do* about gender stratification. This concern leads to another expression of social-conflict theory—feminism.

CHECK YOUR LEARNING State the basic idea of intersection theory. How does this theory help us understand the complexity of social stratification?

Feminism

● **Evaluate**

Feminism is *support of social equality for women and men, in opposition to patriarchy and sexism.* The first wave of feminism in the United States began in the 1840s as women opposed to slavery, including Elizabeth Cady Stanton and Lucretia Mott, drew parallels between the oppression of African Americans and the oppression of women. Their main objective was obtaining the right to vote, which was finally achieved in 1920. But other disadvantages persisted, causing a second wave of feminism to arise in the 1960s that continues today.

Basic Feminist Ideas

Feminism views the everyday lives of women and men through the lens of gender. How we think of ourselves (gender identity), how we act (gender roles), and our social standing as women or men (gender stratification) are all rooted in the operation of society.

Although feminists disagree about many things, most support five general principles:

1. **Taking action to increase equality.** Feminist thinking is political; it links ideas to action. Feminism is critical of the status quo, pushing for change toward social equality for women and men. Many feminists are also guided by intersection theory to seek equality based on race and class as well as gender.

2. **Expanding human choice.** Feminists argue that cultural ideas about gender divide the full range of human qualities into two opposing and limiting spheres: the female world of emotion and cooperation and the male world of rationality and competition. As an alternative, feminists propose a "re-integration of humanity" by which all individuals develop all human traits (French, 1985).

3. **Eliminating gender stratification throughout society.** Feminism opposes laws and cultural norms that limit the education, income, and job opportunities of women. For this reason, feminists have long supported passage of the Equal Rights Amendment (ERA) to the U.S. Constitution, which states, in its entirety, "Equality of rights under the law shall not be denied or abridged by the United States or any State on account of sex." The ERA was first proposed in Congress in 1923. Although it has widespread support, it has yet to become law.

4. **Ending sexual violence.** Today's women's movement seeks to eliminate sexual violence. Feminists argue that patriarchy distorts the relationships between women and men, encouraging violence against women in the form of rape, domestic abuse, sexual harassment, and pornography (A. Dworkin, 1987; Freedman, 2002).

NASCAR racing has always been a masculine world. But Danica Patrick has made a name for herself as an outstanding driver. At the same time, she has made much of her income from trading on her good looks, including appearing in the 2009 *Sports Illustrated* swimsuit edition. Are men as likely to do the same? Why or why not?

5. **Promoting sexual freedom.** Finally, feminism advocates women's control over their sexuality and reproduction. Feminists support the free availability of birth control information. As Figure 10–3 on page 266 shows, about three-quarters of married U.S. women of childbearing age use contraception; the use of contraceptives is far less common in many lower-income nations. Most feminists also support a woman's right to choose whether to have children or to end a pregnancy, rather than allowing men—as husbands, physicians, and legislators—to control their reproduction. Many feminists also support gay people's efforts to end prejudice and discrimination in a largely heterosexual culture (Ferree & Hess, 1995; Armstrong, 2002).

Types of Feminism

Although feminists agree on the importance of gender equality, they disagree on how to achieve it: through liberal feminism, socialist feminism, or radical feminism (Stacey, 1983; L. Vogel, 1983; Ferree & Hess, 1995; Armstrong, 2002; Freedman, 2002). The Applying Theory table on page 266 highlights the key arguments made by each type of feminist thinking.

Liberal Feminism

Liberal feminism is rooted in classic liberal thinking that individuals should be free to develop their own talents and pursue their own interests. Liberal feminists accepts the basic organization of our society but seek to expand the rights and opportunities of women. As they see it, gender should not operate as a form of caste, to the disadvantage of women. As an important step to achieving this goal, they support the passage of the Equal Rights Amendment. Liberal feminists also support reproductive freedom for all women. They respect the family as a social institution but seek changes in society, including more widely available maternity and paternity leave and child care for parents who work.

Given their beliefs in the rights of individuals, liberal feminists think that women should advance according to their individual efforts and merit, rather than by working collectively for change. Both women and men, through personal achievement, are capable of improving their lives, as long as society removes legal and cultural barriers.

Socialist Feminism

Socialist feminism evolved from the ideas of Karl Marx and Friedrich Engels. From this point of view, capitalism increases patriarchy by concentrating wealth and power in the hands of a small number

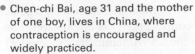

- Achen Eke, age 24 and mother of three, lives in Uganda, where most women do not have access to contraception.

- Chen-chi Bai, age 31 and the mother of one boy, lives in China, where contraception is encouraged and widely practiced.

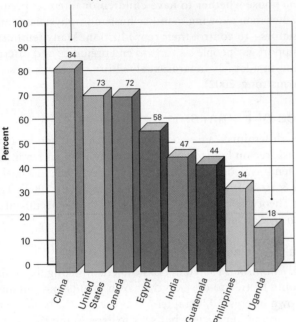

Global Snapshot

FIGURE 10–3 Use of Contraception by Married Women of Childbearing Age

In the United States, most married women of childbearing age use contraception. In many lower-income countries, however, most women do not have the opportunity to make this choice.

Source: Population Reference Bureau (2011).

of men. Socialist feminists do not think the reforms supported by liberal feminists go far enough. They believe that the family form fostered by capitalism must change in order to replace "domestic slavery" with some collective means of carrying out housework and child care. Replacing the traditional family can come about only through a socialist revolution that creates a state-centered economy to meet the needs of all.

Radical Feminism

Like socialist feminism, *radical feminism* finds liberal feminism inadequate. Radical feminists believe that patriarchy is so firmly entrenched that even a socialist revolution would not end it. Instead, reaching the goal of gender equality means that society must eliminate gender itself.

One possible way to achieve this goal is to use new reproductive technology that has been developed by scientists in recent decades (see Chapter 13, "Family and Religion"). This technology has the ability to separate women's bodies from the process of childbearing. With an end to motherhood, radical feminists reason, society could leave behind the entire family system, liberating women, men, and children from the oppression of family, gender, and sex itself (A. Dworkin, 1987). Radical feminism seeks an egalitarian and gender-free society, a revolution much more sweeping than that sought by Marx.

Opposition to Feminism

Because feminism calls for significant change, it has always been controversial. Today, about 20 percent of U.S. adults support the idea that "women should return to their traditional roles in society" (Pew Research Center, 2009). It is also true that only about 20 percent of U.S. adults claim that they are willing to identify themselves as feminists ("The Barrier that Didn't Fall," 2008).

But, over time, the share of the population that opposes feminism has steadily declined. The most dramatic declines took place in the early 1970s; later changes have been far smaller. A larger share of men than women express antifeminist attitudes.

Most men and women who express criticism of feminism hold conventional ideas about gender. Some men oppose sexual equality for the same reason that many white people have historically opposed social equality for people of color: They do not want to give up their privileges. Other men and women, including those who are neither rich nor powerful, distrust a social movement (especially its radical expressions) that attacks

APPLYING THEORY

Feminism

	Liberal Feminism	Socialist Feminism	Radical Feminism
Does it accept the basic order of society?	Yes. Liberal feminism seeks change only to ensure equality of opportunity.	No. Socialist feminism supports an end to social classes and to family gender roles that encourage "domestic slavery."	No. Radical feminism supports an end to the family system.
How do women improve their social standing?	Individually, according to personal ability and effort.	Collectively, through socialist revolution.	Collectively, by working to eliminate gender itself.

the traditional family and rejects patterns that have guided male-female relations for centuries.

Men who have been socialized to value strength and dominance may feel uneasy about feminist ideals of men as gentle and warm (Doyle, 1983). Similarly, some women whose lives center on their husbands and children may think that feminism does not value the social roles that give meaning to their lives. In general, opposition to feminism is greatest among women who have the least education and those who do not work outside the home (Marshall, 1985; Ferree & Hess, 1995; CBS News, 2005).

Race and ethnicity play some part in shaping people's attitudes toward feminism. In general, African Americans (especially African American women) express the greatest support of feminist goals, followed by whites, with Hispanic Americans holding somewhat more traditional attitudes when it comes to gender (Kane, 2000).

Resistance to feminism is also found within academic circles. Some sociologists charge that feminism ignores a growing body of evidence that men and women do think and act in somewhat different ways, which may make complete gender equality impossible. Furthermore, say critics, with its drive to increase women's presence in the workplace, feminism undervalues the crucial and unique contribution women make to the development of children, especially in the first years of life (Baydar & Brooks-Gunn, 1991; Popenoe, 1993b; Gibbs, 2001).

Finally, there is the question of *how* women should go about improving their social standing. A large majority of adults in the United States think that women should have equal rights, but 70 percent also say that women should advance individually, according to their training and abilities; only 10 percent favor women's rights groups or collective action (NORC, 2011:582).

For these reasons, most opposition to feminism is directed toward its socialist and radical forms, while support for liberal feminism is widespread. In addition, we are seeing an unmistakable trend toward greater gender equality. In 1977, 65 percent of all adults endorsed the statement "It is much better for everyone involved if the man is the achiever outside the home and the woman takes care of the home and family." By 2010, the share supporting this statement had dropped sharply, to 36 percent (NORC, 2011: 438).

Gender: Looking Ahead

● Evaluate

Predictions about the future are no more than educated guesses. Just as economists disagree about the likely inflation rate a year from now, sociologists can offer only general observations about the likely future of gender and society.

Change so far has been remarkable. A century ago, women were second-class citizens, without access to many jobs, barred from public office, and with no right to vote. Although women remain socially disadvantaged, the movement toward equality has surged ahead. Two-thirds of people entering the workforce in the 1990s were women, and in 2000, for the first time, a majority of families had both husband and wife in the paid labor force. Today's economy depends a great deal on the earnings of women. In addition, more than one in five married men in the United States have wives who earn more than they do (Fry & Cohn, 2010). As the share of women in higher education continues to rise, women's participation in the labor force has gone up along with the range of work that they perform.

Many factors have contributed to this long-term transformation. Perhaps most important, industrialization and advances in computer technology have shifted the nature of work from physically demanding tasks that favored male strength to jobs that require thought and imagination. This change puts women and men on an even footing. Also, because birth control technology has given us greater control over reproduction, women's lives are less constrained by unwanted pregnancies.

Many women and men have deliberately pursued social equality. For example, sexual harassment complaints in the workplace are taken much more seriously today than they were a generation ago. Another important trend is the increasing share of college degrees that are earned by women. This trend, in turn, is likely to reduce the earnings gap in the years to come as more women assume positions of power in the corporate and political worlds (Foroohar, 2011). As these trends unfold, social change involving gender in the twenty-first century may turn out to be as great as those that have already taken place.

How much do you think conceptions of gender will change over your lifetime? Will there be more change in the lives of women or men? Why?

Seeing Sociology in Everyday Life

CHAPTER 10 **Gender Stratification**

Can you spot "gender messages" in the world around you?

As this chapter makes clear, gender is one of the basic organizing principles of everyday life. Most of the places we go and most of the activities we engage in as part of our daily routines are "gendered," meaning that they are defined as either more masculine or more feminine. Understanding this fact, corporations keep gender in mind when they market products to the public. Take a look at the ads below. In each case, can you explain how gender is at work in selling these products?

Hint Looking for "gender messages" in ads is a process that involves several levels of analysis. Start on the surface by noting everything obvious in the ad, including the setting, the background, and especially the people. Then notice how the people are shown—what they are doing, how they are situated, their facial expressions, how they are dressed, and how they appear to relate to each other. Finally, state what you think is the message of the ad, based on both the ad itself and also what you know about the surrounding society.

There are a lot of gender dynamics going on in this ad. What do you see?

GUCCI

268

Generally, our society defines cosmetics as feminine because most cosmetics are marketed toward women. How and why is this ad different?

FACE

TIME FIGHTER

MENSGROOM

FACE CREAM
CRÈME POUR LE VISAGE

50mL 1.7 fl. oz.

What gender messages do you see in this ad?

DONNAKARAN
NEW YORK

Seeing Sociology in *Your* Everyday Life

1. Look through some recent magazines and select three advertisements that involve gender. In each case, provide analysis of how gender is used in the ad.

2. Watch several hours of children's television programming on a Saturday morning. Notice the advertising, which mostly sells toys and breakfast cereal. Keep track of what share of toys are "gendered," that is, aimed at one sex or the other. What traits do you associate with toys intended for boys and those intended for girls?

3. Do some research on the history of women's issues in your state. When was the first woman sent to Congress? What laws once existed that restricted the work women could do? Do any such laws exist today? Go to the "Seeing Sociology in *Your* Everyday Life" feature on MySocLab to read more about how gender can be changed and learn some of the personal benefits that come from recognizing this fact.

Gender and Inequality

Gender refers to the meaning a culture attaches to being female or male.

- Evidence that gender is rooted in culture includes global comparisons by Margaret Mead and others showing how societies define what is feminine and masculine in various ways.
- Gender is not only about difference: Because societies give more power and other resources to men than to women, gender is an important dimension of social stratification. **Sexism** is built into the operation of social institutions.
- Although some degree of **patriarchy** is found almost everywhere, it varies throughout history and from society to society. **pp. 248–51**

 **Watch** the **Video** on **mysoclab.com**

gender (p. 248) the personal traits and social positions that members of a society attach to being female or male

gender stratification (p. 248) the unequal distribution of wealth, power, and privilege between men and women

matriarchy (p. 250) a form of social organization in which females dominate males

patriarchy (p. 250) a form of social organization in which males dominate females

sexism (p. 250) the belief that one sex is innately superior to the other

Gender and Socialization

Through the socialization process, gender becomes part of our personalities (**gender identity**) and our actions (**gender roles**). All the major agents of socialization—family, peer groups, schools, and the mass media—reinforce cultural definitions of what is feminine and masculine. **pp. 251–53**

gender roles (also known as sex roles) (p. 252) attitudes and activities that a society links to each sex

Gender and Social Stratification

Gender stratification shapes **the workplace:**

- A majority of women are now in the paid labor force, but 39% hold clerical or service jobs.
- Comparing full-time U.S. workers, women earn 77% as much as men.
- This gender difference in earnings results from differences in jobs, differences in family responsibilities, and discrimination. **pp. 253–56**

 **Read** the **Document** on **mysoclab.com**

Gender stratification shapes **family life:**

- Most unpaid housework is performed by women, whether or not they hold jobs outside the home.
- Pregnancy and raising small children keep many women out of the labor force at a time when their male peers are making important career gains. **pp. 255–56**

Gender stratification shapes **education:**

- Women now earn 59% of all associate and bachelor's degrees.
- Women make up 47% of law school students and are an increasing share of graduates in professions traditionally dominated by men, including medicine and business administration. **pp. 256–57**

Gender stratification shapes **politics:**

- Until a century ago, almost no women held any elected office in the United States.
- In recent decades, the number of women in politics has increased significantly.
- Even so, the vast majority of elected officials, especially at the national level, are men.
- Women make up only about 14% of U.S. military personnel. **pp. 257–58**

Explore the **Map** on **mysoclab.com**

minority (p. 258) any category of people distinguished by physical or cultural difference that a society sets apart and subordinates

sexual harassment (p. 259) comments, gestures, or physical contacts of a sexual nature that are deliberate, repeated, and unwelcome

Violence against women and men is a widespread problem that is linked to how a society defines gender. Related issues include

- **sexual harassment**, which mostly victimizes women because our culture encourages men to be assertive and to see women in sexual terms.
- **pornography**, which portrays women as sexual objects. Many see pornography as a moral issue; because pornography dehumanizes women, it is also a power issue. **pp. 258–61**

Theories of Gender

Structural-functional theory suggests that

- in preindustrial societies, distinctive roles for males and females reflect biological differences between the sexes.
- in industrial societies, marked gender inequality becomes dysfunctional and gradually decreases.

Talcott Parsons described gender differences in terms of complementary roles that promote the social integration of families and society as a whole. **pp. 261–62**

Symbolic-interaction theory suggests that

- individuals use gender as one element of their personal performances as they socially construct reality through everyday interactions.
- gender plays a part in shaping almost all our everyday experiences.

Because our society defines men as having more value than women, the sex roles that define how women and men should behave place men in control of social situations; women play a more deferential role. **pp. 262–63**

Social-conflict theory suggests that

- gender is an important dimension of social inequality and social conflict.
- gender inequality benefits men and disadvantages women.

Friedrich Engels tied gender stratification to the rise of private property and a class hierarchy. Marriage and the family are strategies by which men control their property through control of the sexuality of women. Capitalism exploits everyone by paying men low wages and assigning women the task of maintaining the home. **pp. 263–64**

intersection theory (p. 264) analysis of the interplay of race, class, and gender, often resulting in multiple dimensions of disadvantage

Intersection theory investigates the interplay of race, class, and gender, factors that combine to cause special disadvantages to some categories of people.

- Women of color encounter greater social disadvantages than white women and earn much less than white men.
- Intersection theory highlights the ways particular dimensions of difference in women's lives combine in a multi-layered system, creating unique disadvantage for various categories of women. **p. 264**

Feminism

Feminism

- endorses the social equality of women and men and opposes patriarchy and sexism.
- seeks to eliminate violence against women.
- advocates giving women control over their reproduction. **pp. 264–65**

There are three types of feminism:

- Liberal feminism seeks equal opportunity for both sexes within the existing society.
- Socialist feminism claims that gender equality will come about by replacing capitalism with socialism.
- Radical feminism seeks to eliminate the concept of gender itself and to create an egalitarian and gender-free society. **pp. 265–66**

Today, only 20% of U.S. adults say they oppose feminism. Most opposition is directed toward socialist and radical feminism. Support for liberal feminism is widespread. **pp. 266–67**

feminism (p. 264) support of social equality for women and men, in opposition to patriarchy and sexism

Race and Ethnicity

Learning Objectives

Remember the definitions of the key terms highlighted in boldfaced type throughout this chapter.

Understand that both race and ethnicity are socially constructed ideas that are important dimensions of social stratification.

various sociological theories to the concept of prejudice.

Analyze the social standing of various racial and ethnic categories of the U.S. population.

Evaluate recent trends involving prejudice and discrimination.

Create a deeper appreciation for the racial and ethnic diversity of U.S. society, past, present, and future.

CHAPTER OVERVIEW

This chapter explains how race and ethnicity are created by society. The United States is a nation as racially and ethnically diverse as any in the world. Here and elsewhere, both race and ethnicity are not only matters of difference but also dimensions of social inequality. ■

On a cool November morning in New York City, an instructor in a sociology class at Bronx Community College is leading a small-group discussion of race and ethnicity. He explains that the meaning of both concepts is far less clear than most people think. Then he asks, "How do you describe yourself?"

Eva Rodriguez leans forward in her chair and is quick to respond. "Who am I? Or should I say *what* am I? This is hard for me to answer. Most people think of race as black and white. But it's not. I have both black and white ancestry in me, but you know what? I don't think of myself in that way. I don't think of myself in terms of race at all. It would be better to call me Puerto Rican or Hispanic. Personally, I prefer the term 'Latina.' Calling myself Latina says I have a mixed racial heritage, and that's what I am. I wish more people understood that race is not clear-cut."

This chapter examines the meaning of race and ethnicity. There are now millions of people in the United States who, like Eva Rodriguez, do not think of themselves in terms of a single category but as having a mix of ancestry.

The Social Meaning of Race and Ethnicity

● **Understand**

As the story that opened this chapter suggests, people often confuse "race" and "ethnicity." For this reason, we begin with some basic definitions.

Race

A **race** is *a socially constructed category of people who share biologically transmitted traits that members of a society consider important.* People may classify one another racially on the basis of physical characteristics such as skin color, facial features, hair texture, and body shape.

Racial diversity appeared among our human ancestors as the result of living in different geographic regions of the world. In regions of intense heat, people developed darker skin (from the natural pigment melanin), which offers protection from the sun; in

moderate climates, people developed lighter skin. Such traits are literally only skin deep because human beings the world over are members of a single biological species.

The striking variety of racial traits found today is also the product of migration; genetic characteristics once common to a single place are now found in many lands. Especially pronounced is the racial mix in the Middle East (that is, western Asia), historically a crossroads of migration. Greater racial uniformity characterizes more isolated peoples such as the island-dwelling Japanese. But every population has some genetic mixture, and increasing contact ensures even more racial blending of physical characteristics in the future.

Although we often think of race in terms of biological elements, race is a socially constructed concept. It is true that human beings differ in any number of ways involving physical traits, but a "race" comes into being only when the members of a society decide that some particular physical trait (such as skin color or eye shape) actually *matters*.

Because race is a matter of social definitions, it is a highly variable concept. For example, the members of U.S. society consider

 **Read** "The Souls of Black Folk" by W.E.B. Du Bois on **mysoclab.com**

---

race a socially constructed category of people who share biologically transmitted traits that members of a society consider important

ethnicity a shared cultural heritage

The range of biological variation in human beings is far greater than any system of racial classification allows. This fact is made obvious by trying to place all of the people pictured here into simple racial categories.

racial differences more important than people of many other countries. We also tend to "see" three racial categories—typically, black, white, and Asian—while other societies identify many more categories. People in Brazil, for example, distinguish between *branca* (white), *parda* (brown), *morena* (brunette), *mulata* (mulatto), *preta* (black), and *amarela* (yellow) (Inciardi, Surratt, & Telles, 2000).

In addition, race may be defined differently by various categories of people within a society. In the United States, for example, research shows that white people "see" black people as having darker skin color than black people do (Hill, 2002).

The meaning and importance of race not only differ from place to place but also change over time. Back in 1900, for example, it was common in the United States to consider people of Irish, Italian, or Jewish ancestry as "nonwhite." By 1950, however, this was no longer the case, and such people today are considered part of the "white" category (Loveman, 1999; Brodkin, 2007).

Today, the Census Bureau allows people to describe themselves using more than one racial category (offering six single-race options and fifty-seven multiracial options). Our society officially recognizes a wide range of multiracial people (U.S. Census Bureau, 2011).

Racial Types

Scientists invented the concept of race more than a century ago as they tried to organize the world's physical diversity into three racial types. They called people with relatively light skin and fine hair *Caucasoid*, people with darker skin and coarse hair *Negroid*, and people with yellow or brown skin and distinctive folds on the eyelids *Mongoloid*.

Sociologists consider such terms misleading at best and harmful at worst. For one thing, no society contains biologically "pure" people. The skin color of people we might call "Caucasoid" (or "Indo-European," "Caucasian," or more commonly, "white") ranges from very light (typical in Scandinavia) to very dark (in southern India). The same variation exists among so-called "Negroids" ("Africans" or more commonly, "black" people) and "Mongoloids"("Asians"). In fact, many "white" people (say, in southern India) actually have darker skin than many "black" people (the Aborigines of Australia). Overall, the three racial categories differ in just 6 percent of their genes, and there is actually more genetic variation *within* each category than *between* categories. This means that two people in the European nation of Sweden, randomly selected, might have at least as much genetic difference as a Swede and a person in the African nation of Senegal (Harris & Sim, 2002; American Sociological Association, 2003; California Newsreel, 2003).

So just how important is race? From a biological point of view, knowing people's racial category allows us to predict almost nothing about them. Why, then, do societies make so much of race? Such categories allow societies to rank people in a hierarchy, giving some people more money, power, and prestige than others and allowing some people to feel that they are inherently "better" than others.

Because race may matter so much, societies sometimes construct racial categories in extreme ways. Throughout much of the twentieth century, for example, many southern states labeled as "colored" anyone with as little as one thirty-second African ancestry (that is, one African American great-great-great-grandparent). Today, the law allows parents to declare the race of a child (or not) as they wish. Even so, most members of our society are still very sensitive to people's racial backgrounds.

Watch the video "Multiracial Identity, clip 2" on **mysoclab.com**

A Trend toward Mixture

Over many generations and throughout the Americas, genetic traits from around the world have become mixed. Many "black" people have a significant Caucasoid ancestry, just as many "white" people have some Negroid genes. Whatever people may think, race is not a black-and-white issue.

Today, people are more willing to define themselves as multiracial. On the U.S. Census Bureau's American Community Survey (2010), more than 8 million people described themselves by checking two or more racial categories. The number of interracial births in the United States has been increasing. In 2010, some 5.6 percent of children under the age of five were multiracial, compared to less than 1 percent of people age sixty-five and older.

Ethnicity

Ethnicity is *a shared cultural heritage.* People define themselves—or others—as members of an *ethnic category* based on common ancestry, language, and religion that give them a distinctive social identity. The United States is a multiethnic society that favors the English language; even so, almost 60 million people (21 percent of the U.S. population over the age of five) speak Spanish, Italian, German, French, Chinese dialects, or some other language in their homes. In California, 44 percent of the population does so (U.S. Census Bureau, 2011).

With regard to religion, the United States is a predominantly Protestant nation, but most people of Spanish, Italian, and Polish ancestry are Roman Catholic, and many others of Greek, Ukrainian, and Russian descent belong to the Eastern Orthodox Church. More than 6.5 million Jewish Americans have ancestral ties to various nations around the world. The Muslim population is increasing and is estimated to number some 2.75 million people (Pew Research Center, 2011).

Like the reality of race, the meaning of ethnicity is socially constructed, becoming important only because society defines it that way. For example, U.S. society defines people of Spanish descent as "Latin," even though Italy probably has a more "Latin" culture than Spain. People of Italian descent are viewed not as Latin but as "European" and thus less different (Camara, 2000; Brodkin, 2007). Like racial differences, the importance of ethnic differences can change over time. A century ago, Catholics and Jews were considered "different" in the predominantly Protestant United States. This is much less true today.

Keep in mind that race is constructed from *biological* traits and ethnicity is constructed from *cultural* traits. Of course, the two may go hand in hand. For example, Japanese Americans have distinctive physical traits and, for those who maintain a traditional way of life, a distinctive culture as well. Table 11–1 presents the most recent data on the racial and ethnic diversity of the United States.

On an individual level, people either play up or play down their ethnicity, depending on whether they want to fit in or stand apart from the surrounding society: Immigrants may drop their cultural traditions over time or, like many people of Native American descent in recent years, try to revive their heritage. For most people, ethnicity is a more complex issue than race because they identify with several ethnic backgrounds. Rock and roll legend Jimi Hendrix was African American, white, and Cherokee; news anchor Soledad O'Brian considers herself both white and black, both Australian and Irish, and both English and Hispanic.

Minorities

March 3, Dallas, Texas. The lobby of just about any large hotel in a major U.S. city presents a lesson in contrasts: The majority of the guests checking in and out are white; the majority of the employees who carry the luggage, serve the food, and clean the rooms are racial or ethnic minorities.

As defined in Chapter 10 ("Gender Stratification"), a **minority** is *any category of people distinguished by physical or cultural difference that a society sets apart and subordinates.* Minority standing

TABLE 11–1 Racial and Ethnic Categories in the United States, 2010

Racial or Ethnic Classification*	Approximate U.S. Population	Share of Total Population
Hispanic descent	**50,810,213**	**16.4%**
Mexican	32,929,683	10.6
Puerto Rican	4,691,890	1.5
Cuban	1,873,585	0.6
Other Hispanic	11,315,055	3.7
African descent	**40,357,516**	**13.0**
Nigerian	264,550	0.1
Ethiopian	202,715	0.1
Somalian	120,102	<
Other African	39,770,149	12.9
Native American descent	**2,553,566**	**0.8**
American Indian	2,075,554	0.7
Alaska Native Tribes	120,819	<
Other Native American	357,193	0.1
Asian or Pacific Island descent	**15,239,011**	**4.9**
Chinese	3,456,912	1.1
Asian Indian	2,765,155	0.9
Filipino	2,512,686	0.8
Vietnamese	1,625,365	0.5
Korean	1,456,076	0.5
Japanese	774,600	0.3
Cambodian	264,080	0.1
Other Asian or Pacific Islander	2,384,137	0.8
West Indian descent	**2,672,753**	**0.9**
Arab descent	**1,698,570**	**0.5**
Non-Hispanic European descent	**197,380,184**	**63.8**
German	47,911,129	15.5
Irish	34,670,009	11.2
English	25,927,345	8.4
Italian	17,250,211	5.6
Polish	9,569,207	3.1
French	8,761,677	2.8
Scottish	5,460,679	1.8
Dutch	4,645,906	1.5
Norwegian	4,470,081	1.4
Other non-Hispanic European	41,184,996	13.3
Two or more races	**8,398,368**	**2.7**

*People of Hispanic descent may be of any race. Many people also identify with more than one ethnic category. Therefore, figures total more than 100 percent.

< indicates less than 1/10 of 1 percent.

Source: U.S. Census Bureau (2011).

Marcos Chapa attends college in San Diego and lives in a community where most people are in some minority category.

Marianne Blumquist attends a community college in a small town an hour west of Minneapolis, where there are few racial or ethnic minorities.

Percentage of Total Population Consisting of African Americans, Hispanics, Asians, Pacific Islanders, or Native Americans

- 50% or higher
- 40% to 49%
- 30% to 39%
- 20% to 29%
- 10% to 19%
- 9% or lower

Seeing Ourselves

NATIONAL MAP 11–1 Where the Minority Majority Already Exists

Minorities are now in the majority in four states—Hawaii, California, New Mexico, and Texas—and the District of Columbia. At the other extreme, Vermont and Maine have the lowest share of racial and ethnic minorities (about 6 percent each). Why do you think states with high minority populations are located in the South and Southwest?

 Explore the percentage of minority people in your local community and in counties across the United States on **mysoclab.com**

Source: U.S. Census Bureau (2011).

can be based on race, ethnicity, or both. As shown in Table 11–1, white people of non-Hispanic background (63.8 percent of the total) are still a majority of the U.S. population. But the share of minorities is increasing. Today, minorities are a majority in four states (California, New Mexico, Texas, and Hawaii) and also in most of the country's largest cities. By about 2042, minorities are likely to form a majority of the U.S. population (Mather & Pollard, 2008; U.S. Census Bureau, 2008, 2011). National Map 11–1 shows where a minority majority already exists.

Minorities have two important characteristics. First, society imposes on them a *distinctive identity,* which may be based on physical or cultural traits. Second, minorities experience *subordination.* As this chapter shows, U.S. minorities typically have lower income, lower occupational prestige, and limited schooling. Class, race, and ethnicity, as well as gender, are overlapping and reinforcing dimensions of social stratification. The Thinking About Diversity box on page 278 describes the struggles of recent Latin American immigrants to the United States.

Of course, not all members of a particular minority category are disadvantaged. For example, some Latinos are quite wealthy, certain Chinese Americans are celebrated business leaders, and African Americans are among our nation's political leaders. But even job success rarely allows individuals to escape their minority

standing. As described in Chapter 4 ("Social Interaction in Everyday Life"), race or ethnicity often serves as a *master status* that overshadows personal accomplishments.

Minorities usually make up a small proportion of a society's population, but that is not always the case. Black South Africans are disadvantaged even though they are a numerical majority in their country. In the United States, women make up slightly more than half the population but are still struggling for the opportunities and privileges enjoyed by men.

Prejudice and Stereotypes

Apply

November 19, Jerusalem, Israel. We are driving along the edge of this historical city, a holy place to Jews, Christians, and Muslims, when Razi, our taxi driver, spots a small group of Falasha—Ethiopian Jews—on a street corner. "Those people over there," he begins, "they are different. They don't drive cars. They don't want to improve themselves. Even when our country offers them schooling, they don't take it." He shakes his head at the Ethiopians and drives on.

Early in the morning, it is already hot on the streets of Houston as a line of pickup trucks snakes slowly into a dusty yard, where 200 laborers have been gathered since dawn, hoping for a day's work. The driver of the first truck opens his window and tells the foreman that he is looking for a crew to spread boiling tar on a roof. Abdonel Cespedes, the foreman, turns to the crowd, and after a few minutes, three workers step forward and climb into the back of the truck. The next driver is looking for two experienced house-painters. The scene is repeated over and over as men and a few women leave to dig ditches, spread cement, hang drywall, open clogged septic tanks, or crawl under houses to poison rats.

As each driver pulls into the yard, the foreman asks, "How much?" Most of the people in the trucks offer $5 an hour. Cespedes automatically responds, "$7.25; the going rate is $7.25 for an hour's hard work." Sometimes he convinces people to pay that much, but usually not. The workers, who come from Mexico, El Salvador, and Guatemala, know that dozens of them will end up with no work at all this day. Most accept $5 or $6 an hour because they know that when the day is over, $50 is better than nothing.

Labor markets like this one are common in large cities, especially across the southwestern United States. The surge in immigration in recent years has brought millions of people to this country in search of work, and most have little schooling and speak little English.

Manuel Barrera has taken a day's work moving the entire contents of a store to a storage site. He arrives at the boarded-up building and gazes at the mountains of heavy furniture that he must carry out to a moving van, drive across town, and then carry again. He sighs when he realizes how hot it is outside and that it is even hotter inside the building. He will have no break for lunch. No one says anything about toilets. Barrera shakes his head: "I will do this kind of work because it puts food on the table. But I did not foresee it would turn out like this."

These immigrants gather on a New York City street corner every morning hoping to be hired for construction work that pays about $60 a day with no benefits.

The hard truth is that immigrants to the United States do the jobs that no one else wants to do. At the bottom level of the national economy, they perform low-skill jobs in restaurants and hotels and on construction crews, and they work in private homes cooking, cleaning, and caring for children. Across the United States, about half of all housekeepers, household cooks, tailors, and restaurant waiters in the United States were born abroad. Few immigrants make much more than the minimum wage ($7.25 in 2012), and rarely do immigrant workers receive any health or pension benefits. Many well-off families take the labor of immigrants as much for granted as they do their air-conditioned cars and comfortable homes.

What Do You Think?

1. In what ways do you or members of your family depend on the low-paid labor of immigrants?

2. Do you favor allowing the 11 million people who entered this country illegally the opportunity to earn citizenship? What should be done?

3. Should the U.S. government act to reduce the number of immigrants entering this country in the future? Why or why not?

Sources: Based on Booth (1998), Tumulty (2006), U.S. Department of Homeland Security (2011), and U.S. Department of Labor (2011).

Prejudice is *a rigid and unfair generalization about an entire category of people.* Prejudice is unfair because *all* people in some category are described as the same, based on little or no direct evidence. Prejudice may target people of a particular social class, sex, sexual orientation, age, political affiliation, race, or ethnicity.

Prejudices are *prejudgments* that can be either positive or negative. Our positive prejudices exaggerate the virtues of people like ourselves, and our negative prejudices condemn those who are different from us. Negative prejudice can be expressed as anything

---

prejudice a rigid and unfair generalization about an entire category of people

stereotype a simplified description applied to every person in some category

---

from mild dislike to outright hostility. Because such attitudes are rooted in culture, everyone has at least some prejudice.

Prejudice often takes the form of a **stereotype** (*stereo* is derived from a Greek word meaning "solid"), which is *a simplified description applied to every person in some category.* Many white people hold stereotypical views of minorities. Stereotyping is especially harmful to minorities in the workplace. If company officials see minority workers only in terms of a stereotype, they will make assumptions about their abilities, steer them toward certain jobs, and limit their access to better opportunities (R. L. Kaufman, 2002).

Minorities, too, stereotype whites and also other minorities (T. W. Smith, 1996; Cummings & Lambert, 1997). Surveys show, for example, that more African Americans than whites express the belief that Asians engage in unfair business practices and that more

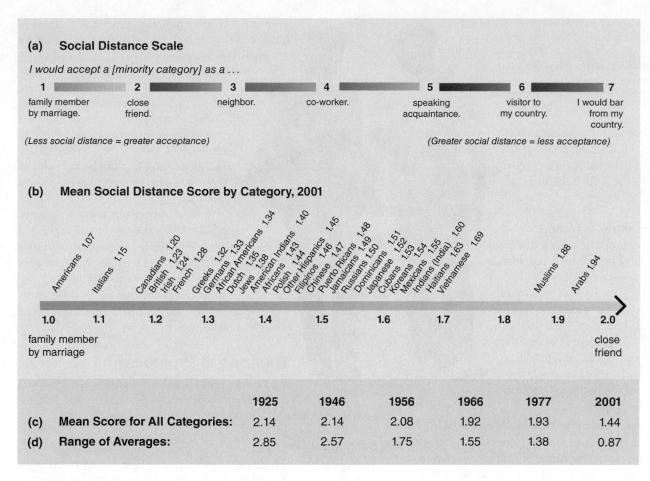

(a) Social Distance Scale

I would accept a [minority category] as a . . .

1	2	3	4	5	6	7
family member by marriage.	close friend.	neighbor.	co-worker.	speaking acquaintance.	visitor to my country.	I would bar from my country.

(Less social distance = greater acceptance)   *(Greater social distance = less acceptance)*

(b) Mean Social Distance Score by Category, 2001

Americans 1.07 · Italians 1.15 · Canadians 1.20 · British 1.23 · Irish 1.24 · French 1.28 · Greeks 1.32 · Germans 1.33 · African Americans 1.34 · Dutch 1.35 · Jews 1.38 · American Indians 1.40 · Africans 1.43 · Polish 1.44 · Other Hispanics 1.45 · Filipinos 1.46 · Chinese 1.47 · Puerto Ricans 1.48 · Jamaicans 1.49 · Russians 1.50 · Dominicans 1.51 · Japanese 1.52 · Cubans 1.53 · Koreans 1.54 · Mexicans 1.55 · Indians (India) 1.60 · Haitians 1.63 · Vietnamese 1.69 · Muslims 1.88 · Arabs 1.94

1.0	1.1	1.2	1.3	1.4	1.5	1.6	1.7	1.8	1.9	2.0

family member by marriage   close friend

	1925	1946	1956	1966	1977	2001
(c) Mean Score for All Categories:	2.14	2.14	2.08	1.92	1.93	1.44
(d) Range of Averages:	2.85	2.57	1.75	1.55	1.38	0.87

Student Snapshot

FIGURE 11–1 Bogardus Social Distance Research

The social distance scale is a good way to measure prejudice. Part (a) illustrates the complete social distance scale, from least social distance at the far left to greatest social distance at the far right. Part (b) shows the mean (average) social distance score received by each category of people in 2001. Part (c) presents the overall mean score (the average of the scores received by all racial and ethnic categories) in specific years. These scores have fallen from 2.14 in 1925 to 1.44 in 2001, showing that students express less social distance toward minorities today than they did in the past. Part (d) shows the range of averages, the difference between the highest and lowest scores in given years (in 2001, for instance, it was 0.87, the difference between the high score of 1.94 for Arabs and the low score of 1.07 for Americans). This figure has also become smaller since 1925, indicating that today's students tend to see fewer differences between various categories of people.

Source: Parrillo & Donoghue (2005).

Asians than whites criticize Hispanics for having too many children (Perlmutter, 2002).

Measuring Prejudice: The Social Distance Scale

One measure of prejudice is *social distance,* how closely people are willing to interact with members of some category. In the 1920s, Emory Bogardus developed the *social distance scale* shown in Figure 11–1. Bogardus (1925) asked students at colleges and universities in the United States how closely they were willing to interact with people in thirty racial and ethnic categories. People express the greatest social distance (most negative prejudice) by declaring that some category of people should be barred from the country entirely

(point 7 in the figure); at the other extreme, people express the least social distance (most social acceptance) by saying they would accept a member of some category into their family through marriage (point 1).

Bogardus (1925, 1967; Owen, Elsner, & McFaul, 1977) found that people felt much more social distance from some categories than from others. In general, students in his surveys expressed the most social distance from Hispanics, African Americans, Asians, and Turks by indicating that they would be willing to tolerate such people as co-workers but not as neighbors, friends, or family members. Students expressed the least social distance from those from northern and western Europe, including English and Scottish people, and also Canadians, indicating that they were willing to include them in their families by marriage.

Recent research measuring student attitudes confirms the trend of declining prejudice toward all racial and ethnic categories. On your campus, does race or ethnicity guide people's choice in romantic attachments? Do some racial and ethnic categories mix more often than others? Explain your answer.

What patterns of social distance do we find among college students today? A recent study[1] using the same social distance scale reported three major findings (Parrillo & Donoghue, 2005):

1. **Student opinion shows a trend toward greater social acceptance.** Today's students express less social distance from all minorities than students did several decades ago. Figure 11–1 on page 279 shows that the mean (average) score on the social distance scale declined from 2.14 in 1925 to 1.93 in 1977 and to 1.44 in 2001. Respondents (81 percent of whom were white) showed notably greater acceptance of African Americans, a category of people that moved up from near the bottom in 1925 to the top one-third in 2001.

2. **People see less difference between various minorities.** The earliest studies found the difference between the highest- and lowest-ranked minorities (the range of averages) equal to almost three points on the scale. As the figure shows, the most recent research produced a range of averages of less than one point, indicating that today's students tend to see fewer differences between various categories of people.

3. **The terrorist attacks of September 11, 2001, may have reduced social acceptance of Arabs and Muslims.** The most recent study was conducted just a few weeks after September 11, 2001. Perhaps the fact that the nineteen men who attacked the World Trade Center and the Pentagon were Arabs and Muslims is part of the reason that students ranked these categories last on the social distance scale. However, not a single student gave Arabs or Muslims a 7, which would have amounted to saying that they should be barred from the country. On the contrary, the 2001 mean scores (1.94 for Arabs and 1.88 for Muslims) show higher social acceptance than students in 1977 expressed toward eighteen of the thirty categories of people studied.

Racism

A powerful and harmful form of prejudice, **racism** is *the belief that one racial category is innately superior or inferior to another.* Racism has existed throughout world history. Despite their many

achievements, the ancient Greeks, the peoples of India, and the Chinese all considered people unlike themselves inferior.

Racism has also been widespread throughout the history of the United States, where ideas about racial inferiority supported slavery. Today, overt racism in this country has decreased because more people believe in evaluating others, in the words of Martin Luther King Jr., "not by the color of their skin but by the content of their character."

Even so, racism remains a serious social problem, as some people still argue that certain racial and ethnic categories are smarter than others. The Seeing Sociology in Everyday Life box explains that these commonsense stereotypes fail to recognize that racial differences in mental abilities result from environment rather than from biology.

Theories of Prejudice

Where does prejudice come from? Social scientists provide several answers to this vexing question, focusing on frustration, personality, culture, and social conflict.

Scapegoat Theory

Scapegoat theory holds that prejudice springs from frustration among people who are themselves disadvantaged (Dollard et al., 1939). Take the case of a white woman who is frustrated by her low-paying job in a textile factory. Directing her hostility at the powerful factory owners carries the obvious risk of being fired; therefore, she may blame her low pay on the presence of minority co-workers. Her prejudice does not improve her situation, but it is a relatively safe way to express anger, and it may give her the comforting feeling that at least she is superior to someone.

A **scapegoat**, then, is *a person or category of people, typically with little power, whom other people unfairly blame for their own troubles.* Because they have little power and thus are usually "safe targets," minorities often are used as scapegoats.

Authoritarian Personality Theory

Theodor Adorno and colleagues (1950) considered extreme prejudice a personality trait of certain individuals. This conclusion is supported by research indicating that people who show strong prejudice toward one minority are usually intolerant of all minorities. People with *authoritarian personalities* rigidly conform to conventional cultural values and see moral issues as clear-cut matters of right and wrong. According to Adorno, people who grow up developing authoritarian personalities also view society as naturally competitive, with "better" people (like themselves) dominating those who are weaker (all minorities).

Adorno and colleagues also found the opposite pattern to be true: People who express tolerance toward one minority are likely to be accepting of all. Such people tend to be more flexible in their moral judgments and treat all people as equals.

---

[1]Parrillo and Donoghue dropped seven of the categories used by Bogardus (Armenians, Czechs, Finns, Norwegians, Scots, Swedes, and Turks), claiming they were no longer visible minorities. He added nine new categories (Africans, Arabs, Cubans, Dominicans, Haitians, Jamaicans, Muslims, Puerto Ricans, and Vietnamese), claiming that these are visible minorities today. This change probably encouraged higher social distance scores, making the trend toward decreasing social distance all the more significant.

Does Race Affect Intelligence?

As we go through an average day, we encounter people of various racial and ethnic categories. We also deal with people who are very intelligent as well as those whose abilities are more modest. But is there a connection between race or ethnicity and intelligence?

Common stereotypes say that Asian Americans are smarter than white people and that the typical white person is more intelligent than the average African American. Throughout the history of the United States, many people have assumed that some categories of people are smarter than others. Just as important, people have used this thinking to justify the privileges of the allegedly superior category and even to bar supposedly inferior people from entering this country.

So what do we know about intelligence? Scientists know that people, as individuals, differ in mental abilities. The distribution of human intelligence forms a "bell curve," as shown in the figure. A person's *intelligence quotient* (IQ) is calculated as the person's mental age in years, as measured by a test, divided by the person's actual age in years, with the result multiplied by 100. An eight-year-old who performs like a ten-year-old has an IQ of $10 \div 8 = 1.25 \times 100 = 125$. Average performance is defined as an IQ of 100.

In a controversial study of intelligence and social inequality, Richard Herrnstein and Charles Murray (1994) claimed that race is related to measures of intelligence. More specifically, they said that the average IQ for people of European ancestry is 100, for people of East Asian ancestry is 103, and for people of African ancestry is 90.

Such assertions go against our democratic and egalitarian beliefs that no racial type is naturally better than another. Because these findings can increase prejudice, critics argue that

intelligence tests are not valid and even that the concept of intelligence has little real meaning.

Most social scientists believe that IQ tests do measure something important that we think of as intelligence, and they agree that *individuals* vary in intellectual aptitude. But they reject the idea that any *category* of people, on average, is naturally smarter than any other. So how do we explain the overall differences in IQ scores by race?

Thomas Sowell (1994, 1995) explains that most of this difference results not from biology but from environment. In some skillful sociological detective work, Sowell traced IQ scores for various racial and ethnic categories throughout the twentieth century. He found that on average, early-twentieth-century immigrants from European nations such as Poland, Lithuania, Italy, and Greece, as well as from Asian countries including China and Japan, scored 10 to 15 points below the U.S. average. But by the end of the twentieth century, people in these same categories had IQ scores that were average or above average. Among Italian Americans, for example, average IQ jumped almost 10 points; among Polish and Chinese Americans, the increase was almost 20 points.

Because genetic changes occur over thousands of years and most people in these

categories marry others like themselves, biological factors cannot explain such a rapid rise in IQ scores. The only reasonable explanation is changing cultural patterns. The descendants of early immigrants improved their intellectual performance as their standard of living rose and their opportunity for schooling increased.

Sowell found that much the same was true of African Americans. Historically, the average IQ score of African Americans living in the North has been about 10 points higher than the average score of those living in the South. Among the descendants of African Americans who migrated from the South to the North after 1940, IQ scores went up, just as they did for descendants of European and Asian immigrants. Thus environmental factors appear to be critical in explaining differences in IQ among various categories of people.

According to Sowell, these test score differences tell us that *cultural patterns matter*. Asians who score high on tests are no smarter than other people, but they have been raised to value learning and pursue excellence. African Americans are no less intelligent than anyone else, but they carry a legacy of disadvantage that can undermine self-confidence and discourage achievement.

What Do You Think?

1. If IQ scores reflect people's environment, are they valid measures of intelligence? Could they be harmful?

2. According to Thomas Sowell, why do some racial and ethnic categories show dramatic short-term gains in average IQ scores?

3. Do you think parents and schools influence a child's IQ score? If so, how?

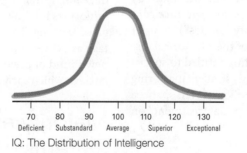

| 70 | 80 | 90 | 100 | 110 | 120 | 130 |
| Deficient | Substandard | | Average | | Superior | Exceptional |

IQ: The Distribution of Intelligence

Adorno thought that people with little schooling and those raised by cold and demanding parents tend to develop authoritarian personalities. Filled with anger and anxiety as children, they grow into hostile and aggressive adults who seek out scapegoats.

Culture Theory

A third theory claims that although extreme prejudice is found in certain people, some prejudice is found in everyone. Why? Because prejudice is part of the culture in which we all live and learn. The Bogardus social distance studies help prove the point. Bogardus found that students across the country had mostly the same

attitudes toward specific racial and ethnic categories, feeling closer to some and more distant from others.

More evidence that prejudice is rooted in culture is the fact that minorities express the same attitudes as white people toward categories other than their own. Such patterns suggest that individuals hold prejudices because we live in a "culture of prejudice" that has taught us to view certain categories of people as "better" or "worse" than others.

Conflict Theory

A fourth explanation proposes that prejudice is used as a tool by powerful people to oppress others. Anglos who look down on Latino

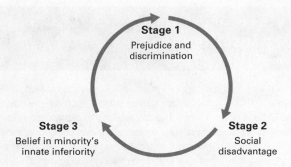

Stage 1
Prejudice and
discrimination

Stage 3
Belief in minority's
innate inferiority

Stage 2
Social
disadvantage

Stage 1: Prejudice and discrimination begin, often as an expression of ethnocentrism or an attempt to justify economic exploitation.

Stage 2: As a result of prejudice and discrimination, a minority is socially disadvantaged, occupying a low position in the system of social stratification.

Stage 3: This social disadvantage is then interpreted not as the result of earlier prejudice and discrimination but as evidence that the minority is innately inferior, unleashing renewed prejudice and discrimination by which the cycle repeats itself.

 FIGURE 11–2 Prejudice and Discrimination: The Vicious Circle

Prejudice and discrimination can form a vicious circle, thereby perpetuating themselves.

immigrants in the Southwest, for example, can get away with paying the immigrants low wages for long hours of hard work. Similarly, all elites benefit when prejudice divides workers along racial and ethnic lines and discourages them from working together to advance their common interests (Geschwender, 1978; Olzak, 1989; Rothenberg, 2008).

According to another conflict-based argument, made by Shelby Steele (1990), minorities themselves encourage *race consciousness* (which is sometimes called "identity politics") in order to win greater power and privileges. Because of their historical disadvantage, minorities claim that they are victims entitled to special consideration based on their race. Although this strategy may bring short-term gains, Steele cautions that such thinking often sparks a backlash from whites or others who oppose "special treatment" on the basis of race or ethnicity.

Discrimination

 Evaluate

Closely related to prejudice is **discrimination,** *unequal treatment of various categories of people.* Prejudice refers to *attitudes;* discrimination is a matter of *action.* Like prejudice, discrimination can be either positive (providing special advantages) or negative (creating obstacles) and ranges from subtle to extreme.

Institutional Prejudice and Discrimination

We typically think of prejudice and discrimination as the hateful ideas or actions of specific people. But Stokely Carmichael and Charles Hamilton (1967) point out that far greater harm results from **institutional prejudice and discrimination,** *bias built into the operation of society's institutions,* including schools, hospitals,

law enforcement, and the workplace. For example, researchers have shown that banks reject home mortgage applications from minorities at a higher rate—or charge higher rates for the same mortgage—compared to white applicants, even when income and quality of neighborhood are held constant (Gotham, 1998; Blanton, 2007).

According to Carmichael and Hamilton, people are slow to condemn or even recognize institutional prejudice and discrimination because it often involves respected public officials and long-established traditions. A case in point is *Brown* v. *Board of Education of Topeka,* the 1954 Supreme Court decision that ended the legal segregation of U.S. schools. The principle of "separate but equal" schooling had been the law of the land, supporting racial inequality by allowing school segregation. Despite this change in the law, more than half a century later, most U.S. students still attend schools in which one race overwhelmingly predominates (KewalRamani et al., 2007). In 1991, the courts pointed out that neighborhood schools will never provide equal education as long as our population is racially segregated, with most African Americans living in central cities and most white people and Asian Americans living in suburbs.

Prejudice and Discrimination: The Vicious Circle

Prejudice and discrimination reinforce each other. The Thomas theorem, discussed in Chapter 4 ("Social Interaction in Everyday Life"), offers a simple explanation of this fact: *Situations that are defined as real become real in their consequences* (Thomas & Thomas, 1928; Thomas 1966:301, orig. 1931).

As Thomas recognized, stereotypes become real to people who believe them and sometimes even to those victimized by them. Prejudice on the part of white people toward people of color does not produce *innate* inferiority, but it can produce *social* inferiority, pushing minorities into low-paying jobs, inferior schools, and racially segregated housing. Then, as white people interpret that social disadvantage as evidence that minorities do not measure up, they unleash a new round of prejudice and discrimination, giving rise to a vicious circle in which each perpetuates the other, as shown in Figure 11–2.

Majority and Minority: Patterns of Interaction

 Analyze

Social scientists describe interaction between majority and minority members of a society in terms of four models: pluralism, assimilation, segregation, and genocide.

Pluralism

Pluralism is *a state in which people of all races and ethnicities are distinct but have equal social standing.* In other words, people who differ

---

discrimination unequal treatment of various categories of people

institutional prejudice and discrimination bias built into the operation of society's institutions

Should we expect people who come to the United States to change their language and other cultural patterns in order to "fit in," or should we expect them to hold onto their own traditions? Why?

in appearance or social heritage all share resources roughly equally.

The United States is pluralistic to the extent that almost all people have equal standing under the law. In addition, large cities contain countless "ethnic villages" where people proudly display the traditions of their immigrant ancestors. These include New York's Spanish Harlem, Little Italy, and Chinatown; Philadelphia's Italian "South Philly"; Chicago's "Little Saigon"; and Latino East Los Angeles. New York City alone has more than 300 magazines, newspapers, and radio stations in more than ninety languages (Paul, 2001; Logan, Alba, & Zhang, 2002; New York Community Media Alliance, 2011).

But the United States is not truly pluralistic, for three reasons. First, although most people value their cultural heritage, few want to live exclusively with others exactly like themselves (NORC, 2011: 667–70). Second, our tolerance for social diversity goes only so far. One reaction to the growing proportion of minorities in the United States is a social movement to make English the nation's official language. Third, as you will see later in this chapter, people of various colors and cultures do *not* have equal social standing.

Assimilation

Many people think of the United States as a "melting pot" in which different nationalities blend together. But rather than everyone "melting" into some new cultural pattern, most minorities have adopted the dominant culture established by the earliest settlers. Why? Because doing so is both the avenue to upward social mobility and a way to escape the prejudice and discrimination directed at more visible foreigners. Sociologists use the term **assimilation** to describe *the process by which minorities gradually adopt patterns of the dominant culture*. Assimilation involves changing styles of dress, values, religion, language, and friends.

The amount of assimilation varies by category. For example, in the United States, Canadians have "melted" more than Cubans, the Dutch more than Dominicans, Germans more than the Japanese. Multiculturalists oppose making assimilation a goal because it suggests that minorities are "the problem" and the ones who need to do all the changing.

Note that assimilation involves changes in ethnicity but not in race. For example, many descendants of Japanese immigrants have discarded their ethnic traditions but retain their racial identity. For racial traits to diminish over generations, **miscegenation**, or *biological reproduction by partners of different racial categories*, must occur. Although interracial marriage is becoming more common, it still amounts to only 7.5 percent of all U.S. marriages (U.S. Census Bureau, 2011).

Segregation

Segregation is *the physical and social separation of categories of people*. Sometimes minorities, especially religious orders such as the Amish, voluntarily segregate themselves. Usually, however, majorities segregate minorities by excluding them. Neighborhoods, schools, occupations, hospitals, and even cemeteries may be segregated. Pluralism encourages cultural distinctiveness without disadvantage; segregation enforces separation that harms a minority.

Racial segregation has a long history in the United States, beginning with slavery and evolving into racially separated housing, schools, buses, and trains. Decisions such as the 1954 *Brown* case have reduced *de jure* (Latin, "by law") discrimination in the United States. However, *de facto* ("in fact") segregation continues in the form of countless neighborhoods that are home to people of a single race.

Despite some recent decline, segregation continues in the United States. For example, Livonia, Michigan, is 90 percent white, and neighboring Detroit is 80 percent African American. Kurt Metzger (2001) explains, "Livonia was pretty much created by white flight [from Detroit]." Research shows that across the country, whites (especially those with young children) continue to avoid neighborhoods where African Americans live (Emerson, Yancey, & Chai, 2001; Krysan, 2002). At the extreme, Douglas Massey and Nancy Denton (1989) document the *hypersegregation* of poor African Americans in some inner cities. Hypersegregation means having little contact of any kind with people beyond the local community. Hypersegregation is the daily experience of about 20 percent of poor African Americans and is a pattern found in about twenty-five large U.S. cities (Wilkes & Iceland, 2004; U.S. Census Bureau, 2011).

Genocide

Genocide is *the systematic killing of one category of people by another*. This deadly form of racism and ethnocentrism violates nearly every recognized moral standard, yet it has occurred time and again in human history.

Patterns of Majority and Minority Interaction

pluralism a state in which people of all races and ethnicities are distinct but have equal social standing

assimilation the process by which minorities gradually adopt patterns of the dominant culture

segregation the physical and social separation of categories of people

genocide the systematic killing of one category of people by another

Genocide was common in the history of contact between Europeans and the original inhabitants of the Americas. From the sixteenth century on, the Spanish, Portuguese, English, French, and Dutch forcibly colonized vast empires. Although most native people died from diseases brought by Europeans, against which they had no natural defenses, many who opposed the colonizers were killed deliberately (Matthiessen, 1984; Sale, 1990).

Genocide also occurred in the twentieth century. Beginning in 1915, more than 1 million Armenians in Eastern Europe perished under the rule of the Ottoman Empire. Soon after that, European Jews experienced a reign of terror known as the Holocaust during Adolf Hitler's rule in Germany. From about 1935 to 1945, the Nazis murdered more than 6 million Jewish men, women, and children, along with gay people, Gypsies, and people with handicaps. The Soviet dictator Josef Stalin murdered on an even greater scale, killing some 30 million real and imagined enemies during decades of violent rule. Between 1975 and 1980, Pol Pot's Communist regime in Cambodia butchered all "capitalists," which included anyone able to speak a Western language. In all, some 2 million people (one-fourth of the population) perished in the Cambodian "killing fields."

Tragically, genocide continues in the modern world. Recent examples include Hutus killing Tutsis in the African nation of Rwanda, Serbs killing Bosnians in the Balkans of Eastern Europe, and the killing of hundreds of thousands of people in the Darfur region of Sudan in Africa.

These four patterns of minority-majority contact have all been played out in the United States. Although many people proudly point to patterns of pluralism and assimilation, it is also important to recognize the degree to which U.S. society has been built on segregation (of African Americans) and genocide (of Native

Americans). The remainder of this chapter examines how these four patterns have shaped the past and present social standing of major racial and ethnic categories in the United States.

Race and Ethnicity in the United States

 Analyze

Give me your tired, your poor,
Your huddled masses yearning to breathe free,
The wretched refuse of your teeming shore,
Send these, the homeless, tempest-tossed to me:
I lift my lamp beside the golden door!

These words by Emma Lazarus, inscribed on base of the Statue of Liberty, express cultural ideals of human dignity, personal freedom, and economic opportunity. Indeed, the United States has provided more of the "good life" to more immigrants than any other nation. About 1.25 million immigrants come to this country every year, and their ways of life create a social mosaic that is especially evident in large cities.

However, as a survey of racial and ethnic minorities in the United States will show, our country's golden door has opened more widely for some than for others. We turn to the history and current social standing of the major categories of the U.S. population.

Native Americans

The term "Native Americans" refers to the hundreds of societies—including Aleuts, Cherokee, Zuni, Sioux, Mohawk, Aztec, and Inca—who first settled the Western Hemisphere. At least 15,000 years before Christopher Columbus landed in the Americas, migrating peoples crossed a land bridge from Asia to North America where the Bering Strait (off the coast of Alaska) lies today. Gradually, they spread throughout North and South America.

When the first Europeans arrived late in the fifteenth century, Native Americans numbered in the millions. But by 1900, after centuries of conflict and acts of genocide, the "vanishing Americans" numbered just 250,000 (Dobyns, 1966; Tyler, 1973). As National Map 11–2 shows, the land they controlled also shrank dramatically.

Columbus first referred to the Native Americans that he encountered as "Indians" because he mistakenly thought he had reached the coast of India. Columbus found the native people passive and peaceful, in stark contrast to the materialistic and competitive Europeans (Matthiessen, 1984; Sale, 1990). Yet Europeans justified the seizure of Native Americans' land by calling them thieves and murderers (Josephy, 1982; Matthiessen, 1984; Sale, 1990).

After the Revolutionary War, the new U.S. government adopted a pluralistic approach to Native American societies and tried to gain more land through treaties. Payment for land was far from fair, however, and when Native Americans resisted surrendering their homelands, the U.S. government simply used its superior military power to evict them. By the early 1800s, few Native Americans remained east of the Mississippi River.

In an effort to force assimilation, the U.S. Bureau of Indian Affairs took American Indian children from their families and placed them in boarding schools like this one, Oklahoma's Riverside Indian School. There they were taught to speak English by non-Indian teachers with the goal of making them into "Americans."

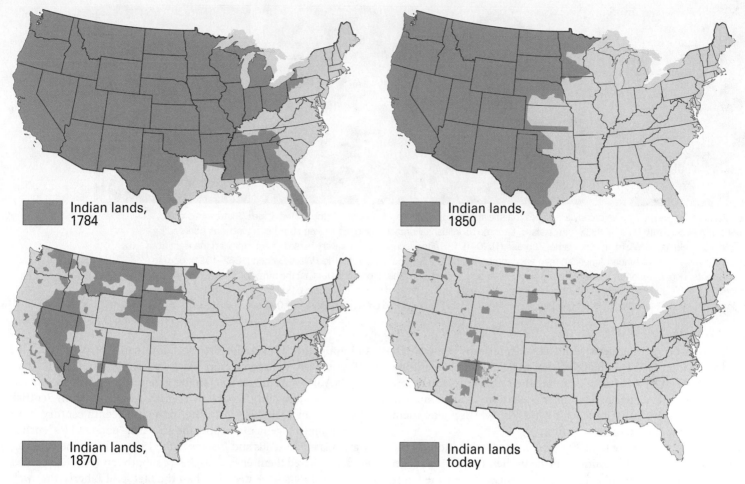

Seeing Ourselves

NATIONAL MAP 11–2 Land Controlled by Native Americans, 1784 to Today

In 1784, Native Americans controlled three-fourths of the land (blue-shaded areas) that eventually became the United States. Today, Native Americans control 436 reservations, scattered across the United States, that account for just 5.3 percent of the country's land area. How would you characterize these locations?

Sources: Waldman (2000) and U.S. Census Bureau (2011).

In 1871, the United States declared Native Americans wards of the government and adopted a strategy of forced assimilation. Relocated to specific territories designated as "reservations," Native Americans continued to lose their land and were on their way to losing their culture as well. Reservation life encouraged dependency on outsiders, replacing ancestral languages with English and traditional religion with Christianity. Officials took many children from their parents and handed them over to boarding schools, where they were resocialized as "Americans." Authorities gave local control of reservations to the few Native Americans who supported government policies, and they distributed reservation land, traditionally held collectively, as private property to individual families (Tyler, 1973).

Not until 1924 were Native Americans entitled to U.S. citizenship. After that, many migrated from the reservations, adopting mainstream cultural patterns and marrying non–Native Americans. Today, one-half of Native Americans consider themselves biracial or multiracial (U.S. Census Bureau, 2011), and many large cities now contain sizable Native American populations. However, as Table 11–2 shows, the income of Native Americans is far below the U.S. average, and relatively few Native Americans earn a college degree.[2]

TABLE 11–2 The Social Standing of Native Americans, 2010		
	Native Americans	Entire U.S. Population
Median family income	$39,664	$60,395
Percentage in poverty	23.7%	15.1%
Completion of four or more years of college (age 25 and over)	13.4%	30.4%

Source: U.S. Census Bureau (2011).

[2]In making comparisons of education and income, keep in mind that various categories of the U.S. population have different median ages. In 2010, the median age for all U.S. people was 37.2 years; for Native Americans, the figure was 31.0 years. Because people's schooling and income increase over time, this age difference accounts for some of the disparities shown in Table 11–2.

The efforts of these four women greatly advanced the social standing of African Americans in the United States. Pictured from left to right: Sojourner Truth (1797–1883), born a slave, became an influential preacher and outspoken abolitionist who was honored by President Lincoln at the White House. Harriet Tubman (1820–1913), after escaping from slavery herself, masterminded the flight from bondage of hundreds of African American men and women via the "Underground Railroad." Ida Wells-Barnett (1862–1931), born to slave parents, became a partner in a Memphis newspaper and served as a tireless crusader against the terror of lynching. Marian Anderson (1902–1993), an exceptional singer whose early career was restrained by racial prejudice, broke symbolic "color lines" by singing in the White House in 1936 and on the steps of the Lincoln Memorial to a crowd of almost 100,000 people in 1939.

From in-depth interviews with Native Americans in a western city, Joan Albon (1971) concluded that their low social standing was a result of cultural factors, including their noncompetitive view of life and reluctance to pursue higher education. In addition, she noted, many Native Americans have dark skin, which makes them targets of prejudice and discrimination.

Members of the more than 200 American Indian nations in the United States today are reclaiming pride in their cultural heritage. Traditional cultural organizations report a surge in new membership applications, and many children can now speak native languages better than their parents. The legal right of Native Americans to govern their reservations has enabled some tribes to build profitable gaming casinos. But the wealth produced from gambling has enriched relatively few Native peoples, and most profits go to non-Indian investors (Bartlett & Steele, 2002). While some prosper, most Native Americans remain severely disadvantaged, with a profound sense of the injustice they have suffered at the hands of white people.

White Anglo-Saxon Protestants

White Anglo-Saxon Protestants (WASPs) were not the first people to inhabit the United States, but they soon dominated the nation after European settlement began. Most WASPs are of English ancestry, but this category also includes people from Scotland and Wales. With some 33 million people claiming English, Scottish, or Welsh ancestry, 10.7 percent of our society has some WASP background, and WASPs are found at all class levels (U.S. Census Bureau, 2011).

Many people associate WASPs with elite communities along the East and West Coasts. But the highest concentrations of WASPs are in Utah (because of migrations of Mormons with English ancestry), Appalachia, and northern New England (also due to historical patterns of immigration).

Looking back in time, WASP immigrants were highly skilled and motivated to achieve by what we now call the Protestant work ethic. Because of their numbers and power, WASPs were not subject to the prejudice and discrimination experienced by other categories of immigrants. In fact, the historical dominance of WASPs has led others to want to become more like them (K. W. Jones, 2001).

WASPs were never one single group; especially during colonial times, hostility separated English Anglicans from Scottish Presbyterians (Parrillo, 1994). But in the nineteenth century, most WASPs joined together to oppose the arrival of "undesirables" such as Germans in the 1840s and Italians in the 1880s. Those who could afford it sheltered themselves in exclusive suburbs and restrictive clubs. Thus the 1880s—the decade when the Statue of Liberty first welcomed immigrants to the United States—also saw the founding of the first country club with exclusively WASP members (Baltzell, 1964).

By about 1950, however, WASP wealth and power had peaked, as indicated by the 1960 election of John Fitzgerald Kennedy, the first Irish Catholic president. Yet the WASP cultural legacy remains. English is this country's dominant language and Protestantism the majority religion. Our legal system also reflects its English origins. But the historical dominance of WASPs is most evident in the widespread use of the terms "race" and "ethnicity" to describe everyone but them.

African Americans

Africans accompanied European explorers to the New World in the fifteenth century. But most accounts trace the beginning of black history in the United States to 1619, when a Dutch trading ship brought twenty Africans to Jamestown, Virginia. Many more ships filled with African laborers followed. Whether these people arrived as slaves or as indentured servants (who paid for their passage by agreeing to work for a period of time), being of African descent on these shores soon became virtually synonymous with being a slave. In 1661, Virginia enacted the first law in the new colonies recognizing slavery (Sowell, 1981).

Slavery was the foundation of the southern colonies' plantation system. White people ran plantations using slave labor, and until 1808, some were also slave traders. Traders—including North Americans, Africans, and Europeans—forcibly transported some

The Congressional Black Caucus represents the increasing political power of African Americans in the United States. Even so, in 2011, African Americans accounted for just forty-four members of the House of Representatives, one state governor, and no members of the U.S. Senate.

10 million Africans to various countries in the Americas, including 400,000 to the United States. On small sailing ships, hundreds of slaves were chained for the several weeks it took to cross the Atlantic Ocean. Filth and disease killed many and drove others to suicide. Overall, perhaps half died en route (Franklin, 1967; Sowell, 1981).

The reward for surviving the miserable journey was a lifetime of servitude. Although some slaves worked in cities at various trades, most labored in the fields, often from daybreak until sunset and even longer during the harvest. The law allowed owners to use whatever disciplinary measures they deemed necessary to ensure that slaves were obedient and hardworking. Even killing a slave rarely prompted legal action. Owners also divided slave families at public auctions, where human beings were bought and sold as property. Unschooled and dependent on their owners for all their basic needs, slaves had little control over their lives (Franklin, 1967; Sowell, 1981).

Some free people of color lived in both the North and the South, laboring as small-scale farmers, skilled workers, and small business owners. But the lives of most African Americans stood in glaring contradiction to the principles of freedom on which the United States was founded. The Declaration of Independence states:

> We hold these Truths to be self-evident, that all Men are created equal, that they are endowed by their Creator with certain unalienable Rights, that among these are Life, Liberty, and the Pursuit of Happiness.

However, most white people did not apply these ideals to African Americans. In the *Dred Scott* case in 1857, the U.S. Supreme Court addressed the question "Are slaves citizens?" by writing, "We think they are not, and that they are not included, and were not intended to be included, under the word 'citizens' in the Constitution, and can therefore claim none of the rights and privileges which that instrument provides for and secures for citizens of the United States" (quoted in Blaustein & Zangrando, 1968:160). Thus arose what the Swedish sociologist Gunnar Myrdal (1944) called the "American dilemma": a democratic society's denial of basic rights and freedoms to one category of people. People would speak of equality, in other words, but then fail to extend the same rights and freedoms to all categories of people. Many white people resolved

this dilemma by defining black people as naturally inferior and therefore undeserving of equality (Leach, 2002).

In 1865, the Thirteenth Amendment to the Constitution outlawed slavery. Three years later, the Fourteenth Amendment reversed the *Dred Scott* ruling, granting citizenship to all people born in the United States. The Fifteenth Amendment, ratified in 1870, stated that neither race nor previous condition of servitude could deprive any (male) citizen of the right to vote. However, so-called *Jim Crow laws*—classic cases of institutional discrimination—segregated U.S. society into two racial castes. Especially in the South, white people beat and lynched black people (and some white people) who challenged the racial hierarchy.

The twentieth century brought dramatic changes for African Americans. After World War I, tens of thousands of women and men fled the rural South for jobs in northern factories. Although most did find economic opportunities, few escaped racial prejudice and discrimination, which placed them lower in the social hierarchy than white immigrants arriving from Europe.

In the 1950s, a national civil rights movement set the climate for a landmark judicial decision that outlawed segregated schools, and in the 1960s, legislation outlawed overt discrimination in employment and public accommodations. The Black Power movement in the 1960s and 1970s gave African Americans a renewed sense of pride and purpose.

Despite these gains, people of African descent continue to occupy a lower social position in the United States, as shown in Table 11–3. The median income of African American families in 2010 ($38,500) was only 56 percent of non-Hispanic white family income ($68,961), a ratio that has changed little in thirty years.[3] Black families remain three times as likely as white families to be poor.

TABLE 11–3 The Social Standing of African Americans, 2010

	African Americans	Entire U.S. Population
Median family income	$38,500	$60,395
Percentage in poverty	27.4%	15.1%
Completion of four or more years of college (age 25 and over)	19.9%	30.4%

Source: U.S. Census Bureau (2011).

[3]Here again, a median age difference (non-Hispanic whites, 42.1; blacks, 32.1) accounts for some of the income and educational disparities. More important is a higher proportion of one-parent families among blacks than whites. If we compare only married-couple families, African Americans (median income $60,772 in 2010) earned 79 percent as much as non-Hispanic whites ($77,416).

The number of African American families securely in the middle class rose by more than half between 1980 and 2010. Today, 40 percent of African American families earn $48,000 or more each year. This means that the African American community is now economically diverse. Even so, a majority of African Americans are still working-class or poor. In recent years, many have seen earnings slip as urban factory jobs, vital to residents of central cities, have been lost to other countries where labor costs are lower. This is one reason that black unemployment is almost twice as high as white unemployment; among African American teenagers in many cities, the unemployment figure exceeds 40 percent. The Great Recession of the past few years has further hurt African Americans, with the wealth of the typical household falling by about half between 2005 and 2010 (R. A. Smith, 2002; Siegel, 2011; U.S. Department of Labor, 2011).

Since 1980, African Americans have made remarkable educational progress. The share of adults completing high school rose from half to 85 percent in 2010, nearly closing the gap between blacks and whites. Between 1980 and 2010, the share of African American adults with at least a college degree rose from 8 percent to almost 20 percent. But as Table 11–3 on page 287 shows, African Americans are still well below the national average when it comes to completing four years of college.

The political clout of African Americans has greatly increased. As a result of both black migration to the cities and white flight to the suburbs, African Americans have gained greater political power in urban places, and many of this country's largest cities have had African American mayors. At the national level, the election of Barack Obama as this country's forty-fourth president—the first African American to hold this office—is a historic and hugely important event. It demonstrates that our society has moved beyond the assumption that race is a barrier to the highest office in the land (West, 2008). Yet in 2011, African Americans accounted for just forty-four members of the House of Representatives (10 percent of 435), no members of the Senate (out of 100), and only one of fifty state governors (National Governors Association, 2011; U.S. House of Representatives, 2011; U.S. Senate, 2011).

In sum, for nearly 400 years, people of African ancestry in the United States have struggled for social equality. As a nation, the United States has come far in this pursuit. Overt discrimination is now illegal, and research documents a long-term decline in prejudice against African Americans (Firebaugh & Davis, 1988; J. Q. Wilson, 1992; NORC, 2011).

On average, Asian Americans have income above the national median. At the same time, however, the poverty rate in many Asian American communities—including San Francisco's Chinatown—is well above average.

Fifty years after the abolition of slavery, W. E. B. Du Bois (1913) pointed to the extent of black achievement but cautioned that racial caste remained strong in the United States. Almost a century later, this racial hierarchy persists.

Asian Americans

Although Asian Americans share some racial traits, enormous cultural diversity marks this category of people. In 2010, the total number of Asian Americans exceeded 15.2 million, or about 4.9 percent of the U.S. population. The largest category of Asian Americans is people of Chinese ancestry (3.5 million), followed by those of Asian Indian (2.8 million), Filipino (2.5 million), Vietnamese (1.6 million), Korean (1.5 million), and Japanese (775,000) descent. Almost one-third of Asian Americans live in California.

Many young Asian Americans command attention and respect as academic high achievers and are disproportionately represented at our country's best colleges and universities. Many of their elders have also made economic and social gains; most Asian Americans now live in middle-class suburbs. Yet despite (and sometimes because of) their achievements, Asian Americans often find that others are aloof or outright hostile toward them (Chua-Eoan, 2000; Lee & Marlay, 2007).

The achievement of some Asian Americans has given rise to a "model minority" stereotype that is misleading because it hides the differences in class standing found among their ranks. We will focus on the history and current standing of Chinese Americans and Japanese Americans—the longest-established Asian American minorities—and conclude with a brief look at the most recent arrivals.

Chinese Americans

Chinese immigration to the United States began in 1849 with the economic boom of California's Gold Rush. New towns and businesses sprang up overnight, and the demand for cheap labor attracted some 100,000 Chinese immigrants. Most Chinese workers were young, hardworking men willing to take low-status jobs that whites did not want. But the economy soured in the 1870s, and desperate whites began to compete with the Chinese for whatever work could be found. Suddenly, the hardworking Chinese were seen as a threat. Economic hard times led to prejudice and discrimination (Ling, 1971; Boswell, 1986). Soon laws were passed barring Chinese people from many occupations, and public opinion turned strongly against the "Yellow Peril."

In 1882, the U.S. government passed the first of several laws limiting Chinese immigration. This action caused domestic hardship because in the United States, Chinese men outnumbered Chinese women by twenty to one. This sex imbalance drove the Chinese population down to only 60,000 by 1920. Because Chinese women already in the United States were in high demand, they soon lost much of their traditional submissiveness to men (Hsu, 1971; Lai, 1980; Sowell, 1981).

TABLE 11–4 The Social Standing of Asian Americans, 2010

	All Asian Americans	Chinese Americans	Japanese Americans	Asian Indian Americans	Filipino Americans	Korean Americans	Entire U.S. Population
Median family income	$75,486	$77,926	$85,894	$100,520	$85,837	$61,683	$60,395
Percentage in poverty	12.1%	13.9%	8.0%	8.5%	6.1%	15.8%	15.1%
Completion of four or more years of college (age 25 and over)	50.3%	51.8%	47.4%	70.8%	48.5%	52.9%	30.4%

Source: U.S. Census Bureau (2011).

Responding to racial hostility, some Chinese moved east; many more sought the relative safety of urban Chinatowns. There Chinese traditions flourished, and kinship networks, called *clans,* offered financial assistance to individuals and represented the interests of all. At the same time, however, living in an all-Chinese community discouraged people from learning English, which limited their job opportunities (Wong, 1971).

A renewed need for labor during World War II prompted President Franklin Roosevelt to end the ban on Chinese immigration in 1943 and to extend the rights of citizenship to Chinese Americans born abroad. Many responded by moving out of Chinatowns and seeking cultural assimilation. In turn-of-the-century Honolulu, for example, 70 percent of the Chinese people lived in Chinatown; today, the figure is below 20 percent.

By 1950, many Chinese Americans had experienced upward social mobility. Today, people of Chinese ancestry are no longer limited to self-employment in laundries and restaurants; many hold high-prestige positions, especially in fields related to science and technology.

As shown in Table 11–4, the median family income of Chinese Americans in 2010 was $77,926, higher than the national average of $60,395. However, the higher income of all Asian Americans reflects a larger number of family members in the labor force.[4] Chinese Americans also have an enviable record of educational achievement, standing significantly above the national average in college graduation.

Despite their success, many Chinese Americans still deal with subtle (and sometimes blatant) prejudice and discrimination. Such hostility is one reason that poverty among Chinese Americans stands near the national average. The problem of poverty is most common among those who remain in the socially isolated Chinatowns working in restaurants or other low-paying jobs, raising the question of whether racial and ethnic enclaves help their residents or exploit them (Portes & Jensen, 1989; Kinkead, 1992; Gilbertson & Gurak, 1993).

Japanese Americans

Japanese immigration to the United States began slowly in the 1860s, reaching only 3,000 by 1890. Most of these immigrants came to the Hawaiian Islands (annexed by the United States in 1898 and made a state in 1959) to take low-paying jobs. After 1900, as the number of Japanese immigrants to California increased (reaching 140,000 by 1915), white hostility increased (Takaki, 1998). In 1907, the United States signed an agreement with Japan limiting the entry of men—the chief economic threat—while allowing Japanese women to immigrate to ease the sex ratio imbalance. In the 1920s, state laws in California and dozens of other states mandated segregation and banned interracial marriage, virtually ending further Japanese immigration. Not until 1952 did the United States extend citizenship to foreign-born Japanese.

Japanese and Chinese immigrants differed in three important ways. First, there were fewer Japanese immigrants, so they escaped some of the hostility directed at the more numerous Chinese. Second, the Japanese knew much more about the United States than the Chinese did, which helped them assimilate (Sowell, 1981). Third, Japanese immigrants preferred rural farming to clustering in cities, which made them less visible. But many white people objected to Japanese ownership of farmland, so in 1913, California barred further purchases. Many foreign-born Japanese (called the *Issei*) responded by placing farmland in the names of their U.S.-born children (*Nisei*), who were constitutionally entitled to citizenship.

Japanese Americans faced their greatest crisis after Japan bombed the U.S. naval fleet at Pearl Harbor, Hawaii, on December 7, 1941. Rage was directed at the Japanese living in the United States. Some people feared that the Japanese here would spy for Japan or commit acts of sabotage. Within a year, President Franklin Roosevelt signed Executive Order 9066, an unprecedented action designed to ensure national security by detaining people of Japanese descent in military camps. Authorities soon relocated 120,000 people of Japanese descent (90 percent of all U.S. Japanese) to remote inland reservations (Sun, 1998; Ewers, 2008).

Concern about national security always rises in times of war, but Japanese internment was sharply criticized. First, it targeted an entire category of people, not one of whom was ever known to have committed a disloyal act. Second, roughly two-thirds of those imprisoned were *Nisei,* U.S. citizens by birth. Third, the United States was also at war with Germany and Italy, but no comparable action was taken against people of German or Italian ancestry.

Relocation meant selling homes, furnishings, and businesses on short notice for pennies on the dollar. As a result, almost the entire Japanese American population was economically devastated. Herded into military prisons, surrounded by barbed wire, and guarded by armed soldiers, families crowded into single rooms, often in buildings that had previously sheltered livestock. The internment ended in 1944 when the Supreme Court declared

---

[4]Median age for all Asian Americans in 2010 was 35.2 years, somewhat below the national median of 37.2 and the non-Hispanic white median of 42.1. But specific categories vary widely in median age: Japanese, 47.6; Filipino, 38.9; Chinese, 37.6; Korean, 36.7; Asian Indian, 32.3; Cambodian, 29.3; Hmong, 20.7 (U.S. Census Bureau, 2011).

In 2010, claiming the federal government is not securing our borders, Arizona officials enacted a new law making law enforcement officials more proactive in determining the immigrant status of people they have a lawful reason to engage. While popular in Arizona, the new law drew the fire of critics who saw the law as an attack on people of Hispanic descent.

it unconstitutional, although the last camp did not close until March 1946 (after the war had ended). In 1988, Congress awarded $20,000 to each of the victims as token compensation for the hardships they endured.

After World War II, Japanese Americans staged a dramatic recovery. Having lost their traditional businesses, many entered new occupations, and driven by cultural values stressing the importance of education and hard work, Japanese Americans have enjoyed remarkable success. In 2010, the median income of Japanese American households was more than 40 percent above the national average, and the rate of poverty among Japanese Americans was well below the national figure.

Upward social mobility has encouraged cultural assimilation and intermarriage. Younger Japanese Americans rarely live in residential enclaves, as many Chinese Americans still do, and most marry non-Japanese partners. In the process, many have abandoned their traditions, including the Japanese language. A large share of Japanese Americans, however, belong to ethnic associations as a way of maintaining their ethnic identity. Still, some appear to be caught between two worlds, no longer culturally Japanese yet, because of racial differences, not completely accepted in the larger society.

Recent Asian Immigrants

More recent immigrants from Asia include Filipinos, Indians, Koreans, Vietnamese, Guamanians, and Samoans. Overall, the Asian American population more than doubled between 1990 and 2010 and currently accounts for 40 percent of all immigration to the United States (U.S. Department of Homeland Security, 2011).

The entrepreneurial spirit is strong among Asian immigrants. In part this reflects cultural patterns that stress achievement and self-reliance, but having one's own small business is also a strategy for dealing with societal prejudice and discrimination. Small business success is one reason that Asian American

family income is above the national average, but it is also true that in many of these businesses, a number of family members work long hours.

Another factor that raises the family income of Asian Americans is a high level of schooling. As shown in Table 11–4 on page 289, for all categories of Asian Americans, the share of adults with a four-year college degree is well above the national average. Among Asian Indian Americans, who have the highest educational achievement of all Asian Americans, more than two-thirds of all men and women over the age of twenty-five have completed college, a proportion that is more than twice the national average. This remarkable educational achievement is one reason that Asian Indian Americans had a median family income of more than $100,000 in 2010, about 66 percent higher than the national average.

In sum, a survey of Asian Americans presents a complex picture. The Japanese come closest to having achieved social acceptance. But some surveys reveal greater prejudice against Asian Americans than against African Americans (Parrillo & Donoghue, 2005). Median income data suggest that many Asian Americans have prospered. But these numbers reflect the fact that many Asian Americans live in Hawaii, California, or New York, where incomes are high but so are living costs (Takaki, 1998). Then, too, many Asian Americans remain poor. One thing is clear—their high immigration rate means that people of Asian ancestry will play a central role in U.S. society in the decades to come.

Hispanic Americans/Latinos

In 2010, the number of Hispanics in the United States topped 50 million (16.4 percent of the U.S. population), surpassing the number of Asian Americans (15.2 million, or 4.9 percent of the U.S. population) and even African Americans (40.4 million, or 13 percent) and making Hispanics the largest racial or ethnic minority. However, keep in mind that few who fall in this category describe themselves as "Hispanic" or "Latino." Like Asian

TABLE 11–5 The Social Standing of Hispanic Americans, 2010

	All Hispanics	Mexican Americans	Puerto Ricans	Cuban Americans	Entire U.S. Population
Median family income	$39,538	$39,264	$41,188	$47,929	$60,395
Percentage in poverty	26.6%	26.6%	26.7%	17.5%	15.1%
Completion of four or more years of college (age 25 and over)	14.1%	9.5%	16.2%	23.4%	30.4%

Source: U.S. Census Bureau (2011).

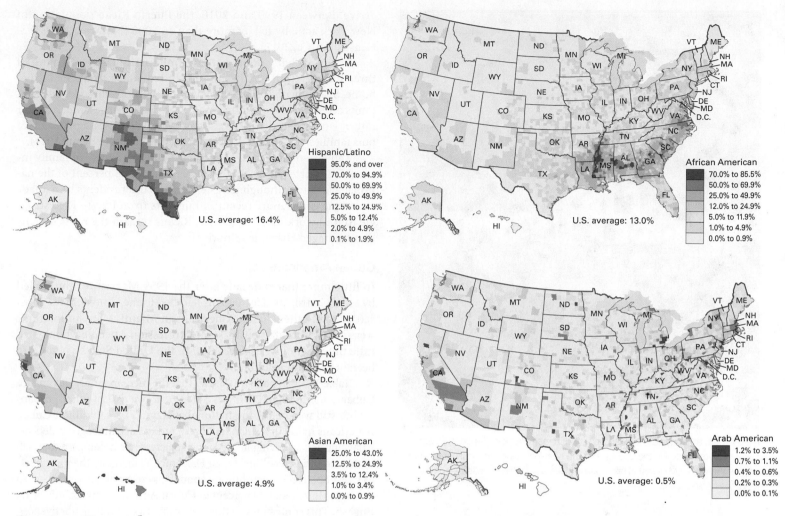

Seeing Ourselves

NATIONAL MAP 11–3 The Concentration of Hispanics or Latinos, African Americans, Asian Americans, and Arab Americans, by County

In 2010, people of Hispanic or Latino descent represented 16.4 percent of the U.S. population, compared with 13 percent African Americans, 4.9 percent Asian Americans, and 0.5 percent Arab Americans. These maps show the geographic distribution of these categories of people in 2010. Comparing them, we see that the southern half of the United States is home to far more minorities than the northern half. But do they all concentrate in the same areas? What patterns do the maps reveal?

Source: U.S. Census Bureau (2010, 2011).

Americans, Hispanics are really a cluster of distinct populations, each of which identifies with a particular ancestral nation (Marín & Marín, 1991). About two out of three Hispanics (some 33 million) are Mexican Americans. Puerto Ricans are next in number (4.7 million), followed by Cuban Americans (1.9 million). Many other nations of Latin America are represented by smaller numbers.

Although the Hispanic population is increasing all over the country, most Hispanic Americans live in the Southwest. One of three Californians is Latino (in Los Angeles, one-half the people are Latino). National Map 11–3 shows the distribution of the Hispanic, African American, Asian American, and Arab American populations across the United States.

Median family income for all Hispanics—$39,538 in 2010—stands well below the national average.[5] As the following sections explain, however, some categories of Hispanics have fared better than others.

Mexican Americans

Some Mexican Americans are descendants of people who lived in a part of Mexico annexed by the United States after the Mexican American War (1846–1848). However, most Mexican Americans

---

[5]The 2010 median age of the U.S. Hispanic population was 27.3 years, far below the non-Hispanic white median of 42.1 years. This difference accounts for some of the disparity in income and education.

Arab American communities can be found in many large cities on the East and West Coasts of the United States, but the heaviest concentrations are found across the upper Midwest. This mosque rises above the cornfields in a rural area near Toledo, Ohio.

are recent immigrants. Today, more immigrants come to the United States from Mexico than from any other country.

Like many other immigrants, many Mexican Americans have worked as low-wage laborers, on farms or elsewhere. Table 11–5 on page 290 shows that the 2010 median family income for Mexican Americans was $39,264, about two-thirds the national average. More than one-fourth of Mexican American families are poor—nearly twice the national average. Finally, despite gains since 1980, Mexican Americans still have a high dropout rate and receive much less schooling, on average, than the U.S. population as a whole.

Puerto Ricans

The island of Puerto Rico, like the Philippines, became a U.S. possession when Spain was defeated at the end of the Spanish-American War in 1898. In 1917, Congress passed the Jones Act, which made Puerto Ricans (but not Filipinos) U.S. citizens and made Puerto Rico a territory of the United States.

New York City is home to nearly 750,000 Puerto Ricans. About one-third of this community is living below the poverty line, including about half of the children. Adjusting to cultural patterns on the U.S. mainland—including, for many, learning English—is one major challenge; one-third of adults over the age of twenty-five have not completed a high-school diploma. In addition, Puerto Ricans with darker skin encounter prejudice and discrimination. As a result, more people now return to Puerto Rico each year than

arrive. Between 1990 and 2010, the Puerto Rican population of New York actually fell by more than 150,000 (Navarro, 2000; U.S. Census Bureau, 2011).

This "revolving door" pattern limits assimilation. Two out of three Puerto Rican families in the United States speak Spanish at home. Speaking only Spanish maintains a strong ethnic identity but limits economic opportunity. Puerto Ricans also have a much higher rate of woman-headed families than other Hispanics, a pattern that puts families at greater risk of poverty (U.S. Census Bureau, 2011).

Table 11–5 on page 290 shows that the 2010 median family income for Puerto Ricans was $41,188, or about 68 percent of the national average. Although long-term mainland residents have made economic gains, more recent immigrants from Puerto Rico struggle to find work. Overall, Puerto Ricans remain the most socially disadvantaged Hispanic minority.

Cuban Americans

In little more than a decade after the 1959 Marxist revolution led by Fidel Castro, 400,000 Cubans had fled to the United States. Most settled with other Cuban Americans in Miami. Many immigrants were highly educated business and professional people who wasted little time becoming as successful in the United States as they had been in their homeland.

Table 11–5 on page 290 shows that the median family income for Cuban Americans in 2010 was $47,929, above that of other Hispanics but still well below the national average. The 1.9 million Cuban Americans living in the United States today have managed a delicate balancing act, achieving in the larger society while holding on to much of their traditional culture. Of all Hispanics, Cubans are the most likely to speak Spanish in their homes: about 82 percent of families do so. At the same time, about 40 percent of Cuban Americans speak little or no English. This contributes to this community's cultural distinctiveness, although living in highly visible communities such as Miami's Little Havana also provokes hostility from some people.

Arab Americans

Arab Americans are another U.S. minority whose numbers are increasing. Like Hispanic Americans, these are people whose ancestors lived in a variety of countries. What is sometimes called "the Arab world" includes twenty-two nations and stretches across northern Africa, from Mauritania and Morocco on Africa's west coast to Egypt and Sudan on Africa's east coast, and extends into the Middle East (western Asia), including Iraq and Saudi Arabia. Not all the people who live in these nations are Arabs, however; for example, the Berber people in Morocco and the Kurds of Iraq are not Arabs.

Arab cultures differ from society to society, but they share widespread use of the Arabic alphabet and language and have Islam as their dominant religion. But keep in mind that "Arab" (an ethnic category) is not the same as "Muslim" (a follower of Islam). A majority of the people living in most Arab countries are Muslims, but some Arabs are Christians or followers of other religions. In addition, most of the world's Muslims do not live in Africa or the Middle East and are not Arabs.

Because many of the world's nations have large Arab populations, immigration to the United States has created a culturally diverse population of Arab Americans. Some Arab Americans are

Muslims and some are not; some speak Arabic and some do not; some maintain the traditions of their homeland and some do not. As is the case with Hispanic Americans and Asian Americans, some are recent immigrants and some have lived in this country for decades or even for generations.

As previously noted in Table 11–1 on page 276, the government gives the official number of Arab Americans as 1.7 million, but because people may not declare their ethnic background, it is likely that the actual number is at least twice as high.[6] The largest populations of Arab Americans have ancestral ties to Lebanon (30 percent of all Arab Americans), Egypt (11 percent), and Syria (9 percent). Most Arab Americans (67 percent) report ancestral ties to one nation, but 33 percent report ancestors in more than one nation, which may include both Arab and non-Arab countries (U.S. Census Bureau, 2011). National Map 11–3 on page 291 shows that the Arab American population is distributed throughout the United States.

Included in the Arab American population are people of all social classes. Some are highly educated professionals who work as physicians, engineers, and educators; others are working-class people who perform various skilled jobs in factories or on construction sites; still others do service work in restaurants, hospitals, or other settings or work in small family businesses. As shown in Table 11–6, median family income for Arab Americans is just above the national average ($61,579 compared to the national median of $60,395 in 2010), but Arab Americans have a higher than average poverty rate (19.6 percent, versus 15.1 percent for the population as a whole). Arab Americans are highly educated; 46 percent have a college degree, compared to 30 percent of the adult population as a whole (U.S. Census Bureau, 2011).

There are large, visible Arab American communities in a number of U.S. cities, including New York, Chicago, Los Angeles, Houston, and Dearborn (Michigan). Even so, Arab Americans may choose to downplay their ethnicity as a way to avoid prejudice and discrimination. The fact that many of the recent terrorist attacks against the United States and other nations have been carried out by Arabs has fueled a stereotype that links being Arab (or Muslim) with being a terrorist. This stereotype, like all stereotypes, is unfair because it blames an entire category of people for the actions of a few individuals. But it is probably the reason that the social distance research discussed earlier in this chapter shows students expressing more negative attitudes toward Arabs than toward any other racial or ethnic category. Its also helps explain why Arab Americans have been targets of an increasing number of hate crimes and why many Arab Americans feel that they are subject to "ethnic profiling" by police officers and security personnel that threatens their privacy and freedom (Ali & Juarez, 2003; Ali, Lipper, & Mack, 2004; Hagopian, 2004).

White Ethnic Americans

The term "white ethnics" recognizes the ethnic heritage and social disadvantages of many white people. White ethnics are non-WASPs whose ancestors lived

---

[6]The 2010 median age for Arab Americans was 30.7 years, below the national median of 37.2 years.

TABLE 11–6 The Social Standing of Arab Americans, 2010

	Arab Americans	Entire U.S. Population
Median family income	$61,579	$60,395
Percentage in poverty	19.6%	15.1%
Completion of four or more years of college (age 25 and over)	45.7%	30.4%

Source: U.S. Census Bureau (2011).

in Ireland, Poland, Germany, Italy, or other European countries. Overall, 53 percent of the U.S. population falls into one or more white ethnic categories.

High rates of emigration from Europe in the nineteenth century first brought Germans and Irish and then Italians and Jews to this country. Despite cultural differences, all shared the hope that the United States would offer greater political freedom and economic opportunity than their homelands. Most did live better in this country, but the belief that "the streets of America were paved with gold" turned out to be a far cry from reality. Most immigrants found only hard labor for low wages.

White ethnics also endured their share of prejudice and discrimination. Many employers shut their doors to new immigrants, posting signs such as "None need apply but Americans" (Handlin, 1941:67). In 1921, Congress enacted a quota system that greatly limited immigration, especially by southern and eastern Europeans, who were likely to have darker skin and different cultural backgrounds than the dominant WASPs. This quota system continued until 1968.

In response to prejudice and discrimination, many white ethnics formed supportive residential enclaves. Some also gained footholds in businesses and trades: Italian Americans entered the

White ethnic communities persist in many U.S. cities, especially in the Northeast region of the country. These communities are primarily home to working-class men and women whose ancestors came here as immigrants. To many more people, areas such as Philadelphia's Italian Market are a source of attractive cultural diversity.

Stephanie: I think Barbara Gruttner got, well, a raw deal. She should have been admitted.

Gina: Perhaps. But diversity is important. I believe in affirmative action.

Marco: Maybe some people do get into college more easily. But that includes guys like me whose father went here.

In a law suit filled against the University of Michigan Law School, Barbara Gruttner, who is white, claimed that she was the victim of racial discrimination. What was the discrimination? She claimed that the Michigan Law School unfairly denied her application for admission while admitting many less qualified African American applicants. In fact, as the court learned, Michigan, a state university, admitted just 9 percent of white students with her grade point average and law school aptitude test scores while admitting 100 percent of African American applicants with comparable scores.

In 2003, the U.S. Supreme Court heard Gruttner's complaint in a review of the admissions policies of both the law school and the undergraduate program at the University of Michigan. In a six-to-three decision, the Court ruled against Gruttner, claiming that the University of Michigan Law School could use a policy of affirmative action that takes account of the race of applicants in the interest of creating a socially diverse student body. At the same time, however, the Court struck down the university's undergraduate admissions policy, which awarded points not only for grades and college board scores but also for being a member of an underrepresented minority. A point system of this kind, the Court ruled, is too close to the rigid quota systems rejected by the Court in the past.

With this ruling, the Supreme Court continued to oppose quotalike systems while at the same time reaffirming the importance of racial diversity on campus. Thus colleges and universities can take account of race in order to increase the number of traditionally underrepresented students as long as race is treated as just one variable in a process that evaluates each applicant as an individual (Stout, 2003).

How did the controversial policy of affirmative action begin? The answer takes us back to the end of World War II, when the U.S. government funded higher education for veterans of all races. The so-called G.I. Bill held special promise for African Americans, most of whom needed financial assistance to enroll in college. By 1960, government funding helped 350,000 black men and women attend college.

There was just one problem: Even with advanced schooling, these individuals were not finding the kinds of jobs for which they were qualified. So the Kennedy administration devised a program of "affirmative action" to provide broader opportunities to qualified minorities. Businesses and universities were instructed to monitor hiring, promotion, and admissions policies to eliminate discrimination against minorities, even if unintended.

Defenders of affirmative action see it, first, as a sensible response to our nation's racial and ethnic history, especially for African Americans, who suffered through two centuries of slavery and a century of segregation under Jim Crow laws. Throughout our history, they claim, being white gave people a big advantage. They see minority preference today as a step toward fair compensation for unfair majority preference in the past.

Second, given our racial history, many analysts doubt that the United States will ever become a color-blind society. They claim that because prejudice and discrimination are rooted deep in U.S. culture, simply claiming that we are or should be color-blind does not mean that everyone will be treated fairly.

Third, supporters maintain that affirmative action has worked. Where would minorities be today if the government had not enacted this policy in the 1960s? Major employers, such as fire and police departments in large cities, began hiring minorities and women for the first time only because of affirmative action. This program has helped expand the African American middle class and increased racial diversity on college campuses and in the workplace.

Only about 10 percent of white people say they support racial preferences for African Americans. Even among African Americans themselves, just 46 percent support this policy (NORC, 2011). Critics point out, first of all, that affirmative action was intended as a temporary remedy to ensure fair competition but soon became a system of "group preferences" and quotas—in short, a form of "reverse discrimination," favoring people not because of talent and effort but because of race, ethnicity, or sex.

Second, critics say, if racial preferences were wrong in the past, they are wrong now. Why should whites today, many of whom are far from privileged, be penalized for past discrimination that was in no way their fault? Our society has undone most of the institutional prejudice and discrimination of earlier times—doesn't the election of an African American president suggest that? Giving entire categories of people special treatment compromises standards of excellence and calls into question the real accomplishments of minorities.

A third argument against affirmative action is that it benefits those who need it least. Favoring minority-owned corporations or holding places in law school helps already privileged people. Affirmative action has done little for the African American underclass that needs the most help.

There are good arguments for and against affirmative action, and people who want our society to have more racial or ethnic equality fall on both sides of the debate. Voters in a number of states, including California, Washington, Michigan, and Nebraska, have passed ballot initiatives banning the use of affirmative action based on gender or race. In 2008, however, voters in Colorado voted down such a proposal. So the country remains divided on this issue. The disagreement is not whether people of all colors should have equal opportunity but whether the current policy of affirmative action is part of the solution or part of the problem.

Join the Blog!

What do you think? Is affirmative action part of the problem or part of the solution? Why? Go to MySocLab and join the Sociology in Focus blog to share your opinions and experiences and to see what others think.

Sources: Bowen & Bok (1999), Kantrowitz & Wingert (2003), Flynn (2008), Leff (2008), and NORC (2011).

construction industry, Irish Americans worked in construction and civil service jobs, Jews predominated in the garment industry, and many Greeks (like the Chinese) worked in the retail food business (W. M. Newman, 1973).

Many white ethnics still live in traditional working-class neighborhoods, although those who prospered have gradually assimilated. Most descendants of immigrants who labored in sweatshops and lived in crowded tenements now make enough money to lead comfortable lives. As a result, their ethnic heritage has become a source of pride.

Race and Ethnicity: Looking Ahead

 Evaluate

The United States has been and will remain a land of immigrants. Immigration has brought striking cultural diversity and tales of hope, struggle, and success told in hundreds of languages.

Most immigrants arrived in a great wave that peaked about 1910. The next two generations brought economic gains and at least some assimilation into the larger society. The government also extended citizenship to Native Americans (1924), foreign-born Filipinos (1942), Chinese Americans (1943), and Japanese Americans (1952).

Another wave of immigration began after World War II and swelled as the government relaxed immigration laws in the 1960s. Today, about 1.25 million people come to the United States from other countries each year—about 1.05 million legally and another 200,000 illegally. This is almost twice the number that arrived during the "Great Immigration" a century ago (although newcomers now enter a country that has five times as many people). Most of today's immigrants come not from Europe but from Latin America and Asia, with Mexicans, Chinese, and Filipinos arriving in the largest numbers.

Immigrants add much to the United States. A larger share of working-age immigrants (30 percent) now have a college degree than lack a high school diploma (28 percent) (Goodwin, 2011). Even so, many new arrivals face much the same prejudice and discrimination experienced by those who came before them. In 1994, California voters passed Proposition 187, which stated that illegal immigrants should be denied health care, social services, and public education; it was later overturned in federal court. More recently, voters there mandated that all children learn English in school. Some landowners in the Southwest have taken up arms to discourage illegal immigrants crossing the border from Mexico. Even so, we continue to debate how to best deal with the almost 11 million illegal immigrants already here.

Even minorities who have been in the United States for generations feel the sting of prejudice and discrimination. Affirmative action, a policy meant to provide opportunities for racial and ethnic minorities, continues to be hotly debated in this country. The Sociology in Focus box describes the debate and invites you to weigh in with your opinions on the Sociology in Focus blog on MySocLab.

Like other minorities, today's immigrants hope to gain acceptance and to take their place in U.S. society without completely giving up their traditional culture. Some still build racial and ethnic enclaves so the Little Havanas and Koreatowns of today stand alongside the Little Italys and Chinatowns of the past. In addition, new arrivals carry the hope that racial and ethnic diversity can be a source of pride rather than a badge of inferiority.

Seeing Sociology in Everyday Life

Does race still matter in people's social standing?

This chapter explores the importance of race and ethnicity to social standing in
the United States. You already know, for example, that the rate of poverty is three
times higher for African Americans than for whites, and you have also learned that
the typical black family earns just 56 percent as much as the typical (non-Hispanic)
white family. But rich people—here, we'll define "rich" as a family earning more than
$75,000 a year—come in all colors. Here's a chance to test your sociological thinking
by answering several questions about how race affects being rich. Look at each of the
statements below: Does the statement reflect reality or is it a myth?

1. In the United States, all rich people are white.
   Reality or myth?
2. Rich white families are actually richer than rich African
   American families. *Reality or myth*?
3. People in rich black families don't work as hard as
   members of rich white families. *Reality or myth*?
4. When you are rich, color doesn't matter. *Reality or myth*?

A

1. *Of course, this is a myth.* But when it comes to being rich, race does matter: About 22 percent of African American families are affluent (Hispanic families, too), compared to about 46 percent of non-Hispanic white families.

2. *Reality.* Rich white, non-Hispanic families have a mean (average) income more than $200,000 per year. Rich African American families average about $127,000 per year.

3. *Myth.* On average, rich black families are more likely to rely on multiple incomes (that is, they have more people working) than their white counterparts. In addition, rich white families receive more unearned income—income from investments—than rich African American families.

4. *Myth.* Rich African Americans still face social barriers based on their race, just as rich whites benefit from the privileges linked to their color.

▌Seeing Sociology in *Your* Everyday Life

1. Give several of your friends or family members a quick quiz, asking them what share of the U.S. population is white, Hispanic, African American, and Asian (see Table 11–1 on page 276). Why do you think most white people exaggerate the minority population of this country? (C. A. Gallagher, 2003)

2. Does your college or university take race and ethnicity into account in its admissions policies? Ask to speak with an admissions officer to see what you can learn about your school's use of race and ethnicity in admissions. Ask whether there is a "legacy" policy that favors children of parents who attended the school.

3. Do you think people tend to see race in terms of biological traits or as categories constructed by society? What about you? Go to the "Seeing Sociology in *Your* Everyday Life" feature on MySocLab to read more about how society constructs the meaning of race and also for some suggestions about how you might think about the meaning of race.

The Social Meaning of Race and Ethnicity

Race refers to socially constructed categories based on biological traits a society defines as important.

- The meaning and importance of race vary from place to place and over time.
- Societies use racial categories to rank people in a hierarchy, giving some people more money, power, and prestige than others.
- In the past, scientists created three broad categories—Caucasoids, Mongoloids, and Negroids—but there are no biologically pure races. **pp. 274–76**

📖 Read the **Document** on **mysoclab.com**

👁 Watch the **Video** on **mysoclab.com**

Ethnicity refers to socially constructed categories based on cultural traits a society defines as important.

- Ethnicity reflects common ancestors, language, and religion.
- The importance of ethnicity varies from place to place and over time.
- People choose to play up or play down their ethnicity.
- Societies may or may not set categories of people apart based on differences in ethnicity. **p. 276**

✳ Explore the **Map** on **mysoclab.com**

race (p. 274) a socially constructed category of people who share biologically transmitted traits that members of a society consider important

ethnicity (p. 276) a shared cultural heritage

minority (p. 276) any category of people distinguished by physical or cultural difference that a society sets apart and subordinates

Prejudice and Stereotypes

Prejudice is a rigid and unfair generalization about a category of people.

- The social distance scale is one measure of prejudice.
- One type of prejudice is the **stereotype**, a simplified description applied to every person in some category.
- **Racism**, a very destructive type of prejudice, asserts that one race is innately superior or inferior to another. **pp. 277–80**

There are four **theories of preducice**:

- **Scapegoat theory** claims that prejudice results from frustration among people who are disadvantaged.
- **Authoritarian personality theory** (Adorno) claims that prejudice is a personality trait of certain individuals, especially those with little education and those raised by cold and demanding parents.
- **Culture theory** (Bogardus) claims that prejudice is rooted in culture; we learn to feel greater social distance from some categories of people.
- **Conflict theory** claims that prejudice is a tool used by powerful people to divide and control the population. **pp. 280–82**

prejudice (p. 278) a rigid and unfair generalization about an entire category of people

stereotype (p. 278) a simplified description applied to every person in some category

racism (p. 280) the belief that one racial category is innately superior or inferior to another

scapegoat (p. 280) a person or category of people, typically with little power, whom other people unfairly blame for their own troubles

Discrimination

Discrimination is treating various categories of people unequally.

- Prejudice refers to *attitudes*; discrimination involves *actions*.
- **Institutional prejudice and discrimination** is bias built into the operation of society's institutions, including schools, hospitals, the police, and the workplace.
- Prejudice and discrimination perpetuate themselves in a vicious circle, resulting in social disadvantage that fuels additional prejudice and discrimination. **p. 282**

discrimination (p. 282) unequal treatment of various categories of people

institutional prejudice and discrimination (p. 282) bias built into the operation of society's institutions

Majority and Minority: Patterns of Interaction

Pluralism means that racial and ethnic categories, although distinct, have roughly equal social standing.

- U.S. society is pluralistic in that all people in the United States, regardless of race or ethnicity, have equal standing under the law.
- U.S. society is not pluralistic in that all racial and ethnic categories do not have equal social standing. **pp. 282–83**

Assimilation is a process by which minorities gradually adopt the patterns of the dominant culture.

- Assimilation involves changes in dress, language, religion, values, and friends.
- Assimilation is a strategy to escape prejudice and discrimination and to achieve upward social mobility.
- Some categories of people have assimilated more than others. **p. 283**

Segregation is the physical and social separation of categories of people.

- Although some segregation is voluntary (for example, the Amish), majorities usually segregate minorities by excluding them from neighborhoods, schools, and occupations.
- *De jure* segregation is segregation by law; *de facto* segregation describes settings that contain only people of one category.
- Hypersegregation means having little social contact with people beyond the local community. **p. 283**

Genocide is the systematic killing of one category of people by another.

- Historical examples of genocide include the extermination of Jews by the Nazis and the killing of Western-leaning people in Cambodia by Pol Pot.
- Recent examples of genocide include Hutus killing Tutsis in the African nation of Rwanda, Serbs killing Bosnians in the Balkans of Eastern Europe, and the systematic killing in the Darfur region of Sudan. **pp. 283–84**

pluralism (p. 282) a state in which people of all races and ethnicities are distinct but have equal social standing

assimilation (p. 283) the process by which minorities gradually adopt patterns of the dominant culture

miscegenation (p. 283) biological reproduction by partners of different racial categories

segregation (p. 283) the physical and social separation of categories of people

genocide (p. 283) the systematic killing of one category of people by another

Race and Ethnicity in the United States

Native Americans, the earliest human inhabitants of the Americas, have endured genocide, segregation, and forced assimilation. Today, the social standing of Native Americans is well below the national average. **pp. 284–86**

White Anglo-Saxon Protestants (WASPs) were most of the original European settlers of the United States, and many continue to enjoy high social position today. **p. 286**

African Americans experienced two centuries of slavery. Emancipation in 1865 gave way to segregation by law (the so-called Jim Crow laws). In the 1950s and 1960s, a national civil rights movement resulted in legislation that outlawed segregated schools and overt discrimination in employment and public accommodations. Today, despite legal equality, African Americans are still disadvantaged. **pp. 286–88**

Asian Americans have suffered both racial and ethnic hostility. Although some prejudice and discrimination continue, both Chinese and Japanese Americans now have above-average income and schooling. Asian immigrants—especially Chinese, Indians, and Filipinos—now account for 40 percent of all immigration to the United States. **pp. 288–90**

Hispanic Americans or **Latinos**, the largest U.S. minority, include many ethnicities sharing a Spanish heritage. Mexican Americans, the largest Hispanic minority, are concentrated in the Southwest and are the poorest Hispanic category. Cubans, concentrated in Miami, are the most affluent Hispanic category. **pp. 290–92**

Arab Americans are a growing U.S. minority. Because they come to the United States from so many different nations, Arab Americans are a culturally diverse population, and they are represented in all social classes. They have been targets of prejudice and hate crimes in recent years as a result of a stereotype that links all Arab Americans with terrorism. **pp. 292–93**

White ethnic Americans are non-WASPs whose ancestors emigrated from Europe in the nineteenth and twentieth centuries. In response to prejudice and discrimination, many white ethnics formed supportive residential enclaves. **pp. 293–95**

Economics and Politics

Learning Objectives

Remember the definitions of key terms highlighted in boldfaced type throughout this chapter.

Understand how three economic revolutions have reshaped human societies.

Apply a global perspective to see how economic and political systems around the world differ.

Analyze the causes and consequences of war and terrorism.

Evaluate both capitalism and socialism in terms of productivity, equality, and individual freedom.

Create a vision of how the world can reduce violent conflict and pursue peace.

SPECULATIO
IS THE
BANKS GOT
Bailed OUT
we GOT
Out
IS
THE 99
WE
ANT
OUR
U SA
BACK

CHAPTER OVERVIEW

This chapter begins a survey of the major social institutions. We begin with the economy, which is widely regarded as having the greatest impact on society as a whole. The chapter explores the operation of the economy and explains how changes in economic production have reshaped society. The chapter then continues by examining politics, a second major social institution, with attention to the character and causes of war and terrorism. ■

Here's a quick quiz about the U.S. economy. (Hint: All seven questions have the same correct answer.)

- Which business do 200 million people in the world visit each week?
- Which business sells the products of more than 100,000 companies?
- Which U.S. company, on average, opens a new or remodeled store every day?
- Which U.S. company buys more than $25 billion worth of goods each year from China, which, if the company were a country, would be China's seventh largest trading partner?
- Which U.S. company is the largest private employer in Mexico?
- Which U.S. company employs more than 2.1 million people worldwide (more than the total population of Botswana or Slovenia)?
- Which single company actually grew in size during the recent economic downturn?

The answer, of course, is Walmart, the global discount chain founded by Sam Walton, who opened his first store in Arkansas in 1962. In 2011, Walmart announced revenues of $419 billion in annual sales through more than 4,400 stores in the United States and 5,200 stores in other countries from Brazil to China, making it the largest corporation in the nation.

But not everyone is pleased with the expansion of Walmart. Across the United States, many people have joined a social movement to keep Walmart out of their local communities, fearing the loss of local businesses and, in some cases, local culture. Critics claim that the merchandising giant pays low wages, keeps out unions, and sells many products made in sweatshops abroad. Beginning in 2010, Walmart has defended itself in the courts against claims of sex discrimination (Saporito, 2003; Walsh, 2007; A. Clark, 2010; Walmart, 2010; Schell, 2011).

This chapter explores the economy and the closely related institution of politics. A number of very large corporations, including Walmart, are at the center of the U.S. economy, raising questions about just how the economy operates, whose interests it ought to serve, and to what extent big business shapes the political life of the United States.

Economics and politics are **social institutions**, *major spheres of social life or societal subsystems organized to meet human needs.* The two chapters that follow consider other social institutions: Chapter 13 focuses on family and religion, and Chapter 14 highlights education, health, and medicine. These discussions explain how social institutions have changed over the course of history, describe how they operate today, and point out controversies that are likely to shape them tomorrow.

The Economy: Historical Overview

 Understand

The **economy** is *the social institution that organizes a society's production, distribution, and consumption of goods and services.* The economy operates, for better or worse, in a generally predictable manner. *Goods* are commodities ranging from necessities (such as food, clothing, and shelter) to luxury items (such as cars, swimming pools, and yachts). *Services* are activities that benefit people (including the work of priests, physicians, teachers, and computer software specialists). Three times in the past, technological revolutions reorganized the economy and, in the process, transformed social life.

The Agricultural Revolution

As Chapter 2 ("Culture") explained, the earliest societies were made up of hunters and gatherers living off the land. In these technologically simple societies, there was no distinct economy; producing and consuming were part of family life.

Harnessing animals to plows around 5,000 years ago permitted the development of agriculture, which was fifty times more productive than hunting and gathering. The resulting surpluses meant that not everyone had to produce food, so many people took on other specialized work: making tools, raising animals, and building dwellings. Soon towns sprang up, linked by networks of traders dealing in food, animals, and other goods. These four factors—agricultural technology, specialized work, permanent settlements, and trade—made the economy a distinct social institution.

As societies industrialize, a smaller share of the labor force works in agriculture. In the United States, much of the agricultural work that remains is performed by immigrants from lower-income nations. These farm workers from Mexico travel throughout Florida during the tomato harvest.

The Industrial Revolution

By the mid-eighteenth century, a second technological revolution was under way, starting in England and spreading to the United States and elsewhere. Industrialization changed the economy in five fundamental ways:

1. **New sources of energy.** Throughout history, "energy" had meant the muscle power of people or animals. Then, in 1765, the English inventor James Watt introduced the steam engine. A hundred times more powerful than animal muscles, early steam engines soon drove heavy machinery.

2. **Centralization of work in factories.** Steam-powered machinery moved work from homes to factories, centralized workplaces that housed the machines.

3. **Manufacturing and mass production.** Before the Industrial Revolution, most people grew or gathered raw materials such as grain, wood, or wool. In an industrial economy, the focus shifts so that most people turn raw materials into a wide range of finished products such as furniture and clothing.

4. **Specialization.** Centuries ago, people worked at home making products from start to finish. In the factory, a laborer repeats a single task over and over, making only a small contribution to the finished product.

5. **Wage labor.** Instead of working for themselves, factory workers became wage laborers working for strangers, who often cared less for them than for the machines they operated.

The Industrial Revolution gradually raised the standard of living as countless new products fueled an expanding marketplace. Yet the benefits of industrial technology were shared very unequally, especially at the beginning. Some factory owners made huge fortunes, while the majority of industrial workers lived close to poverty. Children, too, worked in factories or in coal mines for pennies a day. As time went on, workers formed labor unions to represent their interests collectively to factory owners. In the twentieth century, new laws banned child labor, set minimum wage levels, improved workplace safety, and extended schooling and political rights to a larger segment of the population.

The Information Revolution and Postindustrial Society

By about 1950, the nature of production was changing once again. The United States was creating a **postindustrial economy**, *a productive system based on service work and computer technology*. Automated machinery (and later, robotics) reduced the role of human labor in factory production and expanded the ranks of clerical workers and managers. The postindustrial era is marked by a shift from industrial work to service work.

Driving this economic change is a third technological breakthrough: the computer. Just as the Industrial Revolution did two-and-a-half centuries ago, the Information Revolution has introduced new kinds of products and new forms of communication and has changed the character of work. There have been three significant changes:

1. **From tangible products to ideas.** The industrial era was defined by the production of goods; in the postindustrial era, people work with symbols. Computer programmers, writers, financial analysts, advertising executives, architects, editors, and various types of consultants make up more of the labor force in the information age.

2. **From mechanical skills to literacy skills.** The Industrial Revolution required mechanical skills, but the Information Revolution requires literacy skills: speaking and writing well and, of course, knowing how to use a computer. People able to communicate effectively are likely to do well; people without these skills face fewer opportunities.

3. **From factories to almost anywhere.** Industrial technology drew workers to factories located near power sources, but

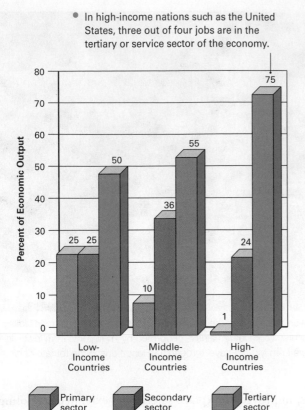

- In high-income nations such as the United States, three out of four jobs are in the tertiary or service sector of the economy.

Global Snapshot

FIGURE 12–1 The Size of Economic Sectors, by National Income Levels of Country

As countries become richer, the primary sector becomes a smaller part of the economy and the tertiary or service sector becomes larger.

Source: Estimates based on World Bank (2011).

computer technology allows people to work almost anywhere. Laptop and wireless computers and cell phones now turn the home, car, or even an airplane into a "virtual office." What this means for everyday life is that new information technology blurs the line between our lives at work and at home.

Sectors of the Economy

The three revolutions just described reflect a shifting balance among the three sectors of a society's economy. The **primary sector** is *the part of the economy that draws raw materials from the natural environment*. The primary sector—agriculture, raising animals, fishing, forestry, and mining—is largest in low-income nations. Figure 12–1 shows that 25 percent of the economic output

of low-income countries is in the primary sector, compared with 10 percent of economic activity among middle-income nations and just 1 percent in high-income countries like the United States.

The **secondary sector** is *the part of the economy that transforms raw materials into manufactured goods*. This sector expands quickly as societies industrialize. It includes operations such as refining petroleum into gasoline and turning metals into tools and automobiles. The globalization of industry means that just about all the world's countries have a significant share of workers employed in the secondary sector. Figure 12–1 shows that the secondary sector now accounts for nearly the same share of economic output in low-income nations as it does in high-income countries.

The **tertiary sector** is *the part of the economy that involves services rather than goods*. The tertiary sector grows with industrialization, accounting for 50 percent of economic output in low-income countries, 55 percent in middle-income countries, and 75 percent in high-income countries. More than 80 percent of the U.S. labor force is in service work, including secretarial and clerical jobs and work in food service, sales, law, health care, advertising, and teaching (U.S. Department of Labor, 2011).

The Global Economy

New information technology is drawing people around the world together and creating a **global economy**, *economic activity that crosses national borders*. The development of a global economy has five major consequences.

First, we see a global division of labor: Different regions of the world specialize in one sector of economic activity. As Global Map 12–1 shows, agriculture represents about half the total economic output of the world's poorest countries. Global Map 12–2 shows that most of the economic output of high-income countries, including the United States, is in the service sector. In short, the world's poorest nations specialize in producing raw materials, and the richest nations specialize in the production of services.

Second, an increasing number of products pass through more than one nation. Look no further than your morning coffee: The beans may have been grown in Colombia and transported to New Orleans on a freighter that was registered in Liberia, made in a shipyard in Japan using steel from Korea, and fueled by oil from Venezuela.

Third, national governments no longer control the economic activity that takes place within their borders. In fact, governments cannot even accurately regulate the value of their national currencies because dollars, euros, pounds sterling, and yen are traded around the clock in the financial markets of New York, London, and Tokyo.

A fourth consequence of the global economy is that a small number of businesses operating internationally now control a vast share of the world's economic activity. Using the latest

---

Sectors of the Economy

primary sector the part of the economy that draws raw materials from the natural environment

secondary sector the part of the economy that transforms raw materials into manufactured goods

tertiary sector the part of the economy that involves services rather than goods

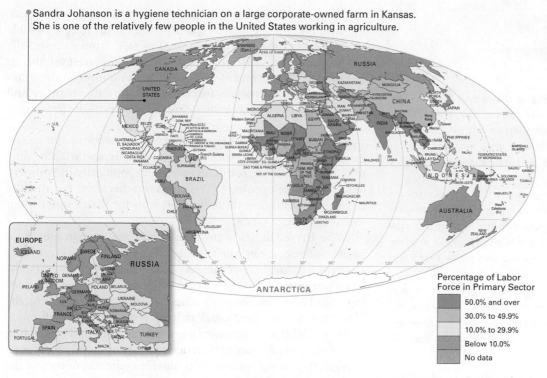

Sandra Johanson is a hygiene technician on a large corporate-owned farm in Kansas. She is one of the relatively few people in the United States working in agriculture.

GLOBAL MAP 12–1 Agricultural Employment in Global Perspective

The primary sector of the economy is largest in the nations that are least developed. Thus, in the poor countries of Africa and Asia, up to half of all workers are farmers. This picture is altogether different in the world's most economically developed countries—including the United States, Canada, Great Britain, and Australia—which have a mere 2 to 3 percent of their labor force in agriculture.

Source: Data from International Labour Organization (2011).

Percentage of Labor Force in Primary Sector

- 50.0% and over
- 30.0% to 49.9%
- 10.0% to 29.9%
- Below 10.0%
- No data

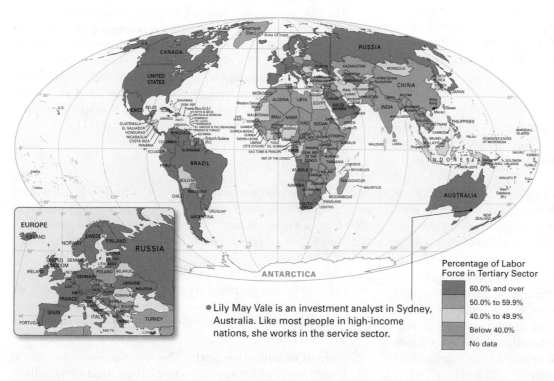

GLOBAL MAP 12–2 Service-Sector Employment in Global Perspective

The tertiary sector of the economy becomes ever larger as a nation's income level rises. In the United States, Canada, the countries of Western Europe, much of South America, Australia, and Japan, about two-thirds of the labor force performs service work.

Source: Data from International Labour Organization (2011).

Lily May Vale is an investment analyst in Sydney, Australia. Like most people in high-income nations, she works in the service sector.

Percentage of Labor Force in Tertiary Sector

- 60.0% and over
- 50.0% to 59.9%
- 40.0% to 49.9%
- Below 40.0%
- No data

available data, the 1,500 largest multinational companies account for half the world's economic output (DeCarlo, 2011; World Bank, 2011).

Fifth and finally, the globalization of the economy raises concerns about the rights and opportunities of workers. Critics of this trend claim that the United States is losing jobs—especially factory jobs—to low-income nations. This means that workers here face lower wages and higher unemployment. At the same time, many workers abroad are paid extremely low wages. As a result, say critics, the global expansion of capitalism threatens the well-being of workers throughout the world.

The world is still divided into 195 politically distinct nations. But the rising level of international economic activity makes nationhood less significant than it was even a decade ago.

Economic Systems: Paths to Justice

 Evaluate

October 20, Saigon, Vietnam. Sailing up the narrow Saigon River is an unsettling experience for anyone who came of age in the 1960s. People like me need to remember that Vietnam is a country, not a war, and that nearly forty years have passed since the last U.S. helicopter lifted off the rooftop of the U.S. embassy, ending our country's presence there.

Saigon is now a boomtown. Neon signs bathe the city's waterfront in color; hotels, bankrolled by Western corporations, push skyward from a dozen construction sites; taxi meters record fares in U.S. dollars, not Vietnamese dong; and Visa and American Express stickers decorate the doors of trendy restaurants and fashionable shops that cater to tourists from Japan, France, and the United States.

There is heavy irony here: After decades of fighting, millions of lives lost on both sides, and the victory of Communist forces, the Vietnamese are doing an about-face and turning toward capitalism. What we see today is what might well have happened had the U.S. forces won the war.

Every society's economic system makes a statement about justice by determining who is entitled to what. Two general economic models are capitalism and socialism. No nation anywhere in the world has an economy that is completely one or the other; rather, capitalism and socialism are two ends of a continuum along which all real-world economies can be located. We will look at each of these models in turn.

Capitalism

Capitalism is *an economic system in which natural resources and the means of producing goods and services are privately owned.* An ideal capitalist economy has three distinctive features:

1. **Private ownership of property.** In a capitalist economy, individuals can own almost anything. The more capitalist an economy is, the more private ownership there is of wealth-producing property such as factories, real estate, and natural resources.

2. **Pursuit of personal profit.** A capitalist society seeks to create profit and wealth. The profit motive is the reason people take new jobs, open new businesses, or try to improve products. Making money is considered the natural way of economic life. Just as important, the Scottish philosopher Adam Smith (1723–1790) claimed that as individuals pursue their self-interest, the entire society prospers (1937, orig. 1776).

3. **Competition and consumer choice.** A purely capitalist economy is a free-market system with no government interference (sometimes called a *laissez-faire economy,* from the French words meaning "leave it alone"). Adam Smith stated that a freely competitive economy regulates itself by the "invisible hand" of the law of supply and demand.

Consumers guide a market economy, Smith explained, by selecting the goods and services offering the greatest value. As producers compete for the customer's business, they provide the highest-quality goods at the lowest possible prices. In Smith's time-honored phrase, from narrow self-interest comes "the greatest good for the greatest number of people." Government control of an economy, on the other hand, distorts market forces by reducing the quantity and quality of goods, shortchanging consumers in the process.

Justice in a capitalist system amounts to freedom of the marketplace, where anyone can produce, invest, buy, and sell according to individual self-interest. The increasing popularity of Walmart, described in the opening to this chapter, reflects the fact that the company's customers think they get a lot for their money when shopping there.

The United States is considered a capitalist nation because most businesses are privately owned. However, it is not completely capitalist because the government plays a large role in the economy. The government owns and operates a number of businesses, including almost all of this country's schools, roads, parks, museums, the U.S. Postal Service, the Amtrak railroad system, and the entire U.S. military. The U.S. government also had a major hand in building the Internet. In addition, governments use taxation and other forms of regulation to influence what companies produce, to control the quality and cost of merchandise, and to motivate consumers to conserve natural resources.

The U.S. government also sets minimum wage levels, enforces workplace safety standards, regulates corporate mergers, provides farm price supports, taxes everyone on what they earn, and also supplements the income of a majority of its people in the form of Social Security, public assistance, student loans, and veterans' benefits. Local, state, and federal governments combined are the nation's biggest employer, with 17 percent of the nonfarm labor force on their payrolls (U.S. Bureau of Labor Statistics, 2011).

Socialism

Socialism is *an economic system in which natural resources and the means of producing goods and services are collectively owned.* In its ideal form, a socialist economy rejects each of the three characteristics of capitalism just described in favor of three opposite features:

1. **Collective ownership of property.** A socialist economy limits rights to private property, especially property used to generate income. Government controls such property and makes housing and other goods available to all, not just to the people with the most money.

2. **Pursuit of collective goals.** The individualistic pursuit of profit goes against the collective orientation of socialism. What capitalism celebrates as the "entrepreneurial spirit,"

---

capitalism an economic system in which natural resources and the means of producing goods and services are privately owned

socialism an economic system in which natural resources and the means of producing goods and services are collectively owned

Capitalism still thrives in Hong Kong (*left*), evident in streets choked with advertising and shoppers. Socialism is more the rule in China's capital, Beijing (*right*), a city dominated by government buildings rather than a downtown business district.

socialism condemns as greed; individuals are urged to work for the common good of all.

3. **Government control of the economy.** Socialism rejects capitalism's laissez-faire approach in favor of a *centrally controlled* or *command economy* operated by the government. Commercial advertising thus plays little role in socialist economies.

Justice in a socialist context means not competing to gain wealth but meeting everyone's basic needs in a roughly equal manner. From a socialist point of view, the common capitalist practice of giving workers as little in wages and benefits as possible to boost company earnings is unjust because it puts profits before people.

The People's Republic of China, Cuba, North Korea, and more than two dozen other nations in Asia, Africa, and Latin America model their economies on socialism, placing almost all wealth-generating property under state control (Miller, 2011). The extent of world socialism declined during the 1990s as countries in Eastern Europe and the former Soviet Union geared their economies toward a market system. More recently, however, voters in Bolivia, Venezuela, Ecuador, and other nations in South America have elected leaders who are moving the national economies in a socialist direction.

Welfare Capitalism and State Capitalism

Most of the nations in Western Europe—especially Sweden, Denmark, and Italy—have market-based economies but also offer broad social welfare programs. Analysts call this third type of economic system **welfare capitalism**, *an economic and political system that combines a mostly market-based economy with extensive social welfare programs.*

Under welfare capitalism, a nation's government owns some of the largest industries and services, such as transportation, the mass media, and health care. In Greece, for example, most economic production is *nationalized*, or state-controlled, and the government provides extensive benefits to the people for education and health care. In Sweden and Italy, although most industry is left in private ownership, almost all economic activity is subject to extensive government regulation. In these nations as well, high taxation (aimed especially at the rich) funds a wide range of social welfare programs, including universal health care and child care, for the benefit of the entire population. Of all the high-income nations of the world, the United States and Iceland have the lowest level of government control of the economy (OECD, 2011).

Another alternative is **state capitalism**, *an economic and political system in which companies are privately owned but cooperate closely with the government.* State capitalism is the rule in the nations along the Pacific Rim. Japan, South Korea, and Singapore are all capitalist countries, but their governments work in partnership with large companies, supplying financial assistance and controlling foreign imports to help their businesses compete in world markets (Gerlach, 1992).

Relative Advantages of Capitalism and Socialism

Which economic system works best? Comparing economic models is difficult because all nations mix capitalism and socialism to varying degrees. In addition, nations differ in cultural attitudes toward work, access to natural resources, levels of technological development, and patterns of trade. Despite such complicating factors, some crude comparisons are revealing.

welfare capitalism an economic and political system that combines a mostly market-based economy with extensive social welfare programs

state capitalism an economic and political system in which companies are privately owned but cooperate closely with the government

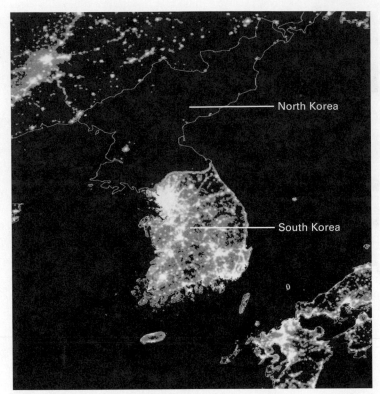

North Korea

South Korea

Directly comparing the economic performance of capitalism and socialism is difficult because nations differ in many ways. But a satellite image of socialist North Korea and capitalist South Korea at night shows the dramatically different electrical output of the two nations, one indication of economic activity.

Economic Productivity

One key dimension of economic performance is productivity. A commonly used measure of economic output is *gross domestic product* (GDP), the total value of all goods and services produced within the nation's borders each year. Per capita (per-person) GDP allows us to compare the economic performance of nations of different population sizes.

The output of mostly capitalist countries in the late 1980s—before the end of socialist economies in the Soviet Union and Eastern Europe—varied somewhat but averaged about $13,500 per person. The comparable figure for the mostly socialist former Soviet Union and nations of Eastern Europe was about $5,000. This means that the capitalist countries outproduced the socialist nations by a ratio of 2.7 to 1 (United Nations Development Programme, 1990). A recent comparison of socialist North Korea (per capita GDP of $1,800) and capitalist South Korea ($29,326) provides an even sharper contrast (Central Intelligence Agency, 2011; United Nations Development Programme, 2011).

Economic Equality

The distribution of resources within the population is another important measure of how well an economic system works. A comparative study of Europe in the mid-1970s, when that region was split between mostly capitalist and mostly socialist countries, compared the earnings of the richest 5 percent of the population and the poorest 5 percent (Wiles, 1977). Societies with mostly capitalist economies had an income ratio of about 10 to 1; the figure for

socialist countries was 5 to 1. In other words, capitalist economies support a higher overall standard of living but with greater income inequality. Said another way, socialist economies generate a lower living standard but with more economic equality.

Personal Freedom

One additional consideration in evaluating capitalism and socialism is the personal freedom each system gives its people. Capitalism emphasizes the *freedom to pursue self-interest* and depends on the ability of producers and consumers to interact with little interference by the state. Socialism, by contrast, emphasizes *freedom from basic want*. The goal of equality requires the state to regulate the economy, which in turn limits personal choices and opportunities for citizens.

Can a single society offer both political freedom and economic equality? In the capitalist United States, our political system offers many personal freedoms, but the economy generates a lot of inequality, and freedom is not worth as much to a poor person as to a rich one. By contrast, North Korea or Cuba has considerable economic equality, but people cannot speak out or travel freely within or outside of the country. Perhaps the closest any country comes to "having it all" is Denmark—the Thinking Globally box takes a closer look.

Changes in Socialist and Capitalist Countries

In 1989 and 1990, the nations of Eastern Europe, which had been seized by the former Soviet Union at the end of World War II, overthrew their socialist regimes. These nations—including the former German Democratic Republic (East Germany), the Czech Republic, Slovakia, Hungary, Romania, and Bulgaria—all moved toward capitalist market systems after decades of state-controlled economies. At the end of 1991, the Soviet Union itself formally dissolved, and many of its former republics introduced some free-market principles into their economies. Within a decade, three-fourths of former Soviet government enterprises were partly or entirely in private hands (Montaigne, 2001).

There were many reasons for these sweeping changes. First, the capitalist economies were far more productive than their socialist counterparts. The socialist economies were successful in achieving economic equality, but living standards were low compared with those of Western Europe. Second, Soviet socialism was heavy-handed, rigidly controlling the media and restricting individual freedoms. In other words, socialism did away with *economic* elites, as Karl Marx predicted, but as Max Weber foresaw, socialism increased the power of *political* elites.

So far, the market reforms in Eastern Europe are proceeding unevenly. During 2010, the nations with the highest rates of economic growth included Turkey, Belarus, and Moldova. But other countries, including Bulgaria, Slovenia, and Latvia, have been buffeted by price increases and falling living standards. Especially in countries that are struggling, public support for market reforms has fallen as people point to lower living standards as well as increasing economic inequality. In Russia, the recent trend has been for government to increase its control over the economy (Ignatius, 2008; Pew Research Center, 2011; World Bank, 2011).

A number of countries, primarily in South America, have recently been heading in a more socialist direction. In 2005, the people

Denmark is a small nation in northwestern Europe with about 5.6 million people. This country is a good example of the economic and political system called welfare capitalism, in which a market economy is mixed with broad government programs that provide for the welfare of all Danish people.

Most Danes consider life in their country to be very good. There is a high standard of living—Denmark's per-person GDP is $35,736, which lags a bit behind the figure of $46,653 for the United States. But Denmark has only half as much income inequality as we have in this country. Its unemployment rate for 2010 was 7.7 percent, lower than the 9.6 percent in the United States.

Low inequality and low unemployment are largely the result of government regulation of the economy. Taxes in Denmark are the highest in the world, with most people paying about 48 percent of their income in taxes and those earning over about $70,000 paying more than 60 percent. That's in addition to a sales tax of 25 percent on everything people buy. These high taxes increase economic equality (by taking more taxes from the rich, who earn and consume more, and giving more benefits to the poor), and they also allow the government to fund the social welfare programs

that provide benefits to everyone. For example, every Danish citizen is entitled to government-funded schooling and government-funded health

To enable men and women to work for income, the government of Denmark grants paid child-care leave to both fathers and mothers.

care, and each worker receives at least five weeks of paid vacation leave each year. People who lose their jobs receive about 75 percent of their prior income (depending on family size) from the government for up to five years.

Many people—especially the Danes themselves—feel that Denmark offers an ideal mix of political freedom (Danes have extensive political rights and elect their leaders) and economic security (all citizens benefit from extensive government services and programs).

What Do You Think?

1. What evidence of less income inequality might you expect to see in Denmark if you were to visit that country?

2. Would you be willing to pay most of your income in taxes if the government provided you with benefits such as schooling and health care? Why or why not?

3. Do you think most people in the United States would like to have our society become more like Denmark? Why or why not?

Sources: Fox (2007), OECD (2011), Population Reference Bureau (2011), United Nations Development Programme (2011), and World Bank (2011).

---

of Bolivia elected Evo Morales, a former farmer, union leader, and activist, as their new president, over a wealthy business leader who was educated in the United States. This election placed Bolivia in a group of South American nations—including Ecuador, Venezuela, Brazil, Chile, and Uruguay—that are moving toward more socialist economies. The reasons for this shift toward socialism vary from country to country, but the common element is a desire to reduce economic inequality. In Bolivia, for example, the economy has grown in recent decades, but most of the benefits have gone to a wealthy business elite. By contrast, more than half the country's people remain very poor (Howden, 2005).

Work in the Postindustrial U.S. Economy

 Analyze

Economic change is occurring not just in the socialist world but also in the United States. In 2011, a total of 141 million people in this country—59 percent of those age sixteen and over—were working for income. A larger share of men (64 percent) than women (53 percent) had jobs, a gap that is holding steady over time. Among men, 57.8 percent of African Americans were employed, compared

with 68.9 percent of whites and 73.7 percent of Hispanics. Among women, 54.0 percent of African Americans were employed, compared with 55.3 percent of whites and 53.2 percent of Hispanics; 59.9 percent of Asian men and women were employed (U.S. Department of Labor, 2011).

The Changing Workplace

In 1900, roughly 40 percent of U.S. workers were farmers. In 2011, 1.7 percent were employed in agriculture. The family farm of yesterday has been replaced by *corporate agribusinesses.* Land is now more productive, but this change has caused painful adjustments across the country as a way of life is lost (Dudley, 2000). Figure 12–2 on page 310 illustrates the shrinking role of the primary sector in the U.S. economy.

A century ago, industrialization swelled the ranks of blue-collar workers. By 1950, however, a white-collar revolution had moved most workers from factories into service occupations. By 2011, some 80 percent of the labor force worked in the service sector, and almost all new jobs were being created in this sector (U.S. Department of Labor, 2012).

As Chapter 8 ("Social Stratification") explained, much service work—including sales, clerical positions, and work in hospitals and restaurants—pays much less than older factory jobs. This

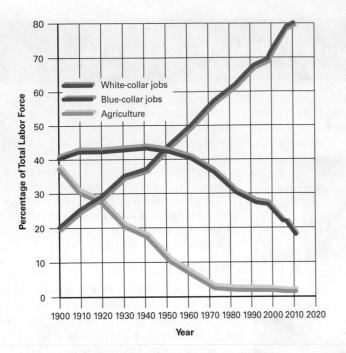

FIGURE 12–2 The Changing Pattern of Work in the United States, 1900–2011

Compared to a century ago, when the economy involved a larger share of factory and farm work, making a living in the United States now involves mostly white-collar service jobs.

Source: Estimates based on U.S. Department of Labor (2012).

means that many jobs in the postindustrial era provide only a modest standard of living. Women and other minorities, as well as many young people just starting their working careers, are the most likely to have jobs doing low-paying service work (Kalleberg, Reskin, & Hudson, 2000; Greenhouse, 2006).

Labor Unions

The changing U.S. economy has seen a decline in **labor unions**, *organizations that seek to improve wages and working conditions through various strategies, including negotiations and strikes.* During the Great Depression of the 1930s, union membership increased rapidly; by 1950, it had reached more than one-third of nonfarm workers. Union membership peaked around 1970 at almost 25 million. Since then, membership has declined to about 11.9 percent of nonfarm workers, or some 14.7 million men and women. Looking more closely, 36.2 percent of government workers are members of unions, compared with just 6.9 percent of private-sector (nongovernment) workers. By 2010, government workers had become a majority of all union members (Clawson & Clawson, 1999; Riley, 2011; U.S. Department of Labor, 2011).

The pattern of union decline holds in other high-income countries, yet unions claim a far smaller share of workers in the United States than elsewhere. Union membership is around 18 percent in Japan, between 20 and 40 percent in much of Europe, 28 percent in

Canada, and it reaches a high of 70 percent in Finland (Visser, 2006; OECD, 2011).

The widespread decline in union membership in the United States reflects the shrinking industrial sector of the economy. Newer service jobs—such as sales jobs at retailers like Walmart, described in the opening to this chapter—are usually not unionized. Citing low wages and worker complaints, unions are trying to organize Walmart employees, so far without winning over a single store. The weak economy of the past few years is giving unions a short-term boost, and the Obama administration is supporting new laws that may make it easier for workers to form unions. But long-term gains probably depend on the ability of unions to adapt to the new global economy. Union members in the United States, used to seeing foreign workers as "the enemy," will have to build new international alliances (Rousseau, 2002; Dalmia, 2008; M. Allen, 2009).

In 2011, the nation's attention was drawn to efforts by several states to limit the power of government employee unions. On one side of the debate were people who claim that high wages and generous benefits for public employees threaten to bankrupt state treasuries. On the other side of the debate were people claiming that such benefits are deserved by people who do important and often dangerous work for modest pay. In addition, critics charge that some political leaders are trying to destroy the union movement. The Sociology in Focus box provides details and offers you a chance to weigh in with your opinion.

Professions

All kinds of jobs today are called *professional*; there are professional tennis players, professional housecleaners, and even professional exterminators. As distinct from an *amateur* (from the Latin for "lover," meaning one who acts out of love for the activity itself) a professional performs some task to earn a living. But what exactly is a profession?

A **profession** is *a prestigious white-collar occupation that requires extensive formal education.* People performing this kind of work make a *profession*, or public declaration, that they are able and willing to work according to certain performance standards and ethical principles. Professions include the ministry, medicine, law, academia, and fields such as architecture, accountancy, and social work. An occupation is considered a profession to the extent that it demonstrates four basic characteristics (W. J. Goode, 1960; Ritzer & Walczak, 1990):

1. **Theoretical knowledge.** Professionals have a theoretical understanding of their field rather than mere technical training. Anyone can master first-aid skills, for example, but doctors have a theoretical understanding of human health. This means that tennis players, housecleaners, and exterminators do not really qualify as professionals according to the formal definition.

2. **Self-regulating practice.** The typical professional is self-employed, "in private practice" rather than working for a company. Professionals oversee their own work and observe a code of ethics.

The Great Union Battle of 2011: Balancing Budgets or Waging War on Working People?

"We're going to reform government," Ohio governor John Kasich told state legislators on March 8, 2011, as he gave his first "state of the state" speech. As he spoke, more than 1,000 firefighters—state employees—crowded the lobby outside the doors of the legislative chamber and chanted in unison, "Kill the bill! Kill the bill! Kill the bill!"

So what was going on? Ohio faces a desperate economic situation—the state government is $8 billion in debt. Governor Kasich believes one major cause of that enormous deficit is past agreements made between state officials and public employee unions, including firefighters, police, and teachers.

As Kasich sees it, the problem is a system that gives public employee unions too much power and threatens to bankrupt the state. Under that system, unions effectively require every public employee to be a union member and to pay hefty dues through payroll deductions. These dues give unions huge political power to elect Democratic leaders who, in the past, have signed off on labor contracts that exceed what workers in the private sector earn and which the state simply cannot afford. The reforms Kasich and the Republican-controlled state government enacted included new laws that would continue collective bargaining by public employee unions for salary but no longer allow it as the means to set benefits. In addition, pay would be linked to a performance-based merit system rather than seniority, and public employee unions would no longer be allowed to strike.

Harold Schaltberger, representing the International Association of Fire Fighters, saw the "reforms" as nothing less than a war on unions. The proposed change, he claimed, "moves us back decades, to when there were no true workers' rights."

In Wisconsin, Governor Scott Walker was elected in 2010 on a platform of reducing that state's budget deficit by cutting the power of public employee unions. On March 11, 2011, he signed a bill passed by that state's legislature limiting collective bargaining by public employees to wages (not benefits), limiting wage increases to the inflation rate, and decreasing the share the government contributes toward health care and retirement pensions. The new law also gave government workers the right to join or not to join a union.

Across the country, thirty-four states mandate that public-employee unions engage in collectively bargaining for their workplace conditions; five states explicitly ban this practice. In most cases, federal workers do not have the right to bargain collectively nor to strike. Many states—as well as the federal government—are facing large budget deficits. So the way this debate plays out in Ohio and Wisconsin may well have even greater importance for the nation as a whole.

Surveys have shown that the public seems to be divided in this debate. Survey data showed public-employee unions receive a favorable rating by 45 percent of the population, with the same share of people claiming an unfavorable view. But the unions mobilized in Ohio, successfully putting Kasich's reform on the ballot in November 2011, when it was soundly defeated by the voters. In Wisconsin, a union-led effort to recall Governor Walker is currently under way.

Join the Blog!

So where do you stand on this issue? Do you support the position taken by Governors Kasich and Walker to reduce union power? Or do you side with these unions and want to see them remain strong? Go to MySocLab and join the Sociology in Focus blog to share your opinions and experiences and to see what others think.

Sources: Gray (2011), Murphy (2011), Rasmussen (2011), Ripley (2011), and Sulzberger (2011).

---

3. **Authority over clients.** Because of their expertise, professionals are sought out by clients, who value their advice and follow their directions.

4. **Community orientation rather than self-interest.** The traditional professing of duty states an intention to serve the community rather than merely to seek income.

In almost all cases, professional work requires not just a college degree but a graduate degree. Not surprisingly, professions are well represented among the jobs beginning college students say they hope to get after graduation, as shown in Figure 12–3 on page 312.

Many occupations that do not qualify as true professions nonetheless seek to *professionalize* their services. Claiming professional standing usually begins by renaming the work to suggest special, theoretical knowledge, moving the field away from its original, lesser reputation. Stockroom workers become "inventory supply managers," exterminators are reborn as "insect control specialists," and cleanup workers describe themselves as "residential rehabilitation experts."

Interested parties may also form a professional association that certifies their skills. This organization then licenses its members, writes a code of ethics, and emphasizes the work's importance in the community. To win public acceptance, a professional association may also establish schools or other training facilities and perhaps start a professional journal. Not all occupations try to claim professional status. Some *paraprofessionals*, including paralegals and medical technicians, have specialized skills but lack the extensive theoretical education required of full professionals.

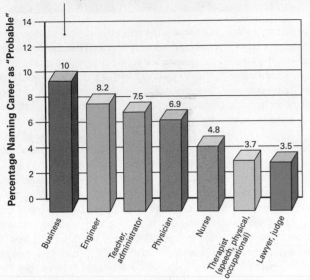

● In a society such as ours, with so many different types of work, no one career attracts the interest of more than a small share of today's students.

Student Snapshot

FIGURE 12–3 The Careers Most Commonly Named as Probable by First-Year College Students, 2010

Today's college students expect to enter careers that pay well and carry high prestige.

Source: Pryor et al. (2011).

Self-Employment

Self-employment—earning a living without being on the payroll of a large organization—was once common in the United States. About 80 percent of the labor force was self-employed in 1800, compared with just 6.7 percent of workers today (7.7 percent of men and 5.5 percent of women) (U.S. Department of Labor, 2011).

Lawyers, physicians, architects, and other professionals are well represented among the ranks of the self-employed in the United States. But most self-employed workers are small business owners, plumbers, farmers, carpenters, freelance writers and editors, artists, and long-distance truck drivers. In all, the self-employed are more likely to have blue-collar than white-collar jobs.

Women own 30 percent of this nation's businesses, and the share is rising. The 7.8 million firms owned by U.S. women employ 6.4 percent of the labor force and generate $1.2 trillion in annual sales (U.S. Census Bureau, 2011).

Unemployment and Underemployment

Every society has some level of unemployment. For one thing, few young people entering the labor force find a job right away; workers may leave their jobs to seek new work or to stay at home raising children; others may be on strike or suffer from long-term illnesses; and still others lack the skills to perform useful work.

But unemployment is not just an individual problem; it is also caused by the economy. Jobs disappear as occupations become obsolete and companies change the way they operate. Since 1980, the 500 largest U.S. businesses eliminated more than 5 million jobs while creating even more new ones.

Generally, companies downsize to become more competitive or close down entirely in the face of foreign competition or economic recession. During the recession that began in 2008 in the United States, millions of jobs were lost, with unemployment rising in just about every part of the economy. Not only blue-collar workers but also white-collar workers who had typically weathered downturns in the past have lost jobs during this recession (U.S. Department of Labor, 2010).

In 2008, just as the country was falling into recession, 7 million people over the age of sixteen were unemployed, about 4.6 percent of the civilian labor force (U.S. Department of Labor, 2008). But by the end of 2011, more than 13 million were officially listed as unemployed, pushing the unemployment rate to 8.9 percent (9.4 percent for men and 8.5 percent for women). This figure was below the high of 10.6 percent at the start of 2010. In some regions of the country, especially rural areas, unemployment rates are usually far worse—as much as double the national average. In addition, counting the people without jobs who have given up looking for work (and, therefore, are not counted in the official unemployment statistics), the number of jobless people almost certainly exceeds 20 million.

Figure 12–4 shows that unemployment among African Americans (15.8 percent) is twice the rate among white people (7.9 percent). Among all categories of people, unemployment is lower among whites than among African Americans, although the gap between white and black teenagers is especially large. For all categories of people, a good way to reduce the risk of unemployment is to earn a college degree: As the figure shows, the unemployment rate for college graduates is around 3.9 percent—less than half the national average.

For those who experience unemployment, finding another job is more difficult than ever. The median length of unemployment has increased to 21.6 weeks, meaning that half of all unemployed people are out of work longer than this. But the mean length of unemployment is 40.9 weeks—an average pulled up by those workers who are out of work for a year or more. In short, our society now faces a problem of *extended unemployment*, with unemployment not only more widespread but also longer lasting than it has been in the recent past (U.S. Department of Labor, 2011).

Underemployment is also a problem for millions of workers. In an era of corporate bankruptcy, the failure of large banks, and downsizing by companies throughout the U.S. economy, millions of workers—the lucky ones who still have their jobs—have been left with lower salaries, fewer benefits such as health insurance, and disappearing pensions. Rising global competition, weaker worker organizations, and economic recession have combined to allow many people to keep their jobs only by agreeing to cutbacks in pay or to the loss of other benefits (K. Clark, 2002; Gutierrez, 2007; McGeehan, 2009).

In addition, the government reports that more than 27 million people work part time, defined as less than thirty-five hours a week. Although most say they are satisfied with this arrangement,

30 percent of part time workers claim that they want more work but cannot find it (U.S. Department of Labor, 2011). In all, as the country struggles to climb out of the recent recession, it is likely that one in five workers is working fewer hours than desired, is out of work and looking for a job, or is a "discouraged worker" who has given up entirely.

The "Jobless Recovery"

The economy operates in cycles, with periods of prosperity followed by periods of recession—what we commonly call "boom and bust." In the past, periods of high job loss during economic recession have typically been followed by a rapid increase in jobs as good times returned, bringing down the unemployment rate within a few years.

This time around, the recovery in jobs has not been as quick. Corporate profits have returned to their pre-recession levels, but U.S. corporations are operating with about 7 million fewer workers. This means that the nation's unemployment remains stubbornly high. One reason for this pattern—sometimes described as the "jobless recovery"—is that, even before the economy went into recession, companies were finding ways to operate with a smaller workforce. Computer technology allows fewer people to do more work; in many cases, too, a smaller number of workers have simply been given more to do. In addition, companies are making more use of temporary workers.

Second, more companies have opened factories and office hubs abroad—often in China, India, or Brazil, where wages and benefits will cost far less. In China, for example, workers earn about 10 percent as much as they do in the United States. For this reason, many global corporations are making record profits while adding almost no jobs here in the United States.

A third issue is that the U.S. economy is simply not growing fast enough—and hasn't been for many years—to absorb all the people looking for jobs. That is why, according to government reports, for every new job that is available, there are almost five people looking for work.

Fourth, and finally, in global terms, U.S. workers are simply too expensive and not highly skilled enough to fare well in today's economy. Perhaps, as some analysts suggest, large investments will have to be made in education and job training in order to get the unemployment rate here in the United States back to pre-recession levels (Faroohar, 2011; Wessel, 2011; Zakaria, 2011).

Workplace Diversity: Race and Gender

In the past, white men were the mainstay of the U.S. labor force. However, the nation's proportion of minorities is rising rapidly. The African American population is increasing faster than the population of non-Hispanic white people. The rate of increase in the Asian American and Hispanic populations is even greater.

Such dramatic changes are likely to affect U.S. society in countless ways. Not only will more and more workers be women and minorities, but the workplace will have to develop programs and policies that meet the needs of a socially diverse

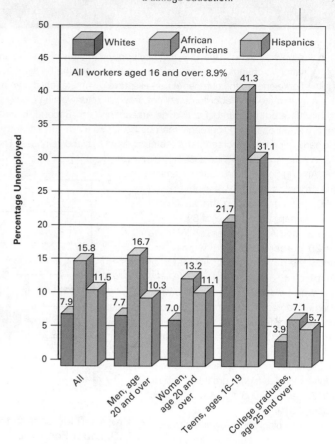

Diversity Snapshot

FIGURE 12–4 **Official U.S. Unemployment Rates for Various Categories of Adults, 2011**

Although college graduates have a low risk of unemployment, race is related to unemployment for all categories of people.

Source: U.S. Department of Labor (2012).

workforce and also encourage everyone to work together effectively and respectfully. The Thinking About Diversity box on page 314 takes a closer look at some of the issues involved in our changing workplace.

New Information Technology and Work

July 2, Ticonderoga, New York. The manager of the local hardware store scans the bar codes of a bagful of items. "The computer doesn't just total the costs," she explains. "It also keeps track of inventory, places orders with the warehouse, and decides which products to continue to sell and which to drop." "Sounds like what you used to do, Maureen," I respond with a smile. "Yep," she nods, with no smile at all.

Another workplace issue is the increasing role of computers and other new information technology. The Information Revolution is

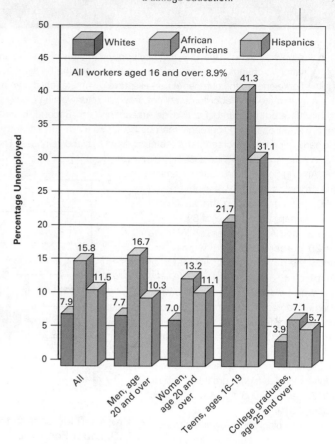 **Watch** the video "Women in the Workplace" on **mysoclab.com**

An upward trend in the U.S. minority population is changing the workplace. As the figure shows, the number of non-Hispanic white men in the U.S. labor force will not grow at all by 2018, but the number of African American men will increase by 8 percent, the number of Hispanic men by 22 percent, and the number of Asian American men will increase by 19 percent.

Among non-Hispanic white women, the projected change is a slight decline of 0.1 percent; among African American women, an increase of 8 percent; and among Asian women, an increase of 20 percent. Hispanic women will show the greatest gains, estimated at 26 percent.

Within a decade, non-Hispanic white men will represent 33 percent of all workers, and that figure will continue to drop. As a result, companies that welcome social diversity will tap the largest pool of talent and enjoy a competitive advantage leading to higher profits (Graybow, 2007; Harford, 2008; U.S. Department of Labor, 2010).

Welcoming social diversity means, first, recruiting talented workers of both sexes and all racial and cultural backgrounds. But developing the potential of all employees requires meeting the needs of women and other minorities, which may not be the same as those of white men. For example, child care at the workplace is a big issue for working mothers with small children.

Second, businesses must develop effective ways to deal with tension that arises from social differences. They will have to work harder to ensure that workers are treated equally and respectfully, which means having zero tolerance for racial or sexual harassment.

Third, companies will have to rethink current promotion practices. At present, 72 percent of the directors of Fortune 100 companies are white men; 28 percent are women or other minorities (Executive Leadership Council, 2008). In a survey of U.S. companies, the U.S. Equal Employment Opportunity Commission (2011) confirmed that non-Hispanic white men, who make up 33 percent of adults aged twenty-five to sixty-four, hold 52 percent of management jobs; the comparable figures are 33 and 29 percent, respectively, for non-Hispanic white women, 13 and 6 percent for non-Hispanic African Americans, and 15 and 6 percent for Hispanics.

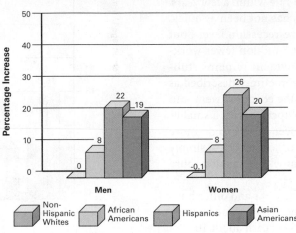

Projected Increase in the Number of People in the U.S. Labor Force, 2011–2018

Looking ahead, the share of minorities in the U.S. labor force will increase much faster than the share of white men and women.

Source: U.S. Department of Labor (2010).

What Do You Think?

1. What underlying factors are increasing the social diversity of the U.S. workplace?

2. In what specific ways do you think businesses should support minority workers?

3. In what other settings (such as schools) is social diversity becoming more important? Why?

---

changing what people do in a number of ways (Rule & Brantley, 1992; Vallas & Beck, 1996):

1. **Computers are deskilling labor.** Just as industrial machines replaced the master craftsworkers of an earlier era, computers now threaten the skills of managers. More business operations are based not on executive decisions but on computer modeling. In other words, a machine decides whether to place an order, stock a dress in a certain size and color, or approve a loan application.

2. **Computers are making work more abstract.** Most industrial workers have a hands-on relationship with their product. Postindustrial workers use symbols to perform abstract tasks, such as making a company more efficient, making software more user-friendly, or hiding risky assets inside financial "derivatives."

3. **Computers limit workplace interaction.** Spending time at computer terminals, workers become isolated from one another.

4. **Computers increase employers' control of workers.** Computers allow supervisors to check employees' output continuously, whether they work at keyboard terminals or on assembly lines.

5. **Computers allow companies to relocate work.** Because computer technology allows information to flow almost anywhere instantly, the symbolic work in today's economy may not take place where we might think. We have all had the experience of calling a business (for instance, a hotel or bookstore) located in our own town only to find that we are talking to a person at a computer workstation thousands of miles away. Computer technology provides the means to outsource many jobs—especially service work—to other places where wages may be lower.

Perhaps in the wake of widespread failures on Wall Street, there will be a trend away from allowing computers to manage risk, putting responsibility for business decisions back in the hands of people (Kivant, 2008). Or perhaps computers, people, and our economic system all have flaws that will always prevent us from living in a perfect world. But the rapidly increasing reliance on computers in business reminds us that new technology is never socially neutral. It changes the relationships between people in the workplace, shapes the way we work, and often alters the balance of power between employers and employees. Understandably, then, people welcome some aspects of the Information Revolution and oppose others.

Corporations

 Understand

At the core of today's capitalist economy is the **corporation**, *an organization with a legal existence, including rights and liabilities, separate from that of its members.* Incorporating makes an organization a legal entity, able to enter into contracts and own property. Of the nearly 32 million businesses in the United States, 5.8 million are incorporated (U.S. Census Bureau, 2011). Incorporating protects the wealth of owners from lawsuits that result from business debts or harm to consumers; it can also mean a lower tax rate on the company's profits.

Economic Concentration

Most U.S. corporations are small, with assets of less than $500,000, so it is the largest corporations that dominate our nation's economy. In 2008, the government listed 2,582 corporations with assets exceeding $2.5 billion, representing 81 percent of all corporate assets (Internal Revenue Service, 2011).

The largest U.S. corporation, measured in terms of sales, is Walmart, with 2011 revenue of $419 billion. This is more money than the combined tax revenues collected by forty-four of the fifty states.

Conglomerates and Corporate Linkages

Economic concentration creates **conglomerates**, *giant corporations composed of many smaller corporations.* Conglomerates form as corporations enter new markets, spin off new companies, or merge with other companies. For example, PepsiCo is a conglomerate that includes Pepsi-Cola, Frito-Lay, Gatorade, Tropicana, and Quaker.

Many conglomerates are linked because they own each other's stock, the result being worldwide corporate alliances of staggering size. Until 2009, General Motors, for example, owned Opel (Germany), Vauxhall (Great Britain), Saab (Sweden), and a share of Daewoo (South Korea) and had partnerships with Suzuki and Toyota (Japan). Similarly, Ford owned Volvo (Sweden) and a share of Mazda (Japan).

In today's corporate world, computers are changing the nature of work just as factories did more than a century ago. In what ways is computer-based work different from factory work? In what ways do you think it is very much the same?

Corporations are also linked through *interlocking directorates,* networks of people who serve as directors of many corporations (Weidenbaum, 1995; Kono et al., 1998). These boardroom connections provide access to valuable information about other companies' products and marketing strategies. While perfectly legal, such linkages encourage illegal activity, such as price fixing, as companies share information about their pricing policies.

Corporations: Are They Competitive?

According to the capitalist model, businesses operate independently in a competitive market. But in light of the extensive linkages that exist between them, it is obvious that large corporations do not operate independently. Also, a few large corporations dominate many markets, so they are not truly competitive.

Federal law forbids any company from establishing a **monopoly**, *domination of a market by a single producer,* because with no competition, such a company could simply charge whatever it wanted for its products. But **oligopoly**, *domination of a market by a few producers*, is both legal and common. Oligopoly arises because the huge investment needed to enter a major market, such as the auto industry, is beyond the reach of all but the biggest companies. In addition, competition means risk, which big business tries to avoid.

The federal government seeks to regulate corporations in order to protect the public interest. Yet as corporate scandals have shown—most recently, involving the housing mortgage business

---

corporation an organization with a legal existence, including rights and liabilities, separate from that of its members

conglomerate a giant corporation composed of many smaller corporations

monopoly the domination of a market by a single producer

oligopoly the domination of a market by a few producers

Controversy & Debate

The Market: Does the "Invisible Hand" Lift Us Up or Pick Our Pockets?

The market or government planning? Governments rely on one or the other to determine the products and services companies will produce and what people will consume. So important is this question that the answer has much to do with how nations define themselves, choose their allies, and identify their enemies.

Historically, U.S. society has relied on the "invisible hand" of the market to make economic decisions. Market dynamics move prices up or down according to the supply of products and buyer demand. The market thus links the efforts of countless people, each of whom—to restate Adam Smith's insight—is motivated only by self-interest. Defenders of the market system—including the economists Milton Friedman and Rose Friedman (1980)—claim that a more or less freely operating market system is the key to this country's high standard of living.

But others point to the contributions government makes to the U.S. economy. First, government must step in to carry out tasks that no private company could do as well, such as defending the country against enemies abroad or terrorists at home. Government (in partnership with private companies) also plays a key role in building and maintaining public projects such as roads, utilities, schools, libraries, and museums.

The Friedmans counter that whatever the task, government usually ends up being very inefficient. They claim that for most people, the least satisfying goods and services available today—public schools, the postal service, and passenger railroad service—are government-operated. The products we enjoy most—household appliances, computers and other electronics, and fashionable clothes—are products of the market. The Friedmans and other supporters of free markets believe that minimal state regulation serves the public interest best.

But supporters of government intervention in the economy make other arguments. First, they claim that the market has incentives to produce only what is profitable. Few private companies set out to meet the needs of poor people because, by definition, poor people have little money to spend.

Second, the market has certain self-destructive tendencies that only the government can curb. In 1890, for example, the government passed the Sherman Antitrust Act to break up the monopolies that controlled the nation's oil and steel production. In the decades since then—and especially after President Franklin Roosevelt's New Deal of the 1930s—government has taken a strong regulatory role to control inflation (by setting interest rates), enhance the well-being of workers (by imposing workplace safety standards), and benefit consumers (by setting standards for product quality). Especially after the failure of the market to prevent a serious economic downturn in 2008, the public voiced support for a larger government presence in the national economy.

To what extent do you think government regulation of the economy is necessary?

Third, because the market magnifies social inequality, the government must step in on the side of social justice. Since capitalist economies concentrate income and wealth in the hands of a few, it is necessary for government to tax the rich at a higher rate to ensure that wealth reaches more of the population.

Does the market's "invisible hand" lift us up or pick our pockets? Although most people in the United States favor a free market, they also support government intervention into the economy. Public opinion shifts back and forth over time. After the economic crisis in 2008, public confidence in corporations fell, and confidence in the federal government went up. Democratic victories in the 2008 elections reflected the public view that government's job is not only to ensure national security but also to maintain economic stability. By 2010, Republicans made electoral gains, suggesting some movement back toward favoring the private sector over government. The outcome of the 2012 election will provide another referendum on the public-private debate. In the years to come, we should expect to see people in the United States, and also around the world, continuing to debate the best balance of market forces and government decision making.

What Do You Think?

1. Do you agree or disagree with the statement that "the government is best that governs least"? Why?

2. What is the view of the Tea Party movement on the best balance of the market system and government? What about the Occupy Wall Street movement?

3. In the 2012 presidential campaign, how and why did the Obama administration defend a larger role for government? How and why did candidate Mitt Romney and the Republican opposition defend a larger role for the private sector?

and the collapse of so many banks—regulation is often too little too late, resulting in harm to millions of people. The U.S. government is the corporate world's single biggest customer, and in 2008 and 2009, it stepped in to support many struggling corporations with multibillion-dollar bailout programs. Especially during tough economic times, the public tends to support a greater role for the government in the economy (Sachs, 2009).

Corporations and the Global Economy

Corporations have grown so large that they now account for most of the world's economic output. The biggest corporations are based in the United States, Japan, and Western Europe, but their marketplace is the entire world. Many large companies such as McDonald's and the chipmaker Intel earn most of their money outside the United States.

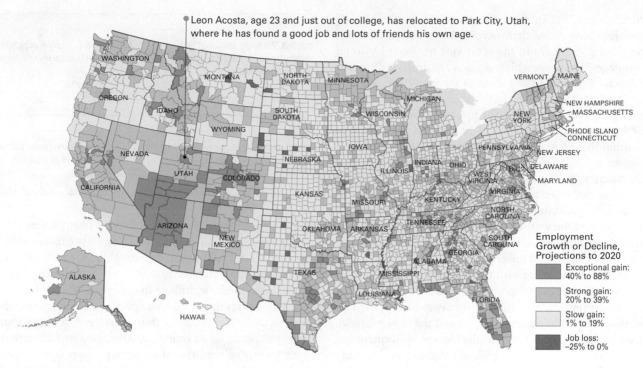

Leon Acosta, age 23 and just out of college, has relocated to Park City, Utah, where he has found a good job and lots of friends his own age.

Employment Growth or Decline, Projections to 2020

Exceptional gain: 40% to 88%

Strong gain: 20% to 39%

Slow gain: 1% to 19%

Job loss: −25% to 0%

Seeing Ourselves

NATIONAL MAP 12–1 Where the Jobs Will Be: Projections to 2020

The economic prospects for people living in counties across the United States are not the same. Gains in jobs are projected to be strong for most areas in the western states as well as for Florida; some areas in the East and the Midwest are also expected to gain jobs. But job growth will be slow at best in the midsection of the country, with a number of counties even projected to lose jobs in the years to come.

 Explore self-employment in your local community and in counties across the United States on **mysoclab.com**

Source: Woods & Poole Economics, Washington, D.C. Copyright © 2007.

Global corporations know that poor countries contain most of the world's people and resources. In addition, labor costs there are attractively low: A manufacturing worker in Mexico, who earns about $5.38 an hour, labors for more than a week to earn what a worker in Japan (who averages about $30.36 an hour) or the United States ($33.53 per hour) earns in a single day (U.S. Department of Labor, 2011).

As Chapter 9 ("Global Stratification") explained, the impact of multinational corporations on low-income countries is controversial. Modernization theorists claim that multinational corporations, by unleashing the great productivity of capitalism, raise living standards in poor nations, offering tax revenues, capital investment, new jobs, and advanced technology that together accelerate economic growth (Berger, 1986; Firebaugh & Beck, 1994; Firebaugh & Sandu, 1998).

Dependency theorists respond that multinationals in fact make global inequality worse by blocking the development of local industries and by pushing poor countries to produce goods for export rather than food and other products for local people. From this standpoint, multinationals make poor nations increasingly dependent on rich nations (Wallerstein, 1979; Dixon & Boswell, 1996; Kentor, 1998).

In short, modernization theory praises the market as the key to progress and affluence for all the world's people. Dependency theory takes a different position, calling for replacing markets with government-based economic policies. The Controversy & Debate box takes a closer look at the issue of whether the market or government should take the lead in guiding the economy.

The Economy: Looking Ahead

Evaluate

Social institutions are a society's way of meeting people's needs. But as we have seen, the U.S. economy only partly succeeds in this mission. As the years go by, our economy experiences alternating periods of expansion and recession. And in both good times and bad, our economy provides for some people much better than for others.

One important trend that underlies change in the economy is the Information Revolution. First, the share of the U.S. labor force engaged in manufacturing is one-third of what it was in 1960; service work, especially computer-related jobs, makes up the difference. For industrial workers, the postindustrial economy has brought unemployment and declining wages. Our society must face up to the challenge of providing millions of men and women with the language and computer skills they need to succeed in the modern economy. Yet in recent years, millions of people in "good" service jobs have found themselves out of work. In addition, there are regional differences in the economic outlook: National Map 12–1 on page 317 shows which regions are projected to gain jobs and which are expected to lose them by the year 2020.

A second transformation of recent years is the expansion of the global economy. Two centuries ago, the ups and downs people experienced reflected events and trends in their own town. One century ago, communities were economically linked so that one town's prosperity depended on producing goods demanded by people elsewhere in the country. Today, we have to look beyond the national economy because, for example, the historical rise in the cost of gasoline at our local gas station has as much to do with increasing demand for oil around the world, especially in China and India. As both producers and consumers, we are now subject to factors and forces that are both distant and unseen.

Finally, analysts around the world are rethinking conventional economic models. The global economy shows that socialism is less productive than capitalism, one important reason behind the collapse of socialist regimes in Eastern Europe and the Soviet Union. But capitalism has its own problems, as the Occupy movement has recently highlighted, including high levels of inequality and a steady stream of corporate scandal. These are two important reasons that the economy now operates with significant government regulation.

What will be the long-term effects of all these changes? Two conclusions seem certain. First, the economic future of the United States and other nations will be played out in a global arena. The new postindustrial economy in the United States has emerged as more industrial production has moved to other nations. Second, it is imperative that we address the urgent issues of global inequality and population increase. Whether the world reduces or enlarges the gap between rich and poor societies may well steer our planet toward peace or war.

Politics: Historical Overview

 **Understand**

There is a close link between economics and **politics** (also known as the "polity"), *the social institution that distributes power, sets a society's goals, and makes decisions.* Early in the twentieth century, Max Weber (1978, orig. 1921) defined **power** as *the ability to achieve desired ends despite resistance from others.* The use of power is the business of **government**, *a formal organization that directs the political life of a society.* Governments typically claim to help people, but at the same time, governments demand that people obey the rules. Yet, as Weber noted, most governments do not openly threaten their people. Most of the time, people respect (or at least accept) their society's political system.

---

politics the social institution that distributes power, sets a society's goals, and makes decisions

government a formal organization that directs the political life of a society

---

power the ability to achieve desired ends despite resistance from others

authority power that people perceive as legitimate rather than coercive

---

No government, Weber explained, is likely to keep its power for very long if compliance comes only from the threat of brute force, because there could never be enough police to watch everyone—and who would watch the police? Every government therefore, tries to make itself seem legitimate in the eyes of the public.

This brings us to the concept of **authority**, *power that people perceive as legitimate rather than coercive.* A society's source of authority depends on its economy. According to Weber, preindustrial societies rely on **traditional authority**, *power legitimized by respect for long-established cultural patterns.* Woven into a society's collective memory, traditional authority may seem almost sacred. Chinese emperors in centuries past were legitimized by tradition, as were aristocratic rulers in medieval Europe. The power of tradition can be so strong that, for better or worse, people typically come to view traditional rulers as almost godlike.

Traditional authority declines as societies industrialize. For example, royal families still exist in ten European nations, but the democratic cultures of countries such as the United Kingdom, Sweden, and Denmark have shifted power to commoners elected to office. Weber explained that the expansion of rational bureaucracy is the foundation of authority in modern societies. **Rational-legal authority** (sometimes called *bureaucratic authority*) is *power legitimized by legally enacted rules and regulations.*

Traditional authority is tied to family; rational-legal authority flows from offices in governments. A traditional monarch passes power on to heirs; a modern president or prime minister takes office and later on gives up power according to law.

Weber described one additional type of authority that has surfaced throughout history. **Charismatic authority** is *power legitimized by extraordinary personal abilities that inspire devotion and obedience.* Unlike its traditional and rational-legal counterparts, charismatic authority depends less on a person's ancestry or office and more on charisma, or personality. Followers see in charismatic leaders some special, perhaps even divine, power. Examples of charismatic leaders include Jesus of Nazareth; Nazi Germany's Adolf Hitler; India's liberator, Mahatma Gandhi; and civil rights leader Martin Luther

---

Types of Authority

traditional authority power legitimized by respect for long-established cultural patterns

rational-legal authority power legitimized by legally enacted rules and regulations (also known as *bureaucratic authority*)

charismatic authority power legitimized by extraordinary personal abilities that inspire devotion and obedience

---

Monarchy is typically found in societies that have yet to industrialize. The recent political unrest throughout the Middle East indicates growing resistance to this form of political system in today's world. Even so, King Abdullah and members of his royal family strengthen their control of Saudi Arabia through their support of Arabic heritage and culture.

King Jr. All charismatic leaders aim to radically transform society, which explains why charismatics are almost always controversial and why few of them die of old age.

Because charismatic authority flows from a single individual, the leader's death creates a crisis. The survival of a charismatic movement, Weber explained, requires the **routinization of charisma**, *the transformation of charismatic authority into some combination of traditional and bureaucratic authority.* After the death of Jesus, for example, followers institutionalized his teachings in a church, built on tradition and bureaucracy. Routinized in this way, Christianity has lasted 2,000 years.

Politics in Global Perspective

 Apply

The world's political systems differ in countless ways. Generally, however, they fall into four categories: monarchy, democracy, authoritarianism, and totalitarianism.

Monarchy

Monarchy (with Latin and Greek roots meaning "one ruler") is *a political system in which a single family rules from generation to generation.* Monarchy is commonly found in agrarian societies; for example, the Bible tells of great kings such as David and Solomon. In the world today, twenty-six nations have royal families;[1] most trace their ancestry back centuries. In Weber's analysis, then, monarchy is legitimized by tradition.

During the Middle Ages, *absolute monarchs* in much of the world claimed a monopoly of power based on divine right (or God's will). In some nations—including Oman, Saudi Arabia, and Swaziland—monarchs (not necessarily with divine support) still exercise virtually absolute control over their people.

With industrialization, however, monarchs gradually pass from the scene in favor of elected officials. All the European societies with royal families today are *constitutional monarchies,* meaning that their monarchs are little more than *symbolic* heads of state; actual governing is the responsibility of elected officials, led by a prime minister and guided by a constitution. In these countries, nobility formally *reigns,* but elected officials actually *rule.*

Democracy

The historical trend throughout most of the world has been toward **democracy**, *a political system that gives power to the people as a whole.* Because it is unrealistic to expect all citizens to be involved in governing, our system is in fact a *representative democracy,* which puts authority in the hands of leaders who from time to time compete for office in elections.

Most high-income countries of the world, including those that still have royal families, claim to be democratic. Industrialization and democracy go together because both require a literate populace. Also, with industrialization, the traditional legitimization of power in a monarchy gives way to rational-legal authority. Thus democracy and rational-legal authority are linked just like monarchy and traditional authority.

---

[1]In Europe: Sweden, Norway, Denmark, Great Britain, the Netherlands, Liechtenstein, Luxembourg, Belgium, Spain, and Monaco; in the Middle East: Jordan, Saudi Arabia, Oman, Qatar, Bahrain, and Kuwait; in Africa: Lesotho, Swaziland, and Morocco; in Asia: Brunei, Tonga, Thailand, Malaysia, Cambodia, Bhutan, and Japan (U.S. Department of State, 2011).

monarchy a political system in which a single family rules from generation to generation

democracy a political system that gives power to the people as a whole

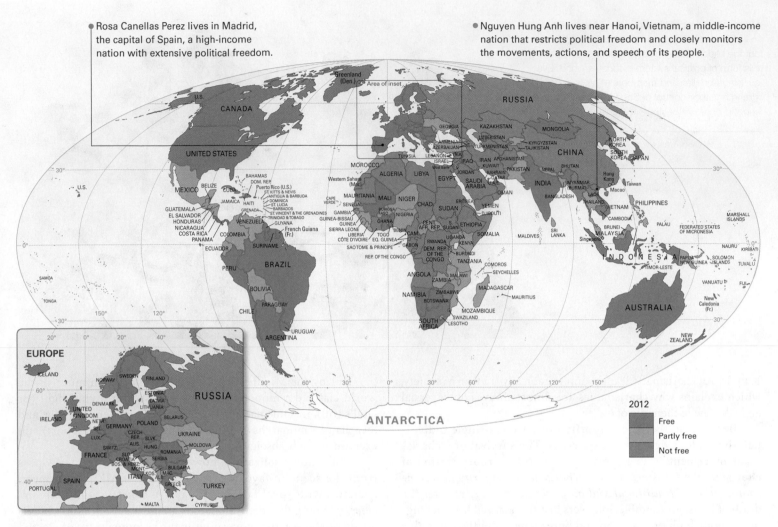

Rosa Canellas Perez lives in Madrid, the capital of Spain, a high-income nation with extensive political freedom.

Nguyen Hung Anh lives near Hanoi, Vietnam, a middle-income nation that restricts political freedom and closely monitors the movements, actions, and speech of its people.

2012

Free

Partly free

Not free

Window on the World

GLOBAL MAP 12–3 Political Freedom in Global Perspective

In 2011, a total of 87 of the world's 195 nations, containing 43 percent of all people, were politically "free"; that is, they offered their citizens extensive political rights and civil liberties. Another 60 countries, which included 22 percent of the world's people, were "partly free," with more limited rights and liberties. The remaining 48 nations, home to 35 percent of humanity, fall into the category of "not free." In these countries, government sharply restricts individual initiative. Between 1989 and 2012, democracy made significant gains, largely in Latin America and Eastern Europe.

Source: Freedom House (2012).

But high-income countries such as the United States are not truly democratic, for two reasons. First, there is the problem of bureaucracy. The U.S. federal government has 2.8 million regular employees and several million more paid for by special funding. Add to this the 1.6 million uniformed service personnel and 64,000 legislative and judicial branch personnel—more than 4.4 million workers in all. Another 19.6 million people work in 90,690 local governments across the country. Most of the officials who run the government are never elected by anyone and do not have to answer directly to the people.

The second problem involves economic inequality: Rich people have far more political power than poor people. Most of our

political leaders have been wealthy men and women, and in politics, "money talks." Given the even greater resources of billion-dollar corporations, how well does our "democratic" system listen to the voices of "average people"?

Still, democratic nations do provide many rights and freedoms. Global Map 12–3 shows one assessment of political freedom around the world. According to Freedom House, an organization that tracks political trends, eighty-seven of the world's nations (with 43 percent of the global population) were "free," respecting many civil liberties, in 2011. This represents a gain for democracy: Just seventy-six nations were considered free two decades earlier (Freedom House, 2012).

Authoritarianism

Some governments prevent their people from having any voice in politics. **Authoritarianism** is *a political system that denies the people participation in government.* An authoritarian government is indifferent to people's needs and offers them no voice in selecting leaders. The absolute monarchies in Saudi Arabia and Oman are authoritarian, as are the undemocratic rulers in Turkmenistan and Uzbekistan.

Totalitarianism

October 30, Beijing, China. Several U.S. students are sitting around a computer in the lounge of a Chinese university dormitory. They are taking turns running Internet searches on keywords such as "democracy" and "Amnesty International." They soon realize that China's government filters the results of Internet searches, permitting only officially approved sites to appear. One Chinese student who is watching points out that things could be worse—in North Korea, she explains, most students have no access to computers at all.

The most intensely controlled political form is **totalitarianism**, *a highly centralized political system that extensively regulates people's lives.* Totalitarianism emerged in the twentieth century as governments gained the ability to rigidly control their populations. The Vietnamese government closely monitors the activities of all of its citizens. Similarly, the government of North Korea uses surveillance equipment and powerful computers to control its people by collecting and storing information about them.

Although some totalitarian governments claim to represent the will of the people, most seek to bend people to the will of the government. As the term "totalitarian" implies, such governments have a *total* concentration of power, allowing no organized opposition. Denying the people the right to assemble and controlling access to information, these governments create an atmosphere of isolation and fear. In the former Soviet Union, for example, most citizens had no access to telephone directories, copiers, fax machines, or accurate city maps. Only in the last few years has the Cuban government allowed ordinary citizens to own personal computers and cell phones.

Socialization in totalitarian societies is highly political, seeking obedience and commitment to the system. In North Korea, one of the world's strictest totalitarian states, pictures of leaders and political messages are everywhere, reminding citizens that they owe total allegiance to the state. Government-controlled schools and mass media present only official versions of events. When that nation's leader Kim Jong-il died in 2011, the official government news agency reported the nation's people were in "utter despair" at the loss of the "Glorious Leader Who Descended from Heaven," but would find comfort in

the "absolute surety that the leadership of [his son] Comrade Kim Jong-un will lead the great task of revolutionary enterprise." Three generations of the same family has tightly controlled this impoverished nation since 1948 (Chance & Kim, 2011; Rogers, 2011).

Totalitarian governments span the political spectrum from fascist (including Nazi Germany) to communist (such as North Korea). In all cases, however, one party claims total control of the society and permits no opposition.

A Global Political System?

Is globalization changing politics in the same way that it is changing the economy? On one level, the answer is no. Although most of today's economic activity is international, the world remains divided into nation-states, just as it has been for centuries. The United Nations (founded in 1945) was a small step toward global government, but its political role in world affairs has been limited.

On another level, however, politics has become a global process. For some analysts, multinational corporations represent a new political order because of their enormous power to shape events throughout the world. In other words, politics is dissolving into business as corporations grow larger than governments.

Also, the Information Revolution has moved national politics onto the world stage. E-mail, text messaging, and Twitter networks mean that few countries can conduct their political affairs in complete privacy. The recent "WikiLeaks" controversy shows that, in the age of computers and hacking, just about anyone can access information—even that guarded by governments—and make it available to anyone and everyone (Gellman, 2011).

Finally, several thousand *nongovernmental organizations* (NGOs) seek to advance global issues, such as human rights

In totalitarian nations, government controls all aspects of people's lives. During the funeral of Kim Jong-il, absolute ruler of North Korea, people were told to line the route used for his public funeral and display appropriate anguish at his death. After the event, government officials examined photographs of the crowds and prosecuted those whose sorrow did not measure up to their demands.

> **authoritarianism** a political system that denies the people participation in government
>
> **totalitarianism** a highly centralized political system that extensively regulates people's lives

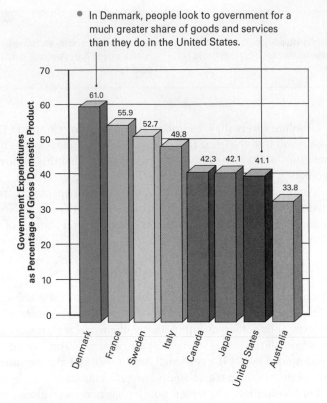

In Denmark, people look to government for a much greater share of goods and services than they do in the United States.

Global Snapshot

FIGURE 12–5 The Size of Government, 2012

Government activity accounts for a smaller share of economic output in the United States than in other high-income countries.

Source: OECD (2012).

(Amnesty International) and environmental protection (Greenpeace). NGOs will continue to play a key role in expanding the global political culture.

In sum, just as individual nations are losing control of their own economies, governments cannot fully manage the political events occurring within their borders.

Politics in the United States

 Analyze

In the eighteenth century, after fighting a war against Britain to gain political independence, the United States replaced the British monarchy with a representative democracy. Our nation's political development since that time reflects its cultural history as well as its capitalist economy.

U.S. Culture and the Rise of the Welfare State

The political culture of the United States can be summed up in one word: individualism. This emphasis is found in the Bill of Rights, which guarantees freedom from undue government interference. It was this individualism that the nineteenth-century

poet and philosopher Ralph Waldo Emerson had in mind when he said, "The government that governs best is the government that governs least."

But most people stop short of Emerson's position, believing that government is necessary to defend the country, operate highway systems and schools, maintain law and order, and help people in need. To accomplish these things, the United States has developed a complex **welfare state**, *a system of government agencies and programs that provides benefits to the population.* Government benefits begin even before birth (through prenatal nutrition programs) and continue into old age (through Social Security and Medicare). Some programs are especially important to the poor, who are not well served by our capitalist economic system; but students, farmers, homeowners, small business operators, veterans, performing artists, and even executives of giant corporations get various subsidies and supports. In fact, a majority of U.S. adults look to government for at least part of their income.

Today's welfare state is the result of a gradual increase in the size and scope of government. In 1789, when the presence of the federal government amounted to little more than a flag in most communities, the entire federal budget was a mere $4.5 million ($1.50 for each person in the nation). Since then, it has steadily risen, reaching $3.7 trillion in 2012 ($11,964 for every person in the country).

Similarly, when our nation was founded, one government employee served every 1,800 citizens. Today, about one in six people in the United States is a government employee—more than are engaged in manufacturing (U.S. Bureau of Labor Statistics, 2011; U.S. Census Bureau, 2011).

Despite this growth, the U.S. welfare state is still smaller than those of many other high-income nations. Figure 12–5 shows that government is larger in most of Europe, especially in Scandinavian countries such as Denmark and Sweden.

The Political Spectrum

Who supports a bigger welfare state? Who wants to cut it back? Answers to such questions reveal attitudes that form the *political spectrum,* which ranges from extremely liberal on the left to extremely conservative on the right. In the United States, about one-fourth of adults fall on the liberal or "left" side, and one-third say they are conservative, placing themselves on the political "right." The remaining 40 percent claim to be moderates, in the political "middle" (NORC, 2011:213).

The political spectrum helps us understand the ways people think about the economy. *Economic issues* focus on economic inequality. On economic issues, liberals support extensive government regulation of the economy and a larger welfare state with the goals of meeting everyone's basic needs and reducing income inequality. Economic conservatives want to limit the hand of government in the economy and allow market forces to operate more freely and also to maximize individual liberty.

The political spectrum can also be applied to *social issues,* which are moral questions about how people ought to live. Social issues include abortion, the death penalty, gay rights, and the treatment of minorities. Social liberals support equal rights and opportunities

Lower-income people have more pressing financial needs, and so they tend to focus on economic issues, such as job wages and benefits. Higher-income people, by contrast, provide support for many social issues, such as animal rights.

for all categories of people, view abortion as a matter of individual choice, and oppose the death penalty because it has been unfairly applied to minorities. The "family values" agenda of social conservatives supports traditional gender roles and opposes gay marriage, affirmative action, and other "special programs" for minorities. Social conservatives condemn abortion as morally wrong and support the death penalty as a just response to the most serious crimes.

Of the two major political parties in the United States, the Republican party is more conservative on both economic and social issues, and the Democratic party is more liberal. But both parties favor big government when it advances their particular aims. During the 2012 presidential campaign, for example, Democrats supported government action to rebuild the nation's infrastructure as well as to provide more benefits to middle-income families. Republicans spoke out in favor of bigger government in the form of a stronger military.

Most people mix conservative and liberal attitudes. With wealth to protect, many higher-income people hold conservative views on economic issues. Yet their extensive schooling and secure social standing lead most affluent people to be social liberals. Lower-income people show the opposite pattern, with most being liberal on economic issues but supporting a socially conservative agenda (Ohlemacher, 2008). African Americans, both rich and poor, tend to be liberal (especially on economic issues) and for half a century have voted Democratic (95 percent cast ballots for the Democratic candidate, Barack Obama, in 2008). Historically, Latinos, Asian Americans, and Jews have also supported the Democratic party (Kohut, 2008).

Women tend to be somewhat more liberal than men. Among U.S. adults, more women lean toward the Democrat party, while more men vote for Republican candidates. In the 2010 elections, for example, 48 percent of women but just 41 percent of men

voted Democratic. Figure 12–6 on page 324 shows how political attitudes have changed over time among college students. Although there have been shifts in student attitudes—moving to the right in the 1970s and moving to the left beginning in the mid-1990s—college women have remained consistently more liberal than college men (Astin et al., 2002; Sax et al., 2003; NORC, 2007; Pryor et al., 2011).

Party Identification

Because many people hold mixed political attitudes, with liberal views on some issues and conservative stands on others, party identification in this country is weak. Surveys show that about 49 percent favor the Democratic party and about 39 percent the Republican party, yet just 19 percent claim to be "strong Democrats" and 10 percent to be "strong Republicans." About 16 percent say they are "independent" (NORC, 2011:196). This lack of strong party identification is one reason each of the two major parties gains or loses power from election to election. Democrats held the White House in 1996 and gained ground in Congress in 1996, 1998, and 2000. In 2002 and 2004, the tide turned as Republicans made gains in Congress and kept control of the White House. In 2006, the tide turned again, with Democrats gaining control of Congress and winning the White House in 2008. By the 2010 elections, however, Republicans had regained a majority in the House of Representatives. Winning the "independent vote" is one key to political success in U.S. politics; in 2008, 52 percent of independents supported Barack Obama, while just 44 percent supported John McCain. In the 2010 Congressional elections, Republican gains reflected the fact that independents broke 56 percent to 37 percent for Republican candidates (Federal Election Commission, 2011).

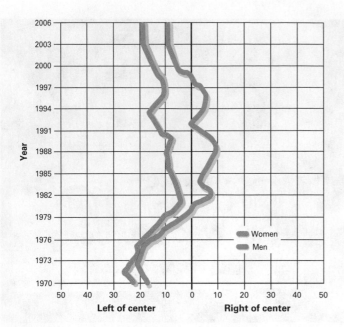

Student Snapshot

FIGURE 12–6 Left-Right Political Identification of College Students, 1970–2006

Student attitudes moved to the right after 1970 and shifted left in the late 1990s. College women tend to be more liberal than college men.

Sources: Astin et al. (2002), Sax et al. (2003), and Pryor et al. (2007).

There is also a rural-urban divide in U.S. politics. People in urban areas typically vote Democratic, and those in rural areas vote Republican. National Map 12–2 shows the county-by-county results for the 2008 presidential election.

Special-Interest Groups

For years, a debate has raged across the United States about the private ownership of firearms. Organizations such as the Brady Campaign to Prevent Gun Violence support stricter gun-control laws; other organizations, including the National Rifle Association, strongly oppose such measures. Each is an example of a *special-interest group*, people organized to address some economic or social issue. Special-interest groups, which include associations of older adults, farmers, fireworks producers, and environmentalists, are strong in nations where political parties tend to be weak. Many special-interest groups employ *lobbyists* to support their goals. Washington, D.C., is home to about 12,220 lobbyists (Center for Responsive Politics, 2011).

Political action committees (PACs) are formed by special-interest groups to raise and spend money in support of political aims. PACs channel most of their funds directly to candidates likely to support their interests. Since they were created in the 1970s, the number of PACs has increased to more than 4,500 (Federal Election Commission, 2011).

Because of the rising costs of campaigns, most candidates eagerly accept support from PACs. In the congressional elections in 2010, a non-presidential election year, 23 percent of all campaign funding came from PACs, and senators who were seeking reelection received, on average, almost $300,000 each in PAC contributions. For members of the House, the average contribution was almost $200,000. In presidential elections, contributions are far greater. In 2008, Barack Obama and John McCain together received and spent more than $1 billion on their presidential campaigns (Pickler & Sidoti, 2008; Center for Responsive Politics, 2008, 2011). Supporters maintain that PACs represent the interests of a vast assortment of businesses, unions, and church groups, thereby increasing political participation. Critics counter that organizations supplying cash to politicians expect to be treated favorably in return, so that in effect PACs try to buy political influence ("Abramoff Effect," 2006; Federal Election Commission, 2009).

Does having the most money matter? The answer is yes: In 95 percent of the 2010 congressional races, the candidate who raised the most money ended up winning the election. Concerns about the power of money led to much discussion of campaign financing. In 2002, Congress passed a modest reform, limiting the amount of unregulated money that candidates can collect. Despite this change, both presidential races since then set new records for campaign spending (Center for Responsive Politics, 2009). And in 2010, the Supreme Court rejected limits on the election contributions of corporations, unions, and other large organizations. Not surprisingly, the money spent in the 2010 elections was five times greater than that spent four years earlier in 2006. Also in 2010, "super PACs" emerged as political action committees that now raise money—without limits—to engage in political activity for or against any candidate for public office (Liptak, 2010; Gorenstrin, 2011).

Voter Apathy

A disturbing fact of U.S. political life is that many people in this country do not vote. In fact, U.S. citizens are less likely to vote today than they were a century ago. In the 2000 presidential election, which was decided by a few hundred votes, only half the registered voters went to the polls. In 2008, participation rose to 63 percent, which was the highest turnout since 1960. But the turnout is still lower than in almost all other high-income countries (Center for the Study of the American Electorate, 2009).

Who is and who is not likely to vote? Research shows that women are slightly more likely than men to cast a ballot. People over sixty-five are much more likely to vote than college-age adults (almost half of whom have not even registered). Non-Hispanic whites are more likely to vote (66 percent voted in 2008) than African Americans (65 percent in 2008, up from 56 percent in 2004) and Hispanics (50 percent). Generally speaking, people with a bigger stake in society—homeowners, parents with young children, people with extensive schooling and good jobs—are more likely to vote. Income matters, too: People earning more

Read "Is Congress Really for Sale?" by Paul Burstein on mysoclab.com

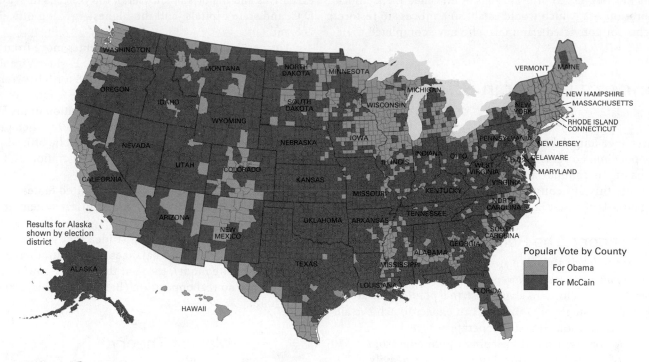

Results for Alaska shown by election district

Popular Vote by County

☐ For Obama
■ For McCain

Seeing Ourselves

NATIONAL MAP 12–2 The Presidential Election, 2008: Popular Vote by County

Barack Obama won the 2008 presidential election with 53 percent of the total popular vote, but he received a majority of the vote in only about one-fourth of the nation's counties. Obama and other Democrats did well in more densely populated urban areas, while John McCain and other Republicans did well in less populated rural areas. Can you explain why urban areas are mostly Democratic and rural areas are mostly Republican? What other social characteristics do you think distinguish the people who vote Democratic from those who vote Republican?

Source: U.S. Department of the Interior (2009).

than $75,000 a year are much more likely to vote (79 percent in 2008) than people earning less than $10,000 (49 percent) (U.S. Census Bureau, 2009).

Of course, we should expect some nonvoting because at any given time, millions of people are sick or disabled; millions more are away from home at college or elsewhere or have moved to a new neighborhood and have forgotten to reregister. In addition, registering and voting depend on the ability to read and write, which discourages the tens of millions of U.S. adults who have limited literacy skills. Finally, people with physical disabilities that limit mobility have a lower turnout than the general population (Schur & Kruse, 2000; Brians & Grofman, 2001).

Conservatives suggest that apathy is really *indifference* to politics on the part of people who are content with their lives. Liberals and especially political radicals on the far left of the political spectrum counter that apathy reflects *alienation* from politics among people who are so deeply dissatisfied with society that they doubt that elections will make any real difference. The fact that the disadvantaged and powerless are least likely to vote and the fact that a candidate such as Barack Obama drew so many new voters into the political process suggest that the liberal explanation for voter apathy is probably closer to the truth.

Should Convicted Criminals Vote?

Although the right to vote is at the very foundation of our country's claim to being democratic, all states except Vermont and Maine have laws that bar people in jail from voting. Thirty states do not allow people to vote if they are on probation after committing a felony; thirty-five states do the same for people on parole. Two states ban voting even after people have completed their sentences, and ten others do so subject to an appeal to restore voting rights. Overall, 5.3 million people (including 1.4 million African American men) in the United States do not have the right to vote (Sentencing Project, 2011).

Should government take away people's political rights as a punishment for criminal acts? The legislatures in most of our fifty states have said yes. But critics point out that this practice may be politically motivated, because preventing convicted criminals from voting makes a difference in the way elections in this country turn out. Convicted felons (who tend to be lower-income people) show better than a two-to-one preference for Democratic over Republican candidates. Even allowing for expected voter apathy, one study concluded that if these laws had not been in force in 2000, Al Gore would have defeated George W. Bush for the presidency (Uggen & Manza, 2002). In 2011, such political considerations led

Democrats in Congress to propose legislation called the Democracy Restoration Act, which would establish a process to restore voting rights for convicted criminals who have completed their sentences.

Theories of Power in Society

 Apply

Sociologists have long debated how power is spread throughout the U.S. population. Power is a very difficult topic to study because decision making is complex and often takes place behind closed doors. Despite this difficulty, researchers have developed three competing models of power in the United States.

Pluralist Theory: The People Rule

Pluralist theory, closely linked to structural-functional theory, is *an analysis of politics that sees power as spread among many competing interest groups.* Pluralists claim, first, that politics is an arena of negotiation. No single organization can expect to achieve all of its goals. Organizations therefore operate as *veto groups,* realizing some goals but mostly keeping opponents from achieving all of theirs. The political process relies heavily on creating alliances and compromises among numerous interest groups so that policies gain wide support. In short, pluralists see power as spread widely throughout society, with all people having at least some voice in the political system (Dahl, 1961, 1982; Rothman & Black, 1998).

Power-Elite Theory: A Few People Rule

Power-elite theory, based on social-conflict theory, is *an analysis of politics that sees power as concentrated among the rich.* The term "power elite" was coined by C. Wright Mills (1956), a social-conflict theorist who argued that the upper class holds most of society's wealth, prestige, and power.

Mills claimed that members of the power elite are in charge of the three major sectors of society: the economy, the government, and the military. The power elite is made up of the "super-rich" (corporate executives and major stockholders); top officials in Washington, D.C. and state capitals; and the highest-ranking officers in the U.S. military.

Further, Mills explained that these elites move from one sector to another, building power as they go. Former Vice President Dick Cheney, for example, moved back and forth between powerful positions in the corporate world and the federal government. General Colin Powell moved from a top position in the U.S. military to become secretary of state. More broadly, when presidents fill cabinet posts, most of these powerful public officials are millionaires. This was true in the Bush administration as it is in the Obama administration.

Power-elite theorists say that the United States is not a democracy because our economic and political systems give a few people so much power that the average person's voice cannot be heard. They reject the pluralist idea that various centers of power serve as checks and balances on one another; according to the power-elite model, those at the top are powerful enough that they face no real opposition (Bartlett & Steele, 2000; Moore et al., 2002).

Marxist Theory: The System Is Biased

A third approach to understanding U.S. politics is the **Marxist political-economy theory**, *an analysis that explains politics in terms of the operation of a society's economic system.* Like the power-elite model, the Marxist approach rejects the idea that the United States is a political democracy. But the power-elite model focuses on the enormous wealth and power of certain individuals; the Marxist model goes further and sees bias rooted in the nation's institutions, especially its economy. Karl Marx believed that a society's economic system (capitalist or socialist) shapes its political system. Therefore, power elites do not simply appear out of nowhere; they are creations of the capitalist economy. From this point of view, reforming the political system—by, say, limiting the amount of money that rich people can contribute to political candidates—is unlikely to bring about true democracy. The problem does not lie in the people who exercise great power or the people who don't vote; the problem is the system itself—what Marxists call the "political economy of capitalism." In other words, as long as the United States has a predominantly capitalist economy, the majority of people will be shut out of politics, just as they are exploited in the workplace.

● **Evaluate** The Applying Theory table summarizes the three models of the U.S. political system. Which model is most accurate? Over the years,

One of the most significant political forces to develop in recent years is the Tea Party movement. Supporters claim that government has grown too big, too expensive, and now threatens the freedom of ordinary people. Do you see government as a "problem" the way many people on the right side of the political spectrum do? Or do you see it as the "solution" the way many people on the left side of the political spectrum do? Why?

Politics

	Pluralist Theory	Power-Elite Theory	Marxist Political-Economy Theory
Which theoretical approach is applied?	Structural-functional approach	Social-conflict approach	Social-conflict approach
How is power spread throughout society?	Power is spread widely so that all groups have some voice.	Power is concentrated in the hands of top business, political, and military leaders.	Power is directed by the operation of the capitalist economy.
Is the United States a democracy?	Yes. Power is spread widely enough to make the country a democracy.	No. Power is too concentrated for the country to be a democracy.	No. The capitalist economy favors the few, so the country cannot be a democracy.

research has shown support for each one. In the end, of course, how you think our political system ought to work is as much a matter of political values as scientific fact.

Classic research by Nelson Polsby (1959) supports the pluralist model. Polsby studied the politics of New Haven, Connecticut, where he found that key decisions involving urban renewal, choosing political candidates, and running the city's schools were made by different groups. Polsby concluded that in New Haven, no one group—not even the upper class—ruled all the others.

Robert Lynd and Helen Lynd (1937) studied Muncie, Indiana (which they called "Middletown," to suggest that it was a typical city), and documented the fortune amassed by a single family, the Balls, from its business producing glass canning jars. Their findings support the power-elite position. The Lynds showed how the Ball family dominated the city's life, pointing to that family's name on a local bank, university, hospital, and department store. In Muncie, according to the Lynds, the power elite boiled down to more or less a single family.

From the Marxist perspective, the point is not to look at which individuals make decisions. Rather, as Alexander Liazos (1982:13) explains, "The basic tenets of capitalist society shape everyone's life: the inequalities of social classes and the importance of profits over people." As long as the basic institutions of society are organized to meet the needs of the few rather than the many—in today's language, the 1 percent rather than the 99 percent—Liazos claims a democratic society is impossible.

Clearly, the political system in the United States gives almost everyone the right to participate in politics through elections. But as the power-elite and Marxist models point out, at the very least, the U.S. political system is far less democratic than most people think. Most citizens have the right to vote, but the major political parties and their candidates typically support only the positions that are acceptable to the most powerful segments of society and in tune with the operation of our capitalist economy.

Whatever the reasons, many people in the United States appear to be losing confidence in their leaders. Only about 60 percent of U.S. adults report having "some" or "a great deal" of confidence that members of Congress and other government officials will do what is best for the country (NORC, 2011:334–36).

CHECK YOUR LEARNING What is the main argument of the pluralist model of power? What about the power-elite model? The Marxist political-economy model?

Power beyond the Rules

 Understand

Politics is always a matter of disagreement over a society's goals and the means to achieve them. A political system tries to settle controversy within a system of rules. But political activity sometimes breaks the rules or even tries to do away with the entire system.

Revolution

Political revolution is *the overthrow of one political system in order to establish another.* Revolution goes beyond *reform,* or change within a system, and even beyond a *coup d'état* (in French, literally, "blow to the state"), as when one leader topples another. Revolution involves change in the type of system itself.

No political system is immune to revolution, nor does revolution produce any one type of government. Our own Revolutionary War (1775–76) replaced colonial rule by the British monarchy with a representative democracy. French revolutionaries in 1789 also overthrew a monarch, only to set the stage for the return of monarchy in the person of Napoleon. In 1917, the Russian Revolution replaced a monarchy with a socialist government built on the ideas of Karl Marx. In 1991, a second Russian revolution dismantled the socialist Soviet Union, and the nation was reborn as fifteen independent republics, the largest of which—known as the Russian Federation—has moved closer to a market system with a somewhat greater political voice for its people.

Despite their striking variety, revolutions share a number of traits (Tocqueville, 1955, orig. 1856; Skocpol, 1979; Tilly, 1986):

1. **Rising expectations.** Common sense suggests that revolution is more likely when people are severely deprived, but history shows that most revolutions occur when people's lives are improving. Rising expectations, rather than bitterness and despair, make

The year 2011 brought sweeping change to many countries in northern Africa and the Middle East. In Libya, a popular protest movement seeking the overthrow of longtime ruler Moammar Gadhafi turned into a civil war. Support for change also comes from high-income nations where large ethnic populations now reside. In London (*at right*), for example, hundreds of people with roots in Libya demonstrated in support of political change.

revolution more likely. Driving the recent uprisings across the Middle East are young people who may be living better than their families did generations ago but not as well as they see people living in other parts of the world.

2. **Unresponsive government.** Revolution becomes more likely when a government is unwilling to reform itself, especially when demands for change being made by powerful segments of society are ignored. In Egypt, for example, the government led by Hosni Mubarak had done little to benefit many people or to reform its own corruption over many decades.

3. **Radical leadership by intellectuals.** The English philosopher Thomas Hobbes (1588–1679) claimed that intellectuals provide the justification for revolution, and universities are often at the center of political change. Students played a key role in China's prodemocracy movement and the uprisings in Eastern Europe in the 1990s and the recent uprisings across the Middle East.

4. **Establishing a new legitimacy.** Overthrowing a political system is not easy, but ensuring a revolution's long-term success is harder still. Some revolutionary movements are held together merely by hatred of the past regime and fall apart once new leaders are installed. This fact is one reason that it is difficult to predict the long-term outcome of recent political changes in the Middle East. Revolutionaries must also guard against counterrevolutionary drives led by overthrown leaders. This explains the speed and ruthlessness with which victorious revolutionaries typically dispose of former leaders.

Scientific analysis cannot declare that a revolution is good or bad. That judgment depends on the personal values of the citizenry, and the full consequences of such an upheaval become evident only after many years.

Terrorism

The terrorist attacks on the United States on September 11, 2001, involving four commercial airliners, killed nearly 3,000 innocent people (from sixty-eight nations), injured many thousands more, destroyed the twin towers of the World Trade Center in New York City, and seriously damaged the Pentagon in Washington, D.C. Not since the attack on Pearl Harbor at the outbreak of World War II had the United States suffered such a blow. This event was the most serious terrorist act ever recorded.

Terrorism refers to *acts of violence or the threat of violence used as a political strategy by an individual or a group*. Like revolution, terrorism is a political act beyond the rules of established political systems. According to Paul Johnson (1981), terrorism has four distinguishing characteristics.

First, terrorists try to paint violence as a legitimate political tactic, despite the fact that such acts are condemned by virtually every nation. Terrorists also bypass (or are excluded from) established channels of political negotiation. Therefore, terrorism is a weak organization's strategy against a stronger enemy. In recent decades, terrorism has become commonplace in international politics. In 2010, there were 11,500 acts of terrorism worldwide, which claimed almost 13,000 lives (including the deaths of 15 U.S. citizens) and injured more than 50,000 people. The country with the largest number of attacks was Iraq, but major terrorist attacks took place in many nations, including Afghanistan, Pakistan, Somalia, India, and Russia (National Center for Counterterrorism, 2011).

Second, terrorism is used not just by groups but also by governments against their own people. *State terrorism* is the use of violence, generally without support of law, by government officials. State terrorism is lawful in some authoritarian and totalitarian states, which survive by creating widespread fear and intimidation. Saddam Hussein, for example, relied on secret police and state terror to protect his power in Iraq.

Third, democratic societies reject terrorism in principle, but they are especially vulnerable to terrorists because they give broad civil liberties to their people and have less extensive police networks. In contrast, totalitarian regimes make widespread use of state terrorism, but their vast police power gives individuals few opportunities for acts of terror against the government.

Fourth and finally, terrorism is always a matter of definition. Governments claim the right to maintain order, even by force, and may label opposition groups who use violence as "terrorists." Political differences may explain why one person's "terrorist" is another's "freedom fighter" (Jenkins, 2003).

Although hostage taking and outright killing provoke popular anger, taking action against terrorists is difficult. Most terrorist groups have no formal connection to any established state, so identifying the parties responsible may be all but impossible. In addition, a military response may risk confrontation with other governments—recall the heightened tensions with Pakistan in 2011 after U.S. soldiers entered the country in a mission to kill Osama bin Laden. Yet as the terrorism expert Brian Jenkins warns, a failure to respond "encourages other terrorist groups, who begin to realize that this can be a pretty cheap way to wage war" (quoted in Whitaker, 1985:29).

War and Peace

 Analyze

Perhaps the most critical political issue is **war**, *organized, armed conflict among the people of two or more nations, directed by their governments.* War is as old as humanity, but understanding it is crucial today because we now have weapons that can destroy the entire planet.

At almost any moment during the twentieth century, nations somewhere in the world were engaged in violent conflict. In its short history, the United States has participated in eleven major wars. From the Revolutionary War to our current engagement in Iraq and Afghanistan more than 1.3 million U.S. men and women have been killed in armed conflicts, as shown in Figure 12–7, and many times that number have been injured. Thousands more have died in undeclared wars and limited military actions around the world.

The Causes of War

Wars occur so often that we might think that there is something natural about armed conflict. But there is no evidence that human beings must wage war under any particular circumstances. On the contrary, governments around the world usually have to force their people to go to war.

Like other forms of social behavior, warfare is a product of society that is more common in some places than in others. The Semai of Malaysia, among the most peace-loving of the world's peoples,

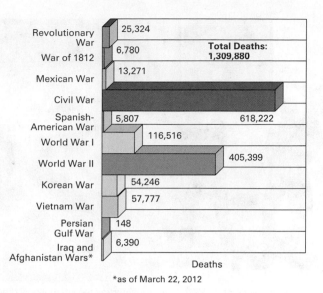

FIGURE 12–7 Deaths of Americans in Eleven U.S. Wars

Almost half of all U.S. deaths in war occurred during the Civil War (1861–65).

Sources: Compiled from various sources by Maris A. Vinovskis (1989) and the author.

rarely resort to violence. In contrast, the Yąnomamö (see the box on page 38) are quick to wage war.

If society holds the key to war or peace, under what circumstances do humans go to war? Quincy Wright (1987) cites five factors that promote war:

1. **Perceived threats.** Nations mobilize in response to a perceived threat to their people, territory, or culture. Leaders justified the U.S.-led military campaign to disarm Iraq, for example, by stressing the threat that Saddam Hussein posed to neighboring countries and also to the United States.

2. **Social problems.** When internal problems cause widespread frustration at home, a nation's leaders may try to divert public attention by attacking an external "enemy" as a form of scapegoating. Although U.S. leaders defended the 2003 invasion of Iraq as a matter of national security, the start of the war effectively shifted the nation's attention away from the struggling national economy and boosted the popularity of President George W. Bush.

3. **Political objectives.** Poor nations, such as Vietnam, have used wars to end foreign domination. Powerful countries such as the United States may benefit from periodic shows of force to increase global political standing.

4. **Moral objectives.** Nations rarely claim that they are going to war to gain wealth and power. Instead, their leaders infuse military campaigns with moral urgency. By calling the 2003 invasion of Iraq "Operation Iraqi Freedom," U.S. leaders portrayed the mission as a morally justified war of liberation from an evil tyrant.

5. **The absence of alternatives.** A fifth factor promoting war is the lack of alternatives. Although the goal of the United Nations is to maintain international peace by finding alternatives to war, the organization has had limited success in preventing conflict between nations.

---

terrorism acts of violence or the threat of violence used as a political strategy by an individual or a group

war organized, armed conflict among the people of two or more nations, directed by their governments

Television shows such as *NCIS: Los Angeles* portray the international drama of terrorism and counter terrorism. How accurately do you think the mass media portray these issues? Why?

the warring parties—which generally involve control of territory—are clearly stated.

Terrorism breaks from these patterns. The identity of terrorist organizations may not be known, those involved may deny their responsibility, and their goals may be unclear. The 2001 terrorist attacks against the United States were not attempts to defeat the nation militarily or to secure territory. They were carried out by people representing not a country but a cause, one not well understood in the United States. In short, they were expressions of anger and hate intended to create widespread fear.

Conventional warfare is symmetrical, with two nations sending armies into battle. By contrast, terrorism is a new kind of war: an asymmetrical conflict in which a small number of attackers—or sometimes a lone individual—use terror and a willingness to die as a means to level the playing field against a much more powerful enemy. Although the terrorists may be ruthless, the nation under attack must use caution in its response to terrorism because little may be known about the identity and location of the parties responsible.

Social Class, Gender, and the Military

In World War II, three out of every four men in the United States in their late teens and twenties served in the military, either voluntarily or by being *drafted*—called to service. Only those who were ruled ineligible due to some physical or mental problem were freed from the obligation to service. Today, by contrast, there is no draft, and fighting is done by a volunteer military. But not every member of our society is equally likely to volunteer.

One recent study concluded that the military has few young people who are rich and few who are very poor. Rather, working-class people look to the military for a job, to become eligible for money to go to college, or simply to get out of the small town where they grew up. In addition, the largest number of volunteers comes from the South, where regional culture is more supportive of the military and where most military bases are located. As one analysis put it, "America's military seems to resemble the makeup of a two-year commuter or trade school outside Birmingham or Biloxi far more than that of a ghetto or barrio or four-year university in Boston" (Halbfinger & Holmes, 2003:1). The Controversy and Debate box asks whether this nation's volunteer army amounts to having a warrior caste.

Throughout our nation's history, women have been a part of the U.S. military. In recent decades, however, women have taken on greater importance in the armed forces. For one thing, the share of women is on the rise, now standing at 14 percent of all military personnel. Just as important, although regulations continue to keep many military women out of harm's way, more women are now engaging in combat. Battle experience is significant because it is widely regarded as necessary for soldiers to reach the highest levels of leadership (Military Diversity Commission, 2011).

Is Terrorism a New Kind of War?

People speak of terrorism as a new kind of war. War has historically followed certain patterns: It is played out according to basic rules, the warring parties are known to each other, and the objectives of

The Costs and Causes of Militarism

The cost of armed conflict extends far beyond battlefield casualties. Together, the world's nations spend more than $1.6 trillion annually for military-related purposes. Spending this much diverts resources from the desperate struggle for survival by hundreds of millions of poor people.

Defense is the U.S. government's second biggest expenditure (after Social Security), accounting for about 20 percent of all federal spending, which amounted to more than $768 billion in the 2012 budget. The United States has emerged as the world's single military superpower, accounting for about 43 percent of the world's military spending. Put another way, the United States spends six times as much on its military than the nation (China) in second place, and nearly as much as the rest of the world's nations combined (Stockholm International Peace Research Institute, 2011; U.S. Office of Management and Budget, 2011).

For decades, military spending went up because of the *arms race* between the United States and the former Soviet Union, which dropped out of the race after its collapse in 1991. But some analysts (who support power-elite theory) link high military spending to the domination of U.S. society by a **military-industrial complex**, *the close association of the federal government, the military, and defense industries.* The roots of militarism, then, lie not just in external threats but also in institutional structures here at home (Marullo, 1987; Barnes, 2002b).

A final reason for continuing militarism is regional conflict. In the 1990s, localized wars broke out in Bosnia, Chechnya, and Zambia, and long-standing conflict continues between Israel and the Palestinians. Even limited wars have the potential to grow and involve other countries, including the United States. India and Pakistan—both nuclear powers—moved to the brink of war in 2002 and then pulled back. In 2003, the announcement by North Korea that it, too, had nuclear weapons raised tensions in Asia.

In 2008, having completed three combat tours in Iraq, Marine Sergeant Alex Lemons returned to the United States. But his arrival did not feel like a homecoming. "I felt as alien here as I felt in Iraq," Lemons explained, sitting in his house in Utah. After getting back, Lemons explained, he saw no signs that this country was engaged in a war. Most people didn't want to think about the War in Iraq. And perhaps that's the problem—the vast majority of our society no longer is directly involved in the military.

It was not always that way. During World War II, about 9 percent of the U.S. population served in the military. Almost everyone else was involved in the war effort by working in defense plants, participating in the rationing of vital materials, and buying bonds to finance the war effort. Today, by contrast, just 0.5 percent of our nation's population is in the military, and most families have no one who has worn a military uniform. Since the September 2001 attacks, just 1 percent of the population over the age of eighteen has served in the military. That leaves 99 percent of us with no direct involvement in military service.

There are many reasons that military service now involves a small slice of the U.S. population. The most important factor is that, in 1973 as the Vietnam War was winding down, the draft was ended, giving rise to today's all volunteer military. A second factor is gender, because 86 percent of today's military personnel are males. Third, the military is overwhelmingly from certain parts of the country—with the South heavily represented. In fact, half of all active-duty military personnel are stationed in just five states: Virginia, North Carolina, Georgia, Texas, and California. Beyond this list, additional factors also come into play: Most people would be ineligible to enlist even if they wanted to due to having criminal records or being overweight.

When all things are considered, today's military personnel are men from rural areas and small towns in more traditional regions of the country, where military values such as honor, discipline, and patriotism are more pronounced. These people are not poor, but generally they are from working class families. Typically, they see in military service a way to gain economic security and work experience.

The burden of military service falls on an ever-thinner slice of U.S. society. This fact is also evident in the country's leadership. After the Vietnam War, almost 80 percent of members of Congress were veterans; today, that share has fallen to 22 percent. As for people who work in the mass media, including newspapers, television, and films, virtually no one has military experience. With that fact in mind, it is easy to understand the frustration of one military wife, who lives in Washington State and has a husband fighting in Afghanistan. The Taliban, she recounts, blew up "a bus last week and killed 17 people, and I didn't know anything about it because it wasn't on the news. It makes me think nobody cares. They're putting on things like Kardashians getting divorced—it's on the news constantly—but we have soldiers over there dying, and you just don't hear about it."

What Do You Think?

1. Should the responsibility of military service be shouldered by just 1 percent of the adult population?

2. Would you support restoring the draft as a means of spreading this responsibility throughout the class structure?

3. Do veterans deserve more than they now receive from our society? Explain.

Source: Thompson (2011).

Iran continues to pursue nuclear technology, raising fears that this nation may soon have an atomic bomb.

Nuclear Weapons

Despite the easing of superpower tensions, the world still contains more than 5,000 operational nuclear warheads, representing a destructive power of several tons of TNT for every person on the planet. If even a small fraction of this stockpile is used in war, life as we know it would end. Albert Einstein, whose genius contributed to the development of nuclear weapons, reflected, "The unleashed power of the atom has changed everything save our modes of thinking and we thus drift toward unparalleled catastrophe." In short, nuclear weapons make unrestrained war unthinkable in a world not yet capable of peace.

The United States, the Russian Federation, Great Britain, France, the People's Republic of China, Israel, India, Pakistan, and probably North Korea all have nuclear weapons. A few nations stopped the development of nuclear weapons—Argentina and Brazil halted work in 1990, and South Africa dismantled its arsenal in 1991. But by 2015, there could be ten new nations in the "nuclear club," and as many as fifty countries by 2025 (Grier, 2006). Such a trend makes any regional conflict very dangerous to the entire planet.

Mass Media and War

The Iraq War was the first war in which television crews traveled with U.S. troops, reporting as the campaign unfolded. The mass media provided ongoing and detailed reports of events; cable television made available live coverage of the war twenty-four hours a day, seven days a week.

Media outlets "frame" the news according to their own politics. Those media outlets that were critical of the war—especially the

Arab news channel Al-Jazeera—tended to report the slow pace of the conflict, the casualties to the U.S. and allied forces, and the deaths and injuries suffered by Iraqi civilians, all of which was information that would increase pressure to end the war. Media outlets that were supportive of the war—including most news organizations in the United States—tended to report the rapid pace of the war and the casualties to Iraqi forces and to downplay any harm to Iraqi civilians as minimal and unintended. In short, the power of the mass media to provide selective information to a worldwide audience means that television and other media are almost as important to the outcome of a conflict as the military forces who are doing the actual fighting.

Pursuing Peace

How can the world reduce the dangers of war? Here are the most recent approaches to peace:

1. **Deterrence.** The logic of the arms race holds that security comes from a "balance of terror" between the superpowers. The principle of *mutual assured destruction* (MAD) means that a nation launching a first strike against another will face greater retaliation. This deterrence policy kept the peace for almost fifty years during the Cold War. Yet it encouraged an enormous arms race and cannot control nuclear proliferation, which represents a growing threat to peace. Deterrence also does little to stop terrorism or to prevent wars that are started by a stronger nation (such as the United States) against a weaker foe (such as the Taliban government in Afghanistan or Saddam Hussein's Iraq).

2. **High-technology defense.** If technology created the weapons, perhaps it can also protect us from them; such is the claim of the *strategic defense initiative* (SDI). Under SDI, satellites and ground installations would destroy enemy missiles soon after they were launched. In a survey shortly after the 2001 terrorist attacks, two-thirds of U.S. adults supported SDI (Thompson & Waller, 2001; "Female Opinion," 2002). However, critics claim that the system, which they refer to as "Star Wars," would be, at best, a leaky umbrella. Others worry that building such a

system will spark another massive arms race. In recent years, the Obama administration has turned away from further development of SDI in favor of more focused defense against short-range missiles that might be launched from Iran.

3. **Diplomacy and disarmament.** Some analysts believe that the best road to peace is diplomacy rather than technology (Dedrick & Yinger, 1990). Teams of diplomats working together can increase security by reducing, rather than building, weapons stockpiles.

    But disarmament has limitations. No nation wants to be weakened by eliminating its defenses. Successful diplomacy depends on everyone involved sharing responsibility for a common problem (Fisher & Ury, 1988). Although the United States and the Russian Federation continue to negotiate arms reduction agreements, the world now faces threats from other nations such as North Korea and Iran.

4. **Resolving underlying conflict.** In the end, reducing the dangers of war may depend on resolving underlying conflicts by promoting a more just world. Poverty, hunger, and illiteracy are all root causes of war. Perhaps the world needs to reconsider the wisdom of spending thousands of times as much money on militarism as we do on efforts to find peaceful solutions (Sivard, 1988; Kaplan & Schaffer, 2001).

Politics: Looking Ahead

 Evaluate

Just as economies are changing, so are political systems. Several problems and trends are likely to be important in the decades to come.

One troublesome problem in the United States is the inconsistency between our democratic ideals and our low turnout at the polls. Perhaps, as conservative pluralist theorists say, many people do not bother to vote because they are content with their lives. On the other hand, the liberal power-elite theorists may be right when they say that people withdraw from a system that concentrates so much wealth and power in the hands of a few people. Or perhaps, as radical Marxist critics claim, people find that our political system offers little real choice, limiting options and policies to those that support our capitalist economy. In any case, the current high level of apathy and distrust in our nation's government, as well as the increasing activism of the "Occupy" movement, reflect a widespread desire for political change.

A second issue is the global rethinking of political models. The Cold War between the United States and the Soviet Union encouraged people to think of politics in terms of two opposing models, capitalism and socialism. Today, however, people are more likely to consider a broader range of political systems that link government to the economy in various ways. Welfare capitalism, as found in Sweden and Denmark, or state capitalism, as found in South Korea and Japan, are just two possibilities. The Thinking Globally box takes a look at the

One reason to pursue peace is the rising toll of death and mutilation caused by millions of land mines placed in the ground during wartime and left there afterward. Civilians—many of them children—maimed by land mines receive treatment in this Kabul, Afghanistan, clinic.

Uprisings across the Middle East:
An End to the Islamic "Democracy Gap"?

The wave of popular political protest that swept across the Middle East in 2011 is the largest global political movement in the two decades since change swept through the former Soviet Union and the nations of Eastern Europe. What's going on? Why are so many nations in this part of the world erupting with political opposition?

Is there a "democracy gap" in the Middle East? Is there a lack of democracy in Islamic nations? Making any assessment of global democracy is more difficult than it may appear. For one thing, in a world marked by striking cultural diversity, can we assume that democracy and related ideas about political freedoms are the same everywhere? The answer cannot be a simple "yes," because with their various political histories, concepts such as "democracy" and "freedom" mean different things in different cultural settings.

What have researchers found? Freedom House is an organization that monitors political freedom around the world by tracking people's right to vote, to express ideas, and to move about without undue interference from government in nations around the world. Freedom House classifies nations in one of three categories: "not free," partly fee," and "free."

Freedom House reports that many of the nations that are classified as "not free" have populations that are largely Islamic. Around the world, 47 of the 195 nations had an Islamic majority population in 2011. Just 11 (23 percent) of these countries had democratic governments, and Freedom House rated only two (4.3 percent)—Indonesia and Mali—as "free." Of the remainder, 19 (40 percent) were considered to be "partly free" and 26 (55 percent) were classified as "not free." Of the 148 nations without a majority Islamic population, 106 (72 percent) had democratic governments, and 84 (57 percent) were rated as "free." When you put these facts together, countries without Islamic majorities were three times more likely to have democratic governments than countries with Islamic majorities. Freedom House concludes that countries with Islamic majority populations display a "democracy gap."

This relative lack of democracy was found in all world regions that have Islamic-majority nations—in Africa, central Europe, the Middle East, and Asia. The pattern is especially strong among the sixteen Islamic-majority states in the Middle East and North Africa that are ethnically Arabic: As of early 2012, only Tunisia was an electoral democracy.

What explains this "democracy gap"? Freedom House points to four factors. First, Islamic-majority countries are typically less developed economically with limited schooling for their people and widespread poverty. Second, these countries have cultural traditions that rigidly control the lives of women, limiting their economic, educational, and political opportunities. Third, although most countries limit the power of religious elites in government, and some (including the United States) even recognize a "separation of church and state," Islamic-majority nations support a political role for Islamic leaders. In just two recent cases—Iran and Afghanistan under the Taliban—Islamic leaders have had formal control

of government; more commonly, religious leaders do not hold office but exert considerable influence on political outcomes.

Fourth and finally, the enormous wealth that comes from Middle Eastern oil plays a part in preventing democratic government. In Iraq, Saudi Arabia, Kuwait, Qatar, the United Arab Emirates, and other nations, this resource has provided astounding riches to a small number of families, money they can use to shore up their political control. In addition, oil wealth permits elites to build airports and other modern facilities without encouraging broader economic development that raises the living standards of the majority.

For all these reasons, Freedom House concludes that the road to democracy for Islamic-majority nations is likely to be long. But today's patterns may not predict those of tomorrow. In 1950, very few Catholic-majority countries (mostly in Europe and Latin America) had democratic governments. Today, however, most of these nations are democratic. Keep in mind that 42 percent of the world's Muslims live in Nigeria, Turkey, Bangladesh, India, Indonesia, and the United States, where they already live under democratic governments. But perhaps the best indicator that change is now under way is the widespread demands for a political voice now rising from people throughout the Middle East.

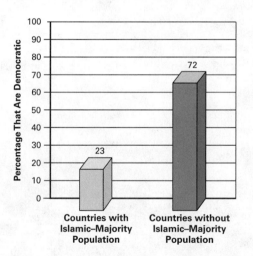

Democracy and Islam
Today, democratic government is much less common in countries with Islamic-majority populations.

What Do You Think?

1. Should the United States try to bring about a democratic political system in other nations of the world? Why or why not?

2. Do you expect to see greater democracy in Islamic-majority countries fifty years from now? Why or why not?

3. Can you point out any reasons that Muslims might object to the kind of political system we call "democracy"? Explain.

Sources: Karatnycky (2002), Pew Forum on Religious and Public Life (2011), and Freedom House (2012).

debate over the chances for the emergence of democratic governments in the world's Islamic countries.

Third, we still face the danger of war in many parts of the world. Even as the United States and the Russian Federation dismantle some warheads, vast stockpiles of nuclear weapons remain, and nuclear technology continues to spread around the world. In addition, new superpowers are likely to arise (the People's Republic of China and India are well on their way), just as regional conflicts and terrorism are likely to continue. We can only hope (and vote!) for leaders who will work toward finding nonviolent solutions to the age-old problems that provoke war, thereby putting us on the road to world peace.

What are the challenges of today's economy?

This chapter explains that the economy is the social institution that organizes the production, distribution, and consumption of goods and services. It's no secret that we are living in tough economic times. Unemployment has been high, earning a living wage is harder than it used to be, and public confidence in a secure future has taken a hit. As C. Wright Mills might have said, the problems we face as individuals are issues that are deeply rooted in the economy. Look at the three photos and ask yourself: What changes in today's economy create challenges for today's labor force?

Hint Industrial production has been moving from the United States to countries where wages are lower. In China, for example, industrial workers earn roughly 10 percent of what a worker is paid in this country. China's economy is still less than half as large as that of the United States, despite having a labor force five times larger. But since 2000, China's industrial production has increased, on average, 15 percent a year. U.S. industrial production has actually declined during five years of this new century and, since 2000, has averaged less than a 1 percent annual increase. Economic activity is also expanding in India, a country that has seen striking growth in service jobs, such as those shown in the photo below of a call-center in the city of Bangalore. Back home in the United States, even highly skilled people such as college professors are facing challenges in today's economy. Computer technology is being used to allow professors to teach larger classes and also to allow a single faculty member to teach students in multiple classrooms in various places at the same time. In short, even when a corporation or organization becomes more productive, it does not always end up employing more people, which helps us to understand why some analysts have been talking about a "jobless recovery."

Have you ever called a toll-free support line and wondered where the person on the other end of the line was located? It is not only manufacturing jobs that have moved overseas. Lower wages have led corporations to relocate many service jobs—including many skilled office jobs—to places such as India, where service employment is skyrocketing. In short, is anyone safe from the trend we call "outsourcing"?

Walk around a big-box store and examine products to see where they are made. It will not take long to see a pattern: What is it? As the share of manufactured goods made abroad rises, what happens to manufacturing jobs here in the United States?

Advancing technology makes our economy more productive, right? Generally, yes. But adopting new technology can make organizations more productive with fewer employees. Have you ever taken a "distance learning" class in which the professor was not in the classroom with you? How can computer technology enable colleges to teach more students using fewer faculty?

Seeing Sociology in *Your* Everyday Life

1. Visit a discount store such as Walmart or Kmart and do a little "fieldwork" in an area of the store that interests you. Pick ten products, and see where each is made. Do the results support the existence of a global economy?

2. Analysis of recent election results, including how gender, race, income, religion, and other variables shaped people's choices, can be found at http://www.cnn.com/ELECTION. Visit this site and develop a profile of the typical Democratic voter and the typical Republican voter. Which variables best predict differences in voting preference?

3. Based on what you have read in this chapter, make three predictions about the nature of work and jobs twenty years from now. That is, what trends have you noted that seem likely to continue? To read more about how information in this chapter can assist you in your own career, go to the "Seeing Sociology in *Your* Everyday Life" feature on MySocLab, where you will find some facts of interest. A second "Seeing Sociology in *Your* Everyday Life" feature helps you think about what a more democratic United States would look like and how you can advance the cause of democracy.

The Economy: Historical Overview

The **economy** is the major social institution through which a society produces, distributes, and consumes goods and services.

- In technologically simple societies, economic activity is simply part of family life.
- The **agricultural revolution** (5,000 years ago) made the economy a distinct social institution based on agricultural technology, specialized work, permanent settlements, and trade.
- The **Industrial Revolution** (beginning around 1750) expanded the economy based on new sources of energy and specialized work in factories that turned raw materials into finished products.
- The **postindustrial economy** is based on a shift from industrial work to service work and computer technology. **pp. 302–4**

Sectors of the Economy

The **primary sector**
- draws raw materials from the natural environment
- is of greatest importance (25% of the economy) in low-income nations **p. 304**

The **secondary sector**
- transforms raw materials into manufactured goods
- is a significant share (24%–36%) of the economy in low-, middle-, and high-income nations **p. 304**

The **tertiary sector**
- produces services rather than goods
- is the largest sector (50%–75%) in low-, middle-, and high-income countries **p. 304**

social institution (p. 302) a major sphere of social life, or societal subsystem, organized to meet human needs

economy (p. 302) the social institution that organizes a society's production, distribution, and consumption of goods and services

postindustrial economy (p. 303) a productive system based on service work and computer technology

primary sector (p. 304) the part of the economy that draws raw materials from the natural environment

secondary sector (p. 304) the part of the economy that transforms raw materials into manufactured goods

tertiary sector (p. 304) the part of the economy that involves services rather than goods

global economy (p. 304) economic activity that crosses national borders

Economic Systems: Paths to Justice

Capitalism is based on private ownership of property and the pursuit of profit in a competitive marketplace. Capitalism results in

- greater productivity ⟷ less productivity
- higher overall standard of living ⟷ lower overall standard of living
- greater income inequality ⟷ less income inequality
- freedom to act according to self-interest ⟷ freedom from basic want **pp. 306–8**

Socialism is grounded in collective ownership of productive property through government control of the economy. Socialism results in

capitalism (p. 306) an economic system in which natural resources and the means of producing goods and services are privately owned

socialism (p. 306) an economic system in which natural resources and the means of producing goods and services are collectively owned

welfare capitalism (p. 307) an economic and political system that combines a mostly market-based economy with extensive social welfare programs

state capitalism (p. 307) an economic and political system in which companies are privately owned but cooperate closely with the government

Work in the Postindustrial U.S. Economy

Jobs
- Agricultural work represents only 1.7% of jobs.
- Blue-collar work has declined to less than 20% of jobs.
- White-collar work represents about 80% of jobs. **pp. 309–10**

Self-Employment
- 6.7% of U.S. workers are self-employed.
- Many professionals fall into this category, but most self-employed people have blue-collar jobs. **p. 312**

Unemployment
- Unemployment has many causes, including the operation of the economy itself.
- At the end of 2011, 8.9% of the country's labor force was unemployed.
- At highest risk for unemployment are young people and African Americans. **pp. 312–13**

👁 Watch the Video on mysoclab.com

✳ Explore the Map on mysoclab.com

labor unions (p. 310) organizations of workers that seek to improve wages and working conditions through various strategies, including negotiations and strikes

profession (p. 310) a prestigious white-collar occupation that requires extensive formal education

Corporations

Corporations form the core of the U.S. economy.

- The largest corporations, which are conglomerates, account for most corporate assets and profits. **pp. 315–16**
- Many large corporations operate as multinationals, producing and distributing products in nations around the world. **pp. 316–17**

corporation (p. 315) an organization with a legal existence, including rights and liabilities, separate from that of its members

conglomerate (p. 315) a giant corporation composed of many smaller corporations

monopoly (p. 315) the domination of a market by a single producer

oligopoly (p. 315) the domination of a market by a few producers

Politics: Historical Overview

Politics is the major social institution by which a society distributes power and organizes decision making. Max Weber claimed that raw power is transformed into *legitimate authority* in three ways:

- Preindustrial societies rely on tradition to transform power into authority. **Traditional authority** is closely linked to kinship.
- As societies industrialize, tradition gives way to rationality. **Rational-legal authority** underlies the operation of bureaucratic offices as well as the law.
- At any time, however, some individuals transform power into authority through charisma. **Charismatic authority** is linked to extraordinary personal qualities (as found in Jesus of Nazareth, Adolf Hitler, and Mahatma Gandhi). **pp. 318–19**

politics (p. 318) the social institution that distributes power, sets a society's goals, and makes decisions

power (p. 318) the ability to achieve desired ends despite resistance from others

government (p. 318) a formal organization that directs the political life of a society

authority (p. 318) power that people perceive as legitimate rather than coercive

traditional authority (p. 318) power legitimized by respect for long-established cultural patterns

rational-legal authority (p. 318) power legitimized by legally enacted rules and regulations

charismatic authority (p. 318) power legitimized by extraordinary personal abilities that inspire devotion and obedience

routinization of charisma (p. 319) the transformation of charismatic authority into some combination of traditional and bureaucratic authority

Politics in Global Perspective

- **Monarchy** is common in agrarian societies; leadership is based on kinship.
- **Democracy** is common in modern societies; leadership is linked to elective office. **pp. 319–20**
- **Authoritarianism** is any political system that denies the people participation in government. **p. 321**
- **Totalitarianism** concentrates all political power in one centralized leadership. **p. 321**

monarchy (p. 319) a political system in which a single family rules from generation to generation

democracy (p. 319) a political system that gives power to the people as a whole

authoritarianism (p. 321) a political system that denies the people participation in government

totalitarianism (p. 321) a highly centralized political system that extensively regulates people's lives

Politics in the United States

- The U.S. government has expanded over the past two centuries, although the *welfare state* in the United States is smaller than in most other high-income nations. **p. 322**
- The *political spectrum*, from the liberal left to the conservative right, involves attitudes on both economic issues and social issues. **pp. 322–23**
- *Special-interest groups* advance the political aims of specific segments of the population. **pp. 324–25**
- *Voter apathy* runs high in the United States: Only 63% of eligible voters went to the polls in the 2008 presidential election. **pp. 324–25**

📖 **Read the Document on mysoclab.com**

welfare state (p. 322) a system of government agencies and programs that provides benefits to the population

Theories of Power in Society

- **Pluralist theory** claims that political power is spread widely in the United States. **pp. 326–27**
- **Power-elite theory** claims that power is concentrated in a small, wealthy segment of the population. **pp. 326–27**
- **Marxist political-economy theory** claims that our political agenda is determined by a capitalist economy, so true democracy is impossible. **pp. 326–27**

pluralist theory (p. 326) an analysis of politics that sees power as spread among many competing interest groups

power-elite theory (p. 326) an analysis of politics that sees power as concentrated among the rich

Marxist political-economy theory (p. 326) an analysis that explains politics in terms of the operation of a society's economic system

War and Peace

- The development and spread of nuclear weapons have increased the threat of global catastrophe. **p. 331**
- World peace ultimately depends on resolving the tensions and conflicts that fuel militarism.

Power beyond the Rules

- **Revolution** radically transforms a political system.
- **Terrorism** employs violence in the pursuit of political goals and is used by a group against a much more powerful enemy. **pp. 327–29**

political revolution (p. 327) the overthrow of one political system in order to establish another

terrorism (p. 328) acts of violence or the threat of violence used as a political strategy by an individual or a group

war (p. 329) organized, armed conflict among the people of two or more nations, directed by their governments

military-industrial complex (p. 330) the close association of the federal government, the military, and defense industries

13 Family and Religion

Learning Objectives

Remember the definitions of the key terms highlighted in boldfaced type throughout this chapter.

Understand the differences in various types of families and religious organizations.

Apply sociology's major theoretical approaches to families and religions.

Analyze how and why family life and religious affiliations are changing.

Evaluate the strengths and weaknesses of traditional families and other family forms.

Create a vision of the choices and challenges that you face in your own family life.

This chapter explores the meaning and importance of two major social institutions. First, the chapter identifies various forms of family life, explores the operations of families, and tracks changes in families over time. Then the chapter explains how religious belief differs from other types of knowledge, identifies types of religious organizations, and analyzes historical change in the importance of religion. ■

Rosa Yniguez is one of seven children who grew up in Jalisco, Mexico, in a world in which families worked hard, went to church regularly, and were proud of having many children. Rosa remembers friends of her parents who had a clock in their living room with a picture of each of their twelve children where the numbers on the clock face would be.

Now thirty-five years old, Rosa is living in San Francisco, attends a local Catholic church, and works as a cashier in a department store. In some respects, she has carried on her parents' traditions—but not in every way. Recalling her childhood, she says, "In Mexico, many of the families I knew had six, eight, ten children. Sometimes more. But I came to this country to get ahead. That is simply impossible with too many kids." As a result of her desire to keep her job and make a better life for her family, Rosa has decided to have no more than the three children she has now.

A tradition of having large families has helped make Hispanics the largest racial or ethnic minority in the United States. The birth rate for immigrant women remains higher than for native born women. But today, more and more Latinas are making the same decision as Rosa Yniguez and opting to have fewer children (Navarro, 2004; U.S. Census Bureau, 2011).

Families have been with us for a very long time. But as this story indicates, U.S. families are changing in response to a number of factors, including the desire of women to have more career options and to provide better lives for their children. It is probably true that the family is changing faster than any other social institution (Bianchi & Spain, 1996).

Religion is changing too as membership in long-established denominations is declining and new religious organizations are flourishing. This chapter examines family and religion, which are closely linked as society's *symbolic institutions*. Both the family and religion guide social life by setting standards of morality, maintaining traditions, and joining people together. With a focus on the United States, and making comparisons to other countries, we will examine why many people consider family and religion the foundations of society while others predict—and may even encourage—the decline of both institutions.

Family: Basic Concepts

 **Understand**

The **family** is *a social institution found in all societies that unites people in cooperative groups to care for one another, including any*

children. Family ties also reflect **kinship**, *a social bond based on common ancestry, marriage, or adoption.* All societies contain families, but exactly who people call their kin has varied through history and varies today from one culture to another. Here and in other countries, families form around **marriage**, *a legal relationship, usually involving economic cooperation, sexual activity, and childbearing.*

Today, some people object to defining only married couples or parents and children as families because it endorses a narrow standard of how to live. Because some business and government programs still use this conventional definition, many unmarried but committed partners of the same or opposite sex are excluded from family health care and other benefits. However, our society is gradually coming to recognize as families people with or without legal or blood ties who feel they belong together and define themselves as a family.

Because the U.S. Census Bureau uses the conventional definition of family,[1] sociologists who use Census Bureau data describing "families" must accept it. But the national trend is toward a broader definition.

---

[1] According to the Census Bureau, there were 118.7 million U.S. households in 2011. Of these, 78.6 million (66 percent) meet the bureau's definition of "family." The remaining living units contained single people or unrelated people living together. In 1950, 90 percent of all households were families.

family a social institution found in all societies that unites people in cooperative groups to care for one another, including any children

extended family a family composed of parents and children as well as other kin; also known as a *consanguine family*

nuclear family a family composed of one or two parents and their children; also known as a *conjugal family*

Families: Global Variations

 Analyze

How closely do people have to be related to consider themselves a "family"? In preindustrial societies, people commonly recognize the **extended family**, *a family composed of parents and children as well as other kin.* This group is sometimes called the *consanguine family* because it includes everyone with "shared blood." With industrialization, however, increasing social mobility and geographic migration give rise to the **nuclear family**, *a family composed of one or two parents and their children.* The nuclear family is also called the *conjugal family*, meaning "based on marriage." Although many people in our society think of kinship in terms of extended families, most people carry out their everyday routines within a nuclear family.

Marriage Patterns

Cultural norms—and often laws—identify people as suitable or unsuitable marriage partners. Some marital norms promote **endogamy**, *marriage between people of the same social category.* Endogamy limits marriage prospects to others of the same age, village, race, ethnicity, religion, or social class. By contrast, **exogamy** is *marriage*

What does the modern family look like? If we look to the mass media, this is a difficult question to answer. In the television series *Modern Family*, Jay Pritchett's family includes his much younger wife, his stepson Manny, his daughter Claire (who is married with three children), and his son Mitchell (who, with his gay partner, has an adopted Vietnamese daughter). How would you define *family*?

between people of different social categories. In rural India, for example, a person is expected to marry someone from the same caste (endogamy) but from a different village (exogamy). The reason for endogamy is that people of similar position pass along their standing to their children, clearly maintaining the traditional social hierarchy. Exogamy, on the other hand, links distant communities, builds alliances, and encourages the spread of culture.

In higher-income nations, laws permit only **monogamy** (from the Greek, meaning "one union"), *marriage that unites two partners.* Global Map 13–1 on page 342 shows that monogamy is the rule throughout the Americas and Europe. But many lower-income countries, especially in Africa and southern Asia, permit **polygamy** (Greek, "many unions"), *marriage that unites a person with two or more spouses.* Polygamy has two forms. By far the more common is *polygyny* (Greek, "many women"), a form of marriage that unites one man and two or more women. For example, Islamic nations in the Middle East and Africa permit men up to four wives. Even so, most Islamic families are monogamous because few men can afford to support several wives and even more children. *Polyandry* (Greek, "many men") unites one woman and two or more men. This extremely rare pattern exists in Tibet, a mountainous land where agriculture is difficult. There, polyandry discourages the division of land into parcels too small to support a family and divides the hard work of farming among many men.

Most of the world's societies at some time have permitted more than one marital pattern. Even so, most marriages have been monogamous (Murdock, 1965, orig. 1949). The historical preference for monogamy reflects two facts of life: Supporting several spouses is very expensive, and the number of men and women in most societies is roughly equal.

Residential Patterns

Just as societies regulate mate selection, they also designate where a couple should live. In preindustrial societies, most newlyweds live with one set of parents who offer protection and assistance. Most often married couples live with or near the husband's family, an arrangement called *patrilocality* (Greek, "place of

marriage a legal relationship, usually involving economic cooperation, sexual activity, and childbearing

endogamy marriage between people of the same social category

exogamy marriage between people of different social categories

monogamy marriage that unites two partners

polygamy marriage that unites a person with two or more spouses

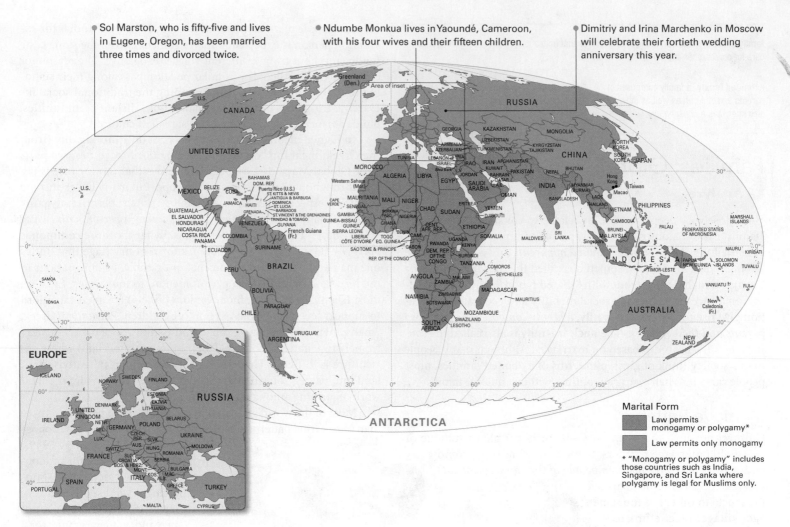

Sol Marston, who is fifty-five and lives in Eugene, Oregon, has been married three times and divorced twice.

Ndumbe Monkua lives in Yaoundé, Cameroon, with his four wives and their fifteen children.

Dimitriy and Irina Marchenko in Moscow will celebrate their fortieth wedding anniversary this year.

Marital Form

Law permits monogamy or polygamy*

Law permits only monogamy

* "Monogamy or polygamy" includes those countries such as India, Singapore, and Sri Lanka where polygamy is legal for Muslims only.

Window on the World

GLOBAL MAP 13–1 Marital Form in Global Perspective

Monogamy is the only legal form of marriage throughout the Western Hemisphere and in much of the rest of the world. In most African nations and in southern Asia, however, polygamy is permitted by law. In many cases, this practice reflects the influence of Islam, a religion that allows a man to have up to four wives. Even so, most marriages in these countries are monogamous, primarily for financial reasons.

Source: *Peters Atlas of the World* (1990), with updates by the author.

the father"). But some societies, including the North American Iroquois, favor *matrilocality* ("place of the mother"), in which couples live with or near the wife's family.

Industrial societies show yet another pattern. Finances permitting, they favor *neolocality* (Greek, "new place"), in which a married couple lives apart from both sets of parents.

Patterns of Descent

Descent refers to *the system by which members of a society trace kinship over generations.* Most preindustrial societies trace kinship through either the father's side or the mother's side of the family. *Patrilineal descent,* the more common pattern, traces kinship through males, so that fathers pass property on to their sons. Patrilineal descent characterizes most pastoral and agrarian societies, in which men produce the most valued resources. *Matrilineal descent,*

by which people define only the mother's side as kin and property passes from mothers to daughters, is found in horticultural societies where women are the main food producers.

Industrial societies with greater gender equality recognize *bilateral descent* ("two-sided descent"), a system tracing kinship through both men and women. In this pattern, children include people on both the father's side and the mother's side among their relatives.

Patterns of Authority

Worldwide, the family patterns discussed so far—polygyny, patrilocality, and patrilineal descent—are dominant and reflect the common global pattern of patriarchy. In industrial societies such as the United States, men are still typically heads of households, and most U.S. parents give children their father's last name. However, more egalitarian families are evolving, especially as the share of women in the labor force goes up.

Theories of the Family

 Apply

As in earlier chapters, applying sociology's three major theoretical approaches offers a range of insights about families. The Applying Theory table summarizes what we can learn from each approach.

Functions of the Family: Structural-Functional Theory

According to the structural-functional approach, the family performs many vital tasks. For this reason, the family is sometimes called the "backbone of society."

1. **Socialization.** As noted in Chapter 3 ("Socialization: From Infancy to Old Age"), the family is the first and most important setting for child rearing. Ideally, parents help children develop into well-integrated and contributing members of society. Of course, family socialization continues throughout the life cycle. Adults change within marriage, and as any parent knows, mothers and fathers learn as much from their children as their children learn from them.

2. **Regulation of sexual activity.** Every culture regulates sexual activity in the interest of maintaining kinship organization and property rights. As discussed in Chapter 6 ("Sexuality and Society"), the **incest taboo** is *a norm forbidding sexual relations or marriage between certain relatives*. Although the incest taboo exists in every society, exactly which relatives cannot marry varies from one culture to another. The matrilineal Navajo, for example, forbid marrying any relative of one's mother. Our bilateral society applies the incest taboo to both sides of the family but limits

Often, we experience modern society as cold and impersonal. In this context, the family can be a haven in a heartless world. Not every family lives up to this promise, of course, but people in families tend to be happier and live longer than those who live alone.

it to close relatives, including siblings, parents, aunts and uncles, and grandparents. Half the states allow first cousin marriages (sometimes with age restrictions), and half the states forbid such marriages.

Why does some form of incest taboo exist in every society? Part of the reason is rooted in biology: Reproduction between close relatives of any species raises the odds of producing offspring with mental or physical damage. But why, of all living species, do only humans observe an incest taboo? The answer is that controlling reproduction among close relatives is necessary for social organization. For one thing, the incest taboo limits sexual competition in families by restricting sex to spouses. Second, because family ties define people's rights and obligations toward one another, reproduction between close relatives would

APPLYING THEORY

Family

	Structural-Functional Theory	Social-Conflict and Feminist Theories	Symbolic-Interaction and Social-Exchange Theories
What is the level of analysis?	Macro-level	Macro-level	Micro-level
What is the importance of the family for society?	The family performs vital tasks, including socializing the young and providing emotional and financial support for members. The family helps regulate sexual activity.	The family perpetuates social inequality by handing down wealth from one generation to the next. The family supports patriarchy as well as racial and ethnic inequality.	Symbolic-interaction theory explains that the reality of family life is constructed by members in their interaction. Social-exchange theory shows that courtship typically brings together people who offer the same level of advantages.

Read "How History and Sociology Can Help Today's Families" by Stephanie Coontz on **mysoclab.com**

hopelessly confuse kinship ties and threaten social order. Third, by requiring people to marry outside their immediate families, the incest taboo serves to tie together the larger society as people look beyond close kin when seeking to form new families.

3. **Social placement.** Families are not needed for people to reproduce, but families do help maintain social organization. Parents pass on their own social identity—in terms of race, ethnicity, religion, and social class—to their children at birth.

4. **Material and emotional security.** Many people view the family as a "haven in a heartless world," offering physical protection, emotional support, and financial assistance. Perhaps this is why people living in families tend to be happier, healthier, and wealthier than people living alone (Goldstein & Kenney, 2001; U.S. Census Bureau, 2009; Fustos, 2011).

● **Evaluate** Structural-functional theory explains why society, at least as we know it, is built on families. But this approach glosses over the diversity of U.S. family life and ignores how other social institutions (such as government) could meet at least some of the same human needs. Finally, structural-functionalism overlooks the negative aspects of family life, including patriarchy and family violence.

CHECK YOUR LEARNING What four important functions does the family provide for the operation of society?

Inequality and the Family: Social-Conflict and Feminist Theories

Like the structural-functional approach, the social-conflict approach, including feminist theory, considers the family central to our way of life. But instead of focusing on ways that kinship benefits society, this approach points out how the family perpetuates social inequality.

1. **Property and inheritance.** Friedrich Engels (1902, orig. 1884) traced the origin of the family to men's need (especially in the higher classes) to identify heirs so that they could hand down property to their sons. Families thus concentrate wealth and reproduce the class structure in each new generation.

According to social-exchange theory, people form relationships based on what each offers to the other. Generally, partners see the exchange as fair or "about even." What do you think is the exchange involved in this marriage?

2. **Patriarchy.** Feminists link the family to patriarchy. To know who their heirs are, men must control the sexuality of women. Families therefore transform women into the sexual and economic property of men. A century ago in the United States, most wives' earnings belonged to their husbands. Today, women still bear most of the responsibility for child rearing and housework (England, 2001; U.S. Bureau of Labor Statistics, 2011).

3. **Race and ethnicity.** Racial and ethnic categories persist over generations only to the degree that people marry others like themselves. Endogamous marriage supports racial and ethnic inequality.

● **Evaluate** Social-conflict and feminist theories show another side of family life: its role in social stratification. Friedrich Engels criticized the family as part and parcel of capitalism. But noncapitalist societies also have families (and family problems). The family may be linked to class inequality, as Engels argued, and to gender inequality, as feminist theory claims. But it carries out societal functions not easily accomplished by other means.

CHECK YOUR LEARNING Point to three ways in which the family supports social inequality.

Constructing Family Life: Micro-Level Theories

Both the structural-functional and social-conflict approaches view the family as a structural system. By contrast, micro-level analysis explores how individuals shape and experience family life.

Symbolic-Interaction Theory

Ideally, family living offers an opportunity for *intimacy,* a word with Latin roots that mean "sharing fear." As family members share many activities and establish trust, they build emotional bonds. Of course, the fact that parents act as authority figures often limits their closeness with younger children. Only as young people approach adulthood do kinship ties open up to include sharing confidences with greater intimacy (Macionis, 1978).

Social-Exchange Theory

Social-exchange theory, another micro-level approach, describes courtship and marriage as forms of negotiation (Blau, 1964). Dating allows each person to assess the advantages and disadvantages of a potential spouse. In

Early to Wed: A Report from Rural India

Sumitra Jogi cries as her wedding is about to begin. Are they tears of joy? Not exactly. The "bride" is an eighteen-month-old squirming in the arms of her mother. The groom? A boy of seven.

In a remote village in India's western state of Rajasthan, the two families gather at midnight to celebrate a traditional wedding ritual. It is May 2, in Hindu tradition an especially good day to marry. Sumitra's father smiles as the ceremony begins; her mother cradles the infant, who has fallen asleep. The groom, wearing a special costume and a red and gold turban on his head, gently reaches up and grasps the baby's hand. Then, as the ceremony ends, the young boy leads the child and mother around the wedding fire three-and-one-half times while the audience beams at the couple's first steps together as husband and wife.

Child weddings are illegal in India, but traditions are strong in rural regions, and laws against child marriage are hard to enforce. As a result, thousands of children marry each year. "In rural Rajasthan," explains one social welfare worker, "all the girls are married by age fourteen. These

are poor, illiterate families, and they don't want to keep girls past their first menstrual cycle."

For now, Sumitra Jogi will remain with her parents. But in eight or ten years, a second ceremony will send her to live with her husband's family, and her married life will begin.

The eighteen-month-old girl on the left is breast-feeding during her wedding ceremony in a small village in the state of Rajasthan, India; her new husband is seven years old. Although outlawed, such arranged marriages involving children are still known to take place in traditional, remote areas of India.

If the reality of marriage is years in the future, why do families push their children to marry at such an early age? Parents of girls know that the younger the bride, the smaller the dowry they must offer to the groom's family. Also, when girls marry this young, there is no question about their virginity, which raises their value on the marriage market. No one in these situations thinks about love or the fact that the children are too young to understand what is taking place.

What Do You Think?

1. Why are arranged marriages common in very traditional communities?

2. List several advantages and disadvantages of arranged marriages from the point of view of the individuals involved.

3. Can you point to ways in which mate selection in the United States is "arranged" by society?

Sources: J. W. Anderson (1995) and Roudi-Fahimi (2010).

---

essence, exchange theory suggests, people "shop around" to make the best "deal" they can.

In patriarchal societies, gender roles dictate the elements of exchange: Men bring wealth and power to the marriage marketplace, and women bring beauty. The importance of beauty in this traditional system explains women's longstanding concern with their appearance and sensitivity about revealing their age. But as women have joined the labor force, they have become less dependent on men to support them, and so the terms of exchange for women and men are becoming more similar.

 Evaluate Micro-level theory balances structural-functional and social-conflict visions of the family as an institutional system. Both the symbolic-interaction and social-exchange approaches focus on the individual experience of family life. However, micro-level theories miss the bigger picture: The experience of family life is similar for people in the same social and economic categories.

CHECK YOUR LEARNING How does a micro-level approach to understanding the family differ from a macro-level approach?

Stages of Family Life

Understand

Members of our society recognize several distinct stages of family life across the life course.

Courtship and Romantic Love

November 2, Kandy, Sri Lanka. Winding through the rain forest of this beautiful island, our van driver, Harry, recounts how he met his wife. Actually, it was more of an arrangement agreed to by their parents: The two families were Buddhist and of the same caste. "We got along well, right from the start," recalls Harry. "We had the same background. I suppose either she or I could have said no. But 'love marriages' happen in the city, not in the village where I grew up."

In rural Sri Lanka, as in rural areas of low- and middle-income countries throughout the world, most people consider courtship too important to be left to the young. *Arranged marriages* are alliances between two extended families of similar social standing and usually involve an exchange not just of children but also of wealth and favors. Romantic love has little to do with marriage, and parents may make such arrangements when their children are very young. A century ago in Sri Lanka and India, half of all girls married before age fifteen. Today, perhaps one-in-nine young women in low income nations is married before the age of fifteen; about one-in-three is married before the age of eighteen (Mayo, 1927; Mace & Mace, 1960; Population Reference Bureau, 2011). The Thinking Globally box takes a closer look at child marriage.

Industrialization both erodes the importance of extended families and weakens traditions. As young people begin the process of choosing their own mate, dating sharpens courtship skills and allows sexual experimentation. Marriage is delayed until young people complete their education, build financial security that will allow them to live apart from their parents, and gain the life experience needed to select a suitable partner.

Our culture celebrates *romantic love*—affection and sexual passion toward another person—as the basis for marriage. We find it hard to imagine marriage without love, and popular culture, from fairy tales such as "Cinderella" to today's television sitcoms and dramas, portrays love as the key to a successful marriage.

Our society's emphasis on romance motivates young people to "leave the nest" to form families of their own; physical passion may also help a new couple through difficult adjustments in learning to live together (W. J. Goode, 1959). On the other hand, because feelings change over time, romantic love is a less stable foundation for marriage than social and economic considerations, one reason that the divorce rate is much higher in the United States than in nations where cultural traditions are a stronger guide in the choice of a partner.

But even in our country, sociologists point out, society aims Cupid's arrow more than we like to think. Most people fall in love with others of the same race who are close in age and of similar social class. Our society "arranges" marriages by encouraging **homogamy** (literally, "like marrying like"), *marriage between people with the same social characteristics.*

The extent of homogamy is greater for some categories of our population (such as older people and immigrants from traditional societies) than for others (younger people and those who live with less concern for cultural traditions).

Settling In: Ideal and Real Marriage

Our culture gives young people an idealized, "happily ever after" picture of marriage. Such optimism can lead to disappointment, especially for women, who have long been taught to view marriage as the key to personal happiness. Also, romantic love involves a lot of fantasy: We fall in love with others not always as they are but as we want them to be.

Sexuality, too, can be a source of disappointment. In the romantic haze of falling in love, people may see marriage as an endless sexual honeymoon, only to face the sobering realization that sex eventually becomes a less-than-all-consuming passion. Although the frequency of marital sex does decline over time, about two in three married people report that they are satisfied with the sexual dimension of their relationship. In general, couples with the best sexual relationships experience the most satisfaction in their marriages. Sex may not be the one key to marital happiness, but more often than not, good sex and good relationships go together (Laumann et al., 1994; T. W. Smith, 2006).

Infidelity—sexual activity by spouses outside marriage—is another area where the reality of marriage does not match our cultural ideal. In a recent survey, 90 percent of U.S. adults said a married person having sex outside of marriage is "always wrong" or "almost always wrong." Even so, about 25 percent of married men and 10 percent of married women indicated (in a private, written questionnaire) that they had been sexually unfaithful to their partners at least once (Lauman et al., 1994; NORC, 2011: 401–11).

Child Rearing

Despite the demands children make on us, U.S. adults overwhelmingly identify raising children as one of life's great joys (NORC, 2011:2317; Wang & Taylor, 2011). Today, about half of U.S. adults say that two children is the ideal number, and few people want more than three (NORC, 2011:405). This is a change from two centuries ago, when *eight* children was the U.S. average.

Big families pay off in preindustrial societies because children supply needed labor. People therefore regard having children as a wife's duty, and in the absence of effective birth control, childbearing is a regular event. Of course, a high death rate in preindustrial societies prevents many children from reaching adulthood; as late as 1900, one-third of children in the United States died by age ten.

Economically speaking, industrialization transforms children from an asset to a liability. It now costs low-income parents almost $200,000 to raise one child, including college tuition; middle-class parents commonly spend about $300,000, and high-income families spend $500,000 and more (Lino, 2011). No wonder the U.S. average steadily dropped during the twentieth century to one child per family![2]

The trend toward smaller families is most pronounced in high-income nations. The picture differs in low-income regions in Latin America, Asia, and especially Africa, where many women have few alternatives to bearing children. In many African nations, as a glance back at Global Map 1–1 on page 4 shows, four or five children is still the norm.

Parenting is a very expensive, lifelong commitment. As our society has given people greater choices about family life, more U.S. adults have decided to delay childbirth or to remain childless. In 1960, 90 percent of women between the ages of twenty-five and twenty-nine who had ever married had at least one child; today, this proportion has declined to 69.5 percent (U.S. Census Bureau, 2011).

About half of parents in the United States claim they would like to devote more of their time to child rearing (Cohn, 2007). But unless we accept a lower standard of living, the need for income demands that most parents

"Son, you're all grown up now. You owe me two hundred and fourteen thousand dollars."

___
[2]According to the U.S. Census Bureau, the mean number of related children per family was 0.93 in 2010. Among all families, the medians were 0.78 for non-Hispanic whites, 1.16 for African Americans, and 1.49 for Hispanics.

pursue careers outside the home, even if that means giving less time to their families. For many families, including Rosa Yniguez's family described in the opening to this chapter, having fewer children is an important step toward resolving the tension between work and parenting (Gilbert, 2005).

Children of working parents spend most of the day at school. But after school, about 4.6 million youngsters (12 percent of five- to fourteen-year-olds) are *latchkey kids* who must fend for themselves (U.S. Census Bureau, 2011). Traditionalists in the "family values" debate charge that many mothers work at the expense of their children, who receive less parenting. Progressives reply that such criticism unfairly blames women for wanting the same opportunities men have long enjoyed.

Congress took a small step toward easing the conflict between family and job responsibilities by passing the Family and Medical Leave Act in 1993. This law allows up to ninety days' unpaid leave from work for either parent to care for a new child or deal with a serious family emergency. Still, most adults in this country have to juggle parental and job responsibilities. When parents work, who cares for the kids? Half of children under age five receive care from a parent (22 percent) or a relative (34 percent). The remaining children include 23 percent who attend day care or preschool, 8 percent who are cared for in a nonrelative's home, 4 percent who are cared for in their own home by a nanny or babysitter, and 9 percent who have no regular arrangement (U.S. Census Bureau, 2011).

The Family in Later Life

Increasing life expectancy in the United States means that couples who stay married do so for a longer time. By age sixty, most have completed the task of raising children. At this point, marriage brings a return to living with only a spouse.

Like the birth of children, their departure—creating an "empty nest"—requires adjustments, although a marriage often becomes closer and more satisfying. Years of living together may lessen a couple's sexual passion, but understanding and commitment often increase.

Personal contact with children usually continues because most older adults live near at least one of their grown children. One-third of all U.S. adults (about 60 million) are grandparents, many of whom help with child care and other responsibilities. Among African Americans (who have a high rate of single parenting), grandmothers have an especially important position in family life. Among all older people, helping out grandchildren and adult children—as well as doing favors for friends and neighbors—is a significant part of daily life (U.S. Census Bureau, 2006; AARP Foundation, 2007; Bianchi, 2011).

The experience of family life changes as we move through the life course. One important responsibility for many people as they move through middle age is caring for aging parents. In what ways does the process of aging change the relationship between parents and their sons and daughters?

The other side of the coin is that adults in midlife now provide more care for aging parents. The "empty nest" may not be filled by a parent coming to live in the home, but many adults find that caring for parents living to eighty, ninety, and beyond can be as taxing as raising young children. The oldest of the baby boomers—now reaching sixty-five—are called the "sandwich generation" because many of them, especially women, will spend as many years caring for their aging parents as they did caring for their children (Lund, 1993).

The final and surely the most difficult transition in married life comes with the death of a spouse. Wives typically outlive husbands because of their greater life expectancy and the fact that women usually marry men several years older than themselves. Wives can thus expect to spend some years as widows. The challenge of living alone after the death of a spouse is especially great for men, who usually have fewer friends than widows and may lack housekeeping skills.

U.S. Families: Class, Race, and Gender

● Understand

Dimensions of inequality—social class, ethnicity, race, and gender—are powerful forces that shape marriage and family life. This discussion addresses each of these factors in turn, but bear in mind that they overlap in our lives.

Social Class

Social class determines both a family's financial security and its range of opportunities. Interviewing working-class women, Lillian Rubin (1976) found that wives thought a good husband was a man who held a steady job, did not drink too much, and was not violent. Rubin's middle-class respondents, by contrast, never mentioned such things; these women simply *assumed* that a husband would provide a safe and secure home. Their ideal husband was someone they could talk to easily, sharing feelings and experiences.

Clearly, what women (and men) hope for in marriage—and what they end up with—is linked to their social class. Much

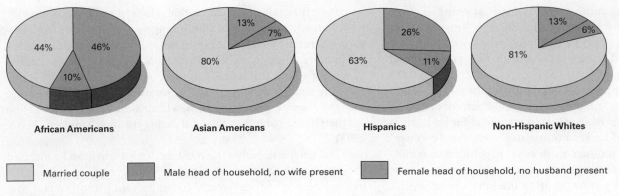

Diversity Snapshot

FIGURE 13–1 Family Form in the United States, 2011

All racial and ethnic categories show variations in family form.

Source: U.S. Census Bureau (2011).

the same holds for children: Boys and girls lucky enough to be born into more affluent families enjoy better mental and physical health, develop more self-confidence, and go on to greater achievement than children born to poor parents (McLeod & Shanahan, 1993; Duncan et al., 1998).

Ethnicity and Race

As Chapter 11 ("Race and Ethnicity") discusses, ethnicity and race are powerful forces that shape family life. Keep in mind, however, that American Indian, Latino, and African American families (like all families) do not fit any single generalization or stereotype (Allen, 1995).

American Indian Families

American Indians display a wide variety of family types. Some patterns emerge, however, among people who migrate from tribal reservations to cities. Women and men who arrive in cities often seek out others—especially kin and members of the same tribe—for help in getting settled. One study tells the story of two women migrants to the San Francisco area who met at a meeting of an Indian organization and realized they were of the same tribe. The women and their children decided to share an apartment, and soon after, the children began to refer to one another as brothers, sisters, and cousins. As the months passed, the two mothers came to think of themselves as sisters (Lobo, 2002).

Migration also creates "fluid households" with changing membership. In another case from this same study, a woman, her aunt, and their children rented a large apartment in San Francisco. Over the course of several months, they welcomed into their home more than thirty other urban migrants, each of whom stayed for a short time while looking for housing of their own. Such patterns of mutual assistance, involving real or fictional kinship, are common among low-income people.

American Indians who leave tribal reservations for the cities are typically better off than those who stay behind. Because people

in reservations have a hard time finding work, they cannot easily form stable marriages, and problems such as alcoholism and drug abuse shatter the ties between parent and child.

Latino Families

Many Latinos enjoy the loyalty and support of extended families. Traditionally, Hispanic parents exercise greater control over children's courtship, considering marriage an alliance of families and not just a union based on romantic love. Some Hispanic families also follow conventional gender roles, prizing *machismo*—strength, daring, and sexual conquest—among men and treating women with respect but also close supervision.

However, assimilation into the larger society is changing these traditional patterns. As the story opening this chapter explained, many women who come to California from Mexico favor smaller families. Similarly, many Puerto Ricans who migrate to New York do not maintain the strong extended families they knew in Puerto Rico. In recent decades, the traditional authority of men over women has also lessened, especially among wealthy Latino families, whose number has more than quadrupled in the past twenty-five years (Navarro, 2004; Raley, Durden, & Wildsmith, 2004; U.S. Census Bureau, 2011).

Overall, however, the typical Hispanic family had an income of just $39,538 in 2010, or 66 percent of the national average (U.S. Census Bureau, 2011). Many Hispanic families suffer the stress of unemployment and other poverty-related problems.

African American Families

The U.S. Census Bureau reports that the typical African American family earned $38,500 in 2010, which was 64 percent of the national average. People of African ancestry are three times as likely as non-Hispanic whites to be poor, and poverty means that parents and children are likely to experience unemployment, substandard housing, and poor health.

Under these circumstances, maintaining stable family ties is difficult. Consider that 32 percent of African American women in their

Dating and Marriage: The Declining Importance of Race

In 1961, a young anthropology student from Kansas named Ann Dunham married a foreign student from Kenya named Barack Obama. This marriage was quite unusual at that time for the simple reason that Dunham was white and Obama was black.

Fifty years ago, barely two of every one hundred marriages involved partners of different racial categories. There were strong cultural forces opposing such unions. Survey data from the 1960s show that 42 percent of adults living in the northern United States said they wanted the law to ban marriage between people of different racial classifications. In the South, almost three-fourths of adults held the same opinion. And, in fact, until 1967 when the Supreme Court declared such laws to be unconstitutional, sixteen states did outlaw interracial marriage.

In 2008, Dunham and Obama's son, Barack Obama Jr., was elected president of the United States. Today, interracial romantic relationships have become much more common. Surveys show that almost all young people between the ages of eighteen and twenty-nine claim that they accept interracial dating and even interracial marriage. Among people who are older, however, a more traditional norm of racial homogamy is still in play: When researchers ask people between the ages of fifty and sixty-four, just 55 percent respond that they would not mind if someone in their family married a person of another racial category. Among those over the age of sixty-five, only 38 percent say the same. Other surveys conducted by Internet dating sites, such as Match.com, confirm that young people express much greater willingness to date a person of another race than older people do.

Even among people who say they accept interracial marriage, most actual marriages still join people of one racial category. Considering both race and ethnicity, 85 percent of U.S. marriages join socially similar partners. Asians are the most likely to "marry out," and about one-third do.

Hispanics are next, with about one-fourth marrying non-Hispanics. About one in six African Americans marries a non–African American. Finally, about one in eleven non-Hispanic whites marries someone of another category.

Even in the "Age of Obama," race and ethnicity continue to guide the selection of a marriage partner, but not as much as they once did. And, in terms of marriage, racial homogamy is certainly no longer the law.

Join the Blog!

What are your views on interracial dating and marriage? What are your personal experiences? What patterns do you see on your campus? Go to MySocLab and join the Sociology in Focus blog to share your opinions and experiences and to see what others think.

Sources: Based on Kent (2010), Taylor (2010), and U.S. Census Bureau (2011).

Watch the video "Economics of the African American Family" on **mysoclab.com**

forties have never married, compared with about 12 percent of non-Hispanic white women of the same age. This means that African American women—often with children—are more likely to be single heads of households. Figure 13–1 shows that women headed 46 percent of African American families in 2011, compared with 26 percent of Hispanic families, 13 percent of non-Hispanic white families, and 13 percent of Asian or Pacific Islander families (U.S. Census Bureau, 2011).

Regardless of race, single-mother families are always at high risk of poverty. Twenty-four percent of U.S. families headed by non-Hispanic white women are poor. The higher poverty rate among families headed by African American women (39 percent) and Hispanic women (42 percent) is strong evidence of how the intersection of class, race, and gender can put women at a disadvantage. African American families with both wife and husband in the home, which represent 44 percent of the total, are much stronger economically, earning

79 percent as much as comparable non-Hispanic white families. But 73 percent of African American children are born to single women, and 39 percent of African American boys and girls are growing up poor today, meaning that these families carry much of the burden of child poverty in the United States (Martin et al., 2011; U.S. Census Bureau, 2011).

Ethnically and Racially Mixed Marriages

Most spouses have similar social backgrounds with regard to class and race. But over the course of the twentieth century, ethnicity came to matter less and less. A woman of German or French ancestry might readily marry a man of Irish or English background without inviting disapproval from their families or from society in general.

Race has been a more powerful barrier in mate selection. Before a 1967 Supreme Court decision (*Loving* v. *Virginia*), interracial marriage was actually illegal in sixteen states. Today, African, Asian, and Native Americans make up 19 percent of the U.S. population; if people ignored race in choosing spouses, we would expect about the same share of marriages to be mixed. The actual

---

For most of our nation's history, interracial marriage was illegal. The last of these laws was struck down forty years ago. Although race and ethnicity continue to guide the process of courtship and marriage, interracial relationships are becoming more and more common.

proportion of racially mixed marriages is 4 percent, showing that race still matters in social relations. Even so, most people claim that race and ethnicity should not matter in choosing a partner. In addition, the age at first marriage has been rising to an average of 28.7 for men and 26.5 for women. Young people who marry a little later in life are more likely to make choices about partners with less input from parents.

One consequence of this increasing freedom of choice is that the share of ethnically and racially mixed marriages is increasing (Rosenfeld & Kim, 2005; Kent, 2011; U.S. Census Bureau, 2011). The most common type of interracial married couple is a white husband and an Asian wife, which accounts for about 21 percent of all interracial married couples. When ethnicity is considered, the most common type of "mixed" couple includes one partner who is Hispanic and one who is not. In nearly half of all "mixed" marriages, one partner claims a multiracial or multiethnic identity. Interracial married couples are most likely to live in the West; in five states—Hawaii, Alaska, California, Nevada, and Oklahoma—more than 10 percent of all married couples are interracial (Passel, Wang, & Taylor, 2010; U.S. Census Bureau, 2011). The Sociology in Focus box on page 349 gives you a chance to share your opinion about the importance of race and ethnicity when it comes to dating and marriage.

Gender

The sociologist Jessie Bernard (1982) says that every marriage is actually two different relationships: the woman's marriage and the man's marriage. The reason is that few marriages have two equal partners. Although patriarchy has diminished, many people still expect husbands to be older and taller than their wives and to have more important, better-paid jobs.

Why, then, do many people think that marriage benefits women more than men? The positive stereotype of the carefree bachelor contrasts sharply with the negative image of the lonely spinster, suggesting that women are fulfilled only through being wives and mothers.

However, Bernard points out, married women actually have poorer mental health, less happiness, and more passive attitudes toward life than single women do. Married men, on the other hand, generally live longer, are mentally better off, and report being happier than single men (Fustos, 2010). These differences suggest why, after divorce, men are more eager than women to find a new partner.

Bernard concludes that there is no better assurance of long life, health, and happiness for a man than having a woman devote her life to taking care of him and providing the security of a well-ordered home. She is quick to add that marriage *could* be healthful for women if husbands did not dominate wives and expect them to do almost all the housework. Survey responses confirm that couples rank "sharing household chores" as one of the most important factors that contribute to a successful marriage (Pew Research Center, 2007a).

Transitions and Problems in Family Life

 Analyze

The newspaper columnist Ann Landers once remarked that one marriage in twenty is wonderful, five in twenty are good, ten in twenty are tolerable, and the remaining four are "pure hell." Families can be a source of joy, but the reality of family life can also fall short of the ideal.

Divorce

Our society strongly supports marriage, and about nine out of ten people in the United States who reach the age of forty have at some point "tied the knot." But many of today's marriages unravel. Figure 13–2 shows that the U.S. divorce rate has more than tripled over the past century. Today, almost four in ten marriages eventually end in divorce (for African Americans, the rate is about six in ten). From another angle, of all people over the age of fifteen, 21 percent of men and 22 percent of women have been divorced at some point. Ours is the highest divorce rate in the world; it is about 1½ times as high as in Canada and Japan and four times higher than in Italy and Ireland (European Union, 2011; OECD, 2011; United Nations, 2011).

Causes of Divorce

The high U.S. divorce rate has many causes (Furstenberg & Cherlin, 1991; Etzioni, 1993; Popenoe, 1999; Greenspan, 2001):

1. **Individualism is on the rise.** Today's family members spend less time together. We have become more individualistic, more concerned with our personal happiness and earning income than about the well-being of our partners and children.

2. **Romantic love fades.** Because our culture bases marriage on

Divorce may be a solution for a couple in an unhappy marriage, but it can be a problem for children who experience the withdrawal of a parent from their social world. In what ways can divorce be harmful to children? Is there a positive side to divorce? How might separating parents better prepare their children for the transition of parental divorce?

romantic love, relationships may fail as sexual passion fades. Many people end a marriage in favor of a new relationship that promises renewed excitement and romance.

3. **Women are less dependent on men.** Women's increasing participation in the labor force has reduced wives' financial dependency on their husbands. Thus women find it easier to leave unhappy marriages.

4. **Many of today's marriages are stressful.** With both partners working outside the home in most cases, people have less time and energy for family life. This makes raising children harder than ever. Children do stabilize some marriages, but divorce is most common during the early years of marriage when many couples have young children.

5. **Divorce has become socially acceptable.** Divorce no longer carries the powerful stigma it did just a few generations ago. Family and friends are now less likely to discourage couples in conflict from divorcing.

6. **Legally, a divorce is easier to get.** In the past, courts required divorcing couples to demonstrate that one or both were guilty of behavior such as adultery or physical abuse. Today, all states allow divorce if a couple simply declares that the marriage has failed. Concern about easy divorce, shared by almost half of U.S. adults, has led a few states to consider rewriting their marriage laws (Phillips, 2001; NORC, 2011:408).

Who Divorces?

At greatest risk of divorce are young couples—especially those who marry after a brief courtship—who tend to lack money and emotional maturity. The chance of divorce also rises if a couple marries after an unexpected pregnancy or if one or both partners have substance abuse problems. People who are not religious are more likely to divorce than those who have strong religious beliefs. Finally, people whose parents divorced also have a higher divorce rate themselves. Researchers suggest that a role-modeling effect is at work: Children who see parents go through divorce are more likely to consider divorce themselves (Amato, 2001). People who live in rural areas of the country are less likely to divorce than people who live in large cities, although this difference is much less than it used to be (Pew Research Center, 2008; Tavernise & Gebeloff, 2011).

Rates of divorce (and remarriage) have remained about the same among people with a college education and those with high-paying jobs. At the same time, divorce rates are increasing (and marriage rates have been declining) among those who do not attend college and among those with low-paying work. Some researchers suggest that more disadvantaged members of our society appear to be turning away from marriage, not so much because they do not wish to be married, but because they lack the economic security needed for a stable family life (Kent, 2011). This trend shows how the recent recession and increasing income inequality in the United States are affecting family life.

Finally, men and women who divorce once are more likely to divorce again. Why? In all likelihood, the reason is that high-risk factors follow them from one marriage to the next (Glenn & Shelton, 1985).

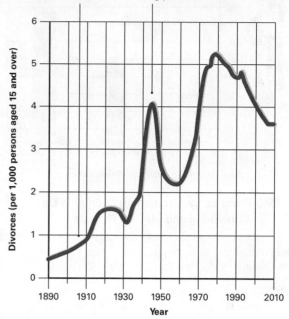

FIGURE 13–2 **Divorce Rate for the United States, 1890–2010**

Over the long term, the U.S. divorce rate has gone up. Since about 1980, however, the trend has been downward.

Source: National Center for Health Statistics (2012).

Divorce and Children

Because mothers usually gain custody of children but fathers typically earn more income, the well-being of many children depends on fathers' making court-ordered child support payments. Courts award child support in 54 percent of all divorces involving children. Yet in any given year, more than half of children legally entitled to support receive only partial payments or no payments at all. Some 3.4 million "deadbeat dads" fail to support their youngsters. In response, federal legislation now requires employers to withhold money from the earnings of fathers or mothers who fail to pay up; it is a serious crime to refuse to make child support payments or to move to another state to avoid making them (U.S. Census Bureau, 2011).

Remarriage and Blended Families

Three out of four people who divorce remarry, most within four years. Nationwide, more than one-quarter of all marriages are now remarriages for at least one partner. Men, who benefit more from wedlock, are more likely than women to remarry (Kreider & Ellis, 2011).

Remarriage often creates *blended families,* composed of children and some combination of biological parents and stepparents. With brothers, sisters, half-siblings, a stepparent—not to mention a biological parent who may live elsewhere and be married to someone else with other children—young people in blended families face the challenge of defining many new relationships and deciding just who is part of the nuclear family. Parents often have trouble defining responsibilities for household work among people unsure of

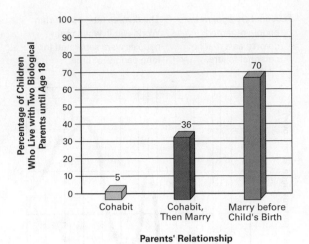

FIGURE 13–3 Parental Involvement in Children's Lives:
Cohabiting and Married Parents

Marriage increases the odds that children will remain in the same household with both biological parents as they grow up.

Source: Phillips (2001).

their relationships to each other. When the custody of children is an issue, ex-spouses can be an unwelcome presence for people in a new marriage. Although blended families require a great deal of new adjustment, they also offer both young and old the chance to relax rigid family roles (Furstenberg & Cherlin, 2001; McLanahan, 2002).

Blended families are also formed when parents have children with more than one partner. As the rate of children in the United States born to unmarried parents rises (in 2010, it was 41 percent), the share of people who live in blended families is increasing. One recent research report stated that more than half of all children born to unmarried parents are born into a family with at least one half-sibling (Scommegna, 2011).

Family Violence

The ideal family is a source of pleasure and support. However, the disturbing reality of many homes is **family violence**, *emotional, physical, or sexual abuse of one family member by another*. With the exception of the police and the military, claims sociologist Richard J. Gelles, the family is "the most violent group in society" (quoted in Roesch, 1984:75).

Violence against Women

Family brutality often goes unreported to police. Even so, the U.S. Bureau of Justice Statistics (2011) estimates that about 510,000 people are victims of domestic violence each year. Family violence harms both sexes, but not equally—women are three times more likely than men to be a victim. In cases of deadly violence, the gender disparity is very large—fully 38 percent of women who are victims of homicide, but just 2 percent of men, are killed by spouses, partners, or ex-partners. In 2010, nationwide, the death toll from family violence was 1,101 women. Overall, women are more likely to be injured by a family member than to be mugged or raped by a stranger or hurt in an automobile accident (Shupe,

Stacey, & Hazlewood, 1987; Blankenhorn, 1995; Durose et al., 2005; U.S. Department of Justice, 2011).

Historically, the law defined wives as the property of their husbands, so no man could be charged with raping his wife. Today, however, all 50 states have *marital rape laws*. The law no longer regards domestic violence as a private family matter; it gives victims more options. Now, even without separation or divorce, a woman can obtain court protection from an abusive spouse, and all states have stalking laws that forbid one ex-partner from following or otherwise threatening the other. Communities across North America have established shelters to provide counseling and temporary housing for women and children driven from their homes by domestic violence.

Finally, the harm caused by domestic violence goes beyond the physical injuries. Victims often lose their ability to trust others. One study found that women who had been physically or sexually abused were much less likely than nonvictims to form stable relationships later on (Cherlin et al., 2004).

Violence against Children

Family violence also victimizes children. Each year, there are roughly 3 million reports of alleged child abuse or neglect. In 2010, 1,530 of these cases involved a child's death, and 80 percent of these deaths involved a child under the age of four. Child abuse involves more than physical injury; abusive adults can also misuse power and trust to damage a child's emotional well-being. Child abuse and neglect are most common among the youngest and most vulnerable children (Besharov & Laumann, 1996; U.S. Department of Health and Human Services, 2011).

Although child abusers conform to no simple stereotype, they are more likely to be women (54 percent) than men (46 percent). But almost all abusers share one trait: having been abused themselves as children. Researchers have found that violent behavior in close relationships is learned; in families, violence begets violence (S. Levine, 2001; U.S. Department of Health and Human Services, 2011).

Alternative Family Forms

 Analyze

Most families in the United States are composed of a married couple who raise children. But in recent decades, our society has displayed increasing diversity in family life.

One-Parent Families

Thirty-one percent of U.S. families with children under eighteen have only one parent in the household, a proportion that has almost tripled since 1970. Put another way, 31 percent of U.S. children now live with only one parent or no natural parent, and about half will do so before reaching eighteen. One-parent families, 85 percent of which are headed by a single mother, result from divorce, death of a partner, or an unmarried woman's decision to have a child.

Single parenthood increases a woman's risk of poverty because it limits her ability to work and to further her education. The opposite is also true: Poverty raises the odds that a young woman will become a single mother. But single parenthood goes well beyond the poor: There are about 1.7 million births to unmarried women each year, which represents 41 percent of all births in this country. In recent decades, the rate of childbirth to younger single women has declined; at the same time, the rate of childbirth to single women over the age of forty is on the rise (Pew Research Center, 2007a; Martin et al., 2011). Looking back at Figure 13–1 on page 348, note that 56 percent of African American families are headed by a single parent. Single parenthood is less common among Hispanics (37 percent), Asian Americans (20 percent), and non-Hispanic whites (19 percent). In many single-parent families, mothers turn to their own mothers for support. In the United States, then, the rise in single parenting is tied to a declining role for fathers and the growing importance of grandmothers.

Research shows that growing up in a one-parent family usually puts children at a disadvantage. Some studies claim that because a father and a mother each make a distinctive contribution to a child's social development, one parent has a hard time doing as good a job alone. But the most serious problem for one-parent families, especially if that parent is a woman, is poverty. On average, children growing up in a single-parent family start out poorer, get less schooling, and end up with lower incomes as adults. Such children are also more likely to become single parents themselves (Popenoe, 1993a; Blankenhorn, 1995; Kantrowitz & Wingert, 2001; McLanahan, 2002; Pew Research Center, 2007; U.S. Census Bureau, 2011).

Cohabitation

Cohabitation is *the sharing of a household by an unmarried couple.* In global perspective, cohabitation as a long-term form of family life, with or without children, is especially common in Sweden and other Scandinavian countries and is gaining in popularity in other European nations. In the United States, the number of cohabiting couples has increased from about 500,000 in 1970 to about 6.8 million today (6.2 million heterosexual couples and 600,000

In 2011, New York became one of eight states that permit lawful marriage joining same-sex couples. The New York law gave a new boost to the movement to legalize same-sex marriage nationwide. How many states do you expect to follow suit in the next few years? Why?

homosexual couples), or about 6 percent of all households. Almost half of people (51 percent of women and 43 percent of men) between twenty-five and forty-four years of age have cohabited at some point (National Center for Health Statistics, 2011; U.S. Census Bureau, 2011).

Cohabiting tends to appeal to more independent-minded people and those who favor gender equality (Brines & Joyner, 1999). Most couples cohabit for no more than a few years. After three years, one in ten couples continues to cohabit, three in ten have decided to marry, and six in ten have split up. Mounting evidence suggests that living together may actually discourage marriage because partners (especially men) become used to low-commitment relationships. For this reason, cohabiting couples who have children—currently representing just 2 percent of all families but 12 percent of all births—are not always long-term parents. Figure 13–3 shows that just 5 percent of children born to cohabiting couples will live until age eighteen with both biological parents if the parents remain unmarried. The share rises to 36 percent among children whose parents marry at some point, but this is still half of the 70 percent figure for children whose parents married before they were born. When cohabiting couples with children separate, the involvement of both parents, especially with respect to financial support, is highly uncertain (Popenoe & Whitehead, 1999; Booth & Crouter, 2002; Scommegna, 2002).

Gay and Lesbian Couples

In 1989, Denmark became the first country to permit registered partnerships with the benefits of marriage for same-sex couples. Since then, more than fifteen countries, including Norway (1993), Sweden (1994), Iceland (1996), Finland (2001), the United Kingdom (2004), Australia (2008), and Ireland (2011), have followed suit. However, only ten countries have extended marriage—in name as well as practice—to same-sex couples: the Netherlands (2001), Belgium (2003), Canada (2005), Spain (2005), South Africa (2006), Norway (2008), Sweden (2009), Argentina (2010), Iceland (2010), and Portugal (2010).

In the United States, Massachusetts became the first state to legalize same-sex marriage in 2004. As of 2012, Iowa, Vermont, Connecticut, New Hampshire, New York, Washington state, Maryland, and the District of Columbia have also changed their laws to allow same-sex marriage. Nine more states, including New Jersey, California, Oregon, and Delaware permit same-sex civil unions or domestic partnerships, with nearly all the rights of marriage.

Back in 1996, Congress passed the Defense of Marriage Act (DOMA), defining marriage as joining one man and one woman. Since then, a total of thirty states have amended their constitutions to permit marriage only between one man and one woman. In February 2011, the Obama administration announced that the Department of Justice will no longer defend the DOMA in court. Soon afterward, Congress began debating whether or not to overturn the DOMA. Critics of the DOMA point to a steady upward trend in public acceptance of same-sex marriage. Currently, about 45 percent of U.S. adults support gay marriage, and 57 percent support civil unions providing the rights enjoyed by married couples (Newport, 2005; Pew Research Center, 2009, 2011; NORC, 2011:2313).

Most same-sex couples with children in the United States live in blended families raising the offspring of previous heterosexual unions; others have adopted children. But many gay parents are quiet about their sexual orientation, not wanting to draw unwelcome attention to their children or to themselves. In several widely publicized cases, courts have removed children from the custody of homosexual couples, citing the "best interests" of the children.

Same-sex couples raising children challenges many traditional ideas. But it also shows that same-sex couples value family life as highly as heterosexuals do.

Singlehood

Because nine out of ten people in the United States marry, we tend to see singlehood as a temporary stage of life. However, increasing numbers of people of all ages are living alone, often by choice. In 1950, only one household in ten contained a single person. By 2011, this share had risen to 28 percent, a total of 32.7 million single adult households (U.S. Census Bureau, 2011).

Most striking is the rising number of single young women. In 1960, some 28 percent of women aged twenty to twenty-four were single; by 2011, the proportion had soared to 81 percent. Underlying this trend is the increasing number of women going to college, which has pushed back the age at first marriage. Women who complete college are more likely to marry and marry later in life than women who do not attend college. The reason is that the more education people have, the more attractive they are as marriage partners (Kent, 2011).

By midlife, many unmarried women sense a lack of available men. Because our society expects women to "marry up," the older a woman is, the more education she has, and the better her job, the more difficulty she has finding a suitable husband.

New Reproductive Technologies and Families

 **Understand**

Medical advances involving new reproductive technologies are also changing families. In 1978, England's Louise Brown became the world's first "test-tube baby"; since then, tens of thousands of children have been conceived outside the womb.

Test-tube babies are the product of *in vitro fertilization,* in which doctors unite a woman's egg and a man's sperm "in glass" (usually not a test tube but a shallow dish) rather than in a woman's body. Doctors then either implant the resulting embryo in the womb of the woman who is to bear the child or freeze it for implantation at a later time.

Modern reproductive technologies allow some couples who cannot conceive normally to have children. These techniques may also eventually help reduce the incidence of birth defects. Genetic screening of sperm and eggs would allow medical specialists to increase the odds for the birth of a healthy baby. But new reproductive technologies also raise difficult and troubling questions: When one woman carries an embryo developed from the egg of another, who is the mother? When a couple divorces, which spouse is entitled to

use, or destroy, their frozen embryos? Should parents use genetic screening to select the traits of their child? Such questions remind us that technology changes faster than our ability to understand the consequences of its use.

Families: Looking Ahead

 Evaluate

Family life in the United States will continue to change in years to come, and with change comes controversy. Advocates of "traditional family values" line up against those who support greater personal choice; the Controversy & Debate box outlines some of the issues. Sociologists cannot predict the outcome of this debate, but based on ongoing research on family patterns, we can suggest five likely future trends.

First, the divorce rate is likely to remain high, even in the face of evidence that marital breakups put children at higher risk of poverty. Today's marriages are about as durable as they were a century ago, when many were cut short by death. The difference is that now more couples *choose* to end marriages that fail to meet their expectations. Although the divorce rate has declined since 1980, it is unlikely that we will ever return to the low rates that marked the early decades of the twentieth century.

Second, family life in the future will be more diverse. Cohabiting couples, one-parent families, gay and lesbian families, and blended families are all on the rise. Most families are still based on marriage, and most married couples still have children. But the diversity of family forms implies a trend toward more personal choice.

Third, men will play a limited role in child rearing. In the 1950s, a decade many people consider the "golden age" of families, men began to withdraw from active parenting (Snell, 1990; Stacey, 1990). In recent years, a countertrend has become evident with some older, highly educated fathers making the choice to stay at home with young children, many using computer technology to continue their work. But we should not overestimate the importance of this trend because the stay-at-home dad represents only about 1 percent of all fathers of young children (U.S. Census Bureau, 2011). The bigger picture is that the high divorce rate in the United States and the increase in single motherhood are weakening children's ties to fathers and increasing children's risk of poverty.

Fourth, families will continue to feel the effects of economic changes. In many homes, both household partners work, increasing income but reducing marriage and family life to the interaction of weary men and women trying to fit a little "quality time" with their children into an already full schedule. The long-term effects of the two-career couple on families as we have known them are likely to be mixed. In addition, in an era of high unemployment and low wages, more and more young people (many of whom continue to live with parents) do not feel that they have the economic security necessary to marry and live on their own.

Fifth and finally, the importance of new reproductive technologies will increase. Ethical concerns about whether what *can* be done *should* be done will surely slow these developments, but new reproductive technologies will continue to alter the traditional experience of parenthood.

Aaron: My parents were really goin' at each other last night. Man, I don't know whether they're going to stay together.

Abdul: I hope they do, my friend. Families are what ties society together.

Tawneesha: Listen to you guys! The important thing is for each person to be happy. If being married does it for you, great. But there are lots of different ways for people to find happiness.

What are "traditional families"? Are they vital to our way of life or a barrier to progress? People use the term *traditional family* to mean a married couple who at some point in their lives raise children. Statistically speaking, traditional families are less common than they used to be. In 1950, 90 percent of U.S. households were families—using the Census Bureau's definition of two or more persons related by blood, marriage, or adoption. By 2011, just 66 percent of households were families, due to rising levels of divorce, cohabitation, and singlehood.

"Traditional family" is more than just a handy expression; it is also a moral statement. Belief in the traditional family implies giving high value to becoming and staying married, putting children ahead of careers, and favoring two-parent families over various alternatives.

"Traditional Families Are the Solution"

On one side of the debate, David Popenoe (1993a) warns that there has been a serious erosion of the traditional family since 1960. At that time, married couples with young children accounted for almost half of all households; today, the figure is 20 percent. Singlehood is up, from 10 percent of households in 1960 to 28 percent today. And the divorce rate has risen by 59 percent since 1960, so that nearly four in ten of today's marriages end in permanent separation. Because of both divorce and the increasing number of children born to single women, the share of youngsters who live with just one parent has almost tripled since 1960 to 27 percent (Martin et al., 2011; U.S. Census Bureau, 2011). Put another way, just one in four of today's children will grow up with two parents and go on to maintain a stable marriage as an adult.

In light of such data, Popenoe concludes, it may not be an exaggeration to say that the family is falling apart. He

sees a fundamental shift from a "culture of marriage" to a "culture of divorce," where traditional vows of marital commitment—"till death do us part"—now amount to little more than "as long as I am happy."

The negative consequences of the cultural trend toward weaker families, Popenoe continues, are obvious and can be found everywhere: As we pay less and less attention to children, the crime rate among young people goes up, along with a host of other problem behaviors including underage smoking and drinking, premarital sex, and teen suicide.

As Popenoe sees it, we must work hard and act quickly to reverse current trends. Government cannot be the solution and may even be part of the problem: Since 1960, as families have weakened, government spending on social programs has soared. To save the traditional family, says Popenoe, we need a cultural turnaround similar to what happened with regard to cigarette smoking. In this case, we must replace our "me first" attitudes with commitment to our spouse and children and publicly endorse the two-parent family as best for the well-being of children.

"Traditional Families Are the Problem"

Judith Stacey (1993) provides a feminist viewpoint, saying "good riddance" to the traditional family. In her view, the traditional family is more problem than solution: "The family is not here to stay. Nor should we wish it were. On the contrary, I believe that all democratic people, whatever their

kinship preferences, should work to hasten its demise" (Stacey, 1990:269).

The main reason for rejecting the traditional family, Stacey explains, is that it perpetuates social inequality. Families play a key role in maintaining the class hierarchy by transferring wealth as well as "cultural capital" from one generation to the next. Feminists criticize the traditional family's patriarchal form, which subjects women to their husbands' authority and gives them most of the responsibility for housework and child care. From a gay rights perspective, she adds, a society that values traditional families also denies homosexual men and women equal participation in social life.

Stacey thus applauds the breakdown of the family as social progress. She does not view the family as a necessary social institution but as a political construction that elevates one category of people—affluent white males—above others, including women, homosexuals, and poor people.

Stacey also claims that the concept of the "traditional family" is increasingly irrelevant. In a diverse society in which both men and women work for income. What our society needs, Stacey concludes, is not a return to some golden age of the family but political and economic change, including income parity for women, universal health care and child care, programs to reduce unemployment, and expanded sex education in the schools. Such measures not only help families but also ensure that people in diverse family forms receive the respect and dignity they deserve.

What Do You Think?

1. To strengthen families, David Popenoe suggests that parents put children ahead of their own careers by limiting their joint workweek to sixty hours. Do you agree? Why or why not?

2. Judith Stacey thinks that marriage is weaker today because women are rejecting patriarchal relationships. What do you think about this argument?

3. Do we need to change family patterns for the well-being of our children? As you see it, what specific changes are called for?

Whether the traditional family is a positive force in U.S. society or a negative one depends on your point of view.

Despite the changes and controversies that have shaken the family in the United States, most people in our society still report being happy in their roles as partners and parents. Marriage and family life will likely remain a foundation of our society for generations to come.

Religion: Basic Concepts

● Understand

Like family, religion plays an important part in human society. Families have long used religious rituals to celebrate birth, recognize adulthood, and mourn the dead.

The French sociologist Emile Durkheim stated that religion involves "things that surpass the limits of our knowledge" (1965:62, orig. 1915). As human beings, we regard most objects, events, and experiences as **profane** (from Latin, meaning "outside the temple"), *included as an ordinary part of everyday life.* But we also consider some things **sacred**, *set apart as extraordinary, inspiring awe and reverence.* Setting the sacred apart from the profane is the essence of all religious belief. **Religion**, then, is *a social institution involving beliefs and practices based on recognizing the sacred.*

There is great diversity in matters of faith, and nothing is sacred to everyone on Earth. Although people regard most books as profane, Jews believe that the Torah (containing the first five books of the Hebrew Bible, also known as the Old Testament) is sacred, in the same way that Christians revere the Old and New Testaments of the Bible and Muslims exalt the Qur'an (Koran).

But no matter how a community of believers draws religious lines, Durkheim (1965:62, orig. 1915) explained, people understand profane things in terms of their everyday usefulness: We log on to the Internet with our computer or turn a key to start our car. What is sacred we reverently set apart from daily life, giving it a "forbidden" or "holy" aura. For example, Muslims remove their shoes before entering a mosque to avoid defiling a sacred place with soles that have touched the profane ground outside.

The sacred is embodied in **ritual**, or *formal, ceremonial behavior.* Holy Communion is the central ritual of Christianity; to the Christian faithful, the wafer and wine consumed during Communion are treated not in a profane way as food but as the sacred symbols of the body and blood of Jesus Christ.

Because religion deals with ideas that transcend everyday experience, neither common sense nor sociology can prove or disprove religious doctrine.

Although rituals take countless forms, all religion deals with what surpasses ordinary or everyday understanding. This man in Los Angeles is part of a dance group taking part in the Day of the Dead, a Mexican celebration involving prayer and remembering those who have passed on.

religion a social institution involving beliefs and practices based on recognizing the sacred

faith belief based on conviction rather than on scientific evidence

Religion is a matter of **faith**, *belief based on conviction rather than on scientific evidence.* The New Testament of the Bible defines faith as "the conviction of things not seen" (Hebrews 11:1) and urges Christians to "walk by faith, not by sight" (2 Corinthians 5:7).

Some people with strong religious beliefs may be disturbed by the thought of sociologists turning a scientific eye on what they hold sacred. However, sociological study is no threat to anyone's faith. Sociologists study religion as a social institution, just as they study the family or the economy. They make no judgments about whether any specific religion is "right" or "wrong." Sociological analysis takes a more worldly approach, seeking to understand what religions have in common and how they differ as well as how religious activity affects society as a whole.

Theories of Religion

● Apply

Sociologists apply the major theoretical approaches to the study of religion just as they do to any other topic. Each provides distinctive insights about the ways religion shapes social life.

Functions of Religion: Structural-Functional Theory

According to Emile Durkheim (1965, orig. 1915), society has a life and power of its own beyond the life of any individual. In a sense, society itself is godlike, shaping the lives of its members and living on beyond them. Practicing religion, people everywhere celebrate the awesome power of their society.

No wonder people around the world transform everyday objects into sacred symbols of their collective life. Members of technologically simple societies do this with a **totem**, *an object in the natural world collectively defined as sacred.* The totem—perhaps an animal or an elaborate work of art—becomes the centerpiece of ritual and symbolizes the power of collective life over the individual. In our society, the flag is a quasi-religious totem that is not to be used in a profane way (say, as clothing) or allowed to touch the ground.

Similarly, putting the words "In God We Trust" on U.S. currency (a practice started in the 1860s at the time of the Civil War) or adding the words "under God" to the Pledge of Allegiance (in 1954) symbolizes widespread beliefs that tie society together. Across the United States, local communities also gain a sense of unity by linking totems to sports teams, from the New England Patriots to the Ohio State Buckeyes to the Iowa State University Cyclones to the San Francisco 49ers.

Durkheim identified three major functions of religion that contribute to the operation of society:

1. **Establishing social cohesion.** Religion unites people through shared symbolism, values, and norms. Religious thought and ritual establish rules of fair play, organizing our social life.

2. **Promoting social control.** Every society uses religious ideas to promote conformity. By defining God as a "judge" of human behavior, many religions encourage people to obey cultural norms. Religion can also be used to back up political systems. In medieval Europe, for example, monarchs claimed to rule by "divine right." Even today, our leaders publicly ask for God's blessing, implying that their efforts are right and just.

3. **Providing meaning and purpose.** Religious belief offers the comforting sense that our lives serve some greater purpose. Strengthened by such beliefs, people are less likely to despair in the face of change or even tragedy. For this reason, we mark major life transitions—including birth, marriage, and death—with religious observances.

Evaluate In Durkheim's structural-functional theory, religion represents the collective life that helps hold society together. The major weakness of this approach is that it downplays religion's dysfunctions, especially the fact that strongly held beliefs can generate social conflict. Terrorists have claimed that God supports their actions, and nations march to war under the banner of their God. Looking around the world, few people would deny that religious beliefs have provoked more violence in the world than differences of social class.

CHECK YOUR LEARNING What are Durkheim's three functions of religion for society?

Constructing the Sacred: Symbolic-Interaction Theory

From a symbolic-interaction point of view, religion (like all of society) is socially constructed (although perhaps with divine inspiration). Through various rituals—from daily prayers to annual events such as Easter, Passover, or Ramadan—people sharpen the distinction between the sacred and the profane. Furthermore, says Peter Berger (1967:35–36), placing our small, brief lives within some "cosmic frame of reference" gives us the appearance of "ultimate security and permanence."

Religion is founded on the concept of the sacred—aspects of our existence that are set apart as extraordinary and demand our submission. Bowing, kneeling, or prostrating oneself are all ways of symbolically surrendering to a higher power. These Filipino Christians seek atonement for their sins in an annual Lenten ritual.

Marriage is a good example. If two people look on marriage as a simple contract, they can agree to split up whenever they want. Their bond makes much stronger claims on them when it is defined as holy matrimony, which is surely one reason for the lower divorce rate among people with strong religious beliefs. More generally, whenever humans face uncertainty or life-threatening situations—such as illness, natural disaster, terrorist attack, or war—we find comfort in our sacred symbols.

Evaluate Using the symbolic-interaction approach, religion gives everyday life sacred meaning. Berger adds that the sacred's ability to give meaning and stability to society depends on ignoring the fact that it is socially constructed. After all, how much strength could we gain from sacred beliefs if we saw them merely as strategies for coping with tragedy? Also, this micro-level view ignores religion's link to social inequality, to which we turn next.

CHECK YOUR LEARNING How would Peter Berger explain the fact that deeply religious people have a low divorce rate?

Inequality and Religion: Social-Conflict Theory

The social-conflict approach highlights religion's support of social inequality. Religion, proclaimed Karl Marx, serves elites by legitimizing the status quo and diverting people's attention from social inequities.

Today, the British monarch is the formal head of the Church of England, illustrating the close ties between religious and political elites. In practical terms, working for political change may mean opposing the church and, by implication, God. Religion also encourages people to accept the social problems of this world while they look hopefully to a "better world to come." In a well-known

---

profane included as an ordinary part of everyday life

sacred set apart as extraordinary, inspiring awe and reverence

	Structural-Functional Theory	Symbolic-Interaction Theory	Social-Conflict and Feminist Theories
What is the level of analysis?	Macro-level	Micro-level	Macro-level
What is the importance of religion for society?	Religion performs vital tasks, including uniting people and controlling behavior. Religion gives life meaning and purpose.	Religion strengthens marriage by giving it (and family life) sacred meaning. People often turn to sacred symbols for comfort when facing danger and uncertainty.	Religion supports social inequality by claiming that the social order is just. Religion supports the domination of women by men. Religion turns attention from problems in this world to a "better world to come."

statement, Marx dismissed religion as "the sigh of the oppressed creature, the sentiment of a heartless world, and the soul of soulless conditions. It is the opium of the people" (1964:27, orig. 1848).

Inequality and Religion: Feminist Theory

Feminist theory explains that religion and social inequality are also linked through gender because virtually all the world's major religions are patriarchal. For example, the Qur'an, the sacred text of Islam, gives men social dominance over women by defining gender roles: "Men are in charge of women. . . . Hence good women are obedient. . . . As for those whose rebelliousness you fear, admonish them, banish them from your bed, and scourge [punish] them" (Qur'an 4:34, quoted in W. Kaufman, 1976:163).

Christianity, the major religion in the Western Hemisphere, has also supported patriarchy throughout history. Although Christians revere Mary, the mother of Jesus, the New Testament contains the following passages:

> A man . . . is the image and glory of God; but woman is the glory of man. For man was not made from woman, but woman from man. Neither was man created for woman, but woman for man. (1 Corinthians 11:7–9)

> As in all the churches of the saints, the women should keep silence in the churches. For they are not permitted to speak, but should be subordinate, as even the law says. If there is anything they desire to know, let them ask their husbands at home. For it is shameful for a woman to speak in church. (1 Corinthians 14:33–35)

> Wives, be subject to your husbands, as to the Lord. For the husband is the head of the wife as Christ is the head of the church. . . . As the church is subject to Christ, so let wives also be subject in everything to their husbands. (Ephesians 5:22–24)

Judaism has also traditionally supported patriarchy. Male Orthodox Jews recite the following prayer each day:

> Blessed art thou, O Lord our God, King of the Universe, that I was not born a gentile.
> Blessed art thou, O Lord our God, King of the Universe, that I was not born a slave.
> Blessed art thou, O Lord our God, King of the Universe, that I was not born a woman.

Despite patriarchal traditions, most religions now have women in leadership roles, and many are introducing more gender-neutral

language in hymnals and prayer books. Such changes involve not just organizational patterns but also conceptions of God. The theologian Mary Daly puts the matter bluntly: "If God is male, then male is God" (cited in Woodward, 1989:58).

 Evaluate Social-conflict and feminist theories emphasize the power of religion to support social inequality. Yet religion also promotes change toward equality. For example, nineteenth-century religious groups in the United States played an important part in the movement to abolish slavery. In the 1950s and 1960s, religious organizations and their leaders were at the core of the civil rights movement. In the 1960s and 1970s, many clergy actively opposed the Vietnam War, and today many support any number of progressive causes such as feminism and gay rights.

The Applying Theory table summarizes the three theoretical approaches to understanding religion.

CHECK YOUR LEARNING How does religion help maintain class inequality and gender stratification?

Religion and Social Change

Apply

Religion can be the conservative force portrayed by Karl Marx. But at some points in history, as Max Weber (1958, orig. 1904–05) explained, religion has promoted dramatic social change.

Max Weber: Protestantism and Capitalism

Weber believed that particular religious ideas set into motion a wave of change that brought about the industrialization of Western Europe. The rise of industrial capitalism was encouraged by Calvinism, a movement within the Protestant Reformation.

Central to the religious thought of John Calvin (1509–1564) is the doctrine of *predestination*: An all-knowing, all-powerful God has selected some people for salvation while condemning most to eternal damnation. Each person's fate, sealed before birth and known only to God, is either eternal glory or endless hellfire.

Driven by anxiety over their fate, Calvinists understandably looked for evidence of God's favor in this world and came to see prosperity as a sign of divine blessing. Religious conviction and a rigid devotion to duty thus led Calvinists to work hard, and many amassed great wealth. But money was not for selfish spending or even for sharing with the poor, whose plight they saw as a mark of God's rejection. As agents for God's work on Earth, Calvinists believed that they could best fulfill their "calling" by reinvesting profits and achieving ever-greater success in the process.

All the while, Calvinists practiced self-denial by living thrifty lives. In addition, they eagerly embraced technological advances that promised to increase their workplace effectiveness. Together, these traits laid the groundwork for the rise of industrial capitalism. In time, the religious fervor that motivated early Calvinists weakened, resulting in a profane "Protestant work ethic." To Max Weber, the spirit that animated industrial capitalism was a "disenchanted" religion, further showing the power of religion to change the shape of society.

Liberation Theology

Historically, Christianity has reached out to suffering and oppressed people, urging all to strengthen their faith in a better life to come. In recent decades, however, some church leaders and theologians have taken a decidedly political approach and endorsed **liberation theology**, *the combining of Christian principles with political activism, often Marxist in character.*

Liberation theology is a social movement that started in the late 1960s in Latin America's Roman Catholic Church. Today, Christian activists continue to help people in poor nations liberate themselves from abysmal poverty. Their message is simple: Social oppression runs counter to Christian morality, so as a matter of faith and justice, Christians must promote greater social equality.

Pope Benedict XVI, like Pope John Paul II before him, condemns liberation theology for distorting church doctrine with left-wing politics. Nevertheless, the liberation theology movement has gained strength in the poorest countries of Latin America, where many people's Christian faith drives them to improve conditions for the world's poor (Neuhouser, 1989; J. E. Williams, 2002).

Types of Religious Organizations

⬤ **Understand**

Sociologists categorize the hundreds of different religious organizations in the United States along a continuum, with *churches* at one end and *sects* at the other. We can describe any religious organization in relation to these two ideal types by locating it on the church–sect continuum.

Church

Drawing on the ideas of his teacher Max Weber, Ernst Troeltsch (1931) defined a **church** as *a religious organization that is well integrated into the larger society.* Churchlike organizations typically persist for centuries and include generations of the same families. Churches have well-established rules and regulations and expect leaders to be formally trained and ordained.

Though concerned with the sacred, a church accepts the ways of the profane world. Church members conceive of God in intellectual terms (say, as a force for good) and favor abstract moral standards ("Do unto others as you would have them do unto you"). By teaching morality in safely abstract terms, church leaders avoid social controversy. For example, many churches celebrate the unity of all peoples but say little about their own lack of social diversity. By downplaying this type of conflict, a church makes peace with the status quo (Troeltsch, 1931).

A church may operate with or apart from the state. A **state church** is *a church formally linked to the state.* For centuries, Roman Catholicism was the official religion of the Roman Empire, and Confucianism was the official religion in China until the early twentieth century. Today, the Anglican Church is the official church of England, and Islam is the official religion of Pakistan and Iran. State churches count everyone in the society as a member, which sharply limits tolerance of religious differences.

A **denomination** is *a church, independent of the state, that recognizes religious pluralism.* Denominations exist in nations, including the United States, that formally separate church and state. This nation has dozens of Christian denominations, including Catholics, Baptists, Episcopalians, Methodists, and Lutherans, as well as various branches of Judaism, Islam, and other traditions. Although members of a denomination hold to their own beliefs, they recognize the right of others to have different beliefs.

Sect

Unlike a church, which tries to fit into the larger society, a **sect** is *a religious organization that stands apart from the larger society.* Sect members hold rigid religious convictions and deny the beliefs of

In global perspective, the range of religious activity is truly astonishing. This woman in Ghana, celebrating the Kokuzahn voodoo festival, throws sand into her open eyes and is not harmed. What religious practices common in the United States might seem astonishing to people living in other countries?

Animism is widespread in traditional societies, whose members live respectfully within the natural world on which they depend for their survival. Animists see a divine presence not just in themselves but in everything around them. Their example has inspired "New Age" spirituality, described on pages 364–65.

others. Compared to churches, which try to appeal to everyone (the term *catholic* also means "universal"), a sect forms an exclusive group. To members of a sect, religion is not just one aspect of life but a formal plan for living. In extreme cases, members of a sect may withdraw completely from society to practice their faith without interference. The Amish community is one example of a North American sect that isolates itself. Because our culture generally considers religious tolerance a virtue, members of sects are sometimes accused of being narrow-minded in insisting that they alone follow the true religion (Kraybill, 1994; P. W. Williams, 2002).

In organizational terms, sects are less formal than churches. Sect members may be highly spontaneous and emotional in worship, compared to members of churches, who tend to listen passively to their leaders. Sects also reject the intellectualized religion of churches, stressing instead the personal experience of divine power. Rodney Stark (1985:314) contrasts a church's vision of a distant God ("Our Father, who art in Heaven") with a sect's more immediate God ("Lord, bless this poor sinner kneeling before you now").

Churches and sects also have different patterns of leadership. The more churchlike an organization, the more likely that its leaders are formally trained and ordained. Sectlike organizations, which celebrate the personal presence of God, expect their leaders to show divine inspiration in the form of **charisma** (from Greek, meaning "divine favor"), *extraordinary personal qualities that can infuse people with emotion and turn them into followers.*

Sects generally form as breakaway groups from established religious organizations (Stark & Bainbridge, 1979). Their psychic intensity and informal structure make them less stable than churches, and many sects form, only to disappear soon after. The sects that do endure typically become more like churches, with declining emphasis on charismatic leadership as they become more bureaucratic.

To sustain their membership, many sects actively recruit, or *proselytize,* new members. Sects value highly the experience of *conversion,* or religious rebirth. For example, Jehovah's Witnesses go door to door to share their faith with others in the hope of attracting new members.

Finally, churches and sects differ in their social composition. Because they are more closely tied to the world, well-established churches tend to include people of high social standing. Sects attract more disadvantaged people. A sect's openness to new members and its promise of salvation and personal fulfillment appeal to people who feel they are social outsiders.

Cult

A **cult** is *a religious organization that is largely outside a society's cultural traditions.* Most sects spin off from a conventional religious organization. However, a cult typically forms around a highly charismatic leader who offers a compelling message of a new and very different way of life. Researchers have counted as many as 5,000 cults in the United States (Marquand & Wood, 1997).

Because some cult principles or practices are unconventional, many people view cults as deviant or even evil. The suicides of thirty-nine members of California's Heaven's Gate cult in 1997—people who claimed that dying was the doorway to a higher existence, perhaps in the company of aliens from outer space—confirmed the negative image the public holds of many cults. In short, calling a religious community a "cult" amounts to dismissing its members as crazy (Shupe, 1995; Gleick, 1997).

This charge is unfair because there is nothing basically wrong with this kind of religious organization. Many religions—Christianity, Islam, and Judaism included—began as cults. Of course, few cults exist for very long. One reason is that they are even more at odds with the larger society than sects. Many cults demand that members not only accept their teaching but also adopt a radically new lifestyle. This is why people sometimes accuse cults of brainwashing their members, although research suggests that most people who join cults suffer no psychological harm (Kilbourne, 1983; P. W. Williams, 2002).

Religion in History

 Understand

Like family, religion is a part of every known society. Also like family, religion shows marked variation over time and from place to place.

Early hunters and gatherers embraced **animism** (from the Latin, meaning "breath of life"), *the belief that elements of the*

---

church a religious organization that is well integrated into the larger society

sect a religious organization that stands apart from the larger society

cult a religious organization that is largely outside a society's cultural traditions

natural world are conscious life forms that affect humanity. Animists view forests, oceans, mountains, and the wind as spiritual forces. Many Native American societies are animistic, which explains their reverence for the natural environment.

Belief in a single divine power responsible for creating the world arose with pastoral and horticultural societies, which first appeared 10,000 to 12,000 years ago. The conception of God as a "shepherd" arose because Judaism, Christianity, and Islam all began among pastoral peoples.

Religion becomes more important in agrarian societies. The huge cathedrals that dominated the towns of medieval Europe—many of which remain standing today—are evidence of the central role of religion in the social life of medieval agrarian society.

The Industrial Revolution introduced the growing importance of science to everyday life. More and more, people looked to physicians and scientists for the knowledge and comfort they used to get from priests. But as Durkheim (1965, orig. 1915) predicted a century ago, religion persists in industrial societies because science is powerless to address issues of ultimate meaning in human life. In other words, *how* this world works is a matter for scientists, but *why* we and the rest of the universe exist at all is a question of faith. In addition, as we shall now see, the United States stands out as a modern society in which religion remains especially strong (McClay, 2007; Greeley, 2008).

Religion in the United States

 Analyze

Compared to almost every other high-income nation in the world, as Figure 13–4 suggests, the United States is a religious country (Inglehart & Welzel, 2010). But measuring the strength of religion in our society turns out to be difficult, as the following section explains.

Religious Affiliation

Not only do about seven in ten people in our society claim that religion is important in their lives, but about 81 percent of adults in

TABLE 13–1 Religious Identification in the United States, 2010

Religion	Share of Respondents Indicating a Preference
Protestant denominations	51.9%
Baptist	18.9
Methodist	6.1
Lutheran	4.4
Presbyterian	3.2
Episcopalian	1.9
All others or no denomination	17.4
Catholic	25.7
Jewish	2.0
Other or no answer	1.1
No religious preference	19.3

Source: *General Social Surveys, 1972–2010: Cumulative Codebook* (Chicago: National Opinion Research Center, March 2011).

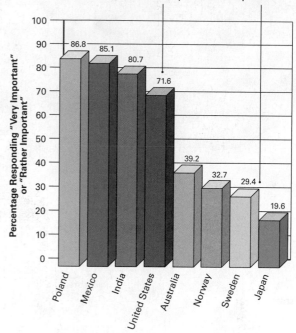

• In general, people in higher-income countries are less religious than those in lower-income nations. The U.S. population is an important exception to this pattern.

Survey Question: "How important is religion in your life?"

Global Snapshot

FIGURE 13–4 Religiosity in Global Perspective

Religion is stronger in the United States than in many other nations.

Source: World Values Survey (2010).

the United States identify with a specific religious tradition (NORC, 2011:256). Table 13–1 shows that more than half of U.S. adults consider themselves Protestants, one-fourth are Catholics, and 2 percent are Jews. Significant numbers of people also hold to dozens of other religions, from animism to Zen Buddhism, making our society not only religious but also religiously diverse (Eck, 2001). The remarkable religious diversity of the United States stems from a constitutional ban of government-sponsored religion and from our historically high numbers of immigrants from all over the world. National Map 13–1 on page 362 shows the share of people across the United States who claim to belong to a religious organization.

National Map 13–2 goes a step further, showing that the religion most people identify with varies by region. New England and the Southwest are predominantly Catholic, the South is overwhelmingly Baptist, and in the northern Plains states, Lutherans predominate. In and around Utah, there is a heavy concentration of members of the Church of Jesus Christ of Latter-Day Saints, whose followers are commonly known as Mormons.

Religiosity

Religiosity is *the importance of religion in a person's life.* However, exactly how religious we are depends on precisely how we operationalize this concept. For example, 90 percent of adults

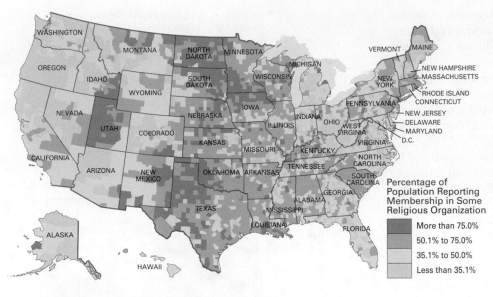

NATIONAL MAP 13–1 Religious Membership across the United States

In general, people in the United States are more religious than people in other high-income nations. Yet membership in a religious organization is more common in some parts of the country than in others. What pattern do you see in the map? Can you explain the pattern?

✳ Explore patterns of religious membership in your local community and in counties across the United States on **mysoclab.com**

Source: Glenmary Research Center (2002).

Percentage of Population Reporting Membership in Some Religious Organization

- More than 75.0%
- 50.1% to 75.0%
- 35.1% to 50.0%
- Less than 35.1%

Seeing Ourselves

NATIONAL MAP 13–2 Religious Diversity across the United States

In most counties, a large share of people who report having an affiliation are members of the same religious organization. So, although the United States is religiously diverse at the national level, most people live in local communities where one denomination predominates. What historical facts might account for this pattern?

Source: Glenmary Research Center (2002).

More than 50 Percent Reported Religious Affiliation

- Baptist
- Catholic
- Christian
- Latter-Day Saints
- Lutheran
- Methodist

in the United States claim to believe in a divine power, although just 58 percent claim that they "know that God exists and have no doubts about it" (NORC, 2011:601). Fifty-eight percent of adults say they pray at least once a day, but just 30 percent report attending religious services on a weekly or almost weekly basis (NORC, 2011:269, 260).

Clearly, the question "How religious are we?" has no easy answer, and it is likely that many people claim to be more religious than they really are. Overall, although most people in the United States claim to be at least somewhat religious, probably no more than one-third actually are. Religiosity also varies among denominations. Members of sects are the most religious of all, followed by Catholics and then "mainstream" Protestant denominations such as Episcopalians, Methodists, and Presbyterians. In general, older people are more religious than younger people. Finally, women are more religious than men: 49 percent of men and 63 percent of women say religion is very important in their lives (Sherkat & Ellison, 1999; Miller & Stark, 2002; Pew Forum, 2009).

What difference does being more religious make? Researchers have linked a number of social patterns to holding strong religious beliefs, including low rates of delinquency among young people and low rates of divorce among adults. More religious people are also more trusting of others, and they are more involved in organizations within their local communities. According to one study, religiosity helps unite children, parents, and local communities in ways that benefit young people, enhancing their educational achievement (Muller & Ellison, 2001; Jansen, 2011).

Religion: Class, Ethnicity, and Race

Religious affiliation is related to a number of other factors, including social class, ethnicity, and race.

Social Class

A study of *Who's Who in America,* which profiles U.S. high achievers, showed that 33 percent of the people who gave a religious affiliation were Episcopalians, Presbyterians, and United Church of

Christ members, denominations that together account for less than 10 percent of the population. Jews also enjoy high social position, with this 2 percent of the population accounting for 12 percent of listings in *Who's Who*.

Research shows that on average, members of other denominations, including Methodists and Catholics, have moderate social standing. Lower social standing is typical of Baptists, Lutherans, and members of sects. Of course, there is considerable variation within all denominations (Keister, 2003; Smith & Faris, 2005; Pyle, 2006).

Ethnicity

Throughout the world, religion is tied to ethnicity, largely because one religion stands out in a single nation or geographic region. Islam predominates in the Arab societies of the Middle East, Hinduism is fused with the culture of India, and Confucianism runs deep in Chinese society. Christianity and Judaism do not follow this pattern; although these religions are mostly Western, Christians and Jews are found all over the world.

Religion and national identity are joined to a certain extent in the United States as well. For example, we have Anglo-Saxon Protestants, Irish Catholics, Russian Jews, and people of Greek Orthodox heritage. This linking of nation and religious belief results from the arrival of immigrants from nations with a distinctive major religion. Still, nearly every ethnic category displays some religious diversity. For example, people of English ancestry may be Protestants, Roman Catholics, Jews, Hindus, Muslims, or followers of other religions.

Race

Scholars claim that the church is both the oldest and the most important social institution in the African American community. Transported to the Western Hemisphere in slave ships, most Africans became Christians, the dominant religion in the Americas, but they blended Christian beliefs with elements of African religions they brought with them. Guided by this religious mix, African American Christians have developed rituals that seem, by European standards, far more spontaneous and emotional (Frazier, 1965; Paris, 2000; McRoberts, 2003).

When African Americans migrated from the rural South to the industrial cities of the North starting around 1940, the church played a major role in addressing problems of dislocation, poverty, and prejudice (Pattillo-McCoy, 1998). Black churches have also provided an important avenue of achievement for talented men and women. Ralph Abernathy, Martin Luther King Jr., and Jesse Jackson have all achieved world recognition for their work as religious leaders.

Today, with 87 percent of African Americans claiming a religious affiliation, this category is somewhat more religious than the population as a whole. The vast majority favor a Protestant denomination. However, there is an increasing number of non-Christian African Americans, especially in large U.S. cities. Among them, the most common non-Christian religion is Islam, with about 400,000 African American followers (Paris, 2000; Pew Forum, 2009).

Religion in a Changing Society

 Analyze

Like family life, religion is also changing in the United States. In the following sections, we look at two major aspects of change: changing affiliations over time and the process of secularization.

Changing Affiliation

A lot of change is going on in the world of religion. In the United States, membership in established, mainstream churches such as the Episcopalian and Presbyterian denominations has fallen by almost 50 percent since 1960. During this time, other religious categories (including both the "New Age" spiritual movement and conservative fundamentalist organizations) have increased in popularity.

Many people are moving from one religious organization to another. A survey by the Pew Forum on Religion and Public Life (2008) reveals that 44 percent of U.S. adults report having switched religious affiliation at some point in their lives. The pattern of being born into and holding one religious affiliation for a lifetime is no longer the case for almost half of the U.S. population.

Such personal changes mean that religious organizations experience a pattern of people coming and going. For some time, for example, Catholics have represented almost one-fourth of the U.S. adult population. But this fairly stable statistic hides the fact that about one-third of all people raised Catholic have left the church. At the same time, about the same number of people—including many immigrants—have joined this church. A more extreme example is the Jehovah's Witnesses: Two-thirds of the people raised in this church have left, but their numbers have been more than replaced by converts recruited by members who travel from door to door spreading their message.

In the last fifty years, traditional "mainstream" religious organizations have lost about half their membership. But during this same period, fundamentalist and new spiritual movements have increased their membership. From another angle, almost half of U.S. adults change their religious affiliation over their lifetime.

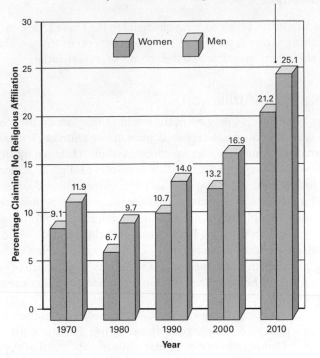

● Although the share has been increasing, only about one-quarter of women and men on U.S. campuses claim no religious affiliation.

Student Snapshot

FIGURE 13–5 Religious Nonaffiliation among First-Year College Students, 1970–2010

The share of students claiming no religious affiliation has risen in recent decades.

Sources: Astin et al. (2002) and Pryor et al. (2011).

This pattern of religious "churn" has created an active and competitive marketplace of religious organizations in the United States. Perhaps one result of this competition for members is that U.S. society remains among the most religious in the world. But it also reflects a loosening of people's ties to the religious organizations they are born into so that men and women now have more choice about their religious beliefs and affiliation.

Secularization

If people are less connected to the religious organization of their childhood, should we conclude that religion is getting weaker? Investigating this question brings us to the concept of **secularization**, *the historical decline in the importance of the supernatural and the sacred*. Secularization (from a Latin word for "worldly," meaning literally "of the present age") is commonly associated with modern, technologically advanced societies in which science is the major way of understanding.

Today, we are more likely to experience the transitions of birth, illness, and death in the presence of physicians (people with scientific knowledge) than church leaders (whose knowledge is based on faith). This shift alone suggests that religion's importance for our everyday lives has declined. Harvey Cox (1971:3) explains:

The world looks less and less to religious rules and rituals for its morality or its meanings. For some [people], religion provides a hobby, for others a mark of national or ethnic identification, for still others an aesthetic delight. For fewer and fewer does it provide an inclusive and commanding system of personal and cosmic values and explanations.

If Cox is right, should we expect religion to disappear someday? Some analysts point to survey data that indicate that the share of our population that claims no religious affiliation is increasing. As Figure 13–5 shows, the share of college students who say they have no religious preference has gone up, nearly tripling between 1980 and 2010. Other analysts point to the fact that large numbers of unaffiliated adults can be found not only in the Pacific Northwest (a longtime secular region) but also in the Northeast, where Christianity first took hold (Meacham, 2009).

But other sociologists are not so sure that religion is going away. They point out that the vast majority of people in the United States still say they believe in God, and nearly as many people claim to pray each day (58 percent) as vote in national elections (63 percent in 2008). In addition, religious affiliation today in this country is higher than it was in 1850. Finally, more people may be switching their religious affiliation from one religious organization to another, but their spiritual life continues all the same (McClay, 2007; Greeley, 2008; Van Biema, 2008; Pryor et al., 2011).

Everyone sees religious change, but people disagree about whether it is good or bad. Conservatives see any weakening of religion as a mark of moral decline. Progressives view secularization as liberation from the dictatorial beliefs of the past, giving people greater choice about what to believe. Secularization has also brought many traditional religious practices, such as ordaining only men, into line with modern social attitudes that support greater gender equality.

According to the secularization thesis, religion should weaken in high-income nations as people enjoy higher living standards and greater security. A global perspective shows that this thesis holds for the nations of Western Europe, where most measures of religiosity have declined and are now low. But the United States—the richest country of all—is an exception, a nation in which, for now at least, religion remains quite strong.

Civil Religion

One dimension of secularization is what Robert Bellah (1975) calls **civil religion**, *a quasi-religious loyalty binding individuals in a basically secular society.* In other words, formal religion may lose power, but citizenship has its own religious qualities. Most people in the United States consider our way of life a force for moral good in the world. Many people also find religious qualities in political movements, whether liberal or conservative (Williams & Demerath, 1991).

Civil religion involves a range of rituals, from standing to sing the national anthem at sporting events to waving the flag at public parades. At all such events, the U.S. flag serves as a sacred symbol of our national identity, and we expect people to treat it with respect.

"New Age" Seekers: Spirituality without Formal Religion

December 29, Machu Picchu, Peru. We are ending the first day exploring this magnificent city built by the Inca people at the top of *the Andes Mountains. Lucas, a local shaman, or religious leader, is leading twelve members of our tour group in a ceremony of thanks. He kneels on the dirt floor of the small stone building and reverently places offerings—corn and beans, sugar, plants of all colors, and even bits of gold and silver—in front of him as gifts to Mother Earth as he prays for harmony, joy, and the will to do good for one another. His heartfelt words and the magical setting make the ceremony a very powerful experience.*

In recent decades, an increasing number of people have sought spiritual development outside of established religious organizations. This trend has led some analysts to conclude that the United States is becoming a *postdenominational society*. In simple terms, more people seem to be spiritual seekers, believing in a vital spiritual dimension to human existence that they pursue more or less separately from any formal denomination.

What exactly is the difference between this so-called New Age focus on spirituality and a traditional concern with religion? As one analysis (Cimino & Lattin, 1999:62) puts it, spirituality is

In this outstanding example of U.S. folk art, Anna Bell Lee Washington's *Baptism 3* (1924) depicts the life-changing experience by which many people enter the Christian faith.

> the search for . . . a religion of the heart, not the head. It . . . downplays doctrine and dogma, and revels in direct experience of the divine—whether it's called the "holy spirit" or "divine consciousness" or "true self." It's practical and personal, more about stress reduction than salvation, more therapeutic than theological. It's about feeling good rather than being good. It's as much about the body as the soul.

Millions of people across the United States today take part in New Age spirituality. Hank Wesselman (2001:39–42), an anthropologist and spiritual teacher, identifies five core values that define this approach:

1. **Seekers believe in a higher power.** There exists a higher power, a vital force that is within all things and all people. Each of us, then, is partly divine, just as the divine spirit exists in the world around us.

2. **Seekers believe we are all connected.** Everything and everyone is interconnected as part of the universal divine force that seekers call "spirit."

3. **Seekers believe in a spirit world.** The physical world is not all there is; more important is the existence of a spiritual reality or "spirit world."

4. **Seekers want to experience the spirit world.** Spiritual development means gaining the ability to experience the spirit world. Many seekers come to understand that helpers and teachers (in some traditions, called "angels") dwell in the spirit world and can touch their lives.

5. **Seekers pursue transcendence.** Various techniques (such as yoga, meditation, and prayer) give people an increasing ability to rise above the immediate physical world (the experience of "transcendence"), which seekers believe to be the larger purpose of life.

From a traditional point of view, this New Age concern with spirituality may seem more like psychology than religion. Perhaps it would be fair to say that New Age spirituality combines elements of rationality (an emphasis on individualism as well as tolerance and pluralism) with a spiritual focus (searching for meaning beyond our everyday concerns). It is this combination that makes New Age seeking particularly popular in the modern world (Tucker, 2002; Besecke, 2003, 2005).

Religious Revival: "Good Old-Time Religion"

At the same time as New Age spirituality is flourishing, a great deal of change has been going on in the world of organized religion. As noted earlier, membership in established, mainstream churches has fallen in recent decades. Since then, not only has interest in New Age spirituality increased, but affiliation with other formal religious organizations, including the Mormons, Seventh-Day Adventists, and especially Christian sects, has risen dramatically.

These opposing trends suggest that secularization itself may be self-limiting: As churchlike organizations become more worldly, many people leave them in favor of sectlike communities offering a more intense religious experience (Roof & McKinney, 1987; Jacquet & Jones, 1991; Warner, 1993; Iannaccone, 1994; Hout, Greeley, & Wilde, 2001).

One striking religious trend today is the growth of **fundamentalism**, *a conservative religious doctrine that opposes intellectualism and worldly accommodation in favor of restoring traditional, otherworldly religion.* In the United States, fundamentalism has made the greatest gains among Protestants. Southern Baptists, for example, are the largest Protestant religious community in the United States.

Cihan: I think someday science will prove religion to be false.

Sophie: You better hope God doesn't prove *you* to be false.

Rasheed: Cool it, both of you. I don't think science and religion are talking about the same thing at all.

About 400 years ago, the Italian physicist and astronomer Galileo (1564–1642) helped launch the Scientific Revolution with a series of startling discoveries. Dropping objects from the Leaning Tower of Pisa, he discovered some of the laws of gravity; making his own telescope, he observed the solar system and found that Earth orbited the sun, not the other way around.

For his trouble, Galileo was challenged by the Roman Catholic Church, which had preached for centuries that Earth stood motionless at the center of the universe. Galileo only made matters worse by responding that religious leaders had no business talking about matters of science. Before long, he found his work banned and himself under house arrest.

As Galileo's treatment shows, right from the start, science has had an uneasy relationship with religion. In the nineteenth century, the two clashed again over the issue of creation. Charles Darwin's masterwork, *On the Origin of Species,* states that humanity evolved from lower forms of life over the course of a billion years—a theory that seems to fly in the face of the biblical account of creation found in Genesis, which states that "God created the heavens and the earth," introducing living things on the third day and, on the fifth and sixth days, animals, including human beings fashioned in God's own image.

Galileo would have been an eager observer of the famous "Scopes monkey trial." In 1925, the state of Tennessee put a small-town science teacher named John Thomas Scopes on trial for teaching Darwinian evolution in the local high school. State law forbade teaching "any theory that denies the story of the Divine Creation of man as

taught in the Bible" and especially the idea that "man descended from a lower order of animals." Scopes was found guilty and fined $100. His conviction was reversed on appeal, so the case never reached the U.S. Supreme Court, and the Tennessee law stayed on the books until 1967. A year later, the Supreme Court, in *Epperson* v. *Arkansas*, struck down all such laws as unconstitutional government support of religion.

Today—almost four centuries after Galileo was silenced—many people still debate the apparently conflicting claims of science and religion. One-third of U.S. adults claim to believe that the Bible is the literal word of God, and many of them reject any scientific findings that run counter to it (NORC, 2011:295). In 2005, all eight members of the school board in Dover, Pennsylvania, were voted out of office after they took a stand that many townspeople saw as weakening the teaching of evolution; at the same time, the Kansas state school board ordered the teaching of evolution to include its weaknesses and limitations from a religious point of view ("Much Ado about Evolution," 2005). And, in 2010, an Ohio middle school science teacher was dismissed from his job based on charges that he was teaching Christianity to his students (Boston, 2011).

But a middle ground is emerging: 43 percent of U.S. adults (and also many church leaders) say the Bible is a book of truths *inspired* by God without being accurate in a literal, scientific sense. In addition, a recent survey of U.S. scientists found that half of them claimed to

believe in God or some form of higher power. So it seems that many people are able to embrace science and religion at the same time. The reason that this is possible is that science and religion are two different ways of understanding that answer different questions. Both Galileo and Darwin devoted their lives to investigating *how* the natural world works. Yet only religion can address *why* we and the natural world exist in the first place.

This basic difference between science and religion helps explain why our nation is both the most scientific and the most religious in the world. As one scientist noted, the mathematical odds that a cosmic "big bang" 12 billion years ago created the universe and led to the formation of life as we know it are even smaller than the chance of winning a state lottery twenty weeks in a row. Doesn't such a scientific fact suggest an intelligent and purposeful power in our creation? Can't a person be a religious believer and at the same time a scientific investigator?

In 1992, a Vatican commission concluded that the church's silencing of Galileo was wrong. Today, most scientific and religious leaders agree that science and religion represent important but different truths. Many also believe that in today's rush to scientific discovery, our world has never been more in need of the spiritual awareness and moral guidance provided by religion.

What Do You Think?

1. Why do you think some scientific people reject religious accounts of human creation? Why do some religious people reject scientific accounts?

2. Does the sociological study of religion challenge anyone's faith? Why or why not?

3. About half of U.S. adults think science is changing our way of life too fast. Do you agree? Why or why not?

Sources: Gould (1981), Huchingson (1994), Applebome (1996), and Greely (2008).

But fundamentalist groups have also grown among Roman Catholics, Jews, and Muslims.

In response to what they see as the growing influence of science and the weakening of the conventional family, religious fundamentalists defend what they call "traditional values." As they see it, liberal churches are simply too open to compromise and change. Religious fundamentalism is distinctive in five ways (Hunter, 1983, 1985, 1987):

1. **Fundamentalists take the words of sacred texts literally.** Fundamentalists insist on a literal reading of sacred texts such as the Bible to counter what they see as excessive intellectualism among more liberal religious organizations. For example, fundamentalist Christians believe that God created the world in seven days precisely as described in the biblical book of Genesis.

2. **Fundamentalists reject religious pluralism.** Fundamentalists believe that tolerance and relativism water down personal faith. Therefore, they maintain that their religious beliefs are true and other beliefs are not.

3. **Fundamentalists pursue the personal experience of God's presence.** In contrast to the worldliness and intellectualism of other religious organizations, fundamentalists encourage a return to "good old-time religion" and spiritual revival. Among fundamentalist Christians, being "born again" and having a personal relationship with Jesus Christ should be evident in a person's everyday life.

4. **Fundamentalists oppose "secular humanism."** Fundamentalists think accommodation to the changing world weakens religious faith. They reject "secular humanism," our society's tendency to look to scientific experts rather than God for guidance about how to live. There is nothing new in this tension between science and religion, as the Controversy & Debate box explains.

5. **Many fundamentalists endorse conservative political goals.** Although fundamentalism tends to back away from worldly concerns, some fundamentalist leaders (including the Christian fundamentalists Pat Robertson and Gary Bauer) have entered politics to oppose the "liberal agenda," which includes feminism and gay rights. Fundamentalists oppose abortion and same-sex marriage; they support the traditional two-parent family, seek a return of prayer in schools, and criticize the mass media for approaching stories from a liberal viewpoint (Manza & Brooks, 1997; Thomma, 1997; Rozell, Wilcox, & Green, 1998).

Opponents regard fundamentalism as judgmental, rigid, and self-righteous. But many believers find in fundamentalism, with its greater religious certainty and emphasis on experiencing God's presence, an appealing alternative to the more intellectual, tolerant, and worldly "mainstream" denominations (Marquand, 1997).

Which religious organizations are fundamentalist? In recent years, the world has become aware of an extreme form of fundamentalist Islam that supports violence directed against Western culture. In the United States, the term is most commonly applied to conservative Christian organizations in the evangelical tradition, including Pentecostals, Southern Baptists, Seventh-Day Adventists, and the Assemblies of God. Several national religious movements, including Promise Keepers (a men's organization) and Chosen Women, have a fundamentalist orientation. In national surveys, 26 percent of U.S. adults describe their religious upbringing as "fundamentalist," 39 percent claim a "moderate" religious upbringing, and 31 percent cite a "liberal" background (NORC, 2011:259).

In contrast to local congregations of years past, some religious organizations, especially fundamentalist ones, have become *electronic churches* dominated by "prime-time preachers" (Hadden & Swain, 1981). Electronic religion is found only in the United States. It has made James Dobson, Joel Osteen, Billy and Franklin Graham, Robert Schuller, and other "televangelists" more famous than all but a few clergy in the past. Perhaps 5 percent of the national television audience (about 10 million people) are regular viewers of religious television, and 20 percent (about 40 million) watch some religious programming every week (NORC, 2011:600).

Religion: Looking Ahead

 Evaluate

The popularity of media ministries, the growth of religious fundamentalism, new forms of spirituality, and the connection of millions of people to mainstream churches show that religion will remain a major part of modern society for decades to come. High levels of immigration from Latin America and elsewhere should intensify as well as diversify the religious character of U.S. society in the twenty-first century (Yang & Ebaugh, 2001).

The world is becoming more complex, and social change seems to move at a faster pace than our capacity to make sense of it all. But rather than weakening religion, this process fires the religious imagination. As new technology gives us the power to alter, sustain, and even create life, we face increasingly difficult moral questions. Against this backdrop of uncertainty, it is little wonder that many people look to their faith for inspiration, guidance, and hope.

How do the mass media portray the family?

Many are familiar with the traditional families portrayed in popular 1950s television shows such as *Ozzie Harriet* and *Leave It to Beaver*. Both of these shows had a working father, homemaker mother, and two (wonderful) sons. But, as the images below suggest, today's television shows are not as family-centered.

Hint The general pattern found in the mass media today is certainly different from that common in the 1950s, the so-called "golden age of families." Today's television shows emphasize that careers often leave little time for family (*House*) or that, for a variety of reasons, stable marriages are the exception rather than the rule (all the shows illustrated here). Does Hollywood have an anti-family bias? This is hard to answer; perhaps script writers find that nonconventional family forms make for more interesting stories. In any case, most television shows make clear that people of all ages (well, maybe not Gregory House) are capable of finding and maintaining satisfying relationships, whether or not those relationships conform to a traditional family form.

One of the most popular television shows in recent years has been *House*, which revolves around a brainy but belligerent physician and his colleagues at an upscale New Jersey hospital. None of the main characters in the show is married; none has children; none gets along well with parents. Why might this be the case?

Courtney Cox plays on the beach with her TV son Dan Byrd as they take a break from the shooting of the show *Cougar Town*. What family patterns appear on this television program?

Another popular television show is *It's Always Sunny in Philadelphia*, in which a group of friends functions in many ways like a family. What can you say about the way this show presents family life?

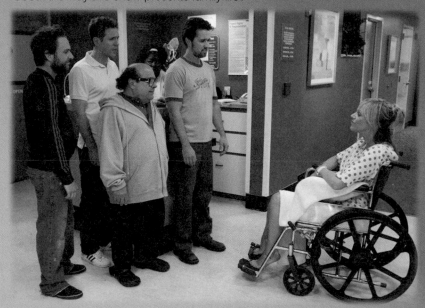

Seeing Sociology in *Your* Everyday Life

1. After reading through the photo essay, list your own favorite television shows and, in each case, evaluate the importance of family life in the show. Is family life included in the show? If so, what family forms are presented? Are families a source of happiness to people or not?

2. Make a list of events, activities, and pastimes that might be considered examples of civil religion. (Start off with Election Day; what about baseball?) Are there any local college events or rituals that might be included? In each case, explain the religious element that you see and the way the event or activity affects members of a family or a community.

3. This chapter explains that family life in today's society is more and more about making choices. What are the underlying reasons that family life is more varied today than it was, say, a century ago? For suggestions about how you can make better choices about relationships and family life in today's world, go to the "Seeing Sociology in *Your* Everyday Life" feature on MySocLab and read more about how what you have learned in this chapter can benefit you. A second feature for this chapter focuses on religion and helps to explain the difference between holding personal religious beliefs and studying religion sociologically.

Families: Basic Concepts

All societies are built on *kinship*. The **family** varies across cultures and over time:

- In high-income nations such as the United States, *marriage* is monogamous.
- Many lower-income nations permit *polygamy*, of which there are two types: *polygyny* and *polyandry*.
- In global perspective, *patrilocality* is most common, but industrial societies favor *neolocality*, and a few societies have *matrilocal residence*.
- Industrial societies use *bilateral descent*; preindustrial societies are either *patrilineal* or *matrilineal*.   **pp. 340–42**

family (p. 340) a social institution found in all societies that unites people in cooperative groups to care for one another, including any children

kinship (p. 340) a social bond based on common ancestry, marriage, or adoption

marriage (p. 340) a legal relationship, usually involving economic cooperation, sexual activity, and childbearing

extended family (p. 341) a family composed of parents and children as well as other kin; also known as a *consanguine family*

nuclear family (p. 341) a family composed of one or two parents and their children; also known as a *conjugal family*

endogamy (p. 341) marriage between people of the same social category

exogamy (p. 341) marriage between people of different social categories

monogamy (p. 341) marriage that unites two partners

polygamy (p. 341) marriage that unites a person with two or more spouses

descent (p. 342) the system by which members of a society trace kinship over generations

Theories of the Family

Structural-functional theory identifies major family functions that help society operate smoothly: socialization of the young, regulation of sexual activity, social placement, and providing material and emotional support.   **pp. 343–44**

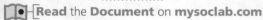 Read the **Document** on **mysoclab.com**

Social-conflict theory and **feminist theory** explore how the family perpetuates social inequality by transmitting divisions based on class, ethnicity, race, and gender.   **p. 344**

Symbolic-interaction theory and **social-exchange theory** highlight the variety of family life as experienced by various family members.   **pp. 344–45**

incest taboo (p. 343) a norm forbidding sexual relations or marriage between certain relatives

Stages of Family Life

Courtship and Romantic Love

- Courtship based on romantic love is central to mate selection in the United States.
- Arranged marriages are common in preindustrial societies.   **pp. 345–46**

Child Rearing

- Family size has decreased over time as industrialization increases the costs of raising children.
- Fewer children are born as more women go to school and join the labor force.   **pp. 346–47**

The Family in Later Life

- Many middle-aged couples care for aging parents, and many older couples are active grandparents.
- The final transition in marriage begins with the death of a spouse.   **p. 347**

homogamy (p. 346) marriage between people with the same social characteristics

U.S. Families: Class, Race, and Gender

- **Social class** s a powerful force that shapes family life. Children born into rich families typically have better mental and physical health and go on to achieve more in life than children born into poor families.   **pp. 347–48**
- **Ethnicity and race** can affect a person's experience of family life, although no single generalization fits all families within a particular category.   **pp. 348–50**
- **Gender** affects family dynamics because husbands dominate in most marriages.   **p. 350**

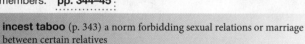 Watch the **Video** on **mysoclab.com**

Transitions and Problems in Family Life

- Nearly four in ten of today's marriages will end in **divorce**. Remarriage creates blended families that include children from previous marriages.   **pp. 350–52**
- **Family violence** is a widespread problem. Most adults who abuse family members were themselves abused as children.   **p. 352**

family violence (p. 352) emotional, physical, or sexual abuse of one family member by another

Alternative Family Forms

Family life is becoming more varied:

- One-parent families, cohabitation, gay and lesbian couples, and singlehood have become more common in recent years.
- Although only eight states and the District of Columbia have lawful same-sex marriage, many gay men and lesbians form long-lasting relationships and, increasingly, are becoming parents.   **p. 353**

New Reproductive Technologies

- Although ethically controversial, new reproductive technologies are changing conventional ideas of parenthood.   **p. 354**

cohabitation (p. 353) the sharing of a household by an unmarried couple

Religion: Basic Concepts

- **Religion** is a major social institution based on setting the *sacred* apart from the *profane*.
- Religion is grounded in *faith* rather than scientific evidence, and people express their religious beliefs through various rituals.   **p. 356**

profane (p. 356) included as an ordinary element of everyday life

sacred (p. 356) set apart as extraordinary, inspiring awe and reverence

religion (p. 356) a social institution involving beliefs and practices based on recognizing the sacred

ritual (p. 356) formal, ceremonial behavior

faith (p. 356) belief based on conviction rather than on scientific evidence

Theories of Religion

- **Structural-functional theory** suggests that religion unites people, promotes social cohesion, and gives meaning and purpose to life; through religion, we celebrate the power of our society (Emile Durkheim).   **pp. 356–57**
- **Symbolic-interaction theory** explains that we socially construct religious beliefs; we are especially likely to seek religious meaning when faced with life's uncertainties and disruptions (Peter Berger).   **p. 357**
- **Social-conflict theory** claims that religion justifies the status quo. In this way, religion supports inequality and discourages change toward a more just and equal society (Karl Marx).   **pp. 357–58**
- **Feminist theory** highlights the fact that major religions have traditionally been patriarchal, supporting the domination of women by men.   **p. 358**

totem (p. 356) an object in the natural world collectively defined as sacred

Religion and Social Change

- Max Weber argued, in opposition to Marx, that religion can encourage social change. He showed how Calvinist beliefs promoted the rise of industrial capitalism.
- **Liberation theology**, a fusion of Christian principles and political activism, tries to encourage social change.   **pp. 358–59**

liberation theology (p. 359) the combining of Christian principles with political activism, often Marxist in character

church (p. 359) a religious organization that is well integrated into the larger society

state church (p. 359) a church formally linked to the state

denomination (p. 359) a church, independent of the state, that recognizes religious pluralism

sect (p. 359) a religious organization that stands apart from the larger society

charisma (p. 360) extraordinary personal qualities that can infuse people with emotion and turn them into followers

cult (p. 360) a religious organization that is largely outside a society's cultural traditions

animism (p. 360) the belief that elements of the natural world are conscious life forms that affect humanity

Types of Religious Organizations

- **Churches** are religious organizations well integrated into their society. Churches fall into two categories: **state churches** and **denominations**.   **p. 359**
- **Sects** are the result of religious division and are marked by charismatic leadership and members' suspicion of the larger society.   **pp. 359–60**
- **Cults** are religious organizations based on new and unconventional beliefs and practices.   **p. 360**

Religion in the United States

The United States is one of the most religious and religiously diverse nations. How researchers operationalize "religiosity" affects how "religious" our people seem to be:

- 81% of adults identify with a religion
- 60% claim to belong to a religious organization
- 58% profess a firm belief in God
- 58% of adults say they pray at least once a day
- just 30% say they attend religious services weekly or almost weekly   **pp. 361–62**

✳️ Explore the **Map** on **mysoclab.com**

Religious affiliation is tied to social class, ethnicity, and race.

- On average, Episcopalians, Presbyterians, and Jews enjoy high standing; lower social standing is typical of Baptists, Lutherans, and members of sects.
- Religion is often linked to ethnic background because people came to the United States from countries that have a major religion (e.g., most Irish Americans are Catholic).
- Transported to this country in slave ships, most Africans became Christians, but they blended Christian beliefs with elements of African religions they brought with them.   **pp. 362–63**

religiosity (p. 361) the importance of religion in a person's life

Religion in a Changing Society

- In the United States, while some indicators of religiosity (like membership in mainstream churches) have declined, others (such as membership in sects) have increased. Almost half of U.S. adults have changed religious affiliation at some point in their lives.   **pp. 363–64**
- **Secularization** is a decline in the importance of the supernatural and sacred.
- Today, **civil religion** takes the form of a quasi-religious patriotism that ties people to their society.
- *Spiritual seekers* are part of the New Age movement, which pursues spiritual development outside conventional religious organizations.
- **Fundamentalism** opposes religious accommodation to the world, interprets religious texts literally, and rejects religious diversity.   **pp. 365–67**

secularization (p. 364) the historical decline in the importance of the supernatural and the sacred

civil religion (p. 364) a quasi-religious loyalty linking individuals in a basically secular society

fundamentalism (p. 365) a conservative religious doctrine that opposes intellectualism and worldly accommodation in favor of restoring traditional, otherworldly religion

14 Education, Health, and Medicine

Learning Objectives

Remember the definitions of the key terms highlighted in boldfaced type throughout this chapter.

Understand why health is not just a matter of biology but a social issue.

Apply sociology's major theoretical approaches to education and health.

Analyze how and why schooling and health vary around the world.

Evaluate how race, class, and gender affect both schooling and health.

Create a vision of how more schooling and better health might become available to a larger share of our society.

This chapter explains the operation of education and health care, which are two major social institutions that emerge in modern societies. The discussions of both education and health include a global perspective and a focus on the United States. ◼

When Lisa Addison was growing up in Baltimore, she always smiled when her teachers said she was smart and encouraged her to go to college. "I liked hearing that," she recalls. "But I didn't know what to do about it. No one in my family had ever gone to college. I didn't know which courses to take in high school. I had no idea of how to apply to a college. How would I pay for it? What would college be like if I got there?"

Uncertain about her future, Addison found herself "kind of goofing off in school." After finishing high school, she spent the next fifteen years working as a waitress in a restaurant and then as a kitchen helper in a catering company. Now, at the age of thirty-eight, Addison has decided to go back to school. "I don't want to do this kind of work for the rest of my life. I am smart. I can do better. At this point, I am ready for college."

Addison took a giant step through the door of the Community College of Baltimore County and, with the help of counselors, set her sights on an associate's degree in business. When she finishes this two-year program, she plans to transfer to a four-year university to complete a bachelor's degree. Then she hopes to go back into the food service industry—but this time as a manager at higher pay (Toppo & DeBarros, 2005).

Education is a social institution that has particular importance to people looking to advance their careers. This chapter explains *why* schooling is more important than ever for success in the United States today and also describes *who* benefits most from schooling. The second half of the chapter examines health and the social institution of *medicine*. Good health, like good schooling, is distributed unequally throughout our society's population. In addition, patterns involving both schooling and education reveal striking differences from society to society.

Education: A Global Survey

 Analyze

Education is *the social institution through which society provides its members with important knowledge, including basic facts, job skills, and cultural norms and values.* Education takes many forms, from informal family discussions around the dinner table to lectures and labs at large universities. In high-income nations, education depends largely on **schooling,** *formal instruction under the direction of specially trained teachers.*

Schooling and Economic Development

The extent of schooling in any society is tied to its level of economic development. In low- and middle-income countries, which are home to most of the world's people, families and local communities teach young people important knowledge and skills. Formal schooling, especially learning that is not directly connected to survival, is available mainly to wealthy people who can afford to pursue personal enrichment. The word *school* is from a Greek root that means "leisure." In ancient Greece, famous teachers such as Plato, Socrates, and Aristotle taught aristocratic, upper-class men who had plenty of spare time. The same was true in ancient China, where the famous philosopher K'ung Fu-tzu (Confucius) shared his wisdom with just a privileged few.

December 30, the Cuzco region, Peru. High in the Andes Mountains of Peru, families send their children to the local school. But "local" can mean 3 miles away or more, and there are no buses, so these children, almost all from poor families, walk an hour or more each way. Schooling is required by law, but in the rural highlands, some parents prefer to keep their children at home where they can help with the farming and livestock.

Today, schooling in low-income countries reflects the national culture. In Iran, for example, schooling is closely tied to Islam. Similarly, schooling in Bangladesh (Asia), Zimbabwe (Africa), and Nicaragua (Latin America) has been shaped by the distinctive cultural traditions of these nations.

All low-income countries have one trait in common when it comes to schooling: There is not much of it. In the poorest nations (including several in Central Africa), more than one-fourth of all children never get to school (World Bank, 2012); worldwide, one-third of all children never make it as far as the secondary grades. As a result, about one-sixth of the world's people cannot read or write. Global Map 14–1 on page 376 shows the extent of illiteracy around the world, and the national comparisons in the text illustrate the link between schooling and economic development.

Schooling in India

India has recently become a middle-income country, but people there still earn only about 7 percent of U.S. average income, and most poor families depend on the earnings of children. Even though India has outlawed child labor, many children continue to work in factories—weaving rugs or making handicrafts—up to sixty hours per week, which greatly limits their opportunities for schooling.

Today, 92 percent of children in India complete primary school, typically in crowded schoolrooms where one teacher may face forty or more children. In comparison, U.S. public school-teachers have an average of thirty students in a class. Sixty percent of students in India go on to secondary school, but very few enter college. As a result, 34 percent of India's people are unable to read and write (UNESCO, 2011; World Bank, 2012).

Patriarchy also shapes Indian education. Indian parents are joyful at the birth of a boy because he and his future wife will both contribute income to the family. But there are economic costs to raising a girl: Parents must provide a dowry (a gift of wealth to the groom's family), and after her marriage, a daughter's work benefits her husband's family. Therefore, many Indians see less reason to invest in the schooling of girls, which is why only 56 percent of girls (compared with 64

percent of boys) reach the secondary grades. So what do girls do if they are not in school? Most of the children working in Indian factories are girls—a family's way of benefiting from their daughters while they can (World Bank, 2012).

Schooling in Japan

Schooling has not always been part of the Japanese way of life. Before industrialization brought mandatory education in 1872, only a privileged few attended school. Today, Japan's educational system is widely praised for training some of the world's highest achievers.

The early grades concentrate on transmitting Japanese traditions, especially a sense of obligation to family. Starting in their early teens, students take a series of rigorous and highly competitive examinations. These written tests, which are like the Scholastic Assessment Test (SATs) in the United States, decide the future of all Japanese students.

More men and women graduate from high school in Japan (95 percent) than in the United States (87 percent). But competitive examinations allow for just 49 percent of high school graduates to enter college—compared to 70 percent in the United States. Understandably, Japanese students take entrance examinations very seriously, and about half attend special "cram schools" to prepare for them.

Japanese schooling produces impressive results. In a number of fields, notably mathematics and science, young Japanese students (who place fourth in the world in mathematics) outperform students in most other high-income nations, including the United States (which is ranked twenty-sixth).

Schooling in the United States

The United States was among the first countries to set a goal of mass education. By 1850, about half the young people between the ages of five and nineteen were enrolled in school. By 1918, all states had passed *mandatory education laws* requiring children to attend school until the age of sixteen or completion of the eighth grade. Table 14–1 on page 377 shows that this country reached a milestone in the mid-1960s, when for the first time a majority of U.S. adults had high school diplomas. In 2010, 87.1 percent of adults had high school educations, and 29.9 percent had a four-year college degree (U.S. Census Bureau, 2011).

The U.S. educational system is shaped by both our high standard of living (which means that most young people do not have to work) and our democratic principles (the idea that schooling should be provided to everyone). Thomas Jefferson thought the new nation could become democratic only if people learned to read. Today, the United States has an outstanding record of higher education for its people: Only one country—Norway—has a higher share of all adults who have earned a university degree (OECD, 2011).

In many low-income nations, children are as likely to work as to attend school, and girls receive less schooling than boys. But the doors to schooling are now opening to more girls and women. These young women are studying nursing at Somalia University in downtown Mogadishu.

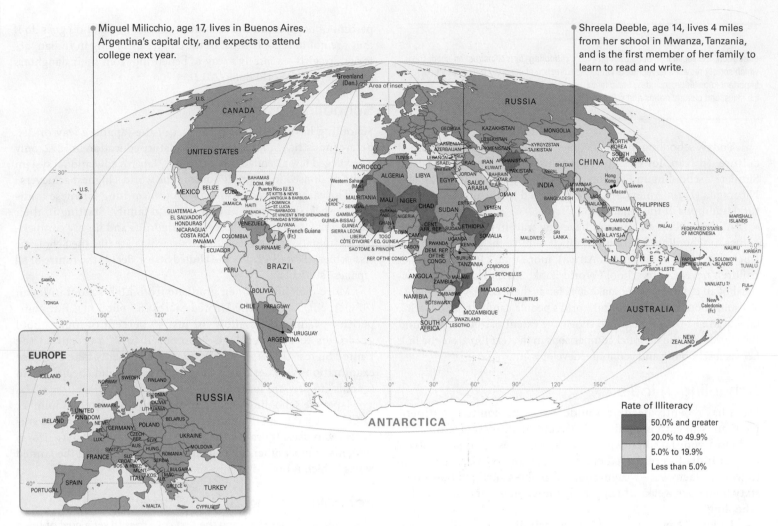

Miguel Milicchio, age 17, lives in Buenos Aires, Argentina's capital city, and expects to attend college next year.

Shreela Deeble, age 14, lives 4 miles from her school in Mwanza, Tanzania, and is the first member of her family to learn to read and write.

Rate of Illiteracy

- 50.0% and greater
- 20.0% to 49.9%
- 5.0% to 19.9%
- Less than 5.0%

Window on the World

GLOBAL MAP 14–1 Illiteracy in Global Perspective

Reading and writing skills are widespread in high-income countries, where illiteracy rates generally are below 5 percent. In much of Latin America, however, illiteracy is more common, one consequence of limited economic development. In thirteen nations—most of them in Africa—illiteracy is the rule rather than the exception; there, people rely on the oral tradition of face-to-face communication rather than the written word.

Source: United Nations Development Programme (2011).

Schooling in the United States also tries to promote *equal opportunity*. National surveys show that most people think schooling is crucial to personal success, and a majority believe that everyone has the chance to get an education consistent with personal ability and talent (NORC, 2011:237, 2244). However, this opinion expresses cultural ideals rather than reality. A century ago, for example, women were all but excluded from higher education; even today, most people who attend college come from families with above-average incomes.

In the United States, the educational system stresses the value of *practical* learning, knowledge that prepares people for their future jobs. This is in line with what the educational philosopher John Dewey (1859–1952) called *progressive education*, having the schools make learning relevant to people's lives. Students seek out subjects of study that they believe will give them an advantage when they are ready to compete in the job market. For example, as concerns about

international terrorism have risen in recent years, so have the numbers of students choosing to study geography, international conflict, and Middle Eastern history and culture (M. Lord, 2001).

The Functions of Schooling

 Apply

Structural-functional analysis focuses on ways in which schooling supports the operation and stability of society:

1. **Socialization.** Technologically simple societies look to families to transmit a way of life from one generation to the next. As societies gain complex technology, they turn to trained teachers to pass on specialized knowledge that adults will need for their future jobs.

TABLE 14–1 Educational Achievement in the United States, 1910–2010

Year	High School Graduates	College Graduates	Median Years of Schooling
1910	13.5%	2.7%	8.1
1920	16.4	3.3	8.2
1930	19.1	3.9	8.4
1940	24.1	4.6	8.6
1950	33.4	6.0	9.3
1960	41.1	7.7	10.5
1970	55.2	11.0	12.2
1980	68.7	17.0	12.5
1990	77.6	21.3	12.4
2000	84.1	25.6	12.7
2010	87.1	29.9	13.0*

Notes: Figures are for people 25 years of age and over. Percentage of high school graduates includes those who go on to college. Percentage of high school dropouts can be calculated by subtracting the percentage of high school graduates from 100 percent.
*Author's estimate.
Source: U.S. Census Bureau (2011).

Graduation from college is an important event in the lives of an ever-increasing number of people in the United States. Look over the discussion of the functions of schooling. How many of these functions do you think people in college are aware of? Can you think of other social consequences of going to college?

2. **Cultural innovation.** Faculty at colleges and universities invent culture as well as pass it along to students. Especially at centers of higher education, scholars conduct research that leads to discoveries and changes our way of life.

3. **Social integration.** Schools mold a diverse population into one society sharing norms and values. This is one reason that states enacted mandatory education laws a century ago when immigration became very high. In light of the ethnic diversity of many urban areas today, schooling continues to serve this purpose.

4. **Social placement.** Schools identify talent and match instruction to ability. Schooling increases meritocracy by rewarding talent and hard work regardless of social background and provides a path to upward social mobility.

5. **Latent functions.** Schooling serves several less widely recognized functions. It provides child care for the growing number of parents who work outside the home. In addition, it occupies thousands of young people in their twenties who would otherwise be competing for limited opportunities in the job market. High schools, colleges, and universities also bring together people of marriageable age. Finally, school networks can be a valuable career resource throughout life.

 Evaluate Structural-functional theory stresses ways in which formal education supports the operation of a modern society. However, this approach overlooks the fact that the classroom behavior of teachers and students can vary from one setting to another, a focus of symbolic-interaction theory, which is discussed next. In addition, structural-functional theory says little about many problems of our educational system and how schooling helps reproduce the class structure in each generation, which is the focus of social-conflict theory.

CHECK YOUR LEARNING Identify five functions of schooling for the operation of society.

Schooling and Social Interaction

● **Apply**

The basic idea of the symbolic-interaction approach is that people create the reality they experience in their day-to-day interactions. We use this approach to explain how stereotypes can shape what goes on in the classroom.

The Self-Fulfilling Prophecy

Chapter 4 ("Social Interaction in Everyday Life") presented the Thomas theorem, which states that situations people define as real become real in their consequences. Put another way, people who expect others to act in certain ways often encourage that very behavior. In doing so, people set up a *self-fulfilling prophecy.*

Jane Elliott, an elementary school teacher in the all-white community of Riceville, Iowa, carried out a simple experiment that showed how a self-fulfilling prophecy can take place in the classroom. In 1968, Elliott was teaching a fourth-grade class when Martin Luther King Jr. was murdered. Her students were puzzled and asked why a national hero had been brutally shot. Elliott responded by asking her white students what they thought about people of color and was stunned to learn that they held many powerful negative stereotypes.

To show the class the harmful effects of such stereotypes, Elliott performed a classroom experiment. She found that almost all of the children in her class had either blue eyes or brown eyes. She told the class that children with brown eyes were smarter and worked harder than children with blue eyes. To be sure everyone could easily tell which category a child fell into, a piece of brown or blue cloth was pinned to each student's collar.

Elliott recalls the effect of this "lesson" on the way students behaved: "It was just horrifying how quickly they became what I told them they were." Within half an hour, Elliott continued, a blue-eyed girl named Carol had changed from a "brilliant, carefree,

How good are you as a student? The answer is that you are as good as you and your teachers think you are. The television show *Glee* demonstrates how the help of an inspiring teacher encourages students toward greater self-confidence and higher achievement.

excited little girl to a frightened, timid, uncertain, almost-person." Not surprisingly, in the hours that followed, the brown-eyed students came to life, speaking up more and performing better than they had before. The prophecy had been fulfilled: Because the brown-eyed children thought they were superior, they became superior in their classroom performance; they also became "arrogant, ugly, and domineering" toward the blue-eyed children. For their part, the blue-eyed children began underperforming, becoming the inferior people they believed themselves to be.

At the end of the day, Elliott explained to the students what they had experienced. She applied the lesson to race, pointing out that if white children thought they were superior to black children, they would expect to do better in school, just as many children of color who live in the shadow of the same stereotypes would underperform in school. The children also realized that the society that teaches these stereotypes, as well as the hate that often accompanies them, encourages the kind of violence that ended the life of Martin Luther King Jr. (Kral, 2000).

Evaluate The symbolic-interaction approach explains how we all build reality in our everyday interactions with others. When school officials define some students as "gifted," for example, we can expect teachers to treat them differently and expect the students themselves to behave differently as a result of having been labeled in this way. If students and teachers come to believe that one race is academically superior to another, the behavior that follows may be a self-fulfilling prophecy.

One limitation of this approach is that people do not just make up such beliefs about superiority and inferiority. Rather, these beliefs are built into a society's system of social inequality, which brings us to social-conflict theory.

CHECK YOUR LEARNING How can the labels that schools place on some students affect the students' actual performance and the reactions of others?

Schooling and Social Inequality

Apply

Social-conflict analysis challenges the structural-functional idea that schooling develops everyone's talents and abilities. Instead, this approach emphasizes three ways in which schooling causes and perpetuates social inequality:

1. **Social control.** As Samuel Bowles and Herbert Gintis (1976) see it, the demand for public education in the late nineteenth century was based on capitalist factory owners' need for an obedient and disciplined workforce. Once in school, immigrants learned not only the English language but also the importance of following orders.

2. **Standardized testing.** Critics claim that the assessment tests widely used by schools reflect our society's dominant culture, placing minority students at a disadvantage. By defining majority students as smarter, standardized tests unfairly transform privilege into personal merit (Crouse & Trusheim, 1988; Putka, 1990).

3. **Tracking.** Despite controversy over standardized tests, most U.S. schools use them for **tracking**, *assigning students to different types of educational programs*, such as college preparatory classes, general education, and vocational and technical training. Tracking supposedly helps teachers meet each student's individual abilities and interests. However, the education critic Jonathan Kozol (1992) considers tracking one of the "savage inequalities" in our school system. Most students from privileged backgrounds get into higher tracks, where they receive the best the school can offer. Students from disadvantaged backgrounds end up in lower tracks, where teachers stress memorization and put little focus on creativity (Bowles & Gintis, 1976; Oakes, 1985; Kilgore, 1991; Gamoran, 1992).

Public and Private Education

Across the United States, about 89 percent of 62.4 million primary and secondary school children attend state-funded public schools. The rest go to private schools.

Most private school students attend one of the more than 7,100 *parochial* (of the parish) *schools* operated by the Roman Catholic Church. The Catholic school system grew rapidly a century ago as cities swelled with immigrants. Today, after decades of flight from the inner city by white people, many parochial schools enroll non-Catholics, including a growing number of African Americans whose families seek an alternative to the neighborhood public school.

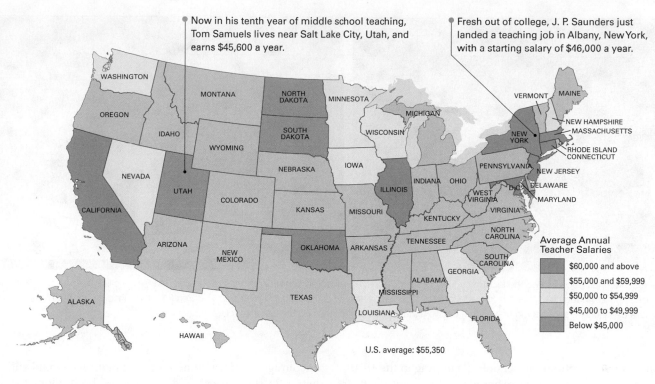

Now in his tenth year of middle school teaching, Tom Samuels lives near Salt Lake City, Utah, and earns $45,600 a year.

Fresh out of college, J. P. Saunders just landed a teaching job in Albany, New York, with a starting salary of $46,000 a year.

Average Annual Teacher Salaries

- $60,000 and above
- $55,000 and $59,999
- $50,000 to $54,999
- $45,000 to $49,999
- Below $45,000

U.S. average: $55,350

Seeing Ourselves

NATIONAL MAP 14–1 Teachers' Salaries across the United States

In 2010, the average public school teacher in the United States earned $55,350. The map shows the average teacher salary for all the states; they range from a low of $35,136 in South Dakota to a high of $71,470 in New York. Looking at the map, what pattern do you see? What do high-salary (and low-salary) states have in common?

Explore the percentage of people without a high school education in your local community and in counties across the United States on **mysoclab.com**

Source: U.S. Department of Education (2011).

Protestants also have private schools, often known as Christian academies. These schools are favored by parents who want religious instruction for their children, as well as parents of all backgrounds who seek higher academic and disciplinary standards.

There are also about 6,900 nonreligious private schools that enroll mostly young people from well-to-do families. These are typically prestigious and expensive preparatory ("prep") schools, modeled on British boarding schools, that not only provide strong academic programs but also teach the way of life of the upper class. Many "preppies" maintain lifelong school-based networks of personal contacts that provide numerous social advantages.

Are private schools better than public schools? Research shows that holding social background constant, students in private schools do outperform those in public schools. The advantages of private schools include smaller classes, more demanding course-work, and greater discipline (Coleman & Hoffer, 1987; Peterson & Llaudet, 2006).

this means that children in more affluent areas receive a better education than children in low-income communities. National Map 14–1 shows one key dimension of difference: Average teacher salaries vary by as much as $36,000 in state-by-state comparisons.

At the local level, differences in school funding can be dramatic. Arlington County, Virginia, one of the richest suburbs in the United States, spends more than $18,500 a year on each of its students, compared to a poor district such as Alpine, Utah, that spends only $5,000 each year. In recent years, these differences have increased (Winter, 2004; U.S. Department of Education, 2011). The Thinking About Diversity box on page 381 shows the effects of funding differences in the everyday lives of students.

Because school funding is most often based on the collection of local property taxes, schools in more affluent areas will offer better schooling than schools in poor communities. This difference also benefits whites over minorities, which is why some districts started a policy of *busing*, transporting students to achieve racial

Inequality in Public Schooling

But even public schools are not all the same. Differences in funding between rich and poor communities result in unequal resources;

Watch the video "Inequities in Education" on **mysoclab.com**

Sociological research has documented the fact that young children living in low-income communities typically learn in classrooms like the one on the left, with large class sizes and low budgets that do not provide for high technology and other instructional materials. Children from high-income communities typically enjoy classroom experiences such as the one shown on the right, with small classes and the latest learning technology.

balance and equal opportunity in schools. Beginning in the 1970s, about 5 percent of U.S. students were bused to schools outside their neighborhoods, and this policy was very controversial. Supporters claimed that given the reality of racial segregation, the only way governments would adequately fund schools in poor, minority neighborhoods was if white children from richer areas attended. Critics responded that busing was expensive and undermines the concept of neighborhood schools. But almost everyone agreed on one thing: Given the racial imbalance of most urban areas, an effective busing policy would have to join inner cities and suburbs—a plan that has never been politically possible. Although racial segregation in U.S. public schools showed a modest decline between 1970 and 1990, there has been little change since then (Logan, Oakley, & Stowell, 2008).

But other policies to address unequal schools have emerged. One policy is to provide money equally across a state. This is the approach taken by Vermont, which passed Act 60, a law that distributes per-student tax money equally to all communities.

Not everyone thinks money is the key to good schooling. Consider, for example, that Youngstown, Ohio, spends about $15,000 a year on each public school student (40 percent above the national average) but manages to graduate barely half of them. Newark, New Jersey, spends double the national average and fewer than half of students graduate (Will, 2011).

What other than money is involved? A classic report by a research team headed by James Coleman (1966) confirmed that schools in low-income communities and with mostly minority populations suffer problems ranging from larger class size to insufficient libraries and too few science labs. But the Coleman report cautioned that more money by itself will not magically improve schooling. More important are the cooperative efforts of teachers, parents, and the students themselves. In other words, even if school funding were exactly the same everywhere (as in Vermont), students who benefit from more *cultural capital*—that is, those whose parents value schooling, read to their children, and

encourage the development of imagination—would still perform better. In short, we should not expect schools alone to overcome marked social inequality in the United States (Schneider et al., 1998; Israel, Beaulieu, & Hartless, 2001; Ornstein, 2010).

Further research confirms the difference the home environment makes in a student's school performance. A research team studied the rate at which school-age children gain skills in reading and mathematics (Downey, von Hippel, & Broh, 2004). Because U.S. children go to school six to seven hours a day, five days a week, and do not attend school during summer months, the researchers calculate that children spend only about 13 percent of their waking hours in school. During the school year, high-income children learn somewhat more quickly than low-income children, but the learning gap is far greater during the summer season when children are not in school. The researchers conclude that when it comes to student performance, schools matter, but the home and local environment matter more. Put another way, schools close some of the learning gap that is created by differences in family resources, but they do not "level the playing field" between rich and poor children the way we like to think they do.

Access to Higher Education

For most people, advanced schooling is the key to a good job. But only 70 percent of U.S. high school graduates enroll in college immediately after graduation. Among young people aged eighteen to twenty-four years old, about 41 percent are enrolled in college (National Center for Education Statistics, 2011).

A crucial factor affecting access to higher education is income. College is expensive: Even at state-supported colleges and universities, annual tuition is about $7,700, and total fees at the most expensive private colleges and universities exceed $50,000 a year. This means that college attendance is more common among families with higher incomes. In the United States, some 6.6 million families have at least one child enrolled in college. Of these

"Public School 261? Head down Jerome Avenue and look for the mortician's office." Off for a day studying the New York City schools, Jonathan Kozol parks his car and walks toward PS 261. Finding PS 261 is not easy because the school has no sign. In fact, the building is a former roller rink and doesn't look much like a school at all.

The principal explains that this is in a minority area of the North Bronx, so the population of PS 261 is 90 percent African American and Hispanic. Officially, the school should serve 900 students, but it actually enrolls 1,300. The rules say class size should not exceed thirty-two, but Kozol observes that it sometimes approaches forty. Because the school has just one small cafeteria, the children must eat in three shifts. After lunch, with no place to play, students squirm in their seats until they are told to return to their classrooms. Only one classroom in the entire school has a window to the world outside.

Toward the end of the day, Kozol remarks to a teacher about the overcrowding and the poor condition of the building. She sums up her thoughts: "I had an awful room last year. In the winter, it was 56 degrees. In the summer, it was up to 90." "Do the children ever comment on the building?" Kozol asks. "They don't say," she responds, "but they know. All these kids see TV. They know what suburban schools are

like. Then they look around them at their school. They don't comment on it, but you see it in their eyes. They understand."

Several months later, Kozol visits PS 24, in the affluent Riverdale section of New York City. This school is set back from the road, beyond a lawn planted with magnolia and dogwood trees, which are now in full bloom. On one side of the building is a playground for the youngest children; behind the school are playing fields for the older kids. Many people pay the high price of a house in Riverdale because the local schools have such an excellent reputation. There are 825 children here; most are white and a few are Asian, Hispanic, or African American. The building is in good repair. It has a large library and even a planetarium.

All the classrooms have windows with bright curtains.

Entering one of the many classes for gifted students, Kozol asks the children what they are doing today. A young girl answers confidently, "My name is Laurie, and we're doing problem solving." A tall, good-natured boy continues, "I'm David. One thing that we do is logical thinking. Some problems, we find, have more than one good answer." Kozol asks if such reasoning is innate or if it is something a child learns. Susan, whose smile reveals her braces, responds, "You know some things to start with when you enter school. But we learn some things that other children don't. We learn certain things that other children don't know because we're *taught* them."

What Do You Think?

1. Are there differences between schools in your city or town? Explain.

2. Why do you think there is so little public concern about schooling inequality?

3. What changes would our society have to make to eliminate schooling inequality? Would you support such changes? Why or why not?

Source: Adapted from Kozol (1992:85–88, 92–96).

families, 44 percent have incomes of at least $75,000 annually (roughly the richest 30 percent, who fall within the upper-middle class and upper class), 46 percent have incomes of at least $20,000 but less than $75,000 (the middle class and working class), and only 10 percent have incomes of less than $20,000 a year (the lower class, including families classified as poor) (U.S. Census Bureau, 2011).

These economic differences are one reason that the educational gap between whites and minorities widens at the college level. As Figure 14–1 on page 382 shows, African Americans are not quite as likely as non-Hispanic whites to graduate from high school and are much less likely to complete four or more years of college. Schooling is an important path to social mobility in our society, but the promise of schooling has not overcome the racial inequality that exists in the United States.

Completing college brings many rewards, including higher earnings. In the past forty years, as our economy has shifted to work that requires processing information, the gap in average income between people who complete only high school and those who earn a four-year college degree has more than doubled. In fact, today, a college degree can add as much as $1 million to a person's lifetime income. Table 14–2 on page 382 gives details. In 2010, men who were high school graduates averaged $40,055, and college graduates averaged $63,737. The ratios in parentheses show that a man with a bachelor's degree earns 2.6 times in annual income as much as a man with eight or fewer years of schooling. Across the board, women earn less than men, although like men, added years of schooling boosts their income. Keep in mind that for both men and women, some of the greater earnings have to do with social background, because the people with the most schooling are likely to come from well-off families to begin with.

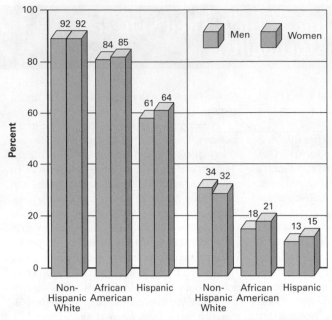

Diversity Snapshot

FIGURE 14–1 Educational Achievement for Various Categories of People, Aged 25 Years and Over, 2010

U.S. society still provides less education to minorities.

Source: U.S. Census Bureau (2011).

Greater Opportunity: Expanding Higher Education

With some 20.5 million people enrolled in colleges and universities, the United States is a world leader in providing a college education to its people. This country also enrolls more students from abroad than any other.

One reason for this achievement is that there are 4,495 colleges and universities in the United States. This number includes 2,774 four-year institutions (which award bachelor's degrees) and 1,721 two-year colleges (which award associate's degrees). Some two-year colleges are private, but most are publicly funded community colleges that serve a local area (usually a city or a county) and charge a low tuition (National Center for Education Statistics, 2011).

Because higher education is a path to better jobs and higher income, the government makes money available to help certain categories of people pay the costs of college. After World War II, the GI Bill provided college funds to veterans, enabling tens of thousands of men and women to attend college. Some branches of the military continue to offer college money to enlistees; in addition, veterans continue to benefit from government grants and scholarships.

Community Colleges

Since the 1960s, the expansion of state-funded community colleges has greatly increased access to higher education. According to the National Center for Education Statistics (2011), the 1,721 two-year colleges across the United States now enroll 41.3 percent of all college undergraduates.

Community colleges provide a number of specific benefits. First, their low cost places college courses and degrees within reach of millions of families who could not otherwise afford them. Many students at community colleges today are the first in their families to pursue a college degree. The low cost of community colleges is especially important during periods of economic recession. When the economy slumps and people lose their jobs, college enrollments soar, especially at community colleges.

Second, community colleges have special importance for minorities. Currently, 40 percent of all African American and 51 percent of Hispanic undergraduates in the United States attend community colleges.

Third, although community colleges serve local populations, some attract students from around the world. Many community colleges recruit students from abroad, and about 15 percent of all foreign students enrolled on a U.S. campus are studying at community colleges (National Center for Education Statistics, 2011).

Fourth, the top priority of faculty who work at large universities is typically research, but the most important job for community college faculty is teaching. So even though teaching loads are heavy (typically four or five classes each semester), community colleges appeal to faculty who find their greatest pleasure in the classroom. Community college students often get more attention from faculty than students at large universities (Jacobson, 2003). Finally, community colleges teach the knowledge and career skills that countless people depend on to find the jobs they want.

Privilege and Personal Merit

If attending college is a rite of passage for rich men and women, as social-conflict theory suggests, then *schooling transforms social privilege into personal merit*. But given our cultural emphasis on individualism, we tend to see credentials as badges of ability rather than as symbols of family affluence (Sennett & Cobb, 1973).

When we congratulate the new graduate, we rarely recognize the resources—in terms of both money and cultural capital—that made this achievement possible. Yet young people from families

TABLE 14–2 Median Income by Sex and Educational Attainment, 2010		
Education	**Men**	**Women**
Professional degree	$115,298 (4.7)	$76,737 (4.2)
Doctorate	101,222 (4.1)	77,392 (4.2)
Master's degree	80,958 (3.3)	59,099 (3.2)
Bachelor's degree	63,737 (2.6)	47,435 (2.6)
1–3 years of college	50,282 (2.1)	33,401 (1.8)
4 years of high school	40,055 (1.6)	29,857 (1.6)
9–11 years of school	29,435 (1.2)	20,883 (1.1)
0–8 years of school	24,453 (1.0)	18,239 (1.0)

Notes: Figures are for persons aged 25 years and over working full time. The earnings ratio, in parentheses, indicates what multiple of the lowest income level a person with the indicated amount of additional schooling earns.
Source: U.S. Census Bureau (2011).

Education

	Structural-Functional Theory	Symbolic-Interaction Theory	Social-Conflict Theory
What is the level of analysis?	Macro-level	Micro-level	Macro-level
What is the importance of education for society?	Schooling performs many vital tasks for the operation of society, including socializing the young and encouraging discovery and invention to improve our lives. Schooling helps unite a diverse society by teaching shared norms and values.	How teachers define their students—as well as how students think of themselves—can become real to everyone and affect students' educational performance.	Schooling maintains social inequality through unequal schooling for rich and poor. Within individual schools, tracking provides privileged children with a better education than poor children.

with incomes exceeding $200,000 a year average almost 400 points higher on the SAT exam than those whose families earn less than $20,000 a year (College Board, 2011). The richer students are thus more likely to get into college; once there, they are also more likely to complete their studies and get a degree. In a *credential society*—one that evaluates people on the basis of their schooling—companies hire job applicants with the best education. This process ends up helping people who are already advantaged and hurting those who are already disadvantaged (Collins, 1979).

 Evaluate Social-conflict theory links formal education to social inequality to show how schooling transforms privilege into personal worthiness and disadvantage into personal deficiency. However, the social-conflict approach overlooks the extent to which finishing a degree reflects plenty of hard work and the extent to which schooling provides upward mobility for talented women and men from all backgrounds. In addition, despite claims that schooling supports the status quo, today's college curricula challenge social inequality on many fronts.

The Applying Theory table sums up what the theoretical approaches show us about education.

CHECK YOUR LEARNING Explain several ways in which education is linked to social inequality.

Problems in the Schools

 Analyze

Intense debate revolves around schooling in the United States. Because we expect schools to do so much—equalize opportunity, instill discipline, and fire imagination—people are divided on whether public schools are doing their job. Although half of adults give their local schools a grade of A or B, just as many give a grade of C or below (Bushaw & Lopez, 2011).

Discipline and Violence

When many of today's older teachers think back to their own student days, school "problems" consisted of talking out of turn, chewing gum, breaking the dress code, or cutting class. Today, schools are grappling with serious issues such as drug and alcohol abuse, teenage pregnancy, and outright violence. Although almost everyone agrees that schools should teach personal discipline, many people think the job is no longer being done.

Schools do not create violence; in most cases, violence spills into schools from the surrounding society. In the wake of a number of school shootings in recent years, many school districts have adopted zero-tolerance policies that require suspension or expulsion for serious misbehavior or bringing weapons on campus.

Deadly school shootings—including the deaths of thirty-three students at Virginia Tech University in 2007, the 2010 death of a student who entered the library at the University of Texas at Austin and shot himself with an AK-47 assault rifle , and the 2012 deaths of six students and one employee at Oikos University in California—have shocked the nation. Such tragic incidents also raise serious questions about balancing students' right to privacy (typically, the law prohibits colleges from informing parents of a student's grades or mental health issues) and the need to ensure the safety of the campus population. In the Virginia Tech case, had the university been able to bring the disturbed young man's mental health problems to the attention of the police or his family, the tragedy might have been prevented (Gibbs, 2007; Shedden, 2008).

Student Passivity

If some schools are plagued by violence, many more are filled with students who are bored. Some of the blame for their passivity can be placed on the fact that electronic devices, from television to iPhones, now claim far more of young people's time than school, parents, and community activities. But schools must share the blame because the educational system itself encourages student passivity (Coleman, Hoffer, & Kilgore, 1981).

Bureaucracy

The small, personal schools that served local communities a century ago have evolved into huge education factories. In a study of high schools across the United States, Theodore Sizer (1984:207–9) identified five ways in which large, bureaucratic schools undermine education:

1. **Rigid uniformity.** Bureaucratic schools run by outside specialists (such as state education officials) generally ignore the cultural

character of local communities and the personal needs of their children.

2. **Numerical ratings.** School officials define success in terms of numerical attendance rates and dropout rates, and teachers "teach to the tests," hoping to increase test scores. Overlooked in the process are dimensions of schooling that are difficult to quantify, such as creativity and enthusiasm.

3. **Rigid expectations.** Officials expect fifteen-year-olds to be in the tenth grade and eleventh graders to score at a certain level on a standardized verbal achievement test. Rarely are exceptionally bright and motivated students permitted to graduate early. Likewise, poor performers are pushed from grade to grade, doomed to fail year after year.

4. **Specialization.** High school students learn Spanish from one teacher, receive guidance from another, and are coached in sports by still others. Students shuffle between fifty-minute periods throughout the school day. As a result, no school official comes to know the child well.

5. **Little individual responsibility.** Highly bureaucratic schools do not empower students to learn on their own. Similarly, teachers have little say in how they teach their classes; any change in the pace of learning or other deviation from the set curriculum risks disrupting the system.

Of course, with 55 million schoolchildren in the United States, schools have to be bureaucratic to get the job done. But Sizer recommends that we "humanize" schools by eliminating rigid scheduling, reducing class size, and training teachers more broadly to make them more involved in the lives of their students. Overall, as James Coleman (1993) has suggested, schools need to be less "administratively driven" and more "output-driven." Perhaps this transformation could begin by ensuring that graduation from high school depends on what students have learned rather than on how many years they have spent in the building.

College: The Silent Classroom

Passivity is also common among college and university students (Gimenez, 1989). Sociologists rarely study the college classroom—a curious fact, considering how much time they spend there. One exception was a study of a coeducational university where David Karp and William Yoels (1976) found that even in small classes, only a few students speak up. Thus passivity is a classroom norm, and students even become irritated if one of their number is especially talkative.

According to Karp and Yoels, most students think classroom passivity is their

For all categories of people in the United States, dropping out of school greatly reduces the chances of getting a good job and earning a secure income. Why is the dropout rate particularly high among Hispanic students?

own fault. But as anyone who watches young people outside of class knows, they are usually active and vocal. It is clearly the schools that teach students to be passive and to view instructors as experts who serve up "knowledge" and "truth." Students see their proper role as quietly listening and taking notes. As a result, the researchers estimate, just 10 percent of college class time is used for discussion.

Faculty can bring students to life in their classrooms by making use of four teaching strategies: (1) calling on students by name when they volunteer, (2) positively reinforcing student participation, (3) asking analytical rather than factual questions and giving students time to answer, and (4) asking for student opinions even when no one volunteers a response (Auster & MacRone, 1994).

Dropping Out

If many students are passive in class, others are not there at all. The problem of *dropping out*—quitting before earning a high school diploma—leaves young people (many of whom are disadvantaged to begin with) unprepared for the world of work and at high risk of poverty.

The dropout rate has declined slightly in recent decades; currently, 8.1 percent of people between the ages of sixteen and twenty-four are high school dropouts, a total of 3.2 million young women and men. Dropping out is least common among non-Hispanic whites (5.2 percent), more likely among non-Hispanic African Americans (9.3 percent), and most common among Hispanics (17.6 percent) (National Center for Education Statistics, 2011).

Some students drop out because of problems with the English language, others because of pregnancy, and some because they must work to support their family. For children growing up in families with income in the bottom 25 percent, the dropout rate is more than six times higher than for children living in high-income families (National Center for Education Statistics, 2011). These data suggest that many dropouts are young people whose parents also have little schooling, revealing a multigenerational cycle of disadvantage.

Dropping out is actually the norm in many large urban school systems. Fewer than half of all children end up graduating from high school in many of this country's largest school districts—including Minneapolis (graduation rate of just 45 percent), Atlanta (44 percent), Los Angeles (44 percent), Baltimore (42 percent), Milwaukee (41 percent), and Detroit (38 percent) (Swanson, 2009).

Academic Standards

Perhaps the most serious educational issue confronting our society is the quality of our nation's schooling. *A Nation at Risk,* a comprehensive study of the quality of U.S. schools conducted by the National Commission on Excellence in Education, begins with this alarming statement:

> If an unfriendly foreign power had attempted to impose on America the mediocre educational performance that exists today, we might well have viewed it as an act of war. As it stands, we have allowed this to happen to ourselves. (1983:5)

Supporting this claim, the report notes that "nearly 40 percent of seventeen-year-olds cannot draw inferences from written material; only one-fifth can write a persuasive essay; and only one-third can solve mathematical problems requiring several steps" (1983:9). Furthermore, scores on the Scholastic Assessment Test (SAT) show little improvement over time. In 1967, median scores were 516 on the mathematic test and 543 on the verbal test; by 2011, the average in mathematics had dropped 2 points to 514, and the verbal average had slipped to just 497. Nationwide, more than one-third of high school students—and more than half of those in urban schools—fail to master even the basics in reading, math, and science on the National Assessment of Educational Progress examination (Marklein, 2000; Barnes, 2002a; College Board, 2011; National Assessment of Educational Progress, 2011).

For many people in this country, even basic literacy is at issue. **Functional illiteracy,** *a lack of the reading and writing skills needed for everyday living,* is a problem for one in three U.S. children. For older people, about 30 million U.S. adults (about 14 percent of the total) lack basic skills in reading and writing.

A Nation at Risk recommended drastic reform. First, it called for schools to require *all* students to complete several years of English, mathematics, social studies, general science, and computer science. Second, it warned schools not to promote students until they meet achievement standards. Third, it stated that teacher training must improve and teachers' salaries be raised to draw talent into the profession. The report concluded that schools must meet public expectations and that citizens must be prepared to pay for a job well done.

What has happened in the years since *A Nation at Risk* was issued? In some respects, schools have improved. A report by the National Center for Education Statistics (2008) noted some decline in the dropout rate, a trend toward schools' offering more challenging courses, and a larger share of high school graduates going to college. At the same time, the evidence suggests that a majority of elementary school students are falling below standards in reading; in many cases, they can't read at all. In short, although some improvement is evident, much remains to be done.

The United States spends more on schooling its children than almost any other nation—half again more than Japan and double the average in Europe. Even so, a recent report comparing the academic performance of fifteen-year-olds in sixty-five countries found that the United States placed twenty-third in science and thirty-first in mathematics. Such statistics fuel fears that our country is losing its leadership in science to other nations, including China, India, and South Korea (OECD, 2011; European Union, 2012).

Cultural values play a part in how hard students work at their schooling. For example, U.S. students are generally less motivated and do less homework than students in Japan. Japanese young people also spend twenty-two more days in school each year than U.S students. Perhaps one approach to improving school performance is simply to have students spend more time in school (IEA, 2009).

Grade Inflation

Academic standards depend on the use of grades that have clear meaning and are awarded for work of appropriate quality. Yet recent decades have seen substantial *grade inflation,* the awarding of ever-higher

grades for average work. Though not necessarily found in every school, grade inflation is evident in both high schools and colleges.

One study of high school grades revealed a dramatic change in the distribution of grades between 1968 and 2010. In 1968, the high school records of students who had just entered college included more grades of C+ and below than grades of A−, A, and A+. By 2010, however, these A grades outnumbered grades of C+ and below by more than eleven to one (Pryor et al., 2011).

A few colleges and universities have enacted policies that limit the share of A grades (generally to one-third of all grades). But there is little evidence that grade inflation will be reversed anytime soon. As a result, the C grade (which used to mean "middle of the pack") may all but disappear, making just about every student "above average."

What accounts for grade inflation? In part, today's teachers are concerned about the morale and self-esteem of their students and perhaps their own popularity. In any case, teachers clearly are not as "tough" as they used to be. At the same time, the ever more competitive process of getting into college and graduate school puts pressure on high schools and colleges to award high grades (Astin et al., 2002).

Current Issues in U.S. Education

 **Understand**

Our society's schools continuously confront new challenges. This section explores several recent and important educational issues.

School Choice

Some analysts claim that our schools teach poorly because they have no competition. Giving parents options for schooling their children might force all schools to do a better job. This is the essence of a policy called *school choice.*

The goal of school choice is to create a market for education so that parents and students can shop for the best value. According to one proposal, the government would give vouchers to families with school-age children and allow them to spend that money at public, private, or parochial schools. In recent years, major cities, including Indianapolis, Minneapolis, Milwaukee, Cleveland, Chicago, and Washington, D.C., as well as the states of Florida and Illinois, have experimented with choice plans designed to make public schools perform better to win the confidence of families.

Supporters claim that giving parents a choice about where to enroll their children is the only sure way to improve all schools. But critics (including teachers' unions) charge that school choice amounts to giving up on our nation's commitment to public education and that it will do little to improve schools in central cities, where the need is greatest (A. Cohen, 1999; Morse, 2002; Hopkinson, 2011).

In 2002, President George W. Bush signed a new education bill that downplayed vouchers in favor of another approach to greater choice. Starting in the 2005–2006 school year, all public schools began testing every child in reading, mathematics, and science in grades three through eight. Although the federal government may provide more aid to schools with students who do not perform well, if those schools do not show improvements in test scores over time, low-income students will have the choice of special tutoring or transportation to

Charter schools are operating in forty-one of the fifty states. These are public schools, but they stand out as centers of innovation for policies and academic programs. As you might expect, the demand on the part of students and their families is greater than the supply of seats in charter school classrooms. As a result, most charter schools—including the SEED school in Washington, D.C., featured in the 2010 documentary film *Waiting for Superman*—employ a lottery system to select those who will be invited to enroll.

another school. This program, called "No Child Left Behind," has helped identify which schools are not doing a good job educating children and has raised some measures of student performance. At the same time, however, little change has occurred in many of the worst-performing schools (Lindlaw, 2002; Wallis & Steptoe, 2007).

By 2012, forty-eight percent of this nation's public schools had been labeled as failing, and public support for the No Child Left Behind Act has declined sharply. Critics claim that, by increasing the importance of test scores, this law encourages schools to "teach to the tests" and to drop their standards of success. The Obama administration supports letting states ask for waivers from key provisions of this policy. In addition, the president has asked Congress to focus attention on the 5,000 schools with the lowest student performance and to shift the goal from raising test scores to raising graduation rates and preparing students for careers (Dillon, 2010, 2011; Gallup, 2011; *New York Times*, 2011; Webley, 2012).

A more modest form of school choice involves *magnet schools,* more than 3,000 of which now exist across the country. Magnet schools offer special facilities and programs to promote educational excellence in a particular field, such as computer science, foreign languages, science and mathematics, or the arts. In school districts with magnet schools, parents can choose the one best suited to their child's particular talents and interests.

Another school choice strategy involves *charter schools,* public schools that are given more freedom to try new policies and programs. There are more than 4,600 such schools in forty-one states, Washington, D.C., and Puerto Rico; they enroll 1.4 million students, 61 percent of whom are minorities. In many of these schools, students have demonstrated high academic achievement—a requirement for renewal of the charter (National Center for Education Statistics, 2011).

A final development in the school choice movement is *schooling for profit.* Supporters of this plan say school systems can be operated more efficiently by private profit-making companies than

by local governments. Private schooling is nothing new, of course; more than 33,000 schools in the United States are currently run by private organizations and religious groups. What is new is that hundreds of public schools, enrolling hundreds of thousands of students, are now run by private businesses for profit.

Research confirms that many public school systems suffer from bureaucratic bloat, spending far too much and teaching far too little. And U.S. society has long looked to competition to improve quality. Evidence suggests that for-profit schools have greatly reduced administrative costs, but the educational results appear mixed. Although some companies claim to improve student learning, some cities have cut back on business-run schools. In recent years, school boards in Baltimore, Miami, Hartford, and Boston have canceled the contracts of for-profit schooling corporations. But other cities have been willing to give for-profit schooling a try. For example, after Philadelphia's public school system failed to graduate one-third of its students, the state of Pennsylvania took charge of that city's schools and turned most of them over to for-profit companies. Although there was some evidence of improvement in student performance, by 2010 school officials were still dissatisfied and so they turned over most of these schools to independent companies that operate as nonprofit organizations. In light of conflicting evidence about the performance of for-profit schools, emotions among both supporters and critics of this policy continue to run high, with each side claiming to speak for the well-being of the schoolchildren caught in the middle (Winters, 2002; Sizer, 2003; Richburg, 2008; Mezzacappa, 2010).

Home Schooling

Home schooling is gaining popularity across the United States. About 1.5 million children (almost 3 percent of all school-age children) have their formal schooling at home.

Why do parents undertake the enormous challenge of schooling their own children? A couple of decades ago, many of the parents who pioneered home schooling (which is legal in every state) did not believe in public education because they wanted to give their children a strongly religious upbringing. Today, however, the majority are mothers and fathers who simply believe that public schools are not doing a good job and who think they can do better. To benefit their children, many parents are willing to change work schedules and relearn algebra or other necessary subjects. Many belong to groups in which parents combine their efforts, specializing in what each knows best.

Advocates of home schooling point out that given the poor performance of many public schools, no one should be surprised that a growing number of parents are stepping up to teach their own children. Even more impressive is that this system works—on average, students who learn at home outperform those who learn in school. Critics argue that home schooling reduces the amount of federal funding going to local public schools, which ends up hurting the majority of students. In addition, as one critic points out, home schooling "takes some of the most affluent and articulate parents out of the system. These are the parents who know how to get things done with administrators" (Chris Lubienski, quoted in Cloud & Morse, 2001:48).

Schooling People with Disabilities

Many of the 6.5 million children with disabilities in the United States have difficulty getting to and from school; once there, many with crutches or wheelchairs cannot negotiate stairs and other obstacles in school buildings. Children with developmental disabilities such as mental retardation need extensive personal attention from specially trained teachers. As a result, many children with mental and physical disabilities have won the right to a public education only after persistent efforts by parents and other concerned citizens (Horn & Tynan, 2001; U.S. Department of Education, 2010).

Most children with disabilities (58 percent) attend public schools and spend most of their time in regular classes. This pattern reflects the principle of *mainstreaming*, which means integrating students with disabilities or special needs into the overall educational program. Mainstreaming is a form of *inclusive education* that works best for physically impaired students who have no difficulty keeping up academically with the rest of the class. A benefit of mixing children with and without disabilities in the same classrooms is allowing everyone to learn to interact with people who are different from each other.

Adult Education

Almost 100 million U.S. adults over twenty-five are enrolled in some type of schooling. These older students range in age from the mid-twenties to the seventies and beyond and make up about 40 percent of students in degree-granting programs. Adults in school are more likely to be women (61 percent) than men (39 percent), and most have above-average incomes.

Why do adults return to the classroom? The most common reasons given are to advance a career or train for a new job, but many are simply seeking personal enrichment (National Center for Education Statistics, 2011). During economic downturns, as we have experienced in recent years, the number of adults returning to the classroom (including many who are out of work) typically goes up.

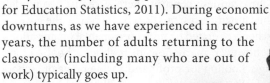

Educators have long debated the best way to teach children with disabilities. On one hand, such children may benefit from separate facilities staffed by specially trained teachers. On the other hand, children are less likely to be stigmatized as "different" if they are included in regular classrooms.

The Teacher Shortage

A final challenge for U.S. schools is hiring enough teachers to fill the classrooms. A number of factors—including low salaries, frustration over extensive bureaucracy, and retirement of aging teachers, as well as rising enrollment and increases in class size—have combined to create about 400,000 teaching vacancies (about 325,000 in public schools and 75,000 in private schools) in the United States in 2012.

How will these slots be filled? About the same number of people graduate with education degrees annually. Most of them do not have a degree in a specific field, such as mathematics, biology, or English, and many have trouble passing state certification tests in the subject they want to teach. As a result, many schools, especially in low-income neighborhoods, are taught by teachers who may be just one chapter ahead of their students. From another angle, almost half of this country's public school teachers have SAT scores that put them in the bottom one-third of all students who took the tests (Quaid, 2008; Kristof, 2011).

What all this adds up to is that the teacher shortage is really a shortage of *good* teachers. For our nation's public schools to improve, two things must happen: First, teachers who do not teach well must receive additional training or lose their jobs, and second, well-qualified people need to be attracted into the classroom by higher pay and greater public respect (Ripley, 2008; Kristof, 2011).

Getting rid of bad teachers (and perhaps bad principals, too) means changing rules that make it difficult or impossible to fire someone after a few years on the job. Gaining well-qualified teachers depends on adopting various recruitment strategies. Some schools offer incentives such as higher salaries (the average salary for a thirty-year-old teacher in public schools is only about $40,000 a year) to draw into teaching people who have already had successful careers. Some schools provide signing bonuses (especially for hard-to-fill positions in disciplines such as chemistry) or give housing allowances (in cities such as New York, where housing is often out of the reach of teachers). President Obama (2007) has written that he believes that school districts should pay highly qualified and effective teachers as much as $100,000 a year—but, he adds, they also should be able to dismiss unqualified and ineffective teachers.

Other policy ideas include having community colleges play a larger role in teacher education and having government and school boards make it easier for good teachers to get the certification they need to enter the classroom. Finally, many school districts are going global, actively recruiting in countries such as Spain, India, and the Philippines to bring talented women and men from around the world to teach in U.S. classrooms (Evelyn, 2002; Ripley, 2008; Wallis, 2008; U.S. Census Bureau, 2011).

Debate about education in the United States

Meg: What's with this campus having so few men?

Tricia: Does it matter? I'd rather focus on my work.

Mark: I think it's, like, really cool for us guys!

A century ago, the campuses of colleges and universities across the United States might as well have hung out a sign that read "Men Only." Almost all of the students and faculty were male. There were a small number of women's colleges, but many more schools—including some of the most prestigious U.S. universities, including Yale, Harvard, and Princeton—barred women outright.

Since then, women have won greater social equality. By 1980, the number of women enrolled at U.S. colleges finally matched the number of men.

In a surprising trend, however, the share of women on campus has continued to increase. As a result, in 2009, men accounted for only 43 percent of all U.S. undergraduates. Meg DeLong noticed the gender imbalance right away when she moved into her dorm at the University of Georgia at Athens; she soon learned that just 39 percent of her first-year classmates were men. In some classes, there were few men, and women usually dominated discussions. Out of class, DeLong and many other women soon complained that having so few men on campus hurt their social life. Not surprisingly, most of the men felt otherwise (Fonda, 2000).

What accounts for the shifting gender balance on U.S. campuses? One theory is that young men are drawn away from college by the lure of jobs, especially in high technology. This pattern is sometimes termed the "Bill Gates syndrome," after the Microsoft founder, who dropped out of college and soon became the world's richest person. In addition, analysts point to an anti-intellectual male culture. Young women are drawn to learning and seek to do well in school, but young men attach less importance to studying. Rightly or wrongly, more men seem to think they can get a good job without investing years of

their lives and a considerable amount of money in pursuit of a college degree.

The gender gap is evident in all racial and ethnic categories and at all class levels. Among African Americans on campus, only 36 percent are men. The lower the income level, the greater the gender gap in college attendance.

Many college officials are concerned about a lack of men on campus. In an effort to attract more balanced enrollments, some colleges are adopting what amounts to affirmative action programs for males. But courts in several states have already ruled such policies illegal. Many colleges are therefore turning to more active recruitment; admissions officers are paying special attention to male applicants and stressing a college's strength in mathematics and science—areas traditionally popular with men. In the same way that colleges across the country are striving to increase their share of minority students, the hope is that they can also succeed in attracting a larger share of men.

Join the Blog!

Why do women outnumber men on the college campus? Is there a gender imbalance on your campus? Does it create problems? What problems? For whom? Go to MySocLab and join the Sociology in Focus blog to share your opinions and experiences and to see what others think.

---

extends beyond the issues noted here. The Sociology in Focus box highlights the declining share of college students who are men.

Schooling: Looking Ahead

 Evaluate

Although the United States still leads the world in sending people to college, the public school system continues to struggle with serious problems. In terms of quality of schooling, this country is falling behind many other nations, a fact that calls into question the future strength of the United States on the world stage.

Many of the problems of schooling discussed in this chapter have their roots in the larger society. We cannot expect schools *by themselves* to provide high-quality education. Schools will improve only to the extent that students, teachers, parents, and local communities commit themselves to educational excellence. In short, educational problems are *social* problems for which there is no quick fix.

For much of the twentieth century, there were just two models for education in the United States: public schools run by the government and private schools operated by nongovernmental organizations. In recent decades, however, many new ideas about schooling have emerged, including schooling for profit and a wide range of "school choice" programs. In the decades ahead, we will probably see some significant changes in mass education, guided in part by the results of social science research into the outcomes of different strategies.

Another factor that will continue to reshape schools is information technology. Today, all but the poorest primary and secondary schools use computers for instruction. Computers prompt students to be more active and allow them to progress at their own pace. Even so, computers will never bring to the educational process the personal insights or imagination of a motivated human teacher.

Nor will technology ever solve all the problems that plague our schools, including violence and rigid bureaucracy. What we need is a broad plan for social change that refires this country's ambition to provide universal schooling of high quality—a goal that we have yet to achieve.

Health and Medicine

● **Understand**

Another institution that expands greatly in modern societies is **medicine,** *the social institution that focuses on fighting disease and improving health.* In ideal terms, according to the World Health Organization (1946:3), **health** is *a state of complete physical, mental, and social well-being.* This definition underscores the important fact that health is as much a social as a biological issue.

Health and Society

Society affects people's health in four major ways:

1. **Cultural patterns define health.** Standards of health vary from culture to culture. A century ago, yaws, a contagious skin disease, was so common in sub-Saharan Africa that people there considered it normal (Dubos, 1980). In the United States, a rich diet is so common that most adults consider overeating to be normal and are now overweight. "Health," therefore, is sometimes a matter of having the same conditions or diseases as one's neighbors (Pinhey, Rubinstein, & Colfax, 1997; CDC, 2011).

    What people see as healthful also reflects what they think is morally good. Members of our society (especially men) think a competitive way of life is "healthy" because it fits our cultural mores, but stress contributes to heart disease and many other illnesses. People who object to homosexuality on moral grounds call this sexual orientation "sick," even though it is natural from a biological point of view. Thus ideas about health act as a form of social control, encouraging conformity to cultural norms.

2. **Cultural standards of health change over time.** Early in the twentieth century, some doctors warned women not to go to college because higher education would strain the female brain. Others claimed that masturbation was a threat to health. We now know that both of these ideas are false. Fifty years ago, on the other hand, few doctors understood the dangers of cigarette smoking or too much sun exposure, practices that we now recognize as serious health risks. Even patterns of basic hygiene change over time. Today, most people in the United States bathe or shower every day; this is three times as often as fifty years ago (Gillespie, 2000).

3. **A society's technology affects people's health.** In poor nations, infectious diseases are widespread because of malnutrition and poor sanitation. As industrialization raises living standards, people become healthier. But industrial technology also creates new threats to health. As Chapter 15 ("Population, Urbanization, and Environment") explains, high-income ways of life endanger health by overtaxing the world's resources and creating pollution.

4. **Social inequality affects people's health.** All societies distribute resources unequally. Overall, the rich have far better physical, mental, and emotional health than the poor.

Health: A Global Survey

● **Understand**

Because health is closely linked to social life, human well-being has improved over the long course of history as societies developed more advanced technology. Differences in societal development are also the cause of striking differences in health around the world today.

Health in Low-Income Countries

Around the world, severe poverty cuts decades off the long life expectancy typical of rich countries. People living in sub-Saharan Africa have a life expectancy of fifty-five years, and in the poorest countries, nearly one in ten newborns dies within a year and one in four people dies before reaching the age of twenty (Population Reference Bureau, 2010; World Bank, 2011).

The World Health Organization reports that 1 billion people around the world—one person in six—suffer from serious illness due to poverty. Poor sanitation and malnutrition kill people of all ages. A lack of safe drinking water is also common, and bad water carries a number of infectious diseases, including influenza, pneumonia, and tuberculosis, which are widespread killers in poor societies today. To make matters worse, medical personnel are few and far between; as a result, the world's poorest people—many of whom live in Central Africa—never see a physician.

In a classic example of a vicious circle, poverty breeds disease, which reduces people's ability to work, increasing poverty. When medical technology does control infectious disease, the populations of poor nations soar. But without enough resources to provide for the current population, poor societies can ill afford population increases. Therefore, programs that lower death rates in poor countries will succeed only if they are coupled with programs that reduce birth rates.

Health in High-Income Countries

As standard of living rises, health generally improves. But, looking back in time, this improvement did not take place immediately. By 1800, as the Industrial Revolution took hold, factory jobs in cities attracted people from the countryside. Cities quickly became overcrowded, causing serious sanitation problems. Factories fouled the air with smoke, and workplace accidents were common.

Gradually, industrialization raised living standards, providing better nutrition and safer housing for most people, so that after about 1850, health began to improve. Also around this time, medical advances began to control infectious diseases. In 1854, for example, a researcher named John Snow mapped the street addresses of London's cholera victims and found that they had all drunk water from the same well. Not long afterward, scientists linked cholera to a specific bacterium and developed a vaccine against the deadly disease. Armed with scientific knowledge, early environmentalists campaigned against common practices such as discharging raw sewage into rivers used for drinking water. By the early twentieth century, death rates from infectious diseases had fallen sharply.

TABLE 14–3 Leading Causes of Death in the United States, 1900 and 2009	
1900	**2009**
1. Influenza and pneumonia	1. Heart disease
2. Tuberculosis	2. Cancer
3. Stomach and intestinal disease	3. Lung disease (noncancerous)
4. Heart disease	4. Stroke
5. Cerebral hemorrhage	5. Accidents
6. Kidney disease	6. Alzheimer's disease
7. Accidents	7. Diabetes
8. Cancer	8. Influenza and pneumonia
9. Disease in early infancy	9. Kidney disease
10. Diphtheria	10. Suicide

Sources: Information for 1900 is from William C. Cockerham, *Medical Sociology*, 2nd ed. (Englewood Cliffs, N.J.: Prentice Hall, 1986), p. 24; information for 2009 is from Kenneth D. Kochanek, Jiaquan Xu, Sherry L. Murphy, Arialdi M. Miniño, and Hsiang Ching Kung, "Deaths: Preliminary Data for 2009," *National Vital Statistics Reports*, vol. 59, no. 4 (Hyattsville, MD: National Center for Health Statistics, 2011).

Table 14–3 shows that the leading killers in 1900—influenza and pneumonia—account for relatively few deaths in the United States today. It is now chronic illnesses, such as heart disease, cancer, and stroke, that cause most deaths, usually in old age.

Health in the United States

 Analyze

Because the United States is a rich nation, health is generally good by world standards. Still, some categories of people have much better health than others.

Who Is Healthy? Age, Gender, Class, and Race

Social epidemiology is *the study of how health and disease are distributed throughout a society's population.* Social epidemiologists examine the origin and spread of epidemic diseases and try to understand how people's health is tied to their physical and social environments. In the United States, a twenty-year gap in average life expectancy separates the richest and poorest communities. This difference can be examined through the lens of age, gender, social class, and race.

Age and Gender

Death is now rare among young people. Still, young people do fall victim to accidents and, in recent decades, to acquired immune deficiency syndrome (AIDS).

Throughout the life course, women have better health than men. First, girls are less likely than boys to die before or immediately after birth. As socialization begins, males become more aggressive and individualistic than females, resulting in double the rate of accidents, triple the rate of violence, and four times the rate of suicide. As the Thinking About Diversity box explains, the combination of chronic impatience, uncontrolled ambition, and

outbursts of hostility that doctors call "coronary-prone behavior" is a fairly close match with our culture's definition of masculinity (Kochanek et al., 2011; Miniño et al., 2011).

Social Class and Race

Government researchers tell us that 82 percent of people in families with incomes over $100,000 think their health is excellent or very good, but only 52 percent of people in families earning less than $35,000 say the same. Conversely, only about 3 percent of higher-income people describe their health as fair or poor, compared with 18 percent of low-income people (CDC, 2011).

Research suggests that African Americans are no different from whites in terms of their desire for good health and willingness to seek medical help. But poverty among African Americans—at almost three times the rate for whites—helps explain why black people are more likely to die in infancy and, as adults, are more likely to suffer the effects of high blood pressure and heart disease as well as violence and drug abuse (Schnittker, Pescosolido, & Croghan, 2005; CDC, 2011; McNeil, 2011; U.S. Census Bureau, 2011).

More than 80 percent of children in the United States can expect to live to the age of sixty-five or beyond. The life expectancy of white children born in 2009 is four years greater than for African American children (78.6 years versus 74.3). Gender is an even stronger predictor of health than race, since African American women outlive men of either race. From another angle, 81 percent of white men but just 68 percent of African American men will live to age sixty-five. The comparable figures for women are 88 percent for whites and 81 percent for African Americans (Arias, 2011; CDC, 2011).

Infant mortality—the death rate among children under one year of age—is twice as high for disadvantaged children in the United States as for children born into privileged families. Although the health of the richest children in our country is the best in the world, our poorest children are as vulnerable to disease as those in low-income nations such as Nigeria and Vietnam.

Cigarette Smoking

Cigarette smoking tops the list of preventable health hazards in the United States. Some 440,000 men and women die prematurely each year as a direct result of cigarette smoking, a figure that exceeds the death toll from alcohol, cocaine, heroin, homicide, suicide, automobile accidents, and AIDS combined. Smokers also suffer more often from minor illnesses such as the flu, and pregnant women who smoke increase the likelihood of spontaneous abortion, prenatal death, and low-birthweight babies. Even nonsmokers exposed to cigarette smoke have a high risk of smoking-related diseases; health officials estimate that second-hand smoke causes 46,000 deaths from heart disease and 3,400 deaths from lung cancer each year (CDC, 2008, 2010).

Only after World War I did smoking become popular in this country. Despite growing evidence of its dangers, smoking remained fashionable until around a generation ago. The adult popularity of cigarettes peaked in 1960, when 45 percent of adults in the United States smoked. By 2010, only 19 percent were lighting up, according to the Centers for Disease Control and Prevention (CDC, 2011).

Jeff: Cindy! If you don't get out of there in ten seconds, I'm gonna break the door down!

Cindy: Chill out! I have as much right to be in the bathroom as you do. I'll come out when I'm ready.

Jeff: Are you going to take *all day*?

Cindy: Why are you guys always in such a hurry?

Doctors call it "coronary-prone behavior." Psychologists call it the "Type A personality." Sociologists recognize it as our culture's concept of masculinity. This combination of attitudes and behavior, common among men in our society, includes chronic impatience ("Get outta my way!"), uncontrolled ambition ("I've gotta have it—I *need* that!"), and free-floating hostility ("Why are people *such idiots?*").

This pattern, although normal from a cultural point of view, is one major reason that men who are driven to succeed are at high risk of heart disease. By acting out the Type A personality, we may get the job done, but we set in motion complex biochemical processes that are very hard on the human heart.

Here are a few questions to help you determine your own degree of risk (or that of someone important to you):

1. **Do you believe you have to be aggressive to succeed?** Do nice guys finish last? For your heart's sake, try to remove hostility from your life. Here's a place to start: Eliminate profanity from your speech. Try replacing aggression with compassion, which can be surprisingly effective in dealing with other people. Medically speaking, substituting compassion and humor for irritation and aggravation—will improve your health.

2. **How well do you handle uncertainty and opposition?** Do you lose patience with other people ("Why won't the waiter take my order?" "This customer just doesn't get it!")? We all like to know what's going on, and we want others to agree with us. But the world often doesn't work that way. Accepting uncertainty and opposition makes us more mature and certainly healthier.

3. **Are you uncomfortable showing positive emotions?** Many men think giving and accepting love—from women, from children, and from other men—is a sign of weakness. But the medical truth is that love supports health and anger damages it.

As human beings, we have a great deal of choice about how we live. Think about the choices you make, and reflect on how our society's idea of masculinity often makes us hard on others (including those we love) and, just as important, hard on ourselves.

What Do You Think?

1. What aspects of masculinity are harmful to health?

2. Why do you think many people are unaware of how masculinity can be harmful to health?

3. How can sociology play a part in changing men's health for the better?

Sources: Friedman & Rosenman (1974) and M. P. Levine (1990).

Another sign of the times is that forty states have banned smoking in most or all public places, such as restaurants and bars.

Quitting tobacco is difficult because cigarette smoke contains nicotine, a physically addictive drug. In addition, many people smoke to cope with stress: Divorced and separated people, the unemployed, and people serving in the armed forces are likely to smoke. Smoking is much more common among working-class people than among those with more income and education. A larger share of men (22 percent) than women (17 percent) smoke. But cigarettes, the only form of tobacco use popular with women, have taken a toll on women's health. By 1987, lung cancer had surpassed breast cancer as a cause of death among U.S. women, who now account for 39 percent of all smoking-related deaths (Pampel, 2006; CDC, 2011).

Tobacco is a $90 billion industry in the United States. In 1997, the tobacco industry admitted that cigarette smoking is harmful to health and agreed to stop marketing cigarettes to young people. Despite the antismoking trend in the United States, research shows that 17 percent of high school students and 33 percent of college students smoke at least occasionally. In addition, chewing tobacco as well as using hookahs to smoke flavored tobacco are gaining popularity among the young, and both practices are threats to health (CDC, 2011; NCSL, 2011; American College Health Association, 2012).

The tobacco industry has increased its sales abroad, especially in low- and middle-income countries where there is less regulation of tobacco products. In many countries, especially in Asia, a large majority of men smoke. Worldwide, more than 1 billion adults (about 25 percent of the total) smoke, consuming some 6 trillion cigarettes annually, and there is as yet no sign of the decline in smoking that we have seen in high-income countries. As a result, the World Health Organization predicts that smoking, which now kills about 6 million people worldwide each year, may end up killing 1 billion people before the end of this century, 80 percent of them in lower-income nations (World Health Organization, 2011).

The harm that can come from cigarette smoking is real. But the good news is that about ten years after quitting, an ex-smoker's health is about as good as that of someone who never smoked at all.

Eating Disorders

An **eating disorder** is *an intense form of dieting or other unhealthy method of weight control driven by the desire to be very thin.* Often, the desire to be thin is itself a symptom of some other underlying mental illness or condition. One eating disorder, *anorexia nervosa,* is characterized by dieting to the point of starvation; another is *bulimia,* which involves binge eating followed by induced vomiting to avoid weight gain.

Eating disorders are not common—less than 1 percent of the adult population is affected. At the same time, 95 percent of people who suffer from anorexia nervosa or bulimia are women. People with eating disorders come from all social backgrounds, although risk levels are highest among whites living in affluent families. For women, U.S. culture equates slimness with being successful and attractive to men. Conversely, we tend to stereotype overweight women (and to a lesser extent, men) as lazy, sloppy, and even stupid (M. P. Levine, 1987; A. E. Becker, 1999; National Institute of Mental Health, 2012).

Research shows that most college-age women believe that "guys like thin girls," that being thin is crucial to physical attractiveness, and that they are not as thin as men would like. In fact, most college women actually want to be thinner than most college men want them to be. Men typically express more satisfaction with their own body shapes (Fallon & Rozin, 1985).

Because few women are able to meet our culture's unrealistic standards of beauty, many women develop a low self-image. Our idealized image of beauty leads many young women to diet to the point of risking their health and even their lives.

People with eating disorders contend with more than their illness. Research indicates that they are also viewed by others not as people with a disorder but as weak individuals who are seeking attention. In fact, the stigma attached to eating disorders was found to be more severe than the stigma attached to depression (Roehrig & McLean, 2010).

Obesity

Eating disorders such as anorexia nervosa and bulimia are serious, but they are not the biggest eating-related problem in the United States. In the population as a whole, obesity is rapidly reaching crisis

The obesity rate for the U.S. population is the highest in the world, and it is increasing. As a nation, we are "big gainers" in terms of body mass. This trend has sparked popular television shows such as *Biggest Loser*, which celebrates individuals who have managed to dramatically drop their weight. But is the solution to the national trend toward obesity simply a matter of personal effort? What changes to our culture would help move the entire population toward a healthier lifestyle?

Read "Let Them Eat Fat: The Heavy Truths about American Obesity" by Greg Crister on **mysoclab.com**

proportions. The United States now has the highest rate of obesity for all the world's nations. The government reports that 64 percent of U.S. adults are overweight, compared to 12 percent for the entire world. Obesity is defined in terms of a *body mass index* (BMI) of 25.0 to 29.9, or roughly 10 to 30 pounds over a healthy weight. Of all overweight people in the United States, 43 percent are clinically obese, with a BMI over 30.0, which means that they are at least 30 pounds over their healthy weight. National Map 14–2 shows the increasing trend toward obesity in the United States.

Being overweight can limit physical activity and raises the risk of a number of serious diseases, including heart disease, stroke, and diabetes. According to the U.S. government, the cost of treating diseases caused by obesity plus the cost of lost days at work due to such illnesses equals almost $150 billion every year. Most seriously, some 112,000 people die each year in the United States from diseases related to being overweight (Ferraro & Kelley-Moore, 2003; R. Stein, 2005; CDC, 2011; Stockdale et al., 2011).

A cause for national concern is the fact that about one in five young people in this country is overweight—triple the share in 1980—and the proportion is still increasing (CDC, 2011). This trend suggests that the members of this new generation will experience more medical problems as they reach middle age and may ultimately reverse the historical trend toward greater life expectancy.

What are the social causes of obesity? One factor is that we live in a society in which more and more people have jobs that keep them sitting in front of computer screens rather than engaging in the type of physical labor that was common a century ago. Even when we are not on the job, most of the work around the house is done by machines (or other people). Children spend more of their time sitting as well, watching television or playing video games.

Then, of course, there is diet. The typical person in the United States is eating more salty, sugary, and fatty food than ever before (Wells & Buzby, 2008). And meals are getting larger: The Department of Agriculture reported that in 2000, the typical U.S. adult consumed 140 more pounds of food each year than was true a decade earlier. Comparing old and new editions of cookbooks, recipes that used to say they would feed six now say they will feed four. The odds of being overweight go up among people with lower incomes partly because they may lack the education to make healthy choices and partly because stores in low-income communities offer a greater selection of low-cost, high-fat snack foods and fewer healthful fruits and vegetables (Hellmich, 2002).

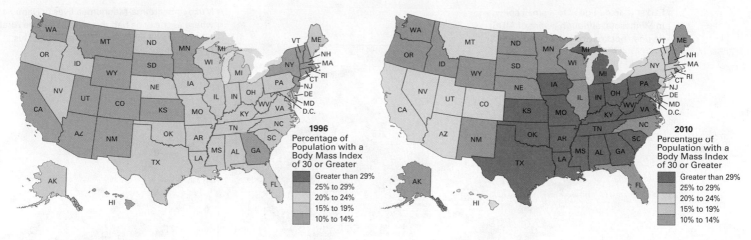

Seeing Ourselves

NATIONAL MAP 14–2 Obesity across the United States, 1996 and 2010

The map on the left shows the percentage of each state's population that was medically obese in 1996; the one on the right shows the figures for 2010. Obesity levels are up in every single state. What factors do you think are responsible for the trend toward more and more obesity in our country?

Source: CDC (2012).

Sexually Transmitted Diseases

Sexual activity, though both pleasurable and vital to the continuation of our species, can transmit more than fifty types of *sexually transmitted diseases* (STDs). Because our culture associates sex with sin, some people regard sexually transmitted diseases not only as illnesses but also as marks of immorality.

STDs grabbed national attention during the "sexual revolution" of the 1960s, when infection rates rose dramatically as people became sexually active at younger ages and had a greater number of partners. This means that STDs are an exception to the general decline in infectious diseases over the course of the past century. By the late 1980s, the rising dangers of STDs, especially AIDS, generated a sexual counterrevolution as people moved away from casual sex (Kain, 1987; Laumann et al., 1994). The following sections briefly describe several common STDs.

Gonorrhea and Syphilis

Gonorrhea and syphilis, among the oldest known diseases, are caused by microscopic organisms that are almost always transmitted by sexual contact. Untreated, gonorrhea causes sterility, and syphilis can damage major organs and result in blindness, mental disorders, and death.

In 2010, some 243,400 cases of gonorrhea and 13,300 cases of syphilis were recorded in the United States, although the actual numbers may be several times higher. Most cases are contracted by non-Hispanic African Americans (68 percent), with lower numbers among non-Hispanic whites (20 percent), Latinos (10 percent), and Asian and Native Americans (2 percent) (CDC, 2011).

Both gonorrhea and syphilis can be cured easily with antibiotics such as penicillin. Thus neither is a major health problem in the United States.

Genital Herpes

Genital herpes is a virus that is fairly common, infecting at least 24 million adolescents and adults in the United States (one in six). Though far less serious than gonorrhea and syphilis, herpes is incurable. People with genital herpes may not have any symptoms, or they may experience periodic, painful blisters on the genitals accompanied by fever and headache. Although it is not fatal to adults, women with active genital herpes can transmit the disease during a vaginal delivery, and it can be deadly to a newborn. Therefore, infected women often give birth by cesarean section (Sobel, 2001; CDC, 2011).

AIDS

The most serious of all sexually transmitted diseases is acquired immune deficiency syndrome (AIDS). Identified in 1981, it is incurable and almost always fatal. AIDS is caused by the human immunodeficiency virus (HIV), which attacks white blood cells, weakening the immune system. AIDS thus makes a person vulnerable to a wide range of diseases that eventually cause death.

AIDS deaths in the United States numbered 16,088 in 2008. But officials recorded some 32,247 new cases in the United States that year, raising the total number of cases on record to 1,108,611. Of these people, 594,496 have died (CDC, 2011).

Globally, HIV infects some 33 million people—2.5 million of them under the age of fifteen—and the number continues to rise. The global death toll now exceeds 25 million, with about 1 percent of the 1.8 million deaths in 2009 here in the United States (UNAIDS, 2011). Global Map 14–2 on page 394 shows that Africa (especially south of the Sahara) has the highest HIV infection rate and accounts for 68 percent of all world cases. A United Nations study found that across much of sub-Saharan Africa, fifteen-year-olds face a fifty-fifty chance of becoming infected with HIV. The risk is especially high for girls,

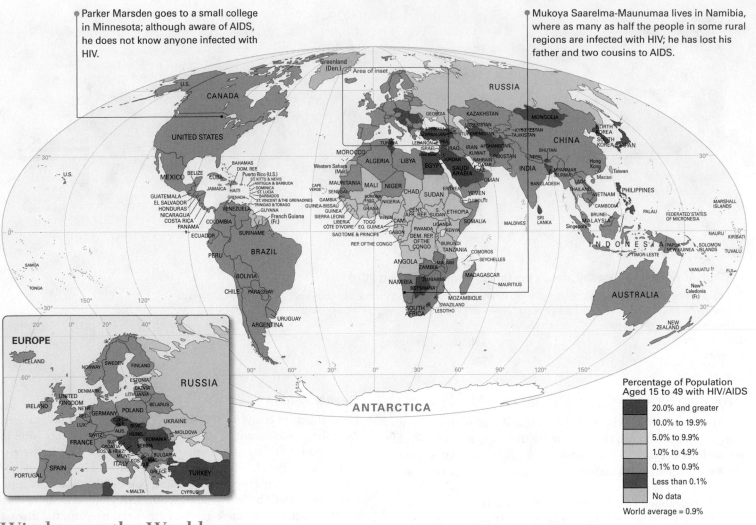

Parker Marsden goes to a small college in Minnesota; although aware of AIDS, he does not know anyone infected with HIV.

Mukoya Saarelma-Maunumaa lives in Namibia, where as many as half the people in some rural regions are infected with HIV; he has lost his father and two cousins to AIDS.

Percentage of Population Aged 15 to 49 with HIV/AIDS

- 20.0% and greater
- 10.0% to 19.9%
- 5.0% to 9.9%
- 1.0% to 4.9%
- 0.1% to 0.9%
- Less than 0.1%
- No data

World average = 0.9%

Window on the World

GLOBAL MAP 14–2 HIV/AIDS Infection of Adults in Global Perspective

Sixty-eight percent of all global HIV infections are in sub-Saharan Africa. In Swaziland, one-fourth of people between the ages of fifteen and forty-nine are infected with HIV/AIDS. This very high infection rate reflects the prevalence of other sexually transmitted diseases and infrequent use of condoms, two factors that promote transmission of HIV. South and Southeast Asia account for about 12 percent of global HIV infections. In Thailand, 1.3 percent of people aged fifteen to forty-nine are now infected. All of North America and South America taken together account for 9 percent of global HIV infections. In the United States, 0.6 percent of people aged fifteen to forty-nine are infected. The incidence of infection in Muslim nations is extremely low by world standards.

Sources: Population Reference Bureau (2011) and UNAIDS (2011).

not only because HIV is transmitted more easily from men to women but also because many African cultures encourage women to be submissive to men. According to some analysts, the AIDS crisis now threatens the political and economic security of Africa, which affects the entire world (Ashford, 2002; UNAIDS, 2011).

Upon infection, people with HIV display no symptoms at all, so most are unaware of their condition. Symptoms of AIDS may not appear for a year or longer, during which time an infected person may infect others. Within five years, one-third of infected people who have gone untreated develop full-blown AIDS; half develop AIDS within ten years; and almost all become sick within twenty years. In low-income countries, the progression of the illness is much more rapid, with many people dying within a few years of becoming infected.

HIV is infectious but not contagious. That means that HIV is transmitted from person to person through blood, semen, or breast milk but not through casual contact such as shaking hands, hugging, sharing towels or dishes, swimming together, or even coughing and sneezing. The risk of transmitting AIDS through saliva (as in kissing) is extremely low. The risk of transmitting HIV through sexual activity is greatly reduced by the use of latex condoms. However, abstinence or an exclusive relationship with an uninfected person is the only sure way to avoid infection.

Specific behaviors place people at high risk for HIV infection. *Anal sex* can cause rectal bleeding, allowing easy transmission of HIV from one person to another. The fact that many homosexual and bisexual men engage in anal sex helps explain why these categories of people account for 48 percent of AIDS cases in the United States.

Sharing needles used to inject drugs is a second high-risk behavior. At present, intravenous drug users account for 27 percent of people with AIDS, so sex with an intravenous drug user is also very risky. Because intravenous drug use is more common among poor people in the United States, AIDS is becoming a disease of the socially disadvantaged. Minorities make up a majority of all people with AIDS: Non-Hispanic African Americans (13 percent of the population) account for 44 percent of people with AIDS, and Latinos (16.4 percent of the population) represent 19 percent of all AIDS cases. Almost 80 percent of all women and children with the disease are African American or Latino. By contrast, Asian Americans and Native Americans together account for only about 1.4 percent of people with AIDS (CDC, 2011).

Use of any drug, including alcohol, also increases the risk of being infected with HIV to the extent that it impairs judgment. In other words, even people who understand the risks may make bad choices regarding sexual activity or intravenous drug use when under the influence of alcohol, marijuana, or some other drug.

In the United States, 47 percent of people with AIDS became infected through homosexual contact, but heterosexual activity can transmit HIV, and the danger rises with the number of sexual partners one has, especially if they fall into high-risk categories. Worldwide, heterosexual relations are the primary means of HIV transmission, accounting for two-thirds of all infections.

Treating just one person with AIDS costs hundreds of thousands of dollars, and the figure tends to rise as new therapies appear. At present, government health programs, private insurance, and personal savings rarely cover more than a fraction of the cost of treatment. In addition, there is the mounting cost of caring for at least 75,000 U.S. children orphaned by AIDS (worldwide, the number is 16.6 million) (Norwood, 2010; UNAIDS, 2011). Overall, there is little doubt that AIDS is both a medical and a social problem of monumental proportions.

In the early 1980s, the U.S. government responded slowly to the AIDS crisis, largely because gays and intravenous drug users were widely viewed as deviant. But funding to combat AIDS has increased (the 2012 federal budget provides $28.4 billion), and researchers have already identified some drugs, including protease inhibitors, that suppress the symptoms of the disease. But educational programs remain the most effective weapon against AIDS because prevention is the only way to stop a disease that so far has no cure.

Ethical Issues Surrounding Death

Now that technological advances are giving human beings the power to draw the line separating life and death, we must decide how and when to do so. In other words, questions about the use of medical technology have added an ethical dimension to health and illness.

In the African nation of Kenya, about 300 people die from AIDS every day. In parts of sub-Saharan Africa, the epidemic is so great that half of all children will eventually become infected with HIV. This Nairobi infant, who already has AIDS, is fighting for his life.

When Does Death Occur?

Common sense suggests that life ends when breathing and heartbeat stop. But the ability to revive or replace a heart and artificially sustain respiration make this definition of death obsolete. So medical and legal experts in the United States now define death as an *irreversible* state involving no response to stimulation, no movement or breathing, no reflexes, and no indication of brain activity (Ladd, 1979; Wall, 1980; D. G. Jones, 1998).

Do People Have a Right to Die?

Today, medical personnel, family members, and patients themselves face the burden of deciding when the life of a terminally ill person should end. Among the most difficult cases are the roughly 15,000 people in the United States in a permanent vegetative state who cannot express their own desires about life and death.

Generally speaking, the first duty of doctors and hospitals is to protect a patient's life. Even so, a mentally competent person in the process of dying can refuse medical treatment or even nutrition either at the time or, in advance, through a document called a *living will* that states the extent of medical care a person would want or not want in the event of an illness or injury that leaves the person unable to make decisions.

Mercy killing is the common term for **euthanasia**, *assisting in the death of a person suffering from an incurable disease.* Euthanasia (from the Greek, meaning "a good death") poses an ethical dilemma, being at once an act of kindness and a form of killing.

Whether there is a "right to die" is one of today's most difficult issues. All people with incurable diseases have a right to refuse treatment that might prolong their lives. But whether a doctor should be allowed to help bring about death is at the heart of today's debate. In 1994, three states—Washington, California, and Oregon—asked voters whether doctors should be able to help people who wanted to die. Only Oregon's proposition passed, and the law was quickly challenged and remained tied up in court until 1997, when voters again endorsed it. Since then, Oregon doctors have legally assisted in the death of more than 525 terminally ill patients. In 1997, however, the U.S. Supreme Court decided that under the U.S.

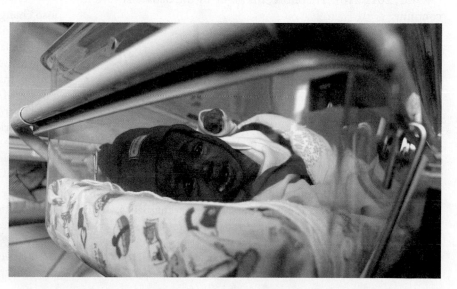

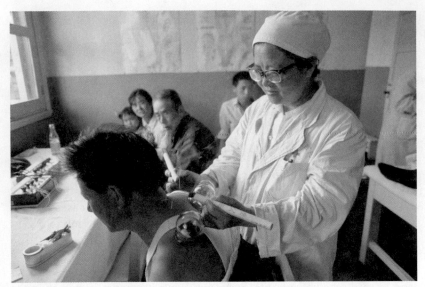

Traditional healers work to improve people's health throughout the world. This patient is receiving a traditional needle therapy in Suining, a city in China's Sichuan province. Do you think people in the United States are accepting of traditional healing practices? Why or why not?

The Rise of Scientific Medicine

In colonial times, herbalists, druggists, barbers, midwives, and ministers practiced the healing arts. But not all were effective: Unsanitary instruments, lack of anesthesia, and simple ignorance made surgery a terrible ordeal, and doctors probably killed as many people as they saved.

Doctors made medicine into a science by following scientific procedures to study the human body and how it works and emphasizing surgery and the use of drugs to fight disease. Pointing to their specialized knowledge, doctors gradually established themselves as self-regulating professionals with medical degrees. The American Medical Association (AMA), founded in 1847, symbolized the growing acceptance of a scientific model of medicine.

Still, traditional practitioners of health care had their supporters. The AMA opposed them by seeking control of the certification process. In the early 1900s, state licensing boards agreed to certify only doctors trained in the scientific programs approved by the AMA. As a result, schools teaching other healing skills began to close, which soon limited the practice of medicine to individuals holding an M.D. degree. Accordingly, the prestige and income of doctors rose dramatically; today, men and women with M.D. degrees earn, on average, $200,000 annually (U.S. Department of Labor, 2011).

Practitioners who did things differently, such as osteopathic physicians, concluded that they had no choice but to fall in line and follow AMA standards. Thus osteopaths (with D.O. degrees), originally concerned with treating illness by manipulating the skeleton and muscles, today treat illness with drugs in much the same way as medical doctors (with M.D. degrees). Chiropractors, herbal healers, and midwives still practice with their own special approaches but have lower standing within the medical profession. Debates between people supporting scientific medicine and those favoring traditional healing practices continue today, both in the United States and in many other countries. An increasing number of U.S. hospitals now mix traditional scientific medicine with various "alternative" medical practices, although many such treatments are not covered by medical insurance (Andrews, 2012).

Scientific medicine, taught in expensive, urban medical schools, also changed the social profile of doctors so that most came from privileged backgrounds and practiced in cities. Women, who had played a large part in many fields of healing, were pushed aside by the AMA. Some early medical schools did train women and African Americans, but with few financial resources, most of these schools ran out of money and closed. Only in recent decades has the social diversity of the medical profession increased, with women and African Americans representing 32 percent and 6 percent of physicians, respectively (U.S. Bureau of Labor Statistics, 2011).

Holistic Medicine

The scientific model of medicine has been tempered by the introduction of **holistic medicine**, *an approach to health care that emphasizes the prevention of illness and takes into account a person's entire physical and social environment.* Holistic practitioners agree on the need for drugs, surgery, artificial organs, and high technology, but they emphasize treating the whole person rather than just

---

Constitution, there is no "right to die," a decision that has slowed the spread of such laws. Only in 2008 did Washington become the second state to allow physician-assisted suicide.

Supporters of *active* euthanasia—allowing a dying person to enlist the services of a doctor to bring on a quick death—argue that there are circumstances (as when a dying person is suffering great pain) that make death preferable to life. Critics counter that permitting active euthanasia invites abuse. They fear that patients will feel pressure to end their lives to spare family members the burden of caring for them and the high costs of hospitalization. Research in the Netherlands, where physician-assisted suicide is legal, indicates that about one-fifth of all such deaths have occurred without a patient's explicitly requesting to die (Gillon, 1999).

In the United States, a majority of adults express support for giving dying people the right to choose to die with a doctor's help (NORC, 2011:416). Therefore, the right-to-die debate is sure to continue.

The Medical Establishment

Understand

Throughout most of human history, health care was the responsibility of individuals and their families. Medicine emerges as a social institution only as societies become more productive and people take on specialized work.

Members of agrarian societies today still turn to traditional health practitioners, including acupuncturists and herbalists. In industrial societies, medical care falls to specially trained and licensed professionals, from anesthesiologists to X-ray technicians. The medical establishment of modern, industrial societies took form over the past 200 years.

symptoms and focus on health rather than disease. There are three foundations of holistic health care (Gordon, 1980; Patterson, 1998):

1. **Treat patients as people.** Holistic practitioners are concerned not only with symptoms but also with how people's environment and lifestyle affect health. Holistic practitioners extend the bounds of conventional medicine, taking an active role in fighting poverty, environmental pollution, and other dangers to public health.

2. **Encourage responsibility, not dependency.** A scientific approach to medicine puts doctors in charge of health, and patients are to follow doctors' orders. Holistic medicine tries to shift some responsibility for health from doctor to patient by emphasizing health-promoting behavior. Holistic medicine favors an *active approach to health* rather than a *reactive approach to illness*.

3. **Provide personal treatment.** Scientific medicine treats patients in impersonal offices and hospitals, both disease-centered settings. Holistic practitioners favor, as much as possible, a personal and relaxed environment such as the home.

In sum, holistic care does not oppose scientific medicine but shifts the emphasis from treating disease to achieving the greatest well-being for everyone. Considering that the AMA certifies more than fifty medical specialties, there is a need for practitioners concerned with the whole patient.

Paying for Medical Care: A Global Survey

As medicine has come to rely on advanced technology, the costs of medical care in industrial societies have skyrocketed. Countries throughout the world have adopted different strategies to meet these costs.

People's Republic of China

This economically growing but still mostly agrarian nation faces the immense task of providing health care for more than 1.3 billion people. China has experimented with private medicine, but the government controls most health care.

China's "barefoot doctors," roughly comparable to U.S. paramedics, bring some modern methods of medical care to peasants in rural villages. Traditional healing arts, involving acupuncture and medicinal herbs, are still widely practiced. The Chinese approach to health is based on a holistic concern for the interplay of mind and body (Kaptchuk, 1985).

Russian Federation

The Russian Federation has transformed what was a state-dominated economy into more of a market system. For this reason, medical care is in transition. But the state remains in charge of medical care, and the government claims that everyone has a right to basic medical care.

As in China, people in the Russian Federation do not choose a doctor but report to a local government health facility. Physicians have much lower incomes than medical doctors in the United States, earning about the same salary as skilled industrial workers (by contrast, U.S. doctors earn roughly five times as much as

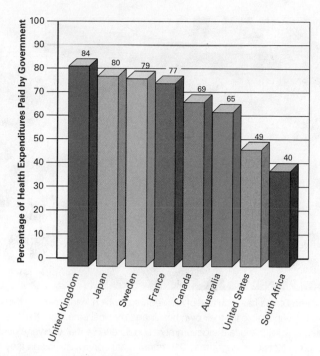

Global Snapshot

FIGURE 14–2 Extent of Socialized Medicine in Selected Countries

The governments of most high-income countries pay a greater share of their people's medical costs than the U.S. government does.

Source: World Bank (2011).

industrial workers in the United States). Also, about 72 percent of Russian doctors are women, compared to 32 percent in the United States. As in our society, occupations dominated by women in the Russian Federation offer lower pay.

In recent years, the Russian Federation has suffered setbacks in health, due in part to a falling standard of living. Rising demand for medical care and cutbacks in government spending on health have strained a bureaucratic system that at best provides highly standardized and impersonal care. The optimistic view is that as living standards rise, the quality of medical service will improve. In Russia's uncertain times, what does seem clear is that inequalities in medical care will increase (Landsberg, 1998; Mason, 2004; Zuckerman, 2006; O'Leary et al., 2009).

Sweden

In 1891, Sweden began a mandatory, comprehensive system of government medical care. Citizens pay for this program with their taxes, which are among the highest in the world. Typically, doctors are government employees, and most hospitals are government-managed. Sweden's system is called **socialized medicine,** *a medical care system in which the government owns and operates most medical facilities and employs most physicians*. Figure 14–2 shows the extent of socialized medicine in specific high-income countries.

Great Britain

In 1948, Great Britain also established socialized medicine by creating a dual system of medical services. All British citizens are entitled

The United States has a culture of individualism, which leads many to think that people should be responsible for their own health and medical care. The 2010 health care reform is a step toward the idea the government should ensure that everyone has at least basic health care. Not surprisingly, the 2010 reforms are controversial, and they are now being reviewed by the U.S. Supreme Court. Where do you stand on this issue?

to medical care provided by the National Health Service, but those who can afford it may go to doctors and hospitals that operate privately.

Canada

Since 1972, Canada has had a "single-payer" model of medical care that provides care to all Canadians. Like a giant insurance company, the Canadian government pays doctors and hospitals according to a set schedule of fees. Like Great Britain, Canada also has some physicians working outside the government-funded system and setting their own fees, although costs are regulated by the government.

Canada boasts of providing care for everyone at a lower cost than the (nonuniversal) medical system in the United States. However, like the British system, the Canadian system uses less state-of-the-art technology and responds more slowly, meaning that people may wait months for major surgery. The Canadian system provides care for all its citizens, regardless of income, unlike the United States, in which lower-income people are often denied medical care (Rosenthal, 1991; Macionis & Gerber, 2008).

> July 31, Montreal, Canada.   I am visiting the home of an oral surgeon who appears (judging by the large home) to be doing pretty well. Yet he complains that the provincial governments in Canada, in an effort to hold down medical costs, cap doctors' annual salaries at several hundred thousand dollars (exact caps vary from province to province). Therefore, he explains, many specialists have left for the United States, where they can earn much more; other doctors and dentists simply limit their practices.

Japan

Physicians in Japan operate privately, but a combination of government programs and private insurance pays medical costs. As shown

in Figure 14–2, the Japanese approach medical care much like the Europeans, with most medical expenses paid through the government.

Paying for Medical Care: The United States

Even after the historic passage of the new health care bill in 2010, the United States stands alone among high-income nations in having no universal, government-sponsored program of medical care. Ours is a **direct-fee system**, *a medical care system in which patients pay directly for the services of physicians and hospitals*. Europeans look to government to fund 70 to nearly 90 percent of medical costs (paid for through taxation), but in the United States the federal, state, and local governments pay just 49 percent of all medical costs (U.S. Department of Health and Human Services, 2012).

In the United States, rich people can buy the best medical care in the world, but poor people are worse off than their counterparts in Europe. This difference translates into relatively high death rates among both infants and adults in the United States compared with many European countries (Population Reference Bureau, 2011).

Several states, including Maine, Vermont, and Massachusetts, have enacted programs that provide health care to everyone. Why does the United States have no national program that provides universal care? First, during World War II, the government froze worker earnings. As a way to increase compensation during the wage freeze, more employers began providing health care benefits. Second, labor unions worked to expand health care from employers rather than go after government programs. Third, the public generally favors a private, worker-and-employer system because our culture stresses individual self-reliance. Fourth, and finally, the AMA and the health insurance industry have strongly and consistently opposed national medical care.

There is no question that medical care in this country is very expensive. The cost of medical care increased dramatically, from $12 billion in 1950 to more than $2.5 trillion in 2010 (U.S. Department of Health and Human Services, 2012). This amounts to more than $8,400 per person, more than any other nation spends for medical care. Who pays the medical bills?

Private Insurance Programs

In 2010, about 169 million people in the United States (55.3 percent) received medical care benefits from a family member's employer or labor union. Another 30 million people (9.8 percent) purchased some private coverage on their own. Combining these figures, 64 percent of the U.S. population has private insurance,

socialized medicine a medical care system in which the government owns and operates most medical facilities and employs most physicians

direct-fee system a medical care system in which patients pay directly for the services of physicians and hospitals

although few such programs pay all medical costs (U.S. Census Bureau, 2011).

Public Insurance Programs

In 1965, Congress created Medicare and Medicaid. Medicare pays some of the medical costs for people over age sixty-five; in 2010, it covered 44 million women and men, 14.5 percent of the population. In the same year, Medicaid, a medical insurance program for the poor, provided benefits to another 48.5 million people, about 16 percent of the population. An additional 12.8 million military veterans (4 percent) can obtain free care in government-operated hospitals. In all, 31 percent of this country's people get medical benefits from the government, but most also have private insurance (U.S. Census Bureau, 2011).

Health Maintenance Organizations

About 75 million people (25 percent) in the United States belong to a **health maintenance organization (HMO)**, *an organization that provides comprehensive medical care to subscribers for a fixed fee.* HMOs vary in costs and benefits, and none provides full coverage. Fixed fees make these organizations profitable if subscribers stay healthy; therefore, many take a preventive approach to health. However, HMOs have been criticized for refusing to pay for medical procedures that they consider unnecessary. Congress is currently debating the extent to which patients can sue HMOs to obtain better care.

In all, 84 percent of the U.S. population has some medical care coverage, either private or public. Yet most plans do not provide full coverage, so serious illness threatens even middle-class people with financial hardship. Most programs also exclude many medical services, such as dental care and treatment for mental health and substance abuse problems. Worse, 50 million people (about 16 percent of the population) have no medical insurance at all, even though 67 percent of these people are working. Almost as many lose their coverage temporarily each year because of layoffs or job changes. Caught in the medical care bind are mostly low- to moderate-income people who cannot afford the cost of the preventive medical care they need to stay healthy (Brink, 2002; U.S. Census Bureau, 2011).

The 2010 Health Care Law

In 2010, Congress passed a law that made significant changes to the way this country pays for health care. The act has a huge cost—estimated at almost $1 trillion over the next ten years—and change will take effect in stages.

Here are some of the most important features of the new law:

1. Starting right away, all families will pay an insurance tax. Lower-income families will receive subsidies to help pay the cost of the insurance; high-income families will pay higher taxes on their income to help fund the program.

2. Six months after enactment of the new law, insurance companies could no longer legally drop customers because they get sick or refuse coverage to children because of preexisting conditions.

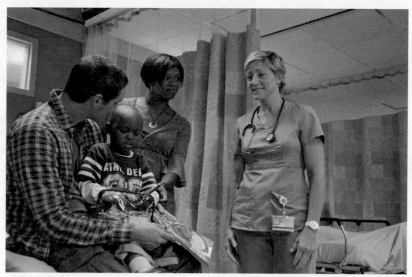

The challenges of nursing in the emergency room of a large, New York City hospital are played out on the television show *Nurse Jackie*. In light of the increasing demand for nurses in the United States, would you consider a career in nursing?

3. Insurance companies cannot set caps on the amount of money they will pay to any individual for medical expenses over a lifetime.

4. Parents can use their health care plans to include children up to the age of twenty-six.

5. By 2014, insurance companies will no longer be able to refuse coverage to anyone of any age due to preexisting health conditions.

6. By 2014, all families will be required to purchase insurance coverage. Government will regulate both the benefits available and the costs.

7. Starting in 2014, the law provides penalties for people who do not buy insurance; these penalties will increase over time.

In all, the 2010 health care law will provide health care insurance to some 32 million people (of the 50 million) in the United States who currently do not have this protection. The Obama administration claims that this law, although providing something short of universal health care coverage, is nonetheless a major step toward that goal.

The Nursing Shortage

Another issue in medical care is the shortage of nurses across the United States. In 2009, there were about 3.1 million registered nurses (people with the degree of R.N.), an increase of 5 percent since 2004. At the same time, more than 100,000 positions for nurses remain unfilled. Looking ahead, the shortage of nurses is projected to increase to more than 250,000 positions by 2025 (American Association of Colleges of Nursing, 2011; U.S. Department of Health and Human Services, 2012).

The increasing demand for nurses is due to several factors. First, technological advances in medicine allow more illnesses to be treated. Second, there has been a rapid expansion in hospital outpatient services, such as same-day surgery, rehabilitation, and chemotherapy. Third, an increasing focus on preventive care, rather than simply treating disease or accidents, means that more people than ever are receiving care. Fourth, and most important of all, the aging population of the United States is consuming more and more medical services.

Almost 500,000 people have entered the field of nursing since 2004. Even so, because the demand for nurses is so great, the supply of new nurses continues to fall short of the need. One reason for the shortage is that nursing schools do not have enough teachers, which limits the number of graduates. A broader reason is that today's young women have a wide range of job choices, and fewer are drawn to the traditionally female occupation of nursing. This fact is evident in the rising median age of working nurses, which is now forty-six. Another is that many of today's nurses are unhappy with their working conditions, citing heavy patient loads, too much required overtime, a stressful working environment, and a lack of recognition and respect from supervisors, physicians, and hospital managers.

The nursing shortage is harming health care. One study estimates that more than 6,000 hospital patients die each year for lack of immediate treatment due to the shortage of nurses. Such facts are bringing change to this profession. Salaries, which range from about $62,000 for general-duty nurses in residential care and child care facilities to $136,000 for certified nurse-anesthetists, are on the rise. Some hospitals and doctors are also offering signing bonuses in an effort to attract new nurses. In addition, nursing programs are trying harder to recruit a more diverse population, seeking more minorities (who are currently 16.8 percent of all nurses) and, especially, more men (now only 7 percent of R.N.s) (Marquez, 2006; U.S. Department of Health and Human Services, 2010; U.S. Bureau of Labor Statistics, 2011; American Association of Colleges of Nursing, 2012).

Theories of Health and Medicine

 Apply

Each of sociology's theoretical approaches helps us organize and understand facts and issues concerning human health.

Role Analysis: Structural-Functional Theory

Talcott Parsons (1951) viewed medicine as society's strategy to keep its members healthy. Parsons considered illness dysfunctional because it reduces people's abilities to perform their roles.

The Sick Role

Society responds to sickness not only by providing medical care but also by allowing people a **sick role**, *patterns of behavior defined as appropriate for people who are ill*. According to Parsons, the sick role releases people from everyday obligations such as going to work or attending classes. However, people cannot simply claim to be ill; they must "look the part" and, in serious cases, get the help of a medical expert. After assuming the sick role, the patient must want to get better and must do whatever is needed to regain good health, including cooperating with health professionals.

The Physician's Role

Physicians evaluate people's claims of sickness and help restore the sick people to normal routines. To do this, physicians use their specialized knowledge and expect patients to follow "doctor's orders" in order to complete treatment.

Evaluate Parsons's analysis links illness and medicine to the broader organization of society. Others have extended the concept of the sick role to some non-sickness situations such as pregnancy (Myers & Grasmick, 1989).

One limitation of the sick-role concept is that it applies to acute conditions (such as the flu or a broken leg) better than to chronic illnesses (such as heart disease), which may not be reversible. In addition, a sick person's ability to assume the sick role (to take time off from work to regain health) depends on the patient's resources. Finally, illness is not completely dysfunctional; it can have some positive consequences: Many people who experience a serious illness consider it an opportunity to reevaluate their lives and gain a better sense of what is truly important (D. G. Myers, 2000; Ehrenreich, 2001).

CHECK YOUR LEARNING Define the sick role. How does turning illness into a role in this way help society operate?

The Meaning of Health: Symbolic-Interaction Theory

Using the symbolic-interaction approach, society is less a grand system than a complex and changing reality. In this view, health and medical care are socially constructed by people in everyday interaction.

The Social Construction of Illness

If both health and illness are socially constructed, people in a poor society may view malnutrition as normal. Similarly, many members of our own society give little thought to the harmful effects of a rich diet.

Our response to illness is also based on social definitions that may or may not square with medical facts. People with AIDS may be forced to deal with prejudice that has no medical basis. Likewise, students may pay no attention to symptoms of real illness on the eve of a vacation but head for the infirmary hours before a midterm examination with a case of the sniffles. In short, health is less an objective fact than a negotiated outcome.

How people define a medical situation may actually affect how they feel. Medical experts marvel at *psychosomatic* disorders (a fusion of the Greek words for "mind" and "body"), when state of mind guides physical sensations (Hamrick, Anspaugh, & Ezell, 1986). Applying the Thomas theorem (presented in Chapter 4, "Social Interaction in Everyday Life"), we can say that once health or illness is defined as real, it can become real in its consequences.

The Social Construction of Treatment

Also in Chapter 4, we used Erving Goffman's dramaturgical approach to explain how doctors tailor their physical surroundings (their office) and their behavior (the "presentation of self") so that others see them as competent and in charge.

Definitions of health are based on cultural standards, including ideas about beauty. Every year, millions of people undergo cosmetic surgery to bring their appearance into line with societal definitions of how people ought to look.

The sociologist Joan Emerson (1970) further illustrates this process of reality construction in her analysis of the gynecological examination carried out by a male doctor. The situation could be seriously misinterpreted because a man touching a woman's genitals is conventionally viewed as a sexual act and possibly an assault.

To ensure that the situation is defined as impersonal and professional, medical personnel wear uniforms, and the examination room is furnished with nothing but medical equipment. The doctor's manner is designed to make the patient feel that to him, examining the genital area is no different from treating any other part of the body. A female nurse is usually present during the examination, not only to assist the physician but also to avoid any impression that a man and woman are "alone together."

Managing situational definitions is rarely taught in medical schools. This oversight is unfortunate, because as Emerson's analysis shows, understanding how medical personnel construct reality in the examination room is as important as mastering the medical skills needed for treatment. One recent study found that physicians who were weak in social skills, even if they were well-trained medically, were much more likely to be the targets of complaints and lawsuits filed by patients (Tamblyn, 2008).

The Social Construction of Personal Identity

A final insight provided by the symbolic-interaction approach is how surgery can affect people's self-image and social identity. The reason that medical procedures can have a major effect on how we think of ourselves is that our culture places great symbolic importance on some organs and other parts of our bodies. People who lose a limb (say, in military combat) typically experience serious doubts about being "as much of a person" as before. The effects of surgery can be important even when there is no obvious change in physical appearance. For example, Jean Elson (2004) points out that one out of three women in the United States eventually has her uterus surgically removed in a procedure known as a *hysterectomy*. In interviews with women who had undergone the procedure, Elson found that the typical woman faced serious self-doubt about gender identity—asking, in other words, "Am I still a woman?" Only 10 percent of hysterectomies are for cancer; most are performed in response to pain, bleeding, or cysts—conditions not dangerous enough to rule out less invasive treatments. Perhaps, Elson points out, doctors might be more willing to consider alternative treatment if they were aware of how symbolically important the loss of the uterus is to many women.

Many women who undergo breast surgery have much the same reaction, doubting their own feminine identity and worrying that men will no longer find them attractive. For men to understand the significance of such medical procedures, it is only necessary to imagine how a male might react to the surgical loss of any or all of his genitals.

● **Evaluate** Symbolic-interaction theory reveals that what people view as healthful or harmful depends on a host of factors that are not, strictly speaking, medical. This approach also shows that in any medical procedure, both patient and medical staff engage in a subtle process of reality construction. Finally, this approach has helped us understand the symbolic importance of limbs and other bodily organs; the loss of any part of the body—through accident or elective surgery—can have important consequences for personal identity.

By directing attention to the meanings people attach to health or illness, the symbolic-interaction approach draws criticism for implying that there are no objective standards of well-being. Certain physical conditions do indeed cause specific changes in people, regardless of how we may view those conditions. People who lack sufficient nutrition and safe water, for example, suffer from their unhealthy environment, whether they define their surroundings as normal or not.

A recent study shows that the share of beginning college students in the United States who described their physical health as "above average" has declined from 74 percent of men and 54 percent of women in 1985 to 68 percent of men and 46 percent of women in 2010 (Astin et al., 2002; Pryor et al., 2011). While these changing perceptions may reflect a real decline in health (due, say, to eating more unhealthy food), might they also be due to changes in the ways students see the world? Can you offer possible explanations for this decline?

CHECK YOUR LEARNING Explain what it means to say that both health and the treatment of illness are socially constructed.

Inequality and Health: Social-Conflict and Feminist Theories

Social-conflict analysis points out the connection between health and social inequality. Following the ideas of Karl Marx, we can link patterns of health to the operation of capitalism. In addition, feminist theory links health and medicine to gender stratification. Most attention has gone to three main issues: access to medical care, the effects of the profit motive, and the politics of medicine.

Social Conflict Theory: Access to Health Care

Health is important to everyone. But by requiring individuals to pay directly for medical care, our society allows the richest people to have the best health. The access problem is more serious in the United States than in most other high-income nations because we do not have a universal medical care system.

Social-conflict theory argues that our society provides excellent health care for the rich but at the expense of the rest of the population. Most of the 50 million people in the United States who lack medical care coverage at present have moderate to low incomes.

Marxist Theory: Capitalism and the Profit Motive

Marxist theory goes further, arguing that the real problem goes beyond access to medical care to the capitalist economy that defines health and medicine. Under a capitalist system, the primary goal of medicine is not health but profit. The profit motive turns doctors, hospitals, and the pharmaceutical industry into multibillion-dollar corporations. The drive for higher profits encourages unnecessary tests and surgery and a reliance on expensive drugs rather than focusing on improving people's lifestyles and living conditions.

Of more than 25 million surgical operations performed in the United States each year, three-fourths are elective, meaning that they are intended to promote long-term health and are not prompted by a medical emergency. Of course, any medical procedure or use of drugs is risky and harms between 5 and 10 percent of patients. Therefore, a Marxist analysis suggests that medical procedures, including surgery, reflect not just the needs of patients but also the financial interests of surgeons and hospitals (Cowley, 1995; Nuland, 1999).

Finally, according to this approach, our society is too tolerant of doctors' having a direct financial interest in the tests and procedures they order for their patients (Pear & Eckholm, 1991). Medical care should be motivated by a concern for people, not profits.

Feminist Theory: Medicine as Politics

Although science claims to be politically neutral, feminist theory claims that scientific medicine often takes sides on significant social issues. For example, the medical establishment has always strongly opposed government medical care programs. In addition, only recently has it allowed a significant number of women to join the ranks of physicians. The history of medicine shows that not only

has sexual and racial discrimination kept women and people of color out of medicine but also that discrimination has been supported by "scientific" opinions about, say, the inferiority of women and other minorities (Leavitt, 1984). Consider the diagnosis of "hysteria," a term that has its origins in the Greek word *hyster,* meaning "uterus." In choosing this word to describe a wild, emotional state, the medical profession suggested that being a woman is somehow the same as being irrational.

Even today, according to the social-conflict approach, scientific medicine explains illness in terms of bacteria and viruses, ignoring the damaging effects of poverty, racism, and sexism. In effect, scientific medicine hides the bias in our medical system by transforming these social issues into simple biology.

● **Evaluate** Social-conflict analysis, including Marxist theory and feminist theory, provides still another view of the relationships among health, medicine, and society. According to this approach, social inequality is the main reason some people have better health than others.

The most common objection to the social-conflict approach is that it minimizes the advances in U.S. health brought about by scientific medicine and higher living standards. Though there is plenty of room for improvement, health indicators for our population as a whole rose steadily over the course of the twentieth century, and they compare well with those in other high-income nations.

CHECK YOUR LEARNING How are health and medical care linked to social classes, capitalism, and gender stratification?

Sociology's three major theoretical approaches, summed up in the Applying Theory table, explain why health and medicine are social issues. The Controversy & Debate box explains how advancing technology, far from solving our health problems, is raising new questions and concerns.

The famous French scientist Louis Pasteur (1822–1895), who spent much of his life studying how bacteria cause disease, said just before he died that health depends less on bacteria than on the social environment in which the bacteria are found (Gordon, 1980:7). Explaining Pasteur's insight is sociology's contribution to human health.

APPLYING THEORY

Health

	Structural-Functional Theory	Symbolic-Interaction Theory	Social-Conflict and Feminist Theories
What is the level of analysis?	Macro-level	Micro-level	Macro-level
How is health related to society?	Illness is dysfunctional for society because it prevents people from carrying out their daily roles.	Societies define "health" and "illness" differently according to their living standards.	Health is linked to social inequality, with rich people having more access to care than poor people.
	The sick role releases people who are ill from responsibilities while they try to get well.	How people define their own health affects how they actually feel (psychosomatic conditions).	Capitalist medical care places the drive for profits over the needs of people.
			Scientific medicine downplays the social causes of illness, including poverty, racism, and sexism.

Felisha: Before I get married, I want my partner to have a genetic screening. It's like buying a house or a car—you should check it out before you sign on the line.

Eva: Do you expect to get a warranty, too?

The liquid in the laboratory test tube seems ordinary enough, like a syrupy form of water. But this liquid is one of the greatest medical breakthroughs of all time; it may even hold the key to life itself. The liquid is deoxyribonucleic acid, or DNA, the spiraling molecule that is found in cells of the human body and contains the blueprint for making each one of us human as well as different from every other person.

The human body is composed of roughly 100 trillion cells, most of which contain a nucleus of twenty-three pairs of chromosomes (one of each pair comes from each parent). Each chromosome is packed with DNA in segments called genes. Genes guide the production of protein, the building blocks of the human body.

If genetics sounds complicated (and it is), the social implications of genetic knowledge are even more complex. Scientists discovered the structure of the DNA molecule in 1952, and in recent years they have made great gains in "mapping" the human genome. Charting our genetic landscape will help us understand how each bit of DNA shapes our being.

But do we really want to turn the key to understanding life itself? And what do we do with this knowledge once we have it? Research has already identified genetic abnormalities that

cause many diseases, including sickle-cell anemia, muscular dystrophy, Huntington's disease, cystic fibrosis, and some forms of cancer. Gazing into a person's genetic "crystal ball," doctors may be able to manipulate segments of DNA to prevent diseases before they appear.

But many people urge caution in such research, warning that genetic information can easily be abused. At its worst, genetic mapping opens the door to Nazi-like efforts to breed a "super race." In 1994, the People's Republic of China began to use genetic information to regulate marriage and childbirth with the purpose of avoiding "new births of inferior quality."

All over the world, many parents will want to use genetic testing to predict the health (or

Scientists are learning more and more about the genetic factors that prompt the eventual development of serious diseases. If offered the opportunity, would you want to undergo a genetic screening that would predict the long-term future of your own health?

even the eye color) of their future children. What if they want to abort a fetus because it falls short of their standards? When genetic manipulations become possible, should parents be able to create "designer children"?

Then there is the issue of "genetic privacy." Can a prospective spouse request a genetic evaluation of her fiancé before agreeing to marry? Can life insurance companies demand genetic testing before issuing a policy? Should employers be allowed to screen job applicants to weed out those whose future illnesses might drain their company's health care funds? Clearly, what is scientifically possible is not always morally desirable. Society is already struggling with questions about the proper use of our expanding knowledge of human genetics. Such ethical dilemmas will multiply as genetic research moves forward in the years to come.

What Do You Think?

1. Traditional wedding vows join couples "in sickness and in health." Do people have a right to know the future health of a partner before tying the knot? Why or why not?

2. Should parents be permitted to genetically "design" their children? Why or why not?

3. Is it right that private companies doing genetic research are able to patent their discoveries so that they can profit from the results, or should this information be made available to everyone? Explain your answer.

Sources: D. Thompson (1999) and Golden & Lemonick (2000).

Health and Medicine: Looking Ahead

 Evaluate

In the early 1900s, deaths from infectious diseases such as diphtheria and measles were widespread. Because scientists had yet to develop penicillin and other antibiotics, even a simple infection from a minor wound might become life-threatening. Today, a century later, most members of our society take good health and long life for granted.

More people in the United States are taking personal responsibility for their health. Even so, there are some grounds for concern. The increasing obesity epidemic is one major problem. If this trend continues, the younger generation may become the first to show a decline in life expectancy. Every one of us can live better and longer if we eat sensibly and in moderation, exercise regularly, and avoid tobacco.

Another health problem that our society faces, discussed throughout this chapter, is the double standard that offers good health to the rich but causes higher rates of disease for the poor. International comparisons reveal that the United States lags in some measures of human health because of the large share of our population who live with low income at the margins of our society. An important question, even after the recent health care reforms, is what our rich society should do about the millions of people who still live with low income and without the security of medical care.

Finally, we find that health problems are far greater in low-income nations than in the United States. The good news is that life expectancy for the world as a whole has been rising—from forty-eight years in 1950 to seventy years today—and the biggest gains have been in poor countries (Population Reference Bureau, 2011). But in much of Latin America, Asia, and especially Africa, hundreds of millions of adults and children lack not only medical attention but adequate food and safe water as well. Improving the health of the world's poorest people is a critical challenge in the years to come.

Seeing Sociology in Everyday Life

How big is our society's inequality in schooling?

All schools, of course, differ in many ways. But there are several tiers of schooling in the United States, and these reflect the social class standing of the students they enroll. The images below provide a closer look at this educational hierarchy.

Hint Private boarding schools provide an outstanding education, and the independent living experience also helps students prepare for success in a good college or university. Although schools like Lawrenceville provide financial aid to many students, the cost of a single year at such a school for most students is about $50,000, which is just about as much as the average family earns in a year. Suburban high schools are supported through tax money; yet the cost of homes in these affluent communities is typically hundreds of thousands of dollars, putting this level of schooling out of reach for a large share of U.S. families. Public schools in the inner city enroll students from families with below-average incomes, which means these schools have the highest percentage of minority students. Liberal Democrats such as the Obamas strongly support public education, but they, like most other residents of the White House (Amy Carter went to public school), have chosen private schooling for their children, whether for educational or security reasons.

At the top of the schooling hierarchy are private boarding schools. The best of these schools, such as the Lawrenceville School in New Jersey, have large endowments, small classes with well-trained and dedicated teachers, and magnificent campuses with facilities that rival those of the nation's top colleges. What do you estimate is the annual cost to attend such a school?

In the middle of the educational hierarchy are the best public high schools, most of which are found in suburban communities. This classroom in Briarcliff High School in Briarcliff Manor, New York, has small classes with good teachers and offers many extracurricular activities. What level of income do you think is typical of the families that are able to send their children to schools such as this?

At the lower end of the hierarchy are the public schools found in our nation's large cities. Thomas Jefferson High School in Los Angeles is better than most, yet compared to suburban and private boarding schools, its classes are larger, its teachers are not as well trained, and the risk of violence within its walls is higher. What can you say about the students who attend inner-city schools?

When Barack and Michelle Obama moved to the White House in 2009, they faced the choice of where to enroll their two young daughters. They chose Sidwell Friends, a private school. What factors might they have considered before making this choice?

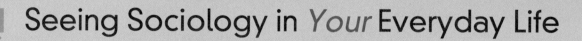

Seeing Sociology in *Your* Everyday Life

1. Make a visit to a public or private secondary school near your college or home. What is the typical social background of students enrolled there? Does the school have a tracking policy? If so, find out how it works. How much importance does a student's social background have in the school's process of making a tracking assignment?

2. Think about the effects of schooling on health. In what ways does getting a college degree (and perhaps a graduate or professional degree) improve a person's likelihood of leading a healthy life?

3. Why are you in college? What benefits do you expect to receive from continuing your education? Go to the "Seeing Sociology in

Your Everyday Life" feature on MySocLab to learn more about the benefits of a college education and also for some suggestions about how to get the most out of college. A second "Seeing Sociology in *Your* Everyday Life" feature asks you to consider how a sociological study of health can benefit your own personal life.

Education: A Global Survey

Education is the major social institution for transmitting knowledge and skills, as well as teaching cultural norms and values.

- In preindustrial societies, education occurs informally within the family.
- Industrial societies develop formal systems of schooling to educate their children. **pp. 374–76**

education (p. 374) the social institution through which society provides its members with important knowledge, including basic facts, job skills, and cultural norms and values

schooling (p. 374) formal instruction under the direction of specially trained teachers

Theories of Schooling

Structural-functional theory highlights major functions of schooling, including socialization, cultural innovation, social integration, and the placement of people in the social hierarchy.

- Latent functions of schooling include providing child care and building social networks. **pp. 376–77**

Symbolic-interaction theory helps us understand that stereotypes can have important consequences for how people act. If students think they are academically superior, they are likely to perform better; students who think they are inferior are likely to perform less well. **pp. 377–78**

Social-conflict theory links schooling to the hierarchy involving class, race, and gender.

- Formal education serves as a means of generating conformity to produce obedient adult workers.

- Standardized achievement tests have been criticized as culturally biased tools that may lead to labeling less privileged students as personally deficient.
- Tracking has been challenged by critics as a program that gives privileged youngsters a richer education.
- The great majority of young people in the United States attend state-funded public schools. A small proportion of students—usually the most well-to-do—attend elite private college preparatory schools.
- Largely due to the high cost of college, only 70% of U.S. students enroll in college directly after high school graduation. **pp. 378–83**

👁 Watch the Video on mysoclab.com

✳ Explore the Map on mysoclab.com

tracking (p. 378) assigning students to different types of educational programs

Problems in the Schools

- *Violence* permeates many schools, especially in poor neighborhoods.
- The bureaucratic character of schools fosters *high dropout rates* and *student passivity*.
- *Declining academic standards* are reflected in today's lower average scores on achievement tests, the functional illiteracy of a significant proportion of high school graduates, and grade inflation. **pp. 383–85**

functional illiteracy (p. 385) a lack of the reading and writing skills needed for everyday living

Current Issues in U.S. Education

The **school choice movement** seeks to make schools more accountable to the public. Innovative school choice options include magnet schools, schooling for profit, and charter schools. **pp. 385–86**

Home Schooling

- The original pioneers of home schooling did not believe in public education because they wanted to give their children a strongly religious upbringing.
- Home schooling advocates today point to the poor performance of public schools. **pp. 386–87**

Schooling People with Disabilites

- Children with mental or physical disabilities have historically been schooled in special classes.

- *Mainstreaming* affords them broader opportunities and exposes all children to a more diverse student population. **p. 387**

Adult Education

- Adults represent a growing proportion of students in the United States.
- Most older learners are women who are engaged in job-related study. **p. 387**

The Teacher Shortage

- About 400,000 teaching vacancies exist in the United States each year due to low salaries, frustration, retirement, and rising enrollments and class size.
- To address this shortage, many school districts are recruiting teachers from abroad. **p. 387**

Health and Medicine

Health is a social issue because personal well-being depends on a society's level of technology and its distribution of resources. A society's culture shapes definitions of health.   **p. 389**

medicine (p. 389) the social institution that focuses on fighting disease and improving health

health (p. 389) a state of complete physical, mental, and social well-being

Health in the United States

Health Facts

- More than 80 percent of U.S. children born today will live to at least age sixty-five.
- Throughout the life course, women have better health than men, and people of high social position enjoy better health than the poor. **p. 390**

Current Issues in **U.S. Health Care Include**

- cigarette smoking, which is the greatest preventable cause of death
- eating disorders and obesity
- the increase in sexually transmitted diseases
- ethical dilemmas associated with advancing medical technology and the right to die   **pp. 393–96**

 **Read the Document** on **mysoclab.com**

social epidemiology (p. 390) the study of how health and disease are distributed throughout a society's population

eating disorder (p. 392) an intense form of dieting or other unhealthy method of weight control driven by the desire to be very thin

euthanasia (p. 395) assisting in the death of a person suffering from an incurable disease; also known as *mercy killing*

Theories of Health and Medicine

Structural-functional theory considers illness to be dysfunctional because it reduces people's abilities to perform their roles (Talcott Parsons). Role analysis explains that society responds to illness by defining roles:

- The *sick role* excuses the ill person from routine social responsibilities.
- The *physician's role* is to use specialized knowledge to take charge of the patient's recovery.   **p. 400**

Symbolic-interaction theory investigates the meanings that people attach to health illness, and medical care. These meanings are socially constructed by people in everyday interaction:

- Our response to illness is not always based on medical facts.
- How people define a medical situation may affect how they feel.   **pp. 400–1**

Social-conflict theory focuses on the unequal distribution of health and medical care. Marxist theory criticizes the U.S. medical establishment for

- its overreliance on drugs and surgery
- the dominance of the profit motive
- overemphasis on the biological rather than the social causes of illness

Feminist theory criticizes the medical establishment for "scientific" statements and policies that effectively allow men to dominate women.   **pp. 401–2**

Health: A Global Survey

Health Varies over Time:

- With industrialization, health improved dramatically in Western Europe and North America in the nineteenth century.
- A century ago, infectious diseases were leading killers; today, most people in the United States die in old age of chronic illnesses such as heart disease, cancer, or stroke.

Health Varies Around the World:

- Poor nations suffer from inadequate sanitation, hunger, and other problems linked to poverty.
- Life expectancy in low-income nations is about twenty-three years less than in the United States; in the poorest nations, more than one in four people die before reaching the age of twenty.   **p. 389**

The Medical Establishment

The Rise of Scientific Medicine

- Health care was historically a family concern but with industrialization became the responsibility of trained specialists.
- The model of scientific medicine is the foundation of the U.S. medical establishment.   **p. 396**

Paying for Medical Care: A Global Survey

- Socialist societies define medical care as a right; governments offer basic care equally to everyone.
- Capitalist societies view medical care as a commodity to be purchased, although most capitalist governments help pay for medical care through socialized medicine or national health insurance.   **pp. 397–98**

Paying for Medical Care: The United States

- Most people have private or government health insurance, but about 50 million people in the United States do not have medical insurance.
- The 2010 health care reforms are a recent effort to move the United States closer to the goal of having everyone covered by health insurance.

holistic medicine (p. 396) an approach to health care that emphasizes prevention of illness and takes into account a person's entire physical and social environment

socialized medicine (p. 397) a medical care system in which the government owns and operates most medical facilities and employs most physicians

direct-fee system (p. 398) a medical care system in which patients pay directly for the services of physicians and hospitals

health maintenance organization (HMO) (p. 399) an organization that provides comprehensive medical care to subscribers for a fixed fee

sick role (p. 400) patterns of behavior defined as appropriate for people who are ill

15 Population, Urbanization, and Environment

Learning Objectives

Remember the definitions of the key terms highlighted in boldfaced type throughout this chapter.

Understand ways in which the natural environment reflects the operation of society.

Apply demographic concepts and theories to see population trends here and around the world.

Analyze the many differences between urban and rural social life.

Evaluate the current global population increase and the state of the natural environment.

Create a vision of how people can live in a way that is environmentally sustainable.

20 DE NOV
F SERVANDO Pte
PINO SUAREZ 7 a 10 hs
F SERVANDO Ote
FRAY SERVANDO PTE
PRECAUCION
20 NOVIEMBRE
40

This chapter explores three dimensions of social change: population dynamics, urbanization, and increasing threats to the natural environment. Not only are all three important, but they are closely linked as well. ■

There's been a lot of talk about what will happen to our planet as we move through 2012, the year the ancient Mayans claimed some great change would take place. At this point, of course, what will actually take place by the end of that year is anyone's guess. But one important milestone has already been passed: By the beginning of 2012, our planet had already become home to 7 billion people—more than ever before in history.

At one level, a record global population seems like a good thing—more people are alive, and living better, than ever before. Yet, warning signs point to a future crisis. For one thing, more and more people demand more and more food. As you have probably noticed, food prices have been going up and, in some parts of the world, the cost of food is already reaching a crisis level. Similarly, most of the planet's people now live in cities, and the populations of the world's largest cities—found in lower-income nations—are now far greater than any time in the past. Finally, the soaring population of our planet means that humanity now consumes more and more oil, water, and other resources; in addition, we are creating unprecedented mountains of waste.

It is hard to imagine what a global population of 7 billion means. But consider this—just fifty years ago, the planet's population was less than half as big. So while we can't be sure exactly what future decades will bring, we can be certain that huge changes are underway.

Demography: The Study of Population

 Apply

When humans first began to raise plants for food some 12,000 years ago, Earth's entire *Homo sapiens* population was about 5 million, or about the number of people living in Colorado today. Very slow growth pushed the total in 1 C.E. to perhaps 300 million, or about the population of the United States today.

Starting around 1750, world population began to spike upward. We are currently adding about 83 million people to the planet each year; the world now holds more than 7 billion people.

The causes and consequences of this drama are the focus of **demography,** *the study of human population.* Demography (from the Greek, meaning "description of people") is a cousin of sociology that analyzes the size and composition of a population and studies how and why people move from place to place. Demographers not only collect statistics but also raise important questions about the effects of population increase and suggest how it might be controlled. The following sections present basic demographic concepts.

Fertility

The study of human population begins with how many people are born. **Fertility** is *the incidence of childbearing in a country's population.* During a woman's childbearing years, from the onset of menstruation (typically in the early teens) to menopause (usually in the late forties), she is capable of bearing more than twenty children. But *fecundity,* or maximum possible childbearing, is sharply reduced by cultural norms, finances, and personal choice.

Demographers describe fertility using the **crude birth rate,** *the number of live births in a given year for every 1,000 people in a population.* To calculate a crude birth rate, divide the number of live births in a year by the total population and multiply the result by 1,000. In the United States in 2010, there were 4 million live births in a population of 309 million, yielding a crude birth rate of 13.0 (Hamilton, Martin, & Ventura, 2011).

> **January 18, Coshocton County, Ohio.** Having just finished off the mountains of meat and potatoes that make up a typical Amish meal, our group of college students has gathered in the living room of Jacob and Anna Raber, members of this rural Amish community. Anna, a mother of four, is telling us about Amish life. "Most of the women I know have five or six children," she says with a smile, "but certainly not everybody—some have eleven or twelve!"

A country's birth rate is described as "crude" because it is based on the entire population, not just women in their childbearing years. In addition, this measure ignores differences among various

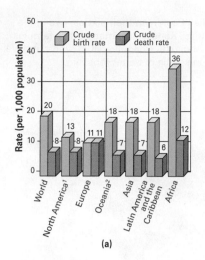
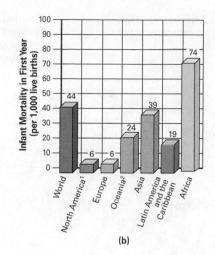
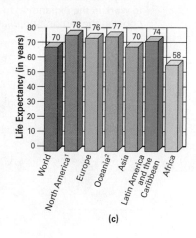

(a)   (b)   (c)

Global Snapshot

FIGURE 15–1 (a) Crude Birth Rates and Crude Death Rates, (b) Infant Mortality Rates, and (c) Life Expectancy around the World, 2011

By world standards, North America has a low birth rate, an average death rate, a very low infant mortality rate, and high life expectancy.

[1] United States and Canada.   [2] Australia, New Zealand, and South Pacific Islands.

Source: Population Reference Bureau (2011).

categories of the population: Fertility among the Amish, for example, is quite high, and fertility among Asian Americans is low. But the measure is easy to calculate and allows rough comparisons of the fertility of one country or region to others. Part (a) of Figure 15–1 shows that compared to the rest of the world, the crude birth rate of North America is low.

Mortality

Population size also reflects **mortality**, *the incidence of death in a country's population.* To measure mortality, demographers use the **crude death rate**, *the number of deaths in a given year for every 1,000 people in a population.* This time, we take the number of deaths in a year, divide by the total population, and multiply the result by 1,000. In 2010, there were 2.47 million deaths in the U.S. population of 309 million, yielding a crude death rate of 8.0 (Murphy, Xu, & Kochanek, 2012). Part (a) of Figure 15–1 shows that in global context, this rate is about average.

A third useful demographic measure is the **infant mortality rate**, *the number of deaths among infants under one year of age for each 1,000 live births in a given year.* To compute infant mortality,

divide the number of deaths of children under one year of age by the number of live births during the same year and multiply the result by 1,000. In 2010, there were 24,548 infant deaths and 4 million live births in the United States. Dividing the first number by the second and multiplying the result by 1,000 yields an infant mortality rate of 6.14. Part (b) of Figure 15–1 indicates that by world standards, North American infant mortality is very low.

But remember the differences among various categories of people. For example, African Americans, with three times the burden of poverty compared to whites, have an infant mortality rate of 11.6, more than twice the rate for non-Hispanic whites of 5.1.

Low infant mortality greatly raises **life expectancy**, *the average life span of a country's population.* U.S. males born in 2009 can expect to live 75.7 years, and females can look forward to 80.6 years. As part (c) of Figure 15–1 shows, life expectancy in North America is twenty years greater than that typical of low-income countries of Africa.

Migration

Population size is also affected by **migration**, *the movement of people into and out of a specified territory.* Movement into a territory,

---

demography the study of human population

fertility the incidence of childbearing in a country's population
crude birth rate the number of live births in a given year for every 1,000 people in a population

mortality the incidence of death in a country's population
crude death rate the number of deaths in a given year for every 1,000 people in a population
infant mortality rate the number of deaths among infants under one year of age for each 1,000 live births in a given year

migration the movement of people into and out of a specified territory

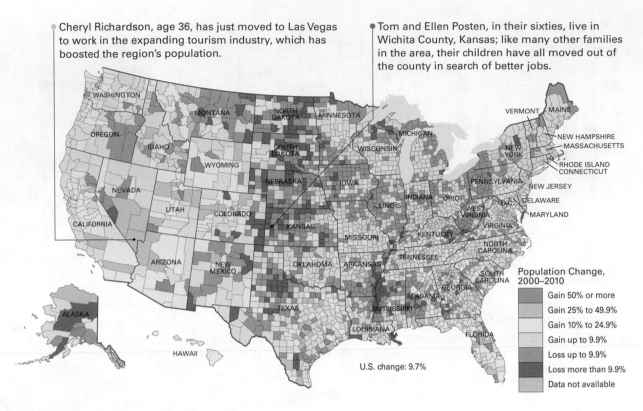

Cheryl Richardson, age 36, has just moved to Las Vegas to work in the expanding tourism industry, which has boosted the region's population.

Tom and Ellen Posten, in their sixties, live in Wichita County, Kansas; like many other families in the area, their children have all moved out of the county in search of better jobs.

Population Change, 2000–2010

- Gain 50% or more
- Gain 25% to 49.9%
- Gain 10% to 24.9%
- Gain up to 9.9%
- Loss up to 9.9%
- Loss more than 9.9%
- Data not available

U.S. change: 9.7%

Seeing Ourselves

NATIONAL MAP 15–1 Population Change across the United States

This map shows that since 2000, population has been moving from the heartland of the United States toward the coasts. What do you think is causing this internal migration? What categories of people do you think remain in counties that are losing population?

✳ Explore population density in your local community and in counties across the United States on **mysoclab.com**

Source: U.S. Census Bureau (2011).

or *immigration,* is measured as an *in-migration rate,* calculated as the number of people entering an area for every 1,000 people in the population. Movement out of a territory, or *emigration,* is measured in terms of an *out-migration rate,* the number leaving for every 1,000 people. Both types of migration usually happen at the same time; the difference is the *net migration rate.*

All nations experience some degree of internal migration, that is, movement within their borders from one region to another. National Map 15–1 shows where the U.S. population is moving and the places being left behind.

Migration is sometimes voluntary, as when people leave a small town to move to a larger city. In such cases, "push-pull" factors are usually at work: A lack of jobs "pushes" people to move, and more opportunity elsewhere "pulls" people to someplace new. For example, cities that have lost jobs in recent decades (such as Detroit, Michigan; Cleveland, Ohio; and Buffalo, New York) have lost population, and regions of the country that offer more jobs (such as the Silicon Valley in California) have gained population (Sauter, 2011). Migration can also be involuntary. One important example of involuntary migration was the forced transport of 10 million Africans to the Western Hemisphere as slaves; a more recent case is Hurricane Katrina forcing tens of thousands of people to flee New Orleans.

Population Growth

Fertility, mortality, and migration all affect the size of a society's population. In general, rich nations (such as the United States) grow almost as much from immigration as from natural increase; poorer nations (such as Pakistan) grow almost entirely from natural increase.

To calculate a population's *natural growth rate*, demographers subtract the crude death rate from the crude birth rate. The natural growth rate of the U.S. population in 2010 was 5.0 per 1,000 (the crude birth rate of 13.0 minus the crude death rate of 8.0), or about 0.5 percent annual growth.

Global Map 15–1 shows that population growth in the United States and other high-income nations is well below the world average of 1.2 percent. Earth's low-growth continents are Europe (currently posting no growth) and North America (increasing by 0.5 percent). Near the global average are Oceania (1.2 percent), Asia (1.1 percent), and Latin America (1.2 percent). The highest-growth region of the world is Africa (2.4 percent).

A handy rule for estimating population growth is to divide a society's population growth into the number 70; this yields the *doubling time* in years. Thus an annual growth rate of 2 percent (found in parts of Latin America) doubles a population in thirty-five years, and a 3 percent growth rate (found in some countries

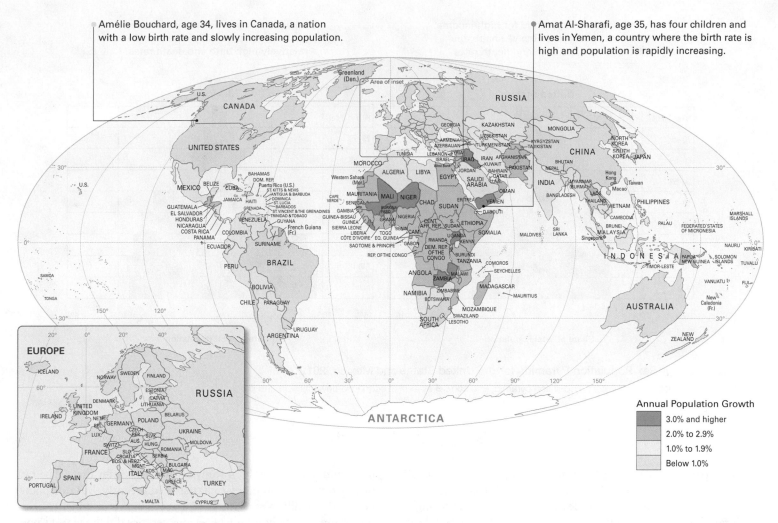

Amélie Bouchard, age 34, lives in Canada, a nation with a low birth rate and slowly increasing population.

Amat Al-Sharafi, age 35, has four children and lives in Yemen, a country where the birth rate is high and population is rapidly increasing.

Annual Population Growth
- 3.0% and higher
- 2.0% to 2.9%
- 1.0% to 1.9%
- Below 1.0%

Window on the World

GLOBAL MAP 15–1 Population Growth in Global Perspective

The richest countries of the world—including the United States, Canada, and the nations of Europe—have growth rates below 1 percent. The nations of Latin America and Asia typically have growth rates around 1.5 percent, a rate that doubles a population in forty-seven years. Africa has an overall growth rate of 2.4 percent (despite only small increases in countries with a high rate of AIDS), which cuts the doubling time to twenty-nine years. In global perspective, we see that a society's standard of living is closely related to its rate of population growth: Population is rising fastest in the world regions that can least afford to support more people.

Source: Population Reference Bureau (2011).

in Africa) drops the doubling time to just twenty-three years. The rapid population growth of the poorest countries is deeply troubling because these countries can barely support the populations they have now.

Population Composition

Demographers also study the makeup of a society's population at a given point in time. One variable is the **sex ratio**, *the number of males for every 100 females in a nation's population*. In 2010, the sex ratio in the United States was 97, or 97 males for every 100 females. Sex ratios are ordinarily below 100 because, on average, women outlive men. In the Great Plains region of the United States, an older population means that the sex ratio is below 100: the small town of Plainville, Kansas, for example, has a sex ratio of only 89, or

89 males for every 100 females. In low-income nations, by contrast, cultural tradition leads parents to value sons more than daughters so that parents may choose to either abort a female fetus or, after birth, give more care to a male infant. In either case, the number of boys exceeds the number of girls, pushing the sex ratio above 100. In India, for example, the sex ratio is 108.

A more complex measure is the **age-sex pyramid**, *a graphic representation of the age and sex of a population*. Figure 15–2 on page 414 presents the age-sex pyramids for the United States and Mexico. Higher death rates as people age give these figures a rough pyramid shape. The share of U.S. "baby boomers" in their fifties and sixties is beginning to decline as they enter old age. The contraction for people in their thirties reflects the subsequent "baby bust." The birth rate of 13.0 in 2010 is still well below its high of 25.3 in 1957.

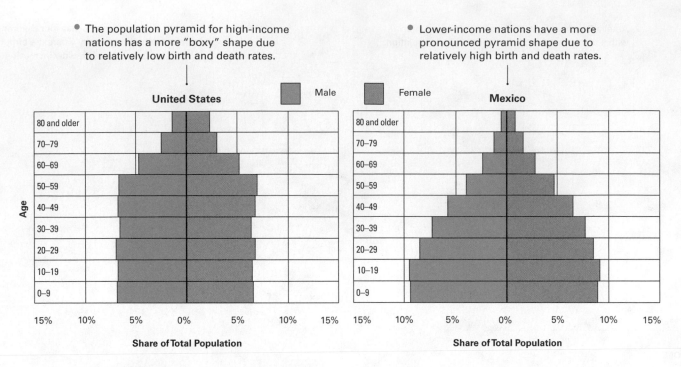

FIGURE 15–2 Age-Sex Population Pyramids for the United States and Mexico, 2012

By looking at the shape of a country's population pyramid, you can tell its level of economic development and predict future levels of population increase.

Source: U.S. Census Bureau (2012).

Comparing the U.S. and Mexican age-sex pyramids shows different demographic trends. The pyramid for Mexico, like that of other lower-income nations, is wide at the bottom (reflecting higher birth rates) and narrows quickly by what we would call middle age (due to higher mortality). In short, Mexico is a much younger society, with a median age of twenty-seven, compared to thirty-seven in the United States. With a larger share of women still in their childbearing years, therefore, Mexico's crude birth rate (19) is half again the size of our own (13), and its annual rate of population growth (1.1 percent) is more than twice the U.S. rate (0.5 percent).

History and Theory of Population Growth

 Analyze

In the past, people wanted large families because human labor was the key to productivity. In addition, until rubber condoms were invented in the mid-1800s, preventing pregnancy was uncertain at best. But high death rates from infectious diseases put a constant brake on population growth.

A major demographic shift began about 1750 as the world's population turned upward, reaching the 1 billion mark by 1800. This milestone (which took all of human history to reach) was matched barely a century later in 1930, when a second billion people were added to the planet. In other words, not only was population increasing, but the *rate* of growth was accelerating as well. Global population reached 3 billion by 1962 (just thirty-two years

later) and 4 billion by 1974 (only twelve years after that). The rate of world population increase has slowed recently, but our planet passed the 5 billion mark in 1987, the 6 billion mark in 1999, and now stands at 7 billion. In no previous century did the world's population even double. In the twentieth century, it *quadrupled*.

Currently, the world is gaining about 83 million people each year; 98 percent of this increase is in poor countries. Experts predict that Earth's population will be more than 9 billion in 2050 (United Nations Population Division, 2011). Given the world's troubles feeding its present population, such an increase is a matter of urgent concern.

Malthusian Theory

The sudden population growth 250 years ago sparked the development of demography. Thomas Robert Malthus (1766–1834), an English economist and clergyman, warned that rapid population increase would lead to social chaos. Malthus (1926, orig. 1798) calculated that population would increase in what mathematicians call a *geometric progression*, illustrated by the series of numbers 2, 4, 8, 16, 32, and so on. At such a rate, Malthus concluded, world population would soon soar out of control.

Food production would also increase, Malthus explained, but only in an *arithmetic progression* (as in the series 2, 3, 4, 5, 6, and so on) because even with new agricultural technology, farmland is limited. Thus Malthus presented a troubling vision of the future: people reproducing beyond what the planet could feed, leading ultimately to widespread starvation and war over what resources were left.

Malthus recognized that artificial birth control or abstaining from sex might change his prediction. But he considered one morally wrong and the other impractical. Famine and war therefore stalked humanity in Malthus's mind, and he was justly known as "the dismal parson."

● **Evaluate** Fortunately, Malthus's prediction was flawed. First, by 1850, the European birth rate began to drop, partly because with industrialization, children were becoming an economic liability rather than an asset and partly because people began using artificial birth control. Second, Malthus underestimated human ingenuity: Modern irrigation techniques, fertilizers, and pesticides increased farm production far more than he could have imagined.

Some people criticized Malthus for ignoring the role of social inequality in explaining patterns of world abundance and famine. For example, Karl Marx (1967, orig. 1867) objected to his view of suffering as a "law of nature" rather than the curse of capitalism. More recently, "critical demographers" have claimed that saying poverty is caused by high birth rates in low-income countries amounts to blaming the victims. On the contrary, they see global inequality as the real issue (Horton, 1999; Kuumba, 1999).

Still, Malthus offers an important lesson. Habitable land, clean water, and fresh air are limited resources, and increased economic productivity has taken a heavy toll on the natural environment. In addition, medical advances have lowered death rates, pushing up world population. Common sense tells us that no level of population growth can go on forever. People everywhere must become aware of the dangers of population increase.

CHECK YOUR LEARNING What did Malthus predict about human population increase? About food production? What was his overall conclusion?

Demographic Transition Theory

A more complex analysis of population change is **demographic transition theory**, *a thesis that links population patterns to a society's level of technological development.* Figure 15–3 shows the demographic consequences at four levels of technological development.

Preindustrial, agrarian societies (Stage 1) have high birth rates because of the economic value of children and the absence of birth control. Death rates are also high due to low living standards and limited medical technology. Deaths from outbreaks of disease cancel out births, so population rises and falls only slightly over time. This was the case for thousands of years in Europe before the Industrial Revolution.

Stage 2, the onset of industrialization, brings a demographic transition as death rates fall due to greater food supplies and

● **Watch** the video "Population Growth and Decline" on **mysoclab.com**

This street scene in Old Delhi, India, conveys the vision of the future found in the work of Thomas Robert Malthus, who feared that population increase would overwhelm the world's resources. Can you explain why Malthus had such a serious concern about population? How is demographic transition theory a more hopeful analysis?

scientific medicine. But birth rates remain high, resulting in rapid population growth. It was during Europe's Stage 2 that Malthus formulated his ideas, which accounts for his pessimistic view of the future. The world's poorest countries today are in this high-growth stage.

In Stage 3, a mature industrial economy, the birth rate drops, curbing population growth once again. Fertility falls because most children survive to adulthood, so fewer are needed, and because high living standards make raising children expensive. In short, affluence transforms children from economic assets into economic liabilities. Smaller families, made possible by effective birth control, are also favored by women working outside the

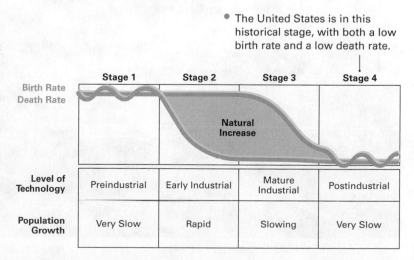

● The United States is in this historical stage, with both a low birth rate and a low death rate.

	Stage 1	Stage 2	Stage 3	Stage 4
Birth Rate / Death Rate			Natural Increase	
Level of Technology	Preindustrial	Early Industrial	Mature Industrial	Postindustrial
Population Growth	Very Slow	Rapid	Slowing	Very Slow

FIGURE 15–3 Demographic Transition Theory
Demographic transition theory links population change to a society's level of technological development.

home. As birth rates follow death rates downward, population growth slows further.

Stage 4 corresponds to a postindustrial economy in which the demographic transition is complete. The birth rate keeps falling, partly because dual-income couples gradually become the norm and partly because the cost of raising and schooling children continues to increase. This trend, coupled with steady death rates, means that population grows only very slowly or even decreases. This is the case today in Japan, Europe, and the United States.

● **Evaluate** Demographic transition theory suggests that the key to population control lies in technology. Instead of the runaway population increase feared by Malthus, this theory sees technology slowing growth and spreading material plenty.

Demographic transition theory is linked to modernization theory, one approach to global development discussed in Chapter 9 ("Global Stratification"). Modernization theorists are optimistic that poor countries will solve their population problems as they industrialize. But critics, notably dependency theorists, strongly disagree. Unless there is a redistribution of global resources, they maintain, our planet will become increasingly divided into affluent "haves," enjoying low population growth, and poor "have-nots," struggling in vain to feed more and more people.

CHECK YOUR LEARNING Explain the four stages of demographic transition theory.

Global Population Today: A Brief Survey

What can we say about population in today's world? Drawing on the discussion so far, we can identify important patterns and reach several conclusions.

The Low-Growth North

When the Industrial Revolution began in the Northern Hemisphere, population growth in Western Europe and North America

Fertility in the United States has fallen during the past century and is now quite low. But some categories of the U.S. population have much higher fertility rates. One example is the Amish, a religious society living in rural areas of Ohio, Pennsylvania, and other states. It is common for Amish couples to have five, six, or more children. Why do you think the Amish favor large families?

was a high 3 percent annually. But in the centuries since, the growth rate has steadily declined, and in 1970, it fell below 1 percent. As our postindustrial society settles into Stage 4, the U.S. birth rate is at about the replacement level of 2.1 children per woman, a point demographers call **zero population growth**, *the rate of reproduction that maintains population at a steady level.* In 2011, eighty nations, almost all of them high-income countries, were at or below the point of zero population growth.

Among the factors that serve to hold down population in these postindustrial societies are a high proportion of men and women in the labor force, the rising costs of raising children, trends toward later marriage and singlehood, and the widespread use of contraceptives and abortion.

In high-income nations, then, population increase is not the pressing problem that it is in poor countries. On the contrary, many governments in high-income countries are concerned about a future problem of *underpopulation* because declining population size may be difficult to reverse and also because the swelling ranks of the elderly will have fewer and fewer young people to look to for support (Population Reference Bureau, 2010; United Nations Development Programme, 2010; El Nasser & Overberg, 2011).

The High-Growth South

Population is a critical problem in poor nations of the Southern Hemisphere. No nation in the world lacks industrial technology entirely; demographic transition theory's Stage 1 applies today to remote rural areas of low-income nations. But much of Latin America, Africa, and Asia is at Stage 2, with mixed agrarian and industrial economies. Advanced medical technology, supplied by rich societies, has sharply reduced death rates, but birth rates remain high. This is why poor countries now account for about 82 percent of Earth's people and 98 percent of global population increase.

In some of the world's poorest countries, such as the Democratic Republic of the Congo in Africa, women still have, on average, about six children during their lifetimes. But in most poor countries, birth rates have fallen from about six children per woman (typical in 1950) to about three. But this level of fertility is still high enough to make global poverty much worse. That is why leaders in the battle against global poverty point to the importance of reducing fertility rates in low-income nations.

Notice, too, that a key element in controlling world population growth is improving the status of women. Why? Because of this simple truth: Give women more life choices and they will have fewer children. History has shown that women who are free to decide when and where to marry, who have access to education and to good jobs, and who bear children as a matter of choice, are women who will choose to limit their own fertility (Axinn & Barber, 2001; Roudi-Fahimi & Kent, 2007).

The Demographic Divide

High- and low-income nations display very different population dynamics, a gap that is sometimes called the *demographic divide.* In Italy, a high-income, very low growth nation, women average about 1.5 children in their lifetimes.

Thinking About Diversity:
Race, Class, and Gender

Where Are the Girls?
China's One-Child Policy

The parents had argued for hours. But Yang, the father, was determined, and Jainying, the mother, was exhausted. Finally, Yang wrested the baby from Jainying's arms. The decision was made; the girl had to go. The father put several extra layers of clothing on his daughter and lay the newborn in a cardboard box lined with blankets. Next to her, he placed a small bottle of milk. Then Yang lifted the box and carried it off into the dark night toward the distant village, leaving behind the sobbing of his wife, "Yang, I beg you, bring back my baby!"

Yet in her heart, she too knew that this must be done. Half an hour later, the father arrived in the village and found his way to the local school. For the last time, he kissed his daughter goodbye. He set her makeshift crib on the steps of the school's front entrance, knowing that when dawn broke she would be found by school officials and cared for. With tears in his eyes, Yang said a quick prayer to his ancestors to keep the baby safe. Then he turned and again disappeared into the night, knowing that he would never see or hear from her again.

This story may be heartbreaking, but it is one that has occurred tens of thousands of times in China. What would prompt parents to give up a child? Why would a father abandon his daughter in a public place? The answer lies in China's population control policy and the nation's cultural traditions.

Back in the 1970s, the high Chinese birth rate was fueling an extremely a rapid population increase. Government leaders could see that the country's economic development depended on controlling population growth. As a result, they passed a law stating that a family can have only one child. Families who follow the one-child policy can expect rewards such as a better job, a higher salary, and maybe even a larger apartment. On the other hand, parents who violate the law by having a second child face a stiff fine, and their second child may not be eligible for educational and health care benefits.

The government actively promotes the one-child message in the mass media, in popular songs, and in classroom lessons. But education is not the government's only tactic—enforcement officials can be found in most neighborhoods and workplaces. The policy may seem highhanded—government telling people how to live as families—but most Chinese willingly comply with the policy. Some praise the law as good for the country. Those who do not know they must obey or face the consequences.

Modern China is determined to control population increase. But China is also a country steeped in a tradition of male dominance. If government rules permit only one child, most families would prefer a boy. Why? Parents see boys as a better investment because sons will carry on the family name and must care for their aging parents. On the other hand, girls will end up caring for their husbands' parents, leading most Chinese to see raising daughters as a waste of precious resources. The Chinese government has expanded women's rights and opportunities, but patriarchal traditions are deeply rooted in the country's history, and attitudes change slowly.

Around the world, the one-child policy has attracted both praise and condemnation. On the positive side, analysts agree that it has succeeded in its goal of reducing the rate of population increase. This trend, in turn, has helped raise living standards and lifted China to the ranks of middle-income nations. Many one-child families are happy with the added income from women who now work outside the home, and parents now have more to spend on a single child's schooling.

China's one-child policy is advertised on billboards throughout the country.

But the one-child policy also has a dark side, shown in the story that began this box. Since the law was passed, as many as 1 million girls have "disappeared." In some cases, parents who learn that the woman is carrying a female fetus may choose abortion so they can "try again." In other cases, family members decide to kill a female infant soon after birth. In still other cases, girls survive but are never recorded in the birth statistics, so that they grow up as "noncitizens" who can never go to school or receive treatment at a local health clinic. Finally, some parents, like those described earlier, give up or abandon their daughter in the hope that the child may find a home elsewhere.

China's one-child policy has certainly held population increase in check. Between 2010 and 2025, China's population is projected to increase by about 10 percent, below the figure of 13 percent in the United States and 22 percent in India. But China's one-child policy has had a dramatic toll on the country's female population. In one recent year, the nation's birth records showed almost 1 million fewer girls than boys. The Chinese population is now about 250 million lower than it would have been without the one-child policy, but the country's population is also steadily becoming more and more male.

What Do You Think?

1. Point to the reasons China's one-child policy has attracted praise and also blame. On balance, do you think this is a good policy? Can you think of a better way to control population? Explain.

2. What about cases where parents think they can afford additional children? Should family size be a couple's decision? Or does government have a responsibility to look out for the entire country's well-being even if it requires regulating people's decision about children?

3. Do you now understand why almost all of the babies U.S. parents adopt from China are girls?

Sources: Hesketh, Lu, & Xing (2005), Baochang et al. (2007), Yardley (2008), and El Nasser & Overberg (2011).

A birth rate this low means that the number of annual births is actually less than the number of deaths. The result: At the moment, Italy is actually *losing* population, and at least some government officials are offering cash to couples who have a child (Frazer, 2011). But such a policy is unlikely to have much effect and, looking ahead to 2050 and even assuming some gains from immigration, Italy's population is projected to be about the same as it is today. The share of elderly people in Italy—now 20 percent compared to 8 percent for the world as a whole—will only increase as time goes on.

Look at how different the patterns are in a low-income nation such as the Democratic Republic of the Congo, where women still have an average of six to seven children. Even with a high mortality rate, this nation's population will more than double by 2050. The share of elderly people is extremely low—about 3 percent—and almost half the country's people are below the age of fifteen. With such a high growth rate, it is no surprise that the problem of poverty is bad and getting worse: About three-fourths of this nation's people are undernourished (Population Reference Bureau, 2011; United Nations, 2011).

In sum, a demographic divide now separates rich countries with low birth rates and aging populations from poor countries with high birth rates and very young populations. Just as humanity has devised ways to reduce deaths around the world, it must now bring down population growth, especially in poor countries where projections suggest a future as bleak as that imagined by Thomas Malthus centuries ago.

China, described in the Thinking About Diversity box on page 417, stands out as a nation that has taken a strong stand on reducing the rate of population increase. Analysts estimate that China's one-child policy, enacted back in the 1970s, has reduced the nation's current population by about 250 million.

Urbanization: The Growth of Cities

 **Understand**

October 8, Hong Kong. The cable train grinds to the top of Victoria Peak, where we behold one of the world's most spectacular vistas—the city of Hong Kong at night. A million bright, colorful lights ring the harbor as ships, ferries, and traditional Chinese junks churn by. Few cities match Hong Kong for sheer energy: This small city is as economically productive as the state of Wisconsin or the nation of Finland. We could sit here for hours entranced by the spectacle of Hong Kong.

Throughout most of human history, the sights and sounds of great cities such as Hong Kong, New York, and Paris were simply unimaginable. Our distant ancestors lived in small, nomadic groups, moving from place to place as they depleted vegetation or hunted migratory game. The small settlements that marked the emergence of civilization in the Middle East some 12,000 years ago held only a small fraction of Earth's people. Today, the largest three or four cities of the world hold as many people as the entire planet did back then.

Urbanization is *the concentration of population into cities.* Urbanization both redistributes population within a society and transforms many patterns of social life. We will trace these changes in terms of three urban revolutions: the emergence of cities beginning 10,000 years ago, the development of industrial cities after 1750, and the explosive growth of cities in poor countries today.

The Evolution of Cities

Cities are a relatively new development in human history. Only about 12,000 years ago did our ancestors begin founding permanent settlements, which paved the way for the *first urban revolution.*

The First Cities

Hunting and gathering forced people to move all the time; however, once our ancestors discovered how to domesticate animals and cultivate crops, they were able to stay in one place. Raising their own food also created a material surplus, which freed some people from food production and allowed them to build shelters, make tools, weave cloth, and take part in religious rituals. The emergence of cities led to both specialization and higher living standards.

The first city that we know of was Jericho, which lies to the north of the Dead Sea in what is now the West Bank. When first settled 10,000 years ago, it was home to only 600 people. But as the centuries passed, cities grew to tens of thousands of people and became the centers of vast empires. By 3000 B.C.E., Egyptian cities flourished, as did cities in China about 2000 B.C.E. and in Central and South America about 1500 B.C.E. In North America, however, only a few Native American societies formed settlements; widespread urbanization did not take place until the arrival of European settlers in the seventeenth century.

Preindustrial European Cities

European cities date back some 5,000 years to the Greeks and, later, the Romans, both of whom formed great empires and founded cities across Europe, including Vienna, Paris, and London. With the fall of the Roman Empire, the so-called Dark Ages began as people withdrew within defensive walled settlements and warlords battled for territory. Only in the eleventh century did Europe become more peaceful; trade flourished once again, allowing cities to grow.

Medieval cities were quite different from those familiar to us today. Beneath towering cathedrals, the narrow, winding streets of London, Brussels, and Florence teemed with merchants, artisans, priests, peddlers, jugglers, nobles, and servants. Occupational groups such as bakers, carpenters, and metalworkers clustered together in distinct sections or "quarters." Ethnicity also defined communities as people sought to keep out those who differed from themselves. The term "ghetto" (from the Italian word *borghetto,* meaning "outside the city walls") was first used to describe the neighborhood in which the Jews of Venice were segregated.

Industrial European Cities

As the Middle Ages came to a close, steadily increasing commerce enriched a new urban middle class called the *bourgeoisie* (French, meaning "townspeople"). Earning more and more money, the bourgeoisie soon rivaled the hereditary aristocracy.

By about 1750, the Industrial Revolution triggered a *second urban revolution,* first in Europe and then in North America. The tremendous productive power of factories caused cities to grow bigger than ever before. London, the largest European city, reached 550,000 people by 1700 and exploded to 6.5 million by 1900 (A. F. Weber, 1963, orig. 1899; Chandler & Fox, 1974).

Cities not only grew but changed shape as well. Older winding streets gave way to broad, straight boulevards to handle the increasing flow of commercial traffic. Steam and electric trolleys soon crisscrossed the expanding cities. Because land was now a commodity to be bought and sold, developers divided cities into regular-sized lots (Mumford, 1961). The center of the city was no longer the cathedral but a bustling central business district filled with banks, retail stores, and tall office buildings.

With a new focus on business, cities became ever more crowded and impersonal. Crime rates rose. Especially at the outset, a few industrialists lived in grand style, but most men, women, and children barely survived by working in factories.

Organized efforts by workers eventually brought improvements to the workplace, better housing, and the right to vote. Public services such as water, sewer systems, and electricity further improved urban living. Today, some urbanites still live in poverty, but a rising standard of living has partly fulfilled the city's historical promise of a better life.

The Growth of U.S. Cities

As noted, most of the Native Americans who inhabited North America for thousands of years before the arrival of Europeans were migratory people who formed few permanent settlements. The spread of villages and towns came after European colonization.

Colonial Settlement, 1565–1800

In 1565, the Spanish founded this country's oldest settlement—Saint Augustine, Florida. In 1607, the English founded Jamestown, Virginia. Later, in 1624, the Dutch established New Amsterdam, which the English later renamed New York.

New York and Boston (founded by the English in 1630) started out as tiny villages in a vast wilderness. They resembled medieval towns in Europe, with narrow, winding streets that still curve through lower Manhattan and downtown Boston. When the first census was completed in 1790, as Table 15–1 shows, just 5 percent of the nation's people lived in cities.

Urban Expansion, 1800–1860

Early in the nineteenth century, towns sprang up along the transportation routes that opened the American West. By 1860, Buffalo, Cleveland, Detroit, and Chicago were all changing the face of the Midwest, and about one-fifth of the U.S. population lived in cities.

Urban expansion was greatest in the northern states; New York City, for example, had ten times the population of Charleston, South Carolina. The evolution of the United States into the industrial-urban North and the agrarian-rural South was one major cause of the Civil War (Schlesinger, 1969).

The Metropolitan Era, 1860–1950

The Civil War (1861–1865) gave an enormous boost to urbanization as factories strained to produce weapons. Especially in the North, waves of people deserted the countryside for cities in hopes of finding better jobs. Joining them were tens of millions of immigrants, mostly from Europe, forming a culturally diverse urban mix.

In 1900, New York's population soared past the 4 million mark, and Chicago, a city that had scarcely 100,000 people in 1860, was closing in on 2 million. Such growth marked the beginning of the **metropolis** (from the Greek, meaning "mother city"), *a large city*

TABLE 15–1 Urban Share of the U.S. Population, 1790–2040

Year	Total U.S. population (in millions)	Urban portion
1790	3.9	5.1%
1800	5.3	6.1
1820	9.6	7.3
1840	17.1	10.5
1860	31.4	19.7
1880	50.2	28.1
1900	76.0	39.7
1920	105.7	51.3
1940	131.7	56.5
1960	179.3	69.9
1980	226.5	73.7
2000	281.4	79.0
2020*	346.3	84.9
2040*	388.9	88.8

*Projection.
Sources: U.S. Census Bureau (2009) and United Nations Population Division (2011).

that dominates an urban area socially and economically. Metropolises became the economic centers of the United States. By 1920, urban areas were home to a majority of the U.S. population.

Industrial technology pushed city populations higher and higher. In the 1880s, steel girders and electric elevators allowed buildings to rise more than ten stories high. In 1930, New York's Empire State Building was hailed as an urban wonder, soaring 102 stories into the clouds.

Urban Decentralization, 1950–Present

The industrial metropolis reached its peak about 1950. Since then, something of a turnaround, called *urban decentralization*, has occurred as people have left downtown areas for outlying **suburbs**, *urban areas beyond the political boundaries of a city*. The old industrial cities of the Northeast and Midwest stopped growing, and some lost considerable population in the decades after 1950. At the same time, suburban populations increased rapidly. The urban landscape of densely packed central cities evolved into sprawling suburban regions.

Suburbs and Urban Decline

Imitating European nobility, some of the rich split their time between town houses in the city and country homes beyond the city limits. But not until after World War II did ordinary people find a suburban home within their reach. With more and more cars to drive along new four-lane highways, government-backed mortgages, and tract homes available at low prices, people flocked to rapidly growing suburbs. By 1999, most of the U.S. population lived in suburbs, where they shopped at nearby malls rather than in the older and more distant downtown shopping districts (Pederson, Smith, & Adler, 1999; Macionis & Parrillo, 2013).

As many older cities of the Snowbelt—the Northeast and Midwest—lost higher-income taxpayers to the suburbs, they struggled to pay for expensive social programs for the poor who remained. Many cities fell into financial crisis, and inner-city decay became severe. Especially to white suburbanites, the inner city

In recent decades, many U.S. cities in the Sunbelt have spread outward in a process called urban sprawl. Los Angeles, for example, now covers about 500 square miles, and even with a vast system of freeways, people moving around the city often find themselves stuck in slow-moving traffic. What are other disadvantages of urban sprawl?

became synonymous with slums, crime, drugs, unemployment, the poor, and minorities.

The urban critic Paul Goldberger (2002) points out that the decline of central cities also led to a decline in the importance of public space. Historically, city life was played out on the streets. The French word for a sophisticated person is *boulevardier,* which literally means "street person"—a term that has a negative meaning in the United States today. The activity that once took place on public streets and in public squares now takes place in shopping malls, the lobbies of cineplex theaters, and gated residential communities—all privately owned spaces. Further reducing the vitality of today's urban places is the spread of television, the Internet, and other media that people use without leaving home.

Sunbelt Cities and Urban Sprawl

As the older Snowbelt cities fell into decline, Sunbelt cities in the South and West grew rapidly. The soaring populations of cities such as Los Angeles and Houston reflected a population shift to the Sunbelt, where 60 percent of people in the United States now live. In addition, most of today's immigrants enter the country in the Sunbelt region. In 1950, nine of the ten largest U.S. cities were in the Snowbelt; in 2010, seven of the top ten were in the Sunbelt (U.S. Census Bureau, 2011).

Unlike their colder counterparts, these cities came of age after urban decentralization began. So while Snowbelt cities have long been enclosed by a ring of politically independent suburbs, Sunbelt

metropolis a large city that socially and economically dominates an urban area

suburbs urban areas beyond the political boundaries of a city

megalopolis a vast urban region containing a number of cities and their surrounding suburbs

cities have pushed their boundaries outward to include suburban communities. Chicago covers 227 square miles; Houston is more than twice that size, and the greater Houston metropolitan region covers almost 9,000 square miles—an area the size of the state of New Hampshire.

The recent housing collapse has certainly slowed suburban sprawl. But, as the economy recovers, the trend may well resume. Although the expansion of cities is one sign of prosperity, this trend has its drawbacks. Many people in cities such as Atlanta, Dallas, Phoenix, and Los Angeles complain that unplanned growth results in traffic-clogged roads leading to unattractive developments and schools that cannot keep up with the inflow of children. Not surprisingly, voters in many communities across the United States have passed ballot initiatives seeking to limit urban sprawl (Lacayo, 1999; Romero & Liserio, 2002; W. Sullivan, 2007; El Nasser, 2009).

Megalopolis: The Regional City

Another result of urban decentralization is urban regions, or regional cities. The U.S. Census Bureau (2010) recognizes 374 *metropolitan statistical areas* (MSAs). Each includes at least one city with 50,000 or more people. The bureau also recognizes 581 *micropolitan statistical areas,* urban areas with at least one city of 10,000 to 50,000 people. *Core-based statistical areas* (CBSAs) include both metropolitan and micropolitan statistical areas.

The biggest CBSAs contain millions of people and extend into several states. In 2010, the biggest CBSA was New York and its adjacent urban areas in Long Island, western Connecticut, northern New Jersey, and eastern Pennsylvania, with a total population of more than 22 million. Next in size is the CBSA in southern California that includes Los Angeles, Riverside, and Long Beach, with a population of almost 18 million.

As regional cities grow, they begin to overlap. In the early 1960s, the French geographer Jean Gottmann (1961) coined the term **megalopolis** to designate *a vast urban region containing a number of cities and their surrounding suburbs.* Along the East Coast, a 400-mile megalopolis stretches all the way from New England to Virginia. Other supercities cover the eastern coast of Florida and stretch from Cleveland west to Chicago.

Edge Cities

Urban decentralization has also created *edge cities,* business centers some distance from the old downtowns. Edge cities—a mix of corporate office buildings, shopping malls, hotels, and entertainment complexes—differ from suburbs, which contain mostly homes. The population of suburbs peaks at night, but the population of edge cities peaks during the workday.

As part of expanding urban regions, most edge cities have no clear physical boundaries. Some do have names, including Las Colinas (near the Dallas–Fort Worth airport), Tyson's Corner (in Virginia, near Washington, D.C.), and King of Prussia (northwest of Philadelphia). Other edge cities are known only by the major highways that flow through them, including Route 1, which runs through Princeton, New Jersey, and Route 128 near Boston (Garreau, 1991; Macionis & Parrillo, 2013).

The Rural Rebound

The 2010 Census showed that 83.7 percent of the country's 309 million people were living in urban places. Over the course of U.S. history, as shown in Table 15–1 on page 419, the urban population of the nation has increased steadily. Immigration has played a part in this increase because most newcomers settle in cities. There has also been considerable migration from rural areas to urban places, typically by people seeking greater social, educational, and economic opportunity.

However, between 2000 and 2010, two-thirds of the rural counties across the United States gained population, a trend analysts have called the "rural rebound." Most of this gain resulted from migration of people from urban areas. This trend has not affected all rural places, however. Many small towns in rural areas, especially in the Plains States, are struggling to stay alive. But even in those areas, the losses have slowed in recent years.

The greatest gains have come to rural communities that offer scenic and recreational attractions, such as lakes, mountains, and ski areas. People are drawn not only to the natural beauty of rural communities but also to their slower pace of life: less traffic, a lower crime rate, and cleaner air. A number of companies have relocated to rural counties as well, which has increased economic opportunity for the rural population (K. M. Johnson, 1999; Johnson & Fuguitt, 2000; D. Johnson, 2001).

Urbanism as a Way of Life

 Analyze

Early sociologists in Europe and the United States focused their attention on the rise of cities. We briefly examine their accounts of urbanism as a way of life.

Ferdinand Tönnies:
Gemeinschaft and *Gesellschaft*

In the nineteenth century, the German sociologist Ferdinand Tönnies (1855–1937) studied how life in the new industrial metropolis differed from life in rural villages. From this contrast, he developed two concepts that have become a lasting part of sociology's terminology.

Tönnies (1963, orig. 1887) used the German word *Gemeinschaft* ("community") to refer to *a type of social organization in which people are closely tied by kinship and tradition*. The *Gemeinschaft* of the rural village, Tönnies explained, joins people in what amounts to a single primary group.

By and large, argued Tönnies, *Gemeinschaft* is absent in the modern city. On the contrary, urbanization creates *Gesellschaft* ("association"), *a type of social organization in which people come together only on the basis of individual self-interest*. In the *Gesellschaft* way of life, individuals are motivated by their own needs rather than by a desire to help improve the well-being of everyone.

The rural rebound has been most pronounced in towns that offer spectacular natural beauty. There are times when people living in the scenic town of Park City, Utah, cannot even find a parking space.

By and large, city dwellers have little sense of community or common identity and look to other people mainly when they need something. Tönnies saw in urbanization the weakening of close, long-lasting social relations in favor of the brief and impersonal ties or secondary relationships typical of business.

Emile Durkheim:
Mechanical and Organic Solidarity

The French sociologist Emile Durkheim agreed with much of Tönnies's thinking about cities. However, Durkheim countered that urbanites do not lack social bonds; they simply organize social life differently than rural people.

Gemeinschaft Tönnies's term for a type of social organization in which people are closely tied by kinship and tradition

Gesellschaft Tönnies's term for a type of social organization in which people come together only on the basis of individual self-interest

Peasant Dance (left, c. 1565), by Pieter Breughel the Elder, conveys the essential unity of rural life forged by generations of kinship and neighborhood. By contrast, Lily Furedi's *Subway (right)* communicates the impersonality common to urban areas. Taken together, these paintings capture Tönnies's distinction between *Gemeinschaft* and *Gesellschaft.*

Pieter Breughel the Elder (c. 1525/30–1569), *Peasant Dance*, c. 1565, Kunsthistorisches Museum, Vienna/Superstock. Lily Furedi, American. *Subway*. Oil on canvas, 99 × 123 cm. National Collection of Fine Arts, Washington, D.C./Smithsonian Institute.

Durkheim described traditional, rural life as *mechanical solidarity,* social bonds based on common sentiments and shared moral values. With its emphasis on tradition, Durkheim's concept of mechanical solidarity bears a strong similarity to Tönnies's *Gemeinschaft.* Urbanization erodes mechanical solidarity, Durkheim explained, but it also generates a new type of bonding, which he called *organic solidarity,* social bonds based on specialization and interdependence. This concept, which parallels Tönnies's *Gesellschaft,* reveals an important difference between the two thinkers. Both thought that the growth of industrial cities weakened tradition, but Durkheim optimistically pointed to a new kind of solidarity. Where societies had been built on *likeness,* Durkheim now saw social life based on *difference.*

For Durkheim, urban society offers more individual choice, moral tolerance, and personal privacy than people find in rural villages. In sum, Durkheim thought that something is lost in the process of urbanization, but much is gained.

Georg Simmel: The Blasé Urbanite

The German sociologist Georg Simmel (1858–1918) offered a micro-level analysis of cities, studying how urban life shapes individual experience. According to Simmel, individuals see the city as a crush of people, objects, and events. To prevent being overwhelmed by all this stimulation, urbanites develop a *blasé attitude,* tuning out much of what goes on around them. Such detachment does not mean that city dwellers lack compassion for others; they simply keep their distance as a survival strategy so that they can focus their time and energy on the people and things that really matter to them.

The Chicago School: Robert Park and Louis Wirth

Sociologists in the United States soon joined the study of rapidly growing cities. Robert Park (1864–1944), a leader of the first U.S. sociology program at the University of Chicago, sought to add a street-level perspective by getting out and studying real cities. As he said of himself, "I suspect that I have actually covered more ground, tramping about in cities in different parts of the world, than any other living man" (1950:viii). Walking the streets, Park found the city to be an organized mosaic of distinctive ethnic communities, commercial centers, and industrial districts. Over time, he observed, these "natural areas" develop and change in relation to one another. To Park, the city was a living organism—a human kaleidoscope.

Another major figure in the Chicago School of urban sociology was Louis Wirth (1897–1952). Wirth (1938) is best known for blending the ideas of Tönnies, Durkheim, Simmel, and Park into a comprehensive theory of urban life.

Wirth began by defining the city as a setting with a large, dense, and socially diverse population. These traits result in an impersonal, superficial, and transitory way of life for city dwellers. Living among millions of others, urbanites come into contact with many more people than residents of rural areas. Thus when city people take notice of others at all, they usually know them not in terms of *who they are* but *what they do*—as, for instance, the bus driver, the pharmacist, or the grocery store clerk. These specialized urban relationships are often pleasant for all concerned, but we should remember that self-interest rather than friendship is the main reason behind the interaction.

The impersonal nature of urban relationships, together with the great social diversity found in cities today, makes city dwellers more tolerant than rural villagers. Rural communities often jealously enforce their narrow traditions, but the heterogeneous population of a city rarely shares any single code of moral conduct (T. C. Wilson, 1985, 1995).

Evaluate In both Europe and the United States, early sociologists presented a mixed view of urban living. Rapid urbanization troubled Tönnies and Wirth, who saw personal ties and traditional morality lost in the anonymous rush of the city. Durkheim and Park emphasized urbanism's positive face, pointing to more personal freedom and greater personal choice.

Minorities Have Become a Majority in the Largest U.S. Cities

According to the latest data from the Census Bureau, minorities—Hispanics, African Americans, and Asians—are now a majority of the population in 66 of the 100 largest U.S. cities, up from 48 in 2000 and 30 in 1990.

What accounts for the change? One reason is that large cities have been losing their non-Hispanic white population. For example, between 1990 and 2000, Detroit lost half of its non-Hispanic, white population; between 2000 and 2010, it lost half of the white population that remained. As a result, by 2010, 92 percent of Detroit's current population was people of various minority categories. The same pattern holds in the Sunbelt. Between 2000 and 2010, the minority population of Garland, Texas rose from 47 percent to 66 percent. In Glendale, Arizona, the minority population rose from 35 percent in 2000 to 51 percent in 2010. Overall, the minority share of the population of the 100 largest cities increased from 47.9 percent in 1990 to 56.2 percent in 2000 and to 60.1 percent in 2010.

But perhaps the biggest reason for the minority-majority trend is the increase in immigration. Immigration, coupled with higher birth rates among new immigrants, resulted in a 25 percent

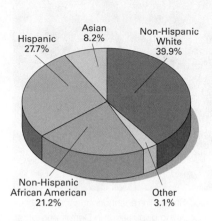

Population Profile for the 100 Largest U.S. Cities, 2010

Racial and ethnic minorities make up a majority of the population of this country's 100 largest cities.

Source: U.S. Census Bureau (2011).

gain in the Hispanic population (about 3.3 million people) of the largest 100 cities between 2000 and 2010. The Asian population also surged by 30 percent (more than 1.1 million people). The African American population decreased by one percent between 2000 and 2010.

Political officials and other policymakers examine these figures closely. Clearly, the future vitality of the largest U.S. cities depends on meeting the needs and taking advantage of the contributions of the swelling minority—and especially immigrant—populations.

What Do You Think?

1. Why are the minority populations of large U.S. cities increasing?

2. What positive changes and challenges does a minority-majority bring to a city?

3. Before Hurricane Katrina, African Americans represented 67 percent of the population of New Orleans; afterward, the share was about 40 percent. What difference might this change make in the city's immediate future?

Sources: Schmitt (2001) and U.S. Census Bureau (2011).

One problem with all of these views is that they paint urbanism in broad strokes that overlook the effects of class, race, and gender. There are many kinds of urbanites—rich and poor, black and white, Anglo and Latino, women and men—all leading distinctive lives (Gans, 1968). As the Thinking About Diversity box explains, the share of racial and ethnic minorities in the largest U.S. cities has increased sharply since 1990. We see social diversity most clearly in cities, where various categories of people are large enough to form visible communities (Macionis & Parrillo, 2013).

CHECK YOUR LEARNING Of these urban sociologists—Tönnies, Durkheim, Park, and Wirth—which were more positive about urban life? Which were more negative? In each case, explain why.

Urban Ecology

Sociologists (especially members of the Chicago School) developed **urban ecology**, *the study of the link between the physical and social dimensions of cities*. One issue of interest to urban ecologists is why cities are located where they are. The first cities emerged in fertile regions where the ecology favored raising crops. Preindustrial people, concerned with defense, built their cities on mountains (ancient Athens was perched on an outcropping of rock) or surrounded by water (Paris and Mexico City were built on islands). With the Industrial Revolution, economic considerations placed all major U.S. cities near rivers and natural harbors that facilitated trade.

Urban ecologists also study the physical design of cities. In 1925, Ernest W. Burgess, a student and colleague of Robert Park, described land use in Chicago in terms of *concentric zones*. City centers, Burgess observed, are business districts bordered by a ring of factories, followed by residential rings with housing that becomes more expensive the farther it is from the noise and pollution of the city's center.

Homer Hoyt (1939) refined Burgess's observations, noting that distinctive districts sometimes form *wedge-shaped sectors*. For example, one fashionable area may develop next to another, or an industrial district may extend outward from a city's center along a train or trolley line.

Chauncy Harris and Edward Ullman (1945) added yet another insight: As cities decentralize, they lose their single-center form in favor of a *multicentered model*. As cities grow, residential areas, industrial parks, and shopping districts typically push away from one another. Few people want to live close to industrial areas, for example, so the city becomes a mosaic of distinct districts.

Social area analysis investigates what people in particular neighborhoods have in common. Three factors seem to explain most of the variation in neighborhood types: family patterns, social class, and race and ethnicity (Shevky & Bell, 1955; R. J. Johnston, 1976). Families with children look for areas with large apartments or single-family homes and good schools. The rich seek high-prestige neighborhoods, often in the central city near cultural

The Industrial Revolution created great cities across the United States. In recent decades, however, the movement of industry abroad resulted in job losses and declining populations in Detroit and other older cities in the "Rustbelt." Yet, today's high levels of immigration are bringing new life to many cities as a new generation of people join the urban mix. In the Detroit metropolitan area, much of a recent gain in population is due to surging Arab immigration.

the result of deliberate decisions by the corporate elite to move their production facilities to the Sunbelt (where labor is cheaper and less likely to be unionized) or to move them out of the country entirely to low-income nations (Molotch, 1976; Castells, 1977, 1983; Lefebvre, 1991; Jones & Wilson, 1999).

 **Evaluate** The fact that many U.S. cities are in crisis, with widespread poverty, high crime, and barely functioning schools, seems to favor the political-economy view over the urban ecology approach. But one criticism applies to both: They focus on U.S. cities during a limited period of history. Much of what we know about industrial cities does not apply to preindustrial towns in our own past or the rapidly growing cities in many poor nations today. It is unlikely that any single model of cities can account for the full range of urban diversity.

CHECK YOUR LEARNING In your own words, explain what the urban ecology theories and the urban political-economy theory teach us about cities.

attractions. People with a common race or ethnic heritage cluster in distinctive communities.

Brian Berry and Philip Rees (1969) tied together many of these insights. They explained that distinct family types tend to settle in the concentric zones described by Burgess. Specifically, households with few children tend to cluster toward the city's center, and those with more children live farther away. Social class differences are primarily responsible for the sector-shaped districts described by Hoyt; the rich occupy one "side of the tracks" and the poor the other. And racial and ethnic neighborhoods are found at various places throughout the city, consistent with Harris and Ullman's multicentered model.

Urban Political Economy

In the late 1960s, many large U.S. cities were rocked by major riots. As public awareness of racial and economic inequality increased, some analysts turned away from the ecological approach to a social-conflict understanding of city life. The *urban political economy* model applies Karl Marx's analysis of conflict in the workplace to conflict in the city (Lindstrom, 1995).

Political economists reject the ecological approach's view of the city as a natural organism with particular districts and neighborhoods developing according to an internal logic. They claim that city life is defined by larger institutional structures, especially the economy. Capitalism, which transforms the city into real estate traded for profit and concentrates wealth in the hands of the few, is the key to understanding city life. From this point of view, for example, the decline in industrial Snowbelt cities after 1950 was

Read "Life and Death in the City: Neighborhoods in Context" by John Logan on **mysoclab.com**

Urbanization in Poor Nations

Understand

November 16, Cairo, Egypt. People call the vast Muslim cemetery in Old Cairo the "City of the Dead." In truth, it is very much alive: Tens of thousands of squatters have moved into the mausoleums, making this place an eerie mix of life and death. Children run across the stone floors, clotheslines stretch between the monuments, and an occasional television antenna protrudes from a tomb roof. With Cairo gaining 1,000 people a day, families live where they can.

Twice in its history, the world has experienced a revolutionary expansion of cities. The first urban revolution began about 8000 B.C.E. with the first urban settlements and continued until permanent settlements were in place on several continents. About 1750, the second urban revolution took off; it lasted for two centuries as the Industrial Revolution spurred rapid growth of cities in Europe and North America.

A third urban revolution is now under way. Today, 75 percent of people in high-income countries are already city dwellers. But extraordinary urban growth is occurring in low-income nations. In 1950, about 25 percent of the people in poor countries lived in cities. In 2008, the world became mostly urban for the first time in history, with more than half of humanity living in cities. By 2050, almost 70 percent of the world's people will be urban (United Nations, 2009; Population Reference Bureau, 2011).

Not only are more of the world's people urban; more and more cities are passing the 10 million mark in population. In 1975, only three cities in the world, Tokyo, New York, and Mexico City, had populations exceeding 10 million, and all of these cities were in high-income nations. In 2010, twenty-one cities had passed this mark, and only five of them were in high-income nations. By 2025, according to projections, eight more mega-cities will be added to the list and none of these eight will be in a high-income nation (five will be in Asia, two in Latin American, and one in Africa) (Brocker-hoff, 2000; United Nations, 2010).

This third urban revolution is the result of many poor nations entering the high-growth Stage 2 of demographic transition theory. Falling death rates have fueled population increases in Latin America, Asia, and especially Africa. For urban areas, the rate of increase is *twice as high* because in addition to natural increase, millions of people leave the countryside each year in search of jobs, health care, education, and conveniences such as running water and electricity.

Cities do offer more opportunities than rural areas, but they provide no quick fix for the problems of escalating population and grinding poverty. Many cities in less developed nations—including Egypt's Cairo, India's Kolkata (formerly Calcutta), and Manila in the Philippines—are simply unable to meet the basic needs of much of their population. All these cities are surrounded by wretched shantytowns, settlements of makeshift homes built from discarded materials. As noted in Chapter 9 ("Global Stratification"), even city dumps are home to thousands of poor people, who pick through the waste hoping to find enough to eat or sell to make it through another day.

Environment and Society

 Analyze

The human species has prospered, rapidly expanding over the entire planet. An increasing share of the global population now lives in large, complex settlements that offer the promise of a better life than that found in rural villages.

But these advances have come at a high price. Never before in history have human beings placed such demands on the planet. This disturbing development brings us to focus on the interplay of the natural environment and society. Like demography, **ecology** is another cousin of sociology, formally defined as *the study of the interaction of living organisms and the natural environment*. Ecology

The environmental movement has gained the support of a number of well-known and influential people. Former president Bill Clinton recently thanked actor Matt Damon for his help in the effort to provide clean water to people around the world. Are you involved in any efforts to protect the natural environment?

rests on the research of natural scientists as well as social scientists. We shall focus on the aspects of ecology that involve familiar sociological concepts and issues.

The **natural environment** is *Earth's surface and atmosphere, including living organisms, air, water, soil, and other resources necessary to sustain life*. Like every other species, humans depend on the natural environment to survive. Yet with our capacity for culture, humans stand apart from other species; we alone take deliberate action to remake the world according to our own interests and desires, for better and for worse.

Why is the environment of interest to sociologists? Environmental problems, from pollution to global warming, do not arise from the natural world operating on its own. Such problems result from the choices and actions of human beings, which means they are *social* problems.

The Global Dimension

The study of the natural environment requires a global perspective. The reason is simple: Regardless of political divisions between nations, the planet is a single **ecosystem**, which encompasses *the interaction of all living organisms and their natural environment*.

The Greek meaning of *eco* is "house," reminding us that this planet is our home and that all living things and their natural environment are interrelated. A change in any part of the natural environment sends ripples through the entire global ecosystem.

Consider, from an ecological point of view, our national love of eating hamburgers. People in North America (and, increasingly, around the world) have created a huge demand for beef, which has greatly expanded the ranching industry in Brazil, Costa Rica, and other Latin American nations. To produce the lean meat sought by fast-food corporations, cattle in Latin America feed on grass, which uses a great deal of land. Latin American ranchers clear the land for grazing by cutting down thousands of square miles of forests each year. These tropical forests are vital to maintaining Earth's atmosphere. Deforestation ends up threatening everyone, including people in the United States enjoying their hamburgers (N. Myers, 1984a).

Technology and the Environmental Deficit

Sociologists point to a simple formula: $I = PAT$, where environmental impact (I) reflects a society's population (P), its level of affluence (A), and its level of technology (T). Members of simpler societies—the hunters and gatherers described in Chapter 2 ("Culture")—hardly affect the environment because they are few in number, are poor, and have only simple technology. Nature affects all aspects of their lives as they follow the migration of game, watch the rhythm of the seasons, and suffer from natural catastrophes, such as fires, floods, droughts, and storms.

Societies at intermediate stages of sociocultural evolution have a somewhat greater capacity to affect the environment. But the environmental impact of horticulture (small-scale farming), pastoralism (the herding of animals), and even agriculture (the use of animal-drawn plows) is limited because people still rely on muscle power for producing food and other goods.

Humans' ability to control the natural environment increased dramatically with the Industrial Revolution. Muscle power gave way to engines that burn fossil fuels: coal at first and then oil. The use of such machinery affects the environment in two ways: Production now consumes more natural resources, and it also releases more pollutants into the atmosphere. Even more important, armed with industrial technology, we are able to bend nature to our will, tunneling through mountains, damming rivers, irrigating deserts, and drilling for oil in the arctic wilderness and on the ocean floor. This explains why people in rich nations, who represent just 23 percent of humanity, account for 46 percent of the world's energy use (World Bank, 2012).

Not only do members of industrial societies use more energy, but we produce 100 times more goods than people living in agrarian societies do. Higher living standards are good in some ways, but they increase the problems of solid waste (because we ultimately throw away most of what we produce) and pollution (industrial production generates smoke and other toxic substances).

The most important insight sociology offers about our physical world is that environmental problems do not simply "happen." Rather, the state of the natural environment reflects the ways in which social life is organized—how people live and what they think is important. The greater the technological power of a society, the greater that society's ability to threaten the natural environment.

From the start, people recognized the material benefits of industrial technology. But only a century later did they begin to see its long-term effects on the natural environment. Today, we realize that the technological power to make our lives better can also put the lives of future generations at risk.

Evidence is mounting that we are running up an **environmental deficit**, *profound long-term harm to the natural environment caused by humanity's focus on short-term material affluence* (Bormann, 1990). The concept of environmental deficit is important for three reasons. First, it reminds us that environmental concerns are *sociological*, reflecting societies' priorities about how people should live. Second, it suggests that much environmental damage—to the air, land, and water—is *unintended*, at least in the sense that most people do not realize all the consequences of cutting down forests, strip mining, or using throwaway packaging. Again, sociological analysis is helpful in making such consequences clearer. Third, in some respects, the environmental deficit is *reversible*. Inasmuch as societies have created environmental problems, societies can undo many of them.

Culture: Growth and Limits

Whether we recognize environmental dangers and decide to do something about them is a cultural matter. Thus along with technology, culture has powerful environmental consequences.

The Logic of Growth

When you turn on the television news, you might hear a story like this: "The government reported some bad economic news today, with the economy growing by only half a percent during the first quarter of the year." If you stop to think about it, our culture defines an economy that isn't growing very fast as "stagnant" (which is bad) and an economy that is getting smaller as a "recession" or a "depression" (which is *very* bad). What is "good" is *growth*—lots of it—which makes the economy get bigger and bigger. More cars, bigger homes, more income, more spending—the idea of *more* is at the heart of our cultural definition of living well (McKibben, 2007).

One of the reasons we define growth in positive terms is that we value *material comfort*, believing that money and the things it buys improve our lives. We also believe in the idea of *progress*, thinking that the future will be better than the present. In addition, we look to *science* to make our lives easier and more rewarding. In simpler terms, "people are clever," "having things is good," and "life gets better." Taken together, such cultural values form the *logic of growth*.

An optimistic view of the world, the logic of growth holds that more powerful technology has improved our lives and that new discoveries will continue to do so in the future. Throughout the history of the United States and other high-income nations, the logic of growth has been the driving force behind settling the wilderness, building towns and roads, and pursuing material affluence.

However, "progress" can lead to unexpected problems, including strain on the environment. The logic of growth responds by arguing that people (especially scientists and other technology experts) will find a way out of any problem placed in our path. If, for example, as the world begins to run short of oil, scientists will come up with new hybrid and electric cars, and eventually hydrogen, solar, or nuclear engines (or some as yet unknown technology) will develop to meet the world's energy needs.

Environmentalists counter that the logic of growth is flawed because it assumes that we can always think our way out of any problem. More important, it incorrectly assumes that natural resources such as clean air, fresh water, and fertile soil will always be plentiful. We can and will exhaust these *finite* resources if we continue to pursue growth at any cost. Echoing Malthus, environmentalists warn that if we call on the planet to support increasing numbers of people, we will surely destroy the environment—and ourselves—in the process.

The Limits to Growth

If we cannot invent our way out of the problems created by the logic of growth, perhaps we need another way of thinking about the world. Environmentalists therefore counter that growth must have limits. Stated simply, the *limits-to-growth thesis* is that humanity must put in place policies to control the growth of population, production, and the use of resources in order to avoid environmental collapse.

In *The Limits to Growth,* a controversial book that played a large part in launching the environmental movement, Donella Meadows and her colleagues (1972) used a computer model to calculate the planet's available resources, rates of population growth, amount of land available for cultivation, levels of industrial and food production, and amount of pollutants released into the atmosphere. The model reflects changes that have occurred since 1900 and projects forward to the end of the twenty-first century. The authors concede that such long-range predictions are speculative, and some critics think they are plain wrong (Simon, 1981). But right or wrong, the conclusions of the study call for serious consideration. The authors claim that we are quickly consuming Earth's finite resources. Supplies of oil, natural gas, and other energy sources are declining and will continue to drop, a little faster or more slowly depending on the conservation policies of rich nations and the speed with which other nations such as China, India, and Brazil continue to industrialize. Within the next 100 years, resources will run out, crippling industrial output and causing a decline in food production.

This limits-to-growth theory shares Malthus's pessimism about the future. People who accept it doubt that current patterns of life are sustainable for even another century. Perhaps we can all learn to live with less. This may not be as hard as you might think: Research shows, for example, that an increase in material consumption in recent decades has not brought an increase in levels of personal happiness (D. G. Myers, 2000). In the end, environmentalists warn, either make fundamental changes in how we live, placing less strain on the natural environment, or widespread hunger and conflict will force change on us.

Solid Waste: The Disposable Society

Across the United States, people generate a massive amount of solid waste—about 1.4 billion pounds *every day.* Figure 15–4 shows the average composition of a typical community's trash.

As a rich nation of people who value convenience, the United States has become a *disposable society.* We consume more products than people living in any other nation, and many of these products

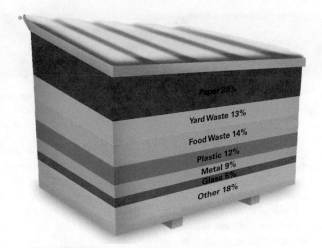

FIGURE 15-4 Composition of Community Trash

We throw away a wide range of material, with paper the single largest part of our trash.

Source: U.S. Environmental Protection Agency (2011).

have throwaway packaging. For example, fast food is served in cardboard, plastic, and Styrofoam containers that we throw away within minutes. But countless other products, from beauty cream to batteries, are elaborately packaged to make them more attractive to the customer and to discourage tampering and theft.

Manufacturers market soft drinks, beer, and fruit juices in aluminum cans, glass jars, and plastic containers, which not only use up finite resources but also create mountains of solid waste. Countless items are intentionally designed to be disposable: pens, razors, flashlights, batteries, even cameras. Other goods, from light bulbs to automobiles, are designed to have a limited useful life, after which they become unwanted junk. As Paul Connett (1991) points out, even the words we use to describe what we throw away—*waste, trash, refuse, garbage, rubbish*—show how little we value what we cannot immediately use. But this was not always the case, as the Seeing Sociology in Everyday Life box on page 428 explains.

Living in a rich society, the average person in the United States consumes twice as much energy, plastics, lumber, and other resources as someone living in many other high-income nations such as Japan, Denmark, or Sweden, and nearly fifty times more than someone living in a low-income nation such as Bangladesh or Tanzania. This high level of consumption means that we in the United States not only use a disproportionate share of the planet's natural resources but also that we generate most of the world's refuse.

We like to say that we throw things "away." But more than half of our solid waste (which totals more than 135 million tons a year) never goes away. It ends up in landfills, which are, literally, filling up. Material in landfills can also pollute groundwater stored under Earth's surface. Although in most places laws now regulate what can be discarded in a landfill, the Environmental Protection Agency has identified 1,302 dump sites across the United States containing hazardous materials that are polluting water both above and below the ground. In addition, what goes into landfills

Why Grandma Macionis Had No Trash

Grandma Macionis, we always used to say, never threw anything away. She was born and raised in Lithuania—the "old country"—where growing up in a poor village shaped her in ways that never changed, even after she came to the United States as a young woman and settled in Philadelphia.

In her later years, when I knew her, I can remember the family traveling together to her house to celebrate her birthday. We never could think of a good gift for Grandma because, although she didn't have all that much, she never seemed to need anything. She lived a simple life and had simple clothes and showed little interest in "fancy things." She had no electric appliances. She used her simple tools until they wore out. Her kitchen knives, for example, were worn narrow from decades of sharpening. The food that was left over from meals was saved. What could not be saved was recycled as compost for her vegetable garden.

After opening a birthday present (often a new sweater that we all knew she would never wear), she would carefully save the box, wrapping paper, and ribbon, which probably meant more to her than whatever gift they surrounded. We all knew the drill and we smiled at each other as we watched her put every piece of the wrapping away, knowing she would find a way to use it all again and again.

As strange as Grandma sometimes seemed to her grandchildren, she was a product of her culture. "Trash" is not natural or inevitable. A century ago, in fact, there was little "trash." If a pair of socks wore thin, people mended them, probably more than once. When they were beyond

Grandma Macionis, in the 1970s, with the author.

repair, they were used as rags for cleaning or sewn, along with other old clothing, into a quilt. For her, everything had value, if not in one way, then in another.

During the twentieth century, as women joined men in working outside of the home, income went up, and families began buying more and more "timesaving" products. Before long, few people cared about the home recycling that Grandma Macionis so carefully practiced. Soon cities sent crews from block to block to pick up truckloads of discarded material. The era of "trash" had begun.

What Do You Think?

1. Just as Grandma Macionis was a product of her culture, so are we. Do you know people who have plenty but never seem to think that they have enough?

2. What cultural values make people today demand timesaving products and "convenience packaging"?

3. Do you think recent decades have made people in our society more likely to recycle? How does today's recycling differ from that practiced by Grandma Macionis?

---

all too often stays there, sometimes for centuries. Tens of millions of tires, disposable diapers, and other items that we bury in landfills each year do not decompose and will be an unwelcome legacy for future generations.

Environmentalists argue that we should address the problem of solid waste by doing what many of our grandparents did: Use less and turn "waste" into a resource. One way to do this is through *recycling*, reusing resources we would otherwise throw away. Recycling is an accepted practice in European nations, where almost half of all waste materials are recycled. This practice is becoming more common in the United States, where we now reuse about 34 percent of what we throw away. The share is increasing as more municipalities pass laws requiring reuse of certain materials such as glass bottles and aluminum cans and as the business of recycling becomes more profitable.

Water and Air

Oceans, lakes, and streams are the lifeblood of the global ecosystem. Humans depend on water for drinking, bathing, cooling, cooking, recreation, and a host of other activities.

According to what scientists call the *hydrologic cycle,* the planet naturally recycles water and refreshes the land. The

process begins as heat from the sun causes Earth's water, 97 percent of which is in the oceans, to evaporate and form clouds. Because water evaporates at lower temperatures than most pollutants, the water vapor that rises from the seas is relatively pure, leaving various contaminants behind. Water then falls to the Earth as rain, which drains into streams and rivers and finally returns to the sea. Two major concerns about water, then, are supply and pollution.

Water Supply

Less than one-tenth of 1 percent of Earth's water is suitable for drinking. It is not surprising, then, that for thousands of years, water rights have figured prominently in laws around the world. Today, some regions of the world, especially the tropics, enjoy plentiful fresh water, using only a small share of the available supply. High demand, coupled with modest reserves, makes water supply a matter of concern in much of North America and Asia, where people look to rivers rather than rainfall for their water. In China, deep aquifers are dropping rapidly. In the Middle East, water supply is reaching a critical level. Iran is rationing water in its capital city. In Egypt, the Nile River provides just one-sixth as

Water is vital to life, and it is also in short supply. The state of Gujarat, in western India, has experienced a long drought. In the village of Natwarghad, people crowd together, lowering pots into the local well, taking what little water is left.

much water per person as it did in 1900. Across northern Africa and the Middle East, people already lack the water they need for irrigation and drinking. About half the world's people live in countries where water scarcity is already reducing food production. With increasing demand for water, such problems will only get worse (United Nations Environmental Programme, 2008; Walsh, 2009; Solomon, 2010).

Rising population and the development of more complex technology have greatly increased the world's appetite for water. The global consumption of water (now estimated at almost 4,000 cubic kilometers, or 140 trillion cubic feet per year) has doubled since 1950 and is rising steadily. As a result, even in parts of the world that receive plenty of rainfall, people are using groundwater faster than it can be replenished naturally. In the Tamil Nadu region of southern India, for example, people are drawing so much groundwater that the local water table has fallen 100 feet over the past several decades. Mexico City—which has sprawled to some 1,400 square miles—has pumped so much water from its underground aquifer that the city has sunk 30 feet in the past century and continues to drop about 2 inches per year. Farther north in the United States, the Ogallala aquifer, which lies below seven states from South Dakota to Texas, is now being pumped so rapidly that some experts fear it could run dry in just a few decades.

In light of such developments, we must face the reality that water is a finite and ever more valuable resource. Greater conservation of water by individuals—the average person in the United States consumes about 100 gallons of water a day, which amounts to about 3 million gallons in a lifetime—is part of the answer. However, households around the world account for just 10 percent of water use. We need to reduce water consumption by industry, which uses 20 percent of the global total, and farming, which consumes 70 percent of the total for irrigation.

Perhaps new irrigation technology will reduce future demand for water. But here again, we see how population increase, as well as economic growth, strains our ecosystem (United Nations World Water Assessment Programme, 2009; U.S. Geological Survey, 2009; Solomon, 2010).

Water Pollution

In large cities from Mexico City to Cairo to Shanghai, many people have no choice but to drink contaminated water. Infectious diseases such as typhoid, cholera, and dysentery, all caused by waterborne microorganisms, spread rapidly through these populations. In addition to ensuring ample *supplies* of water, we must protect the *quality* of water.

Water quality in the United States is generally good by global standards. However, even here the problem of water pollution is steadily growing. Across the United States, rivers and streams absorb hundreds of millions of pounds of toxic waste each year. This pollution results not just from intentional dumping but also from the runoff of agricultural fertilizers and lawn chemicals.

A special problem is *acid rain*—rain made acidic by air pollution—which destroys plant and animal life. Acid rain (or snow) begins with power plants burning fossil fuels (oil and coal) to generate electricity; this burning releases sulfuric and nitrous oxides into the air. As the wind sweeps these gases into the atmosphere, they react with the air to form sulfuric and nitric acids, which turns atmospheric moisture acidic.

This process is a clear case of one type of pollution causing another: Air pollution (from smokestacks) ends up contaminating water (in lakes and streams that collect acid rain). Acid rain is truly a global phenomenon because the regions that suffer the harmful effects may be thousands of miles from the source of the pollution. For instance, British power plants have caused acid rain that has devastated forests and fish in Norway and Sweden, 1,000 miles to the northeast. In the United States, we see a similar pattern as midwestern smokestacks have harmed the natural environment of upstate New York and New England.

Air Pollution

Because we are surrounded by air, most people in the United States are more aware of air pollution than contaminated water. One of the unexpected consequences of industrial technology—especially the factory and the motor vehicle—has been a decline in air quality. In London, fifty years ago, factory smokestacks, automobiles, and coal fires used to heat households all added up to what was probably the worst urban air quality the world has ever known. The fog that some residents jokingly called "pea soup" was in reality a deadly mix of pollutants: In 1952, an especially thick haze that hung over London for five days killed 4,000 people.

Air quality improved in the final decades of the twentieth century. Rich nations passed laws that banned high-pollution heating, including the coal fires that choked London. In addition, scientists devised ways to make factories and motor vehicles operate much more cleanly. In fact, today's vehicles produce only a fraction of the pollutants that spewed from models from the 1950s and 1960s.

If people in high-income countries can breathe a bit more easily than they once did, those living in poor societies face problems of air pollution that are becoming more serious. One reason is that people in low-income countries still rely on wood, coal, peat, and other "dirty" fuels to cook their food and heat their homes. In addition, nations eager to encourage short-term industrial development may pay little attention to the longer-term dangers of air pollution. As a result, many cities in Latin America, Eastern Europe, and Asia are plagued by air pollution as bad as London's "pea soup" back in the 1950s.

The Rain Forests

Rain forests are *regions of dense forestation, most of which circle the globe close to the equator.* The largest tropical rain forests are in South America (notably Brazil), west-central Africa, and Southeast Asia. In all, the world's rain forests cover some 2.8 billion acres, or 8.4 percent of Earth's total land surface (United Nations Environment Programme, 2011).

Like other global resources, rain forests are falling victim to the needs and appetites of the surging world population. As noted earlier, to meet the demand for beef, ranchers in Latin America clear forested areas to increase their supply of grazing land. We are also losing rain forests to the hardwood trade. People in rich nations pay high prices for mahogany and other woods because, as the environmentalist Norman Myers (1984b:88) puts it, they have "a penchant for parquet floors, fine furniture, fancy paneling, weekend yachts, and high-grade coffins." Under such economic pressure, the world's rain forests are now less than half their original size, and they continue to shrink by at least 1 percent (50,000 square miles) annually, which amounts to about an acre every second. Unless we stop this loss, the rain forests will vanish before the end of this century, and with them will go protection for Earth's biodiversity and climate.

Global Warming

Why are rain forests so important? One reason is that they cleanse the atmosphere of carbon dioxide (CO_2). Since the beginning of the Industrial Revolution, the amount of carbon dioxide produced by

Members of small, simple societies, such as the Mentawi in Indonesia, live in harmony with nature; they do not have the technological means to greatly affect the natural world. Although we in complex societies like to think of ourselves as superior to such people, the truth is that there is much we can—indeed, we must—learn from them.

humans (mostly from factories and automobiles) has risen sharply. Much of this CO_2 is absorbed by the oceans. But plants also take in carbon dioxide and in the process expel oxygen. This is why rain forests—our largest concentration of plant life—are vital to maintaining the chemical balance of the atmosphere.

The problem is that production of carbon dioxide is rising while the amount of plant life on Earth is shrinking. To make matters worse, rain forests are being destroyed mostly by burning, which releases even more CO_2 into the atmosphere. Experts estimate that the atmospheric concentration of carbon dioxide is now 40 percent higher than it was 150 years ago (Gore, 2006; United Nations Environment Programme, 2009; National Oceanic & Atmospheric Administration, 2012).

High above Earth, carbon dioxide acts like the glass roof of a greenhouse, letting heat from the sun pass through to the surface while preventing much of it from radiating away from the planet. The result of this *greenhouse effect,* say ecologists, is **global warming**, *a rise in Earth's average temperature due to an increasing concentration of carbon dioxide in the atmosphere.* Over the past century, the global temperature has risen about 1.3° Fahrenheit (to an average of 58° F). The year 2010 (the last one with official data) was the warmest year for the planet since records were started back in 1880. Scientists warn that the planet's average temperature could rise by another 5° to 10° F during this century. Already, the polar ice caps are melting, and scientists predict that increasing temperatures could melt so much ice that the sea level would rise to cover low-lying land all around the world: Water would cover all of the Maldives Islands in the Indian Ocean, most of Bangladesh, and much of the coastal United States, including Washington, D.C., right up to the steps of the White House. Such a change would create perhaps 100 million "climate change refugees." On the other hand, this same process of rising temperatures will affect other regions of the world very differently. The U.S. Midwest, currently one of the most productive agricultural regions in the world, probably would become arid (Gillis, 2011; McMahon, 2011; Reed, 2011).

Some scientists point out that we cannot be sure of the consequences of global warming. Others point to the fact that global temperature changes have been taking place throughout history, perhaps having little or nothing to do with rain forests. A few are optimistic, suggesting that higher concentrations of carbon dioxide in the atmosphere might speed up plant growth (because plants thrive on this gas), and this increase might correct the imbalance and nudge Earth's temperature downward once again. But the consensus of scientists is clear: Global warming is a serious problem that threatens the future for all of us (Kerr, 2005; Gore, 2006; International Panel on Climate Change, 2007; National Oceanic and Atmospheric Administration, 2012).

Declining Biodiversity

Our planet is home to as many as 30 million species of animals, plants, and microorganisms. As rain

Environmental debates typically involve weighing opposing claims. For example, some people claim that the process of "fracking"—using high pressure hoses underground to separate natural gas from shale—promises to give our nation a vast, new source of energy. To others, however, fracking threatens a vital natural resource by poisoning our ground water and perhaps even triggering earthquakes.

forests are cleared and humans extend their control over nature, several dozen unique species of plants and animals cease to exist each day, reducing the planet's *biodiversity*.

But given the vast number of living species, why should we be concerned by the loss of a few? Environmentalists give four reasons. First, our planet's biodiversity provides a varied source of human food. Using agricultural high technology, scientists can "splice" familiar crops with more exotic plant life, making food more bountiful and more resistant to insects and disease. Certain species of life are even considered to be vital to the production of human food. Bees, for example, perform the work of pollination, a necessary stage in the growth of plants. The fact that the bee population has declined by one-third in the United States and by two-thirds in the Middle East is cause for serious concern. Thus biodiversity helps feed our planet's rapidly increasing population.

Second, Earth's biodiversity is a vital genetic resource used by medical and pharmaceutical researchers to provide hundreds of new compounds each year that cure disease and improve our lives. For example, children in the United States now have a good chance of surviving leukemia, a disease that was almost a sure killer two generations ago, because of a compound derived from a tropical flower called the rosy periwinkle. The oral birth control pill, used by tens of millions of women in this country, is another product of plant research, this one involving the Mexican forest yam. Because biodiversity itself allows our ecosystem to control many types of diseases, it is likely that the loss of living species will encourage the transmission of disease.

Third, with the loss of any species of life—whether it is the magnificent California condor, the famed Chinese panda, the spotted owl, or even a single species of ant—the beauty and complexity of our natural environment are diminished. And there are clear warning signs: Three-fourths of the world's 10,000 species of birds are declining in number.

Finally, unlike pollution, the extinction of any species is irreversible and final. An important ethical question, then, is whether people living today have the right to impoverish the world for those who will live tomorrow (E. O. Wilson, 1991; Keesing et al., 2010; Capella, 2011).

Environmental Racism

Social-conflict theory has given rise to the concept of **environmental racism**, *patterns of development that expose poor people, especially minorities, to environmental hazards*. Historically, factories that spew pollution have stood near neighborhoods housing the poor and people of color. Why? In part, disadvantaged people were drawn to factories in search of jobs, and their low incomes often meant they could afford housing only in undesirable neighborhoods. Sometimes the only housing that fit their budgets stood in the very shadow of the plants and mills where they worked.

Nobody wants a factory or dump nearby, but the poor have little power to resist. Through the years, the most serious environmental hazards have been located near Newark, New Jersey (not in upscale Bergen County), in southside Chicago (not in wealthy Lake Forest), or on Native American reservations in the West (not in affluent suburbs of Denver or Phoenix) (Commission for Racial Justice, 1994; Bohon & Humphrey, 2000).

Looking Ahead: Toward a Sustainable Society and World

Evaluate

The demographic analysis presented in this chapter reveals some disturbing trends. We see, first, that our planet's population has reached record levels because birth rates remain high in poor nations and death rates have fallen just about everywhere. Reducing fertility will remain a pressing issue throughout this century.

Nushawn: I'm telling you, there are too many people already! Where is everyone going to live?

Tabitha: Have you ever been to Kansas? Or Wyoming? There's plenty of empty space out there.

Marco: Maybe now. But I'm not so sure there'll be all that room for our children—or their children. . . .

Are you worried about the world's rapidly increasing population? Think about this: By the time you finish reading this box, more than 1,000 people will have been added to our planet. By this time tomorrow, global population will have risen by more than 220,000. Currently, as the table shows, there are four births for every two deaths on the planet, pushing the world's population upward by almost 83 million annually. Put another way, global population growth amounts to adding another Germany to the world each year.

It is no wonder that many demographers and environmentalists are deeply concerned about the future. Earth has an unprecedented population: The 3 billion people we have added since 1974 alone exceed the planet's total in 1900. Might Thomas Malthus—who predicted that overpopulation would push the world into war and suffering—be right after all? Lester Brown and other *neo-Malthusians* predict a coming apocalypse if we do not change our ways. Brown (1995) admits that Malthus failed to imagine how much technology (especially fertilizers and plant genetics) could boost the planet's agricultural output. But, all the same, he maintains that Earth's rising population is rapidly outstripping its finite resources. Families in many poor countries can find little firewood, members of rich countries are depleting the oil reserves, and everyone is draining our supply of clean water and poisoning the planet with waste. Some analysts argue that we have already passed Earth's "carrying capacity" for population and that we need to hold the line or even reduce global population to ensure our long-term survival.

But other analysts, the *anti-Malthusians*, sharply disagree. Julian Simon (1995) points out that two centuries after Malthus predicted catastrophe, Earth supports almost six times as many people who, on average, live longer, healthier lives than ever before. With more advanced technology, people have devised ways to increase productivity and limit population increase. As Simon sees it, this is cause for celebration. Human ingenuity has consistently proved the doomsayers wrong, and Simon is betting that it will continue to do so.

Join the Blog!

Where do you place your bet? Do you think Earth can support 8 or 10 billion people? What do you think should be done about global population increase? Go to MySocLab and join the Sociology in Focus blog to share your opinions and experiences and to see what others think.

Global Population Increase, 2011

	Births	Deaths	Net Increase
Per year	139,558,000	56,611,000	82,947,000
Per month	11,629,833	4,717,583	6,912,250
Per day	382,351	155,099	227,252
Per hour	15,931	6,462	9,469
Per minute	266	108	158
Per second	4.4	1.8	2.6

Sources: Brown (1995), Simon (1995), Scanlon (2001), Smail (2007), Population Reference Bureau (2011), and U.S. Census Bureau (2011).

Even with some recent decline in the rate of population increase, the nightmare of Thomas Malthus is still a real possibility, as the Sociology in Focus box on page 432 explains.

Further, population growth remains greatest in the poorest countries of the world, which cannot support their present populations, much less their future ones. Supporting 83 million additional people on our planet each year, 81 million of whom are in poor societies, will take a global commitment to provide not only food but also housing, schools, and employment. The well-being of the entire world may ultimately depend on resolving the economic and social problems of poor, overly populated countries and bridging the widening gulf between "have" and "have-not" nations.

Urbanization is continuing, especially in poor countries. People have always sought out cities in the hope of finding a better life. But the sheer numbers of people who live in the emerging global supercities, including Mexico City, São Paulo (Brazil), Lagos (Nigeria), Kinshasa (Democratic Republic of Congo), Mumbai (India), and Manila (Philippines), have created urban problems on a massive scale.

Around the world, humanity is facing a serious environmental challenge. Part of this problem is population increase, which is greatest in poor countries. But part of the problem is the high levels of consumption in rich nations such as our own. By increasing the planet's environmental deficit, our present way of life is borrowing against the well-being of our children and their children. Globally, members of rich societies, who currently consume so much of Earth's resources, are mortgaging the future security of the poor countries of the world.

The answer, in principle, is to create an **ecologically sustainable culture**, *a way of life that meets the needs of the present generation without threatening the environmental legacy of future generations.* Sustainable living depends on three strategies.

First, we need to *bring population growth under control.* The current population of 7 billion is already straining the natural environment. Clearly, the higher world population climbs, the more difficult environmental problems will become. Even if the recent slowing of population growth continues, the world will have 9.3 billion people by 2050. Few analysts think that Earth can support this many people; most argue that we must hold the line at about 8 billion, and some argue that we must actually *decrease* population in the coming decades (Smail, 2007).

A second strategy is to *conserve finite resources.* This means meeting our needs with a responsible eye toward the future by using resources efficiently, seeking alternative sources of energy (other than fossil fuels), and in some cases, learning to live with less.

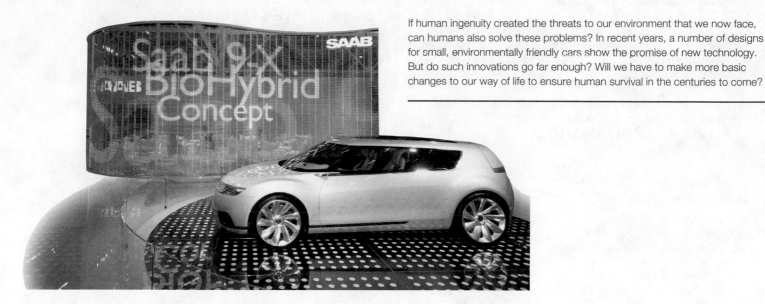

If human ingenuity created the threats to our environment that we now face, can humans also solve these problems? In recent years, a number of designs for small, environmentally friendly cars show the promise of new technology. But do such innovations go far enough? Will we have to make more basic changes to our way of life to ensure human survival in the centuries to come?

A third strategy is to *reduce waste.* Whenever possible, simply using less is the best solution. Learning to live with less will not come easily, especially at a time when economic growth seems to be the way out of high unemployment. But keep in mind that as our society has consumed more and more in recent decades, people have not become any happier (D. G. Myers, 2000). Recycling programs, too, are part of the answer, and recycling can make everyone part of the solution to our environmental problems.

In the end, making all three of these strategies work depends on a more basic change in the way we think about ourselves and our world. Our *egocentric* outlook sets our own interests as standards for how to live; a sustainable environment demands an *ecocentric* outlook that helps us see that the present is tied to the future and that everyone must work together. Most nations in the southern half of the world are *underdeveloped,* unable to meet the basic needs of their people. At the same time, most countries in the northern half of the world are *overdeveloped,* using more resources than Earth can sustain over time. The changes needed to create a sustainable ecosystem will not come easily, and they will be costly. But the price of *not* responding to the growing environmental deficit will certainly be greater (Brown et al., 1993; Population Action International, 2000; Gore, 2006).

Finally, consider that the great dinosaurs dominated this planet for some 160 million years and then perished forever. Humanity is far younger, having existed for a mere 250,000 years. Compared to the rather dimwitted dinosaurs, our species has the gift of great intelligence. But how will we use this ability? What are the chances that humans will continue to flourish 160 million years—or even 160 years—from now? The answer depends on the choices made by just one of the 30 million species living on Earth: human beings.

Why is the environment a social issue?

As this chapter explains, the state of the natural environment depends on how society is organized, especially the importance a culture attaches to consumption and economic growth.

Hint If expansion is "good times," then contraction is a "recession" or perhaps even a "depression." Such a worldview means that it is normal—or even desirable—to live in a way that increases stress on the natural environment. Sustainability, an idea that is especially important as world population increases, depends on learning to live with what we have or maybe even learning to live with less. Although many people seem to think so, it really doesn't require a 6,000-pound SUV to move around urban areas. Actually, it might not require a car at all. This new way of thinking requires that we do not define social standing and personal success in terms of what we own and what we consume. Can you imagine a society like that? What would it be like?

We learn to see economic expansion as natural and good. When the economy stays the same for a number of months, we say we are experiencing "stagnation." How do we define a period when the economy gets smaller, as happened during the fall of 2008?

What would it take to convince members of our society that smaller (rather than bigger) might be better? Why do we seem to prefer not just bigger cars but also bigger homes and more and more material possessions?

Seeing Sociology in *Your* Everyday Life

1. Here is an illustration of the problem of runaway growth (Milbrath, 1989:10): "A pond has a single water lily growing on it. The lily doubles in size each day. In thirty days, it covers the entire pond. On which day does it cover half the pond?" When you realize the answer, discuss the implications of this example for population increase.

2. Each of us generates in our minds a "mental map" of cities in which we have lived. Draw a mental map of a city familiar to you with as much detail of specific places, districts, roads, and transportation facilities as you can. After you complete the map, look at what you considered to be important and try to recognize what you left out. One good way to do this is compare your map to a street map or, better yet, compare it to a map drawn by someone else. If you make comparisons, try to account for the differences.

3. Do you think that the world's increasing population is a problem or not? What about the state of our planet's natural environment? Go to the "Seeing Sociology in *Your* Everyday Life" feature on MySocLab for additional discussion of these issues and suggestions for ways you can become more engaged in promoting a more secure world.

Demography: The Study of Population

Demography analyzes the size and composition of a population and how and why people move from place to place. Demographers collect data and study several factors that affect population

Fertility

- Fertility is the incidence of childbearing in a country's population.
- Demographers describe fertility using the **crude birth rate.**

Mortality

- Mortality is the incidence of death in a country's population.
- Demographers measure mortality using both the **crude death rate** and the **infant mortality rate.**

Migration

The **net migration rate** is the difference between the in-migration rate and the out-migration rate.

✳ Explore the **Map** on **mysoclab.com**

Population Growth

In general, rich nations grow almost as much from immigration as from natural increase; poorer nations grow almost entirely from natural increase.

Population Composition

Demographers use **age-sex pyramids** to show graphically the composition of a population and to project population trends.   **pp. 410–14**

demography (p. 410) the study of human population

fertility (p. 410) the incidence of childbearing in a country's population

crude birth rate (p. 410) the number of live births in a given year for every 1,000 people in a population

mortality (p. 411) the incidence of death in a country's population

crude death rate (p. 411) the number of deaths in a given year for every 1,000 people in a population

infant mortality rate (p. 411) the number of deaths among infants under one year of age for each 1,000 live births in a given year

life expectancy (p. 411) the average life span of a country's population

migration (p. 411) the movement of people into and out of a specified territory

sex ratio (p. 413) the number of males for every 100 females in a nation's population

age-sex pyramid (p. 413) a graphic representation of the age and sex of a population

History and Theory of Population Growth

- Historically, world population grew slowly because high birth rates were offset by high death rates.
- About 1750, a demographic transition began as world population rose sharply, mostly due to falling death rates.
- In the late 1700s, Thomas Robert Malthus warned that population growth would outpace food production, resulting in social calamity.
- **Demographic transition theory** contends that technological advances gradually slow population increase.
- World population is expected to exceed 9 billion by 2050.   **pp. 414–18**

👁 Watch the **Video** on **mysoclab.com**

demographic transition theory (p. 415) a thesis that links population patterns to a society's level of technological development

zero population growth (p. 416) the rate of reproduction that maintains population at a steady level

Urbanization: The Growth of Cities

The **first urban revolution** began with the appearance of cities about 10,000 years ago.

- By about 2,000 years ago, cities had emerged in most regions of the world except North America and Antarctica.
- Preindustrial cities have low-rise buildings; narrow, winding streets; and personal social ties.   **p. 418**

A **second urban revolution** began about 1750 as the Industrial Revolution propelled rapid urban growth in Europe.

- The physical form of cities changed as planners created wide, regular streets to allow for more trade.
- The emphasis on commerce, as well as the increasing size of cities, made urban life more impersonal.   **pp. 418–19**

In the United States, urbanization has been going on for more than 400 years and continues today.

- Urbanization came to North America with European colonists.
- By 1850, hundreds of new cities had been founded from coast to coast.
- By 1920, a majority of the U.S. population lived in urban areas.
- Since 1950, the decentralization of cities has resulted in the growth of suburbs and edge cities and a rebound in rural population.
- Nationally, Sunbelt cities—but not the older Snowbelt cities—are increasing in size and population.   **pp. 419–21**

urbanization (p. 418) the concentration of population into cities

metropolis (p. 419) a large city that socially and economically dominates an urban area

suburbs (p. 420) urban areas beyond the political boundaries of a city

megalopolis (p. 420) a vast urban region containing a number of cities and their surrounding suburbs

Urbanism as a Way of Life

Rapid urbanization during the nineteenth century led early sociologists to study the differences between rural and urban life. These early sociologists included, in Europe, Tönnies, Durkheim, and Simmel, and in the United States, Park and Wirth.

Ferdinand Tönnies built his analysis on the concepts of *Gemeinschaft* and *Gesellschaft*.

- *Gemeinschaft*, typical of the rural village, joins people in what amounts to a single primary group.
- *Gesellschaft*, typical of the modern city, describes individuals motivated by their own needs rather than the well-being of the community.

Gemeinschaft (p. 421) a type of social organization in which people are closely tied by kinship and tradition

Gesellschaft (p. 421) a type of social organization in which people come together only on the basis of individual self-interest

urban ecology (p. 423) the study of the link between the physical and social dimensions of cities

Emile Durkheim agreed with much of Tönnies's thinking but claimed that urbanites do not lack social bonds; the basis of social solidarity simply differs in the two settings.

- **Mechanical solidarity** involves social bonds based on common sentiments and shared moral values. This type of social solidarity is typical of traditional, rural life.
- **Organic solidarity** arises from social bonds based on specialization and interdependence. This type of social solidarity is typical of modern, urban life.

Georg Simmel claimed that the overstimulation of city life produced a blasé attitude in urbanites.

Robert Park, at the University of Chicago, claimed that cities permit greater social freedom.

Louis Wirth saw large, dense, heterogeneous populations creating an impersonal and self-interested, though tolerant, way of life. **pp. 421–24**

📖 Read the Document on mysoclab.com

Urbanization in Poor Nations

- The world's first urban revolution took place about 8000 B.C.E. with the first urban settlements.
- The second urban revolution took place after 1750 in Europe and North America with the Industrial Revolution.
- A third urban revolution is now occurring in poor countries. Today, most of the world's largest cities are found in less developed nations. **pp. 424–25**

Environment and Society

The state of the **environment** is a social issue because it reflects how human beings organize social life.

- Societies increase the **environmental deficit** by focusing on short-term benefits and ignoring the long-term consequences brought on by their way of life. **pp. 425–26**
- The more complex a society's technology, the greater its capacity to alter the natural environment.
- The *logic-of-growth thesis* supports economic development, claiming that people can solve environmental problems as they arise.
- The *limits-to-growth thesis* states that societies must curb development to prevent eventual environmental collapse. **pp. 426–27**

Environmental issues include

- *Disposing of solid waste:* More than half of what we throw away ends up in landfills, which are filling up and which can pollute groundwater under Earth's surface.
- *Protecting the quality of water and air:* The supply of clean water is already low in some parts of the world. Industrial technology has caused a decline in air quality.
- *Protecting the rain forests:* Rain forests help remove carbon dioxide from the atmosphere and are home to a large share of this planet's living species. Under pressure from development, the world's rain forests are now half their original size and are shrinking by about 1% annually.
- *Global warming:* Increasing levels of carbon dioxide in the atmosphere are causing the average temperature of the planet to rise, melting the ice caps and bringing other dramatic changes to the natural environment. **pp. 427–31**

- *Environmental racism:* Conflict theory has drawn attention to the fact that the poor, especially minorities, suffer most from environmental hazards. **pp. 427–31**

ecology (p. 425) the study of the interaction of living organisms and the natural environment

natural environment (p. 425) Earth's surface and atmosphere, including living organisms, air, water, soil, and other resources necessary to sustain life

ecosystem (p. 425) a system composed of the interaction of all living organisms and their natural environment

environmental deficit (p. 426) profound long-term harm to the natural environment caused by humanity's focus on short-term material affluence

rain forests (p. 430) regions of dense forestation, most of which circle the globe close to the equator

global warming (p. 430) a rise in Earth's average temperature due to an increasing concentration of carbon dioxide in the atmosphere

environmental racism (p. 431) patterns of development that expose poor people, especially minorities, to environmental hazards

ecologically sustainable culture (p. 433) a way of life that meets the needs of the present generation without threatening the environmental legacy of future generations

16 Social Change: Modern and Postmodern Societies

Learning Objectives

Remember the definitions of the key terms highlighted in boldfaced type throughout this chapter.

Understand the major causes of social change.

Apply the sociological perspective to a wide range of collective behavior.

Analyze social movements using a number of sociological theories.

Evaluate the benefits and challenges of modern life.

Create the capacity to take advantage of the benefits of modern society and effectively respond to its challenges.

Society does not stay the same. This chapter explores social change, explaining how modern societies differ from earlier, traditional societies. The chapter discusses many causes of change, including collective behavior, disasters, and social movements. ■

The five-story red brick apartment building at 253 East Tenth Street in New York has been standing for more than a century. In 1900, one of the twenty small apartments in the building was occupied by thirty-nine-year-old Julius Streicher; Christine Streicher, age thirty-three; and their four young children. The Streichers were immigrants, both having come in 1885 from their native Germany to New York, where they met and married.

The Streichers probably considered themselves successful. Julius operated a small clothing shop a few blocks from his apartment; Christine stayed at home, raised the children, and did housework. Like most people in the country at that time, neither Julius nor Christine had graduated from high school, and they worked for ten to twelve hours a day, six days a week. Their income—average for that time—was about $35 a month, or about $425 a year. (In today's dollars, that would be about $11,400, which would put the family well below the poverty line.) They spent almost half of their income for food; most of the rest went for rent.

Today, Dorothy Sabo resides at 253 East Tenth Street, living alone in the same apartment where the Streichers spent much of their lives. Now eighty-seven, she is retired from a career teaching art at a nearby museum. In many respects, Sabo's life has been far easier than the life the Streichers knew. For one thing, when the Streichers lived there, the building had no electricity (people used kerosene lamps and candles) and no running water (Christine Streicher spent most of every Monday doing laundry using water she carried from a public fountain at the end of the block). There were no telephones, no television, and of course no computers. Today, Dorothy Sabo takes such conveniences for granted. Although she is hardly rich, her pension and Social Security amount to several times as much (in constant dollars) as the Streichers earned.

Sabo has her own worries. She is concerned about the environment and often speaks out about global warming. But a century ago, if the Streichers and their neighbors were concerned about "the environment," they probably would have meant the smell coming up from the street. At a time when motor vehicles were just beginning to appear in New York City, carriages, trucks, and trolleys were all pulled by horses—thousands of them. These animals dumped 60,000 gallons of urine and 2.5 million pounds of manure on the streets each and every day—an offensive mixture churned and splashed by countless wheels onto everything and everyone within a stone's throw of the streets (Simon & Cannon, 2001).

....

I t is difficult for most people today to imagine how different life was a century ago. Not only was life much harder back then, but it was also much shorter. Statistical records show that life expectancy was just forty-six years for men and forty-eight years for women, compared to about seventy-six and eighty-one years today, respectively (Kochanek et al., 2011).

Over the past 100 years, much has changed for the better. Yet as this chapter explains, social change is not all positive. Even change for the better can have negative consequences too, causing unexpected new problems. Early sociologists were mixed in their assessment of **modernity**, *changes brought about by the Industrial Revolution*. Likewise, today's sociologists point to both good and

bad aspects of **postmodernity**, *the transformations caused by the Information Revolution and the postindustrial economy*. One thing is clear: For better or worse, the rate of change has never been faster than it is now.

What Is Social Change?

Understand

In earlier chapters, we examined relatively fixed or *static* social patterns, including status and role, social stratification, and social institutions. We also looked at the *dynamic* forces that have shaped our way of life, ranging from innovations in technology to the growth of bureaucracy and the expansion of cities. These are all dimensions of **social change**, *the transformation of culture and social institutions over time*. This process of social change has four major characteristics:

1. **Social change happens all the time.** "Nothing is constant except death and taxes" goes the old saying. Yet our thoughts about death have changed dramatically as life expectancy in the United States has nearly doubled in the past century. And back in the Streichers' day, people in the United States paid no taxes on their earnings; taxation increased dramatically over the course of the twentieth century, along with the size and scope of government. In short, even the things that seem constant are subject to the twists and turns of change.

   Still, some societies change faster than others. As Chapter 2 ("Culture") explained, hunting and gathering societies change quite slowly; members of technologically complex societies, by contrast, can witness significant change within a single lifetime.

   It is also true that in any society, some cultural elements change faster than others. William Ogburn's theory of *cultural lag* (see Chapter 2, "Culture") asserts that material culture (that is, things) changes faster than nonmaterial culture (ideas and attitudes). For example, genetic technology that allows scientists to alter and perhaps even create life has developed more rapidly than our ethical standards for deciding when and how to use the technology.

2. **Social change is sometimes intentional but often unplanned.** Industrial societies actively promote many kinds of change. For example, auto manufacturers seek more efficient ways to power our cars, and advertisers try to convince us that life is not complete without a 4G cell phone or some other new electronic gadget. Yet rarely can anyone envision all the consequences of the changes that are set in motion.

   Back in 1900, when the country still relied on horses for transportation, people looked ahead to motor vehicles that would take a single day to carry them distances that used to take weeks or months. But no one could see how much the mobility provided by automobiles would alter everyday life in the United States, scattering family members, threatening the environment, and reshaping cities and suburbs. Nor could automotive pioneers have predicted the 34,000 deaths that occur in car accidents each year in the United States alone (National Highway Traffic Safety Administration, 2011).

3. **Social change is controversial.** The history of the automobile shows that social change brings both good and bad consequences. Capitalists welcomed the Industrial Revolution because new technology increased productivity and swelled profits. However, workers feared that machines would make their skills obsolete and resisted the push toward "progress."

These young men are performing in a hip-hop dance marathon in Hong Kong. Hip-hop music, dress style, and dancing have become popular in Asia, a clear case of cultural diffusion. Social change occurs as cultural patterns move from place to place, but people in different societies don't always have the same understanding of what these patterns mean. How might Chinese youth understand hip-hop differently from the young African Americans in the United States who originated it?

Today, as in the past, people disagree about how we ought to live and what we should welcome as "progress." We see this disagreement every day in the changing patterns of social interaction between black people and white people, women and men, and gays and heterosexuals that are welcomed by some people and opposed by others.

4. **Some changes matter more than others.** Some changes (such as clothing fads) have only passing significance; others (like the invention of computers) have already changed the world. Will the Information Revolution turn out to be as important as the Industrial Revolution? Like the automobile and television, computers have both positive and negative effects, providing new kinds of jobs while eliminating old ones, linking people in global electronic networks while isolating people in offices, offering vast amounts of information while threatening personal privacy.

Causes of Social Change

 **Understand**

Social change has many causes. In a world linked by sophisticated communication and transportation technology, change in one place often sets off change elsewhere.

Culture and Change

Chapter 2 ("Culture") identified three important sources of cultural change. First, *invention* produces new objects, ideas, and social patterns. Rocket propulsion research, which began in the 1940s, has produced sophisticated spacecraft that reach toward the stars. Today we take such technology for granted; during this century, a significant number of people may well have an opportunity to travel in space.

Second, *discovery* occurs when people take notice of existing elements of the world. For example, medical advances offer a growing understanding of the human body. Beyond their direct effects on human health, medical discoveries have extended life expectancy, setting in motion the "graying" of U.S. society (see Chapter 3 "Socialization: From Infancy to Old Age").

Third, *diffusion* creates change as products, people, and information spread from one society to another. Ralph Linton (1937a) recognized that many familiar aspects of our culture came from other lands. For example, the cloth used to make our clothing was developed in Asia, the clocks we see all around us were invented in Europe, and the coins we carry in our pockets were devised in what is now Turkey.

In general, material things change more quickly than cultural ideas. For example, breakthroughs such as the science of cloning occur faster than our understanding of when—and even whether—they are morally desirable.

Conflict and Change

Inequality and conflict within a society also produce change. Karl Marx saw class conflict as the engine that drives societies from one historical era to another. In industrial-capitalist societies, he maintained, the struggle between capitalists and workers pushes society toward a socialist system of production.

In the 130 years since Marx's death, this model has proved simplistic. Yet Marx correctly foresaw that social conflict arising from inequality (involving not just class but also race and gender) would force changes in every society, including our own, to improve the lives of working people.

Ideas and Change

Max Weber also contributed to our understanding of social change. Although Weber agreed that conflict could bring about change, he traced the roots of most social change to ideas. For example, people with charisma (Martin Luther King, Jr. is an example) can carry a message that changes the world.

Weber (1958, orig. 1904–1905) also highlighted the importance of ideas by revealing how the religious beliefs of early Protestants set the stage for the spread of industrial capitalism (see Chapter 13, "Family and Religion"). The fact that industrial capitalism developed primarily in areas of Western Europe where the Protestant work ethic was strong proved to Weber the power of ideas to bring about change.

Demographic Change

Population patterns also play a part in social change. The typical U.S. household was almost twice as large in 1900 (4.8 people) as it is today (2.6 people). Women are having fewer children, and more people are living alone. Change is also taking place as our population grows older. As Chapter 3 ("Socialization: From Infancy to Old Age") explained, 13 percent of the U.S. population was over age sixty-five in 2010, three times the proportion in 1900. By the year 2030, seniors will account for 20 percent of the total (U.S. Census Bureau, 2011). Medical research and health care services already focus extensively on the elderly, and life will change in countless other ways as homes and household products are redesigned to meet the needs of older consumers.

Migration within and between societies is another demographic factor that promotes change. Between 1870 and 1930, tens of millions of immigrants entered the industrial cities in the United States. Millions more from rural areas joined the rush. As a result, farm communities declined, cities expanded, and by 1920 the United States had for the first time become a mostly urban nation. Similar changes are taking place today as people moving from the Snowbelt to the Sunbelt mix with new immigrants from Latin America and Asia.

Where in the United States have demographic changes been greatest, and where have they been less pronounced? National Map 16–1 provides one answer, showing counties where the largest share of people have lived in their present homes for more than thirty years.

Collective Behavior and Change

Sociologists study various types of collective behavior that can bring about social change. **Collective behavior** is *activity involving a large number of people that is unplanned, often controversial, and can bring about change*. Collective behavior involves people in collectivities, which differ from social groups because many people may be involved without most having any direct interaction with others.

Crowds

One type of collective behavior is the **crowd**, which is *a temporary gathering of people who share a common focus of attention and who influence one another*. Crowds are a fairly new development: Most of our ancestors never saw a large crowd. In medieval Europe, for example, about the only time large numbers of people gathered in one place was when armies faced off on the battlefield (Laslettt, 1984). Today, however, crowds of 50,000 or more are common at rock concerts and sporting events, and even the registration halls of large universities.

Given their large numbers, crowds have the power to bring about change. Political demonstrations and rallies, often based on networks supported by computer and cell phone technology, drew together tens of thousands of people in cities of the Arab world during 2011, to bring about unprecedented political change.

Mobs and Riots

Sometimes crowds can turn violent, transforming into a **mob**, which is *a highly emotional crowd that pursues a violent or destructive goal*. In this country's history, lynching was probably the most notorious example of mob behavior. After the Civil War, so-called lynch mobs terrorized newly freed African Americans trying to prevent a breakdown of the race-based caste system that put whites in a position of privilege. Any person of color who challenged white superiority risked death at the hands of hate-filled whites.

Similarly, a **riot** is *a social eruption that is highly emotional, violent, and undirected*. Riots are typically an expression of deep dissatisfaction on the part of people frustrated with the way society is operating. People riot in response to what they see as social injustice, as if to say "We won't take it anymore!" Over the years, workers have rioted over unfair working conditions, just as minorities have rioted in response to a system that harms them.

What does a riot accomplish? One answer is "power." As the recent "Occupy Wall Street" movement illustrates, ordinary people can gain power when they act collectively. The power of the crowd to challenge the status quo and sometimes to force social change is the reason crowds are controversial. Throughout history, defenders of the status quo have feared "the mob" as a threat. By contrast, those seeking change have supported this type of collective action.

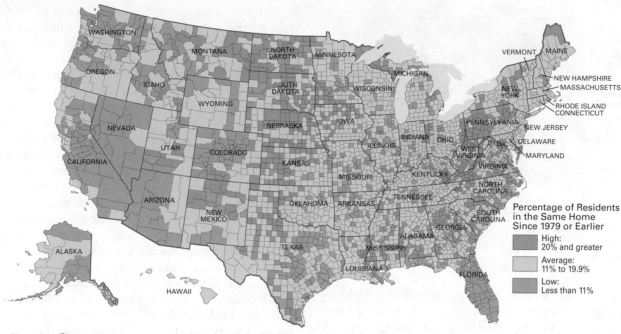

Seeing Ourselves

NATIONAL MAP 16–1 **Who Stays Put? Residential Stability across the United States**

Overall, only about 12 percent of U.S. residents have not moved during the past thirty years. Counties with a higher proportion of "long-termers" typically have experienced less change over recent decades: Many neighborhoods have been in place since before World War II, and many of the same families live in them. As you look at the map, what can you say about these stable areas? What accounts for the fact that most of these counties are rural and at some distance from the coasts?

✳️[Explore residential stability in your local community and in counties across the United States on **mysoclab.com**

Source: U.S. Census Bureau (2010).

Rumor

Collective behavior is sometimes guided by **rumor**, which refers to *unconfirmed information that people spread informally, by word of mouth or by using electronic devices.* Rumor thrives in a climate of uncertainty, when people care about some issue but are not sure of the facts. In a number of cities, for example, rumors about potential police action have spread among supporters of the "Occupy" movements. Rumor is unstable, not only because people are not sure about the facts but also because individuals may give the rumor a "spin" as they pass it along. The mass media and the Internet can quickly spread local issues and events across the country and around the world. Because rumor can trigger the formation of crowds and direct their action, government officials as well as leaders of protest organizations establish rumor control centers during a crisis in order to manage information.

Fashions and Fads

A final way in which collective behavior can influence the process of social change involves fashions and fads. Fashions and fads involve people spread over a large area. **Fashion** refers to *social patterns favored by a large number of people.* People's ideas about polite behavior, their tastes in clothing, music, and automobiles, as well as their political attitudes, are also subject to change over time, going in and out of fashion.

A **fad** refers to *an unconventional social pattern that people embrace briefly but enthusiastically.* Fads, sometimes called *crazes*, are common in high-income societies where many people have the money to spend on amusing, if often frivolous, things. During the 1950s, two young Californians produced a brightly colored plastic hoop, a version of a toy popular in Australia, that you can swing around your waist by gyrating your hips. The "hula hoop" became a national craze. In less than a year, hula hoops all but vanished, only to reappear from time to time. Pokémon cards are another example of the rise and fall of a fad. Justin Bieber probably hopes that he does not turn out to be a fad.

How do fads differ from fashions? Fads capture the public imagination but quickly burn out. Because fashions reflect basic cultural values like individuality and sexual attractiveness, they tend to stay around for a while. Therefore, a fashion—but rarely a fad—becomes a more lasting part of popular culture. Streaking, for instance, was a fad that came out of nowhere and soon vanished; denim clothing, however, is an example of fashion that originated in the rough mining camps of Gold Rush California in the 1870s and is still popular today.

Social Movements and Change

A final cause of social change lies in the efforts of people like us. People commonly band together to form a **social movement**, *an organized activity in which people set out to encourage or discourage social change.* Social movements, such as the political movements that swept across the Middle East in 2011, are common in the modern world. Our nation's history includes all kinds of social movements, from the colonial drive for independence to today's organizations supporting or opposing abortion, same-sex marriage, and legalizing marijuana.

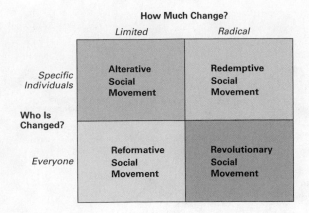

How Much Change?

	Limited	Radical
Specific Individuals	**Alterative Social Movement**	**Redemptive Social Movement**
Everyone	**Reformative Social Movement**	**Revolutionary Social Movement**

Who Is Changed?

FIGURE 16–1 Four Types of Social Movements

There are four types of social movements, reflecting who is changed and how great the change is.

Source: Based on Aberle (1966).

Social movements are about connecting people who share some political goal. Computer technology, including smartphones and social networking Internet sites, has made it easier than ever before for large numbers of people to connect.

Types of Social Movements

Researchers classify social movements according to the type of change they seek (Aberle, 1966; Cameron, 1966; Blumer, 1969). One variable asks, *Who is changed?* Some movements target selected people, and others try to change everyone. A second variable asks, *How much change?* Some movements seek only limited change in our lives; others pursue a radical transformation of society. Combining these variables results in four types of social movements, shown in Figure 16–1.

Alterative social movements are the least threatening to the status quo because they seek limited change in only part of the population. Their aim is to help certain people *alter* their lives. Promise Keepers is one example of an alterative social movement; it encourages men to live more spiritual lives and be more supportive of their families.

Redemptive social movements also target specific individuals, but they seek more radical change. Their aim is to help certain people *redeem* their lives. For example, Alcoholics Anonymous is an organization that helps people with an alcohol addiction achieve a sober life.

Reformative social movements aim for only limited change but target everyone. The environmental movement seeks to interest everyone in protecting the natural environment.

Revolutionary social movements are the most extreme of all, working for major transformation of an entire society. Sometimes pursuing specific goals, sometimes spinning utopian dreams, these social movements, including both the left-wing Communist party (pushing for government control of the entire economy) and right-wing militia groups (seeking the destruction of "big government") seek to radically change our way of life.

social movement an organized activity that encourages or discourages social change

claims making the process of trying to convince the public and public officials of the importance of joining a social movement to address a particular issue

Claims Making

In 1981, the Centers for Disease Control and Prevention began to track a strange disease that was killing people, most of them homosexual men. The disease came to be known as AIDS (acquired immune deficiency syndrome). Although AIDS was clearly a deadly disease, it was given little public or media attention. Only about five years later did the public begin to take notice of the rising number of deaths and start to think of AIDS as a serious social threat.

The change in public thinking was the result of **claims making**, *the process of trying to convince the public and public officials of the importance of joining a social movement to address a particular issue.* In other words, for a social movement to form, some issue has to be defined as a problem that demands public attention. Usually, claims making begins with a small number of people. In the case of AIDS, the gay community in large cities (notably San Francisco and New York) mobilized to convince people of the dangers posed by this deadly disease. Over time, if the mass media give the issue attention and public officials speak out on behalf of the problem, it is likely that the social movement will gain strength.

Considerable public attention has now been given to AIDS, and there is ongoing research aimed at finding a cure for this deadly disease. The process of claims making goes on all the time for dozens of issues. Today, for example, a movement to ban the use of cellular telephones in automobiles has pointed to the thousands of automobile accidents each year related to the use of phones while driving; so far, nine states have passed laws banning the use of handheld phones, thirty states ban cell phones for new drivers, and debate continues in others (McVeigh, Welch, & Bjarnason, 2003; Macionis, 2010; Governors Highway Safety Association, 2011).

Explaining Social Movements

Sociologists have developed several explanations of social movements. *Deprivation theory* holds that social movements arise among people who feel deprived of something, such as income, safe working conditions, or political rights. Whether you feel deprived or not, of course, depends on what you expect in life. Therefore, people band together when they experience **relative deprivation**, *a perceived disadvantage arising from some specific comparison.* This concept helps explain why movements for change surface in both good and bad times: It is not people's absolute standing that counts but how they perceive their situation in relation to the situations of specific other people (J. C. Davies, 1962; Merton, 1968).

Mass-society theory, a second explanation, argues that social movements attract socially isolated people who join a movement in order to gain a sense of belonging, identity, and purpose. From this point of view, social movements have a personal as well as a political agenda (Melucci, 1989).

Resource mobilization theory, a third theoretical scheme, links the success of any social movement to the resources that are available to it, including money, human labor, and the mass media. Because most social movements begin small, they must look beyond themselves to mobilize the resources required for success (Valocchi, 1996; Zhao, 1998; Passy & Giugni, 2001; Packer, 2003).

Watch the video "Defining Social Movements" on **mysoclab.com**

Fourth, *culture theory* points out that social movements depend not only on money and other material resources but also on cultural symbols. People must have a shared understanding of injustice in the world before they will mobilize to bring about change. In addition, specific symbols (such as photographs of the World Trade Center towers engulfed in flames after the September 11, 2001 terrorist attacks) helped mobilize people to support the U.S. military campaigns in Afghanistan and Iraq (McAdam, McCarthy, & Zald, 1996; J. E. Williams, 2002).

Fifth, *new social movements theory* points out the distinctive character of recent social movements in postindustrial societies. Rather than being local matters, these movements are typically national or international in scope, and most focus on quality-of-life issues, such as the natural environment, world peace, or animal rights, rather than more traditional economic issues. This broader scope of contemporary social movements results from closer ties between governments and between ordinary people around the world, who are now linked by the mass media and new information technology (Jenkins & Wallace, 1996; F. Rose, 1997).

Sixth and finally, *political economy theory* is a Marxist approach that claims that social movements arise in opposition to the capitalist economic system, which fails to meet the needs of the majority of people. Despite record corporate profits, U.S. society is in crisis, with tens of millions of people unable to find good jobs, living without health insurance, and living near or below the poverty line. Social movements arise as workers organize to demand higher wages, citizens rally for a health policy that protects everyone, and people march in opposition to spending billions to fund wars while ignoring basic needs at home (Buechler, 2000).

Stages in Social Movements

Social movements typically unfold in four stages: emergence, coalescence, bureaucratization, and decline. The *emergence* of social movements occurs as people begin to think that all is not well. Some, such as the civil rights and women's movements, are born of widespread dissatisfaction. Others emerge as a small group tries to mobilize the population, as when gay activists raised public concern about AIDS.

Coalescence takes place when a social movement defines itself and develops a strategy for attracting new members and "going public." Leaders determine policies and decide on tactics, which may include demonstrations or rallies to attract media attention.

As it gains members and resources, a social movement may undergo *bureaucratization*. As a movement becomes established, it depends less on the charisma and talents of a few leaders and more on a professional staff, which increases the chances for the movement's long-term survival.

Finally, social movements *decline* as resources dry up, the group faces overwhelming opposition, or members achieve their goals and lose interest. Some well-established organizations outlive their original causes and move on to new crusades; others lose touch with the idea of changing society and choose instead to become part of the "system" (Piven & Cloward, 1977; F. D. Miller, 1983).

Claims making is the process of convincing others of the importance of some problem and the need for specific change. The Occupy Wall Street movement has called attention to increasing economic inequality in the United States. In your opinion, how much actual change has this movement caused?

Disasters: Unexpected Change

Sometimes change results from events that are both unexpected and unwelcome. A **disaster** is *an event, generally unexpected, that causes extensive harm to people and damage to property*. Disasters are of three types. *Natural disasters* include floods, earthquakes, forest fires, and hurricanes (such as Hurricane Katrina, which devastated the Gulf Coast in 2005) (Erikson, 2005a). A second type is the *technological disaster,* which is widely regarded as an *accident* but is more accurately the result of our inability to control technology (Erikson, 2005a). The 2011 radiation leak at the Fukushima Daiichi nuclear plant is one recent example of a technological disaster. A third type is the *intentional disaster,* in which one or more organized groups deliberately harm others. War, terrorist attacks, and the genocide that took place in Libya (2011), the Darfur region of Sudan (2003–2010), Yugoslavia (1992–1995), and Rwanda (1994) are examples of intentional disasters.

The full scope of the harm caused by disasters may become evident only many years after the event. The Thinking Globally box on page 446 describes a technological disaster that is still affecting people and their descendants more than fifty years after it occurred.

Kai Erikson (1976, 1994, 2005a) has investigated dozens of disasters of all types and has reached three major conclusions about the social consequences of disasters. First, disasters are *social disruptions*. We all know that disasters harm people and destroy property, but what most people don't realize is that disasters also cause social damage by disrupting human community. When a dam burst and sent a mountain of water down West Virginia's Buffalo Creek in 1972, it killed 125 people, destroyed 1,000 homes, and left 4,000 people homeless. After the waters had gone and help was streaming into the area, the people were paralyzed not only by the loss of family members and friends but also by the loss of their entire way of life. Now five decades later, they have never been able to rebuild the community life that they once knew. We can pinpoint when disasters start, Erikson explains, but we cannot know when they will end. The full consequences of the radiation leak in Japan have yet to be learned.

Second, Erikson explains that the social damage is more serious when an event involves some toxic substance, as is common with technological disasters. As the case of radiation falling on Utrik Island shows

It was just after dawn on March 1, 1954, and the air was already warm on Utrik Island, a small bit of coral and volcanic rock in the South Pacific that is one of the Marshall Islands. The island was home to 159 people, who lived by fishing much as their ancestors had done for centuries. The population knew only a little about the outside world—a missionary from the United States taught the local children, and two dozen military personnel lived at a small U.S. weather station with an airstrip that received one plane each week.

At 6:45 A.M., the western sky suddenly lit up brighter than anyone had ever seen, and seconds later, a rumble like a massive earthquake rolled across the island. Some of the Utrik people thought the world was coming to an end. And truly, the world they had always known was about to change forever.

About 160 miles to the west, on Bikini Island, the United States military had just detonated an atomic bomb, a huge device with 1,000 times the power of the bomb used at the end of World War II to destroy the Japanese city of Hiroshima. The enormous blast vaporized the island and sent a massive cloud of dust and radiation into the atmosphere. The military expected the winds to take the cloud north into an open area of the ocean, but the cloud blew east instead. By noon, the radiation cloud had engulfed a Japanese fishing boat ironically called the *Lucky Dragon*, exposing the twenty-three people on board to a dose of radiation that would eventually sicken or kill them all. By the end of the afternoon, the deadly cloud spilled across Utrik Island.

The cloud was made up of coral and rock dust, all that was left of Bikini Island. The dust fell softly on Utrik Island, and the children, who remembered pictures of snow shown to them by their missionary teacher, ran out to play in the white powder that was piling up everywhere. No one realized that it was contaminated with deadly radiation.

Three-and-one-half days later, the U.S. military landed planes on Utrik Island and informed all the people that they would have to leave immediately, taking nothing with them. For three months, the island people were held at another

military base, and then they were returned home.

Many of the people who were on the island that fateful morning died young, typically from cancer or other diseases associated with radiation exposure. But even today, those who survived consider themselves and their island poisoned by the radiation, and they believe that the poison will never go away. The radiation may or may not still be in their bodies, but it has certainly worked its way deep into their culture. More than half a century after the bomb exploded, people still talked about the morning that "everything changed." The damage from this disaster turns out to be much more than medical—it was a social transformation that left the people with a deep belief that they are all sick, that life will never be the same, and that powerful people who live on the other side of the world could have prevented the disaster but did not.

What Do You Think?

1. In what sense is a disaster like the 2011 radiation leak in Japan never really over?

2. In what ways did the atomic bomb test change the culture of the Utrik people?

3. The U.S. government never formally took responsibility for what happened to the people of Utrik Island. What elements of global stratification do you see in this tragedy?

Source: Based on Erikson (2005a).

us, people feel "poisoned" when they have been exposed to a dangerous substance that they fear and over which they have no control.

Third, the social damage is most serious when the disaster is caused by the actions of other people. This can happen through negligence or carelessness (as in technological disasters) or through willful action (intentional disasters). Our belief that "other people will do us no harm" is a foundation of social life, Erikson claims. But when others act carelessly (as in the case of an oil spill) or intentionally in ways that harm us (as in the case of genocide in Darfur), survivors typically lose their trust in others to a degree that may never go away.

Modernity

 Analyze

A central concept in the study of social change is **modernity**, *changes brought about by the Industrial Revolution*. In everyday terms, modernity (its Latin root means "lately") refers to the present in relation to the past. Sociologists include in this catchall concept all of the social

patterns that were set in motion by the Industrial Revolution, which began in Western Europe in the 1750s. **Modernization**, then, is *the process of social change begun by industrialization*. The timeline inside the back cover of this book highlights important events that mark the emergence of modernity. Table 16–1 provides a summary of change in the United States over the course of the last 100 years.

Peter Berger (1977) identified four major characteristics of modernization:

1. **The decline of small, traditional communities.** Modernity involves "the progressive weakening, if not destruction, of the . . . relatively cohesive communities in which human beings have found solidarity and meaning throughout most of history" (1977:72). For thousands of years, in the camps of hunters and gatherers and in the rural villages of Europe and North America, people lived in small communities where life revolved around family and neighborhood. Such traditional worlds gave each person a well-defined place that, although limiting range of choice, offered a strong sense of identity, belonging, and purpose.

Sociologists classify natural disasters using three types. The 2011 tsunami that brought massive flooding to Japan is an example of a natural disaster. The 2010 Gulf of Mexico oil spill was a technological disaster. The slaughter of hundreds of thousands of people and the displacement of millions more from their homes since 2003 in the Darfur region of Sudan is an example of an intentional disaster.

Small, isolated communities still exist in the United States, of course, but they are home to only a tiny percentage of our nation's people. These days, the isolation of most of these communities is only geographic: Except among those who are extremely poor or who reject modernity on religious grounds, cars, telephones, television, and computers give rural families the pulse of the larger society and connect them to the entire world.

2. **The expansion of personal choice.** People in traditional, preindustrial societies view their lives as shaped by forces beyond human control—gods, spirits, fate. As the power of tradition weakens, people come to see their lives as an unending series of options, a process Berger calls *individualization*. For instance, many people in the United States choose a particular "lifestyle" (sometimes adopting one after another), showing an openness to change. Indeed, a common belief in our modern culture is that people *should* take control of their lives.

3. **Increasing social diversity.** In preindustrial societies, strong family ties and powerful religious beliefs enforce conformity and discourage diversity and change. Modernization promotes a more rational, scientific worldview as tradition loses its hold and people gain more individual choice. The growth of cities, the expansion of impersonal bureaucracy, and the social mix of people from various backgrounds combine to encourage diverse beliefs and behavior.

4. **Orientation toward the future and a growing awareness of time.** Premodern people focus on the past; people in modern societies think more about the future. Modern people are not only forward-looking but also optimistic that new inventions and discoveries will improve their lives.

Traditional people organize their lives around sunlight and seasons. With the introduction of clocks in the late Middle Ages, Europeans began to organize their lives in terms of hours and minutes. Focused on personal gain, modern people demand precise measurement of time and are likely to agree that "time is money." Berger (inspired by Weber) points out that one good indicator of a society's degree of modernization is the share of people who keep track of time by continually glancing at their wristwatches (or nowadays, their cell phones).

Recall that modernization touched off the development of sociology itself. As Chapter 1 ("Sociology: Perspective, Theory, and Method") explained, the discipline originated in the wake of the Industrial Revolution in Western Europe at a point when social change was proceeding rapidly. Early European and U.S. sociologists tried to analyze the rise of modern society and its consequences, both good and bad, for human beings.

TABLE 16–1 The United States: A Century of Change

	1910	2010
National population	92 million	309 million
Share living in cities	46%	84%
Life expectancy	48 years (men), 52 years (women)	76 years (men), 81 years (women)
Median age	24.1 years	37.2 years
Median family income	$8,000 (in 2010 dollars)	$60,395 (in 2010 dollars)
Share of income spent on food	43%	13%
Share of homes with flush toilets	10%	99.4%
Average number of cars	1 car for every 64 households	2.2 cars for every household
Divorce rate	about 1 in 20 marriages	about 6 in 20 marriages
Average gallons of petroleum products consumed	34 gallons per person per year	1,100 gallons per person per year

George Tooker's 1950 painting *The Subway* depicts a common problem of modern life: Weakening social ties and eroding traditions create a generic humanity in which everyone is alike yet each person is an anxious stranger in the midst of others.

Source: George Tooker, *The Subway*, 1950, egg tempera on gesso panel, 18¹/₈ × 36¹/₈ inches, Whitney Museum of American Art, New York. Purchased with funds from the Juliana Force Purchase Award, 50.23. Photograph © Whitney Museum of American Art.

Finally, in the process of comparing industrial societies with those that came before, we find it easy to assume that *everything* in our world is new. This is not the case, as the Seeing Sociology in Everyday Life box explains with an historical look at a favorite type of modern clothing—jeans.

Ferdinand Tönnies: The Loss of Community

The German sociologist Ferdinand Tönnies produced a lasting account of modernization in his theory of *Gemeinschaft* and *Gesellschaft* (see Chapter 15, "Population, Urbanization, and Environment"). Like Peter Berger, whose work he influenced, Tönnies (1963, orig. 1887) viewed modernization as the progressive loss of *Gemeinschaft*, or human community. As Tönnies saw it, the Industrial Revolution weakened the social fabric of family and tradition by introducing a businesslike emphasis on facts, efficiency, and money. European and North American societies gradually became rootless and impersonal as people came to associate with one another mostly on the basis of self-interest—the state Tönnies termed *Gesellschaft*.

Early in the twentieth century, at least some parts of the United States could be described using Tönnies's concept of *Gemeinschaft*. Families that had lived for many generations in small villages and towns were bound together into a hardworking and slowly changing way of life. Telephones (invented in 1876) were rare; not until 1915 could one place a coast-to-coast call (see the timeline inside the back cover of this book). Living without television (introduced commercially in 1933 and not widespread until after 1950), families entertained themselves, often gathering with friends in the evening to share stories, sorrows, or song. Lacking rapid transportation (Henry Ford's assembly line began in 1908, but cars became common only after World War II), many people knew little of the world beyond their hometown.

Inevitable tensions and conflicts divided these communities of the past. But according to Tönnies, the traditional spirit of *Gemeinschaft* meant that people were "essentially united in spite of all separating factors" (1963:65, orig. 1887).

Modernity turns society inside out so that, as Tönnies put it, people are "essentially separated in spite of uniting factors" (1963:65, orig. 1887). This is the world of *Gesellschaft*, where, especially in large cities, most people live among strangers and ignore the people they pass on the street. Trust is hard to come by in a mobile and anonymous society in which people put their personal needs ahead of group loyalty and a majority of adults believe "you can't be too careful" in dealing with people (NORC, 2011:2456). No wonder researchers conclude that even as we become more affluent, the social health of modern societies has declined (D. G. Myers, 2000).

● **Evaluate** Tönnies's theory of *Gemeinschaft* and *Gesellschaft* is the most widely cited model of modernization. The theory's strength lies in its synthesis of various dimensions of change: growing population, the rise of cities, and increasing impersonal interaction. But modern life, though often impersonal, still has some degree of *Gemeinschaft*. Even in a world of strangers, modern friendships can be strong and lasting. In addition, some analysts think that Tönnies favored—perhaps even romanticized—traditional societies while overlooking bonds of family and friendship that continue to flourish in modern societies.

CHECK YOUR LEARNING As types of social organization, how do *Gemeinschaft* and *Gesellschaft* differ?

Emile Durkheim: The Division of Labor

The French sociologist Emile Durkheim shared Tönnies's interest in the important social changes that resulted from the Industrial Revolution. For Durkheim (1964a, orig. 1893), modernization was marked by an increasing **division of labor**, or *specialized economic activity*. Every member of a traditional society performs more or less the same activities; modern societies function by having people perform highly specific jobs.

Durkheim explained that preindustrial societies are held together by *mechanical solidarity*, or shared moral sentiments (see pages 421–22). Members of such societies view everyone as basically alike, doing the same work and belonging together. Durkheim's concept of mechanical solidarity is virtually the same as Tönnies's *Gemeinschaft*.

With modernization, the division of labor (job specialization) becomes more and more pronounced. To Durkheim, this change means less mechanical solidarity but more of another kind of tie: *organic solidarity*, mutual dependency between people engaged in specialized work. Put simply, modern societies are held together not by likeness but by difference: All of us must depend on others to meet most of our needs. Organic solidarity corresponds to Tönnies's concept of *Gesellschaft*.

Despite obvious similarities in their thinking, Durkheim and Tönnies viewed modernity somewhat differently. To Tönnies, modern *Gesellschaft* amounted to the loss of social solidarity because people lose the "natural" and "organic" bonds of the rural

Read "Bowling Alone: America's Declining Social Capital" by Robert Putnam on **mysoclab.com**

Tradition and Modernity: The History of Jeans

Sociologists like to contrast "tradition" and "modernity." Tönnies, Durkheim, Weber, and even Marx developed theories (discussed in the following sections of the chapter) that contrasted social patterns that existed "then" with those that exist "now." Such theories are enlightening. But thinking in terms of "tradition versus modernity" encourages us to conclude that the past and the present have little in common.

All the thinkers discussed in this chapter saw past and present as strikingly different. But it is also true that countless elements of today's society—ranging from religion to warfare—have been part of human society for a very long time. It is also the case that many cultural elements that we think of as "modern" turn out to have been around much longer than many of us realize.

One element of today's culture, popular among today's college students, that we think of as distinctly modern is jeans. This piece of clothing, which is common enough to be considered almost a "uniform" among young people, moved to the center of popular culture when it swept across the college campus in the late 1960s.

But many people would be surprised to learn that jeans have been worn for centuries. To understand more, consider the original meanings of the words used to define this type of clothing. The term *dungarees*, a common name for jeans before the 1960s, is derived from the Hindi word *dungri*, a district of the Indian city Mumbai (formerly Bombay) where the coarse cloth is thought to have originated. From there, the fabric spread westward into Europe. The term *jeans* can be traced back to the name of the Italian city of Genoa, where the cotton fabric was widely worn in the 1650s. Another word for the fabric, *denim*, refers to the French city of Nîmes, reflecting the fact that, somewhat later, people described the cloth as being "de Nîmes."

Art historians have identified paintings from the sixteenth century that show people—typically the poor—wearing jeans. In the 1700s, British sailors used this fabric not only for making sails but also for constructing hammocks to sleep in and for fashioning shipboard clothing.

More than a century later, in 1853, U.S. clothing manufacturer Levi Strauss sold dungarees to miners who were digging for gold in the California gold rush. The familiar blue and white woven fabric is very strong and durable. Jeans became the clothing of choice among people who had limited budgets and who did demanding physical labor.

After gaining popularity among gold miners, jeans became popular among cowboys all across the western United States. By the beginning of the twentieth century, jeans were worn by almost all working people. By the 1930s, most prisoners across the country also wore denim.

This pattern made jeans a symbol of lower social standing. This fact is surely the reason that many middle-class people looked down on such clothing. As a result, especially in higher-income communities, public school officials banned the wearing of dungarees by students.

By the 1960s, however, a youth-based counterculture was emerging in the United States. This new cultural orientation rejected the older pattern of "looking upward" and copying the styles of the rich and famous and, instead, began "looking downward" and adopted the look of working people and even the down and out. By the end of the 1960s, rock stars, Hollywood celebrities, and college students favored jeans as a way to make a statement that they identified with working people—part of the era's more left-leaning political attitudes.

Of course, there was money to be made in this new trend. By the 1980s, the fashion industry was cashing in on the popularity of jeans by promoting "designer jeans" among more well-off people who probably had never entered a factory in their lives. In 1980, a teenage Brooke Shields helped launch Calvin Klein jeans that became all the rage among people who were able to spend three and four times as much as the jeans worn by ordinary people.

By the beginning of this century, jeans had become an accepted form of dress not only in schools but also in the corporate world. Many of the CEOs of U.S. corporations—especially in the high-tech fields—now routinely wear jeans to work and even to public events.

As you can see, jeans turn out to have a very long history. The fact that jeans existed both "then" and "now," all the while taking on new and different meanings, reveals the limitation of characterizing cultural elements as either "traditional" or "modern" in a world in which societies invent and reinvent their way of life all the time.

What Do You Think?

1. Is your attitude toward jeans different from that of your parents? If so, how and why?

2. Do you think the changing trend in the popularity of jeans suggests broader changes in our society before and after the 1960s? Explain.

3. How popular is wearing jeans on your campus? What about among your professors? Can you explain these patterns?

In art from the 1500s, we see poor people wearing "jeans." By the 1800s, jeans had become the uniform for the western cowboy. By the 1960s, jeans became the clothing of choice on the campus. More recently, corporate executives (especially in tech companies) have made jeans acceptable in the workplace.

Source: Based, in part, on Brazillian (2011).

Max Weber maintained that the distinctive character of modern society was its rational worldview. Virtually all of Weber's work on modernity centered on types of people he considered typical of their age: the scientist, the capitalist, and the bureaucrat. Each is rational to the core: The scientist is committed to the orderly discovery of truth, the capitalist to the orderly pursuit of profit, and the bureaucrat to the orderly conformity to a system of rules.

village, leaving only the "artificial" and "mechanical" ties of the big city. Durkheim had a more positive view of modernity, even reversing Tönnies's language to bring home the point. Durkheim labeled modern society "organic," arguing that modern society is no less natural than any other, and he described traditional societies as "mechanical" because they are so regimented. Durkheim viewed modernization not so much as a loss of community as a change from community based on bonds of likeness (kinship and neighborhood) to community based on economic interdependence (the division of labor). Durkheim's view of modernity is thus both more complex and more positive than Tönnies's view.

● **Evaluate** Durkheim's work, which resembles that of Tönnies, is a highly influential analysis of modernity. Of the two, Durkheim was more optimistic; still, he feared that modern societies might become so diverse that they would collapse into **anomie**, *a condition in which society provides little moral guidance to individuals.* Living with weak moral norms, modern people can become egocentric, placing their own needs above those of others and, in their social isolation, find little purpose in life.

Supporting Durkheim analysis, the vast majority of adults report that they see moral questions not in clear terms of right and wrong but as confusing "shades of gray" (NORC, 2011:604). In addition, the suicide rate, which Durkheim considered a good index of anomie, did in fact increase in the United States over the course of the twentieth century. Yet shared norms and values seem strong enough to give most people a sense of meaning and purpose. Whatever the hazards of anomie, most people value the personal freedom modern society gives us.

CHECK YOUR LEARNING Define mechanical solidarity and organic solidarity. In his view of the modern world, what makes Durkheim more optimistic than Tönnies?

Max Weber: Rationalization

For Max Weber, modernity meant replacing a traditional worldview with a rational way of thinking. In preindustrial societies, tradition acts as a constant brake on social change. To traditional people, "truth" is roughly the same as "what has always been" (1978:36, orig. 1921). To modern people, however, "truth" is the result of rational calculation. Because they value efficiency and have little reverence for the past, modern people readily adopt new social patterns that allow them to achieve their goals.

Echoing Tönnies's and Durkheim's claim that industrialization weakens tradition, Weber characterized modern society as "disenchanted." The unquestioned truths of an earlier time had been challenged by rational thinking. In short, said Weber, modern society turns away from the gods just as it turns away from the past. Throughout his life, Weber studied various modern "types"—the scientist, the capitalist, the bureaucrat—all of whom share the forward-looking, rational, and detached worldview that he believed was coming to dominate humanity.

● **Evaluate** Compared with Tönnies and especially Durkheim, Weber was very critical of modern society. He knew that science could produce technological and organizational wonders, yet he worried that science was carrying us away from more basic questions about the meaning and purpose of human existence. Weber feared that rationalization, especially in bureaucracies, would erode the human spirit with endless rules and regulations.

CHECK YOUR LEARNING How did Weber understand modernity? What does it mean to say that the modern world (think scientists, capitalists, and bureaucrats) is "disenchanted"?

Some of Weber's critics think that the alienation Weber attributed to bureaucracy actually stemmed from social inequality. This issue leads us to the ideas of Karl Marx.

Karl Marx: Capitalism

For Karl Marx, modern society was synonymous with capitalism; he saw the Industrial Revolution primarily as a *capitalist* revolution. Marx traced the emergence of the bourgeoisie in medieval Europe to the expansion of commerce. The bourgeoisie gradually displaced the feudal aristocracy as the Industrial Revolution gave it control of a powerful new productive system.

Marx agreed that modernity weakened small communities (as described by Tönnies), increased the division of labor (as noted by Durkheim), and encouraged a rational worldview (as Weber claimed). But he saw these simply as conditions necessary for capitalism to flourish. According to Marx, capitalism draws population away from farms and small towns into an ever-expanding market system centered in the cities; specialization is needed for efficient factories; and rationality is illustrated by the capitalists' endless pursuit of profit.

Earlier chapters have painted Marx as a spirited critic of capitalist society. Unlike Weber, who viewed modern society as an "iron cage" of bureaucracy from which there was no escape, Marx believed that social conflict in capitalist societies would sow the seeds of revolutionary change, leading to an egalitarian socialism. Such a society, as he saw it, would harness the wonders of industrial technology to enrich people's lives and rid the world of social classes, the source of conflict and so much suffering. Although Marx's evaluation of modern capitalist society was highly negative, he imagined a future of human freedom, creativity, and community.

 Evaluate Marx's theory of modernization is a complex theory of capitalism. But he underestimated the dominance of bureaucracy in modern societies. In socialist societies, in particular, the stifling effects of bureaucracy have turned out to be as bad as, or even worse than, the dehumanizing aspects of capitalism. The upheavals in Eastern Europe and the former Soviet Union in the 1990s revealed the depth of popular opposition to oppressive state bureaucracies.

CHECK YOUR LEARNING Of the four theorists just discussed— Tönnies, Durkheim, Weber, and Marx—who comes across as the most optimistic about modern society? Who was the most pessimistic? Explain your choices.

Structural-Functional Theory: Modernity as Mass Society

● Apply

November 11, on Interstate 275. From the car window, we see BP and Sunoco gas stations, a Kmart and a Wal-Mart, an AmeriSuites hotel, a Bob Evans, a Chi-Chi's Mexican restaurant, and a McDonald's. This road happens to circle Cincinnati, Ohio. But it could be in Boston, Saint Louis, Denver, San Diego, or almost anywhere else in the United States.

The rise of modernity is a complex process involving many dimensions of change, described in earlier chapters and reviewed here in the Summing Up table on page 452. How can we make sense of so many changes going on at once? Sociologists have two broad explanations of modern society, one guided by the structural-functional approach and the other based on social-conflict theory.

The first explanation, guided by the structural-functional approach and drawing on the ideas of Tönnies, Durkheim, and Weber, understands modernity as the emergence of a *mass society*

(Kornhauser, 1959; Nisbet, 1966; Berger, Berger, & Kellner, 1974; Pearson, 1993). A **mass society** is *a society in which prosperity and expanding bureaucracy have weakened traditional social ties.* A mass society is productive; on average, people have more income than ever. At the same time, it is marked by weak kinship and impersonal neighborhoods, leaving individuals to feel socially isolated. Although many people have material plenty, they are spiritually weak and often experience moral uncertainty about how to live.

The Mass Scale of Modern Life

Mass-society theory argues, first, that the scale of modern life has greatly increased. Before the Industrial Revolution, Europe and North America formed a mosaic of rural villages and small towns. In these local communities, which inspired Tönnies's concept of *Gemeinschaft,* people lived out their lives surrounded by kin and guided by a shared heritage. Gossip was an informal yet highly effective way of ensuring conformity to community standards. Such small communities tolerated little social diversity—the state of mechanical solidarity described by Durkheim.

For example, before 1690, English law demanded that everyone participate regularly in the Christian ritual of Holy Communion (Laslett, 1984). On the North American continent, only Rhode Island among the New England colonies tolerated any religious dissent. Because social differences were repressed in favor of conformity to established norms, subcultures and countercultures were few, and change proceeded slowly.

Increasing population, the growth of cities, and specialized economic activity driven by the Industrial Revolution gradually altered this pattern. People came to know one another by their jobs (for example, as "the doctor" or "the bank clerk") rather than by their kinship group or hometown. People looked on most others simply as strangers. The face-to-face communication of the village was eventually replaced by the impersonal mass media: newspapers, radio, television, and the computer-based social media that link people throughout the world. Large organizations steadily assumed more and more responsibility for the daily needs that had once been fulfilled by family, friends, and neighbors; public education drew more and more people to schools; police, lawyers, and courts supervised a formal criminal justice system. Even charity became the work of faceless bureaucrats working for various large social welfare organizations.

Geographic mobility, mass communication, and exposure to diverse ways of life all weaken traditional values. People become more tolerant of social diversity, defending individual rights and freedom of choice. Treating people differently because of their race, sex, or religion comes to be defined as backward and unjust. In the process, minorities at the margins of society gain greater power and broader participation in public life. The election of Barack Obama—an African American—to the highest office in the United States is surely one indicator that ours is now a modern society (West, 2008).

The mass media give rise to a national culture that washes over the traditional differences that used to set off one region from another. As one analyst put it, "Even in Baton Rouge, La., the local kids don't say 'y'all' anymore; they say 'you guys' just like on TV" (Gibbs, 2000:42). Mass-society theorists fear that the transformation of

Traditional and Modern Societies: The Big Picture

Elements of Society	Traditional Societies	Modern Societies
Cultural Patterns		
Values	Homogeneous; sacred character; few subcultures and countercultures	Heterogeneous; secular character; many subcultures and countercultures
Norms	Great moral significance; little tolerance of diversity	Variable moral significance; high tolerance of diversity
Time orientation	Present linked to past	Present linked to future
Technology	Preindustrial; human and animal energy	Industrial; advanced energy sources
Social Structure		
Status and role	Few statuses, most ascribed; few specialized roles	Many statuses, some ascribed and some achieved; many specialized roles
Relationships	Typically primary; little anonymity or privacy	Typically secondary; much anonymity and privacy
Communication	Face to face	Face-to-face communication supplemented by mass media
Social control	Informal gossip	Formal police and legal system
Social stratification	Rigid patterns of social inequality; little mobility	Fluid patterns of social inequality; high mobility
Gender patterns	Pronounced patriarchy; women's lives centered on the home	Declining patriarchy; increasing share of women in the paid labor force
Settlement patterns	Small-scale; population typically small and widely dispersed in rural villages and small towns	Large-scale; population typically large and concentrated in cities
Social Institutions		
Economy	Based on agriculture; much manufacturing in the home; little white-collar work	Based on industrial mass production; factories become centers of production; increasing white-collar work
State	Small-scale government; little state intervention in society	Large-scale government; much state intervention in society
Family	Extended family as the primary means of socialization and economic production	Nuclear family still has some socialization functions but is more a unit of consumption than of production
Religion	Religion guides worldview; little religious pluralism	Religion weakens with the rise of science; extensive religious pluralism
Education	Formal schooling limited to elites	Basic schooling becomes universal, with growing share of people receiving advanced education
Health	High birth and death rates; short life expectancy because of low standard of living and simple medical technology	Low birth and death rates; longer life expectancy because of higher standard of living and sophisticated medical technology
Social Change	Slow; change evident over many generations	Rapid; change evident within a single generation

people of various backgrounds into a generic mass provides greater moral freedom but it may also end up dehumanizing everyone.

The Ever-Expanding State

In the small-scale preindustrial societies of Europe, government amounted to little more than a local noble. A royal family formally reigned over an entire nation, but in the absence of swift transportation and efficient communication, even absolute monarchs had far less power than today's political leaders.

As technological innovation allowed government to expand, the centralized state grew in size and importance. At the time of independence, the U.S. government was a tiny organization, its primary function being national defense. Since then, government has assumed responsibility for more and more areas of social life: schooling, regulating wages and working conditions, establishing standards for products of all sorts, providing financial assistance to the elderly, the ill, and the unemployed, providing loans to students, and recently, bailing out corporations facing financial ruin. To pay for such programs, taxes have soared: Today's average worker in

the United States labors about four months each year just to pay for the broad array of services the government provides.

In a mass society, power resides in large bureaucracies, leaving people in local communities with little control over their lives. For example, state officials mandate that local schools must have a standardized educational program, local products must be government-certified, and every citizen must maintain extensive tax records. Although such regulations may protect people and enhance social equality, they also force us to deal more and more with nameless officials in distant and often unresponsive bureaucracies, and they undermine the autonomy of families and local communities.

● **Evaluate** The growing scale of modern life certainly has positive aspects, but only at the cost of our local community life. Modern societies increase individual rights, have greater tolerance of social differences, and raise living standards (Inglehart & Baker, 2000). But they are prone to what Weber feared most—excessive bureaucracy—as well as to Tönnies's self-centeredness and Durkheim's anomie. The size, complexity, and tolerance of diversity of modern societies all but doom traditional values and families, leaving individuals isolated, powerless, and materialistic. As Chapter 12 ("Economics and Politics") noted, voter apathy is a serious problem in the United States. But should we be surprised that individuals in vast, impersonal societies such as ours end up thinking that no one person can make much of a difference?

Critics claim that mass-society theory romanticizes the past. They remind us that many people in the small towns of our past were eager to set out for a better standard of living in cities. This approach also ignores problems of social inequality. Critics say this theory attracts social and economic conservatives who defend conventional morality and are indifferent to the historical inequality of women and other minorities.

CHECK YOUR LEARNING In your own words, state the mass-society analysis of modernity. What are two criticisms of it?

Social-conflict theory sees modernity not as an impersonal mass society but as an unequal class society in which some categories of people are second-class citizens. This Arizona family, like many Native Americans, lives on a reservation, where poverty is widespread and many trailer homes do not have electricity or running water.

Social-Conflict Theory: Modernity as Class Society

Apply

The second explanation of modernity derives mostly from the ideas of Karl Marx. From a social-conflict perspective, modernity takes the form of a **class society**, *a capitalist society with pronounced social stratification*. While agreeing that modern societies have expanded to a mass scale, this approach views the heart of modernization as an expanding capitalist economy, marked by inequality (Habermas, 1970; Harrington, 1984; Buechler, 2000).

Capitalism

Class-society theory follows Marx in claiming that the increasing scale of social life in modern society has resulted from the growth and greed unleashed by capitalism. Because a capitalist economy pursues ever-greater profits, both production and consumption steadily increase.

According to Marx, capitalism rests on "naked self-interest" (Marx & Engels, 1972:337, orig. 1848). This self-centeredness weakens the social ties that once united small communities. Capitalism also treats people as commodities: a source of labor and a market for capitalist products.

Capitalism supports science not just as the key to greater productivity but also as an ideology that justifies the status quo. Modern societies encourage people to view human well-being as a technical puzzle that can be solved by engineers and other experts

rather than through the pursuit of social justice. For example, a capitalist culture seeks to improve health through advances in scientific medicine rather than by eliminating poverty, despite the fact that poverty is a core cause of poor health.

Businesses also raise the banner of scientific logic, trying to increase profits through greater efficiency. As Chapter 12 ("Economics and Politics") explained, capitalist corporations have reached enormous size and control unimaginable wealth as a result of global expansion. From the class-society point of view, the expanding scale of life is less a function of *Gesellschaft* than the inevitable and destructive consequence of capitalism.

Persistent Inequality

Modernity has gradually worn away some of the rigid categories that divided preindustrial societies. But class-society theory maintains that elites are still with us, not as the nobles of an earlier era, but in the form of capitalist millionaires. In short, a few people are still born to wealth and power. In the United States, we may have no hereditary monarchy, but the richest 1 percent of the population controls about 35 percent of all privately held property (Keister, 2005; Wolff, 2010).

What of the state? Mass-society theorists argue that the state works to increase equality and fight social problems. Marx disagreed; he doubted that the state could accomplish more than minor reforms because, as he saw it, real power lies in the hands of the capitalists who control the economy. Other class-society theorists add that to the extent that working people and minorities do enjoy greater political rights and a higher standard of living today, these changes were the result of political struggle, not government goodwill. Despite our pretensions of democracy, they conclude, most people are powerless in the face of wealthy elites.

---

mass society a society in which prosperity and expanding bureaucracy have weakened traditional social ties

class society a capitalist society with pronounced social stratification

Two Interpretations of Modernity

	Mass Society	Class Society
Process of modernization	Industrialization; growth of bureaucracy	Rise of capitalism
Effects of modernization	Increasing scale of life; rise of the state and other formal organizations	Expansion of the capitalist economy; persistence of social inequality

◉ Evaluate Class-society theory dismisses Durkheim's argument that people in modern societies suffer from anomie, claiming instead that most people deal with alienation and powerlessness. Not surprisingly, the class-society interpretation of modernity enjoys widespread support among liberals and radicals who favor greater equality and seek extensive regulation (or abolition) of the capitalist marketplace.

A basic criticism of class-society theory is that it overlooks the increasing prosperity of modern societies and the fact that discrimination based on race, ethnicity, religion, and gender is now illegal and is widely regarded as a social problem. In addition, most people in the United States do not want an egalitarian society; they prefer a system of unequal rewards that reflects personal differences in talent and effort.

Based on socialism's failure to generate a high overall standard of living, few observers think that a centralized economy would cure the ills of modernity. Many other problems—from unemployment, to hunger, to industrial pollution, to war—exist in the United States, but they are also found in socialist nations.

CHECK YOUR LEARNING In your own words, state the class-society analysis of modernity. What are several criticisms of it?

The Summing Up table compares views of modern society offered by mass-society theory and class-society theory. Mass-society theory focuses on the increasing impersonality of social life and the growth of government; class-society theory stresses the expansion of capitalism and the persistence of inequality.

Modernity and the Individual

 Apply

Both mass- and class-society theories look at the broad patterns of change since the Industrial Revolution. From these macro-level approaches, we can also draw micro-level insights into how modernity shapes individual lives.

Mass Society: Problems of Identity

Modernity freed individuals from the small, tightly knit communities of the past. Most members of modern societies have the privacy and freedom to express their individuality. However, mass-society theory suggests that so much social diversity, widespread isolation, and rapid social change make it difficult for many people to

establish any coherent identity at all (Wheelis, 1958; Berger, Berger, & Kellner, 1974).

Chapter 3 ("Socialization: From Infancy to Old Age") explained that people's personalities are mostly a product of their social experiences. The small, homogeneous, and slowly changing societies of the past provided a firm, if narrow, foundation for building a personal identity. Even today, Amish and Mennonite communities that flourish in the United States teach young men and women "correct" ways to think and behave. Not everyone born into an Amish community can tolerate such rigid demands for conformity, but most members establish a well-integrated and satisfying personal identity (Kraybill & Olshan, 1994; Kraybill & Hurd, 2006).

Mass societies are quite another story. Socially diverse and rapidly changing, they offer only shifting sands on which to build a personal identity. Left to make many life decisions on their own, people—especially those with greater wealth—face a confusing range of options. The freedom to choose has little value without standards to guide the selection process; in a tolerant mass society, people may find little reason to choose one path over another. As a result, many people shuttle from one identity to another, changing their lifestyles, relationships, and even religions in search of an elusive "true self." Given the widespread "relativism" of modern societies, people without a moral compass lack the security and certainty once provided by tradition.

To David Riesman (1970, orig. 1950), modernization brings changes in **social character**, *personality patterns common to members of a particular society*. Preindustrial societies promote what Riesman calls **tradition-directedness**, *rigid conformity to time-honored ways of living*. Members of such societies model their lives on those of their ancestors, so that "living a good life" amounts to "doing what people have always done."

Tradition-directedness corresponds to Tönnies's *Gemeinschaft* and Durkheim's mechanical solidarity. Culturally conservative, tradition-directed people think and act alike. Unlike the conformity often found in modern societies, the uniformity of tradition-directedness is not an effort to imitate a popular celebrity or follow the latest trend. Instead, people are alike because they all draw on the same solid cultural foundation. Amish women and men exemplify tradition-directedness; in the Amish culture, tradition ties everyone to ancestors and descendants in an unbroken chain of righteous living.

Today, members of diverse and rapidly changing societies are likely to view a tradition-directed personality as deviant because it seems so rigid. Modern people prize personal flexibility, the capacity

Mass-society theory relates feelings of anxiety and lack of meaning in the modern world to rapid social change that washes away tradition. This notion of modern emptiness and isolation is captured in the photo at the left. Class-society theory, by contrast, ties such feelings to social inequality, by which some categories of people are made into second-class citizens (or not made citizens at all), an idea expressed in the photo at the right.

to adapt, and sensitivity to others. Riesman calls this type of social character **other-directedness**, *openness to the latest trends and fashions, often expressed by imitating others.* Because their socialization occurs in societies that are continuously in flux, other-directed people develop fluid identities marked by superficiality, inconsistency, and change. They try on different "selves" almost like new clothing, seek out role models, and engage in varied performances as they move from setting to setting (Goffman, 1959). In a traditional society, such "shiftiness" marks a person as untrustworthy, but in a changing, modern society, the chameleonlike ability to fit in almost virtually anywhere is very useful.

In societies that value the up-to-date rather than the traditional, people look to others for approval, using members of their own generation rather than elders as role models. Peer pressure can be irresistible to people without strong standards to guide them. Our society urges people to be true to themselves, but when social surroundings change so rapidly, how can people develop the self to which they should be true? This problem lies at the root of the identity crisis so widespread in industrial societies today. "Who am I?" is a nagging question that many of us struggle to answer. In truth, this problem is not so much us as the inherently unstable mass society in which we live.

Class Society: Problems of Powerlessness

Class-society theory paints a different picture of modernity's effects on individuals. This approach maintains that persistent inequality undermines modern society's promise of individual

---

social character personality patterns common to members of a particular society

tradition-directedness rigid conformity to time-honored ways of living

other-directedness openness to the latest trends and fashions, often expressed by imitating others

---

freedom. For some people, modernity serves up great privilege, but for many others, everyday life means coping with economic uncertainty and a gnawing sense of powerlessness (K. S. Newman, 1993; Ehrenreich, 2001).

For racial and ethnic minorities, the problem of relative disadvantage looms even larger. Similarly, although women participate more broadly in modern societies, they continue to run up against traditional barriers of sexism. This approach rejects mass-society theory's claim that people suffer from too much freedom; according to class-society theory, our society still denies a majority of people full participation in social life.

As Chapter 9 ("Global Stratification") explained, the expanding scope of world capitalism has placed more of Earth's population under the influence of multinational corporations. As a result, three-fourths of the world's income is concentrated in high-income nations, where just 23 percent of its people live. Is it any wonder, class-society theorists ask, that people in poor nations seek greater power to shape their own lives?

The problem of widespread powerlessness led Herbert Marcuse (1964) to challenge Max Weber's claim that modern society is rational. Marcuse condemned modern society as irrational for failing to meet the needs of so many people. Although modern capitalist societies produce unparalleled wealth, poverty remains the daily plight of more than 1 billion people. Marcuse added that technological advances further reduce people's control over their own lives. The advent of high technology has generally conferred a great deal of power on a core of specialists—not the majority of people—who now dominate discussion of when to go to war, what our energy policy should be, and how people should pay for health care. Countering the popular view that technology *solves* the world's problems, Marcuse believed that science helps to *cause* them. In sum, class-society theory asserts that people suffer because modern societies have concentrated both wealth and power in the hands of a privileged few.

The firelight flickers in the gathering darkness. Chief Kanhonk sits, as he has done at the end of the day for many years, ready to begin an evening of animated talk and storytelling (Simons, 2007). This is the hour when the Kaiapo, a small society in Brazil's lush Amazon region, celebrate their heritage. Because the Kaiapo are a traditional people with no written language, the elders rely on evenings by the fire to pass along their culture to their children and grandchildren. In the past, evenings like this have been filled with tales of brave Kaiapo warriors fighting off Portuguese traders in pursuit of slaves and gold.

But as the minutes pass, only a few older villagers assemble for the evening ritual. "It is the Big Ghost," one man grumbles, explaining the poor turnout. The "Big Ghost" has indeed descended on them; its bluish glow spills from windows throughout the village. The Kaiapo children—and many adults as well—are watching reality shows on television. Buying a television and a satellite dish several years ago has had consequences far greater than anyone imagined. In the end, what their enemies failed to do with guns, the Kaiapo may well do to themselves with prime-time programming.

The Kaiapo are among the 230,000 native peoples who inhabit Brazil. They stand out because of their striking body paint and ornate ceremonial dress. During the 1980s, they became rich from gold mining and harvesting mahogany trees. Now they must decide if the recent affluence is a blessing or a curse.

To some, material wealth means the opportunity to learn about the outside world through travel and television. Others, like Chief Kanhonk, are not so sure. Sitting by the fire, he thinks aloud: "I have been saying that people must buy useful things like knives and fishing hooks. Television does not fill the stomach. It only shows our children and grandchildren white people's things."

Bebtopup, the oldest priest, nods in agreement: "The night is the time the old people teach the young people. Television has stolen the night" (Simons, 2007:522).

Far to the north, half an hour by ferry from the coast of Georgia, lies the swampy island community of Hog Hammock. The seventy African American residents of the island today trace their ancestry back to the first slaves who settled here in 1802.

Walking past the brightly painted houses that stand among yellow pine trees draped with Spanish moss, a visitor can easily feel transported back in time. The local people, known as Gullahs (or in some places, Geechees), speak a *creole*, a mixture of English and West African languages. They fish, living much as they have for hundreds of years.

But the future of this way of life is now in doubt. Few young people who are raised in Hog Hammock can find work; beyond fishing and making traditional crafts, there are simply no jobs to do. "We have been here nine generations and we are still here," says one local. Then, referring to the nineteen children who live on the island, she adds, "It's not that they don't want to be here; it's that there's nothing here for them—they need to have jobs" (Curry, 2001:41).

Just as important, with people on the mainland looking for waterside homes for vacations or year-round living, the island has become prime real estate. Not long ago, one larger house went up for sale, and the community was shocked to learn of an asking price over $1 million. The locals know only too well that higher property values will mean high taxes that few can afford to pay. In short, Hog Hammock is likely to becomes another Hilton Head, once a Gullah community on the South Carolina coast that is now home to well-to-do people from the mainland.

The odds are that before long, the people of Hog Hammock will be selling their homes and moving inland. But few people are happy at the thought of selling out, even for a good price. On the contrary, moving away will mean the end of their cultural heritage.

The stories of the Kaiapo and the people of Hog Hammock show us that change is not a simple path toward "progress." These people may be moving toward modernity, but this process will have both positive and negative consequences. In the end, both groups of people may enjoy a higher standard of living with better shelter, more clothing, and new technology. But their newfound affluence will come at the price of their traditions. The drama of these people is now being played out around the world as more and more traditional cultures are being lured away from their heritage by the affluence and materialism of rich societies.

What Do You Think?

1. Why is social change both a winning and a losing proposition for traditional peoples?

2. Do the changes described here improve the lives of the Kaiapo? What about the Gullah community?

3. Do traditional people have any choice about becoming modern? Explain your answer.

Modernity and Progress

 Evaluate

In modern societies, most people expect and applaud social change. We link modernity to the idea of *progress* (from the Latin, meaning "moving forward"), a state of continual improvement. We equate stability with stagnation.

Given our bias in favor of change, members of our society tend to regard traditional cultures as backward. But change, particularly toward material affluence, is a mixed blessing. As the Thinking Globally box shows, social change is too complex simply to equate with progress.

Even getting rich has both advantages and disadvantages, as the cases of the Kaiapo and Gullah show. Historically, among people in the United States, a rising standard of living has made lives longer and more comfortable. At the same time, many people wonder whether today's routines are too stressful, with families often having little time to relax or to spend time together. Perhaps this is why, in the United States, measures of happiness over the last twenty-five years have actually gone down (D. G. Myers, 2000; Inglehart, Welzel, & Foa, 2009).

Science, too, has its pluses and minuses. People in the United States are more confident than people living in most other industrial societies that science improves our everyday lives (Inglehart & Welzel, 2010). But surveys also show that many adults in the United States feel that science "makes our way of life change too fast" (NORC, 2011:1762).

New technology has always sparked controversy. Just over a century ago, the introduction of automobiles and telephones allowed more rapid transportation and more efficient communication, improving people's lives. At the same time, such technology also weakened traditional attachments to hometowns and even to families. Today, people might wonder whether computer technology will do the same thing: giving us access to people around the world but shielding us from the community right outside our doors; providing more information than ever before but in the process threatening personal privacy. In short, we all realize that social change comes faster all the time, but we may disagree about whether a particular change is good or bad for society.

Modernity: Global Variation

● Understand

> *October 1, Kobe, Japan.* Riding the computer-controlled monorail high above the streets of Kobe or the 200-mile-per-hour bullet train to Tokyo, we see Japan as the society of the future, in love with high technology. Yet the Japanese remain strikingly traditional in other respects: Few corporate executives and almost no politicians are women, young people still show seniors great respect, and public orderliness contrasts with the relative chaos of many U.S. cities.

Japan is a nation both traditional and modern. This contradiction reminds us that although it is useful to contrast traditional and modern societies, the old and the new often coexist in unexpected ways. In the People's Republic of China, ancient Confucian principles are mixed with contemporary socialist thinking. In Saudi Arabia and Qatar, a love of the latest modern technology is mixed with respect for the ancient principles of Islam. Likewise, in Mexico and much of Latin America, people observe centuries-old Christian rituals even as they struggle to move ahead economically. In short, although we may think of tradition and modernity as opposites, combinations of traditional and modern are far from unusual, and they are found throughout the world.

Postmodernity

● Evaluate

If modernity was the product of the Industrial Revolution, could the Information Revolution be creating a postmodern era? A number of scholars think so, and they use the term **postmodernity** to refer to *the transformations caused by the Information Revolution and the postindustrial economy.*

Precisely what postmodernism is remains a matter of debate. The term has been used for decades in literary, philosophical, and even architectural circles. It has moved into sociology on a wave of social criticism that has been building since the spread of left-leaning politics in the 1960s. Although there are many variations of postmodern thinking, all share the following five themes (Hall & Neitz, 1993; Inglehart, 1997; Rudel & Gerson, 1999):

1. **In important respects, modernity has failed.** The promise of modernity was a life free from want. As postmodernist critics see it, however, the twentieth century was unsuccessful in solving social problems such as poverty. This fact is evident in today's high rates of unemployment and poverty, as well as the widespread sense of financial insecurity.

2. **The bright light of "progress" is fading.** Modern people look to the future expecting their lives to improve in significant ways. Members (and even leaders) of a postmodern society are less confident about what the future holds. The strong optimism that carried society into the modern era more than a century ago has given way to widespread pessimism; almost half of U.S. adults do not expect their children's lives to be better than their own (NORC, 2011:392).

3. **Science no longer holds the answers.** The defining trait of the modern era was a scientific outlook and a confident belief that technology would make life better. But postmodern critics argue that science has failed to solve many old problems (such as poor health) and has even created new problems (such as pollution and global warming).

   Postmodernist thinkers discredit science, claiming that it implies a singular truth. On the contrary, different people see different realities, and there are many ways to socially construct the world.

4. **Cultural debates are intensifying.** Now that the world is capable of producing material abundance, ideas are taking on more importance. In this sense, postmodernity is also a postmaterialist era in which issues such as social justice, the state of the natural environment, and animal rights command more and more public attention.

5. **Social institutions are changing.** Just as industrialization brought sweeping transformation to social institutions, the rise of postindustrial society is remaking society all over again. For example, the postmodern family no longer conforms to any single pattern; on the contrary, individuals are choosing among many new family forms.

● **Evaluate** Analysts who claim that the United States and other high-income nations are entering a postmodern era criticize modernity for failing to meet human needs. In defense of modernity, there have been marked increases in longevity and living standards over the past century. If we take the postmodernist view and reject science as bankrupt and progress as a sham, what are the alternatives?

CHECK YOUR LEARNING In your own words, state the defining characteristics of a postmodern society.

Sociology in Focus

Personal Freedom and Social Responsibility: Can We Have It Both Ways?

Samuel: I feel that being free is the most important thing. Let me do what I want!

Sanji: But if everyone felt that way, what would the world be like?

Doreen: Isn't there a way to be true to ourselves and also take account of other people?

One issue we all have to work out is making decisions that take proper account of other people. But what, exactly, do we owe others? To see the problem, consider an event that took place in New York in 1964.

Shortly after midnight on a crisp March evening, Susan "Kitty" Genovese drove into the parking lot of her apartment complex. She turned off the engine, locked the car doors, and headed across the blacktop toward the entrance to her building. Out of nowhere, a man holding a knife lunged at her, and as she screamed in terror and pain, he stabbed her repeatedly. Windows opened above as curious neighbors looked down to see what was going on. The attack continued for more than thirty minutes until Genovese lay dead in her doorway. As the police conducted an investigation of the killing, they discovered that a number of Genovese's neighbors had heard her screams or witnessed some of the attack yet they did not go to her aid. Only one neighbor called the police. It was only later that police arrested a man on a burglary charge only to have him confess to the Genovese murder. He was convicted by a court and, in 2012, he was still in prison.

The death of this young woman, and the fact that a number of people might have done more to help her, forces all of us to confront the question of what we owe others. As members of a modern society, we prize our individual rights and personal privacy, but we sometimes withdraw from public responsibility and turn a cold shoulder to people in need. When a cry for help is met by indifference, have we pushed our modern idea of personal freedom too far? In a society of expanding individual rights, can we keep a sense of human community?

These questions highlight the tension between traditional and modern social systems, which is evident in the writings of all the sociologists discussed in this chapter. Tönnies, Durkheim, and others

concluded that in some respects, traditional community and modern individualism don't mix. That is, society can unite its members as a moral community only by limiting their range of personal choices about how to live. In short, although we value both community and freedom, we can't have it both ways.

Sociologist Amitai Etzioni (1993, 1996, 2003) has tried to strike a middle ground. The *communitarian movement* rests on the simple idea that with rights must come responsibilities. Put another way, our pursuit of self-interest must be balanced by a commitment to support the larger community.

Etzioni claims that modern people have become too concerned about individual rights. We expect the system to work for us, but we are reluctant to support the system. For example, we believe that people accused of a crime deserve their day in court, but fewer and fewer of us are willing to perform jury duty; similarly, we are quick to accept government services but reluctant to support these services with our taxes.

The communitarians advance four proposals toward balancing individual rights with public responsibilities. First, our society should stop the expanding "culture of rights" by which we put our own interests ahead of social responsibility. The

Constitution, which is quoted so often when discussing individual rights, does not guarantee us the right to do whatever we want. Second, we must remember that, for society to operate all of us must take part in the life of our communities. Third, the well-being of everyone may require limiting our individual rights; for example, pilots and bus drivers may be required to take drug tests in order to protect the public interest. Fourth, no one can ignore key responsibilities such as obeying the law and responding to a cry for help from someone like Kitty Genovese.

The communitarian movement appeals to many people who believe in both personal freedom and social responsibility. But Etzioni's proposals have drawn criticism from both sides of the political spectrum. To those on the left, problems ranging from voter apathy and street crime to increasing poverty and millions without medical care cannot be solved by some vague idea of "social responsibility." As they see it, what we need is expanded government programs to protect people and lessen inequality.

Conservatives, on the political right, see different problems in Etzioni's proposals (Pearson, 1995). As they see it, the communitarian movement favors liberal goals, such as confronting prejudice and protecting the environment, but says little about conservative goals, such as strengthening religious beliefs and supporting traditional families.

Etzioni responds that the criticism coming from both sides suggests he has found a moderate, sensible approach to solving a serious problem. But the debate may also indicate that in a nation as diverse as the United States, people who are so quick to assert their rights are not so ready to agree on their responsibilities.

Join the Blog!

Have you ever failed to come to the aid of someone in need or danger? Why? Do you think members of our society think too much about individual freedom and not enough about social responsibility? Go to MySocLab and join the Sociology in Focus blog to share your opinions and experiences and to see what others think.

In today's world, people can find new ways to express age-old virtues such as extending a helping hand to their neighbors in need. One way that college students in campuses across the country find to lend a hand is by participating in Habitat for Humanity projects. Are there opportunities for you to get involved in your own community?

Looking Ahead: Modernization and Our Global Future

● **Evaluate**

Imagine the entire world's population reduced to a single village of 1,000 people. About 227 residents of this "global village" are from high-income countries. Another 166 people are so poor that their lives are at risk.

The tragic plight of the world's poor shows that some desperately needed change has not yet occurred. Chapter 9 ("Global Stratification") presented two competing views of why 1 billion people around the world are so poor. *Modernization theory* claims that in the past, the entire world was poor and that technological change, especially the Industrial Revolution, enhanced human productivity and raised living standards in many nations. From this point of view, the solution to global poverty is to promote technological development and market economies around the world.

For reasons suggested earlier, however, global modernization may be difficult. Recall that David Riesman portrayed preindustrial people as *tradition-directed* and likely to resist change. So modernization theorists claim that rich nations should help poor countries grow economically. Industrial nations can speed development by exporting technology to poor regions, welcoming students from these countries, and providing foreign aid to stimulate economic growth.

The review of modernization theory in Chapter 9 points to some success for these policies in Latin America and more dramatic results in the small Asian countries of Taiwan, South Korea, and Singapore and in Hong Kong (part of the People's Republic of China). But jump-starting development in the poorest countries of the world poses greater challenges. Even where dramatic change has occurred, modernization involves a trade-off. Traditional people, such as Brazil's Kaiapo, may gain wealth through economic development, but only at the cost of losing their traditional identity and values as they are drawn into a global "McCulture," which is based on Western materialism, pop music, trendy clothes, and fast food. One Brazilian anthropologist expressed optimism about the future of the Kaiapo: "At least they quickly understood the consequences of watching television. . . . Now [they] can make a choice" (Simons, 2007:523).

But not everyone thinks that modernization is really an option. According to a second approach to global stratification, *dependency theory,* today's poor societies have little ability to modernize, even if they want to. From this point of view, the major barrier to economic development is not traditionalism but global domination by rich capitalist societies.

Dependency theory asserts that rich nations achieved their modernization at the expense of poor ones, by taking their valuable natural resources and exploiting their human labor. Even today, the world's poorest countries remain locked in a disadvantageous economic relationship with rich nations, dependent on wealthy countries to buy their raw materials and in return provide them with whatever manufactured products they can afford. According to this view, continuing ties with rich societies will only perpetuate current patterns of global inequality.

Whichever approach you find more convincing, keep in mind that change in the United States is no longer separate from change in the rest of the world. At the beginning of the twentieth century, most people in today's high-income countries lived in relatively small settlements with limited awareness of the larger world. Today, the world has become one huge village because the lives of all people are increasingly interconnected.

The twentieth century witnessed unprecedented human achievement. Yet solutions to many problems of human existence—including finding meaning in life, resolving conflicts between societies, and eliminating poverty—have eluded us. The Sociology in Focus box examines one dilemma: balancing individual freedom and personal responsibility. To this list of pressing matters new concerns have been added, such as controlling population growth and establishing an environmentally sustainable society. In the coming years, we must be prepared to tackle such problems with imagination, compassion, and determination. Our growing understanding of human society gives us reason to be hopeful that we can get the job done.

Seeing Sociology in Everyday Life

CHAPTER 16

Social Change: Modern and Postmodern Societies

Is tradition the opposite of modernity?

Conceptually, this may be true. But as this chapter explains, traditional and modern social patterns combine in all sorts of interesting ways in our everyday lives. Look at the photographs below, and identify elements of tradition and modernity. Do they seem to go together, or are they in conflict? Why?

Hint Although sociologists analyze tradition and modernity as conceptual opposites, every society combines these elements in various ways. People may debate the virtues of traditional and modern life, but the two patterns are found almost everywhere. Technological change always has social consequences—for example, the use of cell phones changes people's social networks and economic opportunities; similarly, the spread of McDonald's changes not only what people eat but also where and with whom they share meals.

These young girls live in the city of Istanbul in Turkey, a country that has long debated the merits of traditional and modern life. What sets off traditional and modern ways of dressing? Do you think such differences are likely to affect patterns of friendship? Would the same be true in the United States?

When the first McDonald's restaurant opened in the city of Kiev in Ukraine, many people stopped by to taste a hamburger and see what "fast food" was all about. As large corporations expand their operations around the world, do they tip the balance away from tradition in favor of modernity? If so, how?

In Riyadh, Saudi Arabia, these young men are shopping for the latest in cell phones. Does such modern technology threaten a society's traditions?

▌Seeing Sociology in *Your* Everyday Life

1. How do tradition and modernity combine in your life? Point to several ways in which you are traditional and several ways in which you are thoroughly modern.

2. Ask people in your class or friendship group to make five predictions about U.S. society in the year 2060, when today's twenty-year-olds will be senior citizens. Compare notes. On what issues is there agreement?

3. What do you see as the advantages of living in a modern society? What are the drawbacks? Go to the "Seeing Sociology in *Your* Everyday Life" feature on MySocLab to learn more about the benefits and challenges of modern living—information you can use to enhance your own life.

What Is Social Change?

Social change is the transformation of culture and social institutions over time. Every society changes all the time, sometimes faster, sometimes more slowly. Social change often generates controversy. **pp. 440–41**

social change (p. 441) the transformation of culture and social institutions over time

Causes of Social Change

Culture

- *Invention* produces new objects, ideas, and social patterns.
- *Discovery* occurs when people take notice of existing elements of the world.
- *Diffusion* creates change as products, people, and information spread from one society to another. **pp. 441–42**

Social Conflict

- Karl Marx claimed that class conflict between capitalists and workers pushes society toward a socialist system of production.
- Social conflict arising from class, race, and gender inequality has resulted in social changes that have improved the lives of working people. **p. 442**

Ideas

- Max Weber claimed that the fact that industrial capitalism developed first in areas of Western Europe where the Protestant work ethic was strong demonstrates the power of ideas to bring about change. **p. 442**

Demographic Factors

Population patterns play a part in social change:

- The aging of U.S. society has resulted in changes to family life and the development of consumer products to meet the needs of the elderly.
- Migration within and between societies promotes change. **p. 442**

✷ Explore the **Map** on **mysoclab.com**

Collective Behavior

- **Crowds**, in the form of political demonstrations and protest rallies, can bring about political change.
- **Mobs** and **riots** are types of crowds that are highly emotional and often violent. By threatening the status quo, they often result in social change.
- **Rumor** thrives in a climate of uncertainty and can trigger the formation of crowds and direct their action.
- **Fashion**, which reflects changes in cultural values, guides people's tastes in clothing, music, and automobiles, as well as their political attitudes. **Fads** are social patterns that people embrace enthusiastically but for a very short period of time. **pp. 442–43**

Disasters

Disasters cause unexpected social change:

- *natural disasters* (example: Hurricane Katrina)
- *technological disasters* (example: nuclear accident at the Chernobyl power plant)
- *intentional disasters* (example: Darfur genocide) **pp. 445–46**

collective behavior (p. 442) activity involving a large number of people that is unplanned, often controversial, and sometimes dangerous

crowd (p. 442) a temporary gathering of people who share a common focus of attention and who influence one another

mob (p. 442) a highly emotional crowd that pursues a violent or destructive goal

riot (p. 442) a social eruption that is highly emotional, violent, and undirected

rumor (p. 443) unconfirmed information that people spread informally, often by word of mouth

fashion (p. 443) a social pattern favored by a large number of people

fad (p. 443) an unconventional social pattern that people embrace briefly and enthusiastically

social movement (p. 443) an organized activity that encourages or discourages social change

claims making (p. 444) the process of trying to convince the public and public officials of the importance of joining a social movement to address a particular issue

relative deprivation (p. 444) a perceived disadvantage arising from some specific comparison

disaster (p. 445) an event, generally unexpected, that causes extensive harm to people and damage to property

SOCIAL MOVEMENTS

Types of Social Movements

- *Alterative social movements* seek limited change in specific individuals (example: Promise Keepers).
- *Redemptive social movements* seek radical change in specific individuals (example: Alcoholics Anonymous).
- *Reformative social movements* seek limited change in the whole society (example: the environmental movement).
- *Revolutionary social movements* seek radical change in the whole society (example: the Communist party). **p. 444**

◉ Watch the **Video** on **mysoclab.com**

Explanations of Social Movements

- *Deprivation theory:* Social movements arise among people who feel deprived of something, such as income, safe working conditions, or political rights.
- *Mass-society theory:* Social movements attract socially isolated people who join a movement in order to gain a sense of identity and purpose.
- *Resource mobilization theory:* Success of a social movement is linked to available resources, including money, labor, and the mass media.
- *Culture theory:* Social movements depend not only on money and resources but also on cultural symbols that motivate people.
- *New social movements theory:* Social movements in postindustrial societies are typically international in scope and focus on quality-of-life issues. **pp. 444–45**

Modernity

Modernity refers to the social consequences of industrialization, which include the decline of traditional communities, the expansion of personal choice, increasing social diversity, and a focus on the future.

- **Ferdinand Tönnies** described modernization as the transition from *Gemeinschaft* to *Gesellschaft*, characterized by the loss of traditional community and the rise of individualism.

  📖 Read the Document on mysoclab.com

- **Emile Durkheim** saw modernization as a society's expanding division of labor. *Mechanical solidarity*, based on shared activities and beliefs, is gradually replaced by *organic solidarity*, in which specialization makes people interdependent.
- **Max Weber** saw modernity as the decline of a traditional worldview and the rise of rationality. Weber feared the dehumanizing effects of modern rational organization.
- **Karl Marx** saw modernity as the triumph of capitalism over feudalism. **pp. 446–51**

modernity (pp. 440, 446) changes brought about by the Industrial Revolution

modernization (p. 446) the process of social change begun by industrialization

division of labor (p. 448) specialized economic activity

anomie (p. 450) Durkheim's term for a condition in which society provides little moral guidance to individuals

Modernity and Progress

- A rising standard of living has made lives longer, and the conveniences brought to us by developments in science and technology have made our everyday lives more comfortable.
- At the same time, many people are stressed and have little time to relax; advancements in transportation and communications technology have weakened traditional attachments to hometowns and families; and there have been no increases in measures of personal happiness over recent decades. **pp. 456–57**

Modernity: Global Variation

Although we often think of tradition and modernity as opposites, traditional and modern elements coexist in most societies. **p. 457**

Postmodernity

Postmodernity refers to the cultural traits of postindustrial societies. Postmodern criticism of society centers on the failure of modernity, and specifically science, to fulfill its promise of prosperity and well-being. **p. 457**

postmodernity (p. 440, 457) the transformations caused by the Information Revolution and the postindustrial economy

Theories of Modernity

Structural-Functional Theory: Modernity as Mass Society

- According to **mass-society theory**, modernity increases the scale of life, enlarging the role of government and other formal organizations in carrying out tasks previously performed by families in local communities.
- Cultural diversity and rapid social change make it difficult for people in modern societies to develop stable identities and to find meaning in their lives. **pp. 451–53**

Social-Conflict Theory: Modernity as Class Society

- According to **class-society theory**, modernity involves the rise of capitalism into a global economic system resulting in persistent social inequality.
- By concentrating wealth in the hands of a few, modern capitalist societies generate widespread feelings of alienation and powerlessness. **pp. 453–54**

mass society (p. 451) a society in which prosperity and bureaucracy have weakened traditional social ties

class society (p. 453) a capitalist society with pronounced social stratification

Modernity and the Individual

Both mass-society theory and class-society theory are macro-level approaches; from them, however, we can also draw micro-level insights into how modernity shapes individual lives.

Mass Society: Problems of Identity

David Riesman described the changes in social character that modernity causes:

- Preindustrial societies exhibit **tradition-directedness:** Everyone in society draws on the same solid cultural foundation, and people model their lives on those of their ancestors.
- Modern societies exhibit **other-directedness:** Because their socialization occurs in societies that are continuously in flux, other-directed people develop fluid identities marked by superficiality, inconsistency, and change. **pp. 454–55**

Class Society: Problems of Powerlessness

- Herbert Marcuse claimed that modern society is irrational because it fails to meet the needs of so many people. He also believed that technological advances further reduce people's control over their own lives.
- People suffer because modern societies have concentrated both wealth and power in the hands of a privileged few. **p. 455**

social character (p. 454) personality patterns common to members of a particular society

tradition-directedness (p. 454) rigid conformity to time-honored ways of living

other-directedness (p. 455) openness to the latest trends and fashions, often expressed by imitating others

These questions are similar to those found in the test bank that accompanies this textbook.

Chapter 1 Sociology: Perspective, Theory, and Method

Multiple-Choice Questions

1. **What does the sociological perspective show us about whom any individual chooses to marry?**
   a. There is no explaining personal feelings like love.
   b. People's actions reflect human free will.
   c. The operation of society guides many of our personal choices.
   d. In the case of love, opposites attract.

2. **The personal value of studying sociology includes**
   a. seeing the opportunities and constraints in our lives.
   b. the fact that it is good preparation for a number of careers.
   c. becoming more active participants in society.
   d. All of the above are correct.

3. **The discipline of sociology first developed in**
   a. countries experiencing rapid social change.
   b. countries with strong traditions.
   c. countries with a history of warfare.
   d. the world's poorest countries.

4. **Which early sociologist coined the term sociology in 1838?**
   a. Karl Marx
   b. Auguste Comte
   c. Adam Smith
   d. Herbert Spencer

5. **Sociology's social-conflict approach draws attention to**
   a. how structure contributes to the overall operation of society.
   b. how people construct meaning through interaction.
   c. patterns of social inequality.
   d. the stable aspects of society.

6. **Empirical evidence refers to**
   a. quantitative rather than qualitative data.
   b. what people consider "common sense."
   c. information we can verify with our senses.
   d. patterns found in every known society.

7. **When trying to measure people's "social class," you would have to keep in mind that**
   a. no measurement can ever be both reliable and valid.
   b. there are several ways to operationalize this variable.
   c. there is no way to measure "social class."
   d. in the United States, everyone agrees on what "social class" means.

8. **Interpretive sociology is a research orientation that**
   a. focuses on people's actions.
   b. sees an objective reality "out there."
   c. seeks to increase social justice.
   d. focuses on the meanings people attach to behavior.

9. **In research using participant observation, the problem of "breaking in" to a setting is often solved with the help of a**
   a. key informant.
   b. research assistant.
   c. bigger budget.
   d. sample.

10. **The critical sociology research orientation is linked most closely to which theoretical approach?**
    a. structural-functional approach
    b. social-conflict approach
    c. symbolic-interaction approach
    d. None of the above is correct.

ANSWERS: 1 (c); 2 (d); 3 (a); 4 (b); 5 (c); 6 (c); 7 (b); 8 (d); 9 (a); 10 (b).

Essay Questions

1. Explain why using the sociological perspective can make us seem less in control of our lives. In what ways does it actually give us greater power over our lives?

2. Guided by the discipline's three major theoretical approaches, come up with sociological questions about (a) television, (b) war, and (c) colleges and universities.

3. Discuss positivist sociology, interpretive sociology, and critical sociology so that you present each orientation clearly. Why might a sociologist prefer one orientation to another? Why is it important for a student of sociology to understand all three?

Chapter 2 Culture

Multiple-Choice Questions

1. **Of all the world's countries, the United States is the most**
   a. multicultural.
   b. culturally uniform.
   c. slowly changing.
   d. resistant to cultural diversity.

2. **Ideas created by members of a society are part of**
   a. high culture.
   b. material culture.
   c. norms.
   d. nonmaterial culture.

3. **Sociologists define a symbol as**
   a. any gesture that creates conflict within a population.
   b. any element of material culture.
   c. anything that has meaning to people who share a culture.
   d. any pattern that causes culture shock.

4. U.S. culture holds a strong belief in
   a. the traditions of the past.
   b. individuality.
   c. equality of condition for all.
   d. "being" rather than "doing."

5. Cheating on a final examination is an example of violating campus
   a. folkways.
   b. symbols.
   c. mores.
   d. high culture.

6. Which of the following phrases describes the concept of ethnocentrism?
   a. taking pride in your ethnicity
   b. judging an unfamiliar culture using the standards of your own culture
   c. seeing another culture as better than your own
   d. judging another culture by its own standards

7. Subculture refers to
   a. a part of the population lacking culture.
   b. elements of popular culture.
   c. people who embrace high culture.
   d. cultural patterns that set apart a segment of a society's population.

8. Which region of the United States has the largest share of people who speak a language other than English at home?
   a. the Southwest
   b. the Northeast
   c. the Northwest
   d. the South

9. In human history, the "dawn of civilization" took place with the development of
   a. hunting and gathering.
   b. pastoralism.
   c. industry.
   d. agriculture.

10. Which theoretical approach focuses on the link between culture and social inequality?
    a. the structural-functional approach
    b. the social-conflict approach
    c. the symbolic-interaction approach
    d. the sociobiology approach

ANSWERS: 1 (a); 2 (d); 3 (c); 4 (b); 5 (c); 6 (b); 7 (d); 8 (a); 9 (d); 10 (b).

Essay Questions

1. In the United States, hot dogs, hamburgers, French fries, and ice cream have long been considered national favorites. What cultural patterns help explain this country's love of these foods?

2. From what you have learned in this chapter, do you think that a global culture is emerging? Do you think the idea of global culture is positive or negative? Explain your answer.

Chapter 3   Socialization: From Infancy To Old Age

Multiple-Choice Questions

1. Kingsley Davis's study of Anna, the girl isolated for five years, shows that
   a. humans have the same instincts found in other animal species.
   b. without social experience, a child never develops personality.
   c. personality is present in all humans at birth.
   d. many human instincts disappear in the first few years of life.

2. Most sociologists take the position that
   a. most human behavior is directed by instincts.
   b. biological instincts develop in humans at puberty.
   c. it is human nature for us to nurture.
   d. All of the above are correct.

3. Lawrence Kohlberg explored socialization by studying
   a. cognition.
   b. the importance of gender in socialization.
   c. the development of biological instincts.
   d. moral reasoning.

4. Carol Gilligan added to Kohlberg's findings by showing that
   a. girls and boys typically use different standards in deciding what is right and wrong.
   b. girls are more interested in right and wrong than boys are.
   c. boys are more interested in right and wrong than girls are.
   d. today's children are far less interested in right and wrong than their parents are.

5. The "self," said George Herbert Mead, is
   a. the part of the human personality made up of self-awareness and self-image.
   b. the presence of culture within the individual.
   c. basic drives that are self-centered.
   d. present in infants from birth.

6. Why is the family so important to the socialization process?
   a. Family members provide necessary care for infants and children.
   b. Families give children social identity in terms of class, ethnicity, and religion.
   c. Parents greatly affect a child's self-concept.
   d. All of the above are correct.

7. Compared to higher-income parents, lower-income parents are more likely to emphasize which of the following as a desirable trait in children?
   a. independence
   b. creativity
   c. obedience
   d. imagination

8. In global perspective, which statement about childhood is correct?
   a. In every society, the first ten years of life are a time of play and learning.
   b. Rich societies extend childhood much longer than poor societies do.
   c. Poor societies extend childhood much longer than rich societies do.
   d. Childhood is defined by being biologically immature.

9. Members of high-income societies typically define people in old age as
   a. the wisest of all.
   b. the most up-to-date on current fashion and trends.
   c. less socially important than younger adults.
   d. All of the above are correct.

10. According to Erving Goffman, the purpose of a total institution is
   a. to reward someone for achievement in the outside world.
   b. to give a person more choices about how to live.
   c. to encourage lifelong learning in a supervised setting.
   d. to radically change a person's personality or behavior.

ANSWERS: 1 (b); 2 (c); 3 (d); 4 (a); 5 (a); 6 (d); 7 (c); 8 (b); 9 (c); 10 (d).

Essay Questions

1. State the two sides of the "nature-nurture" debate. In what important way are human nature and nurture *not* opposed to each other?

2. Point to several common themes in the ideas of Freud, Piaget, Kohlberg, Gilligan, Mead, and Erikson. In what ways do their theories differ?

Chapter 4 Social Interaction in Everyday Life

Multiple-Choice Questions

1. Which of the following concepts defines who we are in relation to others?
   a. role
   b. status
   c. role set
   d. role strain

2. In U.S. society, which of the following is typically a master status?
   a. occupation
   b. age
   c. sex
   d. physical or mental disability

3. Role set refers to
   a. all the roles found in any one society.
   b. a number of roles attached to a single status.
   c. a number of roles that are more or less the same.
   d. the leadership roles within any one organization.

4. Frank excels at football at his college, but with the time sports demands, he doesn't have enough time to study. He is experiencing the problem of
   a. role set.
   b. role strain.
   c. role conflict.
   d. role exit.

5. The Thomas theorem states that
   a. our statuses and roles are the key to our personality.
   b. most people rise to their level of incompetence.
   c. people know the world only through their language.
   d. situations defined as real are real in their consequences.

6. Which of the following is the correct meaning of "presentation of self"?
   a. efforts to create impressions in the minds of others
   b. acting out a master status
   c. thinking back over the process of role exit
   d. trying to draw attention away from others

7. Research supports the conclusion that people around the world
   a. rarely display any emotion when "on the job."
   b. are prompted by the same "triggers" to display emotions.
   c. experience the same six basic emotions.
   d. follow the same rules about when and where to display emotions.

8. In terms of dramaturgical analysis, tact is understood as
   a. helping someone take on a new role.
   b. helping someone "save face."
   c. making it difficult for someone to perform a role.
   d. negotiating a situation to get your own way.

9. In her study of human emotion, Arlie Hochschild explains that many companies
   a. try to regulate the emotions of workers.
   b. want workers to lack all emotion.
   c. encourage workers to express their true emotions.
   d. profit from making customers more emotional.

10. People are likely to "get" a joke when they
   a. know something about more than one culture.
   b. have a different social background than the joke teller.
   c. understand the two different realities being presented.
   d. know why someone wants to tell the joke.

ANSWERS: 1 (b); 2 (d); 3 (b); 4 (c); 5 (d); 6 (a); 7 (c); 8 (b); 9 (a); 10 (c).

Essay Questions

1. Explain Erving Goffman's claim that we engage in a "presentation of self." What are the elements of this presentation? Apply this approach to an analysis of a college professor teaching a class.

2. In what ways are human emotions rooted in our biology? In what ways are emotions guided by culture?

Chapter 5 Groups and Organizations

Multiple-Choice Questions

1. What name did Charles Horton Cooley give to a small social group whose members share personal and lasting relationships?
   a. expressive group
   b. in-group
   c. primary group
   d. secondary group

2. Which type of group leadership is concerned with getting the job done?
   a. laissez-faire leadership
   b. secondary group leadership

c. expressive leadership

d. instrumental leadership

3. **The research done by Solomon Asch, in which subjects were asked to pick lines of the same length, showed that**
   a. groups encourage their members to conform.
   b. most people are stubborn and refuse to change their minds.
   c. groups often generate conflict.
   d. group members rarely agree on everything.

4. **Which of the following concepts refers to a social group that someone uses as a point of reference in making an evaluation or decision?**
   a. out-group
   b. reference group
   c. in-group
   d. primary group

5. **A network is correctly thought of as**
   a. the most close-knit social group.
   b. a category of people with something in common.
   c. a social group in which most people know one another.
   d. a web of weak social ties.

6. **From the point of view of a nurse, a hospital is a**
   a. normative organization.
   b. coercive organization.
   c. utilitarian organization.
   d. All of the above are correct.

7. **Bureaucracy is a type of social organization characterized by**
   a. specialized jobs.
   b. offices arranged in a hierarchy.
   c. lots of rules and regulations.
   d. All of the above are correct.

8. **According to Robert Michels, bureaucracy always means**
   a. inefficiency.
   b. oligarchy.
   c. alienation.
   d. specialization.

9. **Rosabeth Moss Kanter claims that large business organizations**
   a. need to "open up" opportunity to encourage all workers to perform well.
   b. must have clear and stable rules to survive in a changing world.
   c. do well or badly depending on how talented the leader is.
   d. suffer if they do not adopt the latest technology.

10. **The "McDonaldization of society" means that**
    a. organizations can provide food for people more efficiently than families can.
    b. impersonal organizations concerned with efficiency, predictability, uniformity, and control are more and more common.
    c. it is possible for organizations to both achieve their goals and meet human needs.
    d. society today is one vast social network.

ANSWERS: 1 (c); 2 (d); 3 (a); 4 (b); 5 (d); 6 (c); 7 (d); 8 (b); 9 (a); 10 (b).

Essay Questions

1. How do primary groups differ from secondary groups? Give examples of each type of group in your own life.

2. According to Max Weber, what are the six traits that define bureaucracy? What is the advantage of this organizational form? What are several problems that often go along with it?

Chapter 6   Sexuality and Society

Multiple-Choice Questions

1. **What is the term for humans who have some combination of female and male genitalia?**
   a. asexual people
   b. bisexual people
   c. transsexual people
   d. intersexual people

2. **A global perspective on human sexuality shows us that**
   a. although sex involves our biology, it is also a cultural trait that varies from place to place.
   b. people everywhere in the world have the same sexual practices.
   c. people in all societies are uncomfortable talking about sex.
   d. All of the above are correct.

3. **Why is the incest taboo found in every society?**
   a. It limits sexual competition between members of families.
   b. It helps define people's rights and obligations toward one another.
   c. It helps connect members of a family to others in the larger society.
   d. All of the above are correct.

4. **The sexual revolution came of age during the**
   a. 1890s.
   b. 1920s.
   c. 1960s.
   d. 1980s.

5. **Survey data show that the largest share of U.S. adults reject which of the following sexual practices?**
   a. extramarital sex
   b. homosexuality
   c. premarital sex
   d. sex simply for pleasure

6. **According to the Laumann study of sexuality in the United States,**
   a. only one-third of the adult population is sexually active.
   b. there is great diversity in levels of sexual activity, so no one stereotype is correct.
   c. single people have more sex than married people.
   d. most married men admit to cheating on their wives at some point in their marriage.

7. **Which concept refers to sexual attraction to people of both sexes?**
   a. heterosexuality
   b. homosexuality
   c. bisexuality
   d. asexuality

8. Compared to 1950, the U.S. rate of teenage pregnancy today is
   a. higher.
   b. the same, but more teens become pregnant by choice.
   c. the same, but more pregnant teens are married.
   d. lower.

9. By what point in their lives do half of young people in the United States today experience sexual intercourse?
   a. when they marry
   b. by the middle of college
   c. by the end of high school
   d. by age thirteen

10. If we look back in history, we see that once a society develops birth control technology,
   a. social control of sexuality becomes more strict.
   b. the birth rate actually goes up.
   c. attitudes about sexuality become more permissive.
   d. people no longer express concern about incest.

ANSWERS: 1 (d); 2 (a); 3 (d); 4 (a); 5 (b); 6 (c); 7 (d); 8 (c); 9 (c).

Essay Questions

1. What was the "sexual revolution"? What changed? Can you point to reasons for the change?

2. Identify four sexual orientations. Based on what researchers have discovered, how do people take on a sexual orientation?

Chapter 7   Deviance

Multiple-Choice Questions

1. **Crime is a special type of deviance that**
   a. refers to violations of formally enacted criminal law.
   b. always involves punishment.
   c. refers to the violation of any societal norms.
   d. causes the greatest harm to society.

2. Emile Durkheim explains that deviance is
   a. defined by the rich and used against the poor.
   b. harmful not just to victims but to society as a whole.
   c. often at odds with public morality.
   d. found in every society because it has useful consequences.

3. **Using Robert Merton's strain theory, a person selling illegal drugs for a living would fall into which of the following categories?**
   a. conformist
   b. innovator
   c. retreatist
   d. ritualist

4. **Labeling theory states that deviance**
   a. is a normal part of social life.
   b. always changes an offender's social identity.
   c. arises not from what people do as much as from how others respond to the action.
   d. All of the above are correct.

5. When lake's friends began calling him a "dope-head," he left the group and spent more time smoking marijuana. He also began hanging out with others who used drugs, and by the end of the term, he had dropped out of college. Edwin Lemert would say this situation illustrates
   a. a case of primary deviance.
   b. the onset of secondary deviance.
   c. the formation of a deviant subculture.
   d. the beginning of retreatism.

6. A social-conflict analysis links deviance to
   a. who does and does not have power in the society.
   b. a society's moral values.
   c. how often the behavior occurs.
   d. how harmful the behavior is.

7. Stealing a laptop computer from the study lounge in your college dorm is an example of which of the following criminal offenses?
   a. a burglary
   b. motor vehicle theft
   c. robbery
   d. larceny-theft

8. The FBI's criminal statistics used in this chapter reflect
   a. all crimes that occur.
   b. offenses known to the police.
   c. offenses that result in an arrest.
   d. offenses that result in a criminal conviction.

9. Most people arrested for violent crime in the United States are
   a. white.
   b. African American.
   c. Hispanic.
   d. Asian.

10. Which of the following is the oldest justification for punishing an offender?
   a. deterrence
   b. societal protection
   c. retribution
   d. rehabilitation

ANSWERS: 1 (a); 2 (d); 3 (b); 4 (c); 5 (b); 6 (a); 7 (d); 8 (b); 9 (a); 10 (c).

Essay Questions

1. How does a sociological view of deviance differ from the common-sense notion that bad people do bad things?

2. How is social power linked to the creation of crime or other types of deviance? In your response, consider social class and race. Does gender also fit this pattern? Explain.

Chapter 8   Social Stratification

Multiple-Choice Questions

1. **Social stratification refers to**
   a. job specialization in modern societies.
   b. ranking categories of people in a hierarchy.
   c. the fact that some people work harder than others.
   d. inequality of personal talent and individual effort.

2. A caste system is social stratification
   a. based on individual achievement.
   b. based on merit.
   c. based on birth.
   d. in which just two categories of people arc unequal.

3. Sonja has two advanced degrees, an average salary, and is working at a low-prestige job. Which concept best describes her situation?
   a. low status consistency
   b. horizontal social mobility
   c. upward social mobility
   d. high status consistency

4. According to the Davis-Moore thesis,
   a. equality is functional or useful for society.
   b. the more inequality a society has, the more productive it is.
   c. more important jobs must offer enough rewards to draw talent from less important work.
   d. societies with more meritocracy are less productive than those with caste systems.

5. Karl Marx claimed that society "reproduces the class structure." By this he meant that
   a. society benefits from inequality.
   b. class differences are passed on from one generation to the next.
   c. class differences are the same everywhere in the world.
   d. a classless society is impossible.

6. Max Weber claimed that social stratification is based on
   a. economic class.
   b. social status or prestige.
   c. power.
   d. All of the above are correct.

7. The wealthiest 20 percent of people in the United States own about how much of the country's privately owned wealth?
   a. 35 percent
   b. 55 percent
   c. 85 percent
   d. 95 percent

8. Which of the following jobs is an example of high-prestige work?
   a. telephone operator
   b. college professor
   c. child care worker
   d. cashier

9. Which of the following is another term for the working class?
   a. upper-middle class
   b. average-middle class
   c. lower class
   d. lower-middle class

10. Which quintile (20 percent) of the U.S. population has seen the greatest change in income over the last generation?
    a. the top quintile
    b. the middle quintile
    c. the lowest quintile
    d. All quintiles have seen the same change.

11. Change in social position during a person's own lifetime is called
    a. intergenerational social mobility.
    b. intragenerational social mobility.

   c. structural social mobility.
   d. horizontal social mobility.

12. Which age category of the U.S. population has the highest poverty rate?
    a. young people under the age of eighteen
    b. adults in their thirties
    c. middle-aged people in their forties
    d. seniors over age sixty-five

ANSWERS: 1 (b); 2 (c); 3 (a); 4 (c); 5 (b); 6 (d); 7 (c); 8 (b); 9 (d); 10 (a); 11 (b); 12 (a).

Essay Questions

1. Explain why social stratification is a creation of society and not just a reflection of individual differences.

2. How do caste and class systems differ? How are they the same? Why does industrialization introduce a measure of meritocracy into social stratification?

3. What is the extent of poverty in the United States? Who are the poor in terms of age, race and ethnicity, and gender?

Chapter 9   Global Stratification

Multiple-Choice Questions

1. In global perspective, the richest 20 percent of all people earn about what share of the entire world's income?
   a. 17 percent
   b. 37 percent
   c. 57 percent
   d. 77 percent

2. The United States, Canada, and Japan are all
   a. high-income countries.
   b. middle-income countries.
   c. low-income countries.
   d. in different income categories.

3. Low-income nations
   a. are evenly spread in all world regions.
   b. are found mostly in Africa and Asia.
   c. are all in Latin America.
   d. contain a majority of the world's people.

4. China and India are now
   a. the world's two poorest nations.
   b. two of the world's low-income nations.
   c. two of the world's middle-income nations.
   d. two of the world's high-income nations.

5. Which of the following is the range of annual personal income for people living in middle-income nations?
   a. $250 to $1,000
   b. $1,000 to $2,499
   c. $2,500 to $12,000
   d. $12,001 to $25,000

6. How does poverty in poor nations compare to poverty in the United States?
   a. In poor nations, poverty is more likely to involve men.
   b. In most poor nations, the problem of poverty is close to being solved.
   c. Poor nations contain a smaller number of poor people than the United States.
   d. In poor nations, there is far more absolute poverty.

7. Neocolonialism refers to the process by which
   a. rich countries gain new colonies to replace older ones.
   b. multinational corporations dominate the economy of a poor country.
   c. rich countries grant independence to their former colonies.
   d. large corporations do business in many countries at once.

8. Which of the following statements is the basis of modernization theory?
   a. The main cause of poverty in the world is low productivity due to simple technology and traditional culture.
   b. Poor nations can never become rich if they remain part of the global capitalist economy.
   c. The main cause of poverty in the world is the operation of multinational corporations.
   d. Most poor nations were richer in the past than they are today.

9. According to Walt Rostow, which is the final stage of economic development?
   a. drive to technological maturity
   b. traditional
   c. high mass consumption
   d. take-off

10. Dependency theory differs from modernization theory by saying that
   a. poor nations are responsible for their own poverty.
   b. capitalism is the best way to produce economic development.
   c. economic development is not a good idea for poor countries.
   d. global stratification results from the exploitation of poor countries by rich countries.

ANSWERS: 1 (d); 2 (a); 3 (b); 4 (c); 5 (c); 6 (d); 7 (b); 8 (a); 9 (c); 10 (d).

Essay Questions

1. What are the differences between relative and absolute poverty? Describe global social stratification using both concepts.

2. Why do many analysts claim that economic development in low-income countries depends on raising the social standing of women?

Chapter 10   Gender Stratification

Multiple-Choice Questions

1. Gender is not just a matter of personal traits but also a matter of differences in
   a. power.
   b. wealth.
   c. prestige.
   d. All of the above are correct.

2. The anthropologist Margaret Mead studied gender in three societies in New Guinea and found that
   a. all societies define femininity in much the same way.
   b. all societies define masculinity in much the same way.
   c. what is feminine in one society may be masculine in another.
   d. the meaning of gender is changing everywhere toward greater equality.

3. For all of us raised in U.S. society, gender shapes our
   a. feelings.
   b. thoughts.
   c. actions.
   d. All of the above are correct.

4. There is a "beauty myth" in U.S. society that encourages
   a. women to believe that their personal importance depends on their looks.
   b. beautiful women to think they do not need men.
   c. men to improve their physical appearance in order to attract women.
   d. women to disregard beauty in favor of personal achievement.

5. In the United States, what share of women work for income?
   a. 80 percent
   b. 60 percent
   c. 40 percent
   d. 20 percent

6. In the U.S. labor force,
   a. men and women have the same types of jobs.
   b. men and women earn the same pay.
   c. women are still concentrated in several types of jobs.
   d. a majority of working women hold "pink-collar" jobs.

7. For which of the following categories of people in the United States is it true that women do more housework than men?
   a. people who work for income
   b. people who are married
   c. people who have children
   d. All of the above are correct.

8. In the United States, women in the labor force working full time earn how much for every dollar earned by men working full time?
   a. 77 cents
   b. 87 cents
   c. 91 cents
   d. 97 cents

9. Before the 2010 elections, women held about what percentage of seats in Congress?
   a. 7 percent
   b. 17 percent
   c. 37 percent
   d. 57 percent

10. The Equal Rights Amendment, which would expand the rights and opportunities of women, reflects which of the following types of feminism?
   a. socialist feminism
   b. liberal feminism
   c. radical feminism
   d. All of the above are correct.

ANSWERS: 1 (d); 2 (c); 3 (d); 4 (a); 5 (b); 6 (c); 7 (d); 8 (a); 9 (b); 10 (b).

1. How do the concepts "sex" and "gender" differ? Why is the chapter called "Gender Stratification" rather than "Sex Stratification?"

2. Why is gender correctly considered a dimension of social stratification? How does gender intersect other dimensions of inequality, such as class, race, and ethnicity?

Chapter 11   Race and Ethnicity

Multiple-Choice Questions

1. Race refers to _____ considered important in a society, and ethnicity refers to _____.
   a. biological traits; cultural traits
   b. cultural traits; biological traits
   c. our differences; what we all have in common
   d. what we all have in common; our differences

2. People of Hispanic descent make up what share of the U.S. population?
   a. 46.4 percent
   b. 36.4 percent
   c. 26.4 percent
   d. 16.4 percent

3. A minority is denned as a category of people who
   a. at one time were disadvantaged.
   b. are less than half of a society's population.
   c. are defined as different and are disadvantaged.
   d. are below average in terms of income.

4. In the United States, four states have a "minority majority." Which of the following states is *not* one of them?
   a. California
   b. Florida
   c. Texas
   d. New Mexico

5. Research using the Bogardus social distance scale shows that U.S. college students
   a. are less prejudiced than students fifty years ago.
   b. believe that Arabs and Muslims should be kept out of the country.
   c. have the strongest prejudice against African Americans.
   d. All of the above are correct.

6. Prejudice is a matter of _____, and discrimination is a matter of _____.
   a. biology; culture
   b. attitudes; behavior
   c. choice; social structure
   d. social structure; culture

7. The United States is not truly pluralistic today because
   a. part of our population lives in "ethnic enclaves."
   b. this country has a history of slavery.
   c. different racial and ethnic categories are unequal in social standing.
   d. All of the above are correct.

8. Which concept is illustrated by immigrants from Ecuador coming to the United States and learning to speak the English language?
   a. genocide
   b. segregation
   c. assimilation
   d. pluralism

9. When the first Europeans came to the Americas in the late 1400s, Native Americans
   a. followed shortly thereafter.
   b. had just migrated from Asia.
   c. came on ships with them from Europe.
   d. had inhabited this land for 30,000 years.

10. Which is the largest category of Asian Americans in the United States?
    a. Chinese Americans
    b. Japanese Americans
    c. Korean Americans
    d. Vietnamese Americans

ANSWERS: 1 (a); 2 (d); 3 (c); 4 (b); 5 (a); 6 (b); 7 (b); 8 (c); 9 (c); 10 (d); 11 (a).

Essay Questions

1. What is the difference between race and ethnicity? What does it mean to say that race and ethnicity are socially constructed?

2. What is a minority? Pointing to specific facts in this chapter, support the claim that African Americans and Arab Americans are both minorities in the United States.

Chapter 12   Economics and Politics

Multiple-Choice Questions

1. The economy is the social institution that guides
   a. the production of goods and services.
   b. the distribution of goods and services.
   c. the consumption of goods and services.
   d. All of the above are correct.

2. Building houses and making cars are examples of production in which economic sector?
   a. the primary sector
   b. the secondary sector
   c. the tertiary sector
   d. the service sector

3. Which of the following factors is a result of the globalization of the economy?
   a. Certain areas of the world specialize in one sector of economic activity.
   b. Industrial jobs in the United States are being lost to other countries.
   c. More and more products pass through several nations before reaching the consumer.
   d. All of the above are correct.

4. Socialist economies differ from capitalist economies by
   a. being more productive.
   b. creating less economic equality.
   c. creating more economic equality.
   d. making greater use of commercial advertising.

5. The largest 2,582 corporations, each with assets exceeding $2.5 billion, represent about what share of all corporate assets in the United States?
   a. 81 percent
   b. 61 percent
   c. 31 percent
   d. 11 percent

6. Modern societies, including the United States, rely mostly on which type of authority?
   a. charismatic authority
   b. traditional authority
   c. rational-legal authority
   d. no authority at all

7. In which type of political system does power reside in the hands of the people as a whole?
   a. democracy
   b. aristocracy
   c. totalitarianism
   d. monarchy

8. In the 2008 U.S. presidential election, about what share of registered voters actually cast a vote?
   a. 93 percent
   b. 83 percent
   c. 63 percent
   d. 23 percent

9. The Marxist political-economy model suggests that
   a. power is concentrated in the hands of a small "power elite."
   b. an antidemocratic bias is built into the capitalist system.
   c. power is widely spread throughout society.
   d. many people do not vote because they are basically satisfied with their lives.

10. Which of the following wars resulted in the highest loss of life to people in the United States?
    a. Civil War
    b. World War II
    c. Korean War
    d. Vietnam War

ANSWERS: 1 (d); 2 (b); 3 (d); 4 (c); 5 (a); 6 (c); 7 (a); 8 (c); 9 (b); 10 (a).

Essay Questions

1. In what specific ways did the Industrial Revolution change the U.S. economy? How is the Information Revolution changing the economy once again?

2. Discuss the pluralist, power-elite, and Marxist political-economy models of political power, explaining how each differs from the others. Which of these models do you think makes the most sense? Why?

Chapter 13   Family and Religion

Multiple-Choice Questions

1. The family is a social institution that is found in
   a. every society.
   b. low-income nations but typically not in high-income nations.
   c. high-income nations but typically not in low-income nations.
   d. most but not all societies.

2. What is the term sociologists use for a group containing parents, children, and other kin?
   a. extended family
   b. nuclear family
   c. family of affinity
   d. conjugal family

3. Sociologists claim that marriage in the United States follows the principle of homogamy, which means that partners are
   a. people of the same sex.
   b. people who are socially alike in terms of class, age, and race.
   c. people who marry due to social pressure.
   d. selected based on love rather than by parents.

4. Which theoretical approach helps us see that people select partners who have about the same to offer as they do?
   a. the structural-functional approach
   b. the social-conflict approach
   c. the social-exchange approach
   d. the feminist approach

5. In the United States, many Latino families are characterized by
   a. strong extended kinship.
   b. parents exerting a great deal of control over their children's courtship.
   c. traditional gender roles.
   d. All of the above are correct.

6. What term did Emile Durkheim use to describe the everyday aspects of our lives?
   a. religion
   b. sacred
   c. profane
   d. ritual

7. Max Weber's famous thesis states that particular religious ideas set in motion a wave of change that resulted in
   a. increasing social conflict.
   b. a return to the traditions of the Middle Ages.
   c. the Protestant Reformation.
   d. the Industrial Revolution and the rise of capitalism.

8. Which type of religious organization is most integrated into the larger society?
   a. cult
   b. church
   c. sect
   d. counterculture

9. About what share of the U.S. population claims to identify with a religious tradition?
   a. 84 percent
   b. 64 percent
   c. 44 percent
   d. 24 percent

10. The term "secularization" refers to which of the following?
    a. religion becoming more important in people's lives
    b. the increasing popularity of religious fundamentalism
    c. a decline in the importance of religion and the sacred
    d. churches trying to resist social change

ANSWERS: 1 (a); 2 (a); 3 (b); 4 (c); 5 (d); 6 (c); 7 (d); 8 (b); 9 (a); 10 (c).

Essay Questions

1. Sociologists point to ways in which family life reflects not just individual choices but the structure of society as well. Provide three examples of how society shapes family life.

2. Explain Karl Marx's claim that religion tends to support the status quo. Develop a counterclaim, based on Max Weber's analysis of Calvinism and the rise of capitalism.

Chapter 14 Education, Health, and Medicine

Multiple-Choice Questions

1. In the United States and in other countries, laws requiring all children to attend school were enacted following
   a. national independence.
   b. the Industrial Revolution.
   c. World War II.
   d. the invention of computers.

2. Japan differs from the United States in that attending college there depends more on
   a. athletic ability.
   b. race and ethnicity.
   c. scores on achievement tests.
   d. family wealth.

3. According to the structural-functional approach, schooling carries out the task of
   a. linking together a diverse population with common norms and values.
   b. creating new elements of culture.
   c. socializing young people.
   d. All of the above are correct.

4. Social-conflict analysis highlights how education
   a. reflects and reinforces social inequality.
   b. helps prepare students for their future careers.
   c. has both latent and manifest functions.
   d. All of the above are correct.

5. The importance of community colleges to U.S. higher education is reflected in the fact that they
   a. greatly expand the opportunity to attend college.
   b. enroll more than 40 percent of all U.S. college students.
   c. enroll almost half of all African American and Hispanic college students.
   d. All of the above are correct.

6. Health is a social issue because
   a. cultural patterns define what people view as healthy.
   b. social inequality affects people's health.
   c. a society's technology affects people's health.
   d. All of the above are correct.

7. In the very poorest nations of the world today, about one in four people who are born dies before reaching the age of
   a. 20 years.
   b. 40 years.
   c. 60 years.
   d. 80 years.

8. Which is the greatest cause of death among young people in the United States?
   a. cancer
   b. AIDS
   c. accidents
   d. influenza

9. In the United States, the greatest preventable cause of death is
   a. sexually transmitted diseases.
   b. automobile accidents.
   c. cigarette smoking.
   d. AIDS.

10. About what share of U.S. adults are overweight?
    a. two-thirds
    b. one-half
    c. one-third
    d. one-fifth

ANSWERS: 1 (b); 2 (c); 3 (d); 4 (a); 5 (d); 6 (d); 7 (a); 8 (c); 9 (c); 10 (a).

Essay Questions

1. Why does industrialization lead societies to expand their systems of schooling? In what ways has schooling in the United States been shaped by our economic, political, and cultural systems?

2. Using the structural-functional approach, why is schooling important to the operation of society? From a social-conflict point of view, how does schooling reproduce social inequality in each generation?

3. Why is health a social issue as much as a biological issue? What are several ways in which health and medicine are linked to social inequality?

Chapter 15 Population, Urbanization, and Environment

Multiple-Choice Questions

1. Demography is defined as the study of
   a. democratic political systems.
   b. human culture.
   c. human population.
   d. the natural environment.

2. Which region of the world has both the lowest birth rate and the lowest infant mortality rate?
   a. Latin America
   b. Europe
   c. Africa
   d. Asia

3. Typically, high-income nations grow mostly from _____, while low-income nations grow from _____.
   a. immigration; natural increase
   b. emigration; natural increase
   c. natural increase; immigration
   d. internal migration; natural increase

4. In general, the higher the average income of a country,
   a. the faster the population increases.
   b. the slower the population increases.
   c. the lower the level of immigration.
   d. the lower the level of urbanization.

5. In the United States, urban decentralization has caused
   a. the expansion of suburbs.
   b. the development of vast urban regions.
   c. the growth of edge cities.
   d. All of the above are correct.

6. Which of the following concepts did Ferdinand Tonnies use to refer to people coming together on the basis of individual self-interest?
   a. mechanical solidarity
   b. organic solidarity
   c. Gesellschaft
   d. Gemeinschaft

7. The world's third urban revolution is now taking place in
   a. the United States.
   b. Europe and Japan.
   c. middle-income nations.
   d. low-income nations.

8. The environmental deficit refers to
   a. long-term harm to the environment caused by a shortsighted focus on material affluence.
   b. the public's lack of interest in the natural environment.
   c. the fact that natural scientists ignore the social dimensions of environmental problems.
   d. the lack of funding for important environmental programs.

9. Which of the following statements reflects the limits-to-growth thesis?
   a. People are rapidly consuming Earth's finite resources.
   b. Whatever problems technology creates, technology can solve.
   c. Quality of life on Earth is getting better.
   d. Higher living standards today will benefit future generations.

10. Environmental racism is the idea that
    a. few minorities are represented within the environmental movement.
    b. prejudice is the major cause of pollution and other environmental problems.
    c. environmental dangers are greatest for the poor and minorities.
    d. All of the above are correct.

ANSWERS: 1 (c); 2 (b); 3 (a); 4 (b); 5 (d); 6 (c); 7 (d); 8 (a); 9 (a); 10 (c).

Essay Questions

1. According to demographic transition theory, how does economic development affect population patterns?

2. According to Ferdinand Tonnies, Emile Durkheim, Georg Simmel, and Louis Wirth, what characterizes urbanism as a way of life? Note several differences in the ideas of these thinkers.

Chapter 16   Social Change: Modern and Postmodern Societies

Multiple-Choice Questions

1. Sociologists use the term "modernity" to refer to social patterns that emerged
   a. with the first human civilizations.
   b. with the founding of cities.
   c. after the Industrial Revolution.
   d. along with the Information Revolution.

2. Which of the following are common causes of social change?
   a. the invention of things, ideas, and social patterns
   b. diffusion from one cultural system to another
   c. the discovery of existing things
   d. All of the above are correct.

3. Karl Marx highlighted the importance of which of the following factors in the process of social change?
   a. immigration and demographic factors
   b. ideas
   c. social conflict
   d. cultural diffusion

4. Max Weber's analysis of the rise of rational, modern society highlighted the importance of which of the following factors in the process of social change?
   a. invention
   b. ideas
   c. social conflict
   d. cultural diffusion

5. Which term did Ferdinand Tonnies use to describe a modern society?
   a. Gesellschaft
   b. Gemeinschaft
   c. mechanical solidarity
   d. organic solidarity

6. According to Emile Durkheim, modern societies have
   a. respect for established tradition.
   b. widespread alienation.
   c. common values and beliefs.
   d. an increasing division of labor.

7. The 2010 Gulf of Mexico oil spill is one recent case of
   a. a natural disaster.
   b. a technological disaster.
   c. an intentional disaster.
   d. an everyday disaster.

8. Which of the following statements about modernity as a mass society is not correct?
   a. There is more poverty now than in past centuries.
   b. Kinship ties have become weaker.

c. Bureaucracy, including government, has expanded in size.

d. People experience greater moral uncertainty about how to live.

9. **Sociologists who describe modernity in terms of class-society theory focus on which of the following?**

   a. rationality as a way of thinking about the world

   b. mutual interdependency

   c. the rise of capitalism

   d. the high risk of anomie

10. **David Riesman described the other-directed social character typical of modern people as**

    a. rigid conformity to tradition.

    b. eagerness to follow the latest fashions and fads.

    c. highly individualistic.

    d. All of the above are correct.

ANSWERS: 1 (c); 2 (d); 3 (c); 4 (b); 5 (a); 6 (d); 7 (b); 8 (a); 9 (c); 10 (b).

Essay Questions

1. Discuss how Tonnies, Durkheim, Weber, and Marx described modern society. Point out the similarities and differences in their understandings of modernity.

2. What traits lead some people to call the United States a "mass society"? Why do other analysts describe the United States as a "class society"?

glossary

abortion   the deliberate termination of a pregnancy

absolute poverty   a lack of resources that is life-threatening

achieved status   a social position a person takes on voluntarily that reflects personal ability and effort

Afrocentrism   emphasizing and promoting African cultural patterns

ageism   prejudice and discrimination against older people

age-sex pyramid   a graphic representation of the age and sex of a population

agriculture   large-scale cultivation using plows harnessed to animals or more powerful energy sources

alienation   the experience of isolation and misery resulting from powerlessness

anomie   Durkheim's term for a condition in which society provides little moral guidance to individuals

anticipatory socialization   learning that helps a person achieve a desired position

ascribed status   a social position a person receives at birth or takes on involuntarily later in life

asexuality   a lack of sexual attraction to people of either sex

assimilation   the process by which minorities gradually adopt patterns of the dominant culture

authoritarianism   a political system that denies the people participation in government

authority   power that people perceive as legitimate rather than coercive

beliefs   specific ideas that people hold to be true

bisexuality   sexual attraction to people of both sexes

blue-collar occupations   lower-prestige jobs that involve mostly manual labor

bureaucracy   an organizational model rationally designed to perform tasks efficiently

bureaucratic inertia   the tendency of bureaucratic organizations to perpetuate themselves

bureaucratic ritualism   a focus on rules and regulations to the point of undermining an organization's goals

capitalism   an economic system in which natural resources and the means of producing goods and services are privately owned

capitalists   people who own and operate factories and other businesses in pursuit of profits

caste system   social stratification based on ascription, or birth

cause and effect   a relationship in which change in one variable (the independent variable) causes change in another (the dependent variable)

charisma   extraordinary personal qualities that can infuse people with emotion and turn them into followers

charismatic authority   power legitimized by extraordinary personal abilities that inspire devotion and obedience

church   a type of religious organization that is well integrated into the larger society

civil religion   a quasi-religious loyalty linking individuals in a basically secular society

class society   a capitalist society with pronounced social stratification

class system   social stratification based on both birth and individual achievement

cohabitation   the sharing of a household by an unmarried couple

cohort   a category of people with something in common, usually their age

collective behavior   activity involving a large number of people that is unplanned, often controversial, and sometimes dangerous

colonialism   the process by which some nations enrich themselves through political and economic control of other nations

community-based corrections   correctional programs operating within society at large rather than behind prison walls

concept   a mental construct that represents some aspect of the world in a simplified form

concrete operational stage   Piaget's term for the level of human development at which individuals first see causal connections in their surroundings

conglomerate   a giant corporation composed of many smaller corporations

conspicuous consumption   buying and using products because of the "statement" they make about social position

corporate crime   the illegal actions of a corporation or people acting on its behalf

corporation   an organization with a legal existence, including rights and liabilities, separate from that of its members

correlation   a relationship in which two (or more) variables change together

counterculture   cultural patterns that strongly oppose those widely accepted within a society

crime   the violation of a society's formally enacted criminal law

crimes against the person   crimes that direct violence or the threat of violence against others; also known as *violent crimes*

crimes against property   crimes that involve theft of money or property belonging to others; also known as *property crimes*

criminal justice system   the organizations—police, courts, and prison officials—that respond to alleged violations of the law

criminal recidivism   later offenses by people previously convicted of crimes

critical sociology   the study of society that focuses on the need for social change

crowd   a temporary gathering of people who share a common focus of attention and who influence one another

crude birth rate   the number of live births in a given year for every 1,000 people in a population

crude death rate   the number of deaths in a given year for every 1,000 people in a population

cult   a religious organization that is largely outside a society's cultural traditions

cultural integration   the close relationships among various elements of a cultural system

cultural lag   the fact that some cultural elements change more quickly than others, disrupting a cultural system

cultural relativism   the practice of judging a culture by its own standards

cultural transmission   the process by which one generation passes culture to the next

cultural universals   traits that are part of every known culture

culture   the ways of thinking, the ways of acting, and the material objects that together form a people's way of life

culture shock   personal disorientation when experiencing an unfamiliar way of life

Davis-Moore thesis   the functional analysis claiming that social stratification has beneficial consequences for the operation of society

democracy   a political system that gives power to the people as a whole

demographic transition theory   a thesis that links population patterns to a society's level of technological development

demography   the study of human population

denomination   a church, independent of the state, that recognizes religious pluralism

dependency theory   a model of economic and social development that explains global inequality in terms of the historical exploitation of poor nations by rich ones

descent   the system by which members of a society trace kinship

deterrence   the attempt to discourage criminality through the use of punishment

deviance   the recognized violation of cultural norms

direct-fee system   a medical care system in which patients pay directly for the services of physicians and hospitals

discrimination   unequal treatment of various categories of people

division of labor   specialized economic activity

dramaturgical analysis   Erving Goffman's term for the study of social interaction in terms of theatrical performance

dyad   a social group with two members

eating disorder   a disorder that involves an intense form of dieting or other unhealthy method of weight control driven by the desire to be very thin

ecologically sustainable culture   a way of life that meets the needs of the present generation without threatening the environmental legacy of future generations

ecology   the study of the interaction of living organisms and the natural environment

economy   the social institution that organizes a society's production, distribution, and consumption of goods and services

ecosystem   a system composed of the interaction of all living organisms and their natural environment

education   the social institution through which society provides its members with important knowledge, including basic facts, job skills, and cultural norms and values

ego   Freud's term for a person's conscious efforts to balance innate pleasure-seeking drives with the demands of society

empirical evidence   information we can verify with our senses

endogamy   marriage between people of the same social category

environmental deficit   profound long-term harm to the natural environment caused by humanity's focus on short-term material affluence

environmental racism   patterns of development that expose poor people, especially minorities, to environmental hazards

ethnicity   a shared cultural heritage

ethnocentrism   the practice of judging another culture by the standards of one's own culture

ethnomethodology   Harold Garfinkel's term for the study of the way people make sense of their everyday surroundings

Eurocentrism   the dominance of European (especially English) cultural patterns

euthanasia   assisting in the death of a person suffering from an incurable disease; also known as *mercy killing*

exogamy   marriage between people of different social categories

experiment   a research method for investigating cause and effect under highly controlled conditions

expressive leadership   group leadership that focuses on the group's well-being

extended family   a family consisting of parents and children as well as other kin; also known as a *consanguine family*

fad   an unconventional social pattern that people embrace briefly and enthusiastically

faith   belief based on conviction rather than on scientific evidence

family   a social institution found in all societies that unites people in cooperative groups to care for one another, including any children

family violence   emotional, physical, or sexual abuse of one family member by another

fashion   a social pattern favored by a large number of people

feminism   support of social equality for women and men, in opposition to patriarch and sexism

feminization of poverty   the trend of women making up an increasing proportion of the poor

fertility   the incidence of childbearing in a country's population

folkways   norms for routine or casual interaction

formal operational stage   Piaget's term for the level of human development at which individuals think abstractly and critically

formal organization   a large secondary group organized to achieve its goals efficiently

functional illiteracy   a lack of the reading and writing skills needed for everyday living

fundamentalism   a conservative religious doctrine that opposes intellectualism and worldly accommodation in favor of restoring traditional, otherworldly religion

Gemeinschaft   a type of social organization in which people are closely tied by kinship and tradition

gender   the personal traits and social positions that members of a society attach to being female or male

gender-conflict theory (feminist theory)   the study of society that focuses on inequality and conflict between women and men

gender roles (sex roles)   attitudes and activities that a society links to each sex

gender stratification   the unequal distribution of wealth, power, and privilege between men and women

generalized other   Mead's term for widespread cultural norms and values we use as references in evaluating ourselves

genocide   the systematic killing of one category of people by another

gerontocracy   a form of social organization in which the elderly have the most wealth, power, and prestige

gerontology   the study of aging and the elderly

Gesellschaft   a type of social organization in which people come together only on the basis of individual self-interest

global economy   economic activity that crosses national borders

global perspective   the study of the larger world and our society's place in it

global stratification   patterns of social inequality in the world as a whole

global warming   a rise in Earth's average temperature due to an increasing concentration of carbon dioxide in the atmosphere

government   a formal organization that directs the political life of a society

groupthink   the tendency of group members to conform, resulting in a narrow view of some issue

hate crime   a criminal act against a person or a person's property by an offender motivated by racial or other bias

health   a state of complete physical, mental, and social well-being

health maintenance organization (HMO)   an organization that provides comprehensive medical care to subscribers for a fixed fee

heterosexism   a view that labels anyone who is not heterosexual as "queer"

heterosexuality   sexual attraction to someone of the other sex

high culture   cultural patterns that distinguish a society's elite

high-income countries   the nations with the highest overall standards of living

holistic medicine   an approach to health care that emphasizes the prevention of illness and takes into account a person's entire physical and social environment

homogamy   marriage between people with the same social characteristics

homophobia   discomfort over close personal interaction with people thought to be gay, lesbian, or bisexual

homosexuality   sexual attraction to someone of the same sex

horticulture   the use of hand tools to raise crops

hunting and gathering   the use of simple tools to hunt animals and gather vegetation for food

id   Freud's term for the human being's basic drives

ideology   cultural beliefs that justify particular social arrangements, including patterns of inequality

incest taboo   a norm forbidding sexual relations or marriage between certain relatives

income   earnings from work or investments

industry   the production of goods using advanced sources of energy to drive large machinery

infidelity   sexual activity outside one's marriage

in-group   a social group toward which a member feels respect and loyalty

institutional prejudice and discrimination   bias built into the operation of society's institutions

instrumental leadership   group leadership that focuses on the completion of tasks

intergenerational social mobility   upward or downward social mobility of children in relation to their parents

interpretive sociology   the study of society that focuses on discovering the meanings people attach to their social world

intersection theory   analysis of the interplay of race, class, and gender, often resulting in multiple dimensions of disadvantage

intersexual people   people whose bodies (including genitals) have both female and male characteristics

intragenerational social mobility   a change in social position occurring during a person's lifetime

kinship   a social bond based on common ancestry, marriage, or adoption

labeling theory   the idea that deviance and conformity result not so much from what people do as from how others respond to those actions

labor unions   organizations of workers that seek to improve wages and working conditions through various strategies, including negotiations and strikes

language   a system of symbols that allows people to communicate with one another

latent functions   the unrecognized and unintended consequences of any social pattern

liberation theology   the combining of Christian principles with political activism, often Marxist in character

life expectancy   the average life span of a country's population

looking-glass self   Cooley's term for a self-image based on how we think others see us

low-income countries   nations with a low standard of living, in which most people are poor

macro-level orientation   a broad focus on social structures that shape society as a whole

manifest functions   the recognized and intended consequences of any social pattern

marriage   a legal relationship, usually involving economic cooperation, sexual activity, and childbearing

Marxist political-economy theory   an analysis that explains politics in terms of the operation of a society's economic system

mass media   the means for delivering impersonal communications to a vast audience

mass society   a society in which prosperity and bureaucracy have weakened traditional social ties

master status   a status that has special importance for social identity, often shaping a person's entire life

material culture   the physical things created by members of a society

matriarchy   a form of social organization in which females dominate males

measurement   a procedure for determining the value of a variable in a specific case

medicalization of deviance   the transformation of moral and legal deviance into a medical condition

medicine   the social institution that focuses on fighting disease and improving health

megalopolis   a vast urban region containing a number of cities and their surrounding suburbs

meritocracy   social stratification based on personal merit

metropolis   a large city that socially and economically dominates an urban area

micro-level orientation   a close-up focus on social interaction in specific situations

middle-income countries   nations with a standard of living about average for the world as a whole

migration   the movement of people into and out of a specified territory

military-industrial complex   the close association of the federal government, the military, and defense industries

minority   any category of people distinguished by physical or cultural difference that a society sets apart and subordinates

miscegenation   biological reproduction by partners of different racial categories

mob   a highly emotional crowd that pursues a violent or destructive goal

modernity   changes brought about by the Industrial Revolution

modernization   the process of social change begun by industrialization

modernization theory   a model of economic and social development that explains global inequality in terms of technological and cultural differences between nations

monarchy   a political system in which a single family rules from generation to generation

monogamy   marriage that unites two partners

monopoly   the domination of a market by a single producer

mores   norms that are widely observed and have great moral significance

mortality   the incidence of death in a country's population

multiculturalism   a perspective recognizing the cultural diversity of the United States and promoting equal standing for all cultural traditions

multinational corporation   a large business that operates in many countries

natural environment   Earth's surface and atmosphere, including living organisms, air, water, soil, and other resources necessary to sustain life

neocolonialism   a new form of global power relationships that involves not direct political control but economic exploitation by multinational corporations

network   a web of weak social ties

nonmaterial culture   the ideas created by members of a society

nonverbal communication   communication using body movements, gestures, and facial expressions rather than speech

norms   rules and expectations by which a society guides the behavior of its members

nuclear family   a family composed of one or two parents and their children; also known as a *conjugal family*

nuclear proliferation   the acquisition of nuclear weapons technology by more and more nations

oligarchy   the rule of the many by the few

oligopoly   the domination of a market by a few producers

organizational environment   factors outside an organization that affect its operation

organized crime   a business supplying illegal goods or services

other-directedness   openness to the latest trends and fashions, often expressed by imitating others

out-group   a social group toward which a person feels a sense of competition or opposition

participant observation   a research method in which investigators systematically observe people while joining them in their routine activities

pastoralism   the domestication of animals

patriarchy   a form of social organization in which males dominate females

peer group   a social group whose members have interests, social position, and age in common

personality   a person's fairly consistent patterns of acting, thinking, and feeling

personal space   the surrounding area over which a person makes some claim to privacy

plea bargaining   a legal negotiation in which a prosecutor reduces a charge in exchange for a defendant's guilty plea

pluralism   a state in which people of all races and ethnicities are distinct but have equal social standing

pluralist theory   an analysis of politics that sees power as spread among many competing interest groups

political revolution   the overthrow of one political system in order to establish another

politics   the social institution that distributes power, sets a society's goals, and makes decisions

polygamy   marriage that unites a person with two or more spouses

popular culture   cultural patterns that are widespread among a society's population

pornography   sexually explicit material intended to cause sexual arousal

positivism   a scientific approach to knowledge based on "positive" facts as opposed to mere speculation

positivist sociology   the study of society based on systematic observation of social behavior

postindustrial economy   a productive system based on service work and high technology

postindustrialism   the production of information using computer technology

postmodernity   the transformation caused by the Information Revolution and the postindustrial economy

power   the ability to achieve desired ends despite resistance from others

power-elite theory   an analysis of politics that sees power as concentrated among the rich

prejudice   a rigid and unfair generalization about an entire category of people

preoperational stage   Piaget's term for the level of human development at which individuals first use language and other symbols

presentation of self   Erving Goffman's term for a person's efforts to create specific impressions in the minds of others

primary group   a small social group whose members share personal and lasting relationships

primary sector   the part of the economy that draws raw materials from the natural environment

primary sex characteristics   the genitals, organs used for reproduction

profane   included as an ordinary element of everyday life

profession   a prestigious white-collar occupation that requires extensive formal education

proletarians   people who sell their labor for wages

prostitution   the selling of sexual services

queer theory   a body of research findings that challenges the heterosexual bias in U.S. society

race   a socially constructed category of people who share biologically transmitted traits that members of a society consider important

race-conflict theory   the study of society that focuses on inequality and conflict between people of different racial and ethnic categories

racism   the belief that one racial category is innately superior or inferior to another

rain forests   regions of dense forestation, most of which circle the globe close to the equator

rational-legal authority   power legitimized by legally enacted rules and regulations

rationality   a way of thinking that emphasizes deliberate, matter-of-fact calculation of the most efficient way to accomplish a particular task

rationalization of society   Weber's term for the historical change from tradition to rationality as the main type of human thought

reference group   a social group that serves as a point of reference in making evaluations and decisions

rehabilitation   a program for reforming the offender to prevent later offenses

relative poverty   the lack of resources of some people in relation to those who have more

reliability   consistency in measurement

religion   a social institution involving beliefs and practices based on recognizing the sacred

religiosity   the importance of religion in a person's life

research method   a systematic plan for doing research

resocialization   radically changing an inmate's personality by carefully controlling the environment

retribution   an act of moral vengeance by which society makes the offender suffer as much as the suffering caused by the crime

riot   a social eruption that is highly emotional, violent, and undirected

ritual   formal, ceremonial behavior

role   behavior expected of someone who holds a particular status

role conflict   conflict among the roles connected to two or more statuses

role set   a number of roles attached to a single status

role strain   tension among the roles connected to a single status

routinization of charisma   the transformation of charismatic authority into some combination of traditional and bureaucratic authority

rumor   unconfirmed information that people spread informally, often by word of mouth

sacred   set apart as extraordinary, inspiring awe and reverence

Sapir-Whorf thesis   the idea that people see and understand the world through the cultural lens of language

scapegoat   a person or category of people, typically with little power, whom people unfairly blame for their own troubles

schooling   formal instruction under the direction of specially trained teachers

science   a logical system that develops knowledge from direct, systematic observation

scientific management   the application of scientific principles to the operation of a business or other large organization

secondary group   a large and impersonal social group whose members pursue a specific goal or activity

secondary sector   the part of the economy that transforms raw materials into manufactured goods

secondary sex characteristics   bodily development, apart from the genitals, that distinguishes biologically mature females and males

sect   a type of religious organization that stands apart from the larger society

secularization   the historical decline in the importance of the supernatural and the sacred

segregation   the physical and social separation of categories of people

self   George Herbert Mead's term for the part of an individual's personality composed of self-awareness and self-image

sensorimotor stage   Piaget's term for the level of human development at which individuals experience the world only through their senses

sex   the biological distinction between females and males

sexism   the belief that one sex is innately superior to the other

sex ratio   the number of males for every 100 females in a nation's population

sexual harassment   comments, gestures, or physical contacts of a sexual nature that are deliberate, repeated, and unwelcome

sexual orientation   a person's romantic and emotional attraction to another person

sick role   patterns of behavior defined as appropriate for people who are ill

significant others   people, such as parents, who have special importance for socialization

social change   the transformation of culture and social institutions over time

social character   personality patterns common to members of a particular society

social-conflict approach   a framework for building theory that sees society as an arena of inequality that generates conflict and change

social construction of reality   the process by which people creatively shape reality through social interaction

social control   attempts by society to regulate people's thoughts and behavior

social dysfunction   any social pattern that may disrupt the operation of society

social epidemiology   the study of how health and disease are distributed throughout a society's population

social functions the consequences of a social pattern for the operation of society as a whole

social group two or more people who identify with and interact with one another

social institution a major sphere of social life, or societal subsystem, organized to meet human needs

social interaction the process by which people act and react in relation to others

socialism an economic system in which natural resources and the means of producing goods and services are collectively owned

socialization the lifelong social experience by which people develop their human potential and learn culture

socialized medicine a medical care system in which the government owns and operates most medical facilities and employs most physicians

social mobility a change in position within the social hierarchy

social stratification a system by which a society ranks categories of people in a hierarchy

social structure any relatively stable pattern of social behavior

societal protection rendering an offender incapable of further offenses temporarily through imprisonment or permanently by execution

society people who interact in a defined territory and share a culture

sociobiology a theoretical approach that explores ways in which human biology affects how we create culture

socioeconomic status (SES) a composite ranking based on various dimensions of social inequality

sociological perspective the special point of view of sociology that sees general patterns of society in the lives of particular people

sociology the systematic study of human society

state capitalism an economic and political system in which companies are privately owned but cooperate closely with the government

state church a church formally allied with the state

status a social position that a person holds

status consistency the degree of uniformity in a person's social standing across various dimensions of social inequality

status set all the statuses a person holds at a given time

stereotype a simplified description applied to every person in some category

stigma a powerfully negative label that greatly changes a person's self-concept and social identity

structural-functional approach a framework for building theory that sees society as a complex system whose parts work together to promote solidarity and stability

structural social mobility a shift in the social position of large numbers of people due more to changes in society itself than to individual efforts

subculture cultural patterns that set apart some segment of a society's population

suburbs urban areas beyond the political boundaries of a city

superego Freud's term for the cultural values and norms internalized by an individual

survey a research method in which subjects respond to a series of statements or questions on a questionnaire or in an interview

symbol anything that carries a particular meaning recognized by people who share a culture

symbolic-interaction approach a framework for building theory that sees society as the product of the everyday interactions of individuals

technology knowledge that people use to make a way of life in their surroundings

terrorism acts of violence or the threat of violence used as a political strategy by an individual or a group

tertiary sector the part of the economy that involves services rather than goods

theoretical approach a basic image of society that guides thinking and research

theory a statement of how and why specific facts are related

Thomas theorem W. I. Thomas's claim that situations defined as real are real in their consequences

total institution a setting in which people are isolated from the rest of society and controlled by an administrative staff

totalitarianism a highly centralized political system that extensively regulates people's lives

totem an object in the natural world collectively defined as sacred

tracking assigning students to different types of educational programs

tradition values and beliefs passed from generation to generation

tradition-directedness rigid conformity to time-honored ways of living

traditional authority power legitimized by respect for long-established cultural patterns

transsexuals people who feel they are one sex even though biologically they are the other

triad a social group with three members

urban ecology the study of the link between the physical and social dimensions of cities

urbanization the concentration of population into cities

validity actually measuring exactly what you intend to measure

values culturally defined standards that people use to decide what is desirable, good, and beautiful and that serve as broad guidelines for social living

variable a concept whose value changes from case to case

victimless crimes violations of law in which there are no obvious victims

war organized, armed conflict among the people of two or more nations, directed by their governments

wealth the total value of money and other assets, minus outstanding debts

welfare capitalism an economic and political system that combines a mostly market-based economy with extensive social welfare programs

welfare state a system of government agencies and programs that provides benefits to the population

white-collar crime crime committed by people of high social position in the course of their occupations

white-collar occupations higher-prestige jobs that involve mostly mental activity

zero population growth the rate of reproduction that maintains population at a steady level

references

*Blue type denotes reference citations new to this twelfth edition.

Chapter 1 References

AMERICAN SOCIOLOGICAL ASSOCIATION. "Code of Ethics." Washington, D.C.: American Sociological Association, 1997.

———. *Careers in Sociology.* 6th ed. Washington, D.C.: American Sociological Association, 2002.

———. Department of Research and Development. "Research on Jobs and Careers in Sociology." 2011a. [Online] Available at http://www.asanet.org/employment/factsoncareers.cfm

———. "What Can I Do with a Master's Degree?" Washington, D.C.: 2011b. [Online] Available at http://www.asanet.org/research/masters.cfm

BALTZELL, E.DIGBY. "Introduction to the 1967 Edition." In W. E. B. DU BOIS, *The Philadelphia Negro: A Social Study.* New York: Schocken Books, 1967; orig. 1899.

BALTZELL, E.DIGBY. *Puritan Boston and Quaker Philadelphia.* New York: Free Press, 1979.

BENJAMIN, LOIS. *The Black Elite: Facing the Color Line in the Twilight of the Twentieth Century.* Chicago: Nelson-Hall, 1991.

BERGER, PETER L. *Invitation to Sociology.* New York: Anchor Books, 1963.

BOWLES, SAMUEL, AND HERBERT GINTIS. *Schooling in Capitalist America: Educational Reform and the Contradictions of Economic Life.* New York: Basic Books, 1976.

CENTERS FOR DISEASE CONTROL AND PREVENTION, NATIONAL CENTER FOR HEALTH STATISTICS. "Health Data Interactive." [Online] Available at http://www.cdc.gov/nchs/hdi.htm

CENTRAL INTELLIGENCE AGENCY. *The World Factbook.* 2011 (updated biweekly). [Online] Available at http://www.cia.gov/library/publications/the-worldfactbook/index.html

COMTE, AUGUSTE. *Auguste Comte and Positivism: The Essential Writings.* GERTRUD LENZER, ed. New York: Harper Torchbooks, 1975, orig. 1851–54.

DEUTSCHER, IRWIN. *Making a Difference: The Practice of Sociology.* New Brunswick, N.J.: Transaction, 1999.

DU BOIS, W.E.B. *The Philadelphia Negro: A Social Study.* New York: Schocken Books, 1967; orig. 1899.

ECONOMIC POLICY INSTITUTE. "State of Working America 2011." Washington D.C.: Economic Policy Institute. 2011. http://www.stateofworkingamerica.org/

EICHLER, MARGRIT. *Nonsexist Research Methods: A Practical Guide.* Winchester, Mass.: Unwin Hyman, 1988.

FEAGIN, JOE R., AND HERNÁN, VERA. *Liberation Sociology.* Boulder, Colo.: Westview Press, 2001.

FENG HOU, AND JOHN MYLES. "The Changing Role of Education in the Marriage Market: Assortative Marriage in Canada and the United States since the 1970s." *Canadian Journal of Sociology.* Vol. 33, No. 2 (2008):335–64.

GIOVANNINI, MAUREEN. "Female Anthropologist and Male Informant: Gender Conflict in a Sicilian Town." In JOHN J. MACIONIS AND NIJOLE V. BENOKRAITIS, eds., *Seeing Ourselves: Classic, Contemporary, and Cross-Cultural Readings in Sociology.* 2nd ed. Englewood Cliffs, N.J.: Prentice Hall, 1992:27–32.

HANEY, CRAIG, W. CURTIS BANKS, AND PHILIP G. ZIMBARDO. "Interpersonal Dynamics in a Simulated Prison." *International Journal of Criminology and Penology.* Vol. 1 (1973):69–97.

HESS, BETH B. "Breaking and Entering the Establishment: Committing Social Change and Confronting the Backlash." *Social Problems.* Vol. 46, No. 1 (February 1999):1–12.

HOEFER, MICHAEL, NANCY RYTINA, AND BRYAN C. BAKER. "Estimates of the Unauthorized Immigrant Population Residing in the United States: January 2010." U.S. Department of Homeland Security, Office of Immigration Statistics. February 2011. [Online] Available at http://www.dhs.gov/xlibrary/ assets/statistics/publications/ois_ill_pe_2010.pdf

LAPCHICK, RICHARD, WITH WAYNE CLARK, DEMETRIUS FRAZIER, AND CHRISTOPHER D. SARPY. "The 2011 Racial and Gender Report Card: National Football League." Orlando: The Institute for Diversity and Ethics in Sport (TIDES), University of Central Florida. September 15, 2011. [Online] Available at http://www.bus.ucf.edu/documents/sport/RGRC_NFL_2011_FINAL.pdf

LAPCHICK, RICHARD, WITH CHRISTINA CLOUD, AARON GEARLDS, TAVIA RECORD, ELIZABETH SCHULZ, JAKE SPIAK AND MATTHEW VINSON. "The 2011 Racial and Gender Report Card: Major League Baseball." Orlando: The Institute for Diversity and Ethics in Sport (TIDES), University of Central Florida. April 21, 2011. [Online] Available at http://web.bus.ucf.edu/documents/sport/2011_MLB_RGRC_FINAL.pdf

LAPCHICK, RICHARD, WITH CHRISTOPHER KAISER, CHRISTINA RUSSELL, AND NATALIE WELCH. "The 2010 Racial and Gender Report Card: National Basketball Association." Orlando: The Institute for Diversity and Ethics in Sport (TIDES), University of Central Florida. [Online] Available June 9, 2010 at http://web.bus.ucf.edu/documents/sport/2010_NBA_RGRC.pdf

MARÍN, GERARDO, AND BARBARA VAN OSS MARÍN. *Research with Hispanic Populations.* Newbury Park, Calif.: Sage, 1991.

MARTIN, JOYCE A., ET AL. "Births: Final Data for 2009." *National Vital Statistics Reports.* Vol. 60, No. 1 [Online] 2011. Available at http://www.cdc.gov/nchs/data/nvsr/nvsr60/nvsr60_01.pdf

MILLS, C. WRIGHT. *The Power Elite.* New York: Oxford University Press, 1956.

MIÑIÑO ARIALDI M., SHERRY L. MURPHY, JIAQUAN XU, AND KENNETH D. KOCHANEK. "Deaths: Final Data for 2008." *National Vital Statistics Reports.* Vol. 59, No. 10 [Online] Available at http://www.cdc.gov/nchs/data/nvsr/nvsr59/nvsr59_10.pdf

NATIONAL CONFERENCE OF STATE LEGISLATURES. "Same Sex Marriage, Civil Unions and Domestic Partnerships." July 2011. [Online] Available at http://www.ncsl.org/issues-research/human-services/same-sex-marriage.aspx

OAKES, JEANNIE. "Classroom Social Relationships: Exploring the Bowles and Gintis Hypothesis." *Sociology of Education.* Vol. 55, No. 4 (October 1982):197–212.

———. *Keeping Track: How High Schools Structure Inequality.* New Haven, Conn.: Yale University Press, 1985.

PERRUCCI, ROBERT. "Inventing Social Justice: SSSP and the Twenty-First Century." *Social Problems.* Vol. 48, No. 2 (May 2001):159–67.

POPULATION REFERENCE BUREAU. "Datafinder." 2011. [Online] Available at http://www.prb.org/DataFinder.aspx

SCHOEN, ROBERT, AND YEN-HSIN ALICE CHENG. "Partner Choice and the Differential Retreat from Marriage." *Journal of Marriage and the Family.* Vol. 68 (2006):1–10.

SCHWARTZ, CHRISTINE R. AND ROBERT D. MARE. "Trends in Educational Assortative Marriage from 1940 to 2003." *Demography.* Vol. 42, Issue 4, (November 2005):621–646.

SMITH, TOM W. "American Sexual Behavior: Trends, Socio-Demographic Differences, and Risk Behavior." Chicago: National Opinion Research Center. March, 2006. [Online] http://publicdata.norc.org:41000/gss/DOCUMENTS/REPORTS/Topical_Reports/TR25.pdf

TOCQUEVILLE, ALEXIS DE. *The Old Regime and the French Revolution.* STUART GILBERT, trans. Garden City, N.Y.: Anchor/Doubleday, 1955; orig. 1856.

U.S. CENSUS BUREAU. "Current Population Survey." September 2011. http://www.census.gov/cps/

U.S. DEPARTMENT OF HOMELAND SECURITY, OFFICE OF IMMIGRATION STATISTICS. *Yearbook of Immigration Statistics 2010.* 2011. [Online] Available at http://www.dhs.gov/files/statistics/publications/yearbook.shtm

UNESCO. *Literacy Fact Sheet 2010.* 2010. [Online] Available at http://www.uis.unesco.org/template/pdf/Literacy/Fact_Sheet_2010_Lit_EN.pdf

UNITED NATIONS DEVELOPMENT PROGRAMME. *Human Development Report 2011.* Statistical Tables. [Online] Available at http://hdr.undp.org/en/statistics/data/

UNITED NATIONS FOOD AND AGRICULTURE ORGANIZATION. "Food Security Statistics." 2011. http://www.fao.org/economic/ess/food-security-statistics/en/

UPTHEGROVE, TANYA R., VINCENT J. ROSCIGNO, AND CAMILLE ZUBRINSKY CHARLES. "Big Money Collegiate Sports: Racial Concentration, Contradictory Pressures, and Academic Performance." *Social Science Quarterly.* Vol. 80, No. 4 (December 1999):718–37.

WEBER, MAX. *The Protestant Ethic and the Spirit of Capitalism.* New York: Scribner, 1958; orig. 1904–05.

WEITZMAN, LENORE J. *The Divorce Revolution: The Unexpected Social and Economic Consequences for Women and Children in America.* New York: Free Press, 1985.

———. "The Economic Consequences of Divorce Are Still Unequal: Comment on Peterson." *American Sociological Review.* Vol. 61, No. 3 (June 1996):537–38.

WELCH, SUSAN, AND LEE SIGELMAN. "Who's Calling the Shots? Women's Coaches in Division I Women's Sports." *Social Science Quarterly.* Vol. 88 (2007, special issue):1415–34.

WHYTE, WILLIAM FOOTE. *Street Corner Society.* 3rd ed. Chicago: University of Chicago Press, 1981; orig. 1943.

WOLFF, EDWARD N. "Recent Trends in Household Wealth in the U.S., Update to 2007: Rising Debt and the Middle Class Squeeze." March 2010. [Online] Available at http://www.levyinstitute.org/publications/?docid=1235

WORLD BANK. "EdStats." [Online] Available at http://data.worldbank.org/data-catalog/ed-stats

WRIGHT, EARL, II. "The Atlanta Sociological Laboratory, 1896–1924: A Historical Account of the First American School of Sociology." *Western Journal of Black Studies.* Vol. 26, No. 3 (2002a):165–74.

———. "Why Black People Tend to Shout! An Earnest Attempt to Explain the Sociological Negation of the Atlanta Sociological Laboratory despite Its Possible Unpleasantness." *Sociological Spectrum.* Vol. 22, No. 3 (2002b):325–61.

ZAKERIA, FAREED. "The Rise of the Rest." *Newsweek.* Vol. 151, No. 19 (May 12, 2008):24–31.

ZIMBARDO, PHILIP G. "Pathology of Imprisonment." *Society.* Vol. 9, No. 1 (April 1972):4–8.

Chapter 2 References

ASANTE, MOLEFI KETE. *Afrocentricity.* Trenton, N.J.: Africa World Press, 1988.

ASTIN, ALEXANDER W., LETICIA OSEGUERA, LINDA J. SAX, AND WILLIAM S. KORN. *The American Freshman: Thirty-Five Year Trends.* Los Angeles: UCLA Higher Education Research Institute, 2002.

BARASH, DAVID P. *The Whisperings Within.* New York: Penguin Books, 1981.

BARONE, MICHAEL. "Cultures Aren't Equal." *U.S. News & World Report.* Vol. 139, No. 6 (August 22, 2005):26.

BAROVICK, HARRIET. "Tongues That Go Out of Style." *Time* (June 10, 2002):22.

BERTEAU, CELESTE. "Disconnected Intimacy: AOL Instant Messenger Use among Kenyon College Students." Senior thesis. Kenyon College, 2005.

BOULDING, ELISE. *The Underside of History.* Boulder, Colo.: Westview Press, 1976.

CARLE, ROBERT. "Islamists in the 'Rainbow' Coalition." *Society.* Vol. 45, No. 2 (March/April 2008):181–90.

CENTRAL INTELLIGENCE AGENCY. *The World Factbook.* 2012 (updated biweekly). [Online] Available at https://www.cia.gov/library/publications/the-world-factbook/index.html

CHAGNON, NAPOLEON A. *Yanomamö: The Fierce People.* 4th ed. Austin, Tex.: Holt, Rinehart and Winston, 1992.

CRYSTAL, DAVID. *The Cambridge Encyclopedia of the English Language.* 3rd ed. Cambridge: Cambridge University Press, 2010.

DARWIN, CHARLES. *On the Origin of Species by Means of Natural Selection, or the Preservation of Favoured Races in the Struggle for Life.* London: Murray, 1859.

DEUTSCHER, GUY. "Does Your Language Shape How You Think?" *New York Times Magazine.* [Online] Available August 26, 2010, at http://www.nytimes.com/2010/08/29/magazine/29language-t.html?_r=1

FATTAH, HASSAN. "A More Diverse Community." *American Demographics.* Vol. 24, No. 7 (July/August 2002):39–43.

FISHER, ELIZABETH. *Woman's Creation: Sexual Evolution and the Shaping of Society.* Garden City, N.Y.: Anchor/Doubleday, 1979.

GARDYN, REBECCA. "Retirement Redefined." *American Demographics.* Vol. 22, No. 11 (November 2000):52–57.

HARRIS, MARVIN. *Cultural Anthropology.* 2nd ed. New York: Harper & Row, 1987.

HAYDEN, THOMAS. "Losing Our Voices." *U.S. News & World Report* (May 26, 2003):42.

HELIN, DAVID W. "When Slogans Go Wrong." *American Demographics.* Vol. 14, No. 2 (February 1992):14.

IBM. Web site by country/region and language. 2011. [Online] Available at http://www.ibm.com/planetwide/select/selector.html

INGLEHART, RONALD ET AL. "World Values Survey." [Online] Available at http://www.worldvaluessurvey.com

INGLEHART, RONALD, AND CHRISTIAN WELZEL. *Modernization, Culture Change, and Democracy.* New York: Cambridge University Press, 2005.

———. "The WVS Cultural Map of the World." 2010. [Online] Available at http://www.worldvaluessurvey.org/wvs/articles/folder_published/article_base_54

INTERNATIONAL TELECOMMUNICATION UNION. "ICT Database." [Online] Available at http://www.itu.int/ITU-D/ict/statistics

KARRFALT, WAYNE. "A Multicultural Mecca." *American Demographics.* Vol. 25, No. 4 (May 2003):54–55.

KAY, PAUL, AND WILLETT KEMPTON. "What Is the Sapir-Whorf Hypothesis?" *American Anthropologist.* Vol. 86, No. 1 (March 1984):65–79.

KOCHANEK, KENNETH D., ET AL. "Deaths: Preliminary Data for 2009." *National Vital Statistics Reports.* Vol. 59, No. 4. Hyattsville, MD: National Center for Health Statistics. March 16, 2011. [Online] http://www.cdc.gov/nchs/data/nvsr/nvsr59/nvsr59_04.pdf

KRAYBILL, DONALD B. *The Riddle of Amish Culture.* Baltimore: Johns Hopkins University Press, 1989.

KRAYBILL, DONALD B., AND MARC A. OLSHAN, eds. *The Amish Struggle with Modernity.* Hanover, N. H.: University Press of New England, 1994.

LEACOCK, ELEANOR. "Women's Status in Egalitarian Societies: Implications for Social Evolution." *Current Anthropology.* Vol. 19, No. 2 (June 1978): 247–75.

LENHART, AMANDA. "Adults, Cell Phones, and Texting." Pew Research Center Publications. [Online] Available September 2, 2010, at http://pewresearch.org/pubs/1716/adults-cell-phones-text-messages

LEWIS, M. PAUL, ed. *Ethnologue: Languages of the World.* 16th ed. Dallas, Tex.: SIL International, 2009.

LINTON, RALPH. "One Hundred Percent American." *American Mercury.* Vol. 40, No. 160 (April 1937a):427–29.

LIPSET, SEYMOUR MARTIN. "Canada and the United States." CHARLES F. DONAN and JOHN H. SIGLER, eds. Englewood Cliffs, N. J.: Prentice Hall, 1985.

MARX, KARL, AND FRIEDRICH ENGELS. *The Marx-Engels Reader.* 2nd ed. ROBERT C. TUCKER, ed. New York: Norton, 1978; orig. 1859.

MORELL, VIRGINIA. "Minds of Their Own: Animals Are Smarter than You Think." *National Geographic.* Vol. 213, No. 3 (March 2008):36–61.

MURDOCK, GEORGE PETER. "The Common Denominator of Cultures." In RALPH LINTON, ed., *The Science of Man in World Crisis.* New York: Columbia University Press, 1945:123–42.

NOLAN, PATRICK, AND GERHARD E. LENSKI. *Human Societies: An Introduction to Macrosociology.* 11th ed. Boulder, Colo.: Paradigm, 2010.

NORC. *General Social Surveys, 1972–2010: Cumulative Codebook.* Chicago: National Opinion Research Center, 2011. [Online] Available at http://www.norc.org/GSS+Website

OGBURN, WILLIAM F. *On Culture and Social Change.* Chicago: University of Chicago Press, 1964.

PARSONS, TALCOTT. *Societies: Evolutionary and Comparative Perspectives.* Englewood Cliffs, N. J.: Prentice Hall, 1966.

PEW RESEARCH CENTER, INTERNET AND AMERICAN LIFE PROJECT. "Americans and Text Messaging" 2011. [Online] Available at http://www.pewinternet.org/Reports/2011/Cell-Phone-Texting-2011/Summary-of-Findings.aspx

PINKER, STEVEN. *The Language Instinct.* New York: Morrow, 1994.

PROENGLISH. "Official English Map: The 50 States at a Glance." 2011. [Online] Available at http://www.proenglish.org/official-english-state-profiles

PRYOR, JOHN H., ET AL. *The American Freshman: National Norms for Fall 2010.* Cooperative Institutional Research Program at the Higher Education Research Institute. Los Angeles: UCLA Higher Education Research Institute, 2011.

RUBIN, JOEL. "E-Mail Too Formal? Try a Text Message." Columbia News Service. March 7, 2003. [Online] Available April 25, 2005, at http://www.jrn.columbia.edu/student-work/cns/2003-03-07/85.asp

SANG-HUN, CHOE. "Net Addresses to Make Use of Non-Latin Scripts." *New York Times.* Available October 31, 2009 at http://www.nytimes.com/2009/10/31/technology/31net.html

SAPIR, EDWARD. *Selected Writings of Edward Sapir in Language, Culture, and Personality.* DAVID G. MANDELBAUM, ed. Berkeley: University of California Press, 1949.

———. "The Status of Linguistics as a Science." *Language.* Vol. 5, No. 4 (1929):207–14.

STATISTICS CANADA. *Canada Year Book.* 2011. [Online] Available at http://www.statcan.gc.ca/pub/11-402-x/index-eng.htm

STEYN, MARK. "Is Canada's Economy a Model for America?" *Imprimis.* Vol. 37, No. 1 (January 2008):1–7.

STUESSY, JOE, AND SCOTT LIPSCOMB. *Rock and Roll: Its History and Stylistic Development.* 6th ed. Upper Saddle River, N. J.: Pearson Prentice Hall, 2008.

SUMNER, WILLIAM GRAHAM. *Folkways.* New York: Dover, 1959; orig. 1906.

U.S. CENSUS BUREAU. "American Community Survey." 2011. [Online] Available at http://www.census.gov/acs/www

———. "Census 2010." 2011. [Online] Available at http://factfinder2.census.gov/faces/nav/jsf/pages/index.xhtml

———. "Current Population Survey." September 2011. [Online] Available at http://www.census.gov/cps

———. *Statistical Abstract of the United States: 2012,* 131st ed. 2011. [Online] Available at http://www.census.gov/statab/www

U.S. DEPARTMENT OF HOMELAND SECURITY, OFFICE OF IMMIGRATION STATISTICS. "Yearbook of Immigration Statistics 2010." 2011. [Online] Available at http://www.dhs.gov/files/statistics/publications/yearbook.shtm

U.S. DEPARTMENT OF LABOR, BUREAU OF LABOR STATISTICS. "Consumer Expenditure Survey, 2010." September 27, 2011. [Online] Available at http://www.bls.gov/cex

U.S. DEPARTMENT OF LABOR, BUREAU OF LABOR STATISTICS. "Labor Force Statistics from the Current Population Survey." 2011, 2012. [Online] Available at http://www.bls.gov/cps/home.htm

UNESCO. Data reported in "Tower of Babel Is Tumbling Down—Slowly." *U.S. News & World Report* (July 2, 2001):9.

WELCH, WILLIAM M. "English language legislation gathers steam across the USA." *U.S. News and World Report .* [Online] Available June 19, 2008 at http://www.usatoday.com/news/nation/2008-06-18-English-laws_N.htm

WHORF, BENJAMIN LEE. "The Relation of Habitual Thought and Behavior to Language." In *Language, Thought, and Reality.* Cambridge, Mass.: Technology Press of MIT; New York: Wiley, 1956:134–59; orig. 1941.

WILLIAMS, ROBIN M., JR. *American Society: A Sociological Interpretation.* 3rd ed. New York: Knopf, 1970.

Chapter 3 References

ADAMS, PATRICIA F., MICHAEL E. MARTINEZ, AND JACKLINE L. VICKERIE. "Summary Health Statistics for the U.S. Population: National Health Interview Survey, 2009." Vital Health Stat 10(248) Hyattsville, MD: National Center for Health Statistics. December, 2010. [Online] Available at http://www.cdc.gov/nchs/data/series/sr_10/sr10_248.pdf

AMERICAN PSYCHOLOGICAL ASSOCIATION. *Violence and Youth: Psychology's Response.* Washington, D.C.: American Psychological Association, 1993.

BEGLEY, SHARON. "Gray Matters." *Newsweek* (March 7, 1995):48–54.

BERGER, PETER L. *Invitation to Sociology.* New York: Anchor Books, 1963.

BEST, RAPHAELA. *We've All Got Scars: What Boys and Girls Learn in Elementary School.* Bloomington: Indiana University Press, 1983.

CENTERS FOR DISEASE CONTROL AND PREVENTION, NATIONAL CENTER FOR HEALTH STATISTICS. "Health Data Interactive." [Online] Available at http://www.cdc.gov/nchs/hdi.htm

CHODOROW, NANCY. *Femininities, Masculinities, Sexualities: Freud and Beyond.* Lexington: University of Kentucky Press, 1994.

COOLEY, CHARLES HORTON. *Human Nature and the Social Order.* New York: Schocken Books, 1964; orig. 1902.

DAVIES, MARK, AND DENISE B. KANDEL. "Parental and Peer Influences on Adolescents' Educational Plans: Some Further Evidence." *American Journal of Sociology.* Vol. 87, No. 2 (September 1981):363–87.

DAVIS, KINGSLEY. "Extreme Social Isolation of a Child." *American Journal of Sociology.* Vol. 45, No. 4 (January 1940):554–65.

———. "Final Note on a Case of Extreme Isolation." *American Journal of Sociology.* Vol. 52, No. 5 (March 1947):432–37.

DENNISTON, MAXINE M., MONICA H. SWAHN, MARCI FELDMAN HERTZ, AND LISA M. ROMERO. "Associations between Electronic Media Use and Involvement in Violence, Alcohol and Drug Use among United States High School Students." *Western Journal of Emergency Medicine.* Vol. 12, No. 3 (July 2011):310–315. [Online] Available at http://www.ncbi.nlm.nih.gov/pmc/articles/PMC3117607/?tool=pubmed

DONOVAN, VIRGINIA K., AND RONNIE LITTENBERG. "Psychology of Women: Feminist Therapy." In BARBARA HABER, ed., *The Women's Annual, 1981: The Year in Review.* Boston: Hall, 1982:211–35.

EDITOR AND PUBLISHER. "Ongoing Tally of Newspaper Endorsements." October 2008. [Online] Available at http://www.editorandpublisher.com/eandp/news/article_display.jsp?vnu_content_id=1003875230

ELLISON, CHRISTOPHER G., JOHN P. BARTKOWSKI, AND MICHELLE L. SEGAL. "Do Conservative Protestant Parents Spank More Often? Further Evidence from the National

Survey of Families and Households." *Social Science Quarterly*. Vol. 77, No. 3 (September 1996):663–73.

ERIKSON, ERIK H. *Childhood and Society*. New York: Norton, 1963; orig. 1950.

FEDERAL INTERAGENCY FORUM ON AGING-RELATED STATISTICS. "Older Americans 2010: Key Indicators of Well-Being." updated January 2011. [Online] Available at http://www.agingstats.gov/agingstatsdotnet/Main_Site/Data/2010_Documents/Docs/OA_2010.pdf

FELLMAN, BRUCE. "Taking the Measure of Children's TV." *Yale Alumni Magazine* (April 1995):46–51.

FETTO, JOHN. "Me Gusta TV." *American Demographics*. Vol. 24, No. 11 (January 2003):14–15.

GARRISON, MICHELLE M., KIMBERLY LIEKWEG, DIMITRI A. CHRISTAKIS. "Media Use and Child Sleep: The Impact of Content, Timing, and Environment." *Journal of the American Academy of Pediatrics*. (July, 2011):29–35.

GIBBS, NANCY. "What Kids (Really) Need." *Time* (April 30, 2001):48–49.

GILLIGAN, CAROL. *In a Different Voice: Psychological Theory and Women's Development*. Cambridge, Mass.: Harvard University Press, 1982.

————. *Making Connections: The Relational Worlds of Adolescent Girls at Emma Willard School*. Cambridge, Mass.: Harvard University Press, 1990.

GOFFMAN, ERVING. *Asylums: Essays on the Social Situation of Mental Patients and Other Inmates*. Garden City, N.Y.: Anchor Books, 1961.

GOLDBERG, BERNARD. *Bias: A CBS Insider Exposes How the Media Distort the News*. Washington, D.C.: Regnery, 2002.

GOLDSMITH, H. H. "Genetic Influences on Personality from Infancy." *Child Development*. Vol. 54, No. 2 (April 1983):331–35.

GORMAN, CHRISTINE. "Stressed-Out Kids." *Time* (December 25, 2000):168.

HARLOW, HARRY F., AND MARGARET KUENNE HARLOW. "Social Deprivation in Monkeys." *Scientific American* (November 1962):137–46.

HOFFMAN, JAN. "Masculinity in a Spray Can." *New York Times*. January 29, 2010. [Online] Available at http://www.nytimes.com/2010/01/31/fashion/31smell.html

HUMAN RIGHTS WATCH. "Children's Rights: Child Labor." 2006. [Online] Available April 9, 2006, at http://www.hrw.org/children/labor.htm

HYMOWITZ, KAY S. "Kids Today Are Growing Up Way Too Fast." *Wall Street Journal* (October 28, 1998):A22.

INTERNATIONAL LABOUR ORGANIZATION, INTERNATIONAL PROGRAMME ON THE ELIMINATION OF CHILD LABOUR (ILO-IPEC). "Children in Hazardous Work - What we Know, What we Need to Do." 2011. [Online] Available at http://www.ilo.org/ipecinfo/product/viewProduct.do?productId=17035

JORDAN, ELLEN, AND ANGELA COWAN. "Warrior Narratives in the Kindergarten Classroom: Renegotiating the Social Contract?" *Gender and Society*. Vol. 9, No. 6 (December 1995):727–43.

KAO, GRACE. "Group Images and Possible Selves among Adolescents: Linking Stereotypes to Expectations by Race and Ethnicity."*Sociological Forum*. Vol. 15, No. 3 (September 2000):407–30.

KOCHANEK, KENNETH D., ET AL. "Deaths: Preliminary Data for 2009." *National Vital Statistics Reports*. Vol. 59, No. 4. Hyattsville, MD: National Center for Health Statistics. March 16, 2011. [Online] http://www.cdc.gov/nchs/data/nvsr/nvsr59/nvsr59_04.pdf

KOHLBERG, LAWRENCE. *The Psychology of Moral Development: The Nature and Validity of Moral Stages*. New York: Harper & Row, 1981.

————, and CAROL GILLIGAN. "The Adolescent as Philosopher:The Discovery of Self in a Postconventional World." *Daedalus*. Vol. 100, No. 4 (Fall 1971):1051–86.

KOHN, MELVIN L. *Class and Conformity: A Study in Values*. 2nd ed. Homewood, Ill.: Dorsey Press, 1977.

KONIGSBERG, RUTH DAVIS. "New Ways to Think About Grief." *Time* [Online] Available January 29, 2011, at http://www.time.com/time/magazine/article/0,9171,2042372-2,00.html

KÜBLER-ROSS, ELISABETH. *On Death and Dying*. New York: Macmillan, 1969.

LAREAU, ANNETTE. "Invisible Inequality: Social Class and Childrearing in Black Families and White Families." *American Sociological Review*. Vol. 67, No. 5 (October 2002):747–76.

LAROSSA, RALPH, AND DONALD C. REITZES. "Two? Two and One-Half? Thirty Months? Chronometrical Childhood in Early Twentieth-Century America." *Sociological Forum*. Vol. 166, No. 3 (September 2001):385–407.

LICHTER, S.ROBERT, AND DANIEL R. AMUNDSON. "Distorted Reality: Hispanic Characters in TV Entertainment." In CLARA E. RODRIGUEZ, ed., *Latin Looks: Images of Latinas and Latinos in the U.S. Media*. Boulder, Colo.: Westview Press, 1997:57–79.

MEAD, GEORGE HERBERT. *Mind, Self, and Society*. CHARLES W. MORRIS, ed. Chicago: University of Chicago Press, 1962; orig. 1934.

MELTZER, BERNARD N. "Mead's Social Psychology." In JEROME G. MANIS and BERNARD N. MELTZER, eds., *Symbolic Interaction: A Reader in Social Psychology*. 3rd ed. Needham Heights, Mass.: Allyn & Bacon, 1978.

METZ, MICHAEL E., AND MICHAEL H. MINER. "Psychosexual and Psychosocial Aspects of Male Aging and Sexual Health." *Canadian Journal of Human Sexuality*. Vol. 7, No. 3 (Summer 1998):245–60.

NIELSEN MEDIA RESEARCH. "State of the Media 2010." 2011. [Online] Available at http://blog.nielsen.com/nielsenwire/wp-content/uploads/2011/01/nielsen-media-fact-sheet-jan-11.pdf

NORC. *General Social Surveys, 1972–2010: Cumulative Codebook*. Chicago: National Opinion Research Center, 2011. http://www.norc.org/GSS+ Website

PEW RESEARCH CENTER FOR THE PEOPLE & THE PRESS. "Press Widely Criticized, But Trusted More than Other Information Sources: Views of the News Media: 1985–2011." September 22, 2011. [Online] Available at http://www.people-press.org/2011/09/22/press-widely-criticized-but-trusted-more-than-other-institutions/

RIDEOUT, VICTORIA. "Parents, Children & Media, a Kaiser Family Foundation Survey." June 2007. [Online] Available at http://www.kff.org/entmedia/upload/7638.pdf

————, ULLA G. FOEHR, AND DONALD F. ROBERTS. "Generation M2: Media in the Lives of 8- to 18-Year-Olds." Kaiser Family Foundation. January 2010. [Online] Available at http://www.kff.org/entmedia/8010.cfm

ROBINSON, THOMAS N., ET AL. "Effects of Reducing Children's Television and Video Game Use on Aggressive Behavior." *Archives of Pediatrics and Adolescent Medicine*. Vol. 155, No. 1 (January 2001):17–23.

ROTHMAN, STANLEY, STEPHEN POWERS, AND DAVID ROTHMAN. "Feminism in Films." *Society*. Vol. 30, No. 3 (March/April 1993):66–72.

SHUTE, NANCY. "TV Watching Is Bad for Babies' Brains." *U.S. News & World Report Online*. December 9, 2010. [Online] Available at http://health.yahoo.net/articles/parenting/tv-watching-bad-babies-brains

SMITH, TOM W. "Are We Grown Up Yet? U.S. Study Says Not 'til 26." [Online] Available May 23, 2003, at http://news.yahoo.com

SPENCER STUART EXECUTIVE SEARCH FIRM. "Leading CEOs: A Statistical Snapshot of S&P 500 Leaders." December 2008. [Online] Available at http://www.spencerstuart.com/research/articles/975/

TAYLOR, PAUL AND WENDY WANG. "The Fading Glory of the Television and Telephone." Pew Research Center, 2010. [Online] Available at http://www.pewsocialtrends.org/2010/08/19/the-fading-glory-of-the-television-and-telephone/

THRUPKAEW, NOY. "No Minor Issue." *National Geographic*. Vol. 218, No. 5 (November 2010):18.

TREAS, JUDITH. "Older Americans in the 1990s and Beyond." *Population Bulletin*. Vol. 50, No. 2 (May 1995).

TVB. *TV Basics*. December 2011. [Online] Available at http://www.tvb.org/media/file/TV_Basics.pdf

U.S. CENSUS BUREAU. "American Community Survey." 2011. [Online] Available at http://www.census.gov/acs/www

————. "Census 2010." 2011. [Online] Available at http://factfinder2.census.gov/faces/nav/jsf/pages/index.xhtml

————. "Current Population Survey." September 2011. [Online] Available at http://www.census.gov/cps———. "Population Estimates." 2011. [Online] Available at http://www.census.gov/popest/data/index.html

————. "Population Projections." 2008. [Online] Available at http://www.census.gov/population/www/projections/summarytables.html

————. *Statistical Abstract of the United States: 2012, 131st Edition*. 2011. [Online] Available at http://www.census.gov/statab/www

U.S. DEPARTMENT OF HEALTH AND HUMAN SERVICES, SUBSTANCE ABUSE AND MENTAL HEALTH SERVICES ADMINISTRATION (SAMHSA). "Results from the 2010 National Survey on Drug Use and Health." [Online] 2011. Available at http://www.samhsa.gov/data/NSDUH/2k10NSDUH/tabs/TOC.htm

U.S. DEPARTMENT OF JUSTICE, BUREAU OF JUSTICE STATISTICS. "Corrections Statistics." 2011. [Online] Available at http://bjs.ojp.usdoj.gov/index.cfm?ty=tp&tid=1

U.S. DEPARTMENT OF LABOR. Bureau of International Labor Affairs. "Child Labor, Forced Labor and Human Trafficking. 2011. http://www.dol.gov/ilab/media/factsheets/

U.S. DEPARTMENT OF LABOR, BUREAU OF LABOR STATISTICS. "American Time Use Survey." 2011. [Online] Available at http://www.bls.gov/news.release/atus.t01.htm

UNICEF. "State of the World's Children, 2011." 2011. [Online] Available at http://www.unicef.org/sowc2011/fullreport.php

WEITZMAN, LENORE J. *The Divorce Revolution: The Unexpected Social and Economic Consequences for Women and Children in America*. New York: Free Press, 1985.

————. "The Economic Consequences of Divorce Are Still Unequal: Comment on Peterson." *American Sociological Review*. Vol. 61, No. 3 (June 1996):537–38.

WORLD BANK. "Information and Communication (ICT) Tables." [Online] Available November, 2011 at http://data.worldbank.org/data-catalog/ICT-table

Chapter 4 References

BAKALAR, NICHOLAS. "Reactions: Go On, Laugh Your Heart Out." *New York Times* (March 8, 2005). [Online] Available March 11, 2005, at http://www.nytimes.com/2005/03/08/health/08reac.html

BAKER, PATRICIA S., WILLIAM C. YOELS, JEFFREY M. CLAIR, AND RICHARD M. ALLMAN. "Laughter in the Triadic Geriatric Encounters: A Transcript-Based Analysis." In REBECCA J. ERIKSON AND BEVERLY CUTHBERTSON-JOHNSON, eds., *Social Perspectives on Emotion*. Vol. 4. Greenwich, Conn.: JAI Press, 1997:179–207.

BENOKRAITIS, NIJOLE, AND JOE R. FEAGIN. *Modern Sexism: Blatant, Subtle, and Overt Discrimination*. 2nd ed. Englewood Cliffs, N.J.: Prentice Hall, 1995.

DAVIES, CHRISTIE. *Ethnic Humor around the World: A Comparative Analysis*. Bloomington: Indiana University Press, 1990.

EBAUGH, HELEN ROSE FUCHS. *Becoming an Ex: The Process of Role Exit*. Chicago: University of Chicago Press, 1988.

EKMAN, PAUL. "Biological and Cultural Contributions to Body and Facial Movements in the Expression of Emotions." In A. RORTY, ed., *Explaining Emotions*. Berkeley: University of California Press, 1980a:73–101.

————. *Face of Man: Universal Expression in a New Guinea Village*. New York: Garland Press, 1980b.

————. *The Expression of Emotions in Man and Animals*. New York: Oxford University Press, 1998.

————. *Emotions Revealed: Recognizing Faces and Feelings to Improve Communication and Emotional Life*. New York: Tribune Books, 2003.

FARRIS, COREEN, TERESA A. TREAT, RICHARD J. VIKEN, AND RICHARD M. MCFALL. "Perceptual Mechanisms That Characterize Gender Differences in Decoding Women's Sexual Intent." *Psychological Science*. Vol. 19, No. 4 (2008):348–54.

FLAHERTY, MICHAEL G. "A Formal Approach to the Study of Amusement in Social Interaction." *Studies in Symbolic Interaction.* Vol. 5. New York: JAI Press, 1984:71–82.

———. "Two Conceptions of the Social Situation: Some Implications of Humor." *Sociological Quarterly.* Vol. 31, No. 1 (Spring 1990).

GARFINKEL, HAROLD. *Studies in Ethnomethodology.* Cambridge, Mass.: Polity Press, 1967.

GOFFMAN, ERVING. *The Presentation of Self in Everyday Life.* Garden City, N.Y.: Anchor Books, 1959.

———. *Interactional Ritual: Essays on Face to Face Behavior.* Garden City, N.Y.: Anchor Books, 1967.

GOODING, GRETCHEN E., AND ROSE M. KREIDER. "Women's Marital Naming Choices in a Nationally Representative Sample." *Journal of Family Issues.* Vol. 31, No. 5 (May 2010):681–701. [Online] Available at http://0journals.ohiolink.edu.dewey2.library. denison.edu/ejc/issue.cgi?issn=019251 3x&issue=v31i0005

HAMILTON, LAURA, CLAUDIA GEIST, AND BRIAN POWELL. "Marital Name Change as a Window into Gender Attitudes." *Gender & Society.* Vol. 25, No. 2 (2011):145–75.

HENLEY, NANCY, MYKOL HAMILTON, AND BARRIE THORNE. "Womanspeak and Manspeak: Sex Differences in Communication, Verbal and Nonverbal." In JOHN J. MACIONIS and NIJOLE V. BENOKRAITIS, eds., *Seeing Ourselves: Classic, Contemporary, and Cross-Cultural Readings in Sociology.* 2nd ed. Englewood Cliffs, N.J.: Prentice Hall, 1992:10–15.

HOCHSCHILD, ARLIE RUSSELL. "Emotion Work, Feeling Rules, and Social Structure." *American Journal of Sociology.* Vol. 85, No. 3 (November 1979):551–75.

———. *The Managed Heart.* Berkeley: University of California Press, 1983.

JOHNSON, CATHRYN. "Gender, Legitimate Authority, and Leader-Subordinate Conversations." *American Sociological Review.* Vol. 59, No. 1 (February 1994):122–35.

LINTON, RALPH. *The Study of Man.* New York: Appleton-Century, 1937b.

MACIONIS, JOHN J. "A Sociological Analysis of Humor." Presentation to the Texas Junior College Teachers Association, Houston, 1987.

MERTON, ROBERT K. *Social Theory and Social Structure.* New York: Free Press, 1968.

ORLANSKY, MICHAEL D., AND WILLIAM L. HEWARD. *Voices: Interviews with Handicapped People.* Columbus, Ohio: Merrill, 1981.

PIRANDELLO, LUIGI. "The Pleasure of Honesty" (1917). In *To Clothe the Naked and Two Other Plays.* New York: Dutton, 1962:143–98.

POWELL, CHRIS, AND GEORGE E. C. PATON, eds. *Humor in Society: Resistance and Control.* New York: St. Martin's Press, 1988.

PRIMEGGIA, SALVATORE, AND JOSEPH A. VARACALLI. "Southern Italian Comedy: Old to New World." In JOSEPH V. SCELSA, SALVATORE J. LA GUMINA, and LYDIO TOMASI, eds., *Italian Americans in Transition.* New York: American Italian Historical Association, 1990:241–52.

SANSOM, WILLIAM. *A Contest of Ladies.* London: Hogarth, 1956.

SHIVELY, JOELLEN. "Cowboys and Indians: Perceptions of Western Films among American Indians and Anglos." *American Sociological Review.* Vol. 57, No. 6 (December 1992):725–34.

SIMMEL, GEORG. *The Sociology of Georg Simmel.* KURT WOLFF, ed. New York: Free Press, 1950; orig. 1902.

SMITH-LOVIN, LYNN, AND CHARLES BRODY. "Interruptions in Group Discussions: The Effects of Gender and Group Composition." *American Journal of Sociology.* Vol. 54, No. 3 (June 1989):424–35.

SPEIER, HANS. "Wit and Politics: An Essay on Laughter and Power." ROBERT JACKALL, ed. and trans. *American Journal of Sociology.* Vol. 103, No. 5 (March 1998):1352–1401.

SVEBAK, SVEN. Cited in MARILYN ELIAS, "Study Links Sense of Humor, Survival." [Online] Available March 14, 2007, at http://www.usatoday.com

TANNEN, DEBORAH. *You Just Don't Understand: Women and Men in Conversation.* New York: Morrow, 1990.

THOMAS, PIRI. *Down These Mean Streets.* New York: Signet, 1967.

THOMAS, W. I. "The Relation of Research to the Social Process." In MORRIS JANOWITZ, ed., *W. I. Thomas on Social Organization and Social Personality.* Chicago: University of Chicago Press, 1966:289–305; orig. 1931.

THOMAS, W. I., AND DOROTHY SWAINE THOMAS. *The Child in America: Behavior Problems and Programs.* New York: Knopf, 1928.

THORNE, BARRIE, CHERIS KRAMARAE, AND NANCY HENLEY, eds. *Language, Gender, and Society.* Rowley, Mass.: Newbury House, 1983.

TURNER, JONATHAN. *On the Origins of Human Emotions: A Sociological Inquiry into the Evolution of Human Emotions.* Stanford, Calif.: Stanford University Press, 2000.

U.S. DEPARTMENT OF LABOR, BUREAU OF LABOR STATISTICS. "Highlights of Women's Earnings in 2010." 2011. [Online] Available at http://www.bls.gov/cps/cpswom2010. pdf

UNITED NATIONS. *The World's Women 2010: Trends and Statistics.* 2010. [Online] Available at http://unstats.un.org/unsd/demographic/products/Worldswomen/ WW2010pub.htm

YOELS, WILLIAM C., AND JEFFREY MICHAEL CLAIR. "Laughter in the Clinic: Humor in Social Organization." *Symbolic Interaction.* Vol. 18, No. 1 (1995):39–58.

Chapter 5 References

ALLEN, THOMAS B., AND CHARLES O. HYMAN. *We Americans: Celebrating a Nation, Its People, and Its Past.* Washington, D.C.: National Geographic Society, 1999.

"Army Apologizes over Salutation." *USA Today* (January 8, 2009):6A.

ASCH, SOLOMON. *Social Psychology.* Englewood Cliffs, N.J.: Prentice Hall, 1952.

BARON, JAMES N., MICHAEL T. HANNAN, and M. DIANE BURTON. "Building the Iron Cage: Determinants of Managerial Intensity in the Early Years of Organizations." *American Sociological Review.* Vol. 64, No. 4 (August 1999):527–47.

BBC NEWS. "Toyota Beats GM to End 2010 as World's Biggest Carmaker." [Online] Available January 24, 2011, at http://www.bbc.co.uk/news/business-12264396

BEDARD, PAUL. "Washington Whispers." *U.S. News & World Report* (March 25, 2002):2.

BLAU, PETER M. *Inequality and Heterogeneity: A Primitive Theory of Social Structure.* New York: Free Press, 1977.

BLAU, PETER M., TERRY C. BLUM, AND JOSEPH E. SCHWARTZ. "Heterogeneity and Intermarriage." *American Sociological Review.* Vol. 47, No. 1 (February 1982):45–62.

BOBO, LAWRENCE, AND VINCENT L. HUTCHINGS. "Perceptions of Racial Group Competition: Extending Blumer's Theory of Group Position to a Multiracial Social Context." *American Sociological Review.* Vol. 61, No. 6 (December 1996):951–72.

BROOKS, DAVID. *Bobos in Paradise: The New Upper Class and How They Got There.* New York: Simon & Schuster, 2000.

CASTILLA, EMILIO J. "Gender, Race, and Meritocracy in Organizational Careers." *American Journal of Sociology.* Vol. 113, No. 6 (May 2008):1479–1526.

CENTER FOR RESPONSIVE POLITICS. "111th Congress Casualty List." 2011. [Online] Available at http://www.opensecrets.org/bigpicture/casualties.php?cycle=2010

CTIA (THE WIRELESS ASSOCIATION). "Wireless Quick Facts." June, 2011. [Online] Available at http://www.ctia.org/media/industry_info/index.cfm/AID/10323

ETZIONI, AMITAI. *A Comparative Analysis of Complex Organization: On Power, Involvement, and Their Correlates.* Revised and enlarged ed. New York: Free Press, 1975.

FCC (FEDERAL COMMUNICATIONS COMMISSION). "Statistical Trends in Telephony." 2011. [Online] Available at http://www.fcc.gov/wcb/iatd/trends.html

FERNANDEZ, ROBERTO M., AND NANCY WEINBERG. "Sifting and Sorting: Personal Contacts and Hiring in a Retail Bank." *American Sociological Review.* Vol. 62, No. 6 (December 1997):883–902.

GREEN, GARY PAUL, LEANN M. TIGGES, AND DANIEL DIAZ. "Racial and Ethnic Differences in Job-Search Strategies in Atlanta, Boston, and Los Angeles." *Social Science Quarterly.* Vol. 80, No. 2 (June 1999):263–90.

GWYNNE, S. C., AND JOHN F. DICKERSON. "Lost in the E-Mail." *Time* (April 21, 1997):88–90.

HAGAN, JACQUELINE MARIA. "Social Networks, Gender, and Immigrant Incorporation: Resources and Restraints." *American Sociological Review.* Vol. 63, No. 1 (February 1998):55–67.

HALBERSTAM, DAVID. *The Reckoning.* New York: Avon Books, 1986.

HANSON, VICTOR DAVIS. Comment accessed at Townhall.com, June 23, 2011.

HELGESEN, SALLY. *The Female Advantage: Women's Ways of Leadership.* New York: Doubleday, 1990.

HEYMANN, PHILIP B. "Civil Liberties and Human Rights in the Aftermath of September 11." *Harvard Journal of Law and Public Policy.* Vol. 25, No. 2 (Spring 2002):441–57.

HUI, SYLVIA. "Bloomberg Takes Cues from London's Security-Obsessed Security." *The Huffington Post.* [Online] Available May 11, 2010, at http://www.huffingtonpost. com/2010/05/11/bloomberg-taking-cues-fro_n_571359.html

IDE, THOMAS R., AND ARTHUR J. CORDELL. "Automating Work." *Society.* Vol. 31, No. 6 (September/October 1994):65–71.

INTERNATIONAL TELECOMMUNICATION UNION. "ICT Statistics Database." 2011. [Online] Available at http://www.itu.int/ITU-D/ICTEYE/Indicators/Indicators.aspxJANIS, IRVING L. *Victims of Groupthink.* Boston: Houghton Mifflin, 1972.

———. *Crucial Decisions: Leadership in Policymaking and Crisis Management.* New York: Free Press, 1989.

KAMINER, WENDY. "Volunteers: Who Knows What's in It for Them?" *Ms.* (December 1984):93–96, 126–28.

KANTER, ROSABETH MOSS. *Men and Women of the Corporation.* New York: Basic Books, 1977.

KANTER, ROSABETH MOSS, AND BARRY A. STEIN. "The Gender Pioneers: Women in an Industrial Sales Force." In ROSABETH MOSS KANTER and BARRY A. STEIN, eds., *Life in Organizations.* New York: Basic Books, 1979:134–60.

KLEIN, DANIEL B. "Embarrassed as a Non-Left Professor." *Society.* Vol. 47, No. 5 (September/October 2010):377–78.

LEWIS, LIONEL S. "Madoff's Victims and Their Day in Court." *Society.* Vol. 45, No. 5 (September/October 2010):439–50.

LIN, NAN, KAREN COOK, and RONALD S. BURT, eds. *Social Capital: Theory and Research.* Hawthorne, N.Y.: Aldine de Gruyter, 2001.

MADDOX, SETMA. "Organizational Culture and Leadership Style: Factors Affecting Self-Managed Work Team Performance." Paper presented at the annual meeting of the Southwest Social Science Association, Dallas, February 1994.

MARKOFF, JOHN. "Remember Big Brother? Now He's a Company Man." *New York Times* (March 31, 1991):7.

MCDONALD'S CORPORATION. "Annual Report." 2011. [Online] Available at http://www. aboutmcdonalds.com/mcd/investors/financial_highlights.html

MERTON, ROBERT K. *Social Theory and Social Structure.* New York: Free Press, 1968.

MICHELS, ROBERT. *Political Parties.* Glencoe, Ill.: Free Press, 1949; orig. 1911.

MILGRAM, STANLEY. "Behavioral Study of Obedience." *Journal of Abnormal and Social Psychology.* Vol. 67, No. 4 (1963):371–78.

———. "Group Pressure and Action against a Person." *Journal of Abnormal and Social Psychology.* Vol. 69, No. 2 (August 1964):137–43.

———. "Some Conditions of Obedience and Disobedience to Authority." *Human Relations.* Vol. 18, No. 1 (February 1965):57–76.

———. "The Small World Problem." *Psychology Today* (May 1967):60–67.

MILLER, ARTHUR G. *The Obedience Experiments: A Case of Controversy in Social Science.* New York: Praeger, 1986.

MOLLENHORST, GERALD. "Networks in Contexts: How Meeting Opportunities Affect Personal Relationships." Ph.D. Dissertation. University of Utrecht, 2009.

O'HARROW, ROBERT, JR. "ID Theft Scam Hits D.C. Area Residents." [Online] Available February 21, 2005, at http://news.yahoo.com

"Online Privacy: It's Time for Rules in Wonderland." *Business Week* (March 20, 2000):82–96.

OUCHI, WILLIAM. *Theory Z: How American Business Can Meet the Japanese Challenge.* Reading, Mass.: Addison-Wesley, 1981.

PETERSEN, TROND, ISHAK SAPORTA, AND MARC-DAVID L. SEIDEL. "Offering a Job: Meritocracy and Social Networks." *American Journal of Sociology.* Vol. 106, No. 3 (November 2000):763–816.

PHILADELPHIA, DESA. "Tastier, Plusher—and Fast." *Time* (September 30, 2002):57.

PINCHOT, GIFFORD, AND ELIZABETH PINCHOT. *The End of Bureaucracy and the Rise of the Intelligent Organization.* San Francisco: Berrett-Koehler, 1993.

"PLACES WHERE THE SYSTEM BROKE DOWN." *Time* (September 19, 2005):34–41.

PODOLNY, JOEL M., AND JAMES N. BARON. "Resources and Relationships: Social Networks and Mobility in the Workplace." *American Sociological Review.* Vol. 62, No. 5 (October 1997):673–93.

PRYOR, JOHN H., ET AL. *The American Freshman: National Norms Fall 2010.* Los Angeles: Cooperative Institutional Research Program at the Higher Education Research Institute at UCLA, 2011.

RESKIN, BARBARA F., AND DEBRA BRANCH MCBRIER. "Why Not Ascription? Organizations' Employment of Male and Female Managers."*American Sociological Review.* Vol. 65, No. 2 (April 2000):210–33.

RIDGEWAY, CECILIA L. *The Dynamics of Small Groups.* New York: St. Martin's Press, 1983.

RITZER, GEORGE. *The McDonaldization of Society: An Investigation into the Changing Character of Contemporary Social Life.* Thousand Oaks, Calif.: Pine Forge Press, 1993.

SAPORITO, BILL. "Power Steering: How Chrysler's Italian Boss Drives an American Auto Revival." Time. Vol. 178, No. 24. (December 19, 2011):36–41.SCHLOSSER, ERIC. *Fast-Food Nation: The Dark Side of the All-American Meal.* New York: Perennial, 2002.

SHIPLEY, JOSEPH T. *Dictionary of Word Origins.* Totowa, N.J.: Rowman & Allanheld, 1985.

SIMMEL, GEORG. *The Sociology of Georg Simmel.* KURT WOLFF, ed. New York: Free Press, 1950; orig. 1902.

SOUTH, SCOTT J., AND STEVEN F. MESSNER. "Structural Determinants of Intergroup Association: Interracial Marriage and Crime."*American Journal of Sociology.* Vol. 91, No. 6 (May 1986):1409–30.

STEIN, JOEL. "Your Data, Yourself." *Time.* Vol. 177, No. 11 (March 21, 2011):40–46.

STOUFFER, SAMUEL A., ET AL. *The American Soldier: Adjustment during Army Life.* Princeton, N.J.: Princeton University Press, 1949.

SULLIVAN, BARBARA. "McDonald's Sees India as Golden Opportunity." *Chicago Tribune* (April 5, 1995):B1.

TAJFEL, HENRI. "Social Psychology of Intergroup Relations." *Annual Review of Psychology.* Palo Alto, Calif.: Annual Reviews, 1982:1–39.

TANNEN, DEBORAH. *Talking from 9 to 5: How Women's and Men's Conversational Styles Affect Who Gets Heard, Who Gets Credit, and What Gets Done at Work.* New York: Morrow, 1994.

TAYLOR, FREDERICK WINSLOW. *The Principles of Scientific Management.* New York. Harper Bros., 1911.

TAYLOR, PAUL, RICH MORIN, D'VERA COHN, APRIL CLARK, WENDY WANG. "Men or Women: Who's the Better Leader?" Pew Research Center. August 25, 2008. [Online] Available at ttp://pewsocialtrends.org/assets/pdf/gender-leadership.pdf

TINGWALL, ERIC. "Auto Insurance Gets Cheaper but Potentially More Invasive." *Automobile* (December 2008):74.

TORRES, LISA, AND MATT L. HUFFMAN. "Social Networks and Job Search Outcomes among Male and Female Professional, Technical, and Managerial Workers." *Sociological Focus.* Vol. 35, No. 1 (February 2002):25–42.

U.S. CENSUS BUREAU. "Population Estimates." 2011. [Online] Available at http://www.census.gov/popest/data/index.html

U.S. EQUAL EMPLOYMENT OPPORTUNITY COMMISSION. "Job Patterns for Minorities and Women in Private Industry (EEO-1)." 2011. [Online] Available at http://www1.eeoc.gov/eeoc/statistics/employment/jobpat-eeo1/20010/index.cfm

WATTS, DUNCAN J. "Networks, Dynamics, and the Small-World Phenomenon." *American Journal of Sociology.* Vol. 105, No. 2 (September 1999):493–527.

WEBER, MAX. *Economy and Society: An Outline of Interpretive Sociology.* GUENTHER ROTH AND CLAUS WITTICH, eds. Berkeley: University of California Press, 1978; orig. 1921.

WERTH, CHRISTOPHER. "To Watch the Watchers." *Newsweek* (October 20, 2008):E4.

WHITE, RALPH, AND RONALD LIPPITT. "Leader Behavior and Member Reaction in Three 'Social Climates.'" In DORWIN CARTWRIGHT AND ALVIN ZANDER, eds., *Group Dynamics.* Evanston, Ill.: Row & Peterson, 1953:586–611.

WILDAVSKY, BEN. "Small World, Isn't It?" *U.S. News & World Report* (April 1, 2002):68.

YEATTS, DALE E. "Creating the High-Performance Self-Managed Work Team: A Review of Theoretical Perspectives." Paper presented at the annual meeting of the Southwest Social Science Association, Dallas, February 1994.

Chapter 6 References

ALAN GUTTMACHER INSTITUTE. "Facts on Induced Abortion in the United States." August 2011. [Online] Available at http://www.guttmacher.org/pubs/fb_induced_abortion.html

——. "U.S. Teenage Pregnancies, Births and Abortions: National and State Trends and Trends by Race and Ethnicity." January 2010. [Online] Available at http://www.guttmacher.org/pubs/USTPtrends.pdf

ASTIN, ALEXANDER W., LETICIA OSEGUERA, LINDA J. SAX, AND WILLIAM S. KORN. *The American Freshman: Thirty-Five Year Trends.* Los Angeles: UCLA Higher Education Research Institute, 2002.

BARTON, BERNADETTE. *Stripped: Inside the Lives of Exotic Dancers.* New York: New York University Press, 2006.

BEARMAN, PETER S., JAMES MOODY, AND KATHERINE STOVEL. "Chains of Affection." *American Journal of Sociology.* Vol. 110, No. 1 (July 2004):44–91.

BENEDICT, RUTH. "Continuities and Discontinuities in Cultural Conditioning." *Psychiatry.* Vol. 1, No. 2 (May 1938):161–67.

BLACKWOOD, EVELYN, AND SASKIA WIERINGA, eds. *Female Desires: Same-Sex Relations and Transgender Practices across Cultures.* New York: Columbia University Press, 1999.

BOYER, DEBRA. "Male Prostitution and Homosexual Identity." *Journal of Homosexuality.* Vol. 17, Nos. 1–2 (1989):151–84.

CDC (CENTERS FOR DISEASE CONTROL AND PREVENTION). "Youth Risk Behavior Survey 2009." Morbidity and Mortality Weekly Report, Vol. 59, No. SS-5. June 2010. [Online] Available at http://www.cdc.gov/HealthyYouth/yrbs/index.htm

——. *Sexually Transmitted Diseases.* Atlanta: U.S. Department of Health and Human Services. 2010. [Online] Available at http://www.cdc.gov/std/stats/default.htm

——. "Teen Dating Violence." 2010. [Online] Available at http://www.cdc.gov/violenceprevention/pdf/TeenDatingViolence_2010-a.pdf

CHANDRA, ANJANI, WILLIAM D. MOSHER, CASEY COPEN, AND CATLAINN SIONEAN. "Sexual Behavior, Sexual Attraction, and Sexual Identity in the United States: Data from the 2006–2008 National Survey of Family Growth." March 3, 2011. [Online] Available at http://www.cdc.gov/nchs/data/nhsr/nhsr036.pdf

COLTON, HELEN. *The Gift of Touch: How Physical Contact Improves Communication, Pleasure, and Health.* New York: Seaview/Putnam, 1983.

CRACY, DAVID. "Psychologists Repudiate Gay-to-Straight Therapy." *Yahoo News.* [Online] Available August 5, 2009, at http://news.yahoo.com/s/ap/20090805/ap_on_re_us/us_psychologists_gays

CROSSETTE, BARBARA. "Female Genital Mutilation by Immigrants Is Becoming Cause for Concern in the U.S." *New York Times International* (December 10, 1995):11.

DARROCH, JACQUELINE, JENNIFER FROST, AND SUSHEELA SINGH. "Teenage Sexual and Reproductive Behavior in Developed Countries: Can More Progress be Made?" The Alan Guttmacher Institute. November, 2001. [Online] Available at http://www.guttmacher.org/pubs/eurosynth_rpt.pdf

DAVIDSON, JULIA O'CONNELL. *Prostitution, Power, and Freedom.* Ann Arbor: University of Michigan Press, 1998.

DAVIS, KINGSLEY. "Sexual Behavior." In ROBERT K. MERTON AND ROBERT NISBET, eds., *Contemporary Social Problems.* 3rd ed. New York: Harcourt Brace Jovanovich, 1971:313–60.

DICKINSON, AMY. "When Dating Is Dangerous." *Time* (August 27, 2001):76.

DWORKIN, ANDREA. *Intercourse.* New York: Free Press, 1987.

ESTES, RICHARD J. "The Commercial Sexual Exploitation of Children in the U.S., Canada, and Mexico." Reported in "Study Explores Sexual Exploitation." [Online] Available September 10, 2001, at http://dailynews.yahoo.com

FORD, CLELLAN S., AND FRANK A. BEACH. *Patterns of Sexual Behavior.* New York: Harper Bros., 1951.

FOUCAULT, MICHEL. *The History of Sexuality: An Introduction.* Vol. 1. ROBERT HURLEY, trans. New York: Vintage, 1990; orig. 1978.

GAGNÉ, PATRICIA, RICHARD TEWKSBURY, AND DEANNA MCGAUGHEY. "Coming Out and Crossing Over: Identity Formation and Proclamation in a Transgender Community." *Gender and Society.* Vol. 11, No. 4 (August 1997):478–508.

GAVE, ELENI N. "In the Indigenous Muxe Culture of Mexico's Oaxaca State, Alternative Notions of Sexuality Are Not Only Accepted, They're Celebrated." *Travel and Leisure* (November 2005). [Online] Available June 15, 2009, at http://travelandleisure.com/articles/stepping-out/page/2/print

GEERTZ, CLIFFORD. "Common Sense as a Cultural System." *Antioch Review.* Vol. 33, No. 1 (Spring 1975):5–26.

GIDDENS, ANTHONY. *The Transformation of Intimacy.* Cambridge: Polity Press, 1992.

GREENBERG, DAVID F. *The Construction of Homosexuality.* Chicago: University of Chicago Press, 1988.

HAMER, DEAN, AND PETER COPELAND. *The Science of Desire: The Search for the Gay Gene and the Biology of Behavior.* New York: Simon & Schuster, 1994.

HUFFMAN, KAREN. *Psychology in Action.* New York: Wiley, 2000.

KAPSTEIN, ETHAN B. "The New Global Slave Trade." *Foreign Affairs* (November/December 2006). [Online] Available at http://www.foreignaffairs.com/articles/62094/ethan-b-kapstein/the-new-global-slave-trade

KINSEY, ALFRED, WARDELL BAXTER POMEROY, AND CLYDE E. MARTIN. *Sexual Behavior in the Human Male.* Philadelphia: Saunders, 1948.

——, AND PAUL H. GEBHARD. *Sexual Behavior in the Human Female.* Philadelphia: Saunders, 1953.

KLUCKHOHN, CLYDE. "As an Anthropologist Views It." In ALBERT DEUTH, ed., *Sex Habits of American Men.* New York: Prentice Hall, 1948.

KRUKS, GABRIEL N. "Gay and Lesbian Homeless/Street Youth: Special Issues and Concerns." *Journal of Adolescent Health.* Special Issue. No. 12 (1991):515–18.

KUNKEL, DALE, ET AL. *Sex on TV4.* Kaiser Family Foundation. 2005. [Online] Available at http://www.kff.org/entmedia/entmedia110905pkg.cfm

LACEY, MARC. "A Distinct Lifestyle: The Muxe of Mexico." *New York Times* (December 7, 2008):4.

LAUMANN, EDWARD O., JOHN H. GAGNON, ROBERT T. MICHAEL, AND STUART MICHAELS. *The Social Organization of Sexuality: Sexual Practices in the United States.* Chicago: University of Chicago Press, 1994.

LELAND, JOHN. "Bisexuality." *Newsweek* (July 17, 1995):44–49.

LeVay, Simon. *The Sexual Brain*. Cambridge, Mass.: MIT Press, 1993.

Mackay, Judith. *The Penguin Atlas of Human Sexual Behavior*. New York: Penguin, 2000.

Marquardt, Elizabeth, and Norval Glenn. *Hooking Up, Hanging Out, and Hoping for Mr. Right*. New York: Institute for American Values, 2001.

Martinez, Gladys, Casey Copen, and Joyce Abma. "Teenagers in the United States: Sexual Activity, Contraceptive Use, and Childbearing, 2006–2010 National Survey of Family Growth." October 2011. [Online] Available at http://www.cdc.gov/nchs/data/series/sr_23/sr23_031.pdf

Miracle, Tina S., Andrew W. Miracle, and Roy F. Baumeister. *Human Sexuality: Meeting Your Basic Needs*. Upper Saddle River, N.J.: Prentice Hall, 2003.

Murdock, George Peter. *Social Structure*. New York: Free Press, 1965; orig. 1949.

Murray, Stephen O., and Will Roscoe, eds. *Boy-Wives and Female-Husbands: Studies of African Homosexualities*. New York: St. Martin's Press, 1998.

National Conference of State Legislatures. "Marriages." 2011. [Online] Available at http://www.ncsl.org/programs/cyf/cousins.htm

———. "Same Sex Marriage, Civil Unions and Domestic Partnerships." 2012. [Online] Available at http://www.ncsl.org/IssuesResearch/HumanServices/SameSexMarriage/tabid/16430/Default.aspx

NORC. *General Social Surveys, 1972–2010: Cumulative Codebook*. Chicago: National Opinion Research Center, 2011. [Online] Available at http://www.norc.org/GSS+Website

Olyslager, Femke, and Lynn Conway. "On the Calculation of the Prevalence of Transsexualism." 2007. [Online] Available at http://ai.eecs.umich.edu/people/conway/TS/Prevalence/Reports/Prevalence%20of%20Transsexualism.pdf. *Peters Atlas of the World*. New York: Harper & Row, 1990.

Oyez Project at IIT Chicago-Kent College of Law. "America's Sex Statutes - Out of the Closet and Onto the Court's Docket." *On the Docket: U.S. Supreme Court News*. March, 2003.

Population Reference Bureau. "Datafinder." 2010, 2011. [Online] Available at http://www.prb.org/DataFinder.aspx.

Pryor, John H., et al. *The American Freshman: National Norms for Fall 2008*. Los Angeles: UCLA Higher Education Research Institute, 2009.

Rand Corporation. "Does Watching Sex on Television Influence Teens' Sexual Activity?" Rand Health Research Brief, 2004. [Online] Available at http://www.rand.org/pubs/research_briefs/RB9068/index1.html

Reece, Michael, et al.. "National Survey of Sexual Health and Behavior (NSSHB)." 2010. [Online] Available at http://www.nationalsexstudy.indiana.edu

Ritter, Karl. "World Takes Notice of Swedish Prostitute Laws." *Independent*. March 17, 2008. [Online] Available at http://www.independent.co.uk/news/world/europe/world-takes-notice-of-swedish-prostitute-laws-796793.html

Rosenberg, Mica. "Mexican Transvestite Fiesta Rocks Indigenous Town." Reuters, November 23, 2008. [Online] Available June 15, 2009, at http://www.reuters.com/article/lifestyleMolt/idUSTRE4AM1PB20081123

Saint James, Margo, and Priscilla Alexander. "What Is COYOTE?" 2004. [Online] Available May 28, 2008, at http://www.coyotela.org/what-is.html

Smith, Tom W. "American Sexual Behavior: Trends, Socio-Demographic Differences, and Risk Behavior." Version 6.0. Chicago: National Opinion Research Center. March, 2006. [Online] Available at http://publicdata.norc.org:41000/gss/DOCUMENTS/REPORTS/Topical_Reports/TR25.pdf

Snyder, Howard N. "Sexual Assault of Young Children as Reported to Law Enforcement: Victim, Incident, and Offender Characteristics." U.S. Department of Justice. 2000. [Online] Available at http://bjs.ojp.usdoj.gov/index.cfm?ty=pbdetail&iid=1147

Steinhauer, Jennifer. "Sex Sells, So Legislator Urges State to Tax It." *New York Times* (May 26, 2008). [Online] Available November 9, 2008, at http://www.nytimes.com/2008/05/26/us/26porn.html?_r=1&scp=4&sq=pornography%2Dindustry&st=cse& oref=slogin

Stephey, M. J. "A Brief History of Celibacy." *Time*. Vol. 173, No. 20. (May 25, 2009):14.

Storms, Michael D. "Theories of Sexual Orientation." *Journal of Personality and Social Psychology*. Vol. 38, No. 5 (May 1980):783–92.

U.S. Department of Justice, Department of Justice Statistics. "Criminal Victimization in the United States—Statistical Tables." September 15, 2011. [Online] Available at http://bjs.ojp.usdoj.gov/index.cfm?ty=pbdetail&iid=2224———, Federal Bureau of Investigation, Criminal Justice Information Services Division. "Crime in the United States 2010." September 2011. [Online] Available at http://www.fbi.gov/about-us/cjis/ucr/crime-in-the-u.s/2010/crime-in-the-u.s.-2010

United Nations. UN World Contraceptive Use 2007. 2008. [Online] Available at http://www.un.org/esa/population/publications/contraceptive2007/contraceptive2007.htm

———. UNAIDS 2010 Progress Reports by Country, "UNGASS Country Progress Report: Thailand (Reporting Period January 2008–December 2009)." 2010. [Online] Available at http://www.unaids.org/en/dataanalysis/monitoringcountryprogress/2010progressreportssubmittedbycountries

Ventura, Stephanie J., Joyce C. Abma, William D. Mosher, and Stanley K. Henshaw. "Estimated Pregnancy Rates by Outcome for the United States, 1990–2005: An update." *National Vital Statistics Reports*, Vol. 58, No. 4 Hyattsville, MD: National Center for Health Statistics. 2009. http://www.cdc.gov/nchs/data/nvsr/nvsr58/nvsr58_04.pdf

Webley, Kayla. "Brief History: Gays in the Military." *Time*. Vol. 175, No. 6. February 15, 2010:19.

Weinberg, George. *Society and the Healthy Homosexual*. Garden City, N.Y.: Anchor Books, 1973.

Weisberg, D.Kelly. *Children of the Night: A Study of Adolescent Prostitution*. Lexington, Mass.: Heath, 1985.

Women's Justice Center. "Sweden's Prostitution Solution: Why Hasn't Anyone Tried This Before?" 2009. [Online] Available at http://www.justicewomen.com/cj_sweden.html

Wonders, Nancy A., and Raymond Michalowski. "Bodies, Borders, and Sex Tourism in a Globalized World: A Tale of Two Cities—Amsterdam and Havana." *Social Problems*. Vol. 48, No. 4 (November 2001):545–71.

Chapter 7 References

Akers, Ronald L., Marvin D. Krohn, Lonn Lanza-Kaduce, and Marcia Radosevich. "Social Learning and Deviant Behavior." *American Sociological Review*. Vol. 44, No. 4 (August 1979):636–55.

Allan, Emilie Andersen, and Darrell J. Steffensmeier. "Youth, Underemployment, and Property Crime: Differential Effects of Job Availability and Job Quality on Juvenile and Young Adult Arrest Rates." *American Sociological Review*. Vol. 54, No. 1 (February 1989):107–23.

American Gaming Association. "2011 State of the States: the AGA Survey of Casino Entertainment." 2011. [Online] Available at http://www.americangaming.org/files/aga/uploads/docs/sos/aga-sos-2011.pdf

———. "Fact Sheet: Types of Gaming by State." 2011. [Online] Available at http://www.americangaming.org/Industry/factsheets/general_info_detail.cfv?id=15

Amnesty International. "The Death Penalty in 2010." 2011. http://www.amnesty.org/en/death-penalty

Anderson, Elijah. "The Code of the Streets." *Atlantic Monthly* (May 1994): 81–94.

———. "The Ideologically Driven Critique." *American Journal of Sociology*. Vol. 197, No. 6 (May 2002):1533–50.

Anti-Defamation League. "State Hate Crimes Statutory Provisions." 2011. [Online] Available at http://www.adl.org/99hatecrime/state_hate_crime_laws.pdf

Antlfinger, Carrie. "Homicides Down in Some Large U.S. Cities." *Yahoo News*. January 3, 2009. [Online] Available January 3, 2009, at http://news.yahoo.com/s/ap/20090103/ap_on_re_us/urban_homicides

BBC. "Sudan 'Trousers Woman' Released." *BBC Mobile News*. [Online] Available September 8, 2009, at http://news.bbc.co.uk/2/hi/8244339.stm

Becker, Howard S. *Outside: Studies in the Sociology of Deviance*. New York: Free Press, 1966.

Belofsky, Nathan. *The Book of Strange and Curious Legal Oddities*. New York: Penguin, 2010.

Blau, Judith R., and Peter M. Blau. "The Cost of Inequality: Metropolitan Structure and Violent Crime." *American Sociological Review*. Vol. 47, No. 1 (February 1982):114–29.

Bono, Agostino. "John Jay Study Reveals the Extent of Abuse Problem." [Online] Available September 13, 2006, at http://www.americancatholic.org/news/clergysexabuse/johnjaycns.asp

Brady Campaign to Prevent Gun Violence. 2011. [Online] Available at http://www.bradycampaign.org

CAP Index (2011). www.capindex.com

Carlson, Norman A. "Corrections in the United States Today: A Balance Has Been Struck." *American Criminal Law Review*. Vol. 13, No. 4 (Spring 1976): 615–47.

Center for International Policy, Colombia Program. "Mancuso's Accounting of the Drug Economy." January 28, 2010. [Online] Available at http://www.cipcol.org/?p=725

Chiricos, Ted, Ranee McEntire, and Marc Gertz. "Perceived Racial and Ethnic Composition of Neighborhood and Perceived Risk of Crime." *Social Problems*. Vol. 48, No. 3 (August 2001):322–40.

Chopra, Anuj. "Iranian Rap Music Bedevils the Authorities." *U.S. News & World Report* (March 24, 2008):33.

Cloud, John. "A Mind Unhinged." *Time*. Vol. 177, No. 3 (January 24, 2011):32–35.

Cloward, Richard A., and Lloyd E. Ohlin. *Delinquency and Opportunity: A Theory of Delinquent Gangs*. New York: Free Press, 1966.

Cohen, Albert K. *Delinquent Boys: The Culture of the Gang*. New York: Free Press, 1971; orig. 1955.

Cole, George F., and Christopher E. Smith. *Criminal Justice in America*. 3rd ed. Belmont, Calif.: Wadsworth, 2002.

Currie, Elliott. *Confronting Crime: An American Challenge*. New York: Pantheon Books, 1985.

Dang, Alain, and Cabrini Vianney. *Living in the Margins: A National Survey of Lesbian, Gay, Bisexual, and Transgender Asian and Pacific Islander Americans*. New York: National Gay and Lesbian Task Force Policy Institute, 2007.

Death Penalty Information Center. 2011 [Online] Available at http://www.deathpenaltyinfo.org/innocence-and-death-penalty#inn-yr-rc

Defina, Robert H., and Thomas M. Arvanites. "The Weak Effect of Imprisonment on Crime, 1971–1998." *Social Science Quarterly*. Vol. 83, No. 3 (September 2002):635–53.

Demuth, Stephen, and Darrell Steffensmeier. "The Impact of Gender and Race-Ethnicity in the Pretrial Release Process." *Social Problems*. Vol. 51, No. 2 (May 2004):222–42.

Derber, Charles. *The Wilding of America: Money, Mayhem, and the New American Dream*. 3rd ed. New York: Worth, 2004.

Donahue, John J., III, and Steven D. Leavitt. Research cited in "New Study Claims Abortion Is Behind Decrease in Crime." *Population Today*. Vol. 28, No. 1 (January 2000):1, 4.

Durkheim, Emile. *The Division of Labor in Society*. New York: Free Press, 1964a; orig. 1893.

———. *The Rules of Sociological Method*. New York: Free Press, 1964b; orig. 1895.

EBOH, CAMILLUS. "Nigerian Woman Loses Appeal against Stoning Death." 2002. [Online] Available August 19, 2002, at http://dailynews.yahoo.com

ELIAS, ROBERT. *The Politics of Victimization: Victims, Victimology, and Human Rights.* New York: Oxford University Press, 1986.

ELLIOT, DELBERT S., AND SUZANNE S. AGETON. "Reconciling Race and Class Differences in Self-Reported and Official Estimates of Delinquency." *American Sociological Review.* Vol. 45, No. 1 (February 1980):95–110.

ERIKSON, KAI T. *Wayward Puritans: A Study in the Sociology of Deviance.* New York: Wiley, 2005b; orig. 1966.

FERGUSON, ANDREW. "How Marijuana Got Mainstreamed." *Time.* Vol. 176, No. 21 (November 22, 2010):30–39.

FRANK, THOMAS. "Coal Mine Deaths Spike Upward." *USA Today* (January 1, 2007). [Online] Available March 4, 2007, at http://www.usatoday.com

GALLUP. "In U.S., 64% Support Death Penalty in Cases of Murder." November 8, 2010. [Online]. Available at http://www.gallup.com/poll/144298/Support-Death-Penalty-Cases-Murder.aspx

———. "Self-Reported Gun Ownership in U.S. is Highest Since 1993." October 26, 2011. [Online] Available at: http://www.gallup.com/poll/150353/Self-Reported-Gun-Ownership-Highest-1993.aspx

———. "U.S. Schools: Whole Lotta Cheatin' Going On." May 11, 2004. [Online] Available November 12, 2008, at http://www.gallup.com/poll/171644/US-Schools-Whole-Lotta-Cheatin-Going.aspx

GARFINKEL, HAROLD. "Conditions of Successful Degradation Ceremonies." *American Journal of Sociology.* Vol. 61, No. 2 (March 1956):420–24.

GLAZE, LAUREN E. AND THOMAS P. BONCZAR. "Probation and Parole in the United States, 2010." U.S. Department of Justice, Bureau of Justice Statistics. November 2011. [Online] Available at http://bjs.ojp.usdoj.gov/content/pub/pdf/ppus10.pdf

GOFFMAN, ERVING. *Stigma: Notes on the Management of Spoiled Identity.* Englewood Cliffs, N.J.: Prentice Hall, 1963.

GOTTFREDSON, MICHAEL R., AND TRAVIS HIRSCHI. "National Crime Control Policies." *Society.* Vol. 32, No. 2 (January/February 1995):30–36.

GOTTSCHALK, MARIE. *The Prison and the Gallows: The Politics of Mass Incarceration in America.* New York: Cambridge University Press, 2006.

GOTTSCHALK, MARIE. "Prisons Here, There, and Everywhere: Mass Incarceration and Brown V. Plata. *Penn Arts & Sciences Magazine.* (Fall/Winter 2011):12–13.

GREENHOUSE, LINDA. "Supreme Court Allows Lethal Injection for Execution." *New York Times* (April 17, 2008). [Online] Available June 15, 2009, at http://www/nytimes.com/2008/04/17/us/16cnd-scotus.html

HARRIES, KEITH D. *Serious Violence: Patterns of Homicide and Assault in America.* Springfield, Ill.: Thomas, 1990.

HARTOCOLLIS, ANEMONA. "Man Is Convicted of Attempted Murder as Hate Crime in Village Rampage." *New York Times* (March 2, 2007):B6.

HERPERTZ, SABINE C., AND HENNING SASS. "Emotional Deficiency and Psychopathy." *Behavioral Sciences and the Law.* Vol. 18, No. 5 (September/October 2000):567–80.

HINGSON, RALPH W. "Magnitude and Prevention of College Drinking and Related Problems." *NIAA Alcohol Research & Health.* Vol. 33. No. 1 & 2. 2010. http://pubs.niaaa.nih.gov/publications/arh40/toc33-1_2.htm

———, TIMOTHY HEEREN, MICHAEL WINTER, AND HENRY WECHSLER. "Magnitude of Alcohol-Related Mortality And Morbidity Among U.S. College Students Ages 18–24: Changes from 1998 to 2001." U.S. Department of Health and Human Services, National Institute on Alcohol Abuse and Alcoholism: 2005. http://www.collegedrinkingprevention.gov/NIAAACollegeMaterials/magandprev.aspx

HIRSCHI, TRAVIS. *Causes of Delinquency.* Berkeley: University of California Press, 1969.

HOPE, TRINA L., HAROLD G. GRASMICK, AND LAURA J. POINTON. "The Family in Gottfredson and Hirschi's General Theory of Crime: Structure, Parenting, and Self-Control." *Sociological Focus.* Vol. 36, No. 4 (November 2003): 291–311.

INCIARDI, JAMES A. *Elements of Criminal Justice.* 2nd ed. New York: Oxford University Press, 2000.

INTERNAL REVENUE SERVICE. "IRS Updates Tax Gap Estimates." February 14, 2006. http://www.irs.gov/newsroom/article/0, , id=154496, 00.html

JEFFERSON, CORD. "Driving Concerns." *National Geographic* (January 2009):33.

JONES, CHARISSE. "Upon Release from Prison, Some Can Feel Lost." *USA Today* (December 14, 2007):5A.

KING, KATHLEEN PIKER, AND DENNIS E. CLAYSON. "The Differential Perceptions of Male and Female Deviants." *Sociological Focus.* Vol. 21, No. 2 (April 1988):153–64.

KITTRIE, NICHOLAS N. *The Right to Be Different: Deviance and Enforced Therapy.* Baltimore: Johns Hopkins University Press, 1971.

KUBRIN, CHARLES E. "Gangstas, Thugs, and Hustlas: Identity and the Code of the Street in Rap Music." *Social Problems.* Vol. 52, No. 3 (August 2005):360–78.

LANGBEIN, LAURA I., AND ROSEANA BESS. "Sports in School: Source of Amity or Antipathy?" *Social Science Quarterly.* Vol. 83, No. 2 (June 2002):436–54.

LEMERT, EDWIN M. *Social Pathology.* New York: McGraw-Hill, 1951.

———. *Human Deviance, Social Problems, and Social Control.* 2nd ed. Englewood Cliffs, N.J.: Prentice Hall, 1972.

LEMONICK, MICHAEL D. "The Search for a Murder Gene." *Time* (January 20, 2003):100.

LEONARD, EILEEN B. *Women, Crime, and Society: A Critique of Theoretical Criminology.* White Plains, N.Y.: Longman, 1982.

LEVINE, SAMANTHA. "Playing God in Illinois." *U.S. News & World Report* (January 13, 2003):13.

LIAZOS, ALEXANDER. "The Poverty of the Sociology of Deviance: Nuts, Sluts, and Perverts." *Social Problems.* Vol. 20, No. 1 (Summer 1972):103–20.

LIPTAK, ADAM. "More than 1 in 100 Adults Are Now in Prison in U.S." *New York Times* (February 29, 2008):A14.

LISKA, ALLEN E., AND BARBARA D. WARNER. "Functions of Crime: A Paradoxical Process." *American Journal of Sociology.* Vol. 96, No. 6 (May 1991):1441–63.

LITTLE, CRAIG, AND ANDREA RANKIN. "Why Do They Start It? Explaining Reported Early-Teen Sexual Activity." *Sociological Forum.* Vol. 16, No. 4 (December 2001):703–29.

LOHR, STEVE. "In Bailout Furor, Wall Street Salaries Become a Target." *International Herald Tribune* (September 24, 2008). [Online] Available November 6, 2008, at http://www.iht.com/articles/2008/09/24/business/24pay.php

MARTIN, JOHN M., AND ANNE T. ROMANO. *Multinational Crime: Terrorism, Espionage, Drug and Arms Trafficking.* Newbury Park, Calif.: Sage, 1992.

MARTIN, JOYCE A., ET AL. "Births: Final Data for 2009." National Vital Statistics Reports. Vol. 60, No. 1 [Online] 2011. Available at http://www.cdc.gov/nchs/data/nvsr/nvsr60/nvsr60_01.pdf

MARTINEZ, RAMIRO, JR. "Latinos and Lethal Violence: The Impact of Poverty and Inequality." *Social Problems.* Vol. 43, No. 2 (May 1996):131–46.

MERTON, ROBERT K. "Social Structure and Anomie." *American Sociological Review.* Vol. 3, No. 6 (October 1938):672–82.

———. *Social Theory and Social Structure.* New York: Free Press, 1968.

MILLER, WALTER B. "Lower-Class Culture as a Generating Milieu of Gang Delinquency" (1958). In MARVIN E. WOLFGANG, LEONARD SAVITZ, and NORMAN JOHNSTON, eds., *The Sociology of Crime and Delinquency.* 2nd ed. New York: Wiley, 1970:351–63.

MILLER, WILLIAM J., AND RICK A. MATTHEWS. "Youth Employment, Differential Association, and Juvenile Delinquency." *Sociological Focus.* Vol. 34, No. 3 (August 2001):251–68.

MITCHELL, CHRIS. "The Killing of Murder." *New York Magazine* (January 8, 2008). [Online] Available February 9, 2008, at http://nymag.com/news/features/crime/2008/42603

MOFFITT, TERRIE E. ET AL. "A Gradient of Childhood Self-Control Predicts Health, Wealth, and Public Safety." *Proceedings of the National Academy of Sciences of the United States of America.* [Online] Available January 30, 2011, at http://www.pnas.org/content/early/2011/01/20/1010076108

MORIN, RICHARD. "Getting a Grad Degree in Cheating." Pew Research Center. [Online] Available September 27, 2006, at http://pewresearch.org/pubs/68/getting-a-grad-degree-in-cheating

MUNROE, SUSAN. "Abolition of Capital Punishment in Canada." About.com: Canada Online. July 2007. [Online] Available April 16, 2008, at http://canadaonline.about.com/od/crime/a/abolitioncappun.htm

NATIONAL COALITION OF ANTI-VIOLENCE PROGRAMS. "Hate Violence Against Lesbian, Gay, Bisexual, Transgender, Queer and HIV-Affected Communities in the United States in 2010." July 12, 2011. [Online] Available at http://www.avp.org/publications.htm

NATIONAL CONFERENCE OF STATE LEGISLATURES. "State Traffic Safety Legislation." 2011. [Online] Available at http://www.ncsl.org/programs/transportation/trafsafdb.cfm

NORC. *General Social Surveys, 1972–2010: Cumulative Codebook.* Chicago: National Opinion Research Center, 2011. http://www.norc.org/GSS+Website

NOVAK, VIVECA. "The Cost of Poor Advice." *Time* (July 5, 1999):38.

"Our Cheating Hearts." Editorial. *U.S. News & World Report* (May 6, 2002):4.

OZERSKY, JOSH. "Got Raw?" *Time.* Vol. 176, No. 12 (September 20, 2010):69–70.

PEW CENTER ON THE STATES. "One in 100: Behind Bars in America 2008." Washington, DC: The Pew Charitable Trusts. February 2008. [Online] Available at http://www.pewcenteronthestates.org/report_detail.aspx?id=35904

———. "One in 31: The Long Reach of American Corrections." Washington, D.C.: The Pew Charitable Trusts. 2009 [Online] Available at http://www.pewcenteronthestates.org/uploadedFiles/PSPP_1in31_report_FINAL_WEB_3-26-09.pdf

———. "Prison Count 2010." April 2010. [Online] Available at http://www.pewcenteronthestates.org/uploadedFiles/Prison_Count_2010.pdf?n=880

———. "State of Recidivism: The Revolving Door of America's Prisons." Washington, DC: The Pew Charitable Trusts. April 2011. [Online] Available at http://www.pewcenteronthestates.org/uploadedFiles/Pew_State_of_Recidivism.pdf

PEW RESEARCH CENTER. "No Shift Toward Gun Control After Tucson Shootings." [Online] Available January 19, 2011, at http://pewresearch.org/pubs/1864/post-tucson-shooting-gun-control-opinion-broader-problems-isolatedevent

PEW RESEARCH CENTER FOR THE PEOPLE AND THE PRESS. "Poll Database." [Online] Available at http://webapps.ropercenter.uconn.edu/psearch/prc_index.cfm?pid=51

PINKER, STEVEN. "Are Your Genes to Blame?" *Time* (January 20, 2003):98–100.

PRYOR, JOHN H., ET AL. *The American Freshman: National Norms Fall 2010.* Cooperative Institutional Research Program at the Higher Education Research Institute at UCLA: 2011.

QUILLIAN, LINCOLN, AND DEVAH PAGER. "Black Neighbors, Higher Crime? The Role of Racial Stereotypes in Evaluations of Neighborhood Crime." *American Journal of Sociology.* Vol. 107, No. 3 (November 2001):717–67.

QUINNEY, RICHARD. *Class, State and Crime: On the Theory and Practice of Criminal Justice.* New York: McKay, 1977.

RECKLESS, WALTER C., AND SIMON DINITZ. "Pioneering with Self-Concept as a Vulnerability Factor in Delinquency." *Journal of Criminal Law, Criminology, and Police Science.* Vol. 58, No. 4 (December 1967):515–23.

ROGERS, RICHARD G., REBECCA ROSENBLATT, ROBERT A. HUMMER, AND PATRICK M. KRUEGER. "Black-White Differentials in Adult Homicide Mortality in the United States." *Social Science Quarterly.* Vol. 82, No. 3 (September 2001): 435–52.

ROSENFELD, RICHARD. "Crime Decline in Context." *Contexts.* Vol. 1, No. 1 (Spring 2002): 20–34.

SCHEFF, THOMAS J. *Being Mentally Ill: A Sociological Theory.* 2nd ed. New York: Aldine, 1984.

SENTENCING PROJECT. "Felony Disenfranchisement Laws in the United States." September 2008. [Online] Available January 25, 2009, at http://www.sentencingproject.org/Admin%5CDocuments%5Cpublications%5Cfd_bs_fdlawsinus.pdf

SHELDON, WILLIAM H., EMIL M. HARTL, AND EUGENE MCDERMOTT. *Varieties of Delinquent Youth.* New York: Harper Bros., 1949.

SHERMAN, LAWRENCE W., AND DOUGLAS A. SMITH. "Crime, Punishment, and Stake in Conformity: Legal and Informal Control of Domestic Violence." *American Sociological Review.* Vol. 57, No. 5 (October 1992):680–90.

SHOVER, NEAL, AND ANDREW HOCHSTETLER. *Choosing White-Collar Crime.* New York: Cambridge University Press, 2006.

SMITH, DOUGLAS A. "Police Response to Interpersonal Violence: Defining the Parameters of Legal Control." *Social Forces.* Vol. 65, No. 3 (March 1987): 767–82.

———, AND PATRICK R. GARTIN. "Specifying Specific Deterrence: The Influence of Arrest on Future Criminal Activity." *American Sociological Review.* Vol. 54, No. 1 (February 1989):94–105.

———, AND CHRISTY A. VISHER. "Street-Level Justice: Situational Determinants of Police Arrest Decisions." *Social Problems.* Vol. 29, No. 2 (December 1981):167–77.

SPITZER, STEVEN. "Toward a Marxian Theory of Deviance." In DELOS H. KELLY, ed., *Criminal Behavior: Readings in Criminology.* New York: St. Martin's Press, 1980:175–91.

STACK, STEVEN, IRA WASSERMAN, AND ROGER KERN. "Adult Social Bonds and the Use of Internet Pornography." *Social Science Quarterly.* Vol. 85, No. 1 (March 2004):75–88.

STATISTICS CANADA. "Canada Year Book." 2011. [Online] Available at http://www.statcan.gc.ca/pub/11-402-x/index-eng.htm

STEELE, RANDY. "Awful but Lawful." *Boating* (June 2000):36.

SULLIVAN, ANDREW. Lecture delivered at Kenyon College, Gambier, Ohio, April 4, 2002.

SUTHERLAND, EDWIN H. "White Collar Criminality." *American Sociological Review.* Vol. 5, No. 1 (February 1940):1–12.

SWARTZ, STEVE. "Why Michael Milken Stands to Qualify for Guinness Book." *Wall Street Journal* (March 31, 1989):1, 4.

SZASZ, THOMAS S. *The Myth of Mental Illness: Foundations of a Theory of Personal Conduct.* New York: Dell, 1961.

———. *The Manufacturer of Madness: A Comparative Study of the Inquisition and the Mental Health Movement.* New York: Harper & Row, 1970.

———. "Cleansing the Modern Heart." *Society.* Vol. 40, No. 4 (May/June 2003):52–59.

———. "Protecting Patients against Psychiatric Intervention." *Society.* Vol. 41, No. 3 (March/April 2004):7–10.

TERRY, DON. "In Crackdown on Bias, a New Tool." *New York Times* (June 12, 1993):8.

THOMAS, EVAN, AND MARTHA BRANT. "Injection of Reflection." *Newsweek* (November 19, 2007):40–41.

THORNBERRY, TERRANCE, AND MARGARET FARNSWORTH. "Social Correlates of Criminal Involvement: Further Evidence on the Relationship between Social Status and Criminal Behavior." *American Sociological Review.* Vol. 47, No. 4 (August 1982):505–18.

TITTLE, CHARLES R., WAYNE J. VILLEMEZ, AND DOUGLAS A. SMITH. "The Myth of Social Class and Criminality: An Empirical Assessment of the Empirical Evidence." *American Sociological Review.* Vol. 43, No. 5 (October 1978):643–56.

TRUMAN, JENNIFER. "Criminal Victimization in the United States, 2010." September 15, 2011. [Online] Available at http://bjs.ojp.usdoj.gov/index.cfm?ty=pbdetail&iid=2224

UGGEN, CHRISTOPHER. "Ex-Offenders and the Conformist Alternative: A Job-Quality Model of Work and Crime." *Social Problems.* Vol. 46, No. 1 (February 1999):127–51.

U.S. CENSUS BUREAU. "Current Population Survey." 2011. [Online] Available at http://www.census.gov/cps

———. "Population Estimates." 2011. [Online] Available at http://www.census.gov/popest/data/index.html

U.S. DEPARTMENT OF JUSTICE, BUREAU OF JUSTICE STATISTICS. "Capital Punishment, 2010 - Statistical Tables" December 20, 2011. [Online] Available at http://bjs.ojp.usdoj.gov/index.cfm?ty=pbdetail&iid=2236

———. "Federal Criminal Case Processing Statistics." 2011. [Online] Available at http://fjsrc.urban.org/index.cfm

———. "Total Correctional Population." 2011. [Online] Available at http://bjs.ojp.usdoj.gov/index.cfm?ty=tp&tid=11

U.S. DEPARTMENT OF JUSTICE, FEDERAL BUREAU OF INVESTIGATION. "Crime in the United States 2010." September 2011. [Online] Available at http://www.fbi.gov/about-us/cjis/ucr/crime-in-the-u.s/2010/crime-in-the-u.s.-2010

———. "Hate Crime Statistics 2010." November 14, 2011. [Online] Available at # http://www.fbi.gov/about-us/cjis/ucr/hate-crime/2010

———. "Law Enforcement Officers Killed and Assaulted." October, 2011. [Online] Available at http://www.fbi.gov/about-us/cjis/ucr/leoka/leoka-2010

U.S. DEPARTMENT OF LABOR, BUREAU OF LABOR STATISTICS. "Injuries, Illnesses, and Fatalities." 2011. [Online] Available at http://www.bls.gov/iif/

U.S. DEPARTMENT OF LABOR, MINE SAFETY AND HEALTH ADMINISTRATION. "Mine Safety and Health at a Glance." May 13, 2011. [Online] Available at http://www.msha.gov/MSHAINFO/FactSheets/MSHAFCT10.HTM

UNITED NATIONS, OFFICE ON DRUGS AND CRIME. "UNODC Homicide Statistics." 2011. [Online] Available at http://www.unodc.org/unodc/en/data-and-analysis/homicide.html

VALDEZ, A. "In the Hood: Street Gangs Discover White-Collar Crime." *Police.* Vol. 21, No. 5 (May 1997):49–50, 56.

VAN DIJK, JAN, JOHN VAN KESTEREN, AND PAUL SMIT. "Criminal Victimisation in International Perspective: Key Findings from the 2004–2005 ICVS and EU ICS." The Hague, Ministry of Justice, WODC: 2007. http://www.unicri.it/wwd/analysis/icvs/pdf_files/ICVS2004_05report.pdf

VOLD, GEORGE B., AND THOMAS J. BERNARD. *Theoretical Criminology.* 3rd ed. New York: Oxford University Press, 1986.

VON DREHLE, DAVID. "One Madman and a Gun." *Time.* Vol. 177, No. 3 (January 24, 2011):26–31.

WARR, MARK, AND CHRISTOPHER G. ELLISON. "Rethinking Social Reactions to Crime: Personal and Altruistic Fear in Family Households." *American Journal of Sociology.* Vol. 106, No. 3 (November 2000):551–78.

WINSHIP, CHRISTOPHER, AND JENNY BERRIEN. "Boston Cops and Black Churches." *Public Interest* (Summer 1999):52–68.

WITKIN, GORDON. "The Crime Bust." *U.S. News & World Report* (May 25, 1998):28–40.

WITTENAUER, CHERYL. "Saggy Pants May Not Be Lawful." 2007. [Online] Available at http://www.yahoonews.com

WOLFGANG, MARVIN E., ROBERT M. FIGLIO, AND THORSTEN SELLIN. *Delinquency in a Birth Cohort.* Chicago: University of Chicago Press, 1972.

———, TERRENCE P. THORNBERRY, AND ROBERT M. FIGLIO. *From Boy to Man, from Delinquency to Crime.* Chicago: University of Chicago Press, 1987.

WORLD BANK. "Colombia at a Glance." February 25, 2011. [Online] Available at http://devdata.worldbank.org/AAG/col_aag.pdf

WRIGHT, RICHARD A. *In Defense of Prisons.* Westport, Conn.: Greenwood Press, 1994.

XU, JIAQUAN, KENNETH D. KOCHANEK, SHERRY L. MURPHY, AND BETZAIDA TEJADAV-ERA. "Deaths: Final Data for 2007." *National Vital Statistics Reports.* Vol. 58, No. 19. Hyattsville, MD: National Center for Health Statistics, 2010. [Online] Available at http://www.cdc.gov/nchs/data/nvsr/nvsr58/nvsr58_19.pdf

Chapter 8 References

ATLAS, TERRY. "The Human Cost of China's Boom Times." *U.S. News & World Report* (March 12, 2007):21.

BAINBRIDGE, JAY, MARCIA K. MEYERS, AND JANE WALDFOGEL. "Childcare Reform and the Employment of Single Mothers." *Social Science Quarterly.* Vol. 84, No. 4 (December 2003):771–91.

BALTZELL, E. DIGBY. *The Protestant Establishment: Aristocracy and Caste in America.* New York: Vintage Books, 1964.

———. *Sporting Gentlemen: From the Age of Honor to the Cult of the Superstar.* New York: Free Press, 1995.

BECK, RACHEL, AND ELLEN SIMON. "CEOs Who Got Out before Crisis Left with Millions." *Yahoo News* (September 25, 2008). [Online] Available September 25, 2008, at http://news.yahoo.com/s/ap/20080925/ap_on_bi_ge/bailout_ceo_pay&printer=1;_ylt=Ak3o DhhSUwYZqhuaJh10BZ9v24cA

BEEGHLEY, LEONARD. *The Structure of Social Stratification in the United States.* Needham Heights, Mass.: Allyn & Bacon, 1989.

BELLER, EMILY, AND MICHAEL HOUT. "Intergenerational Social Mobility: The United States in Comparative Perspective." *The Future of Children.* Vol. 16, No. 2 (Fall 2006). [Online] Available April 30, 2008, at http://www.futureofchildren.org/information2826/information_show.htm?doc_id=389282

BIAN, YANJIE. "Chinese Social Stratification and Social Mobility." *Annual Review of Sociology.* Vol. 28 (2002):91–116.

BIVENS, JOSH. "Three-Fifths of All Income Growth from 1979–2007 Went to the Top 1%." Economic Policy Institute. October 27, 2011. Accessed at: http://www.epi.org/publication/fifths-income-growth-1979-2007-top-1/

BOHANNAN, CECIL. "The Economic Correlates of Homelessness in Sixty Cities." *Social Science Quarterly.* Vol. 72, No. 4 (December 1991):817–25.

BOTT, ELIZABETH. *Family and Social Network.* New York: Free Press, 1971; orig. 1957.

BRINTON, MARY C. "The Social-Institutional Bases of Gender Stratification: Japan as an Illustrative Case." *American Journal of Sociology.* Vol. 94, No. 2 (September 1988):300–34.

BUCKS, BRIAN K., ARTHUR B. KENNICKELL, TRACI L. MACH, AND KEVIN B. MOORE. "Changes in U.S. Family Finances from 2004 to 2007: Evidence from the Survey of Consumer Finances." February 2009. [Online] Available at http://www.federalreserve.gov/pubs/bulletin/2009/pdf/scf09.pdf

BUSSOLO, MAURIZIO, RAFAEL E. DE HOYOS, AND DENIS MEDVEDEV. "Is the Developing World Catching Up? Global Convergence and National Rising Dispersion." The World Bank Development Economics Prospects Group: September 2008. http://go.worldbank.org/1LFF97ODP0

CDC (Centers for Disease Control and Prevention), National Center for Health Statistics. "Summary Health Statistics for U.S. Adults: National Health Interview Survey, 2008." Vital Health Stat 10(248). August 2010. http://www.cdc.gov/nchs/nhis/nhis_series.htm

CENTRAL INTELLIGENCE AGENCY. *The World Factbook.* 2011 (updated biweekly). [Online] Available at https://www.cia.gov/library/publications/the-world-factbook/index.html

CHANG, LESLIE T. *Factory Girls: From Village to City in a Changing China.* New York: Spiegel & Grau, 2008.

CLARK, MARGARET S., ED. *Prosocial Behavior.* Newbury Park, Calif.: Sage, 1991.

COLEMAN, RICHARD P., AND BERNICE L. NEUGARTEN. *Social Status in the City.* San Francisco: Jossey-Bass, 1971.

COLEMAN, RICHARD P., AND LEE RAINWATER. *Social Standing in America.* New York: Basic Books, 1978.

CONGRESSIONAL BUDGET OFFICE. "Growing Disparities in Life Expectancy." April 17, 2008. http://www.cbo.gov/ftpdocs/91xx/doc9104/04-17-LifeExpectancy_Brief.pdf

CORPORATE LIBRARY, THE. "Executive Compensation." 2010. [Online] Available at http://www.thecorporatelibrary.com/info.php?id=60

CRESWELL, JULIE. "Even Funds that Lagged Paid Richly." *New York Times.* March 31, 2011. [Online] Available at http://www.nytimes.com/2011/04/01/business/01hedge.html?_r=1

DAHRENDORF, RALF. *Class and Class Conflict in Industrial Society.* Stanford, Calif.: Stanford University Press, 1959.

DAVIS, KINGSLEY, AND WILBERT MOORE. "Some Principles of Stratification." *American Sociological Review.* Vol. 10, No. 2 (April 1945):242–49.

DEFENSE FINANCE AND ACCOUNTING SERVICE. "Military Pay Tables." 2011. [Online] Available at http://www.dfas.mil/militarypay/militarypaytables.html

DOMHOFF, G. WILLIAM. *Who Rules America Now? A View of the '80s.* Englewood Cliffs, N.J.: Prentice Hall, 1983.

ECONOMIST, THE. "The Rich and the Rest: What to Do (and Not Do) About Inequality." January 20, 2011. [Online] Available at http://www.economist.com/node/17959590?story_id=17959590&fsrc=rss

EVANS, KELLY. "Smaller Paychecks Having a Big Impact." *The Wall Street Journal.* September 30, 2011:C1.

FEDERAL RESERVE SYSTEM. "2007 Survey of Consumer Finances, Tables Based on the Internal Data and Tables Based on the Public Data." 2010 [Online] Available at http://www.federalreserve.gov/econresdata/scf/scf_2007.htm

FORBES. "Lists and Profiles." 2011. [Online] Available at http://www.forbes.com/lists/

FORBES. "The Forbes 400." 2011. [Online] Available at http://www.forbes.com/forbes-400/

FOROOHAR, RANA. "Your Incredible Shrinking Paycheck." *Time.* Vol. 177, No. 8 (February 28, 2011):24.

FOX, JUSTIN. "Pay Them Less? Hell, Yes." *Time* (March 2, 2009):30.

GERBER, THEODORE P., AND MICHAEL HOUT. "More Shock than Therapy: Market Transition, Employment, and Income in Russia, 1991–1995."*American Journal of Sociology.* Vol. 104, No. 1 (July 1998):1–50.

GROSSMAN, LEV. "2010 Person of the Year: Mark Zuckerberg." *Time.* Vol. 176, No. 26 (December 27, 2010):44–75.

HARFORD, TIM. "The American Dream: Getting to the Starting Line." [Online] Available October 9, 2007, at http://www.forbes.com/entrepreneurs/2007/10/09/income-mobility-opportunity-ent-dream1007-cx_th_1009harford.html

HELMAN, CHRISTOPHER. "America's 25 Highest-Paid CEOs." *Forbes.* October 12, 2011. Accessed at: http://www.forbes.com/sites/christopherhelman/2011/10/12/americas-25-highest-paid-ceos/

HOUT, MICHAEL. "More Universalism, Less Structural Mobility: The American Occupational Structure in the 1980s." *American Journal of Sociology.* Vol. 95, No. 6 (May 1998):1358–1400.

HOUT, MICHAEL, CLEM BROOKS, AND JEFF MANZA. "The Persistence of Classes in Post-Industrial Societies." *International Sociology.* Vol. 8, No. 3 (September 1993): 259–77.

INSTITUTE FOR POLICY STUDIES. " Executive Excess 2011: The Massive CEO Rewards for Tax Dodging." August 31, 2011. [Online] Available at http://www.ips-dc.org/reports-list.php?start=6

INTERNAL REVENUE SERVICE. "Statistics of Income." [Online] Available at http://www.irs.gov/taxstats/indtaxstats/article/0,,id=133521,00.html

JACOBY, RUSSELL, AND NAOMI GLAUBERMAN, eds. *The Bell Curve Debate.* New York: Random House, 1995.

KAISER, EMILY. "Special Report: The Haves, the Have-Nots and the Dreamless Dead." [Online] October 22, 2010 http://finance.yahoo.com/news/Special-Report-The-haves-the-rb-736053606.html?x=0

KAUFMAN, LESLIE. "Surge in Homeless Families Sets Off Debate on Cause." *New York Times* (July 29, 2004). [Online] Available May 4, 2009, at http://www.nytimes.com/2004/06/29/us/surge-in-homeless-families-sets-off-debate-oncause.html?fta=y

KEISTER, LISA A. *Wealth in America: Trends in Wealth Inequality.* Cambridge: Cambridge University Press, 2000.

KOHN, MELVIN L. *Class and Conformity: A Study in Values.* 2nd ed. Homewood, Ill.: Dorsey Press, 1977.

KOHUT, ANDY. "Public and Occupy Wall Street Movement Agree on Key Issues." Pew Research Center. October 19, 2011. Accessed at: http://www.people-press.org/2011/10/19/haves-and-have-nots/

KOZOL, JONATHAN. *Rachel and Her Children: Homeless Families in America.* New York: Crown, 1988.

KRISTOF, NICHOLAS D. "Occupy the Agenda." *The New York Times.* November 19, 2011. Accessed at: http://www.nytimes.com/2011/11/20/opinion/sunday/kristof-occupy-the-agenda.html?_r=1&ref=incomeinequality

KRUGMAN, PAUL. "For Richer: How the Permissive Capitalism of the Boom Destroyed American Equality." *New York Times Magazine* (September 20, 2002):62–67, 76–77, 141–42.

KUZNETS, SIMON. "Economic Growth and Income Inequality." *American Economic Review.* Vol. 14, No. 1 (March 1955):1–28.

———. *Modern Economic Growth: Rate, Structure, and Spread.* New Haven, Conn.: Yale University Press, 1966.

LAREAU, ANNETTE. "Invisible Inequality: Social Class and Childrearing in Black Families and White Families." *American Sociological Review.* Vol. 67, No. 5 (October 2002): 747–76.

LENSKI, GERHARD E. *Power and Privilege: A Theory of Social Stratification.* New York: McGraw-Hill, 1966.

LEWIS, OSCAR. *The Children of Sanchez.* New York: Random House, 1961.

LICHTER, DANIEL T., AND MARTHA L. CROWLEY. "Poverty in America: Beyond Welfare Reform." *Population Bulletin.* Vol. 57, No. 2 (June 2002):3–34.

LICHTER, DANIEL T., AND RUKMALIE JAYAKODY. "Welfare Reform: How Do We Measure Success?" *Annual Review of Sociology.* Vol. 28 (August 2002): 117–41.

LIN, NAN, AND WEN XIE. "Occupational Prestige in Urban China." *American Journal of Sociology.* Vol. 93, No. 4 (January 1988):793–832.

LINO, MARK. "Expenditures on Children by Families, 2010." Miscellaneous Publication Number 1528–2009, U.S. Department of Agriculture Center for Nutrition Policy and Promotion. 2011. [Online] Available at http://www.cnpp.usda.gov/Publications/CRC/crc2010.pdf

LIU, MELINDA, AND DUNCAN HEWITT. "The Rise of the Sea Turtles." *Newsweek* (August 18, 2008):29–31.

LONG, JASON, AND JOSEPH FERRIE. "The Path to Convergence: Intergenerational Occupational Mobility in Britain and the U.S. in Three Eras." *Economic Journal.* Vol. 117, No. 519 (2007):C61–C71.

LORD, WALTER. *A Night to Remember.* Rev. ed. New York: Holt, Rinehart and Winston, 1976.

MABRY, MARCUS, AND TOM MASLAND. "The Man after Mandela." *Newsweek* (June 7, 1999):54–55.

MARTIN, JOYCE A., BRADY E. HAMILTON, PAUL D. SUTTON, STEPHANIE J. VENTURA, T.J. MATHEWS, AND MICHELLE J. K. OSTERMAN. "Births: Final data for 2008." *National Vital Statistics Reports.* Vol. 59, No. 1 Hyattsville, MD: National Center for Health Statistics. December 2010. http://www.cdc.gov/nchs/data/nvsr/nvsr59/nvsr59_01.pdf

MARX, KARL, AND FRIEDRICH ENGELS. "Manifesto of the Communist Party." In ROBERT C. TUCKER, ed., *The Marx-Engels Reader.* New York: Norton, 1972:331–62; orig. 1848.

MASON, DAVID S. "Fairness Matters: Equity and the Transition to Democracy." *World Policy Journal.* Vol. 20, No. 4 (Winter 2003–04). 2004. [Online] Available at http://www.worldpolicy.org/journal/articles/wpj03-4/mason.htm

MCKEE, VICTORIA. "Blue Blood and the Color of Money." *New York Times* (June 9, 1996): 49–50.

MCLEOD, JAY. *Ain't No Makin' It: Aspirations and Attainment in a Low-Income Neighborhood.* Boulder, Colo.: Westview Press, 1995.

MILANOVIC, BRANKO. "Global Inequality of Opportunity." The World Bank, Development Research Group: June 2008. http://go.worldbank.org/AJVRQUZK40

MISHEL, LAWRENCE. "Data on Income Gains Support 99ers' Gripes." Economic Policy Institute. October 19, 2011. Accessed at: http://www.epi.org/publication/data-income-gains-support-99ers/

MOUW, TED. "Job Relocation and the Racial Gap in Unemployment in Detroit and Chicago, 1980 to 1990." *American Sociological Review.* Vol. 65, No. 5 (October 2000):730–53.

MURPHY, JOHN. "Some Rise but Most Sink in Soweto's Sea of Slums." *Baltimore Sun* (October 6, 2002). [Online] Available November 15, 2008, at http://www .baltimoresun.com/news/health/balte.soweto06oct06, 0, 1833961.story

NATIONAL COALITION FOR THE HOMELESS. "How Many People Experience Homelessness?" NCH Fact Sheet No. 2. August 2007. [Online] Available April 30, 2008, at http://www.nationalhomeless.org/publications/facts/How_Many.pdf

NEW YORK TIMES. "Bankers and Their Bonuses." Editorial. [Online] Available February 5, 2011, at http://www.nytimes.com/2011/02/06/opinion/06sun2 .html?_r=1

NEW YORK TIMES. "The Pay at the Top." April 9, 2011. [Online] Available at http://projects.nytimes.com/executive_compensation

NORC. *General Social Surveys, 1972–2010: Cumulative Codebook.* Chicago: National Opinion Research Center, 2011. [Online] Available at http://www.norc.org/GSS+Website

OSTRANDER, SUSAN A. "Upper-Class Women: The Feminine Side of Privilege." *Qualitative Sociology.* Vol. 3, No. 1 (Spring 1980):23–44.

———. *Women of the Upper Class.* Philadelphia: Temple University Press, 1984.

O'TOOLE MOLLY. "White House to Pay $37 Million in Salaries for 2011." Reuters. July 4, 2011. Accessed at: http://news.yahoo.com/white-house-pay-37-million-salaries-2011-041621213.html

PACKARD, MARK. Personal communication (2002).

PERRY, ALEX. "Joburg Gets it Together." *Time.* June 29, 2009. [Online] Available at http://www.time.com/time/magazine/article/0,9171,1905519-1,00.html

———. "South Africa Looks for a Leader." *Time* (April 27, 2009):38–41.

POPULATION REFERENCE BUREAU. "Datafinder." 2011. [Online] Available at http://www.prb.org/DataFinder.aspx

POWELL, BILL. "Postcard: Dongguan." *Time* (December 15, 2008):4.

PYLE, RALPH E., AND JEROME R. KOCH. "The Religious Affiliation of American Elites, 1930s to 1990s: A Note on the Pace of Disestablishment."*Sociological Focus.* Vol. 34, No. 2 (May 2001):125–37.

RAUM, TOM. "High Income Workers' Share of total Wages Grows." Associated Press. October 21, 2011. Accessed at: http://news.yahoo.com/high-income-workers-share-total-wages-grows-231053534.html

RICHBURG, KEITH B. "China's Communist Rulers Find Newly Rich a Headache." *The Richmond Times-Dispatch.* September 14, 2011:A2

ROTH, ZACHARY. "Labor: Lavish CEO Pay Still Rising." *The Lookout* April 20, 2011. Accessed at: http://news.yahoo.com/s/yblog_thelookout/20110420/ts_yblog_thelookout/labor-lavish-ceo-pay-still-rising

ROTH, ZACHARY. "Wall Street Pay Hits New Record." *The Lookout.* [Online] Available February 2, 2011, at http://news.yahoo.com/s/yblog_thelookout/20110202/ts_yblog_thelookout/wall-street-pay-hits-new-record

RUSSELL, CHERYL. "Are We in the Dumps?" *American Demographics.* Vol. 17, No. 1 (January 1995a):6.

SAEZ, EMMANUEL AND THOMAS PIKETTY, "Income Inequality in the United States, 1913–1998" *The Quarterly Journal of Economics*, Vol. 118(1), 2003. Tables and Figures Updated to 2008 [Online] Available at http://www.econ.berkeley.edu/~saez/

SCHERER, RON. "Could Bailout's Pay Caps Launch Wall Street Trend?" *Yahoo News* (September 30, 2008). [Online] Available September 29, 2008, at http://news.yahoo.com/s/csm/20080930/ts_csm/apaycut&printer=1;_ylt=Al3doZ_4Ps07Lcen.QIvU92Oe8UF

SCHWARTZ, NELSON D., AND LOUISE STORY. "Pay of Hedge Fund Managers Roared Back Last Year." *New York Times* [Online] Available March 31, 2010, at http://www.nytimes.com/2010/04/01/business/01hedge.html

SINGH, GOPAL K. "Child Mortality in the United States, 1935–2007: Large Racial and Socioeconomic Disparities Have Persisted Over Time." Rockville, Md.: U.S. Department of Health and Human Services. 2010. [Online] Available at http://www.hrsa.gov/healthit/images/mchb_child_mortality_pub.pdf

SMITH, AARON. "U.S.Millionaire Population Expanded by 8% in 2010."CNN Money. March 16, 2011. Accessed at http://finance.yahoo.com/news/US-millionairespopulation-cnnm-649773567.html?x=0

TUMIN, MELVIN M. "Some Principles of Stratification: A Critical Analysis." *American Sociological Review*. Vol. 18, No. 4 (August 1953):387–94.

UNITED NATIONS DEVELOPMENT PROGRAMME. *Human Development Report 2011*. Statistical Tables. [Online] Available at http://hdr.undp.org/en/statistics/data/

U.S. CENSUS BUREAU. *Statistical Abstract of the United States: 2012, 131st Edition. 2011.* [Online] Available at http://www.census.gov/statab/www

———. "American Community Survey." 2011. [Online] Available at http://www.census.gov/acs/www

———. "Current Population Survey." September 2011. [Online] Available at http://www.census.gov/cps

———. "Voting and Registration." 2009, 2010. [Online] Available at http://www.census.gov/hhes/www/socdemo/voting/index.html

———. "Small Area Income and Poverty Estimates (SAIPE) Program." December 2010. [Online] Available at http://www.census.gov/did/www/saipe/index.html

———. "Families and Living Arrangements." 2011. [Online] Available at http://www.census.gov/population/www/socdemo/hh-fam.html

———. "Housing Vacancies and Homeownership (CPS/HVS)." 2011. [Online] Available at http://www.census.gov/hhes/www/housing/hvs/hvs.html

U.S. CONFERENCE OF MAYORS. "A Status Annual Report on Hunger and Homelessness in America's Cities." December 2010. [Online] Available at http://usmayors.org/pressreleases/uploads/2010HungerHomelessnessReportfinal Dec212010.pdf

U.S. DEPARTMENT OF AGRICULTURE. "Food Security in the United States: Key Statistics and Graphics." 2011. [Online] Available at http://www.ers.usda.gov/Briefing/FoodSecurity/stats_graphs.htm

U.S. DEPARTMENT OF HOUSING AND URBAN DEVELOPMENT, OFFICE OF COMMUNITY PLANNING AND DEVELOPMENT. "The Annual Homeless Assessment Report to Congress." June 2010. [Online] Available at http://www.hudhre.info/index.cfm?do=viewResource&ResourceID=605&topicId=68&productTypeId=2

U.S. DEPARTMENT OF LABOR, BUREAU OF LABOR STATISTICS. "Current Employment Statistics." 2011. [Online] Available at http://www.bls.gov/ces/home.htm

U.S. DEPARTMENT OF LABOR, WAGE AND HOUR DIVISION. 2011. http://www.dol.gov/whd/flsa/index.htm

U.S. HOUSE OF REPRESENTATIVES. *1991 Green Book*. Washington, D.C.: U.S. Government Printing Office, 1991.

U.S. SOCIAL SECURITY ADMINISTRATION. "A Summary of the 2011 Annual Reports: Social Security and Medicare Boards of Trustees." 2011. [Online] Available at http://www.ssa.gov/OACT/TR/2011/

UNITED NATIONS DEVELOPMENT PROGRAMME. Human Development Report 2011. Statistical Tables. [Online] Available at http://hdr.undp.org/en/statistics/data/

VON DREHLE, DAVID. "The Financial Crisis: Who Can Lead Us Out of This Mess?" *Time* (October 6, 2008):32–36.

WALKER, KAREN. "'Always There for Me': Friendship Patterns and Expectations among Middle-and Working-Class Men and Women."*Sociological Forum*. Vol. 10, No. 2 (June 1995):273–96.

WALL STREET JOURNAL. "Market Data Center." 2011. [Online] Available at http://online.wsj.com/mdc/public/page/marketsdata.html?mod=mdc_topnav_2_3051

WARNER,W. LLOYD, AND PAUL S. LUNT. *The Social Life of a Modern Community*. New Haven, Conn.: Yale University Press, 1941.

WEITZMAN, LENORE J. "The Economic Consequences of Divorce Are Still Unequal: Comment on Peterson." *American Sociological Review*. Vol. 61, No. 3 (June 1996): 537–38.

WENDLE, JOHN. "Russia's Millionaires Keep Their Heads Up." *Time* (January 12, 2009):4.

WILLIAMSON, JEFFREY G., AND PETER H. LINDERT. *American Inequality: A Macroeconomic History*. New York: Academic Press, 1980.

WILLIAMSON, SAMUEL H. "Six Ways to Compute the Relative Value of a U.S. Dollar Amount, 1790 to Present." *Measuring Worth*. 2011. [Online] Available at http://www.measuringworth.com/index.html

WILSON, WILLIAM JULIUS. *When Work Disappears: The World of the New Urban Poor*. New York: Knopf, 1996a.

———. "Work." *New York Times Magazine* (August 18, 1996b):26ff.

WINES, MICHAEL, AND IAN JOHNSON. "After a Horrific Crash, a Stark Depiction of Injustice in China." *The New York Times Online*. November 18, 2011. Accessed at: http://www.nytimes.com/2011/11/19/world/asia/a-horrific-crash-sets-off-online-anger-in-china.html?ref=china

WOLFF, EDWARD N. "Recent Trends in Household Wealth in the U.S., Update to 2007: Rising Debt and the Middle Class Squeeze." March 2010. [Online] Available at http://www.levyinstitute.org/publications/?docid=1235

WORLD BANK. "Russian Economic Report #26." September 25, 2011. [Online] Available at http://documents.worldbank.org/curated/en/2011/09/15115904/growing-risks

WORLD BANK. "Russian Federation Partnership, Country Program Snapshot." September 2011. [Online] Available at http://siteresources.worldbank.org/INTRUSSIANFEDERATION/Resources/Russia_Snapshot.pdf

WORLD BANK. "World Development Indicators." 2010, 2011. [Online] Available at http://data.worldbank.org/data-catalog/world-development-indicators

WU, XIAOGANG, AND DONALD J. TREIMAN. "Inequality and Equality under Chinese Socialism: The Hukou System and Intergenerational Occupational Mobility." *American Journal of Sociology*. Vol. 113, No. 2 (September 2007): 415–45.

YEN, HOPE. "Census Shows 1 in 2 People are Poor or Low-Income." Associated Press. December 15, 2011. Accessed at: http://finance.yahoo.com/news/census-shows-1-2-people-103940568.html

ZAGORSKY, JAY. "Divorce Drops a Person's Wealth by 77 Percent." Press release (January 18, 2006). [Online] Available January 19, 2006, at http://www .eurekalert.org/pub_releases/2006-01/osu-dda011806.php

ZAKARIA, FAREED. "A Flight Plan for the American Economy." *Time*. Vol. 177, No. 22 (May 30, 2011):36–38.

ZOGBY, JOHN. "What American Dream?" *Forbes*. [Online] Available March 18, 2010, at www.forbes.com/2010/03/17/american-dream-economy-depression-opinions-columnists-john-zogby.html

ZUCKERMAN, MORTIMER B. "The Russian Conundrum." *U.S. News & World Report* (March 13, 2006):64.

Chapter 9 References

ANTI-SLAVERY INTERNATIONAL. 2011. [Online] Available at http://www.antislavery.org/english/default.aspx

BAJAJ, VIKAS. "Bangladesh Garment Workers Awarded Higher Pay." *New York Times*. [Online] Available July 29, 2010, at http://www.nytimes.com/2010/07/29/business/global/29garment.html

BANGLADESH GARMENT MANUFACTURERS & EXPORTERS ASSOCIATION. Available December 5, 2011 at http://www.bgmea.com.bd/home/pages/aboutus

BAUER, P.T. *Equality, the Third World, and Economic Delusion*. Cambridge, Mass.: Harvard University Press, 1981.

BEARAK, BARRY. "Lives Held Cheap in Bangladesh Sweatshops." *New York Times* (April 15, 2001):A1, A12.

BERGESEN, ALBERT, ed. *Crises in the World-System*. Beverly Hills, Calif.: Sage, 1983.

BERGER, PETER L. *The Capitalist Revolution: Fifty Propositions about Prosperity, Equality, and Liberty*. New York: Basic Books, 1986.

BONANNO, ALESSANDRO, DOUGLAS H.CONSTANCE, AND HEATHER LORENZ. "Powers and Limits of Transnational Corporations: The Case of ADM." *Rural Sociology*. Vol. 65, No. 3 (September 2000):440–60.

BUCKS, BRIAN K., ARTHUR B. KENNICKELL, TRACI L. MACH, AND KEVIN B. MOORE. "Changes in U.S. Family Finances from 2004 to 2007: Evidence from the Survey of Consumer Finances." February 2009. [Online] Available at http://www.federalreserve.gov/pubs/bulletin/2009/pdf/scf09.pdf

BURKETT, ELINOR. "God Created Me to Be a Slave." *New York Times Magazine* (October 12, 1997):56–60.

CENTRAL INTELLIGENCE AGENCY. *The World Factbook*. 2011 (updated biweekly). [Online] Available at https://www.cia.gov/library/publications/the-world-factbook/index.html

CHEN, SHAOHUA, AND MARTIN RAVALLION. "The Developing World Is Poorer than We Thought, but No Less Successful in the Fight against Poverty." 2008. [Online] Available at http://go.worldbank.org/C9GR27WRJ0

CONSORTIUM FOR STREET CHILDREN. "Street Children Statistics." 2011. http://www.streetchildren.org.uk/_uploads/resources/Street_Children_Stats_FINAL.pdf

———. *The Level and Distribution of Global Household Wealth*. September 2009. [Online] Available at http://economics.uwo.ca/centres/epri/wp2009/Davies_Sandstrom_ Shorrocks_Wolff_01.pdf

DELACROIX, JACQUES, AND CHARLES C. RAGIN. "Structural Blockage: A Cross-National Study of Economic Dependency, State Efficacy, and Underdevelopment." *American Journal of Sociology*. Vol. 86, No. 6 (May 1981): 1311–47.

DIXON, WILLIAM J., AND TERRY BOSWELL. "Dependency, Disarticulation, and Denominator Effects: Another Look at Foreign Capital Penetration." *American Journal of Sociology*. Vol. 102, No. 2 (September 1996):543–62.

ECONOMIST, THE. "Paving the Way." [Online] Available January 27, 2011, at http://www.economist.com/node/18013822?story_id=18013822&fsrc=rss

FIREBAUGH, GLENN. "Growth Effects of Foreign and Domestic Investment." *American Journal of Sociology*. Vol. 98, No. 1 (July 1992):105–30.

———. "Does Foreign Capital Harm Poor Nations? New Estimates Based on Dixon and Boswell's Measures of Capital Penetration."*American Journal of Sociology*. Vol. 102, No. 2 (September 1996):563–75.

———. "Empirics of World Income Inequality." *American Journal of Sociology*. Vol. 104, No. 6 (May 1999):1597–1630.

FIREBAUGH, GLENN, AND FRANK D. BECK. "Does Economic Growth Benefit the Masses? Growth, Dependence, and Welfare in the Third World." *American Sociological Review*. Vol. 59, No. 5 (October 1994):631–53.

FIREBAUGH, GLENN, AND DUMITRU SANDU. "Who Supports Marketization and Democratization in Post-Communist Romania?" *Sociological Forum*. Vol. 13, No. 3 (September 1998):521–41.

FISHER, MAX. "The Country Where Slavery is Still Normal." *The Atlantic*. June 28, 2011. [Online] Available at http://www.theatlantic.com/international/archive/2011/06/the-country-where-slavery-is-still-normal/241148/

FORBES. "The World's Billionaires." 2011. http://www.forbes.com/wealth/billionaires

FRANK, ANDRÉ GUNDER. *On Capitalist Underdevelopment*. Bombay: Oxford University Press, 1975.

———. *Crisis: In the World Economy*. New York: Holmes & Meier, 1980.

———. *Reflections on the World Economic Crisis*. New York: Monthly Review Press, 1981.

FRAYSSINET, FABIANA. "Agribusiness Driving Land Concentration." Inter Press Service News Agency. [Online] Available October 5, 2009, at http://ipsnews.net/news.asp?idnews=48734

GALANO, ANA MARIA. "Land Hungry in Brazil." August 1998. [Online] Available December 4, 2008, at http://www.unesco.org/courier/1998_08/uk/somm/intro.htm

Goesling, Brian. "Changing Income Inequalities within and between Nations: New Evidence." *American Sociological Review*. Vol. 66, No. 5 (October 2001):745–61.

Hockenberry, Alison Craiglow. "A Plot of One's Own: The Value of Women's Right to Property." *The Huffington Post*. [Online] Available March 1, 2011, at http://www.huffington post.com/alison-craiglow-hockenberry/a-plot-of-onesown-the-va_b_823227.html

IBGE (Instituto Brasileiro de Geografia e Estatística). Census of Agriculture, 2006. [Online] Available at http://www.ibge.gov.br/english/presidencia/noticias/noticia_visualiza.php?id_noticia=1464&id_pagina=1

International Labour Organization. "Global Child Labour Developments: Measuring Trends from 2004 to 2008." 2010. [Online] Available at http://www.ilo.org/ipecinfo/product/viewProduct.do?productId=13313

———. "Forced Labour." 2011. [Online] Available at http://www.ilo.org/global/topics/forced-labour/lang–en/index.htm

International Monetary Fund. "World Economic Outlook: Globalization and Inequality." October 2007. http://www.imf.org/external/pubs/ft/weo/2007/02/index.htm

Kentor, Jeffrey. "The Long-Term Effects of Foreign Investment Dependence on Economic Growth, 1940–1990." *American Journal of Sociology*. Vol. 103, No. 4 (January 1998): 1024–46.

———. "The Long-Term Effects of Globalization on Income Inequality, Population Growth, and Economic Development." *Social Problems*. Vol. 48, No. 4 (November 2001):435–55.

Landsea Center for Women's Land Rights. 2011. http://www.landesa.org/women-and-land

Lappé, Frances Moore, and Joseph Collins. *World Hunger: Twelve Myths*. New York: Grove Press/Food First Books, 1986.

Lappé, Frances Moore, Joseph Collins, and Peter Rosset. *World Hunger: Twelve Myths*. 2nd ed. New York: Grove Press, 1998.

Leopold, Evelyn. "Sudan's Young Endure 'Unspeakable' Abuse: Report." [Online] Available April 19, 2007, at http://www.news.yahoo.com

Levinson, F. James, and Lucy Bassett. "Malnutrition Is Still a Major Contributor to Child Deaths." Population Reference Bureau. 2007. [Online] Available December 4, 2008, at http://www.prb.org/pdf07/Nutrition2007.pdf

Lindauer, David L., and Akila Weerapana. "Relief for Poor Nations." *Society*. Vol. 39, No. 3 (March/April 2002):54–58.

Maddison Project. "Statistics on World Population, GDP and Per Capita GDP, 1-2008 AD." 2011. [Online] Available at http://www.ggdc.net/maddison/maddison-project/

Milanovic, Branko. "Global Inequality Recalculated: The Effect of New 2005 PPP Estimates on Global Inequality." World Bank. 2009. http://go.worldbank.org/AJVRQUZK40

———. *The Haves and Have-Nots: A Brief and Idiosyncratic History of Global Inequality*. New York: Basic Books, 2010.

———. "Global Inequality: From Class to Location, from Proletarians to Migrants." Policy Research Working Paper 5820. The World Bank. September 2011. Accessed at: http://go.worldbank.org/PWVINQBEH0

Moghadam, Valentine M. "The 'Feminization of Poverty' and Women's Human Rights." July 2005. [Online] Available December 4, 2008, at http://portal.unesco.org/shs/en/files/8282/11313736811Feminization_of_Poverty.pdf/Feminization%2Bof%2BPoverty.pdf

Moore, Wilbert E. "Modernization as Rationalization: Processes and Restraints." In Manning Nash, ed., *Essays on Economic Development and Cultural Change in Honor of Bert F. Hoselitz*. Chicago: University of Chicago Press, 1977:29–42.

———. *World Modernization: The Limits of Convergence*. New York: Elsevier, 1979.

Orhant, Melanie. "Human Trafficking Exposed." *Population Today*. Vol. 30, No. 1 (January 2002):1, 4.

Parsons, Talcott. *Societies: Evolutionary and Comparative Perspectives*. Englewood Cliffs, N.J.: Prentice Hall, 1966.

Populaton Reference Bureau. "Datafinder." 2011. [Online] Available at http://www.prb.org/DataFinder.aspx

Porter, Eduardo. "Study Finds Wealth Inequality Is Widening Worldwide." *New York Times* (December 6, 2006). [Online] Available April 22, 2009, at http://query.nytimes.com/gst/fullpage.html?res=9802E5DB1631F935A35751C1A9609C8B63&sec=&spon=&pagewanted=2

Rostow, Walt W. *The Stages of Economic Growth: A Non-Communist Manifesto*. Cambridge: Cambridge University Press, 1960.

———. *The World Economy: History and Prospect*. Austin: University of Texas Press, 1978.

Sala-I-Martin, Xavier. "The World Distribution of Income." Working Paper No. 8933. Cambridge, Mass.: National Bureau of Economic Research, 2002.

Schaffer, Michael. "American Dreamers." *U.S. News & World Report* (August 26, 2002):12–16.

Thomas de Benitez, Sarah. "State of the World's Street Children: Research." Consortium for Street Children, 2011. [Online] Available at http://www.streetchildren.org.uk/_uploads/publications/State_of_the_Worlds_Street_Children_Research_final_PDF_online.pdf

U.S. Census Bureau. *Statistical Abstract of the United States: 2012, 131st Edition. 2011.* [Online] Available at http://www.census.gov/statab/www

———, Foreign Trade Division. 2011. [Online] Available at http://www.census.gov/foreign-trade/statistics/index.html

U.S. Department of Labor. "List of Goods Produced by Child Labor or Forced Labor." 2011. http://www.dol.gov/ilab/programs/ocft/PDF/2011TVPRA.pdf

U.S. Department of State, Bureau of Intelligence and Research. "Independent States in the World." 2011. http://www.state.gov/s/inr/rls/4250.htm

UNICEF. "ChildInfo Statistics by Area: Child Survival and Health." 2011. http://www.childinfo.org/

UNIFEM. "Women's Land & Property Rights." 2011. http://www.unifem.org/gender_issues/women_poverty_economics/land_property_rights.php

United Nations Development Programme. *Human Development Report 2011*. Statistical Tables. [Online] Available at http://hdr.undp.org/en/statistics/data/

———. *Human Development Report 2008*. 2009. [Online] Available at http://hdr.undp.org/en/statistics/data

United Nations Inter-Agency Group for Child Mortality Estimation. "Levels and Trends in Child Mortality." 2010. [Online] Available at http://www.childinfo.org/files/Child_Mortality_Report_2010.pdf

United Nations, Food and Agriculture Organization, Statistics Division. Food Security Statistics. 2011. [Online] Available at http://www.fao.org/economic/ess/ess-data/ess-fs/ess-fadata/en/

United Nations, Food and Agriculture Organization. "The State of Food Insecurity in the World." Rome: Food and Agriculture Organization of the United Nations. 2011. http://www.fao.org/publications/sofi/en/

United Nations, Population Division. "World Population Prospects: The 2008 Revision." [Online] Available at http://esa.un.org/unpd/wpp2008/peps_mortality-indicators-by-age.htm

———. "World Urbanization Prospects: The 2009 Revision Population Database." [Online] Available at http://esa.un.org/wup2009/unup/index.asp?panel=1

United Nations, Statistics Division. "The World's Women 2010: Trends and Statistics." 2010. [Online] Available at http://unstats.un.org/unsd/demographic/products/Worldswomen/wwPov2010.htm

Vogel, Ezra F. *The Four Little Dragons: The Spread of Industrialization in East Asia*. Cambridge, Mass.: Harvard University Press, 1991.

Wallerstein, Immanuel. *The Modern World-System: Capitalist Agriculture and the Origins of the European World-Economy in the Sixteenth Century*. New York: Academic Press, 1974.

———. *The Capitalist World-Economy*. New York: Cambridge University Press, 1979.

———. "Crises: The World Economy, the Movements, and the Ideologies." In Albert Bergesen, ed., *Crises in the World-System*. Beverly Hills, Calif.: Sage, 1983:21–36.

———. *The Politics of the World Economy: The States, the Movements, and the Civilizations*. Cambridge: Cambridge University Press, 1984.

Weber, Adna Ferrin. *The Growth of Cities*. New York: Columbia University Press, 1963; orig. 1899.

Weber, Max. *The Protestant Ethic and the Spirit of Capitalism*. New York: Scribner, 1958; orig. 1904–05.

World Bank. "Health, Nutrition and Population Statistics." 2011. [Online] Available at http://data.worldbank.org/data-catalog/health-nutrition-and-population-statistics

———. "World Development Indicators." 2008, 2011. [Online] Available at http://data.worldbank.org/data-catalog/world-development-indicators

———. "Bangladesh Economic Update." April 2010. [Online] Available at http://siteresources.worldbank.org/BANGLADESHEXTN/Resources/295759-1271081222839/6958908-1273702902119/BDEconomicUpdateMay2010.pdf

World Health Organization. "Female Genital Mutilation: New Knowledge Spurs Optimism." *Progress in Sexual and Reproductive Health Research*. No.72 (2006). [Online] Available May 13, 2008, at http://www.who.int/reproductivehealth/hrp/progress/72.pdf

———. "The Top 10 Causes of Death (Fact Sheet No 310)." June 2011. [Online] Available at http://www.who.int/mediacentre/factsheets/fs310/en/index2.html

Worsley, Peter. "Models of the World System." In Mike Featherstone, ed., *Global Culture: Nationalism, Globalization, and Modernity*. Newbury Park, Calif.: Sage, 1990:83–95.

Chapter 10 References

American Bar Association. "Legal Education Statistics." 2011. [Online] Available at http://www.americanbar.org/groups/legal_education/resources/statistics.html

Armstrong, Elisabeth. *The Retreat from Organization: U.S. Feminism Reconceptualized*. Albany: State University of New York Press, 2002.

Astin, Alexander W., Leticia Oseguera, Linda J. Sax, and William S. Korn. *The American Freshman: Thirty-Five Year Trends*. Los Angeles: UCLA Higher Education Research Institute, 2002.

"The Barrier That Didn't Fall." *The Daily Beast*. [Online] Available November 18, 2008, at http://www.thedailybeast.com/blogs-and-stories/2008-11-18/thebarrier-that-didnrsquot-fall

Baydar, Nazli, and Jeanne Brooks-Gunn. "Effect of Maternal Employment and Child-Care Arrangements on Preschoolers' Cognitive and Behavioral Outcomes: Evidence from Children from the National Longitudinal Survey of Youth." *Developmental Psychology*. Vol. 27, No. 6 (November 1991): 932–35.

Bem, Sandra Lipsitz. *The Lenses of Gender: Transforming the Debate on Sexual Inequality*. New Haven, Conn.: Yale University Press, 1993.

Bernard, Jessie. *The Female World*. New York: Free Press, 1981.

Bonner, Jane. Research presented in the Public Broadcast System telecast *The Brain #6: The Two Brains*. Videocassette VHS 339. Newark, N.J.: WNET-13 Films, 1984.

Boyle, Elizabeth Heger, Fortunata Songora, and Gail Foss. "International Discourse and Local Politics: Anti-Female Genital-Cutting Laws in Egypt, Tanzania, and the United States." *Social Problems*. Vol. 48, No. 4 (November 2001):524–44.

Catalyst. "Women CEOs of the Fortune 1000." 2011. http://www.catalyst.org/publication/271/women-ceos-of-the-fortune-1000Catalyst. "U.S. Women in Business." 2011. http://www.catalyst.org/publication/132/us-women-in-business

CBS NEWS POLLS. "Poll: Women's Movement Worthwhile." [Online] Available October 23, 2005, at http://www.cbsnews.com/stories/2005/10/22/opinion/polls/main965224.shtml

CECI, STEPHEN J., AND WENDY M. WILLIAMS. "Understanding Current Causes of Women's Underrepresentation in Science." *The Proceedings of the National Academy of Sciences.* 2011. [Online] Available at http://www.human.cornell.edu/hd/loader.cfm?csModule=security/getfile&PageID=60893

CENTER FOR AMERICAN WOMEN AND POLITICS. "Women in Elective Office." 2011. [Online] Available at http://www.cawp.rutgers.edu/fast_facts/levels_of_office/

CENTER FOR WOMEN'S BUSINESS RESEARCH. "Key Facts about Women-Owned Businesses." 2009. [Online] Available at http://www.womensbusinessresearchcenter.org/research/keyfacts/

CHRONICLE OF HIGHER EDUCATION, THE. "A Profile of College Presidents, 1986 and 2006." February 16, 2007. [Online] Available at http://chronicle.com/stats/acesurvey/data.htm#share

COHEN, PHILIP N., AND MATT L. HUFFMAN. "Individuals, Jobs, and Labor Markets: The Devaluation of Women's Work." *American Sociological Review.* Vol. 68, No. 3 (June 2003):443–63.

COLLEGE BOARD, THE. "2011 College-Bound Seniors: Total Group Profile Report." 2011. [Online] Available at http://professionals.collegeboard.com/profdownload/cbs2011_total_group_report.pdf

COLTRANE, SCOTT, AND MELINDA MESSINEO. "Mass Mediated Inequality: Images of Race and Gender in 1990s' Television Advertising."*Sex Roles.* Vol. 42, No. 5/6 (2000):363–89.

CORRELL, SHELLEY J. "Gender and the Career Choice Process: The Role of Biased Self-Assessment." *American Journal of Sociology.* Vol. 106, No. 6 (May 2001):1691–1730.

CORTESE, ANTHONY J. *Provocateur: Images of Women and Minorities in Advertising.* Lanham, Md.: Rowman & Littlefield, 1999.

CROSSETTE, BARBARA. "Female Genital Mutilation by Immigrants Is Becoming Cause for Concern in the U.S." *New York Times International* (December 10, 1995):11.

DAVIS, DONALD M., cited in "TV Is a Blonde, Blonde World." *American Demographics,* special issue: *Women Change Places.* 1993.

DOYLE, JAMES A. *The Male Experience.* Dubuque, Iowa: Brown, 1983.

DWORKIN, ANDREA. *Intercourse.* New York: Free Press, 1987.

EHRENREICH, BARBARA. *The Hearts of Men: American Dreams and the Flight from Commitment.* Garden City, N.Y.: Anchor Books, 1983.

———. "The Real Truth about the Female Body." *Time* (March 15, 1999):56–65.

ENGELS, FRIEDRICH. *The Origin of the Family.* Chicago: Kerr, 1902; orig. 1884.

ENGLAND, PAULA, JOAN M. HERMSEN, AND DAVID A. COTTER. "The Devaluation of Women's Work: A Comment on Tam." *American Journal of Sociology.* Vol. 105, No. 6 (May 2000):1741–60.

FERREE, MYRA MARX, AND BETH B. HESS. *Controversy and Coalition: The New Feminist Movement across Four Decades of Change.* 3rd ed. New York: Routledge, 1995.

FOROOHAR, RANA. "The 100% Solution." *Time.* Vol. 177, No. 21. May 23, 2011:22.

FORTUNE. "25 Highest Paid Women." 2011. [Online] Available at http://money.cnn.com/galleries/2011/fortune/1109/gallery.highest_paid_women.fortune/index.html

FREEDMAN, ESTELLE B. *No Turning Back: The History of Feminism and the Future of Women.* New York: Ballantine Books, 2002.

FRENCH, MARILYN. *Beyond Power: On Women, Men, and Morals.* New York: Summit Books, 1985.

FRIAS, SONIA M., AND RONALD J. ANGEL. "Stability and Change in the Experience of Partner Violence among Low-Income Women."*Social Science Quarterly.* Vol. 88, No. 5 (2007):1281–1306.

FRY, RICHARD, AND D'VERA COHN. "Women, Men and the New Economics of Marriage." Pew Research Center. 2010. [Online] Available at http://pewsocialtrends.org/files/2010/10/new-economics-of-marriage.pdf

FULLER, REX, AND RICHARD SCHOENBERGER. "The Gender Salary Gap: Do Academic Achievement, Intern Experience, and College Major Make a Difference?" *Social Science Quarterly.* Vol. 72, No. 4 (December 1991):715–26.

GEWERTZ, DEBORAH. "A Historical Reconsideration of Female Dominance among the Chambri of Papua New Guinea." *American Ethnologist.* Vol. 8, No. 1 (1981): 94–106.

GIBBS, NANCY. "What Kids (Really) Need." *Time* (April 30, 2001):48–49.

GILLIGAN, CAROL. *In a Different Voice: Psychological Theory and Women's Development.* Cambridge, Mass.: Harvard University Press, 1982.

GOFFMAN, ERVING. *Gender Advertisements.* New York: Harper Colophon, 1979.

GOLDBERG, STEVEN. *The Inevitability of Patriarchy.* New York: Morrow, 1974.

GOUDREAU, JENNA. "*Forbes* 400: The Silent Billionaires." Forbeswoman blog. [Online] Available September 23, 2010, at http://blogs.forbes.com/jennagoudreau/2010/09/23/forbes-400-rich-list-silent-billionaires-bill-gatesmark-zuckerberg-steve-jobs-jay-z

GRAYBOW, MARTHA. "Women Directors Help Boost Corporate's Financial Performance: Study." *International Business Times.* October 2, 2007. [Online] Available December 2, 2008, at http://in.ibtimes.com/articles/20071002/women-directors-help-boost-corporate-financial-performance.htm

GURNETT, KATE. "On the Forefront of Feminism." *Albany Times Union* (July 5, 1998):G-1, G-6.

HANEY, LYNNE. "After the Fall: East European Women since the Collapse of State Socialism." *Contexts.* Vol. 1, No. 3 (Fall 2002):27–36.

HARPSTER, PAULA, AND ELIZABETH MONK-TURNER. "Why Men Do Housework: A Test of Gender Production and the Relative Resources Model." *Sociological Focus.* Vol. 31, No. 1 (February 1998):45–59.

HEATH, JULIA A., AND W. DAVID BOURNE. "Husbands and Housework: Parity or Parody?" *Social Science Quarterly.* Vol. 76, No. 1 (March 1995):195–202.

HENLEY, NANCY, MYKOL HAMILTON, AND BARRIE THORNE. "Womanspeak and Manspeak: Sex Differences in Communication, Verbal and Nonverbal." In JOHN J. MACIONIS AND NIJOLE V. BENOKRAITIS, eds., *Seeing Ourselves: Classic, Contemporary, and Cross-Cultural Readings in Sociology.* 2nd ed. Englewood Cliffs, N.J.: Prentice Hall, 1992:10–15.

HERMAN, DIANNE. "The Rape Culture." In JOHN J. MACIONIS AND NIJOLE V. BENOKRAITIS, eds., *Seeing Ourselves: Classic, Contemporary, and Cross-Cultural Readings in Sociology.* 5th ed. Upper Saddle River, N.J.: Prentice Hall, 2001.

HEWLETT, SYLVIA ANN. "As Careers Paths Change, Make On-Ramping Easy." [Online] Available July 8, 2010, at http://blogs.hbr.org/hbr/hewlett/2010/07/as_careers_paths_change_make_o.html

HEWLETT, SYLVIA ANN, AND CAROLYN BUCK LUCE. "Off-Ramps and On-Ramps: Keeping Talented Women on the Road to Success." Harvard Business Review Vol. 83, Issue 3 (March 2005):43–54.

INTERNAL REVENUE SERVICE. "Statistics of Income." 2010. [Online] Available at http://www.irs.gov/taxstats/indtaxstats/article/0,,id=133521,00.html

INTER-PARLIAMENTARY UNION. "Women in National Parliaments." 2011. [Online] Available at http://www.ipu.org/english/home.htm

JOHNSON, BARRY W., AND BRIAN G. RAUB. "Personal Wealth, 2001." *Statistics of Income Bulletin* (Winter 2005–06). 2006. [Online] Available September 20, 2006, at http://www.irs.gov/pub/irs-soi/01pwart.pdf

KAMINER, WENDY. "Demasculinizing the Army." *New York Times Review of Books* (June 15, 1997):7.

KANE, EMILY W. "Racial and Ethnic Variations in Gender-Related Attitudes." *Annual Review of Sociology.* Vol. 26 (August 2000):419–39.

KARJANE, HEATHER M., BONNIE S., FISHER, AND FRANCIS T., CULLEN. "Sexual Assault on Campus: What Colleges and Universities Are Doing About It." U.S. Department of Justice, National Institute of Justice, Office of Justice Programs: December 2005. http://www.ncjrs.gov/pdffiles1/nij/205521.pdf

KOCHANEK, KENNETH D., ET AL. "Deaths: Preliminary Data for 2009." *National Vital Statistics Reports.* Vol. 59, No. 4. Hyattsville, Md: National Center for Health Statistics. March 16, 2011. http://www.cdc.gov/nchs/data/nvsr/nvsr59/nvsr59_04.pdf

KOCHLAR, RAKESH. "Two Years of Economic Recovery: Women Lose Jobs, Men Find Them." Pew Research Center. July 6, 2011. Accessed at: http://www.pewsocialtrends.org/2011/07/06/two-years-of-economic-recovery-women-lose-jobs-men-find-them/

KRISTOF, NICHOLAS AND SHERYL WU DUNN. *Half the Sky: Turning Oppression into Opportunity for Women Worldwide.* New York: Alfred A. Knopf, 2009.

LAMM, DOTTIE. "Our Boys Are Falling Behind in Education." Denverpost.com. [Online] Available April 18, 2010, at http://www.denverpost.com/opinion/ci_14893585

LENGERMANN, PATRICIA MADOO AND RUTH A. WALLACE. *Gender in America: Social Control and Social Change.* Englewood Cliffs, N.J.: Prentice Hall, 1985.

LEVER, JANET. "Sex Differences in the Complexity of Children's Play and Games." *American Sociological Review.* Vol. 43, No. 4 (August 1978):471–83.

LEWIN, TAMAR. "Girls' Gains Have Not Cost Boys, Report Says." *New York Times* (May 20, 2008). [Online] Available December 7, 2008, at http://www.nytimes.com/2008/05/20/education/20girls.html?partner=permalink&exprod=permalink

Marathonguide.com. 2011. [Online] Available at http://www.marathonguide.com/history/records/index.cfm

MARSHALL, SUSAN E. "Ladies against Women: Mobilization Dilemmas of Antifeminist Movements." *Social Problems.* Vol. 32, No. 4 (April 1985): 348–62.

MARTIN, CAROL LYNN AND RICHARD A. FABES. "The Stability and Consequences of Young Children's Same-Sex Peer Interactions."*Developmental Psychology.* Vol. 37, No. 3 (May 2001):431–46.

McDOWELL, MARGARET A., CHERYL D., FRYAR, CYNTHIA L. OGDEN, AND KATHERINE M. FLEGAL. "Anthropomorphic Reference Data for Children and Adults: United States, 2003–2006." *National Health Statistic Reports,* No. 10 (October 22, 2008). [Online] Available April 21, 2009, at http://www.cdc.gov/nchs/data/nhsr/nhsr010.pdf

McGIRK, TIM. "Crossing the Lines." *Time* (February 27, 2006):36–43.

MEAD, MARGARET. *Sex and Temperament in Three Primitive Societies.* New York: Morrow, 1963; orig. 1935.

MESSINEO, MELINDA. "Does Advertising on Black Entertainment Television Portray More Positive Gender Representations Compared to Broadcast Networks?" *Sex Roles.* Vol. 59, No. 9/10 (2008):752–64.

MURDOCK, GEORGE PETER. "Comparative Data on the Division of Labor by Sex." *Social Forces.* Vol. 15, No. 4 (May 1937):551–53.

NOLAN, PATRICK, AND GERHARD E. LENSKI. *Human Societies: An Introduction to Macrosociology.* 11th ed. Boulder, Colo.: Paradigm, 2010.

NORC. *General Social Surveys, 1972–2010.* Chicago: National Opinion Research Center: March 2011. [Online] Available at http://www.norc.org/GSS+Website

OVADIA, SETH. "Race, Class, and Gender Differences in High School Seniors' Values: Applying Intersection Theory in Empirical Analysis." *Social Science Quarterly.* Vol. 82, No. 2 (June 2001):341–56.

PAPPAS, STEPHANIE. "Americans Like Baby Boys Best." *Live Science.* June 24, 2011. Accessed at: http://news.yahoo.com/s/livescience/20110624/sc_livescience/americanslikebabyboysbest

PARKER, KIM. "The Harried Life of the Working Mother." Pew Research Center. 2009. [Online] Available at http://www.pewsocialtrends.org/2009/10/01/the-harried-life-of-the-working-mother/

PARSONS, TALCOTT. "Age and Sex in the Social Structure of the United States." *American Sociological Review.* Vol. 7, No. 4 (August 1942):604–16.

———. *The Social System.* New York: Free Press, 1951.

———. *Essays in Sociological Theory.* New York: Free Press, 1954.

Paton, Graeme. "Boys Falling Behind Girls at the Age of Five." *The Telegraph*. [Online] Available March 25, 2010, at http://www.telegraph.co.uk/education/education-news/7521315/Boys-falling-behind-girls-at-the-age-offive.html

Paxton, Pamela, Melanie M. Hughes, and Jennifer L. Green. "The International Women's Movement and Women's Political Participation, 1893–2003." *American Sociological Review*. Vol. 71, No. 6 (December 2006):898–920.

Popenoe, David. "Parental Androgyny." *Society*. Vol. 30, No. 6 (September/October 1993b):5–11.

Population Reference Bureau. "Datafinder." 2011. [Online] Available at http://www.prb.org/DataFinder.aspx

———. "Female Genital Mutilation/Cutting: Data and Trends: Update 2010." 2010. [Online] Available at http://www.prb.org/pdf10/fgm-wallchart2010.pdf

Pryor, John H., et al. *The American Freshman: National Norms Fall 2010*. Cooperative Institutional Research Program at the Higher Education Research Institute at UCLA: 2011.

Quota Project. "Global Database of Quotas for Women." 2011. [Online] Available at http://www.quotaproject.org/index.cfm

Raphael, Ray. *The Men from the Boys: Rites of Passage in Male America*. Lincoln: University of Nebraska Press, 1988.

Ridgeway, Cecilia L., and Lynn Smith-Lovin. "The Gender System and Interaction." *Annual Review of Sociology*. Vol. 25 (August 1999):191–216.

Roesch, Roberta. "Violent Families." *Parents*. Vol. 59, No. 9 (September 1984): 74–76, 150–52.

Rosendahl, Mona. *Inside the Revolution: Everyday Life in Socialist Cuba*. Ithaca, N.Y.: Cornell University Press, 1997.

Rossi, Alice S. "Gender and Parenthood." In Alice S. Rossi, ed., *Gender and the Life Course*. New York: Aldine, 1985:161–91.

Sabatini, Joshua. "San Francisco Circumcision Ban Headed for November Ballot." *The Examiner*. [Online] Available February, 18, 2011, at http://www.sfexaminer.com/local/2011/02/san-francisco-circumcision-ban-headednovember-ballot

Saint Jean, Yanick, and Joe R. Feagin. *Double Burden: Black Women and Everyday Racism*. Armonk, N.Y.: Sharpe, 1998.

Schnittker, Jason, Jeremy Freese, and Brian Powell. "Who Are Feminists and What Do They Believe? The Role of Generations." *American Sociological Review*. Vol. 68, No. 4. American Sociological Association: August 2003. http://www.jstor.org/stable/1519741

Seager, Joni. *The Penguin Atlas of Women in the World*. 3rd ed. New York: Penguin Putnam, 2003.

Segal, Mady Wechsler, and Amanda Faith Hansen. "Value Rationales in Policy Debates on Women in the Military: A Content Analysis of Congressional Testimony, 1941–1985." *Social Science Quarterly*. Vol. 73, No. 2 (June 1992):296–309.

Shea, Rachel Hartigan. "The New Insecurity." *U.S. News & World Report* (March 25, 2002):40.

Shellenbarger, Sue. "The Name Change Dilemma." *The Wall Street Journal*. May 13, 2011. Accessed at: http://finance.yahoo.com/family-home/article/112736/name-change-dilemma-women-marriage-wsj?mod=family-love_money

Smolowe, Jill. "When Violence Hits Home." *Time* (July 4, 1994):18–25.

Sommers, Christine Hoff. *The War Against Boys: How Misguided Feminism s Harming Our Young Men*. New York: Simon & Schuster, 2000.

Stacey, Judith. *Patriarchy and Socialist Revolution in China*. Berkeley: University of California Press, 1983.

Stier, Haya. "Continuity and Change in Women's Occupations following First Childbirth." *Social Science Quarterly*. Vol. 77, No. 1 (March 1996): 60–75.

Stratton, Leslie S. "Why Does More Housework Lower Women's Wages? Testing Hypotheses Involving Job Effort and Hours Flexibility." *Social Sciences Quarterly*. Vol. 82, No. 1 (March 2001):67–76.

Tallichet, Suzanne E. "Barriers to Women's Advancement in Underground Coal Mining." *Rural Sociology*. Vol. 65, No. 2 (June 2000):234–52.

Tannen, Deborah. *You Just Don't Understand: Women and Men in Conversation*. New York: Morrow, 1990.

———. *Talking from 9 to 5: How Women's and Men's Conversational Styles Affect Who Gets Heard, Who Gets Credit, and What Gets Done at Work*. New York: Morrow, 1994.

Tavris, Carol, and Carol Wade. *Psychology in Perspective*. 3rd ed. Upper Saddle River, N.J.: Prentice Hall, 2001.

Udry, J. Richard. "Biological Limitations of Gender Construction." *American Sociological Review*. Vol. 65, No. 3 (June 2000):443–57.

U.S. Census Bureau. "Current Population Survey." September 2011. [Online] Available at http://www.census.gov/cps/

———. "Families and Living Arrangements." 2011. [Online] Available at http://www.census.gov/population/www/socdemo/hh-fam.html

———. "Survey of Business Owners." 2010. [Online] Available at http://www.census.gov/newsroom/releases/archives/business_ownership/cb10-184.html

U.S. Department of Defense. "Military Casualty Information." 2011. [Online] Available at http://siadapp.dmdc.osd.mil/personnel/CASUALTY/castop.htm

———. "Military Personnel Statistics." 2011. [Online] Available at http://siadapp.dmdc.osd.mil/personnel/MILITARY/miltop.htm

U.S. Department of Education, National Center for Education Statistics. "U.S. Digest of Education Statistics 2010." 2011. [Online] Available at http://nces.ed.gov/programs/digest/2010menu_tables.asp

U.S. Department of Justice, Bureau of Justice Statistics. "Criminal Victimization in the United States, 2010-Statistical Tables." September 15, 2011. [Online] Available at http://bjs.ojp.usdoj.gov/index.cfm?ty=pbdetail&iid=2224

U.S. Department of Justice, Federal Bureau of Investigation. "Crime in the United States 2010." September 2011. [Online] Available at http://www.fbi.gov/about-us/cjis/ucr/crime-in-the-u.s/2010/crime-in-the-u.s.-2010

U.S. Department of Justice, National Institue of Justice. "Sexual Assault on Campus." 2011. [Online] Available at http://www.nij.gov/nij/topics/crime/rape-sexual-violence/campus/welcome.htm

U.S. Department of Labor, Bureau of Labor Statistics. "Highlights of Women's Earnings in 2010." July 2011. http://www.bls.gov/cps/cpswom2010.pdf"

———. "Employment Characteristics of Families." 2011. http://www.bls.gov/news.release/famee.toc.htm

———. "Labor Force Statistics from the Current Population Survey." 2011. http://www.bls.gov/cps/home.htm

———. "American Time Use Survey, 2010, Unpublished Tables." 2011. [Online] Available at http://www.bls.gov/tus/charts/household.htm.

———. Women in the Labor Force: A Databook. 2011. [Online] Available at http://www.bls.gov/cps/wlf-databook2011.htm

U.S. Department of Labor, Occupational Employment Statistics (OES). "National Occupational Employment and Wage Estimates, United States." 2011. [Online] Available at http://www.bls.gov/oes/current/oes_nat.htm

UNICEF. "ChildInfo Statistics by Area: Child Protection/Female Genital Mutilation/Cutting." November 2009. [Online] Available at http://www.childinfo.org/protection.html

United Nations Development Programme. *Human Development Report 2011. Statistical Tables*. [Online] Available at http://hdr.undp.org/en/statistics/data/

Vogel, Lise. *Marxism and the Oppression of Women: Toward a Unitary Theory*. New Brunswick, N.J.: Rutgers University Press, 1983.

Von Drehle, David. "The Myth About Boys." *Time*. [Online] Available July 26, 2007, at http://www.time.com/time/magazine/article/0,9171, 1647452, 00 .html

Waldfogel, Jane. "The Effect of Children on Women's Wages." *American Sociological Review*. Vol. 62, No. 2 (April 1997):209–17.

Wang, Wendy and Kim Parker. "Women See Value and Benefits of College; Men Lag on Both Fronts Study Finds." Pew Research Center. August 17, 2011. Accessed at: http://www.pewsocialtrends.org/2011/08/17/women-see-value-and-benefits-of-college-men-lag-on-both-fronts-survey-finds/

Wolf, Naomi. *The Beauty Myth: How Images of Beauty Are Used against Women*. New York: Morrow, 1990.

Wolfinger, Nicholas H., Mary Ann Mason, and Marc Goulden. "Problems in the Pipeline: Gender, Marriage, and Fertility in the Ivory Tower." *Journal of Higher Education*, Vol. 79, No. 4 (2008).

World Health Organization. "Female genital mutilation and other harmful practices." 2011. [Online] Available at http://www.who.int/reproductivehealth/topics/fgm/prevalence/en/index.html

Xu, Jiaquan, Kenneth D. Kochanek, Sherry L. Murphy, and Betzaida Tejadavera. "Deaths: Final Data for 2007." *National Vital Statistics Reports*. Vol. 58, No. 19. Hyattsville, Md.: National Center for Health Statistics, 2010. [Online] Available at http://www.cdc.gov/nchs/data/nvsr/nvsr58/nvsr58_19.pdf

Chapter 11 References

Adorno, Theodore W., Else Frenkel-Brunswik, Daniel J. Levinson, and R. Nevitt Sanford. *The Authoritarian Personality*. New York: Harper & Brothers, 1950.

Albon, Joan. "Retention of Cultural Values and Differential Urban Adaptation: Samoans and American Indians in a West Coast City." *Social Forces*. Vol. 49, No. 3 (March 1971):385–93.

Ali, Lorraine, and Vanessa Juarez. "We Love This Country." *Newsweek*. April 7, 2003.

Ali, Lorraine, Tamara Lipper, and Mohammed Mack. "Voters: A Demographic Shift." *Newsweek*. October 25, 2004.

American Sociological Association. *The Importance of Collecting Data and Doing Social Scientific Research on Race*. Washington, D.C.: American Sociological Association, 2003.

Baltzell, E. Digby. *The Protestant Establishment: Aristocracy and Caste in America*. New York: Vintage Books, 1964.

Barbassa, Juliana. "Asian-American Political Profile Rising in U.S." *Yahoo News* (January 18, 2009). [Online] Available January 18, 2009, at http://news.yahoo.com/s/ap/20090118/ap_on_re_us/asian_american_politics

Bartlett, Donald L., and James B. Steele. "Wheel of Misfortune." *Time* (December 16, 2002):44–58.

Blanton, Kimberly. "Borrowers Sue Subprime Lender, Allege Race Bias." *Boston Globe*. July 13, 2007. [Online] Available March 9, 2008, at http://www.boston.com/business/personalfinance/articles/2007/07/13/borrowers_sue_subprime_lender_allege_race_bias/

Blaustein, Albert P., and Robert L. Zangrando. *Civil Rights and the Black American*. New York: Washington Square Press, 1968.

Bogardus, Emory S. "Social Distance and Its Origins." *Sociology and Social Research*. Vol. 9 (July/August 1925):216–25.

———. *A Forty-Year Racial Distance Study*. Los Angeles: University of Southern California Press, 1967.

Booth, William. "By the Sweat of Their Brows: A New Economy." *Washington Post* (July 13, 1998):A1, A10–A11.

Boswell, Terry E. "A Split Labor Market Analysis of Discrimination against Chinese Immigrants, 1850–1882." *American Sociological Review*. Vol. 51, No. 3 (June 1986):352–71.

BOWEN, WILLIAM G., AND DEREK K. BOK. *The Shape of the River: Long-Term Consequences of Considering Race in College and University Admissions*. Princeton, N.J.: Princeton University Press, 1999.

BRODKIN, KAREN B. "How Did Jews Become White Folks?" In JOHN J. MACIONIS AND NIJOLE V. BENOKRAITIS, eds. *Seeing Ourselves: Classic, Contemporary, and Cross-Cultural Readings in Sociology*. 7th ed. Upper Saddle River, N.J.: Prentice Hall, 2007.

CALIFORNIA NEWSREEL. "Race: The Power of an Illusion: Genetic Diversity Quiz." 2003. [Online] Available February 9, 2006, at http://www.pbs.org/race/000_About/002_04_a-godeeper.htm

CAMARA, EVANDRO. Personal communication, 2000.

CARMICHAEL, STOKELY, AND CHARLES V. HAMILTON. *Black Power: The Politics of Liberation in America*. New York: Vintage Books, 1967.

CHUA-EOAN, HOWARD. "Profiles in Outrage." *Time* (September 25, 2000):38–39.

CUMMINGS, SCOTT, AND THOMAS LAMBERT. "Anti-Hispanic and Anti-Asian Sentiments among African Americans." *Social Science Quarterly*. Vol. 78, No. 2 (June 1997):338–53.

DOBYNS, HENRY F. "An Appraisal of Techniques with a New Hemispheric Estimate." *Current Anthropology*. Vol. 7, No. 4 (October 1966):395–446.

DOLLARD, JOHN, ET AL. *Frustration and Aggression*. New Haven, Conn.: Yale University Press, 1939.

EMERSON, MICHAEL O., GEORGE YANCEY, AND KAREN J. CHAI. "Does Race Matter in Residential Segregation? Exploring the Preferences of White Americans." *American Sociological Review*. Vol. 66, No. 6 (December 2001):922–35.

EWERS, JUSTIN. "Saving Symbols of Shame." *U.S. News & World Report*. Vol. 144, No. 7 (March 10, 2008):31.

FIREBAUGH, GLENN, AND KENNETH E. DAVIS. "Trends in Antiblack Prejudice, 1972–1984: Region and Cohort Effects." *American Journal of Sociology*. Vol. 94, No. 2 (September 1988):251–72.

FLYNN, KEVIN. "Colorado Voters Preserve Affirmative Action." *Rocky Mountain News* (November 7, 2008). [Online] Available December 7, 2008, at http://www.rocky-mountain news.com/news/2008/nov/06/colorado-voters-preserveaffirmative-action

FRANKLIN, JOHN HOPE. *From Slavery to Freedom: A History of Negro Americans*. 3rd ed. New York: Vintage Books, 1967.

GALLAGHER, CHARLES A. "Miscounting Race: Explaining Whites' Misperceptions of Racial Group Size." *Sociological Perspectives*. Vol. 46, No. 3 (2003):381–96.

GESCHWENDER, JAMES A. *Racial Stratification in America*. Dubuque, Iowa: Brown, 1978.

GILBERTSON, GRETA A., AND DOUGLAS T. GURAK. "Broadening the Enclave Debate: The Dual Labor Market Experiences of Dominican and Colombian Men in New York City." *Sociological Forum*. Vol. 8, No. 2 (June 1993):205–20.

GOODWIN, LIZ. "College-Educated Immigrants Outnumber Unskilled Immigrants." June 9, 2011. [Online] Accessed at: http://news.yahoo.com/s/yblog_thelookout/20110609/us_yblog_thelookout/college-educated-immigrants-outnumber-unskilled-immigrants

GOTHAM, KEVIN FOX. "Race, Mortgage Lending, and Loan Rejections in a U.S. City." *Sociological Focus*. Vol. 31, No. 4 (October 1998):391–405.

HAGOPIAN, ELAINE C. *Civil Rights in Peril: The Targeting of Arabs and Muslims*. London: Photo Press, 2004.

HANDLIN, OSCAR. *Boston's Immigrants, 1790–1865: A Study in Acculturation*. Cambridge, Mass.: Harvard University Press, 1941.

HARRIS, DAVID R., AND JEREMIAH JOSEPH SIM. "Who Is Multiracial? Assessing the Complexity of Lived Race." *American Sociological Review*. Vol. 67, No. 4 (August 2002):614–27.

HERRNSTEIN, RICHARD J., AND CHARLES MURRAY. *The Bell Curve: Intelligence and Class Structure in American Life*. New York: Free Press, 1994.

HILL, MARK E. "Race of the Interviewer and Perception of Skin Color: Evidence from the Multi-City Study of Urban Inequality." *American Sociological Review*. Vol. 67, No. 1 (February 2002):99–108.

HOEFER, MICHAEL, NANCY RYTINA, AND BRYAN C. BAKER. "Estimates of the Unauthorized Immigrant Population Residing in the United States: January 2010." U.S. Dept. of Homeland Security, Office of Immigration Statistics. February 2011. [Online] Available at http://www.dhs.gov/xlibrary/assets/statistics/publications/ois_ill_pe_2010.pdf

HSU, FRANCIS L. K. *The Challenge of the American Dream: The Chinese in the United States*. Belmont, Calif.: Wadsworth, 1971.

INCIARDI, JAMES A., HILARY L. SURRATT, AND PAULO R. TELLES. *Sex, Drugs, and HIV/AIDS in Brazil*. Boulder, Colo.: Westview Press, 2000.

JIMÉNEZ, TOMÁS R. "Weighing the Costs and Benefits of Mexican Immigration: The Mexican American Perspective." *Social Science Quarterly*. Vol. 88, No. 3 (2007):599–618.

JONES, KATHARINE W. *Accent on Privilege: English Identities and Anglophilia in the U.S.* Philadelphia: Temple University Press, 2001.

JOSEPHY, ALVIN M., JR. *Now That the Buffalo's Gone: A Study of Today's American Indians*. New York: Knopf, 1982.

KANTROWITZ, BARBARA, AND PAT WINGERT. "What's at Stake." *Newsweek* (January 27, 2003):30–37.

KAUFMAN, ROBERT L. "Assessing Alternative Perspectives on Race and Sex Employment Segregation." *American Sociological Review*. Vol. 67, No. 4 (August 2002):547–72.

KEETER, SCOTT AND PAUL TAYLOR. "The Millenials." Pew Research Center, 2009. [Online] Available at http://pewresearch.org/pubs/1437/millennials-profile

KEWALRAMANI, ANGELINA, LAUREN GILBERTSON, MARY ANN FOX, AND STEPHEN PROVASNIK. *Status and Trends in the Education of Racial and Ethnic Minorities, 2005*. National Center for Education Statistics. September 2007. [Online] Available May 19, 2008, at http://nces.ed.gov/pubs2007/minoritytrends

KINKEAD, GWEN. *Chinatown: A Portrait of a Closed Society*. New York: Harper-Collins, 1992.

KRYSAN, MARIA. "Community Undesirability in Black and White: Examining Racial Residential Preferences through Community Perceptions." *Social Problems*. Vol. 49, No. 4 (November 2002):521–43.

LAI, H. M. "Chinese." In *Harvard Encyclopedia of American Ethnic Groups*. Cambridge, Mass.: Harvard University Press, 1980:217–33.

LEACH, COLIN WAYNE. "Democracy's Dilemma: Explaining Racial Inequality in Egalitarian Societies." *Sociological Forum*. Vol. 17, No. 4 (December 2002): 681–96.

LEE, BARRET A., AND MATHEW MARLAY. "The Right Side of the Tracks: Affluent Neighborhoods in the Metropolitan United States." *Social Science Quarterly*. Vol. 88, No. 3 (2007):766–89.

LING, PYAU. "Causes of Chinese Emigration." In AMY TACHIKI ET AL., eds., *Roots: An Asian American Reader*. Los Angeles: UCLA Asian American Studies Center, 1971:134–38.

LOGAN, JOHN R., RICHARD D. ALBA, AND WENQUAN ZHANG. "Immigrant Enclaves and Ethnic Communities in New York and Los Angeles." *American Sociological Review*. Vol. 67, No. 2 (April 2002):299–322.

LOVEMAN, MARA. "Is 'Race' Essential?" *American Sociological Review*. Vol. 64, No. 6 (December 1999):890–98. MARÍN, GERARDO, AND BARBARA VAN OSS MARÍN. *Research with Hispanic Populations*. Newbury Park, Calif.: Sage, 1991.

MARZÁN, GILBERT, ANDRÉS TORRES, AND ANDREW LUECKE. "Puerto Rican Outmigration from New York City: 1995–2000." Centro de Estudios Puertorriqueños, Hunter College (CUNY), *Policy Report*. Vol. 2, No. 2 (2008). [Online] Available at http://www.centropr.org/documents/working_papers/Outmigration091108.pdf

MASSEY, DOUGLAS S., AND NANCY A., DENTON. "Hypersegregation in U.S. Metropolitan Areas: Black and Hispanic Segregation along Five Dimensions." *Demography*. Vol. 26, No. 3 (August 1989):373–91.

MATHER, MARK AND KELVIN POLLARD. "U.S. Population Projected to Hit 400 Million in 2039." Population Reference Bureau, August 2008. [Online] Available at http://www.prb.org/Articles/2008/us400million.aspx

MATTHIESSEN, PETER. *Indian Country*. New York: Viking Press, 1984.

METZGER, KURT. "Cities and Race." *Society*. Vol. 39, No. 1 (December 2001):2.

MONGER, RANDALL AND JAMES YANKEY. "U.S. Legal Permanent Residents: 2010." U.S. Department of Homeland Security, Office of Immigration Statistics. March 2011. [Online] Available at http://www.dhs.gov/xlibrary/assets/statistics/publications/lpr_fr_2010.pdf

MYRDAL, GUNNAR. *An American Dilemma: The Negro Problem and Modern Democracy*. New York: Harper Bros., 1944.

NATIONAL GOVERNOR'S ASSOCIATION. 2010. [Online] Available at http://www.nga.org

NAVARRO, MIREYA. "Puerto Rican Presence Wanes in New York." *New York Times* (February 28, 2000):A1, A20.

NEWMAN, WILLIAM M. *American Pluralism: A Study of Minority Groups and Social Theory*. New York: Harper & Row, 1973.

NEW YORK COMMUNITY MEDIA ALLIANCE. *Many Voices, One City*. 4th ed. 2008. [Online] Available at http://www.indypressny.org

NORC. *General Social Surveys, 1972–2010: Cumulative Codebook*. Chicago: National Opinion Research Center, 2011. http://www.norc.org/GSS+Website

O'HARE, WILLIAM P., WILLIAM H. FREY, AND DAN FOST. "Asians in the Suburbs." *American Demographics*. Vol. 16, No. 9 (May 1994):32–38.

OLZAK, SUSAN. "Labor Unrest, Immigration, and Ethnic Conflict in Urban America, 1880–1914." *American Journal of Sociology*. Vol. 94, No. 6 (May 1989): 1303–33.

OWEN, CAROLYN A., HOWARD C. ELSNER, AND THOMAS R. MCFAUL. "A Half-Century of Social Distance Research: National Replication of the Bogardus Studies." *Sociology and Social Research*. Vol. 66, No. 1 (1977):80–98.

PARRILLO, VINCENT N. "Diversity in America: A Sociohistorical Analysis." *Sociological Forum*. Vol. 9, No. 4 (December 1994):42–45.

PARRILLO, VINCENT, AND CHRISTOPHER DONOGHUE. "Updating the Bogardus Social Distance Studies: A New National Survey." *Social Science Journal*. Vol. 42, No. 2 (April 2005): 257–71.

PATTILLO, MARY. *Black on the Block: The Politics of Race and Class in the City*. Chicago: University of Chicago Press, 2007.

PERLMUTTER, PHILIP. "Minority Group Prejudice." *Society*. Vol. 39, No. 3 (March/April 2002):59–65.

PEW FORUM ON RELIGION AND PUBLIC LIFE. "The Future of the Global Muslim Population: Projections for 2010–2030." 2011. [Online] Available at http://pewforum.org/The-Future-of-the-Global-Muslim-Population.aspx

_____ "Muslims Widely Seen As Facing Discrimination." 2009. [Online] Available at http://www.pewforum.org/Muslim/Muslims-Widely-Seen-As-Facing-Discrimination.aspx

PEW RESEARCH CENTER FOR THE PEOPLE AND THE PRESS. "Muslim Americans: No Signs of Growth in Alienation or Support for Extremism." 2011. [Online] Available at http://www.people-press.org/files/legacy-pdf/Muslim-American-Report.pdf

PORTES, ALEJANDRO, AND LEIF JENSEN. "The Enclave and the Entrants: Patterns of Ethnic Enterprise in Miami before and after Mariel." *American Sociological Review*. Vol. 54, No. 6 (December 1989):929–49.

ROTHENBERG, PAULA. *White Privilege*. 3rd ed. New York: Worth, 2008.

SALE, KIRKPATRICK. *The Conquest of Paradise: Christopher Columbus and the Columbian Legacy*. New York: Knopf, 1990.

SHESKIN, IRA M., AND ARNOLD DASHEVSKY. "Jewish Population in the United States." 2010. [Online] Available at http://www.jewishdatabank.org

SIEGEL, ROBERT. "Black Atlantans Struggle to Stay in the Middle Class." NPR. December 14, 2011. Accessed at: http://www.npr.org/2011/12/08/143378702/black-atlantans-struggle-to-stay-in-the-middle-class

Smith, Ryan A. "Race, Gender, and Authority in the Workplace: Theory and Research." *Annual Review of Sociology*. Vol. 28 (2002):509–42.

Smith, Tom W. "Anti-Semitism Decreases but Persists." *Society*. Vol. 33, No. 3 (March/April 1996):2.

Sowell, Thomas. *Ethnic America*. New York: Basic Books, 1981.

———. *Race and Culture*. New York: Basic Books, 1994.

———. "Ethnicity and IQ." In Steven Fraser, ed., *The Bell Curve Wars: Race, Intelligence, and the Future of America*. New York: Basic Books, 1995: 70–79.

Steele, Shelby. *The Content of Our Character: A New Vision of Race in America*. New York: St. Martin's Press, 1990.

Stout, David. "Supreme Court Splits on Diversity Efforts at University of Michigan." [Online] Available June 23, 2003, athttp://news.yahoo.com

Sun, Lena H. "WWII's Forgotten Internees Await Apology." *Washington Post* (March 9, 1998):A1, A5, A6.

Takaki, Ronald. *Strangers from a Different Shore*. Boston: Back Bay Books, 1998.

Thomas, W. I. "The Relation of Research to the Social Process." In Morris Janowitz, ed., *W. I. Thomas on Social Organization and Social Personality*. Chicago: University of Chicago Press, 1966:289–305; orig. 1931.

Thomas, W. I., and Dorothy Swaine Thomas. *The Child in America: Behavior Problems and Programs*. New York: Knopf, 1928.

Tumulty, Karen. "Should They Stay or Should They Go?" *Time* (April 10, 2006):30–41.

Tyler, S.Lyman. *A History of Indian Policy*. Washington, D.C.: U.S. Department of the Interior, Bureau of Indian Affairs, 1973.

U.S. Census Bureau. "American Community Survey." 2011. [Online] Available at http://www.census.gov/acs/www

———. "Boundary and Annexation Survey." 2012. [Online] Available at http://www.census.gov/geo/www/bas/bashome.html

———. "Census 2010." 2011. [Online] Available at http://factfinder2.census. gov/faces/nav/jsf/pages/index.xhtml

———. "Current Population Survey." September 2011. [Online] Available at http://www.census.gov/cps/

———. "Families and Living Arrangements." 2011. [Online] Available at http://www.census.gov/population/www/socdemo/hh-fam.html

———. "Population Estimates." 2011 [Online] Available at http://www.census .gov/popest/estimates.html

———. *Statistical Abstract of the United States: 2012, 131st Edition*. 2011. [Online] Available at http://www.census.gov/statab/www

U.S. Conference of Mayors. "Meet the Mayors." 2011. [Online] Available at http://usmayors.org/meetmayors/

U.S. Department of Homeland Security, Office of Immigration Statistics. Yearbook of Immigration Statistics 2010. 2011. [Online] Available at http://www.dhs.gov/files/statistics/publications/yearbook.shtm

U.S. Department of Labor, Bureau of Labor Statistics. "Labor Force Statistics from the Current Population Survey." 2011. [Online] Available at http://www.bls.gov/cps/home.htm

U.S. House of Representatives. "African Americans in the 112th Congress." [Online] Available January 24, 2012 at http://www.house.gov/daily/hpg.htm

U.S. Senate. "Minority Senators in the 112th Congress." [Online] Available January 24, 2012 at http://www.senate.gov/galleries/daily/minority2.htm

West, Cornel. "The Obama Moment." *U.S. News & World Report* (November 17, 2008):29.

Wilkes, Rima, and John Iceland. "Hypersegregation in the Twenty-First Century." *Demography*. Vol. 41, No. 1 (February 9, 2004):23–36.

Wilson, James Q. "Crime, Race, and Values." *Society*. Vol. 30, No. 1 (November/December 1992):90–93.

Wong, Buck. "Need for Awareness: An Essay on Chinatown, San Francisco." In Amy Tachiki et al., eds., *Roots: An Asian American Reader*. Los Angeles: UCLA Asian American Studies Center, 1971:265–73.

Chapter 12 References

"Abramoff Effect: Leaping out of Bed with the Lobbyists." *New York Times* (January 16, 2006). [Online] Available May 2, 2009, at http://query.nytimes .com/gst/fullpage.html?res=9D04EEDC143FF935A25752C0A9609C8B63 &sec=&spon=

"Female Opinion and Defense since September 11th." *Society*. Vol. 39, No. 3 (March/April 2002):2.

Allen, Mike. "Card Check Battle Starts Tomorrow." *Politico* (March 9, 2009). [Online] Available May 8, 2009, at http://www.politico.com/news/stories/0309/19786.html

Astin, Alexander W., Leticia Oseguera, Linda J. Sax, and William S. Korn. *The American Freshman: Thirty-Five Year Trends*. Los Angeles: UCLA Higher Education Research Institute, 2002.

Barnes, Julian E. "War Profiteering." *U.S. News & World Report* (May 13, 2002b):20–24.

Bartlett, Donald L., and James B. Steele. "How the Little Guy Gets Crunched." *Time* (February 7, 2000):38–41.

Bell, Jim. "Will Enthusiasm for Democracy Endure in Egypt and Elsewhere?" Pew Research Center. [Online] Available March 8, 2011, at http://pewresearch.org/pubs/1918/enthusiasm-for-democracy-in-egypt-tunisiafragile-eastern-europe-experience-shows?src=prc-latest&proj= peoplepress

Berger, Peter L. *The Capitalist Revolution: Fifty Propositions about Prosperity, Equality, and Liberty*. New York: Basic Books, 1986.

Brians, Craig Leonard, and Bernard Grofman. "Election Day Registration's Effect on U.S. Voter Turnout." *Social Science Quarterly*. Vol. 82, No. 1 (March 2001):170–83.

Carlson, Allan. "Agrarianism Reborn: The Curious Return of the Small Family Farm." *Intercollegiate Review*. Vol. 43, No. 1 (Spring 2008):13–23.

Center for Responsive Politics. "Banking on Becoming President." 2008. [Online] Available April 19, 2009, at http://www.opensecrets.org/pres08/index.php

———. "Lobbying Database." 2011. [Online] Available at http://www.opensecrets.org/lobby

———. "Personal Finances." 2011. [Online] Available at http://www.opensecrets .org/index.php

———. "Politicians and Elections." 2008, 2009 [Online] Available at http://www.opensecrets.org/pres08/index.php

Center for the Study of the American Electorate. "2008 Election Turnout." 2009. [Online] Available January 26, 2009, at Available at http://www.american.edu/spa/cdem/csae.cfm

Central Intelligence Agency. "CIA World Factbook." 2011. [Online] Available at https://www.cia.gov/library/publications/the-world-factbook/index.html

Chance, David and Jack Kim. "North Korea Mourns Dead Leader, Son is 'Great Successor'." Reuters. December 19, 2011. Accessed at: http://news.yahoo.com/north-korea-state-tv-says-kim-jong-il-031257363.html

Clark, Kim. "Bankrupt Lives." *U.S. News & World Report* (September 16, 2002):52–54.

Clawson, Dan, and Mary Ann Clawson. "What Has Happened to the U.S. Labor Movement? Union Decline and Renewal." *Annual Review of Sociology*. Vol. 25 (1999):95–119.

Dahl, Robert A. *Who Governs?* New Haven, Conn.: Yale University Press, 1961.

———. *Dilemmas of Pluralist Democracy: Autonomy vs. Control*. New Haven, Conn.: Yale University Press, 1982.

Dalmia, Shikha. "Obama and Big Labor." *Forbes* (October 29, 2008). [Online] Available May 8, 2009, at http://www.forbes.com/2008/10/28/obama-cardcheck-oped-cx_sd_1029dalmia.html

Decarlo, Scott, ed. "Forbes: The Global 2000." *Forbes* 2011. [Online] Available at http://www.forbes.com/global2000/list

Dedrick, Dennis K., and Richard E. Yinger. "MAD, SDI, and the Nuclear Arms Race." Unpublished manuscript. Georgetown, Ky.: Georgetown College, 1990.

Dixon, William J., and Terry Boswell. "Dependency, Disarticulation, and Denominator Effects: Another Look at Foreign Capital Penetration." *American Journal of Sociology*. Vol. 102, No. 2 (September 1996):543–62.

Dudley, Kathryn Marie. *Debt and Dispossession: Farm Loss in America's Heartland*. Chicago: University of Chicago Press, 2000.

Executive Leadership Council. "2008 Women and Minorities on *Fortune* 100 Boards." January 22, 2008. [Online] Available January 21, 2009, at http://www.elcinfo.com/reports.php

Federal Election Commission. "Campaign Finance Summaries" [Online] Available http://www.fec.gov/press/cf_summaries.shtml

Firebaugh, Glenn, and Dumitru Sandu. "Who Supports Marketization and Democratization in Post-Communist Romania?" *Sociological Forum*. Vol. 13, No. 3 (September 1998):521–41.

Firebaugh, Glenn, and Frank D. Beck. "Does Economic Growth Benefit the Masses? Growth, Dependence, and Welfare in the Third World." *American Sociological Review*. Vol. 59, No. 5 (October 1994):631–53.

Fisher, Roger, and William Ury. "Getting to Yes." In William M. Evan and Stephen Hilgartner, eds., *The Arms Race and Nuclear War*. Englewood Cliffs, N.J.: Prentice Hall, 1988:261–68.

Foroohar, Rana. "Don't Hold Your Breath." *Time*. Vol. 177, No. 25 (June 20, 2011):22–26.

Fox, Justin. "Why Denmark Loves Globalization." *Time* (November 15, 2007). [Online] Available March 15, 2008, at http://www.time.com/time/magazine/article/0, 9171, 1684528, 00.html

Freedom House. "Freedom in the World Comparative and Historical Data." 2012. [Online] Available at http://www.freedomhouse.org/report-types/freedom-world

Friedman, Milton, and Rose Friedman. *Free to Choose: A Personal Statement*. New York: Harcourt Brace Jovanovich, 1980.

Gellman, Barton. "Julian Assange." *Time*. Vol. 176, No. 26 (December 27, 2010–January 3, 2011):90–94.

Gerlach, Michael L. *The Social Organization of Japanese Business*. Berkeley: University of California Press, 1992.

Gibbs, Nancy. "Terrified . . . or Terrorist?" *Time*. Vol. 174, No. 20 (November 23, 2009):28–31.

Goode, William J. "Encroachment, Charlatanism, and the Emerging Profession: Psychology, Sociology, and Medicine." *American Sociological Review*. Vol. 25, No. 6 (December 1960):902–14.

Gorenstrin, Peter. "Don't Call It a Stimulus: 2012 Election Spending Likely to Top $8 Billion." *The Daily Ticker*. April 14, 2011. Accessed at: http://finance.yahoo.com/blogs/daily-ticker/don-t-call-stimulus-2012-election-spending-likely-20110414-084921-208.html

Gray, Stephen. "In Ohio, An Era Nears Its End." *Time*. Vol. 177, No. 11 (March 21, 2011):15.

Graybow, Martha. "Women Directors Help Boost Corporate's Financial Performance: Study." *International Business Times*. October 2, 2007. [Online] Available December 2, 2008, at http://in.ibtimes.com/articles/20071002/women-directors-help-boost-corporate-financial-performance.htm

Greenhouse, Linda. "Many Entry-Level Workers Find Pinch of Rough Market." *New York Times* (September 4, 2006).

Grier, Peter. "How to Slow the Spread of the Bomb." *Christian Science Monitor* (June 5, 2006). [Online] Accessed July 29, 2006, at http://news.yahoo.com/s/csm/20060605

Gutierrez, Carl. "Bear Stearns Announces More Job Cuts." *Forbes* (October 3, 2007). [Online] Available May 28, 2008, at http://www.forbes.com/markets/2007/10/03/bear-stearns-layoffs-markets-equity-cx_cg_1003markets23 .html

Halbfinger, David M., and Steven A. Holmes. "Military Mirrors Working-Class America." *New York Times* (March 20, 2003). [Online] Available May 4, 2009, at http://www.cwalocal4250.org/news/binarydata/Military%20Mirrors %20Working-Class%20America.pdf

Harford, Tim. "The Beauty of Everyday Economics." *U.S. News & World Report* (January 28, 2008):14.

Horwitz, Juliana. "Winds of Political Change Haven't Shifted Public's Ideological Balance." November 25, 2008. [Online] Available January 23, 2009, at http://pewresearch.org/pubs/1042/winds-of-political-change-haventshifted-publics-ideology-balance

Ignatius, Adi. "A Tsar Is Born." *Time* (December 31, 2007):46–62.

Internal Revenue Service. "Statistics of Income, Returns of Active Corporations, Tax Year 2008" 2010. [Online] Available at http://www.irs.gov/taxstats/article/0,,id=170544,00.html

International Labour Organization. *Key Indicators of the Labour Market.* 7th ed. 2011. [Online] Available at http://www.ilo.org/empelm/what/WCMS_114240/lang-en/index.htm

Jenkins, J.Craig. *Images of Terror: What We Can and Can't Know about Terrorism.* Hawthorne, N.Y.: Aldine de Gruyter, 2003.

Johnson, Paul. "The Seven Deadly Sins of Terrorism." In Benjamin Netanyahu, ed., *International Terrorism.* New Brunswick, N.J.: Transaction Books, 1981: 12–22.

Kalleberg, Arne L., Barbara F. Reskin, and Ken Hudson. "Bad Jobs in America: Standard and Nonstandard Employment Relations and Job Quality in the United States." *American Sociological Review.* Vol. 65, No. 2 (April 2000):256–78.

Kaplan, David E., and Michael Schaffer. "Losing the Psywar." *U.S. News & World Report* (October 8, 2001):46.

Karatnycky, Adrian. "The 2001–2002 Freedom House Survey of Freedom: The Democracy Gap." In *Freedom in the World: The Annual Survey of Political Rights and Civil Liberties, 2001–2002.* New York: Freedom House, 2002:7–18.

Kentor, Jeffrey. "The Long-Term Effects of Foreign Investment Dependence on Economic Growth, 1940–1990." *American Journal of Sociology.* Vol. 103, No. 4 (January 1998):1024–46.

Kivant, Barbara. "Reassessing Risk." *Time* (November 17, 2008):Global 1–4.

Kohut, Andrew. "Post-Election Perspectives." November 13, 2008. [Online] Available January 23, 2009, at http://pewresearch.org/pubs/1039/post-election-perspectives

Kono, Clifford, Donald Palmer, Roger Friedland, and Matthew Zafonte. "Lost in Space: The Geography of Corporate Interlocking Directorates." *American Journal of Sociology.* Vol. 103, No. 4 (January 1998):863–911.

Liazos, Alexander. *People First: An Introduction to Social Problems.* Needham Heights, Mass.: Allyn & Bacon, 1982.

Liptak, Adam. "Justices, 5–4, Reject Corporate Spending Limit." *New York Times.* [Online] Available January 21, 2010, at http://www.nytimes.com/2010/01/22/us/politics/22scotus. Html

Lowrey, Ying. "Women in Business, 2006: A Demographic Review of Women's Business Ownership." Office of Economic Research, Office of Advocacy, U.S. Small Business Administration, 2006. [Online] Available at http://www.sba.gov/advo/research/rs280tot.pdf

Lynd, Robert S., and Helen Merrell Lynd. *Middletown in Transition.* New York: Harcourt, Brace & World, 1937.

Marullo, Sam. "The Functions and Dysfunctions of Preparations for Fighting Nuclear War." *Sociological Focus.* Vol. 20, No. 2 (April 1987):135–53.

Mcgeehan, Patrick. "Adding to Recession's Pain, Thousands to Lose Job Benefits." *New York Times* (January 11, 2009). [Online] Available January 12, 2009, at http://www.nytimes.com/2009/01/12/nyregion/12benefits.html.

Military Diversity Commission. "From Representation to Inclusion: Diversity Leadership in the 21st Century Military." Military Diversity Leadership Commission. March 7, 2011. Available at http://mldc.whs.mil/index.php/final-report

Miller, Terry. "2011 Index of Economic Freedom." 2011. [Online] Available at http://www.heritage.org/index

Mills, C. Wright. *The Power Elite.* New York: Oxford University Press, 1956.

Montaigne, Fen. "Russia Rising." *National Geographic.* Vol. 200, No. 5 (September 2001): 2–31.

Moore, Gwen, et al. "Elite Interlocks in Three U.S. Sectors: Nonprofit, Corpgrate, and Government." *Social Science Quarterly.* Vol. 83, No. 3 (September 2002):726–44.

Murphy, Mike. "The Real Stakes in Wisconsin." *Time.* Vol. 177, No. 10 (March 14, 2011):24.

New York Times. "Election Results 2008." November 5, 2008. [Online] Available at http://elections.nytimes.com/2008/results/president/exit-polls.html

Nolan, Patrick, and Gerhard E. Lenski. *Human Societies: An Introduction to Macrosociology.* 11th ed. Boulder, Colo.: Paradigm, 2010.

NORC. *General Social Surveys, 1972–2010.* Chicago: National Opinion Research Center. March 2011. http://www.norc.org/GSS+Website/

NPR. "The Arab Spring: A Year Of Revolution." December 17, 2011. [Online] Available at http://www.npr.org/2011/12/17/143897126/the-arab-spring-a-year-of-revolution

OECD (Organisation for Economic Co-operation and Development). "Economic Outlook No. 90, Annex Tables." November, 2011. [Online] Available at http://www.oecd.org/oecdEconomicOutlook

———. "Product Market Regulation Database." 2011. [Online] Available at http://www.oecd.org/economy/pmr

———. "Revenue Statistics." 2011. [Online] Available at http://www.oecd.org/ctp/revenuestats

———. "Society at a Glance 2011: OECD Social Indicators." 2011. [Online] Available at http://www.oecd.org/els/social/indicators/SAG

———. "Stat.Extracts." 2011. [Online] Available at http://stats.oecd.org/index. aspx

Ohlemacher, Stephen. "Obama's Victory May Show the Way to Win in Future." *USA Today* (November 9, 2008). [Online] Available January 13, 2009, at http://www.usatoday.com/news/politics/2008-11-08-1164297038_x .htm

Pew Research Center. "Confidence in Democracy and Capitalism Wanes in Former Soviet Union." December 5, 2011. Accessed at: http://pewresearch.org/pubs/2139/russia-lithuania-ukraine-former-soviet-union-democracy-capitalism-individualism-economic-conditions?src=prc-newsletter

Pew Research Center. "The Future of the Global Muslim Population: Muslim Population by Country." 2011. [Online] Available at http://features.pewforum.org/muslim-population

Pickler, Nedra, and Liz Sidoti. "Campaigns Unleash Massive Get-Out-Vote Drives." *Yahoo News* (November 2, 2008). [Online] Available November 2, 2008, at http://news.yahoo.com/s/ap/20081102/ap_on_el_pr/campaign_rdp

Polsby, Nelson W. "Three Problems in the Analysis of Community Power." *American Sociological Review.* Vol. 24, No. 6 (December 1959):796–803.

Population Reference Bureau. "Datafinder." 2011. [Online] Available at http://www.prb.org/DataFinder.aspx

Pryor, John H., Sylvia Hurtado, Linda Deangelo, Laura Palucki Blake, and Serge Tran. *The American Freshman: National Norms for Fall 2007.* Los Angeles: UCLA Higher Education Research Institute, 2007.

———. *The American Freshman: National Norms Fall 2010.* Los Angeles: Cooperative Institutional Research Program at the Higher Education Research Institute at UCLA, 2011.

Rasmussen Poll. Reported in the *Dayton Daily News.* [Online] Available February 23, 2011, at http://www.daytondailynews.com/news/dayton-news/americans-split-onunion-issues-1089409.html?cxtype=ynews_rss

Riley, Naomi Schaefer. "Why Unions Hurt Higher Education." *USA Today* (March 3, 2011):9A.

Ripley, Amanda. "Meet Your Government Workers." *Time.* Vol. 177, No. 9 (March 7, 2011):40–44.

Ritzer, George, and David Walczak. *Working: Conflict and Change.* 4th ed. Englewood Cliffs, N.J.: Prentice Hall, 1990.

Rogers, Martin. "In Memory of Kim Jong-Il: Dear Leader, G.O.A.T." *The Daily Take.* December 21, 2011. Accessed at: http://www.thepostgame.com/blog/daily-take/201112/memory-kim-jong-il-dear-leader-and-goat

Rothman, Stanley, and Amy E. Black. "Who Rules Now? American Elites in the 1990s." *Society.* Vol. 35, No. 6 (September/October 1998):17–20.

Rousseau, Caryn. "Unions Rally at Wal-Mart Stores." [Online] Available November 22, 2002, at http://dailynews.yahoo.com

Rule, James, and Peter Brantley. "Computerized Surveillance in the Workplace: Forms and Delusions." *Sociological Forum.* Vol. 7, No. 3 (September 1992): 405–23.

Sachs, Jeffrey D. "The Case for Bigger Government." *Time* (January 19, 2009): 34–36.

Saporito, Bill. "Can Wal-Mart Get Any Bigger?" *Time* (January 13, 2003): 38–43.

Sax, Linda J., et al. *The American Freshman: National Norms for Fall 2003.* Los Angeles: UCLA Higher Education Research Institute, 2003.

Schell, Orville. "How Walmart is Changing China." *The Atlantic.* December 2011 [Online] Available at http://www.theatlantic.com/magazine/archive/2011/12/how-walmart-is-changing-china/8709/3/

Schur, Lisa A., and Douglas L. Kruse. "What Determines Voter Turnout? Lessons from Citizens with Disabilities." *Social Science Quarterly.* Vol. 81, No. 2 (June 2000):571–87.

Sentencing Project. "Felony Disenfranchisement Laws in the United States." 2011. [Online] Available at http://sentencingproject.org/doc/publications/fd_bs_fdlawsinusDec11.pdf

SIPRI (Stockholm International Peace Research Institute). "SIPRI Yearbook 2011." 2011. [Online] Available at http://www.sipri.org/yearbook

Sivard, Ruth Leger. *World Military and Social Expenditures, 1987–88.* 12th ed. Washington, D.C.: World Priorities, 1988.

Skocpol, Theda. *States and Social Revolutions: A Comparative Analysis of France, Russia, and China.* Cambridge: Cambridge University Press, 1979.

Smith, Adam. *An Inquiry into the Nature and Causes of the Wealth of Nations.* New York: Modern Library, 1937; orig. 1776.

Stockholm International Peace Research Institute. "SIPRI Yearbook 2010." June 2010. [Online] Available at http://www.sipri.org/yearbook

Sulzberger, A. G. "Union Bill Is Law, but Debate Is Far From Over." *The New York Times.* [Online] Available March 11, 2011, at http://www.nytimes.com/2011/03/12/us/12wisconsin.html

Thompson, Mark. "The Other 1%." *Time.* Vol. 178, No. 20 (November 1, 2011):33–39.

Thompson, Mark, and Douglas Waller. "Shield of Dreams." *Time* (May 8, 2001):45–47.

Tilly, Charles. "Does Modernization Breed Revolution?" In Jack A. Goldstone, ed., *Revolutions: Theoretical, Comparative, and Historical Studies.* New York: Harcourt Brace Jovanovich, 1986:47–57.

Tocqueville, Alexis De. *The Old Regime and the French Revolution.* Stuart Gilbert, trans. Garden City, N.Y.: Anchor/Doubleday, 1955; orig. 1856.

Tuttle, Brad. "Bounty Hunters." *Time.* Vol. 177, No. 3 (January 24, 2011):52.

U.S. Census Bureau. "2007 Survey of Business Owners" 2010. [Online] Available at http://www.census.gov/econ/sbo/

——. "Federal, State, and Local Governments." 2011 [Online] Available at http://www.census.gov/govs/index.html

——. "Population Estimates." 2011. [Online] Available at http://www.census.gov/popest/data/index.html

——. "Voting and Registration." 2009. [Online] Available at http://www.census.gov/hhes/www/socdemo/voting/index.html

——. *Statistical Abstract of the United States: 2012*, 131st Edition. 2011. [Online] Available at http://www.census.gov/statab/www/

U.S. Department of Defense. "Military Casualty Information." 2011. [Online] Available at http://siadapp.dmdc.osd.mil/personnel/CASUALTY/castop.htm

U.S. Department of Defense. "Military Personnel Statistics." 2011. [Online] Available at http://siadapp.dmdc.osd.mil/personnel/MILITARY/miltop.htm

U.S. Department of the Interior. "National Atlas of the United States." 2011. [Online] Available at http://www.nationalatlas.gov/atlasftp.html

U.S. Department of Labor, Bureau of Labor Statistics. "Employment, Hours, and Earnings (CES)." 2011. [Online] Available at http://www.bls.gov/ces/tables.htm#ee

——. "Employment Situation." 2011. [Online] Available at http://www.bls.gov/news.release/empsit.toc.htm

——. "Employment Projections: Labor Force (Demographic) Data." 2010. [Online] Available at http://www.bls.gov/emp/ep_data_labor_force.htm

——. "International Labor Comparisons." 2011. [Online] Available at http://www.bls.gov/news.release/ichcc.toc.htm

——. "Labor Force Statistics from the Current Population Survey." 2011. [Online] Available at http://www.bls.gov/cps/home.htm

——. "Union Members Summary." 2011. [Online] Available at http://www.bls.gov/news.release/union2.nr0.htm

U.S. Department of Labor. Economic News Release: Unemployed Persons by Duration of Unemployment. December 2011. Accessed at: http://www.bls.gov/news.release/empsit.t12.htm

U.S. Department of State. "Country Background Notes" 2011. [Online] Available at http://www.state.gov/r/pa/ei/bgn/

U.S. Department of State, Bureau of Intelligence and Research. "Independent States in the World." 2011. [Online] Available at http://www.state.gov/s/inr/rls/4250.htm

U.S. Department of State, National Counterterrorism Center. "2010 Report on Terrorism." 2011. [Online] Available at http://www.nctc.gov/witsbanner/docs/2010_report_on_terrorism.pdf

U.S. Equal Employment Opportunity Commission. "Job Patterns For Minorities And Women In Private Industry (EEO-1)." 2011. [Online] Available at http://www1.eeoc.gov/eeoc/statistics/employment/jobpat-eeo1/2010/index.cfm#select_label

U.S. Office of Management and Budget. "The Budget for Fiscal Year 2012." 2011. [Online] Available a t http://www.gpo.gov/fdsys/browse/collectionGPO.action?collectionCode=BUDGET

U.S. Office of Personnel Management. "Employment and Trends." 2011. [Online] Available at http://www.opm.gov/feddata/html/empt.asp

Uggen, Christopher, and Jeff Manza. "Democratic Contraction? Political Consequences of Felon Disenfranchisement in the United States." *American Sociological Review*. Vol. 67, No. 6 (December 2002):777–803.

United Nations Development Programme. *Human Development Report 2011. Statistical Tables. [Online] Available at http://hdr.undp.org/en/statistics/data/*

Vallas, Stephen P., and John P. Beck. "The Transformation of Work Revisited: The Limits of Flexibility in American Manufacturing."*Social Problems*. Vol. 43, No. 3 (August 1996): 339–61.

Vinovskis, Maris A. "Have Social Historians Lost the Civil War? Some Preliminary Demographic Speculations." *Journal of American History*. Vol. 76, No. 1 (June 1989):34–58.

Visser, Jelle. "Union Membership Statistics in 24 Countries." *Monthly Labor Review* (January 2006):38–49. [Online] Available June 2, 2006, at http://www.bls.gov/opub/mlr/2006/01/art3full.pdf

Wallerstein, Immanuel. *The Capitalist World-Economy*. New York: Cambridge University Press, 1979.

Walmart Stores Inc. "Corporate and Financial Facts." August 2011. [Online] Available at http://walmartstores.com/media/factsheets/fs_2230.pdf

——. "Data Sheet: Worldwide Unit Details." January 2011. [Online] Available at http://walmartstores.com/pressroom/news/10532.aspx

Walsh, Bryan. "How Business Saw the Light." *Time* (January 15, 2007):56–57.

Weber, Max. *Economy and Society: An Outline of Interpretive Sociology*. Guenther Roth and Claus Wittich, eds. Berkeley: University of California Press, 1978; orig. 1921.

Weidenbaum, Murray. "The Evolving Corporate Board." *Society*. Vol. 32, No. 3 (March/April 1995):9–20.

Wessel, David. "What's Wrong with America's Job Engine?" *The Wall Street Journal*. July 27, 2011. Accessed at: http://finance.yahoo.com/banking-budgeting/article/113206/americas-job-engine-wsj?mod=bb-budgeting%20&sec=topStories&pos=4&asset=&code=

Whitaker, Mark. "Ten Ways to Fight Terrorism." *Newsweek* (July 1, 1985):26–29.

Wiles, P.J.D. *Economic Institutions Compared*. New York: Halsted Press, 1977.

Woods & Poole Economics Inc. Washington, D.C. [Online] Available at http://www.woodsandpoole.com

World Bank. "Countries and Regions." 2011. [Online] Available at http://go.worldbank.org/9FV1KFE8P0

World Bank. *World Development Indicators*. 2011. [Online] Available at http://data.worldbank.org/data-catalog/world-development-indicators

Wright, Quincy. "Causes of War in the Atomic Age." In William M. Evan and Stephen Hilgartner, eds., *The Arms Race and Nuclear War*. Englewood Cliffs, N.J.: Prentice Hall, 1987:7–10.

Xia, Renee. "In China, Activists Watch and Cheer." *Wall Street Journal*. [Online] Available March 12, 2011, at http://online.wsj.com/article/SB10001424052748704823004576192642010298086.html

Chapter 13 References

AARP Foundation. "GrandFacts." October 2007. [Online] Available July 3, 2008, at http://www.grandfactsheets.org/doc/National%20Resources%20Fact%20Sheet.pdf

Allen, Walter R. "African American Family Life in Social Context: Crisis and Hope." *Sociological Forum*. Vol. 10, No. 4 (December 1995):569–92.

Amato, Paul R. "What Children Learn from Divorce." *Population Today*. Vol. 29, No. 1 (January 2001):1, 4.

Anderson, John Ward. "Early to Wed: The Child Brides of India." *Washington Post* (May 24, 1995):A27, A30.

Applebome, Peter. "70 Years after Scopes Trial, Creation Debate Lives." *New York Times* (March 10, 1996):1, 10.

Association of Religion Data Archives (ARDA). 2011. [Online] Available at http://www.thearda.com

Astin, Alexander W., Leticia Oseguera, Linda J. Sax, and William S. Korn. *The American Freshman: Thirty-Five Year Trends*. Los Angeles: UCLA Higher Education Research Institute, 2002.

Bellah, Robert N. *The Broken Covenant*. New York: Seabury Press, 1975.

Berger, Peter. *The Sacred Canopy: Elements of a Sociological Theory of Religion*. Garden City, N.Y.: Doubleday, 1967.

——. "Faith and Development." *Society*. Vol. 46, No. 1 (January/February 2009):69–75.

Bernard, Jessie. *The Future of Marriage,* 2nd ed. New Haven, Conn.: Yale University Press, 1982.

Besecke, Kelly. "Speaking of Meaning in Modernity: Reflexive Spirituality as a Cultural Resource." *Sociology of Religion*. Vol. 62, No. 3 (2003):365–81.

——. "Seeing Invisible Religion: Religion as a Societal Conversation about Transcendent Meaning." *Sociological Theory*. Vol. 23, No. 2 (June 2005): 179–96.

Besharov, Douglas J., and Lisaa Laumann. "Child Abuse Reporting." *Society*. Vol. 34, No. 4 (May/June 1996):40–46.

Bianchi, Suzanne. "How Older Adults Provide Care for Their Aging Parents, Adult Children, and Friends." Population Reference Bureau. May, 2011. [Online] Available at http://www.prb.org/Journalists/Webcasts/2011/us-aging-family-care-policy-seminar.aspx

——, and Daphne Spain. "Women, Work, and Family in America." *Population Bulletin*. Vol. 51, No. 3 (December 1996).

Blankenhorn, David. *Fatherless America: Confronting Our Most Urgent Social Problem*. New York: HarperCollins, 1995.

Blau, Peter M. *Exchange and Power in Social Life*. New York: Wiley, 1964.

Booth, Alan, and Ann C. Crouter, eds. *Just Living Together: Implications of Cohabitation on Families, Children, and Policy*. Mahwah, N.J.: Erlbaum, 2002.

Boston, Rob. "Ohio Creationism Teacher John Freshwater Fired." *Opposing Views*. [Online] Available January 12, 2011, at http://www.opposingviews.com/i/ohio-creationism-teacher-john-freshwater-fired

Brines, Julie, and Kara Joyner. "The Ties That Bind: Principles of Cohesion in Cohabitation and Marriage." *American Sociological Review*. Vol. 64, No. 3 (June 1999):333–55.

CDC (Centers for Disease Control and Prevention), National Center for Health Statistics. "Cohabitation, Marriage, Divorce, and Remarriage in the United States." 2002. [Online] Available at http://www.cdc.gov/nchs/data/series/sr_23/sr23_022.pdf

——. "Marriage and Divorce Data." 2011. http://www.cdc.gov/nchs/nvss/marriage_divorce_tables.htm

——. "National Survey of Family Growth (NSFG)." 2011. [Online] Available at www.cdc.gov/nchs/nsfg.htm

Cherlin, Andrew J., Linda M., Burton, Tera R., Hart, and Diane M., Purvin. "The Influence of Physical and Sexual Abuse on Marriage and Cohabitation." *American Sociological Review*. Vol. 69, No. 6 (December 2004):768–89.

Clark, Kim. "Bankrupt Lives." *U.S. News & World Report* (September 16, 2002):52–54.

Cohn, D'Vera. "Do Parents Spend Enough Time With Their Children?." Population Reference Bureau. 2007. [Online] Available at http://www.prb.org/Articles/2007/DoParentsSpendEnoughTimeWithTheirChildren.aspx

Cox, Harvey. *The Secular City*. Rev. ed. New York: Macmillan, 1971.

Duncan, Greg J., W. Jean Yeung, Jeanne Brooks-Gunn, and Judith R. Smith. "How Much Does Childhood Poverty Affect the Life Chances of Children?" *American Sociological Review*. Vol. 63, No. 3 (June 1998):406–23.

Durkheim, Emile. *The Elementary Forms of Religious Life*. New York: Free Press, 1965; orig. 1915.

Durose, Matthew R., et al. "Family Violence Statistics Including Statistics on Strangers and Acquaintances." U.S. Department of Justice, Office of Justice Programs, Bureau of Justice Statistics. June 2005. [Online] Available at http://www.ojp.usdoj.gov/bjs/pub/pdf/fvs.pdf

Eck, Diana L. *A New Religious America: How a "Christian Country" Has Become the World's Most Religiously Diverse Nation*. San Francisco: HarperSanFrancisco, 2001.

El-Attar, Mohamed. Personal communication, 1991.

Ember, Melvin, and Carol R. Ember. "The Conditions Favoring Matrilocal versus Patrilocal Residence." *American Anthropologist*. Vol. 73, No. 3 (June 1971):571–94.

——. *Anthropology*. 6th ed. Englewood Cliffs, N.J.: Prentice Hall, 1991.

ENGELS, FRIEDRICH. *The Origin of the Family.* Chicago: Kerr, 1902; orig. 1884.

ENGLAND, PAULA. "Three Reviews on Marriage." *Contemporary Sociology.* Vol. 30, No. 6 (November 2001):564–65.

ETZIONI, AMITAI. "How to Make Marriage Matter." *Time* (September 6, 1993):76.

EUROPEAN UNION, EUROPEAN COMMUNITIES STATISTICAL OFFICE. "Eurostat." 2011. [Online] Available at http://epp.eurostat.ec.europa.eu/portal/page/portal/population/data/database

FRAZIER, E.FRANKLIN. *Black Bourgeoisie: The Rise of a New Middle Class.* New York: Free Press, 1965.

FURSTENBERG, FRANK F., JR., AND ANDREW J. CHERLIN. *Divided Families: What Happens to Children When Parents Part.* Cambridge, Mass.: Harvard University Press, 1991.

———. "Children's Adjustment to Divorce." In BONNIE J. FOX, ed. *Family Patterns, Gender Relations.* 2nd ed. New York: Oxford University Press, 2001.

FUSTOS, KATA. "Marriage Benefits Men's Health." Population Reference Bureau. September 2010. [Online] Accessed at: http://www.prb.org/Articles/2010/usmarriagemenshealth.aspx

GILBERT, NEIL. "Family Life: Sold on Work." *Society.* Vol. 42, No, 3 (2005):12–17.

GLEICK, ELIZABETH. "The Marker We've Been Waiting For." *Time* (April 7, 1997):28–42.

GLENMARY RESEARCH CENTER. *Religious Congregations and Membership in the United States, 2000.* Nashville, Tenn.: Glenmary Research Center, 2002.

GLENN, NORVAL D., AND BETH ANN SHELTON. "Regional Differences in Divorce in the United States." *Journal of Marriage and the Family.* Vol. 47, No. 3 (August 1985): 641–52.

GOLDSTEIN, JOSHUA R., AND CATHERINE T. KENNEY. "Marriage Delayed or Marriage Forgone? New Cohort Forecasts of First Marriage for U.S. Women." *American Sociological Review.* Vol. 66, No. 4 (August 2001):506–19.

GOODE, WILLIAM J. "The Theoretical Importance of Love." *American Sociological Review.* Vol. 24, No. 1 (February 1959):38–47.

GOULD, STEPHEN J. "Evolution as Fact and Theory." *Discover* (May 1981):35–37.

GREELEY, ANDREW M. "Symposium: Neo-Darwinism and Its Discontents." *Society.* Vol. 45, No. 2 (2008):162–63.

GREENSPAN, STANLEY I. *The Four-Thirds Solution: Solving the Child-Care Crisis in America.* Cambridge, Mass.: Perseus, 2001.

HADDEN, JEFFREY K., AND CHARLES E. SWAIN. *Prime-Time Preachers: The Rising Power of Televangelism.* Reading, Mass.: Addison-Wesley, 1981.

HOUT, MICHAEL, ANDREW M. GREELEY, AND MELISSA J. WILDE. "The Demographic Imperative in Religious Change in the United States."*American Journal of Sociology.* Vol. 107, No. 2 (September 2001):468–500.

HUCHINGSON, JAMES E. "Science and Religion." *Miami Herald* (December 25, 1994):1M, 6M.

HUNTER, JAMES DAVISON. *American Evangelicalism: Conservative Religion and the Quandary of Modernity.* New Brunswick, N.J.: Rutgers University Press, 1983.

———. "Conservative Protestantism." In PHILIP E. HAMMOND, ed., *The Sacred in a Secular Age.* Berkeley: University of California Press, 1985:50–66.

———. *Evangelicalism: The Coming Generation.* Chicago: University of Chicago Press, 1987.

IANNACCONE, LAURENCE R. "Why Strict Churches Are Strong." *American Journal of Sociology.* Vol. 99, No. 5 (March 1994):1180–1211.

INGLEHART, RONALD ET AL., "World Values Survey." 2011. [Online] Available at http://www.worldvaluessurvey.com

JANSEN, JIM. "The Civic and Community Engagement of Religiously Active Americans." Pew Research Center, Internet & American Life Project. December 23, 2011. [Online] Accessed at: http://www.pewinternet.org/Reports/2011/Social-side-of-religious/Overview.aspx

KANTROWITZ, BARBARA, AND PAT WINGERT. "Unmarried with Children." *Newsweek* (May 28, 2001):46–52.

KEISTER, LISA A. "Religion and Wealth: The Role of Religious Affiliation and Participation in Early Adult Asset Accumulation." *Social Forces.* Vol. 82, No. 1 (September 2003):175–207.

KENT, MARY MEDERIOS. "U.S. Women Delay Marriage and Children for College." Population Reference Bureau. January 2011. [Online] Available at http://www.prb.org/Articles/2011/usmar riageandchildbirth.aspx

KILBOURNE, BROCK K. "The Conway and Siegelman Claims against Religious Cults: An Assessment of Their Data." *Journal for the Scientific Study of Religion.* Vol. 22, No. 4 (December 1983):380–85.

KRAYBILL, DONALD B. "The Amish Encounter with Modernity." In DONALD B. KRAYBILL and MARC A. OLSHAN, eds., *The Amish Struggle with Modernity.* Hanover, N.H.: University Press of New England, 1994:21–33.

KREIDER, ROSE M., AND RENEE ELLIS. "Number, Timing, and Duration of Marriages and Divorces: 2009." *Current Population Reports*, P70–125 U.S. Census Bureau. 2011. [Online] Available at http://www.census.gov/prod/2011pubs/p70–125.pdf

LACH, JENNIFER. "The Color of Money." *American Demographics.* Vol. 21, No. 2 (February 1999):59–60.

LAUGHLIN, LYNDA. "Who's Minding the Kids? Child Care Arrangements: Spring 2005/Summer 2006." Household Economic Studies, Current Population Reports. 2010. [Online] Available at http://www.census.gov/prod/2010pubs/p70–121.pdf

LAUMANN, EDWARD O., JOHN H. GAGNON, ROBERT T. MICHAEL, AND STUART MICHAELS. *The Social Organization of Sexuality: Sexual Practices in the United States.* Chicago: University of Chicago Press, 1994.

LEE, SHARON M. AND BARRY EDMONSTON. "New Marriages, New Families: U.S. Racial and Hispanic Intermarriage." *Population Bulletin*, Vol. 6, No. 2 (2005) [Online] Available at http://www.prb.org/pdf05/60.2NewMarriages.pdf

LEVINE, SAMANTHA. "The Price of Child Abuse." *U.S. News & World Report* (April 9, 2001):58.

LINO, MARK. "Expenditures on Children by Families, 2010." Miscellaneous Publication Number 1528–2009, U.S. Department of Agriculture Center for Nutrition Policy and Promotion. 2011. [Online] Available at http://www.cnpp.usda.gov/Publications/CRC/crc2010.pdf

LOBO, SUSAN. "Census-Taking and the Invisibility of Urban American Indians." *Population Today.* Vol. 30, No. 4 (May/June 2002):3–4.

LUND, DALE A. "Caregiving." *Encyclopedia of Adult Development.* Phoenix, Ariz.: Oryx Press, 1993:57–63.

MACE, DAVID, AND VERA MACE. *Marriage East and West.* Garden City, N.Y.: Doubleday/Dolphin, 1960.

MACIONIS, JOHN J. "Intimacy: Structure and Process in Interpersonal Relationships." *Alternative Lifestyles.* Vol. 1, No. 1 (February 1978):113–30.

MANZA, JEFF, AND CLEM BROOKS. "The Religious Factor in U.S. Presidential Elections, 1960–1992." *American Journal of Sociology.* Vol. 103, No. 1 (July 1997):38–81.

MARQUAND, ROBERT, AND DANIEL B. WOOD. "Rise in Cults as Millennium Approaches." *Christian Science Monitor* (March 28, 1997):1, 18.

MARQUAND, ROBERT. "Worship Shift: Americans Seek Feeling of 'Awe.'" *Christian Science Monitor* (May 28, 1997):1, 8.

MARTIN, JOYCE A. , ET AL. "Births: Final Data for 2009." *National Vital Statistics Reports.* Vol. 60, No. 1 [Online] 2011. Available at http://www.cdc.gov/nchs/data/nvsr/nvsr60/nvsr60_01.pdf

MARX, KARL. *Karl Marx: Early Writings.* T. B. BOTTOMORE, ed. New York: McGraw-Hill, 1964; orig. 1848.

MAYO, KATHERINE. *Mother India.* New York: Harcourt, Brace, 1927.

McCLAY, WILLIAM M. "Secularism, American Style." *Society.* Vol. 44, No. 6 (2007):160–63.

McLANAHAN, SARA. "Life without Father: What Happens to the Children?" *Contexts.* Vol. 1, No. 1 (Spring 2002):35–44.

McLEOD, JANE D., AND MICHAEL J. SHANAHAN. "Poverty, Parenting, and Children's Mental Health." *American Sociological Review.* Vol. 58, No. 3 (June 1993):351–66.

McROBERTS, OMAR M. *Streets of Glory: Church and Community in a Black Urban Neighborhood.* Chicago: University of Chicago Press, 2003.

MEACHAM, JON. "The End of Christian America." *Newsweek.* [Online] Available April 4, 2009, at http://www.newsweek.com/2009/04/03/the-end-of-christianamerica.html

MILLER, ALAN S., AND RODNEY STARK. "Gender and Religiousness: Can Socialization Explanations Be Saved?" *American Journal of Sociology.* Vol. 107, No. 6 (May 2002):1399–1423.

"Much Ado about Evolution." *Time* (November 21, 2005):23.

MULLER, CHANDRA, AND CHRISTOPHER G. ELLISON. "Religious Involvement, Social Capital, and Adolescents' Academic Progress: Evidence from the National Education Longitudinal Study of 1988." *Sociological Focus.* Vol. 34, No. 2 (May 2001):155–83.

MURDOCK, GEORGE PETER. *Social Structure.* New York: Free Press, 1965; orig. 1949.

NATIONAL CONFERENCE OF STATE LEGISLATURES. "Same Sex Marriage, Civil Unions and Domestic Partnerships." 2012. [Online] Available at http://www.ncsl.org/issues-research/human-services/same-sex-marriage.aspx

NAVARRO, MIREYA. "For Younger Latinas, a Shift to Smaller Families." *New York Times* (December 5, 2004). [Online] Available April 30, 2005, at http://www. researchnavigator. com

NEUHOUSER, KEVIN. "The Radicalization of the Brazilian Catholic Church in Comparative Perspective." *American Sociological Review.* Vol. 54, No. 2 (April 1989):233–44.

NEWPORT, FRANK. "Americans Turn More Negative toward Same-Sex Marriage." Gallup News Service, April 2005. [Online] Available July 3, 2008, at http://www.gallup.com/poll/15889/Americans-Turn-More-Negative-TowardSameSex-Marriage.aspx

NORC. *General Social Surveys, 1972–2010: Cumulative Codebook.* Chicago: National Opinion Research Center, 2011. [Online] Available at http://www.norc.org/GSS+Website

OECD (ORGANISATION FOR ECONOMIC CO-OPERATION AND DEVELOPMENT). "Society at a Glance 2011: OECD Social Indicators." 2011. [Online] Available at http://www.oecd.org/els/social/indicators/SAG

PARIS, PETER J. "The Religious World of African Americans." In JACOB NEUSNER, ed. *World Religions in America: An Introduction.* Revised and expanded ed. Louisville, Ky.: Westminster/John Knox, 2000:48–65.

PASSEL, JEFFREY, WENDY WANG, AND PAUL TAYLOR. "One-in-Seven New U.S. Marriages is Interracial or Interethnic." Pew Research Center. 2010. [Online] Available at http://pewsocialtrends.org/2010/06/04/marrying-out/#fn-755–1

PATTILLO, MARY. "Church Culture as a Strategy of Action in the Black Community." *American Sociological Review.* Vol. 63, No. 6 (December 1998): 767–84.

PEW FORUM ON RELIGION AND PUBLIC LIFE. "U.S. Religious Landscape Survey." 2008. [Online] Available at http://religions.pewforum.org/reports

———. "The Stronger Sex—Spiritually Speaking." [Online] Available February 28, 2009, at http://pewforum.org/The-Stronger-Sex-Spiritually-Speaking.aspx

———. "Gay Marriage Around the World." 2009. [Online] Available at http://www.pewforum.org/Gay-Marriage-and-Homosexuality/Gay-Marriage-Around-the-World.aspx

———. "A Religious Portrait of African Americans." 2009. [Online] Available at http://www.pewforum.org/A-Religious-Portrait-of-African-Americans.aspx

———. "Scientists and Belief." 2009. [Online] Available at http://www.pewforum.org/Science-and-Bioethics/Scientists-and-Belief.aspx

———. "Global Christianity." 2011. [Online] Available at http://www.pewforum.org/Christian/Global-Christianity-exec.aspx

PEW RESEARCH CENTER. "As Marriage and Parenthood Drift Apart, Public Is Concerned about Social Impact." July 1, 2007a. [Online] Available January 31, 2009, at http://pewsocialtrends.org/pubs/542/modern-marriage

Pew Research Center for the People & the Press. "Poll Database." [Online] Available at http://webapps.ropercenter.uconn.edu/psearch/prc_index.cfm?pid=51

Phillips, Melanie. "What about the Overclass?" *Public Interest* (Fall 2001): 38–43.

Popenoe, David, and Barbara Dafoe Whitehead. *Should We Live Together? What Young Adults Need to Know about Cohabitation before Marriage*. New Brunswick, N.J.: National Marriage Project, 1999.

Population Reference Bureau. "Who Speaks for Me? Ending Child Marriage Fact Sheet." May 2011. [Online] Accessed at: http://www.prb.org/pdf11/child-marriage-fact-sheet.pdf

Pryor, John H., et al. *The American Freshman: National Norms for Fall 2010*. Cooperative Institutional Research Program at the Higher Education Research Institute. Los Angeles: UCLA Higher Education Research Institute, 2011.

Pyle, Ralph E. "Trends in Religious Stratification: Have Religious Group Socioeconomic Distinctions Declined in Recent Decades?" *Sociology of Religion*. Vol. 67, No. 1 (Spring 2006):61–79.

Raley, R.Kelly, T. Elizabeth Durden, and Elizabeth Wildsmith. "Understanding Mexican-American Marriage Patterns Using a Life Course Approach." *Social Science Quarterly*. Vol. 85, No. 4 (December 2004):872–90.

Roesch, Roberta. "Violent Families." *Parents*. Vol. 59, No. 9 (September 1984):74–76, 150–52.

Rosenfeld, Michael J., and Byong-Soo Kim. "The Independence of Young Adults and the Rise of Interracial and Same-Sex Unions."*American Sociological Review*. Vol. 70, No. 4 (August 2005):541–62.

Roudi-Fahimi, Farazzeh. "Child Marriage in the Middle East and North Africa." Population Reference Bureau. (April 2010). [Online] Available at http://www.prb.org/Articles/2010/menachildmarriage.aspx

Rozell, Mark J., Clyde Wilcox, and John C. Green. "Religious Constituencies and Support for the Christian Right in the 1990s."*Social Science Quarterly*. Vol. 79, No. 4 (December 1998):815–27.

Rubin, Lillian Breslow. *Worlds of Pain: Life in the Working-Class Family*. New York: Basic Books, 1976.

Scommegna, Paola. "U.S. Parents Who Have Children With More than One Partner." Population Reference Bureau. June 2011. [Online] Accessed at:http://www.prb.org/Journalists/Webcasts/2011/multipartner-childbearing-policy-seminar.aspx

Sherkat, Darren E., and Christopher G. Ellison. "Recent Developments and Current Controversies in the Sociology of Religion."*Annual Review of Sociology*. Vol. 25 (1999):363–94.

Shupe, Anson, William A. Stacey, and Lonnie R. Hazlewood. *Violent Men, Violent Couples: The Dynamics of Domestic Violence*. Lexington, Mass.: Lexington Books, 1987.

Shupe, Anson. *In the Name of All That's Holy: A Theory of Clergy Malfeasance*. Westport, Conn.: Praeger, 1995.

Smith, Christian, and Robert Faris. "Socioeconomic Inequality in the American Religious System: An Update and Assessment." *Journal for the Scientific Study of Religion*. Vol. 44, No. 1 (March 2005):95–104.

Smith, Tom W. "American Sexual Risk Behavior: Trends, Socio-Demographic Differences, and Behavior." March 2006. [Online] Available at http://publicdata.norc.org:41000/gss/DOCUMENTS/REPORTS/Topical_Reports/TR25.pdf

Snell, Marilyn Berlin. "The Purge of Nurture." *New Perspectives Quarterly*. Vol. 7, No. 1 (Winter 1990):1–2.

Stacey, Judith. *Brave New Families: Stories of Domestic Upheaval in Late Twentieth-Century America*. New York: Basic Books, 1990.

——. "Good Riddance to 'the Family': A Response to David Popenoe." *Journal of Marriage and the Family*. Vol. 55, No. 3 (August 1993):545–47.

Stapinski, Helene. "Let's Talk Dirty." *American Demographics*. Vol. 20, No. 11 (November 1998):50–56.

Stark, Rodney, and William Sims Bainbridge. "Secularization and Cult Formation in the Jazz Age." *Journal for the Scientific Study of Religion*. Vol. 20, No. 4 (December 1981):360–73.

Stark, Rodney. *Sociology*. Belmont, Calif.: Wadsworth, 1985.

Stone, Lawrence. *The Family, Sex, and Marriage in England, 1500–1800*. New York: Harper & Row, 1977.

Tavernise, Sabrina, and Robert Gebeloff. "Once Rare in Rural America, Divorce Is Changing the Face of Its Families." *The New York Times*. [Online] Available March 23, 2011, at http://www.nytimes.com/2011/03/24/us/24divorce.html?_r=1&ref=sabrinatavernise

Thomma, Steven. "Christian Coalition Demands Action from GOP." *Philadelphia Inquirer* (September 14, 1997):A2.

Troeltsch, Ernst. *The Social Teaching of the Christian Churches*. New York: Macmillan, 1931.

Tucker, James. "New Age Religion and the Cult of the Self." *Society*. Vol. 39, No. 2 (February 2002):46–51.

U.S. Census Bureau. "Grandparents Day 2010: Sept. 12," *Profile America: Facts for Features*. 2010. [Online] Available at http://www.ccnsus.gov/newsroom/releases/archives/facts_for_features_special_editions/cb10-ff16.html

——. "American Community Survey." 2011. [Online] Available at http://www.census.gov/acs/www

——. "Current Population Survey." September 2011. [Online] Available at http://www.census.gov/cps

——. "Families and Living Arrangements." 2011. [Online] Available at http://www.census.gov/population/www/socdemo/hh-fam.html

——. "Population Estimates." 2011. [Online] Available at http://www.census.gov/popest/data/index.html

——, *Statistical Abstract of the United States: 2012*, 131st Edition. 2011. [Online] Available at http://www.census.gov/statab/www

——. "Survey of Income and Program Participation (SIPP)." 2011. [Online] Available at http://www.census.gov/population/www/socdemo/childcare.html and http://www.census.gov/hhes/socdemo/marriage/data/sipp/index.html

U.S. Department of Health and Human Services, Administration On Children, Youth and Families. "Child Maltreatment 2010." 2011. [Online] Available at http://www.acf.hhs.gov/programs/cb/pubs/cm10/

U.S. Department of Justice, Bureau of Justice Statistics. "Criminal Victimization in the United States, 2010—Statistical Tables." September 15, 2011. [Online] Available at http://bjs.ojp.usdoj.gov/index.cfm?ty=pbdetail&iid=2224

——, Federal Bureau of Investigation. "Crime in the United States 2010." September 2011. [Online] Available at http://www.fbi.gov/about-us/cjis/ucr/crime-in-the-u.s/2010/crime-in-the-u.s.-2010

United Nations Statistics Division. "Demographic Yearbook." December 2010. [Online] Available at http://unstats.un.org/unsd/demographic/products/dyb/default.htm

Wang, Wendy, and Paul Taylor. "For Millennials, Parenthood Trumps Marriage." Pew Research Center. 2011. [Online] Available at http://pewsocialtrends .org/2011/03/09/for-millennials-parenthood-trumps-marriage

Weber, Max. *The Protestant Ethic and the Spirit of Capitalism*. New York: Scribner, 1958; orig. 1904–05.

Weeks, John R. "The Demography of Islamic Nations." *Population Bulletin*. Vol. 43, No. 4 (December 1988):5–54.

Wesselman, Hankv. *Visionseeker: Shared Wisdom from the Place of Refuge*. Carlsbad, Calif.: Hay House, 2001.

Williams, Johnny E. "Linking Beliefs to Collective Action: Politicized Religious Beliefs and the Civil Rights Movement." *Sociological Forum*. Vol. 17, No. 2 (June 2002): 203–22.

Williams, Peter W. *America's Religions: From Their Origins to the Twenty-First Century*. Urbana: University of Illinois Press, 2002.

Williams, Rhys H., and N. J. Demerath III. "Religion and Political Process in an American City." *American Sociological Review*. Vol. 56, No. 4 (August 1991):417–31.

Chapter 14 References

American Association of Colleges of Nursing (AACN). "Nursing Shortage Fact Sheet." 2012. [Online] Available at http://www.aacn.nche.edu/media-relations/fact-sheets/nursing-shortage

American College Health Association. "National College Health Assessment (ACHANCHA-II) Reference Group Data Report." Baltimore: American College Health Association, 2012. [Online] Available at http://www.achancha.org/reports_ACHA-NCHAII.html

American Medical Group Association. "Compensation Survey Data." 2011. [Online] Available at https://www.cms.gov/AcuteInpatientPPS/Downloads/AMGA_08_template_to_09.pdf

Andrews, Michelle. "Hospitals are Making Room for Alternative Therapies." *Los Angeles Times*. January 2, 2012. [Online] Accessed at: http://www.latimes.com/health/la-he-hospitals-alternative-medicine-20120102,0,6660665.story

Arias, Elizabeth. "United States Life Tables, 2007." *National Vital Statistics Reports*, Vol. 59, No. 6. 2011. [Online] Available at http://www.cdc.gov/nchs/data/nvsr/nvsr59/nvsr59_09.pdf

Ashford, Lori S. "Young Women in Sub-Saharan Africa Face a High Risk of HIV Infection." *Population Today*. Vol. 30, No. 2 (February/March 2002):3, 6.

Astin, Alexander W., Leticia Oseguera, Linda J. Sax, and William S. Korn. *The American Freshman: Thirty-Five Year Trends*. Los Angeles: UCLA Higher Education Research Institute, 2002.

Auster, Carol J., and Mindy Macrone. "The Classroom as a Negotiated Social Setting: An Empirical Study of the Effects of Faculty Members' Behavior on Students' Participation." *Teaching Sociology*. Vol. 22, No. 4 (October 1994):289–300.

Barnes, Julian E. "Wanted: Readers." *U.S. News & World Report* (September 9, 2002a):44–45.

Becker, Anne E. "The Association of Television Exposure with Disordered Eating Among Ethnic Fijian Adolescent Girls." Paper presented at the annual meeting of the American Psychiatric Association, Washington, D.C., May 19, 1999.

——. "New Global Perspectives on Eating Disorders." *Culture, Medicine, and Psychiatry*. Vol. 28, No. 4 (December 2004):434–37.

Bowles, Samuel, and Herbert Gintis. *Schooling in Capitalist America: Educational Reform and the Contradictions of Economic Life*. New York: Basic Books, 1976.

Brink, Susan. "Living on the Edge." *U.S. News & World Report* (October 14, 2002):58–64.

Bushaw, William J., and Shane J. Lopez. "Betting on Teachers." *Phi Delta Kappan*. Vol. 93, No. 1 (Sept. 2011): 9–26.

CDC (Centers For Disease Control and Prevention).

"2010 Sexually Transmitted Diseases Surveillance." 2011. [Online] Available at http://www.cdc.gov/std/stats10/tables.htm

——. "Behavioral Risk Factor Surveillance System." 2011. [Online] Available at http://www.cdc.gov/brfss/index.htm

——. "CDC Health Disparities and Inequalities Report — United States, 2011." 2011. [Online] Available at http://www.cdc.gov/mmwr/pdf/other/su6001.pdf

——. "Health, United States, 2010." 2011. [Online] Available at http://www.cdc.gov/nchs/data/hus/hus10.pdf

——. "HIV/AIDS Surveillance Report, 2009." 2011. [Online] Available at http://www.cdc.gov/hiv/surveillance/resources/reports/2009report

——. "Overweight and Obesity." 2011. [Online] Available at http://www.cdc.gov/obesity/data/adult.html

——. "Quitting Smoking Among Adults --- United States, 2001-2010" *Morbidity and Mortality Weekly Report (MMWR)*. November 11, 2011. [Online] Available at http://www.cdc.gov/mmwr/preview/mmwrhtml/mm6044a2.htm

——. "Smoking and Tobacco Use." 2011. [Online] Available at http://www.cdc.gov/tobacco/index.htm

——. "State Tobacco Activities Tracking and Evaluation (STATE) System." 2011. [Online] Available at http://apps.nccd.cdc.gov/statesystem

——. "Summary Health Statistics for the U.S. Population: National Health Interview Survey, 2010." *Vital and Health Statistics*, Series 10, No. 251. September 2011. [Online] Available at http://www.cdc.gov/nchs/data/series/sr_10/sr10_251.pdf

CHRISTLE, CHRISTINE A., KRISTINE JOLIVETTE, and C. MICHAEL NELSON. "School Characteristics Related to High School Dropout Rates." *Remedial and Special Education*. Vol. 28, No. 6 (2007):325–39.

CLOUD, JOHN, AND JODIE MORSE. "Home Sweet School." *Time* (August 27, 2001):46–54.

COHEN, ADAM. "A First Report Card on Vouchers." *Time* (April 26, 1999):36–38.

COLEMAN, JAMES S. "The Design of Organizations and the Right to Act." *Sociological Forum*. Vol. 8, No. 4 (December 1993):527–46.

COLEMAN, JAMES S., AND THOMAS HOFFER. *Public and Private High Schools: The Impact of Communities*. New York: Basic Books, 1987.

COLEMAN, JAMES S., ET AL. *Equality of Educational Opportunity*. Washington, D.C.: U.S. Government Printing Office, 1966.

COLEMAN, JAMES S., THOMAS HOFFER, AND SALLY KILGORE. *Public and Private Schools: An Analysis of Public Schools and Beyond*. Washington, D.C.: National Center for Education Statistics, 1981.

COLLEGE BOARD, THE. "Coming to Our Senses: Education and the American Future." Report of the Commission on Access, Admissions and Success in Higher Education [Online]. Available March 26, 2010, at http://professionals.collegeboard.com/profdownload/coming-to-our-senses-college-board-2008.pdf

——. "2011 College-Bound Seniors: Total Group Profile Report." 2011. [Online] Available at http://professionals.collegeboard.com/profdownload/cbs2011_total_group_report.pdf

——. "Trends in College Pricing 2011." 2011. [Online] Available at http://trends.collegeboard.org/college_pricing

COLLINS, RANDALL. *The Credential Society: A Historical Sociology of Education and Stratification*. New York: Academic Press, 1979.

COWLEY, GEOFFREY. "The Prescription That Kills." *Newsweek* (July 17, 1995):54.

CROUSE, JAMES, AND DALE TRUSHEIM. *The Case against the SAT*. Chicago: University of Chicago Press, 1988.

DEATH WITH DIGNITY NATIONAL CENTER. "Death with Dignity Around the U.S." 2011. [Online] Available at http://www.deathwithdignity.org/advocates/national/

DILLON, SAM "Most Public Schools May Miss Targets, Education Secretary Says." *New York Times* [Online] Available March 9, 2011, at http://www.nytimes.com/2011/03/10/education/10education.html?_r=1

——. "Failure Rate of Schools Overstated, Study Says." *New York Times*. December 15, 2011. [Online] Available at http://www.nytimes.com/2011/12/15/education/education-secretary-overstated-failing-schools-under-no-child-left-behind-study-says.html

DOWNEY, DOUGLAS B., PAUL T. VON HIPPEL, AND BECKETT A. BROH. "Are Schools the Great Equalizer? Cognitive Inequality during the Summer Months and School Year." *American Sociological Review*. Vol. 59, No. 5 (October 2004):613–35.

DUBOS, RENÉ. *Man Adapting*. Enlarged ed. New Haven, Conn.: Yale University Press, 1980.

EHRENREICH, BARBARA. *Nickel and Dimed: On (Not) Getting By in America*. New York: Holt, 2001.

ELSON, JEAN. *Am I Still a Woman? Hysterectomy and Gender Identity*. Philadelphia: Temple University Press, 2004.

EMERSON, JOAN P. "Behavior in Private Places: Sustaining Definitions of Reality in Gynecological Examinations." In H. P. DREITZEL, ed., *Recent Sociology*. Vol. 2. New York: Collier, 1970:74–97. FALLON, A. E., AND P. ROZIN. "Sex Differences in Perception of Desirable Body Shape."*Journal of Abnormal Psychology*. Vol. 94, No. 1 (1985):100–105.

EUROPEAN UNION, EUROPEAN COMMUNITIES STATISTICAL OFFICE. "Eurostat." 2011. [Online] Available at http://epp.eurostat.ec.europa.eu/portal/page/portal/education/introduction

EVELYN, JAMILAH. "Community Colleges Play Too Small a Role in Teacher Education, Report Concludes." *Chronicle of Higher Education Online* (October 24, 2002). [Online] Available October 24, 2002, at http://chronicle.com/daily/2002/10/2002102403n.htm

FERRARO, KENNETH F., AND JESSICA A. KELLEY-MOORE. "Cumulative Disadvantage and Health: Long-Term Consequences of Obesity?"*American Sociological Review*. Vol. 68, No. 5 (October 2003):707–29.

FONDA, DAREN. "The Male Minority." *Time* (December 11, 2000):58–60.

FRIEDMAN, MEYER, AND RAY H. ROSENMAN. *Type A Behavior and Your Heart*. New York: Fawcett Crest, 1974. GILLESPIE, MARK. "Trends Show Bathing and Exercise Up, TV Watching Down." January 2000. [Online] Available April 9, 2006, at http://www.gallup.com

GALLUP. "Americans Lean Toward Revising No Child Left Behind." February 7, 2011. [Online] Available at http://www.gallup.com/poll/145952/Americans-Lean-Toward-Revising-No-Child-Left-Behind.aspx

GAMORAN, ADAM. "The Variable Effects of High-School Tracking." *American Sociological Review*. Vol. 57, No. 6 (December 1992):812–28.

GARLAND, SARAH. "Study Backs Results of For-Profit Schools." *New York Sun Online*. April 11, 2007. [Online] Available March 31, 2008, at http://www2.nysun.com/article/52198

GIBBS, NANCY. "Darkness Falls." *Time* (April 30, 2007):36–52.

GILLON, RAANAN. "Euthanasia in the Netherlands: Down the Slippery Slope?" *Journal of Medical Ethics*. Vol. 25, No. 1 (February 1999):3–4.

GOLDEN, FREDERIC, AND MICHAEL D. LEMONICK. "The Race Is Over." *Time* (July 3, 2000):18–23.

GORDON, JAMES S. "The Paradigm of Holistic Medicine." In ARTHUR C. HASTINGS ET AL., eds., *Health for the Whole Person: The Complete Guide to Holistic Medicine*. Boulder, Colo.: Westview Press, 1980:3–27.

HAMRICK, MICHAEL H., DAVID J. ANSPAUGH, AND GENE EZELL. *Health*. Columbus, Ohio: Merrill, 1986.

HELLMICH, NANCI. "Environment, Economics Partly to Blame." *USA Today* (October 9, 2002):9D.

——. "Premature Death is More Likely in Obese Children." *USA Today* (February 2, 2011). [Online] Available at http://www.usatoday.com/news/health/weightloss/2010-02-11-obesekidsdieearlier11_ST_N.htm

HOPKINSON, NATALIE. "Why School Choice Fails." *The New York Times* (December 4, 2011). Accessed at: http://www.nytimes.com/2011/12/05/opinion/why-school-choice-fails.html

HORN, WADE F., AND DOUGLAS TYNAN. "Revamping Special Education." *Public Interest*. No. 144 (Summer 2001):36–53.

ISRAEL, GLENN D., LIONEL J. BEAULIEU, AND GLEN HARTLESS. "The Influence of Family and Community Social Capital on Educational Achievement." *Rural Sociology*. Vol. 66, No. 1 (March 2001):43–68.

JACOBSON, JENNIFER. "Professors Are Finding Better Pay and More Freedom at Community Colleges." *Chronicle of Higher Education Online*. 2003. [Online] Available March 7, 2003, at http://www.chronicle.com

JONES, D. GARETH. "Brain Death." *Journal of Medical Ethics*. Vol. 24, No. 4 (August 1998):237–43.

KAIN, EDWARD L. "A Note on the Integration of AIDS into the Sociology of Human Sexuality." *Teaching Sociology*. Vol. 15, No. 4 (July 1987):320–23.

KAISER FAMILY FOUNDATION. "U.S. Federal Funding for HIV/AIDS: The President's FY 2012 Budget Request." October 2011. [Online] Available at http://www.kff.org/hivaids/upload/7029-07.pdf

KAPTCHUK, TED. "The Holistic Logic of Chinese Medicine." In BERKELEY HOLISTIC HEALTH CENTER, *The New Holistic Health Handbook: Living Well in a New Age*. SHEPARD BLISS ET AL., eds. Lexington, Mass.: Greene Press, 1985:41.

KARP, DAVID A., AND WILLIAM C. YOELS. "The College Classroom: Some Observations on the Meaning of Student Participation."*Sociology and Social Research*. Vol. 60, No. 4 (July 1976):421–39.

KEIGHER, ASHLEY. "Teacher Attrition and Mobility: Results From the 2008–09 Teacher Follow-up Survey (NCES 2010–353)." U.S. Department of Education. Washington, D.C.: National Center for Education Statistics. 2010. http://nces.ed.gov/pubs2010/2010353.pdf

KILGORE, SALLY B. "The Organizational Context of Tracking in Schools." *American Sociological Review*. Vol. 56, No. 2 (April 1991):189–203.

KOCHANEK, KENNETH D., ET AL. "Deaths: Preliminary Data for 2009." *National Vital Statistics Reports*. Vol. 59, No. 4. Hyattsville, Md: National Center for Health Statistics. March 16, 2011. http://www.cdc.gov/nchs/data/nvsr/nvsr59/nvsr59_04.pdf

KOZOL, JONATHAN. *Savage Inequalities: Children in America's Schools*. New York: Harper Perennial, 1992.

KRAL, BRIGITTA. "The Eyes of Jane Elliott." *Horizon Magazine*. 2000. [Online] Available June 8, 2005, at http://www.horizonmag.com/4/jane-elliott.asp

KRISTOFF, NICHOLAS. "Pay Teachers More." *New York Times*. March 13, 2011. [Online] Available at http://www.nytimes.com/2011/03/13/opinion/13kristof.html?ref=education

LANDSBERG, MITCHELL. "Health Disaster Brings Early Death in Russia." *Washington Times* (March 15, 1998):A8.

LAUMANN, EDWARD O., JOHN H. GAGNON, ROBERT T. MICHAEL, AND STUART MICHAELS. *The Social Organization of Sexuality: Sexual Practices in the United States*. Chicago: University of Chicago Press, 1994.

LEAVITT, JUDITH WALZER. "Women and Health in America: An Overview." In JUDITH WALZER LEAVITT, ed., *Women and Health in America*. Madison: University of Wisconsin Press, 1984:3–7.

LEFF, LISA. "California Gay Marriage Vote Still Undecided." November 5, 2008. [Online] Available November 5, 2008, at http://news.yahoo.com/s/ap/20081105/ap_on_el_ge/ballot_measures

LEVINE, MICHAEL P. *Student Eating Disorders: Anorexia Nervosa and Bulimia*. Washington, D.C.: National Educational Association, 1987.

——. "Reducing Hostility Can Prevent Heart Disease." *Mount Vernon* (Ohio) *News* (August 7, 1990):4A.

LINDLAW, SCOTT. "President Signs Education Bill." 2002. [Online] Available January 8, 2002, at http://news.yahoo.com

LOGAN, JOHN R., DEIDRE OAKLEY, AND JACOB STOWELL. "School Segregation in Metropolitan Regions, 1970–2000: The Impacts of Policy Choices on Public Education." *American Journal of Sociology*. Vol. 113, No. 6 (May 2008):1611–44.

LORD, MARY. "Good Teachers the Newest Imports." *U.S. News & World Report* (April 9, 2001):54.

MACIONIS, JOHN J., AND LINDA GERBER. *Sociology*. 6th Canadian ed. Scarborough, Ontario: Prentice Hall Allyn & Bacon Canada, 2008.

MARQUEZ, LAURA. "Nursing Shortage: How It May Affect You." *ABC News*. January 21, 2006. [Online] Available April 1, 2008, at http://abcnews.go.com/WNT/Health/story?id=1529546

MASON, DAVID S. "Fairness Matters: Equity and the Transition to Democracy." *World Policy Journal*. Vol. 20, No. 4 (Winter 2003). [Online] Available February 21, 2008, at http://www.worldpolicy.org/journal/articles/wpj03-4/mason.html

McNEIL, DONALD G., JR. "Broad Racial Disparities Seen in Americans' Ills." *New York Times*. [Online] Available January 13, 2011, at http://www.nytimes.com/2011/01/14/health/14cdc.html?_r=2

MEZZACAPPA, DALE. "Only Six Providers Approved for 'Turnaround.'" *Philadephia Public Schools Notebook*. 2010. [Online] Available at http://www.thenotebook.org/blog/102296/six-providers-approved-turnaround

MINIÑO ARIALDI M., SHERRY L. MURPHY, JIAQUAN XU, AND KENNETH D. KOCHANEK. "Deaths: Final Data for 2008." *National Vital Statistics Reports*. Vol. 59, No. 10. [Online] Available at http://www.cdc.gov/nchs/data/nvsr/nvsr59/nvsr59_10.pdf

MORSE, JODIE. "A Victory for Vouchers." *Time* (July 8, 2002):32–34.

MOSS, BRIAN G., AND WILLIAM H. YEATON. "Young Children's Weight Trajectories and Associated Risk Factors: Results from the Early Childhood Longitudinal Study—Birth Cohort." *American Journal of Health Promotion*. Vol. 25, No. 3 (January–February 2010):190–98.

MYERS, DAVID G. *The American Paradox: Spiritual Hunger in an Age of Plenty*. New Haven, Conn.: Yale University Press, 2000.

MYERS, SHEILA, AND HAROLD G. GRASMICK. "The Social Rights and Responsibilities of Pregnant Women: An Application of Parsons' Sick Role Model." Paper presented to the Southwestern Sociological Association, Little Rock, Ark., March 1989.

NATIONAL COMMISSION ON EXCELLENCE IN EDUCATION. *A Nation at Risk*. Washington, D.C.: U.S. Government Printing Office, 1983.

NATIONAL CONFERENCE OF STATE LEGISLATURES. "State Smoke-Free Laws and Health." November 2010. [Online] Available at http://www.ncsl.org/issues-research/health/enacted-indoor-smoke-free-laws.aspx

———. "Hookah Hazard." July 2011. [Online] Accessed at: http://www.ncsl.org/default.aspx?tabid=23252

NATIONAL INSTITUTE OF MENTAL HEALTH. "Eating Disorders." 2011. [Online] Available at http://www.nimh.nih.gov/health/publications/eating-disorders/complete-index.shtml

———. "Statistics." 2011. [Online] Available at http://www.nimh.nih.gov/statistics/index.shtml

NIESSE, MARK. "Some Bars Pan Hawaii's Tough Smoking Ban." [Online] Available February 19, 2007, at http://news.yahoo.com

NORC. *General Social Surveys, 1972-2010: Cumulative Codebook*. Chicago: National Opinion Research Center, 2011. [Online] Available at http://www.norc.org/GSS+Website

NULAND, SHERWIN B. "The Hazards of Hospitalization." *Wall Street Journal* (December 2, 1999):A22.

O'LEARY, PATRICK, NATLAIA WHARTON, AND THOMAS QUINLAN. "Job Satisfaction of Physicians in Russia." *International Journal of Health Care Quality Assurance*. Vol. 22, No. 3 (2009): 221–31.

OBAMA, BARACK. *The Audacity of Hope: Thoughts on Reclaiming the American Dream*. New York: Random House, 2007.

OECD (ORGANISATION FOR ECONOMIC CO-OPERATION AND DEVELOPMENT). "Education at a Glance 2011: OECD Indicators." 2011. [Online] Available at http://www.oecd.org/edu/eag2011

———. "Statistical Extracts." 2011. [Online] Available at http://stats.oecd.org/index.aspx

OREGON PUBLIC HEALTH DIVISION. "Death with Dignity Act Annual Report." 2011. [Online] Available at http://public.health.oregon.gov/ProviderPartnerResources/EvaluationResearch/DeathwithDignityAct

ORNSTEIN, ALLAN C. "Achievement Gaps in Education." *Society*. Vol. 47, No. 5 (September/October 2010):424–29.

PAMPEL, FRED C. "Socioeconomic Distinction, Cultural Tastes, and Cigarette Smoking." *Social Science Quarterly*. Vol. 87, No. 1 (March 2006):19–35.

PARSONS, TALCOTT. *The Social System*. New York: Free Press, 1951.

PATTERSON, ELISSA F. "The Philosophy and Physics of Holistic Health Care: Spiritual Healing as a Workable Interpretation."*Journal of Advanced Nursing*. Vol. 27, No. 2 (February 1998):287–93.

PEAR, ROBERT, AND ERIK ECKHOLM. "When Healers Are Entrepreneurs: A Debate over Costs and Ethics." *New York Times* (June 2, 1991):1, 17.

PETERSON, PAUL E., AND ELENA LLAUDET. "On the Public-Private School Achievement Debate." Paper prepared for the annual meetings of the American Political Science Association, August 2006. [Online] Available July 15, 2008, at http://www.hks.harvard.edu/pepg/PDF/Papers/PEPG06-02-PetersonLlaudet.pdf

PHILADELPHIA, DESA. "Rookie Teacher, Age 50." *Time* (April 9, 2001):66–68.

PINHEY, THOMAS K., DONALD H. RUBINSTEIN, AND RICHARD S. COLFAX. "Overweight and Happiness: The Reflected Self-Appraisal Hypothesis Reconsidered." *Social Science Quarterly*. Vol. 78, No. 3 (September 1997):747–55.

POPULATON REFERENCE BUREAU. "Datafinder." 2011. [Online] Available at http://www.prb.org/DataFinder.aspx

PRYOR, JOHN H., ET AL. *The American Freshman: National Norms Fall 2010*. Los Angeles: Cooperative Institutional Research Program at the Higher Education Research Institute at UCLA, 2011.

PUTKA, GARY. "SAT to Become a Better Gauge." *Wall Street Journal* (November 1, 1990):B1.

QUAID, LIBBY. "Study: Math Teachers One Chapter ahead of Students." *Yahoo News* (November 25, 2008). [Online] Available November 25, 2008, at http://news.yahoo.com/s/ap/20081125/ap_on_re_us/qualified_teachers

RAVITCH, DIANE. "Obama's War on Schools." *Newsweek* [Online] Available March 20, 2011, at http://www.newsweek.com/2011/03/20/obama-s-waron-schools.html

RICHARDS, JENNIFER SMITH. "Parents Could Get Club to Fix Bad Schools." *The Columbus Dispatch* (April 4, 2011):A1, A4.

RICHBURG, KEITH B. "School Privatization Plan Sputters." *Washington Post* (June 29, 2008). [Online] Available February 3, 2009, at http://www.boston.com/news/education/k_12/articles/2008/06/29/school_privatization_plan_sputters

RIPLEY, AMANDA. "Can She Save Our Schools?" *Time* (December 8, 2008):36–44.

ROEHRIG, JAMES P., AND CARMEN P. MCLEAN. "A Comparison of Stigma Toward Eating Disorders Versus Depression." *International Journal of Eating Disorders*. Vol. 43, No. 7 (November 2010):671–74.

ROSENTHAL, ELIZABETH. "Canada's National Health Plan Gives Care to All, with Limits." *New York Times* (April 30, 1991):A1, A16.

RUSSELL, DEBORAH. "'Parent Trigger' Laws Give Parents More Power." *The Notebook*. [Online] Available April 1, 2011, at http://www.thenotebook.org/blog/113429/trigger-happy

SCHNEIDER, MARK, MELISSA MARSCHALL, PAUL TESKE, AND CHRISTINE ROCH. "School Choice and Culture Wars in the Classroom: What Different Parents Seek from Education." *Social Science Quarterly*. Vol. 79, No. 3 (September 1998):489–501.

SCHNITTKER, JASON, BERNICE A. PESCOSOLIDO, AND THOMAS W. CROGHAN. "Are African Americans Really Less Willing to Use Health Care?" *Social Problems*. Vol. 52, No. 2 (May 2005):255–71.

SENNETT, RICHARD, AND JONATHAN COBB. *The Hidden Injuries of Class*. New York: Vintage Books, 1973.

SHEDDEN, DAVID. "School Shootings (1997–2008)." Poynteronline. April 16, 2008. [Online] Available July 15, 2008, at http://www.poynter.org/column.asp?id=49&aid=1025

SIZER, THEODORE R. *Horace's Compromise: The Dilemma of the American High School*. Boston: Houghton Mifflin, 1984.

———. "Private Profit, Public Good?" *Frontline* interview. July 3, 2003. [Online] Available May 20, 2006, at http://www.pbs.org/wgbh/pages/frontline/shows/edison/etc/private.html

SOBEL, RACHEL K. "Herpes Tests Give Answers You Might Need to Know." *U.S. News & World Report* (June 18, 2001):53.

SPECTER, MICHAEL. "Plunging Life Expectancy Puzzles Russia." *New York Times* (August 2, 1995):A1, A2.

STEGER, BRIGITTE. "Sleeping through Class to Success." *Time and Society*. Vol. 15, No. 2–3 (2006):197–214. [Online] Available January 17, 2009, at http://tas.sagepub.com/cgi/content/abstract/15/2-3/197

STOBBE, MIKE. "Cancer to Be World's Top Killer by 2010, WHO Says." *Yahoo News* (December 9, 2008). [Online] Available December 10, 2008, at http://news.yahoo.com/s/ap/20081209/ap_on_he_me/mcd_global_cancer

STOCKDALE, CHARLES B., DOUGLAS A. MCINTYRE, AND MICHAEL B. SAUTER. "10 States with the Deadliest Eating Habits." *24/7 Wall Street*. [Online] Available February 9, 2011, at http://finance.yahoo.com/family-home/article/112083/10-states-with-the-deadliest-eating-habits

SWANSON, CHRISTOPHER B. "Cities in Crisis 2009: Closing the Graduation Gap." EPE Research. 2009. http://www.edweek.org/media/cities_in_crisis_2009.pdf

THOMPSON, DICK. "Gene Maverick." *Time* (January 11, 1999):54–55.

TIMMS AND PIRLS INTERNATIONAL STUDY CENTER. "Trends in International Mathematics and Science Study." 2009. [Online] Available at http://timss.bc.edu/index.html

TOPPO, GREG, AND ANTHONY DEBARROS. "Reality Weighs Down Dreams of College." *USA Today* (February 2, 2005):A1.

U.S. CENSUS BUREAU. "Educational Attainment." 2011. [Online] Available at http://www.census.gov/population/www/socdemo/educ-attn.html

———. "Current Population Survey." September 2011. [Online] Available at http://www.census.gov/cps

———. "Families and Living Arrangements." 2011. [Online] Available at http://www.census.gov/population/www/socdemo/hh-fam.html

———. "Population Estimates." 2011. [Online] Available at http://www.census.gov/popest/data/index.html

———. *Statistical Abstract of the United States: 2012*, 131st Edition. 2011. [Online] Available at http://www.census.gov/statab/www

U.S. DEPARTMENT OF EDUCATION, NATIONAL CENTER FOR EDUCATION STATISTICS. "2003 National Assessment of Adult Literacy." 2007. [Online] Available at http://nces.ed.gov/naal/index.asp

———. "National Household Education Surveys (NHES)." 2010. [Online] Available at http://nces.ed.gov/nhes

———. "Common Core of Data (CCD)." 2011. [Online] Available at http://nces.ed.gov/ccd

———. "The Condition of Education." 2011. [Online] Available at http://nces.ed.gov/programs/coe/current_tables.asp

———. "National Assessment of Educational Progress (Nation's Report Card)." 2011. [Online] Available at http://nces.ed.gov/nationsreportcard/naepdata

———. "Private School Universe Survey (PSS)." 2011. [Online] Available at http://nces.ed.gov/surveys/pss

———. "Projections of Education Statistics to 2020." 2011. [Online] Available at http://nces.ed.gov/programs/projections/projections2020/index.asp

———. "U.S. Digest of Education Statistics 2010." 2011. [Online] Available at http://nces.ed.gov/programs/digest/2010menu_tables.asp

U.S. DEPARTMENT OF HEALTH AND HUMAN SERVICES, Centers for Medicare and Medicaid Services. "National Health Expenditure Data." 2011. [Online] Available at http://www.cms.gov/NationalHealthExpendData

———, Health Resources and Services Administration. "The Registered Nurse Population 2008 Survey." 2010. [Online] Available at http://bhpr.hrsa.gov/healthworkforce/rnsurvey2008.html

———, National Institutes of Health, National Institute of Mental Health. 2011. [Online] Available at http://www.nimh.nih.gov/index.shtml

———, Substance Abuse and Mental Health Services Administration (SAMHSA). "Results from the 2010 National Survey on Drug Use and Health." 2011. [Online] Available at http://www.samhsa.gov/data/NSDUH/2k10NSDUH/tabs/TOC.htm

U.S. Department of Labor, Bureau of Labor Statistics. "Census of Fatal Occupational Injuries (CFOI)." 2011. [Online] Available at http://www.bls.gov/news.release/cfoi.nr0.htm

———, "Labor Force Statistics from the Current Population Survey." 2011, 2012. [Online] Available at http://www.bls.gov/cps/home.htm

———, Mine Safety and Health Administration. "Mine Safety and Health at a Glance." 2011. [Online] Available at http://www.msha.gov/MSHAINFO/FactSheets/MSHAFCT10.HTM

———, Occupational Employment Statistics (OES). "National Occupational Employment and Wage Estimates, United States." 2011. [Online] Available at http://www.bls.gov/oes/current/oes_nat.htm

———, Women's Bureau. "Quick Facts on Registered Nurses (RNs)." 2010. [Online] Available at http://www.dol.gov/wb/factsheets/Qf-nursing-08.htm

UNAIDS. "2010 Report on the Global AIDS Epidemic." 2010. [Online] Available at http://www.unaids.org/globalreport/

———. "Fast Facts about HIV Prevention." 2011. [Online] Available at http://www.unaids.org/en/KnowledgeCentre/Resources/FastFacts

UNESCO Institute of Statistics. "Data Centre." 2011. [Online] Available at http://stats.uis.unesco.org/

United Nations Development Programme. Human Development Report 2011. Statistical Tables. [Online] Available at http://hdr.undp.org/en/statistics/data/

United Nations, Population Division. "World Population Prospects: The 2010 Revision." [Online] Available at http://esa.un.org/unpd/wpp/unpp/panel_population.htm

Wall, Thomas F. Medical Ethics: Basic Moral Issues. Washington, D.C.: University Press of America, 1980.

Wallis, Claudia, and Sonja Steptoe. "How to Fix No Child Left Behind." Time. Vol. 169, No. 23 (June 4, 2007):34–41.

Wallis, Claudia. "How to Make Great Teachers." Time (February 14, 2008). [Online] Available March 1, 2008, at http://www.time.com/time/nation/article/0, 8599, 1713174, 00.html

Wells, Hodan Farah, and Jean C. Buzby. Dietary Assessment of Major Trends in U.S. Food Consumption, 1970–2005. Economic Information Bulletin No. (EIB 33). Washington, D.C.: U.S. Department of Agriculture, March 2008.

Will, George F. "Spoiling for a Fight in Ohio." The Berkshire Eagle (February 6, 2011):A6.

Winter, Greg. "Wider Gap Found between Wealthy and Poor Schools." New York Times (October 6, 2004). [Online] Available May 7, 2009, at http://www. nytimes.com/2004/10/06/education/06gap.html

Witt, Louise. "Why We're Losing the War against Obesity." American Demographics. Vol. 25, No. 10 (January 2004):27–31.

World Bank. "Education Statistics." 2011. [Online] Available at http://data.worldbank.org/data-catalog/ed-stats

———. "Health, Nutrition and Population Statistics." 2011. [Online] Available at http://data.worldbank.org/data-catalog/health-nutrition-and-population-statistics

———. "World Development Indicators." [Online] Available at http://data.worldbank.org/data-catalog/world-development-indicators

World Health Organization. Constitution of the World Health Organization. New York:

World Health Organization Interim Commission, 1946.

———. "Highlights on Health in the Russian Federation 2005." 2006. [Online] Available at http://www.euro.who.int/__data/assets/pdf_file/0003/103593/E88405.pdf

———. "Russian Federation." 2007. [Online] Available July 9, 2007, at http://www.who.int/countries/rus/en

———. "The Global Burden of Disease: 2004 Update, Summary Tables." October 2008. [Online] Available at http://www.who.int/healthinfo/global_burden_disease/estimates_regional/en/index.html

———. "WHO Report on the Global Tobacco Epidemic, 2011." 2012. [Online] Available at http://www.who.int/tobacco/global_report/en/index.html

Yin, Sandra. "Wanted: One Million Nurses." American Demographics. Vol. 24, No. 8 (September 2002):63–65.

Zuckerman, Mortimer B. "The Russian Conundrum." U.S. News & World Report (March 13, 2006):64.

Chapter 15 References

Adam, David. "World CO$_2$ Levels at Record High, Scientists Warn." Guardian (May 12, 2008). [Online] Available July 16, 2008, at http://www.guardian.co.uk/environment/2008/may/12/climatechange.carbonemissions

Axinn, William G., and Jennifer S. Barber. "Mass Education and Fertility Transition." American Sociological Review. Vol. 66, No. 4 (August 2001):481–505.

Baochang, Gu, Wang Feng, Guo Zhigang, and Erli Zhang. "China's Local and National Fertility Policies at the End of the Twentieth Century." Population and Development Review. Vol. 33, No. 1 (2007):129–48.

Berry, Brian L., and Philip H. Rees. "The Factorial Ecology of Calcutta." American Journal of Sociology. Vol. 74, No. 5 (March 1969):445–91.

Bohon, Stephanie A., and Craig R. Humphrey. "Courting LULUs: Characteristic of Suitor and Objector Communities." Rural Sociology. Vol. 65, No. 3 (September 2000):376–95.

Bormann, F. Herbert. "The Global Environmental Deficit." BioScience. Vol. 40, No. 2 (1990):74.

Brockerhoff, Martin P. "An Urbanizing World." Population Bulletin. Vol. 55, No. 3 (September 2000):1–44.

Brown, Lester R. "Reassessing the Earth's Population." Society. Vol. 32, No. 4 (May/June 1995):7–10.

Brown, Lester R., et al., eds. State of the World 1993: A Worldwatch Institute Report on Progress toward a Sustainable Society. New York: Norton, 1993.

Capella, Peter. "UN Alarmed at Huge Decline in Bee Numbers." Yahoo.com [Online] Available March 10, 2011, at http://news.yahoo.com/s/afp/20110310/sc_afp/unenvironment speciesanimalfarmbee_20110310124832

Castells, Manuel. The Urban Question. Cambridge, Mass.: MIT Press, 1977.

———. The City and the Grass Roots. Berkeley: University of California Press, 1983.

Central Intelligence Agency. The World Factbook. 2011 (updated biweekly). [Online] Available at https://www.cia.gov/library/publications/the-world-factbook/index.html

Chandler, Tertius, and Gerald Fox. 3000 Years of Urban History. New York: Academic Press, 1974.

Chang, Alicia. "Study: Cleaner Air Adds 5 Months to U.S. Life Span." Yahoo News (January 21, 2009). [Online] Available April 10, 2009, at http://www.newsvine.com/_news/2009/01/21/2339450-study-cleaner-air-adds-5months-to-us-life-span

Commission For Racial Justice. CRJ Reporter. New York: United Church of Christ, 1994.

Connett, Paul H. "The Disposable Society." In F. Herbert Bormann and Stephen R. Kellert, eds., Ecology, Economics, and Ethics: The Broken Circle. New Haven, Conn.: Yale University Press, 1991:99–122.

El Nasser, Haya. "Housing Bust Halts Growing Suburbs." USA Today. (November 20-22, 2009):1A.

El Nasser, Haya, and Paul Overberg. "U.S. Growth Slows, Still Envied." USA Today (January 7–9, 2011):1A.

Frazer, Brian. "The No-Baby Boom." Details. June 28, 2011. [Online] Accessed at: http://shine.yahoo.com/channel/parenting/the-no-baby-boom-2503225/

Gans, Herbert J. People and Plans: Essays on Urban Problems and Solutions. New York: Basic Books, 1968.

Garreau, Joel. Edge City. New York: Doubleday, 1991.

Gillis, Justin. "Sea-Level Science." Conservation. Vol. 12, No. 1 (Spring 2011): 44–45.

Goldberger, Paul. Lecture delivered at Kenyon College, Gambier, Ohio, September 22, 2002.

Gore, Al. An Inconvenient Truth: The Crisis of Global Warming. Emmaus, Pa.: Rodale Books, 2006.

Gottmann, Jean. Megalopolis. New York: Twentieth Century Fund, 1961.

Hamilton, Brady E., Joyce A. Martin, and Stephanie J. Ventura. "Births: Preliminary Data for 2010." National Vital Statistics Reports. Vol. 60, No. 2 . December, 2011. [Online] Available at http://www.cdc.gov/nchs/data/nvsr/nvsr60/nvsr60_02.pdf

Harris, Chauncy D., and Edward L. Ullman. "The Nature of Cities." Annals of the American Academy of Political and Social Sciences. Vol. 242, No. 1 (November 1945):7–17.

Hesketh, Therese, Li Lu, and Zhu Wei Xing. "The Effects of China's One-Child Family Policy after 25 Years." New England Journal of Medicine. Vol. 353, No. 11 (November 2005):1171–76.

Horton, Hayward Derrick. "Critical Demography: The Paradigm of the Future?" Sociological Forum. Vol. 14, No. 3 (September 1999):363–67.

Hoyt, Homer. The Structure and Growth of Residential Neighborhoods in American Cities. Washington, D.C.: Federal Housing Administration, 1939.

International Energy Agency (IEA). "Statistics and Balances." 2011. [Online] Available at http://www.iea.org/stats/index.asp

International Panel On Climate Change. Climate Change, 2007. New York: United Nations, 2007.

Johnson, Dirk. "Death of a Small Town." Newsweek (September 10, 2001):30–31.

Johnson, Kenneth M. "The Rural Rebound." Population Reference Bureau Reports on America. Vol. 1, No. 3 (September 1999). [Online] Available October 9, 2004, at http://www.prb.org/Content/NavigationMenu/PRB/AboutPRB/Reports_on_America/ReportonAmericaRuralRebound.pdf

Johnson, Kenneth M., and Glenn V. Fuguitt. "Continuity and Change in Rural Migration Patterns, 1950–1995." Rural Sociology. Vol. 65, No. 1 (March 2000):27–49.

Johnston, R. J. "Residential Area Characteristics." In D. T. Herbert and R. J. Johnston, eds., Social Areas in Cities. Vol. 1: Spatial Processes and Form. New York: Wiley, 1976:193–235.

Jones, Andrew E. G., and David Wilson. The Urban Growth Machine: Critical Perspectives. Albany: State University of New York Press, 1999.

Keesing, Felicia et al., "Impacts of Biodiversity on the Emergence and Transmission of Infectious Disease." Nature: International Weekly Journal of Science. Vol. 468, Issue 7324. [Online] Available December 2, 2010, at http://www.nature.com/nature/journal/v468/n7324/full/nature09575.html

Kellert, Stephen R., and F. Herbert Bormann. "Closing the Circle: Weaving Strands among Ecology, Economics, and Ethics." In F. Herbert Bormann and Stephen R. Kellert, eds., Ecology, Economics, and Ethics: The Broken Circle. New Haven, Conn.: Yale University Press, 1991:205–10.

Kerr, Richard A. "Climate Models Heat Up." Science Now (January 26, 2005): 1–3.

Kochanek, Kenneth D., et al. "Deaths: Preliminary Data for 2009." National Vital Statistics Reports. Vol. 59 No. 4. [Online] Available March 16, 2011, at http://www.cdc.gov/nchs/data/nvsr/nvsr59/nvsr59_04.pdf

Kuumba, M.Bahati. "A Cross-Cultural Race/Class/Gender Critique of Contemporary Population Policy: The Impact of Globalization."*Sociological Forum.* Vol. 14, No. 3 (March 1999):447–63.

Lacayo, Richard. "The Brawl over Sprawl." *Time* (March 22, 1999):44–48.

Lefebvre, Henri. *The Production of Space.* Oxford: Blackwell, 1991.

Lindstrom, Bonnie. "Chicago's Post-Industrial Suburbs." *Sociological Focus.* Vol. 28, No. 4 (October 1995):399–412.

Macionis, John J., and Vincent R. Parrillo. *Cities and Urban Life.* 6th ed. Upper Saddle River, N.J.: Pearson Prentice Hall, 2013.

Malthus, Thomas Robert. *First Essay on Population, 1798.* London: Macmillan, 1926; orig. 1798.

Marx, Karl. *Capital.* Friedrich Engels, ed. New York: International Publishers, 1967; orig. 1867.

McGurn, William. "The Not So Dismal Science: Humanitarians v. Economists." *Imprimis.* Vol. 40, No. 5 (March 2011):1–7.

McKibben, Bill. *Deep Economy: The Wealth of Communities and the Durable Future.* New York: Times Books, 2007.

McMahon, Bucky. "Vanishing Point." *Conservation.* Vol. 12, No. 1 (Spring 2011):40–48.

Meadows, Donella H., Dennis L. Meadows, Jorgan Randers, and William W. Behrens III. *The Limits to Growth: A Report on the Club of Rome's Project on the Predicament of Mankind.* New York: Universe, 1972.

Milbrath, Lester W. *Envisioning a Sustainable Society: Learning Our Way Out.* Albany: State University of New York Press, 1989.

Molotch, Harvey. "The City as a Growth Machine." *American Journal of Sociology.* Vol. 82, No. 2 (September 1976):309–33.

Mumford, Lewis. *The City in History: Its Origins, Its Transformations, and Its Prospects.* New York: Harcourt, Brace & World, 1961.

Murphy Sherry L., Jiaquan Xu, and Kenneth D. Kochanek. "Deaths: Preliminary Data for 2010." *National Vital Statistics Reports.* Vol. 60, No. 4. 2012. [Online] Available at http://www.cdc.gov/nchs/data/nvsr/nvsr60/nvsr60_04.pdf

Myers, David G. *The American Paradox: Spiritual Hunger in an Age of Plenty.* New Haven, Conn.: Yale University Press, 2000.

Myers, Norman. "Humanity's Growth." In Sir Edmund Hillary, ed., *Ecology 2000: The Changing Face of the Earth.* New York: Beaufort Books, 1984a:16–35.

———. "The Mega-Extinction of Animals and Plants." In Sir Edmund Hillary, ed., *Ecology 2000: The Changing Face of the Earth.* New York: Beaufort Books, 1984b:82–107.

Pacific Institute. "The World's Water." 2011. [Online] Available at http://www.world-water.org/data.html

Park, Robert E. *Race and Culture.* Glencoe, Ill.: Free Press, 1950.

Pederson, Daniel, Vern E. Smith, and Jerry Adler. "Sprawling, Sprawling . . ." *Newsweek* (July 19, 1999):23–27.

Population Action International. *People in the Balance: Population and Resources at the Turn of the Millennium.* Washington, D.C.: Population Action International, 2000.

Populaton Reference Bureau. "2011 World Population Data Sheet." 2011. [Online] Available at http://www.prb.org/Publications/Datasheets/2011/world-population-data-sheet.aspx

———. "Datafinder." 2011. [Online] Available at http://www.prb.org/DataFinder.aspx

Rainforest Foundation. 2010. "Rainforest Facts and Figures." [Online] Available at http://www.rainforestfoundationuk.org/Rainforest_facts

Reed, Brian. "Could People from Kiribati Be 'Climate Change Refugees'?" *The Two-Way.* National Public Radio news blog. [Online] Available February 17, 2011, at http://www.npr.org/templates/archives/archive.php?thingId=131216964

Romero, Francine Sanders, and Adrian Liserio. "Saving Open Spaces: Determinants of 1998 and 1999 'Antisprawl' Ballot Measures."*Social Science Quarterly.* Vol. 83, No. 1 (March 2002):341–52.

Roudi-Fahimi, Farzaneh, and Mary Mederios Kent. "Challenges and Opportunities: The Population of the Middle East and North Africa." *Population Bulletin.* Vol. 65, No. 2 (June 2007). Washington, D.C.: Population Reference Bureau, 2007.

Sauter, Michael B., "American Cities that are Running Out of People." *Yahoo News.* January 1, 2011. [Online] Accessed at http://finance.yahoo.com/family-home/article/111709/us-cities-running-out-of-people

Scanlon, Stephan J. "Food Availability and Access in Less Industrialized Societies: A Test and Interpretation of Neo-Malthusian and Technoecological Theories." *Sociological Forum.* Vol. 16, No. 2 (June 2001):231–62.

Schlesinger, Arthur M., Jr. "The City in American Civilization." In A. B. Callow Jr., ed., *American Urban History.* New York: Oxford University Press, 1969:25–41.

Schmitt, Eric. "Whites in Minority in Largest Cities, the Census Shows." *New York Times* (April 30, 2001):A1, A12.

Shevky, Eshref, and Wendell Bell. *Social Area Analysis.* Stanford, Calif.: Stanford University Press, 1955.

Simon, Julian. ———. "More People, Greater Wealth, More Resources, Healthier Environment." In Theodore D. Goldfarb, ed., *Taking Sides: Clashing Views on Controversial Environmental Issues.* 6th ed. Guilford, Conn.: Dushkin, 1995.

Simon, Julian. *The Ultimate Resource.* Princeton, N.J.: Princeton University Press, 1981.

Singer, S.Fred. "Global Warming: Man-Made or Natural?" *Imprimis.* Vol. 36, No. 8 (2007):1–5.

Smail, J.Kenneth." Let's *Reduce* Global Population!" In John J. Macionis and Nijole V. Benokraitis, eds., *Seeing Ourselves: Classic, Contemporary, and Cross-Cultural Readings in Sociology.* 7th ed. Upper Saddle River, N.J.: Prentice Hall, 2007.

Solomon, Steven. *Water: The Epic Struggle for Wealth, Power, and Civilization.* New York: Harper Collins, 2010.

Sullivan, Will. "Road Warriors." *U.S. News & World Report* (May 7, 2007):42–49.

Tönnies, Ferdinand. *Community and Society (Gemeinschaft und Gesellschaft).* New York: Harper & Row, 1963; orig. 1887.

U.S. Census Bureau. "State and Metropolitan Area Data Book." 2009. [Online] Available at http://www.census.gov/compendia/smadb/SMADBmetro.html

———. "American Community Survey." 2011. [Online] Available at http://www.census.gov/acs/www

———. "Census 2010." 2011. [Online] Available at http://factfinder2.census.gov/faces/nav/jsf/pages/index.xhtml

———. "International Data Base." 2011. [Online] Available at http://www.census.gov/ipc/www/idb

———. "Population Estimates." 2011. [Online] Available at http://www.census.gov/popest/data/index.html

U.S. Department of Commerce, National Oceanic & Atmospheric Administration. "National Climatic Data Center: State of the Climate Annual Global Analysis." 2011. [Online] Available at http://www.ncdc.noaa.gov/sotc/

———. "Trends in Atmospheric Carbon Dioxide." 2012. [Online] Available at http://www.esrl.noaa.gov/gmd/ccgg/trends

U.S. Department of the Interior, U.S. Geological Survey. "Estimated Use of Water in the United States in 2005." 2009. [Online] Available at http://water.usgs.gov/watuse

U.S. Environmental Protection Agency. "Drinking Water Standards and Health Advisory Tables." 2011. [Online] Available at http://water.epa.gov/action/advisories/drinking/drinking_index.cfm

———. "Municipal Solid Waste (MSW) in the United States: Facts and Figures." 2011. [Online] Available at http://www.epa.gov/epawaste/nonhaz/municipal/msw99.htm

———. "National Priorities List (NPL)." 2011. [Online] Available at http://www.epa.gov/superfund/sites/npl/current.htm

U.S. Office of Management and Budget. "Statistical Programs and Standards: Metropolitan Statistical Areas." 2010. [Online] Available at http://www.whitehouse.gov/omb/inforeg_statpolicy/#ms

Unesco, World Water Assessment Programme. "World Water Development Report 3: Water in a Changing World." March 2009. [Online] Available at http://www.unesco.org/water/wwap/wwdr

United Nations Department of Economic and Social Affairs. "World Population Prospects: The 2008 Revision." March 2009. [Online] Available at http://www.un.org/esa/population/unpop.htm

United Nations Department of Economic and Social Affairs. ———. "World Urbanization Prospects: The 2009 Revision." March 2010. [Online] Available at http://esa.un.org/unpd/wup/index.htm

United Nations development Programme, *Human Development Report 2011.* Statistical Tables. [Online] Available at http://hdr.undp.org/en/statistics/data/

United Nations Environment Programme (UNEP). "Vital Water Graphics: An Overview of the State of the World's Fresh and Marine Waters, 2nd Edition." 2008. [Online] Available at http://www.unep.org/dewa/vitalwater/index.html

———. "Vital Forest Graphics: Stopping the Downswing?" 2009. [Online] Available at http://www.grida.no/_res/site/file/publications/vital_forest_graphics.pdf

United Nations Statistics Division. "Environmental Indicators." 2011. [Online] Available at http://unstats.un.org/unsd/ENVIRONMENT/qindicators.htm

United Nations, Food and Agricultural Organization (FAO). "Global Forest Resources Assessment." 2010. [Online] Available athttp://www.fao.org/forestry/fra/fra2010/en

———. "Aquastat Database." 2011. [Online] Available at http://www.fao.org/nr/water/aquastat/main/index.stm

United Nations, Population Division. "World Urbanization Prospects: The 2009 Revision Population Database." [Online] Available at http://esa.un.org/wup2009/unup/index.asp

United Nations, Population Division. "World Population Prospects: The 2010 Revision." [Online] Available at http://esa.un.org/unpd/wpp/unpp/panel_population.htm

Walsh, Bryan. "A River Ran Through It." *Time.* Vol. 174, No. 23 (December 14, 2009):56–63.

Weber, Adna Ferrin. *The Growth of Cities.* New York: Columbia University Press, 1963; orig. 1899.

Wilson, Edward O. "Biodiversity, Prosperity, and Value." In F. Herbert Bormann and Stephen R. Kellert, eds., *Ecology, Economics, and Ethics: The Broken Circle.* New Haven, Conn.: Yale University Press, 1991:3–10.

Wilson, Thomas C. "Urbanism and Tolerance: A Test of Some Hypotheses Drawn from Wirth and Stouffer." *American Sociological Review.* Vol. 50, No. 1 (February 1985):117–23.

———. "Urbanism and Unconventionality: The Case of Sexual Behavior." *Social Science Quarterly.* Vol. 76, No. 2 (June 1995):346–63.

Wirth, Louis. "Urbanism as a Way of Life." *American Journal of Sociology.* Vol. 44, No. 1 (July 1938):1–24.

World Bank. *World Development Indicators.* 2011. [Online] Available at http://data.worldbank.org/data-catalog/world-development-indicators

World Resources Institute. "EarthTrends: Environmental Information." 2008. [Online] Available at http://earthtrends.wri.org

Yardley, Jim. "China Sticking with One-Child Policy." *New York Times* (March 11, 2008). [Online] Available December 23, 2008, at http://www.nytimes .com/2008/03/11/world/asia/11china.html?_r=1

Yemma, John. "As the World's Population Heads Toward a Peak, Malthusian Worries Reemerge." *The Christian Science Monitor.* [Online] Available February 7, 2011, at http://www.csmonitor.com/Commentary/editors-blog/2011/0207/Asworld-population-heads-toward-a-peak-Malthusian-worries-reemerge

Chapter 16 References

ABERLE, DAVID F. *The Peyote Religion among the Navaho.* Chicago: Aldine, 1966.

BERGER, PETER L. *Facing Up to Modernity: Excursions in Society, Politics, and Religion.* New York: Basic Books, 1977.

BERGER, PETER L., BRIGITTE BERGER, AND HANSFRIED KELLNER. *The Homeless Mind: Modernization and Consciousness.* New York: Vintage Books, 1974.

BLUMER, HERBERT G. "Collective Behavior." In ALFRED MCCLUNG LEE, ed., *Principles of Sociology.* 3rd ed. New York: Barnes & Noble Books, 1969:65–121.

BUECHLER, STEVEN M. *Social Movements in Advanced Capitalism: The Political Economy and Cultural Construction of Social Activism.* New York: Oxford University Press, 2000.

CAMERON, WILLIAM BRUCE. *Modern Social Movements: A Sociological Outline.* New York: Random House, 1966.

CDC (CENTERS FOR DISEASE CONTROL AND PREVENTION). "Health, United States, 2010." 2011. [Online] Available at http://www.cdc.gov/nchs/data/hus/hus10.pdf

CURRY, ANDREW. "The Gullahs' Last Stand?" *U.S. News & World Report* (June 18, 2001):40–41.

DAVIES, JAMES C. "Toward a Theory of Revolution." *American Sociological Review.* Vol. 27, No. 1 (February 1962):5–19.

DEWAN, SHAILA. "Ecosystem vs. an Endangered Culture." *New York Times.* [Online] Available July 1, 2010, at http://green.blogs.nytimes.com/2010/07/01/ecosystem-vs-an-endangered-culture/?scp=1&sq=Gullah&st=cse

DURKHEIM, EMILE. *The Division of Labor in Society.* New York: Free Press, 1964; orig. 1893.

EHRENREICH, BARBARA. *Nickel and Dimed: On (Not) Getting By in America.* New York: Holt, 2001.

ERIKSON, KAI T. *Everything in Its Path: Destruction of Community in the Buffalo Creek Flood.* New York: Simon & Schuster, 1976.

———. *A New Species of Trouble: Explorations in Disaster, Trauma, and Community.* New York: Norton, 1994.

———. Lecture at Kenyon College, February 7, 2005.

ETZIONI, AMITAI. "How to Make Marriage Matter." *Time* (September 6, 1993):76.

———. "The Responsive Community: A Communitarian Perspective." *American Sociological Review.* Vol. 61, No. 1 (February 1996):1–11.

———. *My Brother's Keeper: A Memoir and a Message.* Lanham, Md.: Rowman & Littlefield, 2003.

GIBBS, NANCY. "The Pulse of America along the River." *Time* (July 10, 2000):42–46.

GOFFMAN, ERVING. *The Presentation of Self in Everyday Life.* Garden City, N.Y.: Anchor Books, 1959.

GOVERNORS HIGHWAY SAFETY ASSOCIATION. "Cell Phone and Texting Laws." 2011. [Online] Available at http://www.ghsa.org/html/stateinfo/laws/cellphone_laws.html

HABERMAS, JÜRGEN. *Toward a Rational Society: Student Protest, Science, and Politics.* JEREMY J. SHAPIRO, trans. Boston: Beacon Press, 1970.

HALL, JOHN R., AND MARY JO NEITZ. *Culture: Sociological Perspectives.* Englewood Cliffs, N.J.: Prentice Hall, 1993.

HARRINGTON, MICHAEL. *The New American Poverty.* New York: Penguin Books, 1984.

INGLEHART, RONALD. *Modernization and Postmodernization: Cultural, Economic, and Political Change in 43 Societies.* Princeton, N.J.: Princeton University Press, 1997.

———, AND WAYNE E. BAKER. "Modernization, Cultural Change, and the Persistence of Traditional Values." *American Sociological Review.* Vol. 65, No. 1 (February 2000):19–51.

———, CHRISTIAN WELZEL, AND ROBERTO FOA. "Happiness Trends in 24 Countries, 1946–2006." 2009. [Online] Available February 15, 2009, at http://margaux.grandvinum.se/SebTest/wvs/articles/folder_published/article_base_106

———, ET AL. *World Values Survey.* 2011. [Online] Available at http://www.worldvaluessurvey.com

JENKINS, J. CRAIG, AND MICHAEL WALLACE. "The Generalized Action Potential of Protest Movements: The New Class, Social Trends, and Political Exclusion Explanations." *Sociological Forum.* Vol. 11, No. 2 (June 1996):183–207.

KEISTER, LISA A. *Getting Rich: America's New Rich and How They Got That Way.* New York: Cambridge University Press, 2005.

KOCHANEK, KENNETH D., ET AL. "Deaths: Preliminary Data for 2009." *National Vital Statistics Reports.* Vol. 59, No. 4. Hyattsville, Md: National Center for Health Statistics. March 16, 2011.http://www.cdc.gov/nchs/data/nvsr/nvsr59/nvsr59_04.pdf

KORNHAUSER, WILLIAM. *The Politics of Mass Society.* New York: Free Press, 1959.

KRAYBILL, DONALD B., AND JAMES P. HURD. *Horse-and-Buggy Mennonites: Hoofbeats of Humility in a Postmodern World.* University Park: Pennsylvania State University Press, 2006.

———, AND MARC A. OLSHAN, eds. *The Amish Struggle with Modernity.* Hanover, N.H.: University Press of New England, 1994.

KRIESI. 1989.

LASLETT, PETER. *The World We Have Lost: England before the Industrial Age.* 3rd ed. New York: Scribner, 1984.

MACIONIS, JOHN J. *Social Problems.* 4th ed. Upper Saddle River, N.J.: Pearson Prentice Hall, 2010.

MARCUSE, HERBERT. *One-Dimensional Man.* Boston: Beacon Press, 1964.

MARX, KARL, AND FRIEDRICH ENGELS. "Manifesto of the Communist Party." In ROBERT C. TUCKER, ed., *The Marx-Engels Reader.* New York: Norton, 1972:331–62; orig. 1848.

MCADAM, DOUG, JOHN D. MCCARTHY, AND MAYER N. ZALD. "Social Movements." In NEIL J. SMELSER, ed., *Handbook of Sociology.* Newbury Park, Calif.: Sage, 1988: 695–737.

MCVEIGH, RORY, MICHAEL WELCH, AND THORODDUR BJARNASON. "Hate Crime Reporting as a Successful Social Movement Outcome." *American Sociological Review.* Vol. 68 (2003): 843–67.

MELUCCI, ALBERTO. *Nomads of the Present: Social Movements and Individual Needs in Contemporary Society.* Philadelphia: Temple University Press, 1989.

MERTON, ROBERT K. *Social Theory and Social Structure.* New York: Free Press, 1968.

MILLER, FREDERICK D. "The End of SDS and the Emergence of Weatherman: Demise through Success." In JO FREEMAN, ed., *Social Movements of the Sixties and Seventies.* White Plains, N.Y.: Longman, 1983:279–97.

MIRINGOFF, MARC, AND MARQUE-LUISA MIRINGOFF. "The Social Health of the Nation." *Economist.* Vol. 352, No. 8128 (July 17, 1999):suppl. 6–7.

MORRISON, DENTON E. "Some Notes toward Theory on Relative Deprivation, Social Movements, and Social Change." In LOUIS E. GENEVIE, ed., *Collective Behavior and Social Movements.* Itasca, Ill.: Peacock, 1978:202–209.

MYERS, DAVID G. *The American Paradox: Spiritual Hunger in an Age of Plenty.* New Haven, Conn.: Yale University Press, 2000.

NATIONAL HIGHWAY TRAFFIC SAFETY ADMINISTRATION, NATIONAL CENTER FOR STATISTICS AND ANALYSIS. "2009 Traffic Safety Overview." 2010. [Online] Available at http://www-nrd.nhtsa.dot.gov/Pubs/811392.pdf

———. "Fatality Analysis Reporting System (FARS)." 2011. [Online] Available at http://www-fars.nhtsa.dot.gov

NEWMAN, KATHERINE S. *Declining Fortunes: The Withering of the American Dream.* New York: Basic Books, 1993.

NISBET, ROBERT A. *The Sociological Tradition.* New York: Basic Books, 1966.

NORC. *General Social Surveys, 1972–2010.* Chicago: National Opinion Research Center. March 2011. [Online] Available at http://www.norc.org/GSS+Website

OGBURN, WILLIAM F. *On Culture and Social Change.* Chicago: University of Chicago Press, 1964.

PACKER, GEORGE. "Smart-Mobbing the War." *New York Times Magazine* (March 9, 2003):46–49.

PAKULSKI, JAN. "Mass Social Movements and Social Class." *International Sociology.* Vol. 8, No. 2 (June 1993):131–58.

PASSY, FLORENCE, AND MARCO GIUGNI. "Social Networks and Individual Perceptions: Explaining Differential Participation in Social Movements." *Sociological Forum.* Vol. 16, No. 1 (March 2001):123–53.

PEARSON, DAVID E. "Post-Mass Culture." *Society.* Vol. 30, No. 5 (July/August 1993):17–22.

———. "Community and Sociology." *Society.* Vol. 32, No. 5 (July/August 1995):44–50.

PIVEN, FRANCES FOX, AND RICHARD A. CLOWARD. *Poor People's Movements: Why They Succeed, How They Fail.* New York: Pantheon Books, 1977.

RIESMAN, DAVID. *The Lonely Crowd: A Study of the Changing American Character.* New Haven, Conn.: Yale University Press, 1970; orig. 1950.

ROSE, FRED. "Toward a Class-Cultural Theory of Social Movements: Reinterpreting New Social Movements." *Sociological Forum.* Vol. 12, No. 3 (September 1997):461–94.

ROSE, JERRY D. *Outbreaks.* New York: Free Press, 1982.

RUDEL, THOMAS K., AND JUDITH M. GERSON. "Postmodernism, Institutional Change, and Academic Workers: A Sociology of Knowledge." *Social Science Quarterly.* Vol. 80, No. 2 (June 1999):213–28.

SIMON, ROGER, AND ANGIE CANNON. "An Amazing Journey." *U.S. News & World Report* (August 6, 2001):10–19.

SIMONS, MARLISE. "The Price of Modernization: The Case of Brazil's Kaiapo Indians." In JOHN J. MACIONIS AND NIJOLE V. BENOKRAITIS, eds., *Seeing Ourselves: Classic, Contemporary, and Cross-Cultural Readings in Sociology.* 7th ed. Upper Saddle River, N.J.: Prentice Hall, 2007.

TAX FOUNDATION. "America Celebrates Tax Freedom Day." 2011 [Online] Available at http://www.taxfoundation.org/taxfreedomday

TÖNNIES, FERDINAND. *Community and Society (Gemeinschaft und Gesellschaft).* New York: Harper & Row, 1963; orig. 1887.

U.S. CENSUS BUREAU.

———. "Population Projections." 2008. [Online] Available at http://www.census.gov/population/www/projections/summarytables.html

———. "American Community Survey." 2011. [Online] Available at http://www.census.gov/acs/www

———. "Current Population Survey." September 2011. [Online] Available at http://www.census.gov/cps

———. "Population Estimates." 2011. [Online] Available at http://www.census.gov/popest/data/index.html

———. *Statistical Abstract of the United States: 2012,* 131st Edition. 2011. [Online] Available at http://www.census.gov/statab/www

U.S. DEPARTMENT OF HEALTH AND HUMAN SERVICES, ADMINISTRATION ON CHILDREN, YOUTH AND FAMILIES. "Child Maltreatment 2010." 2011. [Online] Available at http://www.acf.hhs.gov/programs/cb/pubs/cm10/

U.S. DEPARTMENT OF LABOR, BUREAU OF LABOR STATISTICS. "Employment Situation." 2011. [Online] Available at http://www.bls.gov/news.release/empsit.toc.htm

VAN DYKE, NELLA, AND SARAH A. SOULE. "Structural Social Change and the Mobilizing Effect of Threat: Explaining Levels of Patriot and Militia Organizing in the United States." *Social Problems.* Vol. 49, No. 4 (November 2002):497–520.

WEBER, MAX The Protestant Ethic and the Spirit of Capitalism. New York: Scribner, 1958; orig. 1904–05.

———. Economy and Society: An Outline of Interpretive Sociology. GUENTHER ROTH AND CLAUS WITTICH, eds. Berkeley: University of California Press, 1978; orig. 1921.

WEST, CORNEL. "The Obama Moment." U.S. News & World Report (November 17, 2008):29.

WHEELIS, ALLEN. The Quest for Identity. New York: Norton, 1958.

WILLIAMS, JOHNNY E. "Linking Beliefs to Collective Action: Politicized Religious Beliefs and the Civil Rights Movement." Sociological Forum. Vol. 17, No. 2 (June 2002):203–22.

WILLIAMSON, SAMUEL H. "Seven Ways to Compute the Relative Value of a U.S. Dollar Amount, 1774 to Present: Measuring Worth." March 2011. [Online] Available at http://www.measuringworth.com/uscompare

WOLFF, EDWARD N. "Recent Trends in Household Wealth in the United States: Rising Debt and the Middle-Class Squeeze—an Update to 2007." March 2010. [Online] Available at http://www.levyinstitute.org/publications/?docid=1235

WORLD BANK. "World Development Indicators." [Online] Available at http://data.world-bank.org/data-catalog/world-development-indicators

ZHAO, DINGXIN. "Ecologies of Social Movements: Student Mobilization during the 1989 Prodemocracy Movement in Beijing." American Journal of Sociology. Vol. 103, No. 6 (May 1998):1493–1529.

photo credits

name index

508

subject index

Note: page numbers followed by "f" indicate figures; "n" indicate notes; "t" indicate tables.

SOCIETY IN HISTORY: TIMELINES

A timeline is a visual device that helps us understand historical change. The timeline at the right represents 5 billion years of the history of the planet Earth. This timeline is divided into three sections, each of which is drawn to a different scale of time. The first section, **The Earth's Origins**, begins with the planet's origins 5 billion years before the present (B.P.) and indicates that another full billion years passed before the earliest forms of life appeared. The second section, **Our Human Origins**, shows that plants and animals continued to evolve for billions more years until, approximately 12 million years ago, our earliest human ancestors came onto the scene. In the third section of this timeline, **Earliest Civilization**, we see that what we call civilization is relatively recent indeed, with the first permanent settlements occurring in the Middle East a scant 12,000 years ago. But the written record of our species' existence extends back only half this long, to the time humans invented writing and first farmed with animal-driven plows some 5,000 years B.P.

Sociology came into being in the wake of the many changes to society wrought by the Industrial Revolution over the last few centuries—just the blink of an eye in evolutionary perspective. The lower timeline provides a close-up look at the events and trends that have defined **The Modern Era**, most of which are discussed in this text. Innovations in technology are charted in the panel below the line and provide a useful backdrop for viewing the milestones of social progress highlighted in the panel above the line. Major contributions to the development of sociological thought are traced along the very bottom of this timeline.

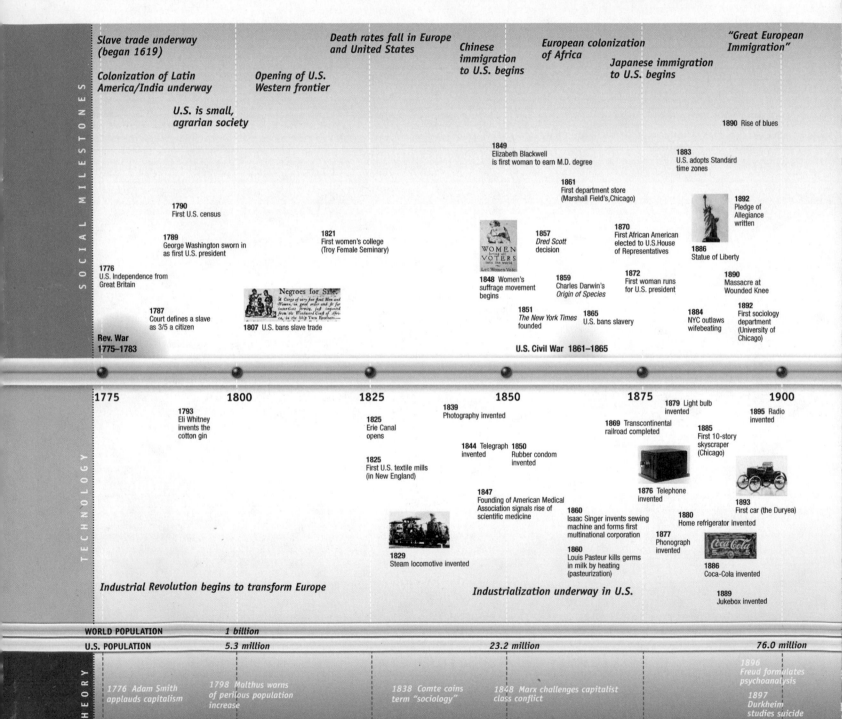